The Information Universe: Issues in Informing Science and Information Technology

Volume 3, 2006

Edited by Eli B. Cohen

Informing Science Institute

Informing Science Press

The Information Universe:
Issues in Informing Science and Information Technology:
Volume 3, 2006

Editor: Eli B. Cohen, Informing Science Institute

Published by

Coastal Publishing International
an imprint of the
Informing Science Press
the publication arm of the
Informing Science Institute
131 Brookhill Court
Santa Rosa, California 95409 USA

Telephone: +1 707 531 4925

Email: Publisher@InformingScience.org

Website: http://ISPress.org

Director of Publications: Peter Baloh

ISBN: 1-932886-00-1
ISSN: 1547-9684

Printed in Canada, United Kingdom, Australia, and USA

The Journal of Issues in Informing Science and Information Technology
Volume 3, 2006

Table of Contents

Remote Method Invocation and Mobil Agent: A Comparative Analysis

G.A. Aderounmu
Obafemi Awolowo University
Ile-Ife, Nigeria

gaderoun@oauife.edu.ng

B.O. Oyatokun
Olabisi Onabanjo
University, Ago-Iwoye,
Nigeria

M.O. Adigun
University of Zululand, Kwadlangezwa,
Republic of South Africa

madigun@pan.uzulu.ac.za

Abstract

This paper presents a comparative analysis of Remote Method Invocation (RMI) and Mobile Agent (MA) paradigm used to implement the information storage and retrieval system in a distributed computing environment.

Simulation program was developed to measure the performance of MA and RMI using object oriented programming language (the following parameters: search time, fault tolerance and invocation cost. We used search time, fault tolerance and invocation cost as performance parameters in this research work.

Experimental results showed that Mobile Agent paradigm offers a superior performance compared to RMI paradigm, offers fast computational speed; procure lower invocation cost by making local invocations instead of remote invocations over the network, thereby reducing network bandwidth. Finally MA has a better fault tolerance than the RMI. With a probability of failure pr = 0.1, mobile agent degrades gracefully.

Keywords: Mobile Agent, RMI, remote object, query, invocation.

Introduction

In the past few years, there has been a growing interest in using mobile agent technology for the next generation enterprises. This is because, the next generation enterprises will require the ability to efficiently retrieve, organize, manage and leverage information and knowledge from widely dispersed sources within and without virtual organization (Seng, 1999). Mobile agents have been specifically proposed to automate the task of retrieving; organizing and filtering information located in widely dispersed sites (Dale and

DeRoure, 1997). Although agent technology is a branch of artificial intelligence, it is believed that mobile agent technology can be employed to build distributed information management tools. There are various reasons for using mobile agent (Lange & Oshima, 1999). This work presents the performance benefits of mobile agent for information storage and retrieval in a distributed computing environment over the exiting client/server (Remote Method Invocation) method.

Several works have been done in developing mobile agent system for information storage and retrieval, but not much has since been done in the area of comparison of the different approaches for distributed information management.

In (Aderounmu, 2004), the use of mobile agent in the control and transfer of data in distributed computing environment was presented against the traditional client-server computing using RPC (Remote Procedure Call). The author explores bandwidth utilization, percentage of denial of service, and network overload with retransmission to show a proof of superior scheme provided by mobile agent as against the client server computing.

Mobile Agent in Distributed Information Retrieval (Brewington, Gray, Moizumi, Kotz, Cybenko, & Rus, 1999) analyzes base performance in terms of response time (the interval between when a request is sent and the time the result is received). The authors made attempt to prove that mobile agent incurs significantly more overhead than RPC due to inter-agent communication and migration when the number of queries and relevant document per query are few; however MA begins to perform excellently as the number of queries and relevant document per query increase.

In (Kunal, 2003), the author simulated the basic behaviour of mobile agent by extending a common general-purpose simulator and a comparison of MA and RPC was carried out using the number of server required to visit to complete a task, the number of records and the number of interaction with agent sizes. Also Ismail and Hagimont, (1999) evaluated the performance of MA paradigm using cost of basic mechanism in the implementation of MA and RPC as the performance metric. Other related works include: Aderounmu, Adagunodo, Ogwu, and Akinde ,2000; Aderounmu, Adekiigbe, and Iyilade, 2004; Ajayi, Aderounmu, and Adigun, 2004; Dilyana and Petya, 2002; Hagimont,and Ismail, 1999; Mawhood-Yunis, Nayak, Nussbaum, and Santoro 2004; Oke, Okelana, and Aderounmu, 2002; Olajubu, Aderounmu, and Akinde, 2004; and Oluwatope, Aderounmu, Akande, and Adigun ,2004.

In this work however, we attempt to compare the mobile agent and client server paradigms both in java environment using RMI for client server. The performance measurements simulated are the invocation cost, search time and fault tolerance.

RMI Communication Model

RMI is the object equivalent of RPC. RPC calls procedure over a network whereas RMI invokes object methods over a network. The server defines objects that client can use remotely and clients can now invoke methods of remote object as if it were a local object running in the same virtual machine as client. RMI possesses the following characteristics

- hides the underlying mechanism of transporting method arguments and return values across network,
- uses a network based registry program to keep track of the distributed object.
- a simple name repository (registry) that acts as a central management point, and
- server makes methods available for remote invocation by binding it to a name in the registry.

The underlying mechanism actually follows the following steps:

- The client invokes a local method called the client stub
- The client stub parcels up the client parameters to the remote procedure, converts them to a standard format and builds network messages (**marshaling**). RMI uses object serialization to marshal and de-marshal messages.
- The network messages are sent to the remote server by the client stub through a previously agreed upon protocol.
- On the remote server, the server skeleton de-marshals the parameters from the network messages and converts them.
- The skeleton invokes local methods to invoke the actual server function, passes the parameters it received on the network messages from the client stub.
- When the server procedure completes, it returns to the skeleton with return values.
- The skeleton converts the return values, if necessary and marshal them into network messages to send back to the client
- The messages are transferred across the network to the client stub
- The client stub de-marshals the return values to the client.

Mobile Agent Paradigm

Mobile agent technology facilitated by recent advances in computers, communications and artificial intelligence, provides an attractive framework for the design and implementation of communicating applications in general and distributed knowledge networks in particular. The computational model based on mobility, can be seen as a replacement, refinement or extension of the traditional client server paradigm. The mobile agent framework emerged in the pursuit of open and decentralized models relevant to the dynamic and distributed nature of computations on the Internet.

Mobile agent is an object that migrates through many nodes of a heterogeneous network of computers under its own control in order to perform tasks using resources of these nodes (Aderounmu, 2004). The user initiates the agent, provides the agent with an itinerary (route), which represents the nodes to visit. The agents take the itinerary data, execution state and necessary code as part of a "bag" for starting its journey on each server. Once the mobile agent finishes its activities on the server, it determines dynamically the next host to visit on the network. As soon as this is done, the mobile agent sets up a client connection routine, which is a subcomponent of the mobility infrastructure in order to establish a link between the current node and its destination node. The distributed mobility infrastructure on each machine serves as the server for the client to establish communication channel that is based on Transmission Control Protocol/internet Protocol (TCP/IP) sockets. After establishing the connection, mobile agent moves through the mobility mat to the destination machine where it is enabled again to perform its activities.

The mobile agent queries the local environment to acquire the necessary information to achieve its objectives. The information retrieval service (corresponding to the current node) interacts with its own database management systems and returns the results to the agent, which adds them to its "bag" and migrates to the next host.

In case a server is disconnected or faulty, the agent skips the node, determine alternative route dynamically and continues its journey. It takes note of any problems and accomplished activities. When all nodes have been visited the agent sends a message to the original host with all results obtained and reports of its itinerary.

Analysis of Performance Parameters

Simulation program was developed to provide performance analysis between the RMI and MA based on communication models explained in section 2. The following parameters were used: search time, fault tolerance, and invocation cost.

Search Time

The time interval between when a query is sent from the source and when the response (data) is found and received at the requesting host is referred to as the search time in this research work. The search time is measured in terms of request time, $\mathbf{t_{req}}$ and response time, $\mathbf{t_{res}}$, relative to the distance between the nodes. In this paper, the sizes of request and response are assumed to be the same and thus request time and response time are the same and correspond to $\mathbf{t_r}$.

With RMI, when a query is generated, client connects to a remote object that was previously registered on the server, searches through the registered object on the server and reports back to the client. If the required information or object is not found on a host, a report is sent to the client before it connects to another server to search for the same object. It reports back to the server again before connecting to yet another server until the object is located or otherwise. If we assume the following:

- the distance between all the nodes is equal.
- the time taken to send a query is t_{req}, and
- the time the response is received at the requesting host is t_{res}

then the search time for one request is the time required to transmit the request from the source node to the destination node and back to the source. This is given by:

$$\mathbf{ST_{rmi}} = t_{req} + t_{res} \qquad 3.1$$

Where

1. $\mathbf{ST_{rmi}}$ is the search time for RMI
2. $\mathbf{t_{req}}$ is the request time
3. $\mathbf{t_{res}}$ is the response time

Each time the RMI visits a node it reports back to the requesting host (client), assuming there are **n** number of nodes in the network, and **m** denotes the number of nodes visited during the search, including the launching (client) node, i.e. the object is found at the $\mathbf{m^{th}}$ mode, where $m \leq n$, then

$$\mathbf{ST_{rmi}} = m\,(t_{req} + t_{res})$$

Assuming size of request is equal to the size of response and equal to t_r

$$\mathbf{ST_{rmi}} = 2*t_r(m-1) \qquad \text{..........(3.2)}$$

Where

- $\mathbf{t_r}$ is the request/response time
- n is the total number of nodes connected on the network, and
- m is the number of nodes visited to locate the object

With mobile agent on the other hand, the client creates an agent which contains the client's request to be executed: this agent moves to server A for local interaction, if the object is not found, the agent moves to the next server, B and yet another server until the object is found. Otherwise, until all the servers are visited, before reporting to the client.

The agent visits each node in t_r time, using the same notations, as with RMI, and let us

assume the size of agent code is **y.** If it takes **ty** units of time to transfer the agent code on the network. The search time of mobile agent paradigm for one request will be equal to the time to transport the request and agent code on the network between the nodes, thus,

$$ST_{ma} = t_r + ty \quad (3.3)$$

Assuming the resource is found at node **m,** which includes the launching node where $m \le n$, the total search time thus becomes

$$ST_{ma} = (m-1)(t_r + ty) \quad (3.4)$$

At the end of the search the agent returns to the source with the response in another $t_r + ty$ time. Such that the total time becomes

$$ST_{ma} = m(t_r + ty) \quad (3.5)$$

Invocation Cost

Cost is estimated in terms of the number and type of invocations involved. The invocations involved in both schemes are classified as either network (remote) invocation or local invocation; we thus generate a cost function for the two schemes.

The RMI scheme involves several invocations between the client and the server on the network. In RMI, once a client object connects to a remote object that was registered on a server, the connection has to be maintained to maintain execution. RMI makes remote invocations as the name implies, every invocation is over the network. The request is sent to the server over the network and the response is sent back to the client the same way. The request is taken one after another and sent to the server with the server sending the response each time across the network. If there are n requests (query) there will be n invocations to the destination and n invocations back to the source.

If we assume a request of size X bytes, response of size Y bytes and the cost of one request over the network (network invocation) is Ni, then, for n number of requests, each has a network invocation to its destination and one response over the network back to its origin, hence the total costs will be

$$C_{rmi} - nX + nY$$

if we assume that the request and response are the same size for the purpose of simplicity, i.e.

$X = Y$, then the total cost becomes:

$$C_{rmi} = 2nX$$

and taking the request and response size to be equivalent to the cost of Network invocation Ni, i.e.

$$X = Ni$$

$$C_{rmi} = 2nNi \quad (3.6)$$

The mobile agent paradigm allows remote invocations to be replaced by local invocations as the agent migrates to the invoked server site. The agent migrates with the execution code and execution thread. The execution thread enables the agent to trace its execution state and execute accordingly, i.e. continues from the last execution state instead of starting execution all over again on another host. In mobile agent scheme, one network invocation would carry all the requests and mobile agent's code and then execute at the remote server. All other invocations are mere local invocations on the server system. The mobile agent system makes fewer remote invocations compared to RMI with a lot of local invocations.

For n number of requests with size X bytes, the cost of network invocation will be nX.

The response to the requesting host is also of size Y bytes

If the cost of one local invocation is Li units, assume each request has one local invocation, n requests will be

nLi units local invocations at the invoked server site.

Since the agent moves with its code and execution thread, the size of the mobile agent code will have to be included.

Let the size of the mobile agent code be C

Then the total cost for the mobile agent system will be the sum of the total cost for network invocations, the total local invocations on the invoked server, the mobile code and the response cost over the network.

$$C_{ma} = nX + nLi + C + Y \text{ -- } (3.7)$$

If the assumption that the size of request and response over the network are equal and equivalent to the cost of network invocations still holds, then, the total cost become:

$$C_{ma} = (n+1)X + C + nLi$$

This gives

$$C_{ma} = (n+1)Ni + C + nLi \ldots\ldots\ldots\ldots\ldots\ldots\ldots\ldots\ldots\ldots\ldots (3.8)$$

Where n is the number of requests

X: the size of request over the network

Y: the size of response over the network

Li: the cost of local invocation

C: the size of t he mobile agent code.

Fault Tolerance

Fault tolerance is the ability of a system to respond gracefully to an unexpected hardware or software failure. A fault tolerant system, as in computer networks, has the ability to continue operation in the event of a network failure.

Fault tolerance is a measure of robustness or adaptability of a system to breakdown. A fault tolerant system degrades gracefully in the face of failure, even though at a lower level of performance (Aderounmu, 2001). When there is a failure of a node in the RMI system or network connection failure, the RMI fails immediately. This is because most of the transactions involved take place over the network. The RMI will have to wait until the link is up again to continue execution.

In mobile agent system however, the agent proactively determines alternative route to the next host or source when failure occurs. The agent dynamically determines alternative path on getting to the host computer. The path is refreshed when moving to a new destination.

In carrying out our performance measure of fault tolerance for MA and RMI schemes, we assume the probability of failure to be 0.1, that is, in every 10 nodes there is likelihood of fault occurring in one out of 10. As in search time analyzed above, if we assume a network with **n** number of nodes, the size of request / response is assumed to be the same and thus the request time and response time are the same and equals t_r. If we take the size of agent code to be **y,** then we assume it would take **ty** units of time to transfer the agent code on the network.

If we further assume that the recovery time for a failure is the same irrespective of the node at which the error occur and is given by t_f, then probability that there is a failure at node **i** on the network is:

Pr (failure at i for i = 1-n) = 0.1

The node at which the fault occurs is generated as a random event that the system does not known a priori.

In MAS, the agent has a predetermined movement pattern at the starting node. The routing table is generated as a random process and it consist of the sequence of nodes on the network that the agent would traverse during its itinerary. However, in the event of a network or node failure, which makes the agent not to follow the original path, an alternative path is generated so as to bypass the failing node. This in effect helps to eliminate the downtime that the system should have experienced while waiting for the link to be up again. This is illustrated below:

Assuming that the mobile agent is moving on a network, with nodes labeled, 1, 2, 3, - ---, 10, and the routing pattern is given as:

$2 \rightarrow 5 \rightarrow 1 \rightarrow 4 \rightarrow 8 \rightarrow 3 \rightarrow 7 \rightarrow 9 \rightarrow 10 \rightarrow 6 \rightarrow 2$

Assuming fault occur between node 4 to 8, then an alternative path is generated at node 4 which may look like this
$4 \rightarrow 7 \rightarrow 3 \rightarrow 10 \rightarrow 6 \rightarrow 8 \rightarrow 2$.

If the resource being searched for is found at node number **m** (where $m \leq n$) then the total search time (T_{ma}) for MA for the resource is the time it takes to transport the requests and agent code on the network between the nodes, which is:

$$T_{ma} = m\,(t_r + ty) \quad \text{.......(3.9)}$$

Where

m is the number of the node at which resource is found,

t_r the request/response time, and

ty the time taken to transfer the agent code

For RMI, there is no way the system can adjust dynamically to the failure. Hence, the system suffers a delay equivalent to the time at which the fault is rectified. Thus, the total search time (T_{rmi}) is equivalent to the time it takes to transmit the request from the source node to the destination node and back to the source. This process is repeated until node **m**.

However, if a faulty node is encountered during the search, the system experience a delay equals to the total failure recovery time kt_f. Where **k** is the no of nodes at which error occur along the itinerary.

Thus:

$$T_{rmi} = 2 * t_r\,(m - 1) + kt_f \quad \text{.......(3.10)}$$

Where

k is the number of node at which failure occurs

t_f is the down time or the total failure recovery time

System Simulation and Result Analysis

Cost versus Number of Requests per Service

In this paper, we measured the invocation cost for varying number for requests per service as discussed in the last section. The result from our simulation also confirms that Mobile Agent approach results in reduced cost overhead than what are obtainable with the RMI scheme.

As shown in Figure1, the cost rises as the number of requests increases, and the cost of RMI increases with a higher gradient compared to mobile agent. The mobile agent paradigm incurs a lower invocation cost compared to RMI at the same or even better efficiency, a desirable quality of any system.

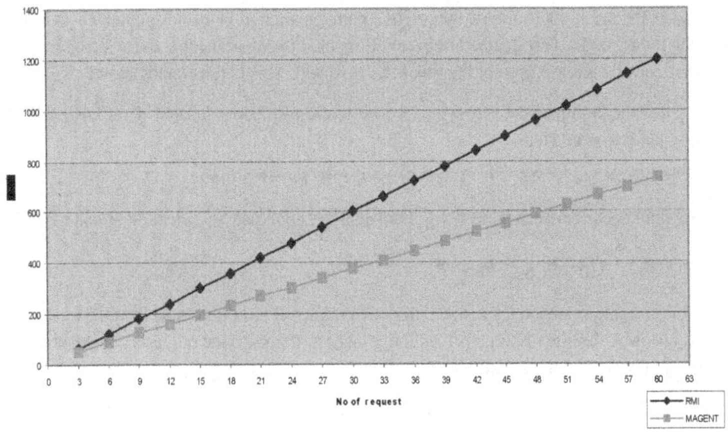

Figure 1 Graph of Cost versus number of requests

Search Time versus Number of Nodes

In measuring the search time involved in using the two approaches, we have compared the time it takes to search and locate a resource on the network. The location of the resource is not known a priori. Using the Mobile Agent approach, it took a shorter time to search for the resource than we have in RMI. Fig.2 shows that mobile agent paradigm offers a lower search time compared to RMI, despite the fact that it travels with the execution code. It should be noted that the search time does not depend on the number of nodes in the network, but the location of the resource being sought.

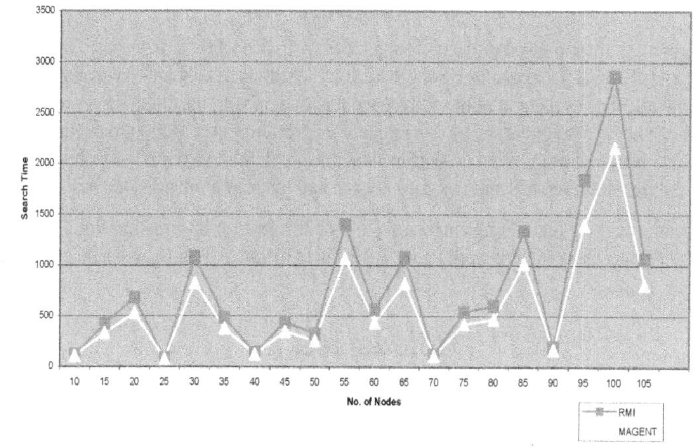

Fig.2 Graph of Search Time Versus Number of Nodes

Query Time versus Number of Nodes

In measuring the response of the MAS and RMI to fault, we measured the time it takes to complete a query for a given number of nodes. Our result indicates that as we have more nodes on the network, the more the likelihood of fault occurring and thus resulting in higher query time as is been experienced in RMI. However, MA is able to adjust in case of a failure and therefore reduce query time because it could dynamically generate alternative path for its itinerary.

Figure 3 shows that the search time for RMI increases in the face of node or network failure due to the down time. The surpassing performance of mobile agent paradigm can be connected to more local invocations it makes as against the RMI which relies heavily on network connections throughout the service, therefore making it more vulnerable to network failure.

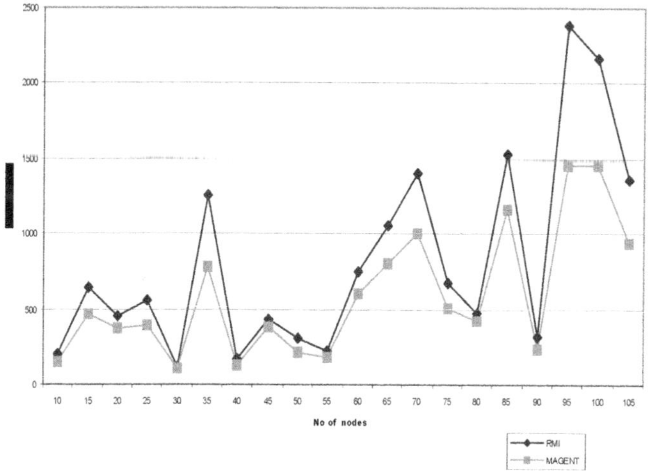

Fig.3 Graph of Query Time for different number of nodes

Conclusion

The authors present a comparison of the performance of MA with RMI for distributed information storage and retrieval. Our conclusion was based on the results of simulation carried out in this research work. The evaluation of the mobile agent paradigm with the client server reveals that the mobile agent paradigm is superior in terms of invocation cost reduction, reduction of search time and better adaptability to failures by dynamically defining alternative route in the face of network failure. However, our analysis does not account for searching large database

We are currently working on full implementation of mobile agent for information storage and retrieval. The perspective of future work in this regard is in the provisioning of adequate security for the mobile agent.

References

Aderounmun, G.A. (2004). Performance comparison of remote procedure calling and mobile agent approach to control and data transfer in distributed computing environment. *Journal of Network and Computer Applications*, 113 – 129.

Aderounmu, G. A., Adagunodo, E. R., Ogwu, F. J., & Akinde, A. D. (2000). On the concept of mobile agent framework for resource management in an enterprise network. *Proceedings of the IASTED International Conference on Artificial Intelligent and Soft Computing*. 168 – 172, July 24-26, Canada.

Aderounmu, G.A, Adekiigbe, A., & Iyilade, J.S.(2004). An evaluation of mobile agent paradigm. *The Journal of Computer Science and Its Applications, 10*(2): 107-116.

Ajayi, A. O., Aderounmu, G. A., & Adigun, M. O. (2004): Web-based expert system for property valuation using mobile agent technology. *Proceedings of the IASTED International Conference on Knowledge Sharing and Collaborative Engineering*, November, 26-31, St. Thomas, Virgin Islands. USA

Brewington, B., Gray, R., Moizumi. K., Kotz, D., Cybenko, C., & Rus, D. (1999). Mobile agents for distributed information retrieval. In M. Klusch (Ed.), *Intelligent information agents* (Chapter 15). Springer-Verlag. 355- 395. Retrieved 29/11/2005 from http://agent.cs.dartmouth.edu/papers/smallbib/brewington:IR.bib

Dale, J. & DeRoure, D. (1997). A mobile agent architecture for distributed information management. *Proceedings of the International Workshop on the Virtual Multicomputer*. Retrieved from http://www.mmrg.ecs.soton.ac.uk/publications/archive/dale1997b/

Dilyana, S. & Petya G., (2002). Building distributed applications with Java mobile agents. *International workshop NGNT* (pp 103- 109). Retreived from http://saturn.acad.bg/bis/pdfs/16_doklad.pdf

Hagimont, D.& Ismail, L. (1999). A performance evaluation of the mobile agent paradigm. *ACM SIGNAL Notices, 34*, 306--313.

Ismail, L. & Hagimont, D. (1999). A performance evaluation of the mobile agent. *Proceedings of the 14th ACM SIGPLAN conference on OOP Systems Languages and Applications*. Denver, Colorado, US. 306- 313.

Kunal, M. S. (2003). Performance analysis of mobile agent in wireless internet application using simulation. (M.Sc Thesis, Faculty of the college of Graduate Studies Lamar University).

Lange, D. B. & Oshima, M. (1999). Seven good reasons for mobile agents. *Communications of the Association for Computing Machinery, 42*(3): 88 - 92

Mawhood-Yunis, A., Nayak, A., Nussbaum, D, & Santoro, N. (2004). Comparing performance of two mobile agent platforms in distributed search. *IEEE/WIC/ACM International Conference On Intelligent Agent Technology* (IAT' 04), pp 425 – 428.

Oke, A. O, Okelana, O. M, & Aderounmu, G. A. (2002). A mobile agent system for electronic shopping. In *Proceedings of the ICT applied to Economic Intelligence* (ICTEI), 105 – 114. August 20-23, Nigeria.

Olajubu, E.A., Aderounmu, G.A., & Akinde, A.D (2004). An agent-based architecture for students' results messanger, Obafemi Awolowo University as case Study. *The Journal of Computer Science and Its Applications, 10*(2): 3-16

Oluwatope, A. O., Aderounmu, G. A., Akande, O. & Adigun, M. O. (2004). An auction scenario in a stock market using mobile agent. *Southern Africa Telecommunication Networks and Applications Conference*, 229 – 234. Western Cape, South Africa.

Seng, W. L. (1999). Mobile agent technology for enterprise distributed applications: An overview and an architectural perspective. *CRC for Distributed System Technology*, Monash University, Caulfield Campus, Caulfield East, Victoria 3145, Australia.

Biographies

G.A. Aderounmu holds a research degree M.Sc./PhD in Computer Science from Obafemi Awolowo University, Ile-Ife, Nigeria (1997 and 2001, respectively). He is a member of the Nigerian Society of Engineers (NSE) and is also a registered computer engineer with Council for the Regulation of Engineering Practice in Nigeria (COREN). He is also a Member of Nigerian Computer Society (NCS) and Computer Professional Registration Council of Nigeria (CPN). He has over 13 years of experience in teaching and research. He is an author of many journal articles in Nigeria and abroad. His special interests include engineering education in Nigeria, curriculum development, and computer communication and network. He is a Visiting Research Fellow to the University of Zululand, Republic of South Africa. He is currently a Senior Lecturer, Deputy Director of the Information Technology and Communication Unit (INTECU) and the Acting Head of the Department of Computer Science and Engineering of the same university.

B. O Oyatokun obtained her research degree M.Sc. Computer Science from University of Ibadan, Ibadan, Nigeria in 2004. Her current research interests are in the areas of computer communications and deployment of mobile agent software management of heterogeneous computer network. She is currently a Ph.D student at the Department of Computer Science , University of Ibadan.

M. O. Adigun holds a research degree PhD in Computer Science from Obafemi Awolowo University, Ile-Ife, Nigeria which he obtained in 1989. Currently, he is a Professor and Head, Department of Computer Science, University of Zululand, Republic of South Africa. He is an author of many journal articles in Nigeria, Republic of South Africa and abroad. His research interests include Software Engineering, Mobile Computing, Modeling and Simulation, and Performance Analysis of Computer System.

The page left blank intentionally.

Performance Modeling of UDP over IP-Based Wireline and Wireless Networks

A. A. Akintola, G. A. Aderounmu, and A. A. Owojori
Obafemi Awolowo University, Ile-Ife, Nigeria

aakintola69@yahoo.com
gaderoun@yahoo.com
folajori2@yahoo.com

M. O. Adigun
University of Zululand, Kwadlangezwa, Republic of South Africa

madigun@pan.uzulu.ac.za

Abstract

The pervasiveness and the seemingly unpopular nature of unidirectional data transfer has greatly necessitated the efforts of this paper. We investigated the performance of User Datagram Protocol (UDP) over IP-based wireline and wireless networks. The conceptual model was developed and tested using Network Simulator 2(NS2) and its bevaviour was monitored over the two networks. The results of the simulation in terms of effective throughput, packet drop/loss, and bandwidth utilization were presented. It reveals that UDP exhibits improved performance degradation on wired networks and that the high throughput is as a result of the fact that UDP does not have flow control protocol as it does not retransmit lost packets.

Keywords: IP networks, UDP, connectionless, bandwidth, throughput, packet drop, unidirectional

Introduction

The ubiquitous nature of IP-based networks has lend credence to the volume of activities and attention accruing to it in the recent times. Driven by the ever-increasing demand for bandwidth and Quality of Service (QoS) guaranteeing, the core of today's network (either wired or wireless) has been evolving. In this research effort, the authors are interested in the behaviour and performance of User Datagram Protocol (UDP) over wired and wireless networks.

UDP is an unreliable protocol because it is unidirectional unlike Transmission Control Protocol (TCP) that is connection-oriented and bi-directional in nature. According to Foster, Kesselman, and Tueke (2001), the rapid increase in network bandwidth and the emergence of new routing and switching technology has made data transfer protocols to become bottlenecks for many applications. Zhang and McLeod (2005) also admitted that the evolving nature of today's Internet has made protocols to be constantly modified in order to optimize performance. Many modifications to the existing protocols have been proposed in the literature to reduce latency. Some of them have been implemented already on the

Internet like pre-fetching web pages the user is likely to access next, while browsing the current displayed page (Crovella & Bardford, 1998) and avoiding the cost of round trip time (RTT) by reducing the number of HyperText Transfer Protocol (HTTP) connections (Padmanabhan & Mogul, 1994).

Motivation

Connectionless Data Transfer is not widely understood as TCP/IP (which is connection-oriented data transfer), it is often difficult in the course of developing service and protocol definitions to adduce a rationale for incorporating UDP, and even more difficult to determine appropriate locations for connectionless service within the layered protocol stack. Since UDP is unidirectional as reproted by Xylomenos and Polyzoz (1999), our aim was to compile a comprehensive set of data describing the performance of UDP over wired and wireless networks in terms of packet loss analysis, bandwidth, and throughput.

There is absolutely no guarantee that the datagram will be delivered to the destination host. Not only the datagram can be undelivered, but it can be delivered in an incorrect order. On the basis of the foregoing, there is the need to carry out a critical analysis of UDP/IP connection on any network; be it wireline or wireless.

Related Research

Network researchers have been improving UDP for many years and have published a series of UDP variations. Although TCP is still dominant in the Internet, the drawbacks inherent in its window based congestion control mechanism prevent its use in high bandwidth-delay product (BDP) environments (Gu, Hong, Mazzuco, & Grossman, 2005). According to Zhang and McLeod (2005), many modifications have been made to the existing protocols in order to reduce latency. Noghani, Kretschmann, and McLeod (2001) suggested the use of multiple TCP connections in conjunction with FTP while the NCSA ("Automatic TCP Window...," 2005) used better estimating bandwidth-delay products by adjusting TCP parameters. However, none of the above mentioned approaches deal particularly with the bevaviour of UDP over various media. Our work will also extend the published results in Eckhardt & Steenkiste (1996) and Nguyen, Katz, Noble, and Satyanarayanan (1996). He & Gary-Chan (2004) reported that packets aggregation was previously proposed for the Internet with the objective to reduce the number of small packets, e.g., the TCP ACKs for web servers (Badrinath & Sudame, 2000), or Voice over IP (VoIP) packets (Tounsi, Tountain, & Kamaoun, 2001).

System Model

In this section, we discuss the conceptual framework for the model of UDP over wired and wireless networks. We also highlighted the model parameters. The model was developed using standard simulation software called Network Simulator 2 (NS2). NS2, an object-oriented simulator, offers the unique capabilities and features required for the system model.

The various networks were defined in NS2 by using nodes and links as building blocks. Nodes are connected by links and contain agents (UDP) and its application CBR (Constant Bit Rate) that are responsible for transmitting and receiving packets. In the process of creating these structures; many of their characteristics are described such as bandwidth, packet drop policy, error rate and other local area network characteristics already present in the simulator. Also, changes that occur in the network at specific times during simulation are scheduled.

The scenario for the Wide Area Network (WAN) model as used in the NS2 environment is as shown in Figure 1. It is worthy of mention that we are only interested in the UDP traffic as shown in the same figure. We abstracted the scenarios of connecting two different networks through wired and wireless means as shown in Figures 2 and 3 respectively. This enabled us to monitor the desired metrics under different conditions.

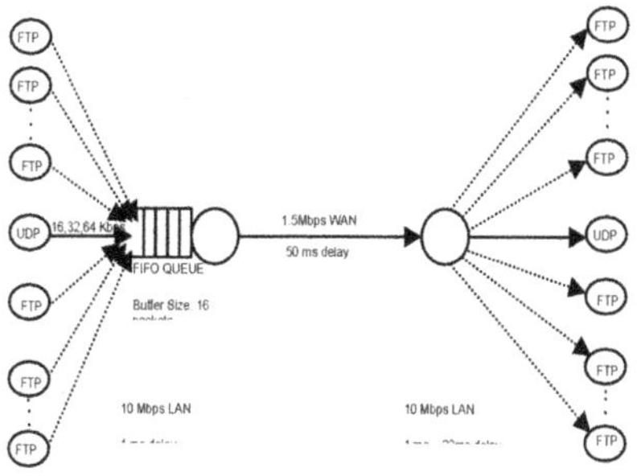

Figure 1: Scenario for Wide Area Network Simulation

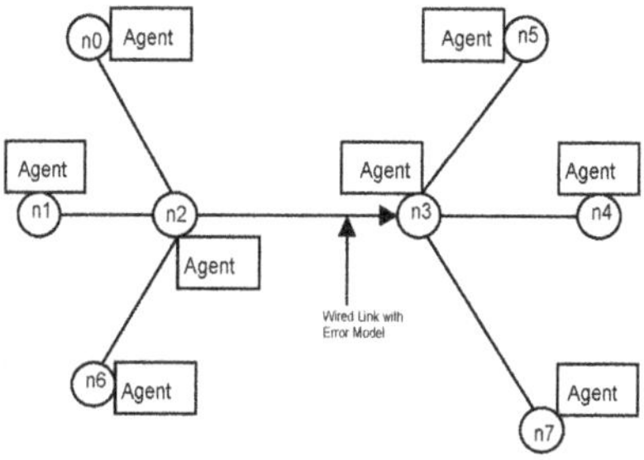

Figure 2: A Model of Two Local Area Networks with Wired Link

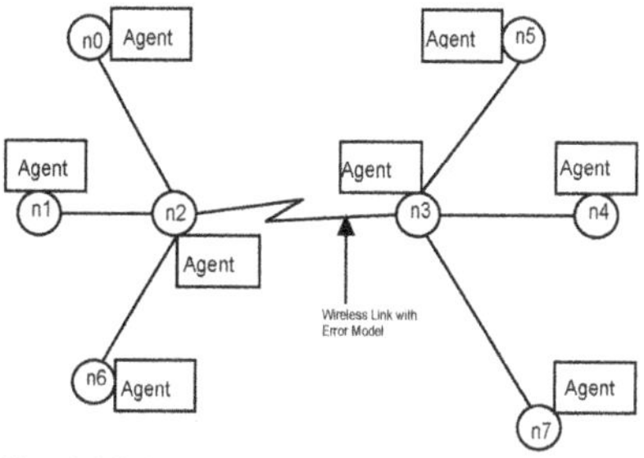

Figure 3: A Model of Two Local Area Networks with Wireless Link

Figure 2 shows a star topology in which n2 and n3 are the main servers between two buildings while the other nodes are located at different points within the buildings. The n2 and n3 are linked together via wired medium. Figure 3 depicts two different networks connected through wireless link; n2 and n3 are the main the servers and are linked via wireless means. The two links; i.e. wired and wireless are with error model.

Model parameters

Here, we specified the model state variables used to describe the abstracted environment in the NS2.

These are:

a) Bandwidth

In this study, it is believed that the bandwidth will be allocated sufficiently to meet the required transmission capacity. In networking, the transmission capacity of a computer or a communication channel is measured in megabits per second (Mbps)

Bandwidth = Packet size / time interval(1)

b) Throughput

This is a measure of the data-transfer rate through a complex communication or networking scheme. Throughput is considered as an indication of the overall performance of the system. In communications, throughput is usually measured as the number of bits or packets processed each second. For the purpose of this work, we used number of packets.

Throughput= Packet (Mb) / time (s)(2)

c) Elapsed Time (sec)

This is the time it takes a packet to travel from the source to the destination;

d) Time Received (sec)

The time at which the destination received each packet sent from the source;

e) Total sent (bytes)

The total packets sent will be determined after the required packets have been sent which will be noted;

f) Total received (bytes)

Due to the features of UDP, packet might be lost during data transfer;

g) Number of packets: total sent / packet size

h) Packet size (bytes)

The packet size will be determined during simulation in which it will be varied;

i) Header size (bytes): header size that the UDP protocol will add to each packet;

j) Total number of packet lost (bytes):

Due to the unreliability nature of UDP, packets could be lost;

k) Packets loss (packets): the system will compute the packet loss through a sink;

l) Percentage received (%): total received / total sent * 100%.

System simulation and results analysis

The simulation was carried out with NS2 in conjunction with MATLAB 6.1. MATLAB 6.1 provides powerful tools for handling data with wide range of parameters under a graphical user interface that allows its objects to be explicitly described. We also used the MATLAB 6.1 to plot the graphs from the data generated from the NS2.

Tracing of Objects

NS2 produced both the visualization trace in a graphical user interface as well as the ASCII text trace corresponding to the events registered at the network when tracing is used; it inserts four objects to the objects in the link: EnqT, DeqT, RecvT and DrpT as shown in Figure 4. EnqT registers information concerning a packet that arrives and is queued at the input queue of the link. If the packets overflow then information concerning the dropped packets is handled by DrpT. DeqT registers information at the instance the packet that is dequeued. RecvT gives information regarding information that has been received at the output of the link.

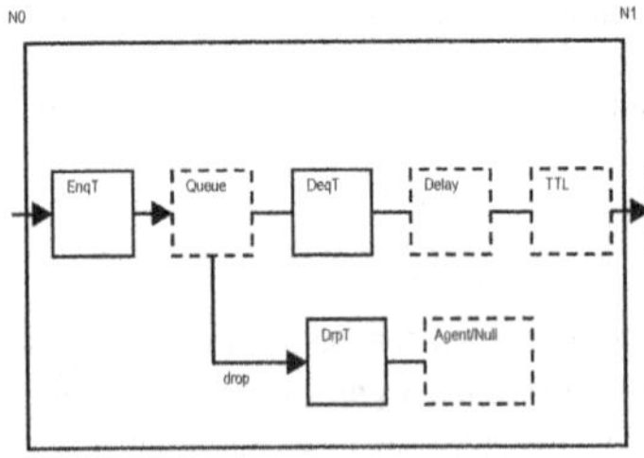

Figure 4: Tracing of Objects

The format of a trace file generated by the simulation follow the sequence below:

- The first field is the event type. It can have the values "r", "+", "-", "d" for "received", "queue", "dequeue", and "dropped" and "r", "s", "f", "D" for "received", "sent", "forward", and "dropped" respectively;

- The second field gives the time at which the event occurs;
- The third field is the node number at which event occurs;
- The next field indicates the packet type, for instance MAC indicates if the packet concerns a MAC layer, AGT indicates the transport layer (for example, udp) packet, RTR indicates a routed packet and IPQ to indicate events related to the inference priority queue (like drop of packets);
- Then following is dashes, which is followed by the global sequence number of the packet;
- The field following gives more information on the packet type such as tcp, ack or udp;
- After this comes the packet size in bytes;
- Then comes the four numbers in square brackets concerning MAC layer information. The first hexadecimal number specifies the expected time in seconds to send the data packet over the wireless channel. The second number indicates the MAC-id of the sending node while the third is that of the receiving node. The fourth number specifies the MAC type (for wireless);
- The next numbers in the second square brackets concerns the IP source and destination addresses, then the "ttl" (Time To Live) of the packet;
- The third square brackets concern the UDP information: its sequence number.

Another information that is also present in the trace data file if the "Movement trace" is turned on has "M" as the first field, which indicates movement. Then the first number is the time, the second is the node number, then followed by the origin and destination locations and then the speed.

Performance Metrics

The system simulation for the network models developed for both the wired and wireless networks are as shown in Figures 5 and 6 respectively. For the purpose of this work, we have used the following parameters to show the behaviour of UDP over IP-based wireline and wireless networks.

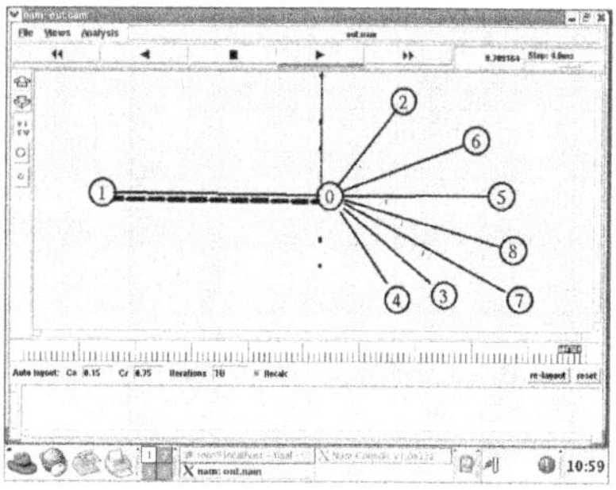

Figure 5: Packet Drop Indication from Wired Network Model

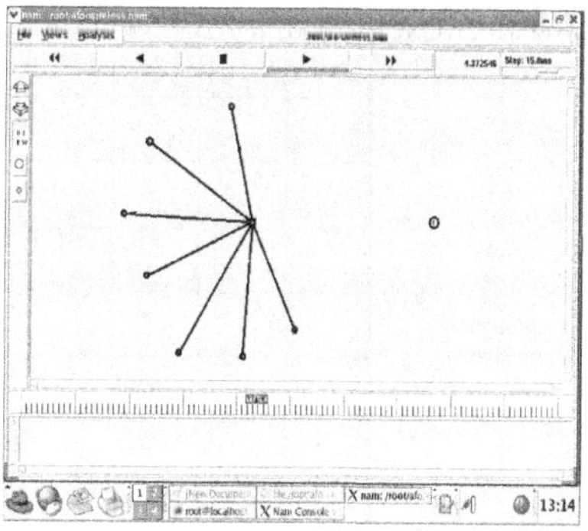

Figure 6: Simulation Interface for a Wireless Network Model

Throughput/Packet Loss Analysis

Packet losses in the wired and wireless networks considered were obtained by extracting the dropped packets in the trace files generated by the simulations. The time at which each packet dropped was also extracted from the trace file and plotted against the effective throughput, which was calculated from the NS2 package called perl. This is as shown in Figure 7.

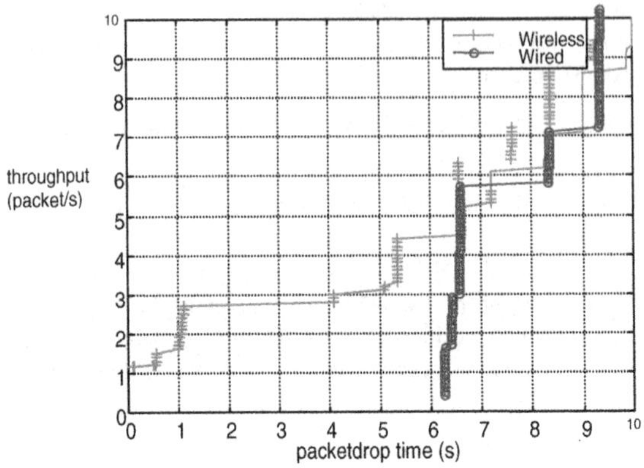

Figure 7: Throughput against Packet Drop on a Wired and Wireless Network

Throughput/Bandwidth

The bandwidth was varied at intervals (i.e. 5, 10, 15. 20, 25, 30, 40, 50, 80, 100 Mbps) and were allocated sufficiently to meet the required transmission capacity. The following parameters were made constant throughout the simulation: packet size, and queue limit. The mean throughputs at each bandwidth intervals were taken into consideration. Figure 8 shows the graph of the effective throughput plotted against the bandwidth.

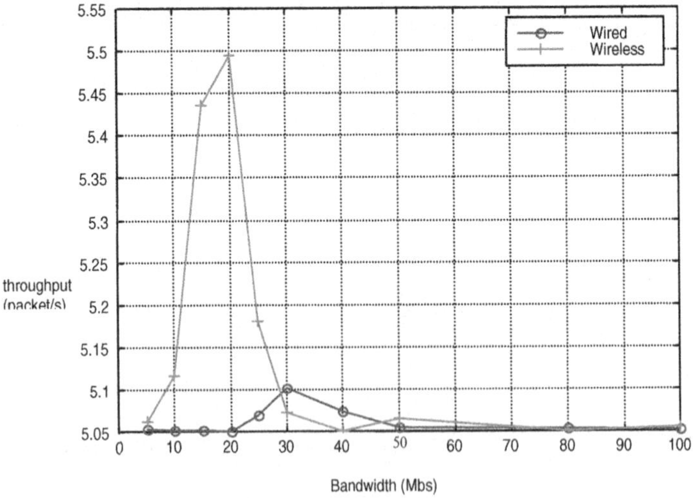

Figure 8: Throughput against Bandwidth on Wired and Wireless network

Interpretation of Results

Effective Throughput vs. Packet drop time

It can be seen clearly from Figure 7 that the packet drop in the wireless network occurred in the early time of 0.365182076s with a gradual increase while the time it occurred for the packet dropped for the wired network was at 6.805292s and thereafter it increases sharply. This shows that wired network has better throughput in terms of packet drop for connectionless data transfer.

Effective Throughput vs. Bandwidth

Wireless network obtained its most effective throughput at 20Mbps; but as the bandwidth increases, a sharp drop in throughput occurred. Wired network obtained its most effective throughput at 30Mbps and thereafter, a linear drop in throughput as the bandwidth increases is observed as shown in Figure 8. This also shows that on wired link, UDP produces a fairly stable and uniform throughput as the bandwidth increases than the wireless network.

Conclusion and Future Work

In this paper, we have investigated the performance of connectionless data transfer over IP-based wired and wireless networks using the Network Simulator 2 and MATLAB 6.1. Carrying UDP traffic over wireless networks often leads to severe degradation in throughput. Our results have amply demonstrated the fact that the most effective throughput for the two networks peaked at different times. In the wireless network, it is unreliable due to its sharp drop after it had reached the maximum. We have also found that the high throughput is as a result of the fact that UDP does not have flow control and it does not retransmit lost packets. In future, we will investigate the performance of UDP over Optical Packet Switched (OPS) networks. We will also consider the behaviour of TCP and more performance metrics will be used.

References

Automatic TCP Window Tuning and Applications. (2005). Retrieved on June 30 from http://www.web100.org/rprojects/

Badrinath, B. R. & Sudame, P. (2000). Gathercast: The design and implementation of a programmable aggregation mechanism for the Internet. *Proceedings of the Ninety International Conference on Computer Communications and Networks*, pp. 206-213.

Crovella, M. & Bardford, P. (1998). The network effects of pre-fetching. *Proceedings of IEEE Infocomm '98*, San Francisco, CA.

Eckhardt, D. & Steenkiste, P. (1996). Measurement and analysis of the error characteristics of an in-building wireless network. *Proceedings of the ACM SIGCOMM '96*, pp. 243-254, August.

Foster, I., Kesselman, C., & Tueke, S. (2001). The anatomy of the grid: Enabling scalable virtual organization. *International Journal of Supercomputer Applications, 15*(3).

Gu, Y., Hong, X., Mazzuco, M, & Grossman, R. (2005). SABUL: A high performance data transfer protocol. Retrieved on June 30 from http://www.rgrossman.com/pdf/sabul-hpdtp-11-02.pdf

He, J. & Gary-Chan, S. H. (2004). TCP and UDP performance for Internet over optical packet-switched networks. *Journal of Computer Networks, 45*, 505-521.

Nguyen, G. T., Katz, R. H., Noble, B., & Satyanarayanan, M. (1996). A trace-based approach for modeling wireless channel behaviour. *Proceedings of the Winter Simulation Conference.*

Noghani, B. S., Kretschmann, S., & McLeod, R. D. (2001). Reducing latency on the Internet using "component-based download" and "file-segment transfer protocol". *PDPTA*, Las Vegas, June.

Padmanabhan, V. N. & Mogul, J. C. (2001). Improving HTTP latency. *Proceedings of the Second International World Wide Web Conference*, Chicago, IL, pp. 995-1005, October.

Tounsi, H, Toutain, L., & Kamoun, F. (2001). Small packets aggregation in an IP domain. *Proceedings of the Sixth IEEE Symposium on Computers and Communications*, pp. 708 – 713.

Xylomenos, G. & Polyzos, G. C. (1999). TCP and UDP performance over wireless LAN. *Proceedings of IEEE INFOCOM '99*, pp. 439-446, March.

Zhang, J. & McLeod, R. D. (2005). A UDP-Based File transfer protocol (UFTP) with Flow Control using a Rough Set Approach. Retrieved on June 30 from http://www.phatpackets.com/papers/jzhang-UFTPpapersubdspac.pdf

Biographies

G.A. Aderounmu holds a research degree M.Sc./PhD in Computer Science from Obafemi Awolowo University, Ile-Ife, Nigeria (1997 and 2001, respectively). He is a member of the Nigerian Society of Engineers (NSE) and is also a registered computer engineer with Council for the Regulation of Engineering Practice in Nigeria (COREN). He is also a Member of Nigerian Computer Society (NCS) and Computer Professional Registration Council of Nigeria (CPN). He has over 13 years of experience in teaching and research. He is an author of many journal articles in Nigeria and abroad. His special interests include engineering education in Nigeria, curriculum development, and computer communication and network. He is a Visiting Research Fellow to the University of Zululand, Republic of South Africa. He is currently a Senior Lecturer, Deputy Director of the Information Technology and Communication Unit (INTECU) and the Acting Head of the Department of Computer Science and Engineering of the same university.

A.A. Akintola obtained his Bachelors and Masters degree in Computer Engineering and Computer Science from Obafemi Awolowo University, Ile-Ife, in 1994 and 2002, respectively. He is a registered computer engineer with Council for the Regulation of Engineering Practice in Nigeria (COREN) and also a member of Nigerian Society of Engineers (NSE). He is an author of many journal articles in Nigeria and abroad. His current research interests are in the areas of teletraffic engineering, mobile/nomadic computing, digital computer networks, hardware system studies, and computer modeling and simulation of streaming video. He is also into the areas of wireless IP networks, error control, and curriculum development. He has over 8 years of experience in teaching and research. He is currently a Ph.D. student and a lecturer at the Department of Computer Science and Engineering of the same university.

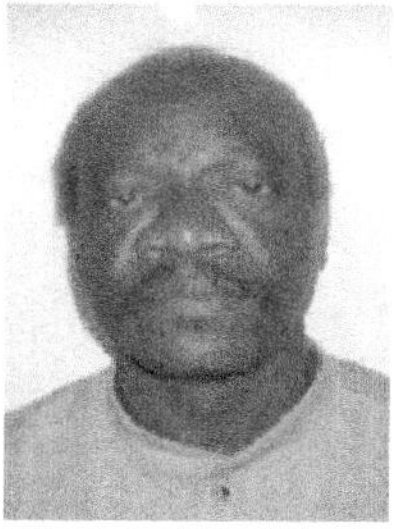

M. O. Adigun holds a research degree PhD in Computer Science from Obafemi Awolowo University, Ile-Ife, Nigeria which he obtained in 1989. Currently, he is a Professor and Head, Department of Computer Science, University of Zululand, Republic of South Africa. He is an author of many journal articles in Nigeria, Republic of South Africa and abroad. His research interests include Software Engineering, Mobile Computing, Modeling and Simulation, and Performance Analysis of Computer System.

A.A. Owojori obtained his Bachelor of Science degree in Computer Engineering from Obafemi Awolowo University, Ile-Ife, in 2005. He is a student member of Nigerian Society of Engineers (NSE). His current research interests are in the areas of computer communications and teletraffic engineering. He is also into protocols design and simulations of wireless communications. Mr. Owojori is currently on National Youth Service.

The page left blank intentionally.

Adding a New Language to VB .NET Globalization – Making the Case for the Kurdish Language

Azad Ali
Indiana University of Pennsylvania
Indiana, PA, USA

azad.ali@iup.edu

Seever Sulaiman
Interthinx
Calabasas, CA, USA

SSulaiman@interthinx.com

Abstract

Starting with the introduction of Visual Studio .NET (VS .NET) application developers can write programs that may be used for different languages listed in VB .NET globalization. However, this globalization list is incomplete and is missing many languages. Among the languages that are missing from VB globalization is the Kurdish language. This paper makes a case for adding the Kurdish language to the list used in VB .NET globalization. The paper starts by explaining about VB .NET globalization, the Kurdish language and then makes a case for adding the Kurdish language. Making the case is based on factors considered in including languages and also on the features of the Kurdish language. A summary and suggested future work is included at the end.

Keywords: VB Globalizations, VB New languages, VB Kurdish, VS Kurdish

Introduction

Developing programs for multiple languages used to be long and daunting tasks. Changing a program so it can be used in another language used to involve making major adjustments to the original program and sometimes used to require writing a totally different program for the new language. For example, developing a program in English and then changing it so it could be used in Arabic would take making major modifications to the original code, adding routines and introducing new tools to make the changes.

The introduction of Visual Studio .NET has changed that drastically. Application developers can write programs in one language (say English) and then with minimum recoding, the programmers can adjust them so they could be displayed in another language (like Arabic). Processing of such changes is helped through the use of a list of languages supported in VS .NET (Finch, 2005). In other words, making modifications from one language to another is made easier because of a list of classes and routines for languages that are supported in VS .NET. However, this list of languages in VS .NET is incomplete and is missing many languages. As a result, missing languages is depriving many from using programs in their own languages. Among the languages that are not available in the VS .NET globalization languages is the Kurdish language.

This paper aims to build a case for introducing the Kurdish language to the list of languages supported in VB .NET globalization. It begins by clarifying the term "Globalization" and the factors that are usually considered when translating programs into different languages. It then explains about the Kurdish language and the features it contains to make it qualify for inclusion in the list of globalization languages. The paper then makes the case based on the factors of the languages supported in the globalization and the features of the Kurdish language. A summary and suggested future work will be included at the end.

About Globalization in VB .NET

The introduction of VS .NET marks a significant increase in the use of "Globalization" term that is used in many programming textbooks (Bradley & Millspauh, 2003; Ekedahl, 2004; Gunderloy, 2003). Newer chapters are introduced in these textbooks to explain about this emerging concept in the programming area. This increase reflects the growing need for writing programs that cover this topic and to explain the concepts associated with it.

Globalization in its simplest term means to be dealing at a global (international) level. It is often referred to when talking about dealings arise across nations at economic levels. But "Globalization" in programming terms refers to a set of roles and procedures related to designing programs for more than one language. Bradely and Millspaugh (2003) explained about this term within the programming context:

> "Globalization is the process of designing your program for multiple cultures and locations. The user interface as well as the output should allow for multiple languages. This is implemented through a set of rules and data for a specific language called culture/locale. A culture/locale contains information about character sets, formatting, currency and measurement rules and methods of sorting (p. 452)".

So the basic purpose of globalization in the programming environment is developing programs so they could be used for more than one language (Mabbut, 2005). As noted before, such writing of programs for more than one language used to be a difficult task, however VB .NET has simplified this process significantly.

The contribution of VB .NET to globalization was through the provision of classes, routines and data that made translating programs into multiple languages simpler. These classes and routines tackled many of the problems that used to make translating programs into multiple languages a difficult process. In other words, VB .NET provides programmers with classes and routines that addressed many of the problematic areas that used to make the task of translating programs into different languages a difficult and daunting undertaking.

Problematic Areas in Globalization

Writers in the programming field identify five specific areas that are potentially problematic when designing a program for multiple languages: First the display of text information. Second, date and time format. Third, formatting numeric and currency data for languages. Fourth, the sort orders for the characters in the languages to be translated to and then the fifth problem is formatting of various other data like phone numbers, postal codes (Ekedahl, 2004; Gunderloy, 2003; Kaplan, 2000).

The first problem is the display of text data for different languages. This may include changing the user interface; display the text information in a particular language, and even different modes of data entries (like right-to-left entries in the Arabic script). This problem can be helped through the "language and globalization settings" in Windows control panel. The introduction of different fonts for various languages helped with this case also. The use of Unicode increased the chances for introducing various fonts that make it possible to virtually include every character in all the languages. VB .NET helped this further through the ability to create resource files and satellite assemblies (Gunderloy, 2003). These last terms refer to the capacity to create multiple user interface files at design time; each file is set up for a different language. Then the users can select the interface they choose for their language.

The second problem is regarding the format for date and time in different languages. This may include the display of month names, days of the week and the various formats for date display and processing. For example, in the US the date is displayed by listing the month first and then the day and year. While in the Arabic world, the day is listed first and then the month and year. The problem gets more complicated when considering different calendar format that may give different dates for starting the year, and different number of days per year. For example, the "Hijri" calendar (Dr. International, 2005; Kaplan, 2000) in Saudi Arabia is a lunar-based calendar and contains smaller number of days per year than the 365 days in the Georgian calendar in the US. Another example is the Baha'i calendar has 19 months each has 19 days (Ekedahl, 2003), which is different than the 12 months and days up to 31 for other calendars. The Thai calendar is another example of a calendar with a different format (Kaplan, 2000).

The third problem is about the display of currency symbols and the formatting for numbers in different languages especially when dealing with number representing monetary values. There are many currency symbols, just to name a few: Dollar in the US, Yen in Japan, and Euro in Europe. These all may need to be displayed when working with a program in different languages. Then, the use of commas and decimal point add more difficulty also. Not all cultures use the same format for numbers regarding the thousand separator and the decimal points. For example, the US uses the comma as a thousands separator and the period for decimal points. The German language uses a period as a thousands separator in numbers and uses a comma to display the decimal points. The French language uses a space as a separator for numbers with thousands and comma for decimal points (Ekedahl, 2003).

The fourth problem that used to make developing international application a difficult task is about the sort order for characters in different cultures. It is customary to use a specific sort order that refers to the order of characters in the alphabet in each of the languages. However, the problem gets complicated when languages add other characters within their alphabet. These characters are called "Diacriticals". Kaplan (2000) lists 23 characters that are used within the alphabet in different languages. Among these characters are included the grave (ã), the acute (é), and the tilde (ň) The French language for example has a grave accent in their alphabet and the German use of an umlaut (Ekedahl, 2004). Turkish language sometimes has up to four versions of the same letter depending on the diacriticals used with the letter (Kaplan, 2000). Further, some languages combine two characters into one letter of the alphabet, thus the term "combining character sequence" is used in some programs (Gunderloy, 2003).

The fifth and last problem regarding international application is the use of postal codes, phone number formats and social security number formats. In some of the applications developed for users in the US, programs allow the entry of five digits postal code (or sometimes nine digits). But not all countries use the same five or nine digits. Some countries do not even use postal codes. The same thing can be said about phone numbers. Not all countries use ten digits for displaying and storing phone numbers and some countries do not use social security numbers in the same way used in the US.

The problems mentioned above are made easier to solve through the use of procedures stored within VB .NET. These procedures use data regarding date, time, sorting sequence and others that are stored in VB .NET for each of the languages that are supported in VB .NET globalization. But entering data for languages can be more complicated when taking into consideration the variety of languages and countries where they are spoken. For example, the English language is spoken in different countries (like US, Britain, Australia) and each country has its own currency symbol, date format and other differences. Another example is that a language can be written in more than one alphabet. The Azeri language in Azerbaijan can use both the Latin and Cyrillic alphabets and each of the alphabets has its own sort order and set of roles. Thus, to solve the problems resulted from these differences, new terms of culture, language and locale have been introduced to VB .NET globalization.

Language, Culture and Locale

The introduction of VB .NET simplified the development of international applications by providing classes that help with the problems listed above. VB .NET stores data about different languages that it has identified to simplify developing programs for these languages. But defining a language runs into newer problems of having multiple languages for each country, multiple alphabets for the language and other issues as noted above. So to solve these newer problems, a newer classification of language, culture and locale has been used in VB .NET.

Language is a general term and refers to the languages spoken and the alphabet they use. But a culture is a more precise term than language. Gunderloy (2003), explained about culture in VB .NET:

> "A culture identifies everything that might need to be localized in an application, which require you to know more than just the language. For example, just knowing that an application uses English as its user interface language doesn't give you enough information to completely localize it: Should you format dates and currency amounts in that application, in a way appropriate to the United States, to the United Kingdom, to Canada, to Australia or to New Zealand (p. 5572)".

While a language is a spoken language, a culture refers to the specific population that speaks the language. A locale is usually noted within the culture. Bradley and Millspaugh (2003) call Locale "the rules and data for a specific language" and explained it further that it "Contains information about character sets, formatting, currency and measurement rules, and methods of sorting (p. 452)". Ekedahl (2004) uses an example in VB .NET to list the data that are stored for various languages and cultures. The display of the output from this program is shown in Figure 1. As a user clicks one of the cultures, the program displays the data specific to that culture.

Figure 1 displays the data about the Arabic language and the Iraqi culture after the user clicked on the language and culture combination. It shows the data about the name, currency, date/time, calendar and others. Note also that the month name is displayed in Arabic. All of these different data are processed and displayed through classes and routines stored in VB .NET for each of the language/culture listed. To standardize the storage and retrieval of data, VB .NET uses a coding for the language/culture similar to the code followed by the International Standardization Organization (ISO).

International Language Standardization

ISO is the International Standards Organizations (or International Organization for Standardization) that develops standards used in different countries. The ISO is responsible also for developing various standards that are used in the computer field. Among ISO standards are two standards for languages and cultures. These standards are termed ISO 639-1 and ISO 639-2. These two standards are used for giving codes to various cultures and languages in VB .NET globalization. Ekedhal (2004) explained about all of this:

> "To identify language uniquely, standards organization, such as the International Organization for Standardization (ISO), has created a standard coding system for

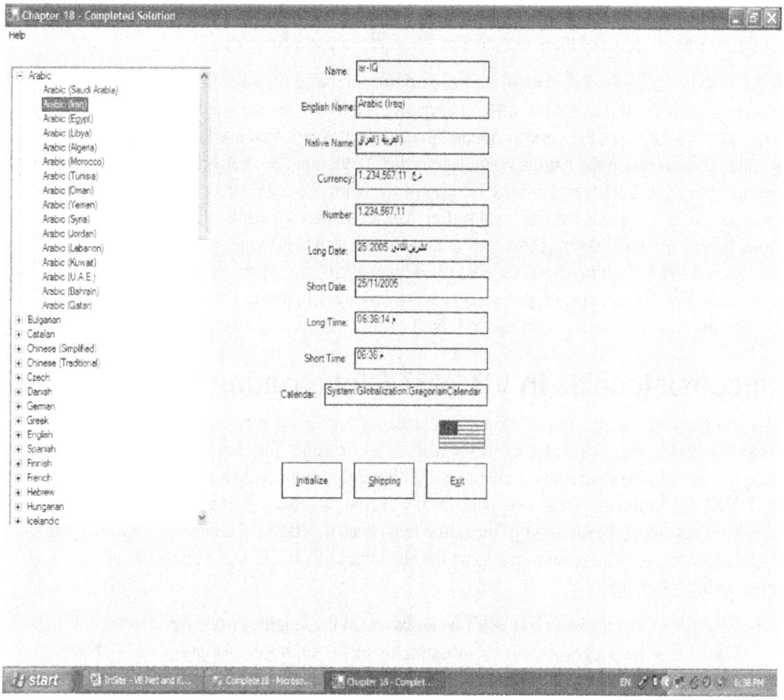

Figure 1 – Display of Data for Languages/Cultures Using a Program in VB .NET (Ekedahl, 2004)

> all languages. The ISO 639-1 standard defines a two-character country code for each language. ISO refers to this two-character code as alpha-2 code. For example "en" is the alpha code for English, "fr" is the alpha code for French.
>
> The ISO standard defines what is called the alpha-3 code. The alpha-3 code contains a 3-character specification where dialectical differences between cultures (countries) are significant" (p. 1052).

So based on the above explanation, the Arabic language is given a code of AR, while the language of Arabic that is spoken in Iraq is given the code "IQ". Thus the code AR-IQ represents the culture code for Arabic in Iraq In the same way, the code Az-Cyrl uses the Azeri language spoken in Azerbaijan that uses the Cyrillic alphabet.

The list of languages that are coded in ISO 639.2 is long and is listed across many pages that exceed hundreds of languages (ISO 639.2, 2005). This list also exceeds the number of languages listed in VB .NET globalization. Among these languages that are included in the ISO 639.2 list of languages is the Kurdish language that is given the code "kur-ku" in ISO.

About the Kurdish Language

Kurdish is the language that is spoken by the Kurdish people. Most of the Kurds live in the area historically know as Kurdistan. The boundaries of Kurdistan extend from Iraq, Iran, Syria, Turkey and some parts of Azerbaijan (Kurdistan, 2005). The total population of the Kurds is varied according to different statistics. Some estimate the population of the Kurds as high as 39 million people (Kurdish Population, 2005) while others give a more conservative number of 26 million (Omniglot, 2005b). Most of the Kurds live in the southern part of Turkey.

The Kurdish language is of the Indo-European origin, similar to the Farsi (Persian) language. However, the different dialects use different scripts. The Kurds in Iraq use the Arabic script while the Kurds in Turkey uses the Latin script and the Kurds in Azerbaijan use the Cyrillic alphabet. The main dialect among the Kurdish language is the Sorani (spoken in Iraq and Iran), and the Kermnji (spoken in Turkey and Syria). Given that the Kurds do not own an independent state, their recognition in various international setting has been often undermined and underrepresented. Among the international settings that they are underrepresented is the globalization list of languages in VB .NET. In other words, the Kurdish language is not among the languages that are supported in VB .NET. Thus, programmers cannot display data that are specific to the Kurdish language and Kurdish users cannot use VB .NET programs that display data in their language.

Inconsistencies in VB .NET Globalization Languages

The list of languages supported in VS .NET globalization does not represent all the languages spoken worldwide and it excludes many languages. We searched the languages that it supports and compared it to the languages available in ISO but did not find a clear pattern that is followed in VB .NET for including certain languages while excluding others. Basically, there are many inconsistencies among the method of including languages in VB .NET globalization list of supported languages. Lack of pattern in adding the languages to VB .NET globalization are explained in the following:

1- The list of languages in VB .NET is not based on the languages presented in the ISO. The ISO list of languages includes a substantially higher number of languages than those listed in VB .NET globalization.

2- The repeated name of countries and nations in VB .NET documentation may give the impression that the list of languages is based on list of countries or nations. However, the VB .NET globalization languages are not based on either countries or nations. The UN lists 191 member-nations (List of member states, 2005) within its charter. The CIA lists 239 countries (CIA – The World Factbook, 2005) that included both members and non-members of the (UN In Brief (2005).

3- The list of languages is not based on population either. There are cultures that are listed with less population than many that are not listed.

4- The list of Arabic languages in VB .NET globalization includes 15 different cultures. The total number of Arabic countries is 21 (Arabic German Consulting, 2005), thus it is missing 6 countries like Sudan, Somalia, Djibouti and others. Again, we did not find a pattern for including these countries while excluding others.

5- There are several cultures that are listed separately, while there is minimal difference in their cultural data. For example, the Arabic culture in Iraq and Syria has similar data except for the currency. Yet these two cultures are listed separately.

6- The Syrian culture is listed twice, once under the Arabic language and the other under the Syriac language. But this does not include similar minorities in other countries like the Barbar in Morocco, the Kurds in Iraq, the Armenian in Turkey and the Hausa in Nigeria (Dr. International, 2005).

Making the Case for Adding the Kurdish Language

Basically, the Kurdish language is not included in the list of languages available in VB .NET globalization thus depriving the Kurdish people from displaying and using VB .NET programs in their own language. This section is to make a case for adding the Kurdish language.

Microsoft grouped the Kurdish with other ones that uses the Arabic script. Dr. International (2005) is a forum provided by Microsoft that answers questions regarding global development and global portal. Dr. International described the process by which the Kurdish language is grouped:

> "The Arabic Windows code page (1256) is actually referring to the Arabic *language,* rather than the Arabic script (which supports many additional languages, such as Baluchi, Berber, Farsi, Kashmiri, Kazakh, Kirghiz, Kurdish, Pashto, Sindhi, Uighur, Urdu, and more). Unfortunately, there is simply not enough room on code page 1256 to support all of the additional characters that these other languages require (p. 1)".

But a closer examination of the list of languages supported in VB .NET globalization reveals that there are many languages listed in the ISO while they do not appear within the languages in VB .NET globalization. Among these missing languages include Abkhazian (abk), Acoli (ch), Caddo(cad), Efik (efi), Kurdish (Kur) and other languages. So basically, people speaking these languages have to view and program in other languages. In the case of the Kurdish language, it can be implied from Microsoft statement (see the statement form Dr. International above), that the Kurds have to view their language in Arabic instead.

But the Arabic and Kurdish are two different languages. Although a portion of the Kurds uses the Arabic alphabet, but there are many differences between the two languages. Also, there are many features within the Kurdish languages that a case can be made to including it within the languages in VB .NET globalization. The case can be made based on the following facts:

1- The Kurdish language uses the same Arabic script but it has different set of alphabet. The number of characters in the Arabic alphabet is 28 letters (Omniglot, 2005a) and the number of letters in the Kurdish language is 36 letters (Omniglot, 2005b). This changes the entire set of text, sort order and others.

2- Different set of fonts are available for the Kurdish language such Ali-K-Samik, Ali-K-Sahifa, K-Dylan and others. Although these fonts can be used in Microsoft Office products, but it still cannot be used in VB .NET globalization. The availability of Kurdish fonts would make changing the display of the interface easier.

3- The use of dates is different from the Kurdish language than the Arabic, including the name of the months and the name of the days.

4- The use of the Arabic script is not limited to the Kurdish language; it is also used in the Farsi (Persian), yet the Farsi is supported in the globalization languages of VB .NET.

5- The population of the Kurds exceeds those of many cultures that are included in the globalization languages. Even if we take only the Kurds in Iraq, by every estimate their population exceeds four million (Kurdistan, 2005; Omniglot, 2005b) many countries (cultures) that are listed in the globalization languages.

6- All Kurdish scripts, whether they will be Arabic, Latin or even Cyrillic have their own set of characters and they are different from their neighboring languages.

7- The Kurdish language sometimes combines two characters into one. This makes sorting the data different than the Arabic characters. In other words, it cannot be assumed that just because both languages have the same alphabet that the names or addresses will be sorted in the same way, they will not.

Summary and Future Work

This paper explained about adding a new language to the VB .NET international language settings. It made the case regarding adding the Kurdish language based on the characters of languages in the globalization settings and the features of the Kurdish language. It further explained about the globalization setting, the problems that were encountered when designing application for multiple languages and then showed how VB .NET helped solving some of these problems through storing data for different languages. We made the case for the addition of the Kurdish language based on these facts and based on a program written in VB .NET 2003.

At the time of this writing, VS .NET 2003 was the latest version of Visual Studio that was available in the market. However, we learned that a new version of VS .NET 2005 is about to be released in the near future. According to our information, the new version of visual studio still does include the Kurdish language among its set of globalization languages. Based also on the inquiries we made that Visual Studio .NET version 2005 contains new classes that enable programmers to add their own customized cultures. So if Microsoft continues on excluding Kurdish from the globalization languages, this may create a situation that it will be helpful to write another paper that shows the technical details and steps of how to add the Kurdish language as a new customized culture to VB .NET programs. It is our intention to write this new paper that will explain about the steps required and program code specifics for adding the Kurdish language.

References

Arabic German Consulting. (2005). Arab countries and links to Arabic web sites. Retrieved November 28, 2005 from http://www.arab.de/arabinfo/arabinfo.htm.

Bradley, J. C. & Millspaugh, A. C. (2003). *Advanced programming using Visual Basic.NET.* Boston: Irwin McGraw Hill.

CIA – The World Factbook. (2005). The world factbook: Rank order – Population. Retrieved November 28, 2005 from http://www.cia.gov/pulications/factbook/rankorder/2119rank.html

Dr. International (2005). Ask Dr. International. Retrieved November 28, 2005 from http://www.microsoft.com/globaldev/DtIntl/columns.

Ekedahl, M. (2004). *Programming guide to developing and implementing Windows-based applications with Microsoft Visual Basic .NET.* Reno, NV: Thomson Course Technology.

Finch, T. (2005). Internationalization. Retrieved November 9, 2005 from http://www.vb-helper.com/essay9.htm.

Global Development and Computing Portal (2005). Frequently asked questions: Locales & languages. Microsoft Corporation. Retrieved November 15, 2005 from http://www.microsoft.com/globaldev/DrIntl/faqs/Locales.mspx

Gunderloy, M. (2003). *MCAD/MCSD Developing and implementing Windows-based applications with Visual Basic .NET and Visual Studion .NET.* Indianapolis: QUE Publishing.

ISO 639.2 (2005). *Codes for representation of names of languages.* Library of Congress. Retrieved November 15, 2005 from http://www.loc.gov/standards/iso639-2/englangn.html

List of Member States. (2005). Retrieved November 28, 2005 from http://www.un.org/overview/unmember.html

Mabbut, D. (2005). Globalization in Visual Basic .NET. Cultural Code: Numbers and VB.NET. Retrieved November 8, 2005 from http://visualbasic.about.com/od/using vbnet/a/blobvbnet1.htm

Kaplan, M. S. (2000). *Internationalization with Visual Basic. The authoritative solution.* Indianapolis, IN: Sams Publishing.

Kurdistan. (2005). Iraqi Kurdistan. Retrieved November 28, 2005 from http://www.unpo.org/member.php?arg=34

Kurdish Population. (2005). The distribution of the Kurdish population. Retrieved November 28, 2005 from http://www.geocities.com/kurdishcommunityofottawa/population.htm.

Omniglot. (2005a). Arabic alphabet, pronunciation and language. Retrieved November 28, 2005 from http://www.omniglot.com/writing/kurdish.htm.

Omniglot. (2005b). Kurdish language, alphabet and pronunciation. Retrieved November 9, 2005 from http://www.omniglot.com/writing/kurdish.htm.

UN In Brief (2005). How the UN works. Retrieved November 28, 2005 from http://www.un.org/overview/brief1.html

Visual Basic and Visual C# Concepts (2005). Introduction to international application in Visual Basic and Visual C#. Microsoft Corporation. Retrieved November 4, 2005 from http://msdn.microsoft.com/library/en-us/vbcon/html/vbinternationalapplication.aspx.

Biographies

Azad Ali, D.Sc., Associate Professor of Technology Support and Training at Eberly College of Business – Indiana University of Pennsylvania has 22 years of combined experience in areas of financial and information systems. He holds a bachelor degree in Business Administration form the University of Baghdad, an M.B. A. from Indiana University of Pennsylvania, an M.P.A. from the University of Pittsburgh, and a Doctorate of Science in Communications and Information Systems form Robert Morris University. Dr. Ali's research interests include object oriented languages, web design tools, and curriculum design.

Seever Sulaiman, MBA, is a Chief Technology Officer of Interthinx which develops fraud detection and compliance tools for the mortgage industry. Interthinx has recently been formed as the merger of the equals between AppIntelligence, Inc. and Sysdome Corporation. Sulaiman possesses over eleven years of experience in the field of information technology, and eight years in the mortgage industry. He now holds the job of Chief Technology Officer and directs the product development and implementation efforts of the organization. Sulaiman holds a master's degree in business administration from Webster University and a bachelor's degree in computer engineering from the University of Baghdad.

The page left blank intentionally.

Preparing Undergraduate Students for IT Certification

Akram Al-Rawi, Faouzi Bouslama, and Azzedine Lansari
College of Information Systems, Zayed University
Abu Dhabi, UAE

akram.alrawi@zu.ac.ae faouzi.bouslama@zu.ac.ae
azzedine.lansari@zu.c.ae

Abstract

Current demand for Information System (IS) graduates requires that they master specific technical skills needed by industry and government institutions. Revising the IS curriculum to keep it up to date while meeting demands of the Information Technology (IT) labor market continues to be a challenging task. In order to graduate students that are competitive, post-secondary educational institutions must adopt a new methodology where IT certification is an integral part of the IS curriculum. The IEEE and ACM recognize the importance of IT certification and provide its members with over 800 online courses that lead to various IT certificates. The selection of the appropriate IT certificate for integration into the IS curriculum is a complex task as it entails a thorough knowledge of the curriculum and the certificate objectives. The goal of this paper is to propose a selection of IT certificates which can be readily integrated into the IS curriculum. Three potential certification tracks for the purpose of this study are identified: Networking, Programming, and IT hardware and software. A list of vendors and non-vendors IT certificates and their exam requirements is developed, and the IS courses which can lead to the listed IT certificates are identified. This identification is based on matching specific course objectives with the IT certificate and the timeline needed for the certificate completion. The selection of the IT certificates for each track is optimized to facilitate both student learning and the completion of the certificate. Integrating IT certification in computing curricula makes IS programs more attractive to students. Moreover, the acquisition of IT certification is a valued asset for graduates seeking employment or advancement in the computing field.

Keywords: Information Systems, IT certifications, Curriculum design, IS courses.

Introduction

Certification establishes a standard of competency in specific area and job roles (Montante & Khan, 2001). This helps industry to determine that employees meet the required credentials for different jobs roles thus requiring less training during the initial employment period. Hence, some job criteria require individuals to be certified in order to be considered for employment. To the certified individual, certification provides a greater sense of confidence in their abilities and a measure of professional expertise and understanding of the job role and products used in that role. It is for these reasons that certification is becoming increasingly popular and in high demand. Many training companies are providing certification-training classes at high costs all across the globe. Unlike traditional academic degrees, some certificates are specific to narrow fields or even to individual products. The aim is to provide targeted skills that have immediate applicability in the workplace.

Cisco, Microsoft, Sun, Novel, Oracle, and other vendors offer certification programs for their own products and related job roles. Third-party companies around the world provide certificate-training classes for these vendors and, increasingly, offer certifications of their own that are venders neutral. Academic institutions, from vocational and technical schools to large universities, are beginning to provide similar training in their curricula to prepare students for certification in special areas (Peterson, Morneau, & Saad, 2003). This paper presents ideas for making changes to the existing IS curricula so that courses would help students prepare for certifications in areas such as Networks, Java programming, Hardware and Software, and Internet Technology.

Certification Consensus

There appears to be a consensus in the community about the importance of certification (Tripp, 2002; Cantor, 2002). In a 2001 IEEE Computer Society survey of software engineering professionals, more than 70% of the respondents agreed that certification would fill a need for improving the software engineering profession and that a software engineering certification program could be used to improve the engineering workforce. More than 67% agreed that certification helps assess an individual's software engineering knowledge and skills. While the role of certification is primarily for the public benefit, individual practitioners may also benefit. The participants in this survey were given a list of eight possible benefits of certification and asked to pick up to three that would best describe the benefits to an individual software engineering practitioner. More than 80% of respondents felt that certification provides recognized evidence of professional capability. Two-thirds felt that certification helps assess an individual's software engineering knowledge and skills, while 44 percent felt that it leads to greater professional recognition. Individuals may also seek certification for personal benefits such as increased opportunity for upward mobility, better ability to compete in the job market, and increased professional credibility, although these benefits were much lower rated by respondents.

In the same survey, respondents identified the benefits of certification to an employer hiring a practitioner. The highest ranking was given to the statement that certification provides confidence in a standard set of knowledge areas with which the individual will be familiar. Employers may also view certification as a means for improving job performance and rewarding employees. Employers may also find that training certified employees take less time. Although the survey targeted software engineering certification the same argument is true for any other IT certification.

Motivation to Include IT Certification in IS Curricula

Certification can be defined as an indicator or confirmation of a person's adequate knowledge and skills in a specified occupation or a particular specialty in that occupation. Certification can be classified into two categories: Vendor specific certification, such as Cisco CCNA or Microsoft MOS, and certification issued by vendor neutral organization or professional associations such as CompTIA and ECDL. Some certificates such as the one issued by Cisco are generally issued for a defined period of time after which there is a need to pass another series of examination to demonstrate continued competency. Other certifications such as the ones issued by CompTIA do not have an expiration date.

Increasingly, employers are turning to certifications as a means to ensure that prospective employees actually do have the required skills for an occupational specialty (Koziniec & Dixon, 2002; Zeng, 2004). Employers are asking educational institutions to incorporate certification exam opportunities into their programs as a further way for students to demonstrate the necessary workplace skills, along with their diplomas. On the other hand, students find that certifications can be earned in a much shorter time period than full associate degree programs take, and that certification often leads to higher starting salaries. There are a numbers of reasons that drive the need to include IT certification as a critical component of IS/IT curricula. A rapid change in workplace technology requirements has increased the burden on workers and employers to maintain workplace skills and to document worker competency. Training students for the workforce and providing them with cutting edge IT skills needed to compete in college education is driving administrators to implement IT certification programs. Students are attracted to colleges that teach leading edge technologies and provide avenues to acquire IT certifications. Employers have a tendency to hire graduates that have acquired IT certification in addition to their degree. Currently University and colleges that offer IT certification often separate IT certification objectives from their undergraduate curricula. It is however important to include IT certification objectives into key IS courses in order to provide an opportunity for students to acquire certification upon completion of these courses.

Certificates That can be Integrated into IS Curricula

There are many IT certificates which can be integrated into various IS curricula. Some of these certificates are vender neutrals such as CompTIA's A+, Network+, i-Net+, and Security+. Other certificates are associated with certain manufacturer such as Cisco CCNA and CCNP. Cisco academy also offers courses that lead to non Cisco certificates such as A+ and Sun Certified Programmer for Java 2. Microsoft also offers a lot of certificates starting from a simple certificate such as MOS to a more complicated certificate such as MCSE. Here, we will address some of the most popular certificates and how they can be integrated into a well established IS curriculum. The proposed IS curriculum is based on the IS 2002 model curriculum, as shown in Figure1.

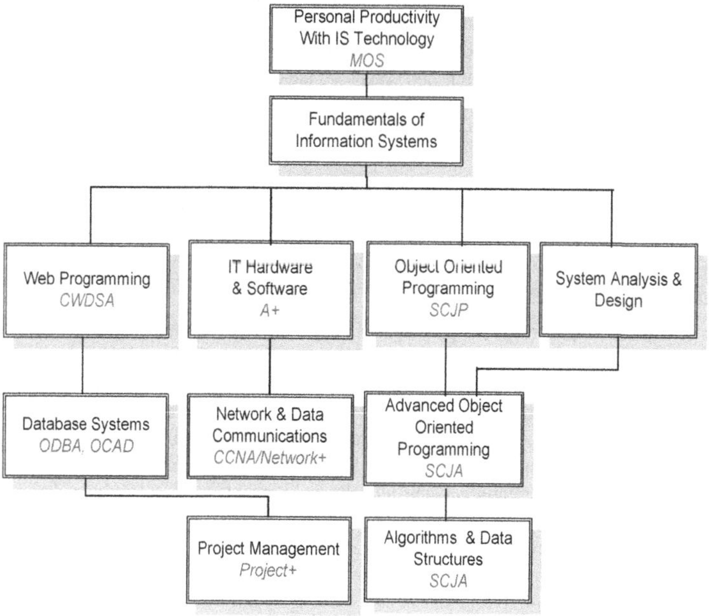

Figure 1: Implementation of the IS 2002 core curriculum with respective IT certificates

Such a curriculum has been developed to fulfill the ABET requirements for accreditation. The IS 2002 model curriculum includes 33 credit hours of IS core courses while a typical degree requires 120 to 126 credit hours. To address the needs of industry for IS graduates to acquire certification the IS 2002 model curriculum is strengthened by including IT certification tracks. Faculty and College administration can provide various tracks to strengthen their IS curriculum. For example a networking track will include courses which lead to MOS, CCNA and possibly CCNP certification; a programming track may include courses which lead to MOS, SCJP and SCJA; a web developer track may include course which lead to the MOS, CWDSA, i-Net+, and Project+; a database administrator track would include courses which lead to the MOS; ODBA and OCAD; and an IT hardware and software track which could lead to the MOS, A+, Network+, and i-Net+. The following certificates are investigated briefly for possible integration into an IS course.

A+ Certificate

A+ certificate is a CompTIA-sponsored testing program that certifies the competency of entry-level computer service technicians. There are two different A+ exams that lead to certification. One exam focuses on Core Hardware and the other on OS Technologies. These tests cover a broad range of technologies but are not vendor-specific. The two exams cost $318. A+ certification signifies that the certified individual possesses the knowledge and skills essentials for a successful entry-level computer service technician. The A+ test is available globally in a variety of languages through testing centers, which are listed on the CompTIA website at http://www.CompTIA.org. The Cisco Networking Academy's IT Essentials I: PC Hardware and Software course helps to prepare students to take both of the exams necessary for this certification. Cisco press also publishes a textbook and a lab manual for this course. Community colleges in the US and Devry University offers a course which prepare students for the A+ certification exams. However, they do not have a mechanism to make the student take the certification exam. IS 2002 (Gorgone, Davis, Valacich , Topi, Feinstein, & Longenecker, 2002) model curriculum has a core course called IT Hardware and System Software (IS 2002.4). This course can be used to integrate the A+ certificate and typically it requires four to five semester hours. Cisco curriculum for this course includes 70 hours of instruction plus a lab component. Besides Cisco textbook and lab manuals there are few textbook from course technology and one textbook from Sybex that can be used for this course. However, one of the main features of our method of offering this course is that in order to pass the course the student must pass the certification exam. This requirement insures that the student has actually mastered the needed skills to pass the course and has also acquired the credentials to show competency at an international level by passing the certification exam.

Network+ Certificate

Network+ Certification is a CompTIA-sponsored testing program, which examines an individual's networking skills. This certification is intended for entry-level network professionals. The Network+ certification certifies that the successful candidate knows the layers of the OSI model, can describe the features and functions of network components and has the skills needed to install, configure, and troubleshoot basic networking hardware peripherals and protocols. The Cisco Networking Academy Program's CCNA1 through CCNA4 helps to prepare students to take the Network+ exam. The test is currently available globally in different languages. However, the CCNA1 through CCNA4 curriculum is designed to cover the objectives of CCNA certificate. Course Technology and Sybex has a textbook that can be used to teach the certificate (Dean, 2004; Grice, 2004). IS 2002 model curriculum has one core course in Networking and data Communications (IS 2002.6) and this course can be used to integrate this certificate. The course can be covered in a 4 semester hour course which has a lab component. The lab component requires few PC's with networking interfacing cards, hubs, switches, and networking operating systems such as Windows 2003 server, Linux, and AppleTalk. There is a single exam for the certificate which consist of 60 multiple-choice question and the cost of the exam is $218. Community colleges in the US offer a course to help the student achieve Network+ certificate. However, they do not require the student to take the certification exam.

Server+ Certificate

Server+ Certification is a CompTIA sponsored testing program that deals with Industry Standard Server Architecture (ISSA) issues, such as RAIDS, SCSI, multiple CPUs, SANs – and more. The level of complexity is above that of the fundamentals of a PC, making the A+ certification a good pre-cursor to Server+. This certification is geared toward mid to upper level technicians responsible for server hardware maintenance. There is one exam, which covers an in-depth understanding of planning, installing, configuring and maintaining servers, including knowledge of server-level hardware implementations, data storage subsystems, data recovery and I/O subsystems. Interrelationships of all parts of the server systems and the transmissions of their actions are also covered. The Cisco Networking Academy Program's IT Essentials II: Network Operating Systems along with IT Essentials I: PC Hardware and Software will help prepare students to take the Server+ exam. The certificate objectives can be integrated in one IS elective course. Course Technology offer textbooks on Server+ and Sybex offer reference book. A course technology textbook (Conrad, 2002) can be used to integrate this certificate in one IS elective course. The exam fee for the certificate is $218.

Linux+ Certificate

Linux+ Certification is a CompTIA sponsored testing program, which measure foundation-level Linux operating system proficiency. This certification is appropriate for individuals who are interested in demonstrating fundamental Linux knowledge and skills. The exam covers basic installation, operation and troubleshooting services for the Linux operating system and hardware on workstations and servers. System administration basics are also part of the Linux+ learning objectives. The Cisco Networking Academy Program's Fundamentals of UNIX along with IT Essentials II: Network Operating Systems will help prepare students to take the Linux+ exam. There are no prerequisites for this certification; however, CompTIA recommends the possession of A+ and Network+ certifications. The cost of the exam is $218 and it consists of multiple-choice questions and covers six domains, these are:

- Installation
- Management
- Configuration
- Security
- Documentation
- Hardware

The certificate objectives can be integrated into a single IS course such as UNIX Operating Systems. Course Technology provides several textbooks for this certification, among them one which can be used to integrate the certification objectives into an IS course (Eckert & Schitka, 2005).

Project+ Certification

Project+ certification is a vendor-neutral credentials recognized worldwide for the management of IT projects. The Project+ was transferred from the Gartner Institute to CompTIA in February 2001, and upgraded in November 2003. The Project+ designation is achieved by passing one conventional exam that covers best practices in project management methods and processes, critical business knowledge and important interpersonal skills. Project+ focuses on people skills much more than the usual technical certification programs. Soft skills incorporated include conflict resolution, negotiation, communication, team building/leadership and setting and mapping expectations. It is also a core requirement for the Novell CNE certification. Sybex has a study guide reference book developed for this certificate. Course Technology also has several reference books from the ILT series. However, this series can be used to study the certificate objectives but can not be used as a textbook. The exam consists of 80 multiple-choice questions and the time allowed is 90 minutes and it cost $218. The exam objectives cover four domains, these are:

- Project Initiation and Scope Definition
- Project Planning
- Project Execution, Control and Coordination
- Project Closure, Acceptance and Support

IS 2002 model curriculum includes one course called Project Management and Practice (IS 2002.10). This course can be used to integrate the Project+ certification objectives.

Sun Certified Programmer for Java2 Platform (SCJP)

Sun Certified Programmer for Java 2 is a Sun Microsystems certification covering the basic syntax and structure of the Java programming language. The current edition of the SCJP exam is based on the Java2 platform, version 1.5. In general, this exam is fairly comprehensive examination of one's knowledge of the latest version of the Java programming language and of few key packages that belong to the Java standard library. It covers concepts, reserved words and language structures and capabilities as well as elements of the standard Java programming environment. Some basic understanding of object-oriented design, development, testing and implementation is absolutely essential for prospective exam candidates. Specifically, these are the seven topics evaluated in this exam:

- Declarations, Initialization and Scoping
- Flow control
- API Contents
- Concurrency
- OO Concepts
- Collections/Generics
- Fundamentals

The CX-310-055 SCJP exam may be taken in any authorized Prometric testing center. It's a multiple choice and drag and drop exam, comprised of 72 questions that must be answered in 175 minutes or less. In order to pass, the candidates must correctly answer at least 43 of the 72 questions (59%). Sun sell the exam voucher for $150 then you need to schedule an appointment at a Prometric testing center, and the certificate is valid for a certain period of time. Cisco Networking Academy Program offers a course called Fundamentals of Java Programming which is designed to prepare the student for this certificate. Sun Microsystems offer three courses in Java to prepare students for this exam. http://www.sun.com/training/certification/objectives/index.html

The IS 2002 model curriculum include one core course in programming and problem solving (IS 2002.5). However, this certificate can not be integrated into a single Java programming course unless the student has taken another course in Object Oriented programming. It can be integrated into a 5 credits hour course in Java or two regular courses such as CS1 and CS2. Ortize (2003) indicated that they offer the certification as an elective course after taking CS1 and CS2 in Java. However, ideally it can be integrated in a second course in Java, and passing the certification exam is a requirement to pass the course. Standard textbook in problem solving using Java does not address all the certification objectives. Mughal & Rasmussen (2000) address the certification objectives, however, this book is not designed as a textbook instead it can be used as a reference in conjunction with another textbook such as Farrell (2006).

Sun Certified Associate for the Java Platform

The Sun Certified Associate for the Java Platform certification exam provides an ideal entry into an application development or a software project management career using Java technologies. This worldwide credential validates basic knowledge of Object Oriented Concepts, UML representation of OO concepts, the Java programming language, and general knowledge of Java Platforms and Technologies. The current version of the exam is CX-310-019 and cost $100. The exam consists of 51 multiple choice/drag and drop questions, the passing score is 68%, and the exam time is 115 minutes. The exam objectives includes eight topics, these are:

- Fundamental Object-Oriented Concepts
- UML Representation of Object-Oriented Concepts
- Java Implementation of Object-Oriented Concepts
- Algorithm Design and Implementation
- Java Development Fundamentals
- Java Platforms and Integration Technologies
- Client Technologies
- Server Technologies

Sun Microsystems offer three online courses to prepare students to pass the certification exam. This certificate cannot be integrated into the first Java programming course of the IS curriculum. It can be integrated into the second course of Object-Oriented programming using Java. Java How to Program (Deitel & Deitel, 2005), covers all the eight topics which are included in the certification objectives. However, this textbook is not dedicated for this certificate, and a search for textbook rather than a reference book is required.

CCNA Certificate

The Cisco Certified Network Associate (CCNA) certification indicates a foundation in and apprentice knowledge of networking for the small office/home office market. CCNA certified professionals can install, configure, and operate LAN, WAN, and dial access services for small networks (100 nodes or fewer), including, but not limited to, use of these protocols: IP, IGRP, IPX, Serial, AppleTalk, Frame Relay, VLANs, RIP, Ethernet, Access Lists. The Cisco Networking Academy Program's CCNA1 through CCNA4 helps to prepare students take the CCNA exam. The certificate can be taken with a single two hours exam that costs $125, or taking two separate exams that each cost $100 and can be taken at a Prometric or Pearson VUE testing center worldwide. Both course technology and Sybex offer textbooks that can be used to teach this certificate. While Cisco Networking Academy has an excellent curriculum for CCNA1 through CCNA4, but it requires four semesters to complete. It also requires some Cisco equipment such as routers and switches that is part of the Cisco Networking Academy Program. The other alternative is to buy the Cisco equipment and teach the CCNA course with out using the academy. This option is more practical and it can be done in one or two semesters rather than four. A textbook such as (Hudson, Caudle, & Cannon, 2003; Cannon, 2003) can be used for this certificate. This certificate can be integrated into IS 2002.6 course (Networking and Data communications) and it requires 5 semester hours.

CCNP Certificate

The Cisco Certified Network Professional (CCNP) certification indicates advanced knowledge of networks. With a CCNP, a network professional can install, configure, and operate LAN, WAN, and dial access services for organizations with networks up to 500 nodes, including, but not limited to, these protocols: IP, IGRP, IPX, Async Routing, AppleTalk, Extended Access Lists, IP RIP, Route Redistribution, RIP, Route Summarization, OSPF, VLSM, BGP, Serial, Frame Relay, ISDN, ISL, X.25, DDR, PSTN, PPP, VLANs, Ethernet, Access Lists, 802.10, FDDI, Transparent and Translational Bridging.

While CCNA curriculum is more on academic, the CCNP curriculum move toward real world networking problems. Cisco Academy offers four courses, CCNP1-CCNP4, to prepare the student for the CCNP certificates. This certificate can be integrated into a networking track or into an Associate degree in networking. Students or professional who does not have access or the patient to go through Cisco Academy can also prepare for this certificate. Though Cisco Academy requires four courses to cover the CCNP curriculum, it can be integrated into two Networking courses. Sybex also has a reference guide that can be used for this certificate. This certificate requires four exams (642-801, 642-811, 642-821, 642-831).

i-Net+ Certificate

i-Net+ Certification is a CompTIA-sponsored testing program, which examines an individual's Internet technology skills. This exam covers a wide range of material about Internet, from using the Internet to demonstrating how the Internet works, using different Internet protocols, programming on the Internet, the Internet infrastructure, security, and e-commerce. Though this certificate can be taught in a single 3 semester hour course but it can be taught only in an elective course geared toward this certificate. Part of the topics addressed in this certificate is pure networking materials such as the OSI model of networking. While the other part is associated with web programming, and it covers wide range topics of both server side and client side programming. The exam consists of 74 multiple-choice questions, the passing score is 665/900 and the exam time is 90 minutes. The exam cost is $218 and it can be taken at any Prometric or Pearson-VUE testing center. Both course technology (Andrews, 2005) and Sybex have textbooks for this certificate, however, the author found the Sybex reference guide (Groth & McGee, 2002) is an excellent one. This certificate is also recommended by the ACM task force for a K-12 model curriculum in computer science (Tucker, Deek, Jones, McCowan, Stephenson, & Verno, 2003). I-Net+ certifies an entry level professional by providing baseline knowledge in six areas:

- Net basics
- Net clients
- Development
- Networking and infrastructure
- Net security
- Business concepts

MOS Certificate

The Microsoft Office Specialist (MOS) is an IT certificate that measures and validates skills in the MS Office suite. The MOS certificate objectives can be easily integrated into the personal productivity with IS Technology course (IS 2002.P0), which is a prerequisite course in the IS

2002 model curriculum. IS 2002.P0 emphasizes personal productivity concepts using functions and features in computer software such as spreadsheets, databases, presentation graphics and web authoring. This course requires prior elementary knowledge of word processing, spreadsheet, email, and web browsing. The IS 2002.P0 objectives can integrate the objectives of the MOS certificate which include the mastery of Microsoft Word, Excel, Access, PowerPoint, and Outlook. The MOS offers various levels of expertise including: Master, Expert and Specialist. The master certification requires the candidates to successfully complete three required exams (Word 2003 Expert, Excel 2003 Expert, and PowerPoint 2003) and one elective exam (either Access 2003 or Outlook 2003). Course technology publishes several textbooks which can be used for this certificate such as Shelly/Cashman (Shelly, Cashman, Pratt, & Last, 2006) series which include modules in Word 2003, Access 2003, Excel 2003, Power Point 2003 and Outlook 2003. Each module comes in three different editions: Introductory, Complete, and Comprehensive. They consist of three, six, or nine projects. The Master certificate requires four modules, two comprehensive and two complete. Microsoft Office Specialist exams are not offered by Pearson VUE or Prometric. The MOS exams are performance based, and require the test-taker to perform specific tasks rather than multiple choice questions and each exam has a fee of $75. The MOS master exam objectives include the following domains:

Word 2003 Expert

- Formatting Content
- Organizing Content
- Formatting Documents
- Collaborating
- Customizing Word

Excel 2003 Expert

- Organizing and Analyzing Data
- Formatting Data and Content
- Collaborating
- Managing Data and Workbooks
- Customizing Excel

PowerPoint 2003

- Creating Content
- Formatting Content
- Collaborating
- Managing and Delivering Presentations

Access 2003

- Structuring Databases
- Entering Data
- Organizing Data
- Managing Databases

Certified Web Designer Associate (CWDSA)

The World Organization of Webmasters (WOW) has created a certification for Certified Web Designer Associate/Apprentice (CWDSA). The certification exam measures fundamental competencies for aspiring or practicing Web designers. The examinee must demonstrate knowledge of Internet concepts, HTML and WYSIWYG editors, Web graphics, Web multimedia, Web site design, Web site management, and basic legal issues. The exam contains 70 multiple-choice questions and the time for the exam is 60 minutes. The passing score may lead to an Associate (70%) or to an Apprentice (50%). Cisco Networking Academy offers a course, the fundamentals of Web design, sponsored by Adobe Systems, to help students to take this certification exam. The certificate can be integrated into one IS course. The WOW organization delivers the exam in partnership with public libraries nationwide (in the US). The certification exam includes the following domains:

- Internet Basics
- Web Multimedia
- HTML and CSS
- HTML and WYSIWYG Editors
- Web Graphics
- Web Site Design
- Web Site Management
- Legal Issues

Discussions and Recommendations

After examination of a number of well-known IT certificates, it was found that most of the CompTIA certificate objectives can be easily mapped and covered into specific courses of the IS curriculum. The Cisco Networking Academy also offers courses that can lead to non Cisco certificates. For example, some courses are designed to lead to the CompTIA A+ certificate. The library of certificates provided by Microsoft is very large. One recommended IT certificate from Microsoft is the MOS, which may be taken by undergraduate students in a general education course.

While Cisco Networking Academy requires their instructor to be certified in the courses they teach, community colleges and universities do not require their faculty to be certified in order to teach a certification course. Ideally, the instructor in charge of IT certification courses should be certified or pass the certification exam to teach that course. Another issue that can be addressed is the integration of the certification exam as part of the final assessment of the course. Currently, neither Cisco nor community colleges require from the student taking the certification exam in order to complete the course. However, to be a Cisco Certified Academy Instructor (CCAI), the instructor must take Cisco training as well as pass the industrial certification exam. It is recommended to make the certification exam as part of completing the course. This provides motivation and quality assurance across the curriculum.

Conclusion

This paper introduced some IT certificates which can be integrated into undergraduate IS curricula. The objectives of each certificate were examined and mapped into core courses from the IS 2002 model curriculum. Three potential certification tracks were identified: Networking, Programming, and IT hardware and software. A thorough investigation of a number of well-known IT certificates led to the identification of certificates which can be integrated in those tracks. For the Networking track, MOS, Network+, CCNA, i-Net+, and possibly CCNP certificate objectives can be mapped into 5 IS courses. For the programming track, MOS, SCJP, SCJA, and Linux+ certificate objectives can be integrated into other 4 IS courses. For the IT hardware and software track, MOS, A+, i-Net+ and Linux+ certificate objectives can be integrated into 4 courses of the IS curriculum. Furthermore, the Project+ certificate can be integrated into the project management course in the IS curriculum. The selection of the IT certificates for each track was optimized to facilitate student learning and the completion of the certificate. Moreover, textbooks and reference books required for courses that integrate IT certification objectives were identified. The cost of taking each certification exam and the number of exams required for each certificate were also identified to help students and administrators account for the additional costs. From an academic point of view, IS programs should be redesigned to educate students on how to adapt to rapid technological changes instead of training students in how to use particular tools. Preparing undergraduate students for certification can help address this paradigm shift. Employers often argue that recent IS graduates lack skills required in "real world" situations and basically support the idea of including IT certification in IS programs. Academics on the other hand argue the need for a broad and balanced education and do not see a need to include IT certification. A reasonable balance can be found between industry needs and academic requirements by integrating various IT certification tracks into the IS curriculum.

References

Andrews, J. & Beck, W. (2005). *i-Net+ Guide to the Internet* (3rd ed.). Course Technology.

Cannon, K. (2003). *Lab manual for CCNA Guide to Cisco networking* (2nd ed.). Course Technology.

Cantor, J. (2002). Skills certifications and workforce development: Partnering with industry and ourselves [Electronic version]. *Leadership Abstracts 15* (1). Retrieved January 24, 2005, from http://www.league.org/publication/abstracts/leadership/labs0102.html

Computing Curricula: Information Technology Volume. (2005). http://www.acm.org

Conrad, J. (2002). *Server+ Guide to advanced hardware support.* Course Technology.

Dean, T. (2004). *Network+ Guide to networks* (3rd ed.). Course Technology.

Deitel, H. & Deitel, P. (2005). *Java how to program* (6th ed.). Prentice Hall.

Eckert, J. & Schitka, J. (2005). *Linux+ 2005 in depth.* Course Technology.

Farrell, J. (2006). *Java programming* (3rd ed.). Course Technology. Retrieved from http://www.course.com

Gorgone, J., Davis, G., Valacich, J. , Topi, H., Feinstein, D. & Longenecker, H. (2002). *IS 2002: Model curriculum and guidelines for undergraduate programs in information systems.* Retrieved November 29, 2005 from, http://www.acm.org/education/is2002.pdf

Grice, M. (2004). *Lab manual for Network+ Guide to networks* (3rd ed.) Course Technology. Retrieved from http://www.course.com/networking/

Groth, D. & McGee, D. (2002). *i-Net study guide.* Sybex.

Koziniec, T., & Dixon, M. (2002). ICT industry certification: Integration issues for post-secondary educational institutions in Australia. *Proceedings of the 2002 Informing Science and IT Education Conference (InSITE)*,Cork, Ireland, pp.831-838. http://proceedings.informingscience.org/IS2002Proceedings

Montante, R., & Khan, Z. (2001). Specialized certification programs in computer science. *SIGCSE*, Charlotte, NC, 371-375.

Hudson, K., Caudle, K., & Cannon. K. (2003). *CCNA guide to Cisco networking* (2nd ed.). Course Technology.

Mughal, K. & Rasmussen, R. (2000). *A programmer's guide to Java certification.* Addison-Wesley.

Ortize, A. (2003). Preparing undergraduate students for Java certification. *OOPSLA '03*, Anaheim, California, October 26-30, 178-183.

Peterson, M., Morneau, K., & Saad, A. (2003). Preparing the new information technology professional in Virginia, *CITC4'03*, Lafayette, IN, October 16-18, 28-30.

Randall, M., & Zirkle, C. (2005). Information technology student-based certification in formal education settings: Who benefits and what is needed. *Journal of Information Technology Education*, *4*, 287-306. Retrieved from http://jite.org/documents/Vol4/v4p287-306Randall78.pdf

Shelly, G., Cashman, T., Pratt, & Last (2006). *Microsoft Office Access 2003: Comprehensive concepts and techniques.* Course Technology.

Tripp, L. (2002). Software certification debate: Benefits of certification. *IEEE Computer*, *35*(6), 31-33.

Tucker, A., Deek, F., Jones, J., McCowan, D., Stephenson, C., & Verno, A. (2003). *A model curriculum for K-12 computer science:* Final Report of the ACM K-12 Education Task Force Curriculum Committee, October 22. Retrieved from http://www.acm.org/education/k12/

Zeng, F. (2004). A new approach to integrate computer technology certifications into computer information system programs, *Proceeding of the 2004 ASEE Annual Conference and Exposition, Salt Lake City, Utah*, June 20-24. Retrieved from http://www.asee.org

Biographies

Akram Al-Rawi is a Professor of CIS at Zayed University, UAE. He has worked at several academic institutions of which the last two were the University of Missouri-Columbia and Columbia College, MO. His teaching interests include programming languages, logic design, and computer architecture. His research interests include computer simulation, web-caching architecture, and curriculum design. He holds certifications in A+, Network+, Sun Certified Java Programmer, ICDL, i-Net+ and CCNA Intro.

Azzedine Lansari received a PhD in Biomedical Engineering from North Carolina State University in 1992. From 1992-1998, he was a senior researcher at MANTECH, NC. He joined Zayed University in August 1998. Currently he is an assistant professor of Information systems. His research interests include systems modeling, educational technology and curriculum design in Information Systems. His teaching interests include instructional technology and statistical modeling.

Faouzi Bouslama received a PhD in Electronics Engineering from Shizuoka University, Japan, in 1992. From 1992-1994, he was a researcher at Toshiba Co., Tokyo. From 1994-2000, he was Associate Professor of Information Systems, Hiroshima City University, Japan. He joined Zayed University, UAE, in August 2000. Currently, he is a Professor of Information Systems, Zayed University, UAE. His research interests include Neuro-fuzzy modeling and control, Signal processing, and IS curriculum design and development.

Honeypot through Web (Honeyd@WEB): The Emerging of Security Application Integration

Nor Badrul Anuar, Omar Zakaria, and Chong Wei Yao
University of Malaya, Kuala Lumpur MY

badrul@um.edu.my omarzakaria@um.edu.my
james_cwy@yahoo.com

Abstract

This paper discusses on the development of the Honeyd@WEB. Honeyd@WEB is a system that can deploy low-interaction, production, dynamic and manageable virtual honeypots via a web interface. It runs open source programs, such as P0f (a passive fingerprinting tool) and Honeyd (a low-interaction honeypot). Honeyd@WEB can automatically determine; how many honeypots to deploy, how to deploy them, and what they should look like to blend in with the environment. The first part of this paper highlights the basic security concepts of honeypot and honeynet. The second part of this paper explains the Honeyd@WEB system. Finally, the strengths and the weaknesses of the system are discussed.

Keywords: Keyword: - Honeypot, honeynet, open source, network security, Honeyd@WEB

Introduction

Today, information is a vital element in every aspect of life. Up-to-date and correct information are the key to any successful in businesses, academia, government, personal finances or leisure activities. While this has been truer for hundreds of years, it has never been as true as in the last half of the 20th century with the invention of the modern digital computer. Security is one of the hottest issues in network today. Worries about security have soared because of the increasing magnitude of electronic commerce occurring over the Internet and the swiftly evolving business trend towards telecommuting. Therefore, more sensitive and critical information is crossing the world than ever before.

The security problem is viewed as a problem to protect information assets, both private and public. Providing solutions and safeguards are fairly straightforward. The greater problem is to educate user about the risks and the consequences if the information is stolen, compromised or lost; user roles in a secure environment and the tools that are available. Administrators find that combining together all security policy that constrains both users and attacks is time-consuming and costly. Users also become irritated at the heavy security policies that make their work more difficult for no obvious reasons and causing bad politics within the company.

Planning an audit policy on huge networks takes up both server time and resources. Most of the time, administrator does not take into account of audited events. A common attitude among users is that if no confidential work is being performed, why bother implementing security. Organisations will need to determine the price they are willing to pay in order to protect their data and other valuable assets. This cost must be weighed against the costs of losing the information, hardware and disrupting services. The solution is to find the correct balance. If the data needs minimal protection and the loss of that data is not going to cost the company, then the cost of protecting the data will be less. If the data is sensitive and needs maximum protection, then the opposite is normally right.

There are organisations dedicated to breaking into computer networks. Besides this, there are literally thousands of computer attackers that roam the Internet and Bulletin Board Systems (BBSs) trading information on how to hack certain systems or networks. The recent expansion of the World Wide Web has provided attackers with nearly unlimited places to play and prey on administrators that are ignorant of basic network security. Administrators and designers must ask themselves the following questions: What is the worst thing that could happen if a malicious person had privileged access to their computer network without any authorisation? Could this event embarrass or compromise the company, the clients, or the country? How much productivity would the company lose if all of its hard drives were erased?

The computer networks of an organisation are considered to be the backbone of the organisation. The information available is crucial to the organisation and will affect its decision-making capability. It is important to secure the organisation's networks as much as possible to prevent hackers from penetrating their networks. If the attacker is able to do so, significant losses in terms of cost will incur and confidential data will be exposed. In some cases, deliberate information compromise has resulted in the loss of lives.

In addition to the basic network security infrastructure like firewall and normal security actions, organisations that have sufficient funds can deploy honeypots and honeynets technologies in their organisations. These emerging technologies play a vital role as it provides some information on the attackers' steps when they are compromising the network. This information is essential and gives us an insight of what an attacker can do to a network that has been compromised. Although every technology created by man has its benefits and disadvantages, it cannot be denied that this technology plays vital roles in our lives. By identifying what the attackers can do and are doing, vulnerabilities of the network can be discovered. Thus, certain precautions can be taken to increase the security of the network to prevent the same attacks from recurring.

Honeypot

The basic idea of a honeypot is quite old and was used already for quite a long time. Prior to honeypots, there was the seminal narrative by Clifford Stoll of monitoring and tracking an intruder (Stoll, 1998). Stoll described how he created a complete but non existent government project with realistic but false files which attackers spent an extended period of time downloading and analysing, thus providing an opportunity to monitor and trace the attackers. The original Honeypot computer systems are documented in the two proceedings that are presented by Bellovin and Cheswick (Bellovin, 1992, Cheswick, 1992). Although, the word "Honeypot" is a new phrase but the technology is not new and is getting more and more crucial. Possible definitions of what a honeypot is:

Spitzner, L. (2003) defines the term "Honeypot" as follows:

> A honeypot is a resource whose value is being in attacked or compromised. This means, that a honeypot is expected to get probed, attacked and potentially exploited. Honeypots do not fix anything. They provide us with additional, valuable information.

Honeypots are important because they allow interaction between the attacker and the honeypot. All traffic from and to a honeypot is considered to be unauthorised activity. Compromised honeypots are not a threat to the security of the network but rather it aids us by collecting the ~~data~~ generated data. All data collected by a honeypot is consequently interesting data. Data gathered by a honeypot is valuable and can lead to a better understanding and awareness which in turn can assist us in increasing overall network security. Ironically, honeypots are not as complex as Honeynets. Honeynet is a network of computer systems consisting of multiple honeypots, intrusion detection systems and firewall components. All inbound and outbound data is controlled, captured and analysed. These systems provide real operating systems and real services that closely resemble the actual conditions found in many organisations today. Each system within the network is really a honeypot, a system designed to be attacked. Exclusively, it is a high interaction honeypot designed primarily for research, to gather information on the enemy. This high interaction can teach us a great deal about intruders, everything from how they break into systems to how they communicate and why they attack systems. Nevertheless, these honeypots are fully functional systems. Therefore, the following aspects need to be considered while setting up the honeypot (Even, 2000; Sink, 2002):

- The honeypot system should appear as generic as possible. This is one reason sniffer based systems are used in conjunction with honeypots. If a Microsoft NT based system is deployed, it should appear to the potential intruder that the system has not been modified or they may disconnect before much information is collected.
- The honeypot is designed so that an attacker cannot easily use the honeypot as a launch point for further attacks against networks.
- The honeypot should appear to contain genuine and interesting information, to entice attackers to stay on the site while tracking their moves.
- Honeypots may be set up in front of a firewall, in the demilitarised zone (DMZ), or behind a firewall. In general, it is best to set up a honeypot behind a firewall. In addition, the closer the honeypot is to actual servers (which are likely behind a firewall), the more likely it is to tempt intruders.
- Being careful in the type of traffic that an intruder can send back out to the Internet is vital as to avoid becoming a possible launch point for attacks against other entities on the Internet. (One of the reasons for installing a honeypot inside of the firewall)
- Making the honeypot an interesting site is necessary by placing "Dummy" information or making it appears as though the intruder has found an intranet server. Expect to spend some time making the honeypot appear legitimate so that intruders will spend enough time investigating and perusing the system so that forensic information can be gathered as much as possible.

System Administration and Networking Security (SANS) Institute (SANS, 2002) also cites Even (2000) and Sink (2002) goals for setting up a honeypot:

- Learns how intruders probe and attempt to gain access to systems. The general idea is that since a record of the intruder's activities is kept, it is possible to gain insight into attack methodologies to better protect the real production systems.
- Gathers forensic information required to aid in the apprehension or prosecution of intruders. This is the sort of information often needed to provide law enforcement officials with the details needed to prosecute. Someone with far superior skills who is out there and poised to attack the system may only take a few hours after it is up, to discover it.

Honeyd@WEB

In order to manage honeypot system using web interface, Honeyd@WEB is created. Through web interface, Honeyd@WEB can deploy low-involvement (low-interaction), production, dynamic and manageable honeypot. It uses a combination of deployment strategies, such as, "Deception Ports on Production Systems" to simulate honeypot services, substituted for well-known services (for instance HTTP, SMTP, POP, DNS and FTP) and "Proximity Decoys" where the honeypot decoys are in close proximity to the production hosts (in the same logical subnet). The risk is minimised because there is no real Operating System present and services are simulated. This deployment is easier to deploy and maintain. Furthermore, the emulated services reduce the risk by containing the attacker's activity. The attacker will never have access to an operating system to do further damage. However, only limited information is logged. It is also easier for an attacker to detect a low-interaction honeypot in this particular architecture. No matter how good the emulation is, a skilled attacker can eventually detect its presence. Another disadvantage is that it will not allow the researcher to capture any additional data associated with the attack other than the initial probe. The honeypots are deployed in the same logical subnet to distract an attacker from the real targets. They are used as a bait to bind attacking attempts as long as possible and protect the productive environment in the meantime. The primary interest here is to protect the real systems. The purpose of running Honeyd@WEB in the intranet is to detect internal attackers. It is also possible to detect a misconfigured firewall using an internal honeypot. In addition, implementation of the Honeyd@WEB is a great way to detect worms or Trojans.

A similar architecture was used by Georgia Institute of Technology for its Honeynet deployment (Levine, Labella, Owen, Contis, & Culver, 2003). Although its type of deployment was somewhat limited in their ability for data capture and data control, they were highly effective in detecting automated attacks or beginner level attacks against targets of opportunity on the network. Their limitations in data control made it possible for a hacker to fingerprint them as a honeynet. They also offered little to a skilled hacker to attract them to target the honeynet.

For Honeyd@WEB, it provides a web-based approach to setting up and deploying low-involvement (low-interaction), production, dynamic and manageable honeypots. Honeyd@WEB makes use of open source programs specifically P0f and Honeyd. The Arp daemon (Arpd) is also used in conjunction with Honeyd (Anuar & Yao, 2004).

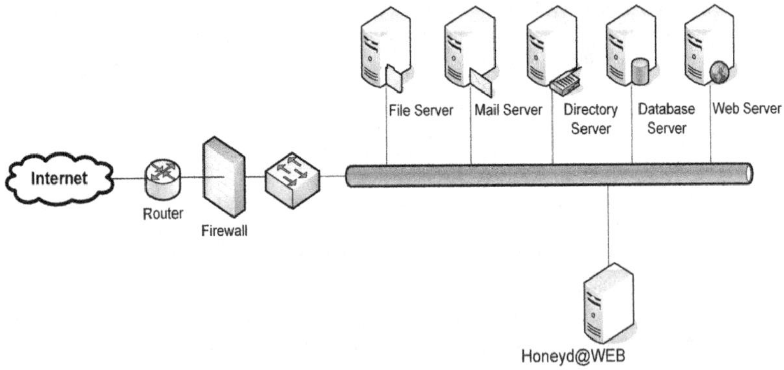

Figure 1: Honeyd@WEB's Placement

Honeyd@WEB sets and deploys the honeypots using a web-based approach. It runs P0f, Arpd and Honeyd through the web interface. The P0f output is used as a guide in setting the honeypots templates. The P0f program (P0f, 2003) used is a useful passive operating system (OS) fingerprinting tool developed by Michal Zalewski. P0f performs a passive fingerprinting technique (Smith & Grundl, 2002) based on information coming from a remote host when it establishes connection to a system. The passive OS fingerprinting technique is based on analysing the information sent by a remote host while performing usual communication tasks, such as, a remote party visiting a web page, connections to a machine, or a connection to a remote host with a browser or by other standard means. In contrast to active fingerprinting with tools such as Nmap (Nmap, 1998), the process of passive fingerprinting does not generate any additional or unusual traffic, as a result this process cannot be detected easily.

Captured packets contain enough information to identify the remote OS, through the subtle differences between Transport Control Protocol/Internet Protocol (TCP/IP) stacks, sometimes certain implementation flaws. Some additional metrics can be used to gather information about the configuration of a remote system or even its ISP and network setup. P0f actually provides three different detection modes:

- Incoming connection fingerprinting (SYN mode, default): whenever you want to know what kind of system, the person who connects to you runs.
- Outgoing connection (remote party) fingerprinting (SYN + ACK mode): to fingerprint systems that you or users around you connect to.
- Outgoing connection refused (remote party) fingerprinting (RST + mode): to fingerprint systems that reject the traffic.

The main advantage of the passive fingerprinting technique is that it can be used in conjunction with the information logged by firewalls and Intrusion Detection System (IDS). This can give valuable information of the systems used by attackers and potentially help track down the attackers without the attacker knowing about it. Active fingerprinting, on the other hand, will most likely be detected and stopped by the network protection tools at the remote network and could, in worst case, lead to legal proceedings. In addition, P0f can run off-line and sift through large amounts of input data from various logs, such as, firewall logs, IDS logs, and router logs for long periods of time. All this information can be extracted and analysed. Interesting information of the systems connecting remotely to the network can be gathered. The information in the packets being analysed by P0f has often not been changed by the remote network's network devices such as proxies and network address translation.

ARP (Address Resolution Protocol) by itself is a protocol that maps Internet Protocol address (IP address) to a physical machine address that is recognised in the local network. An Arp daemon (also known as Arpd) listens on a specified interface and answers ARP requests for some desired IP addresses. Here, Arpd is used to direct network traffic towards the honeypot and to get Honeyd to respond to all unused IP addresses on the network.

Honeyd (Provos, 2003) is a small open source daemon that can create virtual hosts on a network. The hosts can be configured to run random services and their personalities can be modified so that they appear to be running certain versions of Operating Systems. In addition, Honeyd enables a single host to claim multiple addresses on a LAN for network simulation. It is possible to ping the virtual machines or even to run the *traceroute* command to trace the route used. Any type of service on the virtual machine can be simulated based on a simple configuration file. A different architecture was used in the implementation of the Hit@Me honeypot.

The honeypot Hit@Me was a multi-homed host. One network interface card was used for the connectivity to the Internet (the so-called external interface) and the other one served as an administrative interface. However, Hit@Me was a fine high-involvement honeypot. The Hit@Me strength was that the entire honeypot consisted of only one machine. But this was also its weakness. Through this one-machine design, it was not possible to have any influence on the traffic that was targeting or leaving the honeypot. To minimise the risk of becoming an attacking machine, this sort of honeypot should only be run under surveillance. It was then guaranteed that an operator could shutdown or reset a virtual machine if abnormal conditions occurred. A detailed description of the Hit@Me honeypot implementation is available (see Baumann and Plattner, 2002).

Other implementation likes Honeyd is Honeytraps. Honeytraps architecture was discussed by Yasinac and Manzano (2002) through a draft article in the Internet. Honeytraps are systems (honeypots or honeynets) that are designed to be compromised. Honeytraps were developed with two different architectures, serial and parallel. The first is the serial architecture. This architecture works by placing the honeytrap between the Internet and the production systems. In this configuration, the honeytrap acts as a firewall. All recognised users are filtered to the production system while attackers are contained in the honeytrap. The attackers' activities are monitored and all the information collected is routed to another system that is protected by a firewall, to ensure the integrity of the data. The serial architecture forces the attackers to go through the honeytrap to attack the production system thus exposing all attackers to the honeytrap monitoring techniques. Nevertheless the drawback of honeytrap is resource intensive. One of the important characteristics of honeytraps is that they need not deal with real users, thus reducing the volume and complexity of monitoring. However, in the serial connection, the honeytrap must handle all traffic going into the production system and re-route the authorised user to the production system. This architecture runs the fundamental risk that the intruders that are attracted into the honeytrap may subsequently attack the production systems successfully in spite of the best containment efforts of the honeytrap.

The second architecture of the Honeytraps is using parallel architecture. Alternatively, the parallel configuration allows the honeytrap to be independent of the production system. As with the serial configuration, the information gathered about attackers' activities in the honeytrap is re-routed to a separate, protected system. This architecture is less resource intensive so it can be implemented in a system with fewer resources. As with the serial architecture, there are several drawbacks with the parallel honeytrap architecture (Yasinac & Manzano, 2002).

Firstly, for the honeytrap to be useful during the forensic process, Honeytrap and production systems must have been attacked independently. Configuring the honeytrap so that it is likely that an intruder would enter or probe the honeytrap before or shortly after entering the production systems is tricky and again leads us into possible entrapment scenarios (Yasinac & Manzano, 2002).

Secondly, under the parallel honeytrap architecture it is likely to be more difficult to connect an intruder in the honeytrap and the production system using parallel configuration. Honeytrap and the production system are connected using indirect connection (separated connection).

The Web Interface

Honeyd@WEB uses a web-based approach in setting up and deploying the virtual honeypots. The web interface allows the following:

- Run P0f to gather necessary network information.
- Run the arp daemon to listen to a specified range of unused IP addresses.
- Run Honeyd to deploy the virtual honeypots.
- Set and create the honeypots' template for Honeyd to use.

P0f is used to gather network information that may be useful when it comes to setting up the honeypots to match the current environment as much as possible. The output generated by p0f will act as a guide for the next phase; setting up the virtual honeypots. Two options are available when it comes to setting the honeypots.

For the first option, a recommendation of honeypots to be deployed is given. The recommendation given is based on the network information gathered by p0f. Based on this information, certain honeypots are recommended for deployment as to match the current production environment. However, the characteristics of each honeypot have been predefined in a general context. A decision needs to be made whether to deploy the recommended honeypots, which is depending on the requirements. For the second option, the type of honeypots to be deployed can be selected. This allows some form of control over the templates settings; the name of the honeypot can be specified, services to emulate can be selected and the unused IP address that it should take can be assigned. If needed, the honeypots configured can be edited and deleted. In other words, everything will require some form of configuration. Nevertheless, it will take some time and effort when it comes to the configuration of the characteristics of the honeypots.

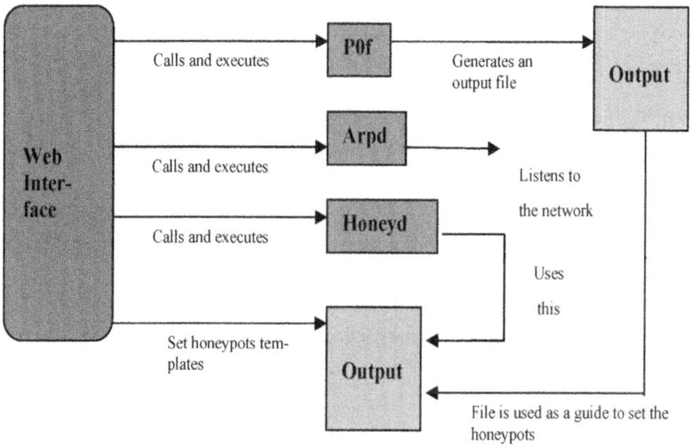

Figure 2: Web Interface's Functions

It is suggested that the recommendation approach be used instead of configuring each of the honeypot. Nonetheless, the final decision is up to the individual using it. For logging and analysis purposes, snort will be used to log the attacks made. Having to have configured the necessary templates and deploying the virtual honeypots through Honeyd@WEB, the Analysis Console for Intrusion Databases (ACID) can be used to view and analyse the attacks attempted on the virtual honeypots. Nevertheless, the level of dynamicity and adaptation that Honeyd@WEB has is quite restricted. Further efforts are being taken to improve the dynamicity and adaptation level of Honeyd@WEB. Figures 3 and 4 illustrate the web interfaces of the Honeyd@WEB.

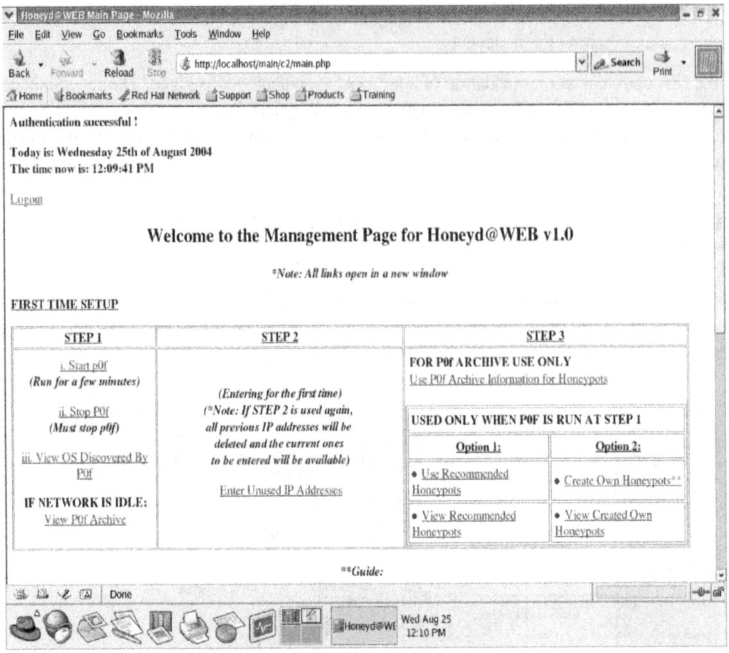

Figure 3: Main Interface (Top Half)

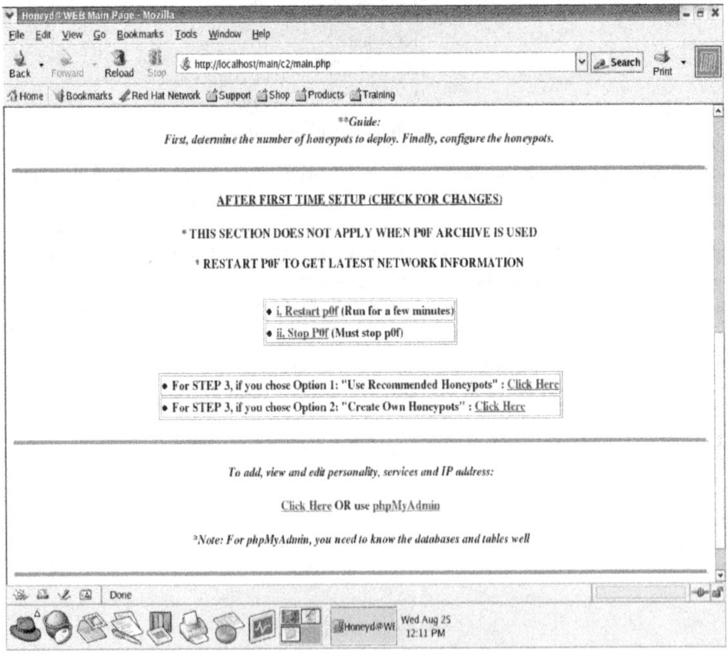

Figure 4 : Main Interface (Bottom Half)

Why is Honeyd@WEB Recommended?

The motivation of developing Honeyd@WEB using open source programs is because they are freely available on the Internet and can be used without any major issues. Honeyd@WEB is just a prototype and has certain limitations but extra efforts are being made to add more features and to enhance it further. It also provides an insight of the possibility of building a dynamic honeypot using a web-based approach. Using a web based approach; Honeyd@WEB is able to provide a web interface to accomplish all that is necessary in deploying virtual honeypots. It is simple in nature and quite straightforward.

Honeyd@WEB will allow virtual honeypots to be deployed through a web interface. Necessary tools and programs can be run as well using the web interface. Virtual honeypots can be deployed either by following the recommendation given; recommended honeypots to deploy or allowing the individual to choose what type of honeypots to deploy and how to deploy it by selecting the services necessary that it should emulate, and giving the individual more flexibility. Analysis and logging of attempted intrusions are also made possible through the use of snort and ACID.

Honeyd@WEB's Strengths

Honeyd@WEB uses a web-based approach to deploy the honeypots, thus allowing everything to be done through the web interfaces from running the necessary tools to configuring the honeypots. It also provides a method of setting up dynamic virtual honeypots through Honeyd that matches the current environment as much as possible. As the network environment changes, the changes are also reflected in the recommended honeypots to be deployed because they are always based on the latest Operating Systems information gathered by P0f that passively monitors the network.

Virtual honeypots can be viewed, added and deleted if desired. Recommended honeypots can be deployed using one of the P0f archive log files or using the current and latest network information gathered by P0f. Honeypots can be managed (configured), where the user can create the preferred honeypots if desired.

Logs generated by Honeyd can also be viewed through the web interface. In addition, certain groups of data can be edited, namely the services to emulate, the personalities (Operating Systems) to mimic and IP addresses available for use. This is made possible as each data group has its own table.

Honeyd@WEB provides flexibility whereby allowing the number of honeypots that can be deployed to be changed easily. Furthermore, the number of services that each honeypot can emulate can be modified as well. Besides that, Honeyd@WEB makes use of open source security tools like Snort. Snort, has a proven track record when it comes to intrusion detection. Snort integrated together with ACID can provide quicker, more efficient and effective analysis of intrusion attempts.

Simplified management and administration is possible using the web interfaces to assist in setting up the virtual honeypots and maintaining them via Honeyd@WEB which can acts like a control centre. Furthermore, Honeyd@WEB can be run from anywhere within a Local Area Network (LAN) via browser.

Honeyd@WEB's Weaknesses

The dynamic property of Honeyd@WEB is limited. This is because if there are certain changes in the network, it requires the user to make a decision whether there is a need to re-deploy the virtual honeypots based on the latest information or not make any changes at all but just keep the current virtual honeypots configuration. Honeyd@WEB uses a simple method when it comes to giving the recommendation of what type of honeypots to deploy.

Honeyd@WEB relies on the open source programs that have been proven and developed by the open source community. Honeyd@WEB utilises quite a number of open source programs; specifically P0f, Honeyd, Snort, MySQL and ACID. Currently, Honeyd@WEB's capabilities are limited to the Linux platform only as Linux can only support open source programs.

Careful configuration and proper installation are essential to ensure the smooth running of Honeyd@WEB. This is due to the fact that it employs a number of open source programs and some of these programs could depend on other open source programs to work correctly. Therefore, it is vital that every single configuration step is followed exactly. If one step is missed or configured wrongly, Honeyd@WEB would not be able to work.

Future Research

The dynamic property of Honeyd@WEB can be further improved which includes; firstly, the gathering of information about the network in terms of the unused IP address range and services running on the network.

Secondly, this development can be enhanced through the algorithm used, which can provide recommendations and options on how the honeypot can be deployed. This algorithm will help the user in deciding what Operating Systems to emulate, what services to emulate, and what IP address it should have. The user just needs to select an option. In addition, the user is able to change or alter any relevant information if desired.

Thirdly, the adding of the number of relevant security tools that can assist in the analysis of intrusions and decision making process. Then, integrating all these security tools to provide more efficient and effective analysis of intrusions; thus allowing reaction time to be much swifter.

Finally, artificial intelligence technique can be used to create dynamic and intelligent honeypot. As a result, the honeypot is able to think and learn by itself and fend for itself. In addition, increasing its ability to be able to operate and adapt in a research environment that tends to have higher levels of interactions.

Conclusion

Honeypots and honeynets are new fields in the sector of network security. At present, there is a lot of ongoing research and discussion all around the world about them. Together, they are indeed an emerging technology that has great potential in the world of network security. To be able to defend networks, hackers' techniques must be learned and identified. This has been made possible through the deployment of honeypots that are less complex compared to honeynets that have varying levels of complexity depending on the deployment technique. As technology continues to strive, many have realized and recognized the importance of honeypots and honeynets in discovering hackers' techniques. Using this technology, vulnerabilities that exist in a computer network can be identified based on the attack methods used.

Although a honeypot does not address and solve a particular problem, it is an instrument that plays a unique part in the overall security architecture. A honeynet is said to be an extremely controlled network with honeypots as part of the honeynet architecture. Systems are set up in such a way that they mimic typical organisations' network environment. Problems and vulnerabilities exposed are very real to the environment. Honeypots provide highly valuable and beneficial data that are much easier to interpret. These data give an insight of what the attack patterns are like, allowing faster analysis and reaction time. Honeypots technology has evolved as time progresses and contributed much to the research of the studies on the blackhat community.

Honeyd@WEB has provided an approach of deploying low-involvement (low-interaction), production, dynamic and manageable honeypots using a web interface; using P0f that passively monitors the network and Honeyd that sets up the virtual honeypots to be deployed. As the network environment changes, the changes are also reflected in the recommended honeypots to be deployed because they are always based on the latest Operating Systems information gathered by P0f. Virtual honeypots deployed using Honeyd can be created automatically or configured through Honeyd@WEB. In addition, Honeyd@WEB has provided a method of running the necessary tools – P0f, Arpd and Honeyd through the use of the web interfaces available. The open source programs used to develop Honeyd@WEB specifically P0f and Honeyd has proven to be excellent tools in their own functional framework. The usage of Snort and ACID has made the analysing of the intrusion attempts made on the virtual honeypots to be quicker, more efficient and effective. There are numerous brilliant open source programs that have made a great deal of contributions to the area of network security such as Snort, Honeyd, P0f, Nmap and many more.

The future of honeypots will be dynamic and intelligent honeypots. Slowly, honeypots that needs configuring will become obsolete. Future honeypots will be a plug-n-play solution. By integrating the capabilities of honeyd with the capabilities of a passive fingerprinting tool such as p0f, dynamic honeypot is not impossible. However, this solution is not entirely perfect; it can be improved further in terms of the level of interaction between these two applications. Besides that, determining what information to use and how to use this information is vital as it will decide the effectiveness and the efficiency of this so known as dynamic honeypot. Dynamic honeypots may not be an entire perfect solution. There are works towards to this potential area of research. Dynamic honeypots can only be improved and enhanced from time to time and slowly but surely it will achieve all the purposes for which it was built (Anuar & Yao, 2004).

References

"ACID" (2003). *Analysis console for intrusion databases.* Retrieved June 20 2005, from http://www.cert.org/kb/acid/

Anuar, N. & Yao, C. W. (2004). Dynamic and manageable honeypot: Honeyd@WEB. *Proceedings of 1st International Conference on Informatics 2004*, Kuala Lumpur, Malaysia, 28 – 30 July 2004.

Baumann, R. & Plattner, C. (2002). *Honeypots.* Diploma Thesis, Swiss Federal Institute of Technology. Retrieved May, 20, 2005 from http://security.rbaumann.net/download/diplomathesis.pdf

Bellovin, S. (1992). There be dragons. *Proceedings of the Third Usenix Security Symposium*, Baltimore MD.

Cheswick, B. (1992). An evening with Berferd in which a cracker is lured, endured, and studied. *Proceedings of the Winter USENIX Conference*, San Francisco.

Even, L. R. (2000). *Honey pot systems explained.* Retrieved May, 20, 2005 from http://www.sans.org/resources/idfaq/honeypot3.php

Levine, J., Labella, R., Owen, H., Contis, D., & Culver, B. (2003) The use of honeynets to detect exploited systems across large enterprise networks. *Proceedings of the 2003 IEEE Workshop on Information Assurance*, 18-20 June 2003, West Point, NY, pp. 92 – 99.

"Nmap." (2005) Nmap - Free Security Scanner for Network Exploration & Security Audits. Retrieved October, 24, 2005 from http://www.insecure.org/nmap

"P0f." (2003). *P0f.* Retrieved October, 24, 2005 form http://lcamtuf.coredump.cx/p0f.shtml

Provos, N. (2003) Honeyd - A virtual honeypot daemon. *10th DFN-CERT Workshop*, Hamburg, Germany.

Sink, M. (2002). The use of honeypots and packet sniffers for intrusion detection. Retrieved November, 5, 2005 from http://www.giac.org/practical/gsec/Michael_Sink_GSEC.pdf

Spitzner, L. (2003). *Honeypots: Tracking hackers*. Addison-Wesley.

Stoll, C. (1998). Stalking the wiley hacker. *Comunications of the ACM, 31*(5), 484-497.

"SANS." (2002). *SANS.* Retrieved May, 20, 2005 from http://www.sans.org.

Yasinac, A. & Manzano, Y. (2002) *Honeytraps, A network forensic tool (Paper Draft)*. Retrieved May, 20, 2005 from http://www.cs.fsu.edu/~yasinsac/Papers/YM02.pdf

Biography

Nor Badrul Anuar obtained his Master of Computer Science from University of Malaya in 2003. Currently, he is a Lecturer at the Faculty of Computer Science and Information Technology in University of Malaya, Kuala Lumpur. His research interests include Computer Network Security, Open Source and IS/ICT.

Omar Zakaria obtained his B Comp Sc from Faculty of Computer Science & Information Techology, University of Malaya, Malaysia in 1994, and his MSc in Information Security from the Information Security Group, Royal Holloway, University of London, UK in 1996. He is currently a PhD candidate at the Information Security Group, Royal Holloway, University of London, UK. His research area is information security management. He has published a number of papers related to information security areas.

Chong Wei Yao obtained his Master of Computer Science from University of Malaya in 2005. At present, he is working as an IT Specialist. His research interests include Computer/Network Security and OpenSource.

Marketable, Unique and Experiential IT-Skills Education for Business Students

Peter Baloh, Talib Damij, and Peter Vrecar
Faculty of Economics, University of Ljubljana, Slovenia

peter.baloh@ef.uni-lj.si, talib.damij@ef.uni-lj.si, peter.vrecar@merkur.si

Abstract

Educational programme for lab-lectures of Business Information Systems module is presented. There, first year undergraduate business students of Faculty of Economics Ljubljana University Business School acquire important hands-on knowledge, which is expected from them by future employers in business practice and by lecturers during their studies. The programme evolved over a course of years of instructors performing both seminars and consulting in real-life businesses and performing lab lectures in afore mentioned institution. The content is strategically rooted in combination of market- and resource-based view of the programme, and nature of performing the lectures is based on experiential education. Content of the programme along with mode of delivery (experiential learning) are presented.

Keywords: IT, Skills, Education, Business Students, Information Technology

Introduction

Most of the employees today are "knowledge workers" – Drucker came up with the term in 1979 (Drucker, 1979) and Sveiby & Lloyd noted in 1987 that knowledge workers replace industrial workers as the largest group of the workforce. "Consequently, businesses should be seen from knowledge perspective" (Sveiby & Lloyd, 1987).

And indeed, we should. Businesses today are being performed "at the speed of thought" (Gates, Bryant, & Dean, 1999) and knowledge workers are using IT to help them solve problems they are faced with. It is therefore absolutely essential for higher education institutions (herein HE) to equip business students with appropriate IT-skills, which match the needs of their future employers, or better said nature of their future work.

Besides, resources (particularly time) for implementing appropriate programme in business HE institutions are usually limited. In our 3+2 year education (undergraduate + postgraduate level - See Baloh (2005) for detailed presentation of the curriculum, which is based on "Managing Information Technology" curriculum. However, it gives brief idea of the content.), less than 4% of the whole programme is constituted by compulsory IT-skills oriented modules, which have to be undertaken by all business students. Naturally, students get these skills in some other modules as well, doing assignments and other coursework; nevertheless, the ratio is far from favorable anyway.

As Naqvi (2005) presents, situation in the rest of the world is fairly similar:

> »Most undergraduate courses in Australian universities designed to develop managers and accountants are structured around 24 subjects, or units, and include a single compulsory unit in information technology, which constitutes less than 5% of the total subjects offered.
>
> In China the business management students are offered a single subject regarding business IT knowledge - "Modern Management Information Systems" - and the credit for this course is only about one-tenth of the total credits.
>
> The BBA students in Finish universities earn at most 7 credits for IT or only approximately 5% of the total credits required for a degree program. This 5% of the total is not sufficient for a future professional in the information society.
>
> In Oman the College of Commerce and Economics at the Sultan Qaboos University offers a 124 credit B.Sc. degree in business discipline. Only six credit hours are allocated for compulsory IT courses, which constitutes only about 5% of the total degree program.« (Naqvi, 2005, pp. 424-425)

The Business Information Systems module is taken by all first year students (1000+ full time students of Business school and School of Economics, and 400+ part time students yearly). At the Faculty of Economics Ljubljana University, we have been trying to develop lab lectures that would fit above mentioned requirement on appropriate skills acquired by our students in the limited time allocated (15-week semester, 2 hours per week).

To succeed in that, we have been posing the *what* and the *how* questions to ourselves over a course of years. Based on performing both seminars and consulting in "real-life" companies, and performing lab lectures at the module, we have reached the programme, we are presenting in this paper.

Lessons Learned: What Did Not Work?

Many approaches on *what* "appropriate" content of such programme would be, and *how* it should be delivered, have been developed and argued for and against. Examples include "Traditional" (Wordprocessor-First-Approach - WFA), "Spreadsheet-First-Approach" (SFA), "Database-First-Approach" (DFA) and "Information-Systems-Approach" (ISA) (see i.e. Naqvi, 2005) for thorough review).

It is not our intention to recognize them all; we however admit that over the years we have considered most of them. The issue we could not get around was applicability of knowledge our students received when course was done in traditional manner. By "traditional" we refer to IT skills education as it is done in most of educational institutions, both public and private. Reviewing our and others' educational programmes we could see that the content had mostly been delivered through review / demonstration of *the tool itself* (i.e. functionalities, menus...). We guess that this approach to knowledge delivery followed contemporary literature approach on the subject. Book-titles in this field seem to follow publishers' need of "not to lag behind" when a new version of a computer package arrives: ("Office XP for dummies" (Chao & Wang, 2001), "Excel 2003 for dummies" (Harvey, 2003), "Access 2003 bible" (Prague, Irwin, & Reardon, 2004) , "Powerpoint 2003" (Denning, 1998)).

However towards the end of 90's and early 00's we have realized that such approach to lecturing does not deliver the value it should. Students knew where a certain tool was located in the programme and could use it if they were told to use it. The most important knowledge was missing, though: they were rarely successful when they were faced with particular problem and they had not been told which application and tool to use. Most of them failed at "real-life-setting" test, as they were not able to solve a particular business problem even though they knew the appropriate tool. When devising "IT for business professionals" educational programme, the latter observation was our starting point. To identify it exactly, we have leaned our thinking in well-known strategic management theories for the *content part*, and on learning theories for the *delivery-method part*.

On Content – "Marketable and Unique"

When devising the *content* of our approach, we combined the "market-based view" and "resource-based-view" of our product, that is, the knowledge we provide to students. Views mentioned are well known in strategic management discipline, and the following two subsections present how they helped us pinpointing the content of our educational programme.

Market-based View of the Programme

In the 1980's Porter developed well known "Five-forces model" to analyze organization's environment, assessing attractiveness of industries, competitive positions, etc (Porter, 1980). Five-forces model forced us to think about the end-results.

As a starting point, we leaned on business practice' requirements. What do businesses expect of our graduates? What kind of skills does he need to bring to the practice? That approach coincides with strategic orientation of our school, whose mission is:

> "FELU [Faculty of Economics Ljubljana University] creates and disseminates knowledge to enable students' successful entry into the business world and offers a rewarding investment opportunity to the business community."

The market requirements were not analyzed using a survey but rather through first-hand education and consulting seminars in companies. One of our findings, when looking at demands of business practice was that we located the applications that are mostly used in businesses (i.e. MS Excel and Database management systems for *data to information* transformation, MS Project for IT support for project management, etc.). However, this was not the only finding.

Resource-based View of the Programme

When developing solutions with our clients we have come to a conclusion that each problem is of complex nature in a sense that only knowledge about the IT tool (i.e. spreadsheet) is not sufficient. The knowledge needed was about modeling the problem itself first (business and analytical knowledge), thinking which IT tool to use and how, and then applying a combination of them all.

This led us to think not only about the knowledge of current products (as it would if we only had the market-based lenses on), but sustainability of what is learned by our students. Business students need to learn how to approach to problem-solving aided by IT, not to know-by-heart every single menu and functionality of particular software. Therefore, we leaned on a resource-based view as well.

In its extreme form, market-based view pays attention only to (outside) market and the product delivered. The resource-base view draws strategic competitive advantages from superior quality of resources (Penrose, 1959; Prahalad & Hamel, 1990; Wernerfelt, 1984). That means, that we had to look at our qualities and *what could be the core competencies of our student*, compared to other IT-skills education institutions.

To elaborate on that: it is of no use to know *about* Word (here we define knowing *about* as user's familiarity with menus, icons, ...), if we do not know how to create a document (including proper content); it is of no use if we know *about* Excel, if we do not know how to create a decision model beforehand in our mind and put it down on paper; it is of no use knowing *about* Access, if we do not know the relational database model and at if we are not at least broadly familiar with working / business process for which database is intended; it is of no use knowing *about* PowerPoint, if we do not know how to perform the presentation properly using PowerPoint.

Based on our experience, employers do not care as to how many certificates an employee had and how many IT software solutions did they claim to know about. That might be a relevant criterion at initial stages of employment process when hundreds of job-applications are screened. What they were actually concerned with and about was whether or not the employee was able to look at a problem and then employ the most appropriate and relevant technologies to solve the problem to add value to the business. IT tools can aid in solving business problems significantly, however, they are merely (yet very powerful) *tools*, not *the brain.*

Findings from business-practice requirements were synthesized in the following motto:

> »Employers do not care what employee "learned" (knows *about*), rather what he "knows" (knows *how* and *why*). Employer cares whether one can efficiently solve business problems which business practice puts forward. «

What business students need to be good at, is ability to draw up on three types of knowledge: business, methodological, and technological (IT); moreover, they need to synthesize all three of them in one coherent piece. This is where business students can show their strengths: understanding and delivering "model-based" approach to business-problem solving. That we elaborated in our next motto:

> »Solving business problems requires using different types of knowledge: business, methodological and IT knowledge, and combination of all three types.«

Combining Market- and Resource- View of the Programme

Future work' requirements don't follow the logic of "certificates of knowledge of this-and-this computer package". Instead of delivering knowledge *about* these tools, knowledge of *how and where* these tools will be applied in practice needs to be transferred to students. Delivering *know-what* is obviously much less effective as delivering *know-how* and *know-why*.

The third motto of our programme is how to deliver such knowledge to our students and educational/consulting seminars:

> »Basic rule about demonstrating the use of a tool is a practical case-example. What doesn't happen in real life, it doesn't exist.«

Solving real-life examples show how to use a particular tool in the context of problem-solving, in which that tool will be used later as well. It is not worth explaining functionalities of IT tools on artificial and made-up trivial examples as the students do not see the real-life context. These principles are summarized in next motto:

> »We do not demonstrate IT tools; rather, we show how to solve business problems using contemporary IT tools.«

Performing lab-lectures in this sense, we find that reduction of "ballast" (in a sense of "old school method" of showing application menus) is significant. Consequently, the most relevant functionalities of IT tools that come handy when solving business problems are learned more efficiently and effectively, as they are used in the course of problem-solving process.

On Delivery Method – "It is all about Experiential Learning"

Background

It is not intention of this paper to ignite epistemological debate on knowledge and learning. We take the view that knowledge is acquired with learning and that knowledge can only reside with a person. What is of interest to us is the process of learning, as understanding them would help improve the role of instructor in that process. Behaviorism and constructivism are two main perspectives in learning theories which help us understand the process of learning.

Behaviorists argue that people need reinforcements to keep them interested and that the use of stimuli can be very effective in controlling behavior. The behaviorist theory of education is probably by far the most commonly practice because the behaviors of the learners can be easily viewed and therefore measured.

Cognitive theorists (starting in cca 1920's by Piaget (see i.e.Furth & Wachs, 1975)) recognize that learning happens inside the brain which therefore needs to be constantly trained. Constructivism views learning as a process in which the learner actively constructs or builds new ideas or concepts based upon current and past knowledge. Learning involves associations established through contiguity and repetition. Cognitive "preachers" therefore teach ex-desk: they set knowledge, learner listens. They hope students will later find ways to apply the knowledge in action. Critics focus on lack of connection of theory to practice.

Constructivists believe that "learners construct their own reality or at least interpret it based upon their perceptions of experiences, so an individual's knowledge is a function of one's prior experiences, mental structures, and beliefs that are used to interpret objects and events." "What someone knows is grounded in perception of the physical and social experiences which are comprehended by the mind." (Jonassen, 1994).

Related to constructivist theory of learning is experiential education. John Dewey (1938) was an early promoter of the idea of learning through direct experience, by action and reflection. Seminal work was done by (Kolb, 1984). According to experiential education theory, students should make discoveries and experiment with knowledge themselves instead of hearing or reading about the experiences of others. Students also reflect on their experiences, thus developing new skills, new attitudes, and new theories or ways of thinking (Kraft & Kielsmeier, 1995; Kraft & Sakofs, 1994). So teachers first immerse students in action and then ask them to reflect on the experience.

Experiential Education 'Our Way'

As external limitations in our case (time, cost) do not allow strict experiential education we added instructors to the learning phases.

1) In the experience-gathering phase, instructor helps (not presents!) students to get experience by mostly explaining, reasoning and solving a business-practice case, and also by role-playing and other activities.
2) That is followed by the experience-reflection phase – a discussion, where instructor helps students to reflect on the experience "What we did? Why we did that? What cases does it also apply"
3) Third phase is help in synthesizing conclusions: "What are we going to do differently in future?"

4) Last phase is applying acquired knowledge and experience to a similar problem. It does not necessarily happen immediately after the third phase; it can be "towards the end of today's lecture" or "next time".

This approach adds the *"how and why"* dimensions of knowledge delivered.

Synthesis

Synthesis of Content and Delivery Method

Based on the above discussed principles the educational programme titled *"Solving business problems with help of information technology tools"* was set up; it is accompanied by a book which includes a CD with all the examples and solutions covered (Baloh et al., 2005).

The programme can be broadly divided into three components, which are shown below, along with description of topics covered. Note that due to time constraints some of the topics listed below are actually performed in the 1st year of Business school. In example, IT support for project management is covered in "Project Management" and "Management of IT Projects" modules.

1) Administrative tasks

We all hate it, however, we all have to do it. It is a component that covers skills that most employees, regardless of their function, position, specialization, need on a regular basis:

- file and workspace (in personal computer sense) management,
- editing complex documents (word processor),
- data processing, table/chart presentation of information (using mostly spreadsheets),
- e-communicating, organizing calendar, contacts (using e-mail client),
- mass mailing (using combination of word processor and customer data base),
- doing presentations.

2) Decision support

The second component's primary audience is employees who make decisions: analytics and managers.("Managers" are considered using the organization- and management-sciences definition; they are the employees whose work includes planning, actuating and controlling; they do that with making decisions and delegating work.) It includes:

- creating decision models, with special section on financial modeling,
- creating databases to support simple business processes,
- creating information using spreadsheets and database-queries,
- finding decision-relevant information on the internet.

3) IT tools for planning and actuating

The third component is intended to support management processes of planning and actuating:

- creating forms and templates for system documents (i.e. directives),
- creating organizational structures,

- business process modeling,
- IT support for project management.

Note, that even though some of the above topics might feel trivial, they are all performed with extensive business-background relevance. I.e. before creating documents, types of business documents according to ISO standard are introduced; required elements of business-documents are introduced and explained, and so on. Doing the e-communication and mass mailing, legal constraints and etiquette for example are discussed. On the topic of presentations IT support for Project Management covers methodological approach to managing projects and IT tool (in our case, Microsoft Project), is used in the context of a particular project that students undertake in a case-study manner.

To sum it up, the main focus of delivery, as discussed in previous section, is practical examples, solved by students, in particular task- and/or process- context.

Results

At the end of each term, a survey about the lab lectures: their content, literature and their execution is done.

Some of the most important questions that we ask, relevant to this paper, are:

1) "Assess practical usefulness of newly acquired skills",

2) "Do you think you have learned more practice-relevant skills as you did at other courses this year?"

3) "Rate the lab lectures in a scale from 1 to 4, 1 being the lowest and 4 being the highest score"

In 2004/05 study year, 183 first year Business school students (out of 420) responded to our on-line questionnaire with 36 questions, most of them using 4-point Likert-style rating scale (to rule out "sit on the fence" stance (Saunders, Lewis, & Thornhill, 2003)), and three of them being open-ended questions. Students were asked to fill out the questionnaire at the last lab lecture with tutor introducing the purpose and explanation of the questions. Students were guaranteed anonymity and have a free-choice of participation.

Results were as presented in Figures 1, 2, and 3. Figure 1 presents the perception of the students about relevancy of newly acquired skills compared to other 1st year subjects. Figure 2 shows in more detail how they feel about practical relevancy; we can see that opinions are skewed in the "proper" direction. Overall assessment in Figure 3 shows a similar picture.

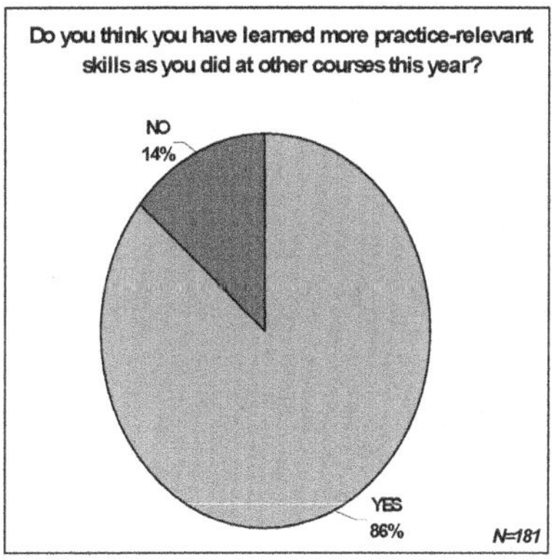

Figure 1: Practical relevance of newly acquired skills compared to other 1st year courses

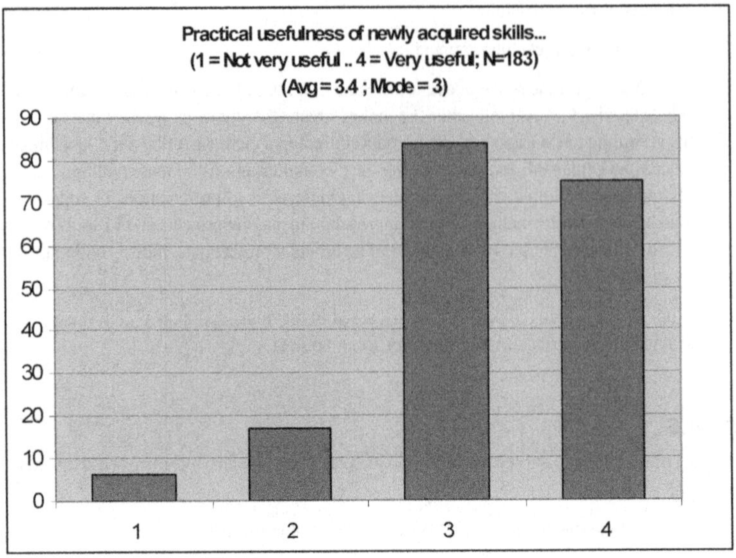

Figure 2: Practical usefulness of newly acquired skills as perceived by students

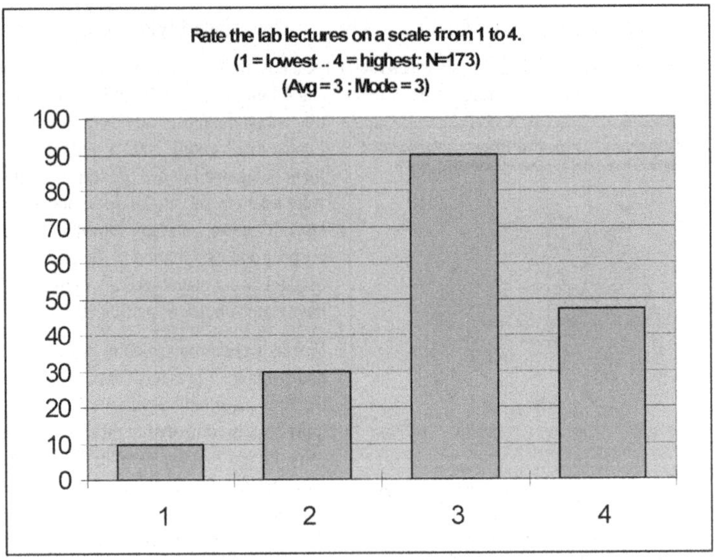

Figure 3: Overall assessment of the lab lectures as perceived by students

Conclusion

Experiential learning with business-process focus are considered to be the most important pillars of presented educational programme. We believe that the concept presented helps our students - both at HEI and from practice - solve business problems using contemporary information tools in a more effective manner. Our experience in business practice shows that even with a high degree of usability of contemporary IT tools, there is much in the "every day work" that can still be improved in this area.

To conclude this paper, we cite the leading motto of the efforts of our programme:

Today knowledge has power. It controls access to opportunity and advancement.
(Peter F. Drucker)

If not today, when? If not you, who? (Anonymous)

References

Baloh, P. (2005). Analysis of information systems management (post)graduate program: Case study of Faculty of Economics, University of Ljubljana, Slovenia. In *Proceedings of IS2005: Informing Science + IT Education Conference*. Flagstaff, AZ, USA, June 19-21 2005: Informing Science Institute, Santa Rosa, CA, USA. Available at http://2005papers.iisit.org/I22f93Balo.pdf

Baloh, P., Cibej, J. A., Popovic, A., Skrinjar, R., Trkman, P., & Vrecar, P. (2005). Resevanje poslovnih problemov s pomocjo informacijskih orodij (Solving business problems using IT tools). Velenje, Pod-plat. (in Slovene).

Chao, P. Y., & Wang, Y. C. (2001). A data exchange framework for networked CAD/CAM. *Computers in Industry, 44*(2), 131-140.

Denning, S. (1998). Building communities of practice. In *Knowledge Management: Lessons from the Leading Edge* (pp. 48-50): APQC.

Dewey, J. (1938). *Experience and education*. New York: Macmillan.

Drucker, P. F. (1979). *Managing for results*. London: Pan Books.

Furth, H. G., & Wachs, H. (1975). *Thinking goes to school: Piaget's theory in practice*. New York; London: Oxford University Press.

Gates, B., Bryant, S., & Dean, M. (1999). *Business @ the speed of thought*. Harlow: Pearson Education.

Harvey, G. (2003). *Excel 2003 for dummies*. Hoboken, N.J.: Wiley.

Jonassen, D. H. (1994). Thinking technology: Toward a constructivist design model. *Educational Technology, 34*(4), 34-37.

Kolb, D. A. (1984). *Experiential learning: Experience as the source of learning and development*. Englewood Cliffs; London: Prentice-Hall.

Kraft, R. J., & Kielsmeier, J. C. (1995). *Experiential learning in schools and higher education*. Boulder, CO: Association for Experiential Education; Dubuque, Iowa : Kendall/Hunt.

Kraft, R. J., & Sakofs, M. (1994). *The theory of experiential education* (2nd ed.). Boulder, Colo.: Association for Experiential Education.

Naqvi, S. J. (2005). An overview: approaches for the development of basic IT skills. In Proceedings of IS2005: Informing Science + IT Education Conference. Flagstaff, AZ, USA, June 19-21 2005: Informing Science Institute, Santa Rosa, CA, USA. Available at http://2005papers.iisit.org/I34f12Naqv.pdf

Penrose, E. T. (1959). *The theory of the growth of the firm*. Oxford: Basil Blackwell.

Porter, M. E. (1980). *Competitive strategy: techniques for analyzing industries and competitors*. New York: Free Press.

Prague, C. N., Irwin, M. R., & Reardon, J. (2004). *Access 2003 bible*. New York; [Great Britain]: Wiley.

Prahalad, C. K., & Hamel, G. (1990). The core competence of the corporation. *Harvard Business Review, 68*(3), 79.

Saunders, M., Lewis, P., & Thornhill, A. (2003). *Research methods for business students* (3rd ed.). Upper Saddle River, NJ: Prentice Hall.

Sveiby, K. E., & Lloyd, T. (1987). *Managing knowhow*. London: Bloomsbury.

Wernerfelt, B. (1984). A resource-based view of the firm. *Strategic Management Journal, 5*(2), 171-180.

Biographies

Peter Baloh, MSc., is full time graduate assistant at Information Management department of Faculty of Economics Ljubljana University, Slovenia. Currently he is on study leave, researching at Informatics Research Institute of University of Salford, Manchester, UK. His main research interest is concentrated in the fields of information systems and knowledge management. He is intrigued by the question of knowledge management strategies and their successful implementation, and by question of supporting businesses with contemporary information technologies. He has authored a good dozen of articles which were presented at conferences and some published in journals. He has co-authored two editions of a book *With practical examples through MS Office* (2001,2002), which have recently been followed by *Solving business problems with help of information technology tools* (2005). Both of them use in-business-practice-affirmed *experiential learning* and are used by future and existing business professionals in Slovene higher-and other-education institutions and industry, to acquire skills for using contemporary IT tools in a more successful manner.

Talib Damij, PhD, received his PhD in Information-Management Science from the faculty of Economics at University of Ljubljana in 1988. He is currently a professor of MIS at the faculty of Economics, University of Ljubljana, Slovenia. Dr. Damij's research interests include Information Systems Development Methodologies, Information Systems Project Management, Business Process Reengineering, and Linear Programming. He lectures at undergraduate and graduate levels the following three courses: Information Systems Development, Information Systems Project Management, and Programming. He has authored numerous articles and books in the mentioned fields, including Springer-published *Tabular Application Development for Information Systems.*

Peter Vrecar, MSc, received his Information management masters degree at Faculty of Economics Ljubljana University, Slovenia. He has been involved in educational process at the University since 1995, firstly as teaching assistant and after graduation as external expert from business practice. Pedagogically he is involved with Business Information Systems, Statistical methods for business, and Organization modules at the Business School. He has co-authored books *With practical examples through MS Office* (2001, 2002) and *Solving business problems with help of information technology tools* (2005), which have been used at numerous educational programmes in higher education and other educational institutions, as well as business practice. His full time position of Manager of Projects at one of Slovenian biggest companies, Merkur d.d., helps bringing business-practice-relevance to modules he is involved with at University. He has pointed his career to project and process management, as well as optimizing everyday business practice with IT tools.

The page left blank intentionally.

Reflecting on an Adventure-Based Data Communications Assignment: The 'Cryptic Quest'

David A Banks
School of Computer and Information Science
University of South Australia, Adelaide, South Australia

david.banks@unisa.edu.au

Abstract

This paper details the development and implementation of an adventure game based assignment exploring the use of ciphers as part of a final year undergraduate data communications course. Students were presented with a document that contained a narrative to help them along the journey to the solution, one section of which required decipherment of a key instruction. The author reflects on the (pre-internet) development, student reactions and the difficulties that may be faced in the use of this type of assignment and upon his perception of the potential impact of changes in educational environments upon the use of 'non standard' themes for assignment work. The paper also considers some of the opportunities afforded by the Web for the development of contemporary assignments based upon the approach outlined here.

Keywords: education, adventure game, data communications, discovery learning, programmed learning

Introduction

This reflective paper was triggered by a conversation with a colleague who currently teaches data communications and networks. The discussion ranged across innovative ways to help students learn what they can perceive as a fairly dry, technical and potentially boring part of the subject area. The author described an assignment he had developed some years ago (around 1987) and some time after the conversation he realised that he had meant to reflect upon and document the design and development work but had never managed to find the time. Even though the paper is based upon work that was carried out almost twenty years ago it is felt that the issues relating to the design and management of 'adventure style' assignments are still valid. This paper is built upon the records of that assignment and around a re-visitation of the literature that originally informed its development. The advent of the Internet raises both opportunities and challenges for the development of a modern incarnation of this assignment.

The paper starts by outlining the broad educational influences that informed the author and then outlines the issues that informed the development of the assignment described later in the paper. This is followed by an explanation of the full 'story' ('The Cryptic Quest') that formed the theme for the assignment. It then presents some student comments and leads into a reflection on the use of such learning vehicles in general and also identifies opportunities afforded by the Web for the development of a contemporary version of the assignment. The paper closes with some personal views of the potential difficulty of using this type of approach in the prevailing educational environment.

The Assignment: Educational Context and Drivers

The assignment described in this paper was developed at a UK university for use with a group of fifty, full-time final year BA (Honours) Business Information System undergraduate students who were studying a Data Communications Networking course.

Much of the material covered in the course was relatively easy to present in the form of lectures and seminars. The lectures were often interactive with, for example, students being brought physically into play to explore the International Standards Organisation (ISO) communication layers. In this session a number of 'volunteers' came to the front of the lecture theatre and collaboratively transformed a given piece of data in accordance with the ISO protocols as the data travelled along the 'human network'. This type of activity alerted students to my non-standard approach and prepared them for what they initially considered to be a 'weird' assignment.

The topic of encryption had previously proved to be somewhat difficult to cover in an interesting and engaging way. Although it was a relatively minor aspect of the overall syllabus it clearly intrigued many students but was typically perceived as being rather complex, dry and mathematical. This perception was aggravated by the topic forming only a small section of a broader subject area that was presented in a traditional lecture format. The author felt that a useful way to learn about this topic would be to provide the students with an opportunity to work individually with an assignment exploring a practical application of codes and ciphers. Although the focus of the activity was to help the students gain an understanding of encryption, an equally important aim was to help them to develop or enhance their individual problem solving skills in a reasonably authentic exercise.

The motivation for the learning approach adopted was largely influenced by the work of Bruner (1960), who suggested that gaining an understanding of the basic ideas of a field involves more than simply memorising general principles and should lead to the development of "an attitude toward learning and inquiry, toward guessing and hunches, toward the possibility of solving problems on one's own ... For if we do nothing else we should somehow give to children a respect for their own powers of thinking, for their power to generate good questions, to come up with interesting informed guesses ... to make ... study more rational, more amenable to the use of mind in the large rather than memorizing." Even though Bruner refers specifically to children rather than adults it was felt that it would be useful to help students re-discover some of their creativity that appeared to have been lost when they moved from earlier education into university study. This issue had been evidenced when a fairly complex packing problem (spheres in cylinders) had been used as a problem solving exercise with a group of computing students on another course. Although they could see that jam jars, marbles and water would offer an excellent way to simulate the problem they were initially extremely reluctant to countenance such 'child-like' investigations.

It is important that a learning environment is created where students felt that they can be creative and try out what may appear to non-standard approaches to problem solving. Combs (1976) considers that an important part of creating effective learning situations is to ensure that learners feel safe and accepted and that they appreciate both the risks and rewards of exploring new knowledge and understanding. In practice this means working closely with students and responding to their questions, however trivial the student may feel it may be, with positive and supportive responses. The responses to questions should be framed in such a way that they encourage the student to recognise new lines of inquiry that will help them solve the problem for themselves. The other thinking that informed the development of the assignment discussed here was largely informed by Programmed Learning (PL) and Discovery Leaning (DL) literature and by the authors' exposure to adult education theory and practice. The ideas taken from these areas were then framed within games-related literature, particularly fantasy role-playing games (Holmes, 1981) and recreational mathematical games (Gardner, 1982). Gardner was particularly interesting because he had included a challenge to the readers of his Mathematical Games column in the Scientific American (Gardner, 1977) offering a $100 prize to anyone who could break an encrypted message using the RSA cryptosystem.

Programmed Learning and Discovery Learning

Thomas, Davies, Openshaw and Bird (1963, p12) identify PL as a combination of methods where learning material is reduced to a series of small, logically related sequences that is then taught by question and answer rather than the more traditional expositional approach. It differs from more conventional teaching in the sense that it is predominantly student-centric, with the student accepting a high level of responsibility for their own learning. The design of the learning material is such that the student operates within a controlled environment, works at their individual rate and must take responsibility for their own learning, forming their own opinions and making their own judgments. PL is designed to be self-pacing with each student working at a speed commensurate with their own ability. (Shirley-Smith, 1986, p41). Thomas et al (1963, p3) note that the teacher should have a low level of intervention in the learning process and should act mainly as a catalyst or facilitator who provides an interesting environment in which the student can learn in a structured way.

Discovery Learning (DL) also takes student-centricity and minimal focus on memorization as its underpinning themes. Belbin (1969) indicates that its success relies upon the ability of the training designer to carefully think out the progression of problems that the trainee is required to solve. As with PL the teaching role is facilitative with low levels of intervention. Students raising questions have these reflected back to them in such a way that they are prompted to carry out further investigation to arrive at their own conclusion. Thus DL differs slightly with PL in the sense that PL more strongly assumes that there is a 'correct' path through the learning and that deviations to secondary paths may be "probably more difficult to traverse" (Davies et al, p6). DL is rather less prescriptive in the learning path, with Belbin emphasizing that students learn by finding out the principles and relationships for themselves.

The PL and DL themes of student-centricity, self-pacing and low level of teacher intervention were used as the key guided the design of the assignment considered in this paper.

Education, Games and Dungeon Masters

At the time when this assignment was developed there was limited reference in educational materials to the use of games in adult education except for the developing area of computer-based approaches. O'Shea and Self (1983, p103), discussing the role of computers in education, offer a brief but attractive description of a computer game as 'a computer-based activity which leads its participants to leap joyfully (from the Indo-European 'ghem', to leap joyfully).' Gilligan (1975, p33) argued that the use of computer-based management games overcame the problems of straightforward lectures to help senior ICL salesmen obtain a better 'feel' for practical problems. Godfrey and Sterling (1982, p54) suggest that if rules are kept hidden it is possible to produce games that encourage inductive thinking. Beard (1976, p173) noted that although the use of a game or simulation does not fully reflect the 'real' world "It almost invariably heightens interest, increases motivation, and may promote reading and study of related subjects." Rogers (1977) reported that "Most groups of adults who have tried discovery learning seem to find it genuinely exciting and enjoyable." but went on to note that "A teacher in adult education wishing to adopt the method for a wider area would immediately come up against difficulties of time and money. Some discovery-type apparatus could be assembled quickly enough, but it is likely that providing something for each student for every lesson would cost more than many institutes could afford." Rogers and Groombridge (1976, p58) identified value in the use of "games, case-studies and simulations for exploring complex problems with no neat solutions", but went on to note that the only educational setting that made consistent use of such approaches "is the privileged, colossally expensive and mostly private management education sector". This suggested that the development of an adventure-based assignment would be extremely time consuming.

Markle (1964, p10), referring to computer-based representations of Programmed Learning, comments that a key aim of the process is to generate an 'active response' to either particular events in the whole process or to the process as a whole. However, he appears to see the response as quite limited when he notes that "An active response is not necessarily a small response to a small bit of information … At the end of an art appreciation program, you might send the student out to spend an afternoon in the local art museum preparing a report on what he saw and felt (This hasn't been done to my knowledge. But I would still call this a response – a very active foot-weary one!)" The intention was that the Cryptic Quest would require students to physically visit several parts of the institution, including the student bar, the computer center and the library, in pursuit of their goal.

Despite these indications that the development of an educational game would be costly in terms of development time and would mean moving into constructivist educational territory it was still felt that it was a worthwhile endeavor in the light of the potential interest in encryption that students had expressed.

Valuable insights were also gained from the broader games literature consulted. Holmes (1981) noted that the 'Dungeon Master' (DM) must "balance the difficulty of his campaign against the abilities of his players characters. Balancing the difficulty of the dungeon to the players is a delicate act for the Dungeon Master, who must avoid the extremes of 'too easy' and 'too difficult'. Rather than offer detailed suggestions for dealing with this difficulty he simply commented that each DM solves this problem in his own special style and must be 'inventive, imaginative and scrupulously fair'.

Holmes also identified the problem that had been of some concern to the author. He commented that "A common DM problem is that, having decided how to deal with some situation during the game, he or she (or one of the players) finds contradictory instructions in the rules." Some initial thinking about the complexity of the assignment problem suggested that it would be difficult to be sure that the story would be coherent, engaging and that all clues would be solvable within the assignment time scale. However, it was still felt that the risk of the whole process failing was worth taking given that the students would not be at risk. In the event that part of the assignment proved to be too complex or convoluted more clues could be given to help the students find their way to the goal.

The Development Process

Consideration was originally given to the idea of building a hyper-text based adventure game using available MSDOS shareware packages (HyperShell and Black Magic) that the author was using for a Technical Authoring Masters. However, further consideration accompanied by some experimentation suggested that the use of a software-based approach could run the risk of being too structured and predictable and this conflicted with the author's wish to provide students with freedom to utilise creative approaches. What began to emerge was an approach based upon the principles of PL and DL but without being structured as a primarily computer-based activity.

The development criteria for the assignment began to emerge as:

- It should be fun, challenging, complex and interesting, having a specific target outcome that could be reached by a semi-structured process that offered room for the exercise of creativity.
- It must be as student-driven as possible with minimum intervention from the member of staff.
- It must be located firmly within the context of data communications.
- It should be an individual assignment (students had strongly expressed the view that they were involved in far too much group work in the whole program).
- It must be achievable within the available time period. This required that sufficient information be made available, but without compromising the need for students to solve problems for themselves.
- It must track and record the development process so that students would have a document that would allow them to reflect on the learning process.

One immediate problem emerged from this list, namely the need for an individual piece of work. The task of designing a complex game that included ciphers with individual outcomes for each of the fifty students initially appeared to be a major problem. Although the basic idea of developing a process that led to a target word or phrase seemed to be moderately straightforward, the trick appeared to be to find a way to include a mechanism that would allow each student to achieve a unique outcome within a common process framework. In practice a compromise was achieved where the material presented to the students *suggested* that the outcome would be unique to each student but in practice there was a common solution. The rationale here was that although students would realise that here was a common outcome this would occur very late in the process. Students were required to keep a 'journal' to document their processes and they were required to include ideas that had been tested and abandoned as well as successful steps. They were required to hand in copies of journal material each week

The approach taken to implying that the work would be unique to each student was to make use of a mathematical trick part way into the solution path. This required students to first convert each letter of their surname into ASCII code (eg A=65 decimal, B=66 and so on), add the numbers together and then follow a mathematical process that almost always generated a outcome of 9 - *almost* always, as I later discovered when the assignment was in operation, because the first step of the process can sometimes generate a palindromic number (eg 121, 202 etc). In this event subsequent steps in the manipulation would provide an outcome of zero rather than the intended 9. When individual students reported that they felt this zero outcome could be a problem they were asked to use a nickname, or add in their middle name and this usually fixed the problem. In practice this 'Dungeon Master' device worked well and most students did assume that the outcome would be unique to them. Iit did not emerge as common knowledge until very late in the assignment that the same target word would be obtained by all students. There was some evidence of a small number of students finding out what the word was very late in the assignment and attempting to reverse-engineer through the solution path, but the requirement for a weekly journal quickly revealed this tactic. Many students refused to reveal the word to those students they considered to be laggards and a number of students still felt that their outcome would be unique even at the close of the assignment.

Having solved this core design problem the idea appeared to be viable and work on the main body of the assignment began. The assignment was labelled 'The Cryptic Quest' and the selected target word was 'Knowledge'. The development process was iterative, progressing from the initial intent to identification of a target word, identification of the possible location of the target word, then working both backwards and forwards through the problem to identify data for the clues. As each piece of relevant data was identified it was wrapped in the text of the Quest at the appropriate point. From vague idea to final product occupied around two months of wandering round the physical university site, deciding on the target word, producing the narrative to support the assignment and planting words and phrases in various computer labs. The narrative took the form of prose (rhyming all the way through began to occupy too much time and was abandoned!) and was framed in a dungeons and dragons type of storyline.

The Assignment: Final Version

The assignment was issued in week three of a 12-week semester. Students were advised that they were seeking a single word as the main outcome of the assignment and that successful identification of that target word would earn them a reward of 1 mark. The remaining 99 marks were available for explaining HOW that word had been located. The explanation was to be demonstrated through the use of a reflective journal with copies of development work handed in each week. Students were advised that this should be a true and accurate record of their work and should therefore include any efforts that did NOT lead them directly to a solution. In practice this journal approach proved to be useful to students as it kept a record of approaches that may have failed for one part of the work but could prove to be useful 'triggers' for later parts of the problem.

The assignment issued to the students was as follows (lines have been numbered here for explanatory reasons):

The Cryptic Quest

1. *Behind the founts of pleasure or pain*
2. *In the cave where companions gather*
3. *There find you some words revealed*
4. *But their message part concealed*
5. *To divine their meaning, imbibe your fill*
6. *Then gather your knapsack to hold all the clues*
7. *And follow the trail to the magic key*
8. *That in the end your goal will be true*
9. *Into Bruce's Kingdom take your venture*
10. *To seek the help of the one-eyed legend*
11. *Use intuition to summon his name*
12. *And heed his words to aid in your quest*
13. *In another cavern, just to the West*
14. *Seek hidden help lying beneath the root*
15. *And from its heart seize the expression*
16. *That is not a stare but almost a gape*

17. *Then onwards to the Castle not quite rounded*
18. *That shelters a treasure most vital*
19. *Cross the open space and down the lane*
20. *Passing the lodge that leads to a copse*

21. *And so to the realm of stone and of paper*
22. *That contains the container containing the key*

23. *Your final clue is your final name*
24. *But summed in the mystic sevenbit way*
25. *Take the result and blend with the potion*
26. *Twisting the key and reflecting the notion*

NOTE: The above four lines were enciphered in the student copy using the Vigenère approach outlined later in the paper. For example the first line (using CYCLOPS as the key) appeared as:

AMWCT XFCJE WITZU WZIGX KLCWB PEG

27. *The treasure you find is but yet a greater key*
28. *Use it well in greater adventures ahead of thee*

Lines 1 to 4 led the students to the bar in the students union. On the wall behind the bar, printed in gothic script of a yellowed and charred piece of card was:

There is magic in the air
And dragons to be fought
A sword and shield provide defence
But the key to mans' true power is
xxxxxxxxx

The number of x's is the same as the number of letters in the word being sought (Knowledge)

Lines 5 to 8 contain one piece of important data and one piece of misinformation. The misinformation was the word 'knapsack' which was a red herring. Students thought that this referred to a specific approach that they had come across in another subject that also included some security material. The other lecturer had been primed to make a strong point of suggesting that this was a useful topic to become familiar with. This allowed him to be sure that students would learn this topic for his course! The important words are 'magic key', suggesting that they will need a key at some stage for the deciphering process.

Lines 9 to 12 referred to the main computer centre (managed by Bruce of course). 'Intuition' indicated that they needed to be in the lab that supported a software package called Intuitive Solution. Students used this software on another course in the program. A file named Cyclops was accessible from this software, Cyclops being the 'one eyed legend'. The Cyclops file was enciphered using a simple 3-letter shift Caesar code and when decoded provided the following text:

Take all of the characters and express them as the fingers of the hands
Tally the values to make the sum
Observe the number and reflect the result
From the larger take the smaller
Tally the result for number new
Tally on until but one is true

This text relates to lines 23 and 24 and is the section where the students convert their names into their 'unique' numeric value. The 'secret of seven' refers to the seven-bit ASCII code. Here 'express them as the fingers of the hands' implies decimal and 'reflect' suggests both 'think about' and number reversal. The full process should always lead to the number 9.

The four personal computer labs in the computer centre were referred to as North, South, East and West and lines 13 to 16 refer to the West lab. Here the student needed to enter DOS, go to the root directory and then identify any directories that appeared significant (eg GRAIL) and work through other subdirectories until they located one named as TREE (reference to 'root'). In that directory was a short text file named READ.ME that contained two numbers, one a Dewey-decimal-style library reference, the other being a 3 digit number (the 'expression'). The Dewey-decimal number had been multiplied by nine. (Nine being the number generated by the mathematical manipulation of the numeric value generated from their name). The text '*...is not a stare but almost a gape*' is a crossword style anagram where gape can be read as page, indicating that the number is a page number.

Lines 17 to 22 took the students on a scenic tour of the university site, across the car parks and tennis courts, and past the building known as the Polygon (*castle not quite rounded*) then down an entry road, passing the gatekeepers lodge and finally onto the large open space with a central island of trees. This was commonly called the 'fishbowl' where students stake out territory using beer can markers, towels etc and go through display routines to attract a mate on those warm summer days. Opposite to the fishbowl was the library - *the realm of stone and of paper that contains the container containing the key.*

Lines 23 to 26 were enciphered using a modern version of the Vigenère cipher (in Kahn, 1973, pp 98-100). This polyalphabetic substitution cipher was developed by Blaise de Vigenère in 1586 and uses a keyword that must be known to both communicating parties plus a *tableau* in which each row corresponds to a Caesar cipher. In the table the first row has a shift of 0, the second has a shift of 1 and so on. The keyword used for this exercise was Cyclops. This is a relatively obscure approach that does not lend itself to simple frequency analysis solution, but the Kahn book was in the library and a number of a number of hints (including a dreadful fake French accent in one of the lectures) was provided to the students.

This is the most complex and error-prone part of the assignment, requiring that the text be deciphered using the keyword and *tableau.* The ciphered text did contain some errors and upon decipherment appeared to be gibberish in some places, suggesting to some students that they were on the wrong track. However 'context dependency' (covered in the lecture/seminar programme) rescued the day and they were still able to construct a meaningful text. The author would like to claim that this was a neat little trick for throwing searchers off the track, but in fact it was totally unplanned and a result of trying to carry out the ciphering too late at night!

Lines 27 and 28 were used to close the narrative.

Successful navigation of the clues provided students with Cyclops, the number 9 derived from the application of a process to their name, a dubious looking Dewey-decimal style number, and a page number. Dividing the Dewey-decimal number by nine allowed identification of a dictionary in the reference section of the library, the page number led to words beginning with 'K' and the first word on the page was 'Knowledge'.

Reflections

Student Comments

The work produced by the students by the end of the semester was of impressive quality in the main, with five students being awarded marks of 100 within a total student group of fifty.

Typical student comments included:

- *Very difficult, in fact it seemed impossible at times, but once you 'saw the light' it was great fun.*

- *Great to have an assignment that was fun for a change!*
- *You fooled me – I was sure we would each end up with a different word. Neat trick*
- *I asked the resident 'spook' at an embassy party I was at if he could help and he said he had never seen that type of code before.*

The students found some aspects of the assignment to be very difficult but generally enjoyed the challenges and a number commented that this was the 'first time we have ever really had to think'. As noted earlier the novelty of the task led to very high levels of engagement, often to the detriment of other subjects. New versions of the assignment were used in the following two years, again with a great deal of success but a re-structure of the program led to this course being absorbed into another part of the program that the author was not involved with.

Educational Issues

One problem in the design of exercises such as this is that the solution is in the developer's head and clues are constructed in that context. There is a danger that more and more convoluted clues are developed with the danger that they can only be understood once the solution is known. It would be possible to insert keywords into the game to allow the reverse engineering of previous sections to help students deal with the rather more tortuous or obscure clues that may be developed. Even so, the developer must be prepared to be flexible and offer significant hints to those students who are not familiar with Greek literature, crosswords, palindromic numbers and so on.

Several colleagues commented that assignments for courses that they taught were arriving late or, extensions were being requested because students were so absorbed by the data communications problem that they were neglecting other subjects. If one member of staff takes innovative approaches to support learning there is a risk that other courses will feel obliged to follow suit, demanding extra development and management time in a world where time is an increasingly scarce resource. Thomas et al (1963, p39), discussing Programmed Learning, suggest that "When preparing a scheme of work apropos the writing of a programme, teachers must bear in mind the interdependency of their subject on others and, as far as is possible, should try to 'dovetail' their work with that being done in other subjects" They comment that appropriate techniques could be used to help students to recognize the interdependence and interrelationships between subject areas and so help to remove the impression that individual subjects exist in their own right. This would have been an excellent aspiration but the development time required would have been even more extensive and would have demanded even more risk and complexity in the management of the process.

Although the focus of this particular game was a specific part of data communications, these games have obvious applications in such areas as project management, systems analysis, human communications and a wide range of other subject areas. The relatively slow and investigative nature of the type of game outlined in this paper may see to be at odds with the faster 'shoot-em-up' genre, but Game Research (2005) comments that 'Adventure games belong in the more thoughtful end of the spectrum. They demand logical thinking and great persistence from the player. Often their loose structures can be compared with a movie that stops at intervals demanding the solution of task or riddles in order for the narrative to progress. But many players seem to find the slow uncovering of adventure game stories appealing.' It would be interesting to structure an entire collection of courses within such a framework, with individual subject areas working around a central theme. This may allow students to make stronger connections between the various subject areas that comprise an entire educational offering.

There is extensive Problem Based Learning (PBL) literature that more broadly encompasses the type of activity discussed in this paper but retains the overall flavour of engagement with the subject, discovery and student-centricity. What PBL has in common with PL and DL is that it deals with messy and complex problems that require student-driven inquiry, information gathering, some trial and error and reflection. Where PBL appears to differ from the PL and DL approach is that it has no single or 'right' solution. Interestingly PBL appears to be currently very much in vogue but Clark (1999) comments that although the concept of DL has appeared several times as part of educational philosophy but has never received overwhelming acceptance.

This type of learning activity may not appeal to every teacher. The approach requires a genuine handing over of the learning to the learner and willingness to deal with unexpected events along the way. There is a potential need to openly admit that part of the process has not been fully thought-through or that a vital piece of data or process is missing. Rogers (1977) recognises this issue when she comments that "A teacher who works on discovery lines and who starts from where the student is will blame himself if students fail; many teachers in conventionally run classes start from where they think the students ought to be and blame them if this is a standard they seem unable to reach." She further comments that a teacher who likes to feel in complete personal control of everything in their classroom may reject discovery methods. Similarly, there will always be some students who want to be told rather than discovery ideas or relationships for themselves.

Contemporary Versions of Quest

The assignment was developed in a pre-internet era and the most significant feature of a modern implementation of the Quest would be extensive use of the web. It is now easy to locate materials relating to, for example a 'quick Google' for Vigenère provides a plethora of explanations (see, for example, http://www.trincoll.edu/depts/cpsc/cryptography/vigenere.html). The benefit of such web-based material is that it provides links to more cryptographic materials for students whose interest may have been triggered. The downside is that the material is so easy to access that a modern version of the Quest would probably have to suggest a reference to a less obvious set of materials (perhaps using the Gronsfield variation of the Vigenère technique) and would require a somewhat more devious (and time-consuming) approach to the design.

At the time the design of the Quest was undertaken the available 'games' literature was somewhat limited but clearly there is a wealth of material now available in the current world of game design. Cavallari, Hedberg and Harper (1992) offer a useful review of adventure games in education. They comment that adventure games are given a variety of names and are categorised according to a variety of criteria including 'Text adventures' and 'graphic adventures'. They note that Balajthy (1986) refers to 'interactive text games, participatory novels, simulations, interactive fiction, fantasy games, strategy games or mystery games'. Quest would probably fit under the 'text adventure' or 'participatory novel' headings even though it was not delivered via computer screen. It was essentially linear, requiring that sub-problems mainly be solved in a sequential fashion (although some reverse thinking could be used), whereas a modern equivalent could use extensive branching approaches. One problem that arises when the possibilities, and complexities, of easily accessible technology are used to replace a simple text based approach is that the time required for development rises dramatically. The Quest developed over a matter of three months even though it is a relatively simple object. The demands for development time for a more complex structure, given that it may be advisable only be used once every few years to avoid plagiarism, as was the Quest, may be impossible to meet in the demanding educational environment that currently prevails. Perhaps what is needed is a team of educators to develop a series of learning objects that could be easily modified and re-configured to extend the usable lifetime of the product in line with the idea of 'learning objects'.

Modern games related learning activities could be built around the WebQuest work of Dodge. Dodge developed and named the concept while teaching a class for preservice teachers in the spring of 1995. He wanted to give his student teachers a format for online lessons that would make the best use of student time while fostering higher-level thinking skills. His comments echo many of those discussed above including the need to find sufficient time for the design and the benefits of working with students as a 'coach' rather than the main source of information.

Other approaches could be built around 'geocaching'. Kidd (2005) outlines the ways that Geocachers bury 'treasure' in a hidden location and upload the GPS coordinates to a website like www.geocaching.com. The treasure may be a log book, further clues, or gifts. When a cache is found, the prize is taken by the seeker, who in turn leaves another gift for a fellow cacher. This moves from the individual approach in Quest to a more collaborative student learning possibility. Incorporation of GoogleEarth co-ordinates could produce a global game that could be used as the basis for exploration of subjects such as geography, politics and so on.

Concluding Reflections

Does the author still develop assignments and learning processes of the types described above? Not to the same extent has to be the honest answer. He currently uses Audience Response Systems, authentic learning exercises, juggling, debates and role-play and strongly believes in deep learning and constructivism - but the level of personal risk taking has been massively reduced. The prevailing educational environment seems to be moving towards a more prescriptive approach where course information books are legal documents and assignments are fully detailed. The author would be very reluctant to even consider the use of a Quest style assignment today. Many students want only the minimum amount of contact time with the university and clearly not everyone enjoys puzzle-based work. Charles and Lester (1982, p9), discussing the teaching of problem solving, observe that "Some people love to work on puzzle problems, whereas many people find them unbearably frustrating and don't like them at all. For people who don't like them, puzzle problems aren't really problems at all because the first and third conditions of our definition of a problem aren't satisfied – that is, the individual does *not* want to find a solution nor does he or she make an effort to find one."

Clear learning outcomes and marking schemes are increasingly demanded, but may also very difficult to produce for creative or process based assignments. Beard (1976, p45) identified this problem and notes that the definition of objectives for 'open-ended' activities is difficult and may stop once the main course objectives have been outlined. She reports that even at this minimal level of objectives definition some teachers of arts subjects indicate that it is impossible, or possibly misleading, to clearly define some of their aims. True discovery based learning implies that the learner will gain insights that were beyond those envisioned by the course designer and may have more intrinsic value to the learner than the 'official' aims. The Quest assignment led to five students being given marks of 100%. This was the first, and only, time that the author has awarded such a mark and, given the somewhat loose and intuitive nature of the 'marking scheme', the examination board was viewed with some trepidation. The response of the external moderators was, however, very supportive and they had no problem appreciating the value of the activity and the worthiness of the high scoring students.

For the learning facilitator the very real risk is that innovative, open ended, ambiguous or seriously challenging approaches often carry risk with them and may lead to negative or even hostile course evaluation by the 'customers' with potential cancellation of the course or, at least, a need to mount a strong defence of the approach used. Even if the risks are taken, the time required to develop different approaches, as indicated earlier, is considerable and time for such activities becomes limited in the contemporary educational environment. However, if time can be made available to develop these types of approach they are valuable learning devices and can also provide some light relief in a busy educators' world, as the following closing stories indicate.

An interesting measure of the impact of the course in terms of student engagement with the problem can be taken from the comments of a student who stopped the author as he was heading for a meal in the refectory and said, in a somewhat accusatory voice, "You are David Banks, aren't you?" I acknowledged that this was the case and the student then commented, at length, on how complex and difficult the assignment was, how much time was required and how it interfered with their social life. Given that I did not recognise her face, I gently pointed out that if they turned up for sessions it might not be so hard as I gave plenty of clues in the lectures and seminars. She replied "Oh, I'm not on your course – but I share a flat with someone who is and they talk about nothing else!"

A flexible approach to marking is required for this type of assignment. One student was awarded 99 marks for his work that demonstrated excellent problem solving and process discussion but eventually arrived at the conclusion that the target word was 'GRIT'. His rationale for this conclusion was as he reached the end of the physical journey round the site he found a large yellow bin with the word 'GRIT' embossed on its side, containing a mixture of salt and coarse sand used for dealing with snow and ice in the car park during winter. This bin was located outside the "realm of stone and of paper" (ie the library) and, as he quite reasonably commented, "You need grit to finish this kind of assignment"!

Designing, implementing and participating in assignments such as the Quest are potentially great fun, for staff and students, but the intensity of design and operation equally demands knowledge and grit on the part of all parties – staff, partners, colleagues, students and even innocent bystanders.

References

Balajthy, E. (1986). *Microcomputers in reading and language arts.* Englewood Cliffs, NJ: Prentice-Hall

Belbin, R. M. (1969). *The discovery method in training*, Training Information Paper 5, Training Services Agency, HMSO, London.

Beard, R. (1976). *Teaching and learning in higher education* (3rd ed.). Bucks, UK: Penguin.

Bruner, J.S. (1960) *The process of education.* Cambridge, MA: Harvard University Press.

Cavallari, B., Hedberg, J., & Harper, B. (1992). Adventure games in education: A review. *Australian Journal of Educational Technology, 8*(2), 172-184.

Charles, R. & Lester, F. (1982). *Teaching problem solving.* Scotland: Edward Arnold.

Clark, D. (1999). A time capsule of training and learning. Retrieved February 2nd, 2006 from http://www.nwlink.com/~donclark/hrd/history/history.html

Combs, A. W. (1976). Fostering maximum development of the individual. In W. Van Til & K.J. Rehage (Eds.). *Issues in secondary education.* (NSSE Yearbook, 1976). Chicago: National Society for the Study of Education.

Dodge, B. (1997). *Some thoughts about WebQuests.* Retrieved February 3rd 2006 from http://webquest.sdsu.edu/about_webquests.html

Game Research. (2005). Retrieved 29 November 2005 from http://www.game-research.com/adventure.asp

Gardner, M. (1977). A new kind of cipher that would take millions of years to break. *Scientific American*, August,120-124.

Gardner, M. (1982). *Mathematical circus.* London: Penguin Books.

Gilligan, J. (1975). Computer assisted learning in ICL. In R. Hopper & I. Toye (Eds.), *Computer assisted learning in the United Kingdom: Some case studies.* Charlesworth, Huddersfield, UK: Council for educational Technology.

Godfrey, D., & Sterling, S. (1982). *The elements of CAL.* Virginia: Reston Publishing.

Holmes, J. E. (1981). *Fantasy role playing games: Dungeons, dragons, and adventures in fantasy gaming,* London: Arms and Armour Press.

Kahn, D. (1973). *The code-breakers.* London: Sphere Books.

Kidd, D. (2005, December). Jargon buster: GPS. *Australian PC Authority*, p114.

Markle, S. M. (1964). *Good frames and bad: A grammar of frame writing.* New York, USA: Wiley and Sons.

O'Shea, T. & Self, J. (1983). *Learning and teaching with computers.* Guildford, UK: Harvester Press.

Rogers, J. (1977). *Adults Learning* (2nd ed.). Milton Keynes, UK: Open University Press

Rogers, J. & Groombridge, B. (1976). *Right to learn: The case for adult equality.* Essex, UK: Arrow Books.

Shirley-Smith, K. (1968). *Guide to programmed techniques in industrial training.* Aylesbury, Bucks, UK: Gower Press.

Thomas, C. A, Davies, I. K, Openshaw, D. & Bird, J. B. (1963). *Programmed learning in perspective: A guide to programme writing.* Barking, Essex, UK: Lamson Technical Products, Adelphi Press.

Biography

David A Banks is a lecturer in Information Systems in the School of Computer and Information Science at the University of South Australia. He worked for a large UK telecommunications company for the first sixteen years of his career, dealing with data, television and video-conferencing systems. During this time he was also a part-time student counsellor with the Open University, taught a variety of adult education classes and produced a series of radio programmes for BBC local radio. Upon gaining a Diploma in Adult Education and a Master of Philosophy from the University of Leeds in the UK he moved into higher education. Subjects taught included computer systems architecture, project management, data communications, database design, and introductory programming. He was seconded to New Zealand in 1993/4 as a Visiting Research Fellow and moved to Australia in 1998 to take up his current post. His research interests include IS education, IS development methodologies and Audience Response Systems. His current teaching includes information systems development methodologies and collaborative information systems.

The page left blank intentionally.

A Virtual Learning Environment for Mobile IP

Laura Bergström, Kaj J. Grahn, and Göran Pulkkis
Arcada Polytechnic, 00550 Helsinki, Finland

laura.bergstrom@arcada.fi kaj.grahn@arcada.fi
goran.pulkkis@arcada.fi

Abstract

This paper presents a virtual learning environment for Mobile IP (Internet Protocol). The learning environment has been produced in a production circle of Virtual Polytechnic of Finland. Protocols and mechanisms for secure mobility in the Internet are surveyed. A detailed description of the development of the learning environment and the content of the Mobile IP animation is given. The chosen didactical approach and the graphical design of the learning platform are presented and motivated. The IT technology and the IT infrastructure needed to implement and use the learning platform are also described and assessed.

Keywords: animation, didactical, learning environment, Mobile IP, security

Introduction

Today, the number of wireless and mobile devices connected to the Internet is strongly growing. Wireless links and networks, mobile users and mobility-related services form an increasing part of the Internet infrastructure. These wireless and mobile parts are normally connected to larger, wired networks. Mastering the key concepts in mobile, wireless and wired technology areas are therefore of increasing importance in the society of today.

There is a distinction between wireless and mobility. You can find many networked environments in which the network nodes are wireless but not mobile. Such examples are wireless home and office networks with stationary workstations. A limited form of mobility that does not require wireless links is the use of a wired laptop at home and in the office. A both wireless and mobile example is the scenario where a mobile user is maintaining a voice-over-IP call while racing down the autobahn. The various degrees of mobility, from the network layer's point of view, can therefore be presented as a user moving only within the same wireless access network, as a user moving between access networks shutting down while moving between network and as a user moving between access networks maintaining ongoing connections (Kurose & Ross, 2005).

Mobile Internet Protocol (IP) is an extension to the standard IP for use in mobile applications. The standard allows users with mobile devices whose IP addresses are associated with one network to stay connected when moving to a network with a different IP address. According to the ISP Glossary 2005:

A common analogy to explain Mobile IP is when someone moves his residence from one location to another. Person moves from Boston to New York. Person drops off new mailing address to New York post office. New York post office notifies Boston post office of new mailing address. When Boston post office receives mail for person it knows to forward mail to person's New York address.

Mobility management skills are needed by practically any user of a mobile device connected to a wireless network. Presently, there is a growing demand for wireless network professionals. Typical areas of interest include mobility management principles, development of wireless network technologies, methodologies and standards, and delivery of support and training to mobile users and professionals in wireless network related issues

A virtual, survey oriented Mobile IP environment, developed for students, will give highly needed, specialized, and also custom designed network education.

The Mobile Internet Protocol

The Mobile Internet Protocol (Mobile IP) was developed for the network layer to support mobility. The Internet architecture and protocols for supporting mobility are defined primarily in the standard RFC 3344 (Perkins, 2002). Objectives related to the development of Mobile IP include (Schiller, 2000):

- *Compatibility*. Mobile IP does not require changes to end-systems, routers, applications and network protocols already in use. Data link layer protocols as IP are also supported. Furthermore, Mobile IP has to ensure that mobile end-systems can communicate with fixed systems.
- *Transparency*. Higher protocols, like TCP (Transport Control Protocol), continue to work even if the mobile unit changes its network attachment point. This implies that mobility remains 'invisible' for higher level protocols and applications.
- *Scalability and efficiency*. Mobile IP has to be scalable over a large number of participants of the Internet. Enhancing mobility must not degrade the efficiency of the network.
- *Security*. Minimum requirements are message replay prevention and authentication of all registration messages.

The Mobile IP standard consists of three main areas (Kurose & Ross, 2005). *Agent discovery* is a procedure where a home or foreign agent advertises its services to be used by the mobile node. When care-of-addresses (COAs) are registered and deregistered with the mobile node's home agent and COA defines the current location of the mobile node from an IP point of view, the procedure is called *registration*. The third main area is *indirect routing of datagrams*, i.e. datagrams (packets) are forwarded to mobile nodes by the home agent. This includes rules for handling error conditions and different forms of encapsulation.

Packet Delivery

Data transfer to/from a mobile node in a typical example network is illustrated in Figure 1. The used terminology is defined below (Schiller, 2000):

- *Mobile node (MN)*. A mobile node is a host or router that changes its point of attachment from one network or subnetwork to another. The mobile node may communicate with other Internet nodes without changing its IP address.
- *Correspondent node (CN)*. A correspondent node is a mobile or stationary peer communicating with a mobile node.

- *Home network.* The network to which the mobile node is normally attached with respect to its IP address.
- *Foreign network.* The network in which the mobile node is currently residing and which is not the home network.
- *Home agent (HA).* The home agent is implemented on a router connected to a mobile node's home network. HA maintains information about the device's current location.
- *Foreign agent (FA).* The foreign agent provides services to the mobile node during its visit in the foreign network. Typically, the foreign agent is implemented on a router connected to the foreign network.
- *Care-of-address (COA).* The care-of-address defines the current position of the mobile node. Packets sent to the mobile node are delivered to the care-of-address using tunnelling, i.e. the care-of-address marks the tunnel endpoint. There are two types of COA:
  - *Foreign agent COA.* The COA is the IP address of the FA
  - *Co-located COA.* An additional IP address which acts as COA is given to the MN
- *Binding cache (BC).* A cache of mobility bindings of mobile nodes, maintained by a node for use in tunneling datagrams to those mobile nodes.

In Figure 1, a CN is connected via a router to the Internet. The HA and the FA are implemented on corresponding routers connected to respective networks. The MN is currently in the foreign

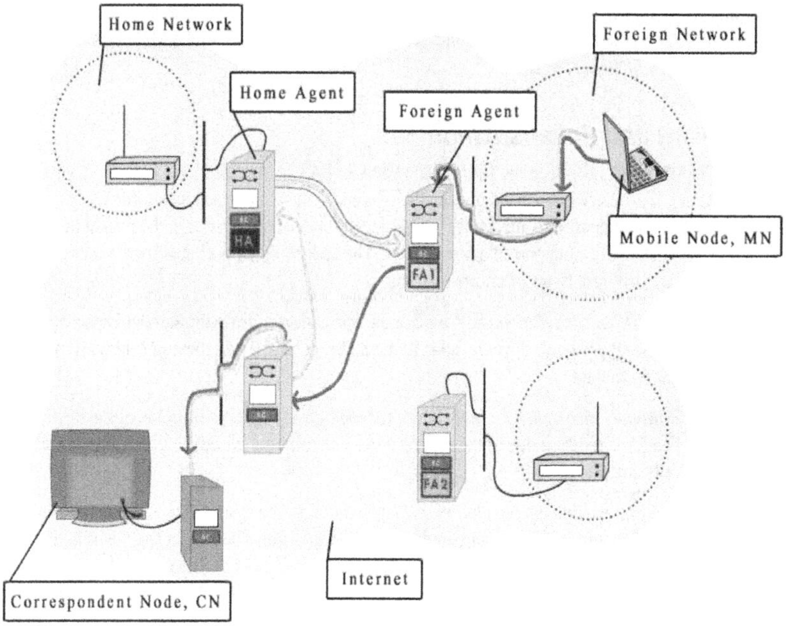

Figure 1: Data transfer to/from the mobile node in an example network.

network. The correspondent node wants to send an IP packet to the mobile node. The ordinary IP address can be used although the current position of the mobile node may not be known. The packet delivery process starts by CN sending the packet to the IP address of the MN. The HA knows that the MN is not in its home network and intercepts the packet. The packet is now encapsulated and tunnelled to the COA in FA. The FA forwards the packet to the MN.

Agent Discovery

After moving the mobile node has to find a foreign agent. The discovery of a new foreign agent and a new network address tells the mobile node that it has moved into a new foreign network. This is called *agent discovery*. This procedure can be accomplished by *agent advertisement* or by *agent solicitation.* In agent advertisement available services are advertised by the foreign or home agent. These beacon broadcast messages are handled by the Internet Control Message Protocol (ICMP) including some mobility extensions. When a mobile node doesn't want to wait for a receiving agent advertisement it can broadcast an agent solicitation message. The agent will then directly unicast an agent advertisement to the mobile node.

Registration

Registration is performed in order to inform the HA of the current location of MN. One role of the foreign agent is to create the COA for the MN. Registration takes part after MN has received the COA. Two addresses are then associated with the MN, its permanent address and it's COA (care-of-address, foreign address). The registration procedures depend on the location of the COA (Schiller, 2000). When the COA is at the FA, the MN sends the registration request with the COA included to the FA, which forwards the registration to the HA. In this case the procedure is accomplished by *registration of a MN via the FA*. When the COA is co-located, the MN sends the request directly to the HA and the HA sends its registration reply back to the MN. This is *direct registration of a MN with the HA*.

Tunneling and Encapsulation

Forwarding of packets between the HA and the COA in FA1 is illustrated in Figure 1. A virtual pipe, a *tunnel*, has been established between the two endpoints. Data packets are forwarded unchanged inside the tunnel. This mechanism is achieved by *encapsulation*, i.e. the packet header and data are put into the data part of a new packet. The encapsulated packet is then routed to the COA. There are different types of encapsulation:

- *IP-in-IP encapsulation*. This type of encapsulation follows the standard specification of the IP protocol. Several fields in the inner (original) and the outer (new) IP header are redundant.
- *Minimal encapsulation*. In this optional method the number of fields of the inner header is reduced due to the redundancy. The minimal encapsulation scheme works only for IP.
- *Generic routing encapsulation (GRE)*. Generally, the system has a packet that needs to be encapsulated and delivered to some destination. The packet (payload) is first encapsulated in a GRE packet, then encapsulated in some other protocol and finally forwarded. This outer protocol is called the delivery protocol.

Optimization of Packet Forwarding

In the basic Mobile IP protocol, packets to the MN go through the HA. In some cases this will cause additional and unnecessary overhead for the network. The packet route is made of three segments, CN to HA, HA to COA/MN, and MN back to CN. This is called *triangular routing* (Schiller, 2000).

The route can be optimized by informing the CN of the current MN location. The update is given by HA. CN makes use of a BC. This cache is a part of the local routing table for the CN. Optimization of the original Mobile IP protocol includes four additional binding messages: request, update, acknowledgement and warning (Schiller, 2000).

Reverse Tunneling

In the solution illustrated in Figure 1, the MN sends directly its packets to the CN according to the standard IP. This solution has some severe problems (Schiller, 2000). A *firewall* can cause problems because it can be set up to filter out malicious addresses. The MN sends packets with a fixed IP address as source which may not be allowed in a foreign network. *Multicast* packets cannot be transmitted by the MN located in a foreign network, a reverse tunnel is needed. When the MN moves to a foreign network, the *TTL (Time To Live)* field may be too low for the packets to reach the destination nodes. Also in this case reverse tunnelling is needed.

Reverse tunnelling can briefly be described by a sequence where the MN is transmitting to the FA, the FA tunnels packets to the HA by encapsulation and finally the HA forwards the packets to the receiver CN in a standard way.

Reverse tunnelling as an extension to Mobile IP is described in RFC 2344 (Montenegro, 1998).

Roaming

Roaming refers to the ability of the MN to move from one access point coverage area to another without interruption in service or loss in connectivity (Webopedia, 2005). This is the case when the MN changes its location from an old FA and registers with a new FA. The HA and the old FA will then receive binding update messages from the new FA/MN. If the CN is sending to the old FA, the FA now notices that the packets have the destination MN and forwards these packets to the COA in the new FA. This procedure provides *smooth handover*. Smooth handover is a kind of handover operation that minimizes data loss during the time that the mobile node is establishing its link to the new access point.

Mobile IP Security

A MN uses wireless data communication. Physical access control to the communication media can only be implemented for wired data communication. Network security issues are therefore especially important for Mobile IP. Security goals and requirements must be defined. Risks, attack possibilities, and vulnerabilities must be thoroughly assessed. Solutions for secure authentication and protected data communication are needed.

Security Goals and Requirements

Two fundamental goals of Mobile IP security have been defined. When the MN visits a foreign network

1. it has the same connectivity and safety as in its home network

2. both the home network and the visited foreign network are protected from active and passive attacks.

To achieve these security goals the following security measures have been considered to be necessary:

1. Mobile IP registration and location update messages must have
    - o *data integrity protection*
    - o *data origin authentication*
    - o *anti-replay protection*
2. *Access control* of resources in foreign networks used by visiting Mobile Nodes
3. IP packet redirecting tunnels must provide
    - o *data integrity protection*
    - o *data origin authentication*
    - o *data confidentiality*

Moreover, MNs should have *location privacy* and *anonymity* (Zao et al., 1999).

Risks, Attacks and Vulnerabilities

Risks of, attacks on and vulnerabilities of Mobile IP are surveyed in Islam (2005) and listed below:

- *Denial-of-Service (DOS).* This attack has two forms, TCP SYN packet flooding or redirection of data packet flow. Strong authentication of all registration messages prevent some DOS attack patterns.
- *Replay Attack.* In this attack a valid Registration Request is tapped and replayed by a malicious node. Use of time stamps or nonces in combination with strong authentication of registration messages give protection against replay attacks.
- *Passive Eavesdropping.* In this attack a malicious node listens to the data communication from a mobile nod. Encrypted data communication gives protection.
- *Session Hijacking.* In this attack an intruder node sends a false registration message to a CN. This message claims that the legal MN has moved to the care-of-address of the intruder node. Encryption of end-to-end or Link Layer data communication gives protection.
- *Malicious Mobile Node Flooding.* In this attack a malicious node is a valid mobile node, which with legal registration request messages redirects data traffic from the CN to a victim node.
- *Other Intrusion Attack.* A malicious node may get physical access to a network socket or use the air interface for intrusion attempts. To prevent this type of attack
    - a visiting MN must be fully registered to the FA before any data packets are routed
    - Link Layer data communication encryption is required from every MN trying to connect to a FA.

Security Solutions

Replay prevention with timestamps or nonces for all messages exchanged within the base Mobile IP protocol is specified in Perkins and Calhoun (2000). Other Mobile IP security solutions specify authentication schemes and protection of data communication.

Secure Mobile IP Authentication with AAA Servers

The base Mobile IP protocol specifies a Mobility Security Association (MSA) between a MN and the HA. This MSA is used to authenticate the Registration Request sent from the MN to the HA. The base Mobile IP protocol also supports an optional MSA between the MN and the FA as well as an optional MSA between a FA and a HA. These two MSAs are used for authenticating of registration messages when a MN connects to a foreign network (Perkins, 2002).

The Authentication, Authorization, and Accounting (AAA) requirements for the base Mobile IP protocol are specified in Glass, Hiller, Jacobs, and Perkins (2000). In Calhoun, Johansson, Perkins, Hiller, & McCann (2005) is specified how these requirement can be fulfilled by the Diameter AAA protocol. Secure Mobile IP registration in a foreign network requires that

- the Foreign Agent is a client of an AAA server of the foreign network of the Mobile Node
- the Home Agent is a client of an AAA server of the home network of the Mobile Node
- both AAA servers have a trust relationship.

Figure 2 shows the request/reply handshake message exchange in the AAA infrastructure, when a MN is registered in a foreign network. AAAF is the foreign network AAA server and AAAH is the home network AAA server.

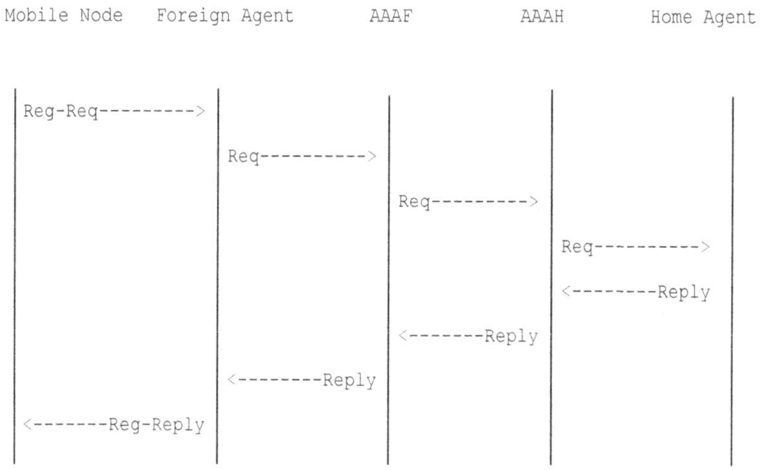

Figure 2: Mobile IP/Diameter Message Exchange (Calhoun & al, 2005).

Secure Mobile IP Authentication with Public Key Cryptography

A Mobile IP authentication extension using a X.509 certificate based PKI has been proposed in an expired Internet Draft (Jabobs & Belgard, 2000). In this scheme all nodes participating in MN registration have a X.509 certified public/private key pair.

Also Mobile IP authentication extensions using an identity based public key cryptosystem, which was first introduced in 1984 (Shamir, 1984), have been proposed (Hwu, Chen, & Lin, in press; Lee, Choi, Kim, Sohn, & Park, 2003). In an identity based public key cryptosystem the public key is derived from public information that uniquely identifies a network user or a network node, for example the email address or telephone number of a network user and node_name@dns_domain_name for an Internet connected node. The corresponding private key is obtained from a trusted Private Key Generator.

An extension of the base Mobile IP protocol specifies authentication based on MN identities and other network host identities in the form of Network Access Identifiers (NAIs). A NAI is derived from hostname.realm, the Fully Qualified Domain Name of a network host, as hostname@realm (Johansson & Johansson, 2004).

Protected Data Communication

A MN often uses a WLAN connection in the home network and in a foreign network. WLAN Link Layer protection is provided by the security protocol WPA or IEEE 802.11i. For protected end-to-end Mobile IP data communication, several IPSec based solutions have been presented (Barun & Danzeisen, 2001; Islam, 2005; Zao & Condell, 1997). Also SSL or SSH encryption or an identity based public key cryptosystem (Hwu et al., 2005) provides protection for end-to-end Mobile IP data communication.

Learning Environment Design

The importance of a well-planned learning environment grows especially in products aimed for learning, as the use of the product must fall into a secondary place and be almost an unnoticeable action. The interface should support the content of the product and lead the user in his/her learning process. A learning environment should not be the cause of any unnecessary frustration and should instead permit an easier interpretation of the study material. In fact, the interface of the product should support direct interaction, in other words, it should let users be able to spend their full cognitive resources on the task, not on the interface. As a result, the interface becomes invisible to users and on the contrary the task becomes transparent. This is achieved by minimization of the *gulfs of execution* and *gulfs of evaluation*, which are created when executing any particular task. More in specific, according to Norman's seven stages of action any activity is composed of many cycles of the following stages of activities: establishing the goal, forming the intention, specifying the action, executing the action, perceiving the system state, interpreting the state and evaluating the system state with respect to the goals and intentions. The gulf of execution in this cycle is the gap between intention and action, and the gulf of evaluation is instead the gap between perception and evaluation (Norman, 1988; as cited in Griffiths, n.d.).

This model brings to evidence the importance of considering principals like

- visibility
- presentation of operations and results in a coherent, consistent system image
- efficient relationships between elements and their effects
- feedback

when designing elements for an interface (Norman, 1988; as cited in Griffiths, n.d.).

The best way to achieve these objectives is to divide the design of the interface, or the learning environment, to two dimensions: to a communicating dimension, *the interface*, which describes the interaction between the user and the learning environment and to an esthetical dimension, *the layout*, which describes the visual style of the product. As communication goals are more easily achieved with a strong esthetical structure (Mullet & Sano, 1995), these two dimensions are very much dependent of each other and only together can they make a learning environment a place where the interface supports the execution of tasks and therefore supports learning.

The functionality of the learning environment can be divided in usability and comprehensibility. The aims of its functions are described in the communicating dimension of the design. In the esthetical dimension topics like the problem of space, harmony of colors, and right font type are confronted.

Didactical Objectives

The "Mobile IP animation" is a learning object, which can be integrated in virtual network courses as well as in traditional network courses.

The chosen didactical approach is a structured animated network environment in which the communication between a CN and a MN can be studied. The communication logistics for all options of the Mobile IP can be studied on the highest level. Communication details, like the data packet header fields, can be interactively studied on lower levels of the animated environment.

Mobile IP Implementation

The learning environment should be a static and scalable framework for the dynamic features of Mobile IP. The underlying visualization model of the Mobile IP animation includes following features:

- communication architecture
- Home Network with HA Router
- two Foreign Networks with FA Router
- a Corresponding Node, CN
- data communication paths
- fundamental data structures
- flow of data packets
- structure of data packets.

Integration of additional Mobile IP features is supported.

The animation is implemented in an environment where a big part of the elements are symbols, in other words they are elements that have a conventional relationship to their referent. This means that the referents, the technical objects, are typically described with these more easily comprehended symbols or graphical elements. Internet is described with the help of a cloud, networks by an area in this cloud, and routers are computers that are labeled with the symbol of a router (⊃⊂). Data packets in data communication are described with rectangular boxes that are similar to packets. Nevertheless there are also elements that are described through their imaginable physical appearance. These elements are the information flow that is described with a packet flow and the radio signals that are described with a flow of waves. Moreover, the correspondent node is an actual person responding to the mobile node that is described through an owl. An owl was chosen as a mobile node as it has the capability to fly, which makes it easy to resolve the problem of the constant moving of the receiver between the networks, and is considered likable, wise and respectable. Animals also often inspire sympathy and therefore give the learning environment, and the very technical contents of it, a humanitarian tone.

All these elements are designed to help the study process and to establish a connection between theory and reality as all the levels of communication are brought to the highest level of abstraction through a physical appearance. The implemented Mobile IP becomes comprehensible for everybody as it is in a recognizable and imaginable environment.

The animation is structured through a division of the learning material into eleven scenes and seven detail scenes. Besides helping the comprehension of the animation and its contents, this division contributes also to reducing the consequences of errors that a user might commit when navigating in the product, and renders the use of the product easier as the search times for particular events is less than in an animation without scenes. A possible future development is an index with a table of contents.

To play all the scenes in the animation with the respective detail scenes takes about 40 minutes. This estimation does not include the additional time of a learning process, which is a difficult variable to count, as it is subjective.

Communicating Dimension – The Interface

The learning environment is designed after an old television with a screen with round edges and on it's left cannel, or here scene, buttons and other control buttons. The motivation of the design is to render the control of the animation familiar and to wake attention and interest combining old and new, traditional media and new media.

For a good usability and comprehensibility of the product the interface has to present clearly the

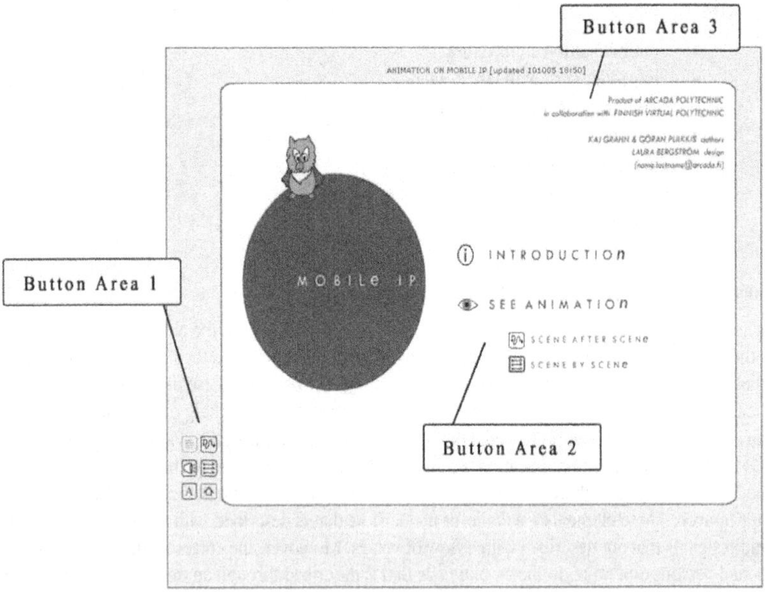

Figure 3: The start composition of the animation. The mouse is over the 'scene-by-scene' option in 'see animation'.

possible operations that may be done in the product and their results. In the start composition of the animation the user has three possibilities of interaction with the product, in other words in this state there are three different button areas on which the user can focus his attention (see Figure 3). Button area 1 is a part of the animations' control panel and will be visible all the time during the use of the product. This property of persistence is described with the fact that it is located outside the television screen, e.g. outside the dynamic animation area, and is therefore available also after changing the contents on the screen. On the contrary, button areas 2 and 3 are located inside the animation area, and are in fact only visible for the user in this particular state of the animation (home page). Button area 3 contains information about the authors of the product and can therefore be easily understood as non-relevant information for the use of the product. Button area 2 initially contains two options, introduction and see animation, and their functionalities as main options are described through a big font and an additional graphical symbol. When bringing the mouse over these options a further description of the user's possibilities is introduced. An observant user can also notice that the same two possibilities for seeing the animation are offered in the control panel on the left. These above mentioned actions are all the possible actions that the user can at this point initialise. Once selected one of the playing modes (see animation) there will appear a list of scenes above the control panel buttons in button area 1 (see Figure 4), which will expand the users possibilities for action.

The learning platform can be divided in three parts, where every part has a particular role (see Figure 4). The screen where the animation is played is the dynamic area of the learning platform, and the text area underneath it is synchronized with the events in it. The control panel on the left of the screen implements the control and comprehension of the platform.

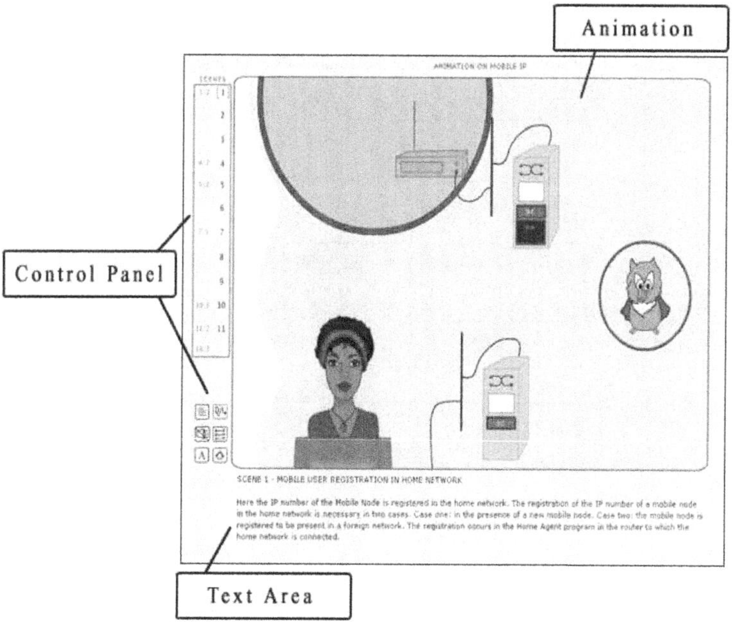

Figure 4: The beginning explanation of scene 1 is playing. The control panel is on the left of the animation meanwhile the text area is below it.

Usability

There are two different animation modes;

1. the main scenes, which are eleven, can be played all in a row with the play mode scene-after-scene and
2. the detail scenes, which are details of a particular event in a determinate scene, can be played only on request.

The study material has been divided in events, or scenes, to render it easier to comprehend, handle and play. This means also that the user is not obliged to see the whole animation when he/she wants to play or replay just a particular event. All scenes, main and detail scenes, start with a beginning explanation that however can be jumped over in the main scenes. This feature allows frequent or material acquainted users to avoid the, for others important, explanations that could for them become elements of frustration. The explanations describe the context, the actions and other necessary information of the scene that is to be played. To render this otherwise difficult listening part, where the user has a passive role, easier to follow, it has been animated in synchronization with the audio and highlighting elements of interest in the environment (see Figure 4).

The main scenes are not interactive, with the exception of the prompt windows that ask the user if he wants to see details, and can therefore only be watched. The detail scenes are on the contrary interactive and divided in multiple steps that the user has to choose between for the animation to play (see Figure 5). Also the introduction to the Mobile IP Environment, which can be accessed from the home page of the learning environment, is interactive (see Figure 6). The introduction permits the user to get acquainted to the all the elements in the animation by bringing the mouse over them and then read (listen) about their significance to the Mobile IP. In the main scenes a constant flow of information was chosen over the activeness of the user as it in this situation helps to establish a connection between small events and the context. Furthermore, this causes less frustration in a frequent user than obligated interventions from his part. On the contrary, it was thought suitable to leave the possibility for an interaction between the product and the user in the detail scenes, where studying chosen features demands its own time.

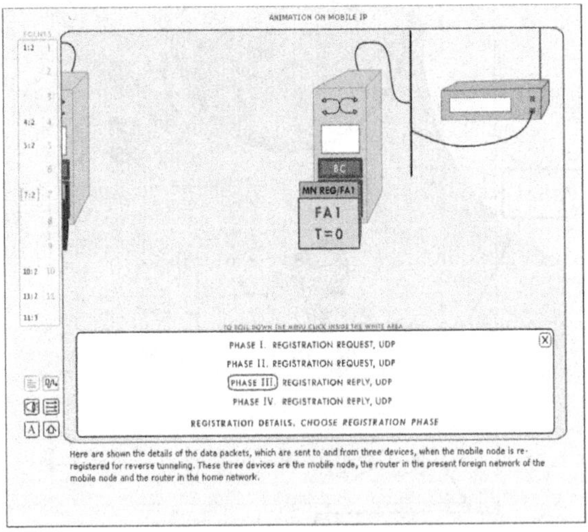

Figure 5: The detail scene of scene 7 is playing. The mouse is over the third option of this detail scene.

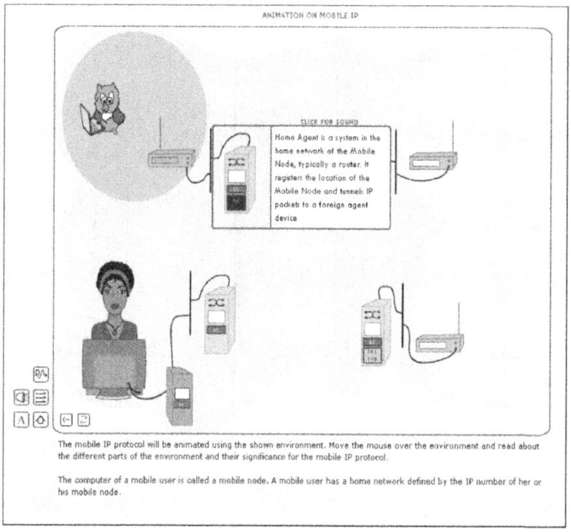

Figure 6: The introduction to the Mobile IP Environment is playing. The mouse is over the Home Agent Router.

The control panel allows the user to navigate inside the learning environment and to control the flow of the animation. In play mode it is composed of a scene area and six control buttons (see Figure 4). In the scene area the numbered scenes are placed in numeric order (see Figure 7). The main scenes are whole numbers meanwhile the detail scenes are composed of two numbers where the first number indicates the main scene it derives from and the second number indicates it being second (or third) part of the particular scene. For example 1:2 is a detail scene of an event in scene 1 (see Figure 8). The six control buttons are placed below the scenes area. These control buttons are home, scene-after-scene, scene-by-scene, sound, authors, and skip explanation (see Figure 9). The last mentioned is active just in the beginning of every scene as it lets the user to jump over the beginning explanation of a scene and to see only the animation without detailed explanations of the material.

The home button brings the user to the home page of the animation, in other words to the start of the animation (see Figure 3). The protagonist of the animation, the flying owl, is introduced directly in the beginning by letting him fly into a scene otherwise non-animated. In this way the user's interest is waked up immediately and he is invited to explore the product. To continue the user has to choose between introduction to the animation or playing the animation. The access to the introduction of the animations environment is only from this home page as it is considered information that the user studies before playing the animation. There are two different modes to play the animation, scene-after-scene and scene-by-scene mode, which can be chosen either from this beginning picture or from the control panel. If the scene-after-scene mode is chosen the animation will automatically continue to the next scene after one scene has ended. In scene-by-scene mode the animation on the contrary will stop at every fully played scene. It was chosen to have these both options because a user who is already familiar with the product or a user who wants to study the animation more slowly than programmed may be motivated to see just a specific part of the animation at a time.

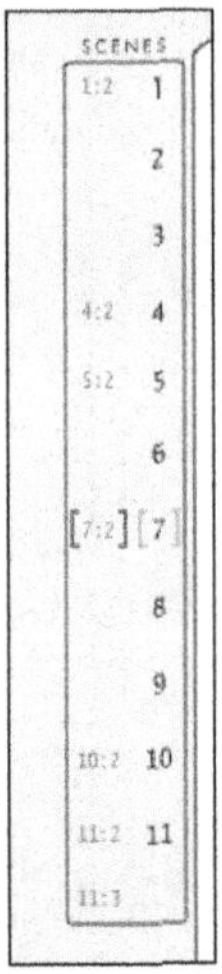

Figure 7: The scenes area in normal mode. Here scene 7 is playing and the mouse is over its detail scene.

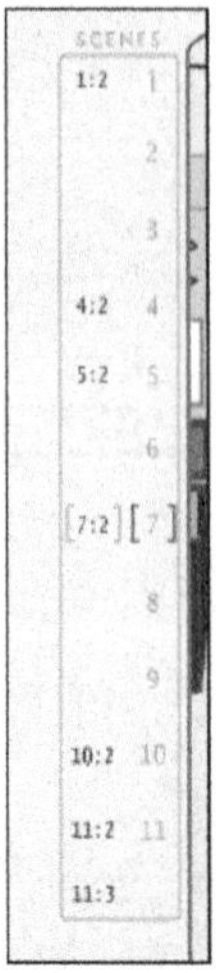

Figure 8: The scenes area when a detail scene is open. Here a detail scene from scene 7 is playing. The mouse is over scene 7.

Figure 9: The control buttons. The significance of the buttons beginning from the top left; skip explanation, scene-after-scene, audio, scene-by-scene, authors and home. Here the scene-after-scene mode is playing and the mouse is over the author's button.

The sound button switches off or on the audio of the animation. The role of this button becomes important at the point where the user wants to switch off the sound of this product without muting his computer. The last element in the control panel, the authors button, opens or closes a small window containing the necessary information of the authors of the product.

The third element of the learning environment is the text area, which is located under the animation, and where all the played audio will appear in the form of text (see Figure 4). This is an important part of the learning environment as all the students have different ways of learning, and it is relevant to include both audio stimulation and text support.

Comprehensibility

A good comprehensibility of a product is achieved when the elements of the interface have an efficient relationships between the interpretation of them and their effects, and when the users actions towards the interface have a feedback from the part of the last mentioned. Here the comprehensibility of the elements in the interface, regarding the signs that they are described through and the feedback that they give to the users actions, is discussed.

A green color indicates to the user where he finds himself in the material, for example when the user is located in the first scene and playing the animation in scene-after-scene mode. Both scene 1 and scene-after-scene buttons are highlighted with a bright green color (see Figure 4). This kind of path indication supports the navigation and makes it clearer. However, an easy comprehensibility is achieved only by combining path indication and action feedback. Action feedback means that when the user brings his mouse over a button or hyperlink this should indicate him its task or its activeness. Here all feedback is given with a dark red color. The same red is used for highlighting the elements of interest during the beginning explanation of the scenes, as its aim is to support the audio and in this way give feedback for thoughts.

The control panel buttons are designed to demonstrate their functions as efficiently as possible (see Figure 9). The signs on the home and audio buttons are symbols, in other words signs that have a conventional relationship to their referent. These kinds of signs are more often easily recognizable as the user is used to the symbols and know their meaning. Therefore, if it is possible, signs as symbols are strongly recommended, especially for learning environment interfaces. The signs on the buttons scene-after-scene, scene-by-scene and skip explanation are icons meaning that the design reflects their referent by appearance. The user is probably able to interpret the meaning of the signs if he applies them to the situation, but it could take him a longer time to interpret an icon compared to a symbol that is familiar to him from advance. However, if the functions of the buttons are not clear to the user, an explanation of what it will do appears on its side when the mouse is brought over the button. This is in fact the only way to understand the signification of the authors button as it is represented with a sign 'A' that stands for 'Authors'. This was considered to be the best option for a referent that doesn't have a conventional sign or is not easily presentable by appearance.

On the home page we can find two buttons, the information and play animation buttons (see Figure 3). The first one is represented with the symbol 'I' that refers to 'Information'. This sign is very commonly used for the referent and can therefore be considered the symbol of 'Information'. Also the second button that is an image of an eye, which refers to the action 'to see', clearly states the function of it.

The scenes area in the control panel has two modes; a main mode for the main scenes and a detail mode for the detail scenes. The second mentioned differs from the main mode for its lower color intensity (see Figure 7 and 8). These two modes are designed to support and enhance the different purposes of the contents in main mode animations and detail mode animations.

Esthetical Dimension – The Layout

The secrets of an elegant and harmonic interface are unity of its elements, contrast that creates tension and interest, and space that helps separate elements earn more attention and/or be grouped (Mullet & Sano, 1995). In other words contrast and space create visibility and unity creates coherence; these are two of the principals that are to keep in mind when designing an interface so that a direct interaction between the user and the product can be achieved (see section *Learning Environment Design*).

All the buttons and also the scenes area, authors window and the screen where the animation is played have rounded corners, which is the unifying element of the learning environment. Another unifying factor is the use of a limited amount of colors in the interface, which are dark gray, red and green. The contrast between elements is created with

1. closure, the element that describes the function of the button is closed inside an defined area (square),
2. colors, the path indication color, the feedback color and the buttons normal color are all easily distinctive, and
3. size, the small size of the control panel buttons compared to the big size of the screen.

Space is used in the control panel between the six buttons and the scenes area to enhance their different functionalities; almost all of the six buttons are for an overall control of the product, while the scenes buttons permits to control the flow of the animation. Also the text area is separated from these elements by a vertical space underneath the buttons that almost seems an explicit and concrete graphical barrier although it is not.

The background color of the learning platform is light gray, which enhances and lifts up the animation that is built on a white background. This is because white, which derives from the unity of red, green and blue (according to the additive color system RGB), has a higher value of light than gray, which is a tint, or a pure color to which has been added white and has therefore a lower value of light than white (Götz, 1998; Larmann, 1995). This causes an effect that pushes the gray on the background and brings the white on top.

All buttons are dark gray and highlighted with a clear green to indicate the path and with dark red to give feedback for users actions. These colors are chosen because green indicates among other things permission or 'go!' and given the situation of its use, an element being used or played, the color corresponds to its function. On the contrary red often stands for stop, alert or attention and is here used as feedback color for user's actions. Often choosing another option means interrupting the one that is playing and therefore the user has to pay attention to his choice as the one playing will stop and/or disappear. These two colors are also the two colors less used in the animation, which makes their use easy as they are not associated to another element in the learning environment.

The font type used in the animation and in the rest of the learning environment is Tw Cen MT. The written audio text is dark gray of the size 11 (points). This is a font without serifs, in other words without end curves in the letters, and because of that it has a better legibility on the computer screen than a font with serifs, like for example Times New Roman.

IT Infrastructure Requirements

Offering the product requires an Apache www server with installed Secure Socket Layer (SSL) support for secure authentication of learning environment users. User authentication to a virtual course, into which the Mobile IP learning environment has been integrated, is necessary. Email address, mobile phone number and Skype address of the user are needed for communication with course teachers.

Requisites for using the product are a high bandwidth Internet connection, a Flash Player that can be downloaded from the website of Macromedia (http://www.macromedia.com), and loudspeakers or headphones. Nevertheless, the animation can be seen without sound as it contains all the audio also as text. A relatively high screen resolution is another important hardware characteristic that is needed for playing the animation properly. In a 800 x 600 pixel resolution screen not even the whole animation area is fully visualized and the user has the scroll both vertically and horizontally to see all corners of the learning platform. With a 1024 x 768 pixel resolution all except the text area is fully visualized. In all screens with 1280 x 1024 pixels and more the learning platform is fully visualized. Therefore a computer screen with at least 1024 x 768 pixel resolution is recommended. In other words at least a laptop is needed for optimal using of this product. A PDA is not sufficient.

The product works with browsers Mozilla Firefox, Netscape 7 and Internet Explorer.

User feedback

A team from the Finnish Virtual Polytechnic (Finnish Virtual Polytechnic, 2006a) has evaluated the learning platform both from a pedagogic and heuristic point of view. The evaluation, which is in Finnish, is available online but requires authentication, e.g. a user account for Finnish Virtual Polytechnic (Finnish Virtual Polytechnic, 2006b).

According to the team the strength of the product, from the pedagogical point of view, is in its context and problem formulation, which are authentic. Also the fact that the user can focus on some details of the Mobile IP is considered particularly good. But on the contrary improvements regarding support for thinking and problem resolving processes of the user could be made. In fact tasks could be associated to the animation in the way that the user has to find answers to them navigating in the animation.

The positive feedback regarding the heuristic evaluation of the platform is its simple navigation that together with an efficient and flexible interface offers the user an easy and, from his part, controlled use of the platform. However some persons from the evaluation team would have wanted more instructions for use before starting the animation. The visualization of the contents in the animation is according to the team expressive and clear, although to fully understand all the elements in it requires having seen the introduction. The introduction is the element that received most critics, as it is not clear and interactive enough. A positive factor is also the fact that the platform is uploaded fast and that it works in many environments.

Conclusions

Mobile IP is – compared to other network protocols – a complex protocol with many options and extensions. The creation of a network learning environment is therefore a demanding challenge. Experts, like graphical designers, have to be included in the production team. Prototypes have to be tested and feedback from students is needed before the learning environment is in its final form. A proper choice of computer software and IT technology is necessary. Furthermore, a sufficient and realistic budget is essential.

The Mobile IP learning environment has proven to be of major importance for the students. In general, the levels of acceptance and satisfaction have been high. The work done during the project has given the authors valuable experience for further work on similar issues.

A future extension of the implemented learning environment will be integration of security schemes in the Mobile IP animation. An example is animation of 'redirection of data packet' DOS attacks with and without strong authentication. The animation should show how the DOS attack succeeds without strong authentication and how it fails with strong authentication. Request/reply messaging to/from AAA servers will be included. Also training exercises should be implemented. A user of the learning environment should have possibilities to trigger DOS attack patterns and study how the attack patterns are handled by different Mobile IP extensions.

References

Barun, T. & Danzeisen, M. (2001). Secure mobile IP communication. *Proceedings of IEE 26th Annual Conference on Local Computer Networks*, 586-593.

Calhoun, P., Johansson, T., Perkins, C., Hiller,T., & McCann, E. P. (2005). Diameter mobile IPv4 application. IETF, RFC 4004. Retrieved March 8, 2006, from http://www.ietf.org/rfc/rfc4004.txt?number=4004

Finnish Virtual Polytechnic (2006a). Portal of Finnish virtual polytechnic. Retrieved March 3, 2006, from http://www.virtuaaliamk.fi/channels/www/eng/etusivu.html

Finnish Virtual Polytechnic (2006b). Production team evaluation page (internal). Retrieved March 3, 2006, from https://www.virtuaaliamk.fi/opintojaksot/041005/1092991850017/1099044944687/1113319626141/1113319658781.html.stx

Glass, S., Hiller, T., Jacobs, S., & Perkins, C. (2000). Mobile IP authentication, authorization, and accounting requirements. IETF, RFC 2977. Retrieved March 8, 2006, from http://www.ietf.org/rfc/rfc2977.txt?number=2977

Griffiths, R. (n.d.) Norman's gulfs of execution and evaluation. Retrieved February 27, 2006, from http://www.it.bton.ac.uk/staff/rng/teaching/notes/NormanGulfs.html

Götz, V. (1998). *Color & type for the screen*. Crans: RotoVision SA.

Hwu, J.-S., Chen, R.-J. & Lin, Y.-B. (in press). An efficient identity-based cryptosystem for end-to-end mobile security. *IEEE Transactions on Wireless Communication*.

Islam, R. (2005). *Enhanced security in Mobile IP communication*. MSc Thesis, Department of Computer and Systems Sciences, Royal Institute of Technology, Stockholm, Sweden.

ISP Glossary (2005). Mobile IP. Retrieved January 20, 2005 from, http://isp.webopedia.com/TERM/M/Mobile_IP.html

Jacobs, S. & Belgard, S. (2001, July). Mobile IP public key based authentication. IETF, Internet Draft (expired). Retrieved November 27, 2005, from http://mirrors.isc.org/pub/www.watersprings.org/pub/id/draft-jacobs-mobileip-pki-auth-03.txt

Johansson, F. & Johansson, T, (2004). Mobile IPv4 extension for carrying network access identifiers. IETF, RFC 3846. Retrieved March 8, 2006, from http://www.ietf.org/rfc/rfc3846.txt?number=3846

Kurose, J. & Ross, K.W. (2005). *Computer networking* (3rd ed.). USA: Pearson.

Larmann, R. M. (1995). *Color saturation and intensity*. University of Evansville, Art Department. Retrieved November 26, 2005, from http://www2.evansville.edu/studiochalkboard/c-saturate.html

Lee, B-G., Choi, D-H., Kim, H-G., Sohn, S-W., & Park, K-H. (2003). Mobile IP and WLAN with AAA authentication protocol using identity-based cryptography. *10th International Conference on Telecommunications ICT 2003*, *1*, 597 - 603

Montenegro, G. (1998). *RFC 2344 -Reverse tunnelling for Mobile IP*. Retrieved November 29, 2005, from http://www.faqs.org/rfcs/rfc2344.html

Mullet, K. & Sano, D. (1995). *Designing visual interfaces*. Mountain View, CA: Sun Microsystems.

Perkins, C. (2002). IP mobility support for IPv4, IETF, RFC 3344. Retrieved March 8, 2006, from http://www.ietf.org/rfc/rfc3344.txt?number=3344

Perkins, C. & Calhoun, P. (2000). Mobile IPv4 challenge/response extensions, IETF, RFC 3012. Retrieved March 8, 2006, from http://www.ietf.org/rfc/rfc3012.txt?number=3012

Shamir, A. (1984). Identity-based cryptosystems and signature schemes. *Advances in Cryptology-CRYPTO'84*, 47-53.

Schiller, J. (2000). *Mobile communications*. Great Britain: Addison-Wesley.

Webopedia (2005). The #1 online encyclopedia dedicated to computer technology. Retrieved November 29, 2005, from http://www.webopedia.com/TERM/r/roaming.html

Zao, J. K. & Condell, M. (1997, November). Use of IPSec in mobile IP. IETF, Internet Draft (expired). Retrieved November 28, 2005, from http://mirrors.isc.org/pub/www.watersprings.org/pub/id/draft-ietf-mobileip-ipsec-use-00.txt

Zao, J., Kent, S., Gahm, J., Troxel, G., Condell, M., Helinek, P., Yuan, N. & Castineyra, I. (1999). A public-key based secure mobile IP. *Wireless Networks*, *5*(5), 393-390.

Biographies

Laura Bergström has a BSc in Media Culture from Arcada Polytechnic, Espoo Finland. Since March 2002 she works for Arcada Polytechnic as graphical designer in virtual education development.

Kaj J. Grahn, Dr. Tech., is presently senior lecturer in Telecommunications at the Department of Business Administration, Media, and Technology of Arcada Polytechnic, Helsinki, Finland. He is also Program Manager of the Electrical Engineering Programme. His current research interests include Wireless and Mobile Network Security.

Göran Pulkkis, Dr. Tech., is presently senior lecturer in Computer Science and Engineering at the Department of Business Administration, Media, and Technology of Arcada Polytechnic, Helsinki, Finland. His current research interests include Network Security and Applied Cryptography

The page left blank intentionally.

Navigating the Virtual Forest: How Networked Digital Technologies Can Foster Transgeographic Learning

Nicole A. Buzzetto-More
University of Maryland Eastern Shore, Princess Anne, MD, USA

Nabuzzetto-more@umes.edu

Abstract

During the past decade the globally networked digital technologies that operate within the realm of the internet have encouraged academicians and educators the world over to communicate, collaborate, and share knowledge. They have stimulated the creation of transgeographic educational initiatives which broaden the opportunities of learners and are an effective means of eradicating ethnocentrism, xenophobia, and cultural divides.

The construction of transgeographic learning communities within the unmapped virtual forest of the internet requires an organized and systematic approach. Success is dependent on committed participants; a shared learning platform; a clear understanding of purpose; extensive student and instructor preparedness towards technology usage; exemplary curricula; a central focus for investigation; interaction with experts; extensive opportunities for intellectual discourse; and collaboration.

The purpose of this paper is to offer an independent examination of a successful technology-dependent transgeographic learning project that serves as a model from which to base future projects. The Summer Ecosystems Experience for Undergraduates (SEE-U) is available to colleges and university students worldwide, operating at three geographically distinct locations concurrently. The program includes global networking, GPS and GIS usage, a shared investigative focus, real-time interactions, data collection, a globally networked geo-referenced digital database that was specifically created for this project, data manipulation, online lectures, bulletin board discussions, Web-based office hours, links to relevant resources, expert presenters, online demonstration videos, networked simulations, collaborative research, and a series of student presentations.

Keywords: Information Communication, e-Learning, Co-operative Learning, Global Education, Distance Education, Global Networking, Instructional Technology

Introduction

The Summer Ecosystems Experience for Undergraduates, otherwise known as SEE-U, is a model of the how information technologies can be used to foster global education. It operates under the auspices of Columbia University's Center for Environmental Research and Conservation, CERC, an organization comprised of world-class scientific institutions. It was created through a collaboration with the Columbia Center for New Media in Teaching and Learning, an instructional technology- development center housed at Columbia University; the Center for International Earth Sciences Information Network, an organization that seeks to use information technology to enhance the worldwide effort to examine the impact of humans on the environment; and the Black Rock Forest Consortium, a unique and powerful amalgamation of distinguished academic institutions and science and cultural centers that successfully collaborate to enhance scientific research and education.

The SEE-U program was piloted in the summer of 2000. Since that time it has attracted students from across the globe. It is offered in three locations concurrently and is an in-depth field and technology-based introduction to ecology, and environmental studies.

Technologies are used in interesting and innovative ways serving as an example for other courses. Students participating in the SEE-U program take advantage of Geographic Position System (GPS) technology to spatially reference data; Geographic Information System (GIS) technology to allow detailed mapping and topographical representation of data; modeling software for the visualization of and experimentation with data; detailed computer networking; online research; digital lectures and demonstration videos; synchronous and asynchronous discussions with students across geographic borders; and an advanced database technology that is multi-query able. Operating across field sites, students use the power of networked digital technologies to compare and analyze data, develop hypothesis, and communicate and collaborate with learners that are geographically distant.

Literature Review

The current impact of technological innovation extends farther and deeper than at any other time in our history. These advances have altered the very constructs of space and time and have changed visibility, making it global in scope. The result has engendered a growing number of international learning communities. These communities open up a world of educational possibilities replete with symbolic interactions that cross geographic borders. Through well-developed globally networked technologies, educators and learners worldwide interact in courses and projects that cross cultural divides, encourage collaboration, develop broader perspectives, and foster intellectual discourse (Buzzetto-More, 2005).

Research conducted by McIsaac (1993) found that the use of information technologies in the fostering of global education is a highly effective means for encouraging educational empowerment. He explained that, although numerous methodologies can be employed in the use of networked digital technologies to create global learning communities, there are issues that must be addressed. According to McIsaac, these issues include language; pedagogy; technological accessibility, usability and reliability; motivation; and project cost and practicality.

Research studies have shown that people learn through meaningful interactions with others (Johnson & Thomas, 1994). A major goal of global education is the creation of learning communities that use technology to stimulate meaningful discourse between and among cultures (McIsaac, 1993). Bhatti, Tubaishat, and El-Quawasmeh (2005) found that technology mediated learning environments can help students overcome social and cultural limitations in higher education.

Technology and global-education partnerships can provide students with nontraditional learning experiences, and perhaps no subject matter is better suited for technology incorporation then science education (Buzzetto-More, 2005).

Skeptics often point out the hands-on nature of scientific study as a deterrent; however, Peter Fenrich (2005) of the British Columbia Institute of Technology found that when simulations, active experimentations, discovery-based learning, interactivity, questioning, feedback, collaboration, and animated models are used, one can successfully teach hands-on skills virtually.

Digital technologies are allowing for more creative and innovative science education that goes beyond the traditional drill and memorization of facts (Lemke in Scalpter, 1998). Kastens (1999) explains that the current goal is to take environmental learning away from the pre-packaged lab and decontextualized textbook-based lessons and transform ecology education by linking science education to scientific practice. Bridging the gaps between learners and scientists is done through the use of real data, hands-on experimentation, the examination scientific processes, modeling, and access to actual working scientists (Buzzetto-More, 2004).

Technology is considered by many to be a means of assisting in the delivery of authentic learning experiences in ecology studies. According to Cheryl Lemke (Scalpter, 1998), technology facilitates the study of science by increasing the scope of available resources, allowing for expedient and reliable access to data and research materials, enhancing collaboration, encouraging systems thinking, and by effectively delivering curriculum.

Kim Kastens of Lamont Doherty Earth Observatory discusses the need to make science education authentic and the role that technology plays in facilitating this effort (1999). Kastens (1999) illustrates that technology helps students imitate the method of inquiry practiced by actual working scientists which in turn makes learning more authentic.

The movement from traditional learning to technology enabled learning has been explained as a move towards the constructivist educational model (Lewis, MacEntee, DeLaCruz, Englander, Jeffrey, Takach, Wilson, & Woodall, 2005) where learning involves collaboration, social discourse, problem solving, exploration, anchored instruction, critical thinking, intellectual discourse, knowledge construction, and scaffolding (Koohang and Harman, 2005).

Kaplan and Black (2001) found that visual mapping technologies help students build effective mental models. Black (1995) explained that through mental models students make observations; engage in visualization; construct interpretations of their observances; use references to contextualize the information; and gain permanence and transferability by being exposed to multiple representations of the knowledge.

Black, Hachey, and Tseui (2001) conducted studies that found that computer-based learning tools enhance student development of scientific reasoning skills by encouraging students to apply skills in meaningful scenarios.

This concept of using technology to immerse students in the scientific process has been echoed by Dede (2000) who noted that the careful design of virtual learning environments that immerse students in the scientific process help build deep understandings of complex scientific knowledge.

Sarapuu (n.d.) has explained the role that technology plays in enhancing the science learning process. He found that computerized learning in science education helps students with memory, comprehension, analysis, and the application of scientific knowledge.

Access to scientific resources and professionals is certainly not equitable. According to White and Frederiksen (2000), technology can serve as an equalizer that makes scientific knowledge more accessible to learners.

The benefits of technology-facilitated global education include: increased exposure to, and understanding of, different cultures so as to combat ethnocentrism; opportunities to prepare learners to enter what is increasingly a global workforce; the fostering of intercultural communications skills; the offering of unique insights through exposure to global perspectives; the development of the preparedness skills that facilitate student collaboration; and the building of necessary technological skills (Buzzetto-More, 2005).

When information communication is used to create global education, it can include a multitude of technologies. Requisite, however, is that the technology is networked; well developed and educationally relevant following student-centered design principles; that it be tested prior to implementation; contain a discussion section and a shared workspace; is user-friendly; includes easily accessible technology support; and has a backup plan in the event of technology failure (Buzzetto-More, 2005).

In order for technology-facilitated global learning experiences to be successful, they should include a central question for investigation; a shared online learning platform; a clear understanding of purpose; extensive student and instructor preparedness for technology usage; interaction with professional experts; a discussion forum; and a collaborative project that is shared among participants (Buzzetto-More, 2005).

Discussion

Curriculum

The five-week SEE-U program is a total immersion course based on the pedagogical concept of anchored instruction. It is held at several locations simultaneously, including the Black Rock Forest in New York State, the Atlantic Forest in Brazil, and Punta Cana in the Dominican Republic, with plans to expand to Kenya. During this field ecology course learners explore biomes globally and locally.

The course is open to undergraduate students across the globe, regardless of college major. Interested students visit the SEE-U website, found at http://www.columbia.edu/itc/cerc/seeu. From the website students can request information or download an application. The website also includes the program's curriculum, field site information, and slide shows. (See Figure 1.)

Figure 1: SEE-U Homepage, courtesy of SEE-U/ CERC

Scientists rarely work independently or in isolation from other scientists. As a result, participants in the SEE-U program conduct scientific research and make discoveries in cooperative learning groups. Collaboratively, the learners create presentations that result in their sharing of findings and entering into discourse with students located remotely. Because success for the students is largely dependent on collaboration, learners develop an understanding that science is a cooperative practice.

The students begin with background information and a shared question for investigation. Throughout the course they research the question by gathering data and testing out different hypotheses in the same manner as professional scientists. The goal of the hands-on experimental aspect of the SEE-U course is designed to help students to develop and build scientific research skills.

The SEE-U curriculum comprises four major sections, namely, biomes, biotic processes, a biotic processes, and contemporary issues. Biomes covers the understanding of the world's major biomes, the different biomes represented by the participating field sites, and provides an in-depth focus on the local biome where the students are immersed. The section on biotic processes includes natural selection and evolution; growth and competition, otherwise known as population dynamics; community ecology; and the basis of ecosystems. A biotic processes, covers the role of light and temperature, geology and soils, chemical and hydrological cycles, and geological disturbances. Contemporary issues, focuses the social, political, and ethical issues that are of concern to their respective biome as well as to the other field sites.

Within each section, topics are broken down into modules. In total there are 16 modules, each taking one or two days to cover. The learning modules include experiments, and throughout the five-week course the learners participate in roughly 20 experiments.

During the experiments, learners enter the field and collect data, later conducting simulations and modeling to analyze their findings. Students work with both archived and new data – seeking, analyzing, and learning from networked information – presenting the total of their work.

Most educational theorists agree that intellectual discussion facilitates learning. The learners in the SEE-U program have symbolic interactions with their counterparts located at the remote field sites. Throughout the program they enter into relevant discourse as they participate in online discussions, take part in collaborative research, share and compare findings, conduct networked simulations, and hear and participate in lectures and discussions given by scientists across the globe.

Technology Use

The SEE-U program uses technology in the acquisition, analysis, modeling, and comparison of data and also to foster communications, collaborations, discussions, debate, and the delivery of curricula. Participating students use Geographic Position System (GPS) technology to spatially reference data; Geographic Information System (GIS) technology for the mapping and topographical representation of data; modeling software for the visualization of and experimentation with data; web based research databases; digital lectures and demonstration videos; synchronous and asynchronous discussions; and an advanced database.

Although the SEE-U program is a field course, it is designed and delivered in many ways as a distance-learning program. Course information is completely delivered online, including lecture notes, slides, text, video, web links, database access, discussion-board availability, live chats, and subscriptions to relevant online scientific publications. The benefits of the online delivery of information are increased access to materials, accuracy in delivery, and the ability for students to visit and revisit course information according to need and interest (Buzzetto-More, 2004).

Global networking allows the learners to communicate and collaborate across all of the program's biological field sites as students share data and work on research projects together. As a result, this course helps illustrate the global nature of the scientific community and the importance of sharing and comparing discoveries with other scientists.

Ebiome

At the core of the Summer Ecosystems Experience is the use of EBiome, which is a geo-spatially referenced database that is available through the global network to all program participants. During the program, participants embark to the field and collect data using GPS instrumentation. GPS technology involves the use of radio signals received from at least four satellites that exist in geo-synchronous orbits circling the Earth. GPS makes it possible to pinpoint exact locations where data is collected. Student use the GPS system to determine the precise latitude and longitude where data are collected.

Upon returning to base station the students input their data into the specially designed EBiome database. Datasets in EBiome can be reference and compared spatially, topically, or by biome. For example, users may search data-sets by any number of characteristics such as data type, by spatial reference, and or by the date or time of the data collection. Users can set parameters for querying data such as soil ph>6.4<3.2. Additionally, Ebiome includes copious amounts of meta-data elements, which help to insure data accuracy and integrity and allow for additional forms of inquiry. According to CERC the benefits of Ebiome are the storage of data for longitudinal study and comparison, the referencing of data and compilation in a digital repository, the geo-referencing of data, the amount of metadata included, and that students take part in the data-collection process. (See Figure 2.)

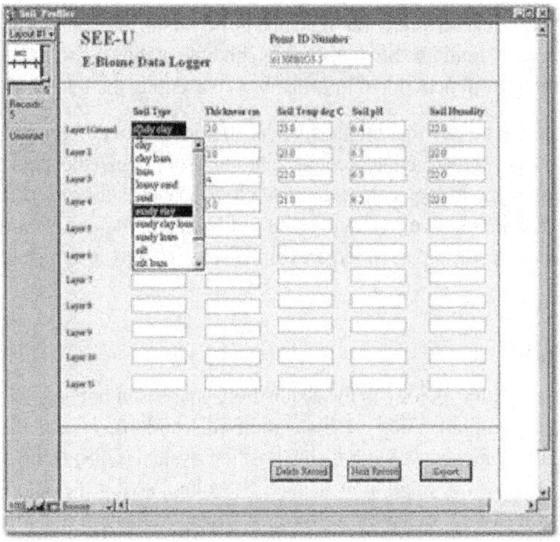

Figure 2: E-Biome Data Logger, courtesy of SEEU/ CERC

EBiome is a unique digital database that is designed to serve as a central repository to what is, increasingly becoming significant and copious amounts of longitudinal data.

EBiome was created specifically for the SEE-U program and is one of the most unique and integral parts of the course. EBiome was created by the Center for Environmental Research and Conservation (CERC), the Columbia Center for New Media in Teaching and Learning (CCNMTL), and the Center for International Earth Sciences Information Network (CIESEN).

All of the data collected as part of the student investigations is entered into EBiome and can be accessed by all who are participating in the program onsite or remotely, as well as by instructors and research scientists the world over.

Students participating in the SEE-U program compare their data to archival data and to data collected by their counterparts at the remote field sites. The students discuss information across locations as they enter into relevant discourse through interactions with learners via the global network at the other biological field sites. At the same time, the students are given the opportunity to assist some of the world's leading scientists in their efforts.

Students enrolled in the SEE-U course are well versed in the use of Ebiome. Prior to working with the technology, students are trained in its proper use and many features. This training is built directly into the course curriculum.

GIS

Ebiome allows data to be represented spatially, using Geographic Information System (GIS) technology. GIS is a dynamic mapping system that allows individuals to collect, manage, and spatially reference volumes of data. GIS involves a series of aerial photos that have been digitized allowing for the construction of elevation models. Additional information is later entered on roads, trails, streams, landmarks, and other features that may not be included in aerial photos. Information displayed in GIS involves the overlaying of maps where individual map layers represent geological characteristics.

The GIS program used by SEE-U was specifically designed and formatted for use by SEE-U. For this project, the information is accessible using the ESRI Arc View Software and a Trimble GeoExplorer mapping system which serves as the field receiver that accepts the GPS information. (See Figure 3.)

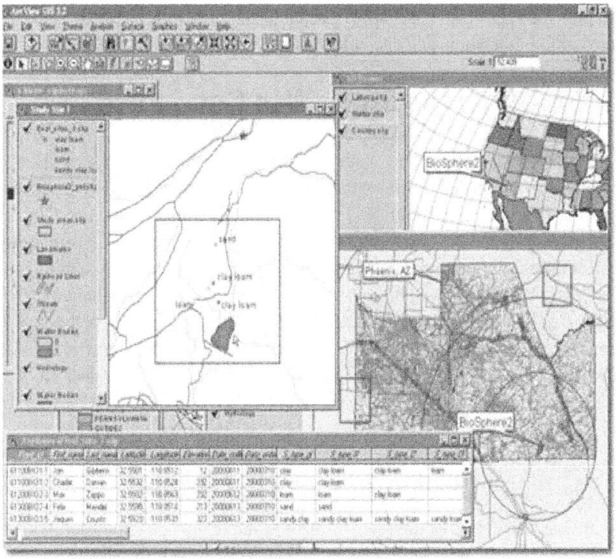

Figure 3: Arc View, courtesy of SEEU/ CERC

Program Goals

According to CERC, when students complete the SEE-U curriculum, they have developed a mastery of several key concepts, including, an understanding of the scientific method and its underlying theory; knowledge of the multilevel interaction of ecological elements and an appreciation of the importance of not disturbing these relationships; an understanding of the human impact on the environment; insight on the interaction of the world's biomes; illustration of ecological and biological diversity; comprehension of population dynamics; knowledge of the chemical cycle within an ecosystem; the ability to work with cutting-edge scientific research technology; an appreciation for human conservation, mediation, and preservation efforts; an appreciation for the global nature of scientific work; and the ability to collaborate and enter into relevant discourse with scientists across the globe.

Not only is the SEE-U program concerned with building knowledge, it is also designed to help students learn several key skills. According to CERC, these skills are a cornerstone of being a successful science student and later in a career as a professional working scientist. They include the ability to implement the scientific method and incorporate it into meaningful experiments; understanding primary statistical methodologies and the ability to conduct and select appropriate simple statistical analyses; knowledge of different field and laboratory techniques; the ability to gather data from a wide variety of sources and determine the relevance of that data; aptitude in preparing and presenting logical oral and written scientific research reports; the understanding of the importance of and the use of technological instrumentation to enhance scientific research; and the ability to communicate and collaborate with scientists across geographic divides.

Contributions

This paper represents an independent examination of an early and sizable transgeographic education project. It outlines a model that has been successful and is worthy of inspection. Although the SEE-U project focuses on global education in the area of science, the program has much broader implications across disciplines. This paper is meant to add to the current discussion of technology facilitated global education, and encourage further research and development.

How the Study Was Conducted

The author of this paper is not affiliated with the SEE-U program. This work represents an independent investigation conducted by an instructional technologist interested in the development and deployment of a technology facilitated transgeographic learning experience. The primary investigation began during the development and pilot testing of the program. The investigation was completed with follow up interviews conducted after the program had been running for a couple of years. The investigation involved the conduction of interviews with key individuals involved with the creation of SEE-U which included individuals affiliated with the Center for Environmental Research and Conservation, the Center for International Earth Sciences Information Network, the Columbia Center for New Media in Teaching and Learning, the Black Rock Forest, and the Black Rock Forest Consortium. Additional information was gathered through the review of internal and external documents.

Limitations of This Study

The most significant limitation of this study is that the author did not administer, nor have access, to student satisfaction surveys. Quantitative data of students' perceived satisfaction with the overall program, curriculum, technological components, and collaborative aspects would have brought to light strengths and weaknesses that were not evident during this examination.

Summary and Future Research

Digital technologies are closing spatial and temporal gaps while engendering expansive new international communities. Replete with symbolic interactions, these transgeographic communities inspire new realms of educational possibility, allowing educators and learners to broaden perspectives through intellectual discourse and collaboration while helping to eradicate cultural divides.

The Summer Ecosystems Experience for Undergraduates (SEE-U) is a model of how technology can be used to this end. The SEE-U program operates at three geographically distinct locations concurrently and includes field research, global networking, GPS and GIS usage, real-time interactions, data collection, a globally networked geo-referenced digital database, data manipulation, online lectures, bulletin board discussions, Web-based office hours, links to relevant resources, expert presenters, online demonstration videos, networked simulations, collaborative research, and a series of student presentations.

The activities included in the SEE-U program have been designed to bridge the gaps between scientific practice and learning and to prepare the next generation of scientists to use cutting edge technologies, be active in global discourse, and collaborate with fellow scientists. As a result of its design, the SEE-U program provides an experience unrivaled in field-science education.

International programs are growing in popularity across the globe. This investigation has helped to inspire the beginning stages of the development of a technology facilitated global education project between the University of Maryland Eastern Shore and several countries located in Sub-Saharan Africa.

References

Bhatti, A., Tubaisahat, A., & El-Qawasmeh, E. (2005). Using technology-mediated learning environment to overcome social and cultural limitations in higher education. *Issues in Informing Science and Information Technology*, 2. Available at http://2005papers.iisit.org/I06f77Bhat.pdf

Black, J. & Kaplan, K. (2001). Computer-based tools for the development and investigation of scientific reasoning skills. In C. Montgomerie & J. Vitelli (Eds.), *Proceedings of EdMedia World Conference On Educational Multimedia, Hypermedia & Telecommunications.* Norfolk, VA: Association for the Advancement of Computing in Education.

Black, J., Hachey, A., & Tsuei, L. (2001). Fostering mental-model thinking during design. In C. Montgomerie & J. Vitelli (Eds.), *Proceedings of EdMedia World Conference On Educational Multimedia, Hypermedia & Telecommunications.* Norfolk, VA: Association for the Advancement of Computing in Education.

Buzzetto-More, N. (2004). The Black Rock Forest consortium: A narrative. Ed.D. dissertation, Columbia University, New York.

Buzzetto-More, N. (2005, June 16-19). The IT Revolution: Applications and strategies for transgeographic learning and academia in the twenty-first century. *Proceedings of the Informing Science and Information Technology in Education Conference 2005.* Flagstaff, AZ. Available at http://proceedings.informingscience.org/InSITE2005/P02f104Buzz.pdf

Dede, C., Ash, K., M. Loftin, B., & Salzman. (2000). In M. Jackobson & R. Kozma, *Innovations in science and mathematics education: Advanced designs for technologies of learning.* Mahwah, NJ: Lawrence Erlbaum Associates.

Fenrich, P. (2005). What you can do to virtually teach hands on skills. *Issues in Informing Science and Information Technology*, 2. Available at http://2005papers.iisit.org/I28f14Fenr.pdf

Frederiksen, J. & White, B. (2000). In M. Jackobson & R. Kozma, *Innovations in science and mathematics education: Advanced designs for technologies of learning.* Mahwah, NJ: Lawrence Erlbaum Associates.

Heterick, R.C., Jr., Mingle, J. R., & Twigg, C. A. (1997). *The public policy implications of a global learning infrastructure.* Paper retrieved August 2003, from http://www.educause.edu/nlii/keydocs/policy.html

Johnson, S. D., & Thomas, R. G. (1994, Winter-Spring). Implications of cognitive science for instructional design in technology education. *Journal of Technology Studies, 20*, 33-45. (EJ 494 218)

Kastens, K. (1999, March 3). *Adding real-time data to the Black Rock Forest digital library to enable students to engage in predictiveiInvestigations.* Unpublished Proposal to the National Science Foundation. New York, NY: Columbia University, Lamont Doherty Earth Observatory.

Koohang, A., & Harmon, K. (2005). Open source: A metaphor for e-learning. *Informing Science Journal*, 8, 75-86. Retrieved from http://inform.nu/Articles/Vol8/v8p075-086Kooh.pdf

Lewis, B., MacEntee, V., DeLaCruz, S., Englander, C., Jeffrey, T., Takach, E., Wilson, S., & Woodall, J. (2005). Learning management systems comparison. *Proceedings of the 2005 Informing Science and IT Education Joint Conference.* Available at http://proceedings.informingscience.org/InSITE2005/P03f55Lewis.pdf

McIssac, M. (1993, January). The global classroom: An international perspective. In: *Proceedings of Selected Research and Development Presentations at the Convention of the Association for Educational Communications and Technology Education.* Educational Resources Information Center. ERIC Identifier: ED3262186

McClintock, R. (1999). *Educators manifesto: Renewing the progressive bond with posterity through the social construction of digital learning communities.* Published Paper. New York, NY: Teachers College, Columbia University, Institute for Learning Technologies.

Sarapuu, T., Adojaan, K., Hirmo, C., Laane, T., Mallo, L., Pata, K., Pedaste, M., & Puusepp, A. (n.d.). *Designing visualized learning process through educational technology.* Retrieved August 2003, from http://www.ut.ee/biodida/e/teadust.htm

Scalpeter, J. (1998). Interview with Cheryl Lemke. Ed Tech Research Forum. *Technology and Learning Magazine.*

Biography

Dr. **Nicole A Buzzetto-More** has a doctorate in communications and instructional technology from Columbia University, a masters in education in communications and instructional technology from Columbia University, a masters of science in communications from the College of New Rochelle, and a bachelor of arts degree from Marist College. Originally from New York, she currently resides on the eastern shore of Maryland where she is a faculty member in the School of Business and Technology at the University of Maryland Eastern Shore. Her intellectual interests include the uses of digital technologies to augment teaching and learning. She has published a number of papers in referred journals and is a frequent presenter at conferences across the globe. In 2005, she was honored by the American Distance Education Consortium. She is currently working on her first book.

Semantics, Ontologies and Information Systems in Education: Concerns and Proposals

Antonio Cartelli
Faculty of Humanities, University of Cassino
Cassino (FR) Italy

cartan@unicas.it

Abstract

The author describes his experience with students interacting with some websites he made for didactics and research and how this led him to an appreciation for the need for better searching tools and strategies for education. The students' difficulties emerging from the above observations were a special case of the more general problem evidenced from people while searching information on the web. Semantic web is then discussed as a way to help people overcome their difficulties in using the web to gain knowledge.

The paper describes some models for knowledge construction and analyzes them in terms of their suitability as instruments for the introduction of semantics on the web. The paper then provides evidence regarding some limits for the systematic use of semantic search engine and ontology domain systems in everyday teaching and knowledge construction.

Finally, the paper reports and explains a hypothesis of an information system for building communities of practice and letting them work on the construction of domain ontology. The paper concludes that this construct is well adapted to the model for knowledge construction firstly hypothesized, and can give good results in teaching-learning planning and carrying out and in helping scientists and scholars to analyze scientific paradigms and to find new trends for research.

Keywords: information system, knowledge construction, learning objects, ontology, semantic web, units of learning

Introduction

More and more, Higher Education (both in high school and University) are benefiting from the Internet and its resources. A variety of systems are used to support teaching-learning activities in the school and the university and to satisfy lifelong learning needs, mostly with the help of the Web. Examples of these systems are: Content Management Systems (CMS), Learning Management Systems (LMS) and Computer Supported Collaborative Learning Systems (CSCLS) (Trentin, 2004). The first two types of systems are primarily content oriented (i.e., scientific and disciplinary topics and teaching-learning activities are their main focus); the last type of system is based on social and situated learning experiences and uses ICT to let students communicate and build social environments for knowledge construction. Furthermore, the comparison of the features of different e-learning platforms (both open source and proprietary) and the evaluation of their performances (Colace, De Santo & Vento, 2003; Graf & List, 2005) shows the importance of systems having all the above features to the success of e-learning contexts in education.

It is also important to note that analysis and explanation of knowledge construction and evolution have great relevance not just for education; corporate and firms are, in fact, strongly interested in the creation of systems for the capture, analysis and development of knowledge and skills, both on an individual and a social basis (communities of practices). The motivation for this interest is the increase in the acquisition of new markets and good performance that organizations can achieve by means of knowledge discovery and knowledge audit systems, knowledge mapping systems, decision support systems, data warehouse and data mining systems, or, in other words, by means of knowledge management systems.

Finally, it has to be noted that special problems or particular needs that emerge in disciplines and in scholars' studies and research can lead to the creation of Web sites and systems for the management of data, information and knowledge. These systems, which are usually self made and can be based on the use of proprietary and/or open source general purpose software, have a relevant place in the management of scientific knowledge together with the above well structured and suitably made platforms.

This paper describes the structure of a web site of this kind and the analysis and results of the teaching-learning experiences the author carried out with it.

The Experience of the Web Site "Didactical Materials for Latin Paleography"

The "Didactical Materials for Latin Paleography" web site was planned and implemented to let students attending Latin paleography lessons easily access and use various kinds of didactical materials (Cartelli & Palma, 2005). It consists of three sections, which are described below, and is still evolving and growing by addition of different documents. Within it one can find:

a) **plates**, reproducing charters in ancient manuscripts (texts written in the various Medieval scripting styles). Together with these images, their translations are reported (i.e., digital full texts where symbols, special signs and abbreviations are clearly written). All documents are organized on the basis of the scripting style used for the plates.

b) **texts**, containing full or partial documents reproducing papers, presentations and articles on different discipline topics, such as book archeology, scripting styles (e.g. beneventana, cancelleresca, carolina, gotica, mercantesca, umanistica), cataloguing, history of paleography etc.

c) **works in progress**, where special documents are placed; they are mostly devoted to work group experiences. These documents are in fact managed by all students attending the course and collect their exercises, analyses and suggestions.

The first and third sections contain materials to be used mostly for everyday work; in the second section texts mostly used for the professor's lectures can be found. New plates and texts are continuously inserted in the site for the enrichment of the scripting reference examples or for reporting the results of studies and research. Texts are summarized or extracted from books and proceedings of conferences and are made available with the authors' approval. Recently there has been an increase in the number of scholars and researchers who propose papers to be published in the site. (Many documents come, in fact, from national and international conferences and are made available only for didactical purposes).

The system was created in 2001 and has been used since then by Professor M. Palma to support his lectures and manage his everyday teaching. On the other hand, while involved in the construction of the site, the author of the paper could analyze and study students' behaviors when they interacted with this new system and could observe how their ways of using site materials changed over time. This last work was very easy to accomplish due to the small number of students involved each time in running of the course. (The academic year 2002-2003 had the biggest class with 19 students attending the lessons. In other academic years, there were from 6 to 17 students attending the lessons.)

The analysis of students' behaviors and the results coming from the use they made of other didactic sites concerning ancient manuscripts led the author to hypothesize the relevant effects of those instruments on the construction of special communities and on the development of new knowledge and skills (Cartelli, 2005b; Cartelli & Palma, 2004, 2005).

We note that how students' accessed didactic materials in the site has changed over time:

a) the students accessing the site in its first stage (i.e., when it was created and there were only a few documents within it), usually read all available texts and did this on their own,

b) now, with more than 72 documents and 211 plates (with their translations) available in the site, students mostly limit their reading to the texts the teacher suggests during the lessons and do this only when they are explicitly invited to do so.

When asked for the reason for their behavior, most of the students state they have difficulty in finding the "right documents" to study or to analyze; in other words, they explain, when they need some information for solving a special problem or studying a particular topic, they go to the site, try to locate the right section, and start reading the document they suppose to be useful. Very often they are forced to read more than one document before finding the right information and, sometimes, this time consuming job prevents them from ending the research and finding what they were searching for. Students experience this difficulty despite the site tree structure (reproducing the structure of the discipline topics), the index pages clearly indicating the available texts, and the systematic use of thumbnails (icons) for giving a preview of plates and other images.

A short survey made at the beginning of the academic year 2005-2006 on a class of 12 students (before lessons started) led to the same results. The students were given a limited time and instructed to browse the site to find documents concerning one or more special topics that were suggested by the professor. Only 25% of them successfully found the right pages in the appointed time, 42% found them after the deadline and 33% did not succeed in finding them and stopped their research after having looked through only a few pages. Table 1 shows the number of students with the percentages.

Tab. 1 – Distribution of students successfully accessing the right pages in the site

Success in accessing the right document in a fixed time	N. of students	%
Succeeded before the deadline	3	25%
Succeeded after the deadline	5	42%
Didn't succeed in finding the right document	4	33%

Further Analyses

The situation described in the above paragraph for the students of paleography seems very similar to a more general question: what kind of difficulty do people encounter while searching materials on the Web? Do they succeed in finding the right data they are searching for? How long and stressful is the searching job?

When search engines were first introduced in the web, people thought that the finding of information would be very easy and that all the above problems were solved. Now, with the increase of the amount of information and the growth of the number of search engines (very different among themselves for their features), we know that things are not so easy and the above problems are far from being solved. The main reason for the difficulties that are reported is the fact that word matching (actually used all over the web to find HTML pages) doesn't guarantee the right result for a given search.

Recently, because of its features, the semantic web has been proposed to offer a good solution to the problem.

To give the semantic web a pedagogical perspective, within which to consider the effects the web can have on individuals' knowledge construction and development, two themes will be deeply analyzed in the following paragraphs: 1) instruments for giving semantics to the web and their possible educational application, 2) models for knowledge construction and evolution in mankind and their consistency with the semantic web.

Semantic Web and Pedagogy

Until now the basic idea of the semantic web has been relatively straightforward: to let the web evolve to enable the automatic processing of its content so that data can be shared and processed both by humans and software (Berners-Lee & Fischetti, 1999; Berners-Lee, Hendler, & Lassila, 2001).

To reach this goal requires instruments and strategies for enabling computers to 'understand' web pages. Users can then be helped in searching for relevant information, in making inferences and calculations, and in combining information in new ways. The reverse side of the coin is that authors must provide explicit and domain specific meaning ('semantics') to allow automatic machine-interpretation.

Today there are several technologies for the semantic web and they are reported and analyzed below:

1. Latent Semantic Analysis (Landauer & Dumais, 1997) is based on programs which can understand natural language so that humans are no longer forced to provide semantic meaning to information (i.e., to type meta-data and use artificial coding schemes). It provides a kind of factor analysis analyzing data (texts) and ordering them on a given underlying dimension; new text can be interpreted by mapping it on the domain specific underlying dimensions it was extracted from (i.e., it provides the interpretation of the meaning of words)

2. OWL (Ontology Web Language) is used when the information in the documents has to be processed by applications, as opposed to the situation where the content has only to be presented to humans. Ontology languages provide machine interpretability of Web content much more than XML, RDF, and RDF-Scheme; this result is obtained by the addition of vocabulary and formal semantics to web content (McGuinness & Van Harmelen, 2003). In other words OWL implements a semantic description of a certain domain by specifying its concepts (terms in vocabularies) and the relationships between them. It has three increasingly-expressive sublanguages: OWL Lite, OWL DL, and OWL Full

3. RDF and RDF-Scheme is the metadata approach from the W3C (RDF, 2003). It does not structure the syntax of the data, but defines semantic meaning for data on the web. Multiple semantic perspectives of the same data are possible. It is based on two lower level technologies: URIs to identify web resources and Namespaces to identify different vocabularies.

4. Software Agents (Jennings, 1998). These are usually regarded as software pieces that can act proactively, can be adaptive and (semi-) autonomous and can communicate with other agents and with their human creators. In other words software agents can be identified with all computer programs which can read and process the coded semantics in the data to help humans to perform their tasks more efficiently and effectively.
5. Topic Maps provide an alternative technology to RDF (Cover, 2003). They let users define arbitrarily complex semantic knowledge structures and allow the exchange of information for collaboratively building and maintaining indexes of knowledge. They provide a more general approach to semantics in documents than RDF, basically because they are not limited to web environment.
6. Unified Modeling Language (UML) (Fowler, 2000) provides a collection of models and graphs for the description of the structural and behavioral semantics of any complex information system. Some of the elements provided are: a) case models and scenarios capturing the user requirements and functionalities of the system (scenarios are instances of cases), b) class and object diagrams specifying the semantic information structure of a system (object diagrams are instances of class diagrams), c) activity diagrams describing workflows, d) state diagrams showing the dynamic behavior of an object in a system, e) interaction diagrams (sequence and collaboration diagrams) modeling collaboration among groups of objects, f) physical diagrams (deployment and component diagrams) simulating the structure of a system.
7. XML and XML Schemes are derived from SGML (XML, 2003). They are used to go beyond the fixed, page structure, oriented vocabulary of HTML. They can structure data and documents according to personal or community defined vocabularies. These vocabularies can have a semantic nature and support the open exchange of data among the communities and tools understanding them.

While looking at the use of the above instruments in teaching and learning activities R. Koper (2004) systematically analyzed the trend in instructional design deriving from their use. He stated that the introduction of the above instruments in education aimed at: (a) increasing the effectiveness of education, (b) increasing the flexibility and accessibility of education, (c) increasing the attractiveness of education and (d) decreasing the workload for educational staff (or more in general: decreasing the institutional costs). On this basis he proposed an educational semantic web, i.e., a strategy representing a course in a formal, semantic way so that it could be interpreted and manipulated by computers as well as humans.

A deeper discussion of Koper's proposals is beyond the scope of this paper, but the following remarks describe, in the author's opinion, some problems and limits in the adoption of semantic web in education as it emerges from the proposals reported as of now:

1. First, it is very difficult to find a correspondence between the representation of knowledge emerging from the use of the instruments described above (building semantics in the web) and the constructivist models for knowledge development reported in the first section (and in the subsequent one); in other words, there is a great difference between knowledge representation and knowledge construction, and the history of last decades with the results of the studies on misconceptions and mental schemes clearly supports this difference (Cartelli, 2003)
2. Second, the use of semantic web for the representation of scientific knowledge introduces less flexibility and adaptability in knowledge evolution and in scientific paradigmatic changes, like the ones hypothesized from Kuhn (1969) in his theory of scientific revolutions. Ontologies and the semantic web more in general, in the author's opinion, create a

static representation of human knowledge, because they represent objects and relations among themselves as they exist at a given moment and they adapt very difficultly to the changes induced by new emerging ideas. If new scientific paradigms are needed for interpreting phenomena the only way to represent them in a given semantic structure is the creation of a new structure (a new ontology).

Knowledge Development Models, ICT and Teaching: A Survey

Human knowledge has been studied since mankind's origins. First of all, philosophy has played a relevant role in interpreting human knowledge; later, especially during the last century, human sciences intervened in explaining phenomena both on an individual and a social perspective. Nowadays many scholars look at constructivist hypotheses as the more suitable ones for the explanation of knowledge construction and evolution in people interpretation of phenomena.

Together with the numerous theories on human knowledge many models for its construction and evolution have been developed over time. In what follows a special model will be analyzed in greater detail, not only because it is very recent, but also for the relevance that ICT plays in it. Figure 1 shows the tri-partition of knowledge phenomena in the model; it shows the importance that different levels of human socialization have on knowledge construction (Cartelli, 2006).

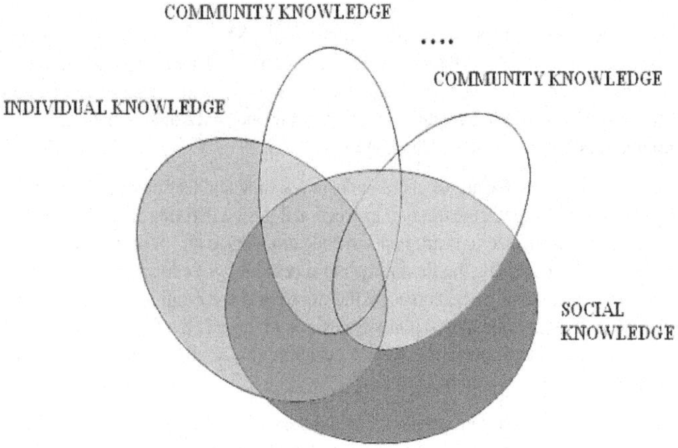

Fig. 1 - Hypothesis for the structure of human knowledge

There are at least three different kinds of knowledge in the model:

a) individual or personal knowledge, i.e., the knowledge a subject has and builds at a given moment, due to his/her interaction with reality.

b) community knowledge, i.e., the knowledge resulting from the interaction of the members of a community; it is the sum and the expression of the know how and the best practices of all the subjects in the community. This kind of knowledge can be identified with the knowledge of a special entity, the community, as it behaves autonomously (maybe differently) from all the subjects it is made of.

c) social knowledge or culture, i.e. the expression of the history and tradition of the society the subjects belong to. Among various elements in this type of knowledge scientific and discipline knowledge play a special role. Subjects and communities can propose new theories and ideas both on the basis of theoretical analyses and experimental results, but sciences in their entirety cannot be considered knowledge constructions of subjects and communities; all ideas and theories in a discipline must be included in commonly accepted scientific paradigms. In other words scientific ideas must be approved from the scientific community to be valid, and only this last step gives them the absolute and objective features and lets them be universally accepted (i.e., lets them become part of human culture).

The main effect of the above tri-partition is, in the author's opinion, the presence of three different ways for knowledge construction:

a) personal interaction with reality and consequent construction of mental schemes for phenomena interpretation (interactive constructivism explains them in several different ways).

b) social interaction among the subjects in a community under the well known E. Wenger's (2004) conditions: 1) presence of a shared identity domain, where membership implies a commitment to the domain, and therefore a shared competence that distinguishes members from other people; 2) community, because in pursuing their interest in their domain, members engage in joint activities and discussions, help each other, and share information; 3) practice, because members of a community of practice are practitioners; they develop a shared repertoire of resources: experiences, stories, tools, ways of addressing recurring problems. These features have been usually assigned to communities of practices but have also been found in communities of learners, fostered communities of learners, virtual communities (Cartelli, 2005a).

c) construction of social models by the subjects immersed in the society and by their living in it, and construction of well structured discipline knowledge (as the highest form of identification of the subjects with the society); school (at all levels) plays a great role in this last way of building knowledge, because it transmits discipline topics to students together with well suited and commonly accepted behavioral models.

It is perhaps too early to say if the above model has the right requisites to be adopted for the description of all knowledge phenomena and for the planning and carrying out of teaching-learning activities. Nevertheless, the increase in the importance of informal education (coming, for example, from subjects' interaction with media, IT and ICT) with respect to formal and non-formal education (school, association etc.), and the influence of other factors all depending from complexity of today society, are showing the inadequacy of old educational models with respect to knowledge society needs. The experiments for the finding of new didactical strategies and the proposal of new regulations for schools all over the world are a good proof, in the author's opinion, for the new emergence in education.

In what follows, two different situations exploring the compatibility of the above model with different contexts explaining knowledge construction are reported.

As regards pedagogical and didactical research it can be stated that the following experiences and theories all agree with the above model:

a) the use of individual and social constructivist strategies in education (Varisco, 2002),

b) the construction of communities of learners or the fostering of communities of learners (Scardamalia & Bereiter, 1996)

c) social knowledge theory (Wenger, 1998).

As regards the impact of ICT on knowledge phenomena and its compatibility with the above model two types of conclusions become possible:

a) when looking at knowledge phenomena from a constructivist perspective the above model can be applied to all contexts: individual, community and society, and succeeds in explaining them.

b) when the application of ICT in education is analyzed and special e-learning experiences are discussed different situations emerge:
- learning objects (LOs), usually adopted for managing students' interaction with discipline structure, have only the individual and the social (scientific) knowledge units as reference element in the model,
- units of learning (UOLs), which implement learning activities within the learning objects (Koper, 2001), have both the individual and the social units of the model as reference elements
- Computer Supported Collaborative Learning Systems (CSCLS) and all e-learning platforms implementing synchronous and asynchronous communication instruments and strategies to support communities of learners (or of practice), have the community unit of the model as reference element
- semantic web and domain ontologies directly refer to scientific (social) knowledge as the corresponding unit of the model.

The main consequence of the above considerations is once again the difference between knowledge representation and knowledge construction. It is clear that when passing from knowledge representation to its construction, of the above instruments no single one is transversal to the model discussed above (i.e., none can be adopted for all the knowledge construction units in the model).

Semantic Web and Information Systems

In one of the above sections it was mentioned that the semantic web, and ontology systems with it, can synthesize and represent knowledge in a given domain with all the concepts and the relations existing among themselves. Furthermore it has been shown that as regards the planning and carrying out of effective didactical activities and the help that people can receive in building the right and meaningful knowledge, there are two different positions on those systems:

1) they are supposed to help teachers in their everyday work due to their features;

2) they don't meet the features of a special knowledge construction and development model and further studies are needed for finding the better way for their introduction in teaching-learning activities.

On the other hand, it has to be noted that information systems never appear among the instruments leading to semantic web also if, in the author's opinion, they can play a relevant role both in introducing semantics in the web and in building effective educational experiences. At the basis of this hypothesis are two kinds or arguments:

a) the experiences the author had with on line information systems (dynamic web sites interfaced with databases), which led to the construction of communities of learners and of practices, and confirmed the structure of the model reported in the above section,

b) the increased awareness of the importance of human interaction with automatic systems for data analysis and management on the web.

With respect to the hypotheses reported up to now, this new idea assigns a great role to humans and to the implementation of their interaction processes for the construction of a domain ontology and semantic web with respect to the strategies for automatically represent scientific information.

In other words, in the author's opinion, a suitable information system, with its databases and selected accesses, can create a semantic network on a given knowledge domain (based or not on pre-existing web pages or any kind of document and bibliography) while integrating in itself the knowledge construction model reported above. The proposal of such an information system letting individuals, communities and disciplines (sciences) analyze and create knowledge follows.

The Information System

As usually happens with all information systems the explanation of the whole project and the description of the system itself both involve the following elements: a) data and their structure, b) subjects and their interactions, c) data flow and processes description.

As regards data (to be managed by a RDBMS) the following elements are hypothesized:

a) system administrator/s, who can create accounts for scientific administrators and students/contributors and manage all information and data in the database,

b) scientific administrator/s, who assign scientific topics to students/contributors for the management of data (compilation of entity and relationship cards) and verify the correctness of the work made by contributors (they are entrusted with the task of validating compiled cards),

c) students/contributors, containing personal data of people cooperating to the construction of the system (including identification and access data; i.e., ID code and password),

d) entities, where concepts, instruments, people, places and times, concerning the topics in the knowledge domain, can be found,

e) relationships, where the links between entities are included; they also contain the description of the links and the references to documents, they can be mono-directional or bi-directional (depending on the type of the connection between entities),

f) reference cards, with data concerning any kind of document (both in printing or on the web) and the links to the documents available in the site (or elsewhere in the web),

g) communication, an electronic blackboard letting people exchange messages in selected ways; i.e., on the basis of the topics they are interested in and in a more general way.

The users accessing the data base have different rights and powers:

a) the user with the least rights on the data is the one who can only query the system to obtain the map of the knowledge domain, the list of available topics, their descriptions and the links to bibliographic materials,

b) at an upper level are the students/contributors who can access a special Web area (by means of their ID and password) with a menu of the allowed operations, i.e. they can see the topics the administrator/s assign them, can manage entity cards, relationship cards and bibliographic cards,

c) the scientific administrator/s follow, they can manage all the data in the data base and write, modify and certify the entity, relationships and bibliographic cards, also if this last operation can be done only once (i.e. when the cards are verified they can no more be accessed from the administrator/s),

d) at the top of the access pyramid is the system administrator who can do all the operations allowed to the scientific administrator/s and can access the verified cards to modify or to delete them.

Once the entity and relationship cards are compiled from the students/contributors and verified from the scientific administrator/s they can be queried from a generic user. People interested in the information contained in the data base and in accessing the ontology domain have two different query systems. First, they have a page containing most relevant topics in the domain; if they select one of the items they find a description of the topic and of the links to related arguments, instruments, people etc. For each element they have in the same page parent and descendant concepts and can browse the discipline tree. Second, they have a traditional search system letting them find pages by means of special fields or terms within them.

When the system starts the data base is empty, and the system administrator has to input the data for at least a scientific administrator. When a scientific administrator is enabled he/she can input the data for one or more students/contributors and make them access the system; he/she can also input the topics to be chosen/assigned to the contributors and can input by him/herself the entity, relationship and bibliographic cards. When the contributor/s can access the materials to work on they can compile the cards. Finally the cards are analyzed and revised from the administrator/s so that they can be read by general users. Figure 2 shows what the various users can do.

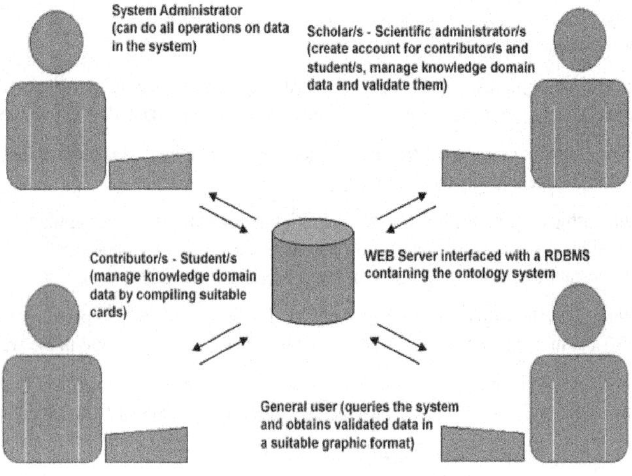

Fig. 2 - Users accessing the system and authorized operations

The key for the success of this system is in the communication subsystem (the electronic blackboard), letting people involved in the creation of the database share their experiences and knowledge, finding support and help from better skilled subject, and so on.

As can be easily shown, the system agrees with the knowledge construction model discussed in the above sections: individual, community and social (science) components of the model are in fact interested in the knowledge construction and evolution process.

Figure 3 synthesizes knowledge construction at the three different levels: individual, community and society.

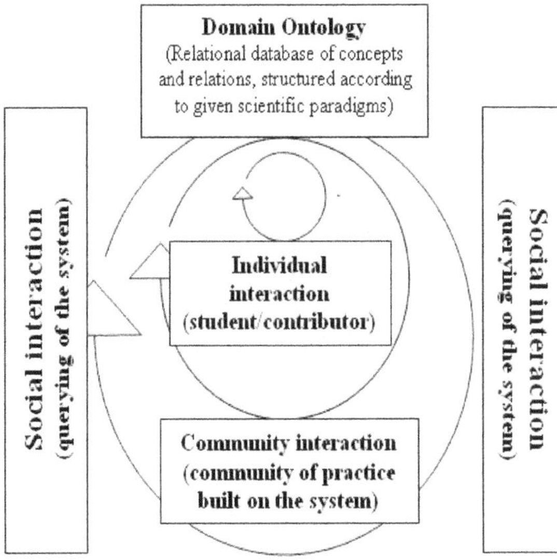

Fig. 3 – Model of knowledge construction according to system's access

Conclusion

Introducing semantics into the web for automatic representation of knowledge is no easy task. But it can be very useful in education for its continuous involving subjects at all their levels of knowledge construction.

The author's experiences led to an information system around which communities of learning and of practices were built. The results of the experiences up to now agree with the knowledge construction model reported in the paper; they led to the introduction of a new element in the SECI knowledge evolution model by Nonaka and Takeuchi (1995) and showed the importance of social-constructivist instruction strategies in today education.

As a conclusion it seems possible that the hypothesized system will be useful for improving teaching-learning strategies even if it will not lead to the automatic management of documents on the Web.

References

Berners-Lee, T., & Fischetti, M. (1999). *Weaving the Web: The original design and ultimate destiny of the World Wide Web by its inventor.* San Francisco: Harper.

Berners-Lee, T., Hendler, J., & Lassila, O. (2001). Il Web Semantico. Quando Internet diventa intelligente: agenti software e rappresentazioni condivise per un'automazione dei servizi in rete … e a casa nostra. *Le Scienze* (Italian edition of *Scientific American*), May (*393*), 77-84.

Cartelli, A. (2003). Misinforming, misunderstanding, misconceptions: What informing science can do. In (E. Cohen, E. Boyds ed.s) *Proceedings of IS + IT Education 2003 International Conference*, pp. 1259-1273. Retrieved on line March 5, 2006 from: http://proceedings.informingscience.org/IS2003Proceedings/docs/156Carte.pdf

Cartelli, A. (2005a). TIC, comunità di apprendimento e modelli di sviluppo della conoscenza. *Journal of e-Learning and Knowledge Society*, 1 (*1*), pp. 75-88.

Cartelli, A. (2005b). ICT and Knowledge Evolution in Learning Organizations the Lesson from Paleographers' Community of Learners. In (F. Malpica, F. Welsch & A. Tremante ed.s) *Proceedings of EISTA International Conference*, Vol. 2, pp. 275-280. Orlando (FL): IIIS.

Cartelli, A. (2006). ICT, Knowledge Construction and Evolution: Subject, Community and Society. In (A. Cartelli ed.) *Teaching in the Knowledge Society: New Skills and Instruments for Teachers*, pp. 33-53. Hershey (PA): Idea-Group Inc.

Cartelli, A., Palma, M. (2004). BMB On Line: An Information System for Paleographic and Didactic Research. In (M. Khosrow-Pour ed.), *Proceedings of IRMA 2004 International Conference: "Innovation Through Information Technology"*, Vol. 1, pp. 45-47. Hershey (PA): Idea-Group Inc.

Cartelli, A., Palma M. (2005). Computer and Information Systems in Latin Paleography Between Research and Didactic Application. In (D. Carbonara ed.) *Technology Literacy Applications in Learning Environments*, pp. 288-298. Hershey (PA): Idea-Group Inc.

Colace, F., De Santo, M., & Vento, M. (2003). Evaluating On-line Learning Platforms: a Case Study. In *Proceedings of the 36th Hawaii International Conference on System Sciences (HICSS'03)*, retrieved on line March 05, 2006 from http://csdl2.computer.org/comp/proceedings/hicss/2003/1874/05/187450154c.pdf

Cover, R. (2003). *(XML) Topic Maps*. Retrieved December 11, 2004, from http://xml.coverpages.org/topicMaps.html

Fowler, M. (2000). *UML distilled (second edition)*. Upper Saddle River (NJ): Addison-Wesley.

Graf, S., & List, B. (2005), *An Evaluation of Open Source E-Learning Platforms Stressing Adaptation Issues*, retrieved on line March 05, 2006 from http://moodle.org/other/icalt2005.pdf

Jennings, N. R. (1998). A Roadmap of Agent Research and Development. *Autonomous Agents and Multi-agent Systems*, 1(*1*), 7-38.

Koper, R. (2001). *Modelling units of study from a pedagogical perspective: the pedagogical meta-model behind EML*. Heerlen: Open University of the Netherlands. Retrieved November 14, 2005, from: http://eml.ou.nl/introduction/docs/ped-metamodel.pdf

Koper, R. (2004). Use of the Semantic Web to Solve Some Basic Problems in Education: Increase Flexible, Distributed Lifelong Learning, Decrease Teachers' Workload. *Journal of Interactive Media in Education, 6*. Retrieved November 14, 2005, from: http://www-jime.open.ac.uk/2004/6

Kuhn, T. S. (1969). *La struttura delle rivoluzioni scientifiche*. Turin: Einaudi.

Landauer, T. K., & Dumais, S. T. (1997). A solution to Plato's problem: The Latent Semantic analysis theory of the acquisition, induction and representation of knowledge. *Psychological Review* (104), pp. 211-240.

McGuinness, D. L., & Van Harmelen, F. (2003). *OWL Web Ontology Language Overview* (W3C Candidate Recommendation 18 August 2003). Retrieved November 14, 2005, from http://www.w3.org/TR/owl-features/

Nonaka, I., Takeuchi, H. (1995). *The knowledge-creating company: how Japanese companies create the dynamics of innovation*. New York (NJ): Oxford University Press.

RDF (2003). *Resource Description Format (RDF)*. Retrieved November14, 2005, from http://www.w3c.org/RDF/

Scardamalia, M., Bereiter, C. (1996). Engaging Students in a Knowledge Society. *Educational Leadership*, 54 (3), pp. 6-10.

Trentin, G. (2004). *Apprendimento in rete e condivisione delle conoscenze*. Milan: Franco Angeli.

Varisco, B.M. (2002). *Costruttivismo socio-culturale*. Rome: Carocci.

Wenger, E. (1998). *Communities of Practice: learning, meaning and identity.* London: Cambridge University Press.

Wenger, E. (2004), *Communities of Practice a brief introduction*, retrieved November 14, 2005, from http://www.ewenger.com/theory/index.htm

XML (2003). *Extensible Markup Language (XML).* Retrieved November 14, 2005, from http://www.w3c.org/XML/

Biography

Antonio Cartelli is a researcher in Didactics. He manages the Laboratory for Teaching-Learning Technologies and the Centre for ICT and on line teaching in the Faculty of Humanities at the University of Cassino - Italy. Among his interests are: misconceptions, mental schemes, Information Systems for research and teaching, Web Technologies in teaching research and their everyday application for the improvement of teaching and learning. He is also author of many papers and books concerning the themes he is interested in.

The page left blank intentionally.

Role of Perceived Importance of Information Security: An Exploratory Study of Middle School Children's Information Security Behavior

S. Chai and S. Bagchi-Sen
University at Buffalo, SUNY, Buffalo, NY, USA
schai2@buffalo.edu
geosbs@buffalo.edu

C. Morrell
University of Maryland at Baltimore County, Baltimore, MD, USA
cmorrell@umbc.edu

H. R. Rao and S.Upadhyaya
University at Buffalo, SUNY, Buffalo, NY, USA
mgmtrao@buffalo.edu shambhu@buffalo.edu

Abstract

Information security and privacy on the Internet are critical issues in our society. Importantly, children and adolescents need to understand the potential risk of using the Internet. In this research, we examine factors that motivate students' Information Security Behavior on the Internet. A pilot survey of middle and junior high school students is the source of the data. This study provides a model that explains students' behavior pertaining to Information Security. A significant research finding is that students' perceived importance of Information Security plays a critical role in influencing their Information Security Behavior.

Keywords: Information Security, Self-efficacy, Internet, Perceived Importance, Information Security Behavior.

Introduction

In recent years a large number of children have started to regularly use the Internet at home, at school, in libraries, and community centers. With this proliferation of use, information and computer security are becoming important issues. We see this in various forms: in the prevention of crime (e.g., physical molestation), harassment and bullying on the Internet, as well AS damage from computer viruses and the breach of privacy.

The Conference Board and TNS, the world's largest custom research company, produced a survey to measure the Consumer Internet Barometer, which covers 10,000 households (2005). This survey shows that approximately 41 percent of online households include school-age children (enrolled in Kindergarten through college). It also reveals that only 56 percent of parents are confident that their kids view only age-appropriate content when logging on from the classroom. Another 50% of parents also worry about privacy and identity theft of their children (2005). Often, the children are, in general, far ahead of their parents in terms of Internet usage since they use blogs and instant messaging to keep in touch with their friends. The teenagers who responded to the Conference Board survey said that they were usually able to circumvent many computer security measures at school (Lemos, 2005). Clearly, this shows that motivating kids to keep their safety on the Internet is more important than supervising and enforcing information security on the Internet.

In this research, we carry out pilot research in order to attempt to understand the factors that motivate school-age children to pay attention to Information Security and motivate them to use the Internet safely. We use social cognitive theory to introduce Information Security Self-Efficacy, Perceived Information Security Importance, and Exposure of Information Security as important factors in influencing the attitude of middle school children's toward information security.

Theoretical Background and Hypothesis

Social Cognitive Theory and Self-Efficacy

Social cognitive theory (Bandura, 1986) is widely used to explain individual behavior. It premises that personal factors in the form of cognitive, affective and biological events, behavior and environmental events all operate as interacting determinants that influence each other (Bandura, 1986). According to this theory, an individual chooses the environment in which they exist in addition to being influenced by that environment. Furthermore, both behavior in a given situation and the environment affect each other. Finally, behavior is influenced by cognitive and personal factors (Compeau & Higgins, 1995). In this reciprocal relationship among environment, behavior and individual, Bandura(1986) introduces self-efficacy as a major cognitive force guiding individual behavior. He defines self-efficacy as people's judgment of their capabilities to perform a task. Self-efficacy is concerned with judgments of what one can do and not with skills (Bandura 1986).

Self-efficacy beliefs perform as an important set of proximal determinants of human motivation and action. They operate on personal behavior through motivational, cognitive, and affective intervening processes (Bandura, 1989). Bandura, Barbaranelli, Caprara, and Pastorelli (1996) show that children's academic self-efficacy is positively associated with their academic performance.

In the context of IT, the research suggests that individuals who possess high self-efficacy toward IT use IT more frequently (Compeau, Higgins, & Huff, 1999). People who have higher level of self-efficacy toward a specific subject are more like to give greater value to that subject. Wisenbaker, Scott and Nasser (2000) show that students' strong cognitive competency toward statistics is related to more value for statistics. In the child development context, children's task-specific beliefs regarding their own ability influence their values regarding a subject (Wigfield & Eccles, 2000).For example, a child, who believes he or she can do well at math, tends to value mathematics more than a child who does not have belief in his or her math competence.

Previous research shows children are much more likely to value math, language, art, and sports when they feel competent in the domain (Jacobs , Lanza, Osgood, Eccles, & Wigfield, 2002). Based on previous research findings, we assume that students who have more opportunity to learn about information security from school, parents and friends would have stronger self-efficacy in information security. Furthermore, if students are exposed to information security, then they tend to have strong perceived importance of information security. In other words, if students hear about information security issues such as how to protect privacy on the Internet or avoid risks from computer viruses, they will develop better perception of information security on the Internet. Based on these assumptions, the hypotheses are:

H1a: Information Security Exposure has positive effect on perceived Information Security Self-Efficacy

H1b: Information Security Exposure has positive impact on Information Security behavior

H1c: Information Security Exposure has positive effect on Perceived Information Security Importance

Based on previous studies regarding self-efficacy, we propose that if students have high self-efficacy toward information security behavior, such as keeping personal information private during Internet use and protecting computers from computer viruses, they will have a strong motivation to implement behavior that shows sensitivity to information security. Furthermore, students are more likely to value information security when they have a high level of self-efficacy in the information security domain. Here we propose the following hypothesis.

H2: Perceived Information Security self-efficacy has positive effect on Perceived Information Security Importance

Perceived Importance of Information Security

As one of the factors driving individual motivation to perform a behavior, such as an academic task, perceived importance has been discussed in numerous studies. Pajares and Graham (1999) observe that middle school students who have high mathematics performance have high perceived importance of mathematics. In evaluating training programs, employee's perceived importance of the training program plays an important role in increasing motivation to join and do well in the training program (Tasi &Tai, 2003). The value, or importance of the object or activity, has positive relationship with individual motivation (Eccles & Wigfield, 2002).

We propose that students who have high perceived importance of information security will have more motivation to be proactive in their information security behavior.

Hypothesis 3: Perceived Information Security Importance has positive effect on Information Security Behavior

Our research model and definitions are presented Figure 1 and Table 1.

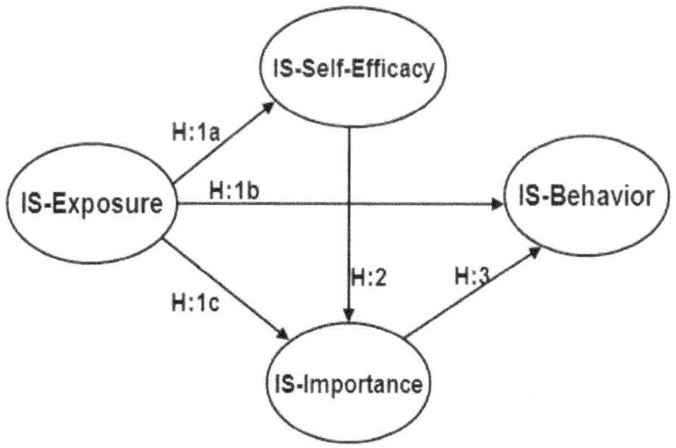

Figure 1 Research Model

Table 1 Construct definition

Construct	Definition
Information Security Exposure (IE)	Experience of learning and hearing about information security and privacy in using internet and computer
Information Security Self-efficacy (IS)	Individuals' judgment of their capabilities to perform information security behavior
Perceived Information Security Importance (ISI)	Individuals' perceived importance of information security behavior
Information Security Behavior (IB)	User's behavior to protect their privacy and computer from virus (e.g., Updating anti-virus software, Never opening e-mail from unknown senders and Updating computer operating system regularly etc.)

Research Design and Methodology

Research design and Sample

This pilot study uses survey methodology to gather data. The sample size is 33. A sample is drawn from 6th to 9th grade students, who attended a summer technology camp at Baltimore, Maryland in July, 2005. 20% of the respondents were male students and 80% of the respondents were female students.

Measures of the construct

We use measures that have been validated in previous research to ensure the control of measurement errors. However, we do construct some measures to reflect the context of information security. Self-efficacy measures are adopted from self-efficacy literature in educational psychology (Bandura et al., 1996; Choi, Fuqua & Griffin, 2001). Perceived importance measures are borrowed from Pajares and Graham (1999). These adopted measures are modified to reflect the context of information security. Other measures in the analysis are newly constructed for this study. Construct validity as well as structural coefficients are analyzed by PLS Graph v.03.

Data Analysis

Model Testing and Construct Validity

To test the model, we used Partial Least Square (PLS), a Structural Equation Modeling (SEM) Technique. PLS enables the specification of both the relationships among the constructs and the measures underlying each construct (Wold 1989).Most of the standardized loadings of individual item were over the acceptable cutoff level of 0.6 (Chin, 1998 a).The only loading lower than 0.6 was 0.5971 out of 15 reflective indicators (Table 2). Therefore, reliabilities of each item are acceptable.

The composite reliabilities, also referred to as a conversant validity, for the multiple reflective indicators in our model ranged from 0.778 (Information security Self-efficacy) to 0.900 (Information Security Exposure). They are well over the recommended acceptable level 0.7 (Fornell &

Larcker, 1981), which means that the measurement model secures construct level reliability. Composite reliability indexes are included in Table 3.

We tested discriminant validity by comparing Average Variance Extracted (AVE) and inter-construct correlation. All AVEs for the latent variables measured by reflective indicators are greater than the required minimum level of 0.5.and every construct had a square root of AVE bigger than its correlations with other constructs. This result presents that our measurement model ensures the discriminant validity (Chin, 1998b). Detailed AVE and inter-construct correlation coefficients are presented in Table 3.

Table 2 Measurement Items and Factor Loadings

Information Security Behavior (IB)	**Factor loadings**
IB1. I never open emails from unknown senders	0.7203
IB2. I never download files (like music, picture, game, movies, etc.) from the Internet if the files are from unknown people.	0.8050
IB3. I never give my personal information (like home/email address, telephone number, school name, etc.) to unknown websites.	0.8297
IB4. I never give my personal information to people I first met on the Internet.	0.8484
IB5. I pay attention to anti-virus updates every time I use a computer	0.8289
Information Security Exposure (IE)	
IE.1 Have you ever heard how to protect your personal information and yourself from other computer (or Internet) users?	0.9091
IE.2 Have you ever heard how to protect important information in your computer from computer viruses?	0.9091
Information Security Self-Efficacy (IS)	
IS1. How good are you at making passwords difficult for others to guess?	0.7173
IS2. How good are you at keeping personal information (like name, photo, email, address, telephone number, etc.) secret from other Internet users you don't trust?	0.5971
IS3. How good are you at protecting computers from computer viruses?	0.7061
IS4. How well are you aware of various computer/information security problems (like virus, privacy breach, bullying on the net, etc.)?	0.7801
Information Security Importance (ISI)	
ISI1.How important is it to keep your personal information (like address, telephone number, etc.) safe while using a computer?	0.8589
ISI2.How important is it to protect computers you use from viruses?	0.6324
ISI3.How important is it to protect your privacy (like giving your name, email, address, telephone number, etc.) on the Internet?	0.8972
ISI4.How important is it for you to stay safe on the Internet?	0.7925

Table 3 Correlations, Composite Reliability and AVE of latent variables

	IB	IE	IS	ISI	Composites Reliability	AVE
IB	1.00				0.896	0.634
IE	0.104	1.000			0.900	0.819
IS	0.085	0.218	1.000		0.778	0.544
ISI	0.244	-0.330	0.359	1.000	0.873	0.634

Results

For the evaluation of the structural model (hypothesized links), the bootstrap resampling procedure was applied to test the significance of the path coefficients. The path coefficient in the PLS model represents standardized regression coefficient. Standardized path coefficients should be around 0.20 and ideally above 0.30 in order to be considered meaningful (Chin, 1998b).

The results reveal that those path coefficients from Information Security Exposure to Information Security Self-efficacy and from Information Security Exposure to Information Security Importance are all positive and significant. In addition, path coefficients from Information Security Self-efficacy to Perceived Information Security Importance and from Perceived Information Security Importance to Information Security Behavior are also positive and significant.

In sum, 19% of the variance in students' Information Security Behavior is explained by our research model. However, Hypothesis H1a: Information Security Exposure has positive impact on information security behavior was not empirically supported in this study. The findings of hypotheses testing are summarized in Figure 2.

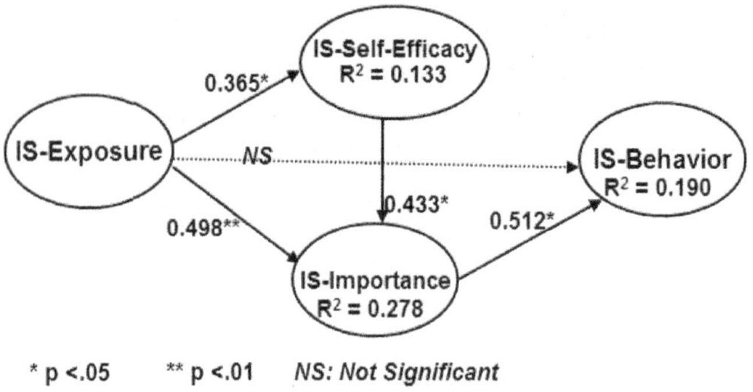

Figure 2 Structural Model Results

Discussion and Limitations

This pilot study focuses on social cognitive and self-efficacy theory to investigate Information Security behavior of 6th-9th grade students. These research findings suggest that students, who have strong self-efficacy toward Information Security on the Internet and have an exposure of information security from school, parents and media, are more likely to practice information security such as updating anti-virus software, not opening e-mails from unknown senders, and protecting personal information on the Internet.

To motivate students' information security behavior, we need to provide more information security education opportunities to students as well as chances for students to be exposed to information security issues. We also need to try to increase their Perceived Importance of information security.

Although we could confirm students' perceived importance toward Information Security on their Information Security Behavior, we fail to explain the direct relationship between Information Security Exposure and Information Security Behavior.

This failure seems to come from the fact that we have a small sample size since this is a pilot research study. The sample size in this study is 33. To generate more statistically rigorous results, we shall conduct a further study using a bigger sample size. Another limitation is that we could not include more factors that can explain student's Information Security Behavior such as years of experience using internet and computer, length of education related with Information Security Issue and gender differences in our model. This limitation also comes from the limited sample size. Future research should be done with larger sample with more diverse demographic characteristic and additional factors.

Acknowledgement

This research has been funded by NSF under grant *0420448. The usual disclaimer applies.*

References

Bagchi-Sen, S, Lee, JK. Rao, H. R., & Upadhyaya, S. J. (2005). A framework for examining skill specialization, gender inequity, and career advancement in the information security field. *Proceedings of the 1st International Conference On Information System Security*. Kolkata, India.

Bandura, A. (1986). *Social foundations of thought and action*. New Jersey: Prentice Hall.

Bandura, A. (1989). *Human agency in social cognitive theory*. New Jersey: Prentice Hall.

Bandura, A., Barbaranelli, C., Caprara, G.V., & Pastorelli, C. (1996). Multifaceted impact of self-efficacy beliefs on academic functioning. *Child Development, 67*(3), 1206-1222.

Banerjee, S., Kang, H., Bagchi-Sen, S., & Rao, H. R. (2005). Gender divide in the use of the Internet applications. *International Journal of E-Business Research, 1*(2), 24-39.

Chin, W.W. (1998a). Issues and opinion on structural equation modeling. *MIS Quarterly, 22*(1), 7 – 16.

Chin, W.W. (1998b). The partial least squares approach for structural equation modeling. In G.A. Marcoulides (Ed), *Modern methods for business research* (pp. 295-336). New Jersey: Lawrence Erlbaum Associates Hillsdale.

Choi, N., Fuqua, D. R., & Griffin, B. W. (2001), Exploratory analysis of the structure of scores from the multidimensional scales of perceived self-efficacy. *Educational and Psychological Measurement, 61*(3), 475-489.

Compeau, D., Higgins, C. A., & Huff, S. (1999). Social cognitive theory and individual reactions to computing technology: A longitudinal Study. *MIS Quarterly, 23*(2), 145-158.

Compeau, D. R. & Higgins, C. A. (1995). Computer self-efficacy: Development of a measure and initial test. *MIS Quarterly, 19*(2), 189-211.

Eccles, J.S. & Wigfield, A. (2002). Motivational beliefs, values, and goals [Learning and performance in educational settings]. *Annual Review Psychology, 53*, 109-132.

Fornell, C. & Larcker, D. (1981). Evaluating structural equation models with unobservable variables and measurement error. *Journal of Marketing Research, 18*, 39-50.

Jacobs, J. E., Lanza, S., Osgood, D. W., Eccles, J. S. & Wigfield, A.(2002). Changes in children's self-competence and values: gender and domain differences across grades one through twelve. *Child Development, 73*(2), 509-522.

Kang, H., Bachi-Sen, S., Rao, H. R., & Banerjee, S.(2005). Internet skeptics: An analysis of intermittent users and net-dropouts. *IEEE Technology and Society Magazine, 24*, 26-31.

Lemos, R. (2005). Teenagers struggle with privacy, security issues. In *SecurityFocus*. Retrieved from http://www.securityfocus.com/news/10940

Pajares, F. & Graham, L. (1999). Self-efficacy, motivation constructs, and mathematics performance of entering middle school students. *Contemporary Educational Psychology, 24*,124–139.

Parents concerned about Internet usage in the classroom. (2005). *Newswise*. Retrieved from http://www.newswise.com/articles/view/515310/

Tsai, W.-C. & Tai, W.-T..(2003). Perceived importance as a mediator of the relationship between training assignment and training motivation. *Personnel Review, 32*(1/2), 151-163.

Wigfield, A. & Eccles, J. S. (2000). Expectancy-value theory of achievement motivation. *Contemporary Educational Psychology, 25*(1), 68-.

Wisenbaker, J. M., Scott, J. S., & Nasser, F. (2000). Structural equation models relating attitudes about and achievement in introductory statistics courses: A comparison of results from the U.S. and Israel. *Ninth International Congress on Mathematics Education*. Tokyo.1-8.

Biographies

Sangmi Chai is a PhD student at the State University of New York at Buffalo. She has an MBA from Seoul National University. Her research interests include information security, human computer interface, productivity of information technology, and women and minority work force in information technology and cyber security.

Sharmistha Bagchi-Sen is a professor of geography at the University at Buffalo (UB) and serves as the director of graduate studies in the Department of Geography. She currently teaches graduate and undergraduate courses in economic geography, labor markets, and international business. She received the Lilly Endowment teaching fellowship in 1991-1992. Her research interests are in the following areas: foreign direct investment; innovation and export market development by small and medium sized firms; geography of innovation in the biotechnology industry; and labor markets. She has published a number of articles on foreign direct investment in the United States export market development strategies by small and medium manufacturing firms (SMFs), and employment patterns. Three articles have been recently completed on the geography of innovation in the biotechnology industry. She has received research funding from the National Science Foundation (1998-1999, 2001-2004, 2004-2006) and the Canadian Embassy (1996-1997 and 1998-1999). She has served as an active member of the research team of three UB centers: Canada-U.S. Trade Center, Baldy Center for Law and Social Policy, and the National Center for Geographic Information Analysis. She is one of the advisory committee members for the Baldy Center for Law and Social Policy, and she served as a member of both the steering and executive committees for the Institute for Research and Education on Women and Gender at the University at Buffalo.

Claudia Morrell is Executive Director of the center for women and information technology at University of Maryland at Baltimore County. Under her leadership, the Center's programs and resources have expanded dramatically, including the development of a CWIT Scholars program which retains 94% of its students; increased funding of $7 million in scholarships, research, and program funding to support girls' and women's participation and advancement in science, technology, engineering, and mathematics (STEM) careers in education and industry; and the expansion of personnel from two to forty-one staff, students, teachers, and faculty. She also served as the executive producer for an international award-winning women and technology video entitled, *You Can Be Anything*. Ms. Morrell effectively maintains an active 25-member advisory board with CEOs, CIOs, and high level executive women and men representing business, education and government leadership across the U.S. Currently she is directing several major initiatives that will increase the participation of girls and women in IT, from middle school through the college and university to the workforce and technology entrepreneurship. Ms Morrell was instrumental in drafting legislation that was signed in to law on May 26, 2004 that established the first statewide Governor's Taskforce on the Status of Women and IT, and she now serves as co-chair of the Taskforce. The Center's award-winning website, www.umbc.edu/cwit, is recognized internationally as "the best resource for women and IT on the web." Ms. Morrell speaks at state, national and international events, including recent presentations at the United Nations and World Bank. CWIT also hosted the first International Symposium on Women and IT in June 2005 in Baltimore, Maryland. Ms. Morrell serves on multiple statewide, national, and international advisory boards. Claudia Morrell received her Bachelor of Science degree from the University of North Carolina at Chapel Hill, a Master of Arts degree from Loyola College of Maryland, and a Master of Science degree from the University of Wisconsin, Madison. She lives in Maryland with her husband and three daughters. Her eldest daughter recently completed a computer science degree and is working in the field.

Dr. H. R. Rao's interests are in the areas of management information systems, decision support systems, and expert systems and information assurance. He has chaired sessions at international conferences and presented numerous papers. He has authored or co-authored more than 100 technical papers, of which more than 65 are published in archival journals. His work has received best paper and best paper runnerup awards at AMCIS and ICIS. Dr. Rao has received funding for his research from the National Science Foundation, the Department of Defense, and the Canadian Embassy, and he has received the University's prestigious Teaching Fellowship. He has also received the Fulbright fellowship in 2004 at York U, Ca. He is a co-editor of a special issue of The Annals of Operations Research, the Communications of ACM, associate editor of Decision Support Systems, Information Systems Research and IEEE Transactions in Systems, Man and Cybernetics, and co-editor- in -chief of Information Systems Frontiers.

Shambhu J. Upadhyaya is an Associate Professor of Computer Science and Engineering at the State University of New York at Buffalo where he also directs the Center of Excellence in Information Systems Assurance Research and Education (CEISARE), designated by the National Security Agency. He is an associate editor of IEEE Transactions on Computers, a member of the editorial board of the International Journal on Reliability, Quality, and Safety Engineering published by the World Scientific Publishers. He was a guest co-editor of the book series Interfaces in OR/CS on Mobile Computing: Implementing Pervasive Information and Communication Technologies, Kluwer Academic Publishers, 2001 and is a guest co-editor of a special issue on Secure Knowledge Management in IEEE Transactions on Systems, Man and Cybernetics, March 2006. He was on the Program Committee of 3rd IEEE International Information Assurance Workshop, Washington DC, March 2005, 6th Annual IEEE Information Assurance Workshop, West Point, NY, June 2005, and Dependable Computing and Communications Symposium of IEEE DSN-2005, among others. He is a senior member of IEEE.

The page left blank intentionally.

Middleware Components for E-commerce Infrastructure: An Analytical Review

Qiyang Chen, James Yao, and Rubin Xing
Department of Management and Information Systems
Montclair State University, Upper Montclair, NJ, USA

cheng@mail.montclair.edu yaoj@mail.montclair.edu
xingr@mail.montclair.edu

Abstract

Embracing inapt infrastructure technology is a major threat in developing extensive and efficient Web-based systems. The architectural strength of all business models demands an effective integration of various technological components. And middleware, the center of all applications, becomes the driver—everything works if middleware does. In the recent times, the client/server environment has experienced sweeping transformation and led to the notion of the "Object Web". Web browser is viewed as a universal client that is capable of shifting flawlessly and effortlessly between various applications over the Net. This paper presents an overview of middleware and the facilitating technologies and point toward the latest developments, taking into account the functional potential of the on-market middleware solutions as well as their technical strengths and weaknesses. The paper classifies and describes various types of middleware technologies such as database middleware, Remote Procedure Call (RPC), application server middleware, message-oriented middleware (MOM), Object Request Broker (ORB), transaction-processing monitors, and Web middleware etc., with on-market technologies.

Keywords: E-commerce Infrastructure, middleware

Introduction

Evolution of Internet-based computing from local area networks (LANs), after transitioning from unconnected computers to networks, is the hallmark of all business models today. The technological backbone of this evolution is the middleware. First connecting, then communicating, and finally seamlessly integrating the distributed systems to external sites, customers, suppliers, and trading partners across the world is the real challenge for the business world. It doesn't stop there. Also required is the talking between client and server over heterogeneous networks, systems architectures, databases, and other operating environment. All this is facilitated by the middleware technologies that offer undercover functions to seamlessly integrate various applications with information instantly to make it accessible across diverse architectures, protocols, and networks. Automation of back-end and front-end operations of business is also effected by the middleware. Middleware binds discrete applications, such as Web-based applications and older mainframe-based systems, to allow companies to hook up with latest systems and developments that drive new applications without making their investments in legacy systems unyielding (Rosencrance, 2002).

The chances of huge returns expected due to enabling middleware technology are, however, controlled—and often diminished—by the fact that the consequence of unpredictability or improper configuration of the middleware technology is extremely severe. Web browser war has given way to the middleware war. Numerous vendors offer various middleware product families—"the operating system of the Web"—with an estimated growth of about 65% for Object Request Broker, 50% for Messaging, and 15% for Transaction Processing Monitor for the year 2001. (CSIRO, 2002),

Functions of Middleware

Middleware functions are generally classified into:

- Application-specific functions to deliver services for different classes of applications such as distributed-database services, distributed-data/object-transaction processing, and specialized services for mobile computing and multimedia,
- Information-exchange functions to manage the flow of information across a network—for tasks like transferring data, issuing commands, receiving responses, checking status, and resolving standoffs, and
- Management and support functions to locate resources, communicate with servers, handle security and failures, and monitor performance.

Database, Web, and legacy application middleware are three basic middleware application types, with database middleware as the major application in most systems and Web middleware is spreading fast and extensively. SQL mainly provides communications between clients and servers in database middleware. Vender-dependent standard such as ODBC is developed to keep apart the client application from database server implementations and can be easily reached from most application programming environments. Non-relational data now can be accessed through Universal Data Access. Remote procedure calls, messaging middleware, transaction process monitors, and object-oriented middleware are four basic middleware communication categories.

Since middleware is a relatively immature technology, the competing standards and fast changing technologies factor into the selection process making it a very complex decision-making area that requires a meticulous insight and analysis of the correlation and interaction between the middleware and applications. The two major issues that concern and influence this process include:

- The types of applications to be carried out by the middleware technology based on the current application environment such as distributed relational database project or non-relational file servers dealing with VSAM and ISAM data and
- The application development environment that is based on if a client application will be written in a traditional procedural language such as COBOL, an event-driven language like Visual BASIC, or an object-oriented environment such as C++ or Java.

Major Types of Middleware

The selection of middleware technology is determined by what information is required to be communicated, for example, database middleware will be the choice if database is the main requirement. However, following are the major categories of middleware:

- Database Middleware,
- Remote Procedure Calls (RPC),

- Object Request Broker (ORB),
- Application Server Middleware,
- Message Oriented Middleware (MOM),
- Transaction Processing Monitor (TP),
- Object Transaction Monitor, and
- Web Application Servers

The most widely used, easy to install, and relatively economical middleware, *Database middleware*, is usually chosen to complement other types of middleware and facilitates communication among applications and local or remote databases but cannot transfer calls or objects. However, database middleware does not allow the two-way communications between servers and clients. SQL type command is generally subjected to the middleware gateway, which would convey the command to the end database to collect and send the reply of the SQL query back. Synchronous point-to-point type of communications is the characteristic of database middleware and can pose problems when multiple demands from multiple users produce huge traffic and congestion. Database middleware is the most mature middleware technology.

Remote Procedure Calls (RPC) permits a client program to call procedures located on a remote server program. Remote procedure calls is not isolated as distinct middleware level and is entrenched into the application with calls embedded into the client portion of the client/server application program. Stubs are developed for both the client and the server to call up synchronously when the client makes a call to the server. The intricacies of distributed processing are reduced by remote procedure calls by maintaining the semantics of a remote call no matter the client and server are located on the same system or not. The synchronous nature of the remote procedure calls makes it most appropriate for smaller applications where all communications are one-to-one and not asynchronous (Slater 2002).

Object Request Brokers (ORB) are language-independent, object-oriented, synchronous remote procedure calls in which an affiliate function of an object can be brought into play remotely by means of the same essential notation. Asynchronous communication suitable to large applications can be made possible by extending the main standards as in CORBA and DCOM, the main competing standards. Java's Remote Method Invocation (RMI) is also like an ORB, but is not language independent. Interfaces between objects can be defined by an IDL (interface definition language). The codes can be recompiled to avoid troubles associated with changing theses interfaces dynamically. ORB technologies are based on the reliability of the transport layer, which is required for the functioning. The application programmer is secured from the details of the client/server approach by using IDL interfaces that allows the application code to call a remote object, as if it were locally supported. Thus, the maintainability is improved as the object communication details are concealed from the application and isolated on the ORB. Hence, ORB-based middleware applications are becoming standard for the multi-tier model. CORBA, enterprise Java Beans, and Active X/COM are among the major technologies. The main limitation of ORB technology is that it goes well only with CORBA, JAVA, or COM oriented applications in the network. However, it can be used with TP Monitor, which supports the client/server communication management; CORBA with TP Monitor tender a good communication middleware in running Web-based business transactions.

Message Oriented Middleware (MOM) or enterprise message technology (EMT), provides asynchronous message delivery. The messages are lined up, just as objects, permitting the application that sends messages, to carry out other tasks without getting blocked till it receives the response. Generally located at a higher level than that of remote procedure calls, MOM assembly provides more than simply passing information. MOM also offers provisions for translating data, security, broadcasting data to multiple program, error recovery, and prioritization of messages and requests. MOM enhances flexibility by allowing applications to switch messages without the requirement of knowing on which platform or processor the other application located. MOM facilitates communications across a range of messaging systems, such as request-response, prolonged conversation, application queues, publishing and subscribing, and broadcasting. Messages are processed asynchronously with appropriate priority levels. Examples of messaging middleware are IBM's MQSeries, BEA's Message Q, and Microsoft's MSMQ.

Transaction Processing Monitor (TP) is over 25 years old technology that controls interactions between a requesting client and databases. It is a database independent technology. TP provides a three-tier client/server model and ensures an appropriate updating of the databases. This technology facilitates and controls the transport of data between numerous terminals and the application programs serving them. It can provide services to thousands of clients in distributed client/server environment by multiplexing client transaction requests by type on to a controlled number of processing routines that support particular services. TP monitor technology can also capture the application transitions logic from the clients. TP monitors are not employed for general-purpose program-to-program communications, but offer an environment for transaction type applications that utilize a database. On initiation of transactions by clients, the TP monitor transports the transaction relating to the database as required and the response is sent back to the client. By the use of TP monitors, the developers can define segments of the application as transactions with a clear start and stop points. TP monitors also offer failure protection and ensure atomic transactions by turning around a transaction back if not completed successfully. TP monitors are often used synchronously to ensure that failures are detected before further transactions take place. This is accomplished by breaking down complex applications into pieces of code called services. Three types of jobs are performed through TP monitors: process management, transaction management, and client/server communication management. Examples of TP monitors include IBM's CICS and BEA's Tuxedo. BEA's Tuxedo is used by some companies as the middle-tier to allow an application developer to write applications as a set of services, each executing a single business function, such as add customer, process orders, and bill customers. Tuxedo supports LAN and Internet-based clients through its Tuxedo IWS and BEA Jolt. C, Cobol, and Java can do programming in Tuxedo applications. Standard Tuxedo communications integrate the business logic proficiently with legacy applications. Tuxedo also supports many security levels, such as the application password, end-user authentication, access control, and mandatory access control.

Object Transaction Monitor (OTM) is a coherent form of middleware consolidated and integrated from discrete technologies available such as TP Monitors, Message Q, and ORB. For instance, the Object Transaction Monitor (OTM) combines the functionality of MOM, TPM and ORB into one product (Boucher & Katz, 1999). BEA's Tuxedo integrates with ORB in one single OTM product known as M3. In addition, Microsoft's MTS, Iona's OrbixOTM, and Inprise's Visibroker ITS also offer OTMs. MTS, COM, and MSMQ are integrated in COM+ and IBM integrates these technologies into the family of WebSphere products. The latest trends in the middleware solutions support the integration of various technologies to increase returns by reducing costs of employing experts for different technologies and applications in the design and functioning of e-business models.

Middleware and the Web Application Servers

With the domination of the Internet over all business models, middleware technology has grown remarkably in the recent years and is expected to grow further. For instance, MOM that is the most potential candidate in middleware technologies is expected to grow at a compound annual growth rate of about 20%. The mission-critical obligation of systems engages far-reaching use of distributed computing to share information across expanding heterogeneous networks. That requires significant diffusion of information consistently across numerous applications on a wide range of machines—embedded in the range from the reproduction of a database to extraordinary push technologies to push required technology over the Internet. By and large, the information traverses throughout the network in the form of messages and the infrastructure entails software development.

HTML pages are served up through the application servers' interaction with back-end databases and applications. However, application servers differ by operation speed, support for component models, programming standards, and database interfaces. Application server software permits originating applications as a set of software components, such as Enterprise JavaBeans or ActiveX controls, and loading these applications on the application server. The components use the features, or the services, of the application server, such as accessing back-end databases, controlling transactions to those databases, interacting with front-end Web server, and even balancing the workload over several copies of the application server. (Cox, 2002)

Sophisticated and easy-to-use Web development tools are being developed by the Web application server vendors. Simplification of coding and integration of distinct tasks allows the next-generation application servers to be developed with much reduced development loads for a successful Web operation, particularly in terms of time. However, one must be careful about increased dependence on the vendor's technology due to several factors: proprietary application components, sizable investments in software and product-specific training, and extensive use of the vendor's own development and consulting services. (Liebmann, 2004)

High vendor-specificity of the application server architecture, infrastructure, and connectivity, as well as increasing business logics being stored in a vendor's application server, lead to increased dependence of a company on vendor's product line. There are two ways to deal with the problem: one way is to create and design applications in a manner that each application function is separated into its own discrete components, so that if any particular feature of the application server becomes outdated, it can be substituted with another technology without breaking down the whole system. The second solution to the problem can be aimed at by integrating standard programming environments such as C++ and Java.

With pervading Web-technology over all business models, the use of application servers as critical components of the infrastructure has become more fundamental than even operating systems and databases. A fast-paced growth of the Net also requires the Web-based applications to be much more scalable, reliable, and transaction supporting. The standard application deployment platform of these applications with the Java 2 Enterprise Edition (J2EE) supports their use as application integrators with XML capabilities. BEA, IBM, and iPlanet/Sun/Netscape/AOL are among the leading vendors of the Web-application servers on-market. These Web-application servers are based on Java and Enterprise Java Beans (EJB) component model and J2EE standards. Each claims leadership in some or the other dimension. BEA, for example, with its WebLogic Server, is the unit volume leader. IBM leads in revenue, a claim supported by its associated implementations of AS/400 and S/390 in traditional enterprises, whereas iPlanet is the leader in the high-growth/high-value Internet sector. (D.H. Brown Associates, Inc., 2001)

BEA's WebLogic Server offers an easy-to-deploy J2EE platform that marks the mainstream market. WebLogic Enterprise builds on this capability, but requires two programming environments to accomplish all of its functions. iPlanet is consistent in almost all areas. IBM's strength in high-end transaction services, application-development tool integration, as well as its leadership in XML and UDDI make a powerful product. IBM's product also requires two programming environments to accomplish all of its capability, bridging CORBA and legacy application systems. BEA WebLogic Enterprise offers strong J2EE conformity, web-presentation services, object services, security, reliability, and scalability. WebLogic is also as good as IBM's offer in management functions and as good as iPlanet Application Server 6.0 in Java Messaging Services (JMS). WebLogic's execution of J2EE is considered cleaner or easier to install. On the other hand, iPlanet and IBM offer integrated implementations of XML. However, WebLogic 6 integrates XML into the package.

The Sun-Netscape-AOL alliance's iPlanet Application Server offers strong capability in J2EE. The first web-application server to be certified J2EE compliant. iPlanet 6.0 has a unique strength in simplified application development at the enterprise level based on its Unified Integration Framework that offers single programming environment to build enterprise applications. By contrast, BEA WebLogic requires the user to dub a separate server, called E-link. IBM's WebSphere EE offers both the Advanced Edition container and CORBA-based Component Broker. However, iPlanet Application Server 6.0 linger in management and transaction functions. IBM's WebSphere EE 3.5 leads the pack in transaction services and development-tool integration. It also is a leader in driving and propagating the XML and UDDI application-integration standards. WebSphere EE includes WebSphere AE as well as IBM's Component Broker technology. However, WebSphere lags in J2EE certification (Moorehead, 2004).

The factors that influence and drive this high-growth market segment characterized by furious competition come from the ever-expanding demand for application integration, growth of services, scalability and reliability, ease of implementation, and security control.

Major Product Families of Middleware Technology in Web Application Servers

BEA's WebLogic integrates EJB with other Java-standard services required for business-critical applications and provides database integration, event management, remote object access, and directory service integration. Additional technologies sustaining the latest version include WML, XML and SNMP, with the add-on software kit offering support for the latest draft of the EJB 2.0 specifications. WebLogic provides see-through replication for automatic load balancing and fail over, strong RSA-based security; rich, graphical management of Enterprise JavaBeans, comprehensive support for the Java Enterprise Standards, and full Java types as arguments to Enterprise JavaBeans.

The WebLogic EJB Deployer tool provides the controls for managing multiple EJB.jar files and for configuring WebLogic Server deployment properties and resources. Deployer tool supports two levels of EJB deployment validation by automatically checking properties and references to make sure they contain the appropriate values and by verifying that key EJB required classes are compliant with the EJB 1.1 specification. WebLogic Zero Administration Client (ZAC) Publish Wizard, a graphical utility, allows creating, publishing, and managing packages containing an application, applet, or library of Java code. ZAC permits building the client-side Java applications and package them for distribution.

IBM's WebSphere can be used for e-business applications in multi-tier client/server environments. WebSphere software platform consists of three layers; WebSphere Foundation—consisting of Application Server and MQ series—and integrates the business processes and applications and transfer them to the Web; Foundation Extension to help the business develop, present, and deploy Web applications and extend the back-end systems to the web; and Application Accelerators that helps the business develop customized solution for collaboration and B2B integration. WebSphere supports every phase of e-business development from the start to the end. The WebSphere provides standards-based Java environment, XML, and XSL support, and support for applications built in Java Servlet specifications, transaction monitor, and message queuing software. It also provides site analysis tools and native language support. (Ling, Yen, & Chou, 2001)

WebSphere Application server includes a HTTP server, user interface logic, the data to construct user interface of the e-business application, the business logic, and the connectors (Conner, 1999). The connectors support the communications with external applications, data, and services. The user interface logic is separated from the business logic and follows the user interface style and mechanisms. The client browser communicates with WebSphere Application server through HTTP, IIOP, and MQ Series. The Application Server integrates e-business applications with data server, existing enterprise resources, and business partners. WebSphere is capable of providing connectivity to many different types of databases and offers high-speed database access using JDBC.

WebSphere Application family includes many products that maintain the existing enterprise systems like the enterprise resource planning (ERP) and aid the integration with business partners. It also makes possible the access of the existing enterprise applications available to the customers, employees, and suppliers through Intranets and Extranets by making these applications securely available to the Web. WebSphere Host Integration Solution makes possible the integration of legacy applications and critical enterprise data with the Web seamlessly. The Transcoding Publisher and WebSphere B2B Integrator enhance B2B data transaction. IBM's MQ Series can be used for flexible and rapid integration of core business process, data and applications, and B2B transactions. IBM also presents MQ Series Integrator that integrates applications originally developed with different systems for supply chain management and customer relationship management. WebSphere's VisualAge for Java offers patterns for expanding ERP systems (SAP R/3) to e-business (Rosencrance, 2000). IBM offers products ranging from simple Web applications to the assorted Transcoding Publisher, a technology that automatically translates and transforms Web-content (HTML) to XML or WML, the markup languages that are currently used in creating content and applications for pervasive devices such as wireless application protocol (WAP) devices, personal digital assistants (PDAs), and so on.

Sun-Netscape's iPlanet Application Server is the result of efforts to remake Netscape's Application Server, combined with NetDynamics technology, to take its place as a foundational piece of the iPlanet Internet Service Deployment Platform. iPlanet is expected to provide an extra level of support. iAS 6.0 meets the requirements of the latest J2EE specification and passed J2EE Certification Test Suite. Basic core services of iAS include a transaction monitor, multiple load-balancing options, full clustering and failover support, an integrated XML parser and Extensible Stylesheet Language Transformations engine, and full internationalization support. iPlanet products including Directory Server, Web Server, and other add-ons for Enterprise Application Integration are well integrated. The iPlanet Application Deployment tool is a Java-based program that leads through the process of deploying an application. Several well-documented sample applications present an overview of creating and organizing real-world applications. iAS offers a separate product, iPlanet Application Builder, that integrates with such third-party tools as WebGain Studio, JBuilder, IBM Visual Age, and Sun Forte for Java Enterprise Edition. iPlanet offers a good e-commerce platform with applications and performance required to successfully deploy today's cutting-edge Web applications. (Astley, Sturman, & Agha, 2001)

iPlanet provides the enterprises with a scalable, high performance platform on which to develop and deploy their large-scale, transactional Web applications. iPlanet provides advanced availability features such as failure recovery and session management and scalability features including dynamic load balancing. Developers can tool their applications in Java or C++, in addition to the offered support to the Client Independent Programming Model (CIPM) for the rapid development of applications for differing client types. iPlanet accomplishes high performance through its fully multi-threaded, multi-process architecture and advanced connection caching and pooling. Scalability is endowed with through dynamic load balancing and point-and-click application partitioning, allowing applications to scale animatedly to support numerous users. New enhancements include a standards based application model supporting Enterprise JavaBeans, JSP, JDBC, and the Java Servlet API. In addition, distributed transaction support enables high performance and centralized management, while "fail over" functionality provides enhanced application availability.

The Table 1 shows a comparison among several products of Web application servers.

Table 1. Comparison of Web Application Servers

Product	Operating systems	Support and Integration.	Legacy Integration	DB Integration	Format Integration	Content Management.
BEA Systems WebLogic Server 5.1	Windows NT/2000, Solaris, HP-UX, Compaq Tru64, SCO Unixware, Siemens MIPS with Reliant Unix, SGI Irix, Dynx, AIX, Linux, AS 400, OS/390	J2EE implementation with certified APIs, native HTML support, integrated HTML, JSP, EJB, O/R mapping development tools, integrates with Macromedia Dreamweaver, Visual Age for Java, Inprise Jbuilder, supports XML, COM, CORBA	More than 30 packaged plug-ins including SAP, Clarify, other mainframe, XML and MQSeries, adaptor developers kit for custom application integration	Oracle, MS-SQL Server, Informix, Sybase, any via JDBC-compliant driver	JMS (API+ SMTP), FTP, TCP/IP, POP, IMAP, SNMP	Workflow and personalization product plus native integration with Documentum, Interwoven and other content managers
IBM WebSphere Application Server 3.5	Windows NT/2000, AIX/6000, Solaris, Red Hat Linux, HP-UX, IBM OS/400, IBM OS/390, IBM OS/2	Supports third-party IDEs, integration with IBM VisualAge for Java and IBM WebSphere Studio IDEs, support for Java and non-Java applications, XML, JSP, EJB, COM, CORBA	IBM DB2, Oracle, Sybase, Informix, SQL Server, Lotus Domino, others, via JDBC, Versant EnJin, eXcelon, IMS, MQ-enabled Systems, MQSeries, CICS, TXSeries/Encina, SAP R/3	Oracle, DB2, SQL Server, Informix, Sybase,Versant , eXcelon, Lotus Domino	SMTP, FTP, LDAP, Telnet, TN3270, TN5250, TCP/IP, JMS, JDBC, JTS, JTA, JNI, XML/XLS, EJB, JNDI, J-IDL, CORBA, RMI, IIOP, RMI/IIOP	Workflow, personalization, rules-based engines, proxy, caching, serving, portal serving
iPlanet E-Commerce Solutions	Windows NT, Solaris, IBM	Includes an integrated J2EE development tool, O/R mapping, integrates	CICS, SAP R/3, PeopleSoft, Tuxedo, MQSeries, Sun JMQ, includes an SDK	Oracle, DB2, Informix, Sybase, SQL Server	JMS, JNDI, XML, RMI, IIOP, RMI/IIOP, JTA, JTS, JDBC, LDAP, NSAPI, ISAPI,	Native J2EE Workflow development tool and runtime, personalization,

iPlanet Application Server 6.0	AIX, HP-UX	with Sun Forte for Java tools and third-party IDEs including WebGain VisualCafe, supports XML, JSP, EJB, Servlets, COM, CORBA	for developing Enterprise Connectors for other Enterprise Information Systems		SMTP, SNMP, HTTP, XML, JNDI, FTP, TCP/IP, EDI	content management

Conclusion

The traditional two-tier client server system can no more manage very large amounts of data and transactions due to a wide range of expanding and diverse operating systems, applications, and environments. What is required now is a translating middle layer that can make these systems, applications, and environments communicate seamlessly at a time. There are many middleware technologies developed to streamline these efforts. An imminent solution is that businesses adopt a multi-tier client/server architecture and infrastructure supported by several middleware technologies.

The choice of technology will be based on the specific needs of the business situation. It has been established now that middleware solutions offered by IBM's WebSphere, BEA's WebLogic, and Sun's iPlanet lent a hand to the businesses by integrating legacy systems to various applications on diverse platforms. These middleware solutions proved to be proficient and cost-effective to construct and support complete e-business models. No organization will be able to compete and survive today's fast-changing, Net-ized, e-business environment characterized by huge data flow unless it adapts and adopts a multi-tier client/server architecture. The middleware solutions, such as WebSphere, WebLogic, or iPlanet not only integrates the Web, client/server, and legacy systems but also supports integration of various middleware technologies to secure investment in existing technologies and skills and incorporate with ERP and business partners.

References

Astley, M., Sturman, D. C., & Agha, G. A., (2001). Customizable middleware for modular distributed software—Simplifying the development and maintenance of complex distributed software. *Communications of the ACM, 44*(5).

Boucher, K. & Katz, F. (1999). *Essential guide to object monitors.* New York: John Wiley & Sons.

Conner, M. H. (2002). Structuring e-business applications, IBM, Library Papers. Retrieved from www.IBM.Com/Software/Developer/Library

Cox, J. (2002). Web app servers bulk up on new features. Retrieved from www.nwfusion.com

CSIRO. (2002). Helping to choose the right middleware. Retrieved from http://www.cmis.csiro.au/adsat/publications.htm

Edwards, J. (1999). *3-tier client server at work.* NY: John Wiley & Sons.

Liebmann, L. (2004 July 28). Web application servers-Are you ready for the commitment? *Internet Week.*

Rosencrance, L. (2002). Middleware. *Computerworld, 34*(41), p. 84.

Slater, D. (2002). Middleware demystified. Retrieved from www2.cio.com/archive/content.html

Ling, R. R., Yen, D. C., & Chou, D. C., (2001). From database to web browser: The solutions to data access. *Journal of Computer Information Systems*, Winter 2000-2001.

Moorehead, K. (2004). Database middleware technologies. Retrieved from http://scis.acast.nova.edu

Rawles, P. T. & Goldman, J. E. (2001). *Local area networks—A business oriented approach*. John Wiley & Sons.

Biographies

Dr. Xing received his Doctor of Global Information Development (Ph.D) in 1992, Master of Computer Science (M.S) in 1989, and Master of Math & Science Education (M.A) in 1987 from Columbia University, New York. Having worked for more than 15 years in the IT industry, Dr. Xing has held senior IT management positions at several large financial conglomerates in metropolitan New York. His current research interests include Broadband and Wireless Communications, the Internet security, Disaster Recover/Business Continuity Planning, and Supply Chain Management.

A Measure of Risk Caused by Information Asymmetry in e-Commerce

This research is partially supported by NFSI-BG, Grant No VU-MI-105/2005

Dimitar Christozov
American University in Bulgaria, Blagoevgrad, Bulgaria

dgc@aubg.bg

Stefanka Chukova
Victoria University of Wellington, Wellington, New Zealand

Stefanka.Chukova@vuw.ac.nz

Plamen Mateev,
University of Sofia "St. Kliment Ohridski", Sofia, Bulgaria

pmat@fmi.uni-sofia.bg

Abstract

The problem of enhancing success in e-Commerce requires reducing or sharing the risk of misinforming. The objectives of this paper is to raise and discuss the difficulties in quantifying the risk of misunderstanding caused by information asymmetry in a communication process; and to propose a mathematical model, developed to measure the risk of misinforming. Usage of warranty, as the most popular tool of sharing risk, is discussed in the light of risks of misinforming. A data set collected in an experiment, was used to illustrate the major ideas proposed as well as to stress on the fact that in particular circumstances this kind of risk is not understood by clients, which often leads to wrong decisions.

Keywords: information asymmetry, misinforming, warranty, risk

Introduction

The success of a business deal in e-commerce, involving the two parties – a seller and a buyer, depends on variety of factors, divided into two major groups:

- **Environmental factors**: properties of the environment in which the seller-buyer relationship operates, such as IT infrastructure, logistic infrastructure, financial infrastructure and government regulations.
- **Communicational factors**: properties of interpersonal relationship between the two parties, such as efficiency and effectiveness of the communication process, trust and confidence, content and acceptance of the exchanged messages, etc.

The information asymmetry, as a natural property of any communication process, may result in misunderstanding between sellers and buyers and therefore may erode the trust between them. **This is critical especially in indirect communication between the two parties, as in e-commerce.** From customer's point of view, missing of adequate knowledge about the product may result in wrong purchase decision. From point of view of the seller, customer's misunderstanding about the properties of the products may result in customer's dissatisfaction and loss of market positions. Often, the customer does not know exactly what s/he is buying and the seller doesn't know why the customer is buying the product. The two parties will benefit from overcoming the information asymmetry as well as from introducing techniques to evaluate and share the risk caused by the information asymmetry. Major instrument used in sharing risk is including a warranty statement into purchase contract.

Information Asymmetry: Risks Caused by Misinforming

What is Information Asymmetry?

In economics, **information asymmetry** occurs when one party to a transaction has more or better information than the other party. Also, it has been called **asymmetrical information** and related markets are called **markets with asymmetrical information**. Typically it is the seller that knows more about the product than the buyer, however, it is possible for the reverse to be true -- for the buyer to be better informed compare to the seller.

Examples, where the seller usually has better information than the buyer are numerous and include used-car salespersons, stockbrokers, real estate and life insurance agents. On the other hand, there are situations where the buyer is usually better informed than the seller, e.g., in insurance, when a buyer purchases insurance for a property with hidden problems.

The informational misbalance was described for the first time by Kenneth J. Arrow (1963), who introduces it as "moral hazard". Later, George Akerlof (1970) used the term asymmetric information, noticing that, in a market with asymmetrical information, the average value of the commodity tends to go down, even for commodities with a perfect quality. Moreover, it is possible for such a market to decay to the point of nonexistence. Because of information asymmetry, unscrupulous sellers can embellish the items (like software or computer games) and defraud the buyer. As a result, many buyers with a risk-averse attitude will avoid certain types of purchases, or will not be willing to spend much on a given item.

Information Asymmetry exists in every communication process. Incorrect, not as intended, interpretation of the received message, as a side effect of the communication process, may cause significant qualitative and quantitave losses to both, the sender and the receiver. These side effects may be described as misunderstanding, misinterpretation, mis-inference, etc. Onwards, we will refer to all of these as misinforming. Reduction of losses caused by misinforming may be achieved either by improving the quality of the message sent or by introducing tools (as warranty) to share this risk between two parties. Sharing risk requires understanding the nature and quantifying the risk of misinforming. Evaluation of the risk caused by information asymmetry is especially important in indirect communication, such as e-commerce.

Quantifying the risks of malfunctioning of the products is relatively well studied (see for example Blischke & Murthy, 1993, 1996; Chukova, Arnold, & Wang, 2004). It uses models, based on information obtained from reliability tests, quality control or other activities carried out by the producer to study product's performance. The comprehensiveness and precision of this assessment is entirely under the control of the producer and the assigned warranty policies fully reflect the objectives of the producer.

On the other hand, measuring the risk of misinforming is based on the failures in the communication process. It is not under the contol of any of the parties involved in the communication and it requires different approaches and new techniques for collecting and processing the relevant data. The primary data source is the customer's feedback on the satisfaction with the product. Studies on the success of information services originate in the area of Information Sciences (see Buckland 1991, page 173), where, in a relatively narrow settings, the impact of a receiver's expertise on the success of the information services was studied. The reciever's expertise was studied by Buckland in the two aspects – subject expertise and expertise to use efficiently the information system providing the servce. The impact of receiver's expertise on both aspects, as defined by Buckland, are of crucial importance for the success in e-commerce. Lack of expertise in using the information system simply excludes these customers from the market. The level of receiver's expertise in the subject area affects the level of information asymmetry – a high expertise in the subject area reduces the level of information asymmetry and vice versa.

The Nature of Misinforming

A communication process represents an exchange of information between two parties – a sender and a receiver – throught a given communication channel. The stages in a communication process are represented in Figure 1.

The sender sends out a message addressing the receiver. The content of the message is a sign of the sender's idea of what is useful to the receiver. The message is composed to represent the meaning as it is understood by the sender. Its structure is influenced by the sender's judgment on the receiver's capability to understand and interpret the message correctly. The message is encoded to make it suitable for transmission through the communication channel and submitted to the receiver.

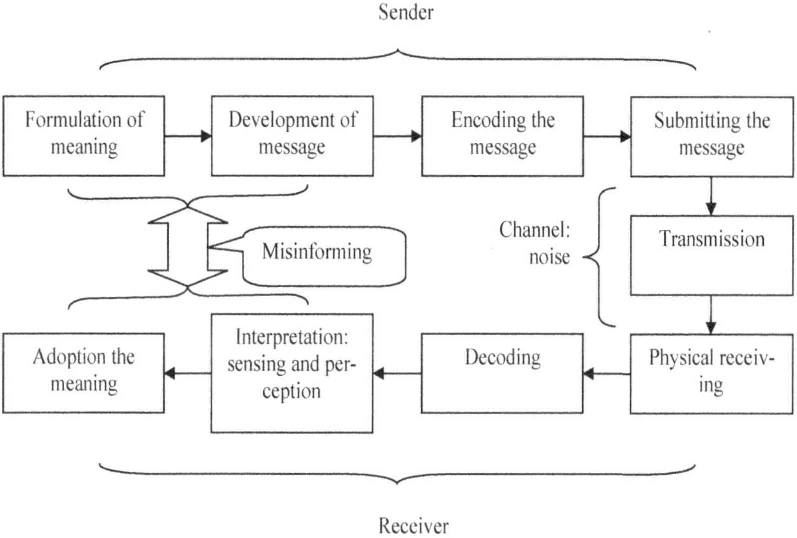

Figure 1. Stages in a communication process

From the receiver's side, the process also includes several stages. It starts with the physical delivery of the message followed by its decoding. The decoding is the ability of the receiver to read the message, which requires an agreement between the two parties on the language used in the message. The understanding, i.e., the proper interpretation of the message is essential for the success of the communication process. The last phase – adoption of the information is successful if the receiver utilises the obtained information in making decisions. It depends on the succes of all of the previous stages in the communication process. Failure in any of them results in a failure in the communication.

Most of the technological tools developed to support the communication are focusing on the physical delivery and correct decoding of the information.

The stage of interpretation the content of the message is critical to whether the message informs or misinforms the receiver. The interpretation is based on receiver's expertise, perceptions, biasness, etc. The success in this stage is seriously influenced by the information assymetry defined as the difference in expertise of the sender and reciever on the subject of the message.

The last stage, the adoption of the information, depends on whether the obtained information, as it is understood, is valuable to the receiver. Also, it is greatly influenced by the level of sender's credability with the receiver. In a face-to-face communication, the trust may be revealed by many factors additional to the content of the message, such as whether the communication takes place in a trustful environment, what is sender's personality, sender's body language, possibilities of clarifying the meaning of the message in an easy and natural dialog, etc. In indirect communication, majority of these factors are irrelevant and they have to be compensated by the structure and the content of the message.

Issues and Possible Solutions

There are many issues and problems naturally arising within an indirect communication environment and, as expected, reflect on the success in e-commerce. Some of these issues are:

1. Whether the meaning of the message intended by the sender matches the meaning understood by the receiver?
2. What is the risk and related business effects due to a wrong interpretation of the meaning of the message from a receiver's point of view as well as from sender's point of view?
3. How should a communication process be modified in order to increase the chance for success?

Better results in an indirect communication process could be achieved by reducing the risk of misinforming for the receiver and by encouraging him/her to utilise the information received.

The reduction of the risk of misinforming may be accomplished in two ways:

- Reducing the information assymetry, by increasing the level of mutual understanding between the two parties.
- Offering a warranty to cover the risk of misinforming, by sharing the risk between the two parties.

Both approaches require collecting and analyzing data related to the feedback on the success of an indirect communication process.

Techniques like Customer Related Management (CRM) or Market Studies address the first of the two approaches. The study of the feedback within a certain commercial activity increases the seller's understanding about the client's expertise. It allows them to compose their messages to target the specifics in the client's backgrounds. Market Studies define groups of customers with similar needs and interests and allow sellers to address the group as a whole at an appropriate level of complexity. CRM allows companies to offer individually customised products and address the clients with specifically designed messages.

Warranty that includes statements like "Money back guarantee if not fully satisfied" is an attempt to solve the problem using the second approach, i.e., to increase the credibility of the seller. This type of warranty promotes:

- an increase in the customer's understanding about the product, by encouraging him/her to experiment with a limited risk,
- an increase in the producer's understanding of customer's language and allows for improvement in communications between the two parties in the future.

This type of warranty provides learning opportunities for both parties. It decreases the information asymmetry and enhances the trust between them. Unfortunately, in the case of indirect communication, the probability of misinforming can be high enough to cause large unexpected losses for the warrantor. Therefore, while designing reasonable warranty coverage, quantifying the risk of misinforming is a significant and often critical task.

Quantitative measures

Next, our goal is to develop a quantitative measure to assess the risk of information asymmetry. We start by introducing certain formalism.

Assume that a particular customer needs to solve a set of problems, say $\{A\}$. Subsequently, we will refer to this customer as a customer with set $\{A\}$. The elements w of $\{A\}$ are disjoined, called tasks, and

$$\{A\} = \{w_i, i = 1,...N\},$$

where N is a positive integer and N < infinity.

Also, let us assume that by applying certain methods, devices or services, a task w_i from $\{A\}$ can be solved. We will call these methods, devices or services **products**. Moreover, we assume that there is a set of products $D=\{d_j\}, j=1,...M$ available on the market, appropriate for solving the tasks in $\{A\}$.

For different customers, who have the same set of tasks $\{A\}$, the complexity and importance of tasks varies and, correspondingly, the **suitability** of the products, available for solving them, also varies. We assume that for each set of tasks $\{A\}$ and each particular customer with set $\{A\}$ a specific threshold of acceptance q, $0 <= q <= 1$, exists and its level (value) is pre-set by the customer. The threshold of acceptance is the lowest level, set by the customer, of product's suitability still acceptable for solving the set $\{A\}$. The threshold of acceptance represents the customer's opinion on how suitable the product should be in order to be considered as a possible solution for the tasks in $\{A\}$. The value of q is independent of the set of products D.

The set of tasks $\{A\}$ can be considered as a sample space of all possible outcomes for a particular customer. Let $P = P(w)$ denotes a probability distribution on $\{A\}$, induced by the customer with set $\{A\}$. This probability distribution is subjective and represents the importance of the tasks to the customer.

Next, our aim is to define the probability that a given product is suitable for a customer with set $\{A\}$. Denote this event as "success" and mark it by S an event. Let $P(S \mid w)$ be the probability that the customer can solve the task $w \in A$ without applying any product. Then, based of the total probability rule, the probability that the customer will successfully solve the set of tasks $\{A\}$ without applying any product is

$$P(S) = \sum_{w \in A} P(S \mid w) P(w)$$

Further, let us apply the product d from D for solving the task $w \in A$. Now, the probability of success is $P(S \mid w, d)$, which is a measure of the suitability of the product d to solve task w. The product d is suitable for solving w if and only if

$$P(S \mid w) < P(S \mid w, d),$$

i.e., the probability to solve the task w with product d is higher then the probability of solving the task without applying any product. We will assume that this inequality holds for product d and at least one of the tasks w, $w \in A$. Otherwise the product d is irrelevant to the needs of the customer with set $\{A\}$.

The suitability of product d for a customer with set $\{A\}$ can be measured with the probability of success when applying this product to all tasks $w \in A$, i.e.,

$$p = P(S \mid d) = \sum_{w \in A} P(S \mid w, d) P(w). \tag{1}$$

Therefore, if a satisfactory estimation for the aforementioned probability is available it can be used to measure the suitability of product d for set $\{A\}$.

The information asymmetry is due to a mismatch between the seller's and the buyer's estimations of the suitability of product d with respect to a set $\{A\}$. The seller is familiar with the product and its suitability to solve a particular task, whereas the seller is better informed on the suitability of the product related to the tasks from $\{A\}$ measured by the probability $P(S \mid w, d)$.

Moreover, the customer is the only one who knows his/her own problems/tasks $\{A\}$ and related distribution $P(w)$. Therefore a customer is identified by the pair $\{(A, P), q\}$, the set of task s/he needs to solve, the measure of the importance of the tasks and the threshold of acceptance for set $\{A\}$. The triple $\{(A, P), q, d\}$ describes how a product d meets customer's needs q in solving tasks w from given (A,P).

Any message from the seller to the customer aims to enrich the customer's information about the product, which will reflect on the value of $P(S \mid w, d)$.

A customer makes his/her purchase decision based on the estimation $\hat{p}$ of $p = P(S \mid d)$, where p given by (1). The estimation $\hat{p}$ summarizes the customer's understanding regarding the suitability of the product to solve his/her set $\{A\}$. In general, there are three categories of customers, optimists with $\hat{p} > p$, pessimists with $\hat{p} < p$ and realists with $\hat{p} = p$. The probability of having $\hat{p} = p$ is negligible, because it refers to exact equality of these two probabilities. In case we refer to realists as those for which $|\hat{p} - p| < \varepsilon$, where ε is a small positive – the difference is negligible, the group of realists deserve attention, but in this case we cannot speak about existence of information asymmetry. That's why we will not discuss the category of realists any further.

The purchase decisions depends on the comparison between q and $\hat{p}$. If $q < \hat{p}$, then the purchase decision should be positive, i.e., customer's estimation of the suitability of the product is greater than the threshold of acceptance and the product is assessed as suitable. If $q > \hat{p}$, the purchase decision should be negative, because customer's estimation of the suitability of the product is less than the threshold of acceptance and the product is not suitable for solving for $\{A\}$. There are six possible scenarios, caused by the information asymmetry:

1. $p < \hat{p} < q$ - the product is not suitable, the customer's estimation of the suitability of the product is **optimistic** and **below the threshold of acceptance,** thus the decision is **negative** and **correct**;

2. $p < q < \hat{p}$ - the product is not suitable, the customer's estimation of the suitability of the product is **optimistic** and **above the threshold of acceptance,** thus the decision is **positive** and **wrong**;

3. $q < p < \hat{p}$ - the product is suitable, the customer's estimation of the suitability of the product is **optimistic** and **above the threshold of acceptance** , thus the decision is **positive** and **correct**;

4. $\hat{p} < p < q$ - the product is not suitable, the customer's estimation of the suitability of the product is **pessimistic** and **below the threshold of acceptance,** thus the decision is again **negative** and **correct**;

5. $\hat{p} < q < p$ - the product is suitable, the customer's estimation of the suitability of the product is **pessimistic** and **below the threshold of acceptance**, thus the decision is **negative** and **wrong**;

6. $q < \hat{p} < p$ - the product is suitable, the customer's estimation of the suitability of the product is **pessimistic** and **above the threshold of acceptance**, thus the decision is **positive** and **correct**.

The first three cases specify the customer as a pessimist and the last three – as an optimist. In each of these categories a **wrong decisions is possible**. For **optimists,** the wrong decision is in case 2 – the product is not suitable, but the purchase decision is positive, whereas, for **pessimists,** the wrong decision is in case 5 – the product is suitable, but the purchase decision is negative.

An Illustrative Example

Next, in order to illustrate the ideas, we consider an example related to the evaluation of the risk of misinforming by selling/buying a personal computer. Usually, the information provided by the **seller,** regarding the configuration of the system is presented in the following form:

Pentium IV/1.6C GHz
Intel 440 - LX Power Pro ATX
256MB DDR RAM
1.44 MB FDD
30GB HDD QUANTUM
16MB SGRAM VGA card AGP
15" Color HANSOL 0.28, LR
N.I. (1024x768), CPU CONTROL

On the other hand, usually the **buyer** is looking for information, regarding the capabilities of the systems to (set of tasks $\{A\}$):

- develop and edit text;
- perform high precision computations;
- use of e-mail;
- easy access to the Internet;
- organize personal data;
- play games;
- watch movies.

In addition, the seller offers warranty coverage, aiming to increase his credibility by sharing the risk of malfunctioning of the computer as well as the risk of misinforming the customers. There are two types of warranty statements and they address the two different sources of the risk.

The standard warranty statement consisting something like "All computers (battery/power adapter excluded) are covered for a period of 1 year warranty from the date of original purchase, except in cases where the manufacturer's warranty exceeds ours. In these cases the manufacturer's warranty will be honored" (see http://www.rjtech.com/notebook_warranty.htm). It addresses the risk caused by the low reliability of the hardware and this is a warranty on the defectiveness and malfunctioning of the item.

On the other hand, the buyer making his/her purchase decision is interested in the following questions:

- What is the meaning of ATX, AGP, etc.?

- Whether this configuration can fit his/her needs in terms of software and computing capabilities?

- Whether s/he needs all of the listed components of the system? and so on.

A warranty statement consisting something like "We guarantee 30-day money back for most items, except CPU and memory are 7-day money back. The exception for the CPU and memory is necessary due to the frequent price fluctuation in these items", (see http://www.directron.com/money-back-guarantee-.html) addresses the risk of miscommunication, misunderstanding, misinforming between the seller and the buyer. In this case, the buyer has an easy task in making his/her decision, because the warranty provides a full protection against any wrong decision for a certain period of time. Also, this type of warranty strongly promotes the sales of the warranted product.

Next, we discuss an illustrative numerical example on evaluation of the risk of misunderstanding. We have designed a simple experiment, collected the relevant data and used them to evaluate the risk of misunderstanding. The original design of the experiment, description of the collected data and their aggregation are described in Christozov and Mateev 2003. The same experiment was repeated twice since Fall 2002 and combined results are presented in Table 1. Designed to illustrate before students the problem of misinforming, the original test did not match perfectly to the need of the current study, but to achieve comparability in repeating experiments we decided to use the same construction of the test, nevertheless that we set further more clearly the objectives of this study.

Target group: a group of sixty students (35 responded), mostly sophomores, were offered to purchase a personal computer (PC). We assumed that these students have a good understanding about their needs regarding the usage of a personal computer, because they actually are facing purchasing computers. The data were collected during the Fall semester of 2002.

The message: the target group was approached with an offer to buy a PC, with powerful computational capabilities, designed to serve professional scientists. It had no communication devices;

no color graphics and the sound capabilities were limited. The offer was presented in the following form:

ASUS A7V333/RA sA, VIA KT333,266,ATA 133,RAID,
3DDR,AGP 4x, USB 2.0, IEE 1394, ATX
AMD XP PALOMINO 2100PR/1.75 GHz
DDRAM 512 MB DDR, PC 333MHz, SAMSUNG
80 GB MAXSTOR / 7200 / ATA 133/2MB
PCI ATI 1MB
17'' SAMSUNG 753S 1280x1024/65Hz 1024x768/85 Hz BW
keyboard, mouse, midi tower case

The offered PC were designed for word processing and complex computations, but not for the use of the Internet and e-mailing, did not have any capabilities for multimedia, playing games, watching movies, etc. The price was realistic, but highly attractive.***The survey***

1. The students were asked to evaluate whether the given PC satisfies their needs, according to the following list of applications:

- word processing,
- complex computations,
- management of personal data,
- Internet,
- e-mail,
- games,
- music,
- movies.

The students had to provide two answers for every item of this list, firstly, whether they need the given application and, secondly, whether the given PC allows for such an application.

2. They were offered two warranty statements: either "**Three years standard warranty**" or "**Three months "money back guarantee" warranty**" and were asked to make their purchase decision.

Table 1. Summary of survey results

Application	Needs		Assessed ability		Actual ability	Wrong decision
1	2		3		4	5
$A = \{w\}$	#	$P(w)$	#	$\hat{p}$	p	$abs(p - \hat{p})$
Word Processing	33	0.143	27	0.77	1.00	0.23
Complex Computations	10	0.043	19	0.54	1.00	0.44
e-mail	35	0.152	25	0.71	0	0.71
Internet	35	0.152	25	0.71	0	0.71
Maintain Personal data	33	0.143	27	0.77	1.00	0.23
Play Games	22	0.095	21	0.60	0	0.60
Movies	28	0.121	21	0.60	0	0.60
Music	35	0.152	20	0.57	0	0.57
Overall Risk:						0.51

The column "Applications" represents the set of tasks $\{A\}$. The column "Needs" consists of subjectively defined needs, which are proportional to the estimates of the probabilities $P(w)$. The third column shows the subjective estimate of product's suitability (expressed by $\hat{p}$) with respect to the tasks as seen by the customers. The fourth column consists of $p = P(S \mid w, d)$, the objective ability of the product to solve the task. The last column shows the share of customers who may do wrong decision, based on misunderstanding the ability of the product to solve the given task, which is computed using the approach discussed on Section 3. In this case p is either 1 or 0 and the threshold q does not play any role, because if we consider a particular w_i, we have the following cases:

1) if $p = 0$, the product is totally unsuitable, then both q and $\hat{p}$ are greater or equal than p and any positive purchase decision is wrong;

2) if $p = 1$, the product is absolutely suitable and both q and $\hat{p}$ are less or equal than p, and any negative purchase decision is wrong.

The risk caused by misunderstanding is calculated as follows: The risk of a wrong decision caused by the information asymmetry is equal to $r = abs(p - \hat{p})$ and depends on p - the objective suitability of the product, described by the seller in the message (seller's information), and on $\hat{p}$ – the suitability of the product as the buyer understands and interprets the message (buyer's information). For the i-task (w_i) the measure of its risk caused by information asymmetry is either $r = (p - \hat{p})$ *if* $p = 1$ and the product is suitable, but purchase decision is negative, or $r = (\hat{p} - p)$ *if* $p = 0$ the product is unsuitable, but purchase decision is positive.

The overall risk of a wrong decision due to misinforming is evaluated by the weighted average of the information asymmetries of the tasks, where the weights set to be equal to the corresponding "needs" $P(w)$, i.e.,

$$R = \sum P(w_i) r_i .$$

The overall risk of misinforming turned out to be a relatively high for this particular case. This could be due to a number of reasons such as a low level of expertise of the buyers (students) regarding computer configurations, lack of easy to read and informative description of the components of the computer system and so on.

Finally, a great majority of students responded positively to the warranty statement addressing malfunctioning of the computer, and lower number to warranty allowing to experiment with the computer and to postpone the final decision until gaining confidence in suitability of the product.

Conclusion

The findings of our study can be summarized in the following way:

The risk caused by information asymmetry could be high enough to incur serious business consequences and it is important to be studied, understood and quantified. A significant percentage of customers do not understand the risk caused by misinforming. The customer's confidence about his/her ability to understand correctly a certain message is often overestimated, which usually leads to poor decisions.

2. E-commerce offers great opportunities for enriching the seller-customer relationship. An indirect business communication emphasizes the trust between the two parties. It requires development of tools to enhance the understanding between them and to overcome the information asymmetry.Sellers/Producers aiming to promote their products by covering the risk of misinforming, usually assume a negligible impact of

this risk on their business. The learning aspects of warranty related to misinforming are underestimated as well. Warranty is a mechanism for sharing the risk between the seller and the buyer. On one hand, the seller receives customer's feedback regarding this risk and, on the other hand, it allows for an increase of customer's understanding about the product, by encouraging them to experiment with a limited risk. Growing customer's awareness and requirements towards quality in the marketplace forces producers/sellers to pay special attention to the risk of misinforming and to develop and apply techniques for the evaluation and sharing of this risk, similarly to what has been done for the risk of malfunctioning.

References

Akerlof, G. A. (1970). The market for 'lemons': Quality uncertainty and the market mechanism. *Quarterly Journal of Economics, 84*(3), 488-500.

Arrow K. (1963). Uncertainty and the welfare economics of medical care. *AER*.

Blischke W., & Murthy, D.N.P. (1993). *Warranty cost analysis*. Marcel Dekker.

Blischke W., & Murthy D.N.P. (1996), *Product warranty handbook*. Marcel Dekker.

Buckalnd, M. (1991). *Information and information systems*. NY: Preager.

Christozov, D., & Mateev P. (2003). Warranty as a factor for e-commerce success. *Proceedings of Informing Science and IT Education Conference*, Pori, Finland, June 2003. Available at http://proceedings.informingscience.org/IS2003Proceedings/docs/068Chris.pdf

Chukova, S., Arnold, R., & Wang, D. (2004) Warranty analysis: An approach to modelling imperfect repairs. *International Journal of Production Economics, 89*(1), 57-68.

Biographies

Dimitar Christozov is a Professor of Computer Science at the American University in Bulgaria, Blagoevgrad 2700, Bulgaria since 1993. He has more than 25 years of experience in areas as computer science, quality management and information systems. He graduated Mathematics from Sofia University "St. Kliment Ohridski" in 1979. He completed his PhD thesis "Computer Aided Evaluation of Machine Reliability" in 1986. In ICTT "Informa" (1986-1993) Dr. Christozov was involved in establishing the national information network for technology transfer and research in the areas of technologies assessment, integral quality measures and information systems for quality management. In these areas he was recognized as one of the leading experts in Bulgaria. Professor Christozov has more than 50 publications as separate volume, journal papers and papers in refereed procideengs. He is a founding member of Informing Science Institute and chair of Bulgarian Informing Science Society; and member of the Bulgarian Statisyical Society.

Dr. **Stefanka Chukova** is a Reader in Statistics and Operations Research at the School of Mathematics, Statistics and Computer Science, Victoria University of Wellington, Private Bag 600, Wellington, New Zealand, e-mail: schukova@mcs.vuw.ac.nz. She has a PhD and MSc in Mathematics (concentration in Probability and Statistics) and BSc in Mathematics from University of Sofia, Sofia, Bulgaria. Her research interests are in applied stochastic models, warranty analysis, reliability and queueing. She has more than 50 publications and has presented papers at national and international conferences and workshops. She is a member of ORSNZ, AWIS and ASA.

Dr.**Plamen S. Mateev** is Associate professor in Faculty of Mathematics and Informatics, Sofia University "St.Kliment Ohridski", Department "Probability, Operation research, Statistics", Bulgaria, 1164 Sofia, 5, J.Boucher str., e-mail: pmat at fmi.uni-sofia.bg.

His MSc in Mathematical Statistics is from Sofia University and his PhD is from Moscow State University. The research interests are in communication theory, applied statistics, statistical software and applications. More than 70 papers are published in scientific journals and proceedings of scientific conferences. He is a member of Bulgarian Statistical Society , ENBIS and InSITE Bulgaria..

Will It Work? An Initial Examination of the Processes and Outcomes of Converting Course Materials to CD-ROMs

Rob Connoley
Deakin University, Geelong, Australia

rob.connoley@deakin.edu.au

Abstract

The Faculty of Business and Law at Deakin University (Victoria, Australia) decided to dispense of all printed post-graduate learning materials and replace them with CD-ROMs from the commencement of the 2006 academic year. In addition, CD-ROMs were developed for a limited number of undergraduate units as part of a future delivery plan for this cohort of students. The following paper describes this project, the reasons underpinning it, and the processes the Faculty adopted to implement the project. The project is ongoing and part of a broader agenda for change that will see an even greater application of electronic technology to teaching and learning within the Faculty. Although only initial findings and observations are possible at this stage, the project provides a basis for longitudinal reporting and, potentially, a guide for other institutions who may be considering such a move. The paper reports on these observations and on those in the educational development arena and suggests that the Faculty will need to learn from these initial experiences and evaluate the project in greater depth to guarantee a smooth transition for all stakeholders.

Keywords: Distance education, educational development, online education

Introduction

In 2005 the Faculty of Business and Law at Deakin University (Victoria, Australia) decided to dispense of all printed post-graduate learning materials and replace them with enhanced CD-ROMs or other electronic formats. In addition, CD-ROMs were to be developed for a limited number of undergraduate units as part of a similar future plan for this cohort of students. Although this conversion is not revolutionary (see: for example, Savenye, Olina & Niemczyk 2001; Van der Vyver & Lane 2004), the initiative signals the future direction to be taken by the Faculty to course development and teaching and learning in general. This paper commences with a description of the project and then explores the reasons underpinning the Faculty's decision to move to electronic delivery of learning materials. This is to be followed by an examination of the processes that the Faculty employed to implement the project. As this project is relatively new, only preliminary observations can be made at this stage. However, it provides an opportunity to track progress over time and hopefully provide assistance to other institutions considering such a venture. A number of areas, such as student and staff reaction, have been identified that will require further analysis and evaluation in the next year. A separate section also identifies the implications for educational development, highlighting the need for a greater integration with other online developments planned in the Faculty and across the university.

Project Description

The project consisted of three components or sub-projects, all based on delivery by CD-ROM or directly online. The first was the development of a CD-ROM on post-graduate courses offered by the Faculty. It was anticipated that this CD-ROM would primarily have a marketing and information disseminating focus. It was planned to be distributed to all enrolled postgraduate students and to prospective students. Initial discussions determined that the contents of this CD-ROM should include:

- A Faculty-level page - Welcome from the Dean of the Faculty, links to course areas on the CD-ROM, links to university and faculty web pages, search facility across all units (assuming a set of CD-ROMs is provided as part of the second project).
- Course-level pages – A page for each course, with overviews provided by course-team chairs (voice-over PowerPoint slides), employment opportunities, information about professional associations, and links to unit-level pages.
- Unit-level pages – A page for each unit, with an overview/welcome message provided by unit chairs (for example, voice-over PowerPoint slides), how the unit develops graduate attributes, unit-level search facility, and a description of the learning resources.

The second sub-project was the provision of post-graduate unit learning resources on CD-ROM. From semester 1, 2006, all print materials normally supplied to students are to be replaced by a set of CD-ROMs containing all relevant learning materials, including the previously supplied print-only readers. Similar to the third sub-project explained below, only those units offered in semester 1, 2006 were to appear on the first set of CD-ROMs. Thus, 45 Postgraduate units were to be delivered on CD-ROM to approximately 6,500 students in Semester 1, 2006 (and then every semester following). It should be noted at this stage that the Faculty of Business and Law is already delivering a number of units with additional (non-text based) learning resources; some of which are currently provided online and some delivered on unit-specific CD-ROMs. Enrolled students also received a CD-ROM containing the study guides for all post-graduate units offered in a particular semester and had access to study guides and lecture material online. As explained below, the Faculty has been at the forefront in utilising available technology for course delivery and this sub-project illustrates further the Faculty's directions in respect of course development. The basic level of enhancement anticipated to be undertaken was the hyper linking to readings from within study guides. However, additional enhancements, such as audio and video files were also expected to be included.

The third sub-project was the provision of the core units of the undergraduate Bachelor of Commerce onto CD-ROM(s), commencing from semester 1, 2006. The undergraduate program requires the completion of 24 units over three years of equivalent full-time study, of which ten are compulsory or core units. Of these core units one is already offered in a fully on-line mode and another is supplied on CD-ROM along with a printed study guide. Similar to post-graduate students, off-campus students had received print-based study guides and readers, whilst on-campus students had the option of purchasing these materials. In addition, all students have online access to study guides, lecture materials and discussion forums. Although this sub-project was an afterthought, its importance lay in the message it has signalled for the future. The inclusion of these units in this initiative has forewarned students, academics and other key stakeholders of the Faculty's future directions for course material delivery, that is, the eventual replacement all print materials. As for the post-graduate units, academics were encouraged to go beyond the hyper linking to readings from within study guides to include audio and video files.

In addition to this project, academics are actively encouraged to progressively enhance their learning materials and place them online for all students.

The Reasons Underpinning the Project

The project to convert from print-based learning resources to an electronic format can be viewed as a logical extension to developments that have occurred within Deakin University and the Faculty of Business and Law since the early 1990s. Deakin has moved progressively to introduce and expand its online learning resources for more than a decade. For instance, in 1995 Deakin expanded the use of e-mail for academic communication and support services, introduced the FirstClass computer conferencing facilities and expanded its use of the WWW (Calvert 2001, p. 2). In addition, the university has implemented WebCT Vista as its online Learning Management System, known locally as Deakin Studies Online (DSO), since 2003.

The Faculty of Business and Law is one of Australia's most experienced provider of quality distance education programs offering programs by distance education and face-to-face since the 1970s. It is also the largest provider of post-graduate and distance education units in Deakin University. The Faculty has been at the forefront of developments in course delivery, continuing to update delivery methods for this cohort of students, from print-only delivery in the 1970s and 1980s, to print being supplemented by electronic access to study guides on CD-ROMs and via online technologies since the mid-1990s. Currently, the Deakin Business School, in conjunction with other schools within the Faculty of Business and Law, offers postgraduate programs in a wide variety of disciplines including business administration, commerce and international business.

Electronic learning material delivery is a world-wide occurrence and advances in technology have provided educational institutions with greater means to adopt more sophisticated methods of course delivery. These developments have been particularly beneficial for Deakin University, which has approximately 40 per cent of students studying in an off-campus mode. Similar to other higher education institutions, online technologies at Deakin are aimed at enriching learning experience, adding flexibility and complementing traditional teaching methods. Deakin has also pursued this path to better prepare students in using online technologies, particularly when they enter the workforce. This direction has been supported by a number of key decisions. In 2004 all Deakin units were required to have at least a basic online environment (see table 1) for information, resources and communication, with some units increasing their online presence to include more interactive learning resources (levels 2 and 3). The university also decided that all commencing undergraduate students from 2004 are expected to successfully complete at least one unit of study in a fully online mode at some point in their program of study.

The university has also imposed targets on faculties to increase the number of units they offer at an extended online mode (or level 2). This follows feedback that the level 1 online requirement did not represent a major transformation of teaching and learning at Deakin. For instance, prior to 2004, the university already had 68 percent of units meeting a level 1 requirement. Faculty management realised that only a small number of under-graduate and post-graduate units had an online presence at levels 2 and 3. The production of print-based readers meant most units were non-compliant with these levels. Thus, the conversion to CD-ROM was a means of meeting the new online targets.

A move to an electronic format required a shorter lead time to produce, resulting in fewer delays in getting material to off-campus students. It also was cheaper for the faculty to produce. Like other higher education institutions in Australia, Deakin, and consequently its faculties, is facing a constantly tighter financial environment, commonly requiring action to reduce costs. In the past the Faculty provided students with both a CD-ROM and a hard copy of study guides and readings at no additional charge. The hard copies were provided in high-quality binders and cost the faculty around $250,000 each year. In contrast, the cost of providing each student with material on CDROM would cost around $20,000 per semester. A CD-ROM was also seen to more easily exploit resources from a wide range of sources and in many formats compared to print-based materials.

The decision to favour CD-ROMS, relative to DSO, was due to the difficulties of online access in the more remote areas. This was an important consideration for the Faculty as many students enrolled in post-graduate units reside in regional and remote locations. The placement of all learning resources onto CD-ROM format could free students from downloading large files, such as audio and video files, some of which were prohibitive from being efficiently sourced from DSO. Though online technology has become increasingly sophisticated, download times continue to limit effective delivery, particularly in geographical areas serviced by Deakin University. (See Table 1.)

Table 1: Deakin Categories of Online Activity

Category	Features
Level 1: Basic Online	A Deakin Studies online (DSO) site established. The DSO site will include, where appropriate and feasible and where they exist, the unit guide, a 'resources area' where an electronic version of the readings (where appropriate) and other resources might be placed, and the opportunity for the teaching staff to communicate with students through a noticeboard (one-many communication e.g. announcements). A facility for structured online interaction between teacher and students will also be available to use at the choice of the lecturers involved in the unit, with the proviso that all students in unites that do not meet face-to-face at least once a week will have such opportunities for facilitated online interaction. The unit chair must be prepared to report to their unit community through the DSO site established for their unit. This may include complementary use of email in the first instance. Student expectations about communication should be managed (i.e. they are told how they should communicate with teaching staff, and how soon they should expect a reply).
Level 2: Extended Online Unit	In addition to the above: The study guide for that unit Additional DSO options included in the unit and available for students Additional resources available to students (e.g. additional electronic content, CD ROMs with additional material, video and audio streaming, etc.) Additional and/or compulsory use of advanced communication and instruction facilities More advanced and diverse pedagogies imbedded.

Level 3: Wholly Online Unit	All content (either commercial print-based textbooks or commercial e-texts may be used as supplementary material) All communication and interaction with students Assignment submission and feedback (examinations will move online when the University is administratively ready) Each unit will have at least ONE session of interactive communication (synchronous, asynchronous, or both) between teacher and students online at least weekly or as established at the beginning of the course. Such interactive sessions will have an assessable component where appropriate. To ensure access for all students until bandwidth issues in Australia are addressed, additional resources such as video and audio will be provided on CD-ROMs for off-campus students where appropriate. (This will be reviewed annually.)

The move was not devoid of risk and the Faculty took these into consideration in their deliberations. The major risk is the reaction by students (see: for example, Van der Vyver & Lane 2004). At the stage of the project, it is still an unknown variable. Informal discussions with academics noted some apprehension by students and the risk of student discontent was potentially high. Faculty management also perceived the provision of readings in addition to study guide material as a significant and immediate enhancement. In addition, the course level CD-ROM (the first sub-project) was also an added advantage. In anticipation of potential student dissatisfaction, the Faculty provided an option for students to purchase a hard copy of study guides and readers where applicable at cost. In addition, the third sub-project was a deliberate move by the Faculty of Business and Law to prepare all stakeholders of the future direction of the university.

A further risk was in the responses from academics. This is a very real concern, as academics had already shown some reluctance to enhance materials beyond the level 1 requirement on DSO. Faculty management were aware that the short time frame meant it would be impossible to enhance all unit resources on the first set of CD-ROMs. Resource constraints also meant that the scope of value adding to existing learning resources would most likely be limited in the first run, even with strong encouragement from the Dean and Associate Dean. Academics were subsequently encouraged to continue to develop learning enhancements and place them directly onto DSO.

The Process

Faculty teaching and learning representatives and representatives from the university's Knowledge Media Division (KMD) initially met in February 2005 to discuss the possibility of converting learning materials to CD-ROM. However, it was not until April 2005 that the Faculty formally presented its project to the University's Teaching and Learning Committee. From that time onwards, a number of measures were taken to see this project to fruition.

The decision to move to CD-ROM required a change to the traditional course development processes. The first area to be changed was the Faculty's learning materials planning cycle. Prior to this project, the Faculty had a three- year cyclical process for learning material updates. The planning cycle was constructed on advice from unit teams or from the unit chair as to the extent to which learning materials were to be updated, generally ranging from either no revision, a minor revision or a major re-write. Unit Chairs (academics responsible for coordinating the curriculum, teaching and assessment in a unit) coordinate the development of learning resources for the unit. There are many models for the way units are presented and developed. Under this cyclical approach, the Unit Chair is to keep the Faculty Production Manager informed of plans for unit development so that the necessary Faculty and university resources could be assigned. For minor updates, the Faculty Production Manager publishes a schedule stating when different units should complete the work ready for the next offering of the unit. If a unit is undergoing a minor update, the Unit Chair must ensure that a study guide and other learning resources are downloaded (from the Faculty web site), updated and uploaded (again via the Faculty web site) by the due date. For cases where there is a major redevelopment of learning resources, the Unit Chair must coordinate these. The Faculty Production Manager also provides academics with templates in a Word format on study and unit guide preparation and production.

A previous entitlement to a number of units (approximately 10) that would receive 'above-the-line' or high level KMD support continued, as this generally meant constructing units for the fully online (or level 3) mode. The role of KMD is to provide a range of support services to assist faculties in developing learning materials through such services as audio production (plan, record, edit, format and post produce most types of audio content for delivery via CD-ROM, Audio CD, DVD and online systems), CD-ROM production, copyright advice, desktop publishing, graphic design, lecture streaming, and multimedia and website development. This Division also undertakes quality checks on course materials such as checking whether materials meet accessibility requirements. KMD has also recently provided access to showcase exemplars on electronic learning from staff across the university.

The Faculty and KMD personnel realised that the production of multimedia learning objects was not necessarily a straightforward process, requiring a range of skills and personnel including academics (subject experts), multimedia producers, educational developers, and production staff working together in order to meet the Faculty expectations (see also Brett & Nash 1999, p.19). Regular meetings were consequently conducted between representatives from the Faculty's Teaching and Learning unit and personnel from KMD throughout 2005. These meetings covered issues such as design features, level of support necessary, technical and system requirements, timelines, quality checks and procedures for enhancing learning materials. Key responsibilities were also allocated at these meetings. KMD was responsible for the technical specifications and the Faculty responsible for managing the conversion of learning materials. KMD was also ultimately responsible for ensuring the materials were burned to CD-ROMs.

Faculty management were cognisant of the need to gain examples of enhancements from staff, particularly given the short time frame for development and the challenge to the traditional development cycle where resources are allocated for such pursuits. To assist, the Faculty decided to give more discretion to academics and unit teams to convert learning resources to CD-ROM. This bottom-up approach had a significant potential advantage of creating a greater number of enhancements relative to the limited number that could be provided with KMD support.

Initial meetings were held between the Dean, the Associate Dean – Teaching & Learning and the Heads of Schools (HoS). These meetings were aimed at providing the HoS with details about the process for enhancement and their expected contributions to the first CD-ROM. They were also strongly encouraged to ensure unit teams within their Schools commenced enhancing materials as soon as possible. Meetings with affected staff across all campuses followed these initial meetings with the HoS. Although face-to-face meetings were preferable, minimal turnout meant most information was subsequently distributed to staff via email and telephone. Staff were advised that they would be doing students a disservice by forcing them to read long pages of text on a computer screen and so should be examining ways to reduce content in favour of other learning objects, such as digital photos, audio files, video files, streamed lectures, interactive demonstrations, and text-based readings.

Educational development support was also available to academics. The Faculty currently has two dedicated educational development staff in addition to the Associate Dean to assist academics. Although it was not feasible for these persons to work with all unit teams, they were able to assist with some and also provide assistance through the development and distribution of examples being used in other unit teams. Educational developers were also able to start to provide unit teams with access to instructions and guidelines for creating learning objects.

The Faculty also took a more unique step of creating a shared site for learning resources development. The shared site provided individual folders for all units and these contained all the current learning resources (except those specifically designated for DSO). This shared site was designed to allow unit teams to manage the redevelopment of their learning resources of CD-ROM contents whilst in development. As noted above, there was a concerted effort on behalf of the Faculty to ensure ownership for development rested with unit teams. This site was established to enable continuous development and access to examples from other units.

Once updated, academic unit teams could revisit the updated resources prior to signing-off for final production by KMD. Unit teams were also advised that after they had reviewed and signed off on the unit's materials, a copy of the resources in editable form was to be placed into a new site folder in the shared drive. This enabled academics to continue to develop their learning resources in readiness for the next offering of the unit or onto DSO.

The Outcomes to Date

A full and extensive analysis of the project has not been possible at the time of writing as the unit material is now being returned to academics for a final examination prior to be burned on to CD-ROMs. In addition, no feedback from students has been possible. However, some initial thoughts can be presented in readiness for a more in-depth analysis during the next few months. The findings are important to identify at this initial stage since the project has mapped out the future path for all learning materials development within the Faculty. The first set of findings report on outcomes of the three sub-projects and the processes employed by the Faculty. This will be followed by an identification of the implications for educational development practices within the Faculty.

Project Outcomes

Project outcomes are presented for the three sub-projects.

Sub-project 1: Development of a CD-ROM on post-graduate courses offered by the Faculty

This sub-project was relatively straight forward from a Faculty's perspective, compared to the other two sub-projects. Apart from the audio presentations from the Dean and from course directors, many other resources such as, program details, course structures and study assistance, were already available for burning onto CD-ROM. Throughout the development of this sub-project, progressive details were placed online for Faculty staff to view and provide feedback to KMD via the Faculty's Associate Dean Teaching and Learning. This CD-ROM contained much of what was planned. A home page was developed which included a welcome message from the Dean (along with a printable online transcript). A copy of the home page of sub-project 1 CD-ROM is provided in Figure 1.

From the home page links were provided to a range of other pages/locations including post-graduate programs, methods of applying, money matters, study assistance, and instructions for how to use the CD-ROM. All the post-graduate programs can be examined from the links on the programs home page. Students will be able to access each program via the hyperlinks on the home page. Each program page provides at least a text-based course overview and course structure. Some program pages have also added audio recordings and transcripts explaining additional features including employment opportunities and the relevant professional associations (see Figure 2).

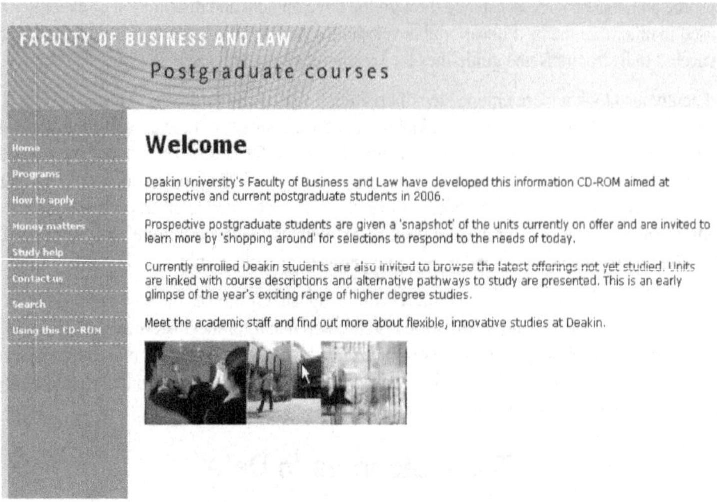

Figure 1: Sub-Project 1 - Home Page CD-Rom

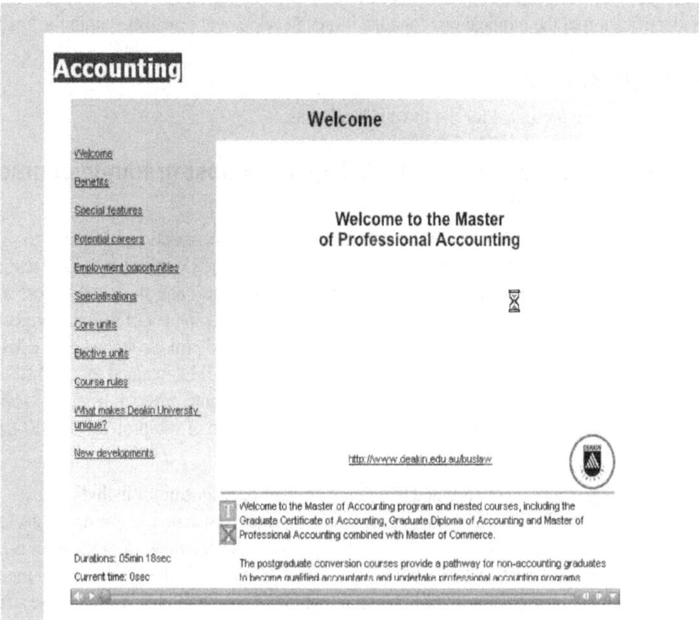

Figure 2: Sub-Project 1 – Program Page

Sub-project 2: Conversion of post-graduate learning materials to CD-ROMs

This sub-project was by far the most challenging for the Faculty. As noted above, the Faculty had been gradually increasing its adoption of electronic formats in the delivery of learning materials for many years. However, the number of units voluntarily moving to an electronic format only was quite slow. This sub-project sought to complete this push and signal a future push for electronic feedback. So what has been the result at this point in time? The level of enhancement in this, the first run, can be described as variable, with most semester 1, 2006 units (75 per cent) enhanced to the Faculty's basic level, where readings have been hyperlinked to a text-based study guide. This was not an unanticipated outcome, given the cultural change required, the tight timelines set to complete the conversion, and the limited funds to devote to developing learning enhancements. It is also reflective of the traditional text-heavy approach taken by academics to post-graduate learning materials development. This is an issue raised later in the paper in terms of implications for educational development. In response, the Faculty has strongly encouraged unit teams to continue to work on developing additional learning objects for either placement on their DSO site in readiness for semester 1, 2006.

The majority of units had a basic home page interface, listing topics and hyperlinking to pdf-version study guides (Figure 3). From the study guide, further links were added to pdf-version readings.

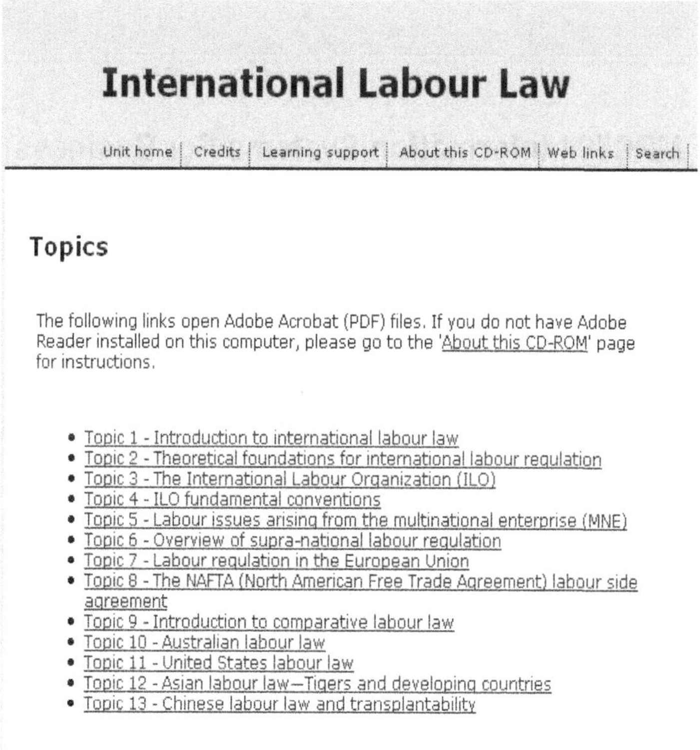

Figure 3: Sub-Project 2 – Common Home Page

The units that enhanced learning resources beyond this basic level were either converted to HTML (Figure 4) or redesigned using PowerPoint or Roadmap Tools, the latter tools being developed in-house by the Associate Dean of Teaching and Learning (Figure 5). The units prepared on these bases generally restructured the previously heavy text-based study guides and added additional features such as video and audio clips. Lecture slides were used to replace study guides in most of the units that used the Roadmap Tools.

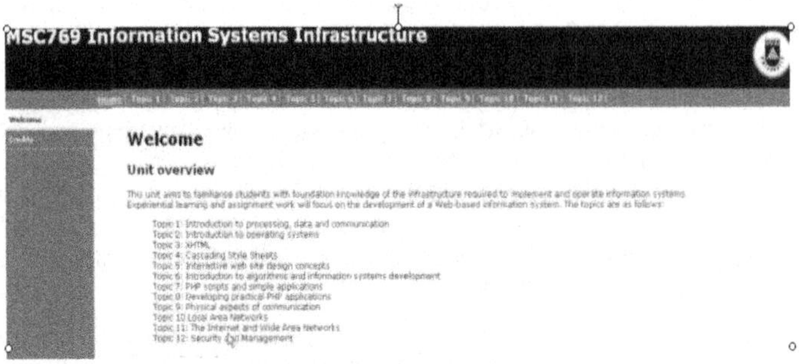

Figure 4: HTML Structure

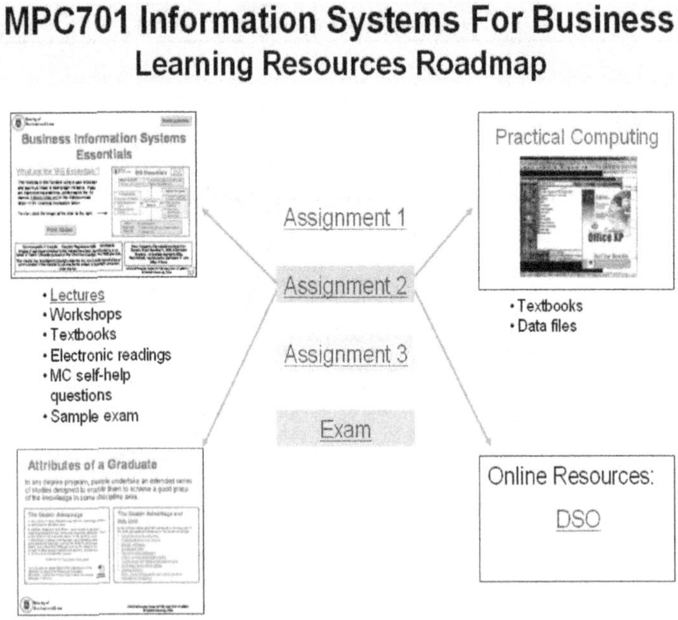

Figure 5: Structure Using Roadmap Tools (PowerPoint)

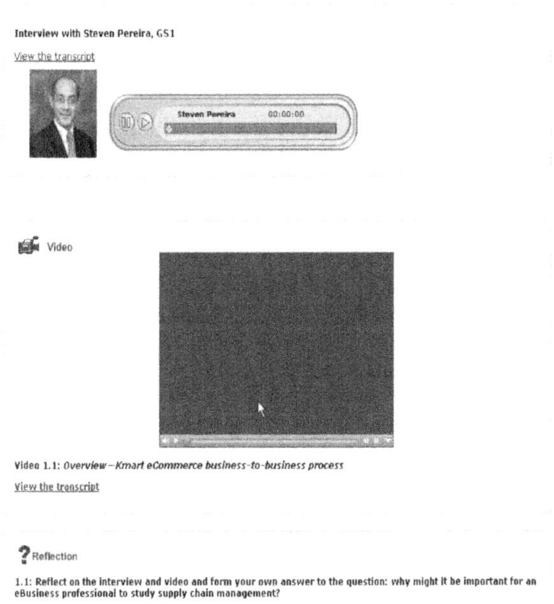

Figure 6: Sub-Project 2 – Example of Enhancements From HTML

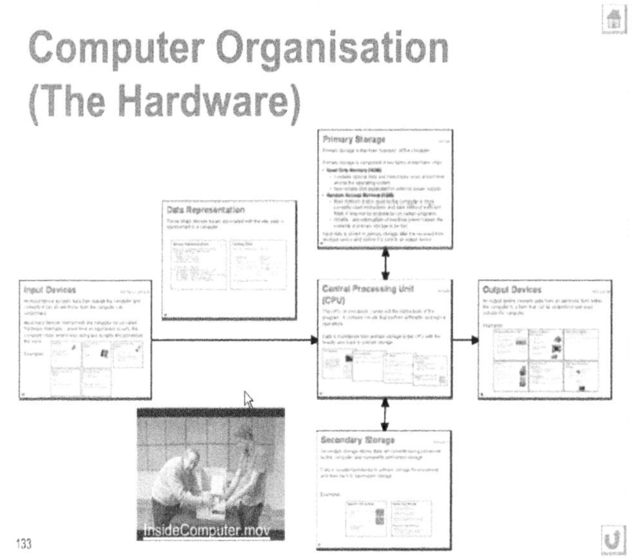

Figure 7: Sub-Project 2 – Example of Enhancement using Roadmap Tools

The enhancements ranged from a complete overhaul of study materials to the addition of videos and audio learning objects. Examples of the inclusion of enhancements are presented in Figures 6 and 7. The learning objects were able to be viewed from links within the redesigned learning materials.

Sub-project 3: Provision of the core units of the undergraduate Bachelor of Commerce onto CD-ROM(s)

Although the core units of the Bachelor of Commerce degree attracted less attention from Faculty management than the post graduate level units, the conversion represents the start of a future plan for course materials. This future is one where all undergraduate print-based learning materials will be replaced by electronic formats.

As noted earlier, one core unit is already offered entirely online and one was delivered on CD-ROM (along with a printed study guide). During the conversion process this unit opted to replace the print study guide with an updated version and be placed onto the CD-ROM. Of the eight remaining units, only three were unable to be enhanced, primarily due to staffing changes. Five units underwent more extensive changes, with four adopting a concept mapping approach using the Roadmap Tools (see Figure 5) and one received KMD support to convert their existing learning materials to a HTML format (see Figure 4). Similar to the post-graduate units, these undergraduate units also provided features such as audio and video clips, lecture streaming, and a range of publisher learning objects (such as online topic multiple choice tests). In is anticipated the remaining core units will undergo extensive modifications before the end of 2006.

Process outcomes

Some initial observations can also be presented about the processes used by the Faculty to implement these sub-projects. This is an important area for evaluation as the process will commence again in January/February 2006 for semester 2 offerings. The change was far more complicated than originally anticipated by Faculty management, and many more unit teams than had been anticipated were not enhancing their materials beyond a basic level. It appears that the level of enhancement was primarily dependent upon the level of support directly provided to individual units by KMD or by the Faculty's teaching and learning staff and to a limited extent on the pressures applied by the HoS. The limited enhancement by the majority of units is also indicative of the major cultural change to course development that this project entailed. Although meetings were held with academic teams, the benefits of conversion were not self-evident in informal discussions with individual academics.

Short comings were also evident in the areas of project management and in the level of resources required to effectively enhance learning. An overall project plan would have mapped out key tasks, responsibilities and issues to address prior to the project's implementation. It would have also anticipated constraints in the conversion process and in the level of resources required. However, limited time and resources resulted in the project management tasks generally being done 'on the fly'.

The level of resources dedicated to the project also needs to be planned. Multimedia enhancements are time consuming, sometimes involving many programming hours and material writing by academics. The Faculty cannot dedicate educational development resources to each individual unit meaning that in future the necessary tools need to be made more readily accessible by unit teams. The establishment of the shared development site has provided an avenue for an efficient distribution of required technology. Although the establishment of a shared site for unit development did not result in a major redevelopment at the local level or in the sharing of learning objects, it still appears to offer considerable advantages for future educational development. A key factor in its success will be determined by the extent to which the Faculty is able to convince academics of the ways in which electronic learning materials can enhance student learning and be able to provide the necessary technological tools and training in their application.

Implications for Educational Development

Both the time span and the extensive number of units offered by the Faculty of Business and Law limited the level of direct educational development support available to individual unit teams. Also the establishment of the shared development site has meant that academics can progressively develop resources for their unit and these not be analysed as to appropriate fit within their learning resources. Since the Faculty is pursuing the conversion of units at the undergraduate level, opportunities for educational developers to work individually with all unit teams will be even more unlikely in the future. This will necessitate developers to use other means of skilling up academics in their conversion of learning materials to an electronic format. In addition, as academics are also required to complete other tasks related to learning, such as preparing course and unit outlines and unit guides, some means of integration of these to this project is also pressing.

A first task will be for educational developers to increase the level of academic understanding of appropriate instructional design principles for electronic learning materials. Observations to date have indicated that academics require a foundation of knowledge of instructional principles and be provided with examples that could be adapted or applied to suit their units. In addition, standards for accessibility and other matters will also need to be communicated to academics. People's first instinct is to use it to do what they already do and consequently it is important for educational developers to work on assisting changing this mind set. The current mind set is one of producing substantial bodies of print-based resources. The move to electronic delivery will place pressure on this mind set. The anticipated introduction of additional electronic learning requirements, such as the introduction of electronic feedback during 2006, will also challenge existing practices of assessment and feedback currently used by academics.

Developers will also need to keep abreast of advances made available by new technologies and assist in spreading these to academics. Technology provides opportunities for the development of innovative and powerful interactive educational material (Aldrich, Rogers, & Scaife, 1998, p.321). These technologies provide new ways of delivering content, and they often promote learner-centred environments that can motivate students and add variety to learning. In this environment, instructional units are often accompanied by a liberal use of multimedia that is intended to add excitement to the lesson and hold the learner's attention. However, visual and auditory components that are intended to stimulate do not always make for sound instructional design in multimedia delivery and can quickly become counter-productive to learning (Sorden, 2005, p.264). A central problem is that the CD-ROMs could be simply a mishmash of images sounds and video offering little more than light entertainment (Aldrich et al., 1998, p.321). Time did not permit an analysis of the educational value of the enhancements provided by unit teams. Post graduate materials have also been very text-heavy and a major implication for educational developers to encourage unit teams to put the interactivity provided by the new technology to good use. Academics need an understanding of a range of media/technologies, their sources and possible educational uses, including the benefits of integrative approaches. This may involve developers assisting in the preparation of online tutorials for unit teams in how to apply particular tools to their learning materials. Through the consideration of a range of cases, participants should develop and/or review the current media/technologies mix in their teaching area with a view to suggesting enhancements associated with the use of digital media, via the mapping of learning resources, and new styles of student learning guides. The creation of a shared development site provides an ideal location for educational developers to direct academics to relevant exemplars.

Throughout 2006, it is planned to develop resources to instruct academics on capturing demonstrations on computer screen, including audio voice-overs and for tools to create and edit web pages.

Educational developers will also need to maintain an awareness of current and future trends in electronic delivery, particularly in identifying good practices from institutions following this path and particularly those which are providing electronic assessment and feedback. This will add value to decision makers about the development and delivery of courses in the future, particularly as the Faculty seeks to extend the application of electronic means of learning.

Conclusion

Higher education institutions are likely to continue to face pressure to deliver high-quality education to many learners at a reasonable cost (Savenye, Olina, & Niemczyk, 2001, p.381). Advances in technology have made the production of CD-ROMs an efficient and potentially effective educational strategy to meet this need. The Faculty of Business and Law at Deakin University decided to move to CD-ROM format in late April 2005 for its study materials, replacing the weighty paper-based format familiar to most students. It also decided to initiate undergraduate students to a CD-ROM delivery format in the core units of their Bachelor of Commerce degree.

At this stage, the Faculty has placed considerable faith that students and academics will accept this initiative and has also indicated there will be 'no going back'! Given previous studies of similar conversions (Van der Vyver & Lane, 2004), feedback from students and academics is essential. In respect of students we need data on learning styles and whether the learning materials cater for different styles. A project to evaluate the learning styles of law students is planned for 2006 and this will assist in informing the Faculty on approaches to use in the post-graduate level. An inquiry is warranted into how academics can learn about the educational value of technological enhancements, whether their developments are being shared with colleagues, and importantly the extent to which educational principles are informing the development of these enhancements. In addition, learning from the practices of other institutions pursuing similar forms of learning is essential, particularly assessment practices and the provision of feedback to students. An analysis of these areas will ensure the Faculty of Business and Law can gain the maximum advantages from this delivery format. It will also hopefully provide other interested parties with advice of how to guide, encourage and organise teachers to develop educationally valuable learning materials and methods with new technology.

References

Aldrich, F., Rogers, Y. & Scaife, M. (1998). 'Getting to grips with "interactivity": helping teachers assess the educational value of CD-ROMs', *British Journal of Educational Technology*, Vol. 29, No. 4, pp. 321-332

Brett, P. A. & Nash, M. 1999. 'Multimedia language learning courseware: a design solution to the production of a series of CD-ROMS', *Computers & Education*, Vol. 32, pp.19-33

Calvert, J. 2001. 'Deakin University: Going Online At A Dual Mode University', *International Review of Research in Open and Distance Learning*, Vol. 1, No. 2, pp.1-20

Savenye, W. C., Olina, Z. & Niemczyk, M. 2001. 'So you are going to be an online writing instructor: issues in designing, developing, and delivering an online course', *Computers and Composition*, Vol. 18, pp. 371-385

Sorden, S. D. (2005). A cognitive approach to instructional design for multimedia learning, *Informing Science Journal, 8*, 263-279. Available at http://inform.nu/Articles/Vol8/v8p263-279Sorden34.pdf

Van der Vyver, G. & Lane, M. S. (2004). Higher education course content: Paper-based, online or hybrid course delivery? Paper presented at the *Informing Science & Information Technology Education Joint Conference*, Rockhampton, Queensland, Australia, June 25 – 28. Retrieved 24 November 2005 from http://proceedings.informingscience.org/InSITE2004/109vande.pdf

Biography

Rob Connoley has been employed in the Faculty of Business and Law as a Lecturer in Teaching and Learning/Educational Developer since 2004, for the provision of educational development in the areas of assessment, flexible teaching and learning, and online learning resources development and delivery. Previous to 2004, Rob has worked as an instructional designer, held various management positions in government/semi-government organisations and has taught in universities and secondary schools. Rob is currently completing his PhD.

The page left blank intentionally.

Workflows without Engines: Modeling for Today's Heterogeneous Information Systems

Cristina Chuva Costa
Instituto Politécnico de Coimbra/Centro de Informática e Sistemas da Universidade de Coimbra, Coimbra, Portugal

chuva@isec.pt

Paulo Rupino da Cunha
Centro de Informática e Sistemas da Universidade de Coimbra, Coimbra, Portugal

rupino@dei.uc.pt

Abstract

Workflow modeling has been able to handle requirements down to the point where the specification gets executed on a specialized engine. Present day information systems, however, pose new challenges. Data and decision logic are spread out across a collection of heterogeneous applications of different ages, provided by various vendors, supported on diverse technologies. "Running" a business workflow thus means orchestrating several applications that were not designed to work together. Middleware and other technological solutions can be used to engineer coordination and communication between the systems, but, at a higher level, modeling techniques must be adjusted so that their inputs and deliverables fit this new "engineless" execution environment. We describe an approach we have used to bring together generic information systems design and workflow-specific concerns to produce an architecture that easily maps into today's heterogeneous scenarios. Special care has been taken to ensure that end-users are able to contribute throughout the process.

Keywords: workflow, heterogeneous systems, requirements, modulation

Introduction

A series of phenomena have changed the nature of information systems. Instead of the traditional heavy reliance on custom programming, common off-the-shelf (COTS) software is now purchased to satisfy most business needs. On the other hand, companies have accumulated several applications throughout the years, effectively creating a portfolio of systems that interact as business processes are carried out. Finally, the emergence of intranets provides means of leveraging the information stored in these various applications in a uniform and distributed manner.

This new reality means that business data and business logic are spread through dozens or even hundreds of autonomous applications "wired" together to meet the organization's diverse needs. This heterogeneous collection of systems, supported on disparate technologies, provided by various vendors, at different times of the organization's life, is the supporting infrastructure for the high-level business workflows. For instance, a request made by a client using the company's call center may be recorded in the underlying customer relationship management system (CRM) from vendor A and forwarded to the relevant department to process it using the enterprise resource management system (ERP) supplied by vendor B.

The transfiguration of information systems into highly heterogeneous portfolios of applications rendered traditional design methodologies inadequate, since their deliverables – clean architectures of data and logic to be coded – ceased to be in sync with actual field reality (Avison & Fitzgerald, 1999; Baskerville & Fitzgerald, 1995). Workflow modeling faces similar challenges. Although high-level analysis and planning must still be conducted, this process must now acknowledge as input the "fragmentation" of information and processing logic across several heterogeneous applications, and produce results that can be deployed in these "engineless" environments.

We describe how we extended a recent information systems design methodology, conceived to handle heterogeneous portfolios of applications (Cunha, 2000), to include workflow modeling.

The remaining of this paper is organized in the following way: in section "Approaches to Workflow Modeling" we briefly review various existing approaches to workflow modeling, looking for practices or aspects that remain adequate when handling heterogeneous information systems. These aspects were considered when developing our proposal, which is presented in section "Taking on Heterogeneity". The paper closes with a discussion of the results.

Approaches to Workflow Modeling

To avoid blindly proposing a new approach, we identified and reviewed several, quite distinct, workflow modeling techniques, to understand to which extent they could cope with the new reality of heterogeneous information systems. The detailed analysis has been published in (Costa & Cunha, 2002). In this section we merely summarize it and draw brief conclusions, pointing out which characteristics in each approach remain useful in today's information systems.

Function Modeling Techniques

Although not originally intended to model workflows, dataflow diagrams (DFD) were adopted for this purpose by some authors (Sadiq, Marjanovic, & Orlowska, 2000). The main appeal of this approach is the effective way in which it represents data circulation and processing. Another similar technique – the integration definition for function modeling (IDEF0) diagrams (Air Force Wright Aeronautical Laboratories, 1981) – also uses simple graphical elements to represent the flow of information between activities. However, both types of diagram pose a serious handicap: in their original form they are unable to represent time, and need supplementary specification techniques to clarify control logic details. The notations also exhibit some limitations when applied to ill-structured situations and to scenarios with many interactions. Finally, DFDs and IDEF0 diagrams are hard to understand by end-users, whose knowledge of business process is fundamental to the correct specification of workflows.

Graphs and Petri Nets

Several authors suggested the use of graphs to model workflow processes (Aalst, 1995; Casati, Ceri, Pernici, & Pozzi, 1995). A proposal by Sadiq and Orlowska, 1996 includes different types of objects: flows, tasks, conditions and synchronizers. These objects enable the specification of workflows by building and joining different constructs, such as ordering, alternative, exclusive join, concurrency, synchronization and iteration.

Different researchers preferred Petri nets over graphs (Peterson, 1997). The order in which the tasks are to be executed can be modeled by Petri Nets using constructs for sequential, conditional, parallel, and iterative routing. Despite its simplicity, Petri nets are not succinct and manageable enough to be useful in modeling complex business processes (Leyman & Roller, 1999). In order to surpass these difficulties, several extensions have been proposed in the last few years. Three well-known ones are color, time and hierarchy, to address, respectively, data, temporal aspects and large models. A Petri net extended with these characteristics is called a high-level Petri net (Aalst, 1999).

In their formal semantics, graphs and Petri nets emphasize the graphical representation of the sequence of workflow activities over the specification of the data. Modeling with graphs and Petri nets may, however, result in complex and less intuitive structures that, as it happened with DFDs and IDEF0 diagrams, inhibit an effective dialog with non-specialists.

The Language Action Paradigm

The Language Action paradigm (Medina-Mora, Winograd, Flores, & Flores, 1992) is quite different from the techniques described so far. It is based on the speech-act theory, and elects natural language as the tool for the planning and coordination of actions.

Using this approach, a business process is seen as a conversation between two actors (customers and providers of a service) (Medina-Mora et al., 1992) and it is represented as a closed-loop, ending with explicitly stated customer satisfaction (Carlsen, 1997).

The dialogs between customers and providers consist of four phases: "Proposal", "Agreement", "Performance" and "Acceptance". In any of the four phases new actions can be added, such as clarifications or additional negotiation details related with the commitments between the participants (Medina-Mora, et al., 1992). This decomposition of dialogs creates a network of actions and commitments.

Language Action assumes that the participation of end-users and their expectations are extremely important in modeling workflow processes. This concern leads to the use of natural language, trading off formalism for easiness of communication. A potential pitfall of this approach resides in the assumption of a very explicit communication between all actors, which is not always achieved.

Unified Modeling Language Extensions

Since the Unified Modeling Language (UML) – used in software engineering to graphically depict the architecture of a system – established itself as a standard, some authors proposed adapting and extending it to encompass workflow modeling (Eshuis & Wieringa, 2001). One such example is the WIDE methodology (Baresi & Casati, 1999) that puts strong emphasis on the requirements phase and describes the business process using three perspectives:

Functional – represents the operational structures of the business processes by means of UML use cases, interaction diagrams, class diagrams and activity diagrams.

Organizational – models aspects related to roles, actors and organizational units (e.g. departments) involved in a business process. The organization, as a whole, can be described as a set of UML packages that cooperate between them, each having its own actors.

Business – models goals to be achieved by the business processes, decomposing them into subprocesses that are closely related to UML activities.

The UML diagrams used by the WIDE methodology represent data, control sequences and interactions. By explicitly identifying organizational units (such as departments) the WIDE methodology enables a global awareness over the context of the various existing flows. However, this methodology doesn't represent the workflows between those organization units.

Since WIDE makes use of UML, it is not particularly suited to engage in dialog with end-users, in view of the fact that its modeling elements are highly technical.

Use of Patterns

The pattern concept was originally introduced by the architect Christopher Alexander, to describe how several autonomous elements (such as "front porch" or "courtyard") could be joined together to create a harmonious building (Alexander, 1979). The idea was picked up in software engineering by (Gamma, Helm, Johnson, & Vlissides, 1994), to describe the context of common situations or problems, together with the algorithms to handle them.

The high level of abstraction associated with pattern descriptions is also an effective means of identifying, generalizing and modeling recurrent workflow scenarios in a manner independent from technology or specific of a particular application.

Currently, many workflow design patterns have been identified, ranging from fairly simple constructs available in any workflow language (such as sequence, parallel split or exclusive choice), to complex primitives (synchronizing merge, implicit termination or deferred choice) not yet supported by today's generation of workflow management systems (Aalst, Hofstede, Kiepuszewski, & Barros, 2000).

By holding solutions to common situations, patterns promote the reuse of knowledge. The analyst must, however, be familiar with the catalog of pre-identified patterns in order to match them to the situation at hand. The construction of such catalogs of solutions is also a significant endeavor.

Summing up

Recently, information systems have been transfigured from quite homogeneous software solutions into an entangled web of applications from different vendors that are used to support different parts of the business. Frequently, business workflows must be run on top of this heterogeneous multi-vendor, multi-technology, multi-era network, instead of on top of a "proper" specialized engine. The workflow modeling techniques we just briefly reviewed were introduced at different points in time, and shaped to provide answers to diverse challenges. Although present reality calls for new adjustments or proposals, the following characteristics, of the various approaches, remain important:

- The specification of information flow between activities (Function Modeling Techniques);
- The representation of the workflow control perspective (Graphs and Petri Nets);
- The participation of end-users in the requirements analysis (Language Action);
- The representation of the organizational structure (Unified Modeling Language extensions);
- The reuse of existing solutions (Patterns).

In the next section we will introduce a workflow modeling extension that we have added to a recent information systems design methodology (EISD) (Cunha & Figueiredo, 2001), already conceived to handle heterogeneous portfolios for today's applications.

Taking on Heterogeneity

In our effort to address workflow modeling over heterogeneous systems, we departed from a methodology, called Evolutionary Information Systems Design (EISD) recently conceived to cope with new challenges posed by the growing use of common-off-the-shelf software (COTS), the use of intranets and extranets, and the need to integrate and evolve legacy systems (Cunha, 2000; Cunha & Figueiredo, 2000, 2001). We extended it to encompass the specificity of workflow modeling. Although generic information systems design traditionally uses concepts different than those of workflow modeling (i.e.: data models and procedures or objects vs. activities, roles and documental flows), EISD narrows this semantic gap by using higher granularity concepts – entities and responsibilities – that closely model organizations' departments or teams and the services they are accounted for, respectively.

By systematically identifying and documenting all business entities and their interactions via responsibilities, this modeling approach affords an organizational model that blends in the information system. Full-scale applications, or ERP modules, such as financial, human resources or employee relationship management, may support the inner workings of a responsibility.

The EISD methodology uses business entity cards to document each business entity (consisting of a name, a list of its responsibilities and its client entities). On the other hand a responsibility card is used to detail information about each service: name, purpose, importance, main rules, exchanged data, business procedure to carry out and available information systems support are specified.

Figure 1 exemplifies how EISD would model a typical tendering system, with the relationships between all involved entities (identified with the bold designations and represented by large rectangles) and their responsibilities (smaller grey rectangles with their designation on the right side). Being external to the organization, supplier's responsibilities are not assigned an id.

As can be observed in Figure 1, the Marketing Team schedules a meeting with several Suppliers to obtain quotations for the desired items (R1). After analyzing the information, the Marketing Team asks for a final budget from suppliers that offered better conditions (R2). The Suppliers submit their proposals to the Administrative Services, which collect and deliver the proposals to the Executive Committee (R4).

The Executive Committee produces a ranked list of proposals (R6) and forwards it to the Administrative Services that subsequently send a notification of the acceptance to the selected Supplier. Finally, the chosen Supplier delivers the requested goods to the Marketing Team, which, after verifying conformance (R3), sends the invoice to the Administrative Services to process payment (R5)

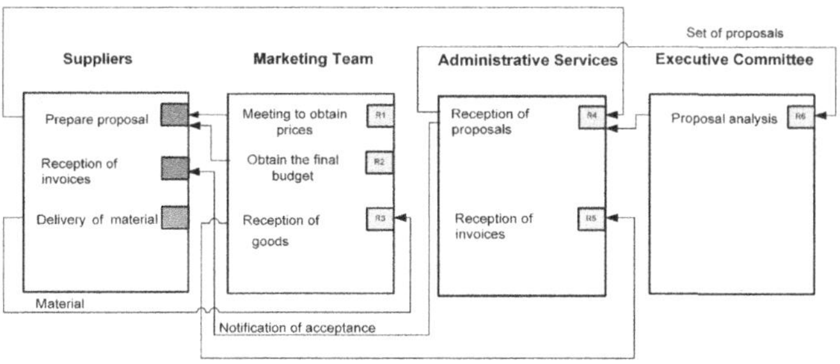

Figure 1. Acquisition process modeled by the EISD methodology

EISD doesn't have a specific technique to model all the complexities related with the "interaction protocol" (i.e.: the specification of how the information is supplied), but gathers all the information necessary to specify the data circulation between entities, typical of workflow modeling.

Considering the potential offered by the EISD, we developed a new workflow requirements approach that represents the documents circuits between entities/responsibilities and describes their business procedures. This extension focuses on the responsibility interface, through which interaction with an entity is possible.

After constructing the organizational model according to the original EISD methodology recommendations, it's possible to identify scenarios where workflow mechanisms should be included to specify in detail all the protocols between the responsibilities. We propose to address this issue in the workflow extension to EISD according to three perspectives:

- Intra-responsibility workflow - describes rules and document-related conditions inherent to a given responsibility.
- Document descriptions - provides detailed information about every document.
- Inter-responsibility workflow - describes the connections between responsibilities that cooperate in the execution of a business process and the documental circuit of that cooperation.

Intra-responsibility Workflow

Regarding the flow of documents inside a responsibility, five possible alternatives were identified:

- Documents created in a responsibility;
- Documents that end their flow in a responsibility;
- Documents for which the responsibility is an intermediary point in their overall circuit;
- Joining of documents in a responsibility;
- Splitting of documents in a responsibility.

To describe these cases, two forms were created that identify the responsibility being analyzed, using a title and a code.

The first form (Figure 2) describes the relation between each responsibility and each document it processes, namely, the responsibility position in each document flow (creation, terminus or intermediary point), the activities performed by the responsibility on the documents, the conditions associated with those activities and the way the responsibility handles the document (e.g., digital or paper format).

RESPONSIBILITY NAME: *RECEPTION OF GOODS*		***RESPONSIBILITY ID:*** *R3*	
Document name		*Requisition form*	
Intermediary Points ☐		Source	
Creation ☒		Creation condition	*Issue a Request For Proposal (RFP)*
		Responsible	*Marketing Team*
Terminus ☐		Termination condition	
		Responsible	
		Source	
Actions to perform			
A_1	*Check the delivery and sign the "Requisition form"*	Pre-condition	*All the goods specified in the RFP being delivered*
		Post-condition	
		Responsible	*Marketing Team*
		Destiny	*Supplier*
		Duration	*5 minutes*
		Maximum of duration	*15 minutes*
		Frequency of use	*1 time per month*
$?_x$		Responsible	
Procedure		*Paper forms are physically moved between entities*	
Observations		*Nothing to declare*	

Figure 2. Form describing the creation of the "Reception of goods" document

The simple case, depicted in Figure 2, illustrates how the document "Requisition form" is created in the responsibility "Reception of Goods" ("R3") by the Marketing Team. The activities (represented by "Ax") performed on the document are also described. If conditional activities existed, they should be written in the field marked "?x".

The second form characterizes operations of joining or splitting of documents in a responsibility, identifying the responsible for that operation and describing the condition that originates it. In the example presented in Figure 3, several supplier proposals are joined in the responsibility "Proposal Analysis" by, the Executive Committee, to originate the document "Ranked list of proposals".

RESPONSIBILITY NAME: PROPOSAL ANALYSIS		RESPONSIBILITY ID: R10
Junction ☒	Documents involved	- Model Design INC Proposal - 3LM INC proposal
	Resulting document	Ranked list of proposals
Disjunction ☐	Document's source	
	Resulting documents	
Responsible	Executive Committee	
$?_{1jd}$	All the fields necessary to originate the "Process of candidature" being filled in the two proposals	
Procedure	If the two proposals have all the information necessary to produce the process of candidature, this should be created by the executive committee	
Observations		

Figure 3. Form describing the joining of proposals into a new "Ranked List" document

This form is needed only for operations of joining or splitting documents inside a responsibility.

The joining or splitting operations originate new documents, new flows and also the circuit ending of the incoming documents. These modifications must be reflected not only in the form responsible for describing these operations (Figure 3), but also in the first form (Figure 2). For this reason, it's necessary to establish a relation between both forms used in the intra-responsibility perspective. The linkage between the two forms is provided by the "?xjd" field – the joining or splitting condition represented in the form of Figure 3 by "?1jd". The "x" was substituted by "1" since the field in question was the first joining or splitting condition in that responsibility. This field should be used as the "Creation condition" or "Termination condition" in a form identical to the one in Figure 2.

It is possible to identify several responsibilities in a business model, like the one described in Figure 5. For this reason an index is attributed (represented by x) to the acronym "R", used to represent the number of the responsibilities. The acronyms "A" (Activity) and "?" (Conditions) also have indexes associated.

Textual descriptions (in natural language) were used in the forms to promote more effective communication with end-users. The aim is to encourage their participation in the analysis of workflow requirements.

Description of Documents

The necessary information to characterize documents isn't restricted to items related with the specification of circuits and with the execution of activities, mentioned previously. It's also important to describe document's properties such as deadlines, formats, priority levels, passwords and attachments.

The form illustrated in Figure 4 was developed with the purpose of gathering all the information related with a specific document, by means of achieving a complete description of all the items relevant to its workflow requirements specification.

The replication of information that exists between the form responsible by the description of a document (Figure 4) and the forms that characterize the document's flow among organizations (exemplified in Figure 2 and 3) is justified by the advantages of having in just one analysis tool all the necessary information to specify the workflow requirements of a document.

DOCUMENT NAME: REQUISITION FORM	DOCUMENT ID: D1
Date of creation	08/06/2005
Document source	Entity: Marketing Team Responsibility: Reception of materials
Intermediary point(s)	Non existent
Document destiny(ies)	Entity: Supplier (External entity)
Fields required	All
Existing dependencies	Non existent
Activities performed on the document	Entity: Marketing Team Responsibility: Reception of materials ▪ Check the delivery and sign the "Requisition form"
Document conditions	Creation condition - Issue a Request for Proposal (RFP) A_1 Pre-condition - All the goods specified in the RFP being delivered
Deadlines of the activities	Supplier - 08/07/2005
Possible operations on the data	Register and lecture operations
Document format	Web pages
Attach	Non existent
Priority of the document	Median
Passwords	Non existent
Access frequency and number of users	Access numbers -4 times per month Number of users - 2
Importance of the supporting information system	Reduce the bureaucracy related with the reception of material
Informatics knowledge of the users that interact with the document	Median
Description of how the support systems should represent the document behavior	The Marketing Team may access the form "Requisition form" via an intranet, checking automatically the reception.
Observations	The Marketing Team didn't show many interest in developing a support system to the document

Figure 4. Form used to describe a document

With this specification process it is possible to access in a straightforward and centralized way all the details that characterize a particular document.

Inter-responsibility Workflow

Tests and interviews with end-users revealed the necessity of representing graphically the flow of documents between entities, as well as the activities performed over the documents by the responsibilities involved in a business process. Figure 5 illustrates this representation for the previous example.

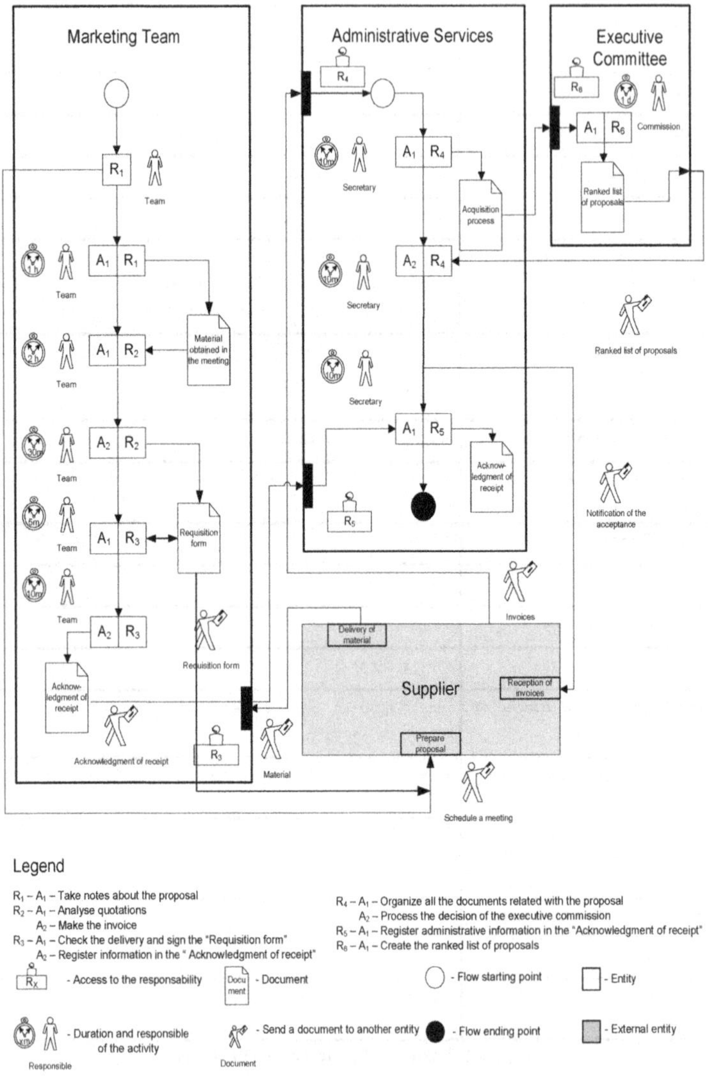

Figure 5. Intra-responsibility form for the acquisition of materials

In this diagram, the entities from Figure 1 (large rectangles) are retained, together with their responsibilities (smaller, grey rectangles). Extra detail, regarding the inner workings of these elements is added. This perspective allows for perception over dataflow as well as control issues.

After the Marketing Team schedules a meeting with several Suppliers (external entity), the document "Material obtained in the meeting" is created and subsequently analyzed with the purpose of creating a "Requisition Form", which will be delivered to the suppliers that offered better conditions. The Suppliers submit their proposals to the Administrative Services, which organize all the documents related with the proposal in a folder/document designated "Acquisition Process" and send it to the Executive Committee.

The Executive Committee establishes a "Ranked list of proposals" and delivers it to the Administrative Services that processes the decision of the Committee and sends a notification of the acceptance to the selected Supplier. Finally, the chosen Supplier delivers the requested goods to the Marketing Team, which, after verifying conformance and filling the "Acknowledgment of receipt", sends the invoice to the Administrative Services that finish completing the fields in the "Acknowledgment of receipt" document.

The functionalities executed by each responsibility are represented independently of the technological solution adopted, providing the specification of requirements that may involve the integration of different workflow technologies, including the solutions used by external entities.

The symbols used in the diagram are simple, encouraging communication with end-users and reinforcing their participation in the specification of the requirements of a workflow management system.

All the analysis tools illustrated in section "Taking on Heterogeneity" should be used together, since they approach different perspectives of the specification of heterogeneous workflow requirements. To maintain the consistency between these tools the nomenclature used is always the same.

Conclusion

The extension we propose in this article entails a solution, which encloses in a single methodology the design of information systems and its workflow components, examining the adjacencies of these two worlds and, consequently, minimizing the effort expended on the specification of systems.

To achieve this proposal the most widespread techniques for the specification of workflows have been reviewed, in order to identify characteristics that should be retained. Those characteristics are: data and sequence representation, the importance of client participation in the analysis phase, the representation of document's flows in the organization and the advantages of software reuse in the development of heterogeneous workflow management systems.

We departed from the EISD methodology because its underlying concepts were already close to those required by workflow. Its use of entities and responsibilities emphasized relationships and the encapsulation of functionalities. Furthermore, the collected information could easily be expanded to fully specify workflow management systems. As it happened with the original EISD, there is a separation between business process description and technological solutions that support them. This enables the use of Enterprise Application Integration techniques to articulate various heterogeneous systems on top of which the designed workflow must run.

References

Aalst, W. (1995). *A class of Petri net for modelling and analysing business processes*. Eindhoven, Eindhoven University of Technology.

Aalst, W. (1999). Interorganizational Workflows: An Approach based on Message Sequence Charts and Petri Nets. *Systems Analysis - Modelling - Simulation, 34*(3), 335-367.

Aalst, W., Hofstede, A., Kiepuszewski,V., & Barros, A. (2000). *Workflow patterns*. Eindhoven, Eindhoven University of Technology.

Air Force Wright Aeronautical Laboratories. (1981). *Integrated computer- aided manufacturing (ICAM) architecture - Function modeling manual (IDEF0)*. Ohio, Air Force Wright Aeronautical Laboratories.

Alexander, C. (1979). *The timeless way of building*. New York: Oxford University Press.

Avison, D. & Fitzgerald, G. (1999). Information systems development. In W. Currie & R. Galliers, *Rethinking management information systems*. New York, Oxford University Press: 250-278.

Baresi, L. & Casati, F. (1999). *WIDE workflow development methodology*. Milano, Politecnico di Milano.

Baskerville, R. & Fitzgerald, B. (1995). Beyond systems development methodologies: Time to leave the lamppost? In *Information Technology and Changes in Organisational Work, Proceedings of the IFIP 8.2 Conference*, UK.

Carlsen, S. (1997). Conceptual modeling and composition of flexible workflow models. *Department of Computer Science and Information Science*. Trondheim, Norwegian University of Science and Technology.

Casati, F., Ceri, S., Pernici, B. & Pozzi, G. (1995). Conceptual modeling of workflows. In *Proceedings of the 14th International Object-Oriented and Entity-Relationship Modelling Conference*, Gold Cost.

Costa, C. & Cunha, P. (2002). Especificação de workflows num contexto de aplicações heterogéneas: reflexão sobre as técnicas existentes. In *Actas da 3ª Conferência da Associação Portuguesa de Sistemas de Informação*, Coimbra, Portugal.

Cunha, P. R. (2000). Projecto de sistemas de informação para a realidade emergente: proposta baseada num modelo de carteira de soluções. Departamento de Engenharia Informática da Universidade de Coimbra. Coimbra, Universidade de Coimbra.

Cunha, P. & Figueiredo, A. (2000). Information systems design under a different light. In *AMCIS*, California, USA.

Cunha, P. & Figueiredo, A. (2001). Information systems development as flowing wholeness. In *IFIP WG8.2*, Idaho, USA.

Eshuis, R. & Wieringa, R. (2001). A formal semantics for UML activity diagrams - Formalising workflow models. Twente, Department of Computer Science - University of Twente.

Gamma, E., Helm, R., Johnson, R. & Vlissides, J. (1994). *Design patterns - Elements of reusable object-oriented software*. Massachusetts: Addison-Wesley.

Leyman, F. & Roller, D. (1999). *Production workflow: Concepts and techniques*. New Jersey: Prentice Hall.

Medina-Mora, R., Winograd, T., Flores, R., & Flores, F. (1992). The action workflow approach to workflow management technology. In *ACM Conference Supported Cooperative Work (CSCW'92) - Emerging technologies for cooperative work*, Toronto, Ontario.

Peterson, J. (1997). Petri Nets. *Computing Surveys, 9*(3), 223-252.

Sadiq, S., Marjanovic, O., & Orlowska, M. (2000). Managing change and time in dynamic workflow process. *The International Journal of Cooperative Information Systems, 9*(1&2), 93-116.

Sadiq, S. & Orlowska, M. E. (1996). *Modelling and verification of workflow*. Queensland, University of Queensland.

Biography

Cristina Chuva Costa obtained her BSc. in Computer Science at the University of Coimbra in 1998 and her MSc, in the area of Workflow Specification, from the same University in 2002. She has been teaching classes of computing programming, systems analysis, computational architectures and simulation in the Computer Science Department of the Polytechnic of Coimbra since 1999.

Currently she is working on her PHD at the University of Coimbra. Her studies are related with the use and contribution of social theories, like Actor Network Theory, in the specification of requirements in information systems.

Paulo Rupino da Cunha is an Assistant Professor of Informatics Engineering and Information Systems at the Faculty of Science and Technology of the University of Coimbra, Portugal, where he lectures since 1993. He holds a Ph.D. (2001) and an M.Sc. (1997) in Informatics Engineering - Information Systems from the University of Coimbra. His main research interests centre on Information Systems Design, Quality Management and Information Systems, Design of Business Models and Strategy, Enterprise Application Integration and IT Investment Valuation. He is the Vice-President of Instituto Pedro Nunes, an Innovation and Technology Transfer organization providing specialized consulting, training and business incubation. He is the Scientific Director of the informatics volume of the Portuguese encyclopedia Nova Activa Multimédia and a member of the board of the Portuguese Information Systems Association. For a period of three years, he was the elected Coordinator of the Informatics Engineering Chapter for the center region of Portugal of the Portuguese Engineering Association and for a two year term he held the Vice-Presidency of the Department of Informatics Engineering of the University of Coimbra. He also served as Deputy Director of the Informatics Lab at Instituto Pedro Nunes.

Paulo is the author of various papers. He serves in the Program Committee or as a reviewer for various international conferences. He is currently a member of the editorial review board of the International Journal of e-Collaboration. He was a member of the editorial board of the journal ofthe Portuguese Engineering Association.

The page left blank intentionally.

Interactive On-line Formative Evaluation of Student Assignments

Heinz Dreher
School of Information Systems, Curtin University of Technology Perth, Western Australia

h.dreher@curtin.edu.au

Abstract

Automated Essay Grading (AEG) technology has been maturing over the final decades of the last century to the point where it is now poised to permit a transition in 'assessment-thinking'. The administrative convenience of using objective testing to attempt to assess deep learning, learning at the conceptual level, has now been obviated by efficient and effective automated means to assess student learning. Further, the new generation AEG systems such as MarkIT deliver an unprecedented interactive formative assessment feedback capability, which is set to transform individualized learning and instruction as implemented in existing Learning Management Systems (LMS).

Keywords: AEG; Automated Essay Grading; automated formative assessment; conceptual learning; deep learning; formative evaluation; interactive assessment feedback; Latent Semantic Analysis, MarkIT; Normalised Word Vector; NWV.

Introduction

Assessment of student assignments has been an important part of the teaching and learning process long before the advent of desktop computers, Learning Management Systems, and the Internet. Whether the education is traditional format or facilitated in on-line mode, typically, assignments are submitted, assessed or graded, and returned, with a mark or grade, and some comments explaining the possible improvements and applauding the assignment's positive aspects. At times the assignment is returned with an assessment pro-forma or template containing the assessment criteria and weightings, with details of component marks and specific comments in addition to a summary. Creating such feedback is time-consuming and laborious. On the other hand, detailed feedback can be valuable for students wishing to improve, tracking student progress, or for multi-stage assessments in which the successful completion of earlier stages are required for later stages. When there are many students and time is short, feedback detail is reduced, assessment quality may be compromised, and in extreme cases, a 'tick and flick' approach may seem a tantalizing option.

Numerous techniques are available to support carrying out the assessment task to a high standard, but the greatest gain by far is afforded by utilizing computer based augmentation of the assessment process. Often it is the sheer volume of assignments that poses the greatest challenge to the assessment task. In recent years we have seen the development and refinement of Automated Essay Grading Systems originating with the work of Ellis B. Page (1966) which he carried forward through the 1990s (Page 1994) and which spawned numerous competitor systems such as the Intelligent Essay Assessor (IEA) (Foltz, Laham, & Landauer, 1999), e-rater® (Attali & Burstein, 2004), and MarkIT (Williams & Dreher, 2004).

The Intelligent Essay Assessor's developers describe it as "a set of software tools for scoring the quality of essay content" (Foltz et al. 1999). The IEA has been commercialized by Knowledge Analysis Technologies, which company has recently been acquired by global publisher Pearson Education. Another competitive system, e-rater® is being used by the Educational Testing Service (http://www.ets.org). Whilst IEA and e-rater® are now clearly a commercially competitive products, on the other side of the globe in Perth, Western Australia, a new generation of AEG system has been taking shape since the turn of the century, and is now at what may be termed a pre-competitive stage.

The developers of MarkIT have been successful in devising a semantic representation method which has been termed *Normalised Word Vector* (NWV) (Williams, 2006) – it is interesting from the view of deployment in Learning Management Systems because it is computationally more efficient than prior systems, while still performing at the level of human graders. Another innovative aspect of MarkIT is the integral interactive formative assessment component that provides immediate feedback to students and teachers. For an evaluation of various conceptual models used in AEG technology see Williams (2001). Valenti, Neri, and Cucchiarelli (2003) provide a description of AEG research up to the turn of the century. Williams (2006) analyses the NWV technology relative to Latent Semantic Analysis (LSA). The interactive formative assessment feedback aspect of this technology is the focus of this paper.

In summary, we can see that there is growing interest in finding some way to support the educator in assessment of deep, conceptual learning as distinct from the relatively more superficial learning so easily checked with computer based objective testing mechanisms. Despite the interest, the educational community has in main remained ignorant of the all important advances in the Automated Essay Grading domain which Ellis B. Page (1966) introduced us to some 40 years ago.

Contemporary LMS Assessment Support Capability

When Learning Management Systems are compared and evaluated, scrutinized criteria include: usability and navigation; content development; discussion space; group interaction; communication; calendar and other study tools; multimedia; site administration; and of course monitoring student participation and progress (Lewis et al., 2005). However, even this last mentioned criterion, monitoring, is bereft of learning appraisal in a qualitative sense, never mind the all important formative evaluation aspect with its feedback cycle to promote further learning. Are we to conclude formative evaluation is unimportant? Serious educators know that immediate feedback on student learning is central to success. What we may conclude is that computer based formative evaluation of deep learning, as demonstrated in the writing of essays, has been too difficult and demanding relative to the leverage obtained by supporting the other mentioned LMS evaluation criteria. The problem has been that the required technological breakthrough is just now emerging as this new century begins. And even as the technology emerges, the issue of communicating the news and winning over the skeptics cannot be ignored.

In their article on supporting formative assessment with e-Learning tools, Heinrich and Lawn (2004) admit defeat when it comes to automating formative assessment, but are highly motivated to investigate support for human markers performing such assessments. Their MarkTool system provides assistance in document management, and very importantly some provision for feedback annotations and marks, although these are pixel-level objects and cannot be subjected to semantic manipulation. Whilst their motivation is clearly consistent with good educational theory, practice, and intentions, one might say, sadly their implementation efforts have been progressed in ignorance of the AEG technology in general and MarkIT in particular.

Paul Blayney (2005), was also ignorant of AEG when he developed his spreadsheet-based formative and summative assessment system, but as he works in a quantitative discipline, the need for automated support for free-text grading is not needed. His system had its roots in the same decade – a learning technology 20th century fin de siècle as it were – that AEG technology was being proven. What makes his system so dramatically effective is that accounting student assignments have numbers or formulae as answers, and these are of course simply checked by automatic means. Actually, the Blayney system is far from simple. It is very sophisticated in its design intent, which is to provide timely, and interactive constructive formative feedback via iterations of individualized assignments. The system is spreadsheet based and able to infer deep understanding of accounting concepts by tracking formulae that must be entered and used in a particular logical sequence to complete the non-trivial questions he sets his students. Out of the entire literature that has been accumulated on the matter of "interactive assessment and feedback" his system (apart from MarkIT) is the only one which automatically provides truly interactive real-time formative assessment feedback to students.

The considerable interest in deploying computer based formative assessment systems has produced some curious solutions. For example, Yasuko (2004) describes his system of "formative assessments" which relies on objective testing, but adds a contextual and temporal analysis of learning object accesses as stored in activity logs. The advantage claimed is that by analyzing logs of e-Learning sessions and comparing them with test results "it is possible to know the transition of the level of comprehension of each student" (Yasuko, 2004). Presumably, this indirect but automated approach permits one to appraise the deep learning. Some insight into deep learning may be derived from such a convoluted analysis and tenuous link (at best) between "transition of the level of comprehension" (Yasuko, 2004) and deep conceptual learning. One may contemplate whether Yasuko would persist with such a scheme if essay-type assignments, which contain the evidence of deep learning, could be automatically assessed. There is no degree of interactivity in the Yasuko system.

In their article "Thematic driven Learning", Dreher, Scerbakov, and Helic (2004) explain how their Learning Management System, WBT-Master, was endowed with assignment assessment and feedback support functions, but this still required the evaluator to read through hundreds of assignments. The system did however place prior assessments (assignment, marks and feedback) in an onscreen window juxtaposed with the current assignment being assessed. This permitted the current assignment to be assessed in the light of previous feedback in addition to the usual considerations, consistent with the incremental improvement goal of formative evaluation.

Advances in technology support embedded in alternate paradigms as compared with those adopted by the majority of LMS are beginning to emerge. For example, D'Mello et al. (2005) at the University of Memphis have developed "a fully automated computer tutor that simulates human tutors and holds conversations with students in natural language". This of course requires an ability to 'understand' or assess free-text or essay-type student responses, albeit in the form of short dialogue components. AutoTutor, as their system is known, uses the LSA technology mentioned earlier, and since the textual elements are restricted to tens of words, a paragraph or two, computational efficiency is less of an issue as in the case of grading thousand-word essays in real time, as is possible with MarkIT. Another important feature of the AutoTutor system is its interactivity, which its authors remark was inspired by the constructivist theories of learning and the commonsense knowledge that collaboration and feedback iterations are observable in the work of good teachers.

The Transition in 'Assessment-Thinking'

The so called objective testing schemes – short answer, true/false, and multiple-choice, were devised entirely as a matter of convenience. It is acknowledged they cannot readily assess the degree of deep learning that is evident from an essay-type assessment item, and yet objective testing is deployed in most educational settings, and especially where large numbers of students are being catered for. This is not to say that objective testing is not useful, but rather that its use has often been determined by administrative convenience, in contradistinction to educational imperative. Few Learning Management Systems (e.g. WebCT, and Blackboard, being the most popular) offer any technological support for essay grading, whilst they offer excellent support for objective testing. Large educational book publishers and their prominent textbook authors, orient their products to objective testing.

The assessment of written assignments or essay-like answers to exam questions is such a laborious task that for large student cohorts, educators have been forced into choosing computer-scored assessments. The argument has been that speed, accuracy, and consistency of such assessment outweighs the major drawback – the difficulty of assessing deep learning as opposed to knowledge recall and recognition. Even prior to the prevalence of desktop computers and online systems it was relatively straightforward to arrange a computer-scored test, even for thousands of students. Users of such systems and products are prepared to trade the quality of feedback against convenience. The result is inferior learning outcomes relative to what is possible by utilizing more educational resource or by deploying superior educational technology.

When students learn, they need to know how they have progressed with respect to some standard or benchmark. Teachers also need to know about their students' performance so they may devise progression or remedial strategies as necessary, or certify performance – the former being formative and the latter summative in intent. Our concern here is the formative evaluation of learning. That is, we would like to be able to provide relevant feedback so as to permit further learning, or re-learning as necessary. Since learning is individual – with reference to content, process, and time, it would be useful to have an assessment system that is tailored to individual students. Such a system is called "teacher", actually, one would need to qualify that perhaps and specify "good teacher". There are more qualifications required however in today's educational setting – minimizing cost, and maximizing efficiency, student numbers, teacher performance, and return on educational investment are at least as important as quality of educational outcomes. The problem with the system known as "teacher" is that it is expensive.

The skeptic will need to imagine, whilst others may take it on faith (at least for the moment), that AEG systems can now perform as good as humans (Palmer, Williams, & Dreher, 2002) when it comes to assessing or grading essays, in addition to providing feedback which is superior to that which humans can provide within realistic resource constraints. Williams and Dreher (2005) have given an insight in how the MarkIT system provides formative assessment feedback at the semantic and conceptual level. Guetl, Dreher, and Williams, (2005) have described the significance of the advantage of deploying auto-generated essay-type question and answer assessment.

The New Wave – Automated Formative Evaluation

Clearly, the old thinking is giving way to the new. As explained above, the new technology known as Automated Essay Grading (AEG) is now available commercially and is beginning to find its way into educational practice. In the years ahead one may witness the adoption of AEG to an extent similar to that of the now relatively predominant use of technology to create assignments – Word-processing technology has replaced the pen and paper method. The collegiate question "what are you doing this weekend?" will no longer induce a response of "assignment grading!", but rather some response which indicates that the onerous educational imperative of formative assessment has been supported by AEG leaving the teacher to relax in preparation for meaningful educational activities the new week may bring.

One may well ask what are these "meaningful educational activities" if technology can now do so much of the teacher's work. A typical scenario with the use of the Western Australian system MarkIT (www.essaygrading.com) follows:

Students write their essays as usual. Naturally they must be in computer readable form, and at this juncture in English (plans for a European languages version of MarkIT are well advanced). Preparatory arrangements need to have been made so that the MarkIT web-site is configured to cater to the particular essay assignment. Clearly, considerable work goes into generating a model answer (a teacher activity, although this may also be supported with technology, and is a MarkIT project agenda item for 2006), administrative and workflow functionality to support assignment upload, and feedback access by both student and teacher, and other necessary arrangements relating to 'return-on-investment matters'.

Essays are submitted according to an agreed schedule, assessed on-the-fly or in batch mode, and results made available via the same interface, a standard Java enabled browser, as was used for assignment upload. The results comprise the usual quantitative parameters (assignment score according to pre-supplied criteria and weighting scheme – model answer; and via generally available technology, length, readability, spelling, grammar, and similar characteristics).

However, far more important for formative evaluation, MarkIT produces an interactive graph comparing the assignment concepts as represented in the model answer with that of an individual student. Students and teachers may see at a glance why the particular assessment or grade has been suggested or assigned by MarkIT. More, they may interact with the bars in the graph probing into the detail relating to each concept represented by the graph, which interaction yields the corresponding structured thesaurus entry. Interested readers are encouraged to visit www.essaygrading.com and explore the demonstration under menu <MY ACCOUNT> then <Guest Account> and experience the interactivity at the level of assignment and model answer concept representation and explanation.

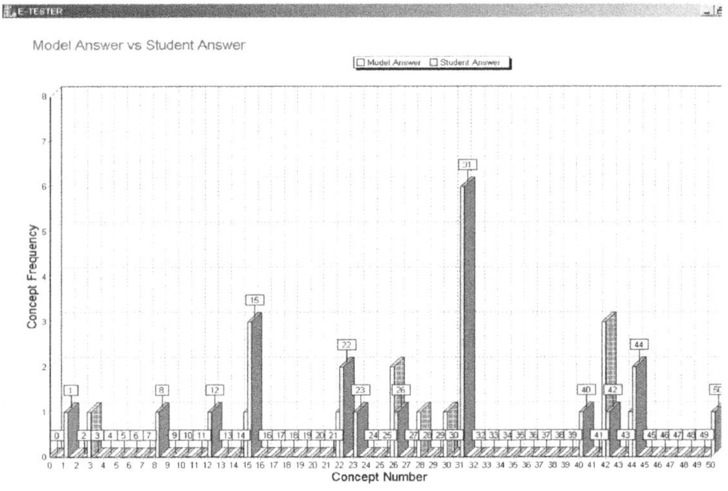

Figure 1: Concept frequencies: student answer and **course content**

In ***Error! Reference source not found.***, a graphical feedback element as designed into MarkIT, juxtaposes the 'concepts' associated with model answer and student answer. Naturally, the better the correspondence between the concept representation in both, the better the score. For example, the tallest bar (Concept_Number 31) reveals a concept_frequency of 6 (vertical axis) for the student answer (dark bar), where the model answer called for no discussion on this topic or concept. One may conclude that the student has introduced irrelevancies into the answer; or perhaps this is what can be termed an error on the student's part. MarkIT concludes likewise. Concept_Number 26 has a better match between model and student answer, indicating the student has learned relevant material. It is important to understand that MarkIT is not performing simple word matching, but rather employs the Normalised Word Vector technology devised by Williams (2006) to make comparisons at the semantic level, and thus allows one to assign a grade to conceptual learning.

There are three cases where the model answer concepts are not matched by a student contribution (3, 28, 30) – this we would call "ignorance" or a deficit in knowledge. Such visual feedback is rather informative to student and teacher alike. It is intended to further develop such visual feedback into a dynamic object that responds to inquiry for concept name (associated with Concept_Number), and the possibility of linking back to the sections of the student assignment which are good, and those needing improvement.

Error! Reference source not found. shows the graph produced by MarkIT when a user is exploring the reason for the mismatch between concept representation in student and model answers. In this case the concept labeled "Working Class" is being explored (see the shaded pair of bars in

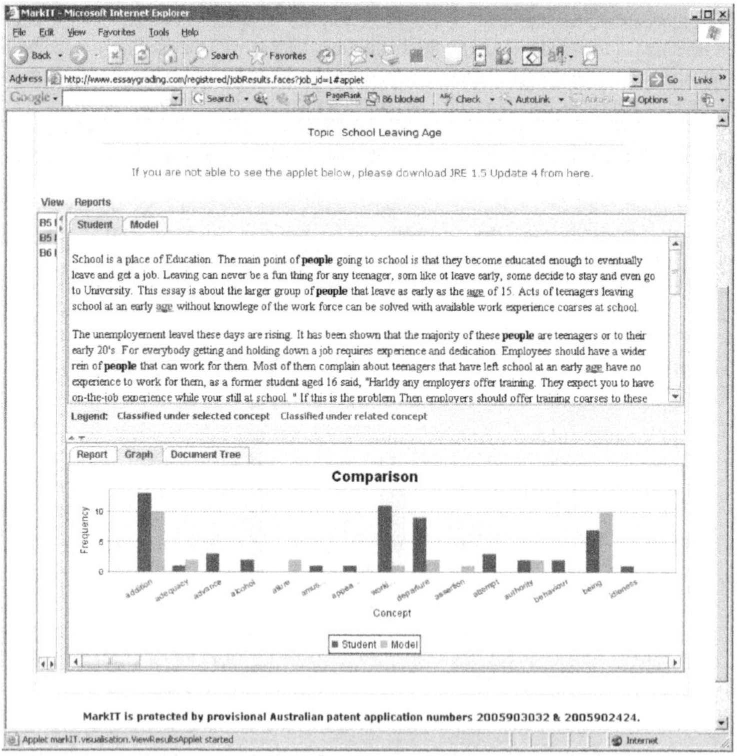

Figure 2: Interactive concept comparison (student vs model)

the middle of graph with label "worki..." just above the word "Concept" used as the legend for the horizontal axis.

There is a large mismatch between student (concept_frequency = 11) and model (concept_ frequency = 1) and the user wishes to see an explanation. Some activation method, for example a double-click, produces the window depicted in ***Error! Reference source not found.***. Now, the student, perhaps in conjunction with the teacher can review what may have been a conceptual error. Obviously not all the words reproduced from the thesaurus would be relevant and further refinement of this aspect of MarkIT, using the technique of ontological filtering for example, is being pursued. In the interim, users need to be discerning in the use of feedback. As with any technology, it is produced in the 'service of mankind' and in our case, is made to augment teachers so that this special resource may be applied to the truly human aspects of students and learning.

The MarkIT designers have provided for interactivity at the within-assignment-concept level, a

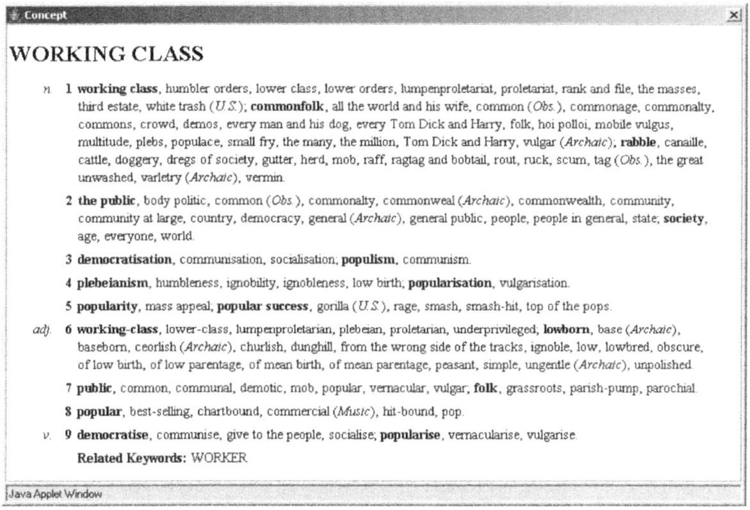

Figure 3: Within-assignment-concept level interactive explanation

feature already implemented as described above, but one can readily imagine an iterative cycle of assignment submission, improvement, resubmission, where MarkIT provides feedback based on the model answer and the series of repeated assignment submissions. Under these conditions a student's rate of learning may also be appraised. Such ideas, and more, remain for further discussion and development. Ideas from interested readers are welcomed.

Never before has there been such a level of feedback available to students and teachers – in such detail and interactively, except perhaps in one-on-one student-tutor situations. We all know such arrangements are beyond the financial reach of the vast majority of students.

Conclusion

The proposition that human teachers can now be relieved of, or strongly supported in, the essay grading task is a reality in this new century. Skeptics still abound, but as AEG systems become embedded in the new wave of LMS, they too will experience the actual results of automated support for assessing essays and generating interactive visual and formative feedback for their students. In time, the skeptics will surely make the transition in assessment-thinking and help their students perform to maximize individual potential within reasonable resource constraints. As explained in this paper, the *New Wave of Automated Formative Evaluation of Student Assignments* is here.

References

Attali, Y. & Burstein, J. (2004). Automated essay scoring with E-rater V.2.0. Paper presented at the *Conference of the International Association for Educational Assessment (IAEA)*, June 13-18, 2004, Philadelphia, USA. Retrieved from http://www.ets.org/research/dload/IAEA.pdf

Blayney, P. (2005). Interactive assignments used for formative & summative assessment. In *Proceedings of World Conference on E-Learning in Corporate, Government, Healthcare, and Higher Education 2005* (pp. 1209-1214). Norfolk, VA: AACE. Retrieved from http://www.editlib.org/index.cfm

D'Mello, S., Craig, S., Witherspoon, A., Sullins, J., McDaniel, B., Gholson, B., & Graesser, A. (2005). The relationship between affective states and dialog patterns during interactions with AutoTutor. In *Proceedings of World Conference on E-Learning in Corporate, Government, Healthcare, and Higher Education 2005* (pp. 2004-2011). Norfolk, VA: AACE. Retrieved from http://www.editlib.org/index.cfm

Dreher, H., Scerbakov, N., & Helic, D. (2004). Thematic driven learning. In *Proceedings of World Conference on E-Learning in Corporate, Government, Healthcare, and Higher Education 2004* (pp. 2594-2600). Norfolk, VA: AACE. Retrieved from http://www.editlib.org/index.cfm

Foltz, P., Laham, D. & Landauer, T. (1999). Automated essay scoring: Applications to educational technology. Retrieved from http://www-psych.nmsu.edu/~pfoltz/reprints/Edmedia99.html

Guetl, C., Dreher, H. & Williams, R. (2005). E-TESTER: A computer-based tool for auto-generated question and answer assessment. In *Proceedings of World Conference on E-Learning in Corporate, Government, Healthcare, and Higher Education 2005* (pp. 2929-2936), October. E-Learn 2005. Retrieved from http://www.editlib.org/index.cfm

Heinrich, E., & Lawn, A. (2004). Onscreen marking support for formative assessment. In *Proceedings of World Conference on Educational Multimedia, Hypermedia and Telecommunications 2004* (pp. 1985-1992). Norfolk, VA: AACE. Retrieved from http://www.editlib.org/index.cfm

Lewis, B. A., MacEntee, V. M., DeLaCruz, S., Englander, C., Jeffrey, T., Takach, E., Wilson, S., & Woodall, J. (2005). Learning management systems comparison. Proceedings of the *2005 Informing Science and IT Education Joint Conference*, Flagstaff, Arizona, USA – June 16-19. Retrieved from http://proceedings.informingscience.org/InSITE2005/P03f55Lewis.pdf

Page, E. B. (1994). Computer grading of student prose, using modern concepts and software. *Journal of Experimental Education, 62*, 127-142.

Page, E. B. (1966). The imminence of grading essays by computer. *Phi Delta Kappan, January*, 238-243.

Palmer, J., Williams, R., & Dreher, H. (2002). Automated essay grading system applied to a first year university subject – How can we do it better? *Proceedings of Informing Science 2002 Conference*, Cork, Ireland, June 19-21. Retrieved from http://proceedings.informingscience.org/IS2002Proceedings/papers/Palme026Autom.pdf

Valenti, S., Neri F., & Cucchiarelli, A. (2003). An overview of current research on automated essay grading. *Journal of Information Technology Education*, *2*, 19 – 330. Retrieved from http://jite.org/documents/Vol2/v2p319-330-30.pdf

Williams, R. & Dreher, H. (2004). Automatically grading essays with Markit©. *Issues in Informing Science and Information Technology, 1*, 693-700. Retrieved from http://articles.iisit.org/092willi.pdf

Williams, R. & Dreher, H. (2005). Formative assessment visual feedback in computer graded essays. *The Journal of Issues in Informing Science and Information Technology*, *2*, 23-32. Retrieved from http://2005papers.iisit.org/I03f95Will.pdf

Williams, R. (2001). Automated essay grading: An evaluation of four conceptual models. In M. Kulski & A. Herrmann (Eds.), *New horizons in university teaching and learning: Responding to change*. Curtin University of Technology, Perth, Australia. Retrieved from http://lsn.curtin.edu.au/tlf/tlf2001/williams.html

Williams, R. (2006). The power of normalised word vectors for automatically grading essays. Paper to be presented at InSITE 2006, Manchester, England, June 25-28. http://2006.informingscience.org

Yasuko, N. (2004). Innovation of the formative assessments approach using WBT. In *Proceedings of World Conference on E-Learning in Corporate, Government, Healthcare, and Higher Education 2004* (pp. 453-460). Norfolk, VA: AACE. Retrieved from http://www.editlib.org/index.cfm

Biography

Heinz Dreher is senior lecturer and research fellow in the School of Information Systems, part of the Curtin Business School at Curtin University in Perth, Western Australia. He has published in the educational technology and information systems domain through conferences, journals, invited talks and seminars; is currently the holder of Australian National Competitive Grant funding for a 4 year E-Learning project; is collaborating on Automated Essay Grading technology development, trial usage and evaluation, resulting in the creation of MarkIT (www.essaygrading.com); has received numerous industry grants for investigating hypertext based systems in training and business scenarios; and is an experienced and accomplished teacher, receiving awards for his work in cross-cultural awareness and course design. In 2004 he was appointed Adjunct Professor for Computer Science at Graz University of Technology, and continues to collaborate in teaching & learning and research projects with European partners.

The page left blank intentionally.

Development of the Web Users Self-Efficacy Scale (WUSE)

Peter Eachus and Simon Cassidy
Directorate of Psychology, University of Salford, Salford, UK

p.eachus@salford.ac.uk s.cassidy@salford.ac.uk

Abstract

The aim of this research was to develop a scale that could evaluate an individuals confidence in using the Internet. Web-based resources are becoming increasingly important within higher education and it is therefore vital that students and staff feel confident and competent in the access, provision, and utilisation of these resources. The scale developed here represents an extension of previous research (Cassidy & Eachus, 2002) that developed a measure of self-efficacy in the context of computer use. An iterative approach was used in the development of the Web User Self-Efficacy scale (WUSE) and the participants were recruited from the student body of a large University in the North West of the United Kingdom, and globally via a web site set up for this purpose. Initial findings suggest that the scale has acceptable standards of reliability and validity though work is continuing to refine the scale and improve the psychometric properties of the tool.

Keywords: Psychology, self-efficacy, teaching and learning

Introduction

In their exploration of factors affecting the success of online learning, Blocher, Sujo de Momtes, Willis & Tucker (2002) considered whether online learners need specific skills and strategies to be successful. They examined factors including cognitive and metacognitive learning strategies and motivation and found that the online programme included in their study tended to attract students who were young and who were confident in their technology skills. Cassidy and Eachus (2002) have also identified confidence, or self-efficacy, as a pertinent factor in the context of computer use, with higher levels of computer user self-efficacy associated with greater self-rated computer competency and experience. Computer user self-efficacy relates specifically to an individual's judgement of their capabilities to use computers and is derived from Bandura's (1986) social cognitive theory in which he defines the general construct of self-efficacy as "peoples judgements of their capabilities to organize and execute courses of action required to attain designated types of performances. It is concerned not with the skills one has but with the judgements of what one can do with whatever skills one posses" (p.391). Simplified, self-efficacy represents an individual's beliefs regarding their perceived capability to successfully complete a particular behaviour or task. The impact of positive and negative self-efficacy beliefs has been demonstrated in a range of contexts including academic achievement (; Cassidy & Eachus, 2000; Eachus, 1993; Eachus & Cassidy, 1997), health behaviour (Bandura, 1986; Schwarzer, 1992), stock market investment (Eachus, 1994) as well as more recently computer use (Cassidy & Eachus, 2002).

Within the context of computer use, positive self-efficacy has been shown to be related to willingness to choose and participate in computer-based activities, expectations of success, perseverance when faced with difficulties and computer-based performance (Holcomb, Brown, Kulikowich & Zheng, 2003). The effects of both gender and experience with computers have also been reported, with males and experienced computer users showing higher levels of computer user self-efficacy (Cassidy & Eachus, 2002).

According to Bandura (1986), self-efficacy beliefs develop is response to four sources of information: previous experience (success and failure), vicarious experience; (observing others successes and failures); verbal persuasion (from peers, colleagues, relatives); and affective state (emotional arousal, e.g. anxiety). Because self-efficacy is based on self-perceptions regarding particular behaviours, the construct is considered to be situation specific or domain sensitive (Cassidy & Eachus, 2002). To illustrate domain sensitivity Cassidy & Eachus (2002) provide the example of an individual who may exhibit high levels of self-efficacy (indicating a high level of confidence) within one domain, for example sport, whilst simultaneously exhibiting low levels of self-efficacy within another domain such as academic ability. Bandura (1986) suggests that the perception that one has the capabilities to perform a task will increase the likelihood that the task will be completed successfully.

It is within the specific context of information and communication technologies and e-learning that the current paper examines self-efficacy beliefs, with specific reference to Internet or web-based resources. We are amidst a revolution involving virtual learning environments and identifying, measuring and manipulating any factor that might impede our access to, utilisation of, or success with virtual learning should be a principal concern of educational research and pedagogical practice.

There are many reasons or factors that make both access to, and utilisation of the Internet both desirable and necessary. Its ubiquitous nature has deemed access to and familiarity with the Internet an assumption of the modern age; not using the net may even be, as suggested by Wolfinbarger, Gilly & Schau (2005), socially undesirable. However, although the human computer interface is becoming increasingly intuitive, for inexperienced users there are still formidable problems. The Internet has the potential to impact on many facets of our daily lives, but for many people the ability to exert that power is limited by an inability to control that potential. This inability may be real – in that the individual genuinely may not have the necessary skills or abilities – or it may simply be a belief which results in incapacity and poor motivation, as in the case of self-efficacy expectations (Cassidy & Eachus, 2002). In their study examining Internet usage in older individuals, Wolfinbarger et al. (2005) have already demonstrated the effect of self-efficacy beliefs in determining propensity and intensity of Internet use, with positive beliefs associated with earlier adoption of and increased use of the Internet.

The nature of self-efficacy as an ego-centric construct demands that it be measured directly, rather than indirectly and for this reason self-efficacy is usually measured using self-report scales (Cassidy & Eachus, 2002). Over the past decade a number of scales have been developed to measure various aspects of Internet self-efficacy. The early measures tended to focus on a few specific types of Internet behaviour, for example creating bookmarks or entering the address of a web page correctly (Nahl, 1996). Similarly Ren (1999) reports on a self-efficacy scale designed to evaluate searches for government information. A more general measure of Internet self-efficacy was developed by Eastin and LaRose (2000) and although the psychometric properties of this scale were adequate, the domain of behaviours examined was very limited and the scale itself only contained 8 items.

The purpose of the research described here is to extend the work on Internet self-efficacy by developing a scale that will have broad utility. If students, and others who choose to learn online, are to gain maximum benefit from the experience it is important that tutors know something of their perceived capabilities before they embark on this form of learning. In this way it will be possible for tutors to identify students who could benefit from additional support before they face the frustrations of trying to tackle course material via a medium for which they are not best prepared.

Method

The construct of web user self-efficacy was sampled using items suggested by Nahl (1996), Ren (1999) and Eastin and LaRose (2000). In addition it was felt important that the items reflect four domains of Internet self-efficacy i.e. Information Retrieval, Information Provision, Communication, and Internet Technology. It was suggested that these four domains would cover aspects of Internet self-efficacy from the simplest retrieval of a web page up to the more complex issues associated with the design and construction of whole web sites. Examples of items from the four domains are shown in Table 1. The first item is worded positively and the second negatively in each case:

Table 1: Examples of items from the four domains

Information Retrieval:

I rarely have problems finding what I am looking for on the Internet
I sometimes find using search engines like Google and Yahoo can be difficult

Information Provision:

I wouldn't have any problems creating a simple web page.
Using ftp to upload web pages to a server is quite complicated.

Communication

I find using email easy.
I much prefer using letters or the telephone to communicate with people rather than the Internet.

Internet Technology

I can usually sort out any Internet access problems I may have.
I am not really sure what a modem does.

From the items generated a 40-item scale was constructed where respondents were required to indicate their level of agreement/disagreement to each statement along a 5-point Likert scale. Affirmation bias was controlled for by wording half of the statements in a negative manner so that a disagree response was needed to add positively to the composite self-efficacy score. Hence a high score would indicate high self-efficacy on each of the four domains, which in turn could be totalled to provide an overall Web Users Self-Efficacy (WUSE) score.

In addition to the main scale items, data was also collected on age, gender, Internet expertise (novice, intermediate or advances), and Internet education (i.e. how the user had learned to access the Internet). This data was used for validation purposes.

Sampling

Since the study was concerned with web user self-efficacy it seemed relevant to sample from the population of web users. This does create certain sampling problems, for example nothing is known about non-responders, and those who do respond obviously require a certain degree of Internet expertise and therefore completely naive respondents will probably be missed. However with the judicious use of target populations, in this case Usenet news groups, it is suggested that many of these problems were minimised. The aim was to achieve a sample with a wide age range, adequate gender representation, and a good cross section of experience. In order to achieve this a number of specific newsgroups were targeted, designed to give a balance between people who were likely to be very active on the Internet and those who were less so. The final newsgroups selected were: comp.internet.net-happenings; uk.people.silversurfers; misc.consumers; soc.senior.issues; alt.computer; talk.politics.misc; misc.rural; alt.internet; misc.activism.progressive; alt.education; and humanities.classics.

In addition to the web-based sample, students from a large University in the North West of the United Kingdom were also recruited for the study. These students were not studying computer or Internet based courses and therefore their experience with these technologies would be expected to be somewhat less than the sample recruited via the web. It was felt that this would make the whole sample more balanced and therefore more representative of web users.

Procedure

The 40 item scale was converted into an html form and uploaded onto the University server. To recruit participants for this study a message was posted on the selected newsgroup explaining the nature of the research and inviting people to participate. The URL of the web site was also provided allowing would be participants direct access.

On entering the web site and after reading the brief instructions and a statement assuring anonymity the participants were required to express the extent of their agreement with the items in the scale by clicking on one of five radio buttons ranging from Strongly Disagree through to Strongly Agree. After completing all 40 items the participant was presented with a "submit" button that on clicking sent the data to the University server. The server then responded with a "Thank You" screen before stripping the data of any identifying features and then emailing the data to the researchers.

For student participants a paper version of the scale was prepared and after explaining the purpose of the research the students were asked to complete the questionnaire by expressing their agreement/disagreement with the statements provided using a five point Likert scale.

Results

A total of 141 completed questionnaires were returned, 68 from the web based sample and 73 from the student participants. The mean age of the web group was 46 years with a range from 13 to 72 years (standard deviation 16.3). Of these, 52 were male, 15 female and one did not specify. For the student group the mean age was 21 with a range of 18-53 years (standard deviation 7.6), 13 male and 60 female. For the sample as a whole the mean age was 33 years with a range of 13-72 (standard deviation 17.5) and the gender split was 65 males and 75 females. Preliminary analysis examined the data from the two samples separately and the findings are presented below.

Reliability

Table 2 shows the means, standard deviations and alpha coefficients for the four domains and the WUSE scale as a whole. For each domain the minimum and maximum scores are 10 and 50 respectively. For the WUSE scale the minimum is 40 and the maximum 200. The reliability of each domain was measured using Cronbach's alpha.

Table 2. Web User Self-Efficacy Scores

Domain	Mean		Standard Deviation		Alpha	
	Web	Students	Web	Students	Web	Students
Information Retrieval	45.19	36.63 *	4.90	7.59	0.778	0.852
Information Provision	39.29	23.12 *	9.84	8.94	0.909	0.883
Communications	38.24	31.91 *	5.70	7.09	0.617	0.755
Internet Technology	41.12	28.25 *	5.41	8.36	0.685	0.822
WUSE	165.53	119.95 *	20.34	28.17	0.907	0.943

* $p < 0.001$

It can be seen from Table 2, using an alpha of 0.80 as a criterion (Howitt & Cramer, 2005) that the domains of Information Retrieval, Information Provision and the WUSE scale as a whole all reach acceptable levels of reliability. In the case of Communications and Internet Technology only the students achieve Alpha's that meet this criterion.

Comparing the two sample groups across the five domains found significant differences in all cases (Information Retrieval, $t = 7.739$, $df = 134$ $p < 0.001$; Information Provision, $t = 10.075$, $df = 135$, $p < 0.001$; Communications, $t = 5.489$, $df = 128$, $p < 0.001$; Internet Technology, $t = 10.435$, $df = 134$, $p < 0.001$; WUSE, $t = 9.956$, $df = 123$, $p < 0.001$).

For the two sample groups combined, summary statistics are shown in Table 3.

Table 3. Web User Self-Efficacy Scores for combined group

Domain	Mean	Standard Deviation	Alpha
Information Retrieval	40.59	7.70	0.880
Information Provision	30.67	12.36	0.937
Communications	34.69	7.22	0.747
Internet Technology	34.23	9.59	0.876
WUSE	138.92	33.76	0.960

Validity

In order to assess the discriminant validity of the WUSE scale, participants had been asked to rate their level of expertise on a three point scale: Novice, Intermediate and Advanced. It was predicted that there would be significant differences in the WUSE scores obtained by these three groups. ANOVA was used to confirm this prediction ($F=72.60$, $p<0.001$). It was also predicted that similar differences would be obtained for the four domains and this was also confirmed (Table 4).

Table 4. Mean Self-Efficacy Scores and Level of Expertise

Domain	Novice	Intermediate	Advanced	F
Information Retrieval	27.72	38.40	46.45	59.84 *
Information Provision	15.63	25.47	41.88	80.41 *
Communications	25.81	33.22	38.75	24.48 *
Internet Technology	20.36	30.41	42.18	60.84 *
WUSE	89.54	127.51	169.40	72.60 *

* $p < 0.001$

Post hoc tests on the four domains and the WUSE scores all proved to be significant in the way predicted, i.e. the Advanced group achieved the highest scores, the Intermediate the next highest and the Novice group had the lowest scores.

Intuitively the four domains would appear to represent different levels of web user self-efficacy. It seems probable that most Internet users simply retrieve information or perhaps use it for communications, e.g. email. Only the more experienced and skilled user will be providing information in the form of web site design. It seems likely that these people will also be more knowledgeable as far as Internet technology is concerned. To examine this, a repeated measures anova was performed comparing the data from the four domains and this was found to be significant ($F= 86.14$, $p < 0.001$). A paired sample t-test was used to compare each of the domains with the others. Multiple comparisons using a t-test in this way can be problematic and to correct for this the procedure suggested by Dancy and Reidy (2002) was followed. This suggests that the chosen significance level (0.05) should be divided by the number of comparisons (6) to give a corrected level of significance, in this case 0.008. When the self-efficacy scores on the four domains are all compared with each other in this way, with the exception of Communications compared with Internet Technology, all the other comparisons proved to be statistically significant with $p < 0.001$ for each comparison.

Stereotypically, Internet users are usually perceived as young and male. In this study the gender split was almost equal with 65 males and 75 females. However it was also hypothesised that there would be significant gender differences obtained on the WUSE scores and the four domains with males would scoring more highly. This prediction was confirmed (Information Retrieval, $t = 6.188$, $df= 133$, $p < 0.001$; Information Provision, $t = 7.091$, $df= 134$, $p < 0.001$; Communications, $t = 3.646$, $df= 127$, $p < 0.001$; Internet Technology, $t = 8.147$, df 137, $p < 0.001$, WUSE, $t = 7.068$, $df = 122$, $p < 0.001$).

Just why males should score more highly than females on all dimensions of the scale is perhaps revealed when gender differences in accessing the Internet is examined. In this study males report that they have been using the Internet regularly for significantly longer than females, 7.9 and 4.1 years respectively ($t = 5.923$, $df= 137$, $p < 0.001$). Males also spend more hours per week on the Internet than do females, 24.1 and 10.8 hours respectively, ($t = 4.182$, $df= 135$, $p < 0.001$).

If the Internet really is a plaything of the young then we would expect to find that younger people score more highly on the WUSE and its sub scales than would older people. To test this it was predicted that there would be a negative correlation between age and WUSE scores i.e. older people would exhibit lower levels of Internet self-efficacy when compared with young users. One difficulty in testing this hypothesis is that the Web sample is on average considerably older than the student sample, 33 and 21 years respectively. For this reason partial correlation coefficients were calculated controlling for the source of the data, i.e. web or student. The predicted relationships were tested using Spearman's rho and found to be supported. WUSE ($r = -0.253$, $p<0.005$). Similar findings were confirmed for three of the four domains; Information Provision ($r = -0.205$, $p<0.02$), Communications ($r = -0.358$, $p< 0.001$) and Information Retrieval ($r = -.196$, $p < 0.03$). No significant correlation with age was obtained for Internet Technology ($r = -0.132$, ns).

Further validation of the WUSE scale was sought by asking participants where they were most likely to access the Internet, from home, at work, or both. It was hypothesised that those who access the Internet from home would probably use the Internet less and therefore would have the lowest self-efficacy scores, those who access the Internet from both home and work would score the highest, and those who mainly access it from work would fall somewhere in between. This hypothesis was tested using oneway analysis of variance and the results can be seen in Table 5. This table shows the mean self-efficacy scores for each domain and the WUSE as a whole. All reach statistical significance in the direction predicted. Post hoc analysis revealed that for Information Retrieval and the WUSE as a whole the differences between the three access groups were statistically significant. However for the Information Provision and Internet Technology domains the difference between home and work access was not significant. Similarly for the Communications domain the difference between access from work and access from both home and work, also failed to reach significance. This data therefore can only be said to partly support the proposed hypothesis.

Table 5: Influence of Internet Access on Self-Efficacy

Domain	Home	Work	Both	F Significance
Information Retrieval	32.33	40.11	43.42	5.343 0.006
Information Provision	23.33	29.41	35.71	4.965 0.008
Communications	28.00	34.69	36.07	3.118 0.048
Internet Technology	25.88	33.28	37.61	4.394 0.014
WUSE	109.55	137.50	152.82	6.360 0.002

In developing the WUSE scale it was suggested that Internet use could be divided into four domains, Information Retrieval, Information Provision, Communications, and Internet Technology. To test the proposition that these four domains are independent constructs the responses to the forty items of the scale were subject to factor analysis using principal component analysis and varimax rotation. The factor analysis produced seven factors with eigenvalues over one which accounted for 64% of the variance. The factor loadings did not allow any clear distinctions to be made in terms of the predicted domains. Indeed when the intercorrelations of the domain scores are examined, Table 6, it can be seen that there is considerable overlap between the four domains suggesting that Web User Self-Efficacy is best explained as a unitary construct rather than multi-dimensional.

Table 6: Domain Intercorrelations

Domain	Information Retrieval	Information Provision	Communications	Internet Technology
Information Retrieval	1.00	0.791	0.713	0.868
Information Provision		1.00	0.650	0.850
Communications			1.00	0.709
Internet Technology				**1.00**

All the correlations were calculated using Spearman's rho (2-tailed) and are statistically significant ($p < 0.01$).

Discussion

The principal aim of the study was to develop a psychometric instrument capable of measuring the self-efficacy construct in the context of Internet use. This aim relates to similar instrument development within the context of computer user self-efficacy (Cassidy & Eachus, 2002). Given the centrality of electronic communication and resources in everyday functioning, professional competence, education and training, and the inhibitory effects of negative self-efficacy beliefs reported by Eachus & Cassidy (1997) and facilitatory effects of positive self-efficacy beliefs (Holcomb et al. 2003), the development of an instrument to assess perceived capabilities around internet use was considered a worthwhile pursuit.

The Web User Self-Efficacy Scale (WUSE) was therefore developed on this basis and this first phase of development has been largely successful in demonstrating acceptable psychometric properties and utility of the instrument.

Reliability

Internal reliability of both the total WUSE scale and the composite sub-domains was assessed using Cronbach's Alpha. An alpha coefficient of 0.96 was reported for the total scale, while alphas for the four subscales ranged between 0.75 and 0.94, which—according to developmental criteria suggested by Kline (1986) indicates acceptable levels of internal item consistency and reliability at both sub-scale and total scale levels. As the sample was derived from what could be considered two distinct populations, separate alpha coefficients were calculated for participants who completed the WUSE online and those who completed an off-line paper version. Results indicated similarly acceptable internal reliability for both groups on the total WUSE and sub-scales with the exception of Communications and Internet Technology subscales for the web-based group, where alpha levels were reported at marginally below the set criteria, i.e. Communications 0.62 and Internet Technology 0.69. Although further refinement of the scale is planned to address this issue, it is suggested that the tool is appropriate for both on-line and off-line completion. External (test-re-test) reliability was not assessed as this stage of development.

Validity

Previous work (Cassidy & Eachus, 2002) reports experience with computers as a significant factor in determining computer user self-efficacy, with increased experience leading to positive self-efficacy beliefs. The validity of the WUSE was demonstrated by significant differences in both total and subscale scores between groups reporting themselves as novice, intermediate and advanced Internet users. Advanced participants achieved higher WUSE (and subscale) scores than intermediate participants who, in turn, achieved higher WUSE (and subscale) scores than novice participants. This fits with earlier reports by Wolfinbarger et al. (2005) that self-efficacy is associated with intensity of Internet use.

According to the rationale that the prevailing function for most Internet users is information retrieval and communication, these two subscales should record higher levels of self-efficacy on the basis that participants will be more 'practised' in these domains. Although not all permutations of subscale comparisons proved significant, sufficient evidence was reported to support the proposition and thus further support the validity of the WUSE and its subscales.

In line with previous reports of gender differences in computer user self-efficacy (Cassidy & Eachus, 2002), validity of the WUSE was examined according to the known groups method. The WUSE (and its subscales) successfully distinguished between groups of males and females, with males scoring significantly higher on total scale scores and all subscales. It is suggested that the gender difference reported here may be an artefact of experience and expertise as, males reported themselves as regular users for significantly longer than females.

In addition, some evidence was reported for an age dependent effect, with older participants having lower WUSE scores than younger participants, and for place of Internet access, with home only access group scoring lower than work only, and home plus work gaining the highest scores. Both of these effects were anticipated on the basis of the findings reported by Cassidy and Eachus (2002) and Wolfinbarger et al. (2005) and can be considered further evidence for the validity of the scale.

Although the authors remain confident of the content validity of the instrument, factor analysis did not produce a convincing four factor solution in accordance with those domains nominated: Information Retrieval; Information Provision; Communications; and Internet Technology. Instead a seven factor model accounting for 64% variance was reported. That factor loadings were not clearly indicative of source domains, and that inter-correlations between the originally proposed domains were high, means that it is not helpful to consider web-user self-efficacy in multidimensional terms. Instead, the construct should be treated as unidimensional, pending further investigation.

Conclusion

Although a programme of further development and refinement is planned, preliminary results do provide strong support for the utility of the existing 40-item WUSE scale. Like computer user self-efficacy, assessing web user self-efficacy will allow some insight into the implications and impact of positive and negative belief systems for individuals in many areas including both personal and professional functioning, and enable consideration to be given to interventions which will alleviate the effects of inhibitory beliefs systems such as low or negative web-user self-efficacy. Specific examples might include tutors or trainers who are thinking of using Internet based resources as either part or even the whole of a course, and who wish to evaluate web-user self-efficacy in their students as either a criterion for recruitment or to identify the need for further skill development. There is sufficient evidence within the self-efficacy literature to support the argument which suggests that negative web-user self-efficacy beliefs will inhibit successful internet use and thus limit utility of ICT in such areas as virtual learning. As further evidence is gathered—both practice-based and through research activity—the authors are optimistic that the WUSE will establish itself as robust, domain-specific tool for assessment of self-efficacy in the context of internet use.

References

Bandura, A. (1986). *Social foundations of thought and action: A social cognitive theory*. Englewood Cliffs, NJ: Prentice Hall.

Blocher, J. M.; Sujo de Momtes,L., Willis, E. M., & Tucker, G. (2002). Online learning: Examining the successful student profile. *The Journal of Interactive Online Learning, 1*(2), 1-12.

Cassidy, S. & Eachus, P. (2000). Learning style, academic belief systems, self-report student proficiency and academic achievement in higher education. *Journal of Educational Psychology, 20*(3), 307-322.

Cassidy, S & Eachus, P. (2002). Developing the computer user self-efficacy (CUSE) scale: Investigating the relationship between computer self-efficacy, gender and experience with computers. *Journal of Educational Computing Research, 26*(2), 169-189, 2002.

Dancy, C. P., & Reidy, J. (2002). *Statistics without maths for psychology: Using SPSS for Windows*. Pearson:Prentice Hall.

Eachus, P. (1993). Development of the health student self-efficacy scale. *Perceptual and Motor Skills, 77*, 670.

Eachus, P. (1994). *Locus of control, self-efficacy and attributional style of investment professionals*. Unpublished PhD Thesis. Manchester Metropolitan University.

Eachus, P. & Cassidy, S (1997). Self-efficacy, locus of control and styles of learning as contributing factors in the academic performance of student health professionals. *Proceedings of First Regional Congress of Psychology for Professionals in the Americas - Interfacing the Science and Practice of Psychology*, July 27-August 2, 1997, Mexico City, Mexico.

Eastin, M.S. & LaRose, R. (2000). Internet self-efficacy and the psychology of the digital divide. *Journal of Computer-Mediated Communication, 6*(1). Retrieved from http://www.asusc.org/jcmc/vol6/issue1/eastin.html

Howitt, D. & Cramer, D. (2005). *Introduction to statistics in psychology* (3rd ed.). Pearson: Prentice Hall.

Holcomb, L. B., Brown, S. W., Kulikowich, J. M. & Zheng, D. (2003). Raising educational technology self-efficacy through assessment. *American Psychological Association Conference*, 30th May –2nd June 2003, Altanta, USA. Retrieved online at: http://teachtech.education.uconn.edu/holcomb_asp.pdf

Kline, P. (1986). *A handbook of test construction: Introduction to psychometric design*. London: Methuen.

Nahl, D. (1996). Affective monitoring of Internet learners: Perceived self-efficacy and success. *Journal of American Society for Information Sciences, 33*, 200-209.

Ren, W. (1999). Self-efficacy and the search for government information. *Reference & User Service Quarterly, 38*, 283-291.

Schwarzer, R. (1992). *Self-efficacy: Thought control of action*. London: Hemisphere.

Wolfinbarger, M., Gilly, M. C. & Schau, H. J. (2005). Keeping up with the times: Innovation and usage of the Internet among later adopters. CRITO Consortium Project. Accessed online February 2006 from: www.crito.uci.edu/consortium

Biographies

Peter Eachus is a Senior Lecturer in Psychology at the University of Salford. As well as his interests in the psychological aspects of Internet use, he also has research interests in robotics and the psychology of tourism. He has published extensively and has presented papers at conferences in North America, Spain, Italy, Belgium and the United Kingdom. Outside interests include running marathons and skydiving.

Simon Cassidy is a Chartered Psychologist and Senior Lecturer and Researcher based at the University of Salford, UK. Principle areas of teaching and research include in applied social psychology, health psychology, health promotion and educational psychology. He has an established national and international research profile which includes paper presentations in South America, Europe and the UK and publications in international journals such as Educational Psychology, Educational Computing Research and Perceptual and Motor Skills.

The page left blank intentionally.

A Principled Methodology for Information Retrieval on the Web

Martin Eayrs
University of Salford, Manchester, UK

m.eayrs@salford.ac.uk

Abstract

The World Wide Web provides a wealth of information - indeed, perhaps more than can comfortably be processed. But how does all that Web content get there? And how can users assess the accuracy and authenticity of what they find? This paper will look at some of the problems of using the Internet as a resource and suggest criteria both for researching and for systematic and critical evaluation of what users find there.

Keywords: critical thinking, www, unprincipled surfing, principled surfing, accuracy, authority, objectivity, currency, coverage

Introduction

"It's not what you don't know that'll hurt you - it's what you do know, that isn't so"

(Arase, 2003)

Is there a danger that over reliance on the Internet as a source of information for academic purposes might result in a degradation of the integrity of data acquired? Is the anarchical and pioneering nature of much of the Internet compatible with the provision of reliable and authoritative resource material? This paper considers these questions, and suggests that balanced and critical consideration of the origin and purpose of web texts may be beneficial to students, and may constitute a useful study skill for teachers to provide students with.

Content

The Importance of Critical Thinking

The ability to think critically is what allows a reader to see beyond the literal meaning of discourse and give balanced, reasoned and well-grounded responses. The same evaluative criteria should be brought to bear on the selection of appropriate resources for teaching or research purposes.

Critical thinking is, in short, the ability to perceive and respond appropriately to a great deal that is - and is not - immediately apparent to the casual reader or viewer. Critical thinking takes the learner beyond the literal, surface aspects of any given piece of material into the motivation and purpose of the writer.

This paper will not attempt to define 'critical thinking', but does suggest that certain principles – in particular, the ability to evaluate - can be applied to the evaluation of material found everywhere, and particularly, for the purpose of this paper, on the WWW.

Reading in the Offline World

When people pick up something to read they already have certain expectations. To use examples from UK newspapers, one tends to approach The Sunday Telegraph rather differently from The News of the World. Previous reading experience has led readers to identify each as a separate 'type' and the reader reacts to each on the basis of this experience.

'Periodicals', to take a category at random, can be divided into four categories:

- Scholarly - 'concerned with academic study, especially research'
- Substantive News / General Interest - 'having a solid base, being substantial'
- Popular - 'fit for, or reflecting the taste and intelligence of, the people at large'
- Sensational - 'arousing or intending to arouse strong curiosity, interest or reaction'

(Merriam-Webster's Online Dictionary, 2006)

It is experience and familiarity with these broad genres that enable readers to assign a publication to one of these categories, and although there will be borderline cases readers on the whole feel confident about so assigning them. What is interesting, however, is how they are able to do this. This paper suggests that critical thinking plays an important part.

This 'grading' system works well for printed periodicals, where on opening the publication the reader's expectations are largely met. However, when following the results of a search engine or a link on a web page it is not always clear what lies in store, and all may not always be what it seems. For example, it is uncommon to find advertising placed alongside the text of printed academic articles, and flashing sprites or animated gifs that waltz across the page to the accompaniment of midi or other sound files, are not a feature of academic journals. And whereas academic journals tend to be produced by distinguished scholars in the ivory towers of academe, all the world and his brother seems to be producing web-pages, some built and maintained by children as young as seven or eight.

Put at its simplest, when readers open a book or journal they generally have a clear idea where their reading will take them. When the same reader clicks on a hypertext link on the World Wide Web they can't really be sure exactly where they are going, and even when they get there they can't always be sure exactly where they are. But there are clues, as shall be seen.

The Dangers of Unprincipled Sourcing and Referencing

As has been stated, academics all have to learn how to distinguish 'scholarly' journals from other periodicals. In fact these might be divided these into such areas as: 'academically respectable', 'professionally solid', 'popular' and 'sensationalist' - as was done above - but how does a reader do this? What criteria is brought to bear?

When evaluating traditional printed material there are certain points one would do well bear in mind. These are well known and generally taught as part of an academic skills programme. They are presented below in the form of questions one might wish to ask, drawing on Susan Beck (1997).

Accuracy

- Is the information reliable?
- Has the information been checked for errors of fact? By whom?
- Is there an editor who assumes authority for this?
- Are there people entrusted with the specific duty of checking all the facts?
- Is it clear who these people are?

Authority

- Is the author really 'qualified' to write on this subject?
- Is the author a recognised authority in this field?
- Is the publisher a 'reputable' publisher?
- Is the book published privately, perhaps even by the author himself?

Objectivity

- Is bias kept to a minimum?
- Is the information trying to influence the opinion of the audience?
- Is theory supported by data or coherent argument?
- Is unsupported theory built on to produce subsequent argument?

Currency

- Is the content of the work up-to-date?
- Is the date of publication clearly marked?
- Can one be satisfied that the given date is genuine?

Coverage

- Is the range of topics included in the work adequate?
- Is the range of topics included in the work relevant?
- Is the range of topics included in the work explored in reasonable depth?

Criteria for Web Evaluation

These criteria, remember, are used for evaluating printed material. Now these same points will be applied to publishing on the World Wide Web.

Accuracy

The truth – for good or bad - is that anyone with the right software and who knows how to type and navigate can publish on the Web. Statistically, few Web resources are verified by editors or fact checkers and there are as yet no internationally accepted Web Standards to ensure the accuracy of information displayed. In the worst of cases, there is nothing whatsoever to prevent the malicious posting of totally false (or, what is far worse, partially false) information.

Authority

It is usually difficult and often impossible to determine real authorship of material posted on the Web. In cases where an author's name is listed his/her qualifications are usually not, and responsibility for accuracy or truthfulness of content is very rarely stated. The fact that an article is attributed to, say, Noam Chomsky, is no guarantee that Chomsky himself wrote it or that it even reflects his views.

Objectivity

It is not claimed here that writers should not attempt to be persuasive their writing, but there is an academic tradition of presenting alternative arguments and interpretations, and in most writing the literature revue will refer widely to the field. In. But in many cases the aims of persons or groups who post material on the web are often unclear. The Web has a tendency to act as a "virtual soapbox" where anybody can get up and say what they want - indeed this is one of its strengths - but it certainly attracts a fair share of eccentrics along with the altruistically motivated. Which of these is which is not always clear.

Currency

Any active Internet user is aware of the number of dead pages littering the Web; sites, for example, saying 'last modified August 1995'. 1995 is in fact an interesting date, as it was about then that postgraduate students started to have university web pages, Would that the universities had been as quick to close these sites down when the students left as they were to put them up, but it seems that many 10 year old sites are still out there, untouched, unmodified and with their content long superseded.

There has in any case been no obligation to include dates on Web pages and in cases where a date is included it may variously be the date the information was first written, the date the information was posted or the date the information was last modified. And the fact that a page bears a date does not mean that the date is genuine, nor is there any way of authenticating it.

Coverage

It is hard to determine the extent of Web coverage because of the nature of the hypertext links that join web pages and web sites together. It is not technically possible to prevent one site linking to another, and with a little skill it is possible in most cases to link to any part of any site, thus implying an authoritative and authorised link, when in fact no such tacit connection was intended by the author(s) of the site so targeted. For this reason, any one web page should in principle be evaluated independently of any other, especially when leaving the 'home' site.

Further Issues

Advertising

In printed material the distinction between advertising and information is usually made explicit, or if not immediately so the reader learns over time which parts of a publication with which he or she is familiar is likely to contain each. On the web it is not always easy to discern, especially when advertising on so many sites nowadays – as an intricate and intrinsic part of web site economics – is wholly incorporated into the page and site design.

Furthermore, while it is clear in a printed publication what is advertising and what is editorial copy, on the Web it is usually impossible to know whether the advertising and informational content are being supplied by the same person or organisation. If they are, the advertising is likely to bias the informational content, and the reader needs to be aware of this.

Customisation

What each user can see on their screen and how they see it, and what they can print or download to their computer will often vary from user to user, according to the user's platform, system and browser configuration and the software and plug-ins they have installed. Indeed the server may serve different page content according to the country of access, modem bandwidth or user-defined preferences.

Furthermore many sites are dynamic, with constantly changing content, some being randomised on user access. And even respected sites change their content regularly – for example the concept of a 'daily' newspaper doesn't exist on the Web, where 'breaking news' breaks at any time of day or night.

All these factors can mean in essence that two people can go to the same website at the more or less the same time and see very different pages, with different content, which is not helpful when you want to cite a fixed reference and lead others to it.

URL structure

Today's search engines and indexes are extremely powerful for those that have learned how to use them. Still, they are far from perfect and can retrieve Web Pages totally out of context, frequently directing the user to somewhere wholly inappropriate. To quote Huw Jarvis, "Search engine 'hits' are no indication of 'quality', nor is the numerical list any true indication of the importance of the site" (Jarvis 2003, p.209).

Sometimes you can work back through the URL, stripping off sub-directories backslash by backslash, to get to a relevant home page, but equally frequently users will be bewildered by the plethora of pop-up windows and aliased web addresses that ambush them from all sides, with the result that they end up not knowing where they are.

Site managers are frequently to blame for the inability to find previously visited and bookmarked files, or files cited in another document, and it would certainly be helpful if web managers would leave files in the same place on the site and not restructure web content every few months.

An ability to understand the way URLs are constructed and the principles of directory systems is helpful here, but even then a savvy hacker can dump a directory on some one else's system which may go undetected for a while, leaving the user believing he is on one site while in truth he is somewhere else.

Accessibility

Web Pages are notoriously unstable and not only can they become temporarily unavailable (web maintenance, too much traffic, server down, etc.) but they are likely to move or disappear without notice. Far worse, they can be altered without their owners knowing, either accidentally or intentionally. Many sites are not protected by firewalls and a competent hacker may still penetrate those that are. After all, for a skilled and dedicated hacker who can work his way into the Pentagon a University web site is hardly likely to present much of a challenge.

Online publications

Many online journals are available nowadays. Some of these are online versions of printed journals, carrying much the same content. Others, however, are wholly electronic. In this latter case, articles which are 'refereed' are far more likely to be reliable sources that those which have just arrived from nowhere to fulfil the editor's publication schedules. Check carefully to see if there is a review board and what the publishing policy of the journal is.

Caution should also be taken when quoting from electronic lists and discussion forums. Just because someone posts a message citing the words or opinions of a third party does not automatically mean that the 'quote' is accurate – it should, as in all such cases, be independently verified.

Data entry

It is also useful to reflect on how information gets into digital form in the first place. Web resources are often keyboarded or scanned. Keyboarding of long texts is often farmed out as piecework to people who may be unfamiliar with technical texts – or even in extreme cases, the language. Like humans, OCR (optical character recognition) engines have an unfortunate tendency to make sense of unfamiliar words by changing them to something within their repertoire. Spell checkers don't always help here, merely checking that each word typed corresponds to a word in the language, and not necessarily to the one intended by the author. Given this potential for error, along with the high costs of professional proofreading, it is hardly surprising that web sites have so many inaccurate texts and data.

Possible Solutions

One solution to the problem of site integrity has arrived in the shape of the portal – a web site that purports to guarantee the integrity of its content and that any outgoing links on its pages are acceptable to the site administrators. No site administrator can stop incoming links but once users arrive at the portal they know (in theory at least) where they are and what they can expect.

The down side for the user is that many such sites are passworded. There are many reasons (legal, commercial, protection of data, etc.) why academic or commercial institutions are unable or unwilling to share all their content with the world at large. Most reach a compromise and make some of their information generally available and limit other areas to their own Intranet, available only to their own staff and students, and accessible only through their own onsite terminals and with a personalised password.

Another emerging solution may lie in Extensible Markup Language (XML), which provides flexible and customisable identification of information through standardised, embedded databases. One expert in the field writes that XML "… provides a robust, non-proprietary, persistent, and verifiable file format for the storage and transmission of text and data both on and off the Web' (Flynn 2002).

XML is actually a metalanguage and, put simply, using XML means that in addition to page content a web page can also contain identification and categorisation data – in the form of data base fields - that will define its content and provenance more precisely. These data can include classification information (such as the Library of Congress subject areas), institution identification (verifying an institution as a member of one of a number of professional bodies), etc., but can also include user-defined fields for whatever purposes may serve the user(s).

It is not the purpose of this paper to discuss XML in any level of detail, and indeed beyond the competence of this author to do so,. The system is still in development, and at present is not 'foolproof', but if or when fully implemented will be a great boon to academics keen to separate the wheat from the chaff.

Other low-tech solutions include restricting a search to pre-defined domains by using a limiter (such as host: ac.uk) that will instruct the search engine to search in a limited area, in this case UK university sites.

In addition to these technological solutions, as has been said earlier, it is of course vital that users demanding data integrity apply rigorous criteria not only where they look but also in evaluating what they stumble upon on in their wanderings around the Web.

Beyond Web Texts

It has been the purpose of this paper to suggest the caution in the evaluation of printed pages on the web that one would with printed resources. However, many of the same criteria can be applied to other media that can be embedded in or called up from a web page. The content of embedded or streamed audio or video files should be given the same measure of healthy prudence, as should content of blogs, pod casts and other material of uncertain origin.

It is in fact increasingly hard to define what a 'web page' is, when so much of its content is stored in different locations. Typically, routines call on such diverse sources as scripts, includes, media files, dynamic data bases, and many others to present the user with a viewing experience that may indeed be unrepeatable, even on a screen refresh. Variables that determine what viewers actually see may include the geographical location of a user's ISP, the software configuration on the computer being used, the time of day, current server traffic, a user's previous browsing experience, and many others.

Political considerations may also be a factor controlling what a web user may and may not access. The recent entry of Google into mainland China may be a useful reference point here, although it is worth noting that as early as 2004 technology was finding solutions to provide access for Chinese web users (BBC News, 2004).

Conclusion

The Web is only one source of information, not always reliable, which can be very useful for researching certain topics on certain sites, and of little value – and possibly dangerous - for others. Judicious use of the critical faculty will improve the chances that the data accessed will be genuine and useful.

Students should be taught that to research a topic thoroughly they should use a variety of sources, both Web and non-Web. As a work-around, and if available, 'hard' material (available as CDs and DVDs), if printed by responsible institutions and reasonably up-to-date, may be more reliable than the Web in some respects. But beyond these, this paper suggests there is still very much a place for the old fashioned 'dead-tree' library, both as a source of authoritative texts and also as a means of honing study and referencing skills that might otherwise atrophy if students rely exclusively on electronic sources..

Many of the points made above are perhaps obvious to a mature, adult user of the Web. However, as the Web is increasingly being recommended for educational research projects and may - in the more developed world at least – be in the process of replacing the use of printed resources, younger users need to be warned of the limitations too. A new module in a study skills programme to this effect might not go amiss.

References

Arase, V. (2003). Message posted to "Has anyone bought Norton Systemworks 3?" In *MacUseNet* discussion Group. Retrieved 11 February 2006 from http://www.macusenet.com/archive/index-t-8972.html

BBC News [UK version]. (2006). Accessed 5 February 2006 at http://news.bbc.co.uk/1/hi/technology/3548035.stm

Beck, S. (1997). Evaluation criteria. In *The Good, The Bad & The Ugly: or, Why It's a Good Idea to Evaluate Web Sources.* Accessed 5 February 2006 at http://lib.nmsu.edu/instruction/evalcrit.html

Flynn, P. (Ed.) (2002). *The XML FAQ v. 2.1.* Accessed 15 September 2003 at http://www.ucc.ie/xml/faq.xml

Jarvis, H. (2001). Internet usage of English for academic purposes courses. In *Recall, 13*, Cambridge University Press.

Merriam-Webster's Online Dictionary. (2006). Accessed 5 Feb 2006 at http://www.m-w.com/

Biography

Martin Eayrs is a lecturer at the University of Salford, UK. He has previously worked at the University of Essex, UK, and at the Universidad de Los Andes in Venezuela. He was for seventeen years director of a private language school in Buenos Aires, and latterly language consultant to the British Council in Argentina. After twenty-three years in Latin America he returned to the UK in 2000.

Information Systems Success in the Public Sector: Stakeholders' Perspectives and Emerging Alignment Model

Ivana Elpez and Dieter Fink
Edith Cowan University, Perth, Australia

d.fink@ecu.edu.au

Abstract

There have been many attempts to define Information Systems (IS) success but they have mostly been in the private sector. This paper reviews existing IS success models and then takes into account stakeholders as well as public sector perspectives in conducting qualitative case studies of 3 major Western Australian government agencies. Findings of the study identified key IS success variables relevant to the public sector and characteristics that distinguish the public from the private sector. By aligning success variables with these characteristics, it was possible to conceptualise an early theoretical IS success model for the sector.

Keywords: IS success, IS success models, IS in public sector, IS case studies, Public sector

Introduction

It is commonly accepted that Information Technology (IT) has become a tool with which to produce accurate, reliable and timely information through the development of Information Systems (IS). For an IS to be judged successful, however, it has to satisfy additional criteria in today's competitive world. For example, at a broad level, it is expected that it becomes a key component in achieving the organisation's mission (Drury & Farhoomand, 1998 referenced by Garson, 1999) and more narrowly, improve productivity and facilitate service delivery (Brown, 1999 cited by Garson, 1999). Even a cursory examination of the IS literature reveals that organisations have utilised numerous surrogate measures for IS success (see Hwang, Windsor, & Pryor, 2000).

What is also evident is that IS Success studies have been conducted mostly in the private sector (Specht, 1999 cited by Garson, 1999) while research into IS success within the public sector has been greatly neglected (Seneviratne, 1999). Overall, it has been concluded that little progress has been made in how to achieve IS success within the public sector (Brown, 1999 cited by Garson, 1999). Yet IS are critical to increase effectiveness and efficiency in the delivery of public services, the management of critical information sources for decision making affecting the population, and formulation of public policy (Lynn, 1999 cited by Garson, 1999). The spectacular growth of public investment in IT further reflects an enormous potential for improving the performance of public organisations (Lynn 1998 cited by Garson, 1999). As such, understanding what contributes to IS success is of great importance and value to public sector agencies (Seneviratne, 1999).

The objective of this study was to establish what IS success is within the Western Australian (WA) government sector. A stakeholder perspective was adopted since it was argued that success of an IS project is what stakeholders perceive it to be. To achieve this outcome, the views on how the public sector differs from the private sector were also captured. This would lead to an early model of IS success within the public sector in which key IS success variables would be aligned with public sector characteristics. In this way the study seeks to add to the current lack of research into IS success in the public sector thereby providing new insights to both the researcher and IS professional working in the sector.

Background Literature

When reviewing background literature, three key perspectives were encountered; they are outlined below and provided the basis for designing our research.

The IS Success Model Perspective

Much of the work done in IS success has its origin in the well-known DeLone and McLean (D&M) IS Success Model (DeLone & McLean, 1992). This model provided a comprehensive taxonomy on IS success based on the analysis of more then 180 studies on IS success and identified over 100 IS success measures during the analysis. It established that System Quality, Information Quality, Use, User Satisfaction, Individual and Organisational Impact were the most distinct elements of the IS success equation. In a later work, the authors confirmed the original taxonomy and their conclusion, namely that IS success was "a multidimensional and interdependent construct" (DeLone & McLean, 2003, p. 12).

Seddon (1997) proposed a respecified and extended version of the original D&M IS Success model with the purpose of clarifying confusion caused by the integration of process and casual explanation of IS success measures. According to Seddon (1997), DeLone and McLean (1992) "tried to do too much in their model, and as a result, it is both confusing and misspecified" (p. 240). Seddon used literature on IS success to theoretically evaluate IS success measures and proposed the extended IS Success model. His model focused on measures of information and system quality and net benefits of IS use. As a result, IS success variables were: System Quality, Information Quality, Perceived Usefulness, User Satisfaction, Net Benefits to Individuals, Net Benefits to Organisations and Net Benefits to Society.

An alternative model is the 3-D Model of IS success, introduced by Ballantine Bonner, and Levy (1998) as an attempt to restructure the original D&M model. They identified the need to restructure existing relationships between identified dimensions, identified the lack of accountability for the systemic nature of organisations and the need for critical awareness of identified dimensions and their limitations. The name of the 3-D Model of IS success comes from the three IS dimensions included in the model: Development, Deployment and Delivery. Ballantine et al. (1998) identified factors for each level in the model that determine the quality of the IS. Those factors are either endogenous or exogenous. Exogenous factors include those that cannot be predicted, such as economic and political factors, while endogenous factors, on the other hand, include items that are controllable.

More recently, Hwang et al. (2000) claimed that success of an IS project is directly related to environmental factors related to the organisation, users, IS operations, IS development, IS and external environment. They influence Use, Satisfaction, and the Individual and Organisational Impact of IS. The five environmental variables provided in their System Success Model come from the Ives et al (1980) model which included three process variables, which have been replaced by four success measures from the DeLone and McLean IS Success Model of 1992.

The Stakeholder Perspective

From a 'stakeholder' perspective, each stakeholder is in the position to view the project outcome from various perspectives and arrive at different conclusions. To obtain a comprehensive perspective on IS success these views have to be considered. In the IS discipline, relevant stakeholders can readily be identified as those that will ultimately use the system (end-users) and those charged with delivering those systems (IS professionals). From an end-user perspective, high usability of the system is logically linked to IS success. "If users cannot use the system effectively and efficiently it cannot be deemed to be a success" (Fisher, 2001, p. 25). Several factors have greatly contributed to the usability of an IS; they were identified by Fisher (2001) as shown in Table 1.

Table 1: Variables for IS usability

User expectations of a system
Task-technology fit
Understanding the user's perspective. The system reflects the cognitive style and mental model of the users
Meeting user expectations or perceptions of the system
System usability
Quality and effectiveness of the interface design
Quality and effectiveness of user documentation and information
Ease of use
User acceptance and ownership of a system
Level of user involvement in the development process
Participation in the development leading to greater commitment
The extent of user involvement and participation
The quality of user-developer communication
The quality of the system and system reliability

As shown in Table 1, the user's expectations of a system is important in gaining an understanding of the user's perspective on IS success. Users with realistic expectations of an IS have higher levels of satisfaction and are more likely to engage in the use of the IS when compared to users with unrealistic expectations (Ginzberg, 1981; Szajna & Scamell, 1993). System usability refers to "the degree to which a person believes that using a particular system would enhance his or her job performance" (Davis, 1989, p. 320). In this category, the quality and effectiveness of the user interface, documentation of information as well as ease of use are indicators of IS success. Ease of use has been defined as "the degree to which a person believes that using a particular system would be free from effort" (Davis, 1989, p. 320). It contributes significantly to user satisfaction (Seddon & Kiew, 1996). User acceptance and ownership of the system can be defined as "a subjective psychological state reflecting the importance and personal relevance of a system to the user" (Barki & Hartwick, 1989, p. 53). This can be refined further into user participation which is "a set of behaviors or activities performed by users in the system development process" (Barki &

Hartwick, 1989, p. 53). Both user involvement and participation have been linked to the success of an IS project (Hwang & Thorn, 1999; Kappleman & McLean, 1991; Saleem, 1996).

Besides satisfying end-users, IS also have to receive senior management's commitment and support (Bloom, 1996). However, this stakeholder group has its own perspectives on what makes a successful IS. A study by Adelakun and Jennex (2002) revealed that IT executives, CIO's and IS managers assess success of an IS project by focusing on costs, savings, user satisfaction, value to the organisation and how well the IS interacts within the organisational infrastructure. These perceptions have been ranked in a recent study by CIO (2003) in which 118 executives participated. Internal customer/user satisfaction was considered one of the top three measures for determining the value and success of an IS project by 78% of participants. Staying at or under budget was the second most popular determining factor of IS project success (57% of participating executives), followed by external customer satisfaction, employee productivity, improvements in competitive advantage, system uptime, organisational and IT department productivity, service level agreements and generating revenue.

Project managers are those involved in developing and implementing IS. It has been found that they are expected to reconcile the expectations of end-users and those of senior management as outlined above. They are expected to "see the big picture...be aware of the results expected...and look for long term benefits" (Shenhar, Levy, Dvir, 1997). For project managers, managing user expectations within the IS field has become a critical factor for delivering successful IS projects (Staples, Wong, & Seddon, 2002). However, Wateridge (1998) found that project managers, although being aware of the importance of meeting user requirements, were focusing on time and budget more than on long term criteria such as delivering a system users are happy with. The reason for the emphasis on short term criteria is linked to ongoing appraisals by project manager's superiors on their ability to deliver projects within a defined time period and budget (Wateridge, 1998). This was confirmed in a recent study which found that IS success from a project management perspective was mainly associated with items such as organisational fit and business performance, cost, time and quality components (White & Fortune, 2002).

The Public Sector Perspective

The term public sector in Australia refers to "enterprises which the Commonwealth Government, State/Territory and local governments, separately or jointly have control over. It includes local government authorities and all government departments, agencies and authorities created by, or reporting to, the Commonwealth Parliament and State parliaments. It also includes public trading enterprises such as Australia Post" (Australian Statistics, 1998). The sector has a unique purpose since "government serves all citizens through the exercise of its powers, authorities and roles, including those who are direct recipients of its services. Government therefore governs in the public interest, a role which is unique to government" (Crawford, 1996, p. 5).

Although making profit and maximising shareholder value is not the main objective of public sector agencies nor do they depend upon outperforming its competitors (DeLoof, 1996), the accountability of an IS project team within the public sector is often much wider than in the private sector (Briner, Hastings, Geddes, 1996). Furthermore, changes within the stakeholders group can create much organisational turbulence concerning political, legal, public, financial, managerial and professional issues. Public sector organisations are therefore strongly political and institutionalised (Dowse, 2003). Organisational turbulence, for example, can be very high within an election period (Campbell, 2003). As a result, CIO's and IT staff members can find themselves working for two different governments in quick succession who dislike and distrust each other and have a different attitude towards the importance of IS within the agency. As a result, a change in stakeholders of an IS project has a direct flow on effect on 'success' attainment.

Campbell (2003) looked at financial flexibility within the public sector and concluded, somewhat paradoxical to the above, that government agencies don't have financial flexibility for quick changes like private sector organisations do. This is mainly due to budgets being planned at least a year in advance yet systems may have to respond in the short term as a result of a ministerial request. Within the Australian public sector, accountability for decision making in most cases lies with the government and its ministers (Williams, 1998). Having to deal with the requirements of legislature as well as ministerial expectations (for example a system may have to change 'overnight') adds to the complexity of system delivery and hence to the achievement of IS success.

Procurement policies are critical in most government agencies and typically require that IS within an agency need to deliver value for money, be very efficient, innovative, responsive, customer focused and provide a high quality service at optimal cost to taxpayers (Marriott, 2002). IT departments within the public sector operate with very tight budgets and decisions at every step must be justified. As Marriott (2002) states, "it is imperative that public-sector bodies are demonstrably open and fair. In addition, senior public servants need to constantly ask themselves what their decision would look like if they had to defend it to their parliamentary public-expenditure scrutiny committee" (p. 1).

Flowers (1996) believes that delivering successful IS projects within the public sector is associated with situationally specific constraints when compared to the private sector. Those constraints are outlined in Table 2 and include the politics surrounding the creation and operation of the IS, highly bureaucratic decision making processes, management, technology led, uniqueness and cost.

Table 2: Typical Government IS Characteristics

Factor	Typical Government IS Development
Politics	Priorities may be refocused: for instance as a result of changes in government policy. Impositions of external deadlines: primarily for political reasons
Decision making	Highly bureaucratic decision-making processes. High level of public interests and oversight
Management	Short-term tenures of managers overseeing projects
Lead from	Technology led
Uniqueness	Custom systems rather than packaged preferred
Cost	Low-cost solutions not sought

(Adapted from Al-Wohaibi, Masoud, & Edwards, 2002, p. 6)

Research Design

The study adopted the stakeholder approach in order to capture the opinions of those involved with IS in the Western Australian public sector. The approach conforms with Seddon's (1997) view, namely that IS success can be defined as "a measure of the degree to which the person evaluating the system believes that the stakeholder in whose interest the evaluation is being made is better off" (p. 246). Stakeholders are in a position to view the IS from various perspectives (Belassi & Tukel, 1996). As such, end-users, project managers, project leaders, project sponsors, IT managers and CIO's were interviewed.

Given the nature of this research study (i.e. the subjective meaning of 'IS success' as perceived by the participating stakeholders), the qualitative research method was considered as more appropriate than the quantitative research method. According to Myers (1997), trends within the IS research field show that there has been a general shift away from technological issues towards managerial and organisational issues, thus increasing the application of qualitative research methods. Hammersley (1992, cited in Travers, 2001) suggests that qualitative data is reliable because it captures the issue from the point of view of the research participants rather than from the view of the researcher. The case study research method was chosen as the appropriate qualitative research method. This method is particularly well suited to research within the IS field, as the objects of the study are linked to Information Systems within organisations (Myers, 1997).

The study covered three large IS projects developed and implemented within three Western Australian government agencies. When conducting qualitative case studies it is recommended that between 20 and 40 participants are part of in-depth interviews (Walker, 1985). Thus, 21 participants from the three government agencies were chosen who were either part of the development processes of IS or end-users of that IS depending on their availability, accessibility and the willingness to participate. Semi-structured in-depth interviews were conducted to identify what participants of the study perceived IS success within the Western Australian government sector to be. As such, the interviews followed a specific and focused agenda in alignment with the research objectives and to ensure that similar type of data was collected from participants (Holloway, 1997).

The interview agenda was pre-tested before the data collection phase by three participants who were not part of the study for reliability purposes (Yin, 2003). The interview guide consisted of three distinct parts, namely background information about the participant and the IS project being used, importance of identified IS success variables and the differences between the private and public sector within an IS context.

Findings and Discussion

Background Data

The purpose of the Case Study 1 IS project was to implement a new Document Management System and enable staff members to control, organise, access and disseminate corporate information. A team consisting of a project sponsor, project manager, project leader, two business analysts, expert programmer and programmer analyst was put together to implement and customise a common off-the-shelf records/document management package. The package was subject to several modifications and took one year and three months to implement. Participants of this case study included the project sponsor, project manager, business analyst, two end-users and one project team member.

The purpose of the Case Study 2 IS project was to upgrade the existing IT systems of electoral offices. A new computer image was created and installed on all machines. A computer image, as explained by the project manager of the Case Study 2 IS project, is "a collection of software on a computer consisting of the operating system and all of its software and drivers". The main scope of the project was the conversion of the email system to bring the electoral office email systems in line with the Ministerial offices. A team consisting of a project sponsor, project manager, project leader, business consultant and three IT support officers was put together to complete the project. Participants of this case study included the project sponsor, business consultant, IT support officer and three end-users.

The purpose of the Case Study 3 IS project was to amalgamate previously old and separate systems within the participating agency into one. Due to confidentiality reasons the main function of this IS cannot be stated as it would reveal the agency the IS was developed at. Nevertheless, the cost of the project was at around $13 million and the IS was subsequently sold to one interstate jurisdiction. Participants of this case study included one project manager, one business analyst, one analyst programmer and three end-users of the IS.

IS Success Factors

An integrated account of findings is provided in Table 3. Importance ratings by participants have been used to rank IS success variables. The most important variables are highlighted in bold as explained below.

Table 3: IS Success Variables

Rk	Case Study 1	Case Study 2	Case Study 3
1	**Meeting user requirements**	**Meeting user requirements**	**Meeting user requirements** **Information Quality** **Use**
2	**System usability and performance**	**Information Quality** **Use**	System Quality User participation and involvement **System usability and performance** **User acceptance and IS ownership**
3	**User acceptance and IS ownership**	**Interaction with rest of IT infrastructure**	**Interaction with rest of IT infrastructure**
4	User participation and involvement Interaction with rest of IT infrastructure	Improvements in employee productivity	Improvements in employee productivity Improvements in business performance
5	Information quality	Satisfying user expectations System quality	Satisfying user expectations
6	System quality Use	User participation and involvement	Meeting budgeted criteria
7	Improving business performance	System usability and performance	
8	Satisfying user expectations	Meeting budgeted criteria	
9	Meeting budgeted criteria	User acceptance and IS ownership	
10	Improvements in employee productivity	Improving business performance	

When examining items ranked in the top three levels, it can be observed that meeting user requirements was the only variable for all three case studies and it was in first position. Those ranked twice in the top three rankings in two case studies were system usability and performance (ranked second, twice), information quality and use (both ranked first and second), user acceptance and IS ownership (ranked second and third), interactions with the rest of IT infrastructure (ranked third, twice).

Meeting user requirements has long been considered as a significant indicator of IS success (e.g. Wateridge, 1998) and this study again provides evidence for this. Comments were along the line of "a system that doesn't meet user requirements won't be used by users", expressed in Case

Study 3 by Participant 3 (CS3 – P3). Statements such as "if you don't meet user requirements they won't be happy and ultimately won't use the system" (CS1 – P1) and "no matter how wonderful it is if people don't use it it will fail" (CS1 – P1) exemplified general views. Participants also claimed that "in the end we are trying to provide a service to those people and if we don't keep them happy we haven't done the job" (CS2 – P2). "If you don't meet the requirements what is the purpose of the project?" (CS2 – P1) one participant asked. The participant further expanded on the response by highlighting that meeting user requirements was essentially achieving the purpose of the project. "User requirements represent the business itself. If you are not meeting that you are not achieving the goal" (CS3 – P1).

Consistency in ranking was found between the views held by Case Study 1 and Case Study 3 participants in terms of the second most critical IS success variable, that of *system usability and performance*. As indicated by Davis (1989) system usability and performance are a large part of "the degree to which a person believes that using a particular system would enhance his or her job performance" (p.320). It was stated that "A system has to be fit for a purpose at the level of usability and quality, which is required to achieve the objectives." (CS1 – P2) Participants explained that unless usability and performance benchmarks are met users simply won't use the IS. As stated by CS3 – P6: "Once performance is not good enough, users start being not happy and kick up the sting because of it."

As seen in Table 3, case Study 3 participants placed *use* as one of the most critical IS success variables together with meeting user requirements. The comment below made by a participant summarises the general perceptions towards the 'use' IS success variable. CS3 – P4: "We use it constantly and it is an indication of success." CS3 – P5: "Otherwise it is just a waste of time and money and effort." Expanding on the comment, the participant associated use of an IS with *information quality,* which was another IS success variable receiving high importance ratings by participants. Case Study 3 participants placed information quality in the same category as meeting user requirements and use of the IS for achieving success while participants in Case Study 2 perceived information quality as the second most critical IS success variable. As one participant explained, "members of Parliament are expected to get up and be 100% accurate on what they are talking about. The information has to be 100% accurate" (CS2 – P4).

For *user acceptance and ownership* participants claimed that "users have to accept it and if they don't you go to the same old story. They won't use it and they'll find ways of sabotaging it or making sure that the thing is not successful" (CS1 –P1). As such, participants promoted user acceptance and IS ownership as mechanisms for achieving voluntary IS use by end-uses. For *interaction with rest of IT infrastructure,* participants argued that within the West Australian government sector most systems accept and process data from other agencies and as such all systems needed to integrate.

Public Sector Characteristics

In terms of the difference between the public and the private sector within an IS context the majority of participants (16/21) claimed that the two sectors are uniquely identifiable. The key differences were accountability, expenditure control and taking a long-term perspective. Theses are reflected in the comments made by participants, examples of which are reproduced below.

Accountability

- "There is not much difference except the government uses taxpayers money and is more accountable" (CS3 – P2)

- "The government sector is more accountable for everything including the process of evaluation, what is being purchased and budgets are not as flexible. Selection process of employees and getting skilled people is also different." (CS1 – P4)

Expenditure control

- "Working environments are different, there tends to be greater scrutiny on public sector organisations in terms of expenditure. Investors certainly do scrutinise private sector expenditure but not to the same extent. If you have a really big public sector project that fails then it is all over newspapers." (CS1 – P1)
- "Money and time are more important in the private sector. The government wants things to be on time and budget but can always find little bit of extra money." (CS3 – P5)
- "The government has access to more money. If it is a critical project like this one the government will provide lots of money for it. In smaller private sector organisations there is a greater emphasis on costs, even with bigger organisations although they can afford to go for the latest." (CS3 – P6)

Long-tem perspective

- "The need for good, reliable and comprehensive information and not, I guess, so much cost driven when compared to the private sector where the IS might be designed to reduce and cut costs. Plus lots of agencies are providing services that private sector wouldn't provide. Services that are based on information needs." (CS1 – P8)
- "From a general perspective, my general understanding would be that they [private sector] would be more focused on productivity improvements and financial benefits whereas the public sector is more focused on customer service and quality of the system that they put so that they are able to last for a long time." (CS3 – P1)
- "With the private sector tenders are put out. Major emphasis is costing and time where cost and time within the government are not as emphasised." (CS2 – P2)

Although the majority of participants claimed that the differences between the public and the private sectors impact on the success of an IS project, five participants (5 out of 21) disagreed. According to these participants, the criteria on whether a project is successful or not is not related to whether the project is being undertaken within the public or the private sector. Participants claimed that the underlining reasons for success or failure would be the same regardless of whether the IS project is completed within the public or the private sector. Four out of six participants were previously employed within the private sector and drew upon their experiences while commenting on this item. Participants stated the following:

- "I don't think that there is a difference because any IS project is governed by the same needs, dollars and usability." (CS2 – P4)
- "It shouldn't differ at all. The government should be just as efficient as the private sector." (CS2 – P5)
- "I don't believe there is any, not even in the accountability aspect." (CS2 – P6).

Emerging Model

From the study's findings it is possible to provide a preliminary model that aligns IS success variables with public sector characteristics as shown in Figure 1. The design of the model reflects the views expressed by participants (see above discussion) of each of the most highly ranked variables. The design of the model is therefore based on the following key arguments. It is argued that 'meeting user requirements', the highest ranked variable, reflects the user's expectation for 'system usability and performance' (e.g. ease of use) and 'information quality' (e.g. accuracy). In other words, without having access to a suitable system which provides the appropriate information, the user's needs are not met. These variables, together with 'user acceptance and IS ownership' (e.g. using systems without resistance) determine 'use'.

Use in turn enables public sector employees to be 'accountable' (e.g. to their ministers) and to exercise 'expenditure control' (e.g. over the budget). The emergence of the variable 'interaction with the IT infrastructure' of other government departments not only improves use (e.g. by providing the public with a whole of government service approach) but also 'meets long term needs'. As mentioned in an earlier section, the study by Adelakun and Jennex (2002) of IT executives, CIO's and IS managers revealed a similar finding, namely that success of an IS project is determined in a large part of how well the IS interacts within the organisational infrastructure.

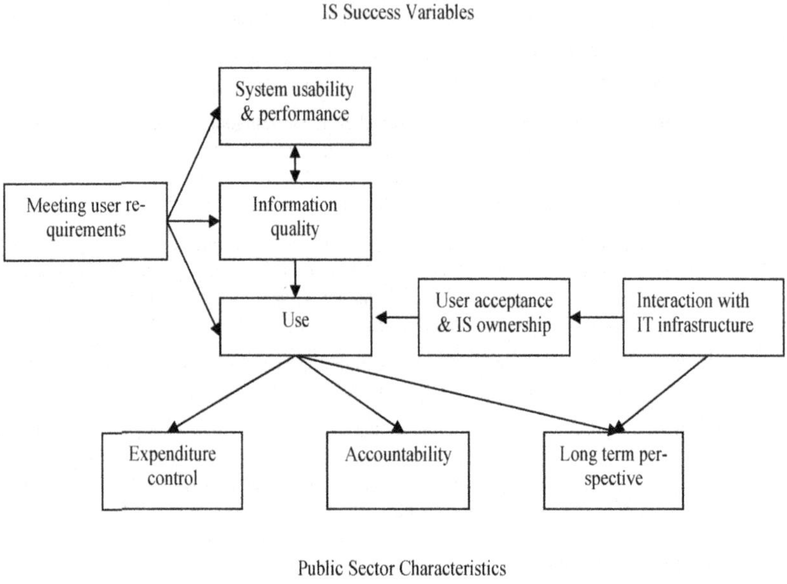

Figure 1: Aligning WA Public Sector IS Success Variables and Characteristics

Conclusion

IS success is a topic widely researched as evident from the IS success models that have emerged over recent years and the well known perspectives that various stakeholders have on what they regard as successful IS. However, it has been recognized that research is under represented in the public services sector despite the importance of this sector. The sector is a major investor in IS and relies heavily on IS to stay efficient and effective. This study provides one of few attempts that have been made to explore the characteristics of the sector and to establish associated IS success factors.

When the study asked participants to identify IS success factors, a full range of variables were identified but after ranking the responses and taking into account the highest ranked ones the following emerged: meeting user requirements, system usability and performance, information quality and use, user acceptance and IS ownership, and interactions with the rest of IT infrastructure. These findings differ from those shown in the IS success models reviewed earlier. Compared to that of DeLone and McLean (1992, 2003) and its respecified version (Seddon, 1997), the variables found to be used in assessing success by earlier IS were most prominent. In other words, they emphasised perspectives of the user, use and information quality. They did not emphasise the overall effect on the organization, except for interaction with the organisation's IT infrastructure. This could be a key difference between the two sectors, i.e. the need for the private sector to remain viable while such a concern is not highly visible in the public sector. It is recommended that further research be carried out in this respect.

In this study, the majority of participants from the Western Australian government agencies held the view that the public sector differs from the private sector. In particular they identified three key areas, namely accountability, expenditure control and taking a long term perspective that provides the differentiation. The proposed model shown in Figure 1 is an early attempt to link IS success variables with public sector characteristics. It needs, however, to be remembered that the model took into account only the three highest ranked IS variables which is a subjective decision. Using different approaches to interpreting the findings (e.g. taking further variables into account) will lead to different IS success models. The model, unlike the DeLone and McLean style models, takes into account organisational characteristics. In this way the approach resonates with those of Ballantine et al. (1998) and Hwang et al. (2000) who recognised environmental factors, and also with Seddon (1997) who recognized benefits to society.

The study took place in Western Australia and hence the findings and conclusions cannot be generalised across the entire publics sector. They represent the opinions of those stakeholders that participated in the study and relate to the particular types of IS on which they expressed their opinions. The findings, therefore, may be situational specific (see Flowers, 1996) and as such, the study should be regarded as an exploratory one but one which hopefully encourages other researchers to consider the public services sector in their endeavours.

References

Adelakun, O. & Jennex, M. E. (2002). Stakeholder process approach to information systems evaluation. *Eighth America's Conference on Information Systems*, Dallas.

Al-Wohaibi, M., Masoud, F.A., & Edwards, H.M. (2002). Fundamental risk factors in deploying IT/IS Projects in Omani government organisations. *Journal of Global Information Management, 10*(4), 1 – 22.

Australian Bureau of Statistics (1998). *Australian social trends 1998.* Retrieved 30 June 2004 from http://www.abs.gov.au

Ballantine, J., Bonner, M., & Levy, M. (1998). Developing a 3-D model of information systems success. In E. J. Garrity & G. L Sanders (Eds.). *Information Systems Success Measurement.* Hershey, PA: Idea Group Publishing.

Barki, H. & Hartwick, J. (1989). Rethinking the concept of user involvement. *MIS Quarterly, 13*(1), 53–63.

Belassi, W., & Tukel, O. (1996). A new framework for determining critical success/ failure factors in projects. *Project Management, 14*(3), 141-151.

Bloom, N. L. (1996). Select the right IS project manager for success. *Personnel Journal, 75*(1).

Briner, W., Hastings, C., & Geddes, M. (1996). *Project leadership* (2nd ed.). Guildford: Biddles Ltd.

Campbell, W. (2003). How to survive in the public sector. *CIO, 16*(18), 1.

Crawford, P. (1996). *The serious business of governing.* RIPAA(NSW). Sydney: Hale and Iremonger.

Davis, F. D. (1989). Perceived usefulness, perceived ease of use, and user acceptance of information technology. *MIS Quarterly, 13*(3), 319-340.

DeLone, W. H. & McLean, E. R. (1992). Information systems success: The quest for the dependent variable. *Information Systems Research, 3*(1), 60-95.

DeLone, W. H. & McLean, E. R. (2003). The DeLone and McLean model of information systems success: A ten-year update. *Journal of Management Information Systems, 19*(4), 9 – 30.

DeLooff, L. A. (1996). *IS outsourcing by public sector organisation.* International Federation for Information Processing.

Dowse, A. (2003). The benefits, limitations and governance implications of federated public sector systems. *14th Australasian Conference on Information Systems*, Perth.

Fisher, J. (2001). User satisfaction and system success: Considering the development team. *Australian Journal of Information Systems, 9*(1), 21 – 29.

Flowers, S. (1996). *Software failure: management failure.* West Sussex, UK: John Wiley & Sons.

Garson, G. D. (1999). *Handbook of public information systems.* Retrieved 10 April 2005 from http://hcl.chass.ncsu.edu/garson/dekker.htm

Ginzberg, M. J. (1981). Early diagnosis of MIS implementation failure: Promising results and unanswered questions. *Management Science, 27*(4), 459-478.

Holloway, I. (1997). *Basic concepts for qualitative research.* Oxford: Blackwall Science.

Hwang, H. I. & Thorn, R. G. (1999). The effect of user engagement on system success: A meta-analytical integration of research findings. *Information & Management, 35*(4), 229 – 236.

Hwang, M. I., Windsor, J. C., & Pryor, A. (2000). Building a knowledge base for MIS research: A meta-analysis of a systems success model. *Information Resources Management Journal, 13* (2), 26 – 32.

Ives, B., Hamilton, S., & Davis, G. B. (1980). A framework for research in computer-based management information systems. *Management Science, 26*(9), 910 – 934.

Kappleman, L. & McLean, E. (1991). The respective roles of user participation and user involvement in the information system implementation success. *ICIS Conference Proceedings*, New York.

Marriott, I. (2002). *Public sector: The search for quality and value for money.* Gartner COM-17-5685.

Myers, M. D. (1997). Qualitative research in information systems. *MIS Quarterly, 21*(2), 241-242.

Saleem, N. (1996). An empirical test of the contingency approach to user participation in information systems development. *Journal of Management Information Systems, 13*(1), 145 – 166.

Seddon, P. B. (1997). A respecification and extension of the DeLone and McLean model of IS success. *Information Systems Research, 8*(3), 240- 253.

Seddon, P. B. & Kiew, M. Y. (1996). A partial test and development of DeLone and McLean's model of IS success. *Australian Journal of Information Systems, 4*(1), 90-109.

Seneviratne, S. J. (1999). *Is technological progress social progress?* University of Southern California, Los Angeles.

Shenhar, A. J., Levy, O., & Dvir, D. (1997). Mapping the dimensions of project success. *Project Management Journal, 28*(2), 5 – 13.

Staples, D. S., Wong, I., & Seddon, P. B. (2002). Having expectations of information systems benefits that match received benefits: Does it really matter? *Information & Management, 40*,115-131.

Szajna, B. & Scamell, R. W. (1993). The effects of information system user expectations on their performance and perceptions. *MIS Quarterly, 17*(4), 493 – 514.

Travers, M. (2001). *Qualitative research through case studies.* California: Sage Publications.

Walker, R. (1985). *Applied qualitative research.* England: Aldershot.

Wateridge, J. (1998). How can IS/IT projects be measured for success? *International Journal of Project Management, 16*(1), 59 – 63.

White, D. & Fortune, J. (2002). Current practice in project management - An empirical study. *International Journal of Project Management*, January *20*(1), 1-11.

Williams, A. H. (1998). *The future of public sector management – The public interest.* Retrieved 2 March 2005 from http://www.apsc.gov.au/media/williams200898.htm

Yin, R. K. (1994). *Case study research: design and methods.* Thousand Oaks, CA: Sage.

Yin, R. K. (2003). *Applications of case study research.* Thousand Oaks, CA: Sage.

Yin, K. R. (2003). *Case study research design and methods.* Thousand Oaks, CA: Sage.

Biographies

Ivana Elpez is currently working as a Co-ordinator of Corporate Systems within the Western Australian public sector. Prior to this role she has worked as a Programmer Analyst and a Business Systems Analyst. Ivana has completed a First Class Honours degree in Management Information Systems at Edith Cowan University.

Dr Dieter Fink is an Associate Professor and co-ordinator for the DBA in Information Systems in the School of Management Information Systems at Edith Cowan University in Perth, Western Australia. Prior to joining academe he worked as a Systems Engineer for IBM and as Manager, IS Consulting for Arthur Young (now Ernst & Young). He has been a visiting academic at a number of universities: Australian National University, University of Cape Town, Canterbury University, and Free University of Berlin. His primary interest is in IT Governance which includes establishing and measuring the value of IT investments, IT adoption, and minimising the risk of e-commerce and e-business. Further details about him are provided at http://myprofile.cos.com/fink22

The page left blank intentionally.

Getting Practical with Learning Styles in "Live" and Computer-based Training Settings

Peter Fenrich
British Columbia Institute of Technology, Burnaby, Canada

peter_fenrich@bcit.ca

Abstract

Learning styles are relatively-stable characteristic behaviors that indicate how students prefer to learn. To maximize student learning, it is important for instructors to address learning styles when designing their lessons. What does the research say about learning styles? What should instructors do to factor learning styles into traditional lessons? What should be done differently with respect to learning styles when designing computer-based training software? This summary paper answers these questions. In this presentation, through discussion and demonstration, participants will be given practical suggestions for addressing learning styles in both traditionally-delivered lessons and computer-based training applications.

Keywords: learning styles, cognitive styles, learning preferences, computer-based training, instructional design

Introduction

This summary paper describes what the research says about learning styles, suggests how instructors can factor learning styles into their traditional lessons, and presents what should be done with respect to learning styles in computer-based training applications.

Learning styles, also known as cognitive styles or learning preferences, are characteristic behaviors that indicate how students prefer to learn. Learning styles tend to be relatively stable over time, in other words are predictable, but are not static in that there can be some variation from day-to-day, week-to-week, and as one ages (Ayersman, 1993; Davidson & Savenye, 1992; Guild & Garger, 1985; Price, 2004). To maximize student learning, it is important for instructors (used as a general term that includes teachers, instructors, professors, lecturers...) to address the variety of learning styles when designing and delivering their lessons.

Some of the numerous learning style categorizations and preferences include:

- concrete thinkers who prefer details, specifics, structure, and organization versus abstract thinkers who like to think about things, analyze, and visualize (Butler, 1986; McCarthy, 1987)
- active learners who like to try things first versus reflective learners who prefer to first watch and reflect on things (McCarthy, 1987)
- holists who, for example, like to understand the overall idea first and then learn details versus serialists who like to work step-by-step to gradually learn the whole idea (Ellis, Ford & Woods, 1993; Geisert & Dunn, 1991)

- visually-based versus text-based versus audio-based activities (Ayersman, 1993; Enochs, Handley & Wollenberg, 1986; Suits & Lagowski, 1994)
  - Simply put, individuals have different media preferences. Note that some references refer to these as right-brained versus left-brained activities. However, the original research was flawed. In reality, both halves of the brain are involved in processing both visual and text-based material. Ayersman (1993) stated, "Both sides of the brain are necessary to reach higher-ability levels in certain skill areas such as language."
- sociological factors such as introversion, extroversion, and working alone, in pairs, in groups, or with or without an authoritative or collegial adult (Enochs, Handley & Wollenberg, 1986; Hoffman & Waters, 1982)
- environmental considerations (Ayersman, 1993; Billings & Cobb, 1992; Dunn & Bruno, 1985; Geisert & Dunn, 1991; Ross, Drysdale & Schulz, 2001)
  - There are preferences for differing amounts of light and sound in the room.
  - Learning position preferences can vary greatly. Choices include learning in a hard chair, in a soft chair, on a pillow, on a carpet, and lying on one's back.
  - Some learners perform better when the room temperature is cold or cool while others like it warm.
  - There can be differences in performance simply from food or drink being present or not.
  - Mobility can be important for learners who like to get up and move around periodically.
  - The time of day can have an impact. As stated by Dunn and Bruno (1985), "No matter when a teacher is teaching, it is the wrong time of day for at least one-third of that class."

Research has not concluded that there is only one way to categorize students with respect to learning styles. In other words, research has supported many learning style classification systems.

Learning Style Research

For learning styles in general, research has shown that:

- Each learning style is equal in terms of overall achievement (Ayersman, 1993; Butler, 1988; Davidson & Savenye, 1992; Guild & Garger, 1985). However, depending on the material taught and how it is taught, one specific learning style can be better than another (Crosby & Iding, 1997; Davidson & Savenye, 1992).
- Matching learning style with the instructional design can lead to increased achievement and better attitudes (Ayersman, 1993; Carlson, 1991; Dunn & Bruno, 1985; Geisert & Dunn, 1991; Miller, 2005; Price, 2004; Ross & Shultz, 1999; Shivers, Nowlin & Lanouette, 2002; Smith & Renzulli, 1984; Suits & Lagowski, 1994; Takacs, Reed, Wells & Dombrowski, 1999; Yung-Bin, 1992).
  - For example, learners who prefer a structured approach to learning and to use their senses, such as sight and sound, tend to learn effectively with those types of instructional strategies. Students who prefer to learn by experimenting or by using intuition, common sense, or imagination should be taught with lessons and activities that encourage those preferences.
  - Note that effective learning can still occur when the student's preferred learning style does not match the instructional design. Most students have learned how to learn from a variety of instructional approaches. This does not imply that their learning is as effective as possible.
  - There is some value in occasionally mismatching learning style with instructional design. This can help students learn to adapt to other instructional styles. However, mismatching can be harmful to both teachers and students if done over extended periods of time (Smith & Renzulli, 1984).

- Conversely, some studies have shown no differences in test scores when matching learning styles with instructional strategies (Billings & Cobb, 1992; Carlson, 1991; Davidson-Shivers, Nowlin & Lanouette, 2002; Ellis, Ford & Woods, 1993; Miller, 2005; Steele, Palensky, Lynch, Lacy & Duffy 2002; Suits & Lagowski, 1994). There are numerous explanations for this. For example, it may be that most students adapt to the nature, context, and difficulty of the task and can learn effectively from a variety of methods (Ayersman, 1993; Butler, 1986; Ross, Drysdale & Schulz, 2001; Smith, 2004; Takacs, Reed, Wells & Dombrowski, 1999). Other factors could depend on how well the learning style assessment tool matches the context in which it is used and how accurately students assess themselves (Miller, 2005; Price, 2004).
- Within each learning style categorization and preference, students generally fall somewhere along the continuum between two opposite extremes. Few students are found at the extremes (McCarthy, 1987).
- Learning style is only one of the variables affecting learner achievement. Other factors, such as the quality and content of a course can be more important (Engleberg, Schwenk & Gruppen, 2001).

With respect to computer-based training (CBT) applications, students who are more likely to have problems are those who cannot easily concentrate, cannot stay with a task until it is completed, do not pay attention to details, have poor memories for facts, and have poor reading skills (Dunn & Bruno, 1985; Enochs, Handley & Wollenberg, 1986; Hoffman & Waters, 1982; Ross & Shultz, 1999). However, these students would likely have problems with other types of instructional presentations. It can be argued that many of these students would benefit most from well-designed CBT lessons (Ayersman, 1993; Fitzgerald, 1990). For example, the ability of students to proceed at their own pace and to review as much and as often as they wish in CBT lessons can help students who have trouble concentrating or not staying with tasks until completion. CBT lessons with a variety of media can help students remember details and facts as well as learners with poor reading abilities.

Getting Practical with Learning Styles

From a practical perspective, instructors will not be able to individually address all of the learning style categorizations in each lesson they teach. The issue is what should be done for students who have some difficulties with an instructional strategy. If students are not learning effectively in the way they are taught, they should be taught in the way they learn best. The instructional design must revolve around how the students learn rather than the instructor's preferred teaching approach. There are a number of strategies that instructors can use to teach students in the way they learn best:

- Conduct a learner analysis, through questions and observations, to determine the student's learning styles, motivational factors, and interests (Fenrich, 2005). From a practical perspective, if the instructor's time is limited, the instructor should assume that there is significant variation among the students and that the instructor's teaching (and learning) style preferences will not be the same as all of the students.
- Include a variety of instructional activities (Ayersman, 1993; Takacs, Reed, Wells & Dombrowski, 1999) so that each student is likely to have a preferred activity some of the time. As Magoulas, Papanikolaou, and Grigoriadou (2003) said, "No single instructional strategy is best for all students."
  - For example, lessons throughout a course or in a CBT application could include theoretical approaches, drill and practice, simulations... Instructors can get ideas by watching others teach. Creators of CBT materials should view lessons created by others. This will likely give both "good" and "bad" ideas.

- The planned instructional activities must include interactivity (Ghaoui & Janvier, 2004; Takacs, Reed, Wells & Dombrowski, 1999), defined as active learner participation in the learning process. This is essential for effective learning. Learners retain more if they see, hear, and do something than if they just see and hear something than if they just see or just hear something. "Live" lessons and CBT applications have the potential of enabling learners to "see, hear, and do". In CBT applications, interactivity can take the form of learners answering questions that require thinking, students being actively involved with a simulation or an educational game, providing feedback, utilizing the learner's existing knowledge and experience, students making comments and annotations, learners modifying the computer program, and/or students discussing the content in pairs or groups of three (Fenrich, 2005).
- Different question types and questioning techniques help provide variation.
- Note that serialists tend to do much better than holists in typical CBT programs (Geisert & Dunn, 1991). So, also include activities that holists prefer. For example, allow students to see the whole idea at the beginning of the lesson. This can be done in a detailed overview. Similarly, learners who prefer to learn material sequentially tend to learn better from typical CBT programs than learners who prefer thinking in abstract ways (Ross, Drysdale & Schulz, 2001; Ross & Shultz, 1999). Abstract thinkers can be supported through variety, overviews, learner control of pace and sequence, motivating them, meaningful and relevant content, and enabling them to work with others.

• Use different instructional strategies to teach the varied learning outcomes of the different learning domains. The learning domains are verbal information where students learn skills such as stating, listing, describing, and naming, intellectual skills including discriminating, identifying, classifying, demonstrating, generating, originating, and creating, psychomotor skills entailing tasks such as making, drawing, adjusting, and assembling, and attitudes including learners making choices (Dick & Carey, 1990).

When teaching verbal information:
- Organize the material into small easily retrievable chunks.
- Link new information to knowledge the learner already possesses. For example, use statements such as "Remember how" or "This is like..." Linking information helps the learner to store and recall the material.
- Use memory devices like forming images or using mnemonics for new information. For example, the musical notes of the treble clef staff lines can be remembered with the mnemonic Every Good Boy Deserves Fudge.
- Use meaningful contexts and relevant cues. For example, relating an example to a sports car can be relevant for some learners.
- Have the learners generate examples in their minds, "do" something, such as create a song or game, with the information, or apply the knowledge to the real world. If the student only memorizes facts then the learning will only have minimal value.
- Avoid rote repetition as a memorization aid. Rote repetition has minimal effectiveness over time.
- Provide visuals to increase learning and recall.

(Fenrich, 2005)

When teaching intellectual skills:
- Link new knowledge to previously learned knowledge. This can be explicitly done (e.g., the bones in your feet are comparable to the bones you have learned about in your hands) or implicitly done (e.g., compare the bones in your feet to other bone structures you have learned about).
- Use memory devices like forming images or mnemonics for new information. For example, help students remember rules by using rhymes such as "i before e except after c".

Remember that rules often have exceptions. Learners need to be told about the exceptions.
- Use examples and non-examples that are familiar to the student. For example, when classifying metals, iron and copper are examples while glass and plastic are non-examples.
- Use discovery-learning techniques. For example, let students see the consequences of decisions they make. This can be done very effectively in CBT applications.
- Use analogies that the learners know. However, be careful that learners do not overgeneralize or create misconceptions.
- Provide for practice and immediate feedback.

(Fenrich, 2005)

When teaching psychomotor skills:
- Provide directions for completing all of the steps.
- Provide repeated practice and feedback for individual steps, then groups of steps, and then the entire sequence.
- Remember that, in general, practice should become less dependent on written or verbal directions.
- Consider visuals to enhance learning.
- Consider job aids, such as a list of steps, to reduce memory requirements. This is especially important if there are many procedures or if the procedures are infrequently used.
- After a certain point, allow learners to interact with real objects or do the real thing. How much can students learn about skydiving while standing on the ground?
- Note that some psychomotor skills involve other learning domain classifications. For example, when learning how to drive a standard transmission car, many of the skills are psychomotor. However, deciding when to shift gears is an intellectual skill. Also, note that the required proficiency level can affect the instructional strategy. There is a significant difference between imitating a skill and automatically doing a skill.

(Fenrich, 2005)

When teaching attitudes:
- Try to show a human model. The students should easily relate to the model. For example, it may be better if the model is of the same race and socio-economic class. For practical reasons, instructors can use video clips to show human models.
- Show realistic consequences, such as through a simulation, to appropriate and inappropriate choices.
- Instructors can use role-playing to reinforce the attitudes taught.
- Remember that attitudes taught "live" or through computer technology are not guaranteed to transfer to the real world. If appropriate and possible, consider also arranging for practice opportunities to make the choice in real life.
- Note that it can be difficult to test whether the attitudes taught have transferred to real situations. For example, learners may not behave as they naturally would if they know that they are being observed. If learners have not voluntarily permitted observations to be made then the instructor must determine whether it is ethical to make the observations.

(Fenrich, 2005)

- Use instructional strategies, such as simulations and discovery-learning techniques, that go beyond basic teaching methods, as is appropriate. A pitfall of some instructors is that they only teach in the way they were taught. As Emile Chartier said, "Nothing is more dangerous than an idea, when it is the only one you have."
- Include a variety of media, as is appropriate for learning, so that all students can learn from media they prefer.

  - For example, some students prefer visuals while others prefer to read text. If instructors include both, they are likely to reach more students (Enochs, Handley & Wollenberg, 1986). This is particularly easy to do with CBT applications and computer-managed presentations (e.g., as can be done with PowerPoint®).
  - Instructors can reach most learners by providing both visual and text-based content.
  - Learning through more than one medium involves more of the brain in learning. However, if too much mental processing is required, learning can be compromised (Muthukumar, 2005). One way to limit the mental processing requirements is to ensure the learners only focus on one medium at a time.
- Let students choose how to present their knowledge, at least some of the time.
  - Knowledge can be demonstrated in group discussions, debates, speeches, computer presentations, written assignments... Activities like these can be combined with CBT materials.
- Let learners have some input in how they would like to be taught (Smith & Renzulli, 1984).
  - For example, let students choose whether to receive a generalization and then examples or vice versa, whether to receive a different version of the content or supplementary information, how much practice they should get, and even the material's level of difficulty. Assuming that students can make good decisions about these choices, a practical problem remains of whether instructors would be able to design and develop these alternatives. Since it could be hard to justify the costs for creating these alternatives, particularly for CBT applications, instructors should simply provide variation for different learning outcomes.
  - Note that students will not necessarily make the best choices with respect to their learning style (Davidson & Savenye, 1992). Students may choose to do what they think is easy or activities with which they are already familiar.
  - Instructors must be willing to incorporate strategies in which they have less comfort, if learners can influence how they are taught.
  - Instructors must remember to utilize their natural teaching strengths, while accommodating learners.
- Create learning materials that help ensure success.
  - Success may help make mismatches in teaching style and learning style less important.
  - Ensure success through organizing the material into small incremental steps and by providing numerous practice opportunities with immediate and detailed feedback (Fenrich, 2005).
  - With CBT applications, designers can help ensure success by allowing students to have control over the instruction's pace and sequence (Fitzgerald, 1990).
- Encourage students to cooperatively work in pairs while learning.
  - Working in pairs can help increase performance (Cavalier & Klein, 1998; Enochs, Handley & Wollenberg, 1986; Fitzgerald, 1990; Hoffman & Waters, 1982; Hooper, Temiyakarn & Williams, 1993) since students who work in pairs or groups tend to discuss and thus think about the material and questions more than when they are working alone.
  - With "live" teaching and particularly with CBT programs, working in pairs can help those who do not like to work alone (extroverts).
- Allow for flexibility.
  - Let students learn where they prefer (in a hard chair, on a lounge, on the floor, in a noisy area, in a quiet area, where it is bright, where the light is low, in warm areas, in cool areas …). For CBT applications, a laptop can provide this flexibility.
  - For CBT applications, make the program available so that students can work when they prefer. This also lets them take breaks when they need.

- For CBT applications, include a workbook with summaries of the multimedia material so that students do not have to take detailed notes, which can become tedious (Fenrich, 2005). This particularly affects students who are inclined to copy everything presented by the computer.

Instructors can also help students by having them assess their learning styles and then teaching them strategies to accommodate their individual learning styles (Ross, Drysdale & Schulz, 2001). However, it is not essential that instructors categorize and label a student into a particular learning style, especially since many individuals incorrectly identify elements of their learning style (Geisert & Dunn, 1991). Labeling students with a learning style could have negative consequences if the information is incorrect, not used properly, or abused (Butler, 1986).

Discussion

Given, it is important for instructors to address learning styles when designing their lessons and instructors will not have the time or receive funding to develop each lesson specifically for each learning style, instructors must deal with learning styles in practical ways. To address learning styles when creating lessons for both "live" and CBT applications, instructors should:

- Conduct a learner analysis to determine the students' learning styles, motivational factors, and interests.
- Include a variety of instructional activities so that each student experiences at least one preferred activity.
- Teach different earning outcomes with different instructional strategies.
- Use instructional strategies that go beyond basic teaching methods.
- Include a variety of media so that all students can learn from media they prefer.
- Let students choose how to present their knowledge.
- Let learners have some input in how they would like to be taught.
- Create learning materials that help ensure success.
- Encourage students to work in pairs.

Specifically for CBT applications:

- Include activities that holists prefer such as allowing students to see the whole idea at the beginning of the lesson.
- Support abstract thinkers and others through variety, overviews, learner control of pace and sequence, motivating them, meaningful and relevant content, and enabling them to work with others.
- Interactivity can take the form of learners answering questions that require thinking, students being actively involved with a simulation or an educational game, providing feedback, utilizing the learner's existing knowledge and experience, students making comments and annotations, learners modifying the computer program, and/or students discussing the content in pairs or groups of three.
- Use discovery-learning techniques.
- Include a variety of media (video, audio, still images, and text).
- Allow for flexibility.
- Let students use a laptop so that they can learn where they prefer.
- Include a workbook with summaries of the material.

Instructors should remember that:

- In general, each learning style is equal in terms of achievement.
- Matching learning style with the instructional design can lead to increased achievement and better attitudes.
- Effective learning can still occur when the student's preferred learning style does not match the instructional design.

- Within each learning style categorization and preference, most students generally fall somewhere along the continuum between two opposite extremes.
- Students can benefit from assessing their learning styles if they are then taught strategies to accommodate their individual learning styles.
- No one single teaching method or medium is perfect for all learners.

Well-designed CBT applications have the potential to help students who cannot easily concentrate, cannot stay with a task until it is completed, do not pay attention to details, have poor memories for facts, and have poor reading skills.

References

Ayersman, D. (1993). An overview of the research on learning styles and hypermedia environments. Paper presented at the 1993 *Annual Convention of the Eastern Educational Research Association*, Clearwater Beach, Florida.

Billings, D., & Cobb, K. (1992). Effects of learning style preferences, attitude and GPA on learner achievement using computer assisted interactive videodisc instruction. *Journal of Computer-Based Instruction, 19* (1), 12-16.

Butler, K. (1986). *Learning and teaching style: In theory and practice.* Columbia, CT: The Learner's Dimension.

Butler, K. (1988). *It's all in your mind: A student's guide to learning style.* Columbia, CT: The Learner's Dimension.

Carlson, H. (1991). Learning style and program design in interactive multimedia. *Educational Technology Research and Development, 39* (3), 41-48.

Cavalier, J., & Klein, J. (1998). Effects of cooperative versus individual learning and orienting activities during computer-based instruction. *Educational Technology Research and Development, 46*(1), 5-17.

Crosby, M., & Iding, M. (1997). The influence of cognitive styles on the effectiveness of a multimedia tutor. *Computer Assisted Language Learning, 10* (4), 375-386.

Davidson, G., & Savenye, W. (1992, Spring). How do learning styles relate to performance in a computer applications course? *Journal of Research on Computing in Education, 24* (3), 348-357.

Davidson-Shivers, G., Nowlin, B., & Lanouette, M. (2002, March). Do multimedia lesson structure and learning styles influence undergraduate writing performance? *College Student Journal, 36* (1), 20-31.

Dick, W., & Carey, L. (1990). *The systematic design of instruction* (3rd ed.). Glenville, IL: Harper Collins Publishers.

Dunn, R., & Bruno, A. (1985, September). What does the research on learning styles have to do with Mario? *The Clearing House, 59* (1), 9-12.

Ellis, D., Ford, N., & Wood, F. (1993, February). Hypertext and learning styles. *The Electronic Library, 11* (1), 13-18.

Engleberg, N., Schwenk, T., & Gruppen, L. (2001). Learning styles and perceptions of the value of various learning modalities before and after a 2nd-year course in microbiology and infectious diseases. *Teaching and Learning in Medicine, 13* (4), 253-257.

Enochs, J., Handley, J., & Wollenberg, J. (1986). Relating learning style, reading vocabulary, reading comprehension, and aptitude for learning to achievement in the self-paced and computer-assisted instructional modes. *Journal of Experimental Education, 54*, 135-139.

Fenrich, P. (2005). *Creating Instructional Multimedia Solutions: Practical Guidelines for the Real World.* Santa Rosa, CA: Informing Science Press.

Fitzgerald, G. (1990, November). *Using the computer with students with emotional and behavioral disorders. Tech use guide: Using computer technology*. Reston, VA: The Council for Exceptional Children.

Geisert, G., & Dunn, R. (1991, March/April). Effective use of computers: Assignments based on individual learning styles. *The Clearing House, 64* (4), 219-224.

Ghaoui, C., & Janvier, W. (2004). Interactive E-Learning. *Journal of Distance Education Technologies, 2* (3), 26-35.

Guild, P., & Garger, S. (1985). *Marching to different drummers*. Alexandria, VA: Association for Supervision and Curriculum Development.

Hoffman, J., & Waters, K. (1982, March). Some effects of student personality on success with computer-assisted instruction. *Educational Technology, 22* (3), 8-14.

Hooper, S., Temiyakarn, C., & Williams, M. (1993). The effects of cooperative learning and learner control on high- and average-ability students. *Educational Technology Research and Development, 41* (4), 5-18.

Magoulas, G., Papanikolaou, K., & Grigoriadou, M. (2003). Adaptive web-based learning: accommodating individual differences through system's adaptation. *British Journal of Educational Technology, 34* (4), 511-527.

McCarthy, B. (1987). *The 4MAT system: Teaching to learning styles with right/left mode techniques*. Barrington, IL: Excel, Inc.

Miller, L. (2005). Using learning styles to evaluate computer-based instruction. *Computers in Human Behavior, 21*, 287-306.

Muthukumar, S. (2005, March). Creating interactive multimedia-based educational courseware: Cognition in learning. *Cognition, Technology & Work, 7* (1), 46-50.

Price, L. (2004, October). Individual differences in learning: Cognitive control, cognitive style, and learning style. *Educational Psychology, 24* (5), 681-698.

Ross, J., Drysdale, M., & Schulz, R. (2001, Summer). Cognitive learning styles and academic performance in two postsecondary computer application courses. *Journal of Research on Computing in Education, 33* (4), 400-412.

Ross, J., & Schulz, R. (1999). Can computer-aided instruction accommodate all learners equally? British *Journal of Educational Technology, 30* (1), 5-24.

Smith, L., & Renzulli, J. (1984, Winter). Learning style preferences: A practical approach for classroom teachers. *Theory Into Practice, 23* (1), 44-50.

Steele, D., Palensky, J., Lynch, T., Lacy, N., & Duffy, S. (2002). Learning preferences, computer attitudes, and student evaluation of computerized instruction. *Medical Education, 36*, 225-232.

Suits, J., & Lagowski, J. (1994). Chemistry problem-solving abilities: Gender, reasoning level and computer-simulated experiments. Paper presented at the *Annual Meeting of the National Association for Research in Science Teaching*, Anaheim, California.

Takacs, J., Reed, W., Wells, J., & Dombrowski, L. (1999, Summer). The effects of online multimedia project development, learning style, and prior computer experiences on teacher's attitudes toward the Internet and hypermedia. *Journal of Research on Computing in Education, 31* (4), 341-355.

Yung-Bin, B. (1992). Effects of learning style in a hypermedia instructional system. Proceedings of *Selected Research and Development Presentations at the Convention of the Association for Educational Communications and Technology*, pp. 506-508.

Biography

Peter Fenrich is a Project Leader/Instructional Multimedia Designer at the Technology Centre of the British Columbia Institute of Technology (BCIT). Since 1984, Peter has been solving challenging instructional problems through the creation of innovative instructional multimedia products at BCIT. He leads projects, designs instructional multimedia software, writes proposals, conducts applied research, gives presentations and leads training workshops both locally and internationally, and evaluates software. His work is recognized with national and international awards.

In Peter's book entitled, "Creating Instructional Multimedia Solutions: Practical Guidelines for the Real World", he provides practical information that he has gained through years of experience in the field.

Peter taught secondary school in Nigeria for two years. He continues to support developing countries through a number of initiatives. His goal is to make the world a better place through his instructional multimedia productions and training workshops.

Practical IT Education. Deepening of Technology, Expansion of Work, and Development into Headwaters: A Systematic Effort to Achieve Higher Levels

Yoshinori Fujio
Prefectural University of Kumamoto, Kumamoto, Japan

fujio@pu-kumamoto.ac.jp

Abstract

A practical IT education is a combination of lectures and exercises, as well as learning and putting into practice the theory of a fundamental system technology. The following is presumed. It is important to execute such education by directing the accumulation of knowledge and the expansion of knowledge through the spiral model, making it more educationally effective.

The present treatise considers the efficacy of education when supplemented with working examples of graduate research that direct the accumulation and expansion of knowledge through a spiral model, and lectures accompanied by graduate research. Further examples are shown of the development into headwaters and systematic effort through a spiral model as a plan for increasing the efficacy of the education. This effort relates to "practical IT education", for which new directionality is suggested.

Keywords: Education, Spiral model, Skill, Measurement, Graduate research, Headwaters

Introduction

In the thesis (Fujio, 2000) the author provided the necessary knowledge needed to analyze, design, and build information systems. Since the combination of lectures and exercises is important (Felder & Silverman, 1988), the author provided specific examples of sales management design. In thesis (Fujio, 2002), the author provided the technological development format of the basic system of a 3-tier e-business. Further, in thesis (Fujio, 2003), the author performed a study on the theme of "activating the local community using IT", giving 4 specific examples, as well as measuring the efficacy of education.

Regarding graduate research carried out on the basis of the thinking in theses (Fujio, 2000, 2002, 2003), the present treaties shows the measurement results of an analysis of student questionnaires over the past 3 years, and suggests directionality for "practical IT education" through supplemental fieldwork for areas in which the efficacy of education is low.

Deepening of Technology and Expansion of Work

Science and technology have advanced from the past to present with the accumulation and expansion of technology. In education, is it also possible to accumulate and expand knowledge? Specific examples of graduate research are examined hereafter and the possibilities are investigated. Considering Kolb's spiral model (Kolb, 1984), a lifecycle in Barry Boehm's spiral model (Barry, 1988) using Object-Oriented Analysis/Design, is applied in the present treatise. The accumulation of knowledge, the vertical axis of the spiral model (Figure 1), is defined as the deepening of technology. The expansion of knowledge, the horizontal axis, is replaced by the expansion of work. The effect of education in graduate research was also measured according to the level of the students.

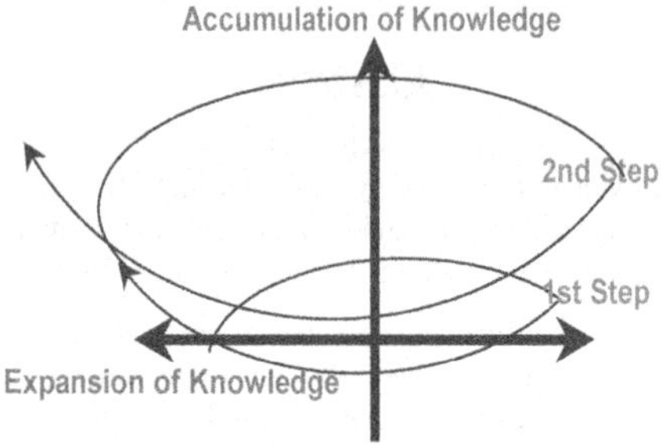

Figure1: Spiral Model

Deepening of Technology

Application was made of the accumulation of knowledge, or in other words, the deepening of technology, to the design and manufacturing phase of the lifecycle of an information system construct. The research lifecycle of 1-year is divided into four phases, "Planning", " Environment Development", "Construction", "Evaluation and Paper/Design Specification". The next year research is succeeded by the late research. The technology is deepening step-by-step. The vertical axis of Figure 1 represents the accumulation of knowledge. In order to understand the trial manufacturing system of the previous year, students first acquired basic knowledge about servers, Java, databases, etc., and solved problems from texts and reference books to gain understanding. Next, an understanding was obtained of the architecture used in the trial manufacturing system of existent graduate research, which was developed by its application to the future systems designed in graduate research. Table 1 shows 4 years of examples.

"Year-No." in Table 1 refers to the students, wherein "01-1" refers to the first student graduating in 2001, and "01-2" refers to the second student graduating in 2001. The author extracted the research of two students from each year. It can be seen that student "01-1" in Table 1 designed a client-centered system, using Windows as the OS and Access as the database, and programmed it using Java.

Generally, the student designed trial manufacturing system started as a client centered system and later as a server centered system. The OS on the server was mainly Windows, but Linux was also used. The Java language started with Java and was expanded to JSP and Servlet, and Access was used mainly for the database, but MySQL and PostgreSQL were also used. For the client computers, use was made of mainly Windows PCs, but i-mode cellular phones were also used. As can be seen, as the years passed, the technology deepened and knowledge was accumulated.

Table1: Deepening of Technology

Year-No.	Client centered system		
	Client side		
	OS	**Java Language**	**Database**
	Windows	**JAVA**	
01-1	o	o	o

Year-No.	Server centered system									
	Server side								Client side	
	OS		**Java Language**			**Database**			**PCs**	**Cellular Phone**
	Windows (Tomcat)	**Linux (Apache-Tomcat)**	**JAVA**	**JSP**	**Servlet, JavaBeans**	**Access**	**MySQL**	**Post-gre SQL**	**Windows**	**i-mode**
01-2	o		o							o
02-1	o		o			o				o
02-2	o		o	o		o			o	
03-1	o		o				o		o	
03-2	o		o	o	o	o			o	o
04-1	o		o	o		o			o	
04-2		o	o	o				o	o	

The Expansion of Work

The system domain of design and a trial manufacturing in application was applied to the work processed by the information system. Even work for the trial manufacturing system was expanded with the spiral model, which has a 1-year cycle. The horizontal axis in Figure 1 represents the expansion of knowledge. Students with ability and volition understand the basic work, and can expand it to the entire system. It is important that social science students have an understanding of information, money, and the distribution of goods in order to build a complete system (Dhamija, Heller, & Hoffman, 1999). Examples of work expansion are shown in Table 2.

"Year-No." in Table 1 is made to correspond to the students. Specially mentioned items in Table 2 describe the characteristics of the applications. For instance, student "01-1" has a client centered design, in which the work of the client is customer management. Student "01-2" has customer management on the server, student "02-1" has added sales management, student "03-2" has added product management, and student "04-1" has added accounting, expanding the work. Even the i-mode function is expanded from the schedule referred to in "01-2" to the stock browsing referred to in "02-2"'. As each year passes, the work expands, and knowledge increases.

Measurement of the Efficacy of Education

Graduate research was preceded as follows. Third year students spend one day a week in class (90 minutes), 30 times in all, learning the "IT basics" and "System design basics using database/Java". Fourth year students individually decide on a theme for graduate research for which they accomplish "research and design a trial manufacturing system". Main themes are how to solve the local communities' problems using information systems. Once a week (90 minutes) they report on their study progress, receiving the guidance of the instructor.

Table2: Expansion of Work

Year No.	Client centered system	
	Client side (Work)	Notes
	Customer management	
01-1	o	**1)**

Year - No.	Server centered system										
	Server side (Work)								Client side(Work)		Notes
	i-mode server function		**Customer management**	**Sale management**		**Product management**		**Accounting**	**PCs**	**Cellular Phone**	
	Schedule table	**Stock browsing**	**Customer list**	**Order**	**Stock**	**Buy**	**Stock**	**Profit**	**Online terminal**		
01-2	o		o							o	**2)**
02-1			o	o					o		**3)**
02-2		o		o						o	**4)**
03-1			o	o	o				o		**5)**
03-2		o				o	o		o	o	**6)**
04-1			o	o	o	o	o	o	o		**7)**
04-2			o	o	o				o		**8)**

1)Customer's record, discount by record points 2) i-mode design 3) Basic sales management
4) i-mode & database 5) Expansion of sales management 6) i-mode & PCs
7) Expand to sales, product management & accounting 8) Complicated Regional e-commerce

Figure 2 shows the skills of 22 students graduating from 2001 to 2004, after the completion of their graduate research, and was compiled based on questionnaires. The Appendix shows a sample skill level questionnaire. It investigates skill level (A) that students have only acquired in lectures and laboratories. About the same skill level items, using the same format questionnaire, are used to investigate skill level (B) after graduate research. To measure the graduate research effect, the research structures are classified and shown with explanatory remarks. "High level" indicates students who willfully researched reference materials and created an advanced trial manufacturing system. 9 applicable students are distilled. 8 students in Table 1/2 are included in this high level. "Mid level" indicates those students who researched reference materials and created an average trial manufacturing system. 9 applicable students are distilled. "Research level" refers to the other 4 students who mainly researched reference materials, but did not make a trial manufacturing system.

The vertical axis indicates skill levels (Lethbridge, 2000) that were acquired, wherein "0" represents students who have no knowledge, "1" means he is familiar with the material, "2" means he has acquired a basic knowledge, "3" means he can apply his knowledge, "4" means he has learned a lot, and "5" means he has learned deeply and is an expert.

The horizontal axis shows items learned relating to administration/management (administration and information, management and information), research methods (how to proceed with research, how to write a thesis), system building techniques (Lethbridge, 2000) (acquisition of requirements, analysis/design techniques, database design, network design, software design, algorithm

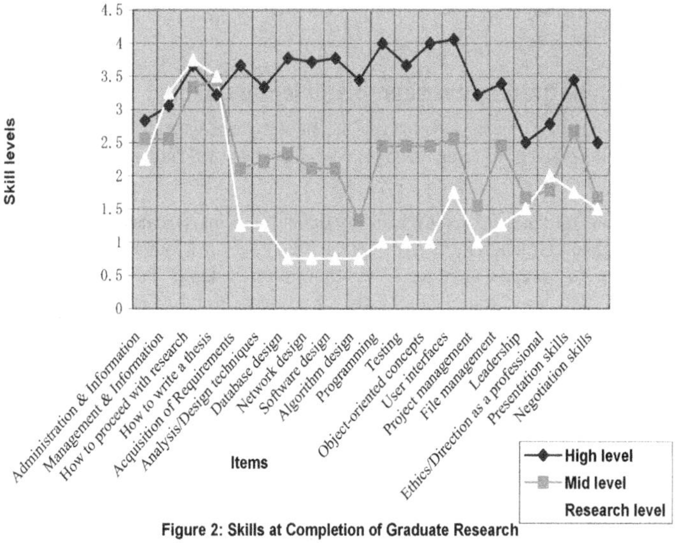

Figure 2: Skills at Completion of Graduate Research

design, programming, testing), system architecture (object-oriented concepts, user interfaces), development management (project management, file management), SE skills/morals (leadership, ethics/direction as a professional, presentation skills, negotiation skills).

Skills at completion of graduate research

Items relating to administration/management in Figure 2 are studied to learn how to solve problems of administration and management in information systems. Basic knowledge can be applied regarding "Administration and Information," wherein "high level" skill is 2.8, "mid level" skill is 2.5, and "research level" skill is 2.2, and for "Management and Information," "high level" skill is 3, "mid level" skill is 2.5, and "research level" skill is 3.2.

"High level" skill for "how to proceed with research" as a method of doing research is 3.7, "mid level" skill is 3.3, and "research level" skill is 3.7, with 3.3-3.5 for all skill levels being appropriate for applying knowledge on "how to write a thesis."

Students of social science have attained the basic skills for all skill levels "high," "mid," and "research" for skills relating to administration/management as well as for how to proceed with research.

The skills for the 8 items of system building techniques and the 2 items of system architecture are for a "high level" of 3.4-4, and high for students who willfully made a trial manufacturing system. "Mid level" skills are 2—2.5 and the "research level" is 0.7-1.2. Students who only did research with reference materials are low. However, 1.4 is low for "mid level" in "Algorithm Design," and 1.8 is high for "research level" in "User Interface." A great difference in skills can be seen between the "high level," "mid level," and "research level" for these items.

A "high level" skill for "project management" in development management is 3.2, "mid level" is 1.5 and "research level" is 1.0, which is low in comparison to other items, since it relates to individual research. The SE skills/morals and presentation skills are higher due to the holding of presentations for graduate research with a "high level" skill being 3.5, "mid level" being 2.6 and "research level" being 1.7.

Comparison of graduate research and lecture skills

Figure 3 is a comparison of skills after the completion of lectures, with the skills existent up to the point when the graduate research is completed. "High level" and "mid level" skills were investigated.

"Management and Information" skills relating to administration/management increased from 2.7 to 3 for the "high level," and from 1.9 to 2.5 for the "mid level." In addition, skills in research methods on "how to proceed with research" and "how to write a thesis" increased in both the "high level" and "low level" from 2.4 to 3.4, showing a great effect from graduate research.

In system building techniques, the following items showed a great increase in skill. "Database design" increased from 2.8 to 3.8 for the "high level" and from 1.9 to 2.4 for the "mid level." "Network design" increased from 2.6 to 3.8 for the "high level" and from 1.5 to 2.2 for the "mid level." "Programming" increased from 3.8 to 4.0 for the "high level" and from 2.1 to 2.4 for the "mid level," and "testing" increased from 3.3 to 3.7 for the "high level" and from 2 to 2.4 for the "mid level." As can be seen from above, the breadth of improvement in the "high level" is greater in comparison to that of the "mid level."

"Object-oriented concepts" in system architecture skills showed greatly improved breadth from 3.2 to 4 for the "high level" and from 2.1 to 2.4 for the "mid level," and "User Interface" increased from 3.8 to 4.1 for the "high level" and from 2.2 to 2.6 for the "mid level" because the

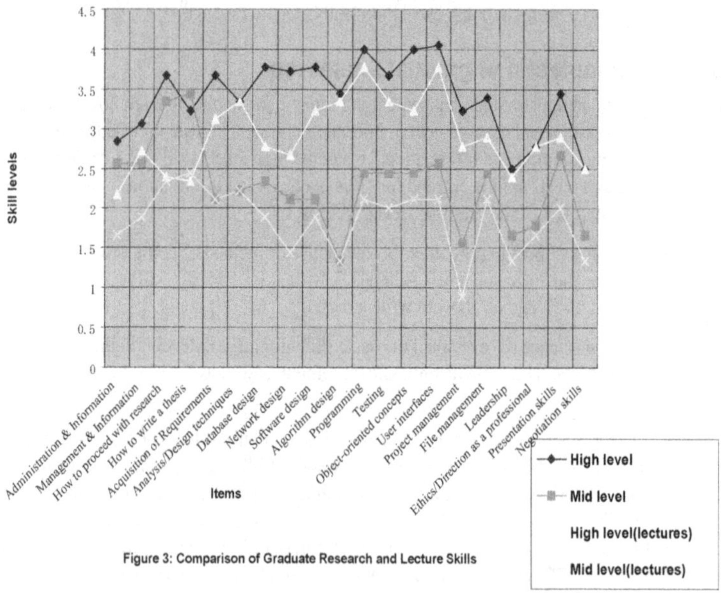

Figure 3: Comparison of Graduate Research and Lecture Skills

students had hands-on experience in an actual system.

An increase can be seen in "project management" in development management skills from 2.8 to 3.2 for the "high level" and from 0.9 to 1.5 for the "mid level." "Presentation ability" in SE skills/morals increased from 2.8 to 3.5 for the "high level" and from 2 to 2.7 for the "mid level."

The supplemental effect of graduate research can be seen overall. The efficacy of education, where graduate research supplements lectures, is understood to be especially great in "high level" students.

Development into Headwaters and the Systematic Effort

The vertical axis of the Spiral Model in Figure 1 represents the accumulation of knowledge toward development into headwaters and the horizontal axis represents the expansion of knowledge as a systematic initiative. In industry, information strategies are proposed with a current survey or analytical phase, in order to plan the desired information system images. In the University, desired system images are drawn, designed and created by students primarily based on bibliographic research, primarily because of the time or cost required to execute field surveys and to examine the current situation.

So far the philosophy, importance of experience, has been mentioned on Cone of Experience (Dale, 1946), but was not embodied in the universities. As an embodiment for higher-level development, examples are cited of field studies for building sightseeing information systems relating to current surveys or analytical phases constructing the upper level information systems. Next, as an example of an organizational initiative, an introduction is made of fieldwork, which has been started by the university.

Sightseeing Information System

This is an extracurricular activity in which research examination of regions is accomplished by planning independent fieldwork in which the students can freely participate. The students propose a plan to be executed, and if there is agreement, the expenses are provided by a support group. In addition to achieving an understanding of the current situation, problem points are educed, and resolution measures are proposed and created using an information system. Examining the current situation comprising the source point of IT education, consideration is given as to whether or not the problem areas can be resolved.

The first test is to undertake the following types of survey, to educe the problem points, and to propose measures for their resolution.

Survey (fieldwork)

1) The ASO region was made the subject region in which survey items were established in relation to the sightseeing characteristics of the region.

(1) Hot springs; (2) Points of nature; (3) Lodging establishments; (4) Product development; (5) Shopping sites

2) The survey method comprises the accumulation of information through the Internet, the use of fieldwork (on site surveys), and survey questionnaires.

Diverse surveys were undertaken in multiple locations, giving rise to the overall characteristics.

(1) Fieldwork

- On site, surveys of lodging and sightseeing facilities were conducted.

- Collection of many still pictures and moving pictures

(2) Questionnaire Survey

- Responses: survey items were created for each object facility.

- Lodging facilities: information was collected relating to location, client information characteristics and peripheral sports. Pictures were taken of the external environment and the inside of rooms and baths. Collected materials included lodging guides and peripheral maps and the like.

Presentation

Survey materials were compiled to be visually self-explanatory.

e-Map System

Surveyed and analyzed hot springs or lodging facilities were displayed by hand on electronic maps.

Owing to temporal limitations, and the lack of experience in the use of scientific survey methods, the survey was restricted to a limited region, and the anticipated results could not be obtained. However, the upper-level field survey obtained was an information system otherwise unavailable through the construct of only the University, and the fact that the current state of the region could be ascertained on the basis of individual experiences is a significant achievement.

"Moyaisuto" Education Program

"Moyai" is a slogan used when rebuilding the relationship between man, nature, and regional society. Beginning with this year, the objective of this program will build upon individual experiences by constructing a career from among the large number of experienced successes and failures, and from among many human relationships with nature, touching upon the actual regional problems and creating proposals for their resolution. The initiative will involve all students, including graduate students.

The anticipated results will build upon (the strength of cooperation between the regions and the universities and the like), and include publications extended to the regions (relating to discovered regional problems and resolutions), educational effects (individual re-discoveries and edification, relating to an understanding of the regional economies and administrations, and their cultures and traditions and succession, etc.), and education/research.

Hereafter, we would like to establish the position of "Education in IT Survey Research Region" within the education program of this type of organizational "fieldwork".

Conclusion

The author has given actual proof applying the accumulation and expansion of knowledge through the spiral model to the education of information system building.

The deepening of technology and the expansion of work (Table 1 and Table 2) is regarded as having been successful, as shown by the actual results of 4 years of students. In addition, measurements of the effectiveness of education (Figure 3) provide actual proof of the effectiveness of education supplemented by a combination of lectures and graduate research. However, the increase in the amount of skill for such things as the "acquisition of requirements" and "analysis/design techniques" in system building techniques, and "leadership, ethics/direction as a professional," and "negotiation skills" in SE skills/morals has been limited. In order to strengthen this area, consideration is given to the development of upper classes for the fieldwork referred to in item 3, which has become the primary body. Furthermore, through the organizational accomplishment of the fieldwork, a single layer educational effect can be anticipated. This is a place in which students can experience for one selves a method for independent discovery and resolution of problems points, and correction of the regional views.

Hereafter, studies will be accelerated for methods of initiative and guidance for building an information system for increasing the efficacy of education.

References

Barry, W. B. (1988). A spiral model of software development and enhancement. *IEEE Computer, May,* 61-72.

Dale, E. (1946). *Audio visual methods in teaching.*

Dhamija, R., Heller, R., & Hoffman, L. (1999). Teaching e-commerce. *Communications of the ACM, 42*(9), 50-55.

Fedler, R. M. & Silverman, L. K. (1988). Learning and teaching styles in engineering education. *Engineering Education, 78*(7), 674-681.

Fujio, Y. (2000). Information system design of undergraduate education. *Proceedings of SITE 2000, Society for Information Technology & Teacher Education International Conference*, 359-364.

Fujio, Y. (2002). Education of overall IT system design. *2002 Proceedings Informing Science + IT Education Conference*, 507-511. Available at http://proceedings.informingscience.org/IS2002Proceedings/papers/Fujio047Educa.pdf

Fujio, Y. (2003). Building a regional community with IT. *2003 Proceedings Informing Science + IT Education Conference*, 7-16. Available at http://proceedings.informingscience.org/IS2003Proceedings/docs/010Fujio.pdf

Kolb, D. A. (1984). *Experiential learning.* Englewood Cliffs. NJ: Prentice Hall.

Lethbridge, T. C. (2000). What knowledge is important to a software professional? *Computer, 33*(5), 44-50. *IEEE Computer Society.*

Biography

Yoshinori Fujio is a professor at Prefectural University of Kumamoto, where he teaches Information Administration, Software Design, Information System Development and Web related courses. He has authored papers on Education in Information Technology & Computer Science, CASE and 4 books on the subject of Information Processing Engineering.

From 1966 to 1994, he belonged to NEC, Nippon Electric Company, where he engaged in design of magnetic tape controls on NEC's computer and managed the Technical Support Center for SE. In the meantime, he had contributed to the national Σ project for increasing software productivity in Japan.

Appendix

Skill evaluation questionnaire for information science & technology

Research Day XX Day, XX Month, XX Year

School register Name Faculty

About skill level that only you have acquired in lectures/laboratories; ***before graduate research***

Please write sign ○ on your attained skill level in Table.

"0": you have no knowledge "1": you are familiar with the material "2": you have acquired the fundamental knowledge "3": you can apply your knowledge "4": you have learned a lot "5": you have learned deeply and are an expert

Items	0	1	2	3	4	5	Notes
#Relating to administration/management							
1.administration and information							
2.management and information							
#Research methods **3.how to proceed with research**							
4.how to write a thesis							
#System building techniques **5.acquisition of requirements**							
6.analysis/design techniques							
7.database design							
8.network design							
9.software design							
10.algorithm design							
11.programming							
12.testing							
#System architecture **13.object-oriented concepts**							
14.user interface							
#Development management							
15.project management							
16.file management							
#SE skill/morals **17.leadership**							
18.ethics/direction as a professional							
19.presentation skills							
20.negotiation skills							

Issues in Informing Science and Information Technology Volume 3, 2006

The Development, Use and Evaluation of a Program Design Tool in the Learning and Teaching of Software Development

Stuart Garner
Edith Cowan University, Joondalup, Australia

s.garner@ecu.edu.au

Abstract

The learning of software development is difficult for many students. Given a problem statement, students have to be able to: design a solution to the problem; implement a solution in a programming language; and test the solution. Often students miss out the design step and start writing programming code immediately. And yet instructors aim to encourage their students to develop a design in, for example, pseudocode. This helps students think carefully about their program designs without getting bogged down in the intricacies of a programming language. However students do not like writing pseudocode. Reasons for this include: it is another language to learn; they do not think that they are actually programming; they cannot test their designs as the designs are not executable; there is not a rigid syntax and so students are unsure whether their pseudocode meets an instructor's expectations. This paper concerns the development of a simple tool that helps students create pseudocode. The tool has been used and evaluated in an introductory programming unit of study. The results suggest that the tool was easy for students to use and that it helped support their learning.

Keywords: learning, programming, design, pseudocode, tools.

Introduction

This paper concerns the development, use and evaluation of a tool that helps novice programmers generate pseudocode designs for programming problems. It discusses: the difficulties of learning to program; what is meant by pseudocode; the development of the tool; and the evaluation of the tool with students.

Difficulty of Learning to Program

Learning to write computer programs is not easy (e.g., Scholtz & Wiedenbeck, 1992) and this is reflected in the low levels of achievement experienced by many students in first programming courses. Jenkins (2002) suggests that the learning of programming is a perennial problem. Students struggle as they try to master the subject and it is not uncommon for a student's first experience of programming to be so negative and stressful that it leads to academic failure or withdrawal. In a study into the teaching and learning of first year programming, it was found that the main concerns were high failure rates, a low flow of students into higher degrees, and a perception of a wide variation of teaching skills (Carbone et al, 2000).

Programming is a complex process involving many steps (e.g., Winslow, 1996). The process comprises:

- Studying a given problem statement / set of requirements and producing an algorithm, often in pseudocode, to solve that problem;
- Translating the algorithm into the programming code of a certain programming language; and
- Testing and amending the program until it meets the original set of requirements.

Frequently students combine steps one and two above and attempt to produce algorithms in the programming language that is being utilised in their course of study rather than in a design language such as pseudocode. Many instructors do not encourage the use of pseudocode with students and the majority of introductory programming texts include few, if any, references to pseudocode.

What is Pseudocode?

Pseudocode is:

> *A detailed yet readable description of what a computer program or algorithm must do, expressed in a formally-styled natural language rather than in a programming language. Pseudocode is sometimes used as a detailed step in the process of developing a program. It allows designers or lead programmers to express the design in great detail and provides programmers a detailed template for the next step of writing code in a specific programming language* (TechTarget, 2005).

The following are two examples of pseudocode used to stipulate the algorithm for converting a Celsius temperature to Fahrenheit (Villanova University, 2005).

Example 1

```
prompt user for a celsius temperature to be converted
get input from user and store in a variable called celsiusTemp
calculate: (celsiusTemp * (5/9)) + 32 and store in a variable called
          fahrenheitTemp
display fahrenheitTemp
```

Example 2

```
BASE = 32
CONVERSION_FACTOR = 9/5
prompt user for celsius temperature
input celsiusTemp
fahrenheitTemp = (celsiusTemp * CONVERSION_FACTOR) + BASE
output fahrenheitTemp
```

As seen above, the algorithms differ in the syntax that is used to describe the particular algorithm. Robertson (2003, p.7) points out that:

> *There is no standard pseudocode at present. Authors seem to adopt their own special techniques and sets of rules, which often resemble a particular programming language.*

The fact that there is no standard is one of the reasons that many students bypass using it in their program designs and move directly to coding their solutions. Another reason for students disliking pseudocode is that the code is not executable and direct feedback of a design cannot therefore be obtained.

There are also reasons why some instructors do not use pseudocode. The first reason is that an instructor may have their own "standard" pseudocode syntax that they wish to use and yet that standard is probably different to the format used in the available textbooks. A second reason is that many of pseudocode languages do not reflect the event driven nature of programming that is in use today.

However research suggests that the use of pseudocode in the design of programs helps students in their learning of software development. Ramadhan (2000) synthesised certain empirical results (Gilmore & Green, 1988; Jones, 1984; Norman, 1983) and concluded:

- *The underlying programming constructs can be learned independently of the surface structure or syntax of the programming language; and*
- *When users are introduced to programming using a pseudocode language they perform more accurately during problem solving and their programming knowledge is more transferable to other programming languages, and the languages that involve simple and few programming concepts to be learned reduce the mental load on users and help them in the process of program understanding and debugging.*

Development of a Program Design Tool

A technology supported tool to help students create pseudocode for the design of programs was developed by the author. The main aims of the tool were that:

- It should be easy to use.
- It should include a library of "standard" constructs to reduce the amount of typing required. An example of such a construct is the IF/Then/Else/EndIf construct.
- There should be a facility to change the "standard" constructs so that an instructor or students can utilise a different syntax.
- There should be a facility to gradually add pseudocode constructs to the tool thereby allowing for a reduced cognitive load on students in the earlier stages of their learning.

The inspiration for the pseudocode tool came from a tool that is being used to help students learn scripting languages (Gibbs, 2002). The tool developed by Gibbs makes use of a freeware text editor named NoteTab (2005). NoteTab is much more than a text editor as it includes: a "clipbook" feature that lets a user create and organize textual clips; and macros that can range from text replacement to complete mini-applications that use a simple built-in scripting language.

Such a "clipbook" library was created by the author for use with NoteTab. The library was specifically designed to support the production of pseudocode for introductory programming in an event driven environment, eventual implementation being in Visual BASIC. The interface of NoteTab with the pseudocode library loaded is shown in Figure 1.

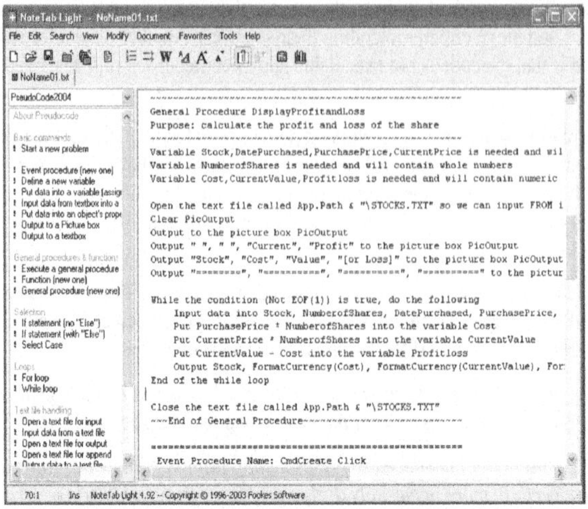

Figure 1: Program Design Tool Interface

The left-hand window contains the pseudocode library and the right-hand window contains an example of the pseudocode that can be "generated". When students use the system, they double click on an item in the library and a macro is executed. The macros prompt the user for relevant information, generates text and then places that text in the right-hand window. For example, double clicking on the library item "**Input data from textbox into a variable**" causes the dialogue box shown in Figure 2 to be displayed. Note that data has been entered into the dialogue box. When the "**OK**" button is clicked, pseudocode is generated as shown in Figure 3.

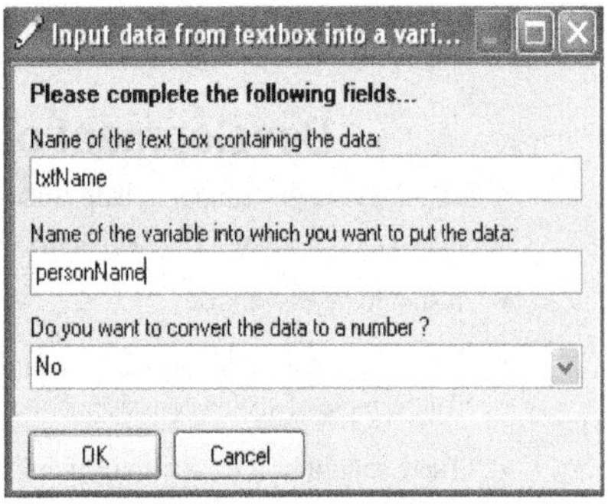

Figure 2: Dialogue Box

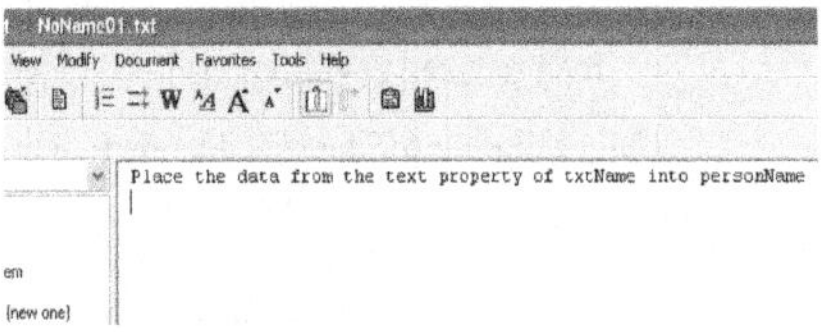

Figure 3: Generated Line of Pseudocode

The design tool supports the standard statements that are necessary to create algorithms that will eventually be implemented in a programming language including: input and output statements; assignment statements; the selection and control structures; procedures and functions; etc. A complete example of the pseudocode that was created by a student in an introductory programming class is shown below.

```
=======================================================
Event Procedure Name: cmdClassify_Click
Purpose: Classify the yob

This code is to be executed when the Click event takes place
on the object called cmdClassify
=======================================================

Variable personName is needed and will contain string data
Variable yob is needed and will contain whole numbers
```

```
Open the text file called YOB.TXT so we can input FROM it
Open the file called SENIORS.TXT so we can output TO it
Open the file called JUNIORS.TXT so we can output TO it
While the condition (it is not the end of file of YOB.TXT) is true, do the following
   Input data into personName, yob from the text file YOB.TXT
   If yob > 1940 Then
     Output the data personName, yob to the text file JUNIORS.TXT
   Else
     Output the data personName, yob to the text file SENIORS.TXT
   End If
End of the while loop
Close the text file called SENIORS.TXT
Close the text file called JUNIORS.TXT
Close the text file called YOB.TXT
```

There is also a library item "**Convert to VB Comments**" that, when double clicked, places a single quote in front of every line of pseudocode. The pseudocode can then be copied and pasted into a Visual BASIC program for self-documentation purposes.

The pseudocode shown above uses a syntax that has been created by the author. The aim of the particular syntax utilised is to help students gain a better understanding of what particular statements in an algorithm "do". A selection of statements, their Visual BASIC equivalent, and the rationale for the syntax chosen is shown in Table 1.

Table 1: Selection of Pseudocode Statements

<table>
<tr><th>Pseudocode Statement</th><th>Visual BASIC Statement</th><th>Rationale</th></tr>
<tr><td>Variable price is needed and will contain numbers with decimal places</td><td>Dim price As Double</td><td>There is a need for students to understand the types of data to be used in an algorithm</td></tr>
<tr><td>Place the data from the text property of txtPrice into price after converting it to a number</td><td>Price = CDbl(txtPrice.Text)</td><td>Students have problems understanding assignment statements and the need to change string data to numeric data</td></tr>
<tr><td>Put counter + 1 into the variable counter</td><td>counter = counter + 1</td><td>Students have difficulty with this type of assignment statement and its mechanism needs to be made explicit as to what is happening</td></tr>
<tr><td>While the condition (X = 9) is true, do the following

End of the while loop</td><td>Do While X = 9

Loop</td><td rowspan="2">Loop mechanisms need to be made more explicit</td></tr>
<tr><td>For counter going from 1 To 5 in steps of 1

Next value of counter</td><td>For counter = 1 To 5

Next</td></tr>
<tr><td>Open the text file called yob.txt so we can input FROM it</td><td>Dim sr As IO.StreamReader = IO.File.Opentext("yob.txt")</td><td>Some students have difficulties understanding the different modes that files can be opened in</td></tr>
</table>

As mentioned earlier in the paper, it should be possible to amend the macros so that the generated syntax meets the requirements of different instructors. The macros are programmed in an interpreted "Clip" language. Examples of the macros for two statements are shown in Table 2.

Table 2: Examples of the "Clip" Programming Language

<table>
<tr><th>Library Statement</th><th>Macro</th></tr>
<tr><td>Define a new variable</td><td>^!SET %variableName%=^?{What is the name of the new variable?=^%variableName%};
%variabletype%=^?{What type (kind) of data will the variable contain=String|Number (with decimal values)|Integer (whole number)}
;Do the testing
^!IF ^%variabletype% = "String" stringPart
^!IF ^%variabletype% = "Number (with decimal values)" numberPart
;Must be integer</td></tr>
</table>

<table>
<tr><td></td><td>Variable ^%variableName% is needed and will contain whole numbers
^!GoTo end
:stringPart
Variable ^%variableName% is needed and will contain string data
^!GoTo end
:numberPart
Variable ^%variableName% is needed and will contain numeric data
:end</td></tr>
<tr><td>Input data from textbox into a variable</td><td>^!Set %textBoxName%=^?{Name of the text box containing the data=^%textBoxName%}; %variableName%=^?{Name of the variable into which you want to put the data=^%variableName%}; %convertToNumber%=^?{Do you want to convert the data to a number ?=Yes|_No}
^!IF ^%convertToNumber% = "No" NoConvert
Place the data from the text property of ^%textBoxName% into ^%variableName% after converting it to a number</td></tr>
</table>

The above table suggests that the "Clip" language is not the easiest to use, however it would be expected that a programming instructor should be able to make any necessary changes.

Initial Evaluation of the Program Design Tool

The tool has been used over a number of semesters in an introductory programming unit at an Australian university. The unit is within a major in Information Systems and the programming language used is Visual BASIC. An initial evaluation was conducted via a questionnaire with a group of 21 students and Table 3 contains some initial results together with their interpretation.

Table 3: Questionnaire Results and Interpretation

Question	Result	Comment
How easy was the pseudocode generator to use?	76% of students indicated that the pseudocode generator was straightforward or easy to use.	Any tool, especially one designed for novices, should be easy to use and have a small learning curve.
How often did you create the pseudocode before you created the Visual BASIC code?	67% of students indicated that they usually created the pseudocode before the Visual BASIC code.	It is well documented that a majority of students do not create pseudocode before they create their programming code. In this context, the result of this question is pleasing.
How often did you feel that the creation of pseudocode before the Visual BASIC code helped your understanding?	82% of students indicated that the creation of pseudocode usually helped their understanding.	This confirms the usefulness of good algorithm design that is encouraged by the use of the pseudocode generator.
Did a pseudocode statement such as: "Put 6 into the variable hours" help your understanding of how the assignment statement works?	76% of students indicated that the syntax of this statement helped their understanding of how the statement worked.	One of the aims of the pseudocode generator was to help students gain an understanding of the purpose and mechanism of statements required in computer implementable algorithms and this appears to have been successful.
Did a pseudocode statement such as: "Put the data "Bob" into the property named text of the object txtName" help you understand how assigning data to properties worked?	90% of students indicated that the syntax of this statement helped their understanding of how the statement worked.	
Did a pseudocode statement such as: "Execute the general procedure AddNumbers passing arguments X, Y" help you understand how general procedures worked?	62% of students indicated that the syntax of this statement helped their understanding of how the statement worked.	
Would you have preferred NOT to use the pseudocode generator?	35% of students replied "Yes" to this question.	It was pleasing that around two thirds of students were comfortable using the generator. It still appears however that a sizeable minority prefer coding algorithms

Question	Result	Comment
		directly in a programming language.

Students were also asked to comment on the use of the pseudocode generator. The positive comments included:

> *It helped me go through all the things needed in the question.*
>
> *The pseudocode in general was very straightforward and easy to follow. The indentation of certain statements was useful as it reminded me to indent the statement when writing the actual Visual BASIC code.*
>
> *It helps you to think about the sequence of the program statements;*
>
> *It forces you to organise your thoughts in a clear logical manner. Without this I find I tend to go back and forth between deciding what I do and do not want in my code. The creation of the pseudocode gave me the necessary preparation time before commencing the programming task.*
>
> *Using the pseudocode helps in understanding what is needed to do in the VB code.*
>
> *It makes me think more carefully about the question and the variables I need for each question.*
>
> *Well... lets me organize a bit in computer instead of the brain. It reduced the typing work required.*

The comments strongly support the use of the pseudocode generator as a tool that helps in the design process of algorithms that can then be implemented in a programming language. It seems to have helped students think about the problems to be solved and organise their solutions and designs in a coherent manner.

There was one negative comment:

> *It is useless!! Because, if we get the pseudocode wrong, we will not know if the program is correct. Using VB directly, we can monitor our mistake.*

This comment concerns the fact that pseudocode is not executable and clearly this student believed that the cycle of coding and testing in a program development environment was more useful in his or her learning. This reflects the fact that some students always prefer to skip the careful thought processes required in program design and use trial and error techniques in their algorithm design.

Conclusions

This paper has discussed the design and use of a tool to support the generation of pseudocode for novice programmers. It has been used and evaluated with students in an introductory programming unit within an Information Systems major at an Australian university. The tool has been well received by students who believe that it is very useful in their learning and that is helps scaffold them in the program design process.

The results of the evaluation suggest that possible changes to the tool and its use might include:

- The actual programming language statements could be generated in addition to the pseudocode statements.
- A help file that includes information on all of the pseudocode statements could be included.

- A facility could be made available that allows students to easily change the wording, or syntax, of statements generated by the macro library. Such a facility should not require students to have to amend scripts that form the basis of the macro library.

References

Carbone, A., Hurst, J., Mitchell, I. & Gunstone, D. (2000). Principles for designing programming exercises to minimise poor learning behaviours in students. *Paper presented at the Fourth Australasian Computing Education Conference,* Melbourne, Australia.

Gibbs, D. C. (2002). An interactive introductory programming environment using a scripting language. Paper presented at the *Ed-Media 2002*, Denver, Colorado.

Gilmore, D. & Green, T. (1988). Programming plans and programming expertise. *Journal of Experimental Psychology, 40A*(3), 67-82.

Jenkins, T. (2002). On the cruelty of really teaching programming. Paper presented at the *2nd LTSN-ICS one day conference on the teaching of programming*, University of Wolverhampton, UK.

Jones, A. (1984). How novices learn to program. Paper presented at the *First IFIP Conference on Human-Computer Interaction*, London.

Norman, D. (1983). Some observations on mental models. In D. Gentner & A. Stevens (Eds.), *Mental models* (pp. 34-39). NJ: Erlbaum.

NoteTab (2005). *NoteTab*. Retrieved November 16, 2005 from http://www.notetab.com

Ramadhan, H. A. (2000). Programming by discovery. *Journal of Computer Assisted Learning,* (16), 83-93.

Robertson, L. (2003). *Simple program design*. Thomson.

Scholtz, J. & Wiedenbeck, S. (1992). The role of planning in learning a new programming language. *International Journal of Man-Machine Studies, 37*, 191-214.

TechTarget (2005). *TechTarget*. Retrieved November 14, 2005 from http://whatis.techtarget.com/definition/0,,sid9_gci213457,00.html

Villanova University (2005). *Villanova University*. Retrieved November 14, 2005 from http://www.csc.villanova.edu/~map/1051/pseudocode.html

Winslow, L. (1996). Programming pedagogy - A psychological overview. *SIGCSE Bulletin, 28*(3).

Biography

Stuart Garner has been a college and university lecturer for over 30 years and has also spent time working in industry as an analyst programmer. His main research interests include: the teaching and learning of programming; the teaching and learning of systems analysis and design; eLearning; personal knowledge management; and web based development.

Stuart is currently a senior lecturer in information systems at Edith Cowan University, Western Australia. His profile is available at: http://www.business.ecu.edu.au/schools/mis/staff/sgarner.htm

Virtual Medical Campus (VMC) Graz Innovative Curriculum meets Innovative Learning Objects Technology

Volkmar Haase
HM&S IT-Consulting GmbH, Graz, Austria

vhaase@ist.tugraz.at

Josef Smolle
Medical University Graz (MUG), Austria

josef.smolle@meduni-graz.at

Stefan Vejda
HM&S IT-Consulting GmbH, Graz, Austria

stv@hms.org

Reinhard Staber
Medical University Graz (MUG), Austria

reinhard.staber@meduni-graz.at

Christian Steinmann
HM&S IT-Consulting GmbH, Graz, Austria

cs@hms.org

Ingomar Wascher
HM&S IT-Consulting GmbH, Graz, Austria

iw@hms.org

Abstract

Experience with a large scale virtual university learning system is presented. A newly designed curriculum for medical studies is made available in electronic multimedia form and is serving the needs of 2500 students per semester. We describe the concept, the technology based on a 3-layer-software system, and especially problems and solutions in connection with mapping medical knowledge onto a multimedia learning objects repository including metadata. The résumé is that virtualised teaching is a successful method to manage high numbers of students and to organize a fair selection process. When we proceed with face-to-face communication in later phases of the education virtual teaching is still used as a powerful support function.

Keywords: Virtual campus; medical curriculum; learning objects technology; metadata

The Story

The Federal Republic of Germany executes a strict "numerus clausus" scheme for students of Medicine. Austria did not in the recent years, but: foreign (i.e. German) students were not allowed to enter unless they were eligible for studies in their home country. Because of this there was no chance for German numerus-clausus-victims in Austria.

In July 2005 the European Court of Justice stopped this practice. Now German students are able to inscribe medical studies at Austrian (German speaking) universities. The size of a typical class for beginners will rise from approximately 250 to 2500.

The Medical University of Graz (MUG) can handle this situation by using virtual teaching in the first semester. Everybody is free to start medical studies, and we select the "best" students in examinations after the first semester. In autumn 2005, more than 3000 students started Medicine at MUG – our largest lecture hall has 375 seats but VMC can handle almost unlimited numbers by means of electronic multimedia teleteaching.

In 2002 MUG had introduced a new curriculum for Medicine, concentrating on thematic issues crossing classical borderlines of medical disciplines (Glasgow, 1997; Maerz, 1998). The new contents had to be backed by a university-wide information system as a guidebook for students and an orientation system for lecturers.

The project VMC ("Virtual Medical Campus") started in 2002: all relevant learning contents of the new curriculum had to be mapped into an electronic system and should be accessible for all MUG students without charge and without technical problems. Contents were (and are still) provided by MUG, the technology was (and is continuously) developed by HM&S IT-Consulting and partner companies, the overall design was a task of the whole team. (Smolle, 2004)

At present VMC is "the" learning system for students of the first semester. They get all the necessary information from there, while later in the curriculum VMC has rather a tutorial function complementary to lectures, seminars and bedside experience.

Educational Background

Two decisions mark the beginning of the project: the design of a new curriculum coping with the requirements of the 21st century (Stuko, 2002), and the idea that this curriculum had to be "available" in electronic form for everybody. (Ecker, 2000) Two project groups working closely together developed the table of contents of the curriculum and the e-learning system, respectively. The new courses had to be "implemented" in electronic form. In parallel with that, the MUG lecturers were educated and supported in the use of the new medium.

In our VMC competence centre four persons are responsible for this process. The means were planning workshops, now support is provided individually on demand. There are approx.600 lecturers at MUG. 50 of them were members of the development process of the curriculum, and 10 cooperated in new media issues. At present 180 active authors are providing contents (learning objects) for VMC. Personal contacts of members of the project team with potential authors have proved to be the best way to success.

Students receive a one-hour introduction and a consultation hour is held once a month. Our experience is that there are no problems from this side: they mainly work at home using internet connection.

The whole curriculum is divided into four levels: Modules, Topics, Learning Units and Learning Objects. The Study of Human Medicine on the Medicine University of Graz is divided into 29 Modules, about 10 Tracks and about 20 "Special Study Modules". Each of these modules has its own topics. The Learning Units on the next level hold the Learning Objects for up to four lessons (45 minutes each). This arrangement is working well because there is a hundred percent compatibility to the study "in real life" and so the students don't get confused because of more than 4000 Learning Objects and find the important ones for their term very fast.

Each learning object (LO) has to cover the maximum contents of a 45 minutes lecture. It is possible to assemble different courses from a pool of learning objects of this size. Authors are free as to the contents, didactical norms, formats and structures within the objects are not provided either. LOs are mainly presentations in MicrosoftWord, Powerpoint, PDF and HTML formats. Powerful didactical possibilities like video and simulation are consecutively produced by the members of the competence centre in close cooperation with the responsible lecturers.

Virtual seminars and exercises are obligatory complemented with Computer Based Training Objects (CBT). So there is a structure in the Learning Object where the students learn in a guided way. The feedbacks for this Learning Objects were very positive in the first term. The lecturers could build a LO in the way they used to teach in their lecture (e.g. questions and answers) and the students found it very easy to learn with CBTs because the handling is very easy and clear. Furthermore, the students got an Email after working through a CBT giving the percentage of right and wrong answers. This procedure was also used by the university to log the result of each CBT (test) and if there was a positive grade on the Test the students got a certification for it.

At the end of each CBT there is also a possibility for the students to send a feedback to the author. This was, for the students the important link to the lecturers. It was used very often for questions on the learning matter and also for criticism (positive and negative).

The CBTs could be created online; so for the lecturers, there was no need to install any Software for creating their LOs. They just needed to open the Internet Browser and to write their questions and answers into the system.

Technological Background

The challenge was that conventional textbooks do not fulfil the requirements of an integrated curriculum (overlapping special disciplines). There is a necessity of an electronic learning system.

vmc.meduni-graz.at has been implemented by an international group of software companies under the leadership of HM&S and coordinated by MUG. The 3-layer-system consists of a front-end with its user interface for students and lecturers which is accessible via Web-Browsers, a middleware layer as the functional heart and a multimedia repository which is the LO data base.

The system is designed to handle 2000 concurrent users. Software technology is based on Microsoft's **.NET** suite.

The Clustering of the Front end was handled by the integrated Software-Cluster of the Windows 2003 Server Enterprise Edition, the Clustering of the back-end was realised by a SQL-Server-Cluster from Microsoft. With this technology there was not one problem to handle the massive count of requests from the students.

All LOs are accompanied by metadata (LOM = learning object metadata) following the SCORM standard (sharable content objects reference model) version 1.2.2.

LO metadata are a key issue for any computer based university training system. They allow the flexible construction of various courses out of "LO-atoms", re-use of LO content – also in different languages, and the handling of accompanying question/answer modules for self evaluation. Metadata are inevitable for the ongoing exchange of LO based courses with the Faculty of Medicine of the University of Maribor and the Medical University of Vienna.

The middle layer organizes all interactions of the Learning Management System: access to LOs using subject/discipline or module identification, the question – answer - system for the students' self assessment, and the management of users: students, authors, and administrators. Another main task is the setup and control of the LO – course – subject – structure (using LO metadata), and the release of individual LOs.

Experience

Since autumn 2005, VMC is in full operation handling the needs of 2500 students – beginners of their medical studies. More than 6000 learning objects are available and are being used. 500 to 600 concurrent users are not causing technological problems. Students can use any Browser (in the newest version) they want. Authors have to use the Internet Explorer as a standard.

Each LO contains a clear reference to the corresponding textbook, and represents the topic in adequate electronic form from text and diagrams to video, animation and simulation. Interactive LOs are provided to allow the student to check her/his knowledge. Seminars and practical work are mapped onto elaborated Computer Based Training (CBT) objects, which can be sent to professors/tutors. They are an integral part of our examination system.

While students regard VMC as a "no problem"-issue, authors, i.e. lecturers/professors, had to learn their new job: a new curriculum that is neglecting traditional discipline borders, and its presentation in electronic form – creation of interactive, "life" textbooks. As the VMC team did not prescribe presentation standards the content was and is growing fast. On the other hand we can see an abundance of pure presentation LOs – mimicking traditional classroom teaching. We are trying to promote the creation of interactive objects via support, training and consultancy. Also discrepancies in the didactical quality are visible. LOs range from textbook copies – not to be understood without explanation – to didactically excellent teleteaching objects. As a third observation we found that different authors use different internal structures in their contents. This led to some confusion on the side of the students.

We therefore initiated a review process including the students – with considerable success in form of quality improvement. Last but not least, some guidelines for LO and course structures were issued (Smolle, 2005).

At the end of the virtual semester, more than 1000 students attended the examinations, which were held in Graz on two consecutive days. These tests covered all topics that were taught through the VMC during the virtual semester. It turned out that the examination results in particular multiple choice questions were significantly related to the mode and intensity of presentation in the VMC. Topics which were entirely covered by interactive computer-based training learning objects yielded significantly better examination results than those which depended mainly on presentation and visualization learning objects or textbook references.

In the evaluation, the overwhelming majority of the students agreed that they would prefer face-to-face teaching in the first semester, and that they would prefer a selection process prior to admission rather than at the end of the first semester. They found, however, the VMC easy to use. They particularly valued the computer-based training learning objects as useful and efficient tools for learning and self-assessment.

Ongoing Development

Apart from the ongoing improvement of VMC contents both in quantitative and in qualitative respects (as described above), and the introduction of both examinations and student feedback considerations, we have to continue developing the system in technological respect.

The main issue is the enhancement of both hardware and software to handle up to 5000 concurrent users. In the new system which is introduced step by step without any interruption of the continuous use by students and authors, we run 11 server computers: 5 for the presentation layer, user interface and web communication, 4 for the middle layer managing all important functions, and two to hold the database: our repository. The whole task is performed by HM&S. Programming of the Front end is done by using ASP.NET from Microsoft (Visual Studio.NET, 2005). The repository is fully compatible with the Content Repository for Java technology API (jsr 170, http://www.jcp.org/en/jsr/detail?id=170) and written in Java.

Authoring tools (Musch, 1999) have not been an integral part of the system for some time. The most common external tool used is a CBT-tool, mainly an intelligent text processing system including the possibility to construct learning (or even diagnostic) paths. For special medical applications a "virtual microscope" is used: the student works with the Internet browser in the same way as he would do with a real microscope.

Recently an authoring tool for presentation and visualisation objects has been integrated into VMC so that authors and administrators can provide new contents more easily and make better use of interactive features.

Multi language features that are necessary for international exchange of courses are in the beta testing stage. Collaborative work in the web has not the same priority in Medicine than in other fields – face-to-face communication will play the main role but will be heavily supported by virtual learning of necessary facts.

One important interface will soon be implemented: the connection of the VMC to the new "Med-Online"-Software which organises the whole study for each student, providing a timetable, an overview of class rooms and so on.

Apart from classical medicine, other curricula at MUG are virtualised e.g. the curriculum for dentists and postgraduate studies.

In the future there will be more universities integrated in the VMC-Infrastructure. The University of Maribor and the Medical University of Vienna will be online in autumn this year and some other universities asked for an account to test the system and may want one or more own study courses in the future. Some meetings with very concrete conceivability have already been held.

Final Remarks

High quality curricula for future medical doctors and for dentists at MUG require large amounts of resources of persons, rooms, infrastructure and money. They cannot be made available for extraordinarily large numbers of students. Our view on "numerus clausus" is a fair, transparent selection system solely based on the medical knowledge and skill of the candidate. Virtual teaching in the first half year of study is a very good way to provide large numbers of students with clearly defined and structured subject matter. They get equal chances in the following examination/selection process.

Teaching medicine cannot be fully virtualised. Our curriculum provides workshops and tutorials, early bedside experience which can only be organized for small numbers. This will start in the second semester after the selection. Virtual teaching via VMC will play an important role also in the later phases of the curriculum. VMC is support; it helps both students and lecturers to concentrate on the important activities in their time budget, namely personal communication!

Without VMC, either a random, "casino-type" selection process would eliminate many of the best candidates, or when we take everybody, the medical curriculum would nearly impossible to put into practice.

Thus virtual teaching at the beginning is the key to get the best students and to have the most excellent medical doctors in the future.

References

Ecker, A. (2000). Handbook –New media in teaching at universities and polytechnics in Austria. Austrian Federal Ministry for Education, Vienna.

Glasgow, N. A. (1997). *New curriculum for new times*. Corwin Press: Thousand Oaks

Maerz, R. (1998). Medizinstudium. *Zeitschrift für Hochschuldidaktik, 22*(4), 3-140

Musch, J. (1999). Die Gestaltung von Feedback in computergestützten Lernumgebungen. *Zeitschrift fuer Pädagogische Psychologie, 13*,148-160.

Smolle, J. (2004). 100 Stunden virtuell. In Neue Medien in Lehre und Forschung an der Universität Graz.

Smolle, J. (2005). Aufbau eines universitätsweiten Lerninformationssystems. In Tavangarian/Nölting (Eds.), Auf zu neuen Ufern 217-226. Waxmann Berlin.

Stuko. (2002). Studienkommision (MUG): Studienreform der Medizin Graz. http://www.uni-graz.at/skmedwww/skm/skmed.html

Biographies

Ao. Univ.-Prof. Dr. Volkmar Haase. A formerly at the Institute for applied computer science and formal description procedures (AIFB) of the University of Karlsruhe in Germany. Emeritus on the Institute of Software Technology of the Technical University of Graz.

Scientific Work: applications in terms of artificial intelligence and improvements of processes in software development.

Prof. Dr. Josef Smolle. Born on 1958, married, four children.

Medical Education: 1976 - 1981 University of Graz, Faculty of Medicine. Qualified as Dr. med. on March 30th, 1981. Internship in Internal Medicine 1981 - 1982. 1982 - 1987 resident in the Department of Dermatology, University of Graz. Qualified as dermatologist since 1987. Associate Professor since 1988, Full Professor since 2006.

Scientific Work: Concerns quantitative morphology, tumor biology and medical education. 210 original publications and 500 oral and poster presentations. Membership and leading functions in national and international scientific societies, including the Austrian Forum New Media in tertiary education. Director of the Virtual Medical Campus Graz.

Stefan Vejda. Study of Telematik at the Technical University in Graz from 1989 until 1995. Graduation at the pedagogical academy of Diözese Graz-Seckau in June 1999 as a teacher in mathematics, sports and informatics. Since 1998 employee of Haase, Mülleitner & Steinmann GmbH. Now Co-owner, authorized officer, and chief of development of HM&S IT-Consulting GmbH (successor of Haase, Mülleitner & Steinmann GmbH).

Since 2000 assistant lecturer for programming 1 and from 2002 to 2004 for Messaging- and Workflow-Systems at the FH JOANNEUM in Graz at the degree programme Information Management.

Since 2004 Certified Spice Assessor (ISO 15504).

Reinhard Staber. Industrial plant technician, Study of Human Medicine, special skills in pathology in 2001; 2000 - 2003: employee at the institute of pathology in Graz as Image Editor and IT - specialist; Design of tissue databases and responsible for the first e-Learning developments at the institute of pathology. Since 2003 employee at the bureau of the Vice-Rector for Teaching and Studies of the Medical University of Graz as consultant and content mediator, since May 2005 technical director and head of further development of the VMC Graz.

Since January 2006: dedicated to the newly formed Department of VMC Graz at the Medical University of Graz in the same duties.

DI Christian Steinmann. Christian Steinmann is the managing director of HM&S IT-Consulting in Graz, Austria. His thesis at the TU-Graz in 1994 deals about the approach for efficient software process assessments and was the basis for his ongoing consulting in the area of software engineering (automotive industry & finance, mainly). He is the author of the SPiCE 1-2-1 assessment tool and he has lead several IT projects for knowledge management, balanced business scorecards, benchmarking and e-learning. Since 1997 he is also teaching computer science for automotive engineers at the University of Applied Sciences FH JOANNEUM.

The page left blank intentionally.

Software Agents for Managing Learning Plans

I. T. Hawryszkiewycz
Department of Information Systems,
University of Technology, Sydney

igorh@it.uts.edu.au

Abstract

Support for personalized learning requires further assistance than currently available with most learning management system. Software agents have been proposed as one way of providing such assistance. The paper identifies three kinds of software agents, pedagogical, function and process agents. The paper then concentrates on process agents, which guide learners to develop personalized preferred learning plans that match learner needs and then manage progress through such plans. Agent support will only be practical if widely applicable generic agents, which can be re-used in many plans, can be identified. Such agents can then be adapted to particular learner needs without extensive programming. The paper identifies some generic agents for this purpose and concentrate on agents that manage progress through the learning plans.

Keywords: Learning process, software agents, modelling

Introduction

Demands for more customized learning will require new ways to support learning processes. Such demands may be to acquire particular competencies (Hezemans and Ritzen, 2002) or knowledge of new subject areas. Educational approaches are also placing more emphasis on constructivist learning approaches (Jonassen, 2002), where learners construct knowledge in their preferred ways. A learner sets their learning goal and develops a learning plan and is provided with learning materials. In educational institutions, the learning plan is usually a set of lectures and assessments that is followed by all the students taking a subject. We address ways to customize such plans to specialized learner needs for large numbers of learners. The learners are then guided through their specialized plan using support systems to minimize the effort needed to manage the plans by teachers. Such guidance can take many forms. It may be to identify a lack of some elementary knowledge and provide ways to build familiarity of this knowledge before continuing with the main learning plan. One further advantage in formulating plans is support constructivist learning, which some writers (Petraglia, 1998) suggest are not effectively supported in current systems.

New kinds of support systems are needed for personalized learning. It will be prohibitively expensive to use current techniques. One teacher obviously is limited in the number of students, each following their personal program that they can support. Agent systems can provide better support here as they can provide greater flexibility in the way learners utilize services provided by learning management systems. Agent systems have been suggested earlier. One are the pedagogical agents (Baylor, 2003) such as expert, motivator or mentor. Another are agents that support specific functions (McArdle, 2005), such as interface or navigational agents. The paper proposes a third class of agents, namely process agents. Process agents guide users through a process and are generic in the sense that they are domain independent. They do not contain domain knowledge but simply assist learners and teachers to proceed through the learning process. They assist learners to get access to materials, and where necessary create their learning plans.

Two classes of process agents have been identified earlier (Hawryszkiewycz, 2005a). One are agents that assist a learner to construct a learning plan. The other are agents that manage the learning plan and dynamically amend the plan as needed. Earlier work has described agents that assist learners to create their learning plans. The paper concentrates on agents that manage learning plans.

Defining the Process

Our first step in defining generic agents is to define a taxonomy, or grammar, for describing leaning processes. The grammar or taxonomy will provide a fundamental set of concepts that serve as the framework for generic agent systems. The main elements, or learning process concepts, of such a grammar for the learning process are shown in Figure 1. These include:

Learning environment, or where learning takes place. This may be a University of a person's place of work.

Learning goal, which describes the learning objective,

Learning plan, which defines the sequence of learning activities to be followed to achieve the learning goal.

Learning activity, which describes a step of the learning plan; this may be create a report, evaluate a problem,

Subject metadata, which provides explicit references to information needed in the activity,

The learning method, which will be used in the learning step,

Support services provided for the learning method.

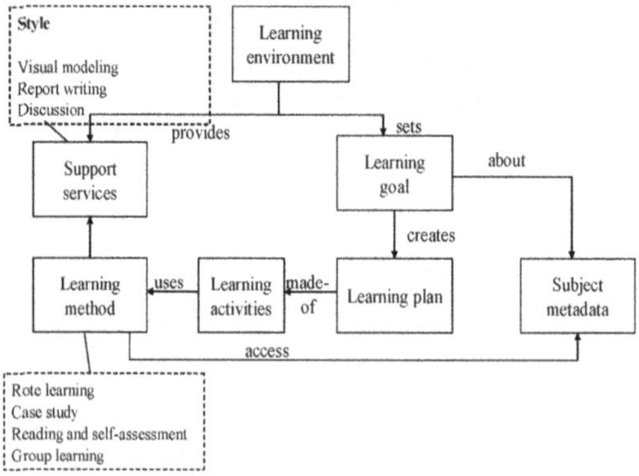

Figure 1 –Learning Process Concepts

The general semantic here is that a learner specifies a learning goal. A plan, which is made up of a number of learning activities, is then constructed by the learner with assistance from an agent. Each activity has a learning subgoal and specifies the preferred learning method to be used by the learner. Wang (2005) defines a similar set made up of units (corresponding to our learning plans), activities (corresponding to our learning activities), and facilities (corresponding to our methods).

Figure 2 shows an outline of the learning process that is made up of the elements shown in Figure 1. Here the learner sets a goal. An agent then assists the learner to set up a learning plan. The agent uses the learner profile to select the necessary learning activities to address learner knowledge gaps. It also uses the learner's preferred learning style to select the best learning method. The learner is then assisted by managing agents to proceed through a number of planned activities. The activity results in the creation of activity records, which can be artifacts that must be produced as part of the activity. It also includes an evaluation step. The plan can of course be changed to do some additional catch up work if indicated during the evaluation.

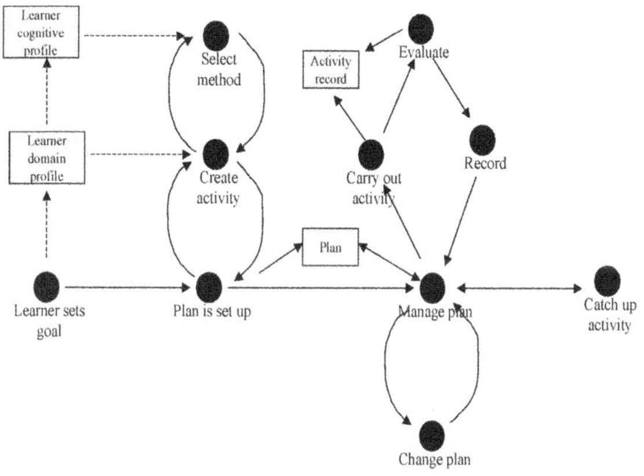

Figure 2 – General framework for agent support

The Learning Plan

There can of course be more than one alternate plan for the same learning goal. Figure 3, for example, shows alternate plans for learning on how to integrate knowledge management into e-business applications. One approach is the case study approach, whose goal is to identify and generalize ways in where knowledge management has been shown to provide advantages. Thus one step here is to read a number of case studies to identify successful implementation and from these develop some conclusions about ways to use knowledge to advantage in a variety of business situations.

The other plan is a standard modeling approach. Here a system model is developed followed by design, which stresses innovations in the use of knowledge management. A new design is then proposed and evaluated.

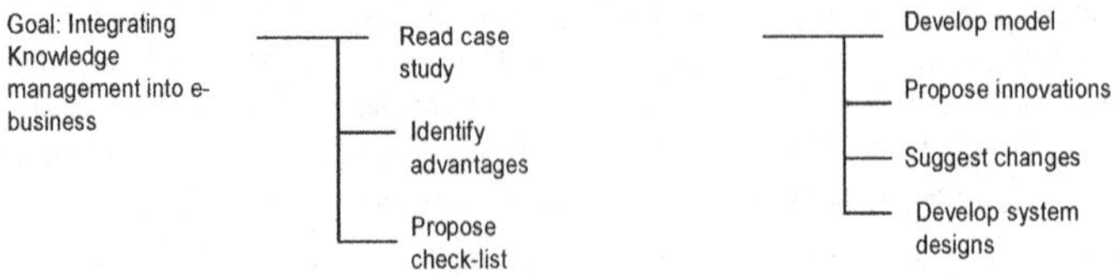

Figure 3 – Alternate plans, an example

In either case, the learning plan is made up of a number of learning activities. This plan is then implemented as a learning plan on the computer support system. Figure 4 shows an example learning plan for the second option in Figure 3. It shows the steps of the plan and their particular start and finish times. Each step also includes the materials needed in the step and the outcomes to be produced.

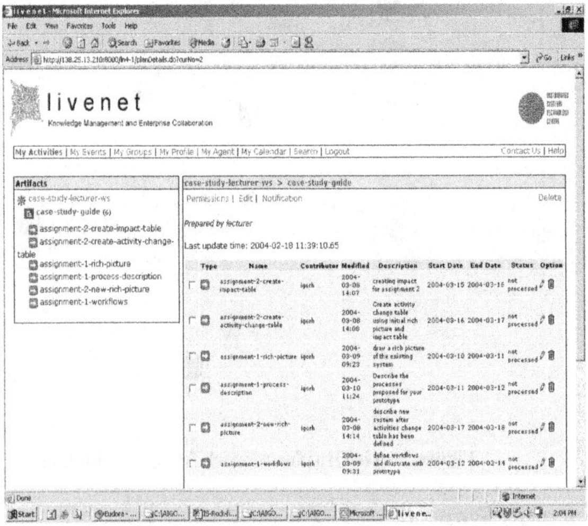

Figure 4 – The learning plan

Managing the Learning Plan using Process Agents

This paper concentrates on using agents for learning plan management. The goal is not to define specific agents for each learning plan but to have a set of generic agents that can be put together to support any learning process. Thus there will be a generic agent to support any learning activity, a generic agent to support a learning plan, and so on. This theoretical approach here is illustrated in Figure 5.

It is based on our learning process concepts defined in Figure 1. It then uses the metamodel of collaboration defined in earlier work, which identified the concepts to describe collaborative processes. These included roles, groups, work-items, work-activities among others (Hawryszkiewycz, 2005b). The collaborative metamodel concepts identify candidates for generic agents (Hawryszkiewycz & Lin, 2003) and typical multi-agent architectures. Typical agents here include a role agent, a group agent, a work-item agent or an activity agent.

Any process can then be expressed in collaborative concepts. Generic agents are chosen to correspond to these concepts. In our case, a learning process can then be converted into a model expressed in terms of collaborative concepts. The corresponding generic agents can then be selected and customized for each element of the learning process. These generic agents are then combined in a multi-agent architecture to support a learning environment. They are then implemented on our system, LiveNet (http://livenet4.it.uts.edu.au).

Based on such conversions, the following generic agents have been selected (Hawryszkiewycz, 2005a) to assist in managing the learning process:

An activity agent, which manages a learning plan,

Work-item agents, each of which manage one learning activity,

Work-item agents, each of which manage one learning method,

An artifact agent, which manages an artifact that may be produced as part of learning and which serves as a check-list for building knowledge,

A personal agent that supports the learner.

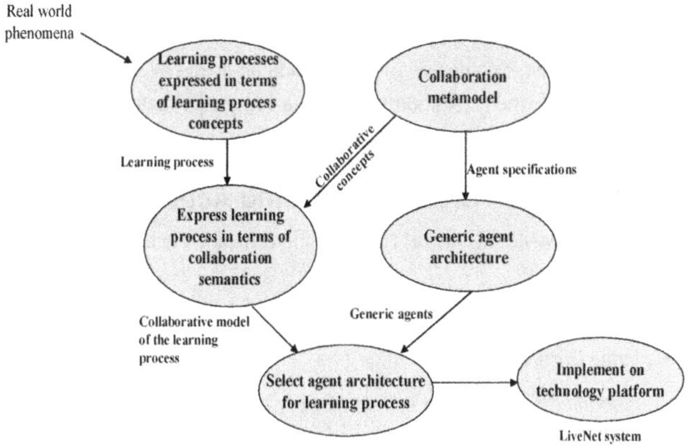

Figure 5 – Theoretical approach

The way that agents interact with each other in a multi-agent architecture is shown in Figure 6 as follows:

The learning plan agent delegates work to learning activities by creating a workspace for the learning activity and its agent,

The learning plan agent monitors progress on the learning activity task,

The artifact agent serves as the collection of knowledge developed by the learner. It interacts with the learning plan agent to identify knowledge needs. The learning plan agent then sets up a learning activity to acquire this knowledge,

The learning activity agent can interact with the learner agent to find the learner's background when choosing the next learning activity,

The learning activity agent can initiate any support activity such as situation assessment as needed.

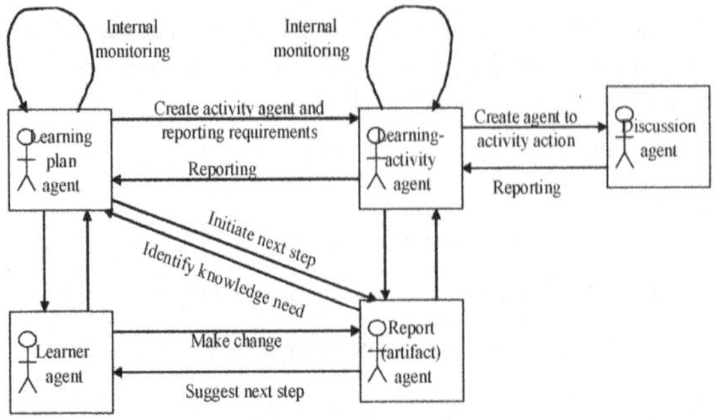

Figure 6 – Multi-agent structure for learner support

We use the usual reasoning model of agents where an agent goal leads to a plan, which is defined in terms of rules that lead to actions. The plan itself can have lower level goals. The reasoning model is implemented using the three-layer architecture (Müller, 1996) chosen from a number of alternative architectures (Wooldridge, 1999). Agents are used to achieve goals using plans defined by agent users. A plan is composed of event-condition-action rules, each of which specifies the actions to be executed when condition is true. We can predefine the goal, belief, plan, rule, and action for an agent or define them at run time.

Learning Plan Agent - Creating Learning Activities

The learning plan agent would include the rules of actions to take when progress is not as expected. These would include:

Goal: Complete the learning plan;

Plan: for completing learning plan.

Subgoal g1: determine if next activity is to be started;

Subgoal g2: determine if additional learning activity is needed;

Subplan: for identifying additional activity

Rule: if next artifact step needs 'a' and learner has no 'a' knowledge then action start activity to learn 'a';

Subgoal g3: determine if expert advice is needed;

The agent that manages the plan creates workspaces for each activity. The workspace in Figure 7 shows a learning activity on design. It provides background material, guidelines for completing the key artefacts, that describe the outcomes of this learning activity, as well as contact information to group members and instructors.

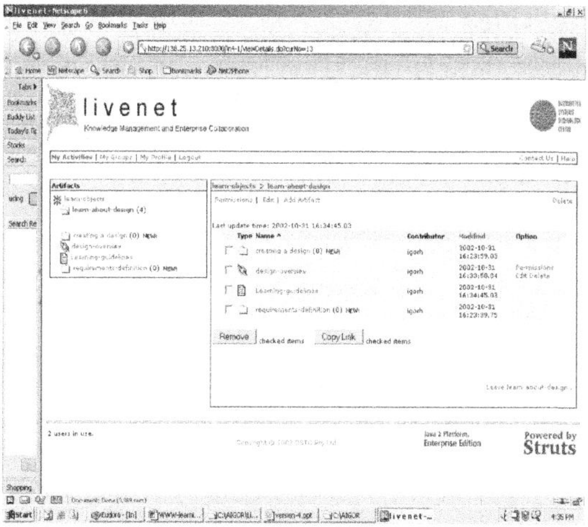

Figure 7 – A workspace for a learning activity

Selecting Services

The services to support the chosen learning method can be chosen from those available in the learning environment. Figure 8 describes one such set of services. These can be selected as needed and placed in the learning activity workspace. The type of service selected depends on the learning method. Thus a learning method where a group jointly carries out a case study would require services such as chatrooms or discussion systems.

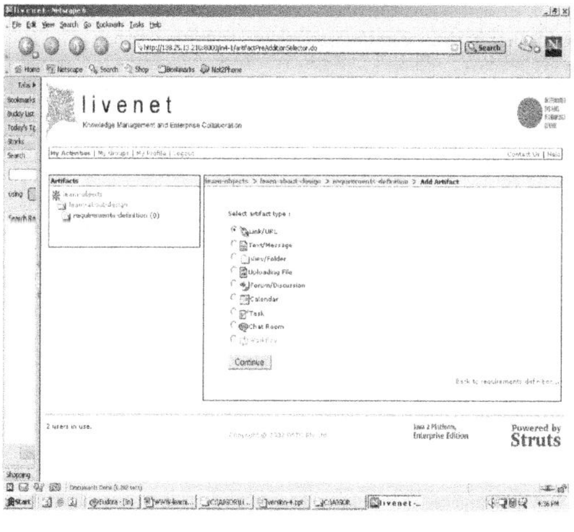

Figure 8 – Available support services

Managing Activities

The primary goal of this agent is to expedite the completion of this activity. The learning activity agent primarily encourages participation in the group activity and maintains awareness of progress among group members. It keeps track of changes made to documents, participation in group discussion. Typical rules for this agent include:

Goal: Complete learning-activity on time

Plan: for completing learning-activity on time

Subgoal g1: determine if action is needed to *correctly assign role responsibility*

Sub plan P1: for g1

Rule R1: on timer alter if no role assigned **then** action A1

Action A1: send e-mail message to learner and instructor "you should meet and choose someone as the coordinator for learning activity <learning-activity-name>"

Subgoal g2: determine if action needed *for work to proceed in a steady manner*

Sub plan P2: for g2

Rule R2: on timer alter if today is later than two days after last update and today is not after the task end date **then** take action A2

Action A2: send the following message to participant in coordinator role "There seems to be no progress on the key document – should it be updated?"

Rule R3: on timer alter if accesses larger than 15 and no updates to key artifact **then** action A3. (probably disagreement).

Action A3: send the following message to participants in team-member "You should begin to make changes to the key document"

Subgoal g3: determine if action is needed to *improve interaction between team members*

Subgoal g4: determine if lack of progress *requires some additional learning*

The actions to be taken would be derived from rules that evaluate reported outcomes from current learning-activities.

Summary

The paper described the importance of personalizing learning experiences and ways that agents can be used to manage learning processes. It described the need to have generic agents that can be used to support a large number of learning processes. It then described a way to identify such generic agents using a collaborative metamodel. Learning processes expressed in terms of collaborative concepts can then be supported by such generic objects.

References

Baylor, A. & Kim, Y. (2003). Validating pedagogical agent roles: Expert, motivator, and mentor. *ED-Media 2003, 15th. Annual Conference on Educational Multimedia, Hypermedia and Telecommunications,* Hawaii, June.

Hawryszkiewycz, I. T. (2005a). An agent framework for learning systems. *Proceedings of the Fourth IASTED International Conference on Web-based Education,* Grindelwald, pp. 142-147.

Hawryszkiewycz, I. T. (2005b). A metamodel for modeling collaborative systems. *The Journal of Computer Information Systems*, Spring.

Hawryszkiewycz, I. T. & Lin, A.(2003). Process knowledge support for emergent processes. *Proceedings of the Second IASTED International Conference on Information and Knowledge Management*, Scottsdale, Arizona, November, pp. 83-87.

Hezemans, M. & Ritzen, M. (2002). Learning environments: Three types of learning environment. *Tele-Learning: The Challenge for the Third Millennium, IFIP Congress,* Montreal, August 2000, Kluwer Academic Publishers, Boston, pp. 185-192.

Hiltz, R. & Turoff, M. (2002). What makes learning networks effective? *Communications of the ACM, 45*(4), 56-59.

Jonassen, D. (1999). Constructivist learning environments on the Web: Engaging students in meaningful learning. *EdTech99*.

Jonassen, D. & Rohrer-Murphy, L. (1999). Activity theory as a framework for designing constructivist learning environments. *ETR&D, 47*(1), 61-59.

Koper, R. (2000). Modeling units of study from a pedagogical perspective: The pedagogical model behind EML. Retrieved from http://eml.ou.nl/articles

McArdle, G., Monahan, T., Bertolotto, M., & Mangina, E. (2005). Conceptual agent models for a virtual reality and multimedia e-learning environment. *Proceedings of the Fourth IASTED International Conference on Web-based Education*, Grindelwald, pp. 119-124.

Müller, J. P. (1996). *The design of intelligent agents.* Springer Verlag.

Petraglia, J. (1998). The real world on a short term lease: The (Mis)Application of constructivism to the Design of Educational Technology. *ETR&D, 46*(3), 53-65.

Wang, F. H. (2005). Developing web-based virtual classroom based on IMS learning design specification. *Proceedings of the Fourth IASTED International Conference on Web-based Education*, Grindelwald, pp. 267-272.

Wooldridge, M. (1999). Intelligent agents. In G.Weiss (Ed), *Multiagent systems*. K. M. Carley & L. Gasser Chapter 1: Computational organization theory.

Biography

Prof. **Hawryszkiewycz** is the research leader in the area of collaborative systems at UTS. He completed BE and ME degrees in Electrical Engineering at the University of Adelaide, and a PhD degree at the Massachusetts Institute of Technology. His early research covered the design of databases and information systems for business. Since 1987 his work has focused on collaborative work including the design of collaborative systems with emphasis on knowledge management, including small business networks, or research planning at the World Health Organization (WHO). His team has developed the prototype LiveNet workspace system, which supports collaborative applications. He has over 150 research publications and 3 text books.

The page left blank intentionally.

What Makes Valuable Pre-experience for Students Entering Programming Courses?

Edward Holden and Elissa Weeden
Golisano College of Computing and Information Sciences, Rochester Institute of Technology, Rochester, NY, USA

eph@it.rit.edu emw@it.rit.edu

Abstract

For the past several years, the authors have been studying the impact of prior experience on performance in introductory Information Technology (IT) courses. Since 2002, data has been collected on all incoming freshmen and performance has been measured by the grade received in initial courses. The grades are expressed in the traditional four-point scale used at most US colleges and universities.

Prior studies (Holden & Weeden, 2003, 2004, 2005) have used an experience index to determine the level of prior experience possessed by students entering the IT undergraduate program. The index has also been used to place students in appropriate classes. This study looks at the components of the formula used to calculate this index as well as some informal experience information that is collected as part of the survey. It concludes with a revised version of the experience index formula which will be used to place students into cohorts in the future.

Keywords: Computers, Education, Information Technology (IT), Information Science Education, Computer Science Education, Curriculum, Information Systems Education

Introduction

In the Information Technology (IT) department at Rochester Institute of Technology (RIT), the authors started looking at retention in initial programming courses in the IT undergraduate program. It was observed that certain students seemed to be unintentionally intimidated by other students who appeared to have more experience. This caused the students without prior experience to not become fully engaged in the course. A formula was developed to predict performance in the first course in the programming sequence (Holden & Weeden, 2003).

It was then decided to group incoming students into cohorts based on their score using the formula, under the assumption that the students without experience would not be intimidated. This series of studies was used to examine student performance as measured by the grade received in the class (Holden & Weeden, 2003, 2004, 2005). An earlier study by Wilson and Shrock (2001) indicated that students performed better when they are comfortable in class. One way to increase comfort would be to have a more homogeneous group.

Since 2002, data has been collected on all incoming freshmen students beginning the Information Technology program at RIT. This data has shown the types and level of experience possessed by these students. Course performance has been measured by the grade received in initial courses. These grades are expressed in the traditional four-point scale used at most US colleges and universities.

The formula was developed and used in our prior studies (Holden & Weeden, 2003, 2004, 2005) to analyze the experience level of students entering the program. The formula has been used to determine the depth of experience of each incoming freshman. The formula focused on the formal experience that a student can encounter before entering the program. The formula included formal high-school courses, college courses, work experience and exposure to object-oriented concepts only and is documented in Appendix A. It did not include informal activities. This is similar in concept to the formula developed by Wilson and Shrock (2001) to determine experience level except that they included other factors that we did not consider relevant for our study. Other factors are evaluated separately later in this paper. These include other ways to gain experience that are not included in the formula and include programming for enjoyment, self teaching, summer camps or other short programs, and clubs.

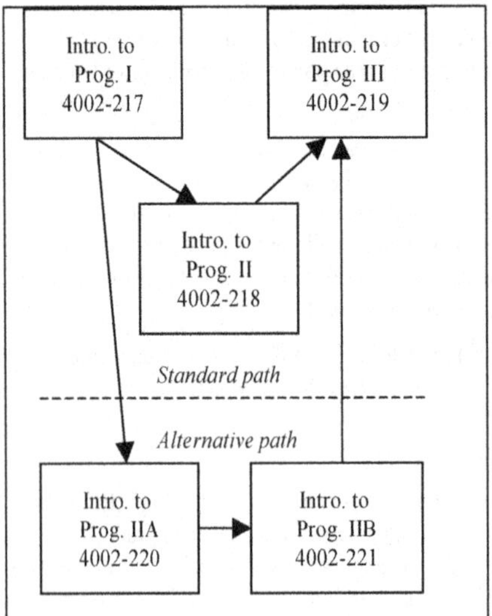

Figure 1: Introductory Programming Sequences

This paper will layout the results of prior studies (Holden and Weeden, 2003, 2004, 2005) and report on the sources of prior experience both inside and outside the formula mentioned above, and how this experience impacts the performance, as measured by grade in the first programming course, Introduction to Programming I (4002-217). This course is the first of a three or four course sequence, as documented in prior studies (Holden and Weeden, 2003) and is illustrated in Figure 1.

Methodology

Since 2003, a survey has been sent to all students in the summer before their freshman year. Students were asked to return the survey before they would be registered for their programming courses. This survey investigated five areas.

- General computing background
- Computer programming experience
- RIT and program affiliation
- About yourself
- Learning styles

Only the first two areas are covered in this study. This study was aimed at gaining insight into prior student experience in programming and individual motivation to program. The survey data was collected for later analysis when course grades were available. The questions related to this study are included in Appendix B.

Part I of the survey was designed to determine the students' comfort using computers and asked if they had any prior programming experience, either academically, in a work environment or for fun. Students with no prior experience did not complete part II of the survey. Students with experience completed part II, which gave more insight into the nature of that experience.

Student performance as measured by grade on a four point scale in the first courses in the programming sequence was compared to the data gathered in the survey.

The remainder of the survey is used in other studies.

The 2002 survey was less formal and contained only the first two sections. It was conducted during the first quarter of the freshman year.

Results of Prior Studies

In anecdotal discussion of the impact of prior experience, faculty members have been mixed on their attribution of value of prior experience. Some say that it is a good predictor of success while others have said that it was actually detrimental because students had to unlearn bad practices.

Other studies have looked at the impact of experience on performance in computing courses, but most of theses have been focused on Computer Science courses rather than IT (Byrne & Lyons, 2001; Franklin, 1987; Hagen & Markham, 2000; Taylor & Luegina, 1989).

Several studies have concluded that prior experience does have an impact on student performance (Byrne & Lyons, 2001; Hagan & Markham, 2000), while others have had the opposite result (Bergin & Reilly, 2005; Ventura & Ramamurthy, 2004)

Wilson and Shrock (2001) differentiated between programming experiences from formal course work compared to informal experience. In earlier studies (Holden & Weeden, 2003, 2004, 2005), only formal and work experience was considered, not informal experience. Informal experience will be considered as a separate item in this report. Wilson and Shrock found that programming experience, both formal and informal, as part of their model, did not have a significant impact, but previous programming coursework did.

Prior results found by Holden and Weeden (2003, 2004, 2005) include:

- Prior programming experience has an impact on student performance in the first course in the programming sequence; however it does not have a significant impact on student performance in subsequent courses. By the end of the sequence, students seem to have equivalent performance.
- Students with prior experience are more likely to complete a faster three course sequence than their inexperienced peers. The alternative is a four course sequence covering the same material.
- The hurdle in learning programming appears to be learning the basic concepts such as sequence, iteration, and decision. Once these are learned, students are able to master the more advanced concepts covered in later courses.
- The depth of programming experience does have an impact in the first course although there are diminishing marginal returns for going from minimal experience to higher levels, but these returns are not statistically significant. Once the key hurdles mentioned above are overcome, other material is more easily learned.
- Students exposed to the concepts of inheritance, encapsulation and polymorphism have significantly better performance in the first course. This may be because these students had a more rigorous prior programming experience.
- This study has shown that there is a positive difference in performance for students who have prior experience, particularly if the experience covered more advanced concepts.

This has some broad implications for IT programs. Institutions should consider designing their early curriculum around the experience level of their entering students. They may consider designing more intense courses for experienced students or transitional courses for those who do not have experience.

- They may also want to organize students into cohorts, based on experience. This could eliminate the frustration of early students who complain that a course is either too fast or too slow. It may also eliminate the frustration felt by students who believe that they are the only ones who have difficulty with the material. This latter point is currently being investigated.
- Students' indication of "comfort level" with computers is not an indication of future performance in programming courses.
- One programming language used in the prior experience does not seem to indicate future success more than others.
- Formal educational experience does improve performance in the first course in the sequence.

In this paper, the authors examine the components of the formula used in the prior studies to see if one component has more impact than others. It will also be used to modify the method of determining experience as outlined in Appendix A.

Where Do Students Get Prior Experience?

A survey done in 1987 found the 34% of 321 students had prior experience in a high school course (Franklin, 1987). In 2002 Holden and Weeden (2003) found that 53% of 159 students sampled had prior experience through a high school course, an increase of 19% in fifteen years.

In the combined survey from 2002 to 2005, the authors have surveyed 525 students. Many of these students indicated that they had prior experience in programming. It was found that 56% of the incoming freshman gained programming experience in a high school course.

In addition 10% had experience in a college course before entering our first programming course.

The Information Technology department also had 8% of incoming students entering with programming experience from work.

The surveys used also included questions about informal experience that has not until now been analyzed. The questions asked if the incoming students programmed for enjoyment, taught themselves to program, learned to program as part of a club, or learned to program at a summer camp or other short program.

From this data it was found that 38% of our incoming students programmed for enjoyment, 31% taught themselves to program, 6% learned to program as part of a club, and 6% learned to program as part of a summer camp or other short program. These results are summarized in Table 1.

All-in-all a large percentage of the incoming students have some experience before they arrive in the Introduction to Programming I course.

Prior studies by Holden and Weeden (2003, 2004, 2005) have indicated that the formal experience does have a positive impact on performance. We will now isolate the types of experience to see what the impact of each component is.

Table 1: Where students get prior programming experience. Note that students may have more than one type of experience.		
Student Category	**Number of Students**	**Percentage of Students**
Total students in survey	525	
Formal experience		
High school experience	294	56%
College experience	50	10%
Work experience	41	8%
Informal experience		
Programmed for enjoyment	197	38%
Self taught	165	31%
Clubs	32	6%
Summer camp or other short program	33	6%

Dissecting the Experience Formula

The experience formula documented in Appendix A is broken down into four parts, high school experience, college experience, work experience and exposure to advanced concepts. The analysis began by looking at the first three parts since advanced concepts exposure was a result of the first three. When the formula was dissected, some interesting results were found.

A total of 525 students who entered the Introduction to Programming I course, using Java, from 2002 through 2005 were included in the study. Of these students, 318 fell into the experienced categories while 207 had no experience. The average grade of students in the experienced group was 2.86 while those with no experience only averaged 2.33, 0.53 points lower than the experienced. An independent sample *t*-test showed a significant difference (p=0.000) between the non-experienced group and the experienced group in the first course and is consistent with the results of the prior research.

To isolate the components, the experienced group was further broken down into the type of experience used in the experience formula, high school only, college only, work only and a mixture of high school, college or work. An ANOVA comparing the grades earned in the Introduction to Programming I course showed no significant difference between the experience types used in the experience formula (p=.336).

A total of 233 students had only high school experience. These students averaged 2.91, which was also consistent with the overall experienced students. Similarly, the 64 students with a mixture of experience had a 2.75 average, again consistent with the experienced group.

The 12 students in the college only group only scored an average of 2.25. These results are not significant due to the small sample size. The evaluation of experience was done from the students' perspectives. The sample size is low here due to two factors. First, most of the students who enter this course are first-time college students who have not taken a college programming course. Second, students who have had a college experience equivalent to this course, as determined by the department's undergraduate coordinator, are allowed to waive this course. This would cut the number of students even further. The lower average is explained by the fact that the undergraduate coordinator determined that students taking this course had a less rigorous experience than the other students who had a college-only experience.

The nine students who had work-only experience scored higher than the overall experienced group, with an average grade of 3.11. This result however is not significant due to the small sample size. Again, the sample is small because most entering students come from high school, and have not entered the work force as programmers. These students often represent non-traditional students who have entered our program. These results are shown in Table 2.

Table 2: Average grade in Introduction To Programming I by type of experience		
Type of Experience	**Number of Students**	**Average Grade in Introduction to Programming I (4.0 scale)**
High School Only	233	2.91
College-Only	12	2.25
Work-Only	9	3.11
Mixture	64	2.75
Total Experienced	***318***	***2.86***
No Experience	207	2.33
All Students	***525***	***2.65***

The fourth factor in the experience formula was exposure to the advanced, object-oriented programming (OOP), concepts of polymorphism, encapsulation and inheritance. The 2002 survey had a slightly different question than the 2003 though 2005 surveys. The 2002 survey only asked if the students had "learned" the concepts (Yes or No). The 2003 through 2005 survey asked students to describe their level of understanding: not at all, weak, moderate, or strong. The 2002 students were considered to have had exposure to OOP if they selected "Yes", while the 2003 through 2005 students were considered to have had exposure to OOP if they selected a moderate or strong understanding.

The results showed that all experience categories had higher average grades if they had exposure to OOP concepts than those who did not. Of the 233 students who had high school only experience, 42 had exposure to OOP concepts. Those 42 had an average grade of 3.23, 0.32 above their peers without the OOP exposure. A 1-tailed independent sample *t*-test indicated that a students that had programming experience in high school and were exposed to OOP concepts performed significantly higher in Introduction to Programming I than students that had programming experience in high school but were not exposed to OOP concepts (p=.04).

The students with college-only experience who had exposure to OOP concepts averaged 2.33, 0.08 above their inexperienced peers. The sample was small (3/12) and the difference between the groups was not significant (p=.46) given a 1-tailed independent sample t-test. Likewise, those with only work experience and exposure to OOP concepts finished with a 4.00, 0.89 above their peers without OOP exposure. But again, the sample is small (2 / 9) and the results using a 1-tailed independent sample *t*-test indicated that there was no significant difference (p=.051). College-only experience will no longer be included because of the introduction of the undergraduate coordinator's process mentioned earlier, which causes a downward bias on the grades.

The 16 students who had a mixture of types of experience, who also had exposure to OOP concepts had a significant improvement over their 64 peers without exposure to OOP concepts. The former averaged 3.31, 0.56 above the latter. The results where shown to be significant through a 1-tailed independent sample t-test (p=.038).

In general, the 318 experienced students averaged 2.86. The 63 students who had exposure to OOP concepts demonstrated better performance (3.24) than the 255 who did not (2.76). This difference is shown to be significant through a 1-tailed independent sample *t*-test (.005). These results are summarized in Table 3.

Table 3: Average grade in Introduction To Programming I for experienced students with and without exposure to advanced OOP concepts.				
Type of Experience	**Number of Students w/Advanced Concepts**	**Average Grade in Intro to Prog I (4.0 scale)**	**Number of Students w/o Advanced Concepts**	**Average Grade in Intro. to Prog. I (4.0 scale)**
High School Only	42	3.24	191	2.83
College-Only	3	2.33	9	2.22
Work-Only	2	4.00	7	2.86
Mixture	16	3.31	48	2.56
All Types	*63*	*3.24*	*255*	*2.76*

Other Factors Outside the Experience Formula

The experience formula detailed in Appendix A does not include informal experience like self training, clubs, summer camps or other activities. The surveys did collect information on these areas.

When looking at these informal factors, some interesting results were found. Of the 318 experienced students, 217 students (68%) were involved in one or more of the informal activities. The experienced students had an overall average of 2.86. Of these students, 174 said that they wrote programs for enjoyment. These students had an overall average of 2.97, 0.11 above the average for the experienced group. Similarly the 142 experienced students who taught themselves to program had an average of 2.99, 0.13 above the experienced group.

The opposite results were seen when the non-experienced group was examined. Only 27 (13%) of the 207 students took part in these informal activities. The 207 students who had no prior experience had an average of 2.33. The 23 students who programmed for enjoyment had an average of 2.48, 0.15 above the non-experienced group. The 23 students who were self-taught had an average of 2.65, 0.32 above the non-experienced group.

This may have indicated that these students had more motivation than the others to learn to program.

The 31 experienced students who belonged to a club fared no better in the first programming course that their experienced group as a whole. They averaged 2.87 compared to 2.86 for the larger group.

The questions concerning learning to program at a summer camp or other short term program were not included in the 2002 survey, so these results are from the later surveys.

The experienced students who learned to program as part of a summer camp or other short program actually fared worse than the whole experienced group. These 30 students averaged 2.47, 0.39 less than the larger group.

The sample was too small for the non-experienced students who belonged to a club or attended a summer camp or other short program to make judgments about the results. Only one of these students belonged to a club and three went to a summer camp or other short program. Table 4 summarizes these results.

Table 4: Average grade in Introduction To Programming I by type of informal experience		
Experience Type	Number of Students	Average Grade in Intro. To Prog. I
All Experienced	318	2.86
Experience - Program for Enjoyment	174	2.98
Experience - Self Taught	142	2.99
Experience - Club	31	2.87
Experience - Summer Camp	30	2.47
No Experience - Program for Enjoyment	23	2.48
No Experience - Self taught	23	2.65
No Experience - Club	1	2.00
No Experience - Summer Camp	3	3.67
All No Experience	207	2.33

Restating the Experience Formula

When the components of the experience formula documented in Appendix A were examined more closely for possible refinement, it was noted that various weights based on the type of experience that the student had were not always appropriate. For example, more weight was given to college courses than high school and much more weight was give to work experience over high school. The formula was based on some assumptions derived from discussions with faculty and students. The assumptions were then added together. One assumption was that these factors were additive, implying that the more, different types, of experience the better. The data suggest that for placement in an introductory programming course, these factors are not always be additive as can be seen in Table 2.

As shown in Table 2, all 318 students that indicated they had programming experience received an average grade of 2.86, 0.53 above 2.33 that the non-experienced students received. The average for the 233 students who had only high school experience was 2.91, slightly above the total experienced group, but consistent with the overall average for the whole experienced group. The group of nine students who only had work experience had an even higher average (3.11). The 64 students who had a mixture of experience averaged 2.75, slightly below the average for the total experienced group, but consistent with the experienced group.

One conclusion that can be drawn from this is that experience is not additive since the average grade for students who had only one type of experience was consistent with those with a mixture of experience.

Students with only college experience were left out of this discussion. This was because of the way transfer credit is handled within the department by the undergraduate coordinator, as described earlier.

Based on this analysis, either high school or work experience will be counted as determining an experienced student, but not both, since they do not appear to be additive. College experience will no longer be used in this situation, as it does not apply for the reasons mentioned earlier. This exclusion of college experience may not apply at other institutions.

The old formula added one point if the student had experience with the advanced concepts of polymorphism, encapsulation and inheritance. The new formula will continue this. This is based on the results shown in Table 3. In all types of experience the students averaged higher that those without the concepts.

The old formula did not include the informal activities shown in Table 4. Experienced students that programmed for enjoyment or taught themselves to program averaged 0.12 and 0.13 higher than the overall average for experienced students, respectively. These additional factors will be included in the new formula.

The New Formula

With this new information, a new formula has been developed to assess the experience level of each individual in the sample.

- The high school experience will continue to be assessed the same way. Students received a maximum of two points for their high school experience. If they had a one semester course, they received one point. For two or more semesters they received two points. If the programming was only part of another course, the score was multiplied by 0.5.
- For the reasons mentioned above, college experience will not be included. For other universities, this may be a factor that should be included if they do not do the same screening that is done by the undergraduate coordinator.
- Work experience will continue to be assessed the same way but with the weights assigned for time worked reduced. First, a factor was assigned based on the type of position: Full time = 1 point, part time = 0.5 point, and less than part time = 0.25. This was multiplied by a factor reflecting the number of years they held a job: Less than six months = 0.5, 6 months or more but less than 18 months = 1, 18 months or more = 2.
- The experience index will be the maximum of the high school score or the work score, plus one point if the student had learned about the object-oriented programming concepts of polymorphism, encapsulation and inheritance.
- One-half point will be added if the student has informal experience from programming for enjoyment or being self-taught. This was not included in the original formula.
- This index will be used as the experience index for each individual, with a maximum possible total of 3.5.

This formula is closer to the reality that different types of experience are not as radically different as indicated in the old formula. It recognizes that students with college experience are removed from the sample by the undergraduate coordinator if their experience is equivalent to the introductory course. It also recognizes that the different types of experience are not necessarily additive as shown through the ANOVA performed across the experience types shown in Table 3.

We defined student experience levels differently in terms of the calculated experience index as follows:

- No experience: experience index = 0
- Average experience: 0 < experience index <=2
- High experience: 2 < experience index

Using this new formula, the experience levels for students in the sample ranged from 0 to 3.5 out of the maximum possible index of 3 points. The average is 1.1. Out of the 404 students, 142 had no experience, 178 had an average level of experience and 84 had a high level of experience

Conclusion

Based on the new evaluation of this analysis, IT departments may want to consider cohorting students into groups based on the new experience formula, which gives a more realistic view of the students' prior experience. This will allow tailoring of course material and pace to individual student needs.

This, of course, will depend on the number of course sections being offered. In some situations it may be necessary to combine groups for logistical reasons.

Future Study

In future studies we will continue examine and refine the experience formula. In addition, other experiences that may impact student performance should be examined and considered. This includes the items in Table 3 as well as other factors that are included in the survey.

Also, a separate study is examining the cohort data to determine if cohorted students actually perform better than non-cohorted students.

References

Bergin, S., & Reilly, R. (2005). Programming: Factors that influence success. *Proceedings of the 36th SIGCSE Technical Symposium on Computer Science Education, 37*(1), 411-415. Retrieved February 9, 2006, from ACM Digital Library database.

Byrne, P., & Lyons, G. (2001). The effect of student attributes on success in programming. *Proceedings of the 6th Annual Conference on Innovation and Technology in Computer Science Education, 33*(3), 49-52. Retrieved February 9, 2006, from ACM Digital Library database.

Franklin, R. E., Jr. (1987). What academic impact are high school computing courses having on the entry-level college computer science curriculum? *Proceedings of the Eighteenth SIGCSE Technical Symposium on Computer Science Education, 19*(1), 253-256. Retrieved February 9, 2006, from ACM Digital Library database.

Hagan, D., & Markham, S. (2000). Does it help to have some programming experience before beginning a computing degree program? *Proceedings of the 5th Annual SIGCSE/*SIGCUE ITiCSE Conference on Innovation and Technology in Computer Science Education, 32(3), 25-28. Retrieved February 9, 2006, from ACM Digital Library database.

Holden, E., & Weeden, E. (2003). The impact of prior ecperience in an information technology programming course sequence. In *Conference on Information Technology Education. Proceedings of the 4th conference on information technology education* (pp. 41-46). New York: ACM Press. Retrieved February 9, 2006, from ACM Digital Library database.

Holden, E., & Weeden, E. (2004). The experience factor in early programming education. In *Conference on Information Technology Education. Proceedings of the 5th conference on information technology education* (pp. 211-218). New York: ACM Press. Retrieved February 9, 2006, from ACM Digital Library database.

Holden, E., & Weeden, E. (2005). Prior experience and new IT students. *The Journal of Issues in Informing Science and Information Technology, 2*(1), 189-204. Retrieved February 9, 2006, from http://iisit.org/IssuesVol2v2.htm

Taylor, H. G., & Mounfield, L. C. (1989). The effect of high school computer science, gender, and work on success in college computer science. *Proceedings of the Twentieth SIGCSE Technical Symposium on Computer Science Education, 21*(1), 195-198. Retrieved February 9, 2006, from ACM Digital Library database.

Ventura, P., & Ramamurthy, B. (2004). Wanted: CS1 students, no experience required. *Proceedings of the 35th SIGCSE Technical Symposium on Computer Science Education, 36*(1), 240-244. Retrieved February 9, 2006, from ACM Digital Library database.

Wilson, B. C., & Shrock, S. (2001). Contributing to the success in an introductory computer science course: A study of twelve factors. *Proceedings of the 32nd SIGCSE Technical Symposium on Computer Science Education, 33*(1), 184-188. Retrieved February 9, 2006, from ACM Digital Library database.

Appendix A - The Current Experience Formula Used in this Study

People with prior programming experience filled in part II of the survey included in Appendix B. This data was used to examine the depth of their programming experience. The following questions on the survey were used to assess how deep the experience was.

- Did you learn about the concepts of encapsulation and inheritance?
- High School – Did you learn to program as part of a high school class (either formal or informal)? If yes, how many semesters did you take courses involving programming? Was this programming experience part of another course (e.g. Math, Business, Science…)?
- College – Did you learn to program as part of a college course? If yes, how many semesters (quarters) did you take courses involving programming? Was this programming experience part of another course (e.g. Math, Business, Science…)?
- Work – Did you program as part of your work? If yes, was your work programming experience full time, part time or less that part time? Roughly how long did you have this work programming experience?

With this data, a formula was developed to assess the experience level of each individual in the sample.

- Students received a maximum of two points for their high school experience. If they had a one semester course, they received one point. For two or more semesters they received two points. If the programming was only part of another course, the score was multiplied by 0.5.
- A similar approach was used for college experience. The students could score a maximum of three points for college coursework. For one semester they received 1.5, for two or more, they received three points. Again, if the programming was only part of another course, the score was multiplied by 0.5.
- Work experience was handled a little differently. First, a factor was assigned based on the type of position: Full time = 1 point, part time = 0.5 point, and less than part time = 0.25. This was multiplied by a factor reflecting the number of years they held a job: Less than one year = 1.5, one year = 3, Greater than one year but less than or equal to two years = 4, Greater than two years = 6.
- Finally, students who had learned about the object-oriented programming concepts of polymorphism, encapsulation and inheritance received an additional point.
- The sum of these scores was used as the experience index for each individual, with a possible total of 12.

The formula is somewhat arbitrary, but is designed to reflect the assumptions that work experience (application) is worth more than educational experience alone and that there were diminishing marginal returns for additional experience over a certain level. The extra point for studying encapsulation and inheritance reflects the assumption that courses covering this material would be more rigorous than other courses.

The experience levels for students in the sample ranged from 0 to 7.0 out of the maximum possible index of 12 points.

Student experience levels were defined in terms of the calculated experience index as follows:

- No experience: experience index = 0
- Minimal experience: 0 < experience index <=2
- Medium experience: 2 < experience index <=4
- Very experienced: experience index > 4

Appendix B - Survey Questions

Part I – General Computing Background

1. Choose the statement that best describes your level of comfort with using computers.
   a) I am very comfortable and have used computers extensively.
   b) I am comfortable but have not used them extensively.
   c) I am moderately comfortable with computers.
   d) I am a little uncomfortable using computers.
   e) I am very uncomfortable using computers.

Enter your level of experience on each of the following computer platforms:

2. Windows (any version)	a) none	b) a little	c) some	d) a lot
3. Macintosh	a) none	b) a little	c) some	d) a lot
4. Linux/Unix	a) none	b) a little	c) some	d) a lot
5. Other	a) none	b) a little	c) some	d) a lot

6. Do you have programming experience (<u>excluding</u> HTML)? a) YES b) NO

If you answered NO to question #6, please skip to Part III of the survey now.

If you answered YES to question #6, please continue with Part II of this survey.

Part II – Computer Programming Experience

Do <u>not</u> answer these questions unless you answered YES to question #6 in Part I above.

Choose the phrase that best describes your level of experience with each of the following languages:

7. C Language	a) none	b) a little	c) some	d) a lot
8. C++	a) none	b) a little	c) some	d) a lot
9. Java	a) none	b) a little	c) some	d) a lot
10. Visual Basic	a) none	b) a little	c) some	d) a lot
11. Pascal	a) none	b) a little	c) some	d) a lot

12. Fortran	a) none	b) a little	c) some	d) a lot
13. Other (excluding HTML)	a) none	b) a little	c) some	d) a lot

Choose the phrase that best describes your understanding of the programming language topics below.

14. variables, constants and data types	a) not at all	b) weak	c) moderate	d) strong
15. logic structures: sequence	a) not at all	b) weak	c) moderate	d) strong
16. logic structures: decision (if)	a) not at all	b) weak	c) moderate	d) strong
17. logic structures: iteration (loop)	a) not at all	b) weak	c) moderate	d) strong
18. methods or procedures	a) not at all	b) weak	c) moderate	d) strong
19. arrays	a) not at all	b) weak	c) moderate	d) strong
20. encapsulation, inheritance & polymorphism	a) not at all	b) weak	c) moderate	d) strong

<u>**High School**</u>

21. Did you learn to program as part of a high school class (either formally or informally)?
    a) YES b) NO

If you answered YES to question # 21, please answer the following three questions about your high school classes.

22. How many courses did you take that involved some computer programming?
    a) one
    b) two or three
    c) more than three

23. Did you have at least one course that focused primarily on computer programming?
    a) YES b) NO

24. Did you take an Advanced Placement (AP) Computer Science course?
    a) YES b) NO

<u>**College**</u>

25. Did you learn to program as part of a college course?
    a) YES b) NO

If you answered YES to question # 25, please answer the following two questions.

26. How many courses did you take involving programming?
    a) one
    b) two to three
    c) more than three

27. Was this programming experience part of another course (e.g. Math, Business, Science, etc.)
    a) YES b) NO

Other Educational Experiences

28. Did you learn to program as part of a summer camp or other short program?
    a) YES b) NO

If you answered YES to question # 28, please answer the following question about your experience.

29. Estimate how many days you spent programming.
    a) less than 3 days
    b) 3 to 5 days
    c) 7 to 14 days
    d) more than 14 days

30. Did you teach yourself to program? a) YES b) NO

31. Did you program as part of a computer club? a) YES b) NO

32. Do you program for enjoyment? a) YES b) NO

Job Experiences

33. Did you have a job that involved programming? a) YES b) NO

If you answered YES to question #33, please answer the following two questions about your work.

34. How many hours a week did you program?
    a) full time (roughly 30 hours or more per week)
    b) half time (roughly 20 to 30 hours per week)
    c) less than half time (less than 20 hours per week)

35. How long did you program at work?
    a) less than 3 months
    b) 3 to less than 6 months
    c) 6 to less than 12 months
    d) 12 to less than 18 months
    e) 18 months or more

Biographies

Ed Holden is an Assistant Professor in the Information Technology Department of the Golisano College of Computing and Information Sciences at Rochester Institute of Technology (RIT). He teaches courses in programming, database management, technology transfer, needs assessment, e-commerce and process management. Prior to joining RIT full-time, Ed spent 28 years in the Information Systems business at a major corporation. In his last positions he served as the manager of Global Infrastructure Development for Messaging and Groupware and worked on a special assignment to integrate digital business efforts with back office systems and operations. Prior to this he was the manager of Messaging and Groupware for US and Canada where he supervised the outsourcing of email and groupware and the migration of 30,000 users to a new email and groupware system. He also worked on the preliminary design and requirements definition for the company's business-to-business e-commerce initiative.

Ed has performed all phases of the systems life cycle from proposal through continued support and the negotiation and management of outsourcing contracts. His clients have included finance, marketing, sales, research and development, and supply chain management.

Ed holds a BA in Mathematics from SUNY Oswego (1972) and an MBA, Finance, from RIT (1995).

Elissa Weeden is an Assistant Professor in the Information Technology Department of the Golisano College of Computing and Information Sciences at Rochester Institute of Technology (RIT). Her areas of expertise are in database design and implementation as well as applications programming. She consults professionally and regularly within those areas. Her research and teaching interests include: data modeling, database implementation and administration, active learning, and assessment methods.

Elissa holds a BS in Information Technology and a MS in Software Development and Management, both from RIT. She is currently working towards her Ph.D. in Computing Technology in Education from Nova Southeastern University.

The page left blank intentionally.

Information Access for Development: A Case Study at a Rural Community Centre in South Africa

SJ Jacobs and ME Herselman
Tshwane University of Technology, South Africa

jacobssj@tut.ac.za herselmanme@tut.ac.za

Abstract

This paper examines the theoretical linkage between ICT and advances within a business in a rural community in the North West Province of South Africa. Various aspects are addressed like services and service delivery mechanism, locally adapted content and context, realistic approach to technologies and financial sustainability. A rural community centre in Itsoseng was investigated regarding the above aspects and the results are provided. It became apparent that if these above aspects are not seen as integrated activities within a rural community, success is difficult to achieve. Success in providing human and institutional capacities that harness information and knowledge is imperative.

Keywords. digital divide, CT hub model, rural areas, South Africa

Introduction

Interaction between humans and computers has greatly increased as we embark on the 21st century. Ability to access computers and the Internet has become increasingly important to completely immerse oneself in the economic, political and social aspects of the world. However not every business have access to this technology. In the global digital information age those who are unable to access the Internet through ICTs are increasingly disadvantaged in their access to information. Government policies in South Africa (ICT charter) are being established which attempt to ensure that all citizens have the opportunity to access and effectively use ICT in order to enable them to participate fully in the educational, social and economic activities and democratic processes (Cullen, 2002, p.2). New and powerful technologies can also promote efficiency of enterprises competing in the global economy and public sector service delivery (CIDAs strategy, 2005, p. 5). ICTs are now a standard operating tool in today's information society and the information that ICTs carry is increasingly becoming an important factor of production. Moreover teledensity and power supply are generally accepted as drivers of economic growth in developing countries (Saunders, Warford & Wellenius, 1994 as cited in CIDA 2005). In the poor and underdeveloped regions or countries one has the gap that exist between those who have access to technologies and those who do not, commonly referred to as the digital divide. This divide can result in information and knowledge poverty. However it has to be noted that technology in itself does not solve social and economic discrepancies within societies and can often exacerbate them. Massive growth in the use of ICTs in India for instance has had no impact at all on what has been described as "the highest concentration of poverty in the world" (Rao, 2003, p. 3). Also new technologies do not always replace the old. They may co-exist and in doing so enhance the range of human experience without necessarily diminishing the experience of those who do not use them, preferring older technologies (telephone, radio) to achieve the same ends. The contribution of using the Internet in rural communities seems to be on sharing global knowledge and expertise to help support their initiatives against poverty and disease, better communication with trading partners through e-commerce and the ability to trade opportunities and to use low wage economy and different time zones to monitor and process transactions around the globe (Cullen 2002:3).

Finances and ICTs Adoption in Rural Businesses

In 1990s Cosh & Hughes (2000) indicated that the financial and employment performance of small rural businesses deteriorated relative to urban ones. This climate has stimulated the debate on how best to support rural business activity. Roberts (2002) and Smallbone, North, Baldock, and Ekamen (2002) list barriers to growth in rural businesses and indicate that there is a slower adoption of ICTs among these type of businesses. Friedlander (2001), Roberts (2002) and Warren (2000) emphasize the importance of limited access to communications networks and technology, high usage costs and limited relevant content as reasons for the slow adoption to ICTs in these businesses. Smallbone et al. (2002) and Freshwater (2001) acknowledge an alternative case that there are gaps in labour force skills and reluctance on the part of rural business owner-managers to adapt to the changing environment. In these papers rural businesses are slow to understand the benefits of ICT adoption.

According to Cullen (2002) and Rao (2003) the following factors can be highlighted for preventing rural businesses for reaping the benefits of ICTs and can also be seen as barriers to using technology:

- Physical access (lack of a robust telecommunications infrastructure, computers and connectivity) and costs it involves
- Lack of awareness of the benefits of ICTs
- Lack of ICT skills and support
- Attitudinal barriers like cultural and behavioral attitudes towards technology
- Language barriers in using the Internet especially if English is not the first language
- Lack of local language information products or content, especially tailored to the assimilation capacities of rural people or interesting and relevant to them
- Non-availability of governmental information online
- Lack of motivation to use information over the Internet

These above factors can play a role in a rural community and governments also need to be informed of these in order to ensure they are diminished for better results.

Low demand in rural businesses can be result of information failures and market conditions. Deakins, Galloway & Mochrie (2004) further state that global orientation is the best predicator of rural business growth and rapid ICT adoption is also much more likely within globally orientated businesses. Rural businesses therefore have to strategise themselves for the global market and ensure that information is distributed correctly in order to ensure financial sustainability. Apart from the finances and slow adoption in rural communities, innovation, taking risks and policy issues further hampers development.

Innovation, Risks and Policy

The conventional model of small business behaviour which underpin most rural policy interventions treats innovation generally as the driver of employment and income growth. Thus ICT adoption deserves support because of its potential impact on the health of both individual businesses and the rural economy. Yet, the previous discussion of the role of global or growth orientation of rural businesses suggest that ICTs are more likely to have an important role in terms of transforming businesses' behaviour if their role is innovative, at least at the level of the firm. This argument is also appearing in the policy literature. Fuller and Southern (1999) and Naidoo (2005) criticize those governmental policies based on 'technology push' as being unlikely to engage with the business development needs of rural businesses. Despite the governmental intervention the value of imaginative ICT adoption in rural businesses cannot be underestimated. Friedlander (2001) and Cullen (2002) argue that the content of technologies must engage with potential users' needs in order for it to be adopted. Mitchell and Clark (1999, p. 45) has found in their studies that locally orientated rural businesses make very little use of computing facilities, typically using computers for 'word processing, financial management and producing accounts". These limited usages of ICTs limit the possibility of ICTs being used in innovative ways. Warren (2000) argues that for micro-businesses in particular, limited use of ICTs can be a rational response to the business environment. Thus policy interventions are more likely to be successful where they meet the clients of rural businesses, are easily accessible, have flexible delivery mechanisms, provide services from a one-stop-shop and achieve sustainability, so that they are not reliant upon continued public funding (Deakins, Galloway & Mochrie, 2004, p. 7).

As Ramirez (2001) states that for communities to be sustainable they need to define what they want to be, where they want to go and ICT are tools to be harnessed towards those agreements. The value of ICTs should be found in community-owned activities and communication spaces where issues of importance (content) to the community are addressed.

Huggins and Izushi (2002) argue that the sort of imaginative and innovative way of using ICTs that enable businesses to obtain the full benefit of adoption is more likely to occur in environments in which ICTs are ubiquitous. Facilities like community centers can assist by increasing user's familiarity with technology in non-threatening, social settings. The design of policy interventions should therefore be guided by analysis of the nature of the causes of slow adoption as well as an understanding of the environment within which rural businesses work. Evidence of the following can be found: slow roll-out of high bandwidth networks in rural areas, limited training facilities, the paucity of exemplars of rapid adoption and the uncertainty of how to use ICTs to transform business activity. Such failures of demand are likely to prove more intractable for policy makers. Rather than simply presenting rural businesses with a menu of technologies to choose from, public agencies have to assist businesses identify ways in which ICTs adoption and use can enhance their ongoing activities, so that limited process innovation may occur.

The role of infrastructure upgrades to assist rural businesses in becoming economically viable is only possible through regulatory mechanisms, governmental support and partnerships (Ramirez, 2001). A community development approach to rural and remote ICT development, calls for the integration of economic and social development goals. In other words, while the benefits of ICTs for rural businesses must be presented as economically feasible, at the same time they must engage social and regional developmental policy dimensions. The focus on the infrastructure should also therefore include a focus on the info-structure where access to technology can allow for rural businesses to supply their communities with information that they might be interested about.

Information is critical to development; thus ICTs as means of sharing information are not simply a connection between people, but a link in the chain of the development process itself. There is now considerable evidence that telecommunications contributes to socio-economic development

(Conradie, Morris & Jacobs, 2003; Gómez & Hunt 1999; Mncube, 2003); studies have shown that access to information through telecommunications can facilitate many development activities including agriculture, fisheries, commerce, tourism, shipping, education, health care and social services (Gómez & Hunt ,1999, p. 149; Sebusang & Masupe, 2003).

In general, the ability to access and share information can contribute to the development process by improving:

- *efficiency,* or the ratio of output to cost;
- *effectiveness,* or the quality of products and services;
- *equity*, or the distribution of development benefits throughout the society.

The purpose of the paper was to establish which information access a rural community needs in order to develop itself to become self sustainable. A community centre is a means to provide access to tools to create, access, and share information. Thus, if the contribution of a centre to the development of a community is understood, the need exist to understand what information is needed in the communities, and what other factors may influence the initiation and impact of activities that may be considered developmental (from economic, social, cultural and/or political perspectives).

Research Methodology

In order to determine whether a rural community centre can support the community with relevant content and service delivery in an ICT based environment with financial success, a qualitative research methodology approach was selected. The research data was obtained through the interview process, site visits and questionnaires used during this study at the Ikageng community centre in Itsoseng. This is a rural community located between Lichtenburg and Mafikeng in the North West Province of South Africa.

The data collection process utilise questionnaire sets to acquire information on the current services offered and problems experienced with the delivery process of these services.

The content of the questionnaires (step 3) focused on the main operational components and/or business areas of a community centre, namely: telecentre services, desktop publishing services, training services and business support services. The information gathered was used to design a specific management model for the Itsoseng community (for the use in the Ikageng rural community centre) based on the needs identified from the questionnaires.

The last step was to discuss the proposed management model with the community centre management and staff before computerising the paper model. The data obtained during this process through interviews and informal discussions was used to support the concept multi-media prototype model. The concept prototype model was tested within the same community centre and the data obtained through questionnaires and interviews was used as inputs towards refining the prototype. The prototype should be adaptable to any other community centre with similar needs.

The participants for this study included both the management (n=4) and the staff (n=9) at the Ikageng community centre in Itsoseng in South Africa. They had to each complete a questionnaire and focus group interviews were conducted in order to clarify and verify certain information. It is important to understand that what was done during this study was to conduct interviews and questionnaires in order to determine needs of the community and to create a prototype that was responsive to a specific community's needs and circumstances.

This means it is not necessarily applicable to other community centres, unless exactly the same needs and circumstances apply. What exists is an electronic model that can be introduced into a new community and then fine-tuned to the needs and circumstances of that new community by means of a similar process.

The Results

The services offered within the rural community centre are listed in Table 1 according to the key operational areas.

Table1: Current Services Offered by the Ikageng Community Centre

Key Operational Area	Services Offered within this Operational Area
Telecentre Services	• Sent Faxes • Receive Faxes • E-mail • Internet
Desktop Publishing Services	• Content Creation • Publication • Photo Copying • Typing • Printing
Business Support Services	• Compile Business Plans • Marketing Services • Financial Services
Government Services	• Skills Development
Training Services	• Introduction to Computers • Microsoft Word • Microsoft Excel • Microsoft Power Point • Microsoft Access • Junior Training (school kids - mathematics)
Other Services	• Complete Tender Applications for Government Tenders

Management and staff of the community centre were asked: "What other forms of support could be offered through the centre to meet the community members' needs and expectations?". The responses were the following:

- The centre needs a support system that can assist with the management of training material, training courses, store of standard templates to support customers' requirements (e.g. curriculum vitae and fax templates), etc.
- The centre could do with an information management system that contains general information concerning basic health care, educational, and agricultural content. This could be in the form of links to websites or a software packages that contain some of these basic content.

The Table 2 summarizes the information needs of the centre staff and management with regards to services offered to the community members. It is categorized according to the operational components as identified above.

Table 2: Summary of Information needs from Ikageng Community Centre Management and Staff

Centre Operational Component	Centre Management Response	Centre Staff Response
Telecentre Services	• Standard calculation sheets for example computer and Internet usage, faxing and phone call services. • Daily general checklist when opening and closing the Centre.	• Standard templates to add customer content. • Standard financial recording and reporting forms. • Information with regard to the Internet and e-mail terminologies (ex. WWW, using search engines, etc.)
Desktop Publishing Services	• Not sure, ask the staff working with those services.	• Standard CV templates • Interview tips on for example "what an interview looks like for the candidate?" or "how to act during an interview" or "asking the right questions during the interview" etc. • List of shortcut keys for word processors and spreadsheets. • Short description on what a computer, word processor, spreadsheets publishing and presentation is that they can give to their clients when confronted with these terminologies.
Training Services	• Need more Computer Based training material to assist the Centre staff with training and continuous improvement of skills.	• Content with regard to training on Microsoft Office, Internet and e-mail Usage, etc. • List of Computer Based Training material on the market that they could use to train customers on operating systems, Web Page Publishing, Business Analysis, Project Management and Presentation Skills. • Software packages that can assist children in the community to develop their mathematical skills.
Business Support Services	• Need a step-by-step instruction sheet that could be used when analysing customers business and drawing up business plans. • Information regarding trademarks, copyright and patents.	• Standard business plans. • Templates for financial analysis for clients. • Need a marketing plan template to assist customers to draw up a customized marketing plan. • Template to assist customer in preparing a financial statement.

Technology Support	• Maintenance on equipment in the Centre.	• Need Computer Based Material to assist staff and clients on PC support and maintenance aspects. • Books and software that could assist with technical aspects on computer and networks.
Government Information	• Government Tenders. • Funding opportunities for the Centre.	• Government information on funding programmes. • Government Tenders.
Specific Content	• Basic Agricultural Content to expose the children to farming practices. • Basic first aid content.	• Educational content to assist school kids with mathematics and perceptual skills on Saturdays. • Agricultural content on sustainable farming practices.
Operational Management (Day-to-Day issue)	• Guidelines for the staff on managing the centre operations on a daily basis.	• Need standard checklist to ensure a quality service to the community.

Based on the above feedback a business model was developed electronically to assist them.

The Business Model

The operational and business model is based on defining the income-generating potential of the main operational components. The main operational components are:

- Telecentre Components with an income generating potential;
- Desktop Publishing Components with an income generating potential;
- Training Components with an income generating potential;
- Business Support (SMME) Components - with an income generating potential.
- Technology to support the main operational component.

The basic income generating components of an ICT equipped community centre could be illustrated graphically as in Figure 1.

Each major component provides a range of services to the community at a fee. The typical transaction value of the components of service delivery follows an exponential increase from R1 through to R500 as illustrated in Figure 1.

The low-cost, high volume business found in the first two components (Telecentre and Desktop Publishing services) can create the fundamental cash flow needed to support the higher-level activities (Training and Business support). These elements have been combined with anticipated volumes of transactions to arrive at the target income and other aspects of the business plan, to analyse the potential for the rural community centre to support itself as a self-sustaining business. It could also reduce the *digital divide* (Jacobs, 2003, pp. 108-138).

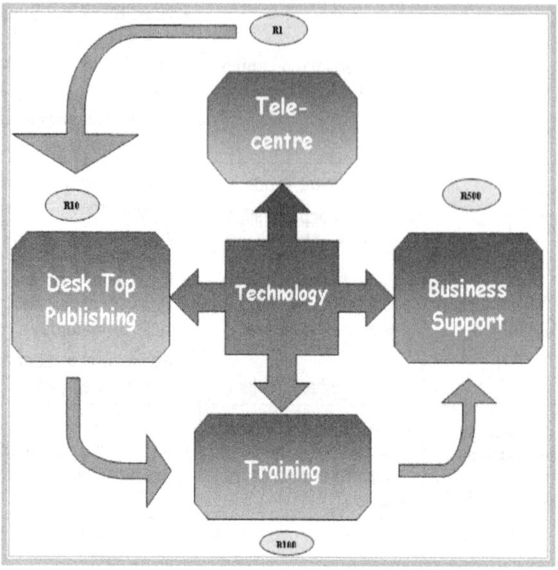

Figure 1: ICT-Hub Income Generating Components
Source: Adapted from Conradie, Morris & Jacobs (2003:212)

Figure 2 is the electronic version of the business model for rural community centres as illustrated in Figure 1 above.

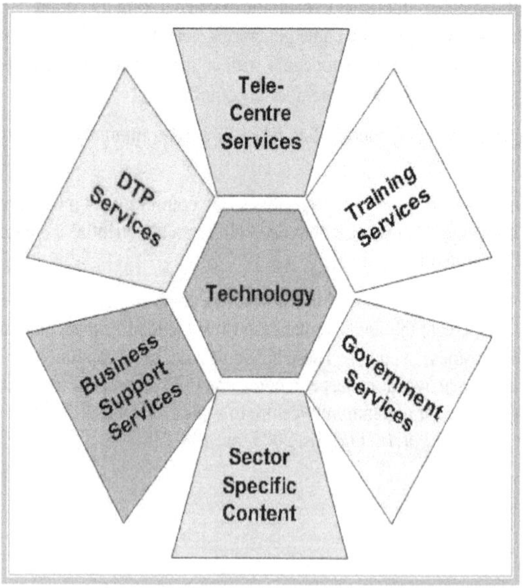

Figure 2: Community centre Operational Components
Source: Adapted from Jacobs (2003:197).

The electronic business model was designed to be a user-friendly information system and support tool for the management, staff and users within a rural community centre. The operational and business model was based on defining the income-generating potential of the various operational service delivery components of a rural community centre as previously discussed. The main operational components of the electronic version are the same as for the illustration in Figure 2; accept for adding two extra operational components to support the need of the community, namely:

- *Sector Specific Content* containing information regarding agricultural, health and educational aspects identified by the community centre staff and management (locally adapted content and context).
- *Government Services* contain links to government related websites for information purposes (content).

Throughout the research it became evident that a need exist within the Ikageng community centre to develop an electronic system that are fully interactive and easy to use by the centre staff and management. The level of complexity of the information in the system as well as the usage of the system must be equal to the level that the users at the community centre.

Conclusion

The results from the research indicated that a need exist for an electronic system that can support community centre staff and management to provide a more repeatable service to the customers (community members) to improve service delivery. It is important to note that this study was only conducted at one centre and that needs of communities differ when it comes to access to information for their own development or advancement. The results from this study further indicated that such a system must have a logical or systematic approach to service customer and staff needs and focus on relevant local content.

It is evident from the results obtained in this study that information contained in any type of electronic system must take care of two sets of information, namely:

- *customer* support content and
- centre support content for *staff* and *management.*

It is therefore evident that ICT-equipped community centres can be instrumental in the development and well-being of a community. Not only can they provide people with access to information related to health, nutrition, education, agriculture and other social basic necessities, they can support local entrepreneurs with various business services, market information, and e-commerce opportunities; they can help people connect with distant family, friends, and government officials; and they can provide a setting for entertainment and social affairs. It is important to note that not all information should be electronic and that rural community centre's should also make use of posters or billboard displays to communicate valuable information.

It is therefore essential that ICTs be demystified and deployed with the interests of local communities in mind. An example of a success in this regard was the Information Kerala Mission of 1997 in India where the State-level Informatics System for Strengthening the Decentralized Plan Implementation (SLIDE), government decision-makers throughout India realized the important role that ICTs would play in modern governance. Focused on creating efficient and responsive mechanisms for governance at the local level, the SLIDE project employed a variety of ICTs to help local institutions mitigate the transition to a decentralized governing system that is unique to the State. It was seen as one of the biggest technology literacy-building programmes in India.

By engaging Government officials and members of civil society, the electronic business model initiative promises to strengthen the Ikageng community centre's position as a high-technology centre in the country, while enhancing the states' profile in the global economy just as the Kerala project in India.

References

Burns, B.R. (2000). *Introduction to research methods.* London: SAGE Publications.

CIDA strategy on Knowledge for development through information and communication technologies. (2005). Accessed: 2005/03/03 at http://www.acdi-cida.gc.ca/ict

Conradie, D.P. & Jacobs, S.J. (2003). Challenges encountered when using ICTs (Information and Communication Technologies) in support of development in rural African communities. *Engineering Management, February*, 30-33.

Cosh, A. & Hughes, A. (2000). The British enterprise in transition: Growth, innovation and public policy in the small and medium sized enterprise sector 1994-1999, *ESRC Centre for business research*, University of Cambridge.

Cullen, R. (2002). Addressing the digital divide. *Online Information Review, 25*(5), 311-320.

Deakins, D. Galloway, L. & Mochrie, R. (2004). *The use and effect of ICT on Scotland's rural business community.* Accessed: 2005/03/08 at http://scholar.google.com/scholar?hl=en=lr=&safe=off&q=cache:03MvBO7w_4MJ:ww

Freshwater, D. (2001). *Delusions of grandeur: The search for a vibrant rural Merica.* University of Kentucky, TVA rural studies programme. Kentucky Publishers.

Friedlander, A. (2001). *Networked technologies and the Internet: A brief historical perspective.* Washington, DC: Benton Foundation.

Fuller, E. & Southern, A. (1999). Small firms and information and communication technologies: Policy issues and some words of caution. Environment and planning: *Government Policy, 17*, 287-302.

Gómez, R. & Hunt, P. (1999). *IDRC Telecentre Evaluation: A Global perspective.* Report of an International Meeting on Telecentre Evaluation. Far Hills Inn, Quebec, Canada, 28-30 September 1999.

Harris, R. W. Sa. (2005). *Evaluating Telecentre within National Policies for ICTs in Developing Countries.* Accessed 2005/11/20 at http://www.idrc.ca/telecentre/evaluation/nn/18_Eva.html

Heeks, R. (1999). *Information and communication technologies, poverty and development.* Development Informatics Working Paper Series Working Paper No. 5 (ISBN: 1 9025 1826 8). Accessed 2005/11/23 at http://www.man.ac.uk/idpm/di_wp5.htm

Huggins, R & Izushi, H. (2002). The digital divide and ICT learning in rural communities: Examples of good practice service delivery. *Local Economy, 17*, 111-122.

ITU. (2002). Bridging the digital divide in rural and remote communities: The Canadian Experience. *World telecommunication development conference*, Istanbul, Turkey, 18-27 March 2002. Accessed 2005/03/03 at www.wtdc-02/info/006V3E.doc

Jacobs, S.J. (2003). *An information and communication technology hub for rural communities.* (Unpublished: M Tech Dissertation) Pretoria: Tshwane University of Technology.

Mitchell, S. & Clark, D. (1999). Business adoption of information and communications technologies in the two-tier rural economy: Some evidence from the South Midlands. *Journal of Rural Studies, 15*, 447-455.

Mncube, S.S. (2003). *The role of information in development.* Development Bank of Southern Africa. Halfway House, South Africa.

Naidoo, K. (2005). Civil society. *Sangonet Conference*, 103 March 2005, Fourways, Johannesburg.

Olivier, M. S. (2004). *Information technology research: A practical guide for computer science and informatics* (Second Edition). Pretoria: Van Schaik Publishers.

Ramirez, R. (2001). A model for rural and remote information and communication technologies: A Canadian exploration. *Telecommunications Policy, 25*(5), 315-330.

Rao, S.S. (2003). Information systems in Indian rural communities. *Journal of Computer Information Systems, 44*, 48-56.

Roberts, S. (2002). *Key drivers of economic development and inclusion in rural areas.* London: DEFRA.

Sebusang, S.E.M. & Masupe, S. (2003). ICT development in Botswana: Connectivity for rural communities. *The South African Journal of Information and Communication, 4*, 41-51. LINK Centre, Witwatersrand University, South Africa, Johannesburg.

Smallbone, D., North, D., Baldock, R. & Ekamen, I. (2002). *Encouraging and supporting enterprise in rural areas.* Middlesex University Business School Research report for the DTIs small business service, London.

Sparks, A. & Thomas, B. (2001). The use of the Internet as a critical success factor for the marketing of Welsh agri-food SMEs in the twenty-first century. *British Food Journal, 103*, 331-347.

Warren, M. (2000). *Farmers, computers and the Internet in contrasting areas in the UK: Implications for rural development.* Plymouth: University of Plymouth.

Welman, J.C. & Kruger, S.J. (2004). *Research methodology.* Oxford, New York: Oxford University Press.

United Nations Development Programme (UNDP). (1996). Report on the Workshop on Governance for Sustainable Human Development. MDGD, New York. April 1996.

United Nations Development Programme (UNDP). (1999). Human Development Report 1999: Globalisation with a human face. UNDP, Geneva.

World Bank. (1998). Harnessing Information for Development. World Bank, Washington D.C.

Yin, R.K. (1994). *Case study research: Design and methods.* London: Sage Publications.

Biographies

SJ Jacobs studied Electrical Engineering (Light Current) at the School of Electronic and Electrical Engineering at the Cape Technikon from 1988 till 1991, where he obtained a National Diploma in Electrical Engineering in 1990, and a National Higher Diploma in Electrical Engineering in 1991.

In 2003 he obtained his Master's Degree (cum laude) at the Faculty of Information and Communication Technology (ICT) at the Tshwane University of Technology. The title of his dissertation was: *An Information and Communication Technology Hub (ICT-Hub) for Rural Communities.* He received an award from the ICT Faculty in the category for bridging the digital divide.

In 2004 SJ enrolled for a Doctorate in Technology at the Tshwane University of Technology, and successfully completed his qualification, with the title of his thesis: *A Quality Management System for Rural Community Centers.*

Throughout his post graduate studies at TUT, SJ received bursaries from the National Research Foundation (NRF) to support his research activities.

Since 2000, he has received 8 merit awards, published 6 articles in peer-review/accredited journals, and presented 6 papers at various national/international conferences. Presently he supervises two master's students and one doctorate student at TUT.

SJ started his career at the Council for Scientific and Industrial Research (CSIR) as a student in training in 1989.

In 2002 he left the CSIR as a senior project manager, responsible for managing multi-disciplinary and multimillion rand rural development projects, to join the then Technikon Pretoria as a project manager, responsible for technology transfer.

At present he is the Director of the Technology Station in Electronics (TSE) at TUT's Faculty of Engineering. The TSE's focus is to stimulate SME development and technology transfer in the electronic/electrical and ICT sectors.

Prof **Marlien Herselman** is an Associate Research Professor of the Faculty of Information and Communication Technology. She assists lecturers and postgraduate students in research projects, National Research Foundation (NRF) projects, in writing research articles, and in other research-related activities. She obtained her PhD at the University of Pretoria in 1999. Her PhD studies focused on the use of computer games. She is currently busy with research on ICT usage in rural communities in South Africa with a National Research Foundation funded project.

In 2000, Prof Herselman was awarded a scholarship of the Deutsche Akademischer Austauschdienst (DAAD) of the International Women's University (IFU) to attend a summer semester at the University of Hamburg, in the project field of information.

In 2005 she received the prize as Women Researcher of the Year 2004 at Tshwane University of Technology.

Research outputs:

- Thriteen accredited journal publications
- Nine peer-reviewed published conference proceedings
- Four technical reports
- Fifteen contributions at international conferences
- One Chapter in a book

Field of expertise

- Technology in Higher Education
- ICT bridging the digital divide
- E-learning and ICT
- Business Information Systems

Principals, Agents and Prisoners: An Economical Perspective on Information Systems Development Practice

Karlheinz Kautz and Bjarke Nielsen
Copenhagen Business School, Department of Informatics, Frederiksberg, Denmark

Karl.Kautz@cbs.dk Bjarke.Nielsen@tiscali.dk

Abstract

Information systems development takes place within an economical context. However, the economical conditions, which shape systems development in practice, are hardly researched. In this paper we are investigating the question how a given price structure influences systems development projects. Our analysis is based on a multi case study and a Grounded Theory inspired research approach. Our work is informed by economic theories, which deal with the relationship of suppliers and customers and their mutual dependency. We thus apply principal-agent theory and economic game theory in form of the prisoner's dilemma. As a result we provide three interlinked models for understanding the impact of pricing structure on systems development practice. The main elements of these models are pricing structure, risk distribution and price level, and opportunistic behavior. We discuss how these elements are interrelated and examine their impact on information systems development in practice.

Keywords: information systems development, pricing structure, principal-agent theory, prisoner's dilemma.

Introduction

Information systems development takes place within an economical context. Cost overruns are frequently reported and the delivery of information systems within appropriate time and cost limits has even been given as one justification for the utilization of information systems development methodologies (Avison & Fitzgerald, 1995). However, the economical conditions, which shape systems development practice are – beyond studies of IT service outsourcing (see for an overview f. ex. Dibbern, Goles, Hirschheim, & Jayatilka, 2004; Lacity & Hirschheim, 1993) - rarely researched by the information systems and the software engineering communities.

The term software economics has been coined by the software engineering community (Boehm & Sullivan), which mostly concentrates on questions related to effort estimation (see f. ex. Boehm, 1981, Boehm et al. 1995, Jørgensen & Carelius, 2004; Jørgensen & Grimstad, 2005; Jørgensen, Teigen, & Moløkken-Østvold, 2004).

Ciborra (1996) takes a contractual view on information systems development and based on transaction cost theory discusses the market, bureaucracy and hierarchy, and the clan with their differing levels of trust and task uncertainty as a basis for different forms of systems development approaches. A number of other IS-related studies (see f. ex. Ang & Beath, 1993; Banerjee & Duflo, 2000; Banker & Kemerer, 1992; Richmond & Seidelmann, 1993; Richmond, Seidmann, & Whinston, 1992; Wang, Baron, & Seidmann, 1997; Whang, 1992) describe features of contracts, contract types and pricing structures and investigate their economical role, but do not relate them to actual systems development practice.

Lichtenstein and McDonnell (2003) and Lichtenstein (2004) are an exception. Considering software development as outsourcing and based on an economical perspective they formulate a number of hypotheses about the relationship between frequency of milestones, project risk, uncertainty and price structure as determined in systems development contracts, but they do not obtain any clear results.

Sabherwal (1999) and Bjerknes and Mathiassen (2000) discuss the antithetic relation between trust and control with regard to supplier-customer interactions and contracts. Based on this work a case study carried out by Madsen and Kautz (2002) found that information systems development encounters difficulties when performed in an iterative way acknowledging uncertainty, but according to a fixed price contract.

On this background we studied how a given price structure affects information systems development in practice. We collected data in a multi case study and applied economic theories, which deal with the relationship of suppliers and customers and their mutual dependency, namely principal-agent theory and economic game theory in form of the prisoner's dilemma. As our investigation is a first attempt of understanding the relationship between pricing structure and systems development in practice it is exploratory and we have limited it to the development of new information systems for a particular customer.

The remainder of the paper is structured as follows: Section 2 presents our research method and section 3 describes our theoretical background. In section 4 we provide our research findings in form of three interrelated models explaining the impact of pricing structure on systems development practice. We finish with discussing implications and conclusions in the sections 5 and 6.

Research Method

Our research question implies that we are investigating how practice behaves instead of investigating if practice behaves in a specific way. Because of its explorative and emergent nature, our study leaves us with no specific hypothesis and advocates an open method. Thus, we adopted an approach with many explanatory variables. Without hypotheses to be verified or invalidated, the data collection had to be more extensive than a search for the impact of already known factors and implied that our study would be narrower without a number of observation units. We therefore opted for a multiple case study. Based on our experience from earlier studies (Hansen & Kautz, 2005; Kautz, Hansen, & Jacobsen, 2004; Kjærgaard & Kautz, 2005) we chose an analysis, which utilizes an approach inspired by the Grounded Theory methodology (Glaser & Strauss, 1967; Strauss & Corbin, 1998). As there exists no specific theory on contract types, pricing structure and systems development in practice Grounded Theory is particularly appropriate as it does not require an existing theory, on the contrary it grounds an emerging theory on the collected data. To secure the validity of our work we largely followed Klein and Myers's (1999) seven principles for interpretive field research and Eisenhardt's (1989) seven steps for case study research.

The data collection is based on twelve semi-structured qualitative interviews with representatives from 7 companies. To avoid any sector or product specific bias we chose organizations, which covered as diverse sectors as aerospace, banking & finance, media & advertisement, health and public administration and which provide content management, document handling, e-business, process management and many other kinds of information systems. The sample includes companies with as few as 10 employees as well as 40 000 employees. The companies were between 6 and 40 years old. As the project aimed at understanding the impact of a chosen price structure on systems development projects we were interested in data from those stakeholders involved in the tasks spanning from the actual sales to the delivery of the final product. Thus, we interviewed 2 sales personnel, 4 project managers and 6 developers across the different companies with 3 to 25 years of experience in the field. The questions in the individual interviews were based on existing literature within the subject, and for this purpose we worked out interview guides for the individual interviews. As we worked with semi-structured interviews, the interview guide was used as a checklist for issues that had to be covered during the interview and not as an actual outline for the interviews. The nature of the interviews had been open, and when the conversation moved towards new and interesting areas relevant to the subject, we pursued and probed the new directions. All interviews lasted between 60 and 75 minutes and were tape recorded and transcribed. The interviewees had the opportunity to see and approve the transcripts.

With the collected data from the interviews we performed an analysis based on Grounded Theory. The Grounded Theory framework describes a way to search relevant topics and relations through three sequential steps: the purpose of open coding is to open the data material. This is done by looking for different meanings in the statements and classifying part-statements with labels to explain the meanings of the different parts. The result is a range of different codes and concepts comprising the thoughts, ideas and meanings of the text. The purpose of axial coding is to find the categories into which the discovered codes/concepts can be classified. The meanings behind the concepts are compared and categorized in main and subcategories or concepts, which together present patterns or a set of axes to explain the data material and relationships between the concepts. Thus, the located axes reflect the parameters that are important for the study's subject. Based on the axes categories, the purpose of selective coding is to explain relationships and contexts to refine the overall explanation into a coherent picture of the observations. The overall picture is based on central categories and represents a complete framework of explanations for the field in focus.

In general, we can describe our approach as follows: In parallel with the actual data collection during the interviews, we reflected on possible categories and relations and in a brainstorm session after the 4th interview, we wrote down our first impressions and ideas. With the results from the brainstorm in mind, we afterwards performed the remaining interviews, transcribed them all and then read and coded the transcribed interviews and subsequently gathered the codes. Subsequently, we searched for coincidences and patterns in the codes and evaluated them in relation to each other. In this way, we achieved a general picture of the statements from the interviews grouped around important axes and categories in the data material. Next, we arranged the categories into main and subcategories and described and explained the main categories based on the data material. Informed by economic theory we identified three main categories, which were mutually related to each other, and as a final result we developed three interlinked models, which explain the mutual impact of pricing structure and systems development in practice. These are described in the following. First, we however introduce the theoretical background in more detail.

Theoretical Background

Although no specific theory relating pricing structure and systems development in practice exists, by taking an economic perspective, our study is informed by the existing literature and in particular by economic writings concerning pricing structures and theories of supplier-customer relationships.

As such Ciborra's (1996) work on transaction cost theory with its possible implications for information systems development and use builds the general background for our study. With regard to pricing the literature distinguishes between fixed price and time and material approaches and variations of these such as fixed price with payment for extra efforts or time and material with an upper limit (see f. ex. Overby, Vang, & Mahnke, 2003).

With regard to the relationship between suppliers and customers principal-agent theory provided a suitable background for our study. It describes how a principal, a customer, should build up an incentive structure, a pricing structure or scheme, to achieve a desired behavior from an agent, a supplier. Principal-agent theory is based on the assumption that people do not always fulfill the contracts and do not always stick to the agreements they have made. Such behavior, which might lead to advantages at the expense of others, is called opportunistic behavior (Douma & Schreuder, 2002). Characteristic for opportunistic behavior is that only some people and also they only some times, exhibit it. It is difficult, if not impossible to distinguish honest from dishonest people before they actually show opportunistic behavior. Principal-agent theory deals with the avoidance of opportunistic behavior. In this context two concepts are important, namely risk, in particular the possibility of loss, and here especially the suppliers' relationship to risk, and observability, in particular the customers' possibility to observe a supplier.

The prisoner's dilemma is a behavioral theory, which formalizes situations of mutual dependency such as those of principals and agents and it is part of the economical game theory (Douma & Schreuder, 2002). The classical prisoner's dilemma can be illustrated by the situation to arrested suspects of a crime find themselves in. If both of them confess the crime they will be sentenced for 5 years each. They also know that if they are silent they can not be imprisoned for more than 3 years and they have made deal that they will not confess to minimize their sentence. During the interrogation the police create a mutual dependency between them by offering them a deal. If one testifies for the prosecution against the other and this one remains silent or denies the crime, this accomplice receives a 6 year sentence and the betrayer will get 1 year for a minor charge. The aim of the police with the mutual dependency is to create a dilemma for the suspects and thus the basis for mistrust. Complete trust between the suspects and thus both silence and rejection of the police's offer will result in the lowest joint degree of penalty. However the dilemma for both suspects is, that independently of what the other chooses, they would be better off admitting the crime. Thus there is an incentive to act opportunistically. The police hope that both suspects are tempted to show opportunistic behavior, which means they will break their contract and seek a personal advantage at the expense of the other. If this happens both of them will be sentenced for 5 years each. In a more general form the theory can be used to characterize co-operation and deviation from a contract, also termed as opportunistic behavior by two business partners, where co-operation of both parties is considered a win-win situation, co-operation of one party and deviation from the contract as a win-loose or loose win situation, respectively and a situation where both parties deviate from the contract as a loose-loose situation. There, the following four outcomes can be distinguished: Punishment for the naivety to co-operate (PN), Reward for co-operation (RC), Temptation to act opportunistically (TO), and Punishment for mutually opportunistic behavior (PO). This leads to the situation described in Table 1:

Table 1: The Prisoner's Dilemma

		Business Partner 1	
		Co-operation	Deviation from Contract
	Co-operation	RC, RC	PN, TO
Business Partner 2	Deviation from Contract	TO, PN	PO, PO

The model depicted in Table 1 is based on the subsequent relationship between the four outcomes: Punishment for the nativity to co-operate < Punishment for mutually opportunistic behavior < Reward for co-operation < Temptation to act opportunistically, where

- Punishment for the nativity to co-operate < Punishment for mutually opportunistic behavior means that the reward to act opportunistically is larger, in case one partner acts opportunistically;
- Punishment for mutually opportunistic behavior < Reward for co-operation means that the reward for mutually opportunistic behavior is smaller than the reward for mutual co-operation;
- Reward for co-operation < Temptation to act opportunistically means that the reward to act opportunistically is larger, in case the other partner co-operates.

Findings

As a background for our further analysis we identified the pricing structures our respondents used during the contract negotiations and realisation of new systems development projects. In line with the literature we found the following pricing structures. A fixed price comprises all costs of a development project and the suppliers' profit depends on their ability to provide the desired system within time and budget. With its origin in a given task with fixed scope, a fixed deadline and a fixed price, fixed price with payment for extra effort contains an explicit mechanism for dealing with changed or additional requirements. Time and material bills the actual effort, while time and material with an upper limit sets a threshold for the maximum expenses. Finally, we came across a 5th structure called framework agreements. Framework agreements comprise a maximum number of hours, for which a customer can book a supplier within a given time frame. This might give a customer a lower price per hour and gives both parties the liberty to negotiate the actual use of the hours according to all available pricing structures.

Suppliers as Agents and Customers as Principals

Applying principal-agent theory, we recognize customers as principals and suppliers as agents, and a model (see Figure 1) describing the relationship of opportunistic behavior, risk distribution and price level and the choice of pricing structure emerged from the data.

Pricing structures have an embedded distribution of risk between both the supplier and the customer. Choice of pricing structure has an impact on risk distribution and price level. Fixed price contracts shift the risk to the supplier. If, in contrast a time and material pricing structure is used, the risk moves to the customer. We found that the suppliers are rather risk averse, thus the price level increases with risk supplements, which reflect the risks that the suppliers perceive.

Distribution of risk and price level has an impact on the opportunistic behavior, which both suppliers and customers show. When suppliers carry the risk their opportunistic behavior is derived from the experienced time pressure they work under to reach the deadline. They might then try to fulfil the customers' requirements with as little functionality as possible and sometimes even leave out some of them. They might also insist on the requirement specification as originally developed and not accept any changes of the requirements after the contract was signed. In any case, the supplier compromises the functionality of the product to be delivered as well as the customer expectations and as such the system's quality. When the customer carries the risk, the suppliers' behavior is influenced by the fact that their earnings will be higher the more time they use for an assignment. Thus, project management sometimes relaxes with regard to keeping deadlines, and progress and the customers' effort are not steered and monitored to the same extent as if the suppliers themselves carry the risk. Suppliers also extend and let the scope of a project slip by experimenting with new functionality and even technology. Unauthorised further development

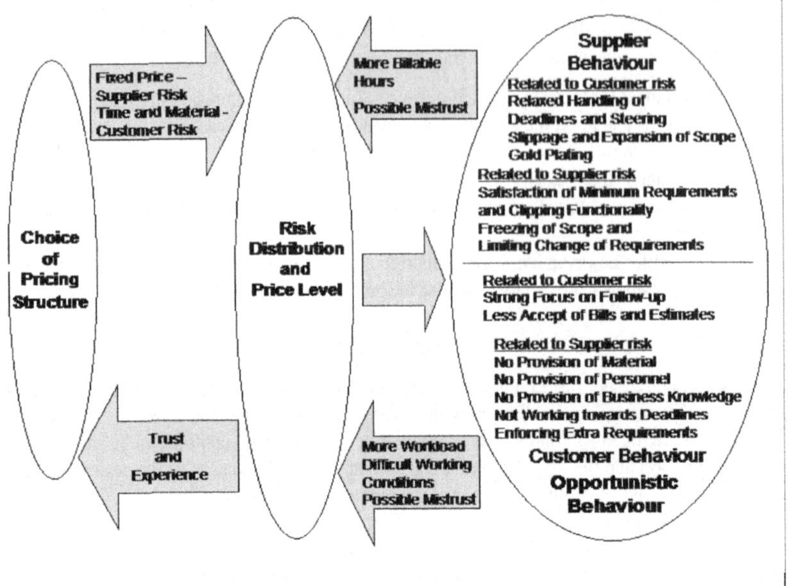

Figure 1: Model of the Mutual Impact of Pricing Structure and Systems Development Practice

and attempts for perfection, known as gold plating, happen more often. Ultimately, the customers might not get the systems they want and as a consequence might choose another supplier in the future. The customers' opportunistic behavior differs depending on which party is carrying the risk. When the suppliers hold the risk, their earnings depend on the customers' efforts. However, suppliers experience that they are not provided by the customer with the material, the personnel and the business knowledge they need. They also complain that the customers do not work dedicatedly towards agreed deadlines and that they try to press new requirements into the projects. This is a problem for them, because denying these demands might have an impact on future business with the customer, while accepting them results in extra hours, time pressure and changes of deadlines. When the customers themselves carry the risk they tend to demand more documentation with regard to the hours the suppliers use in the project, which leads to larger administrative expenses for those. In addition, customers are to a lesser extent appreciative of the suppliers' use of time, which sometimes results in a reluctance to pay for the suppliers' efforts. In that situation it can be hard for the suppliers to collect the charges for some provided development work.

The suppliers' and customers' behavior in return has an impact on the distribution of the risk between the two parties and on the price for a project. As described above lacking customer efforts might lead to increased workload and economical strain for the suppliers and relaxed project steering and handling of deadlines might cause more billable hours and thus higher costs for the customer. The same is true for slippage and expansion of scope as well as for gold plating.

The customers' experiences from previous projects with regard to distribution of risk and price level have an impact on the choice of pricing structure for future projects. The basis for trust is created when suppliers live up to the customers' expectations, which means that the customers will be more willing to choose a pricing structure, where they carry more of the risk. However, when suppliers abuse this trust either by decreasing functionality or raising prices, mistrust develops and customers will not accept the same degree of risk in future projects.

As principal-agent theory describes how a principal, the customer should put together a reward structure, i.e. pricing structure, to achieve the desired behavior from an agent, the supplier, in this context observability of the suppliers' efforts plays an important role. The customers are usually not able to observe the suppliers' efforts directly and often realise that it is too expensive and unrealistic, f. ex. as project leaders in severe technical projects, to directly observe the suppliers. They therefore leave the management of the projects to the suppliers, but then demand some signals as indication for the actual effort. The suppliers also see the necessity to send these signals and meet the demanding by providing them in form of project plans and follow-ups.

In order to give the supplier the biggest possible incentive to deliver an effective effort, this puts the customers in a situation where they can choose between shifting the risk over to the supplier in form of demanding a fixed price contract or remunerating the supplier in accordance with the provided signals. The choice between these two possibilities is made on the basis of the extra costs, which are implied by a shift of risk.

Suppliers and Customers as Prisoners

The above analysis has shown a mutual dependency of the suppliers and the customers. Applying the prisoner's dilemma we can now illustrate, which behavior leads to what the suppliers and the customers experience as win-loose and loose-win situations. When the suppliers carry the risk (see Table 2), customers experience fulfillment of minimum requirements and the clipping of functionality as well as the freezing of scope and limitation of requirement changes as opportunistic supplier behavior, in which they loose and the suppliers win. When they hold the risk themselves the suppliers experience the customer behavior of no provision of material, no provision of personnel and no provision business knowledge as well as those not working towards deadlines and enforcing extra requirement as opportunistic behavior with a win for the customers and a loss for the supplier.

Table 2: Opportunistic Behavior and Win-Loose/Loose Win Situation during Supplier Risk

Supplier Risk		Customer	
		Co-operation	Opportunistic Behavior Win-Loose/ Loose-Win Situation
Supplier	Co-operation		No Provision of Material No Provision of Personnel No Provision of Business Knowledge Not Working towards Deadlines Enforcing Extra Requirements
	Opportunistic Behavior Win-Loose/ Loose-Win Situation	Satisfaction of Minimum Requirements and Clipping Functionality Freezing of Scope and Limiting Change of Requirements	

When the customers carry the risk (see Table 3) they see relaxed handling of deadlines and steering, slippage and expansion of scope and gold plating as a win for the suppliers and a loss for themselves while the suppliers see the customers' strong focus on follow-ups and the lesser accept of bills and estimates as a loose-win situation for themselves. If none of the parties show opportunistic behavior they will achieve a win-win situation, if they both show opportunistic behavior they will end up in a loose-loose situation. This is described in more detail below.

Table 3: Opportunistic Behavior and Win-Loose/Loose Win Situation during Customer Risk

Customer Risk		Customer	
		Co-operation	Opportunistic Behavior Win-Loose/ Loose-Win Situation
Supplier	Co-operation		Strong Focus on Follow-up Less Accept of Bills and Estimates
	Opportunistic Behavior Win-Loose/ Loose-Win Situation	Relaxed Handling of Deadlines and Steering Slippage and Expansion of Scope Gold Plating	

The opportunistic behavior of both suppliers and customers has a number of impacts (see table 4). Dependant on which of the parties shows opportunistic behavior it can lead to an increase of costs and price, changes in the product functionality, scope and ultimately quality or an reimbursed or non-reimbursed increase of the supplier's development expenses. Opportunistic behavior might also lead to mistrust between the parties. However, in cases where both parties observe the terms of earlier contracts, are they able to build up trust to each other and hereby create the possibility to co-operate under a less strict framework. Suppliers and customers experience a mutual dependency which satisfies the conditions of the general model for the prisoner's dilemma. This means that the collective benefit will be highest when both parties co-operate to reach a win-win situation. In such a situation the customers will get a product, which satisfies their expectations and with the quality as agreed in the contract. Likewise, the suppliers will get the earnings as agreed in the contract and both parties will develop trust to each other.

Table 4: Ultimate Consequences of Opportunistic Behavior

		Customer	
		Co-operation	Opportunistic Behavior
Supplier	Co-operation	Supplier: Earnings as agreed in contract Trust in customer Customer: Product quality as agreed in contract Trust in Supplier	Supplier: Minimization of earnings Mistrust in customer Customer: Maximization of product quality
	Opportunistic Behavior	Supplier: Maximization of earnings Customer: Minimization of product quality Mistrust in supplier	Supplier: Minimization of earnings Mistrust in customer Customer: Minimization of product quality Mistrust in supplier

The relationship between suppliers and customers is however characterized by the temptation, which each party experience, to think or work towards achieving a win-loose situation. In case the suppliers work towards such a situation and the customers work towards a win-win situation, the suppliers will be able to maximize the earnings from the respective project. The profit will be of such a magnitude that the suppliers will earn more from the project by acting opportunistically than they would earn in a win-win situation for that one project. This happens at the expense of the customers, who either get a product, which does not meet their expectations, has lesser functionality and thus quality or has to pay more. In any case the customers develop mistrust.

If, in contrast, the customers work for a win-loose situation and the suppliers for a win-win situation, the customers will experience a fulfillment of their expectations and the quality of the product. The maximization will have such an extent that the customer will achieve a better system by acting opportunistically than by working for a win-win situation. This happens at the expense of the supplier, who will be forced to use more resources and thus will have a smaller profit for that respective project as agreed. It will however also lead to mistrust by supplier for the customer.

Finally, when both parties act opportunistically, they end up in a loose-loose situation. Both parties will gain less than in a win-win situation. Beyond less profit for the suppliers, less product quality and fewer fulfilled expectations for the customer, both parties will also develop a mutual mistrust for each other.

The win-loose and loose-loose situations are characterized by that one or both parties think 'me' and 'them', while in a win-win situation both parties think 'we' and 'us' and take care of the mutual dependency and relationship and work to achieve their shared objectives.

Implications

Our analysis and our models of the mutual impact of pricing structures and information systems development practice show that suppliers and customers are mutually dependant on that none of the parties shows opportunistic behavior to secure that the suppliers' earnings and the customers' expectations concerning the systems' functionality and ultimately quality turn into what was agreed upon in the contract.

In line with Bjerknes and Mathiassen (2000), who found that while trust promotes creativity and mutual learning, necessary elements of systems development, contracts promote decisions and monitoring of progress according to the agreement we argue that to enhance practice it is necessary to reconsider the customer-supplier relationship and to change the current form of pricing structures and contract. This argument is supported by Madsen and Kautz's (2002) case study which indicates that iterative development with its explicit focus on learning is problematic, when information systems development has to be performed according to a fixed price contract. Ciborra (1996) has argued that if task uncertainty, as is often the case in information systems development, is high the most efficient work arrangement is one based on a high level of trust. The question then arises how to handle the contradiction between trust and control and how to develop trust.

We agree with Highsmith (2002) who promotes as one way of creating trust what he calls 'delivered-feature' contracts and pricing structures, where the supplier makes operational features available to the customer at the end of each iterative delivery cycle. They provide visibility and observability and allow for the continuous determination of value, and of the contract, but they require a development approach and model that support short iterations as promoted more recently under the label agile software development (Cockburn, 2002; Highsmith, 2000), but already advocated since more then a decade known as f. ex. evolutionary systems development (Budde, Kautz, Kuhlenkamp, & Züllighoven, 1992).

Conclusions

Our study demonstrates the merits of principal-agent theory and the prisoner's dilemma for the information systems development research and confirms the literature on pricing structures, but goes beyond reporting the mere distribution of the different contract types and pricing structures as well as abstract economic reflections.

The analysis of the pricing structures' influence on information systems development practice has provided new insights and resulted in three explanatory models of the phenomenon, describing 1) the mutual influence of pricing structures and information systems development practice 2) the involved parties' perception of opportunistic behavior as win-loose/loose-win situations, and 3) the ultimate consequences of opportunistic behavior.

The models contribute with a cumulative treatment of the interrelationship of pricing structures, distribution of risk, price level and the opportunistic behavior of suppliers and customers. This provides a solid basis for future studies. We have limited our study to the development of new information systems and excluded operation, maintenance and further development as well as the development and adjustment of off-the-shelf products and have not researched whether there is any relationship between particular pricing structures and development models. These issues and the defendable limitation - as we were in particular interested in their perspective - that we only interviewed supplier and not customer organizations should be considered when performing future investigations.

References

Ang, S. & Beath, C. M. (1993). Hierarchical elements in software contracts. *Journal of Organisational Computing, 3*(3), 329-361.

Avison, D.E., & Fitzgerald, G. (1995). *Information systems development: Methodologies, techniques and tools.* Maidenhead, UK: McGraw-Hill.

Banerjee, A. & Duflo, E. (2000). Reputation effects and the limits of contracting: A study of the Indian software industry. *Quarterly Journal of Economics, 15*(3), 989-1017.

Banker, R. D. & Kemerer, C. F. (1992). Performance evaluation metrics for information systems development: A principal-agent model. *Information Systems Research, 3*(4), 379-401.

Bjerknes G. & Mathiassen L. (2000). Improving the customer-supplier relation in IT development, In *Proceedings of the 33rd Hawaii International Conference on Systems Sciences (HICSS-33).*

Boehm, B. W. (1981). *Software engineering economics.* Prentice Hall.

Boehm, B. W. & Sullivan, K. J. (2000). Software economics: A roadmap. In *Proceedings of the International Conference on Software Engineering*, Conference on The Future of Software Engineering, IEEE-CS: Computer Society, Irish Computer Society, 319-343.

Boehm, B. W., Clark, B., Horowitz, E., Westland, J. C., Madachy, R. D. & Selby, R. W. (1995). Cost models for future software life cycle processes: COCOMO 2.0. *Annuals of Software Engineering, 1*, 57-94.

Buddde, R., Kautz, K., Kuhlenkamp, K. & Züllighoven, H. (1992). *Prototyping -- An approach to evolutionary systems development.* Berlin, Germany: Springer Verlag.

Ciborra, C. (1996). *Teams, markets and systems.* Cambridge, UK: Cambridge University Press.

Cockburn, A. (2002). *Agile software development.* Boston, USA: Addison-Wesley.

Dibbern, J., Goles, T., Hirschheim, R., & Jayatilka, B. (2004). Information systems outsourcing: A survey and analysis of the literature. *ACM SIGMIS Database, 35*(4), 6-102.

Douma S. & H. Schreuder (2002). *Economic approaches to organizations* (3rd ed.). Prentice Hall.

Eisenhardt, K. M. (1989). Building theories from case study research. *Academy of Management Review, 14*(4), 532-550.

Glaser, B. G. & Strauss, A. L. (1967). *The discovery of grounded theory - Strategies for qualitative research.* New York, USA: Aldine De Gruyter.

Hansen, B. & Kautz, K. (2005). Grounded theory applied –Studying information systems development methodologies in practice. In *Proceedings of the Hawaii International Conference on System Sciences* (HICSS-38).

Highsmith, J. (2000). *Adaptive software development: A collaborative approach to managing complex systems.* New York, USA: Dorset House.

Highsmith, J. (2002). *Agile software development ecosystems.* Boston, USA: Addison-Wesley, Pearson Education.

Jørgensen, M. & Carelius, C. G. (2004). An empirical study of software project bidding. *IEEE Transactions of Software Engineering, 30*(12), 953-969.

Jørgensen, M., Teigen, K. H. & Moløkken-Østvold, K. J. (2004). Better sure than safe? Overconfidence in judgment based software development effort prediction intervals. *Journal of Systems and Software, 70*(1-2), 79-93.

Jørgensen, M. & Grimstad, S. (2005).Over-optimism in software development projects: "The winner's curse". In *Proceedings of IEEE ConieleComp*, Puebla, Mexico. IEEE Society Press, pp. 280–285.

Kautz, K., Hansen, B. & Jacobsen, D. (2004). The utilization of information systems development methodologies in practice. *Journal of Information Technology Cases and Applications, 6* (4).

Kjærgaard, A. & Kautz, K. (2005). Knowledge management as an autonomous venturing process: A process model of establishing knowledge management. In *Proceedings of the International Conference on Information Systems*, Las Vegas, USA, December 11 – 14, 2005

Klein, H. & Myers, M. (1999). A set of principles for conducting and evaluating interpretive field studies in information systems. *MIS Quarterly, 23*(1), 67-93.

Lacity, M.C. & Hirschheim, R. (1993). The information systems outsourcing bandwagon. *Sloan Management Review*, Fall, 73-86.

Lichtenstein, Y. & McDonnell, A. (2003). Pricing software development services. In *Proceedings of the European Conference on Information Systems*, Naples, Italy, June 16 -21, 2005.

Lichtenstein, Y. (2004) Puzzles in software development contracting. *Communication of the ACM*, *47*(2), 61-65.

Madsen, S. &Kautz, K. (2002). Applying system development methods in practice - The RUP example. In *Proceedings of 11th International Conference on Information Systems Developments, Methods & Tools - Theory & Practice*, Riga, Latvia, September, 12-14, 2002.

Overby, M. L., Vang, J. & Mahnke, V. (2003). *Strategic IT outsourcing* (In Danish), Copenhagen, DK: Thomsen.

Richmond, W., Seidmann, A. & Whinston, A. (1992). Incomplete contracting issues in IS development outsourcing. *Decision Support Systems*, *8*(5), 459-477.

Richmond, W. & Seidmann, A. (1993). Software development outsourcing contract: Structure and business value. *Journal of Management Information Systems, 10*(1), 57-72.

Sabherwal, R. (1999). The role of trust in outsourced IS development projects. *Communications of the ACM*, *42* (2), 80-86.

Strauss, A. & Corbin, J. (1998). *Basics of qualitative research*. London, UK: SAGE Publications.

Wang, E. T. G., Baron, T. & Seidmann, A. (1997). Contracting structures for custom software development: The impacts of informational rents and uncertainty on internal development and outsourcing. *Management Science*, *43*(12), 1726-1744.

Whang, S. (1992). Contracting for software development. *Management Science*, *38*(3), 307-324.

Biographies

Karlheinz Kautz is professor in systems development and software engineering at the Department for Informatics He holds a PhD in systems development and MSc in software development. He is the chair of the IFIP TC 8 WG 8.6 on the adoption and diffusion of IT. His work has been published internationally on conferences and in journals including Information Systems Journal, Informing Science Journal, Information Technology and People, IEEE Software, Journal of IT Cases and Applications, Information and Software Technology, Scandinavian Journal of Information Systems, Journal of IT Education and Journal of Knowledge Management.

Bjarke Nielsen has been a student in the degree program in Computer Science and Business Administration at Copenhagen Business School and has been a research assistant for the project, which builds the basis for the research described here.

E-learning: Incorporating Information Security Governance

E. Kritzinger
University of South Africa, Pretoria, SA

kritze@unisa.ac.za

S.H von Solms
University of Johannesburg, Johannesburg, SA

basie@krw.rau.ac.za

Abstract

The global society is living in the electronic age where electronic transactions such as e-mail, e-banking, e-commerce and e-learning are becoming more and more prominent. This paper primarily focuses on e-learning and how important it is to ensure that proper Information Security measures are put in place to ensure that all information within the e-learning environment is properly protected. This paper highlights four Information Security pillars that could be used to achieve this.

Keywords: electronic learning, e-learning, information security, countermeasures

Introduction

Education methods within the education environment have undergone a paradigm shift of over the last few years. This is primarily due to the introduction of newer and better technologies for example the Internet. One new education method that emerged from using these new technologies is Electronic Learning (E-learning). E-learning can be defined as technology-based learning in which learning material is delivered electronically to remote learners via a computer network (Zhang, Zhao, & Nunamaker, 2004). A great deal of research has already been done in the e-learning environment. However, one aspect that has not received much attention is the important role *Information Security* plays within the e-learning environment.

The primary reason why *Information Security* is so important within the e-learning environment is that e-learning is mainly dependent on information as well as communication technologies (ICT). The use of ICT however, could lead to many possible Information Security risks that could compromise information. These Information Security risks are not necessarily unique to the e-learning environment but should however be addressed as if it where. It is therefore vital that all necessary steps be taken by educational institutions to ensure information is properly secured within the e-learning environment.

Possible Information Security Risks Regarding E-Learning

Let us envisage the following scenario where an e-learning environment allows students to access a system from remote access points. This scenario is not uncommon and many such scenarios could already be found in educational institutions all around the globe. A comprehensive e-learning environment exists, where lecturers (L) and students (S) can do the following:

- (L) : Load course material onto course web sites for students to retrieve,
- (S) : Retrieve course material and lectures from a course web site,
- (S) : Submit assignments to a course web site from where lecturers retrieve and mark such assignments,
- (L) : Store assignment marks on a course web site,
- (S) : Access a course web site to retrieve their marks for assignments,
- (L) : Store tests to be written directly on the course web site,
- (S) : Write different types of tests directly on their work stations with results marked by the system and stored on a course database, and
- (S) : Access course web sites to get the results of tests.

Please note that the examples above are not the only actions with in e-learning, however it is sufficient enough to illustrate the scenario. Information Security risks that can arise from the above mentioned examples without proper Information Security include the following:

- Course material may be altered by unauthorized people,
- Bogus course material may be loaded on course web sites, or web sites may be defaced,
- Submitted assignments can be copied from course web sites by unauthorized parties,
- Submitted assignments can be changed or deleted by unauthorized parties,
- Marks can be changed/deleted,
- Access to test papers may be gained, test contents can be changed, or the test can be deleted before the scheduled test date,
- People may masquerade as students and write tests on behalf of such students,
- Students may get unauthorized help during the writing of tests,
- The destruction of course web sites and course databases containing marks
- Denial of service attempts against course web sites preventing authorized students from accessing the web site.
- Logon information (student/user ID and passwords) of lecturers and students can be intercepted and misused.

The Information Security risks identified above should be addressed by ensuring that the e-learning Information Security countermeasures are implemented thought out the e-learning environment. This paper proposes four e-learning pillars that could help institutions in securing their information against harmful attacks.

E-Learning Information Security Pillars

The four main pillars that the authors claim to be essential for proper Information Security within the e-learning environment are as follows:

- Ensuring e-learning Information Security Governance
- Creating e-learning Information Security Policies and Procedures
- Implementation of e-learning Information Security countermeasures
- Monitoring the e-learning Information Security countermeasures

A combination of these four pillars will have a significant effect on implementing and maintaining a good and secure e-learning environment. These four pillars are depicted in Figure 1.

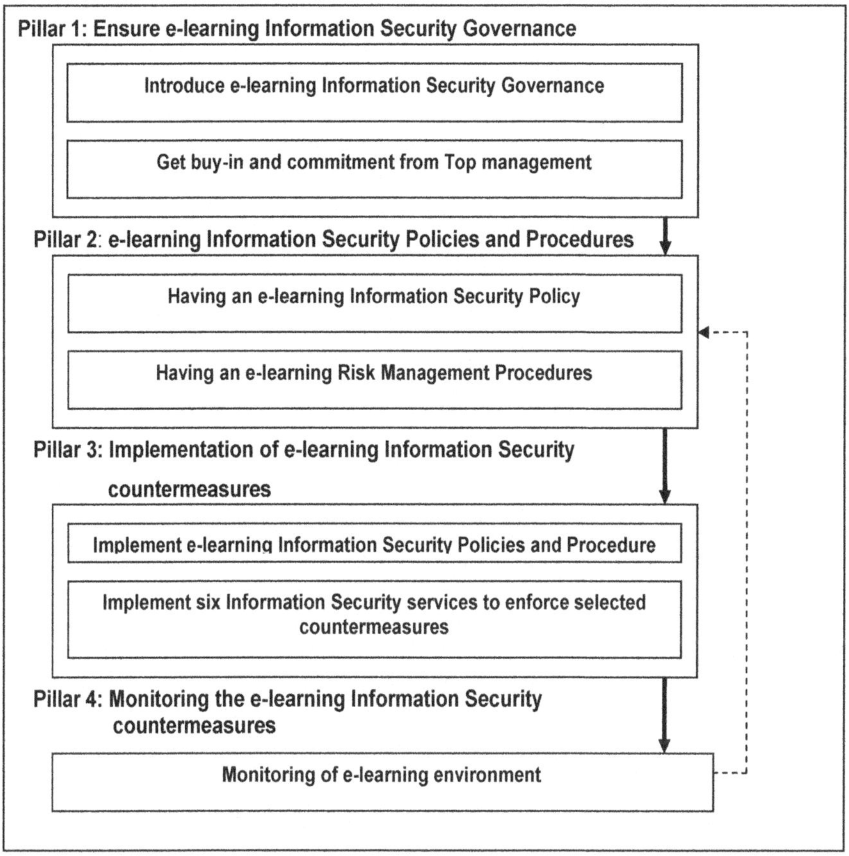

Figure 1: Four Pillars of e-learning

Each of the four pillars consists of one or more actions that will help the institution in implementing that specific pillar. Each of the pillars as well as the actions (depicted in Figure 1) will be separately looked at in the rest of this paper.

Ensuring E-Learning Information Security Governance

The first pillar highlights the significance of Information Security Governance within the e-learning environment and consists of two actions. The first action is to ensure proper Information Security Governance and the second actions is about the buy-in and commitment from Top management.

Introduce e-learning Information Security Governance

Information Security Governance consists of the leadership, organizational structure, processes and technologies that ensure that information is never compromised (Von Solms, 2001b). From this definition it is clear that in general, the main purpose of Information Security Governance is to protect against the risks that can impact on the confidentiality, integrity and availability of all electronic resources. In most cases information is processed using Information and Communications Technologies (ICT) systems, this means the information is stored in databases and transmitted over networks. This is naturally just as important for educational institutions, where ICT is used for such information processing, and where risks can arise with regard to the confidentiality, integrity and availability of the following types of data and information, usually stored in centralized databases:

- student information like course marks and study records,
- staff information like salaries and pension information,
- intellectual property,
- etc.

All educational institutions should therefore enforce Information Security Governance, at least to protect and secure the types of sensitive information and data referred to above.

Get buy-in and commitment from top management

The second action in this pillar highlights how important it is to obtain the buy-in and commitment from Top management. Top management is ultimately the responsibly to ensure that Corporate Governance is implemented within the institution. This responsibility is enforced by law in many countries and in many cases Top management can be taken to court and held accountable if the integrity, availability or confidentiality of information is compromised in any way (Lindup, 1996). Top management should therefore protect information through effective management, which is assured only through effective board oversight (Von Solms, 2001a). Only if Top management takes Information Security seriously will the rest of the institution will follow.

E-learning Information Security Policies and Procedures

The second pillar is about ensuring that proper e-learning Information Security policies and procedures are designed and implemented within the institution. This pillar also consists of two actions which include policies and risk management procedures. Both of these actions is vital in ensuring information is secured.

Having an e-learning information security policy

Before any institution can start managing Information Security, they should have an e-learning Information Security policy in place. This e-learning Information Security policy should be used as a guideline as to **what** must be managed and **how** this should be done. An e-learning Information Security policy (like any other policy) should be a document that addresses the rules and regulations regarding e-learning within the institution and should directly relate to the institution's e-learning policy.

This e-learning Information Security policy should address how security decisions can be made with regard to hardware, software, networks and information. The primary purpose of an e-learning Information Security policy is to protect the institution's information assets from all possible threats. Such an e-learning Information Security policy should comprise of a maximum of 2 to 3 pages, very generic, and non-technical, and must be signed by the most senior official in the company.

Having an e-learning risk management procedures

The second action in this pillar is to prevent the Information Security incidents within the e-learning environment. Top management of educational institutions should provide platforms for integrated educational, learning and assessment environments. This could be done by following at least, the following steps:

- Perform a proper risk analysis to identify all the ICT and business-related risks involved in the implemented, or intended, system. Ensure that this risk analysis is driven by international best practices in the field of ICT and Information Security governance.
- Determine the potential impact of these risks on the institution if they should materialize.
- Determine how to handle these risks, i.e. ignore them, transfer them or accept and manage them.
- Determine the Information Security countermeasures needed to manage those risks which are accepted.
- Create a proper Enterprise Information Security Management (EISM) system to continuously manage these risks. Such a system should include the relevant policies, procedures, technical measures as well as the necessary compliance measurement and monitoring mechanisms to monitor and enforce compliance with the relevant policies, and to report the level of risk to top management on a regular basis.
- Review the risk situation on an annual basis and adapt the EISM system as necessary.

Implementation of E-Learning Information Security Countermeasures

The third pillar highlights the implementation of different Information Security countermeasures. This pillar consists of two actions, the first is about the implementation of policies and procedures (see also section 3.2). The second action identifies six countermeasures that are vital for overall security within e-learning.

Implement e-learning information security policies and procedures

It is essential that all institutions ensure that their e-learning Information Security policy is not only properly designed but also properly implemented. An e-learning Information Security policy has no value if it is stored somewhere on a shelf and is not used to secure information. If an e-learning Information Security policy is not implemented within the institution, it is just as bad as not having one at all. However, the implementation of the e-learning Information Security policy however is ultimately the responsibility of Top management.

Implement six information security countermeasures

The second action in this pillar is to identify and implement six Information Security countermeasures. When implementing Information Security countermeasures within the e-learning environment it is essential that the implemented countermeasures should enforce the following six Information Security services:

1. Identification and Authentication. The first service, identification and authentication, is put in place to ensure that only authorized users can gain access to a system (or part of a system). The first part of this service is about determining whether or not a person who is trying to gain access to a system is cleared for access. This process is called identification and is usually done by entering a user ID into the system. Once the user has been identified, the system must ensure that the user is truly who he/she claims to be. This process is called authentication. Authentication can be done by means of something the user knows, such as passwords, something the user has, such as an access card or something the user is, such as fingerprints (Von Solms & Eloff, 2004). Examples of the Information Security countermeasures for identification and authentication include proper unique passwords and login IDs.

2. Authorization. The next step towards enforcing Information Security is authorization. This involves determining whether or not the authenticated party has the right to access the information in question (Von Solms & Eloff, 2004). An example of the Information Security countermeasures for authorization is *accesscControl.*

3. Confidentiality. The third service, confidentiality, is an Information Security characteristic as well as a service and is put in place to protect data from unauthorized access. The purpose of confidentiality is to ensure that information and data are not disclosed to any unauthorized person or entity (International Federation of Accountants, 2000). An example for the Information Security countermeasure for confidentiality is *encryption*.

4. **Integrity**. The fourth service is integrity. The purpose of integrity is to ensure that information is still in its original form and that no tampering or alteration has taken place. In other words, only authorized parties may change the content of information and unauthorized modification must be prevented. An example of a countermeasure that will help to ensure integrity is m*essage authentication codes.*

5. **Non-Repudiation**. The last step towards enforcing Information Security is non-repudiation or non-denial. This service ensures that no action taken that affects Information Security can be denied at a later stage (Von Solms & Eloff, 2004). An example of the Information Security countermeasure for non-repudiation *is digital signatures*.

6. **Availability**. This service ensures that all electronic resources and services are available to authorized users when they want to use such services. Availability means that data and information is accessible at any time to authorized parties (International Federation of Accountants, 2000). An example of the Information Security countermeasures for availability is regulator b*ackups*.

Monitoring the E-Learning Information Security Countermeasures

The fourth and last pillar is about Information Security compliance monitoring to establish if procedures and processes that are implemented in an organization are working as they should. The objects that are monitored can differ from organization to organization and include products, systems, processes, security program effectiveness and personal competence (Katzke, 2001). This monitoring process should therefore be extended to include the e-learning environment and include aspects such as validation of information, evaluating of the operating capacity as well as overall impact of the e-learning environment on learners' success.

This monitoring process will ensure that institutions know their Information Security situation within the e-learning environment at any given time. This will also help Top management in their decision making process to ensure that if there is a security incident, it can be resolved before the availability, integrity and confidentiality of information is compromised. If any difficulty is identified by the monitoring process it is essential that the e-learning Information Security policies and Risk Management procedures are updated at regular intervals (as depicted in Figure 1).

Conclusion

This paper highlighted how important it is to ensure that information within the e-learning environment is secured at all times. The authors identified four pillars that should be put in place to enhance the overall Information Security as regards to e-learning. Each of these pillars and its actions should be individually addressed and implemented. However, all four pillars should be seen as a top-down approach that Top management could use for guidelines to ensure that Information is secured within the e-learning environment.

References

Deloitte. (2005): 2005 global security survey. Available at: http://www.deloitte.com

International Federation of Accountants (2000). *Managing security of information.*

Katzke, S. (2001). Security metric. Available at: http://www.acsac.org/measurement/position-papers.

Kwok, L. & Longley, D. (1997). Code of practice: A standard for information security management. In *Proceedings of IFIP TC11, 13th International Conference on Information Security.*

Lindup, K. (1996). The role of information security in corporate governance. *Computers & Security, 15*(6): 477-485.

Von Solms, S. H. (2001a). Information security - A multidimensional discipline. *Computers & Security, 20*(6): 504-508.

Von Solms, S. H. (2001b). Corporate governance and information security. *Computers & Security, 20*(3): 215-218.

Von Solms, S. H. & Eloff, J. H. P. (2004). *Information security*, Johannesburg, South-Africa.

Zhang, J., Zhao, L. & Nunamaker, J. F. (2004). Can e-learning replace classroom learning? *Communications of the ACM, 47*(5): 75-79.

The page left blank intentionally.

Strategies to Enhance Student Learning in a Capstone MIS Course

Anil Kumar
Central Michigan University, Mt. Pleasant, MI, USA

anil.kumar@cmich.edu

Abstract

The information systems marketplace is changing rapidly requiring students to be well versed in skills that go beyond traditional IT skills. To achieve this, management information systems (MIS) instructors in MIS programs across the country need to design courses that reflect these changes. Failure to incorporate these changes in the MIS program will lead to graduating MIS students who are not competitive in the marketplace. While curriculum changes are often times a time consuming process, the capstone course in an MIS program can be used effectively to reflect these changes. This paper highlights different strategies that can be used in a capstone MIS course to help students synthesize, analyze, and apply knowledge acquired over different courses in the program.

Keywords: Capstone MIS course, student learning, systems approach, assessment, integrated learning

Introduction

The capstone course in any program of study provides a student the opportunity to synthesize, analyze, and apply knowledge acquired over different courses in the program. This course enhances the overall education experience of students by helping them understand the big picture, i.e. how knowledge acquired from all the courses in their curriculum converges together. For example a management information system (MIS) student learns several concepts and acquires multiple technology skills in different courses that are a part of the MIS program and then learns how to apply all these concepts and use the skills to design and develop an information system. Knowledge integration and application in a capstone MIS course can be a challenging task. An instructor designing the capstone course needs to ensure that critical components from all the courses in a program are integrated.

Designing a capstone MIS course is challenging due to factors such as the need to integrate business concepts and technology concepts & skills, the diversity of IT skills and the rapid rate of change in the IT industry. Scholars (Lopes & Morais, 2002; Neville & Adam, 2003) have highlighted the need to provide an integrated (business and information technology) experience to information technology students in a capstone course. Neville and Adam (2003) state that this enables students to develop skills that they can use immediately to "contribute to the organizations that hire them." Lopes and Morais (2002) point out that IS courses need to be "frequently updated to remain effective" due to the nature of the evolution and advancement in the IT industry. Noll and Wilkins (2002) highlight the diversity of skills needed by the IS industry and the fact that a generic IS program cannot provide these skills to students. They recommend "distinct concentrations" such as "programming, analyst and user support" that provide diverse skills to students.

MIS capstone course studies highlight using the project experience as a pedagogical approach to teaching the capstone course. Studies like Myers (2003) and Tuttle (2001) provide useful insights from using the project-based approach to increase student learning in a capstone IS course. Tuttle (2001) does go beyond the project experience and describes the course structure, methodology and student feedback. These studies fail to take a comprehensive view of the MIS capstone experience and this is the gap the present study is trying to address. Students need to learn about the integration and convergence of not just the MIS curriculum but the complete academic experience. They need to learn how to successfully synthesize, analyze, and apply knowledge acquired in an academic program in the capstone course. This will help them gain an advantage in the highly competitive MIS marketplace, leading to successful careers in the MIS discipline. MIS programs across the nation can highlight these success stories leading to increased student enrollment in the MIS programs. The challenge for educators is to design a capstone MIS course that provides students the opportunity to learn and succeed in their chosen field. This paper shares strategies that have helped students synthesize, analyze, and apply knowledge in a capstone MIS course. The author is a MIS faculty and has taught the MIS capstone course at both the undergraduate and graduate level for several years in a Midwestern university.

Strategies for Teaching a Capstone MIS Course

A capstone course in any discipline requires that students are provided the opportunity to synthesize and integrate their knowledge acquired over several years. This creates unique challenges for the designer of the course as one has to ensure that students walk away from this course with a good understanding of how knowledge acquired from all their courses in their curriculum fits together and how they can apply this knowledge to design and develop an information system.

Using the Systems Approach

It is critical to start the capstone course by a discussion of the systems approach to designing and developing information systems. The systems approach encourages students to look at different courses as elements that need to interact rather than be studied as individual courses. As Friedman (2005) points out "the world is moving from a place where value was created in vertical silos of command and control to a world where value is increasingly going to be created horizontally by how you connect and collaborate – how you synthesize this with that… It's great to have people who can forge dots, it's even better to have people who can connect them." The ability to understand how different courses are building blocks (dots) in the process of acquiring integrated (connecting) MIS knowledge can help students understand and relate the diverse concepts and skills used to design and develop information systems.

Using the systems approach the course content was divided into several modules. Concepts discussed and learned in a course module were reinforced by a project milestone helping students apply the concepts. A project management approach was used for managing these projects where each student in the group was made responsible for managing the project for a milestone. This exposed students to the challenges of managing an Information System project. The capstone project was designed keeping in view the systems theory approach to designing and developing an information system.

Using a Student-Centered Rather than a Teacher-Centered Approach to Enhance Student Learning in the Classroom

A student-centered teaching approach was used to actively engage students in the learning process. Student learning is the focal point of my teaching and in pursuing this effort the goal has been to answer how will students learn rather that how do I teach them? A conscious effort was made to increase student involvement in the classroom to promote student learning. Instead of using a teacher-centered approach where students receive information passively and tend to lose interest, a student-centered approach was used. To achieve active participation in the classroom, class lectures were made available to students on Blackboard a week before class. The students were expected to read the assigned chapters and presentations and come prepared to class. Classroom time was used for discussions and problem solving exercises to learn the theory and concepts of MIS. This strategy facilitated the transition to student-centered learning and also ensured active participation from students.

This approach enhanced the overall learning experience for the students as indicated by their comments provided as part of the end of the semester evaluations:

> "Presents the material in a way that helps us learn, by asking questions and getting our thoughts instead of just lecturing."
>
> "He structured the class around the students. It was the only class I enjoyed coming to."
>
> "Good open discussions. Good use of examples. It was good that he was open to student suggestions."
>
> "I liked how the teacher got us involved through group discussions and presentations. The class was lively and as a result I was very motivated in attending every single class. The teacher is very approachable and makes students comfortable."
>
> "Lots of questions and interactivity during lecture."

To use the student-centered approach a significant effort was made every semester to know individuals in the class. This was achieved by using several ice-breaking activities in the first class to know more about the students-their names, hobbies, background etc. In the first class I shared experiences with them and encouraged them to do the same. This process is critical and often leads to motivating students. Motivated students tend to be more receptive to learning. When designing the course make sure that the first class meeting is planned for developing the rapport with students. This prepares students to interact actively with the instructor and other students leading to an environment that promotes active learning in the classroom.

Use Multiple Assessment Methods to Ensure that Students with Diverse Learning Styles have an Opportunity to Demonstrate their Learning

Every semester students were required to complete a questionnaire at the beginning to identify their learning styles, and multiple course assignments & projects were designed to accommodate diverse student learning styles. The Grasha-Riechmann Student Learning Style Scale (Hruska-Riechmann & Grasha, 1982) that identifies six types of student learners, Independent, Collaborative, Dependent, Participative, Competitive, and Avoidant was used to identify student learning style. This was done with a view to ensure that students with diverse learning styles in my classroom had an opportunity to demonstrate their learning. A critical part of the assessment process was to provide ongoing feedback to students about their performance. This enhanced student learning as they were always aware of the progress they were making and could focus on things that they needed to improve.

Students' ability to comprehend concepts of management information systems design and development were assessed using a two-phased approach. Initially classroom discussions were used for assessing student understanding of concepts and their ability to demonstrate this understanding orally in a group setting. As a follow up measure to reinforce their understanding individual students were asked to write up a reflective paper for each course module completed in class. This reflective paper required students to answer questions on the different concepts discussed in the module. For example, the module on logical design required them to discuss the significance of modeling (data and process), and students were required to discuss the concepts using examples from their project. In addition, students were asked to create a concept map that allowed them to depict pictorially how concepts in each module were related to each other. The concept map enabled students to see the big picture from an integrated learning perspective. Instant feedback was provided to students in the classroom during discussions. Reflective papers were graded and returned to students with comments before the next class period. All course grades were posted on Blackboard and students were able to track their progress throughout the semester.

The following end of semester student comments indicated that usage of multiple assessment methods promoted student learning.

> "The whole project milestone idea was great and it made me have a first-hand development of a system. The reflective paper was also good."
>
> "Gives examples. Sits down w/students & explains the material. Posts documents on Blackboard. Uses email to communicate with students."
>
> "By dividing the system work into Milestones and also asking students write reflective papers make it easy on me to really know what is going on step by step."

Integrate Technology to Promote Student Learning

Technology usage was a critical component of my teaching. Technology was used as a tool to support and promote active student learning. Blackboard (BB) was used as a course management system to support student learning. All course materials such as course syllabus, course content presentations, assignments, announcements, student grades etc. were made available to students on BB. Further, BB group communications features have been used consistently to promote active student learning. Students have been required to interact with their peers electronically to exchange ideas on different topics being discussed in class. This promoted collaboration within and among groups in the class and prepared students for the real-world where electronic collaboration is highly desired.

Numerous technology tools such as MS-Project, MS-Visio, MS-IIS 6.0 web server, MS Office Suite, MS SQL Server, Oracle, HTML, MS-FrontPage, Active Server Pages, Cold Fusion, Dreamweaver etc. were used in the class to help students develop skills required for designing and developing computer-based information systems. Students used these tools to develop systems that simulate real world organizations. Examples from previous semesters include: day care registration & information management system, student flea market system, and entertainment & dining information system for a small community among others. Students were encouraged to use technology tools extensively to enhance their learning and provide an opportunity for them to manage and operate technology for their projects. For example, at the beginning of the semester, all systems development software was provided for free from Microsoft through the University Alliance. It provided the students the opportunity to practice working with the software in their own time outside of class throughout the first half of the semester and finally use it to implement their systems in the second half of the semester. Partnering with the College of Business Administration technology department, students were provided access to virtual MS-Windows servers. To enhance the learning process students were provided the opportunity to build and maintain IIS

6.0 web servers to host their systems. A unique feature of this process was that these web servers were developed and maintained by students using virtual server management tools. All students in the course were given administrative rights to these virtual servers and responsibility for running, maintaining and security was delegated to the students. This unique feature enabled students to understand how organizations create an IT infrastructure to manage their systems and the associated challenges that MIS professionals face in managing them. Though technologically frustrating at times, the students enjoyed the "power" they had in managing their systems. The MIS design and development projects used for application of concepts in the capstone MIS course need to address the complexity of the process, yet should be simple enough so that students can complete them in a semester's time.

Integrating Student Learning, Assessment & Feedback and Technology Usage to Enhance Student Learning

The key to my teaching strategy was the integrated approach that was used to design the capstone course. Student learning, assessment & feedback and technology usage were integrated for course design to achieve alignment with the mission of the University and the College of Business Administration. The integrated approach was implemented by first listing the three components, i.e., student learning outcomes, assessment procedures & feedback, and technology usage and then ensuring that these three components were aligned with each other and supported each other. The benefit of using this integrated approach was that the focus of the course was on achieving student learning outcomes.

Student comments indicated that they liked the integrated learning approach that was used in the classroom.

> "Lectures are interactive. Extensive use of Blackboard helps too. Instructor also involves students in design of class & making decisions about assignments, tests, quizzes etc."
>
> "The format of the class was excellent-discussions were well paced. Papers/case analysis to test knowledge is more "real-world" than testing."

Collaborating with Students on Multiple Research Projects

I am a strong believer in encouraging my capstone course students at both the undergraduate and graduate level to conduct quality research as part of their academic career. In pursuit of this goal during the past three years I have co-authored peer review journal articles, research monographs, and presented multiple papers at International conferences with my students.

Inviting Recent Graduates to Speak to Capstone Course Students

In an attempt to help capstone students understand the IS industry environment, recent MIS graduates were invited to speak to the class. This helped calm students' fears about entering the workplace and prepare them for the transition. Speakers that have participated have come from companies such as Deloitte Consulting, Eli Lilly, EDS, and Dow Chemical etc. These speakers were in addition to senior industry professionals that have visited the capstone classes from time to time to talk about job potential in the IS discipline.

Conclusion

As discussed in the previous sections, this paper highlights multiple strategies used to actively involve students in the learning process leading to enhanced student learning and engagement in their capstone MIS course. Students, individually and in groups, always participated in both classroom and online discussions. The prompt feedback provided to students on their performance helped them assess their own knowledge on a specific topic before moving to the next topic in class. Technology was integrated as a critical component of the classroom to extend the learning environment beyond the traditional classroom. Since students learn in different ways it was ensured that multiple opportunities were provided to students to demonstrate their learning. I believe that using these innovative approaches has challenged the students to set high expectations for them to excel in the classroom. Student opinions indicate that they liked the challenge and the high expectations set for them in the course and their performance in the form of grades, research publications, and international conference presentations etc. indicates the success of these innovative approaches.

References

Friedman, T. (2005). *The world is flat: A brief history of the twenty-first century.* New York: Farrar, Straus and Giroux.

Hruska-Riechmann, S., & Grasha, A. F. (1982). The Grasha-Riechmann student learning style scales. In J. Keefe (Ed.), *Student learning styles and brain behavior.* Reston, VA: National Association of Secondary School Principals.

Lopes, F. & Morais, P. (2002). Lessons learnt from the teaching of IS development. *Journal of Information Technology Education, 1*(2), 103-112. Retrieved from http://jite.org/documents/Vol1/v1n2p103-112.pdf

Myers, M. (2003). An IS capstone project: The Mywick property management system, *Journal of Information Systems Education, 14*(3), 235-239.

Neville, K. & Adam, F. (2003). Integrating theory and practice in education with business games. *Informing Science Journal, 6*, 61-73. Retrieved from http://inform.nu/Articles/Vol6/v6p061-073.pdf

Noll, C.L. & Wilkins, M. (2002). Critical skills of IS professionals: A model for curriculum development, *Journal of Information Technology Education, 1*(3), 143-154. Retrieved from http://jite.org/documents/Vol1/v1n3p143-154.pdf

Tuttle, S.M. (2001). A capstone course for a computer information systems major, *Proceedings of the Second Annual CCSC on Computing in Small Colleges Northwestern Conference*, 42-49.

Biography

Dr. Anil Kumar is an Associate Professor in the Business Information Systems Department at Central Michigan University. He has published more than 40 articles on global IT management, technology-mediated learning and IS education. His current research focuses on globalization & technology, and technology-mediated learning. Prior to his academic appointment, he spent several years working in the IS industry. He is active in several professional organizations and serves on the editorial board of the Journal of Global Information Technology Management and the International Board of Reviewers of the Journal of Information Technology Education.

The Emergence of Modern Biotechnology in China

Shaheen Emmanuel Lakhan
Global Neuroscience Initiative Foundation, Los Angeles, USA

slakhan@gnif.org

Abstract

Science and technology of Republican China (1912-1949) often replicated the West in all hierarchies. However, in 1949 when the Chinese Communist Party (CCP) declared the nation the People's Republic of China, it had assumed Soviet pseudo-science, namely neo-Lamarckian and anti-Mendelian Lysenkoism, which led to intense propaganda campaigns that victimized intellectuals and natural scientists. Not until the 1956 Double Hundred Campaign had China engaging in meaningful exploration into modern genetics with advancements of Morgan. The CCP encouraged discussions on the impact of Lysenkoism which cultivated guidelines to move science forward. However, Mao ended the campaign by asserting the Anti-Rightist Movement (1957) that reinstated the persecution of intellectuals, for he believed they did not contribute to his socialist ethos of the working people. The Great Leap Forward (1958-1959), an idealist and unrealistic attempt to rapidly industrialize the nation, and the Cultural Revolution (1966-1976), a grand attempt to rid China of the "technological elite," extended China's lost years to a staggering two decades. Post-Mao China rapidly revived its science and technology frontier with specialized sciences: agricultural biotechnology, major genomic ventures, modernizing Traditional Chinese Medicine, and stem-cell research. Major revisions to the country's patent laws increased international interest in China's resources. However, bioethical and technical standards still need to be implemented and locally and nationally monitored if China's scientific advances are to be globally accepted and commercialized.

Keywords: history, stem cell, bioethics, agriculture, intellectual property, Lysenkoism

Abbreviations: CCP: Chinese Communist Party; PRC: People's Republic of China; CAS: Chinese Academy of Sciences; NNSF: National Natural Science Foundation; CNCBD: China National Center for Biotechnology Development; HGP: Human Genome Project; MoST: Ministry of Science and Technology; BAC: bacterial artificial chromosome; HB: Hepatitis B; TCM: Traditional Chinese Medicine; CATCM: China Academy for Traditional Chinese Medicine; ES: embryonic stem; MPH: Ministry of Public Health; GMO: genetically modified organism; UCSD: University of California, San Diego; CQMHTIO: Chongqing Municipality High-Technology Industrialization Office.

Introduction

China has been a pioneer in science, discovery, and invention since its early history. In the 6th century BC, Chinese farmers were using a form of agricultural row cultivation and intensive hoeing that was not practiced in Europe until the 18th century. While Dr. William

Harvey is often credited with discovering the circulatory nature of the human blood system in 1628, indisputable and abundant textual evidence from the 2nd century demonstrates China's extensive knowledge on this subject (Temple, 1986). China has utilized traditional forms of manipulating living organisms - agricultural biotechnology - including grain cultivation, soy sauce and vinegar production, and bacterial maceration, for centuries.

Despite these achievements, China has failed to undergo the biotechnology revolution experienced in the West during the twentieth century. Republican China (1912-1949) did make a significant effort to achieve scientific prominence, including establishing the Central Academy of Sciences in 1928. However, the Chinese Communist Party's (CCP) indiscriminate acceptance of Soviet pseudo-science, namely anti-Mendelian Lysenkoism, led to intense propaganda campaigns that victimized intellectuals and natural scientists who spoke out against the Party or practiced Mendel-Morgan science.

After years of anti-Mendelian Soviet pseudoscience and decades of anti-intellectual propaganda and persecution, China's biotechnology industry was undeveloped, even backwards. In the post-Mao era, China instituted a novel modernization and high-technology plan to redress these problems with national science and technological advancement. Deng Xiaoping was instrumental in conveying the idea to the Chinese people that science and technology were key to generating economic wealth and improving the country's international reputation. He instituted many of the biotechnical programs in the universities and medical and agricultural institutes that are responsible for China's well-known achievements in the field today.

This article traces the emergence of modern biotechnology in the People's Republic of China, particularly in the agricultural, genomic, and stem-cell sciences and traditional Chinese medicine. The paper begins with a review of the significant events in biology and genetics education and research in China's modern history. The future directions of the biotechnology industry in the country, such as transparent and peer-reviewed funding mechanisms, bioethical and biosafety standards with proper enforcement, and international collaboration in education and multi-faceted sciences, are also discussed.

History of Science & Technology in China (1911-2005)

The collapse of the Chinese monarchial system with the toppling of the Qing dynasty in 1911 marked a turning point in China's science policies. The new Republic of China, under the guidance of the revolutionary leader Dr. Sun Yat-Sen, established local, regional, and national scientific societies and scholarly journals, reinstated study abroad education programs, and founded higher education science departments in evolution, population genetics, and the life sciences. Realizing that science and technology were key to China's economic and political stability and development, the central government actively fostered and protected the fledgling scientific community. The founding of the Central Academy of Sciences (Academia Sinica) in 1928 characterized the culmination of modern Chinese scientific exploration. In addition, the China Science Service was published in cooperation with the US Department of State to educate and inform Chinese scientists about important scientific developments in the West (Fairbank, 1976). In fact, Chinese science often replicated the West.

Sino-Soviet Scientific Philosophy (1949-1956)

After the defeat of the Nationalists by the CCP in the 1949 Civil War, the People's Republic of China (PRC) uniformly adopted the prevailing Soviet pseudo-scientific philosophical doctrines and theories of the day, particularly those postulated by Lysenko and Michurin. Ukrainian agronomist Trofim Lysenko (1898-1976) condemned the work of Gregor Mendel (1822-1884),

August Weismann (1834-1914), and Thomas Morgan (1866-1945) because their theories contradicted Marxist doctrine. His anti-Mendelian theories held that acquired traits could be inherited, a notion that was not based on statistical research, a field that Lysenko detested. [This notion was originally proposed by French naturalist Jean-Baptiste Lamarck and later advocated by Soviet scientist Ivan Michurin (1855-1935).] Lysenko dismissed "genes" and "chromosomes" as mere figments of "bourgeois" and "reactionary" idealism. His views found favor with Soviet dictator Joseph Stalin, and he was made President of the Lenin Academy of Agricultural Sciences (1938) and Director of the Department of Genetics at the USSR Academy of Science (1940). [The American pioneering geneticist and socialist Hermann Muller advocated Mendelian genetics, eventually proposing to Joseph Stalin that the Soviet Union establish a eugenics program involving artificial insemination ((Glad, 2003)). Muller's Soviet career ended when he compared Lysenko's neo-Lamarckian thinking to alchemy and astrology in his 1936 address to the Soviet Academy of Agricultural Sciences. A decade later, Muller was awarded the Nobel Prize in Physiology/Medicine for his discovery of x-ray irradiation-induced mutations.]

Genetics in the Soviet Union and Communist China was governed by ideology rather than systematic research and experimentation. Simply put, science was relegated to being a tool of dogma. The Lysenko and Michurin theories, collectively termed "creative Darwinism," severely hindered progress in genetics and molecular biology in the Soviet Union and China. Communist doctrine held that social rather than genetic etiologies were responsible for human inequality. Lysenko's research focused on manipulating an organism's environment to induce a phenotypic alteration that could be inherited in its offspring. His findings led him to extrapolate that the creation of a socialist environment would dictate future human success as their achievements were passed to succeeding generations.

Most Chinese biologists supported orthodox genetics in the 1940s, and few had worked in the liberated areas of North China and Yan'an, the de facto capital of the CCP during the Sino-Japanese War (Peishan, 1988). The scientists in these areas were not Western-educated, and they subsequently accepted the major tenets of Lysenkoism without much opposition. The Central Academy of Sciences and two other academies formed the Chinese Academy of Sciences (CAS) in November 1948, standing as the country's highest academic and research institution. Lysenko's 1948 report to the Lenin Academy of Agricultural Sciences, *The Situation of Biological Science*, was translated into Chinese in 1949 and became a mandatory text for biology departments in higher education institutions (Peishan, 1988). The work attacked and rejected Darwin's theories, particularly gradual evolution, natural selection, and "definite-indefinite" variations. Most Chinese biology texts during this period were translations of Soviet works that contained some additional Chinese cultural and environmental subject material.

Lysenkoism and Michurian biology was adopted as the official party science doctrine in late 1949 (CCP, 1952). Intellectuals and scholars that continued to practice the Mendel-Morganian life sciences were persecuted. Ultimately, under intense pressure to conform, many scientists stopped pursuing such research or switched fields. For example, Dr. Tan Jiazhen, a PhD student of Morgan at the California Institute of Technology and now considered the "Father of China's Genetics," stopped teaching genetics and focused on evolution (particularly paleontology and evolutionary mechanisms), and his infamous Drosophila population studies (Schneider, 2003).

Double Hundred Campaign (1956-1957)

Although scientists were often unable to reproduce Lysenko's "experiments," his ideology dominated scientific inquiry in the PRC until Sino-Soviet tensions rose in 1956. In a "secret speech" at the 20th Congress of the Communist Party of the Soviet Union, Nakita Khrushchev denounced Stalin as a brutal despot and accused him a several crimes (Peishan, 1988). Khrushchev also supported the production of hybrid-corn seeds, a practice that had been banned in the Soviet Union until 1952 and remained forbidden in China (Schneider, 2003). Finally, Lysenko stepped down as President of the Lenin Academy of Agricultural Sciences in April 1956 after hundred of petitioners requested his removal (Hossfeld & Olsson, 2002).

Chinese representatives at the Congress learned of Khrushchev's speech and reported it to Beijing. Li Zhisui, Mao Zedong's personal physician, has stated that Mao considered Khrushchev "unreliable," and that he would never forgive the attack on Stalin. In fact, Mao believed that the Soviets wanted to "control China" (Garver, 2003). These dramatic changes forced the CCP to evaluate its once uncritical acceptance of transplanted Soviet scientific ideology to "prevent the abuses of Stalin's Russia from being duplicated in China" (MacFarquhar, 1974).

The CCP used the Lysenkoism vs. Mendel-Morganian quandary as the model for future relations between the Party and the Chinese scientific community. In response to Khrushchev's destalinization program, Mao delivered the speech "On the Ten Major Relationships" in April 1956. It spoke of uniting the Chinese people and mobilizing all available resources to build a socialist country in opposition to imperialism and bureaucratic-capitalism (Zedong, 1977). He acknowledged the backwardness of the natural sciences in China and, most importantly, emphasized the need to "learn critically, not blindly" from other countries, neither indiscriminately rejecting nor imitating what is foreign. Soon after, Premier and Foreign Minister Zhou Enlai reported a comprehensive analysis of Mao's speech to the general public in the People's Daily (E. Zhou, 1957).

Lu Dingyi, Director of the Propaganda Department of the CCP Central Committee, summarized Mao's "Double Hundred - Hundred Flowers, Hundred Schools" policy with the famous slogan: "Let a hundred flowers blossom and a hundred schools of thought contend" (Peishan, 1988). The goal was to strengthen party-intellectual relations through open discussion and criticism. Improving the state's treatment of intellectuals was emphasized rather than granting academic freedoms or individual rights. Lu Dingyi also echoed Mao's call to learn from the objective approaches to education practiced abroad.

Lu Dingyi's pronouncements formed the framework for the Double Hundred Campaign. He initiated discussions among members of the Chinese scientific community in an effort to promote the new policy, eventually leading to the Qingdao Symposium on the genetics dilemma. (Peishan, Qingzhe, Qinghe, & Shun'e, 1985) The symposium commenced on August 10, 1956 with 130 attendees (50 of whom presented) representing both the Mendel-Morgan and the Lysenko schools. Tong Dizhou (1902-1979), Director of the Department of Biology of the CAS, chaired the opening and closing ceremonies. The main subjects of discussion were heredity, embryology, evolution, and genetics education and research.

The two-week symposium revealed that most Chinese biologists were "shielded" from the biotechnological breakthroughs that had occurred in the West because they were denied access to the relevant literature. However, some were aware of the relatively poor progress of China's scientific community in comparison to Western genetics research. The Morganists shared the results and implications of their experiments in identifying and characterizing genes and RNA. They criticized the CCP for forcing them to abide by Soviet "colonial science" and the government's failure to trust or support the Chinese scientific community (Schneider, 2003). While the Qingdao Symposium inspired similar discussions in other sciences, including physiology, pathology, chemistry, and quantum mechanics, the Double Hundred Campaign lost direction after 1956.

Anti-Rightist Movement (1957)

The Double Hundred Campaign permitted intellectuals to openly discuss national problems, including Lysenkoism and Michurin biology. However, as a result of this new openness, harsh criticism and complaints were directed against the Party, with some even published in newspapers and journals. Simply put, scientists did not want the Party to impose restrictions on their work - they believed that the direction and conduct of scientific inquiry was best left to them.

Mao and the CCP did not foresee the massive discontent the Double Hundred Campaign generated. In July 1957, under intense pressure from the CCP, Mao initiated an Anti-Rightist Movement that resulted in the condemnation, imprisonment, and death of many intellectuals. It also marked the start of the "Two Lost Decades, " a period that saw no attempt to foster scientific talent or education to further China's national development.

The persecution of intellectuals and their families began just weeks after criticism of state policies and methods was first permitted. Thousands of "rightists," mostly literary intellectuals and some natural scientists, were exiled to rural areas, sent to labor camps, or jailed (Hao, 1997). The backlash was directed at those who directly spoke against the Party or socialism; critics of Lysenkoism were often spared (Peishan, 1988). In five months, over 300,000 people (the "rightists" and their families) were persecuted in some way (Spence, 1990).

Great Leap Forward (1958-1959)

The Anti-Rightist Movement was followed by an ill-fated socialist program of economic development and independence known as the Great Leap Forward (1958-1959). Mao and the CCP interpreted the Soviet Union's weakening economic situation in the 1950s as an opportunity for China to rapidly industrialize. This involved a massive shift of the country's human resources from agriculture to industry. While the Anti-Rightist Movement sought to suppress intellectuals that opposed absolute control by the Party, the Great Leap Forward planned to end China's reliance on a technological elite. The underlying principle was summarized by Mao's slogan: "The masses must make themselves masters of culture and science" (Meisner, 1999).

Over 100 million peasants were mobilized to construct water-conservation systems while other agricultural tasks were neglected. Some peasants were even sent to the CAS Institute of Agricultural Sciences and, in turn, scientific experts were forced to work on farms (Schneider, 2003). The purpose of this switch was to force the technological elite to "learn from the farmers [and] sum up their invaluable experiences to lead to higher yields" (Schneider, 2003).

Envisioning a true communist society, Mao claimed China would surpass Britain in steel production within 15 years; in reality, production quotas were often aligned to his revolutionary goals. The Great Leap Forward proved to be a total failure - its legacy was economic ruin, widespread famine, environmental degradation, and the collapse of modern and professional specialized scientific research and inquiry in the PRC.

The natural sciences were partially rescued after the Great Leap Forward through Mao's promotion of the "science of the people." Although conflict continued, the country's reliance on high technology and scientific developments necessitated the return of leading economists, central planners, and proponents of professional science to the Party. After Mao resigned as Chairman of the PRC, Liu Shaoqi became his successor.

The CCP Central Committee sponsored a national conference in Canton in 1960 to improve China's poor record of scientific innovation and education. Lu Dingyi restarted the Double Hundred Campaign for specialized fields, including genetics. Dr. Tan Jiazhen (P. Chen, 1962) stated that the Canton Genetics Conference genuinely attempted to rebuild genetics research by reinstituting the principles of the 1956 Qingdao Symposium. As a result, Chinese scientific societies, scholarly journals, and major experiments were briefly revived.

Mao also sought educational reforms known as the Socialist Education Movement (1962-1965) to restore ideological purity and prevent the creation of a technological elite. Under this new system, schools adopted work-study programs that required students to participate in manual labor activities. This policy generated conflict within the Party, particularly between PRC Chairman Liu Shaoqi and CCP General Secretary Deng Xiaoping. While the controversy over the Social Education Movement and the devastating consequences of the Cultural Revolution caused Liu's downfall, Deng was ultimately credited with reviving China.

Cultural Revolution (1966-1976)

Many studies have chronicled the devastating events of the Cultural Revolution (MacFarquhar, 1974). Suffice it to say, the Cultural Revolution had severe negative consequences for the Chinese science community. On June 1, 1966, the *People's Daily* announced that all "imperialists" and "intellectuals" must be purged from the country. This "Cultural Revolution" was intended to rescue China from the treacherous "rightists" who were seeking a "bourgeois restoration." In practice, intellectuals and their families were subjected to humiliation, violence, and even killed. Some chose to escape the cruel persecution by committing suicide. Not even the communist leadership was spared: Liu Shaoqi was imprisoned, eventually dying in 1969 from starvation and poor sanitation; Deng Xiaoping was forced to perform manual labor in an engine factory.

The Cultural Revolution halted educational and scientific progress in China through the closure of all schools and research institutions. The CAS was disbanded in 1967, and the State Science and Technology Commission was abolished in 1969, with the members of education faculties "sent down" to rural areas to work as manual laborers (Schneider, 2003). Dr. Tan Jiazhen noted that the only positive aspect of the Cultural Revolution was that "some old Lysenkoites were sent down with the rest of the biologists, and finally got a taste of their own medicine" (Schneider, 2003). The revolutionary committee also relocated the Beijing Agricultural University to the countryside because they believed that agricultural sciences should not be taught in a city. The former university campus was subsequently transformed into barracks and offices for the People's Liberation Army.

In 1976, the end of the Cultural Revolution was marked by Chairman Mao's death and the arrest of political radicals instrumental to extending the revolution. However, severe damage had been done to Chinese science by that time. There were three principle consequences: First, students who had been denied access to educational institutions became a "lost generation." Second, scientists were ignorant of scientific advances because they had been barred from laboratories and unable to read the literature. Finally, the understanding and practice of science had been completely removed from the working class, creating a new and dangerous bourgeoisie. Facing these problems, the post-Mao leadership engaged in reformist campaign to restore the capabilities and standing of the scientific community.

Science Reformation Post-Cultural Revolution (1976-2005)

After two decades of gross interruptions - the Anti-Rightist Movement, the Great Leap Forward, and the Cultural Revolution - science in China was slowly put on a permanent pathway of reform. In the post-1976 era, political leaders like Deng Xiaoping actively implemented modernization, globalization, and high-technology policies and programs in an attempt to revive scientific thought, systematic experimentation, and biotechnology research in the country. Party leaders even condemned the attacks on science and scientists that occurred during the Cultural Revolution. Deng realized that scientific research and technological development, as well as interaction with the international academic community, had to be pursued in the long-term. Remarkably, prominent intellectuals such as Dr. Tan Jiazhen joined the CCP in the hope of influencing the reform process and improving conditions in the nation (Saich, 1989).

Deng's Four Modernization plan called for a national movement in science and technology, agriculture, national defense, and industry (Deng, 1977). Mao's focus on class struggle and self-reliance was disregarded in favor of individuals using their hands or brains to build a powerful socialist state. At the National Science Conference on March 18 1978, Deng stated: "Without the rapid development of science and technology, there can be no rapid development of the country" (Deng, 1978).

Deng Xiaoping revitalized the spirit of the people, instilling a sense of unity between the peasantry (i.e. farmers) and intellectuals (i.e. academicians, artists, scholars, scientists). It was also acknowledged that a comprehensive survey of China's scientific output and higher education resources was necessary. The results were presented in the State Science and Technology Commission's 1986 "Sci-Tech White Paper" (Commission, 1986). In addition, the newly formed Beijing University Center for the Study of Science and Society addressed China's history of intellectual persecution through an intensive examination of the Double Hundred Campaign and the events that followed (Schneider, 2003). Lysenkoism was used a cautionary example of the danger of permitting politics and ideology to violate intellectual independence and integrity.

The CAS research institutes also restarted their experiments and education programs during this period. In 1982, the CAS created the Science and Technology Fund to support research in the universities through competitive grants, which had largely been absent since 1956. In the first three years, 120.33 million *yuan* was provided to conduct 2,433 approved projects. In 1986, the Fund became the National Natural Science Foundation (NNSF), which was independent of the CAS and funded directly by the Ministry of Finance. The Frontiers in High Technology Program, emphasizing the potential of the applied sciences, was eventually replaced by the larger 863 Program

The China National Center for Biotechnology Development (CNCBD) was established in 1983 to manage and distribute funds for biotechnology research in agriculture, food processing, and pharmaceutical manufacturing. The CNCBD also provided consultative and promotional services for China's burgeoning biotechnology industry. In 1986, Deng Xiaoping ordered the formation of the High Technology Research and Development (863) Program in response to international strategic programs using novel sophisticated technologies. With a total budget of 10 billion *yuan*, the program was tasked with providing 15 years of research and development promotion (1986-2000). To reduce the science and technology gap between China and other nations, the 863 Program provided millions of *yuan* per year for applied agriculture, medicine, and protein engineering projects. Although the grant system was peer-reviewed, there was a "complex negotiation process" involving various government committees and centers (Hamer & Kung, 1989).

The CAS and the US National Academy of Sciences jointly sponsored *Biotechnology in China*, an evaluation of China's state-of-the-field analysis between 1986 to 1989 (Hamer & Kung, 1989). The study noted that the allocation of biotechnology research funding was decentralized, with only 1.7% of funding in 1989 provided to applicants that directly requested financial backing. While the study stated that China's biotechnology sector improved significantly in the preceding decade, it was still far behind the developed nations.

China's Specialized Biotechnology

In 1973, Stanford medical professor Stanley Cohen and UCSF biochemist Herbet Boyer made landmark discoveries in modern biotechnology: Cohen found that plasmids, or circular DNA, can be cloned and propagated in *E. coli* bacteria, while Boyer identified the restriction enzyme *EcoRI* that had DNA cleaving activity. Together, these two discoveries could be used to engineer cellular DNA (genetic engineering). Scientists eventually synthesized somatostatin in bacteria, the first human protein made using recombinant technology.

Despite the obvious importance of these new methodological discoveries, several factors delayed the transmission of recombinant DNA technology to China's scientific institutions until the early

1980s. First, the Cultural Revolution resulted in a deficit of trained personnel who were capable of performing such complicated experiments. Second, China lacked the proper facilities and reagents to proceed with recombinant experimentation. Finally, financial support was limited to scarce foreign sources that relied on scientists willing to engage in such biotechnology work. In later years, the 863 High Technology Program and the National Basic Sciences (973) Initiative, with a total budget of 2.5 billion *yuan* (1997-2002), were willing to provide substantial funding for such research. The CAS, State Science and Technology Commission, and other Chinese academies eventually reversed China's shortfalls by launching rapid exploration into the new frontier of modern biotechnology.

Agricultural Biotechnology

The forces driving China's agricultural biotechnology research are food security (Zhang, 1999), scientific progression, and health. Early biotechnology developments in China focused on cell engineering and tissue culture, and emphasized work on plants such as rice, wheat, and cotton. However, funding from the 863 Program made the development and utilization of transgenic techniques common. Chinese research institutions, including the CAS and the Chinese Academy for Agricultural Sciences, prioritized plant biotechnology research funding for cotton, rice, wheat, maize, soybean, potato, rapeseed, cabbage, and tomato. Genetic engineering to achieve insect resistance, disease resistance, stress tolerance, quality improvement, and herbicidal resistance were sought by Chinese agricultural biotechnologists in the mid-1980s. As a result, China rapidly became a global leader in the field.

China's success is amply illustrated by its development of the enormously successful *Bacillus thuringiensis* (Bt) resistant cotton. The breakthrough occurred in the search for alternatives to using pesticides to control common insects that were decimating certain types of agriculture. For example, pesticide expenditures had skyrocketed in an effort to protect cotton production from the bollworm. Moreover, the widespread use of pesticides jeopardized farmers' health and limited biodiversity in the cotton fields. Using the pollen-tube pathway transformation technique, China's scientists transferred a modified Bt gene into major cotton cultivars. After greenhouse studies, mutation and lineage analyses, and biosafety inquiries, the genetically modified (GM) crop was approved in 1997 for commercial distribution (Xu & Bai, 2002). Today, China's Bt cotton is the world's most prevalent transgenic crop for small farmers. Chinese scientists have since modified hundreds of plant varieties, although very few have been approved for commercial use. A Chinese university greenhouse is shown in **Error! Reference source not found.**.

In the 1990s, China's agrobiologists transferred techniques learned while studying in the West to the domestic biotechnology industry (e.g., marker-assisted breeding, selection, and introgression, and chimeraplasty). Subsequently, many novel transformation methodologies using *Agrobacterium* and gene-gun particle bombardment technology have been used to study transgene inheritance (Yin, Plader, & Malepszy, 2004), bacterial blight resistance in transgenic rice (Zhai et al., 2004), cotton fiber quality (D. M. Li et al., 2003; X. Li, Wang, Zhao, & Dutt, 2004), and aphid resistance in transgenic tobacco (J. Yao et al., 2003; J. H. Yao et al., 2003).

China is projected to continue to develop its specialized molecular plant sciences and has even recently ventured into oral immunization research, or "edible vaccinations." China's plant molecular biologists realize that crops can be genetically modified to produce disease-like, yet harmless, antigens that can stimulate humoral immunity after ingestion. Most plant-based antigen protein expression system studies are currently in the experimental animal testing phase, including hepatitis B immunity via transgenic cherry tomatoes (Y. Gao et al., 2003) and rotaviral immunity using transgenic potatoes (Wu et al., 2003). Edible vaccines would be cheap to produce, easy to transport, and act as an ideal vector for resistance to human pathogens. However, problems with oral immunization include variance in production causing irregular antigen concentration, the

Figure 1. An example of a greenhouse facility in China.

potential for accidental ingestions, and the inability to mediate essential post-translational modifications that trigger the immunity response.

China now possesses the largest plant biotechnology capacity outside of North America (Huang, Rozelle, Pray, & Wang, 2002), with over 100,000 research staff in well-equip laboratories as shown in **Error! Reference source not found.**. A substantial pool of well-trained scientists, relatively inexpensive research experimentation, and access to a variety of plant germplasm and cell lines provides China with many advantages compared to other countries. Agricultural research and development in China is likely pursue many potential transgenesis paths, such as metabolic engineering and the manipulation of plant biochemistry for the production of non-protein based products (e.g., antipyretic quinine, unsaturated fatty acids, pigments, and biodegradable plastics).

Major Genomic Projects

China has made a major leap forward by collaborating with renowned universities around the world on the most ambitious and intensive genome study, the Human Genome Project (HGP). Sponsored by the US Department of Education and the National Institute of Health, the HGP began in 1988 with the objective of developing the methodology to successfully sequence the entire human genetic code. In 1997, the newly established National Human Genome Research Institute noted that recently developed methodologies would be essential to sequencing human DNA.

Despite skepticism about the ability of a developing country to effectively participate in the HGP, China joined the International Human Genome Sequencing Consortium in 1998 to work alongside France, Germany, Great Britain, Japan, and the United States. China's State Science and Technology Commission became the Ministry of Science and Technology (MoST) the same year. The MoST established two institutions under the direction of the CAS to spearhead China's role

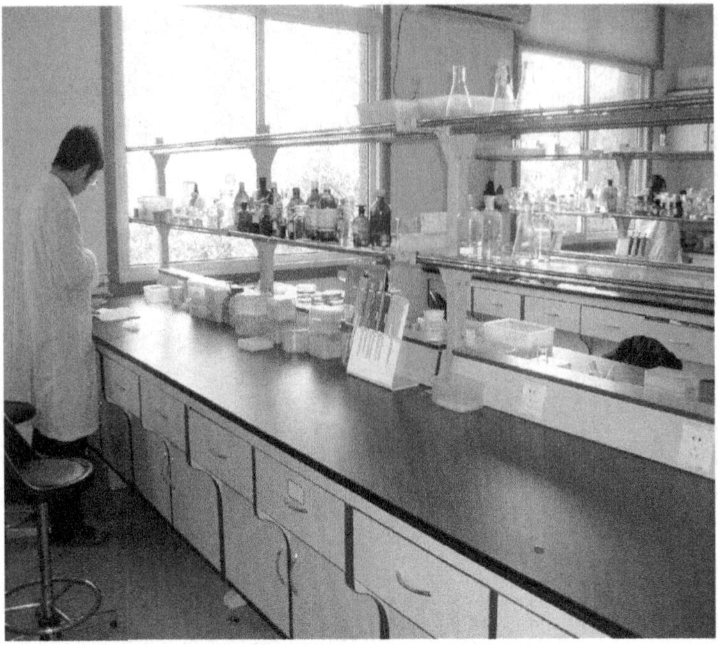

Figure 2. An example of a research laboratory in China.

in the project: the Beijing and Shanghai Human Genome Centers. Zhu Chen, then Vice President of the Chinese Academy of Sciences, and Prof. Boqin Qiang, an academician of the CAS, were appointed to run the Shanghai and Beijing divisions, respectively. The Beijing Center was better equipped to perform high-throughout and quantity genome sequencing and bioinformatics analysis, while the Shanghai Center was more oriented to functional medical genomics. A third institution, the Beijing Genome Center/Bioinformatics Center, was established later.

In 2001, the International Human Genome Sequencing Consortium published their landmark construction of the whole-genome bacterial artificial chromosome (BAC) map with limited annotations (McPherson et al., 2001). China contributed to 1% of the published sequence, particularly the short-arm of chromosome 3, labeled the "Beijing region."

Chinese institutions engaged in another major genomic venture in 2003, the International HapMap Project, which is trying to determine shared patterns of DNA variation in the human genome from populations with ancestry from Africa (Nigeria), Asia (Japan and China), and Europe (Utah residents of northern or western European decent) (Consortium, 2003). The Beijing and Shanghai Human Genome Centers, University of Hong Kong, Hong Kong University of Science and Technology, and the Chinese University of Hong Kong will haplotype and screen an estimated 10% of the human genome on chromosomes 3, 8p, and 21. Beijing Normal University and Beijing Genomics Institute will aid in community engagement and procuring samples, respectively.

China is also participating in the ten-country International Rice Genome Sequencing Project that is promoting the development of rice and cereal genomics. Remarkably, the Beijing National Genome Center published the draft sequence of the rice genome *Oryza sativa* - the most important crop for human consumption -in *Science* (Yu et al., 2002). The Beijing Center had succeeded at the task after only a few months work, while competitors who had dedicated intensive amounts of time and effort failed to produce large-scale published genomic data.

China will continue to generate sequence data on human, rice, and experimental organism genomes, and enrich the annotation profiles of the identified genes. In addition, Chinese scientists sponsored by the MoST are proposing a Human Proteome Project and the Human Liver Proteome Project (H. Jia & Louet, 2004). The latter project is in direct response to the Hepatitis B (HB) pandemic that has infected nearly 170 million people in China (Sun, Ming, Zhu, & Lu, 2002). The nationwide HB vaccination campaign and the universal immunization of newborns initiated by the Ministry of Public Health and World Health Organization has decreased the rate of new infections; however, the Human Liver Proteome Project could reveal new diagnostic and therapeutic options for current suffers.

Profiling, identifying, and creating anti-bodies for the entire human proteome is a greater feat than the HGP, as proteins are subject to multiple structure levels, various expression and interaction pathways, and a host of possible modifications. Thus, China is rapidly becoming a leading nation in the quest to understand basic human biology and the mechanisms of disorders.

Modernizing Traditional Chinese Medicine

China has a long - even ancient - history of using herbological and acupuncture intervention to treat a variety of medical disorders. Theories of *Qi*, a neuroendocrinological regulatory substance, state that it is the life and vital force of the body. Qi circulates the body in a systemic pattern, stimulating and regulating organ systems. Interruptions of flow induce disease by way of *Qi* antagonists (e.g., physical or emotional trauma, radiation, thermo instability, nutritional imbalance, environmental pollutions, or intoxicants). Health is ultimately defined as equilibrium established and controlled by the Yin/Yang theory of opposites and interdependent processes and systems.

Mao understood the power of Traditional Chinese Medicine (TCM), avidly supporting its widespread use on the rural masses after the 1949 CCP victory. He referred to TCM as the nation's "treasurehouse," and urged the Chinese people to "raise its standards" (Unschuld, 1985). In 1955, the China Academy for Traditional Chinese Medicine (CATCM) was established in Beijing as the center of TCM research, healthcare, and academics in the country. The CATCM was tasked with developing mass production methods, creating viable strains of herbs, and offering quality control policies.

The Institute of Chinese Materia Medica (a division of the CATCM) had been responsible for performing basic research into herbological compounds. While the staff lacked adequate training into biochemical experimentation, they assisted in a discovery that benefited the international community. During the Cultural Revolution, Mao chose to spare a group of scientists in the Materia Medica in a bold attempt to find a domestic compound with anti-malarial properties, or even a cure. Mao recognized the destructive impact of malaria on the country, and perhaps he also realized that such a discovery would generate enormous respect for TCM. After an intensive search through thousands of ancient medicinal recipes, the scientists isolated artemisinin from *qinghao* (Artemisia annua, sweet wormwood). Ancient literature noted that the herb produced thermostability when administered to patients with fevers. The researchers found that artemisinin could combat resistant strains of the malaria parasite (H. H. Chen, Zhou, & Fang, 2003; Efferth, Dunstan, Sauerbrey, Miyachi, & Chitambar, 2001) and recent work suggests it has anti-cancer properties as well. Derivatives of artemisinin are the most rapid acting of the known anti-malarial agents, and they have been administered to more than one million patients around the world (White, 1996).

Chinese biotechnology companies are also developing computerized instrumentation that can provide TCM doctors with greater diagnostic capabilities. For example, Chongqing Tianhai

Medical Equipment Inc. has developed a tongue reader with an integrated CCD video system and image analysis software to detect discoloration and textural changes (useful for diagnosing conditions like psoriasis, which produce a crimson tongue with a yellow coating; see **Error! Reference source not found.** for an image of this bioinstrument).

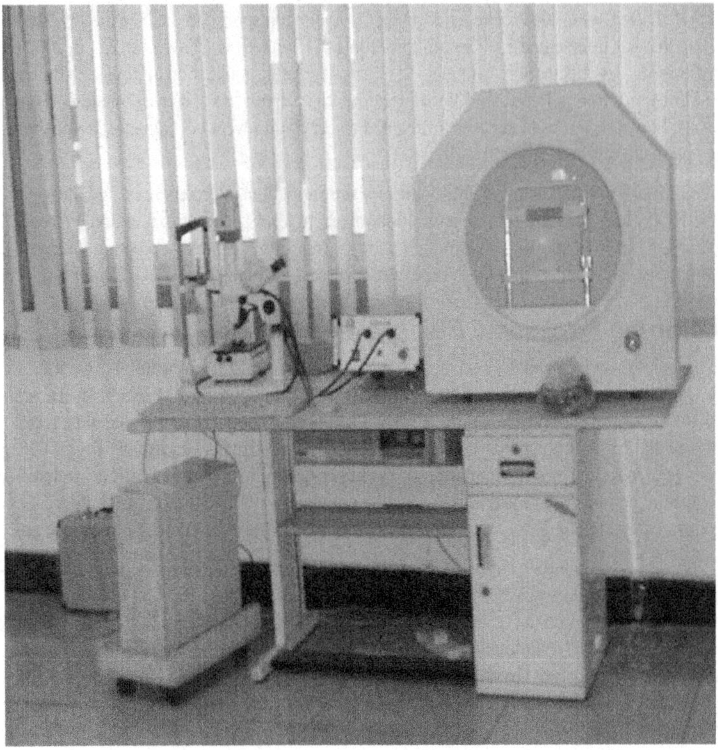

Figure 3. Instrumentation used by TCM doctors to observe facial and oral features for clinical diagnosis.

Deng Xiaoping's modernization program called for research into the biochemical mechanisms of herbal compounds and extended trade with the outside world. Other TCM compounds with potential clinical effectiveness have been noted for diabetes (W. Jia, Gao, & Tang, 2003), improper blood circulation (F. W. Li et al., 2001), and hypertension (C. Zhou, Yu, Li, & Tian, 2001). However, the lack of acceptance of TCM by the Western medical and scientific community remains a central concern of TCM health professionals and researchers.

Stem-Cell Research & Regenerative Medicine

China's 1979 One-Child Policy will eventually create a disproportionately elderly population that receives an uneven provision of support, particularly in poorly developed rural areas (Joseph & Phillips, 1999). Chinese scientists are exploring stem cell research, therapeutic developments, and regenerative medicines as potential solutions to the aging crisis. In the United States and Germany, stem cell research was proceeding rapidly until government sanctions prohibited federal funding for human embryonic stem (ES) cell research conducted after August 2001 and January

2002, respectively (Gershon, 2003). In contrast, China, the United Kingdom, Australia, India, Israel, Singapore, and Sweden have established more liberal research policies.

All tissues and cells of the embryo and adult organism trace their origin to the pluripotent cells with developmental plasticity of the early mammalian embryo (Hogan, Beddington, Costantini, & Lacy, 1994). Tissue defects, including cellular loss and/or function, can be treated with stem cell regenerative therapy. Contending with the HBV epidemic made China a pioneer in the advancement of allogeneic hematopoietic stem cell transplantation for the prevention or deferral of hepatitis (Lau et al., 2002; Ma et al., 2004). As a result of high incidence of insulin resistance in China, researchers at the Third Military Medical University in Chongqing are investigating the plasticity and transdifferentiation potential of adult pancreatic ductal cells as potential stem cells into insulin producing islet cells with positive findings (Yao, Qin, Liu, Chen, & Zhou, 2004).

The Shanghai Second Medical University has demonstrated that scientists may be able to bypass human embryos for harvesting human ES cells by nuclear fusion of the human somatic nuclei from skin cells into enucleated rabbit eggs (Y. Chen et al., 2003). The procedure may help avoid immune incompatibility for future cell therapies. After electrofusion and cell culture, the reconstituted cell undergoes normal embryological development. The scientists collected ES cells from an embryo at blastocyst stage, and found that the somatic cell nuclear transfer procedure generated ES cells that retained traits similar to those of conventional human ES cells. Most importantly, the cells could undergo multi-lineage cellular differentiation; however, self-renewal capabilities were not addressed. This study demonstrates the progress of China's cellular engineering technology, but also hints at a lack of ethical regulation in the biomedical sciences.

Concerns for China

Scientific discovery and technological development has occurred rapidly in China in the past twenty years, with certain applied science fields now on par with the West. Concentrated funding programs from the MoST have boosted genomic exploration and stem cell research. Areas of particular national concern, such as food insecurity, hepatitis B, and a disproportionately aging population, have led China to develop specialized forms of science. However, China must pursue active reforms and intensive development in other sectors if it is to achieve a long-term reputation for innovation. First, China's bioethics system fails to meet accepted international standards. Second, grant funding is highly specialized and review policies are ambiguous. Finally, China must increase its willingness to seek international participation and collaboration in scientific endeavors that require expertise in many sectors (e.g. stem cell therapies).

Bioethics, Biosafety, & Regulation

Policy makers in China are beginning to understand the positive implications of developing and implementing ethical and technical standards. Recent biotechnological regulations indicate progression towards the fostering of an ethical scientific and medical community; this is not surprising given China's membership in the World Trade Organization in 2001. Scientists often study abroad and return to China, bringing with them the bioethical standards of their post-doctoral institution. Nevertheless, ethical science is certainly not practiced by all scientists in China. In fact, bioethical standards are often maintained only because violations can prevent publication in prominent Western journals or halt participation in international research projects or pharmaceutical marketing.

Sex selection has been practiced in China for long time. Modern technology (e.g., amniocentesis, ultrasound, and chorionic villi sampling) has empowered couples seeking to manage sex selection and family size. In response, the Maternal and Infant Health Care Law of 1995 forbade prenatal genetic diagnosis that may lead to sex selection, and demanded full basic health for the entire population (Doring, 2003). However, the legislation also permits the use of a highly controversial eugenics statute that facilitates the systematic abortion of offspring with mental diseases. Although the Chinese people believe in individual autonomy, they also hold that autonomy is guided by social needs.

In 1998, the Ministry of Public Health (MPH) formally banned human cloning, with no exception granted for therapeutic cloning (Doring, 2003). In fact, the public showed little opposition to such practices, and China is considered the world's most liberal nation in terms of embryo research. To halt the operation of numerous unlicensed *in-vitro* fertilization centers that conducted artificial insemination from unknown donors, the MPH implemented further restrictive policies in late 2001. China has now instituted tightly controlled systems of assisted reproduction and sperm-bank licensing to halt substandard operations.

Many Chinese research institutions have yet to implement or enforce ethical standards, particularly governing the humane treatment of animals. The China Wildlife Conservation Association and International Fund for Animal Welfare have unsuccessfully lobbied the Chinese government to institute laws protecting animal welfare. The Beijing Municipal Government considered a draft proposal for four days in 2004, but eventually rejected it without providing a reason (Xinhuanet, 2004). Given that more than 100 countries have instituted animal protection laws, including many developing countries in Africa, China is lagging significantly behind the international norm.

As genetically modified organisms (GMOs), plant medicines, and embryological manipulation become increasingly common, ethical and biosafety questions are naturally raised and must be addressed. The potential ecological risks associated with transgene escape through gene flow or cross-pollination has already been noted. For instance, transgenes may propagate within weedy or wild plant varieties through sexual reproduction or asexual vegetative propagation. Traits such as antibiotic, pesticide, and temperature resistance may significantly enhance the ecological fitness of weedy and wild populations or destroy endangered species. Risks from GM crops should be closely monitored and measured. Regulatory agencies, as established in the US (e.g., Food and Drug Administration and Environmental Protection Agency) perform monitoring, approval, and assessment tasks, a practice that China must adopt.

Chinese scientists must realize that their studies may not be published, their access to foreign funding restricted, international collaboration halted, or the nation's reputation jeopardized if legally binding and effective monitoring systems are not established for bioethical research. Furthermore, ignorance of agricultural biosafety could cause the production of transgenic weeds that are resistant to pesticides or cause the extinction of endangered species in local ecosystems.

Patenting Biotechnology

The Patent Office of the PRC was founded in 1980 as a component of Deng Xiaoping's globalization program. China revised its Patent, Trade Mark, and Copyright Laws in 1992 and 2000, and they are now similar to those in the European Patent Convention. An invention is clearly defined as patentable if it possesses novelty, inventiveness, and industrial applicability. The revisions also made it easier to determine the court jurisdiction of an infringement lawsuit and raised the maximum intellectual property remedies to 500,000 *yuan*. Genetic technologies rely on main patent protection, while new species of plants and animals fall under special protections.

These new intellectual property protections in coverage and enforcement were established to promote investment in the Chinese market, improve international collaboration, and reward technical innovation. More than 250,000 applications were filed between 1985 and 1999, mostly for Chinese herbal medicines, foodstuffs, and pharmaceuticals (Lui, 2001). Since 2003, China's patent agency has reviewed nearly three million applications, many of which are for new genetic engineering techniques and methods for modernizing TCM. As a result of these changes, foreign companies are finally starting to trust China's life science intellectual property systems.

Funding Mechanisms

There are major problems with China's current funding approval and dispersal mechanisms. The optimal system would be similar to that implemented by the US National Institute of Health, which is characterized by a transparent review process, equitable scoring system, and mandatory reviewer comments for every application.

In some ways, the traditional Chinese work system is responsible for some of the problems in this area. Until the 1960s, the Chinese urban workforce was governed by a "work-unit system" called *danwei*. The workplace was a relatively regimented and controlled environment, providing the principle means of support for workers, including their room and board. Budgets were allocated to the work-unit rather than to individual scientists, often resulting in redundancy and poor information distribution. While post-Cultural Revolution reforms have reduced the use of *danwei*, it continues to harm the scientific inquiry. For example, it is still common for a scientist to remain at one institution for their entire career, and this lack of mobility can seriously impede effectiveness. Moreover, the procedure for dismissing government workers remains lengthy and troublesome; it is therefore often avoided by administrators.

While the 863 Program peer-reviewed funding applications for high-technology research, the process involved many different government organizations and the policies were unclear. The 973 National Basic Sciences Initiative made significant improvements to this review procedure; in fact, 15 new projects funded by this program in 2003 were published in *Science* (Lei, 1998). The remaining concerns that need to be addressed include the artificial inflation of grant budgets to keep the surplus for personal use and the implementation of a transparent and accountable application review process.

Conclusion

The CCP's blind acceptance of Lysenkoism from 1949 to 1956 was detrimental to the development of the Chinese scientific community and the welfare of the population. Its doctrinaire assertion that genes and chromosomes are mere fabrications of "bourgeois" and "reactionary" idealism has caused untold suffering. How much grain was lost by failing to utilize well-known hybrid crop techniques? How many millions of Chinese people died from starvation as a result? How much did this philosophy prevent or impede China's industrialization, economic progress, and scientific competence?

Modern Chinese history clearly illustrates how social-political philosophies can affect natural sciences and, by extension, the development of an entire society. Mao Zedong's attempt to control science and scientists decimated China's economy and halted technological progress. By actively seeking to repress and eliminate intellectuals and the "technological elite" to achieve a socialist ideal, Mao paralyzed the ability of the country to adapt to the modern world. Deng Xiaoping's effort to regenerate scientific exploration and technological development was an acknowledgement that progress in these fields is the driving force of modernization, whether scientific, economic, military, or agricultural. The establishment of dedicated national biotechnology centers such as the NNSF and CNCBD facilitated the development and organization of important applied science projects in China. Progress was also driven by the Frontiers in High Technology Program, High Technology Research and Development (863) Program, and National Basic Sciences (973) Initiative. In fact, the 873 funding program has allowed China to develop specialized biotechnology sectors that now make it globally competitive.

Advancements in plant biotechnology, TCM, and embryological biology in application-oriented and fundamental mechanisms will occur rapidly in China over the next five years. Important research in the basic sciences has already occurred, for instance, regulation of smooth muscle contractility (Yang et al., 2002), human Bim proapoptotic activity (J. Z. Chen et al., 2004), novel regulators of NF-kappaB pathways (H. Gao et al., 2004), heterotic effects at the single-locus level (Hua et al., 2003), and bHLH-Zip gene role in human spermatogenesis (Sha et al., 2003).

Instead of merely transplanting Western science - a problematic practice from the Republican era - China has now begun to utilize modern biotechnology to solve indigenous and national problems. The country's access to diverse plant germplasm, foreign educated and trained scientists, and substantial government support has facilitated the integration of recombinant DNA technology into China's research and development environment. In fact, China's experience with traditional medicines and its pool of transgenic plant varieties make the country enormously attractive to international businesses and collaborative research projects. Major revisions to the country's patent laws have only increased international interest in China's resource treasurehouse. However, bioethical and technical standards must be implemented and monitored countrywide if China's scientific advances are to be globally accepted and commercialized.

Note on International Collaboration

China must increase its participation in international collaborative biotechnology education programs and high-technology research, particularly regarding clinical trials for stem cell therapies and any subsequent commercialization of the results.

The knowledge of Chinese science graduate students is often limited to specialized areas (e.g., biomedical engineering). My observations and research noted that the primary complaint made by Chinese university students related to their lack of knowledge in bioinstrumentation, experimental biology, and other scientific sectors outside their major. These gaps are problematic because survey knowledge of medical, agricultural, aquatic, microbial, genomic, and proteomic biotechnology is essential to making biotechnology advances. Although students learn some of these techniques while studying or conducting research abroad, such practical knowledge would be optimally employed before research is undertaken.

I underwent an academic and instructional trip to Beijing and Chongqing in March of 2004 with Prof. Gin Gee of Miramar College. I was part of an instructional team to deliver a collegiate distance education course, "Biotechnology from a Global Perspective," that utilized a WebCT online educational platform to reach an international student body. The course instructed and stimulated discussion about the biotechnological sciences and its impact on the global economy, business practices, public health, social society, and ethical considerations. Using Internet based video-streaming technology, the students viewed guest lectures and resources delivered or prepared by prominent industrialists and academics from well-known institutions such as Harvard, Invitrogen, University of California – San Diego, Illumina, and Chongqing University. In addition, the instructors and external contributors developed *Biotech World*, a comprehensive web resource on the latest bioscience research and business and societal culture of "biotechnologically-active" countries.

After establishing a Memorandum of Understanding with China's prestigious universities, several students enrolled in the "Global Biotech" course for the spring 2004 term. The participants included graduate and post-doctoral students and faculty members of Chongqing University, Sichuan University, Fourth Military Medical College, and the China Academy of Tradition Chinese Medicine (see **Error! Reference source not found.** for students during an orientation lecture). During the course, the participants openly expressed their opinions on the progress of China's biotechnology sector and the need for bioethical standards, proper funding, and elective graduate

Figure 4. Global Biotechnology distance learning students in China at a computer laboratory in the spring 2004 term.

education courses. This experience demonstrates that further collaborative education systems should be established with Chinese universities and research institutions, particularly faculty/student exchange programs.

In 1999, the Municipality of Chongqing established a High-Technology Industrialization Office (CQMHTIO) to monitor adherence to national policies and strategies. The organization represents over 150 biotech companies and research institutes, as well as administering important projects in the highly applied sciences. The CQMHTIO views the government as the "head" and enterprise the "main body." Currently, the primary concerns of biotechnology industry executives are commercialization, collaboration with the US, and access to competent scientists. Furthermore, collaborative efforts can be initiated as sponsorship by Western institutions, however, the concern is China's implementation of bioethical practices that are backed by firm financial support. Industry executives may serve as advisory committee members for nearby colleges and universities, and university officials may act on the consulting board for the CQMHTIO. Moreover, our online courses may establish links between the international biotech academic and industry communities, which can facilitate the open exchange of ideas and future collaboration.

Most high-technology projects require expertise in many subjects (e.g., molecular biology, biochemistry, immunology, genetics, transplantation biology, pathology, and clinical medicine). The Chinese government should promote international research and publication because such collaboration will attract scientists to China and increase its scientific reputation. During my visit to China, I met with Dr. Fulong Liao, the Director of Pharmacology at the Institute of Materia Medica, CATCM. I was invited to lecture their doctoral students, staff, and faculty on global biotechnology and on developing collaborative diploma programs (see **Error! Reference source not**

Figure 5. Doctoral students, staff, and faculty of the China Academy of Traditional Chinese Medicine attending Lakhan's lecture on biotechnology.

found.). They have tremendous interest in mass spectrometry and other proteomic experimentations on an ancient TCM herb with specific properties, for example, thermostability.

Collaborative endeavors should be encouraged to bridge China's scientific quest with proper resources, namely, bioinstrumentations and technologies of the West. Moreover, international training programs should be established to impart essential knowledge about experimental design to Chinese researchers who have not studied abroad.

References

CCP. (1952). The struggle to persist in the Michurinist direction in biological science. *People's Daily*.

Chen, H. H., Zhou, H. J., & Fang, X. (2003). Inhibition of human cancer cell line growth and human umbilical vein endothelial cell angiogenesis by artemisinin derivatives in vitro. *Pharmacological Research, 48*(3), 231-236.

Chen, J. Z., Ji, C. N., Gu, S. H., Li, J. X., Zhao, E. P., Huang, Y., et al. (2004). Over-expression of Bim alpha3: A novel isoform of human Bim, result in cell apoptosis. *International Journal of Biochemistry & Cell Biology, 36*(8), 1554-1561.

Chen, P. (1962). *Communist China 1961* (Vol. 1). Hong Kong: Union Research Institute.

Chen, Y., He, Z. X., Liu, A., Wang, K., Mao, W. W., Chu, J. X., et al. (2003). Embryonic stem cells generated by nuclear transfer of human somatic nuclei into rabbit oocytes. *Cell Research, 13*(4), 251-263.

Commission, S. S. a. T. (1986). *White paper on science and technology No. 1*. Beijing: Joint Publications Research Service - China Science & Technology.

Consortium, I. H. (2003). The international HapMap project. *Nature, 426*(6968), 789-796.

Deng, X. (1977). Respect knowledge, respect trained personnel. In P. s. D. Online (Ed.), *Selected works of Deng Xiaoping* (Vol. II). Beijing: People's Daily Online.

Deng, X. (1978). Speech at the opening ceremony of the National Conference on Science. In P. s. D. Online (Ed.), *Selected Works of Deng Xiaoping* (Vol. II). Beijing: People's Daily Online.

Doring, O. (2003). China's struggle for practical regulations in medical ethics. *Nature Review Genetics, 4*(3), 233-239.

Efferth, T., Dunstan, H., Sauerbrey, A., Miyachi, H., & Chitambar, C. R. (2001). The anti-malarial artesunate is also active against cancer. *International Journal of Oncolology, 18*(4), 767-773.

Fairbank, W. (1976). *Americas cultural experiment, Publication No. 8839*. Washington DC: Department of State.

Gao, H., Sun, Y., Wu, Y., Luan, B., Wang, Y., Qu, B., et al. (2004). Identification of beta-Arrestin2 as a G protein-coupled receptor-stimulated regulator of NF-kappaB pathways. *Molecular Cell, 14*(3), 303-317.

Gao, Y., Ma, Y., Li, M., Cheng, T., Li, S. W., Zhang, J., et al. (2003). Oral immunization of animals with transgenic cherry tomatillo expressing HBsAg. *World Journal of Gastroenterology, 9*(5), 996-1002.

Garver, J. (2003). Review article: Mao's Soviet policies. *The China Quarterly, 173*, 199-213.

Gershon, D. (2003). Complex political, ethical and legal issues surround research on human embryonic stem cells. *Nature, 422*(6934), 928-929.

Glad, J. (2003). Herman J. Muller's 1936 letter to Stalin. *The Mankind Quarterly, XLIII*(3).

Hamer, D., & Kung, S.-d. (1989). *Biotechnology in China*. Washington DC: National Academy Press.

Hao, Z. (1997). May 4th and June 4th compared. *Journal of Contemporary China, 6*(14), 79-100.

Hogan, B., Beddington, R., Costantini, F., & Lacy, E. (1994). *Manipulating the mouse embryo*. New York: Cold Spring Harbor Laboratory Press.

Hossfeld, U., & Olsson, L. (2002). From the modern synthesis to Lysenkoism, and back? *Science, 297*, 55-56.

Hua, J., Xing, Y., Wu, W., Xu, C., Sun, X., Yu, S., et al. (2003). Single-locus heterotic effects and dominance by dominance interactions can adequately explain the genetic basis of heterosis in an elite rice hybrid. *Proceedings of the National Academy of Sciences of the United States of America, 100*(5), 2574-2579.

Huang, J., Rozelle, S., Pray, C., & Wang, Q. (2002). Plant biotechnology in China. *Science, 295*(5555), 674-676.

Jia, H., & Louet, S. (2004). China pushes liver proteomics. *Nature Biotechnology, 22*(2), 136.

Jia, W., Gao, W., & Tang, L. (2003). Antidiabetic herbal drugs officially approved in China. *Phytotherapy Research, 17*(10), 1127-1134.

Joseph, A. E., & Phillips, D. R. (1999). Ageing in rural China: Impacts of increasing diversity in family and community resources. *Journal of Cross-Cultural Gerontology, 14*(2), 153-168.

Lau, G. K., He, M. L., Fong, D. Y., Bartholomeusz, A., Au, W. Y., Lie, A. K., et al. (2002). Preemptive use of lamivudine reduces hepatitis B exacerbation after allogeneic hematopoietic cell transplantation. *Hepatology (Baltimore, Md.), 36*(3), 702-709.

Lei, X. (1998). 15 new projects bolster basic research. *Science, 282*(5397), 2171.

Li, D. M., Xiao, Y. H., Luo, M., Hou, L., Luo, X. Y., Luo, K. M., et al. (2003). [Cloning and characterization of the PTS2 receptor gene (GhPex7) from cotton (Gossypium hirsutum L.)]. *Yi Chuan Xue Bao, 30*(9), 823-829.

Li, F. W., Zhang, L. S., Liu, H., Cai, Y. C., Pan, J. H., Jia, X. Y., et al. (2001). [Study of protective effect of leech, radix Salviae miltiorrhizae and its composite recipe on vascular endothelial cells in rats with blood stasis syndrome]. *Zhongguo Zhong Yao Za Zhi, 26*(10), 703-706.

Li, X., Wang, X. D., Zhao, X., & Dutt, Y. (2004). Improvement of cotton fiber quality by transforming the acsA and acsB genes into Gossypium hirsutum L. by means of vacuum infiltration. *Plant Cell Reports, 22*(9), 691-697.

Lui, J. (2001). Patenting biotechnology inventions in China. *Nature Biotechnology, 19*(1), 83-84.

Ma, S. Y., Au, W. Y., Ng, I. O., Lie, A. K., Leung, A. Y., Liang, R., et al. (2004). Hepatitic graft-versus-host disease after hematopoietic stem cell transplantation: Clinicopathologic features and prognostic implication. *Transplantation, 77*(8), 1252-1259.

MacFarquhar, R. (1974). *The origins of the cultural revolution* (Vol. 1). New York: Columbia University Press.

McPherson, J. D., Marra, M., Hillier, L., Waterston, R. H., Chinwalla, A., Wallis, J., et al. (2001). A physical map of the human genome. *Nature, 409*(6822), 934-941.

Meisner, M. (1999). *Mao's China and after*. New York: The Free Press.

Peishan, L. (1988). Genetics in China: The Qingdao Symposium of 1956. *ISIS, 79*, 227-236.

Peishan, L., Qingzhe, M., Qinghe, H., & Shun'e, H. (1985). *Hundred schools contending - The road that must be followed for the development of science*. Beijing: Commercial Press.

Saich, T. (1989). *China's science policy in the 1980s*. Atlantic Highlands, NJ: Humanities Press.

Schneider, L. (2003). *Biology and revolution in twentieth-century China*. Lanham, MD: Rowman & Littlefield Publishers, Inc.

Sha, J. H., Zhou, Z. M., Li, J. M., Lin, M., Zhu, H., Zhou, Y. D., et al. (2003). Expression of a novel bHLH-Zip gene in human testis. *Asian Journal of Andrology, 5*(2), 83-88.

Spence, J. D. (1990). *The search for modern China*. New York: WW Norton.

Sun, Z., Ming, L., Zhu, X., & Lu, J. (2002). Prevention and control of hepatitis B in China. *J Medical Virology, 67*(3), 447-450.

Temple, R. (1986). *The genius of China*. New York: Simon and Schuster.

Unschuld, P. U. (1985). *Medicine in China: A history of ideas*. Berkeley: University of California Press.

White, N. J. (1996). Current concepts: The treatment of malaria. *The New England Journal of Medicine, 335*(11), 800-806.

Wu, Y. Z., Li, J. T., Mou, Z. R., Fei, L., Ni, B., Geng, M., et al. (2003). Oral immunization with rotavirus VP7 expressed in transgenic potatoes induced high titers of mucosal neutralizing IgA. *Virology, 313*(2), 337-342.

Xinhuanet. (2004). Beijing suspends draft animal welfare rule. *China View*.

Xu, Z.-H., & Bai, S.-N. (2002). Impact of biotechnology on agriculture in China. *Trends in Plant Science, 7*(8), 374-375.

Yang, Y., Wang, W., Cleaves, R., Zahurak, M., Cheng, L., Civin, C. I., et al. (2002). Acceleration of G(1) cooperates with core binding factor beta-smooth muscle myosin heavy chain to induce acute leukemia in mice. *Cancer Research, 62*(8), 2232-2235.

Yao, J., Pang, Y., Qi, H., Wan, B., Zhao, X., Kong, W., et al. (2003). Transgenic tobacco expressing Pinellia ternata agglutinin confers enhanced resistance to aphids. *Transgenic Research, 12*(6), 715-722.

Yao, J. H., Zhao, X. Y., Liao, Z. H., Lin, J., Chen, Z. H., Chen, F., et al. (2003). Cloning and molecular characterization of a novel lectin gene from Pinellia ternata. *Cell Research, 13*(4), 301-308.

Yao, Z. X., Qin, M. L., Liu, J. J., Chen, X. S., & Zhou, D. S. (2004). In vitro cultivation of human fetal pancreatic ductal stem cells and their differentiation into insulin-producing cells. *World Journal Gastroenterology, 10*(10), 1452-1456.

Yin, Z., Plader, W., & Malepszy, S. (2004). Transgene inheritance in plants. *Journal of Applied Genetics, 45*(2), 127-144.

Yu, J., Hu, S., Wang, J., Wong, G. K., Li, S., Liu, B., et al. (2002). A draft sequence of the rice genome (Oryza sativa L. ssp. indica). *Science, 296*(5565), 79-92.

Zedong, M. (1977). On the ten major relationships. In M. Zedong (Ed.), *Selected works of Mao Zedong* (Vol. 5, pp. 299-300). Beijing.

Zhai, W., Chen, C., Zhu, X., Chen, X., Zhang, D., Li, X., et al. (2004). Analysis of T-DNA- Xa21 loci and bacterial blight resistance effects of the transgene Xa21 in transgenic rice. *Theoretical and Applied Genetics.*

Zhang, Q. (1999). *China: agricultural biotechnology opportunities to meet the challenges of food production.* Paper presented at the Agricultural Biotechnology and the Poor, Washington, DC.

Zhou, C., Yu, Z., Li, R., & Tian, Z. (2001). The principle and technique of using Chinese drugs in the treatment of hypertension. *Journal of Traditional Chinese Medicine, 21*(1), 7-11.

Zhou, E. (1957, June 19). On the correct handling of contradictions among the people. *People's Daily.*

Biography

Dr. **Shaheen Emmanuel Lakhan** is a biotechnology educator, global philanthropist, biomedical research scientist, and administrator of a host of projects in bioethics, psychiatry, proteomics, emergency response, and open-access policy -- to name a few disciplines. He underwent extensive didactic and research based training, completing undergraduate and graduated programs in biochemical sciences, education (educational technology), applied proteomics, medical sciences, and several interdisciplinary fields. He has a well-rounded educational palate from an international perspective by studying in Saint Petersburg - Russia, Queensland - Australia, Haifa - Israel, and in Los Angeles, Boston, New Britain, and New York - USA.

As the Executive Director of the Global Neuroscience Initiative Foundation, Dr. Lakhan oversees the operations, charitable interests, affiliations, and sponsorships of the non-profit charity organization established for the sole benefit of furthering neurological and psychiatric research, patient welfare, and education -- psychological, biochemical, sociological or historical in nature.

During an academic mission to China, Dr. Lakhan collaborated with many government sponsored and private research institutions to further international biotechnology. He was instrumental in co-implementing a multiphase scheme for international biotechnology education and business entrepreneurship. Currently, he is cooperating with the Chinese FDA for distance science education and revamping his course offerings.

The page left blank intentionally.

Processes for *Ex-ante* Evaluation of IT Projects - Case Studies in Brazilian Companies

Fernando José Barbin Laurindo and Renato Oliveira Moraes
Production Engineering Department of Polytechnic Engineering School - University of São Paulo, São Paulo, Brazil and Federal University of Ouro Preto. Ouro Preto & FEAD – Business Studies College of Minas Gerais - Belo Horizonte, Brazil

fjblau@usp.br renato.moraes@perceptron.com.br

Abstract

In the highly competitive nowadays markets, many companies actions assume the project form. In special, Information Technology (IT) projects assume great importance, enabling the dynamic actions that organisations need (Porter, 2001; Tapscott, 2001). However, IT applications assume different roles, from operational support to strategic, according to companies' strategies and operations, besides the peculiarities of the industry in which they compete (McFarlan, 1984; Porter & Millar, 1985). According to this role (appraised by McFarlan's Strategic Grid), ex-ante evaluation practices for selecting IT projects to be implemented can vary (Jiang & Klein, 1999). The objective of this paper is to analyse practices for selecting IT projects in Brazilian companies classified in different quadrants of the Strategic Grid and to observe any differences in *ex-ante* evaluation practices among them. The adopted methodological approach was qualitative research, more specifically case study (Claver, Gonzalez & Llopis, 2000; Yin, 1991) performed in four companies.

Keywords: Information Technology, IT projects, Project Management, IT effectiveness, IT Strategy, Ex-ante Evaluation, Project Selection

Introduction

The current competitive scenery is characterised by the dynamism of business operations. As a consequence, many plans assume the form of projects, which compete for scarce and disputed resources. Among these projects, Information Technology (IT) projects can play a very important role, by enabling dynamic actions that organisations need to stay competitive (Porter, 2001; Tapscott, 2001). Therefore, IT projects management can present strong links with companies operations and strategies.

Although some authors argue about the actual benefits of IT applications, like Carr (2003, 2005), decisions concerning which IT applications should be implemented are still important for operations and, in many situations, for business strategy (Brynjolfsson & Hitt, 1998). It is largely discussed in the literature that IT role in organisations can vary from simple administrative support to a strategic position (Farrel, 2003; Henderson

& Venkatraman, 1993; McFarlan, 1984). Internet has increased this potential and also the reach and impact of IT applications, especially in the most competitive markets (Porter, 2001).

Several authors have studied the strategic impact of IT applications (specially information systems - IS), both on single firms and on industries. The Strategic Grid is a widely known model proposed by McFarlan (1984), which allows the visualization of the relationship between IT strategy and the business strategy, considering both present and future situations. Henderson & Venkatraman (1993) pointed out the importance of the alignment among IT and business strategies, as well as they analysed the different forms for such alignment occurs.

Thus, there is a need for an appropriate IT management that should include adequate evaluation and selection of which IT projects would be implemented and if internal resources and competences are sufficient for these projects or if it is necessary to outsourcing them.

The way the selection process is performed in different companies present differences regarding the extension of its formalisation and also the criteria adopted to choose and to prioritize possible alternative solutions for implementation. However, the form of these selection and prioritisation processes depends on the role that IT carries out in the organisations. Jiang & Klein (1999) studied how companies classified in different quadrants of Strategic Grid select their IT projects, and they found significant distinctions.

McFarlan (1981), in another work, analysed how to select new IT applications projects considering individual project risks, as well as the risks of a project portfolio. Thus, the companies would decide just based on the analysis of each project (Laurindo, Carvalho, & Shimizu, 2003) or taking into account a group of alternatives of new possible IT projects, i.e., considering IT projects portfolio (Moraes & Laurindo, 2003).

The adopted methodological approach was qualitative research, more specifically case study (Claver, Gonzalez & Llopis., 2000; Yin, 1991) performed in four companies.

The aim of this paper is to analyse *ex-ante* evaluation practices for selecting IT projects in companies in activity in Brazil. Besides, the research searches for differences among these practices, although there has been an intense outsourcing of IT activities, as well as a wide use of 'packages' and standardized software.

In order to investigate the concepts above and the central question "How companies selects IT projects", the adopted methodological approach was a multiple case study (Claver, Gonzalez & Llopis, 2000; Yin, 1991).

Four companies were selected for this study. Each of these companies would be classified in different quadrants of McFarlan's Strategic Grid, in a preliminary analysis. Besides, companies should present an important set of IT projects, as well as regular processes for project management. The information was obtained through semi-structured interviews with different players of the company, including IT professionals and the users from different hierarchical levels.

Information Technology Projects Strategic Impacts

The role of IT in organisations has changed in many ways along the years. Initially, hardware and software imposed many restrictions to the spectrum of possible IT applications, limiting them to more structured and less complex situations, like, typically, payroll, stock control and accounting. However, technological advances gradually brought new and far more including possibilities (Zwass, 1998). On the other hand, the wider range of these possibilities also brought greater difficulties on the decisions about which projects should be implemented (Laudon & Laudon, 2004; Moraes & Laurindo, 2003).

At this point, efficiency and effectiveness concepts are very useful for understanding IT role in organisations (Laurindo, 2002).

Efficiency is associated to the use of resources, while effectiveness is associated to achieving goals and objectives and with requirements satisfaction. Efficiency is related to internal aspects of IT management and the appropriate use of resources, while effectiveness confronts results of IT applications with their impact on business operations and also in business strategy and organisational structure (Laurindo et al, 2003). IT effectiveness means to use it to leverage company business competitiveness.

In the discussion about IT effectiveness, it is necessary to understand several different approaches for analysing the strategic role of IT in the organisations, in order to build a broad vision of this role.

One of the first proposals to solve the problem of choosing and prioritizing IT projects was the Critical Success Factors (CSF) method developed by Rockart (1979) and that is still widespread used nowadays. This method aimed especially management and executive information systems and it was based on the definition by top executives of their current needs, expressed by the CSF. Rockart defines CSF as the areas where satisfactory results 'ensure successful competitive performance for the organization'. This author states that CSF prime sources are structure of industry, competitive strategy, industry position, geographic location, environment and temporal factors. Although primarily conceived for information systems design, this method had an important impact on managerial and strategic planning practices. It is usual to define CSF for different functions of the company, like marketing CSF, manufacturing CSF, projects CSF, among others.

McFarlan (1984) proposed the Strategic Grid that allows understanding the relationship between IT and business strategies. This model analyses the impacts of IT existent applications (present situation) and of IT applications portfolio (future situation), defining four boxes (or quadrants), each one representing one possible role for IT in the enterprise: 'Support', 'Factory', 'Turnaround' and 'Strategic' (Figure 1).

- 'Support': IT has little influence in present and future IT application will not affect company strategies.
- 'Factory': existent IT applications are important for company's operations success, but there is no new strategic IT application planned for the future.
- 'Turnaround': IT is changing from a situation of little importance ('support' box) to a more important status in business strategy.
- 'Strategic': IT is very important in business strategy in the present and new planned IT applications will maintain this strategic importance in the future.

In order to assess these strategic impacts of IT, McFarlan proposed to analyse IT applications effects on the five competitive forces (Porter, 1979).

Porter (1979) emphasizes the importance of positioning a firm in its industry, in order to achieve a sustainable competitive advantage through the choice of one of three alternative generic strategies: cost leadership, differentiation and focus. Meanwhile, the competitiveness of an industry results from the interaction of five competitive forces: buyers bargain power, suppliers bargain power, threat of substitute products or services, threat of new entrants and rivalry among existent competitors.

According to McFarlan, IT can alter the balance of the competitive forces of an industry, since it can establish barriers to the entrance of new competitors, it can change the relationship among suppliers and customers, it can enlarge the basis of potential suppliers or strengthening existent relationships and finally it can create new businesses.

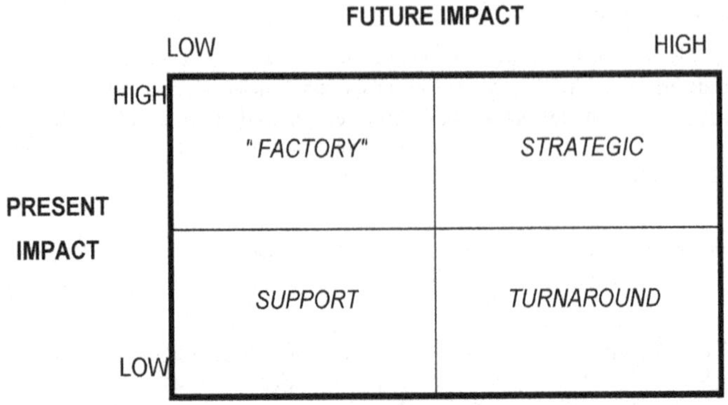

Figure 1: Strategic Grid, strategic impact of IT applications (adapted from McFarlan, 1984)

Nolan & McFarlan (2005) have recently updated the Strategic Grid, changing the two "axis" to "Need for Reliable IT" (instead of "Present Impact") and "Need for new IT" (instead of "Future Impact"). These authors stated that companies in "Support" and "Factory" quadrants adopt a Defensive approach regarding IT, meanwhile companies in "Turnaround" and "Strategic" quadrants can be considered Offensive in IT use.

Henderson & Venkatraman (1993) proposed the "Strategic Alignment Model", which analyses IT strategic importance in the companies. This model is based not only on company internal factors (infrastructure) but also on external factors (strategy).

Therefore, according to this model, in order to plan IT, four important factors should be considered: (i) business strategy; (ii) IT Strategy; (iii) organizational infrastructure and processes; (iv) infrastructure of information systems and processes.

The basic premise of the Strategic Alignment Model is that an effective IT requires a balance between the decisions in all these four factors. An important novelty of this model is that it considers that IT strategy can change a company's business strategy, when usually business strategy is considered as the starting point for IT planning.

Since external factors are constantly changing, this planning should be a continuous process. If the company does not follow these changes, it can be in serious disadvantage in the fierce competition of nowadays markets. That is particularly true when a new technology is adopted by almost all companies of an industry; in this situation, this technology does not represent a competitive advantage for their users but is a clear disadvantage factor for non users (Luftman, Lewis & Oldach, 1993).

Henderson & Venkatraman (1993) and Luftman et al. (1993) presented four main perspectives of strategic alignment, considering business strategy or IT Strategy as driver of this process, as follows:

I – Strategy Execution

Business strategy directs choices of organizational infrastructure and, as consequence, the decisions about IT infrastructure; it corresponds to the classic model of hierarchical vision of strategic management.

Business strategy ⇒ Business Infrastructure ⇒ IT Infrastructure

II – Technology Transformation

Technological leadership is the basis for competing. The implementation of business strategy depends on a new IT Strategy, which demands for an appropriate IT infrastructure and processes

Business strategy ⇒ IT Strategy ⇒ IT Infrastructure

III - Competitive Potential

Business Strategy and business infrastructure are consequences of the adoption of a new IT Strategy, capable to bring impacts in products and services, influencing strategy and relationships in the market.

IT Strategy ⇒ Business Strategy⇒ Business Infrastructure

IV - Service Level

The aim of this perspective is to provide world class Information System services to business infrastructure. IT performance criteria are based on the satisfaction of IT users.

IT Strategy ⇒ IT Infrastructure ⇒ Business Infrastructure

McFarlan (1981) analysed the selection process of new IT applications projects considering the risks associated with each project and also the risks of projects portfolio. These risks encompass costs, time, technical performance, overestimation of IS benefits and incompatibility of hardware and/or software for the IS.

Selection of IT projects was also studied by Jiang & Klein (1999), which took into consideration the four different possibilities of the Strategic Grid. Enterprises classified in the 'strategic' and 'turnaround' quadrants usually are more prone to assume risks and have more rigorous controls for IT projects. On the other hand, enterprises classified as 'support' consider costs as the primary criterion for selecting and conducting IT projects.

Moraes & Laurindo (2003) presented a procedure for building a portfolio IT development projects, considering the strategic impact of these projects and an evaluation of the risks associated to each project. It uses a typology of projects that supports this analysis and it also provides elements for building a portfolio that balances IT efficiency and effectiveness demands in the organization.

Several authors proposed methods based on portfolio concept for ex-ante evaluation or selection of IT projects, as Bedell (1985), Luehrman, (1998a, 1998b) and Tjan (2001). Khalifa et al. (2001) affirmed that there is a consensus that there is no IT evaluation method that can be applied in all situations. Farbey et al. (1993) suggested that the evaluation presents better results when an appropriate method is applied to an also appropriate organizational context.

The evaluation of IT projects should consider, simultaneously, efficiency (use of resources) and effectiveness (obtaining results for the organization) aspects, and also the analysis of their risks. These criteria are very important in highly competitive markets of the globalised economy. In this paper, practices adopted by the companies to evaluate IT projects to be implemented are investigated, observing the relationship of the concepts described in this item.

Methodology

As previously mentioned, the aim of this paper is to analyse *ex-ante* evaluation practices for selecting IT projects in companies in activity in the Brazilian market and that can be classified in different quadrants of the Strategic Grid. The investigation searches for differences among these companies, although there has been an intense outsourcing of IT activities, as well as the use of 'packages' and standardized software (as ERP - Enterprise Resource Planning - Systems).

In order to investigate the concepts above and the central question "How companies evaluate and select new IT projects ", the adopted methodological approach was qualitative research, more specifically a multiple cases study (Claver et al., 2000; Yin, 1991).

Based on the discussion about project selection practices in companies classified in different quadrants of Strategic Grid, specially by MFarlan (1984); Jiang and Klein (1999), Nolan and McFarlan (2005), the following propositions should be investigated:

- (p1) companies classified in quadrants "Support" and "Turnaround" of the Strategic Grid should present less systematic procedures to select IT projects;
- (p2) there is a bigger involvement of business personnel in IT projects selection in companies classified in the "Strategic" and "Factory" quadrants of the Strategic Grid;
- (p3) criteria of strategic nature are more frequently used to select IT projects in companies classified in the "Strategic" and "Turnaround" quadrants" of the Strategic Grid.

The criteria for selecting the companies to be studied were the following:

- Business and operations in Brazilian market;
- An important portfolio of IT projects;
- Regular processes for project management;
- Each of these companies should be classified in different quadrants of McFarlan's Strategic Grid, in a preliminary analysis.

This preliminary classification in the Grid was based on a brief analysis of secondary data about the companies and on short contacts by email and/or telephone, regarding the present importance of IT applications and the plans for new significant projects. During the case study, these classifications were re-analysed based on the collected data.

Data was obtained through semi-structured interviews with different players of the company, including IT professionals and the users from different hierarchical levels. The main points of the questionnaire used in these interviews are the following:

- Company Characteristics: businesses, products, competitive strategy, organisational structure, operations, presence of business unit, recent results, industry competitive forces.
- IT organisation: IT position in the company hierarchy, IT history in the company
- IT projects selection and evaluation in the company: formal methods for evaluating IT projects, decision making process regarding IT issues, IT projects risk analysis process, IT project financial viability process, IT committee existence, IT discussion forums, IT company position in relation to main competitors, IT in the organisation in the vision of IT professionals, IT in the organisation in the vision of users, existence of periodic meetings among IT and user areas, process for building IT projects portfolio.
- Critical Success Factor identification: is there formal CSF defined for the company, definition of CSF if they were not previously defined relationship of CSF with strategic objectives.
- Strategic Grid: identification of the main existent IT applications, identification of the main planned IT applications.
- Strategic Alignment Model: identification of the perspective relative to company situation, importance of new technologies, definition of the driver of IT implementation processes.

- IT importance for competitiveness: strategic, operational, present and future

Four Brazilian companies were selected for this study. Each of them was classified in different quadrants of McFarlan's Strategic Grid, in the preliminary analysis (see Figure 2). Their characteristics were:

- Case A: a company operating in the transport of medical and pharmaceutical products.
- Case B: a clothes retailer that, since some years ago, made significant IT investments that have been very important for its competitiveness.
- Case C: a worldwide supplier operating in Brazil in distribution, transportation and logistics services.
- Case D: a worldwide manufacturer (also operating in Brazil) of components for automobile industry.

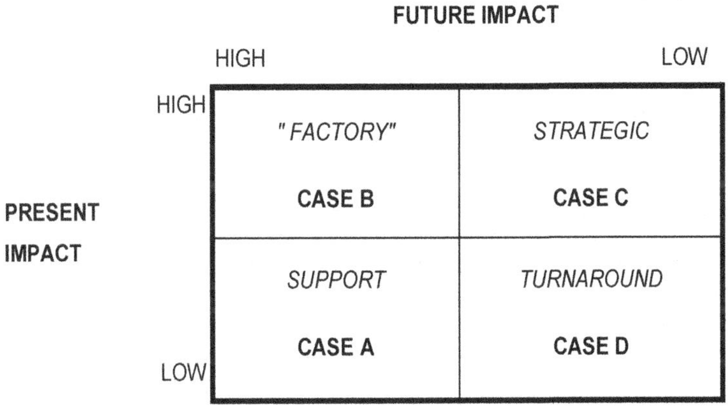

Figure 2. Preliminary classification of studied companies in McFarlan's Strategic Grid

Case Studies

Case A

Case A is a company operating in the transport of pharmaceutical and medical products. It is part of a conglomerate of companies in medical and, mainly, pharmaceutical industries. It should be highlighted that nowadays, most of its revenue comes from services provided to companies of the same group.

Its generic competitive strategy is focus with differentiation (to provide service to pharmaceutical companies). The provided services can be considered complex, because its fleet is specially equipped to transport this type of products, the vehicles present special devices for the shipment of sensitive and fragile materials. The differential of the company relies on its great operational specialisation to carry out this function.

The critical success factors of this company are:

- Operational excellence and services reliability;
- Integrated business in order to offer a complete array of services as a logistics operator.
- High service level, minimizing rates of claiming, misleading and mishaps.

Although operating in an industry in which IT has been very important, IT area of company A presents little impact in the business strategic planning. It is limited to support company operations, providing managerial tools, hardware maintenance and implementation of projects that automate operations and to enhance stronger linking with branches and partners.

Thus, IT applications have the purpose of improving operations of other departments and areas of this company. There are no plans of new IT applications that could change this situation by bringing significant strategic impacts. Therefore, this company can be classified in "Support" quadrant. In other words, IT applications have low strategic influence as much in the present as in the planned future.

The vision is that IT should supply the necessary support to operations in order to achieve company strategic objectives. This indicates that the perspective of strategic alignment, as proposed by Henderson and Venkatraman (1993), would be "Strategy Execution".

The selection of IT projects is just a reaction to IT operational needs, and the basic performance criterion is based on financial factors, reflecting a vision of IT as cost and not as investment.

In company A, there is an intense sharing of risks and responsibilities between IT and business. The IT area is demanded to offer support for implementation of projects that look for achieving goals stated by stakeholders and top management during strategic planning phase. Risks and responsibilities are strictly controlled by top management. IT projects are considered as part of other projects involving the main activities end of this company. There is a rigid control of IT projects regarding costs and time for implementation. Projects with high risk and out of strategic planning scope are simply discarded.

Case B

Company B has operated since the 40´s as clothing retailer, especially women's wear, but also men's and children's wear and accessories for Bed, Tableware & Bathing. It presents a constant concern to be updated to market trends and it is always innovating as a strategy for growing.

The company is quite aware of fashion tendencies, by researching new releases in the whole world, keeping in touch and negotiating with both national and foreigner suppliers, specially those with notorious brands.

It holds approximately 150 stores and three distribution centres, dispersed through different Brazilian regions.

Purchases from their main suppliers are made in its central office in São Paulo, since supply policy privileges centralisation. This supply policy allows buying well in order to be able to sell their products at more accessible prices, which is considered fundamental in its adopted competitive strategy.

From the point of vision of the CIO (Chief Executive Officer, main IT executive) and confirmed with businesses executives, the critical success factors for company B would be:

- Relationship with suppliers - it is important in order to the company be able to implement one of their main strategies: competitive prices.

- Following fashion tendencies (world and national) since in clothing business this is a crucial aspect, with emphasis in following the main European tendencies, which always are a season ahead of national fashion;
- Products Disposition in the stores - clothes retailers need to have their products appropriately available and presented to the consumers.

Since Company B has looked for integration among the several company areas in the last years, the importance of IT role has increased. IT role passed from just a support area to a strategic factor, operating closely and in alignment with its business. IT is subordinated to the Executive Vice-President (in the same hierarchical level of another areas, like sales and marketing), and its executives considered that it is fundamental that IT teams understand company business and not only technical aspects, so that IT can be strategically aligned with company objectives.

In the last years, company B made significant IT investments that impacted positively its competitiveness and that placed this company in advantage in IT utilisation in comparison to their competitors. The focus was to support business needs, looking for, when necessary, forms to develop or to acquire technologies that the firm do not dominate. So, the IT and business strategic alignment started from this moment and on and was an important mark to the company since IT had changed its role and also users perception of this importance had modified. Another important mark was the great investments in e-commerce, with over than 300 products sold through its Virtual Store.

Thus, in this process, this company built a much more comprehensive IS infrastructure, effective and efficient, capable to monitor and to support properly the critical success factors mentioned above. Decisions concerning to IT issues passed to be taken in partnership between IT and users areas, with focus in possible strategic impacts, which shows that IT started to play a far more important role than merely support.

After this qualitative breakthrough, there has been no forecast of new IT applications with strategic impact in the planned future. This situation confirms company classification in the "Factory" quadrant of the Strategic Grid.

Many of the presently available technologies in the company are provided by outsourcing. Although this practice may cause some dependence, it provides agility to be the pioneer in the adoption of new IT solutions in its industry. Considering this situation, this company can be classified in the "Technology Transformation" perspective, according to the typology of Henderson and Venkamatran (1993).

It must be emphasised that IT projects portfolio is quite diversified in this company, varying from projects that demand only one IT professional allocated in partial time until big projects that involve several areas and a full time dedication team. IT projects are selected by a committee composed by members from IT and users areas; this composition can vary according to the nature of the projects in evaluation. This committee evaluates the proposals without following a specific procedure. The result from the evaluation process indicates to the top management and to the shareholders which projects should be considered critical.

In cases of adoption of new technologies, the company hires specialized consultancies to aid in the search for solutions and in the evaluation of the proposals. Finally, the company has demonstrated the first initiatives in terms of implementation of concepts about IT governance, although without formal procedures, focusing in the guarantee of the consistence of results of the projects with their proposed objectives.

Case C

Case C is a worldwide supplier (also operating in Brazil) of distribution and logistics services. It can be considered one of the great logistic operators in the world, with special emphasis in its performance in foods industry. It is a 50 years old company that operates in 10 different countries (including Brazil) through 29 distribution centres. It provides among others services: customers stocks planning, transport, storage and logistic planning.

Its global strategy concentrates in the following objectives: to be considered the best supplier by its customers; to develop a world class organization; to promote businesses growth; to obtain effective results. It is separated in 4 business areas:

- corporate services (Human resources, IT and Finances);
- a joint venture with another multinational company that work with commodities, offering services for restaurants, hotels, hospitals and bars;
- a provider of storage, transports and distribution services, besides consultancy and support in Supply Chain Management; and
- a business area specifically dedicated to assist its main customer worldwide.

IT area, therefore, is subordinated to "Corporate Services", but supports all other business areas.

IT has been one of the greatest integration factors, a differentiation enabler and consequently a factor of company's competitiveness increase in the logistics market. Company C, in fact, has been highlighted in these aspects, and has been considered benchmark not only in its industry. In the vision of company IT users, there is a clear relationship between IT and company business. Investments in IT allowed a larger speed in providing services to its customers, as well as they make possible a better stocks management and optimization of distribution routes.

In this context, critical success factors for this company can be considered the following:

- Capacity for changing: flexibility, innovation, proactive posture and disposition to assume risks.
- To act as only one company: thought and global performance and solid help among all to obtain success.
- Relationships: durable relationships with respect, integrity and mutual trust with employees, suppliers and communities.
- Execution: accomplishment of agreements terms.

Nowadays, existent IT applications present, as previously mentioned, big strategic importance for this company. There is a great dependence on an integrated information system that allows providing safe and efficient services, seeking to optimize resources use and to maximize information flow along Supply Chain. There is an expectation that new IT applications would be implemented, fundamentally based on the Internet potential, that would allow a growing and increasingly richer information flow between customers and suppliers.

In company C industry, many firms constantly look for costs reduction and customers' pressure for more aggregated value services; this indicates that new IT applications will also play a significant strategic impact in the future. Thus, this company can be classified in the "Strategic" quadrant, since IT performance in the company should be aligned with organization goals, due to its strategic role.

Although there are constant technology changes applicable to this industry, this company privileges internal development of IT applications.

IT structure and strategy satisfy the necessary requirements in order to put strategy in practice; this indicates that, nowadays, this company follows the " Strategy Execution" perspective, according to Henderson and Venkamatran (1993) model. IT is strongly guided by company business strategy and IT management is the implementer of the formulated strategy, enabling alternatives and allowing monitoring of organization strategic objectives.

IT area makes monthly meetings with Business Executives in order to discuss on going and planned IT projects. However, there is no formal method for evaluating IT applications to be implemented. The process usually includes an analysis of projects alignment with company strategy and also return on investment (ROI) estimates. So, decisions concerning IT applications are driven by company business strategy. Usually projects are developed according to costs estimates, although their duration are not seldom underestimated.

Case D

Case D is a worldwide supplier parts to automobile industry. It belongs to a multinational corporation that operates in different industries: building materials, glasses, plastics and industrial ceramics. This group is present in 46 countries, with more than 1.200 companies and 171.000 employees. In Brazil, this group has 11.000 employees in 43 dispersed industrial units in 36 cities of 8 Brazilian states.

Two great business areas exist in company D: (i) large scale production of original parts to automobile industry and (ii) replacement market. The first is subjected to high time and quality demands. The second business area faces a larger competition, with diversity of brands and competitors.

The critical success factors for the company D, according to its executives, are:

- Process Technology;
- Integration to the supply-chain;
- Quality;
- Original parts markets: on time deliveries, with the required quality and in the right quantity;
- Replacement market: availability of demanded products.

IT area is subordinated to financial area, providing support to business development

After the implementation of an ERP system that allowed the global integration of the company, this company started to be more dependent on their information systems to compete successfully.

However, there is a distinction of this dependence on IT in each of the two business areas. In original pieces market, all the complexity of necessary information for a repetitive intermittent production was already reached and stabilized; so IT role can be classified in "Factory" quadrant.

On the other hand, in replacement market, that was first analysed for the preliminary classification, there is a demand for a increasingly growing integration with the various customers and for flexibility and promptness in service providing, which makes IT a source of differentiation and fundamental for the success in this kind of operations. These IT applications are still being planned, because nowadays IT plays just a support role. This change in the near future allows characterizing IT role for this business area in the "Turnaround" quadrant, as previously indicated.

Once top management has established strategies and business objectives in both business areas, IT should provide the required applications and services. Therefore, company IT does look for technological leadership or the creation of new business forms, but to supply to each unit the required tools to each respective strategy. In this way, strategic alignment in this company is classified in the "Strategy Execution" perspective.

There is none systematic forum to discuss aspects of strategic alignment between IT and business. However, it is not uncommon that IT area participate in meetings that discuss strategic issues, because users understand IT strategic role as a crucial factor.

IT projects selection is made through a financial viability evaluation executed by IT area. Besides, there is an analysis that compares advantages and disadvantages of each proposal and a calculation of implementation and maintenance costs involved. Frequently, projects are discussed additionally through business cases. After the decision for the implementation, the amount of resources is discussed that would be made available for the approved projects. Project teams can include professionals from user areas, besides IT people.

Synthesis of the Studied Cases

The cases showed different realities in relation to the selection of IT projects, as it can be observed in Table 1.

Table 1: Comparison among the studied companies

FACTOR	*CASE A*	*CASE B*	*CASE C*	*CASE D*
Industry	Focused logistics	Clothes Retail	Logistics	Manufacture
Strategic Grid	Support	Factory	Strategic	Turnaround
Strategic alignment	Strategy Execution	Technology transformation	Strategy Execution	Strategy Execution
Focus in the selection of IT projects	Financial (costs) and low risk	Strategic	Strategic and financial	Strategic and financial
Systematic procedure in the selection of IT projects	Does not exist. *Ad hoc* costs calculation process	Although there is evaluation of the projects, it does not always follow the same systematic. Eventually it uses consultancies.	Although there is projects evaluation, it does not always follow the same systematic.	There is a Procedure, which includes technical and financial aspects, besides business cases
Systematic forum in the selection of IT projects	Does not exist. IT projects are considered as part of projects relative to company operations	IT Committee exists, composed by IT area and by the user areas involved in the projects	IT Committee exists, composed by IT area and Business Executives	Does not exist, but it is common to IT team to discuss alternatives with user areas

Conclusions

The objective of this paper was to analyse practices for projects ex ante evaluation and selection in companies operating in the Brazilian market and that would be classified in different quadrants of the Strategic Grid, in order to observe if any differences exist. The multiple cases study showed that there is no uniformity in the form that IT projects are selected, as previously expected. However, there was a better understanding of the involved factors, and the objectives can be considered reached.

The following considerations about the investigated propositions can be presented:

(p1) companies classified in quadrants "Support" and "Turnaround" of the Strategic Grid should present less systematic procedures to select IT projects;

The company classified "Support" quadrant, in fact, didn't show systematic procedures, but company D ("Turnaround" quadrant) was the only one that presented systematic procedures. However, it must be stand out that this company operate in two different business areas and that such procedures were transmitted by the business area that can be classified in "Factory" quadrant. It should be noticed that projects selection concerns basically to future applications; as in the case of the "Factory" quadrant there is no expectation of new strategic IT applications; this can lead to less rigid procedures for evaluation of future applications. Meanwhile, in the "Turnaround" quadrant, there is this expectation of new IT applications that would change IT role in the future situation of the company. In this way, it makes sense that there are more systematic procedures to evaluate new IT projects. Thus, this proposition can be considered as just partially confirmed.

(p2) there is a bigger involvement of business personnel in IT projects selection in companies classified in the "Strategic" and "Factory" quadrants of the Strategic Grid;

This proposition was verified, since both in companies B and C it is clear the users' and the business management's involvement in the IT projects selection. However, it must be pointed out that company D also showed this characteristic, although in a less systematic way. A possible explanation would be the fact of the role of IT would be changing ("Turnaround" quadrant). Company D must be "learning" how to proceed about IT evaluation in these new conditions. Therefore, this proposition could be enlarged, to include organisations classified in the "Turnaround" quadrant.

(p3) criteria of strategic nature are more frequently used to select IT projects in companies classified in the "Strategic" and "Turnaround" quadrants" of the Strategic Grid.

The third proposition was verified for companies classified in the "Strategic" and "Turnaround" quadrants of the Strategic Grid, because both companies C and D present this characteristic. As projects selection defines future initiatives in the company, it was reasonable to expect that such fact would happen, since in these quadrants there is, by definition, strategic impact of future IT applications. Similarly to the previous proposition, this situation can also be observed in company B ("Factory quadrant).

It is interesting to notice that, unlike it was expected, this company does not adopt systematically financial criteria in the evaluations. A possible explanation would be that in this company the perspective of strategic alignment "Technology Transformation" was identified, and in this perspective, companies look fundamentally for technological leadership. Hence, there would be a larger predisposition for IT investments without many concerns to justification of financial returns. Still about company B, maybe the "instantaneous picture" of the Strategic Grid has captured a specific moment in that there were not new IT applications that could bring strategic advantages, i.e., maybe company B could be classified in the "Strategic" quadrant in a new analysis performed in a new moment.

Maybe the study has captured indications of the ways that led IT to assume today this role in organization B. In conclusion, the concern and the dedication to compose past IT applications portfolio allowed IT applications presenting a strategic role nowadays.

Another interesting point is that, except for company D, many professionals mentioned that formal and complex procedures for evaluating IT projects would be harmful to the agility of the decisions required in turbulent markets.

In spite of the observed results showed an alignment between theory and observed practice, futures studies should contemplate a larger number of companies and/or an observation of the same companies studied in another instant in the time.

References

Bedell, E. F. (1985). *The computer solution: Strategies for success in the information age*. Homewood: Dow –Jones, Irwin.

Brynjolfsson, E. & Hitt, L. M. (1998). Beyond the productivity paradox. *Communications of the ACM, 41*(8), 49-55.

Carr, N.G. (2003). IT doesn't matter. *Harvard Business Review, 81*(5), 41-49.

Carr, N.G. (2005). The end of corporate computing. *Sloan Management Review, 46*(3), 67-73, Spring.

Claver, E; Gonzalez R.; Llopis, J. (2000). An analysis of research in information systems (1981-1997), *Information & Management, 37*, 181-195.

Farbey, B.; Land, F. F.; Targett, D. (1995). A taxonomy of information systems applications: the benefits evaluation ladder. *European Journal of Information Systems, 4*(1), 41-50.

Farrell, D. (2003). The real new economy. *Harvard Business Review. 81*(10), 104-112, October.

Henderson, J. C.; & Venkatraman, N. (1993). Strategic alignment: Leveraging information technology for transforming organizations. *IBM Systems Journal. 32*(1), 4-16.

Jiang, J. J. & Klein, G. (1999). Project selection criteria by strategic orientation. *Information & Management, 36*, 63-75.

Khalifa, G., Irani, Z., Baldwin, L. P & Jones, S. (2001). Evaluating information technology with you in mind. *The Electronic Journal of Information Systems Evaluation, 4*(1), March.

Laudon, K. C. & Laudon, J. P. (2003). *Essentials of management information systems: Managing the digital firm.* Upper Saddle River, NJ: Prentice Hall, 512p.

Laurindo, F. J. B., Carvalho, M. M. & Shimizu, T. (2003). Information technology strategy alignment: Brazilian cases. In K. Kangas (Ed.), *Business Strategies for Information Technology Management* (p. 186-199). Hershey, PA: Idea Group.

Laurindo, F. J. B. (2002). Tecnologia da Informação: Eficácia nas organizações. São Paulo: Editora Futura, 248 p.

Luehrman, T. A. (1998a). Investment opportunities as real options: Getting started on the numbers. *Harvard Business Review*, July–August.

Luehrman, T. A. (1998b). Strategy as a portfolio of real options. *Harvard Business Review*, September–October.

Luftman, J. N., Lewis, P. R., & Oldach, S. H. (1993). Transforming the enterprise: The alignment of business and information technology strategies. *IBM Systems Journal, 32*(1), 198-221.

McFarlan, W. E. (1981). Portfolio approach to information systems. *Harvard Business Review,* September-October, pp. 142-150.

McFarlan, W. E.(1984). Information technology changes the way you compete. *Harvard Business Review, 62*(3), 98-103, May/June.

Moraes, R. O. & Laurindo, F. J. B. (2003). Um Estudo de Caso de Gestão de Portfolio de Projetos de Tecnologia da Informação. *Revista G&P: Gestão e Produção, 10*(3), 311-328.

Nolan, R. L. & McFarlan, W. E. (2005). Information technology and the board of directors. *Harvard Business Review, 83*(10), 96-106, October.

Porter, M. E. (1979). How competitive forces shape strategy. *Harvard Business Review*, Nov-Dec, 137-145.

Porter, M. E. (2001). Strategy and the Internet. *Harvard Business Review*, March, p.63-78.

Porter, M. E. & Millar, V.(1985). How information gives IT competitive advantage. *Harvard Business Review,* Jul-Aug, 149-160.

Rockart, J. F. (1979). Chief executives define their own data needs. *Harvard Business Review, 57*(2), 81-92, Mar./Apr.

Tapscott, D. (2001). Rethinking strategy in a networked world. *Strategy + Business, 24*, 8.

Tjan, A. K. (2001). Finally, a way to put your Internet portfolio in order. *Harvard Business Review, 79*(2), 76-85.

Yin, R. (1991). *Case study research: Design and methods*. Newbury Park. Sage Pub.

Zwass, V. (1998). *Foundation of information systems*. Boston: Irwin McGraw-Hill.

Biography

Fernando José Barbin Laurindo is associate professor at Polytechnic School, University of São Paulo - USP (since1997). He holds Production Engineering degree (Polytechnic School of University of São Paulo). He is M.Sc. and Ph.D in Production Engineering from Polytechnic School of University of São Paulo. He also graduated in Law (University of São Paulo) and made Extension Course in Business Administration from Fundação Getúlio Vargas. He belongs to Information Technology Management Group (GTI) of the Production Engineering Department. He is the research vice-coordinator of GTI group (listed in CNPq Research Group Files). During more than ten years, he worked in Information Technology, Project and Product Management in companies of the industrial, financial and service sectors. Its main research interests are in Information Technology Management and Strategy, Competitive Strategy and Project Management.

Renato de Oliveira Moraes is an associated professor of Business Administration College (FEAD) of Minas Gerais and Federal University of Ouro Preto. He holds Production Engineering degree (Polytechnic School of University of São Paulo). He is Ph.D in Business Administration Business School of University of São Paulo. He is a researcher in the GTI group (listed in CNPq Research Group Files). He worked in many manufacturing companies, in Information Technology and Project Management areas. Its main research interests are in Information Technology Management and Strategy and Project Management.

The page left blank intentionally.

Oracle Database Workload Performance Measurement and Tuning Toolkit

Sai Peck Lee and Džemal Zildžić
Faculty of Computer Science and Information Technology
University of Malaya, Kuala Lumpur, Malaysia

saipeck@um.edu.my

Abstract

Database tuning practice is mainly conducted as a consequence of user's complaints on the performance. There is a need for a reactive monitoring and tuning tool enabling a real-time overview of the main resource consumers in order to detect and solve performance bottlenecks. With an assessment of the Oracle's high-availability database, in terms of the main architectural components and their impact on performance, we have developed a Java tool for the efficient and resource-effective tuning of Oracle databases. Our tool, called Workload Performance Monitoring and Tuning (WPMT), enables proactive and reactive database tuning. By combining today's best monitoring and tuning practices with our metrics management, we have designed a unique approach to illustrate the efficiency of the Oracle database memory segments responsible for handling the workload. This approach consists of developing database memory delta charts, illustrating the efficiency of memory initialization parameters versus component's workload performance.

Keywords: database management systems, tuning, workload performance

Introduction

Regardless of IT environment-specific requirements for running mission-critical database-driven applications, the two basic requirements are always requested: firstly, high availability, in terms of database accessibility and resource availability; and secondly, a high performance, in terms of access and code efficiency (Silberschatz, Korth & Sudarshan, 2002). These database management systems, i.e. the most demanding systems with 24x7 availability (24 hours a day, 7 days a week), require regular or proactive maintenance practice in order to achieve and maintain the optimal database workload performance. Although Oracle, IBM, and Microsoft provide a solution for a high availability (or multi-node) computing environment, availability, scalability, and manageability among them differ significantly (Buch & Cheevers, 2002; Chandrasekaran, & Kehoe, 2003; MSDN, 2004).

Ultimately responsible for database tuning, the most inconvenient situation for a database administrator (DBA) is when users submit complaints about the database performance. Forced to act immediately (reactive tuning), for the DBA it is a critical task due to the fact that it often happens during the peak database activity. A common solution would be to optimize the SQL (Structured Query

Language) statement's Execution Plan that improves the execution performance. However, performing the object optimization during the peak database activity shall decrease the overall performance, since the optimization process consumes resources (CPU and RAM), and may even bring some objects temporary unavailable. Identifying the cause of performance overhead is not an easy task. For example, knowing that excessive disk I/O operations may bring down the database performance up to 2500 times (Burleson, 2003), a DBA must have a real-time overview of major I/O users, as well as the most expensive user's SQL statements causing the slowdown. The root cause can be inaccurate SQL's Execution Plan, or unbalanced memory allocation due to inappropriate initialization of database, or because the database server has no more resources to handle the workload and requires the upgrade. In any case, the DBA must be able to assess the current database resource consumption and to proceed with investigation to discover the root of the problem and to solve the problem.

Based on conducted on-line survey and an interview with Oracle Support Manager (Zildžić, 2005), we may conclude that database memory and index tuning practice needs an improvement. Since it is mainly conducted as a consequence of database performance overhead, i.e. when the user submits a complaint, a proactive monitoring of database performance should be implemented to anticipate performance leakage and ultimately avoid severe performance degradation.

The above considerations led to a custom developed monitoring and tuning tool which delivers a unique solution for the efficient and resource-effective Oracle database workload performance measurement and tuning. This tool, called Workload Performance Monitoring and Tuning (WPMT), is developed in Java. It can proactively and reactively be used during Oracle database tuning in order to measure the current workload performance of the main database components, anticipate resource shortage, and optimize database objects for the achievement of the optimal database performance (Zildžić, 2005).

Oracle's Monitoring and Tuning Tools

Effective data collection and analysis is essential for identifying and correcting system performance problems. Oracle provides tools, such as Statspack and Oracle Enterprise Manager (OEM) packs allowing a DBA to gather information on database performance (Metalink A87503-02, n.d.). These tuning tools, recommended by Oracle corporation and currently the most often used, use data dictionary views to capture database activity metrics. In this section, a part from Oracle Company designed tools, we shall assess the third-party tuning tool, i.e. the MGA's EagleEye, developed by a recognized Oracle database expert Mark Gurry.

Statspack Utility

Statspack utility consists of a set of Programming Language/Structured Query Language (PL/SQL) scripts, executed against the database, in order to gather, store data and metrics, and generates reports of the database activity. These metrics (Table 1), collected from dynamic performance tables, are automatically recorded in utility-created tables within a database with the DBA's choice of collection and threshold level to be used (Metalink 228913.1, n.d.). Bundled with the Oracle Server, it is also known as Utlbstat/Utlestat and as of database release version 8.1.6, it is renamed as Statspack.

Table 1: Statspack utility collection levels

Collection level*	Description
0 to 4	General performance metrics on all memory areas, latches, pools, and events.
5 to 9	Same metrics from the lower levels, plus the most resource-intensive SQL statements.
10 +	Same metrics from the lower levels, plus parent/child latch data.

*By default and recommended value of the collection level is 5, but it depends on the scope of the tuning.

Statspack tool has been designed by the Oracle Server architects, and it generates a set of reports based on user-defined collection level. With a higher collection level, metrics capturing consisting of almost all database performance activity related segments. Executing this utility has high costs in terms of space usage and query performance. For example, just for STATS$SYSSTAT table, Oracle will generate 255 rows for each snapshot, and there are 35 tables more. Whether required or not, the thousands of rows will be generated anyway with this utility. Managing historical metrics (dozen of snapshots) requires significant space allocation. The reports are generated in text format only, and it is difficult to establish "chain" conclusion-analysis with dependent parameters. Report analysis is a time consuming task due to non self-intuitive and complex report presentation. Statspack is not supported with database releases earlier than 8.1.6, and storing data from multiple databases in one PERFSTAT user account is currently not supported.

Oracle Enterprise Manager (OEM) tools

Oracle Enterprise Manager (OEM) is Oracle's single, integrated solution for managing, administering and monitoring global enterprises. OEM management framework consisting of three tiers: The Console (client tier) and its integrated tools provide a graphical interface for administrators to manage the complete Oracle environment. Management Servers and a database repository provide a scalable middle tier for processing system management tasks. Intelligent Agents are installed on each network node (database) to monitor the services that node provides, and to execute tasks from the Management Server (Metalink A96674-01, n.d.).

Oracle offers several tools to administer the complete Oracle environment, including: databases, Internet Application Servers (iAS), applications, and services. For this research we have assessed two types of tools that help the DBA to tune and monitor Oracle database: Performance Tuning pack (Metalink A86647-01. n.d.) with Oracle Expert tool for automated database tuning, and Diagnostics pack (Metalink A88748-02, n.d.) with a tool called Performance Manager that provides a set of graphical charts to monitor the performance of the database.

Oracle Expert provides a methodology that is used to collect, evaluate, verify, and implement database tuning changes (Metalink 93490.1, n.d.). Tuning areas cover instance parameter tuning, database structure and placement, index tuning, and SQL statement reuse evaluation. During the tuning session, Oracle Expert collects metrics from dynamic performance views, processes this input through the various rules and algorithms, and creates recommendations, tuning scripts, and reports.

Before creating a tuning session, Oracle establishes a current workload baseline (application SQL data and statistics or SQL History) of the database environment. Tuning session consists of five steps: defining the scope (SGA tuning, SQL reuse, storage management, data access – I/O), metrics collection, metrics review, recommendations based on built-in rules, and generating the SQL scripts based on the recommendations.

Observation. Oracle Expert tool, with 900 tuning rules built-in, sub-applications SQL Analyze and Index Wizard, represents Oracle's most enhanced graphical tool, especially with the release 9i. To host and manage collected metrics, this tool creates near 700 objects: 249 tables, 270 indexes, and 63 views. Algorithms for processing recommendations based on the collected metrics are high memory and CPU consumers. Using this tool with a repository installed on a production (main) database would not be an advantage due to its negative impact on the overall database performance.

Performance Manager, available as a part of Oracle Diagnostic pack, Performance Management and Overview, provides a set of charts on the current state of the database. This tool is designed to give an immediate feedback on the state of all tuning areas. With an Overview option selected, this tool displays several charts simultaneously. Dynamic monitoring of the database state is enhanced with user defined snapshot time interval, and various type of chart formats (Metalink 169551.1, n.d.).

Observation. This tool provides a complete overview of Oracle database state, in the form of multiple-choice charts in HTML format. Also it can monitor Microsoft SQL server database. It is available for UNIX, and Windows platforms only. For the database release prior to 9i, tool is available only with OMS repository connection. With 9i release, without OMS only the current activity can be monitored. Collection and review of historical data is available with OMS repository connection exclusively. With a frequent refresh rate (snapshot time interval), the database has drawbacks in the overall performance due to increased activities (CPU and RAM consumption) necessary to calculate all performance metrics.

MGA's EagleEye

MGA EagleEye is a third-party software tool developed by Mark Gurry & Associates (MGA) that monitors the performance of Oracle databases and provides real-time diagnostic information to allow for immediate rectification of performance problems (http://maxdbt.com/eagleeye.htm) (Gurry, 2001; Gurry & Corrigan, 1996). This tuning tool is reviewed by 'SELECT' magazine, Australian Oracle Users Group, and recommended for users experiencing extensive problems with performance and robustness on their mission critical database.

Observation. The tool runs a set of SQL statements and records tuning information when expected response times are exceeded, including details of logged on users, the applications and specific actions they are running, and where the contention is occurring. It also produces graphical information on:

- Shared Pool Problems
- Analysis (and not rebuilt) of tables and indexes
- Waits in tables and indexes
- Sort efficiency
- Disk I/O analysis

Eagle Eye is a product that has been developed to help DBAs to quickly identify where the performance problems are occurring and the cause of the problems. When used with the Mark Gurry's books Oracle Performance Tuning and Oracle SQL Tuning, the tool enables the DBA to get performance problems under control. This tool does not provide a solution for recording historical metrics. It is designed to give an instant overview of database performance, and therefore is not suitable for a long-term proactive database maintenance. Also, it does not enable object optimization nor cache hit-ratio analysis.

Workload Performance Measurement and Tuning

Workload Performance Measurement and Tuning (WPMT) is a custom developed monitoring and tuning tool enabling a DBA to perform reactive and proactive Oracle database tuning, with an efficient and resource-effective solution for managing the memory related historical resource and performance metrics. With an assessment of the high-availability Oracle database architectural components and their impact on workload performance, we have designed a tool with following features:

- Database connections assessment. A feature required for the successful implementation of developed tuning strategy for administrating efficiently mission-critical Oracle database-driven applications.
- Database workload assessment. Capturing and displaying in real-time the database users with the most demanding resource allocations, in terms of top memory and CPU consumers, as well as the most expensive SQL statements in terms of I/O executions.
- Instance memory allocation assessment. In order to determine the efficiency of allocated memory to manage the workload, the current memory allocation breakdown, calculated cache hit ratios using a ratio-methodology, memory sort ratio, and a redo log space requests, are calculated and displayed in real-time as well.
- Bottleneck or Wait Event assessment. With wait-methodology, we have determined total instance session's wait time and corresponding event description, required to identify the root causes of session's hang-up.
- Storage or space allocation assessment. In order to anticipate space shortage and eliminate unnecessary database performance overhead or downtime, we have developed a feature to provide an overview of the currently free/used space. Furthermore, with calculated fragmentation index, the efficiency of the overall datafile free space has been determined and displayed.
- Disk or I/O activities assessment. A real-time assessment feature detecting inappropriate or unbalanced throughput of physical storage allocation has been developed in terms of highest physical reads/writes per datafile.
- RAC inter-node performance assessment. An overview of top wait events related to instance cache has been determined using RAC's dictionary views. The efficiency of inter-instance intercommunication component has been assessed using average current block time metric.
- Memory metrics management. Instead of recording metrics in database tables, and as a consequence additionally increase the database workload; we have developed a solution that uses a flat file for recording and reviewing current/historical metrics. Recorded memory related performance metrics keep track of database performance achieved with historical initialization parameters, and enable a DBA to continuously measure the efficiency of allocated memory compared to the component's workload performance (delta metrics).
- Automated object optimization feature updates the database data dictionary with the current table and index statistics required by the Oracle's Cost Based Optimizer to calculate the best SQL Execution Plan. With accurate table and index statistics, a database workload performance will be improved.

These features successfully integrated in a user-friendly Java application (WPMT tool), enable a DBA to continuously measure, resource-effectively and efficiently, the workload performance excellence of high-availability Oracle databases.

WPMT Tool's Testing

Our tool has been tested with three workload setting criteria: Low, Medium, and High, as described in Table 2. Transactions have been executed by each user independently and simultaneously against a single CPU P-IV 1.8GHz/512 MB of RAM, on Personal edition Oracle 9i database. These transactions, containing a mixture of SQL commands such as INSERT, UPDATE, SELECT, and DELETE, are executed via sql scripts from Oracle SQL Plus editor.

Table 2: Workload criteria

	Low	Medium	High
Users	2	5	13
Transactions	12000	19500	43000
Exec. Time	1h00	1h15	2h00

A Low workload criteria is defined as two (2) users executing 12 000 transactions in one hour. A Medium workload criteria is defined as five (5) users, executing 19 500 transactions within an hour and fifteen minutes. A High workload criteria is defined as thirteen (13) users, executing 43 000 transactions within two (2) hours.

Hit ratios at the beginning (start) and at the end (end) of the simulation, as well as adjusted initialization parameters SHARED_POOL_AREA (SPA) and DB_CACHE_SIZE (CACHE), are illustrated in Tables 3, 4, 5 for Low, Medium, and High workload settings respectively.

Table 3: Low Workload*

	start	end
Dic. Hit	83,7	95,8
Lib. Hit	99,3	100,0
Buff. Hit	76,9	99,5
SPA	8MB	12MB
CACHE	4MB	4MB

*2 users/12 000 trans./1h

Table 4: Medium Workload**

	start	end
Dic. Hit	83,6	95,8
Lib. Hit	99,3	99,9
Buff. Hit	78,1	99,4
SPA	8MB	16MB
CACHE	4MB	8MB

**5 users/19 500 trans./1h10m

Table 5: High Workload***

	start	end
Dic. Hit	83,9	95,7
Lib. Hit	99,3	99,6
Buff. Hit	76,7	99
SPA	8MB	20MB
CACHE	4MB	8MB

***13 users/43 000 trans./2h

Low Workload results, as illustrated in Table 3, show that for the achievement of an optimal database performance in case of dictionary hit (95.8%) and a peak performance in case of library hit (100%), a size of shared pool area initialization parameter (SPA) had to be increased from 8 to 12 MB. Furthermore, there was no need to increase a buffer cache parameter size (CACHE) since almost a peak database performance (99.5%) has been achieved with an initial size of 4 MB (Figure 1).

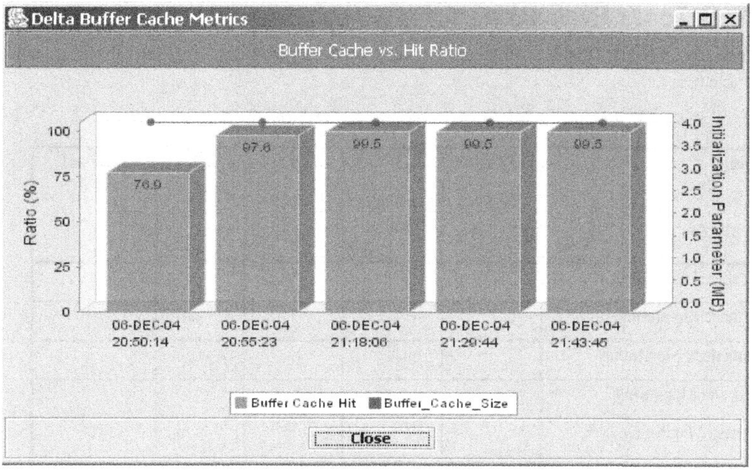

Figure 1: Buffer Hit Ratio – Low workload

Medium Workload results, as illustrated in Table 4, show that bigger values for both initialization parameters: shared pool area size (SPA) and buffer cache (CACHE), were required to achieve optimal/peak database workload performance. In case of buffer cache ratio a CACHE size was increased from 4 to 8 MB achieving 99.4 %; dictionary hit ratio achieving 95.8% with 16 MB, and a peak performance for library hit ratio (99.9%) with 16 MB (Figure 2).

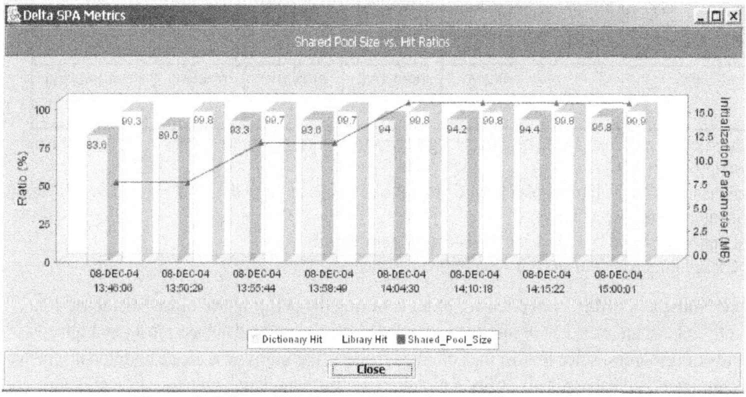

Figure 2: Library/Dictionary Hit Ratio – Medium Workload

High Workload results, as illustrated in Table 5, describe requirements, in terms of parameters size, for an achievement of optimal database workload performance. A 20 MB of memory allocated to shared pool area (SPA) were needed to achieve 95.7% and 99.6% hit ratios for dictionary and library respectively. A buffer cache size (CACHE) was increased from 4 to 8 MB in order to achieve 99% buffer hit ratio.

As illustrated in Tables 3,4, and 5, and as demonstrated in Figure 1 and 2, we may conclude that our WPMT tool, can be used efficiently and resource-effectively to tune database initialization parameters in order to achieve optimal/peak workload performance regardless the current database workload.

WPMT Tool's Evaluation

Comparison between Oracle tuning tools and custom developed WPMT tool has been described in Table 6.

Table 6: Oracle database monitoring and tuning tools evaluation

Tools / Features	1.Oracle's Statspack	2. OEM's Tuning pack (2.1)	3. OEM's Diagnostic pack	4. MGA's EagleEye	5. WPMT v1.0
Workload Monitoring	√	√	√	√ (4.1)	√
Instance Monitoring	√	√	√	√ (4.2)	√
Bottleneck Monitoring	√	√	√		√
Disk I/O Monitoring	√	√	√	√	√
Storage Monitoring	√	√	√	√	√
RAC Monitoring	√	√	√		√
Object Optimization		√			√
Cumulative metrics	√	√	√	√	√
Historical metrics		√	√		√ (5.1)
Metrics presentation	text	recomm	graph	graph	graph/delta
Metrics storage	database	repository	repository		file
Recommended tuning script		√			
Maintenance	reactive	proactive	proactive	reactive	Proactive and reactive

(2.1)Metrics are hidden and used by internal algorithms to provide recommendations in the form of tuning scripts

(4.1)Enhanced with the Explain plan feature (trace the execution of the SQL in order to discover all objects involved in the execution)

(4.2)Limited to Shared Pool Area, and no cache-hit ratio analysis

(5.1)Cache hit-ratio metrics and top initialization parameters

Oracle Statspack utility is an effective tool measuring the performance of each database component. To have an overview of metrics generated by this tool, the database must pay high costs in terms of resources, since to host the collected metrics, the utility will create additional schema in the production database. This utility maintains only the cumulative metrics, since all collected and recorded metrics are automatically deleted when the instance is restarted.

The main disadvantage of this Oracle's recommended tool for proactive maintenance, in our opinion, is an additional performance overhead created with an each utility's snapshot that collects metrics from almost all database performance views (default and recommended is level 5). For example, if we want to apply Oracle's recommended tuning methodology, i.e. one-by-one parameter, and to evaluate the effect of change on one component, Statspack's snapshot will capture metrics for other components anyway, thus increasing unnecessary database workload. Furthermore, the generated text file (report) is very complex to analyze and understand. For example, to evaluate the efficiency of hit ratios compared to dependent initialization parameters, the DBA must browse txt report from the beginning until the end since the information is provided on separate locations within a same report file.

Oracle Enterprise Manager (OEM) tools, i.e. tuning and diagnostic packs are effective tools but should be used jointly with a repository on a remote database (separately from production database) due to high cost in resources. Using these tools independently would not be an advantage since tuning pack provides only recommendations and not an overview of performance metrics. Algorithms (rules) are hidden, and the DBA has no insight of how and why did Oracle server draw the conclusions and which parameter should be changed.

A tuning pack in combination with diagnostic pack provides a complete monitoring and tuning mechanisms to measure overall and independently database component's workload. For example, when Oracle Expert (tuning pack) recommends altering SHARED_POOL_SIZE parameters with optimal value, it will generate the script, and the DBA, after executing the script, may monitor the library and dictionary hit ratio through performance manager (diagnostic pack). Maintaining the OEM repository and tools high financial costs (new database on new server) are the main disadvantages in our opinion.

MGA's EagleEye is an efficient tool to optimize SQL statements for the best Execution Plan. The Author's book (Gurry, 2001) and EagleEye tool focus on database component that mainly measures SQL execution efficiency, i.e. Shared Pool Area. Although it is enhanced with storage and I/O metrics, the tool is quite limited with features for measuring overall database workload performance. User-friendly GUI, low cost in resources, and a quick overview of the performance is an advantage of this tool. In our opinion, it is suitable only for proactive database maintenance.

With **WPMT tool**, we have combined the best practices to monitor and measure the overall database workload performance.

These best practices are the recommendations from Oracle Support Services (http://metalink.oracle.com/), combined with our 5 years expertise in maintaining the Oracle database. With a lean and portable Java user-friendly GUI, the tool has the lowest possible requirements in terms of resources. It does not create any additional table in production or remote instance, and metrics are saved in *RandomAccessed* flat file on the local or remote machine. Furthermore, with the most important instance related initialization parameters, recorded together with related performance metrics, we enabled historical overview of delta metrics.

Summary and Conclusion

A custom developed Java application (WPMT v1.0) combines the best practices of the most common Oracle tuning tools. WPMT's user-friendly GUI enables a DBA to efficiently perform proactive and reactive database tuning regardless of the current database workload.

Our tool combines two approaches for gauging database workload performance hit-ratio and wait (or bottleneck) analysis. Measuring a workload performance with wait analysis enables the DBA to have an insight where a database is spending time, and with hit-ratio, the efficiency of instance memory allocation is instantly detected.

Overcoming the limitations of measuring only the current (cumulative) metrics is achieved with a cost-effective and efficient solution, i.e. the flat-file metrics management. With this solution the burden of performance overhead created with a historical metrics is completely removed from a production database. Measurement with delta metrics and monitoring of memory allocation for each SGA component enables the DBA to efficiently readjust the memory for optimal database workload performance. Effective combination of the memory allocation with initialization parameter and overall efficiency of the related component responsible to manage the current workload is an advantage compared to all Oracle tools. In case of reported performance overhead (for example, low hit-ratios), based on available SGA memory, a DBA can reallocate additional memory to area(s) with low performance (SPA or Buffer Cache).

Acknowledgements

We thank Mr. Bazran Bin Md Bahe, Oracle Support Manager Malaysia, for providing the information regarding Oracle database implementation and maintenance.

References

Buch, V. & Cheevers, S. (2002). Database architecture: Federated vs. clustered. (Oracle white paper.) Online library: http://otn.oracle.com

Burleson, K. D. (2003). *Creating a self-tuning Oracle database*. Kittrell, North Carolina, USA: Rampant TechPress.

Chandrasekaran, S. & Kehoe, B. (2003). Technical comparison of Oracle real application clusters vs. IBM DB2 UDB ESE. (Oracle white paper.) Online library: http://otn.oracle.com

Gurry, M. (2001). *Oracle SQL tuning*. O'Reilly & Associates.

Gurry, M. & Corrigan, P. (1996). *Oracle performance tuning, Database management systems* (2nd ed.). O'Reilly & Associates.

Metalink A87503-02. (n.d.).*Oracle9i database performance guide and reference, release 1 (9.0.1)*. On-line: http://download-west.oracle.com/docs/cd /A91202_01/ 901_doc/server.901/a87503/toc.htm

Metalink 228913.1. (n.d.). *Systemwide tuning using StatsPack reports*. Oracle Support Services. On-line library: www.metalink.oracle.com

Metalink A96674-01. (n.d.). *Oracle enterprise manager concepts guide release 9.2.0*. On-line: http://download-west.oracle.com/docs/html/A96674_01/toc.htm

Metalink A86647-01. (n.d.). *Oracle enterprise manager database tuning with the Oracle tuning pack release 9.0.1*. On-line library: http://download-west.oracle.com/docs/cd/A91202_01/901_doc/em.901/a86647/tun_ovw.htm#1001025

Metalink A88748-02. (n.d.). *Oracle enterprise manager getting started with the Oracle diagnostics pack release 9.0.1*. On-line: http://download-west.oracle.com/docs/cd/A91202_01/901_doc/em.901/a88748/toc.htm

Metalink 93490.1. (n.d.). *How to use Oracle Expert*. Oracle Support Services. On-line library: www.metalink.oracle.com

Metalink 169551.1. (n.d.). *FAQ Oracle diagnostics pack 9.0.1*. Oracle Support Services. On-line library: www.metalink.oracle.com

MSDN. (2004). Federated SQL Server 2000 Servers, MSDN. *Microsoft library*. On-line: http://msdn.microsoft.com/library/default.asp?url=/library/en-us/architec/8_ar_cs_4fw3.asp

Silberschatz, A., Korth, H. F. & Sudarshan S. (2002). *Database system concepts* (4th ed.). McGraw – Hill.

Zildžić, Dž. (2005). *Workload performance measurement and tuning of high-availability Oracle databases*. Masters Dissertation. University Malaya, Malaysia.

Biographies

Sai Peck Lee is currently an associate professor at Faculty of Computer Science & Information Technology, University of Malaya. She obtained her Master of Computer Science from University of Malaya, her Diplôme d'Études Approfondies (D. E. A.) in Computer Science from University of Pierre et Marie Curie (Paris VI) and her Ph.D. degree in Computer Science from University of Panthéon-Sorbonne (Paris I). Her current research interests include Software Engineering, Object-Oriented (OO) Methodology, Software Reuse and Framework-based Development, Information Systems and Database Engineering, OO Analysis and Design for E-Commerce Applications and Auction Protocols. She has published an academic book and more than 70 papers in various local and international conferences and journals. She had also served as the executive editor of a journal for 2 years, and has been in the programme and reviewer committees of several local and international conferences.

M.Sci. **Dzemal Zildzic**, born on 26.08.1975, Sarajevo, Bosnia and Herzegovina. Diplome Universitaire de Technology (DUT)-1997, Paris XI, France; Master of Software Engineering (MSE)-2005, Faculty of Computer Science and Information Technology (FCSIT), University Malaya, Kuala Lumpur, Malaysia. Working experience consists of OOT/Java programming and Oracle database administration (Oracle division manager - digiNET d.o.o. 2000-2002), consultant (Datapower Sdn Bhd 2004), and managerial positions (Head of IT department - Bosnia Bank International 2002-2003). Since April 2005, employed as managing director of IN2 d.o.o. Sarajevo - one of the largest software development companies in the region of South-Eastern Europe.

The page left blank intentionally.

An Information Assurance and Security Curriculum Implementation

Samuel P. Liles and Reza Kamali
Purdue University Calumet, Hammond, IN, USA

sliles@purdue.edu kamalir@calumet.purdue.edu

Abstract

A holistic approach to security education is important to providing practitioners the scope of learning necessary for integration of their skills into the enterprise. Specifically domains of knowledge can easily be identified that allow for this holistic approach to be implemented into a new program of study or curriculum for information assurance and security. Within the Purdue Calumet CIT Department a new curriculum has been written and the program of study has been approved for implementation and the first students have applied to the program. The domains of systems assurance, software assurance, and operations assurance are as critical to the success as the overall goal of ABET accreditation of the program to the ACM SIGITE draft specifications when finalized.

Keywords: Information Assurance, Security, Curriculum, SIGITE, ACM

Introduction

The benefits and responsibilities having been fully weighed by *the Purdue Calumet CIT Department,* a strong case for positive acceptance was made for aligning *the Purdue Calumet CIT Department* with the ACM SIGITE (Curriculum) guidelines. The ACM SIGITE group has been working on a ABET accrediting program for information technology education in a four year program. These guidelines were mapped to multiple information technology disciplines, and specifically to a new information assurance and security program that is now accepting students. This document shows how the new program was designed and how it aligns with a variety of different certifying bodies and specifically with NTISSI 4011(NTISSI).

The process utilized wove a tapestry of the guidelines as proposed by SIGITE. The topics when given were processed into outcome based learning objectives (Bloom, 1956). These objectives were then processed as requirements against the NTISSI 4011 certification standard as a prerequisite of the program. One of the basic outcomes of this new curriculum was at the two year level all information technology students would attain the NTISSI 4011 certification as well as a broad based information technology education. This is one of the closest implementations to the newly proposed SIGITE guidelines.

Domains of knowledge

Domain areas for the entire curriculum were addressed and knowledge area requirements were examined as found in previous papers (Davis, 2003; Laswell, 1999). These were invaluable resources and allowed *the Purdue Calumet CIT Department* to evaluate and concentrate on the most likely areas of specialization for undergraduate instruction. Having a pattern of courses put together that would advance students quickly from novice to subject matter expert was a goal. Having a framework for knowledge to be wrapped around also was part of the success strategy for *the Purdue Calumet CIT Department*.

Each of the outcome base learning objectives was processed for level of skill based on the Bloom Taxonomy (Bloom, 1956) for education. The objectives were then looked at for area of expertise as applied to the individual curricula guidelines. Balance of instructional expectation was attained by insuring that freshman and sophomore classes were balanced strongly towards the lower levels of Blooms taxonomy with fewer upper level objectives. Consequently upper level courses have higher level objectives and significantly fewer lower level objectives with an expectation that prior courses prepared the student sufficiently. As part of the preparation of that expectation course designers met and built a map of the course objectives and knowledge requirements.

Before beginning the mapping of objectives, the role of a student completing the course was discussed. What would a successful student from this program do as a career? Was the objective to create practitioners, scholars, or graduate school aspirants? These objectives were addressed within *the Purdue Calumet CIT Department* and a plan was put in place.

The Proposed Process for Certification

Starting with the documents provided by NTISSI, *the Purdue Calumet CIT Department* set up learning objectives that coincided. The first goal was to attain 4011 certification at the two year level even though *the Purdue Calumet CIT Department* is currently a four year program. Truly utilizing ad hoc methods, the learning objectives were split between the four courses known as platform technologies, operating system administration, networking, and fundamentals of information assurance and security. These four courses are split out from the objectives as set in the accreditation guidelines for 4011 certification and the outcome based learning objectives basically mirror 4011. Added to this and coinciding nicely with the draft ACM SIGITE guidelines (Curriculum) the courses also serve to help with this accreditation goal. Both of these programs sincerely support each other and help in the curriculum design process.

Inclusive Modularity

Multiple domains of information assurance knowledge were identified and three knowledge domains were taxonomically derived and provided the structure for the curriculum modules as areas of interest (Maconachy, 2001). The first module is systems assurance. This module is inclusive of the operating systems, networks, hardware systems, and the other mature sciences of securing systems. The second module is the software assurance module. This second module, though less holistic, is inclusive of the sub disciplines of software auditing, secure coding practices, analysis of software, and implementing software in the enterprise. The third module is a well defined module of operations assurance where the concepts of physical security, policies, procedures, risk analysis, and the other organizational non-technical controls exist.

The three domains as discussed can be sliced and defined differently depending on the perspectives of the evaluators for defining threads of knowledge through the program. The domains became increasingly important for sequencing courses and providing knowledge dependencies for curriculum design. The three domains of information assurance as identified also allow for future growth of the program as cohesive specializations. Pursuant to the goal statements of the Purdue Calumet CIT Department the final outcome of the program is to provide a student that has a well rounded information technology background with a broad based specialization in information assurance and security.

Systems Assurance

Systems assurance is the practice of hardening operating systems from known threats, analyzing and auditing hardware and devices for known threats, and remeditating the devices and computing platforms within the enterprise (Maconachy, 2001). For instance, proper configuration and defensive strategies employed for protecting a network and specifically a router would be considered systems assurance. Ensuring that user accounts are active and properly used with permissions inside of the enterprise would be considered systems assurance.

Table 1 Systems Assurance Courses

Systems Assurance Courses
Fundamentals of Information Assurance: This course covers security mechanisms, fundamental aspects, operational issues, policy, attacks, security domains, forensics, information states, security services, threat analysis, vulnerabilities, and other topics.
Systems Assurance: This course covers the implementation of systems assurance with computing systems. Topics include confidentiality, integrity, authentication, non-repudiation, intrusion detection, physical security, and encryption. Extensive laboratory exercises are assigned.
Assured Systems Design and Implementation: This course covers the design and implementation of assured systems in an enterprise environment. Topics include hardening of operating systems, choice of platforms, design criteria within the assured systems domain. Extensive laboratory exercises are assigned.
Computer Forensics: This course covers the techniques used in the forensic analysis of computerized systems for gathering evidence to detail how a system has been exploited or used. Extensive laboratory exercises are assigned.

Software Assurance

Software assurance is a selection of sub disciplines merged into a practice. Software assurance is the practice of requirements gathering, secure coding, testing, auditing, and implementation of software in the enterprise protecting against known vulnerabilities. Software assurance is the preparation of source code such that known vulnerabilities are excluded from the product. Software assurance is also about preparing robust source code so that unknown vulnerabilities create secure failure conditions (Software, 1992). Preparation can include auditing of commercial off the shelf software (COTS), or free open source software (F/OSS) being implemented within the enterprise, or third party prepared/contracted source code.

Software assurance includes normally associated computer science topics such as Software Engineering (SE), Software Quality Assurance (SQA), Highly Assured Computing (HAC), Capability Maturity Model (CMM), and other development lifecycle issues. Further software assurance elements include domain crossing topics such as end of life cycle, maintenance, retirement, reusability, and legacy adaptation strategies. Software assurance definitively includes practice oriented computing concepts including secure coding, threat modeling, vulnerability analysis, implementation, auditing, and defensive integration of software within the enterprise.

Table 2 Software Assurance Courses

Software Assurance Courses
Programming Fundamentals: This course covers fundamental data structures, fundamental programming constructs, object-oriented programming, algorithms and problem-solving, event-driven programming, recursion, and other topics.
Advanced Programming: This course covers advanced topics in programming languages, GUI development, threaded applications, components, testing and debugging methods and advanced topics in event-driven and object oriented programming techniques. Extensive laboratory exercises are assigned.
Software Assurance: This course covers defensive programming techniques, bounds analysis, error handling, advanced testing techniques, detailed code auditing, and software specification in a trusted assured environment. Extensive laboratory exercises are assigned.

Operations Assurance

Operations assurance advocates the tools of physical security and operational characteristics found in a cohesive information technology organization (Software,1999). Within the curriculums scope are the concepts of physical security, data center design, and legal and procedural reporting. Items that are of great concern to the enterprise that would be found here include disaster recovery and planning. The concept of business continuity and risk analysis are threads of knowledge that run through the domain area of operations assurance.

Within operations assurance you would find for example the implications of HIPPA, DMCA, or the concepts of physical security. Paradoxically items often overlooked as part of information assurance would be the concept of back up and recovery testing procedures, insurance, and other litigation aspects of operations. The ability to define, categorize, and apply financial loss expectation documents to management of an enterprise is a valuable skill.

Table 3 Operations Assurance Courses

Operations Assurance Courses
Ethical and Legal Issues of IT: This course covers professional communications, social context of computing, teamwork concepts and issues, intellectual properties, legal issues in computing, organization context, professional and ethical issues, responsibilities, privacy and civil liberties, and other topics.
Disaster recovery and planning: This course covers risk management and business continuity. Topics include disaster recovery strategies, mitigation strategies, risk analysis, and development of contingency plans for unexpected outages and component failures. Extensive laboratory exercises are assigned.
Information Assurance Risk Assessment: This course covers industry and government requirements and guidelines for information assurance and auditing of computing systems. Topics include risk assessment and implementation of standardized requirements and guidelines.

Conclusion

Developing a holistic approach to information assurance and security curriculum was an onerous task. As defined in other publications (Laswell, 1999) there are a variety of approaches to the concept of information assurance and security. With only a relatively small number of courses to deal with in developing a curriculum and not wanting to follow a standard computer science model the solution at *the Purdue Calumet CIT Department* is to focus on implementations of security strategies. These implementation strategies fit within the overall goal for *the Purdue Calumet CIT Department* to attain accreditation through SIGITE.

Developing courses that split into three domains was in consideration arbitrary but definitely necessary for defining the knowledge areas. Other divisions were considered along these same lines, or even further devolvement of the topics into common knowledge areas as defined in other people's work. Keeping in mind the practitioner approach these three domain areas served quite well at helping meet the overall goals. Further the three domain areas fit nicely at segmenting the courses and though some would argue with a particular course filling a slot often the flexibility is overlooked. This flexibility is part of the final solution to the curriculum modules and allows for growth in the overall courses.

References

Bloom, B. S. (1956). *Taxonomy of educational objectives: Handbook I: Cognitive domain*. Longmans, Green & Company

Curriculum: Proposed standards for IT curriculum. Retrieved 6/12/2005 from http://sigite.acm.org/activities/curriculum/downloads/IT%20Volume-April%202005.pdf

Crowley, E. (2003). Information system security curricula development. *Proceeding of the 4th Conference on Information Technology Curriculum*, pp. 249-255

Davis, J. & Dark, M. (2003). Defining a curriculum framework in information assurance and security. *ASEE Annual Conference*, Nashville, TN, June.

Laswell, B., Simmel, D., & Behrens, S. (1999). Information Assurance Curriculum and Certification: State of the Practice. CMU/SEI-99-TR-021, *Software Engineering Institute*, Carnegie Mellon, Pittsburg, PA, Sept.

Maconachy W. V., Schou C. D., Ragsdale D., & Welch D. (2001). A model for information assurance: An integrated approach. *Proceedings 2001 IEEE Information Assurance Workshop* , West Point, NY, 2001, pp. 306 - 310.

National Information Systems Security (INFOSEC) Glossary. (1997). NSTISSI No. 4009, National Security Telecommunications and Information Systems Security Committee, August.

NSTISSI, (1994). No. 4011 - National Training Standard for Information Systems Security (INFOSEC) Professionals.

Software Assurance Standard. (1992). NASA-STD-2201-93, NOVEMBER 10, 1992.

Biographies

Samuel P. Liles III is an Assistant Professor of Computer Information Technology at Purdue University Calumet. He is currently involved in research identifying the knowledge skills and abilities of cyber adversaries and mitigation strategies.

Dr. **Reza Kamali** is an Associate Professor and Department Head of Computer Information Technology at Purdue University Calumet, Hammond, Indiana. He was a founding member of SITE, which later became ACM's SIGITE. He was a member of the IT2006 Task Force and a member of The Joint Task Force for Computing Curricula 2005

The page left blank intentionally.

Readiness to Communicate in a Digital World

Kathy Lynch
Faculty of IT, Monash University, Australia

kathy.lynch@infotech.monash.edu.au

Abstract

Communicating with friends, family, peers and colleagues has always underpinned work and social behaviour. However, the devices that act as conduits to this communication have changed over time, and differ across the globe. People in industralised corners of the world are more and more frequently using advances in information and communication technologies (ICTs) to assist both the senders and receivers to have more timely, synchronous and value-added communiqués. *Well, that is what the promotional material is telling us.*

The primary role of undergraduate education is to best prepare graduates for the workforce that they are being primed. To this end, educators need to be knowledgeable in what students already know, do, and their perceptions of what is required and is of value in assisting them to communicate with colleagues or peers.

This paper presents a study that aimed to identify directions for undergraduate IT curriculum in developing the information and communication technology (ICT) readiness of beginning IT (in particular Information Systems) professionals to work in a collaborative team.

Three hundred undergraduate Information Systems (IS) students were invited to participate in the study, one-hundred and sixty responded. The results indicate that there is a definitive relationship between frequency of use and the perceived value of an information and communication technology, and that the use of an ICT as a communication device in a social situation does not guarantee its use or even its perceived value as a communication device in a work situation: Visa versa is also true. Findings from the research could be used to influence IS curriculum developers in preparing undergraduate students' readiness for communicating (and collaborating) in the digital workforce of today.

Keywords: information and communication technologies, information systems, skill development, curriculum

Background

Information technology workers of the 21st century need to be conducive to new ways of working within the workplace; a workplace that revolves around communication, specifically, communication technologies. Not only is skill required in effectively using communication technologies becoming paramount, but the effective use of these communication technologies is also critical.

Work colleagues, social acquaintances, and family have a strong human need to maintain communications with each other even when in different temporal or spatial locations. Advancements in telecommunication technologies can facilitate and accommodate these new spaces through dissolving the boundaries or restrictions between them, according to Lipnack and Stamps (2000) "electronic media are dissolving the historic connection between physical place and social place" (p.16). These spaces are an integral part of today's workplace of today as it adopts a more collaborative format; and one that is less dependant on the location of its workers (Castells, 2001; Rice & Mitchell-Ketzes, 2002; Wajcman, 2004). A common theme in the literature of today is expressed clearly by Wajcman (2004); "life is now mediated by technology" (p.1).

The industralised, 'third wave' (Toffler, 1980) IT worker is often part of a global team (Lynch, 2004); a team that has a strong reliance on technology. The use of technologies to assist in collaboration is not new; it has been reported by such researchers as Mankin, Cohen and Bikson (1996, p.6) who expressed the relationship as a synergy, however the reliance on ICTs to assist in the development of this synergy, is relatively recent. This synergy develops where the contribution of the two is greater than the sum of the parts in the development and improving the performance of the team. To develop this synergy, there needs to be an acceptance and adoption of the value of using communication technologies on collaborative projects. If a technology is to have a chance of improving a team's performance, individual team members need to be skilled in their use, and organizations need to address and manage the changes associate with adopting the new technologies and procedures.

ICTs are more than communication tools, they enable numerous interactions between team members that could otherwise not happen easily (Furst, Blackburn & Rosen, 1999; Gould, 1998; Mankin, Cohen & Bikson, 1996), and have been reported to enable the team to work "better, faster, cheaper and smarter" (Furst, Blackburn & Rosen, 1999 p.249). Their use can compress space and time (Lurey & Raisinghani, 2000), and through their creation of shared understandings, develop a shared trust (Schrage, 1990).

Castells (2001) argues that technology not only influences how we work, but the use of it is recursive; that is, technology is transformed by society, and society is transformed by technology therefore creating a new socio-technical interaction (pp.4-5). Bijker and Law's (1997) work is somewhat in agreement with Castells in that technologies have social implications in so much as teams using ICTs also have the ability to shape the technology to suit themselves and the organisation in which they work. This interaction can have implications that are advantageous (or not). The key is to manage and use the technology to its fullest advantage through interweaving it into society and work (Bijker & Law, 1997; Casey, 1999; Castells, 2001). Technology should not constrain the development and creativity of team members, but rather enhance the work and allow the team members to develop in creativity and skill (Bijker & Law, 1997 p.105).

The information technology profession is the focus of this study, and as in numerous other professions there is an increasing expectation that the new recruit will be part of a collaborative team to complete the tasks of the job. As an effective member of a collaborative team, the beginning IT professional needs to be proficient in the technologies that permit and encourage support between team members.

Information technology professionals therefore, need to be familiar, comfortable and confident with the technology that they use to complete their work in their, often global, workplace. Using the ICTs as an effective means to an end requires not only training in the technologies themselves, but the users require educating in the ubiquitous nature of the technologies and the decisions associated with their selection, use, appropriateness, modification and evaluation. Before an IT team can benefit from the use of ICTs for the greater team effort, individual team members need to be confident, efficient and value the worth of the ICT in enabling the collaboration.

The Research Study

Given that ICTs are important for effective collaboration, collaborative teams underpin the way IT professionals work and will continue to work, and individuals are at the nucleus of a team, there is a need for the individual team members to be proficient in the use of the ICTs that underpin the effectiveness of the collaboration. To this end, a preliminary study was designed to investigate the perceived value or worth, and the frequency of use of popular ICTs by undergraduate information technology students in their everyday student life. The outcomes of this study can be used to direct curriculum enhancements that would better prepare students for the collaborative, ICT rich IT professional workforce.

Method

The study was conducted through the dissemination of a questionnaire to Information Systems undergraduate students enrolled at a large Australian university.

Participants

The participants selected for the study were from core units in each of the three year levels in the Bachelor of Information Systems. The students had been with their fellow students in these units for eleven weeks prior to the data collection. Each unit was selected on the premise that students had undergone some instruction on team work in previous weeks or previous years of their course, and that the students are expected to collaborate effectively in group work. During their development of team skills in these units the students are often exposed, though one cannot say with what regularity or level across classes in the one year or from one year to the next, to the use of ICTs for collaboration. Three hundred students were invited to participate in the study, one-hundred and sixty questionnaires were returned. The responses, were from a mix of first (63), second (42) and third year (55) IS students.

Data Instrument

A questionnaire was devised to elicit responses regarding the respondents' perceptions as to the value of a particular ICT for work practices and for social interactions, plus their frequency of use of the selected ICTs. The use of ICTs in social situations was deemed an important aspect for investigation, so as to determine if there was any misalignment between the students' use of an ICT for one situation over another (for example, social rather than academic). The ICTs from which the respondents were asked to make comment on were ICTs that are used frequently by IS practitioners. It is acknowledged that there is a paradox between devices and services here, and that there is an unclear differentiation between 'The Device' and 'The Service'. This could create participate confusion in participant's responses to the questionnaire. However, as it is a presumption that the students are familiar with these terms, it did not seem to be a flaw in the instrument.

The ICTs selected for the study were:

- Voice and text messaging using a mobile phone
- Email
- Synchronous chat (e.g. MSN,ICQ) using the Internet
- Video/audio chat using the Internet
- Asynchronous discussion areas using the Internet.

The questionnaire (Table 1) captured data regarding the respondents' frequency of use of the selected ICTs. A six point Likert-type scale was presented for the respondent to select the most appropriate answer, these were then coded as 5 = "Lots-every day use", 4 = "Frequently-a few times a week", 3 = "once a week", 2 = "a few times a month", 1 = "rarely", 0 = "never", and a null data entry was made if the question was unanswered.

To establish the perceived value of an ICT in an academic and social context, the questionnaire also included questions using a five point Likert-type scale was presented for the respondent to select the most appropriate answer, these were then coded as 5 = "highly valued", 4 = "moderately valued", 3 = "of little value", 2 = "unsure", 1 = "no value", and a null data entry was made if the question was unanswered.

Table 1. Questionnaire

Tick the technologies that you feel you are comfortable in using (you can select more than one). AND tick your frequency of use	**Lots (every day)** [5]	**Frequent (a few times every week)** [4]	**Maybe once a week** [3]	**A few times a month** [2]	**Rarely** [1]	**Never** [0]
❑ Voice and text messaging (Mobile Phone)						
❑ Email						
❑ Internet synchronous text chat						
❑ Internet video or audio chat						
❑ Internet asynchronous chat						

2A. Tick the technologies that you have used use when working on **group projects**?

2B. Rate your perception of their value to team members in working on **group projects**. Where 5 is "highly valued", 4 is "moderately valued", 3 is "unsure", 2 is "little value" and 1 is of "no value at all".

3A. Tick the technologies that you use for **entertainment or social contact**?

3B. Rate your perception of their value to the participants engaged in the **entertainment or social contact**. Where 5 is "highly valued", 4 is "moderately valued", 3 is "unsure", 2 is "little value" and 1 is of "no value at all"

2A. Tick the technologies that you have used use when working on **group projects**?	**2B.** Rating	**3A.** Tick the technologies that you use for **entertainment or social contact**?	**3B.** Rating
❑ Mobile voice/text	5,4,3,2,1	❑ Mobile voice/text	5,4,3,2,1
❑ Email	5,4,3,2,1	❑ Email	5,4,3,2,1
❑ Internet synchronous text chat	5,4,3,2,1	❑ Internet synchronous text chat	5,4,3,2,1
❑ Internet video or audio chat	5,4,3,2,1	❑ Internet video or audio chat	5,4,3,2,1
❑ Internet asynchronous chat	5,4,3,2,1	❑ Internet asynchronous chat	5,4,3,2,1

Data Analysis

To allow for comparison between the frequency and the value data, the frequency scores of 5 to 0 were transposed in to scores in the range of 5 to 1 to match the range for the value data (5 to 1). These transpositions are shown in Table 2.

Table 2. Re-coding of frequency of use

Old	New (frequency)
5	5.0 (lots, every day)
4	4.2 (few times a week)
3	3.4 (maybe once a week)
2	2.6 (a few times a month)
1	1.8 (rarely)
0	1.0 (never)
Null	No response

It is acknowledged that as students progress through the years of their degree, they develop and master the skills and techniques that they are exposed to: Therefore one should expect 3rd year students to be more knowledgeable and proficient in the use of ICTs than first year students, therefore the data presented has been displayed according to year levels so as to see if there is a transition from year to year.

Though there was an area in the questionnaire for the participants to add open comment, this option was not taken up by enough participants to make a rigorous analysis of the data, and therefore have not been included in the paper.

Results and Findings: Frequency of Use

The questionnaire asked participants to select from a list of phrases, the one that best described their use of the selected ICT in any context. To determine if there were any trends in the frequency of use of a particular technology, the mean score to two significant figures was calculated for the frequency of use for each ICT. The mean scores are presented in Figure 1.

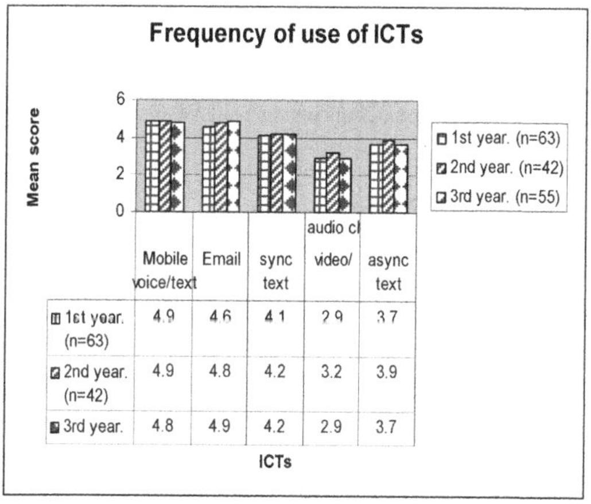

Figure 1. Frequency of use of ICTs

Voice and text using a mobile phone is typically the most frequently used ICT, and are used everyday across the three year levels of participants. The use of email is the next most frequently used ICT from the given list, with 2nd and 3rd year students frequency of use just a little above that of 1st year students surveyed. Of the remaining ICTs listed all but synchronous video/audio chat are also used everyday by the survey respondents. The lower level of use for synchronous Internet video/audio chat could be due to a number of reasons, such as, the non-availability of hardware to interact with users, and the relative small number of users of the technology. The use of mobile phones and email are two common technologies that have become ubiquitous in many western societies, in particular university settings. It is interesting to note that the number of responses relating to the frequency of use of synchronous video/audio chat and asynchronous chat were lower than for the other ICTs (74% and 71% respectively). This indicates less skill and or knowledge in the technologies, and it seems, therefore, a lower level of use.

Overall, there is little variation in typical responses for the top three ranked ICTs; mobile voice and text, email and synchronous Internet chat, therefore it is educationally difficult to differentiate between them. Nevertheless, the analysis was done to separate the ICTs, but as the results indicate, there is no claim that statistically they mean anything. Furthermore, and more importantly, educationally and in terms of the consequences of the research, there is very little significant difference in the ranking.

Third year students appear to use email and synchronous chat more frequently than respondents from the other two years. This could be due to the type of communications (such as long messages, attaching files, scheduled meeting times), their familiarity with the technology, no cost to send or receive messages, and the readily availability of the technology. The technologies associated with synchronous Internet text chat (for example MSN, ICQ) are widespread, popular, cheap, and have reached many households and workplaces over the last three years. Furthermore, mobile phones are 'wearable' and often easier to use than email as they do not require plugging in or shared access. However, the sending and receiving of messages costs more than email, and this could possibly be of a greater consideration to students who have become more independent as they progress through their course.

It could be argued that the use of less popular technologies, such as synchronous Internet video and audio chat is not yet common or accepted as the technologies associated with the more obtainable synchronous Internet text chat. However, second year respondents use these technologies more frequently than respondents from the other two years. This could be due to first year students being overwhelmed with the ICTs before them and having to become accustomed to much in a short period of time, and third students having explored numerous technologies, and are now more likely to use their preferred methods of communications - that is, email, mobile voice/text and synchronous Internet chat.

Results and Findings: Perceived Value

To investigate if there were any trends in the respondents' perceived value of the listed ICTs when working in groups for academic purpose and for social purposes, the questionnaire asked respondents to select from a list of terms, the one that best described their perceived value of the listed technology. The mean score to two significant figures was calculated for the perceived value of each ICT in an academic and social setting, and are presented in **Error! Reference source not found.**.

The perceived academic value of email and mobile voice/text is typically high with little variance. The most typical response for the perceived value of synchronous Internet video/audio chat for academic group work varies between no value to little value. This, together with the low response rate for this particular question indicates that the respondents may not understand the technology or may not have had the opportunity to use the technology in an academic setting, and therefore they had trouble perceiving its value.

The ICTs that are typically perceived as most highly valued are mobile voice/text, email and synchronous text chat. The use of mobile voice/text services using a mobile phone are unanimously perceived as of high valued for social communications. It is not surprising that email and synchronous Internet text chat are both valued and ranked highly, as they use the Internet as their

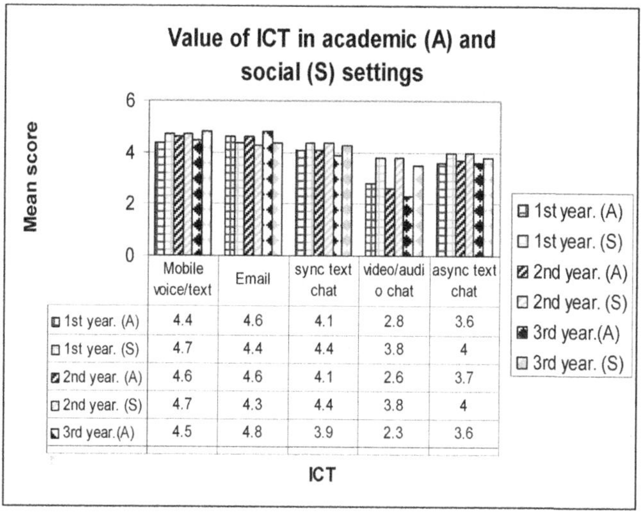

Figure 2. Perceived value in academic and social settings

underpinning technology, are free, and are in generally popular no matter the location of the sender or receiver.

Once again, as in the frequency of use, the number of responses relating to the perceived value of synchronous video/audio chat and asynchronous chat were lower than for the other ICTs, with the average of responses for academic and social, 40% and 55% respectively. This indicates a significant lack of skill and or knowledge in the technologies, and it seems, therefore, leading to a low level of not only their use but participants' perceived value of synchronous video/audio chat in particular for academic work. This seems to be in direct contract to what has been found in the literature which argues that we are social beings and require face-to-face contact (Becker & Sims, 2001. p5).

Results and Findings: Frequency of Use / Perceived Value

The questionnaire allowed for an exploration of correlations between the frequency of use of an ICT and its perceived value in academic or social settings. The ICTs explored were based on the results of frequency and perceived value as presented above, in so far as those that displayed a positive response where used to explore the possibility of correlations. The ICTs that were investigated further were voice and text from a mobile phone, email and synchronous Internet text chat. It is not surprising that these three ICTs produced a response rate of 65 per cent or above in all questions. The level of statistical significance also influenced the selection for analysis of the findings and therefore a Chi-square test was conducted on only the relationships that showed a level of significance at 0.05 or 0.01 were explored.

Chi-square (or Pearson's chi-square) is a non-parametric technique used to explore relationships or the "goodness of fit" (Cramer & Howitt, 2004) between two categorical variables. Neuman (2000 p.340) states that cross tabulations between at least two variables using chi-square is a valid inferential statistical measure. When interpreting the chi-square results, one needs to look at the percentage of cells that violate the expected value (less than 5). If this value is greater that zero per cent, then the assumptions of the chi-square test are violated, and therefore confidence is reduced in the chi distribution. As a result the test can only be interpreted as an indication rather than statistically conclusive (Neuman, 2000). After conducting the chi-square technique on the listed variables, it was found that all results had some cells that had an expected count greater than five, therefore the results can only be used as an indication rather than statistically conclusive. Regardless, the results do have some educational relevance and therefore add to fulfilling the research aims.

The following relationships met the criteria in both an academic and social setting:

- frequency of use * value of mobile voice/text using a mobile phone,
- frequency of use * value of email,
- frequency of use * value of synchronous Internet text chat.

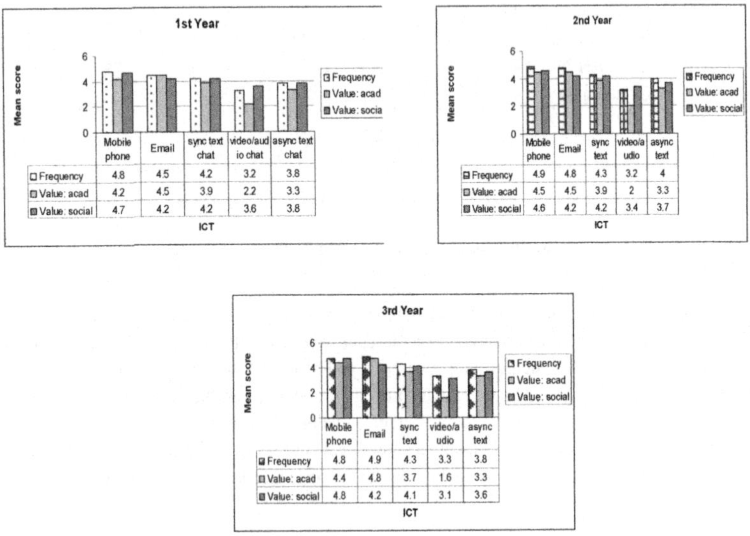

Figure 3. Frequency and perceived value of ICTs

To further explore the relationship between the above variables, mean scores were calculated on each of the above variables for each year level. These results are presented in **Error! Reference source not found.**.

Of a possible maximum mean of 5.0, the use of mobile phones, email and synchronous Internet text chat stand out as the most prominent technologies and of the greatest value in both academic and social settings. Asynchronous Internet text chat, though not used as frequently as email, mobile phones or synchronous Internet text chat, appears to be perceived as valuable in both contexts. It can be seen that often an ICT has a higher social value than academic value, and that there is a high correlation of transfer of value in the ICTs for academic and social context apart from when using video/audio chat. The respondents indicted that they use video/audio chat frequently and value it in a social content, but rated its value as low in an academic context. It could be argued that this indicates that the students have not yet learnt the flexibility of the technology; an area that should be addressed during their undergraduate studies so as to better prepare them for the workforce.

The results indicate clearly that an ICT that is used frequently is also perceived as valuable to the setting in which it is used. There is little differentiation between the results for voice/text using a mobile phone, email and synchronous Internet text chat.

Typically the respondents who use mobile phones for voice and text messaging, and email a number of times every day, perceive their value as high in assisting with academic and social interactions. What is surprising is the relatively high percentage of respondents who frequently use and value synchronous Internet text chat in academic settings. This leads the researcher to believe that students are familiar with some of the newer ICTs, and value and use the technologies for group work.

Conclusion

The trend that is evident in the results is that the less frequently used ICTs are perceived to be lower in value in either academic or social settings, with video/audio chat ranking last and mobile voice/text ranking first. What is interesting to note is the overall commonality in ranking between the three years; that is mobile voice/text, email, synchronous text chat, asynchronous text chat then video chat. I also it appears that third year students do not use nor value (overall) the selected ICTs anymore than the first year students. This could be interpreted as over the duration of their program, the students do not see any additional value nor do they increase their frequency in use of the selected ICTs. Educationally this is of concern, as the ubiquitous use of ICTs is fundamental to the skills and attributes required of beginning IS graduates to be productive members of the IS profession, and effective members of collaborative IS teams (Lynch, 2004). This finding further supports the need to educate these students in the use and value of ICTs in their IT-rich lives.

Emerging from the results there is evidence that the students see and use the technologies according to two categories, with one technology bridging the two:

Category 1 (high use and high value) – voice/text chat using mobile phones, and email,
bridging synchronous Internet text chat,

Category *2* (low use and low value) - synchronous Internet video/audio chat, asynchronous Internet text chat.

The ICTs that fall into the first category are used frequently and are highly valued in both academic and social group settings. The respondents overwhelmingly perceived that the social value of synchronous Internet text chat is just as good as using a mobile phone for voice/text chat, and the value of email for academic group work is equal to the value of using a mobile phone for voice/text chat. These three ICTs are accepted as valuable communication technologies regardless of context.

The second group of ICTs is more diversified in the respondents' frequency of using them and their perceived value. The technologies underpinning synchronous Internet video/audio chat and asynchronous Internet text chat are still relatively new and their use is not yet a part of everyday life. However, with the advancement in technology, and in particular, mobile technologies, there is a likelihood that these ICTs will become aligned in use and value with the ICTs listed in group one.

Together with the advancement of multimedia technology, its convergence with telephony and advancements in Internet video and audio chat, there is a probability that the merger of these technologies will supersede any single technology on its own. This will be further intensified through the lower costs of the devices and services that accommodate the need to faster, better, smarter ways of collaborating on projects.

However, without a concerted effort in the development and implementation of curriculum, and in particular IS curriculum, that has a focus on developing students' ubiquitous use of ICTs in their work and social contexts, in general they will not develop the required skills and attributes informally (or through osmosis). Further research needs to be conducted to confirm the results of the study, and to extend it to include a study of both curriculum and IT students from more diverse and global locations.

Acknowledgements

The author would like to thank Professor Dick Gunstone and Associate Professor Julie Fisher (Monash University) for their valued assistance during this project.

References

Bijker, W. & Law, J. (1997). *Shaping technology/building society*. Cambridge, Massachusetts: MIT Press.

Casey, C. (1999). The changing contexts of work. In D. B. J. Garrick, *Understanding learning at work*. Routledge, London

Castells, M. (2001). *The Internet galaxy: Reflections on the Internet, business, and society*. Norfolk: Oxford University Press.

Cramer, D. & Howitt, D. (2004). *The SAGE dictionary of statistics*. London: SAGE Publications.

Furst, S., Blackburn, R. & Rosen, B. (1999). Virtual team effectiveness: A proposed research agenda. *Information Systems Journal, Special issue on virtual teamworking, 9* (4), 249-270.

Gould, D. (1998). *Virtual organization: Virtual teams*, Retrieved May 2001 from http://www.seanet.com/~daveg/vrteams.htm

Lipnack, J. & Stamps, J. (2000). *Virtual teams: People working across boundaries with technology*. New York: John Wiley & Sons.

Lurey, S. & Raisinghani, M. (2000). *An empirical study of best practices in virtual teams*, Retrieved May 2003 from http://citm.utdallas.edu/Publications/Whitepapers/BestPractices.html

Lynch, K. (2004), Collaborative work skills for beginning IS professionals. In Iss*ues in Informing Science and Information Technology, 1*, 417-429. Available at http://articles.iisit.org/066lynch.pdf

Mankin, D., Cohen, S. & Bikson, T. (1996). *Teams and technology: Fulfilling the promise of the new organisation*. Boston: Harvard Business School Press.

Neuman, W. L. (2000). *Social research methods: Qualitative and quantitative approaches*. Boston: Allyn & Bacon.

Rice, J. & Mitchell-Ketzes, S. (2002). Success stories from new workplace. Retrieved May 2003 from http://www.facilitiesnet.com/bom/Aug02/Aug02facility.shtml

Schrage, M. (1990). *Shared minds: The new technologies of collaboration*. New York; Random House.

Toffler, A. (1980) *The third wave: A classic study of tomorrow*. Bantam Books

Wajcman, J. (2004). *Technofeminism*. Cambridge, UK: Polity Press.

Biography

Dr Kathy Lynch is a senior lecturer in the Faculty of Information Technology at Monash University,Australia. Her current research interests encompass collaborative work, enabling and emerging technologies, HCI, usability and IS/ICT education. She has a Doctor of Philosophy (Education), and numerous other qualifications in the both the disciplines of IT and Education.

(http://www.sims.monash.edu.au/staff/klynch/)

Evolution of the Philosophy of Investments in IT Projects

Ram B. Misra
Montclair State University, Montclair, NJ, USA

misrar@mail.montclair.edu

Abstract

This paper discusses the changes in Information Technology (IT) investment philosophy of both private and public sector companies. Based on the available published material in scholarly journals and magazines, our analysis is focused on the USA and the UK. The paper analyzes the past and current behaviors of business investments in technology and the factors that have prompted companies to change their IT investment patterns. The paper discusses how the success of IT can not be measured with traditional methods of calculating return on investments (ROI) but must be evaluated in other ways. It highlights specific points proving that IT has slowly evolved over the years from an uncontrollable technological change to a strategic management tool that creates and increases competitiveness. In this strategic role, investment in IT has become a tool of meeting business objectives for the companies.

Keywords: IT Investments, ROI, Information Technology, Failed IT Projects

Introduction

For the past decade, economists and information technology specialists have argued back and forth whether IT investments have generated return on investments and increased national output of goods and services. Businesses, fueled by high expectations on productivity growth generated by IT investments, heavily invested into computing power between the mid 1980s and the 1990s. It was generally accepted that IT spending would prove to be a valuable investments and would pay for itself in the long run. Growth and high return on investment were expected. A few years later, managers and business leaders were beginning to question the gains in productivity, which at best seemed to be in a state of status quo (Brynjolfsson, 1993). Though a few success stories were recorded and praised, for most, information technology became a source of frustration and disillusion. The notion of the productivity paradox emerged. Companies, learning from the wasted billions in questionable IT investments, had to reinvent the way they did business to integrate their IT investments into their strategic planning. Today IT resources are specialized, tailored and customized to the needs of the company, and optimized to maximize companies' efficiency and output level. This transition has been slow, lengthy, and painfully costly.

This paper presents an analysis of the evolution of the philosophy of investments in IT projects - by both pubic as well as private sector companies. The paper discusses the empirical evidence – both at macro and micro levels - that led to questioning of the contribution of IT investments to productivity gains and other measurable returns such as ROI (return on investment), an analysis of three major examples of high profile failed IT projects, and four periods of evolution of IT investments starting from the time of euphoria when no one questioned IT investments to the current (fourth) period of the total (IT) integration management.

Questioning the Return on IT Investments

In recent years computers have revolutionized the way companies do business with customers and other businesses; yet business data and other productivity statistics do not reflect any added growth. To solve this mystery, academic economists and scholars began collecting macro-economic data.

The focus of the research mainly concerned many factors and labor productivity statistics. Economists discovered that both indices and the GDP dropped after 1973 when the first main-frame was introduced in the business world (Hubbard, 2003). In the late 1990s, the threatening Y2K bug forced companies to invest even more in IT resources to prevent a massive loss of data that many IT specialists predicted. Nothing happened and companies had more technology than needed and productivity growth was not seen.

Many have written books and articles explaining this paradox. A great deal of time was also spent on detailing how to measure productivity. Economists just could not assess whether technology contributed to growth or negatively affected it. Productivity and GDP were still growing but at a much slower pace. Many argued that most analysts measured macro data when computer contribution can only be noticed on a micro level (Devaraj & Kohli, 2002). Finally, the argued theories of the old economy and the new economy did not answer the problem or explain the paradox.

Researchers came to the conclusion that this paradox exists due to seven factors that mask proper measurements and analysis. These factors are: (1) IT investments only represent a small share of GDP. (2) Computers have a rapid rate of depreciation and obsolescence. (3) Old measurements do not apply in the new economy. (4) Poor analogy exists between the service sector (where productivity slowed down the most) and its heavy reliance on computers. (5) Computers have provided many intangible benefits. (6) A time lag exists between technology arrival and productivity benefits. (7) Web surfing, instant messaging and other nonproductive computer related activities have offset gains (Misra, 2003).

The attention given to measurements and assessments of IT contributions to the economy has changed the attitude towards investments in IT related projects. In the beginning, IT expenditures were not subjected to major scrutiny. In the nineties, the bullish market pushed companies and businesses into a spending euphoria stage and expansion phase. IT spending was expensive, but due to the state of growth of the economy between mid-eighties and late nineties, few analysts, financial advisors and investors questioned the estimated payoffs of the IT investments. Today, however, growth has been succeeded by need to survive, and companies' strategic goals, choices and overall expenditures are under constant scrutiny from investors, shareholders and regulatory institutions. Time calls for conservation, savings and management to achieve economic profit. In order to remain solvent companies have had to optimize all factors of production and resource allocation. Most companies have adopted the "do more with less" policy and many have restructured, laying-off employees and changing or adjusting their business strategies and goals. Most companies strived to yield positive earnings in the past couple of years. Many industries such as the airline industry or the general retail industry have consolidated, strengthened and developed new strategic alliances to achieve such goals; yet only few have succeeded. The bearish economy increased the level of competition in a given industry, forcing each business to focus on increasing (at least holding) its market share rather than its size. New strategies have developed to establish, strengthen and augment a company's competitive advantage. This has resulted into a greater coupling of IT strategy with the business strategy.

At the micro level, a long history of failed IT projects world wide (Bupa, 2005; Chua & Lam, 2005; Pearce, 2003) has cast a further shadow on the return of these projects in the face of completing these projects well above the original estimated costs.

Research Method

We conducted initial search in two popular online databases, ProQuest (ABI/INFORM) and Emerald, using the search terms "Failed IT Projects" The ProQuest search yielded 54 results and the Emerald search yielded 1052 results. A closure examination revealed a few noteworthy papers. One scholarly paper (Ewusi-Mensah, 1997) on failed IT projects discussed what could have been done to avoid the failure and what some of the critical issues were. The two others were related to the related fields such as Knowledge Management (Chua & Lam, 2002) and Project Management (Aiyer, Rajkumar, and Havelka, 2005); hence, had a discipline specific angle to the analyses. Another paper (Duggal, 2002) discussed the global issues with technology management. Then, we expanded our search to trade magazines (CIO in particular) and government publications. We found all three cases discussed in the next section in these publications. Also we found a wealth of information on the UK government websites regarding failed public sector projects.

Multi-Case Analysis of Failed IT Projects

In order to understand the conditions that created changes in the attitude towards IT investment decision making, one needs to understand the causes of IT projects failures. We will discuss three prominent failed IT projects pointing out the key factors potentially responsible for their failure.

The Case of Medicare Processing System in the Health Care Financing Administration

"Medicare Transactions: A $50 Million Lesson in Project Management," (Friel, 2000) reported the case of the Health Care Financing Administration (HCFA) which spent six years, from 1991 to1997, developing a new IT system. This system was supposed to combine 14 Medicare systems located at 60 different sites and operated by more than 70 contractors. Each system was developed in different computing languages, different computing platforms and by different service providers between the 1960s and 1980s. After several years of debate, the agency concluded the systems were becoming unmanageable and decided to build one large, integrated system, which would handle all the agency's systems and programs. The new system was expected to generate huge cost savings over time once the system was implemented 5 years down the road. Although the inspector general of the HCFA warned the administration to develop a clearer strategy for MTS (Medicare Transaction System) before jumping into building a system, the administration went ahead and granted the development of the new system to GTE Government Services. GTE developed a strategy to link these systems together; however, it became rapidly evident that HCFA was not clear on the needs and wants of the new system. In addition, GTE was not given enough information about Medicare complex processing. In 1994 and 1995 HCFA ignored the recommendations of the inspector general who warned of the danger of not giving GTE enough information. In 1996, due to considerable over-budget spending, Congress scheduled a hearing. HCFA ordered GTE to stop working on the project. The General Accounting Office estimated that HCFA spent $80 million on project and the projected costs ballooned from $151 million to $1 billion. Furthermore, GTE estimated the project completion date not to be before the year 2000. In August of 1997, HCFA canceled the contract with GTE, and the MTS project was scrapped. During the congressional hearing, the General Accounting Office attributed the failure of the project to HCFA's lack of planning, strategic management, performance measurement and cost benefit analysis which would have allowed the administration to continually track the progress of GTE. HCFA was incapable of keeping track of its spending on the project while maintaining that it only spent $50 million of the project.

The Case of Russ Berrie and Company

Russ Berrie & Company, the New Jersey based teddy bear manufacturer, also suffered from failed IT implementation (Songini, 2003). In 1999, the bear maker contracted SAP AG to develop and implement a system that would migrate old applications such as homegrown distribution, financial and customer service systems toward Y2K compliant packaged ERP applications. The implementation of the project failed. As a consequence, the company was forced to "resurrect its aging Digital Equipment Corp system." and had to ensure that it was Y2K compliant. This process greatly strained both the IT department and the business units. The ordeal lasted three years and the total estimated cost of the failed project was $10.3 million. This represented quite an investment for a company that had annual revenues averaging only $230 million. In 2002 the company needed a working ERP and had to allocate new funds to the development of a new project. Even though it is not clearly stated in the case, one can easily conclude that the lack of strategic planning especially through the implementation phase was one of the key elements leading to failure.

F.B.I.'s $170 Million Virtual Case System

FBI Director Mueller told the Congressional subcommittee hearings on March 8, 2005 that the virtual case system project suffered from technical, management and scheduling problems. If the system were allowed, he said, to be completed, it would have been an outdated system. He did not elaborate on what he meant by this. But, it can be safely assumed that the system would not have worked. He pointed out that the agency underestimated the required level of project/contract management skills and hence failed to assign the right people for the project. The Virtual Case File project was the third and last phase of a $581 million effort to overhaul the embedded computer systems. Representative Frank R. Wolf of Virginia, chair of the subcommittee that oversees F.B.I. financing, has announced that his staff was opening a formal investigation into why the project failed. As the investigation of this case goes on, it will be interesting to find out the level of actual losses. Previously, Office of Inspector General has issued an audit report in February 2005 ("The Federal Bureau of Investigation's," 2005).

United Kingdom's Public Sector 25 IT Projects

Going back to 2000, the failure of many public sector (government) projects led to many investigations ("Getting IT Right for Government," 2000; "Review of Major Government IT Projects," 2000). These projects were either delivered late or not at all, came over budget, did not have the required functionalities. The first report was prepared by IT companies (part of the Computing Services and Software Association (CSSA)) that do business with the UK government. It concluded that a strong connection is needed between the business objectives and IT Projects (something we discuss in the next section). Report also pointed out that the public sector lacks business oriented project managers. What is most frustrating is that a decade of the steps (Cross, 2000) undertaken to better manage IT projects has not yielded satisfactory results. 28% of the UK government IT projects are in the red, 50% are amber and only 22% are green.

Analysis

Unfortunately these scenarios of failed IT projects are not unusual. A study of IT Projects in the 1980's and 1990's (Johnson, 1995) made by the Standish Group of the IT projects in the 1980's and 1990s reported that 31% of new IS projects were canceled before completion, costing a combined bill of $81 billion. In addition, nearly 53% of completed projects were 189% over the estimated budget, costing companies an excess of $59 billion.

Another analysis of failed projects (Ewusi-Mensah, 1997) identified some major and recurrent factors leading to project cancellation and implementation problems. The first was the lack of a clear statement of the new system's purpose and objectives, which changed during the project development, decreasing further the chance of satisfying the need of the organization. The second element leading to project cancellation was an inherent problem rooted deep into the organization of the development team. Three sub-components were identified as part of the problem: (1) lack of structure and organizational purpose in the teams' efforts, (2) lack of leadership in the team and (3) lack of interaction between team members, often due to unclear lines of communication that created misunderstanding about requirements and design decisions, which encouraged individualism instead on team effort and synergy. The third element was the lack of system development methodology, which encompassed phase lifecycle approach and which guided project team members through the development of each stages of the project. The absence of rigorous structures led to a status quo in the development of the project. Loose management and control of the development team was the forth reason for development and implementation failure.

Often managers and executives (Ewusi-Mensah, 1997) did not monitor and assess the progress of the task. Problems were not identified early and only became bigger as the project development advanced. For obvious reasons, the technical knowledge and aptitude of the team should have been a must in the development of such project; yet many teams were under-qualified to develop the projects or the size of the project was too big for their competencies. He further stated that the size of the project was directly related to its level of difficulty. As the difficulty increased, so did the risks undertaken by the development team. Lastly, one of the last reasons for failure was the lack of cooperation and involvement from senior management executives in the development, assessment and progress of the project. Sufficient information and data were not given to the development team, and too often objectives were changed or new options were added considerably increasing the complexity of the projects and the risks of failure.

These failed IT projects quickly became a source of discontent and unease among senior executives and chief information officers. The main problem came from their inabilities to evaluate return on investment effectively as well as their failures to strategically plan and manage such project. The lack of "adult supervision" (Cramm, 2001) of IT projects was responsible for their failure. Not enough attention was given to the payback of the IT investments. Executives adopted the "build it and revenue will come" philosophy for investment in technology. The executives' lack of understanding of the technology and their excessive faith in it gave them the authority to hold information technology above the common investments code of conducts which always required investment justification and measurements of expected returns.

Many books and articles began referring to IT investment as a necessary evil rather than a strategic management tool. Unquestioned faith (Cramm, 2001) on the virtues of technology made managers ignore the well established rules of justifying the investments. However, after billions of dollars were wasted on failed projects and uncontrolled budgets, companies were more than ever dependent on computers and the needed information technology systems were still needed. Disclosures of many failed IT projects led to the questioning by the researchers and practitioners of the approval process used by the executives... Between the 1980s and mid 1990s, non-IT executive were in charge of approving IT projects. Due to subjective performance assessments, lack of relevant ROI measurements and investment management framework, IT became an expense to be minimized instead of an investment to be optimized (Cramm, 2001). Incompatibility, lack of training or incurred mainframe upgrades cascaded into one problem or another. As a consequence $5,000 software expenses lead to a $50,000 or $100,000 decision ("Folio: Plus," 1999). Realizing that IT investments were complicated and could not be treated as one time decisions, senior executives designated CIO's to be responsible for IS developments. "It fell to them to wrestle back into reality the overblown promises and overrun budgets of information technology (Varon, 2003)." Project development became for the first time an incalculable risk. Uncertainty and incalculable risks forced IT development managers to rely less on science to evaluate potential value. It became an art. This new concept was the beginning of the so-called revolution (Andrew & Johnson, 2002) in making IT investment decisions.

(R)Evolution of Investment Decision Making in IT Projects

After reviewing many of the failed projects, we observe that IT investment decisions have evolved through four eras. The first era was the age of euphoria and extreme optimism when not much attention was given to the return. Their success was taken for granted. The first era evolved to the second era in the aftermath of failed projects and disappointments. IT projects in order to get approved had to have detailed ROI justifications; life cycle costs (LCC) and total costs of operations (TCO) had to be accounted for. However, this did not improve the success of IT projects and people started to question the assumptions behind the calculations of ROI, LCC and TCO. The whole notion of justifying IT projects on financial returns came under attack. They did not do justice to the contribution of IT projects since they did not include (IT's) strategic contributions to company's business. The second era evolved to yet another era - the third era. The decision matrix of IT investments included, in addition to the quantitative measures, an assessment of the impact on strategic factors (GAO, 2000). The IT industry is still in this era even though there are signs to expand the scope of the era three decision matrix. We are calling it era four – the era of total integrated (IT) Impact. "It involves linking and influencing every segment of a firm's supply, production, distribution and service chains into a coherent whole using information technology," (Rapp, 2002). We are going to expand on each of these eras next.

This revolution of information strategy management has been a long and very costly process. Billions of dollars have been wasted and more than a decade passed before companies realized that they could not sustain such frivolous spending and not rely on the subjective art of senior executives' evaluation system to assess the added value of their investments. IT investment became a necessary evil. Due to their high development failure rate, companies faced serious doubt concerning the actual and real value of such projects.

The lack of success and the billions spent on IT development raised many questions. Many tried to understand this phenomenon however asked the wrong questions: Why doesn't this work? What's the problem? How can we fix it? Most of these questions were reactive questions and lacked scope and perspective. The projects were poorly designed and structured and as consequence, implementation could not be executed or completed. It became apparent that strategic planning and strict project management were necessary to get control of these exuberant spending over the project life cycles. Projects needed to become highly structured. First hand managers had to strictly review and closely supervise goals, scope, target and logic behind the strategy. Companies came to the conclusion that there was no alternative to IT and was necessary for the company to remain competitive. Now companies desperately tried to reduce failure rates of IT projects, overall costs, increase viability and gain (or sustain) competitive advantage through information technology.

The primary driving force that resulted in revolutionizing IT investment decisions came from analyzing the managers' past wrong doings. The Waterfall effect (Andrews & Johnson, 2002, pp. 19, 31-35, 177) comprised of five "unrealistic assumptions" which managers tend to make during the development of an IT project. The first assumption was the expectations that the business environment would remain constant during the project. In the new information era, such conditions were unrealistic. The Internet has opened the doors to instant communication and access to desired information, considerably reducing the bounded rationality effect. As a consequence the business environment has constantly changed and evolved. Such assumption could have been made prior to the late 80s but not after that. Many managers still kept the same mentalities and failed to realize this constant evolution. The second assumption was that end users could exactly define in advance what they needed. Project failures and over budgeting cases have one common trend: users always want more. The third managerial assumption was that intricate problems could be entirely resolved on the first attempt. According to these authors, "classic methodologies assume a linear process where the problem is defined, a plan is created, the solution is implemented and victory is declared." Complex problems require much more than a linear solving process and are much more demanding on the knowledgeable people and resources. An answer might not be found right away or not at all depending on the complexity of the problem. The fourth assumption implied that managers expected requirements to be known and defined before the software could be selected. Due to assumptions one and two, these requirements often changed and one specific type of software bundle could not be defined. Managers often choose one specific package and had to modify it due to the changing environment and customers' needs. The switching costs were tremendous. The fifth and final assumption was that changes would be universally and happily accepted in the company. Once again experience and common sense should have dictated otherwise.

Over the past two decades, managers have had tremendous trouble linking IT projects to positive financial growth. Typical return on investment measurements does not seem to apply to IT projects. Return on investment has been in center of the economic debate that raged between economists and analysts during the 1980s and 1990s. Measurements along with the various factors affecting those measurements were scrutinized and criticized; yet no one gave tangible reasons why IT benefits could not be aggregately measured. IT returns (Solovy & Chaiken, 2003) could be of three different types. The first type is financial, which either directly increases revenue or reduces overall cost. Operation returns are the second type of returns. Processes are done more efficiently, various errors are eliminated and the company's overall daily operations are improved. The third type is structural. It resembles the operation type. It is slightly different because it involves improvement of customer care and services. These different types of returns render ROI method obsolete and require managers to re-evaluate what they expect from a project.

For many years the classical ROI calculations have limited the field of visions of managers. Specifically, two major shortcomings presented significant concerns from tactical and strategic points of view. ROI calculations (Northrop, 2003) are based on "assumptions of possible project revenues and are often baseless, inflated or inaccurate," and "the ability to accurately predict the investment component is highly questionable." Due to these shortcomings, a transformation of ROI analysis was required. ROI are based on assumptions that often are not true. These assumptions were often based on an assumption of a static business environment. Furthermore, ROI analysis has proved to be of little use due to the failure and cost overruns in developing IT projects in the 1990s.

These traditional assumptions, which are the basis of ROI, cannot be applied to IT project development due to the simple fact that IT investment creates and improve many intangible benefits that cannot be measured. Mindsets are however in general difficult to change. Today, some managers still believe that if a strategy cannot show a positive return within the first three years, it is a failure. IT has constantly challenged these managerial perceptions and expectations of various projects and development, therefore many managers have been forced to change their classical project evaluation methods.

We contend that there was no "IT revolution", as claimed by some (Guidoni, 1993). A revolution is a spontaneous and sudden change in behavior, patterns or regime. Changes in IT project management were slow, costly and have not been completely achieved. Undeniably, the environment and mentalities have changed and so have expectations of IT returns and use. However, IT project development processes and financial return measurements have not been revolutionized they have evolved and transformed. Evolution is a slow and rigorous process constituted of trials and errors. It comes after chaos and brings stability. Stability is achieved due to drastic control measures. The survival of the fittest has been evolution's main control tool for billion of years. From a business viewpoint, IT investments and IT project development were chaotic between the mid 1980s and the 1990s. As previously mentioned, billions of dollars were wasted on failed projects and over budgeting. The explosion of the technology bubble and the following world wide recession brought rigorous control on project developments.

The evolution of IT investments has left many business managers discontented and burned because it has come at great financial costs. After the billions spent, no one can deny that IT investment has generally brought little tangible returns. At this point one may wonder the use of IT investments is and why one would spend more IT development. These questions are legitimate and many managers may wonder the same; yet it is very difficult to conceive the business world without technology and information technology. It is clear that information technology investments brought new elements; however, it is hard to pin point exactly what and measure it. One may look at the evolution of the business environment in the past two decades and may conclude that most of the IT contributions to the business environment are intangible elements.

A few examples are Internet banking, supply chain management, the music industry and information accessibility. Undeniably, technology has become a greater part of our lives over the years. IT investments have not brought financial returns but have certainly brought value, growth, knowledge and increased customer care in more than one way. These intangible elements are extremely important in today's economy and can create sustainable competitive advantage over competitors. It is very difficult to evaluate the impact and benefit of IT investments on Wal-Mart's supply chain; yet it is undeniable that the company has managed to save billions in inventory costs and logistics. These savings have been passed on to customers who enjoy the company's everyday low price strategy. Such IT investments create distinct and sustainable competitive advantage for Wal-Mart. K-mart back in the late 1990's could not compete on such low margin and had to declare bankruptcy.

The business management strategy called Balanced Score Card (Kaplan & Norton, 1996) could help answer these questions. This business strategy favors growth and emphasizes business improvement through development of intangible assets. The balance score card helps company develop competitive advantage and create real customer value. It "provides executives with a comprehensive framework that can translate a company's vision and strategy into a coherent and linked set of performance measures...used to articulate the strategy of the business, to communicate the strategy of the business and to help align individual, organizational and cross departmental initiatives to achieve a common goal." Over the years, companies' focuses changed from revenue growth and beating the street's analysis to meeting and exceeding customers' expectations through learning, internal and customer strategic goals. These goals are then linked to financial elements to ensure the viability of such initiatives.

Only a handful of companies focused on future value and customers' needs during the 80's and 90's. The trend was one of revenue growth and beating analysts' forecasts to increase shareholder's equity. Today revenue and economic profits are difficult to achieve, and companies must find different ways of growing. Companies have turned there attention toward intangible assets. "Branding, knowledge, customers and innovation are nearly impossible to numerically quantify, yet have a very significant impact on an organization's success and growth" (Northrop, 2003). Information technology has developed and increased many of these areas for example online banking or logistics and many others. Managers are beginning to understand this concept and are now developing new strategy to integrate IT into increasing customer value and customer service. For instance, Wendy's recently announced that it would allow customers to use credit card to purchase hamburgers and fries. Customers will be allowed to use technology to simplify their transactions for their convenience. Wendy's strategy is to attract new customers and retain a greater number to ultimately increase market share and overall revenue.

Companies have taken proactive measures to link IT projects and business strategies. To fulfill this purpose, IT steering committees have been formed in many companies and have become widespread in the business world. These committees, while providing CEOs with information about IT usefulness, contribution and linkage to the company, ensure that "CEOs agree that IT has strategic importance to their company" (Varon, 2003). These committees help decision makers to analyze more relevant data and simplify and clarify the decision making process. Overall, they help IT organization to concentrate on better execution of strategies.

Steering committees are not the only way CIOs and top managers can reach better decisions when it comes to IT investments and how to use IT to enhance strategies. In the mid 1980s, Congress was growing wary of the lack numerical proof of economical growth due to IT involvement. Many were concerned of the IT paradox. Considerable amount of government investment were spent on IT projects; yet no empirical data proved the investment to be worthwhile. Congress passed the Information Technology Management Reform Act on February 10, 1996. It is also know as the Chief Information Officers Act. It was enacted to reduce IT projects financial waste and "provide CIOs with several identified set of realistic and attainable actions to be taken to show American Tax Payers that IT investment are having a clear positive impact on outcomes."

In the recent years, the notion of Total Integrated (IT) Impact has emerged. "It involves linking and influencing every segment of a firm's supply, production, distribution and service chains into a coherent whole using information technology," (Rapp, 2002). Such integration allows for cost cutting as well as better designed and more efficient delivery of products and increased customer satisfaction. It affects a firm's environment through increase relationship between its suppliers and customer care after sale and provides a tool to tie both sides closer to the firm's strategies to create new strategic partnership. Competitive advantage is gained through that process due to increased shared information between suppliers and the firm, reducing inventory cost. Customers' needs and expectations can be assessed faster and the company can adapt quicker and more efficiently its products to the tastes of consumers.

Conclusion

In conclusion, this paper has shown that information technology investment decisions have evolved over the past twenty years. Some called it an IT revolution; however, we disagree because it delivered results only three decades after its development. Through various examples we have shown that the transition was not only extremely costly to companies but also very slow and lengthy. Revolutions are spontaneous and involve radical changes. Gradual change over several decades cannot be revolutions. It is clear that much can still be done to further improve its effectiveness and efficient use throughout an organization to further improve every aspect of the current business operations of companies. Return on investment will undoubtedly be difficult to evaluate and analyzed because IT mostly benefits companies' intangible assets such as customers service or brand recognition. Information technology investment should get the same level of scrutiny like any other financial investment. Its scope and impact should be well diversified. Managers should however not expect a fifteen percent return on investment. They should focus their attention instead on increasing market share, brand recognition, customer satisfaction and care as well as overall length reduction of their supply chains and its management.

References

Aiyer, J., Rajkumar, T. M. & Havelka. D. (2005). A staged framework for the recovery and rehabilitation of troubled IS projects. *Project Management Journal, 36*(4), 32-43.

Andrews, D.H. & Johnson K.R. (2002). *Revolutionizing IT: The art of using information technology effectively*. John Wiley & Sons.

Brynjolfsson, E. (1993). The productivity paradox of information technology: Review and assessment. *Communications of the ACM, 36*(12), 67-77.

Bupa, S. H. (2005). Why do so many major IT projects fail? *Computer Fraud & Security*, 15-17.

Chua, A. & Lam W. (2005). Why KM projects fail: A multi-case analysis. *Journal of Knowledge Management, 9*(3), 6-17.

Cramm, S. M. (2001). IT project planning: Adult supervision required. *CIO, 14*(9), 74 – 76.

Cross, M. (2005). Public sector IT failures. *Prospect, 15*, October.

Devaraj, S. & Kohli R. (2002). *The IT payoff: Measuring the business value of information technology investments*. New York: Prentice Hall.

Duggal, S. M. (2002). Global information technology management. *Proceedings of Informing Science 2002 Conference*. Retrieved from http://proceedings.informingscience.org/IS2002Proceedings/papers/Duggal19Globa.pdf

Ewusi-Mensah, Kweku (1997). Critical issues in abandoned information systems developments projects, *Communications of the ACM, 40*(9), 75.

Folio: Plus (1999, July 15). *Folio: The Magazine for Magazine Management, 28*(9), 9.

Friel, B. (2000, April). Medicare transactions: A $50 million lesson in project management. *Government Executive, 32*(4), 68-70.

GAO/AIMD-10.1.23 (2000, May). Information technology investment management. Retrieved from http://www.gao.gov/special.pubs/ai10123.pdf

Getting IT right for government: A review of public sector IT projects (2000 June). Report available on http://www.intellectuk.org/

Guidoni, G (1993). A joyless recovery. *Canadian Packaging, 56*(11), 5.

Hubbard, G. (2003, February 4). Prepared testimony of Glenn Hubbard chairman, council of economic advisers before the senate budget committee. *Federal News Service 1.*

Information Technology Management Reform Act. (1996). *Congressional Records*, February 10, 1996

Ives, M. (2005). Identifying the contextual elements of project management within organizations and their impact on project success. *Project Management Journal, 36*(1), 37-50.

Johnson, J. (1995). CHAOS: The dollar drain of IT project failures. *Application Development Trends*, January.

Kaplan, R. S. & Norton, D. P. (1996, Fall). Linking the balanced scorecard to strategy. *California Management Review, 39*. 1.

Misra, R. (2003). The productivity paradox and the value of IT investments. *Proceedings of Global Information Technology Management (GITM) 2003.*

Northrop R. (2003, June 17). The hidden cost of ROI. *E-Business Developers*, 46.

Pearce, S. (2003). Government IT projects post report 200 July 2003. Available on http://www.parliament.uk/post/

Rapp, W. V. (2002). *Information technology strategies: How leading firms use IT to gain an advantage.* New York: Oxford University Press.

Review of Major Government IT Projects; Successful IT: Modernizing Government in Action. (2000 April). A UK Public Accounts Committee. Available on http://www.ogc.gov.uk/

Solovy, A. & Chaiken B. (2003, Spring). ROI under scrutiny: The radical redefinition of a core concept/reply. *Frontiers of Health Services Management, 19*(3), 17-28.

Songini, M. L. (2003, August). Teddy bear maker prepares for second attempt at ERP rollout. *Computerworld, 36*(6), 16.

The Federal Bureau of Investigation's management of the trilogy information technology modernization project. (2005). *Audit Report No. 05-0, Office of Inspector General*, February 2005.

Varon, E. (2003, April 1). Organize an IT steering group: How a cross-functional steering committee can make better spending decisions. *CIO, 16*(12), 1.

Biography

Ram B. Misra is an associate professor of Management and Information Systems in the School of Business, Montclair State University. Prior to joining Montclair in 2002, Ram spent over 20 years in telecom industry that spanned Bell Labs, and Bell Communications Research. Ram got his Ph.D. from Texas A&M University, and a bachelor from Indian Institute of Technology Kanpur. He also has an executive MBA from the Columbia School of Business, New York. Ram's research interests include valuation of IT investments, outsourcing, and systems analysis.

The page left blank intentionally.

Video Learning Object Application System: Beyond the Static Reusability

Xiangming Mu and Alex Koohang
University of Wisconsin – Milwaukee
Milwaukee, WI, USA

mux@uwm.edu koohang@uwm.edu

Abstract

This paper presents an advanced an innovative Video Learning Object (VLO) application model for optimal dynamic VLO reusability. The model contains three essential elements – the metadata, the links, and a learning center. Each element of VLO application system is configured for a specific assignment. The model allows for dynamic reconfigurability of VLO metadata based on usage profile. This leads into easy adaptation of VLOs to various contexts thus attaining optimum reusability. Two multimedia application cases are presented that further demonstrate the application of the proposed model and its use for optimal dynamic reusability of VLOs. Conclusion and recommendation for future development of VLO application systems are made. `

Keywords: Video learning objects, video learning object application system, reusability, reconfigurability, dynamic reusability

Introduction

Learning objects are increasingly becoming popular in e-learning settings. A learning object is an independent piece of instruction that can be reused in various instructional contexts.

Wiley (2000) defines learning object as "any digital resource that can be reused to support learning. This definition includes anything that can be delivered across the network on demand, be it large or small. Examples of smaller reusable digital resources include digital images or photos, live data feeds (like stock tickers), live or prerecorded video or audio snippets, small bits of text, animations, and smaller web-delivered applications, like a Java calculator. Examples of larger reusable digital resources include entire web pages that combine text, images and other media or applications to deliver complete experiences, such as a complete instructional event."

The Learning Technology Standards Committee (LTSC LOM, 2002) defines learning objects as "any entity, digital or non-digital, which can be used, re-used or referenced during technology supported learning. Examples of technology supported learning include computer-based training systems, interactive learning environments, intelligent computer-aided instruction systems, distance learning systems, and collaborative learning environments. Examples of Learning Objects include multimedia content, instructional content, learning objectives, instructional software and software tools, and persons, organizations, or events referenced during technology supported learning."

Harman and Koohang (2005, p. 68) concluded that "a learning object is not merely a chunk of information packaged to be used in instructional settings. A learning object, therefore, can include anything that has pedagogical value - digital or non-digital such as a case study, a film, a simulation, an audio, a video, an animation, a graphic image, a map, a book, or a discussion board so long as the object can be contextualized by individual learners. The learner must be able to make meaningful connections between the learning object and his/her experiences or knowledge he/she previously mastered."

Although all the above definitions include the term *video* as a learning object; Mu (2005) specifically refers to video object as a Video Learning Object with unique features such as hierarchical structure and video surrogates.

Mu (2005) advanced a VLO model of *three-tier information infrastructure* that substituted the traditional two-tier VLO structure, i.e., user interface tier and video data tier. The new model overcame the limitations of the two-tier structure, mainly the lack of standards essential for interoperability and the direct link between video metadata and the video application which limits the reusability of VLO. The three-tier information infrastructure contained *video metadata tier, video learning object tier, and video application tier.*

Today, VLOs are increasingly being used in distance education/e-learning programs. The use of VLOs is mainly for workshops, training, and education in the industry, business, government, healthcare, K-12, and post secondary educational settings. Examples of entities providing these videos for workshops, training, and education are Microsoft Multi University Research Laboratory which serves as a digital repository for universities' lectures and seminars (http://murl.microsoft.com/default.asp , Stanford Center for Professional Development (SCPD) program at Stanford University (http://scpd.stanford.edu) which provides distance education using digital videos recorded from live classes, MIT Open Courseware which is a free and open educational resource for faculty, students, and self-learners (http://ocw.mit.edu/index.html), and eduCommons, a project of the Center for Open and Sustainable Learning, is a free and open Content Management System used for Open Courseware creation and use (http://cosl.usu.edu/cosl/projects/eduCommons) among others.

Most of today's current VLO application systems are still based on the similar organization and representation strategies developed for adopting static video metadata. These systems lack suitable reusability. The static nature of the VLO's reusability makes it difficult for optimal reuse in various contexts. Even though initial efforts have been taken towards the integration of user profile and usage information (Houten, Setten, & Enschede, 2000), very little research has been done to develop innovative video organization models that overcome the limitations of current VLO application retrieval systems.

The purpose of this paper is to present an advanced model that contains essential elements, i.e., learning center, metadata, and links, leading to optimal VLO reusability. Compared to previous three-tier reusable learning object model based on metadata (Mu 2005), the new model goes beyond the static reusability. It is a dynamic model that allows for VLO's reconfigurability. Each element of VLO application system is configured to accomplish a particular task. These elements can then be reconfigured based on usage profile (e.g., who the users are, how they are using the VLOs, what the frequent links between components are, etc.) to adapt VLOs to various contexts (e.g., distance learning, video conference, collaborative project, or medical video analysis) thus achieving optimal dynamic reusability.

The paper is organized in a manner consistent with its purpose. The introductory remarks define the term learning object and the use of video as a learning object. The focus is then shifted in defining VLO and their use in distance education settings. Next, the discussion focuses upon presenting the proposed VLO Model. This presentation follows by presenting two short cases that further illustrate the application of the proposed model. Conclusions and recommendations round out the paper.

The Video Learning Object Retrieval Model

The Video Learning Object (VLO) retrieval model is composed of three components: 1) the metadata, 2) the links, and 3) a learning center (see Figure 1).

The VLO metadata is an integration of both the concept-based (textual) and content-based (audiovisual) video metadata, including: a) video clips, b) video structure, c) video textual metadata, d) video visual metadata, and e) video audio metadata.

The VLO links refer to the internal VLO links (i.e., connections among various video components within the VLO) and external VLO links (i.e., connections between the VLO and other related VLOs.)

The VLO learning center is the mechanism enabling the VLO to dynamically update its VLO links and interface for applications that are based on the usage profile. In other words, a VLO can learn from the historical applications and changes of its content and structure accordingly.

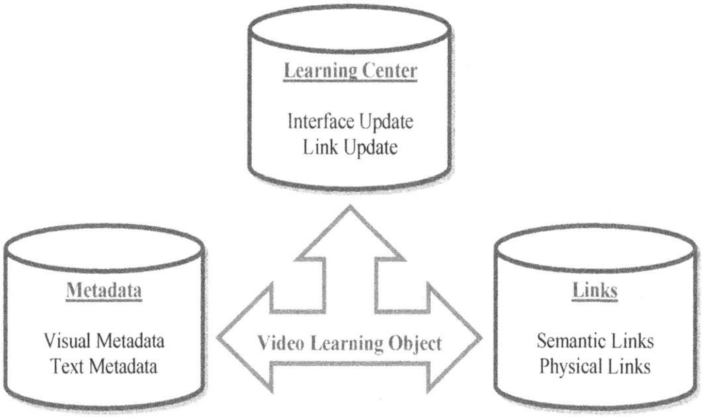

Figure 1: VLO Retrieval System Model

The VLO Metadata

Textual and visual video metadata

The VLO Metadata contains both textual and visual Metadata. Metadata is also called "data about data" – any data that promotes the identification, description, and location of resources. This includes both physical and electronic formats. Metadata is utilized to describe the content, quality, condition, and other appropriate characteristics of the original data. For example, metadata for a book may include title, subject, description, publisher, etc.

The textual metadata for a digital video clip contains all the metadata that a book possesses (i.e., title, description, author, publisher, etc.) with additional metadata unique to the VLO, i.e., the length (how many seconds or minutes), the format (MPEG, QuickTime, etc.) and possibly other features exclusive to VLO. Textual metadata is widely used to facilitate a wide range of video related applications, particularly in video retrieval. Video retrieval is a specific Information Retrieval (IR) process that focuses on finding video documents. One example of the video IR application is the video-based search engines. Textual video metadata are the basis for Google video engine (http://video.google.com) and Yahoo video retrieval search engine (http://video.search.yahoo.com).

Visual metadata refers to any metadata that directly relates to the visual contents of the video. Visual metadata may include: video key frames, video shots, Automatic Sound Reorganization (ASR), Machine Translation (MT), low-level camera movement features (i.e., zoom, tilt, and pan), and high-level semantic features. Naphade et al. (2005) defined a light-scale-concept ontology for the 2005 TRECVID project (http://www-nlpir.nist.gov/projects/tv2005/tv2005.html). The ontology defined seven dimensions: Program Category, Setting/Scene/Site, People, Objects, Activities, Events, and Graphics. A total of 40 individual features included in the ontology that can be utilized in the VLOs.

Visual metadata can be very helpful for content-based video information seeking and retrieval. The following illustrates visual metadata:

- *"A video that can demonstrate the structure and evolution of a category 5 hurricane" (see picture on right)*
- *"Video clips that illustrate how to effectively control the AIDS in Africa for public health training program"*
- *"A Video that demonstrates how to effectively lower cholesterol"*
- *"Video clips that teach about how to use a course management system in a distance learning setting"*

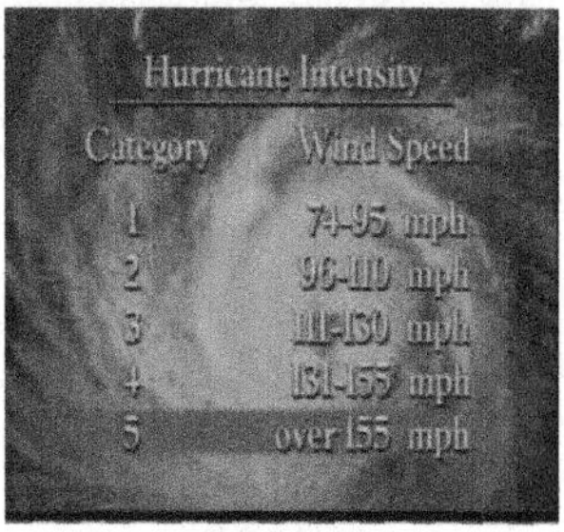

VLO metadata and IR infrastructure

Most of the current digital video retrieval systems are based on a typical two-tier infrastructure, i.e., *digital video archive tier and user interface tier*. The digital archive tier is composed of a collection of indexed digital videos and the associated metadata. The user interface tier provides support to various video related services such as video searching, ranking, and presentation. However, Mu (2005) has demonstrated that a three-tier infrastructure would improve the VLO reusability in video-based applications. For this reason, the proposed model adds a new VLO metadata tier in the traditional IR infrastructure - the VLO metadata tier bridges the traditional video archive tier and user interface tier.

Both textual and visual metadata are incorporated in the VLO metadata tier. XML markup language is utilized to code the hierarchy of the metadata. The model chooses MPEG-7 as the metadata standard. An example portion of XML code adapted from TRECVID 2005 project (http://www-nlpir.nist.gov/projects/tv2005/tv2005.html) is as follows:

```
<?xml version="1.0" encoding="UTF-8"?>

<Mpeg7 xmlns="urn:mpeg:mpeg7:schema:2001"
xmlns:mpeg7="urn:mpeg:mpeg7:schema:2001"
xmlns:xsi="http://www.w3.org/2001/XMLSchema-instance">

<Description xsi:type="ContentEntityType">

<MultimediaContent xsi:type="VideoType">
```

```
&lt;Video id="VLO_TEST_1"&gt;
&lt;MediaLocator&gt;
&lt;MediaUri&gt;20041116_110000_CCTV4_NEWS3_CHN.mpg&lt;/MediaUri&gt;
&lt;/MediaLocator&gt;
&lt;MediaTime&gt;
&lt;MediaTimePoint&gt;T00:00:00:0F30000&lt;/MediaTimePoint&gt;
&lt;MediaDuration&gt;PT00H28M19S29949N30000F&lt;/MediaDuration&gt;
&lt;/MediaTime&gt;
&lt;TemporalDecomposition gap="false" overlap="false"&gt;
&lt;VideoSegment id="shot1_1"&gt;
&lt;MediaTime&gt;
&lt;MediaTimePoint&gt;T00:00:00:0F30000&lt;/MediaTimePoint&gt;
&lt;MediaDuration&gt;PT00H00M03S26116N30000F&lt;/MediaDuration&gt;
&lt;/MediaTime&gt;
...
&lt;/Video&gt;
&lt;/MultimediaContent&gt;
&lt;/Description&gt;
&lt;/Mpeg7&gt;
```

The VLO Links

The VLO links are defined as connections between components within a VLO or connections across different VLOs. The VLO links allow different dimensions of video metadata to be integrated into a video metadata object space. In such a space, each video shot (associated with a metadata object) can be accessed from any specific dimensions: indexed words (from Automatic Speed Recognition - ASR transcript), sample image (key frame), or a specific feature (i.e., A video shot with multiple vehicles. In addition, these dimensions are linked with each other through a mechanism called "Smartlinks" proposed by Mu, Marchionini, and Patte (2003) in video collaboration project (see the example portion of XML code above). Furthermore, Christel, Hauptmann, Wactlar, and Ng (2002) demonstrated the effectiveness of the integration of related video shots retrieved along the temporal and spatial dimensions. The authors coined a word collage, which refers to the combination of text and images derived from multiple video sources, to facilitate video retrieval. The combination is based on user context, e.g.,, an originating query, coupled with automatic processing to refine the potential images.

There are two levels of links: 1) the semantic links and 2) the physical links. The semantic links are defined as connections of two or more VLOs or components with VLOs due to semantic relationships. For example, a video shot about route of the hurricane Katrina (with a map or illustration) in 2005 is linked to another shot that illustrates route of hurricane Andrew in 1992. Semantic similarities are used to decide the semantic links. Similarity between the target shot and shots in the same or different videos are calculated based on some specific criteria (the choices of the criteria is beyond the scope of this paper).

The physical links are defined as connections of the VLO components through video's time-stamps. For example, a video shot is linked to its neighbor shots through the physical links. A video script obtained from the audio channel will be linked to the associated video shot. Unlike the semantic links, the VLO's physical links are built-in. They are created automatically.

The VLO links can be created by either automatic or manual approaches. Nevertheless, they are normally created by automatic approaches. Examples of the physical links include, but are not limited to, neighboring shots, shot and its associated transcript, shot and its key frame, shot and its associated audio clip, and shot and its associated text metadata such as description, genre, length, and format. A large number of the semantic links are still created for quality consideration. The following four video shots from a video "Hurricane Force - a Coastal Perspective" (provided by Informedia Project at Carnegie Mellon University (http://www.informedia.cs.cmu.edu/team/index.html), See Figure 2) are linked with each other for their common topic of hurricane routes along the Mexico Golf coast.

In fact, automatic approaches (based on modern data mining and clustering technologies) are being applied in the creation of VLOs. For example, collages (linked videos) are used for creation of new videos Christel, Hauptmann, Wactlar, and Ng (2002).

The VLO links are closely related to the VLO metadata. A number of VLO physical links are defined as connections between different VLO metadata components. Timestamps are usually used to link video surrogates, including both visual and textual metadata, with the raw video shots. The VLO links provide "short cuts" to *direct access* of related video metadata in various video applications.

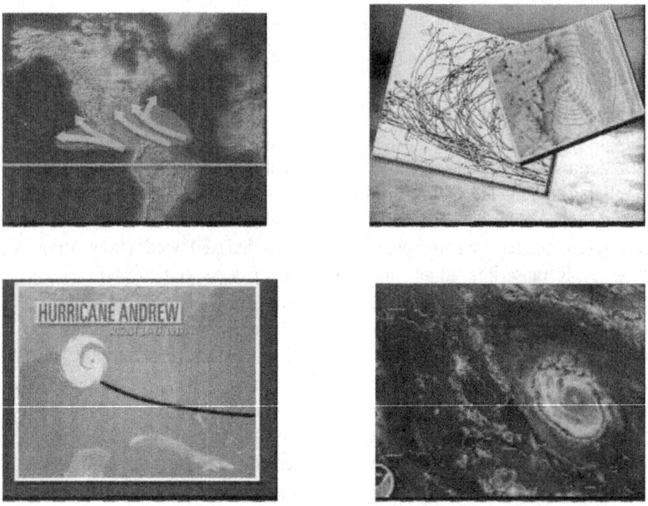

Figure 2: Hurricane Force - a Coastal Perspective (provided by Informedia Project at Carnegie Mellon University)

The VLO Learning Center

The VLO learning center is a dynamic update mechanism embedded in a VLO. The VLO learning center can update both VLO metadata and VLO links based on its application profile. An application profile refers to a summary of the utilizations of a specific VLO in various applications.

A VLO learning center is an interactive *self-learning* module in the VLO retrieval system. A small database that tracks all historical applications is created inside the VLO to provide support for the VLO learning center. Each time the VLO is accessed by a specific application, the usage information will be added to the tracking database and the new information will further be utilized to update the current status of the VLO metadata and VLO links based on a pre-defined algorithm. (The predefined algorithm is beyond the scope of this paper). For example, a video search with the query "Hurricane Katrina" and the final list of user-selected video shots will lead the VLO learning center to update the metadata of those video shots to adjust the weight variables for all key words containing "Hurricane Katrina" to reflect the current status. In addition, the new application information in which a set of video shots are selected (grouped) will also trigger the VLO leaning center to adjust its semantic links to reflect the newest status. No information related to user's identification and privacy will be collected in this process.

The Cases

In this section, two short cases are presented to further exemplify the application of the proposed model and its use for optimal dynamic reusability of VLOs. Case one includes the Video Annotation and Summarization Tool (VAST) developed by Mu and Marchionini (2001). Case two uses the Interactive Shared Educational Environment (ISEE) developed by Mu and Marchionini (2002). Both cases integrated links into the traditional video learning objects to leverage the video metadata.

Case One: Implementation of VLO Model in VAST project

The Video Annotation and Summarization Tool (VAST) developed by Mu and Marchionini (2001) is a novel middleware video application environment (Figure 3). Implemented in Java which enables the interoperability across the operating systems and platforms, VAST allows users to generate, modify, and deploy video annotations on several levels: clips, segments, scenes, shots, and frames. The VLO created by the VAST provides an enriched collection of visual metadata and links. Fast-forward version of the original video clips is used as a type of video summaries. VAST extracts the frames from the raw video in an interval configured by the user and stores them in sequence which can be used directly by some tools to produce the fast-forward version of the video.

To balance the efficiency and accuracy of the key frame extracting, a unique VLO metadata authorization approach (a semi-automatic two-phase key frame authoring approach) is adopted by the VAST system. First, the automatic signal processing approach (which is not appropriate for some specific genres such as the educational "talking head" videos). Second, the manual selection approach, which is usually time-consuming, will be adapted to refine the selection of video metadata. Our strategy is to use the first phase to narrow down the selecting pool to a small number of candidates so as to dramatically improve the efficiency and effectiveness in the second manual selection stage.

Visual metadata (key frames) and semantic metadata (outlines, annotations) are both important. They are two perspectives of the same video content. Visual metadata can keep the visual gist, while the semantic metadata provides information about concepts and abstract relationships. A mapping between these two kinds of metadata is supported in VAST through the VLO links coordinated by the video timestamp. Fast forward version of the video enables user to quickly browse the video and to grasp the visual gist effectively. A re-configuration mechanism in VAST is introduced in the VAST user interface to control the time compression ratio. The *image size* parameter can be adjusted by users to produce customized sized frames. The links were embedded in the application with the creation of video annotation. The links were automatically generated with the input of each annotation item (see two-way arrows in Figure 3).

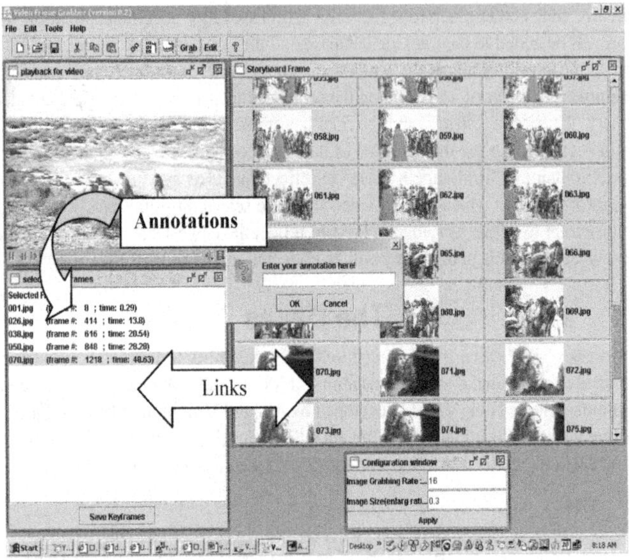

Figure 3: User interface of VAST

Case Two: Implementation of VLO Model in ISEE project

The Interactive Shared Educational Environment (ISEE) developed by Mu and Marchionini (2002) is an advanced real-time multimedia application that supports highly interactive collaboration and distance learning activities within a heterogeneous network context. The ISEE takes full advantage of fast LAN campus networks or the Internet2 Wide Area Networks to provide peer-to-peer multicast support. In addition, it can be used in the less advanced settings of home users. Media (e.g., digital video) are integrated into a desktop style interface in the ISEE. The ISEE allows users to interact with live multicasts, a shared web browser, shared video/audio with thumbnails for quick navigation, and text chat.

Collaborative work is supported via a shared time line across the multiple ISEE tools. With pre-buffering and a novel collaboration protocol, ISEE not only supports dynamic user-media interactions in real time, but also guarantees synchronization across participants.

The VLO metadata in the ISEE application (Figure 4) includes both textual and visual metadata. Different from generic VLO, hypertext documents are embedded into the VLO metadata to provide direct access through a component called "Shared Web Browser" in the ISEE interface. Other metadata displayed on the ISEE interface are the video storyboard, which is composed of a set of selected key frames.

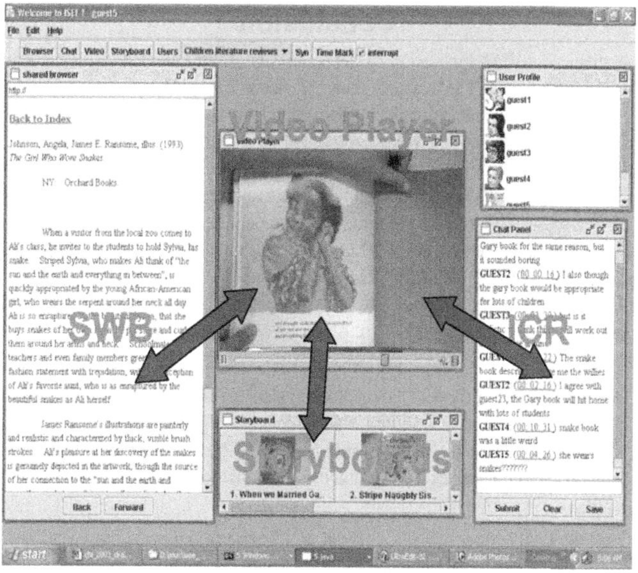

Figure 4: User Interface of ISEE

The VLO links (see the two-way arrows in Figure 4) are widely adopted in the ISEE systems. Each of the learning and communication components in the ISEE, including Interactive Chat Room (ICR), Shared Web Browser (SWB), video player, and storyboards, are "smartly" linked through the video timestamps or hypertext URLs. In ISEE, the Interactive Chat Room (ICR) is different from the generic online text chat tools in terms of supporting interaction between users via messages. Each message sent by a user contains not only the sender's username and the message content, but also the sender's video timestamp representing the point when the message was sent. A single click on the timestamp by a particular user immediately updates that user's local video player with the same value of the timestamp. Thus any user who is interested in a particular message is able to share both the text message and the video context associated with the message. Such a mechanism is based on the VLO links and brings convenience to users who want to discuss topics that are tightly associated with the video context. For example, when discussing a video picture book, a message such as "look at the little thing sitting at the table, is it a mouse?" makes no sense to another user if he/she cannot share the same scene. For a list of current links implemented in the ISEE system refer to Mu (2005).

Integration of the Learning Center in VAST and ISEE

Both the VAST and the ISEE implemented links (primary internal links) in their VLOs, which made the VLO in both applications "smarter" than the traditional *Video plus Metadata* model. The VAST and ISEE do not possess the VLO learning center proposed in this study. Therefore, currently these systems lack the dynamic reconfigurability. Our next attempt is to integrate the learning center component in the VLOs that used for both VAST and ISEE. The learning center will leverage the application context and can be used directly by multiple multimedia applications including VAST and ISEE without introducing any extra intermediary.

Conclusion

This paper advanced a VLO application model consisting of three elements - the metadata, the links, and a learning center. The metadata contains video clips, video structure, video textual metadata, video visual metadata, and video audio metadata. The VLO links are the internal links such as connections among various video components within the VLO and the external links such as connections between the VLO and other related VLOs. The VLO learning center is the key to dynamically update the VLO links and the interface for applications that are based on the usage profile. The three essential elements work together and complement one another in a dynamic system that maximizes the reusability of VLOs in various contexts. Our model goes beyond the traditional static reusability in which the VLOs are reused in various contexts with no consideration to their adaptation to new situations. In other word, the VLOs are reused without any changes or modifications to the new contexts. The reusability is achieved, but the VLOs are not adapted to the new situation.

In our model the elements of the VLO application system are allowed for reconfigurability. Reconfigurability creates dynamic reusability. Each element of VLO retrieval system is responsible for a specific task. The elements can be reconfigured based on usage profile to adapt VLOs to various contexts (each context has its own unique situation), consequently arriving at optimal dynamic reusability.

Our model is a first stride in advancing an innovative model for VLO retrieval system that optimizes dynamic reusability. While the implementation of this model is underway by the authors of this study, it is recommended that the model be further explored. The exploration should focus upon key issues affecting the dynamic reusability of VLO retrieval systems. These issues are standards, and reconfigurability.

Standards make way for the interoperability of VLOs. There are several entities who are actively working on learning objects standards in general. Examples of these entities are IEEE LO Metadata (http://ltsc.ieee.org), Advanced Distributed Learning (ADL) Initiative - Shareable Courseware Object Reference Model (SCORM) (http://www.adlnet.org), IMS (Instructional Management System) Global Learning Consortium (http://www.imsproject.org), and the Dublin Core: Metadata for Electronic Resources (http://dublincore.org). The key questions that merit attention for standards are:

1. Which standard should be used for VLOs?
2. Will there be a common standard for VLOs?

The key questions that merit attention for reconfigurability are:

1. A VLO application system must be flexible. Can flexibility be easily embedded into reconfigurability in a VLO application system?
2. Dynamic functionality is referred to extensibility that works in concert with reconfigurability. Dynamic functionality means that functionality can be added to an implemented VLO application system without an impact on the rest of the system. What measures should one take to assure inclusion of dynamic functionality in a VLO application system?
3. While reconfigurability brings about advantages in a VLO application system, how can one address its economical feasibility?

This paper has presented an innovative model for VLO application system. The focus of this model is optimum VLO reusability. The static reusability is substituted by dynamic reusability in which VLOs are adapted by means of dynamic reconfigurability and specifically tailored to various contexts.

References

Christel, M. Hauptmann, A. Wactlar, H. & Ng, T. (2002). Collages as dynamic summaries for news video, *MM'02*, Dec, 1-6, 2002, France.

Harman, K. & Koohang, A. (2005). Discussion board: A learning object. *Interdisciplinary Journal of Knowledge and Learning Objects, 1*, 66-77. Retrieved from http://ijklo.org/Volume1/v1p067-077Harman.pdf

Houten, V., Setten, V., & Enschede, E. O. (2000). *Video browsing & summarization: User interaction techniques for video browsing & summarization.* Retrieved September 30, 2006 from https://doc.telin.nl/dscgi/ds.py/Get/File-12409/user_interaction.pdf

IEEE (2002). *IEEE Standard for Learning Object Metadata.* 1484.12.1-2002.

Mu, X. (2005). Decoupling the information application from the information creation: Video as learning objects in three-tier architecture. *Interdisciplinary Journal of Knowledge and Learning Objects, 1*, 109-125. Retrieved from http://ijklo.org/Volume1/v1p109-125Mu.pdf

Mu, X. & Marchionini, G. (2001). An architecture and prototype interface for an online statistical table browser. *Proceedings of the 64th annual meeting of the American Society for Information Science and Technology*, 38, 156-170.

Mu, X. & Marchionini, G. (2002). *Interactive shared educational environment (ISEE): Design, architecture, and user interface.* Technical Report, School of Information and Library Science, University of North Carolina at Chapel Hill, TR-2002-01.

Mu, X., Marchionini,G., & Pattee,A., (2003). The Interactive Shared Educational Environment: User interface, system architecture and field study. *Proceedings of the third ACM/IEEE-CS joint conference on Digital libraries*, Houston, Texas, May 27-31, 291-300

Naphade, R., Kennedy, L., Kender, R.,, Chang, S., Smith, R., Over, P., & Hauptmann, A. (2005). *A light scale concept ontology for multimedia understanding for TRECVID 2005.* Retreived September 30, 2006 from http://www-nlpir.nist.gov/projects/tv2005/LSCOMlite_NKKCSOH.pdf

Wiley, D. (2000). Connecting learning objects to instructional design theory: A definition, a metaphor, and a taxonomy, in *The instructional use of learning objects.* Retrieved June 15, 2005 from http://reusability.org/read/chapters/wiley.doc

Biographies

Xiangming Mu, an assistant professor from School of Information Studies, University of Wisconsin—Milwaukee, earned his PhD in Information and Library Science from University of North Carolina. He worked in multiple research projects supported by National Science Foundation (NSF) and developed a suite of new information systems: Interactive Shared Educational Environment (ISEE) to support the Video-based Collaborative Distance Learning, Browser for Enriched Statistical Tables (BEST) to help non-specialists access and use statistical data in tabular form, Video Annotation and Summarization Tool (VAST) to facilitate the creation of both semantic and visual metadata, and Table-Hunter to support context + focus view of a complex web site. His current research interests include: learning technology and learning objects, digital library, multimedia information retrieval, human-computer interaction, and data mining.

Alex Koohang is a faculty member and the director of undergraduate program in the School of Information Studies at University of Wisconsin - Milwaukee, USA. Dr. Koohang has designed, developed, and implemented various traditional, non-traditional, hybrid, and on-line courses/programs. He has been involved in the development of on-line education, having initiated and administered some of the earliest asynchronous learning networks. Dr. Koohang's current research interests are in the areas of learning objects, open education, open access, open source, e-learning, usability, and knowledge management.

M-Learning Management Tool Development in Campus-Wide Environment

Anang Hudaya Muhamad Amin, Ahmad Kamil Mahmud, Ahmad Izuddin Zainal Abidin, and Miziana Abdul Rahman
ICT/BIS Program, Universiti Teknologi PETRONAS, Bandar Sri Iskandar, Perak Darul Ridzuan, Malaysia

ananghudaya@petronas.com.my kamilmh@petronas.com.my
izuddin_z@petronas.com.my mizeeana@yahoo.com

Abstract

Mobile learning (M-Learning) integrates the current mobile and wireless computing technology with education primarily to enhance the effectiveness of the traditional learning process. One of the difficulties in implementing M-Learning is to deliver the content efficiently. This paper focuses on the development of M-Learning management tool in campus-wide environment using the Microsoft .NET infrastructure. User acceptance study was carried out to measure the feasibility of the M-learning management application development. The results of the study indicate a tendency towards the M-Learning acceptance in campus-wide environment. The main objective of the works that have been carried out is to develop a server-side M-Learning application using the Microsoft .NET infrastructure. The works that has been carried out act as preliminary work for future development of M-Learning application in campus-wide environment.

Keywords: M-Learning, E-Learning, Management Tool, Application Development, User Acceptance

Introduction

Education is the cornerstone of economic development in any nations (Ruttenbur, Spickler, & Lurie, 2000). Traditionally, formal classroom-based education has been adopted, allowing a teacher and students to have face-to-face interactions (Moneta & Moneta, 2002). However, this approach has noticeable drawbacks. Firstly, students' physical presence and participation in group discussions in a learning centre are virtually required and form an integral part of the institution's curriculum (Bouras & Philopoulos, 2001; Goodison, 2003). Secondly, the teacher has to adhere to the classroom schedules (Boyle, 1997; Jansen, Hooven, Jägers, & Steenbakkers:, 2002). With the advancement of mobile technology, the traditional classroom-based learning has been supplemented by other forms of education capable of reaching out to a larger audience. Mobile learning (M-Learning) offers possible solutions that address the shortcomings of the traditional classroom-based education. Since the use of mobile phones and handheld devices among students has dramatically increased, implementing M-Learning in academic institutions is of common interest (Keegan, 2002).

M-Learning is the teaching and learning processes through the use of mobile and handheld devices such as mobile phones, Personal Digital Assistants (PDAs), laptops, and tablet PCs. M-Learning is usually referred to as an extension of the existing e-learning applications. There is a suggestion that M-Learning enables learners the ability to receive learning on any device practically anywhere and anytime (Chabra & Figueiredo, 2002). Hence, the mobility factor is the ultimate means of providing M-Learning services to the students or teachers. While the existing electronic learning (E-Learning) extends learning beyond physical classroom, M-Learning promises continued extension of learning process in a context-awareness manner. The key difference between E-Learning and M-Learning would be that M-Learning offers greater flexibility in where and when learning happens (Valentine, 2005). Moreover, M-Learning has the ability of providing rich mobile Internet experiences that are ubiquitous, accessible, rich in content, efficient, flexible, secure, reliable, and interactive (Wagner, 2005). The term E-Learning is analogous to online education. It is characterized by the separation of teachers and learners distinguishing it from face-to-face interaction, the influence of an educational organization differentiating it from self-study and private tutoring, the use of a computer network to present or distribute educational contents, and the provision of two-way communication via a computer network to enable students benefit from communication with each other, teachers, and staff (Geddes, 2005). Most of the E-Learning applications exploit the availability of the World Wide Web (WWW) as a means of content delivery (IBM Mindspan Solution, 2002). One of the great advantages of the WWW is that it is platform-independent and able to support such media types as audio and video. From an educational perspective, teaching could now take place both synchronously and asynchronously (Keegan, 2002). With E-Learning, time and place are no longer restrictions as the learning experience can be tapped anywhere provided that one has a computer and access to the Internet (IBM Mindspan Solution, 2002; Jansen et al., 2002; Ruttenbur et al., 2000). It should be noted here that in E-Learning implementation, students would be able to receive services through the E-Learning system, and at the same time would be able to communicate with others via the system.

With the existence of wireless and mobile communication technology, the initiative towards providing mobility in E-Learning has started (Heath et al., 2005). The M-Learning system, which exploits the use of mobile and handheld devices, becomes a new approach in providing content delivery and assistance to the students (Heath et al., 2005; Holzinger, Nischelwitzer, & Meisenberger, 2005). Figure 1 illustrates how M-Learning works. By means of wireless Internet/intranet connection, students can receive course content located on a remote server, student support services and other materials that constitute the overall educational package.

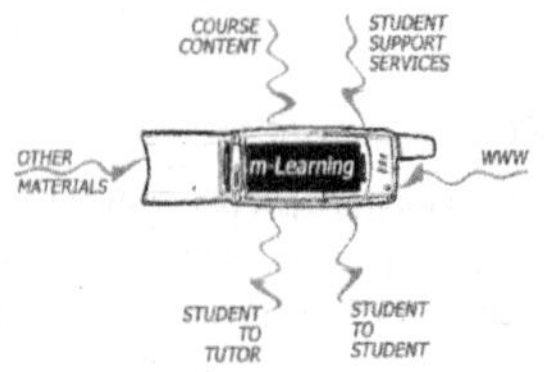

Figure 1: Mobile Learning Environment

In the development of any M-Learning applications, there are several challenges that should be observed. M-Learning should not convert the existing PC-based learning content into a mobile format, but to make a consideration on how the mobile devices can be used to strengthen the overall learning strategy (Ting, 2005). M-Learning should be able to provide complete independence of both location and time for users to use the application (Holzinger et al., 2005). Some of the challenges that should be taken into consideration in developing M-Learning application include the ability to provide adaptive learning environment, limited text display to support learning, and characteristics of instant communication in mobile network (Holzinger et al., 2005; Ting, 2005).

Related Works

M-Learning is often defined as E-Learning through mobile devices (G Vavoula & Karagiannidis, 2000). In this context, mobile device is considered as small, autonomous, and obtrusive enough to accompany people in every moment of their daily life, and that can be used for some form of learning (Griswold et al., 2004). These small tools can be seen as instruments for accessing contents, either stored locally on the device or reachable through interconnection. They can also be a tool for interacting with people, via voice and through the exchange of written messages, still and moving images.

There are many properties differentiating mobile devices from desktop computers. The former have impact on what is reasonable, useful, and even pleasant to do on such devices (Bae, Lim, & Lee, 2005; Holzinger et al., 2005). For example, the output (screen size and resolution capabilities), input (keypad, touch-screen), processing power and memory size, and supported applications.

The concept of mobility – the anytime, anywhere capabilities of mobile devices encourage learning experiences outside classroom-based environment. Inside the classroom, mobile devices provide students with the capabilities to link to activities that do not correspond with either the teacher's agenda or the curriculum (Sharples, 2003). Apart from that, lifelong learners would also need effective tools to record, organise, and reflect on their mobile learning experiences (Vavoula, 2004; Vavoula & Karagiannidis, 2000). The concept of mobility is related to how the design of the M-Learning application should be adopted. M-Learning should be simple to use and has value-added functionality. It should be possible to use M-Learning system without reading a user manual and the experience of studying with the help of such devices should be interesting and engaging (Trifonova & Ronchetti, 2003). An initiative that has been carried out by (Bae et al., 2005) include the modeling and development of M-Learning application using the existing WAP and HTML infrastructure. The works that have been carried out in this paper will be focusing on the development of server-side M-Learning application that will support the mobility factor, which include the content delivery method.

Another issue that has been identified by the authors, with regards to the M-Learning concept is the flexibility of the M-Learning application. M-Learning application should be developed in the sense that it would be able to be supported by different devices, such as smart phones, PDAs, and laptops. There are several initiatives that have been carried out by other researchers in developing M-Learning applications. Project Numina (Heath et al., 2005) is one of the examples of such development. In this project the full-course content and management system was developed using the existing Mobile Learning Engine (MLE). MLE is a Java-based Mobile Learning Development Tool. Similarly, the initiative carried out by (Holzinger et al., 2005) in developing M-Learning application for Healthcare domain using Mobile Interactive Learning Objects (MILOs). These initiatives show that the development of M-Learning application has been established by other researchers. The main difference that has been carried out by the authors as compared to these related works is such that the development of M-Learning Management Tool is developed using .NET environment introduced by Microsoft. The main reason behind this adoption of .NET environment is such that the architecture would be able to provide flexibility to the user to use the system. With the contents being delivered using ASP.NET format, it would be readable by not only mobile devices, but other existing desktop-based web browsers. The development of this M-Learning management tool also revealed that the development of server-side M-Learning application is possible. Furthermore, this work heavily focuses on the management tool, rather than the contents delivery. Figure 2 shows the architecture of this M-Learning Management Tool.

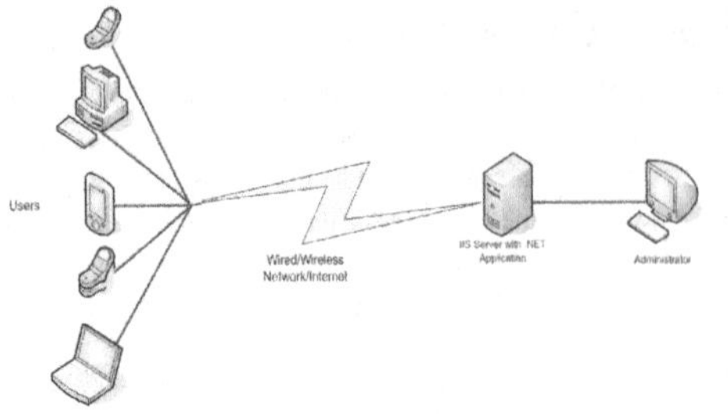

Figure 2: M-Learning Management Tool Architecture

Another challenging issue in M-Learning is the device ownership (Wagner, 2005). Both personal and group learning are most effectively supported when each student has access to a device. The ownership of the device is thus a key consideration. Both tangible and intangible benefits can accrue through the use of mobile devices. Intangible benefits include the sense of belonging with the device and personal commitment and comfort. Ownership is stated as a prerequisite for engagement allowing students to have the potential to go beyond the necessary and play with it to explore its potential. Personal ownership does, however, present a challenge to the institutional control of the technology (Savill-Smith & Kent, 2003).

This paper focuses on the development of M-Learning management tool in campus-wide environment. The tool has been developed for the use of students in the campus. The management tool enables students to view the contents for courses they enroll in, the timetables, assessment reports, and assignments anywhere, and anytime on campus. The main issues to be discussed include the mobility factor, as well as the flexibility of M-Learning application. These issues have been explored, with regards to the development of server-side M-Learning management tool using the .NET architecture. The works that has been carried out act as a preliminary work for future development of M-Learning application in campus-wide environment. The paper consists of several sections namely, Related Works, M-Learning Management Tool Development, Results and Discussion, and Conclusion.

M-Learning Management Tool Development

In developing M-Learning tool for this study, the normal system development methodology has been adopted, which include four main phases: planning, analysis, design, and implementation. Figure 3 shows the conceptual flow model that has been developed for this M-Learning management tool. It should be noted that there are four core modules that have been included: My Courses, My Schedule, My Grade, and My Assignment. Each of these modules has been built on mobile web form, which is different from the normal web forms. Each mobile web form can have multiple forms, while normal web form can have a single form per page. In developing this ap-

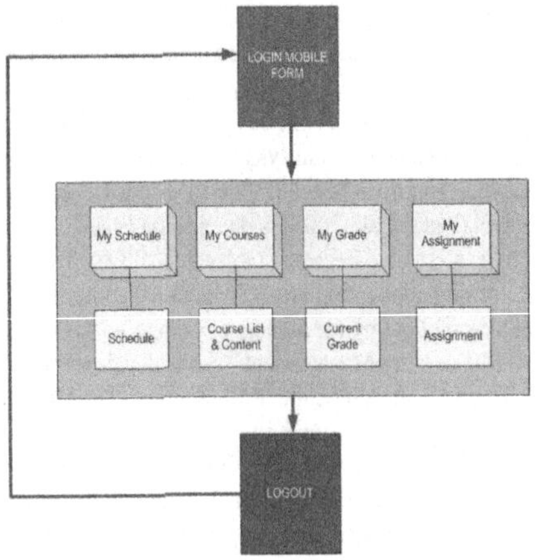

Figure 3: Conceptual Flow Model of M-Learning Management Tool

plication, the authors have adopted Microsoft .NET architecture and uses Microsoft Visual Studio as the development tool. In achieving the mobility factor, the authors have adopted the Microsoft Mobile Internet Toolkit (MMIT) as the means to develop this M-Learning application. The authors also found out that MMIT can generate different mark-up language for different devices. This actually simplifies the development process in the sense that application would only need to be written once and the different languages would be generated by the .NET framework. The toolkit has been tested with multiple devices including Nokia 6210, Pocket PC with Microsoft Internet Explorer v.4.5., and Sony Ericsson R380.

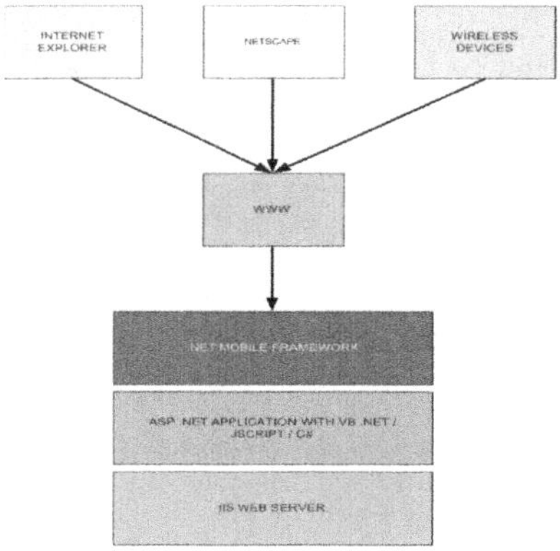

Figure 4: Microsoft Mobile Internet Architecture

MMIT is built on Microsoft ASP .NET Web Forms. Since the toolkit is an extension of ASP .NET, it supports languages like VB.NET, C#, and JScript.NET. The toolkit is also integrated with Microsoft Visual Studio .NET. Figure 4 shows the MMIT Framework in mobile computing applications. The advantage of implementing this M-Learning Management Tool over MMIT is such that it will be able to support other means of access. For example, the user would not only be able to access the tool by using mobile devices. This system would only able to be accessed via desktop-based web browsers (Internet Explorer, Netscape).

Throughout the development of the M-Learning management tool, the authors discovered that although M-Learning is a revolution of E-Learning, to effectively build and deliver, it requires rethinking, reinvestigating, and re-evaluating the human-computer interaction in the mobile environment. The existing E-Learning frameworks may not work very well with M-Learning: the interaction experience in M-Learning is different from other types of learning.

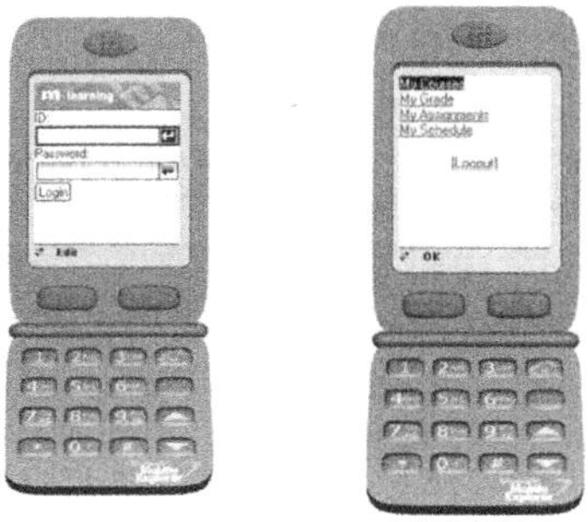

Figure 5: Login Page and Default Page of M-Learning

Figure 5 shows the login page and the default page of the system. Once user has been logged in, they will be directed to the main page of the system.

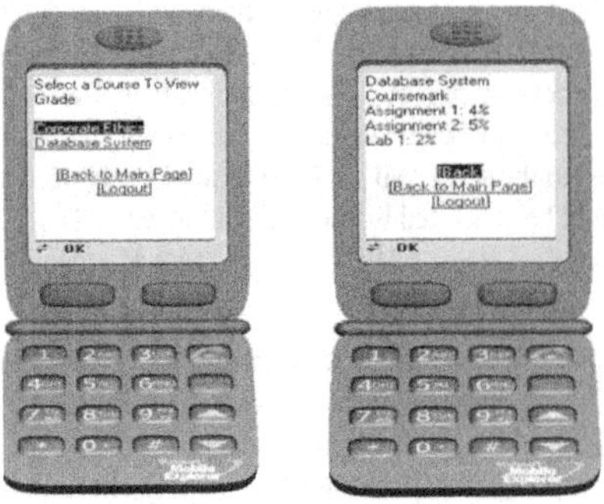

Figure 6: Course Grade Module

The main page consists of four modules that have been previously explained. It should be noted that the development has been done using the emulator provided by the MMIT. Figure 6 shows the page for the grades module. This module shows the marks for labs, projects and tests. This module allows the students to be informed of their performance in the course.

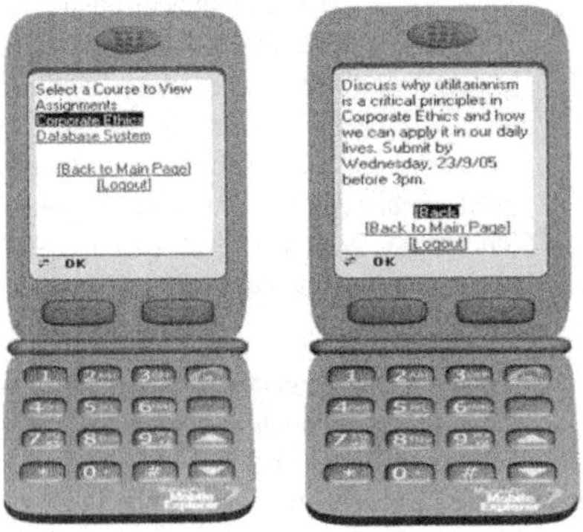

Figure 7: Course Assignment Module

The assignment module shown in Figure 7 enables students to open text file from lecturers to view the assignments that has been given.

Results & Discussion

Generally, the authors' research was also aimed at the understanding interaction experience in M-Learning by examining a broad range of aspects of M-Learners and their environment. In achieving this, acceptance study has been adopted. The user acceptance study for M-Learners has been sub-categorized into two main areas including interaction experience in the mobile environment as well as the usability of M-Learning management tool. To understand the interaction experience in the mobile environment, three important characteristics were examined: understanding of the mobile learners (including their characteristics, psychological, and physical capability), understanding of the M-Learning environment (the motivations and circumstances surrounding mobile device usage and adoption), and understanding of mobile experience which differs from desktop computing. This study has adopted a survey method by the means of questionnaire to obtain the feedbacks from the users, on the M-Learning tool that has been developed, as well as to obtain the data that reflects towards the study on the acceptance of users for M-Learning method.

The purpose of the questionnaire is to elicit information on the effectiveness of M-Learning as a learning management tool. It is an excellent way of obtaining either quantitative or qualitative data, since the user responses are written and can be tallied to illustrate user preferences. Questionnaires can only evaluate users' opinions about the user interface, not their behavior while using the M-Learning management tool.

For these reasons, the authors decided to adopt a variant of the Delphi survey approach. In the early 1950s, the term Delphi was used to describe a reliable consensus of opinion, obtained from group of experts by a series of intensive questionnaires interspersed with controlled opinion feedback (Linstone & Turoff, 1975). This approach is characterized as 'a method for the systematic solicitation and collation of judgments on a particular topic through a set of carefully designed sequential questionnaires interspersed with summarized information on feedback of opinions derived from earlier responses' (Delbecq, 1975). Delphi is particularly useful when accurate information is unavailable or expensive to obtain, or where evaluation models require subjective inputs to the point where they become the dominating parameters (Linstone & Turoff, 1975). The survey is the most common technique of Delphi application.

For the purpose of this study, we selected 30 students as the evaluators for the M-Learning tool, and they also involved in the survey that has been conducted.

At first, responses to the idea of M-Learning were mixed, as many were immediately accepting, while some were immediately rejecting. Irrespective of their initial views, most responded with questions about the nature, format and purpose of M-Learning. Respondents were quite difficult to adapt to the term M-Learning due to its new concept in education. The initial tendency was for the respondents to consider the benefits and drawbacks of M-Learning for themselves as individuals. Those initially most favorable towards the idea argued that they would benefit from it. However, the ones who disagreed towards the idea argued that they would benefit more from the traditional learning system.

Generally, students were interested in the technology that M-Learning could offer them. Another plus factor was that most of them owned at least one mobile device, the most common being mobile phones. Figure 8 shows that 11 percent strongly agreed and 38 percent agreed while 25 percent strongly disagreed. Another 18 percent disagreed while the remaining was uncertain. These obtained data show that the acceptance level of respondents is still cannot be considered high. This may due to the inexperience use of mobile devices for course management, as well as the lack of proper documentation on how the system should be used.

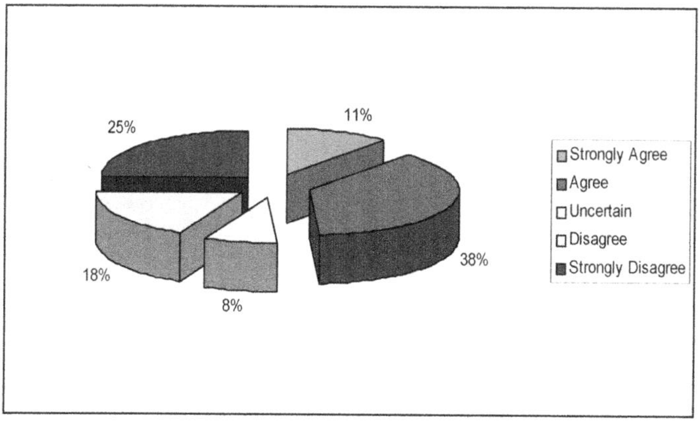

Figure 8: Responses on User Acceptance

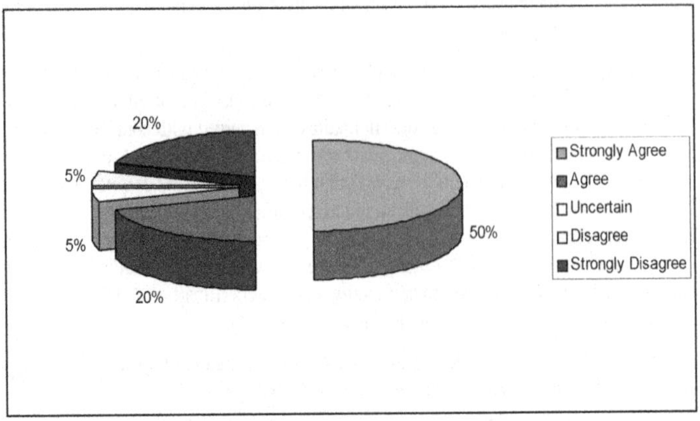

Figure 9: Responses on User-Friendliness

Based on Figure 9, the authors found that 50 percent strongly agreed that the system was user friendly and easy to use. Another 20 percent agreed, while 5 percent were uncertain about the management tool's user friendliness. Both 5 percent and 20 percent disagreed and strongly disagreed on the user friendliness of the system. The result shows that the M-Learning management tool developed has a good navigation and users would be able to use it without any difficulties.

Figure 10 shows an imbalanced distribution between those who agreed and those who did not. About 62 percent strongly agreed that M-Learning could improve educational efficiency while 9 percent strongly disagreed and still preferred the current learning styles. The rest showed that 18 percent agreed, 9 percent disagreed while another 2 percent are uncertain. The result obtained revealed that the respondents believed that there is a tendency on which the M-Learning would be able to improve the educational efficiency, with regards to the usage of M-Learning management tool.

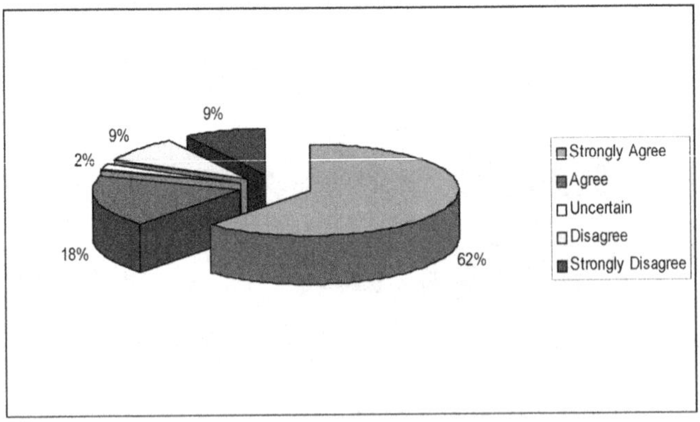

Figure 10: Responses on Didactic Efficiency

Figure 11 shows that 33 percent disagreed on the feasibility of the system, with most of them disagreed that it was not necessary to use graphics and illustrations in order for M-Learning to be effective, considering the screen limitation factor. About 20 percent strongly disagreed while 8 percent remained uncertain. Both 22 percent and 17 percent strongly agreed and agreed on technical feasibility. This shows the mixed reactions of users with regards to the use of visual elements in M-Learning management tool.

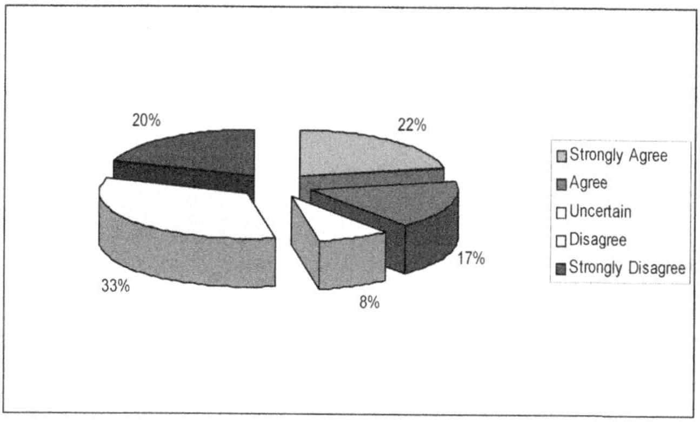

Figure 11: Responses on Feasibility of the System

Conclusion

The development of M-Learning management tool has been completed. From the development process, as well as the results of the development, the issues on mobility and flexibility of M-Learning application has been identified. The development of server-side M-Learning management tool using .NET architecture has shown that the mobility and flexibility issues could be resolved. The .NET architecture has the capability to provide easy access from mobile devices to the application server, as well as the flexibility, in terms of different devices used as the front-end of the system. This M-Learning management tool provides users with a new look on learning style, where they can access information they want using a mobile device, anywhere and anytime.

The authors also discovered that understanding interaction experience is not an entirely new area in human computer interaction (HCI), but there is no agreed framework that can actually guide designers and developers towards the development of usable M-Learning systems. There is considerable work to be accomplished on many fronts - HCI, mobile technology, learning communities, and content development before the potential of M-Learning comes to fruition. In addition, the implementation of M-Learning Management tool using .NET architecture has been able to provide greater flexibility for the users to use the system, regardless whether the mobility is required or not.

After analyzing the survey data, the authors found out that the concept of M-Learning might be of an interest to the users specifically in a campus-wide environment, provided that it can assist them in their learning process. Apart from that, it seems that M-Learning can be more easily acceptable if it is able to provide at least the same learning experience based on the current educational style, and able to provide an interactive learning environment for the users. Those who disagree prefer to stick to the current learning style or might be resistant to technology changes. Users are very concerned with the usability of the system as this will be the determining factor in feasibility of the system.

References

Bae, Y. K., Lim, J. K., & Lee, T. W. (2005, July 5-8). Mobile learning system using the ARCS strategies. *Proceedings of the 5th International Conference on Advanced Learning Technologies*, Taiwan.

Bouras, C., & Philopoulos, A. (2001). e-Learning through distributed virtual environments. *Journal of Network and Computer Applications, 24.* Available online at http://citeseer.nj.nec.com/456858.html

Boyle, T. (1997). *Design for multimedia learning.* London: Prentice Hall.

Chabra, T., & Figueiredo, J. (2002). How to design and deploy handheld learning. Retrieved December 8, 2002 from http://www.empoweringtechnologies.net/eLearning/eLearning_expov5_files/frame.htm

Delbecq, A. L. (1975). *Group techniques for program planning: A guide to nominal group and Delphi processes.* Scott, Foresman & Co.

Geddes, S. J. (2005). Mobile learning in the 21st century: Benefit for learners. *The Knowledge Tree, 6.* Available at http://knowledgetree.flexiblelearning.net.au/edition06/download/geddes.pdf

Goodison, T. (2003). Integrating ICT in the classroom: A case study of two contrasting lessons. *British Journal of Educational Technology, 34*(5), 549-566.

Griswold, W. G., Shanahan, P., Brown, S. W., Boyer, R., Ratto, M., Shapiro, R. B., Truong, T. M. (2004). ActiveCampus: Experiments in community-oriented ubiquitous computing. *Computer, 37(10),* 73-81.

Heath, B. P., Herman, R. L., Lugo, G. G., Reeves, J. H., Vetter, R. J., & Ward, R. W. (2005). Project Numina: Enhancing student learning with handheld computers. *IEEE Computer Society, 38*(6), 46-53.

Holzinger, A., Nischelwitzer, A., & Meisenberger, M. (2005, March 8-12, 2005). Mobile phones as a challenge for M-Learning: Examples for mobile interactive learning objects (MILOs). *Proceedings of the 3rd International Conference on Pervasive Computing and Communications Workshop 2005*, Hawaii, USA.

IBM Mindspan Solution. (2002). E-Learning: Implementing the 4-tier blended learning model. Retrieved from http://www.ibm.com/Mindspan

Jansen, W., Hooven, H. M. V. D., Jägers, H. P. M., & Steenbakkers, G. C. A. (2002). The added value of e-learning. *Proceedings of the Informing Science and IT Education Conference: InSITE 2002*, June 19-21, 2002, Cork, Ireland. Retrieved from http://proceedings.informingscience.org/IS2002Proceedings/papers/Janse124Added.pdf

Keegan, D. (2002). The future of learning: From E-Learning to M-Learning. Retrieved September 7, 2005 from http://learning.ericsson.net/leonardo/thebook/chapter4.html#milearn

Linstone, H. A., & Turoff, M. (1975). *The Delphi method: Techniques and applications.* Addison-Wesley.

Moneta, S. K., & Moneta, G. B. (2002). E-Learning in Hong Kong: Comparing learning outcomes in online multimedia and lecture versions of an introductory computing course. *British Journal of Educational Technology, 33*(4), 423-433.

Ruttenbur, B. W., Spickler, G. C., & Lurie, S. (2000). *E-Learning: The engine of the knowledge economy.* Memphis: Morgan Keegan.

Savill-Smith, C., & Kent, P. (2003). The use of palmtop computers for learning. Learning and Skills Development Agency. Retrieved May 20, 2005, from http://www.m-learning.org/docs/the_use_of_palmtop_computers_for_learning_sept03.pdf

Sharples, M. (2003). Disruptive devices: Mobile technology for conversational learning,. *International Journal of Continuing Engineering Education and Lifelong Learning, 12*(5/6), 504-520.

Ting, R. Y. (2005). Mobile learning: Current trend and future challenges. *Proceedings of the Fifth IEEE International Conference on Advanced Learning Technologies 2005.*

Trifonova, A., & Ronchetti, M. (2003). A general architecture for M-Learning. Paper presented at the *M-ICTE 2003 Conference*, USA.

Valentine, E. (2005). Unplugged learning: A report on the rise of mobile technology in learning. *14th National VET Research Conference,* Albury - Wodonga, July, 2005. Retrieved from http://cms.steo.govt.nz/NR/rdonlyres/6C03CDFA-70E7-4179-90E5-7637BA267D7C/0/UnpluggedLearningFinalNovember04.doc

Vavoula, G. (2004). *KLeOS: A knowledge and learning organization system in support of lifelong learning.* Unpublished PhD, University of Birmingham.

Vavoula, G., & Karagiannidis, C. (2000). *Designing mobile learning experiences.* Institute of Educational Technology.

Wagner, K. (2005). Enabling mobile learning, *Educause Review.* May/June.

Biographies

Anang Hudaya Muhamad Amin is currently working as lecturer and researcher at Universiti Teknologi PETRONAS, Malaysia. His research interests include mobile applications development, agent-based computing and Quality of Service (QoS) in network environment. Received his Master of Network Computing from Monash University, Australia and BTech(Hons.) in Information Technology from Universiti Teknologi PETRONAS, Malaysia.

A Kamil Mahmood is a Senior Lecturer at Universiti Teknologi PETRONAS. He earned his PhD from the University of Salford, UK while his M Sc and B Sc from the University of Iowa, USA. He was a system analyst, associate lecturer to Manchester Metropolitan University, UK and external examiner to a number of academic institutions in Malaysia. His research has focused on the socio-technical issues including e-commerce and the use of embodied agents. Currently, he is heading ICT/BIS program and supervising 4 post graduate students.

Ahmad Izuddin Zainal Abidin is currently working as a lecturer and a researcher at Universiti Teknologi PETRONAS, Malaysia. His research interests include mobile applications development, e-business, and algorithms. He graduated with MS Computer Science and BS Computer Science from State University of New York and University of Pittsburgh, respectively.

Miziana Abdul Rahman is currently pursuing undergraduate studies at Universiti Teknologi PETRONAS, Malaysia. Her research interests include human-computer interaction (HCI) and mobile applications development.

Attitudes toward WebCT and Learning: An Omani Perspective

Syed Jafar Naqvi and Manzur Ali Ajiz
Sultan Qaboos University, Al-Khod, Sultanate of Oman

cce3249@squ.edu.om manzur@squ.edu.om

Abstract

This study investigated the students attitudes toward the use of World Wide Web Course Tools (WebCT) and its influence on learning taking a course Introduction to Computers in Business offered at the College of Commerce and Economics in Sultan Qaboos University in Oman. Sultan Qaboos University is a co-educational institution where in most computer classes the male and female students are equally distributed. Omani society is a segregated society where male and female students have some how different life style and have different attitudes towards learning Information Technology.

This research is exploring the difference if any of their attitudes toward WebCT, where WebCT was introduced in their "Introduction to Computers in Business" course as a supplementary learning tool. The finding showed that though male students have little more exposure of WebCT at the beginning of the course than the females, but towards the end of the course the male and female students have appreciated almost equally the importance and the use of WebCT as it is easily accessible from any Internet enabled location and at any time in addition it helps them in better understanding and learning the course material.

Keywords: WebCT, learning, Information Technology, student attitudes

Introduction

Oman, is a developing nation striving to improve her education through their national reforms. Sultan Qaboos University is the only national university in the country, serving to more than 10000 male and female students at a time. Recently the Center for Education Technology (CET), of Sultan Qaboos University has provided access to WebCT to all colleges in the University. At the College of Commerce and Economics the instructor has introduced WebCT for students to have access the digital contents of the Introduction to Computers in Business course along with the traditional course teaching.

The moving from traditional learning to using digital learning environment like WebCT may have some implications on students' attitudes. This study investigating their overall attitudes toward WebCT based on gender differences when taking "Introduction to Computers in Business" course.

One of the most apparent trends affecting education is the advancement of technology. Infrastructures are growing stronger as computers double in speed while decreasing in cost, and high-speed network connections continue to expand. Computer, fax, picture phone, duplication, and other modalities are merging and becoming available at ever cheaper prices (Cetron, 2003).

"New technology will transform higher education as we know it today" (Oblinger, Barone, & Hawkins, 2001), one example being the changes caused by broader use of e-texts and PDAs (Chick et al., 2002). By the year 2012, schools and colleges will routinely use "computerized teaching programs and interactive television lectures and seminars, as well as traditional methods" (World Future Society, 2003). Videoconferencing and other technologies will also help enrich distance media and provide many benefits for face-to-face instruction.

Dunn (2000) projected changes in higher education's landscape over the next 20 years. "The number of degree-granting institutions will continue to grow, while the number of traditional campuses will decline."

The current technology may continue to increase the options available for distributing distance education to more people in a scalable fashion, especially if it is accompanied by technological fluency. Several universities have started offering courses using WebCT, Moodle, Blackboard or similar packages mainly for their distance education programs. Sultan Qaboos University has recently started using WebCT as a supportive tool to its traditional teaching.

What is WebCT?

WebCT is a course management system that enables the delivery of online education. With a complete set of teaching and learning tools for course development, course delivery, and course management, WebCT provides a system for student learning and an efficient solution for faculty of all experience levels (Williams, 2003). It allows educators to design the appearance of course pages, it provides a set of educational tools that can easily be incorporated into any course, and it provides a set of administrative tools that assist the educator in the task of course administration (Goldberg, Salari, & Swoboda, 1996).

The advantages of WebCT include a simple interface that can be accessed from anywhere a network-connected computer is available. While this is important for all users of WebCT who enjoy time and location independent access to their learning resource (Williams, 2003).

Purpose of the Study

The purpose of this study was to explore attitudes and gender differences toward WebCT and its effects on understanding and learning in the course "Introduction to Computers in Business" offered at the Sultan Qaboos University where WebCT is recently introduced.

Methodology

The sample for this study consisted of seventy one students enrolled for the course where male students were 37 (52%) and female were 34 (48%). These students had similar educational background and having no or little initial IT skills. All students were allowed to have access to the course on campus or else where with a uniform access procedure.

A questionnaire was developed for this study. It comprised of fourteen questions designed covering four major domains related to accessing WebCT, Attitudes toward WebCT, WebCT helps in acquiring IT skills and WebCT in teaching. The questionnaire was administered in the similar way to all students in the course. There were two stages for data collection Prior and After. The Prior data collection point was at the beginning of the course, while After data collection point was at the end of the course. The course lasted for one semester of sixteen weeks.

Responses to each item were based on Likert scale ranging from 1 to 5, where 1 = Strongly Disagree, 2 = Disagree, 3 = Uncertain (never used WebCT before), 4 = Agree, 5 = Strongly Agree, as shown in Appendix 1.

The same course outline, syllabus, data collection and processing tools were used in the study. The responses-means prior to the course and after the course were compared to see if there was any marked difference between male and female students attitudes toward WebCT and its effects on learning the course material.

Simple analysis of the data was done by comparing the means to assess the size of change in the male and female students. The results of these comparisons were incorporated to examine the effects on issues like students accessibility to WebCT, attitudes toward WebCT, learning and understanding the course material.

Results and Findings

WebCT Accessibility

The WebCT accessibility was found to be low for both male and female students prior to the course. In fact it is lower for female students (M=2.65) as compared to the male students (M=3.20). It might be that only few students had taken a course prior to this requiring to use WebCT while others had not used it before.

But after the enrollment in the course each student was given user account to access the WebCT. Most students responded very high as the mean response for male students were (M = 4.48) and female students were (M=4.45). There is no significant difference between male and female students on issue of WebCT accessibility during or After the course as compared Prior to the course.

The means of the survey of both the groups at Prior and After stages along with the change from Prior to After are tabulated in Table 1 and the graphical representations of Prior vs. Prior and After vs. After is shown in Figure 1 and Figure 2 correspondingly, showing at After stage both male or female students had better access to WebCT.

Table 1. Accessing WebCT

		Mean		Size of Change
	Gender	Prior	After	After-Prior
Accessing WebCT Comfortably	Male	3.04	4.46	1.42
	Female	2.60	4.52	1.92
Accessing WebCT from any location	Male	3.00	4.46	1.46
	Female	2.64	4.48	1.84
Accessing WebCT at any time.	Male	3.50	4.39	0.89
	Female	2.76	4.44	1.68
Accessing WebCT any length of Time	Male	3.29	4.61	1.32
	Female	2.60	4.36	1.76
Overall (WebCT Accessibility)	Male	3.20	4.48	1.28
	Female	2.65	4.45	1.80

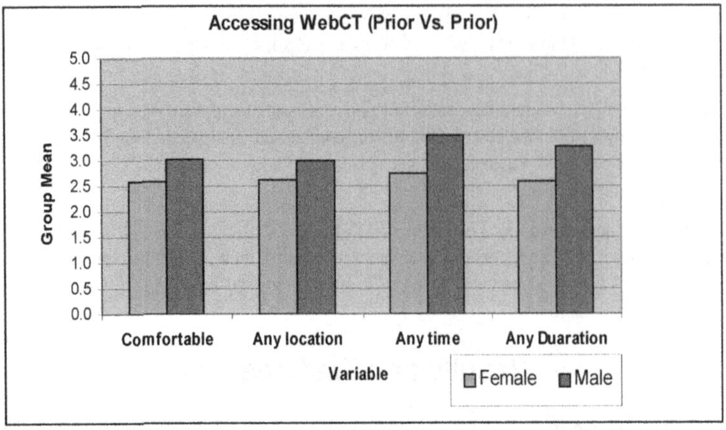

Figure 1: Accessibility of WebCT (Prior Vs. Prior)

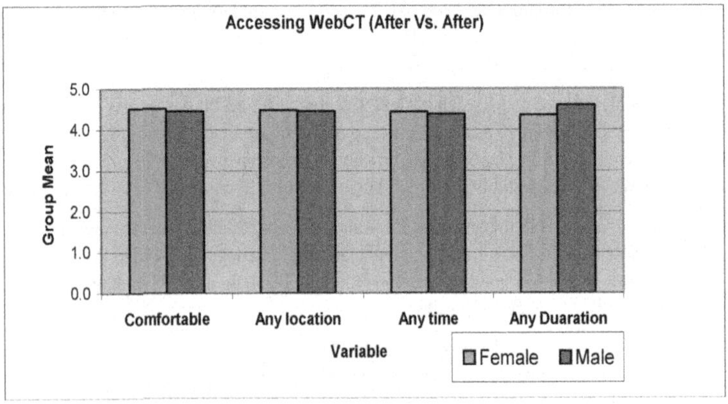

Figure 2: Accessibility of WebCT (After Vs. After)

Attitudes toward WebCT

The overall attitudes toward the WebCT was found to be less positive or like neutral for all students prior to the course as it could be seen by comparing the means for females (M=2.70) and males (M=3.33). This could be because of lack of access to WebCT by all students especially the females at the beginning of the course.

But at the end of the course, when the WebCT was more easily accessible to all students their attitudes toward the WebCT had improved. When considering the size of change from Prior to After, both groups have indicated a significant difference between the attitudes at the After stage versus the Prior stage of the course. However, this change is more among female students as compared to male students, might be because of the lack of accessibility of WebCT.

In general, both male and female students have indicated more positive attitudes toward WebCT when surveyed at the After stage of the course. This is shown in Table 2 and graphically presented in Figure 3 and Figure 4. It is interesting to note that the same pattern is shown with

WebCT accessibility. It appears that those students who got more accessibility of WebCT had more positive attitudes toward WebCT.

Table 2. Attitudes toward WebCT

Dependent Variables	Gender	Mean		Size of Change
		Prior	After	After-Prior
Feel Friendly using WebCT	Male	3.29	4.54	1.25
	Female	2.84	4.52	1.68
Feel at Ease Using WebCT	Male	3.21	3.93	0.72
	Female	2.96	4.52	1.56
Feel relaxed with WebCT Interaction	Male	3.43	4.43	1.00
	Female	2.96	4.68	1.72
Feel WebCT is Important	Male	3.39	4.57	1.18
	Female	3.04	4.64	1.60
Overall(Attitude towards WebCT)	Male	3.33	4.37	1.04
	Female	2.96	4.59	1.63

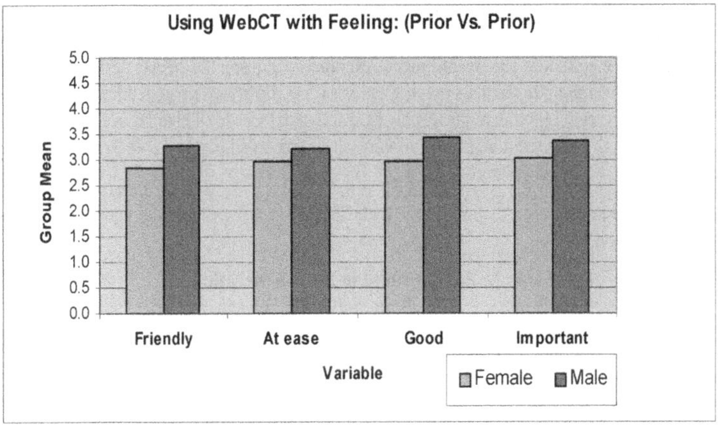

Figure 3: Attitudes towards WebCT (Prior Vs. Prior)

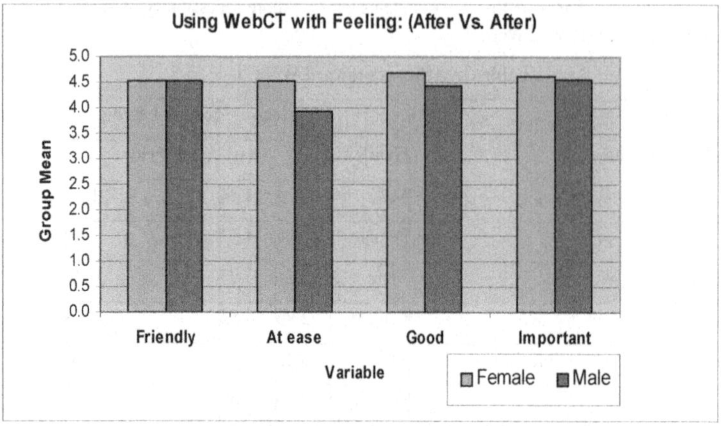

Figure 4: Attitudes towards WebCT (After Vs. After)

Learning through WebCT

The overall perception of male and female students towards the WebCT as a tool for learning was poor Prior to the course. When comparing the overall mean responses given by male students (M=2.94) while for female students was (M=2.92), showing no significant difference.

But when asked at After stage of the course both male and female students have really appreciated the effects of WebCT on their learning. The students got more accessibility of WebCT using it with more positive attitudes. The overall mean responses regarding the effects of the WebCT on their learning, the overall male students mean was (M=4.53) while for female students was (M=4.84) showing very high but similar responses. But when the size of change from Prior to After were compared, indicated a highly significant difference as shown in Table 3 and graphically presented in Figure 5 and Figure 6.

All students regardless of gender believed that WebCT improved their learning, understanding and exam preparation.

Table 3. WebCT helps in the course with:

		Mean		Size of Change
	Gender	Prior	After	After-Prior
Better understanding	Male	3.00	4.39	1.39
	Female	2.72	4.88	2.16
Better learning	Male	2.96	4.54	1.58
	Female	3.04	4.80	1.76
Better preparation for exams	Male	2.86	4.68	1.82
	Female	3.00	4.84	1.84
Overall(Helps in the course learning)	Male	2.94	4.53	1.59
	Female	2.92	4.84	1.92

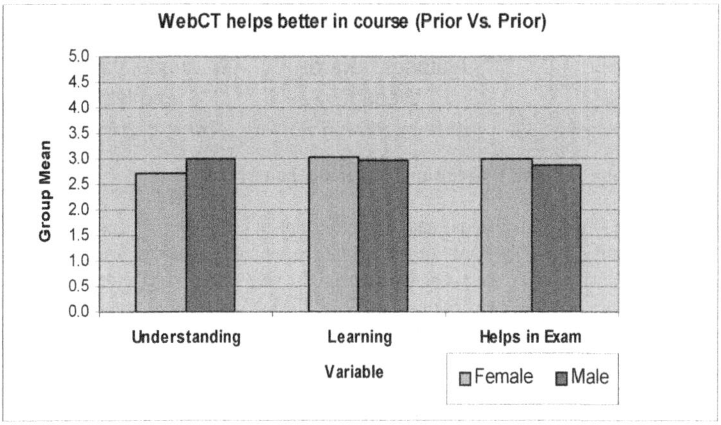

Figure 5: WebCT and Learning (Prior Vs. Prior)

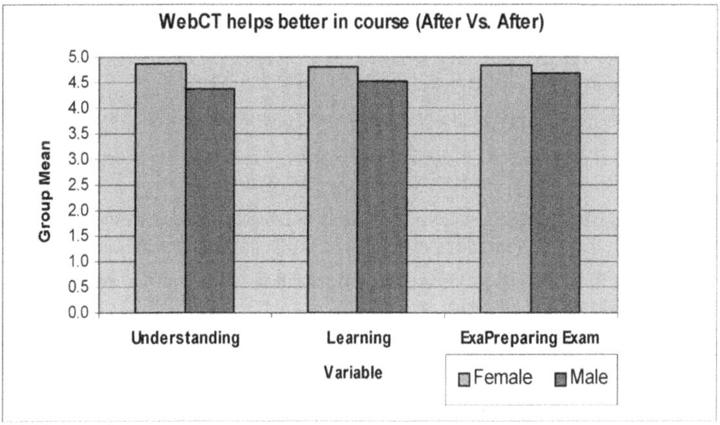

Figure 6: WebCT and Learning (After Vs. After)

Conclusion

The results of the survey showed that most students had little exposure to WebCT prior to the course and did not appreciate its benefits. After completing the course students expressed a more positive attitude towards WebCT. This positive change in their attitudes appears have contributed towards better understanding and learning the course material through WebCT as it was made easily accessible from any Internet enabled location at any time of the day for any duration.

In summary, those students who had access to WebCT had more positive attitude towards it and reported better understanding and learning of the course material (Figure 7).

The findings of this study are also in line with Koohang (1989), Hunt and Bohlin (1993), and Gressard and Loyd (1985), in that greater use of IT brings about more positive attitudes and hence greater confidence in the users. This enhanced confidence, in turn, results in more use, which may lead to even greater learning.

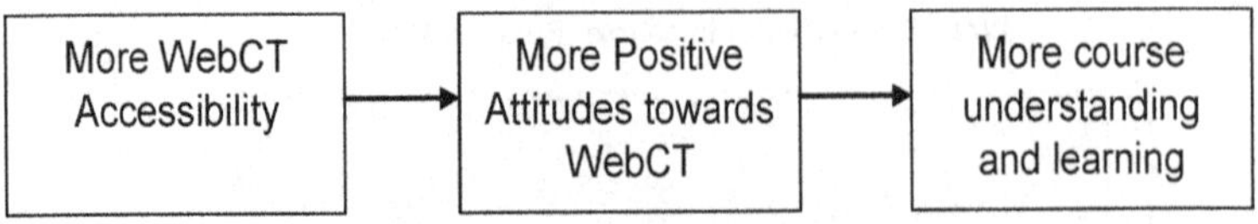

Figure 7: WebCT (accessibility, attitudes and learning)

With the increasing spread of the Internet and the proliferation of computing devices, technological literacy is becoming more vital. Distance education is becoming more widespread, especially online, and location independent, increasing the need for effective course-management systems and teaching strategies that utilize technology. The WebCT, Moodle or similar packages may continue play a major role influencing the students learning and meet students need and also overcome the funding challenges that traditional institutions could not offer.

References

Cetron, M. J., & Daview, O. (2003). 50 trends shaping the future. *Special Report Published by the World Future Society.*

Chick, S., Day, R., Hook, R., Owston, R., Warkentin, J., Cooper, P. M., Hahn, J., & Saundercook, J. (2002). *Technology and student success in higher education: A research study on faculty perceptions of technology and student success.* Toronto, Ontario McGraw-Hill Ryerson.

Dunn, S. (2000), The virtualizing of education. *The Futurist, 34*(2), 34-38.

Goldberg, M. W., Salari, S. & Swoboda, P. (1996), *World Wide Web Course Tool: An Environment for Building WWW-Based Courses*, Computer Networks and ISDN Systems.

Gressard, C. P. & Loyd, B. H. (1985). Validation studies of a new computer attitude scale. Paper presented at the *Annual Meeting of the American Educational Research Association, Chicago.*

Hunt, N. P. & Bohlin, R. M. (1993). Teacher education students attitudes towards using computers. *Journal of Research on Computing in Education, 25*(4), 487-497.

Koohang, A. A. (1989), A study of attitudes toward computers: Anxiety, confidence, liking and perception of usefulness. *Journal of Research on Computing in Education, 22*(2), 137-50.

Oblinger, D., Barone, C.A., & Hawkins, B.L. (2001). Distributed education and its challenges: An overview. American Council on Education (ACE). Retrieved June, 2003 from http://www.acenet.edu/bookstore/pdf/distributed-learning/distributed-learning-01.pdf

West, G.B. (1999). Teaching and technology in higher education: Changes and challenges. *Adult Learning*, 16-18.

Williams, P.E. (2003). Roles and competencies for distance education programs in higher education institutions. *The American Journal of Distance Education, 17*(1), 45-57.

The World Future Society. (2003). *Emerging technologies and ground-floor investment opportunities*. Special Report: Forecasts for the Next 25 Years. Bethesda, Maryland.

Appendix 1

College of Commerce and Economics

Questionnaire form

Introduction to Computers in Business (INFS 1411)

Spring, 2005

Please Tick

Male	Female

Dear Student:

The purpose of this form is to get your feedback regarding the course. Your input will help us in understanding and improving the course delivery process and will not at all affect the assessment of your work. Evaluate the following statements by selecting:

1 = Strongly Disagree 2 = Disagree 3 = Uncertain (Never used WebCT) 4 = Agree 5 = Strongly Agree

Please circle your response;

Thanks for your help

	Before Course	After Course
1. I access WebCT comfortably.	1 2 3 4 5	1 2 3 4 5
2. I access WebCT from any location.	1 2 3 4 5	1 2 3 4 5
3. I can access WebCT at any time.	1 2 3 4 5	1 2 3 4 5
4. I can be on WebCT as long as I wish.	1 2 3 4 5	1 2 3 4 5
5. I feel WebCT is friendly.	1 2 3 4 5	1 2 3 4 5
6. I feel at ease while using WebCT.	1 2 3 4 5	1 2 3 4 5
7. I feel comfortable interacting with computers.	1 2 3 4 5	1 2 3 4 5
8. I feel that WebCT is an important part of this course.	1 2 3 4 5	1 2 3 4 5
9. I prefer this course be taught by the instructor only.	1 2 3 4 5	1 2 3 4 5
10. I prefer this course be taught through WebCT only.	1 2 3 4 5	1 2 3 4 5
11. I prefer this course be taught by Instructor and supported through WebCT.	1 2 3 4 5	1 2 3 4 5
12. Overall, WebCT helped me in understanding better the course material.	1 2 3 4 5	1 2 3 4 5
13. Overall, WebCT helped me in learning more the course material.	1 2 3 4 5	1 2 3 4 5
14. Overall, WebCT helped me in scoring more in the course exams.	1 2 3 4 5	1 2 3 4 5

Biographies

Syed Jafar Naqvi is an Assistant Professor in the Department of Information systems, College of Commerce and Economics, Sultan Qaboos University, Muscat, Sultanate of Oman. He received M.S. from East Texas State University and a Ph.D. from University of Birmingham. His teaching interests include programming languages, Web applications development and e-commerce with research interest in computer education.

Manzur A. Ajiz is presently working as an Assistant Professor in the Department of Information Systems, College of Commerce and Economics, Sultan Qaboos University, Muscat, Sultanate of Oman. Prior to this he worked at many other prestigious universities and published widely on programming languages, e-commerce and systems development methodologies in national and international journals.

A Second Opinion on the Current State of Affairs in Computer Science Education – An Australian Perspective

V. Lakshmi Narasimhan
School of Electrical Engineering and Computer Science
The University of Newcastle, NSW, Australia

lakshmi.narasimhan@newcastle.edu.au

Abstract

This paper presents a critical look at the likely demise of Computer Science (CS) as a discipline, in the light of various mishaps that academics in Universities have met with due to trial and error. We trace the issues of the past and present and, identify the reasons why computer science as a discipline in many Universities has not moved with time – in particular why it is not kept up with the pace required by the field. The loss of computer science is also well-reflected in the huge downturn in CS student enrolment across the Anglo-Saxon world. The paper also details some steps on how to change the ways and means of CS academics. We record that some of the arguments and recommendations presented in this paper can be controversial and may not necessarily relate to scenarios that exist in other countries. Further, some of the assertions made are without comprehensive statistical data, as we could not gather them, besides gathering anecdotal evidences.

Keywords: Academic morality, Relationship management in CS, Multi-disciplinary approach, Change management and Downturn in CS education

Introduction

Many Universities have reported considerable decline in the enrolment of Computer Science (CS) majors around the Anglo-Saxon world and, many Australian Universities are also no exception to this down-turn (see Figures1-3 adapted from Higher Education Research Institute, n.d.). Briefly, the following observations can be made: i) student uptake of Computer Science has declined (Figure1) by over 60% between 2000-2004 and is now 70% lower than its peak in the early 1980, ii) interest in CS among women fell 80% between 1998-2004 (Figure 2) and 93% since its peak in 1982 and iii) the degree of production of CS female graduates is dwindling fast (Figure 3). However, some Universities have managed to fill-up their intake and some even managed to increase their student numbers. The following questions therefore beget the observer:

1. Why did the downturn happen in CS education?
2. What are the real contributing factors to the downturn in CS education?
3. What actions could CS educators taken to prevent the falling enrolment?

Figure 1. Computer Science Listed as Probable Major Among Incoming Freshmen
Source: HERI at UCLA

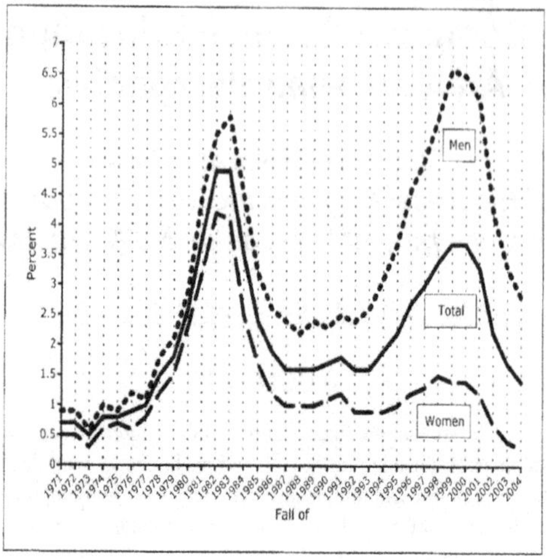

4. Why did the CS educators not take the required actions?
5. Why are some Universities able to attract full enrolment or even over-enrolment despite the downturn?
6. What lessons can be learnt from this downfall?
7. What are the real underlying issues?
8. Why are that comparative perspectives on CS education in the non-Anglo-Saxon world?

Figure 2. Probable Majors Indicated by Incoming Freshmen
Source: HERI/UCLA

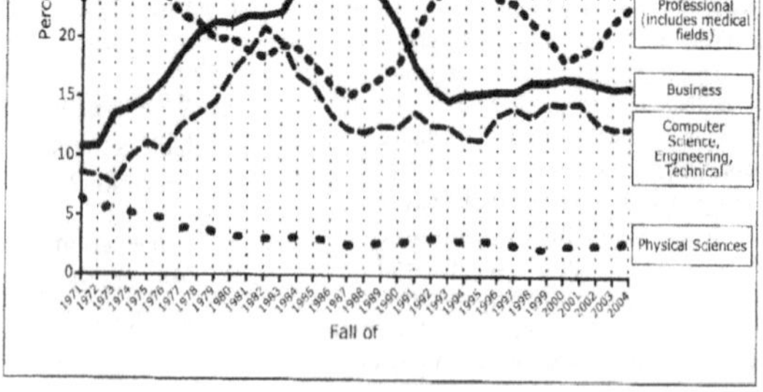

Figure 3. Portion of Bachelor's Degrees Granted to Women
Source: National Science Foundation. Data were not reported for 1999.

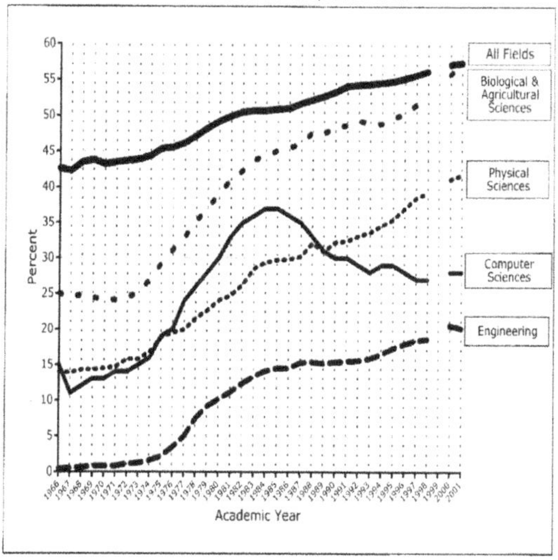

This paper addresses some of these questions and provides some pointers for introspection. The rest of the paper is organised as follows: the next section provides the context and perspectives on Computer Science, followed by the analysis of the list of issues raised in section 3. We discuss the lessons learnt in section 4 and give some pointers for further work in section 5. The conclusion summarises the paper and raises further investigative ideas.

As a special note, we record here that some of the arguments and recommendations presented in this paper can be controversial and may not necessarily relate to scenarios that exist in other countries. In addition, some of the assertions made are without comprehensive statistical data, as we could not gather them; however, the assertions and conjectures we make do have anecdotal, verbal and document-based support, some of which cannot be identified due to privacy reasons.

Perspectives on Computer Science

It is well accepted that computer science has its foundations in Logic, Mathematics, Electrical Engineering and Linguistics and according to Wikipedia (n.d.), its ideals are about "*Finding eternal truths about problems and algorithms for posterity*". Its emphasis is on analysing various problems, finding out their complexities, correctness and algorithms that yield the best solution. When the problems are solved, they do not change in a major way, except for "*changes around the frills*". Thus for example, the solution to the famous matrix multiplication problem has been found by many people with different degrees of complexities for different applications and their underlying contexts (e.g., sequential, parallel, etc). Formal theory, most often based on (computational) logic, have also been developed to understand and get a handle on problems in computer programming language, natural language, database structures and artificial intelligence.

Most Computer Science departments have their origins traceable to schools belonging to either Mathematics (most often) or Electrical Engineering (mostly in technology dominated Universities). In general, mathematics-originated CS departments (which we will call CSM departments) tend to be strong in theoretical aspects, while technology background CS departments (which we will call CST department) tend to be strong in practical aspects.

Computer science finds its niche by finding association with other disciplines and fields. Indeed Edsger Dijkstra, renowned computer scientist, said, "*Computer science is no more about computers than astronomy is about telescopes*". It is worth noting in this context there are Universities in which CS departments trace their origins to such diverse disciplines as medicine, fashion design, business, finance, mechanical engineering, library science, pure artistic design and pure linguistics. Such CS departments (which we will call CSO departments) tend to have a finer focus compared to other CS departments and have been generally successful in maintaining their focus. The CSOs have indeed maintained their links with their origins and have taken considerable efforts to diverse their efforts in teaching, research and application focus.

We take the proposed issues in this context in the next section and provide a second opinion on why CSM and CST departments have not fared well in relation to the handling of student education.

Analysis of Issues

Why did the Downturn Happen in CS Education?

Many educators in CS have attributed the downturn in student numbers in CS departments as something to do with the downturn in IT jobs available on the market. The negative publicity has some how permeated to the level of high school leavers and this has led to the consequent reduction in student numbers at the Universities. The Dotcom burst added to this vows considerably and somehow the charm that kept CS students numbers on the upward profile for a decade or so seem to have evaporated. The potential to make "*a quick buck*" also appeared to have been lost in this process and this has led some parents to think that CS is no longer a commercially good proposition for their progenies. Added to these, is the fact that outsourcing of IT jobs to third world countries such as India and China have contributed significantly to the job losses and the consequent loss of interest in IT education. It is noted that these perceptions – to a degree - have their origins to academics, who belong to CSM and CST departments and other vested interests. If enrolments stabilise at the current level, it will still be 40% below that of two years ago (Wilson, n.d.).

What are the Real Contributing Factors to the Downturn in CS Education?

We contend that none of the reasons quoted in the previous section, namely, Dotcom burst, loss of jobs, job migrations, etc, are tenable towards justifying such a profound loss in student numbers in CS Departments in Australia and the Anglo-Saxon world. We believe that the real contributing factors are as follows.

Profound Lack of Good Mathematics Education at High School Level

It is well recognised that school leavers in Australia (in particular) do not necessarily have sufficient mathematics background that justifies their entry into CS. We recognise this as a serious problem, particularly since mathematics is somehow not considered/marketed as a "*cool and interesting subject*" at the school level. The lack of good mathematics teachers and the dilution of the rigour required for learning the subject are two other reasons for poor mathematical background for high school leavers. Universities seem to do an *ad hoc* job of patching the skill set requirement with bridge courses, which are once again inadequate.

Untrained CS Educators at the University Level

A number of CS educators at the University level have obtained their terminal degrees from the University at which they are currently teaching. While a degree of "*incest*" may be good in that the person may already be part of a research group with "*a known culture of operation*", this could be detrimental for the broad development of the CS discipline in the University. This also impedes cross-fertilisation of ideas and thoughts. Anecdotal evidences suggest that a number of Universities in Australia have this problem. In contrast leading Universities in the USA (e.g., MIT, UC Berkeley) have policies for appointing internal Phds into their faculty stream. Usually they expect at least a period of activity being spent outside of their *alma mater* after completion of their Phds, before they could be considered for faculty positions.

Other serious issues include, limited amount of formal training in current CS related educational issues *per se.* Indeed most of the CS educators trace their background to (pure) mathematics and quite a number of them still continue to insist that CS is an extension of mathematics. Further, some of these academics do not realise that the field of CS has its origins in fields other than mathematics, i.e., in linguistics, logic and engineering. These issues coupled with the fact that most academics have little or no industrial experience in IT related areas, lead to poorly trained CS educators at the University level.

Unprepared CS Educators at the University Level

CS educators at many Universities in general have little industrial background or training (This has been observed by borrowing through a number of websites for academic resumes). A large majority of academics seem to have obtained their Phds straight after a series of course-based degrees (BS and MS typically) and with little IT industrial exposure, have joined academia to pursue typically academic research and teaching with little relevance to industry. Their PhDs are in advanced topics, which have little relevance to common teaching materials required to be addressed at the undergraduate level. Indeed at one University in Australia most of the CS academics have background in graph theory – not even in its applications. These CS educators, while they do teach well to CS students, do not do justice to the field in that they have little passion in teaching the materials; instead they teach out of necessity. Indeed in most Universities around Australia, very few academics spend their sabbatical leave at IT industries and further, spending quality time with industry is considered "*less than optimal*" by such academics too.

Inappropriate Marketing of CS Education to High School Leavers

CS courses are being marketed inappropriately at the high school level. Most of the high school leavers decide their career/course options by the time they reach their year 10 level. Unfortunately, Universities tend to market their courses at the year 12 level and consequently, with major failures. Anecdotal evidences suggest that Universities also do not articulate the differences between their various course offerings clearly to prospective students. Indeed a number of Universities have more than one CS (or related) Departments in various Faculties, which tend to compete with each other, rather than co-operate -- all to the detriment their very existence.

Fears and Dreams of High School Leavers have not been Studied well in the Context of CS Education

Most students who choose CS have "*potential for better job opportunities*" as the major reason for their choice. With the downturn in the IT industry, the fears and dreams of high school leavers have not been studied and understood well. Indeed if only the educators address the very concerns of prospective students, their field would considerably improve in terms of industrial relevance and student numbers too (Arora & Chazelle, 2005). Unfortunately, a number of CS academics appear to be really out of touch with market forces that drive the field.

Significant Semantic Gap between CS Education Offered by the University and that Required by Industry

As noted before, there exists a sharp and significant semantic gap between what are taught at the University and what are required by industry. Several industries have taken the task of re-training the recruited employees to fit into the industrial mould. On the other hand, there appears to be some value in the popular comment offered by academics that industries want only immediate technology knowledge, while Universities teach the theory that underpins not only a particular technology behind a product, but also whole raft of technologies that are still being attempted. However, if one looks at the market penetration of Windows, it is around 94%, but very few institutions offer Windows as the basis for teaching a course on operating systems!

Lack of Exposure of CS Students to Industrial Practices and Procedures

In general, CS educators have provided minimal insight to students on industrial practices and procedures, while software engineering students do get some exposure on these issues in the recent curriculum. While some would dispute this, the overwhelming evidence in industry indicates that CS students do need considerable re-training in the industry, prior to joining a major project. This could also be due to the fact that CS educators – a considerable number of them – come from mathematics background with little knowledge or respect for best-case practices and procedures.

During the Dotcom peak, the attrition rate in the IT industry was around 15%-27% per year, depending on the sub-field. Notwithstanding this, the attrition rate at SAS Institute (which produces such quality statistical packages like SAS) had an attrition rate of less than 1% per year and they attributed this low attrition rate to the profound efforts of their HRD (Human Resources Department (Harvard Business Review, 1996)). Indeed a typical successful employee has to undergo nearly 1.5 years of training, before s/he can be placed in a team that manages a project. During the training period, the person is "*unproductive*" to the company. The HRD places considerable emphasis on moulding the person and "*fitting*" the person into a team. They thus create champion teams that work on project. The old adage, "*A champion team will beat a team of champions*" holds good for SAS Institute and success follows them.

Lack of Recognition of CS Educators

Indeed in the current "*publish or perish*" environment, there is very little recognition for CS educators' plight. The field changes by the day and its application potential (to other fields) increases by the day, but there is very little time given to the academics to explore the open world; they are instead forced to teach unduly long hours on worthless courses. Further, the publication rates and their nature (e.g., journal, conference, etc) of typical CS academics are often compared with engineers[1]. The facts in the CS field, which are conveniently ignored, include: i) conference publications have more relevance to current research, ii) journal publications are mainly for archival purposes only and iii) by the time journal publication comes in print, it has little relevance to current

[1] This comparison is worse for Software Engineering academics.

research. The publication rates and their citation rates of various sub-fields in CS are also vastly different. Typically graph theorists tend to publish a number of papers, also with considerable citation rates, but this is not the case with experimental CS scientists, where the gestation time is at least three years for a significant paper to be published in a serious journal (e.g., IEEE Transactions on Software Engineering). With a systematic lack of understanding of the CS discipline, administrators often resort to unfair comparison. As a consequence, a number of CS departments have skewed profiles of academics, mostly with non-CS trained academics dominating over properly CS-trained academics.

Lack of Administrative Will to let the CS Educators do their Job

We have also noticed that there is a lack of will on the part of administrators to let the CS educators do their job. For example, CS educators are frowned upon when they engage in paid consultancy. Somehow paid consultancy is considered "*work for personal benefit*". On the contrary, paid consultancy must be made mandatory, just as it applies to General Practice in the field of Medicine. It is through consultancy, an academic can "*preach what s/he practices*[2]" and this has profound impact on the way CS courses are being taught. Consultancy also results in better education and understanding of current practices and procedures in the industry, besides providing knowledge in the state-of-the-art technology. Unfortunately, this issue is very much side-stepped by University administration.

"Fill the class with sheep heads" Syndrome to Justify Existence of CS Department

A lack of recognition and administrative will has other implications too. In the CS heyday, most Universities considered CS Departments as "*cash cows*" into which a considerable number of students could be pushed into in order to get their quota of monies from the Federal Government. These "*sheep heads*" (as one of the academics described succinctly his/her students) had neither background nor interest in the CS field; their only hope was the possibility of jobs. Furthermore, the academics had more than one reason to give a certain percentage of pass rates in the field in order to protect themselves. As a consequence, some Universities produced CS graduates with extremely poor quality and indeed some industries would not even interview graduates from certain Universities. Along with the considerable number of courses a typical CS academic has to teach, s/he is left with little time to keep themselves abreast of the field. This downward spiral has led to continued reduction in the quality of CS education and erosion of moral and ethical standards.

Lessons Learnt from Past Experience

What actions could CS educators have taken to prevent the falling enrolment? Before we look into what actions CS educators can take to prevent the falling enrolment, it is worth looking at what is happening in the current "*CS-boom countries*", such as India and China. We trace their successes and the underlying causes, before we give present our recommendations.

---

[2] Indeed the great management guru, Prof. Peter Drucker, mentions in his recent book that the reason he did not take up the professorship at the Harvard University (in their famous School of Business) was precisely because Harvard would not allow him to practice management through paid consultancy. According to Drucker, he could not preach what he could not practice. Harvard changed the policy much later, admitting their failure to do so much earlier was indeed a mistake.

A Brief Inspection of India, China, Japan and Other Asian & Third World Countries

Currently there is a boom in IT education in India, thanks primarily to the significant change in geopolitical equations around the world and the consequent IT in-sourcing into that country. An off-shoot of one of the largest Indian IT companies in India, viz. Hindustan Computers Limited (HCL, India), is the NIIT (National Institute for IT; http://www.niit.com/), which is now the largest IT education service provider in the world. NIIT has even started a private University in the USA specifically aimed at IT education and research. NIIT currently operates in 42 countries around the world, including China. Similarly the Indian Government has started another institution, called the Indian Institute of Information Technology (IIIT) at Hyderabad (http://www.iiita.ac.in/) (now being fondly called Cyberabad) with the specific aim to foster IT education and research. Another institution, called the Indian Institute of Banking and Finance (IDBF) (http://www.utiicm.com/fac_members.htm), has also been started recently to foster IT applications research into the financial sector. Both IIIT and IBDR are deemed Universities, which compare at par with the famous Indian Institute of Technologies (IITs, http://www.iitd.ernet.in/) and Indian Institute of Science (IISc, http://www.iisc.ernet.in/) in their quality of student in-take and educational services.

Broad and important observations that have been noted in India include the following:

1. High level of mathematics is being taught at the high school level and further, mathematics is still considered fundamental towards learning all scientific, engineering and various other fields.

2. High level of professionalism among teachers has been observed in teaching mathematics, formal logic and other analytical skills at the high school level.

3. Competition to get into good and reputed educational institutions is quite high and this competition in turn drives higher the quality of students seeking to study at the University level. In a recent ***60 minutes*** program (produced in 2005), one leading industrialist, Mr. Narayana Murthy (CEO of InfoSys Pty Ltd, currently the leading software outsourcing company in the world) remarked that his son could not get into one of the IITs despite very good preparations and hence he admitted him into Cornell University. A recent US Senate resolution singled out its praise for the profound contributions made by IITs to the economy of the USA.

4. A great degree of interaction exists among students with the spirit of "*co-operate to compete*". Indeed at most IITs and equivalent institutions, a very substantial database of questions and answers for various types of examinations are available to students at their living quarters[3]. These datasets have been collected over a period of time by the student themselves. So much so, one academic remarked that if he wants to look for variations and novel ideas for a question, s/he gets into one of these databases to explore further. Another academic commented that these databases typically appear to be better than the Schaum's Outline Series published by the McGraw Hill!

5. A good number of books are relatively cheaply available on fundamental topics of mathematics, computer science, linguistics and logic, thanks to most publishers printing exclusive "*India Only*" printed versions. These have since had a profound effect on CS education.

6. Having missed the "*Manufacturing Bus*" to China, the Indian Government decided to open up the economy for the software sector, which led to the extensive contracts in software outsourcing into India.

---

[3] The author has first hand experience on this, having graduated from the Indian Institute of Science.

7. The emphasis on good English language skills has led to numerous jobs being opened to CS graduates. Indeed English is a compulsory second language in almost all schools in India.

8. The availability of heterogeneous mix of people in India, particularly with vastly different linguistics skills, means that the thought processes during the various stages of the software life cycle (i.e., requirements elicitation, analysis, design, implementation, testing and maintenance) are diverse. This leads to a multitude of issues being documented and attempted during software development.

9. The "*publish or perish*" syndrome has not affected the Indian CS education environment considerably yet. This has resulted in good teaching being considered a major part of an academic activity. Further, good teachers are being recognised by the government and other NGO (Non-Governmental Organisations) organisations periodically.

10. The participation of private organisations in CS/IT education has been profound and their quality has also been quite good, thanks to the vibrant competition in this sector. The most notable one is the NIIT, which has now become the world's largest CS/IT education service provider, covering some 42 countries around the globe. Indeed admission to NIIT Diploma courses is through several screening exams in which the selection rate is around 30% or less.

11. Industry participation even in Government section CS/IT education has been very good, as industries are willing to actively supervise final year project students. Their aim appears to be two fold: i) to get part of their work done at low or no cost and ii) to identify potential employees, that could have been well-trained. Several organisations have reported good success in this type of active involvement.

12. Various programs in mass media (e.g., television, radio and even local Women's weeklies) have started educational columns on computing, which has revolutionised the way moms' and dads' thinking on computers. Nearly every village of India has at least one computer and this has transformed businesses and their requirements considerably. Thus farmers and fishermen are selling their products for the best prices they can fetch, instead of through the local middlemen. Indeed requirements by such customers have now forced various types of e-Commerce and related technologies to come to the forefront.

13. The multitude of languages in India[4] has made computer-linguistics develop rapidly. This is a field which is likely to have the next stage of growth and a company like Verity Inc. is likely to be the next Microsoft, because their products are highly sought after by companies involved in the fields of Finance, Marketing, Advertising and Media. A number of companies (notably CDAC – Centre for Development of Advanced Computing) have taken up the technical challenges in computer-linguistics from an international perspective and are fast competing with Multinationals.

The situation appears to be similar in China and other third world countries. In particular, the cost of "*intellectual labour*" is considerably less than in the Anglo-countries. While China is still struggling to cope with India in CS/IT area, mainly due to the lack of English skills among its service providers, it is nonetheless catching up fast. Indeed several self-learning English kiosks are operating in China, in addition to private organisations involved in teaching English.

[4] India has 18 official languages and 50+ actual languages and over 500 dialects. The two mother languages are Tamil and Sanskrit.

What are the Real Underlying Issues?

IT is now going through what "*manufacturing*" was going through some 40 years ago. There was big hue and cry, when mass manufacturing migrated to Japan, particularly a decade after World War II. American "*jobs were being lost*", as it was portrayed then, unfortunately did happen. However, America moved on to other areas, particularly in computer systems manufacturing, popularly known as "*Silicon Manufacturing*". Later even silicon manufacturing moved to Japan. Presently, most types of manufacturing are happening in China and other Dragon countries, while the majority of high-end manufacturing is happening in Japan. Whereas the United States still maintains a comfortable edge in high-end CPU (Central Processing Unit) manufacturing and related R&D areas.

Another important issue that is happening in the IT sector is the consolidation of major companies – i.e., big fish eating small fish – just as it happened to railways in the 1930s in the USA. As a consequence, a few multinational companies are dominating several areas of IT and the Internet and related services. Their Standards are over-riding Standards set by such organisations, as the IEEE (Institute of Electrical and Electronics Engineers), ISO (International Standards Organisation) and OMG (Object Management Group), particularly so in the software services area. CS educators who are not following these and adapting to the current state-of-the-art are doing so at their own peril.

There is a crying need to open up new and innovative areas in CS and IT. As mentioned before, CS/IT owns their continued existence to identifying and substantiating on-going relations with many other disciplines. One such area (besides a number of others), where such issues are dominating is the area of Information Management and Information Fusion, particularly due to information overload that is currently happening. However, few academic institutions are offering formal courses or degrees in these upcoming areas. In particular, media technologies will become an important IT application focus area in the future to come.

Why didn't the CS Educators Take the Required Actions?

It is our contention that one of the reasons that CS educators did not take the required actions is that they were driven by blind competition to fill-up seats so that their positions are safe. It is also true that the process was partially driven by greed to expand the CS faculty at a time when opportunity prevailed. Furthermore, Government regulations have limited University finances to such an extent that this opening provided a good opportunity get further funding in a "*growth area*". However, little or no efforts were made at planned growth. It is not that issues were not unknown to CS educators, but the syndromes persisted as to "*Who will bell the cat?*" and "*Why should we do that?*" We also contend that there was a systematic lack of vision to "*foresee, accept and act*" on the future on the part of CS educators. Given the ground realities of CS and IT, the educators need to pull up the socks – particularly at high school level education.

Why are Some Universities able to Attract Full Enrolment or Even Over-Enrolment Despite the Downturn?

There are a number of reasons as to why some Universities are able to attract full enrolment or even over-enrolment despite the downturn, which include, but not limited to the following:

- Mainly because of their historically well-known high profile (e.g., MIT, UC Berkeley, etc).
- Active fostering of foreign students – foreign students are not considered as "*necessary evils, but as affirmative good*". A number of G8 Universities in Australia (the top 8 Universities are called G8) have nearly failed in this area.

- Understanding and appreciating foreign student culture, learning mechanisms (particularly learning by examples and group learning), delivery of lectures and linguistic requirements.
- Industry involvement and participation.
- Addressing the issues mentioned in this paper and others in a logical manner taking into considerations the market realities.

Indeed we believe that less than 10% of the Universities in the Anglo-Saxon world are taking these issues seriously and attempting to find their way ahead.

What Lessons can be Learnt out of this Downfall?

Sound planning is required to support CS/IT education. Key industrialists and lobby groups must be fostered to keep the relevant Minister and their Departments to be in-tune with ground realities and latest market conditions. In a recent conference, Bill Gates mentioned that funding from the American NSF (National Science Foundation) has nearly halved for CS/IT research and he has voiced profound concerns it will have on almost all fields of research. In Australia, the Tourism industry advisory group lobbies and obtains funding to the tune of 400+ million dollars, but the IT lobby is poorly represented. The IT education lobby is even more poorly represented – perhaps, it may even be non-existent.

Periodic re-learning is fundamental to CS/IT education. This has been one of the key deficiencies of the current environment. Engaging in on-going industrial consultancies and learning current state-of-the-art technology is of paramount importance.

Actively diversifying CS/IT into other areas, establishing and sustaining their R&D is very important.

Creating a core body of knowledge in CS/IT that can be easily replicated using automation is the foundation to the success of this profession – just in as much as Civil and other Engineers have done in their worlds. Prof. David Parnas (a pioneer in software engineering) in his keynote address at the ASWEC conference (Parnas, 2005), specifically mentioned the lack of core body of knowledge in CS/IT/SE as a major impediment to further progress in these fields. As a consequence, people keep on re-inventing the wheel.

Exposing future students to such opportunities will be the key to increasing student numbers.

What are the Comparative Perspectives on CS Education in the Non-Anglo-Saxon World?

Lacking a core body of knowledge in CS/IT, most of the non-Anglo-Saxon world is placing considerable emphasis on fundamental subjects like Mathematics, Statistics, Physics and others. This approach provides their students with critical analytical abilities to think logically and to handle complex problems, which in turn help these countries establish a sound environment for software in-sourcing. China and Korea, for example, have created several Universities and Schools, where English is the medium of instruction, particularly in IT related areas.

These countries are trying to understand and come to terms with the global white collar labour market, their potentials and their added-value to their economies. They have created a new stream of high value employment. As a consequence, these countries are providing substantial tax concessions or subsidies to ICT industries to start new venture companies.

Several countries are also encouraging professionals from IT industries to actively participate in educational programs; they offer grants and aids-in-support to encourage such transitional arrangements.

It is recognised that the Digital Divide still persists, particularly in the third world countries, but these countries are developing useful mechanisms to bridge the divide through their sheer "*knowledge power*" that is inherent in their people.

Recommendations for Managing Future CS Departments

We present below a list of recommendations that CS Departments should consider for their future:

1. Allow teaching staff to undergo at least one month of industrial training per year. Attending "*academic/s (dominated) conferences*" is not at all a substitute in this case.
2. Allow teaching and tutorial staff to be active participants in consultancy programs. Indeed this activity must be made mandatory to the extent that their corresponding educational institutions must provide avenues for staff to perform consultancies. Note that this is a win-win situation for both the staff and their Institution.
3. Encourage academic staff to spend their sabbatical (study) leave at relevant IT industries, rather than in another academic institution.
4. Encourage industry based professionals to offer serious academic equivalent courses at the University. Their participation is vital for the robustness of the entire program.
5. Provide mandatory summer-term bridge courses in advanced mathematics (make this a prerequisite, if necessary) that high school leavers must undergo and pass, before they can take their CS program. Do not allow unprepared students into the CS course. Avoid the temptation to fill the class with poor students just for the sake of money. They will become a drain to the staff, the University and the society. This will also lead to greater intellectual competition leading to better quality of outputs.
6. Create or be part of lobby groups that advise the relevant Minister (or their Cabinet Secretary) on IT related issues and, in particular, on the corresponding skill shortages and related educational issues.
7. Accept that CS/SE/IT is different to traditional Science and/or Engineering and allow them to be evaluated on their performance differently, particularly since the area is still evolving. This will give academics the much-needed confidence (particularly in rural sectors) to compete on a "*level playing field*". CS staff performance must also include the fact that the field keeps changing all the time (in particular in IT and SE areas). Their preparation times are grossly under-valued currently. Their research outputs, which appear mostly in conferences (as opposed to other fields, where they tend to prefer journal publications), are often disparaged. This attitude must change and a concerted effort is required to educate the people around.
8. Allow private participants to offer relevant CS/IT programs. Their quality can be monitored and adjudicated through accreditation programs from the ACS (Australian Computer Society), IEAust (Institution of Engineers, Australia) and other similar bodies.
9. Allow research and academic staff to develop broader field research profile and give them suitable avenues and opportunities to explore newer areas. During this period suitable funding and performance measures (not the traditional measures) must be applied.
10. Use appropriate marketing strategies to educate high school leavers; "*catch them young*" a popular advertisement slogan from the McDonalds is very relevant here. Involve student participation in CS/IT/SE related areas at various levels and let Universities employ a suitable (paid) person as high school liaison officer to address prospective students' fears and dreams.

11. The curriculum must be amended to include real world industrial input. This means even some of the Microsoft[5] specific technical issues must be addressed and discussed in the curriculum.

12. While emphasis must be placed on programming skills, it is very essential that a greater emphasis must be placed on design, maintenance and testing of software systems. The latter issues determine the success of products better. While coding will become a routine job, design will still require advanced cognitive skills.

13. Emphasise good English language[6] and oral and written communication skills. Longer term team-based projects are also essential. Allow "*incubators*" to be set-up within the University system, with proper academic and industry joint supervisions.

14. Develop University-based "*Continuing Education in IT*" and "*Advanced Professional Development Programs*" so that the community and industry professionals can be engaged with the University system on an on-going basis. The "*Quality Improvement Program (QIP)*" conducted at the Indian Institute of Science, Bangalore, has been an outstanding success (on a number of factors) for over 30 years.

15. Aim to develop a corporate body of knowledge. This cannot be done in isolation, but in partnership with Universities and industries around the world. One approach is to foster "*sister University*" concept further.

16. Be not alarmed by the "*invasion of skilled professionals*" from other parts of the world. The resulting heterogeneous talent pool will only enhance the quality of software systems. Accept that while collar jobs are globally re-locatable and that too at short notice.

Conclusions

This paper presents a number of issues that have been plaguing the CS education environment in the Anglo-Saxon world over the recent past, with particular reference to Australia. We argue – some times controversially - that most of the issues and problems were predictable, but CS educators failed to admit, accept and act on them. We present in this paper a list of issues that could have been addressed wisely, at least in hindsight. There are a number of lessons to be learnt from the past and also from other countries, wherein CS education is really booming. Two of the key issues we argue are i) the lack of recognisable private CS/IT education providers in Australia and ii) significant lack of industry participation in CS/IT educational scenario.

We argue that all is still not lost. History has shown a number of scenarios from which several lessons can be learnt. We identify some of these issues in this paper and also the ways to look forward to the future of CS/IT education in Australia. Even though some of our arguments and assertions may be controversial, they do form pointers for brainstroming the underlying problem in the CS Educational Community. It is a pity that we could not provide some of the real information due to privacy reasons; consequently they are mentioned as anecdotal.

References

Arora, S. & Chazelle, B. (2005). Is the thrill gone?. Communications of the ACM, 48(8), 31-33.

[5] The author does not own any shares in Microsoft, but if any one wishes to bequeath some to the author, he will gladly accept -;)

[6] English is still the preferred language, while addressing various issues that arise during software development across international boundaries.

Harvard Business Review, 1996.

Higher Education Research Institute at the University of California at Los Angeles (HERI/UCLA).

Parnas, D. (2005). Keynote address at the Australian Software Engineering Conference (ASWEC'05).

Wikipedia. (n.d.). entry on comparing software engineering with other disciplines: http://en.wikipedia.org/wiki/Comparing_software_engineering_and_related_fields.

Wilson, B. (n.d.). Possible consequences of reduced student numbers for CSE teaching. Retrieved from http://www.cse.unsw.edu.au/~teachadmin/tc/downturn.html

Biography

Prof. **Lakshmi Narasimhan** obtained his Bachelor's degrees in Physics and Electronics Engineering from the University of Madras and Indian Institute of Science respectively. He also obtained his Master's and Phd degrees respectively from the Madras Institute of Technology and University of Queensland, Australia. He worked at his *alma mater* in Australia as a lecturer and senior lecturer and was also the Director of the PA3SE (Parallel Algorithms, Architectures And Software Engineering) Research Laboratory. In 1995 he moved to the Australian Defence and Science and Technology Organisation (DSTO) as a Principal Research Scientist and was leading the program on Information Management and Information Fusion. He has been instrumental in initiating few key computer information systems projects with strategic clients within the Australian Defense Force, which have since led to the deployment of several mission critical systems at various customer sites. Later he moved to the USA, where worked as a full professor at the Computer Science Department, University of North Texas at Denton. Currently he is the Professor and Chair in Software Engineering at the University of Newcastle, Australia.

Prof. Narasimhan has published over 120 papers in the areas of Software Engineering and Information Engineering. In particular, his research interests are in computer architecture, parallel and distributed computing, software testing, text & audio processing, E-Commerce, Software process, and information management & fusion. His papers have appeared in such archival journals as the various IEEE Transactions and IEE Proceedings. Prof. Narasimhan was the founding chair of the IEEE Computer Society, Queensland Chapter and initiated the International Conference series ICA3PP (IEEE International Conference on Algorithms And Architectures) and acted as its Inaugurating Chair. He has also been the technical chair of two other conferences and has been on the technical panel of over 30 leading International Conferences. Currently his research interests are the areas of large-scale system engineering, testing & visualization, Agent technology for Decision Support System design and distributed object computing. He has consulted to a number of industries and educational institutions on various IT and Software Engineering projects. Presently he is also associated with two Co-Operative Research Centres (CRC on Construction Innovation and CRC on Integrated Engineering Asset Management). He is also the Director of the MESTEC Research Centre at the University of Newcastle, which specialises in the applications of mobile technology to medical information management and patient care. Prof. Narasimhan is a Senior Member of the IEEE, ACM, Fellow of ACS and IEAust. He is an (technical) Expert Panel Member of ISO (International Standards Organisation) and MIMOSA (Machinery Information Management Open Standards Organisation, USA).

Issues in Informing Science and Information Technology Volume 3, 2006

Cheating or 'Collaborative Work': Does it Pay?

E. Naude & T. Hörne
University of South Africa, Pretoria, South Africa

naudeej@unisa.ac.za hornet@unisa.ac.za

Abstract

Being a distance education institution, our current infrastructure does not allow group or collaborative work on undergraduate level. Although students are allowed to work together and assist each other, each student is required to submit individual attempts for assignments and/or projects. Assignments that are so similar that we could not accept them as individual attempts are considered cheating. According to the literature, cheating in assignments and projects is a problem in educational institutions at all levels. Students often use ingenious ways to disguise dishonesty. It is not always possible to determine the extent of the problem due to the inability to identify all instances, especially in modules with large student numbers. We investigated this problem in a second-level computing module. The examination results of students suspected of cheating were analysed and compared with the results of the rest of the students (the control group). This was done for 2004 and 2005. In this paper we report on our findings in this regard.

Keywords: cheating, assignments, examination results, programming education

Introduction

It is clear from the literature that student cheating is a serious problem in educational institutions at all levels throughout the world (McCabe, Treviño, & Butterfield, 2001; Sheard, Dick, Markham, MacDonald, & Walsh, 2002; Smith, 2005). We were hesitant to use such a strong word for this phenomenon but, even if one uses a synonym that 'sounds' less crude, this does not change the fact that cheating remains a serious offence which should be addressed urgently. Dick et al. (2003) state that student behaviour could be regarded as cheating if one or more of the following apply:

- the behaviour violates the accepted standard of the particular institution;
- the behaviour violates the rules laid down by the institution for the particular assessment task.

Using this as a guideline, the behaviour of students as described in this paper can be considered cheating.

This study is part of a long-term project where various ways in which the pass-rate of students in computer programming modules could be improved are investigated (Naudé & Hörne, 2003, 2004). In this paper we look at the phenomenon of cheating in assignments and how this affects the examination results of individual students. We identified a number of students that cheated in their assignments and looked at their examination results.

In the next section we discuss general reasons for students cheating in assignments, projects and examinations. We then discuss the methodology used for our research, the various ways in which the students tried to disguise the fact that they were cheating and the methods we used for detecting it. We present research results for the 2004 and 2005 academic years and in the final section we draw some conclusions and discuss further research. Note that we use the terms 'he', 'his' and 'him' to indicate both male and female students.

Reasons for Cheating

One could consider students cheating to be a three-layered event. Cheating is, in most cases, the result of a combination of factors or reasons. Firstly, there has to be the *necessity to cheat.* If a student could complete a sufficiently good assignment in time, and the perceived effort of the student is worth the benefit derived from it, then it is unlikely that he would even consider cheating. There would be no need to do so. Cizek (1999) supports this view by stating that students cheat to get a better grade. Drake, as quoted in (Cizek, 1999), found a clear relationship between cheating and grades. The weaker students were more prone to cheating. In our case, where assignments generally do not count towards the final mark of a student, this would mean that students cheat merely to achieve admission to the examination with less effort. Thus it has to be beneficial to the student to cheat.

Research (Cizek, 1999; Dick et al., 2003; McCabe et al., 2001) has identified a number of reasons related to the necessity layer. The following reasons can be assumed to be relevant to our students:

- external pressures to perform well (e.g. from parents and employers), thus the need for high marks;
- financial pressures;
- overly difficult assignments;
- time pressures;
- a heavy workload.

As far as the last two (related) reasons are concerned, it should be kept in mind that most of our students study part time. Their study time competes with family time, work time and time to socialise. Students often overestimate their own capabilities as well as the available time for studying, and also underestimate the amount of time needed to master a specific module. Thus they burden themselves with too heavy a work load. Unexpected events in the life of a UNISA student, such as starting a new job, job transfers, family matters such as unexpected pregnancies and illness may also encourage a student to cheat.

When a necessity to cheat has arisen, the next layer, namely the opportunity to cheat, needs to be present. Like a mountaineer that climbs a mountain 'because it is there', a student will cheat only if it is possible to do so. The following factors could be considered relevant:

- the availability of fellow students whose assignments can be copied;
- a person (e.g. friend, daughter, father, colleague) who can do all or part of the assignment for the student;
- chat groups, discussion forums and the Internet;
- a tutor doing large parts of the assignments for his students;

- availability of the solutions to questions asked in previous years: either the model solutions despatched by the University, or obtained from students that completed the module in a previous year;
- availability of a solution done by another student on a shared computer, e.g. in the computer laboratory of the University.

Technological advances have led to an increase in cheating (Dick et al., 2003) simply because it facilitates cheating and because of the increased availability of material on the Internet. The easier it is to cheat, the more prevalent cheating can be expected to be.

Many students that have both the need and the opportunity to cheat, still do not yield to the temptation. This brings us to the third layer, i.e. the internal influences that result in the final decision to cheat. Here we turn our attention to the student himself. The final decision to cheat is a personal choice made by weighing internal values and beliefs against the external factors discussed earlier. Some students consider cheating to be a 'victimless crime' – no one gets hurt, so it is acceptable (Dick et al., 2003). Related to this, is the belief that it really is not wrong to cheat in assignments as it has little or no influence on the final mark. Educators should clearly state what is and what is not acceptable behaviour and why. Students may find it difficult to understand the difference between helping a fellow student, and actually doing his work for him.

In the School of Computing at the University of South Africa one of the purposes of assignments is to provide students with the opportunity to obtain examination admission by earning a specified number of credits through the submission of assignments throughout the academic year. Some students might feel that, since they pay their fees, they are actually entitled to automatic admission to the examination and thus they are justified in cheating. Related to this is the issue of repeated assignments. 'If my lecturer does not bother setting a new assignment, why should I bother doing it. I might as well use last year's model solution.' These are forms of *neutralisation* which is defined as the denial of responsibility for improper actions because of the improper actions of others (Cizek, 1999).

Lack of character and integrity, and no pride in a job well done, as well as pure laziness, are more reasons mentioned by McCabe et al. (2001).

The decision to cheat may become easier if a student observes cheating by fellow students. 'Everybody else does it, so I might as well join in.' McCabe et al. (2001) have in fact found that peer behaviour showed the most significant relationship to cheating. This is another example of neutralisation.

The decision of a student to cheat will inevitably also depend on the perceived reaction of lecturers and the institution if he is found out. Especially in cases where an assignment contributes towards the final mark, a message that cheating will not be tolerated must be clearly stated.

Although in most cases all three of the layers discussed above are present when a student cheats, there may be the exception where a student cheats although there is no real necessity to do so. However, the opportunity and inclination still exist. An example may be when a student cheats because he does not see the educational benefits of assignments. Lecturers should emphasise the fact that assignments are not merely opportunities for gaining admission to the examination, but should rather be seen as opportunities for mastering the study material at a steady pace. This also means that the assignments should be relevant, geared to reaching the specific learning outcomes of the module, and neither too easy nor too difficult.

We may conclude that the decision to cheat is almost never the result of one reason only, but rather a combination of various factors.

Research Methodology

This study ran for two years: 2004 and 2005. We used a second-level module on computer organisation for this study. This module has a theoretical component as well as a practical component in which students have to write relatively small programs in assembly language. We clearly state in our tutorial letters that, since we are a distance learning institution, group work does not form part of our assessment programme and thus that students are not allowed to submit group efforts. We also emphasise the fact that students will be penalised if their assignments are so similar that they cannot be considered individual attempts.

There are four assignments for this module; two written and two multiple-choice. With the multiple-choice assignments we could not determine whether students cheated or not. Where cheating was detected in the first written assignment, students were given a strict warning that this is not acceptable and that they will be penalised in future.

The second written assignment consisted of a number of theoretical questions as well as an assembly language program which the students had to submit electronically. During the marking process, the programs were evaluated by testing the executable code and assessing a printout of the program to evaluate the structure, etc. of the programming effort. We only used one external marker for this assignment. With her help we were able to identify groups of students that cheated by submitting either identical assignments or assignments that were so similar that we could not accept them as individual efforts. For 2004, these groups were combined to form an experimental group and the rest of the students who were admitted to the examination for this module were the control group. The χ^2-test of independence is often used in research to compare two independent groups. For this reason we used this test to compare the examination results of the two groups mentioned above. Due to our findings, we decided to use two experimental groups and the control group for 2005.

Ways of Cheating

There were some cases where the students simply submitted exactly the same assignment, spelling mistakes and all. In several other cases the students used various techniques to disguise the fact that they were submitting the same assembly language code. A number of these could be identified:

- search and replacing variable and label names. This was also reported by Carter (1999) in a Java programming course;
- using different fonts in the printout they present as part of the written assignment;
- not submitting a program listing;
- changing the comments in the program;
- submitting programs without any comments.

Detecting Incidences

Cheating is not easy to identify if the program executes perfectly and does nothing unexpected. We suspect that several such incidents of cheating went undetected.

However, if the program does not produce the correct results and/or displays a message that catches the attention of the marker, e.g. a spelling mistake, it is easy for the marker to detect similarities. Such students also tend to submit their assignments on the same date so the marker gets them in the same batch. This was also reported by (Cizek, 1999; Dick et al., 2003).

Research Results

Results for 2004

We were able to identify 4 groups of students that cheated in the practical assignment. Groups 1, 2 and 3 simply submitted identical assignments. However, a relatively large number of the students in Group 4 used some of the techniques discussed earlier to disguise the fact that they were cheating. The students in this group differ from the others in the sense that they are all registered at one of the business schools that offer Unisa courses while the students write the official Unisa examinations. Since these students attend lectures, the possibility exists that the tutor 'assisted' the students with the programming assignment.

Table 1 contains a summary of the examination results of the four groups plus the results of the control group.

Table 1: Examination results 2004

	No of students Admitted	No of students absent from exam	Passed	Failed	Total
Group 1	3	1/3 = 33.3%	1/3 = 33.3%	1/3 = 33.3%	100%
Group 2	2	0/2 = 0%	0/2 = 0%	2/2 = 100%	100%
Group 3	7	0/7 = 0%	1/7 = 14%	6/7 = 86%	100%
Group 4	35	6/35 = 17%	11/35 = 32%	18/35 = 51%	100%
Experimental group (total)	**47**	**7/47 = 15%**	**13/47 = 28%**	**27/47 = 57%**	**100%**
Control group	**253**	**54/253 = 21%**	**120/253 = 48%**	**79/253 = 31%**	**100%**

The results of Groups 1 and 3 could be an indication that one person in the group did the actual work while the others merely copied the program and submitted it as their own. The result was that one student mastered the work and subsequently passed the exam while the others in the group did not master the practical work and were consequently unsuccessful in the examinations. The higher pass rate of Group 4 with respect to Groups 1-3 could be ascribed to the students being tutored. One may expect the pass rate of this particular group to be higher than the pass rate for the average UNISA student who does not attend lectures. However, this is not the case for the 2004 results (32% vs. 48% of the control group).

We used the χ^2-test of independence to compare the pass rate of the experimental group to that of the control group. Based on Table 1, $\chi^2_{(1, N=239)} = 5.37$ which is larger than the corresponding test statistic $\chi^2_{0.05} = 3.84$. Thus we can conclude that there is a statistically significant difference between the results of the experimental group and that of the control group. This indicates that cheating is not beneficial to the student since it does not contribute to the learning process. It also confirms the results reported by Drake as quoted in (Cizek, 1999) (see section on reasons for cheating).

Results for 2005

As shown in Table 2, we identified seven groups of students that cheated in the practical assignment with Group 7 once again the tutored group.

Table 2: Examination results 2005

	No of students Admitted	No of students absent from exam	Passed	Failed	Total
Group 1	2	2/2 = 100%	0/2 = 0%	0/2 = 0%	100%
Group 2	2	1/2 = 50%	0/2 = 0%	1/2 = 50%	100%
Group 3	2	1/2 = 50%	0/2 = 0%	1/2 = 50%	100%
Group 4	2	1/2 = 50%	1/2 = 50%	0/2 = 0%	100%
Group 5	2	0/2 = 0%	0/2 = 0%	2/2 = 100%	100%
Group 6	2	2/2 = 100%	0/2 = 0%	0/2 = 0%	100%
Group 7	17	7/17 = 41%	9/17 = 53%	1/17 = 6%	100%
Experimental group (total)	**29**	**14/29 = 48%**	**10/29 = 35%**	**5/29 = 17%**	**100%**
Control group	**288**	**60/288 = 21%**	**113/288 = 39%**	**115/288 = 40%**	**100%**

As mentioned earlier, Group 7 should actually be considered separately from the rest of the experimental group. This is summarised in Table 3 with Experimental group 1 comprising Groups 1 to 6 of Table 2 and Experimental group 2 the tutored students.

Table 3. Summarisation with regrouping

	No of students Admitted	No of students absent from exam	Passed	Failed	Total
Experimental Group 1	12	7 = 58.3%	1 = 8.3%	4 = 33.3%	100%
Experimental Group 2	17	7 = 41%	9 = 53%	1 = 6%	100%
Control group	288	60 = 21%	113 = 39%	115 = 40%	100%

When comparing the results from Experimental group 1 to the results of the control group, there is a significant difference in the pass rate (8.3% vs. 39%). Thus the same trend was observed in both year groups.

Contrary to the results for 2004, the tutored group, i.e. Experimental Group 2 in Table 3, did in fact outperform the control group in 2005 as far as the pass rate is concerned (53% vs. 39%). In Experimental Group 2, only 1 student failed. This probably collates with the higher percentage of absentees for this group (41% vs. 21% for the control group). This may be due to a tutor advising students who were not properly prepared to rather stay away from the exam.

Conclusion and Further Research

According to (Dick et al., 2003) one should consider cheating to be a serious problem if one or more of the following, amongst others, is/are true:

- many students are involved, not only one or two;
- students try to disguise the fact that they are cheating;
- the students did not achieve a satisfactory learning outcome; and
- the assessment task contributes to the final outcome of the course.

From the points listed above, it is clear that all of the above are relevant in this study:

- nearly 20% of the students that were admitted to the examinations were involved.

As stated earlier, we suspect that this number may be significantly higher;

- students used various techniques to disguise the fact that they were cheating;
- the examination results are significantly lower on average for the cheaters than for the control group;
- although the year mark counts only 10% of the final mark of a student, the marks for this particular assignment carries the most weight in establishing the year mark of a student for this module.

In a study conducted by McCabe et al. in 2001, it was found that 'some forms of cheating have increased dramatically in the last 30 years' (Dick et al., 2003). It is clear from the results in this study that, as is the case in most educational institutions over the world, cheating is a serious problem in our School and probably in the University as a whole. Apart from being dishonest, this study also indicates that it may have a strong negative influence on the pass rate.

As professed by (Dick et al., 2003) and (Rittman, 2005), a clear set of rules and standards should be set out for students registered for modules offered by the School of Computing. This should clearly state the policy of the School regarding cheating and the steps that will be taken if students do not abide by these rules and standards. Because of the high incidence of cheating and the low pass-rate of students in the School of Computing, this policy should not merely form part of the mountain of material the student is presented with on registration but rather sent out as a separate tutorial letter. A clear policy from the University as well as strict regulations for enforcing it is also needed.

Although this study provided some answers, a few important questions that require further research surfaced. We have a very high percentage of repeaters in this specific module. We would like to conduct a longitudinal study to determine what becomes of students that cheated and failed when they repeat the module. We also want to establish whether repeaters are more prone to cheating than students taking the module for the first time. The attitude of the students in our School with respect to cheating in assignments may be determined by means of questionnaires. Our student body is composed of different societies, each with its own set of norms. Do the social norms of a given society influence the incidence of cheating or is cheating universal? Does the IT environment have a sound ethical framework that could be enforced on students about to enter the profession?

Does informal group work encourage cheating in assignments? Formal group work and collaborative learning are often compulsory in undergraduate final year projects. Will all the members of the group necessarily develop the same set of skills required by the project to the same extent? For example, one person may solely be responsible for system specifications and documentation, another might do all the programming and a third the graphics or the final presentation.

Technology exists for identifying plagiarism but may not be so readily available for determining 'plagiarism' of executable program code.

Acknowledgement

We would like to express our appreciation to MC Pistorius who played a major part in the assessment of the assignments for this project.

References

Carter, J. (1999). Collaboration or Plagiarism: What happens when students work together? *ITiCSE, 1999*, Cracow, Poland.

Cizek, G. J. (1999). *Cheating on tests: How to do it, detect it, and prevent it*. Mahwah, N.J.: L. Erlbaum Associates.

Dick, M. Sheard, J., Bareiss, C., Carter, J., Joyce, D., Harding, T. & Laxer, C. (2003). Addressing student cheating: Definitions and solutions. *ACM SIGCSE, 35*(2), 172-184.

McCabe, D. L., Treviño, L. K. & Butterfield, K. D. (2001). Cheating in academic institutions: A decade of research. *Ethics & behaviour, 11*(3), 219-232.

Naudé, E. J & Hörne, T. (2004). The role played by assignments in computer programming education. *Proceedings of SAARMSTE 2004*. Cape Town.

Naudé, E.J & Hörne, T. (2003). Investigating suggestions for increasing the throughput rate of IS students. *Proceedings of INSITE 2003*, Pori, Finland. Available at http://proceedings.informingscience.org/IS2003Proceedings/docs/116Naude.pdf

Rittman, A.L. (2005). Academic dishonesty among college students. Retrieved April 30, 2005 from http://www.mwsc.edu/psychology/research/psy302/fall96/andi_rittman.html

Sheard, J., Dick, M., Markham S., MacDonald, I. & Walsh, M. (2002). Cheating and plagiarism: Perceptions and practices of first year IT students. *Proceedings of the ITiCSE 2002*, Denmark.

Smith, S. L. (2005). At what age do children start cheating? Retrieved April 30, 2005 from http://clearinghouse.missouriwestern.edu/manuscripts/45.asp

Biographies

Tertia Hörne is a Senior Lecturer in the School of Computing at the University of South Africa. She did her BSc at the University of Johannesburg and her Hons BSc and MSc at the University of South Africa. She is currently registered for a PhD at the same university, working in the field of model checking. Her research interests include knowledge representation and automated reasoning, functional programming, logic programming and constraint logic programming, and artificial intelligence in general. In her spare time she loves reading and playing golf.

A Memory Optimized Public-Key Crypto Algorithm Using Modified Modular Exponentiation (MME)

A. O. Oluwatope, B. A. Ojo, and G. A. Aderounmu
Comnet Laboratory, Computer Science And Engineering, Obafemi Awolowo University Ile-Ife. Nigeria

M. O. Adigun
Computer Science, University of Zululand. South-Africa

aoluwato@oauife.edu.ng, ojo_d@yahoo.com, gaderoun@oauife.edu.ng & madigun@pan.uzulu.ac.za

Abstract

Since the advent of data communication over networks, it has become imperative to ensure security of information. Cryptography is a technique that is being employed. This paper takes a look at an important aspect of the public key encryption scheme, the modular exponentiation technique, with the view of optimizing it. Taking a look at some public key encryption schemes, it would be observed that the modular exponentiation process is primal to achieving high speed algorithms in data encryption. With special emphasis on the Montgomery exponentiation algorithm, a blend of this algorithm with the sliding window method of exponentiation is proposed. A detailed complexity analysis of the proposed and selected algorithms was carried out. Both algorithms were implemented and simulated using MATLAB 6.5. While the proposed algorithm did not prove to be faster than the classical Montgomery exponentiation algorithm, it was rather observed that it makes lesser number of calls to the Montgomery reduction sub-function. This means 10% lesser number of loops during execution and thus better optimized for lower memory applications.

Keywords Public-key encryption, modular multiplication, modular exponentiation, sliding window, algorithm

Introduction

With the awareness that the world is fast becoming a global village due to the increased application of the internet especially in the area of e-commerce and m-commerce, information security is an issue that cannot be overemphasized. Since the onset of e-commerce in the mid 90s, statistics have it that e-commerce is expected to generate a total sales of about $105 billion in the United States alone by 2007. Statistics further shows that as of 2001, over $700million has been lost to online sales (Holcombe, 2006). Most often times, ecommerce customers are often concerned about the authenticity of the online trader they are dealing with (data origin authenticity) and more importantly, the privacy of their information (data confidentiality); such as credit card details, which is being used for the transaction.

Based on these statistics, it has become very important to improve techniques used for information security. New techniques have been developed and newer techniques are evolving. Cryptography is one of such techniques being used to ensure information security. It would be pertinent to seek ways of improving this technique as adversaries are daily developing newer techniques of breaking information security systems. Based on this, it has become pertinent to ensure security of information. Data encryption using cryptographic techniques is a means of achieving this.

Furthermore, with respect to an already developed application in our laboratory- (the M^2 agent for the stock market) (Oluwatope, Aderounmu, Akande, & Adigun, 2004), an important aspect yet to be added is security of data traversing the network. The mobile agent in the stock market application traverses the Internet searching for stock deals based on certain criteria set by the stock broker. When such criteria are met, the mobile agent reports back to the static agent. Whenever a mobile agent is reporting back to the static agent, the data it is carrying along can be intercepted and altered if proper encryption scheme is not put in place. It will not be a out-of-place to mention that the proposed algorithm is applicable in digital signal processing (DSP) (Tang et al, 2003). In DSP, coding of digitised signals for optimised transmission, higher bandwidth utilisation and efficient processor-time utilisation is highly desirable. The outcome of this work will form a baseline input into algorithms used for coding and decoding in DSP.

Cryptography is about communication in the presence of adversaries (Rivest, 1990). The reason for cryptography is to ensure security as information traverses an unsecured channel. Some of the objectives of information security include privacy, confidentiality, data integrity, data origin authentication, entity authentication, non-repudiation (Rivest, 1990). Basically, cryptography seeks to address these objectives in theory and in practice. Cryptography is defined as the study of mathematical techniques related to aspects of information security such as confidentiality, data integrity, entity authentication, and data origin authentication (Menezes, Van Oorschot, & Vanstone, 1997).

Motivation

As mentioned earlier, in the course of trying to achieve security of information, some cryptographic tools are used. These tools transform the information such that the encrypted information becomes meaningless to an adversary. The transformation process involves the execution of some computational steps. It has also been observed that the computational speed of some of these public-key cryptosystems is based on the speed of the modular exponentiation algorithm, especially when considering public-key encryption schemes such as RSA, Rabin and ElGamal. Furthermore, based on the fact that part of the security of these systems is the use of very large integers in the range of 1024bits and above, it usually requires enormous amount of processor time to complete these computational steps.

In the study of complexity theory (classification of computational problems based on the resources required to solve them), one of the resources used to classify computational problems is time. It is a thing of interest to look for the most efficient algorithms for solving computational problems because time is a very critical resource. More so in the e-commerce world that deals with transaction of businesses over the internet, *time can be equated to money*. This serves as the basis of motivation for this work.

Public-key encryption is slower than symmetric-key encryption which is been used for bulk data encryption. This is also due to the encryption/ decryption processes. It would be pertinent to optimize the former because if it has a comparable speed to symmetric-key encryption, lesser resources would be utilized in the transportation of private information over the Internet. In Tang Tsui, and Leong (2003) montgomery multiplier and a semi-systolic pipeline scheme have been used to increase the clock rate and enhanced parallelism in Field-Programmable Gate Arrays (FPGAs) devices. In Hachez and Quisquater (2001) the authors showed from software perspective montegomery exponentiation speed can be increased as well. In Joseph and Penzhorn (2004), the authors extended analysis to previous works and reduced running time of modular exponentiation step required for public–key encryption algorithms. Yesufu and Amao (2004) succeeded in producing a hybrid scheme of Knapsack algorithm, symmetric key cipher and pseudo-random sequencing. We will show, from a software view, a modified montgomery exponentiation that makes lesser number calls to sub-functions. Also, we will show analytically that the algorithm is optimized arithmetically.

Hence, this paper seeks to develop an optimized public-key crypto algorithm. In order to achieve our goal, we set these tasks: - propose and model an optimized montgomery exponentiation algorithm, and compare the proposed algorithm with the classical montgomery exponentiation.

Review of Selected Public-Encryption Schemes

To show the relevance of this work to the optimization of public-key encryption schemes, a review of selected public-key encryption schemes was carried out. It would be noticed that the modular exponentiation process is a core aspect these encryption schemes. The encryption schemes are RSA, Rabin and ElGamal public-key encryption schemes.

RSA Public-key Encryption Scheme

The algorithms used for the RSA public-key encryption are shown below (Menezes et al, 1997)

Key generation algorithm

Each entity is expected generate a key pair (public and private key). Ayo does the following:

1. Generate two large random (and distinct) primes p and q, each roughly the same size.
2. Compute $n = pq$ and $\Phi = (p - 1)(q - 1)$.
3. Select a random integer e, $1 < e < \Phi$, such that gcd $(e, \Phi) = 1$.
4. Use the binary extended gcd algorithm to compute the unique integer d, $1 < d < \Phi$, such that $ed \equiv 1 \pmod{\Phi}$.
5. Ayo's public key is (n, e); the corresponding private key is d.

Encryption/ Decryption algorithm

---

1. *Encryption:* Ben does the following:
   a) Obtain an authentic copy of Ayo's public key (n, e).
   b) Represent the message as an integer m in the interval $(0, n - 1)$.
   c) Compute $c = m^e \bmod n$.
   d) Send the ciphertext c to Ayo.
2. *Decryption:* To recover plaintext m from c, Ayo should do the following:
   a) Use the private key d to recover $m = c^d \bmod n$.

Rabin Public-key Encryption Scheme

The algorithms used for the Rabin public-key encryption are shown below (Menezes et al, 1997).

Key generation algorithm

Each entity is expected generate a key pair (public and private key). Ayo does the following:

1. Generate two large random (and distinct) primes p and q, each roughly the same size.
2. Compute $n = pq$.
3. Ayo's public key is n; his corresponding private key is (p, q).

Encryption/ Decryption algorithm

1. *Encryption:* Ben does the following:
   a) Obtain an authentic copy of Ayo's public key n.
   b) Represent the message as an integer m in the range $\{0, 1, \ldots, n-1\}$.
   c) Compute $c = m^2 \bmod n$.
   d) Send the ciphertext c to Ayo.
2. *Decryption:* To recover plaintext m from c, Ayo does the following:
   a) Use an algorithm for finding square root modulo n to find the four square roots m_1, m_2, m_3, and m_4 of c modulo n.
   b) The message sent was either m_1, m_2, m_3, or m_4. Ayo somehow determines which is m.

ElGamal Public-key Encryption Scheme

The algorithms of this scheme as regards to its functionality are shown below.

Key generation algorithm

Each entity is expected generate a key pair (public and private key). Ayo does the following:

1. Generate a large random prime p and a generator α of the multiplicative group Z^*_p of the integers modulo p.
2. Select a random integer a, $1 \le a \le p-2$, and compute $\alpha^a \bmod p$.
3. Ayo's public key is (p, α, α^a); his corresponding private key is a.

Encryption/ Decryption algorithm

1. *Encryption*: B should do the following:
   a) Obtain an authentic copy of Ayo's public key (p, α, α^a).
   b) Represent the message as an integer m in the range $\{0, 1, \ldots, p-1\}$.
   c) Select a random integer k, $1 \le k \le p-2$.
   d) Compute $\gamma = \alpha^k \bmod p$ and $\delta = m \cdot (\alpha^a)^k \bmod p$.
   e) Send the ciphertext $c = (\gamma, \delta)$ to Ayo.
2. *Decryption*: To recover plaintext m from c, Ayo should do the following:
   a) Use the private key a to compute $\gamma^{p-1-a} \bmod p$ (note: $\gamma^{p-1-a} = \gamma^{-a} = \alpha^{-ak}$).
   b) Recover m by computing $(\gamma^{-a}) \cdot \delta \bmod p$.

As seen in the algorithms described above, the modular exponentiation process plays an important role in the speed of these algorithms.

Review of Exponentiation Methods

In order to get a proper understanding of the subject matter of this paper, we are taking a look at some of the existing exponentiation methods.

M-ary Method

The *m*-ary method is an optimization of the binary method. Bits of the exponent are scanned in groups as against the binary method in which a bit is scanned per iteration. A *t*-bit exponent is divided into *s* words of length *r* bits each. If r doesn't divide *t*, the exponent is padded with at most $(r-1)$ 0s just before the leftmost bits. The actual *t*-bit word is defined in equation (1).

$$f_i = \left(e_{ir+r-1}, e_{ir+r-2}, \ldots, e_{ir}\right) = \sum_{j=0}^{t-1} e_{ir+j} 2^j \qquad (1)$$

This method does a precomputation of $g^w \pmod n$ for all $w = 2, 3, \ldots, m-1$ after which the bits of the exponent are scanned *r* bits per iteration from left to right. For each iteration, modular multiplications are performed based on the bits scanned (Koc, 1994). The algorithm for this technique is shown below.

---

m-ary modular exponentiation

INPUT: positive integer *g*, exponent $e = (e_{t-1}, \ldots, e_1, e_0)_2$ and a modulus *n*.

OUTPUT: $A = g^e \bmod n$.

1. Precomputation
   1a. Compute and store $g^w \pmod n$ for all $w = 2, 3, \ldots, m-1$.
   1b. Decompose *e* into *r*-bit words f_i for i from 0 to $s-1$.
2. $A \leftarrow g^{f_{s-1}} \pmod n$.
3. For *i* from $s-2$ down to 0, do;
   3a. $A \leftarrow A^{2^r} \pmod n$
   3b. If $f_i \neq 0$, $A = A \cdot g^{f_i} \pmod n$.
4. Return (A).

This technique can be optimized to do precomputations in the powers of only the partitioned exponent bit value. This helps to save unnecessary precomputations that are not used. A generalized analysis can be given as follows; for a *t*- bit exponent, with the assumption that $2^r = m$ and $^t/r$ is always an integer, this method requires;

- $2^r - 2$ number of precomputations,
- $(^t/r - 1)\, r = (t - r)$ number of squarings (step 3a),
- $(^t/r - 1)(1 - 2^{-r})$ number of multiplications.
- $2^r - 2 + t - r + (^t/r - 1)(1 - 2^{-r})$ average number of multiplications.

Drawbacks – Each iteration step involves costly multiple precision modular multiplications. Also for larger exponent values, it would involve too many iterations.

Sliding Window Method

Siding window method attempts to partition the exponent bits into zero and nonzero words (window) f_i. It then does as many multiplications as there are nonzero words (windows). The windows could be of variable length but its least significant bit must be equal to 1. For an exponent partitioned into d-bit words, the longest window length is $d = \max L(f_i)$ for $i = 0$ to $(t-1)$. This method also reduces the number of precomputations by computing only g^w for only odd values of w. (Koc, 1994). The algorithm is shown below where p is the number of windows.

Sliding Window modular exponentiation

INPUT: positive integer g, exponent $e = (e_{t-1}, \ldots, e_1, e_0)_2$ and a modulus n.

OUTPUT: $A = g^e \bmod n$.

1. Precomputation
   1a. $g_1 \leftarrow g$, $g_2 \leftarrow g^2$.
   1b. For i from 1 to $(2^{d-1} - 1)$, do; $g_{2i+1} \leftarrow g_{2i-1} \cdot g_2$.
   1c. Decompose e into zero and nonzero windows f_i of length $L(f_i)$ for i from 0 to $p-1$.
2. $A = g^{f_{p-1}} \pmod{n}$
3. For i from $p-2$ down to 0,
   3a. $A = A^{2^{L(f_i)}} \pmod{n}$
   3b. If $f_i \neq 0$, then $A = A \cdot g^{f_i} \pmod{n}$.
4. Return (A)

In partitioning the bit, two techniques are being proposed; constant length nonzero windows and variable length nonzero windows (Koc, 1994).

Montgomery's Method

Montgomery method allows the implementation of modular multiplication without directly dividing by the modulus. Instead, it replaces that division operation of the modulus by a power of 2 which is much faster because of the binary representation used by computers (Koc, 1994). This is known as the Montgomery reduction technique. For a k-bit modulus, $2^{k-1} \leq n < 2^k$, r is defined to be 2k. This technique requires that gcd (r, n) = 1. It computes the n-residue of the product of two integers whose n-residues are given. The n-residue of an integer $a < n$ with respect to r is given as;

$$\bar{a} = a \cdot r \bmod n.$$

Thus the Montgomery reduction is defined as;

$$\bar{R} = \bar{a} \cdot \bar{b} \cdot r^{-1} \bmod n,$$

where r^{-1} is the multiplicative inverse of r modulo n and $\bar{R}$ is the n-residue of the product

$$R = a \cdot b \bmod n$$

An additional quantity n' is required to describe the Montgomery reduction algorithm. It has the property

$$r \cdot r^{-1} - n \cdot n' = 1 \text{ and } n' = -n^{-1} \bmod r$$

r^{-1} and n' are computed using the binary gcd algorithm. The Montgomery reduction algorithm is stated as follows (Koc, 1994);

Montgomery reduction

INPUT: n-residues $\bar{a}$ and $\bar{b}$, integer $n = (n_{k-1}, \ldots, n_1, n_0)_2$, $r = 2^k$ with $\gcd(r, n) = 1$ and n'.

OUTPUT: $u = \bar{a} \cdot \bar{b} \cdot r^{-1} \bmod n$.

1. $t = \bar{a} \cdot \bar{b}$.
2. $m = t \cdot n' \bmod r$.
3. $u = (t + m \cdot n) / r$.
4. If $u \geq n$ then return $u - n$ else return u.

This Montgomery reduction can be used to obtain a faster algorithm for computing modular multiplication.

Montgomery exponentiation

Montgomery reduction is very suitable for computations that involve several modular multiplications with a fixed modulus. Based on this idea, the Montgomery reduction algorithm is now incorporated into the square and multiply binary algorithm to give an optimized method of computing modular exponentiations called the Montgomery exponentiation. This method circumvents the costly multiple precision multiplications involved in the binary square and multiply method (Koc, 1995). The algorithm is shown below.

Montgomery exponentiation

INPUT: $n = (n_{k-1}, \ldots, n_1, n_0)_2$, $r = 2^k$ with $\gcd(r, n) = 1$, $n' = -n^{-1} \bmod r$, $e = (e_{t-1}, \ldots, e_1, e_0)$, and integer $g, 1 \leq g < n$.

OUTPUT: $A = g^e \bmod n$

1. $\bar{g} \leftarrow g \cdot r \bmod n$
2. $\bar{A} \leftarrow 1 \cdot r \bmod n$
3. For i from $t - 1$ down to 0, do;
   - 3a. $\bar{A} = mont(\bar{A}, \bar{A})$
   - 3b. if $e_i = 1$, then $\bar{A} = mont(\bar{g}, \bar{A})$
4. $A = mont(\bar{A}, 1)$
5. Return (A)

Proposed Algorithm: Montgomery Exponentiation Using Sliding Windows

The proposed algorithm is an improvement on the classical Montgomery exponentiation technique. The classical Montgomery exponentiation carries out the exponentiation operation based on the bits of the exponent in a bitwise fashion. The algorithm been proposed, combines the Montgomery reduction algorithm with the sliding windows exponentiation algorithm. The exponentiation process is carried out in groups of bits (synchronously), thus reducing the number of iterations and improving on the speed of the exponentiation process. The algorithm is shown below.

Montgomery exponentiation using sliding windows

INPUT: $n = (n_{k-1},...,n_1,n_0)_2$, $r = 2^k$ with gcd(r, n) = 1, $n' = -n^{-1} \bmod r$, $e = (e_{t-1},...,e_1,e_0)$, integer $g, 1 \leq g < n$, and integer $d \geq 1$.

OUTPUT: $A = g^e \bmod n$

1. $\overline{g} \leftarrow g \cdot r(\bmod n)$.
2. Precomputation
   a) $\overline{g_1} \leftarrow \overline{g}, \overline{g_2} \leftarrow mont(\overline{g}, \overline{g})$.
   b) For i from 1 to $(2^{d-1} - 1)$, do; $\overline{g}_{2i+1} \leftarrow mont(\overline{g}_{2i-1}, \overline{g}_2)$.
   c) Decompose e into zero and nonzero windows f_i of length $L(f_i)$ for i from 0 to $p - 1$.
3. a) $\overline{A} \leftarrow r(\bmod n)$
   b) $\overline{A} = mont(\overline{A}, \overline{g}_{f_{p-1}})$
4. For i from $p - 2$ down to 0,
   a) For $j = L(f_i) - 1$ down to 0, do;

      $$\overline{A} \leftarrow mont(\overline{A}, \overline{A})$$

   b) If $f_i \neq 0$, then $\overline{A} \leftarrow mont(\overline{A} \cdot \overline{g}_{f_i})$.
5. $A = mont(\overline{A}, 1)$.
6. Return (A).

A performance comparison of this algorithm is not given in this paper. This is because work is still in progress with respect to the algorithm.

Montgomery Exponentiation (Analysis)

A generalized analysis can be given as follows; for an n-bit exponent, this method requires, where Single Precision Multiplication (SPM) and Multiple Precision Modular Multiplication (MPMM);

Step 1:	One MPMM = $(2n^2 + 2)$ SPMs,
Step 3a:	$n - 1$ mont-red calls and,
Step 3b:	wt(e) -1 mont-red calls, where wt(e) is the hamming weight (number of 1s in the binary representation) of the exponent.
Step 4:	One mont-red call = $(n^2 + n)$ SPMs

For $0 \leq$ wt(e) -1 $\leq n - 1$, there can be a maximum of $n - 1$ ones and a minimum of 0 ones in the binary representation of e. Assuming $e_{n-1} = 1$, this implies that we can have;

- $(n-1)+(n-1)=2(n-1)$ maximum number of mont-red calls,
- $(n-1)+0=(n-1)$ minimum number of mont-red calls,

$\frac{1}{2}[2(n-1)+(n-1)]=\frac{3}{2}(n-1)$ average number of mont-red calls (for step 3a).

Since one mont-red call is made up of n^2+n SPMs, then the total number of SPM calls would be;

$$\left(2n^2+2\right)+\left(\left(\tfrac{3}{2}(n-1)\right)*\left(n^2+n\right)\right)+\left(n^2+n\right)$$

$$=1.5n^3+3n^2-0.5n+2 \text{ SPMs}$$

Montgomery Exponentiation Using Sliding Windows (Proposed Algorithm)

A generalized analysis can be given as follows; for an n-bit exponent, this method requires;

Step 1: One MPMM = $\left(2n^2+2\right)$SPMs,

Step 2a: One mont-red call = $\left(n^2+n\right)$ SPMs,

Step 2b: $\left(2^{d-1}\right)$ mont-red calls = $\left(\left(2^{d-1}\right)*\left(n^2+n\right)\right)$ SPMs,

Step 3b: One mont-red call = $\left(n^2+n\right)$ SPMs,

Step 4a: $(n-d)$ mont-red calls = $\left((n-d)*\left(n^2+n\right)\right)$ SPMs,

Step 4b: C_1 mont-red calls = $\left(C_1*\left(n^2+n\right)\right)$ SPMs (where C_1 is average number of transitions from state 0 to state 1 after n iterations (constant length non-zero window) as modeled using Markov chain (Koç, 1995)).

Step 5: One mont-red call = $\left(n^2+n\right)$ SPMs.

Total number of SPMs =

$$\left(\left(2^{d-1}\right)*\left(n^2+n\right)\right)+\left(n^2+n\right)+\left((n-d)*\left(n^2+n\right)\right)+\left(C_1*\left(n^2+n\right)\right)$$

$$=n^3+5n^2+2^{d-1}n^2-dn^2+C_1n^2+2n+2^{d-1}n-dn+C_1n+2^{d-1}+2$$

In comparing the various exponentiation techniques analyzed, the coefficients of the highest degree of the various polynomials are considered. This is so because all exponentiation algorithms are polynomial time algorithms of the cubic order.

Experimental Results and Discussion

The algorithms were implemented in MATLAB 6.5 codes, run on Pentium III 500Mhz IBM PC. The Classical and the modified algorithms were run for 100 times each for four different exponent bit sizes. This gives a total of 400 runs for each of the algorithms. The execution time for each run was recorded and used to compute the mean and standard deviation for both algorithms. Contrary to expectation, the Classical Montgomery algorithm was seen to have a shorter execution time than the Montgomery modular exponentiation using sliding windows. Figure 1 shows a graph of exponent bit size against the mean execution time. All graphs were also plotted using MATLAB.

Apart from the execution times of the algorithms, an interesting observation was made which forms the strength of this paper. Despite the fact the classical algorithm was seen to run faster than the modified one, the modified algorithm was seen to make lesser number of calls to the Montgomery reduction sub-function than the classical algorithm. This observation is shown in Figure 2. This implies that although the Montgomery exponentiation using sliding windows algorithm could be slower than the Classical Montgomery algorithm, it makes use of lesser memory space (space complexity). Further statistical analysis revealed that Montgomery exponentiation with sliding windows algorithm required 10% lesser memory referencing. Lesser number of calls to the Montgomery reduction sub-function implies lesser number of loops but why it does not translate to a reduced execution time is yet to be ascertained. In other word, we can say that the Montgomery exponentiation using sliding windows algorithm is arithmetically optimized

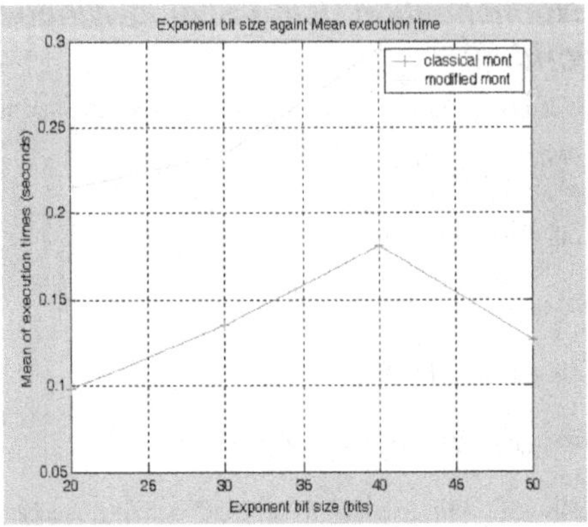

Figure 1: Graph of Exponent bit size against mean execution time

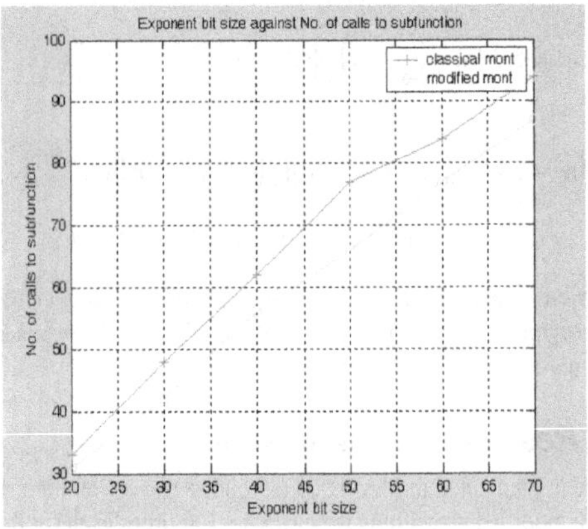

Figure 2: Exponent bit size against No. of calls to sub- function

Conclusion

In large computer complexes, information security becomes a very pertinent issue. Furthermore in applying layers of security, it is also crucial to conserve network resources such as processor time and memory. This project work attempted to propose an optimized algorithm for a core process in cryptographic procedures (exponentiation). As it can be seen from the simulation results, contrary to expectation, the Classical Montgomery modular exponentiation algorithm was seen to run faster than the proposed Montgomery modular exponentiation using sliding windows. On the other hand, the proposed algorithm was seen to make lesser number of calls to the Montgomery reduction sub-function. This implies it carries out lesser number of memory activities (storage and retrieval) and thus it is optimized for smaller memory applications.

It should be noted that exponentiation is only one of the many algorithms involved in cryptography. In spite of the optimization of this algorithm, it would be imperative to look into the optimization of other algorithms involved. In future, we will find out why the new algorithm did not run faster, despite reduced number of sub-function calls. Thereafter modified the Montgomery exponentiation with sliding windows algorithm for higher speed.

References

Hachez & Quisquater, J. J. (2001). Exponentiation with no final subtractions: Improved results. *Lecture Notes in Computer Science, 1965*, 293-301.

Holcombe C. (2006). What is ecommerce? Retrieved from www.ecommerce-digest.com/tut.html

Joseph, G. & Penzhorn, W. T. (2004). High-speed algorithms for public-key cryptosystems in an e-commerce environment. Proceedings of the *Southern African Telecomunication Networks and Applications Conference SATNAC 2004, 2*, 205-210.

Koç, Ç. K. (1994). High-speed RSA implementation, Version 2.0. *RSA Laboratories*, November 1994.

Koç Ç. K. (1995). Analysis of sliding window techniques for exponentiation. *Computer and Mathematics with Applications, 30*(10), 17-24.

Menezes, P., Van Oorschot, & Vanstone, S. (1997). *Handbook of applied cryptography.* CRC Press.

Oluwatope, A. O., Aderounmu, G. A., Akande, O. O. & Adigun, M. O. (2004). An auction scenario in a stock market using M^2 Agent. Proceedings of *Southern Africa Telecommunication Networks and Applications Conference (SATNAC). 1*, 229 – 234.

Rivest, R. L. (1990). *Cryptology.* MIT Laboratory for Computer Science.

Tang, S. H., Tsui, K. S. & Leong, P. H. W. (2003). Modular exponentiation using parallel multipliers. *Proceedings of the 2003 IEEE International Conference on Field Programmable Technology (FPT)*, Tokyo, 52-59.

Yesufu, T. K. & Amao, O. R. (2004). A cryptosystem based on a combination of three computationally secure algorithms. *Southern African Telecomunication Networks and Applications Conference SATNAC 2004 Proceedings, 2*, 199-204.

Biographies

A. O. Oluwatope obtained his Bachelors and Masters degree in Computer Engineering and Computer Science from Obafemi Awolowo University, Ile-Ife, in 1995 and 2003, respectively. He is a registered computer engineer with Council for the Regulation of Engineering Practice in Nigeria (COREN), a member of Nigerian Society of Engineers (NSE) and an Associate member of Nigeria Computer Society (NSC). He has co-authored several articles published in Nigeria and abroad. His current research interests include internet congestion control, internet protocol development, algorithm modeling and simulation and grid computing. He has about seven years of teaching and research experience. He is currently a doctoral student and a lecturer in the Department of Computer Science and Engineering of the same university.

A.A. Owojori obtained his Bachelor of Science degree in Computer Engineering from Obafemi Awolowo University, Ile-Ife, in 2005. He is a student member of Nigerian Society of Engineers (NSE). His current research interests are in the areas of computer communications and teletraffic engineering. He is also into protocols design and simulations of wireless communications. Mr. Owojori is currently on National Youth Service.

G.A. Aderounmu holds a research degree M.Sc./PhD in Computer Science from Obafemi Awolowo University, Ile-Ife, Nigeria (1997 and 2001, respectively). He is a member of the Nigerian Society of Engineers (NSE) and is also a registered computer engineer with Council for the Regulation of Engineering Practice in Nigeria (COREN). He is also a Member of Nigerian Computer Society (NCS) and Computer Professional Registration Council of Nigeria (CPN). He has over 13 years of experience in teaching and research. He is an author of many journal articles in Nigeria and abroad. His special interests include engineering education in Nigeria, curriculum development, and computer communication and network. He is a Visiting Research Fellow to the University of Zululand, Republic of South Africa. He is currently a Senior Lecturer, Deputy Director of the Information Technology and Communication Unit (INTECU) and the Acting Head of the Department of Computer Science and Engineering of the same university.

M. O. Adigun holds a research degree PhD in Computer Science from Obafemi Awolowo University, Ile-Ife, Nigeria which he obtained in 1989. Currently, he is a Professor and Head, Department of Computer Science, University of Zululand, Republic of South Africa. He is an author of many journal articles in Nigeria, Republic of South Africa and abroad. His research interests include Software Engineering, Mobile Computing, Modeling and Simulation, and Performance Analysis of Computer System.

End-to-End Performance Evaluation of Selected TCP Variants across a Hybrid Wireless Network

A.O. Oluwatope, A. B. Obabire, and G. A. Aderounm
Comnet Laboratory, Obafemi Awolowo University. Ile-Ife, Nigeria

aoluwato@oauife.edu.ng gaderoun@oauife.edu.ng

M. O. Adigun
University of Zululand. South-Africa

madigun@pan.uzulu.ac.za

Abstract

Reliable transport protocols such as TCP are tuned to perform well in traditional networks where packet losses occur mostly because of congestion. TCP is intended for use as a highly reliable end-to-end transport protocol for transporting applications such as World-Wide Web (WWW) between hosts in packet-switched computer communication networks. TCP was originally designed for wired links where the error rate is really low and actually assumed that packet losses are due to congestion in the network. However, the increasing popularity of wireless networks indicates that wireless links will play more important role in future internetworks but TCP performance in such networks suffers from significant throughput degradation and very high interactive delays. TCP responds to all losses by invoking congestion control and avoidance algorithms, resulting in degraded end-to-end performance in wireless and lossy systems. Thus, in a bid to show and determine the possibility of adapting TCP protocol for optimal performance on the wireless link, this paper reviews and models the behaviors of TCP variants with a view to evaluate the end-to-end performance analysis of TCP versions: TCP Reno, TCP SACK and TCP Westwood (TCPW), which are designed to improve the performance of TCP in lossy networks. A wireless network model was developed using NS-2 network simulator which and the model was simulated. The results were analyzed in MATLAB 6.5 using throughput as a metric for comparison. The overall results indicate that TCP Westwood (TCPW) demonstrates better performance indices over other versions in a hybrid wireless network environment.

Keywords: tcp, tcpwestwood, tcpreno, tcpsack, bandwidth, ns-2

Introduction

With rapid growth in the number of nomadic users that access the Internet using wireless technology it has been established that wireless links will play more important role in future internetworks. Many popular Internet applications including World-Wide Web (WWW), File Transfer Protocol (FTP) and email require reliable data delivery over the network. The Transmission Control Protocol (TCP) is the most widely used transport protocol for this purpose and has become the predominant transport protocol in the Internet today. TCP is a large expended transport layer protocol that provides connection oriented, reliable service to the application layer. It is intended for use as a highly reliable end-to-end protocol between hosts in packet-switched computer communication networks and was originally designed for wired links where the error rate is really low and actually assumes that packet losses are due to congestion in the network. Quality of Service On the fixed wired networks, less than 1% of the packet losses is considered being due to link errors (Lefevre & Vivier, 2003), a missing packet means, in most cases, that the network is congested and in reaction TCP triggers the congestion algorithm aimed at reducing throughput. In a wireless network, however, packet losses occur more frequently due to link error because of the unreliability of the physical link. This implies the unnecessary invocation of the congestion algorithm which reduces the throughput drastically and causes severe performance degradation. The congestion avoidance mechanism is mainly the origin of the poor QoS of TCP over wireless.

However, with the increase in wireless data applications, there is a growing need to adapt TCP to wireless networks. Thus, it is necessary to extend TCP features to be efficient on a wireless interface while taking into account the characteristics of a wireless channel.

The Existing Possible Solutions

There are two different approaches to improving TCP performance in wireless lossy networks. The first approach hides any non-congestion related losses from the TCP sender which requires no change to existing sender implementations. Protocols that adopt this approach attempt to make the lossy link appear as a higher quality link with a reduced effective bandwidth. As a result, most of the losses seen by the TCP sender are caused by congestion.

The second approach attempts to make the sender aware of the existence of wireless hops, and realize that some packet losses are not due to congestion. The sender can then avoid invoking congestion control algorithms when non-congestion related losses occur. We classify the many schemes into three basic groups based on their fundamental philosophy: end-to-end proposals, split-connection proposals, and link-layer proposals. (Lefevre & Vivier, 2003).

End-to-end Proposal

The end-to-end protocols attempt to make the TCP sender handle losses through the use of two techniques. First, the use of selective acknowledgment (SACKs) that allows the sender recovers from multiple packet losses in a window without resorting to a coarse timeout. Second, the attempt to have the sender distinguishes between congestion and other forms of losses using an Explicit Loss Notification (ELN) mechanism.

End-to-end protocols

TCP Sack (Selective Acknowledgments): Since standard TCP uses a cumulative acknowledgment scheme, it often does not provide the sender with sufficient information to recover quickly from multiple packet losses within a single transmission window. Study (e.g., Fall & Floyd, 1996; Hoe, 1996) has shown that TCP enhanced with selective acknowledgments performs better than standard TCP in such situations. SACK's were added as an option to TCP by RFC 1072 (Jacobson & Braden, 1988). The SACK RFC proposes that each acknowledgment contain information about up to three noncontiguous blocks of data that have been received successfully by the receiver. Each block of data is described by its starting and ending sequence number. Due to the limited number of blocks, it is best to inform the sender about the most recent blocks received. The RFC does not specify the sender behavior, except to require that standard TCP congestion control actions be performed when losses occur.

TCP Reno: The Reno TCP assumes a packet has been lost (due to congestion) when it observes 3 duplicate ACKs (DUPACKS), or when a retransmission timer expires. In either case, it reacts by setting *ssthresh* to half of the current window size (the minimum of *cwnd* and window). It then initializes *cwnd* back to the value of 1. This will typically cause the TCP to enter slow-start (Fall & Floyd, 1996; Naito, Okada, Saito, Yamazaato, & Katayama, 2002; Padhye, Firoiu, & Towsley, 1999; Padhye, Firoiu, Towsley, & Kurose, 2000).

TCP Westwood: The key innovative idea in TCP Westwood is that the TCP sender continuously computes the connection BandWidth Estimate (BWE) which is defined as the share of bottleneck bandwidth available to the connection i.e. the packet rate of the connection by properly averaging the rate of returning ACKs. BWE is equal to the rate at which data is delivered to the connection destination. The delivery rate estimate is based on information in the ACKs, and the rate at which the ACKs are received (Claudio et al., 2002). After a packet loss indication, which is mostly due to congestion but could also be due to link errors, through packets loss symptoms which include the reception of 3 duplicates acknowledgment (DUPACKS) or coarse timeout expiration, the sender uses the estimated bandwidth to properly set the congestion window and the slow start threshold. In contrast to TCP Reno, which "blindly" halves the congestion window after three duplicate ACKs, TCP Westwood (TCPW) attempts to select a slow start threshold and a congestion window which is consistent with the effective connection rate at the time congestion is experienced.

Bandwidth Estimation Mechanism

When an ACK is received at the source at time t_k such that d_k bytes have been received at the TCP receiver, the sample bandwidth used by this connection can be measured as (Claudio et al, 2002):

$$b_k = d_k / (t_k - t_{k-1}) \text{.........................} (1)$$

where t_{k-1} is the time the previous ACK was received.

Letting $\Delta t_k = t_k - t_{k-1}$,

Then $b_k = d_k / \Delta t_k$ .... (2)

Since congestion occurs whenever the low-frequency input traffic rate exceed the link capacity, a low-pass filter is employed to average sampled measurements and to obtain the low-frequency components of the available bandwidth.

The low-pass filter is proposed as follows: b_k is the bandwidth sample, and $\hat{b}_k$ the filter estimate of the bandwidth at time t_k. Also, α_k is the time varying exponential filter coefficient at t_k. The TCPW filter is then given by:

$$\hat{b}_k = \alpha_k \hat{b}_{k-1} + (1-\alpha_k)\left(\frac{b_k + b_{k-1}}{2}\right) \text{......} (3)$$

where

$$\alpha_k = \frac{2\tau - \Delta t_k}{2\tau + \Delta t_k} \text{..........................} (4)$$

and $1/\tau$ is the filter cut-off frequency.

The coefficients α_k are made to depend on Δt_k to counteract the effect of non-deterministic inter-arrival times. When the inter-arrival time Δt_k increases, the last value $\hat{b}_{k-1}$ should have less significance. On the other hand, a recent $\hat{b}_{k-1}$ is given higher significance. The coefficient α_k decreases when the inter-arrival time increases, and thus the previous value b_{k-1} is accorded less significance with respect to the last two recent samples which are weighted by:

$$(1-\alpha_k)/2 \quad \text{..............................} \quad (5)$$

Since the TCPW filter has a cut-off frequency equal to $1/\tau$, all frequency components above $1/\tau$ are filtered out.

Work Done

Architecture of the Hybrid Wireless Network

We considered a sample campus area network setup in Obafemi Awolowo University (OAU) Ile-Ife Nigeria that connects to the UNIVERSITY of ZULULAND campus network via the Internet. At the OAU campus network end, several local area networks are linked to the central control via wireless links. To simplify the architecture, we built and simulated only one wireless link connecting two sub-nets. This wireless link is a full-duplex data communication link. The sub-nets traffic are transported over wire-line LAN. OAU campus wireless network is the largest university network in Nigeria. It is known as OAUNet. It records over 2,000 users log-on per day from 13 sub-networks connected by wireless (packet radio frequency) links. Figure 1 depicts our simple model.

A sub-net gateway runs a dynamic host configuration protocol (DHCP) service that allocates internet protocol (IP) address numbers to the workstations-clients. Sub-net gateways also acts as routers between a particular local area network (LAN) and the central university network (CUN). The mode of connectivity between a sub-net gateway and the central university network is a wireless radio link whose bandwidth is 2Mbps. At the CUN is an omni-directional antenna concentrating 13 wireless links from different directions of the campus.

Limitations

The modifications on TCP in this work will be preferably processed without implying an entire alteration to the widespread TCP protocol. The simulation study was carried out on the OAU wireless network using only one sub-net gateway out of a total of 13 sub-nets. Also, this work is limited to the accuracy of the model developed using the NS simulator (NS2) (Altman & Jimenez, 2002; Kevin & Kannan, 2003). The application assumed to be running on the OAU network model is HTTP, although, in future, VOIP is a likely application being considered.

Development Tools

The development tool used in this work includes:

- **NS simulator (NS2):** NS2 is a discrete event simulator that operates in virtual time and supports various flavors of TCP and other transport protocols NS uses NAM, an animation tool, developed in Tcl/Tk, to visualize the simulation packet traces which are created when running NS scripts (ns-2) (Allman & Paxson, 2000).

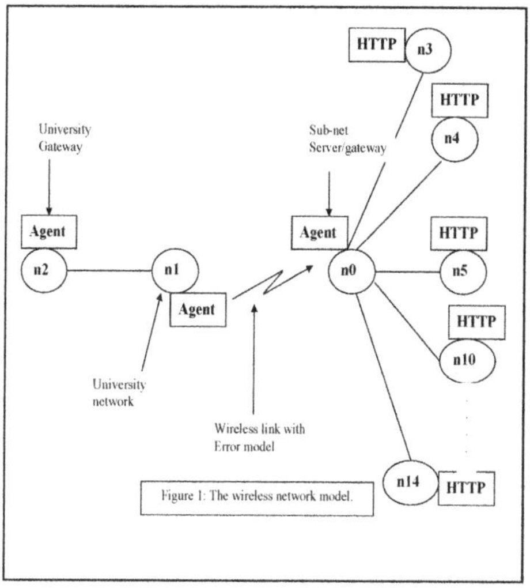

Figure 1: The wireless network model.

- **MATLAB 6.5:** The data collected, based on performance measures, were saved in an output trace file and afterwards plotted and analyzed using MATLAB 6.5

Simulation scenario

NS-2 network simulator ran on a Linux operating system installed on a Pentium III 1.33GHz, 256MB RAM system. The simulation was run several times within the range of 15ms - 20ms. Our simulation environment parameters setting of 5% wireless packet error rate, 2Mbps bottleneck bandwidth and two-way propagation time of 5ms were set as standard. The simulated wireless network model is as shown in Figure 1.

Results of the Simulation

Simulation of the Model at Constant Packet Error Rate 5%

The result obtained is shown in Figure 3. At 5% PER, there was a transient behavior in which all the TCP protocol versions were in the slow start phase (first 10s). Here, TCPs window size initially increased exponentially with TCPWestwood exhibits a very high throughput, in excess of .45Mbps as against TCPReno and TCPSACK that recorded throughput of about .35 and .38Mbps respectively. Also during the slow start phase, at time 3.5s, there were losses traceable to time-out making TCPReno and TCPSACK to suddenly half their window size, therefore reducing

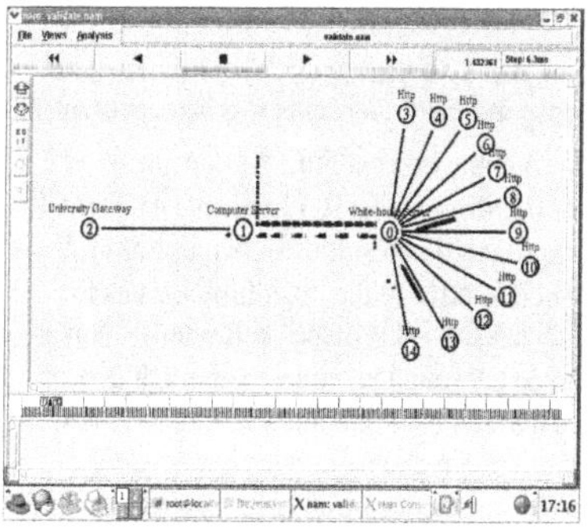

Figure 2: OAU Wireless Network Model showing the link between computer

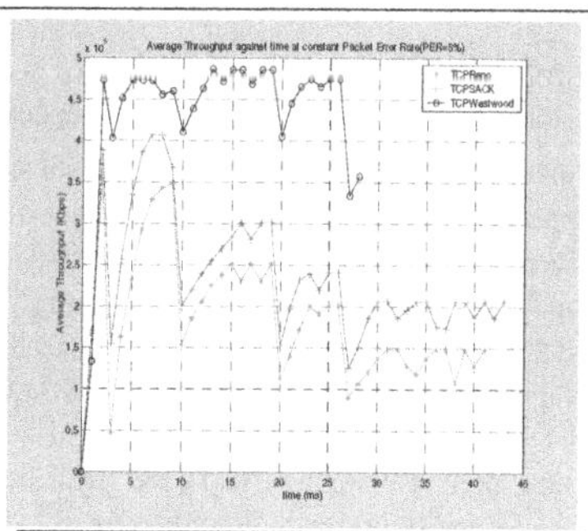

Figure 3: Shows the graph of Average Throughput gained by the TCP versions against time at constant

throughput to about 0.4 and 1.5 respectively. While TCPWestwood reduced its window size by setting it to the measured rate currently experienced by the connection using bandwidth estimation mechanism, contrary to the conventional multiplicative decrease scheme (i.e., divide the current window by half) which caused the throughput to only reduced by 0.05Mbps. After time 10s all TCP versions switched into congestion avoidance phase and their window size increases almost linearly until losses occurred again at time 20 and all TCP versions entered into slow start phase again. The other control mechanisms (i.e., slow start after timeout, exponential/additive increase in slow start/congestion avoidance, etc.) are identical to all the TCP versions. The transmission continued in this order with TCPWestwood exhibiting the highest and most regular throughput of approx. 0.5Mbps all through the transmission phases.

Simulation of the Model at Random Packet Error Rate

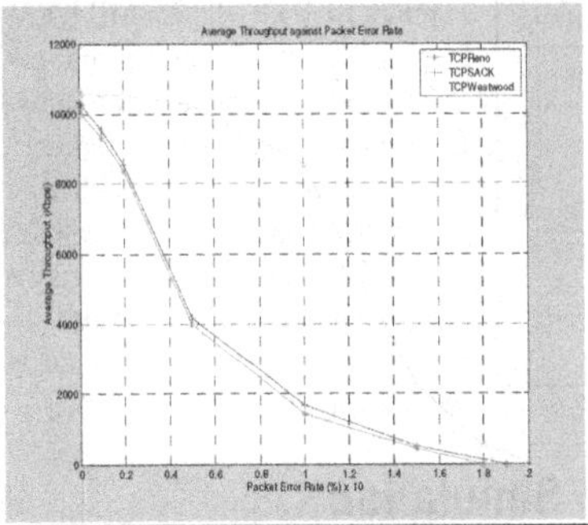

Figure 4: Shows the graph of Average Throughput gained by the TCP versions as a result of variation in Packet Error Rate (%) at constant packet size, bottleneck bandwidth and propagation time.

A bottleneck bandwidth was set to 2Mbps, and a two-way propagation time set at 5ms. At 0% PER, the performances of TCP protocols were virtually identical at a throughput of about 10000 Kbps (1Mbps) approximately 50% link utilisation At 85 PER, TCPWestwood remained within the neighbourhood of 1Mbps while TCPReno and TCPSACK had dropped below 0.4Mbps. At 10 % error rates, appropriate for wireless links, the throughput TCPWestwood just dropped slightly below 0.9Mbps as against 0.2Mbps recorded for TCPReno and TCPSACK. This shows an improvement is about 400%. However, as the error rate increases beyond 10%, the improvement obtained via TCPWestwood decreases. At very high error rates of about 20 % and above, TCPWestwood as well as TCPReno and TCPSACK suffer low bandwidth utilization which results to zero throughput due to outrageous packet drop.

Simulation of the Model at Random Transmission Speed (Mbps) (Bottleneck Link Speed)

Here, the channel errors rate are independent and correspond to a 5 % packet loss rate, equivalent to a BER in the order of 10^{-50} and round trip propagation time is set at 5ms. At transimission speed of 2Mpbs, TCPWestwood was operating at over 0.2Mbps while TCPReno and TCPSACK were operating at 0.15 and 0.12Mbps respectively. The simulation result as shown in Figure 5 indicates significant gain in throughput in TCPWestwood relative to the other protocols as the bottleneck link transmission speed increases. Thus, TCPWestwood provides better utilization at higher link speeds. At 10 Mbps, TCPWestwood achieved a throughput equal to about 300 % of TCPReno and TCPSACK. This graph also establishes that retransmission rate is a function of link speed. This shows that TCPW, while less conservative in reducing congestion window (*cwin*) and slow start threshold (*ssthresh)*, did not have a significantly higher retransmission rate than TCP Reno.

Simulation of the Model at Random Propagation Time (ms)

A random propagation time with the channel error fixed at 0.05% packet error rate and bottleneck link transmission speed at 2Mbps was used in order to compare impact of the propagation time on the performance of TCP versions. The simulation results are presented in Figure 6. TCPWestwood throughput remained uniformed from 0ms to 5ms propagation time and had dropped by 0.1% at 15ms. In the case of TCPReno and TCPSACK average throughput had by 60% of the starting throughput. There was a steep reduction immediately propagation time increased to 20 and 25ms. The reason may not be unconnected delay in bandwidth estimation processes of TCPwestwood at such propagation times.

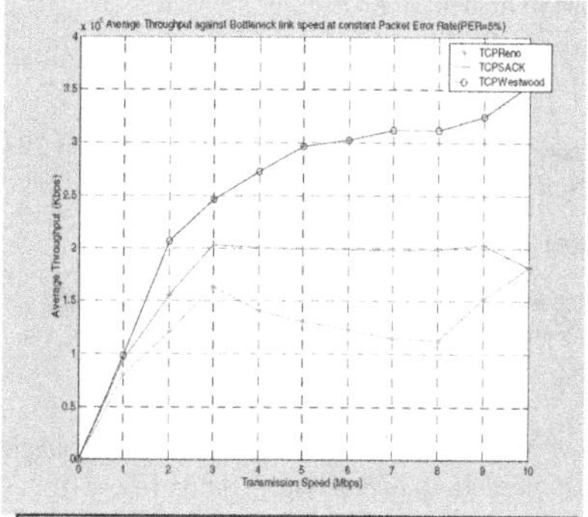

Figure 5: Shows the graph of Average Throughput gained by the TCP versions as a result of variation in Transmission Speed (Mbps) at constant Packet Error Rate (PER).

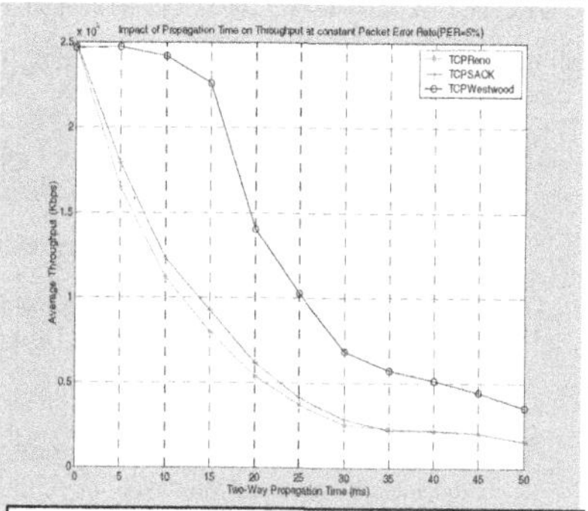

Figure 6: Shows the graph of Average Throughput gained by the TCP versions as a result of variation in two-way propagation time (ms) at constant Packet Error Rate (PER).

Conclusion

When packets are lost in the wireless network for reason other than congestion, it results to unnecessary reduction in end-to-end throughput and hence, in suboptimal performance. This project studies the behavior and performance of TCP when applied over wireless network by surveying the TCP versions based on End-to-End scheme which have been designed for best-effort traffic in wireless network. Various result obtained from the simulation analysis using performance parameters when TCP versions were applied over the wireless network shows the expected performance level.

Thus, TCPWestwood showed superior performance and improved throughput over the wireless network. In particular, the throughput performance of TCPWestwood over a lossy wireless network exhibited a 100 % improvement over TCPReno and TCPSACK.implementations. In future we hope to scale upward the applications running the network with particular interest in real-time applications (VOIP and Streaming multimedia).

References

Allman, M. & Paxson, V. (2000). TCP congestion control. *IEEE Communications Surveys & Tutorials, 4*(5). Retrieved from http://www.comsoc.org/pubs/surveys

Altman, E. & Jimenez, T. (2002). NS Simulator for beginners. Retrieved from http://www-mash.cs.berkeley.edu/ns

Balakrishnan, H. (1998). Challenges to reliable data transport over heterogeneous wireless networks. PhD thesis, Computer Science Division, University of California at Berkeley, Berkeley, CA. pp 25-30.

Claudio, C., Mario, G., Scott, L., Saverio, M., Sanadidi, M. Y. & Ren, W. (2002). TCP Wwood: end-to-end bandwidth estimation for enhanced transport over wireless links. *ACM/Baltzer Wireless Networks Journal, 8*, 467-479.

Fall, K. & Floyd, S. (1996). Simulation-based comparisons of Tahoe, Reno, and Sack TCP. *Computer Communications Review, 26*(3), 5-21.

Hoe, J. C. (1996). Improving the start-up behavior of a congestion control scheme for TCP. Proceedings of the *ACM SIGCOMM Conference on Applications, Technologies, Architectures, and Protocols for Computer Communications, 26*(4), 270-280. ISBN 0-89791-790-1.

Jacobson, V. & Braden, R. T. (1988), TCP extensions for long delay paths. RFC, RFC-1072.

Kevin, F. & Kannan, V. (2003). The ns manual. Retrieved from http://www.isi.edu/nsnam/ns/

Lefevre, F. & Vivier, G. (2003). Understanding TCP's behavior over wireless links. Motorola Labs-Centre de Recherche de Motorola-Paris, pp 1-3.

Naito, K., Okada, H., Saito, M., Yamazaato, T., & Katayama, M., (2002). New analytical model for TCP in wireless environment. *IEICE Trans.Journal, E85-A*(7).

ns-2 network simulator, version 9, LBL. Retrieved from http://www-mash.cs.berkeley.edu/ns

Padhye, J., Firoiu, V., & Towsley, D. (1999). A stochactic model TCP Reno congestion avoidance and control. CMPSCI Technical Report 99-02.Dept. of Computer Science, University of Massachusetts Amherst, MA.

Padhye, J., Firoiu, V., Towsley, D. F. & Kurose, J. F. (2000). Modeling TCP Reno performance: A simple model and its empirical validation. *IEEE ACM Transactions on Networking, 8*(2), 133-145.

TCP Westwood modules for *ns*-2. Retrieved from http://www.telematics.polito.it/casetti/tcp-westwood

Biographies

A. O. Oluwatope obtained his Bachelors and Masters degree in Computer Engineering and Computer Science from Obafemi Awolowo University, Ile-Ife, in 1995 and 2003, respectively. He is a registered computer engineer with Council for the Regulation of Engineering Practice in Nigeria (COREN), a member of Nigerian Society of Engineers (NSE) and an Associate member of Nigeria Computer Society (NSC). He has co-authored several articles published in Nigeria and abroad. His current research interests include internet congestion control, internet protocol development, algorithm modeling and simulation and grid computing. He has about seven years of teaching and research experience. He is currently a doctoral student and a lecturer in the Department of Computer Science and Engineering of the same university.

A. B. Obabire obtained his Bachelor of Science degree in Computer Engineering from Obafemi Awolowo University, Ile-Ife, in 2004. He is a student member of Nigerian Society of Engineers (NSE). His research interest is in internet protocol simulation. Mr. Obabire has since completed a one year National Youth Service.

G.A. Aderounmu holds a research degree M.Sc./PhD in Computer Science from Obafemi Awolowo University, Ile-Ife, Nigeria (1997 and 2001, respectively). He is a member of the Nigerian Society of Engineers (NSE) and is also a registered computer engineer with Council for the Regulation of Engineering Practice in Nigeria (COREN). He is also a Member of Nigerian Computer Society (NCS) and Computer Professional Registration Council of Nigeria (CPN). He has over 13 years of experience in teaching and research. He is an author of many journal articles in Nigeria and abroad. His special interests include engineering education in Nigeria, curriculum development, and computer communication and network. He is a Visiting Research Fellow to the University of Zululand, Republic of South Africa. He is currently a Senior Lecturer, Deputy Director of the Information Technology and Communication Unit (INTECU) and the Acting Head of the Department of Computer Science and Engineering of the same university.

M. O. Adigun holds a research degree PhD in Computer Science from Obafemi Awolowo University, Ile-Ife, Nigeria which he obtained in 1989. Currently, he is a Professor and Head, Department of Computer Science, University of Zululand, Republic of South Africa. He is an author of many journal articles in Nigeria, Republic of South Africa and abroad. His research interests include Software Engineering, Mobile Computing, Modeling and Simulation, and Performance Analysis of Computer System.

The page left blank intentionally.

Journey to the Center of the Core: Computers and the Internet in the Core Curriculum

Jorge Pérez and Meg Murray
Kennesaw State University, Kennesaw, Georgia, USA

jperez@kennesaw.edu mcmurray@kennesaw.edu

Abstract

Computers, digitalization and the Internet have transformed modern society. Commerce, education, communication and socialization will never be the same. Surprisingly, many universities do not require a computing course in the core curriculum. Critical information technology (IT) competencies are often taken for granted, to the detriment of students who lack computing and Internet skills. This paper describes an initiative undertaken by a computer science and information systems department to assess and remediate IT skills needed by all university students, regardless of major. The project is evolving along several dimensions: identification of discipline-independent IT competencies, assessment of IT skills among current and incoming students, and curriculum development.

Keywords: assessment, curriculum, education, computer skills, information systems, computer science, Internet.

Introduction

No industry is untouched by the information technology revolution. Commerce, education, communication and socialization are among the areas that are undergoing radical transformations. At most universities, fundamental IT skills have not risen to the level of must-have competencies such as math and English. Surprisingly, many universities do not assess IT skills or require a computing course in the core curriculum. Critical IT competencies are often taken for granted, to the detriment of students who lack computing and Internet skills.

Not too many years ago, requiring students to demonstrate a basic level of computer competency was an issue on many college campuses. Several institutions developed computer literacy courses that all students were required to take. The primary focus of these courses was developing basic skills in the use of applications such as word processing, spreadsheet and presentation software. Eventually, these computer skill-based courses began to disappear as many educators believed that students were entering the university well-versed in basic computer usage.

While most students today have exposure to computers and experience using the Internet, a gap is emerging between functional and analytical uses of computing technologies. Students may be able to word process and surf the Internet, but they often do not understand the fundamentals of how and why these technologies work. An analogy is often put forth that relates using a computer to driving a car. Certainly, one does not need to know the engineering principles or mechanical processes that make an automobile work to be a successful driver. But the comparison of the automobile to the computer is incomplete. Whereas the results of driving a car are distinct and finite, the outcomes of using the resources and information that emanate from computer technologies are infinite and complex. Cars get us from point A to point B; information technology allows us to reinterpret the journey.

We have entered the age of ubiquitous and pervasive computing. Universities are again pondering what defines computer literacy and what specific skills are needed to effectively utilize computer technologies. Computer literacy has traditionally been defined as the ability to use computers to perform a variety of tasks, but that definition is no longer adequate. Computer literacy no longer simply means viewing a computer as a collection of applications; it also means using the computer as a means of communication and a source of information (Hoffman, Blake, McKeon, Leone, & Schorr, 2005). These same authors provide an expanded definition of computer literacy. Specifically, they state that computer literacy includes both "information literacy, the ability to evaluate information found online, and critical computer literacy, the ability to incorporate computing technology in support of critical thinking" (p. 164). Moreover, computer literacy must now be extended to digital literacy, as students are increasingly expected to interact with information and content made omnipresent by the fact that it is digitized and available on a cadre of devices.

The challenge of redefining a core course in computing lies in operationalizing the expanded definition of computer literacy. This is a major undertaking as the functional definition of computer literacy is expansive. This paper describes an initiative undertaken by two computer science and information systems professors to assess and remediate IT skills needed by all students at one regional university, regardless of major. The project is evolving along three dimensions: identification of discipline-independent IT competencies, assessment of IT skills among current and incoming students, and curriculum development. Each dimension is elaborated upon below.

Identifying IT Competencies

Preliminary Research

A preliminary investigation was undertaken to formulate a framework upon which a special topics course offering could be developed. The first phase of this investigation involved reviewing current literature and related course offerings in the areas of computer literacy and information literacy, as well as engaging in introspection with experienced faculty members. This investigation resulted in the identification of a set of exploratory questions that serve as the basis for identifying critical IT competencies that should be included in a computing course offered as part of a core curriculum. The set of questions include:

- What computing skills should any incoming college student possess?
- What should students know about purchasing a computer or upgrading an existing system?
- What does a college student need to know to effectively use a computer as a problem-solving tool?
- What should any student know about using the Internet for research and assessing the reputability of Internet sources?
- What should a college graduate know about computers and the Internet to succeed in any chosen profession?

- What do computer and Internet users need to know about ethics, privacy, security, globalization and diversity?
- What does one need to know about digital photography, music and video to enrich one's life with these technologies?

An exploratory survey of junior and senior IS majors in a required capstone course showed that a majority viewed familiarity with the Internet and World Wide Web as among the most important IT skills. Also rated as highly important was the ability to use applications such as Word, PowerPoint, Excel and Access, in that order.

Focus Group

The next phase of the preliminary investigation was to share the exploratory questions with interested stakeholders for the purpose of facilitating more in-depth discussions. Two primary groups of stakeholders were identified. These included faculty who teach in the computer science and information systems department and industry professionals who serve on the department's Industry Advisory Board. Approximately 20 faculty and 12 industry experts participated in the focus group discussion. Several general observations and specific suggestions arose from the focus group. First, the focus group perceived that many college students have only superficial IT skills. One participant remarked that while it was once enough for students to be casual computer users, they now need to become power users. Another focus group member mentioned that universities should prepare students for life-long learning about IT.

In the area of computer usage, the group identified the need for students to understand the "total cost of ownership" of computing devices. Specifically, students should engage in an exercise of specifying the configuration of a computer that meets their specific needs. Then they need to develop a maintenance plan for software and operating system updates, as well as a security plan that addresses protection from viruses, spyware and intrusions on privacy.

Related to information literacy, the group felt that students need to learn to manage information overload by developing skills in searching, applying filters and data reduction techniques. Specifically, they identified that students need to be able make sense of the vast amount of information available online. Moreover, students should be able to make critical value judgments about the sources of any specific information that they access online.

Another area that was explored was the need to understand and assess student perceptions of how computing impacts their lives and how confident they feel in their interactions with information technologies. Computing technologies are becoming more pervasive, not only in school and work related applications, but also as mediums for social interactions. Consequently, it is important for universities to identify and assess critical IT competencies and provide opportunities for students to remediate these IT skills.

Finally, the focus group identified the need for students to engage in conversations about ethical issues in computing and the Internet. Students need to be aware of matters related to privacy and security, and understand basic concepts about intellectual property, copyright and standards of ethical use.

Symposium

The authors have organized a symposium at an upcoming annual conference on university teaching. The symposium will cultivate a dialogue with colleagues across disciplines and institutions. Another objective of the symposium is to move the discussion of IT skills to the high school level, where remediation of math and English skills is well established, but assessment of IT competencies is not. Panelists in the symposium include the authors, a professor of communications, and a teacher at a private high school.

Future Directions for Identifying IT Competencies

The authors are developing a number of survey instruments. Questionnaires will be administered to high school and university students, educators and administrators. In addition, IT practitioners and recruiters for general, non-IT positions will also be surveyed. The intent of the surveys is to continue to refine the findings of the previous stages in which core IT skills were identified. The authors will also proceed with exploration of the IT skills addressed in the curricula of high schools and universities.

Assessment of IT Competencies

For quite some time, institutions of higher education have espoused the need to create graduates who demonstrate a set of IT competencies. While there is no standard set of computer skills that clearly define the IT competent individual, many institutions have implemented assessment measures that attempt to ascertain the specific computer skills students possess. For the most part, these assessments focus on basic computer operations, use of functional software such as word processors and basic skills in searching the Internet and using e-mail. A typical computer literacy assessment instrument evaluates student skill levels in such tasks as creating a document in a word processor, naming the parts of a computer, sending an e-mail, participating in a chat session and using a search engine on the WWW. Some instruments even include sections related to creating a Web page and setting up a small network.

Perhaps one of the best examples of a widely available computer literacy assessment instrument for undergraduate students is known as the Tek.Xam. Tek.Xam is a partnership between the Virginia Foundation for Independent Colleges, and ACT, Inc, an internationally known educational assessment corporation. Tek.Xam tests student proficiency in seven areas, including General Computing, Knowledge and Use of the Internet, Word Processing, Spreadsheets, Presentations, Databases and Web Authorship. Another widely available assessment instrument is sponsored by the International Computer Driving License (ICDL) (http://www2.icdlus.com/icdlus-lms-webclient/), an international essential IT skills certification in use by over 50 countries. The ICDL assesses skills in the areas of basic IT concepts, operating environments, word processing, spreadsheets, databases, presentation graphics and the Internet and e-mail. Each of these instruments assesses needed and worthwhile IT skills, but they represent only one aspect of computer literacy. They focus on the functional use of computers; they do not attempt to evaluate the analytical skills students need to be able to use computing technologies to support critical thinking activities.

George Mason University instituted a "Technology Across the Curriculum" program that has received national and international recognition. The purpose of the program is "to promote the most effective uses of technology to enhance learning" (George Mason University, 2005). As part of this program, they have identified ten IT skills and knowledge areas that are most important for liberal arts students. The knowledge areas attempt to expand upon functional computer based literacy to include outcomes of computer use. For instance, the goals are stated in terms such as "Students are expected to be able to use information technology for data presentation and communication, for data organization and search, and for data analysis. In addition, students are expected to possess a basic understanding of legal and ethical issues related to IT and of basic computing concepts" (Holisky, n.d.).

In the area of critical computer literacy skills, the Association of American Colleges and Universities has identified the importance of technology in higher education (Ehmann, 2004). Specifically, they identify five key educational outcomes of a liberal education and how computing technologies are necessary to support the attainment of these objectives. Their outcomes focus on the development of strong analytical skills, inquiry practices through hands-on experiences, developing intercultural knowledge and collaborative problem-solving skills, developing civic responsibility through the connection of knowledge, skills, values and action, and fostering integrative thinking and the ability to transfer skills and knowledge. For each of these areas they suggest activities that can be used to facilitate the attainment of student outcomes, and they suggest the use of an online portfolio as an assessment instrument. The focus is away from teaching functional computer usage skills towards integrating the use of technology as a means to achieve critical computer literacy.

What has become apparent when considering what constitutes a core course in computer literacy is that the notion cannot be defined from simply a functional or a critical perspective. Obviously, one cannot be a critical computer user without having functional usage skills. On the other hand, simply being able to master basic computer functions is not enough to describe one as computer literate. A course focused on meeting the needs of today's students in the area of critical IT competencies must, therefore, provide a bridge between these two extremes.

Imparting IT Competencies: Curriculum Development

Based upon the preliminary investigations and research on assessments, a special topics course was developed. The purpose of the course is to address IT competencies identified as critical to the success of any university student. However, it should be noted that the development of this course is an iterative process. The course will be subjected to an extensive evaluation process. In addition, the authors are developing a number of survey instruments that will be administered to high school and university students, educators and administrators. Moreover, IT practitioners and recruiters for general, non-IT positions will also be surveyed. The intent of the surveys and the course evaluation is to incorporate the findings into the development of the curriculum for a course that facilitates student development of critical IT competencies.

In order to synthesize the findings of the initial investigations, guiding principles for the evolution of the course were defined. These principles help to categorize the many competency areas and skills sets previously identified. The basic premise of the guiding principles recognizes that many of the students who participate in such a course will be college freshmen who have at least casual experience as computer and Internet users. The goal is to empower students with the skills necessary so that they can effectively use these technologies to support critical thinking activities.

Guiding Principles:

- Know Yourself
    - Know your strengths and limitations as a computer and Internet user
- Inform Yourself
    - Be resourceful and know where to locate useful, relevant information
    - Manage your learning about computers and the Internet
- Protect Yourself
    - Protect your identity on the Internet
    - Know who knows what about you
    - Protect your computer and network from common attacks

- Express Yourself
  - Communicate what you know about computers and the Internet
  - Share and present ideas using the Internet and common computer applications
- Enjoy Yourself
  - Have fun with digital music, photography and video
  - Participate in blogs, vlogs and other virtual communities
- Empower Yourself
  - Be confident in what you know and can learn about computers and the Internet

Course Objectives

Drawing from the guiding principles, general learning objectives were articulated and are outlined below.

Students who complete the course will (be able to):

- become a well-rounded, confident user of PCs and the Internet.
- use PC applications to solve common problems encountered at home, school or work.
- protect a networked PC from various security and privacy threats.
- conduct research on the Internet, assessing reputability of Internet sources.
- be aware of the social impacts of computers and the Internet.
- articulate a position on ethical issues regarding computers and the Internet.

Specific Learning Modules

The course content is under development and refinement. At the time of this writing, the specific course modules are as follows:

1. General computing and hardware
   a. Configure a PC desktop or notebook system for purchase
   b. How to purchase computers and PC components
   c. Replace or install components such as RAM modules, hard drives, CD-ROMs and expansion cards
2. Operating system and applications
   a. Set up a logical file folder structure
   b. Manage files and encrypt sensitive data
   c. Control panel functions and administrative tools in Windows
   d. Search for files on a PC system
   e. Solve a real-world problem using common applications such as spreadsheet, database, presentation and word processing software
   f. Communicate and present ideas using common PC applications
3. Recovery

   a. Reinstall an operating system to a reformatted hard drive
   b. Create and boot from a bootable floppy or CD
   c. Back up documents and data to CD-R, USB key, or other media

4. Internet and networking
   a. Recognize the difference between scholarly sources and news, practitioner publications, and un-edited articles that are available via the Internet
   b. Know what constitutes plagiarism and how to avoid it
   c. Find a computer's MAC address and IP address
   d. Set up a wireless router, including WEP and MAC filter
   e. Use PING, TRACERT and IPCONFIG at the command prompt
   f. Use FTP to upload files to a Web server
   g. Cookie settings to achieve an acceptable balance between privacy and utility
   h. Protect against spyware, viruses and exploits
   i. Create and upload a basic web site (e-portfolio)
5. Music, photography and video
   a. Uses of the JPG and GIF file formats
   b. Edit a photograph and attach a photo to an e-mail message
   c. Using MP3 and other audio compression options
   d. Common video formats
   e. Streaming audio and video
   f. Legal issues regarding copyrights and file sharing
6. Domain-specific knowledge – What you should know about how computers and the Internet are used in diverse fields:
   a. Business
   b. Psychology
   c. Biology
   d. Education
   e. Nursing
   f. Others

Course Description

With the general objectives and specific learning modules in mind, the course description was developed:

Start | Run | Learn. Computers and the Internet have revolutionized society. Every profession is affected. Communication, education and commerce have been transformed. Music, films, photography and books are digitized. Students who enroll in this course will rip a music CD, edit and e-mail a digital photograph, reinstall an operating system, design a database, conduct research on the web, secure a wireless router, participate in an online community and create a web site. Issues explored include security, privacy, globalization, diversity and ethics. Be a well-rounded user of computers and the Internet. Don't get left behind by the information technology revolution.

Conclusion

There is a well-established history of assessment and remediation of math and English skills at all levels of education. This paper argues that the age of pervasive computing dictates that core IT competencies rise to the level of math and English as universal skills that are evaluated, imparted and nurtured by all institutions of higher education. The iterative three-dimensional program designed by the authors of the paper flows from identification of critical IT competencies, to assessment, to remediation via curriculum development. The program is iterative because whereas basic math remains basic math, new computing applications are introduced at an accelerating pace.

There is a continuum of institutional approaches toward assessment and delivery of IT competencies. Some institutions, such as George Mason University, have developed extensive programs to infuse IT competencies throughout the curriculum. Other institutions have at least one IT course that is a requirement for all students. The university at which the authors teach does not require an IT course in its core curriculum, but encourages students to take free computing workshops that are sponsored by the institution's IT department. Basic, intermediate and advanced workshops are offered in popular word processing, spreadsheet, and presentation applications, and students may also take a workshop in which they learn how to create a basic Web page. Self-remediation works for some students but might leave others behind. At the other extreme, one can imagine that at least some institutions are grappling with how to establish and deliver a baseline of core IT competencies.

The program described in this paper is in its early stages. The course outlined above will be offered for the first time in an upcoming term. In the short run, assessments will be conducted, the course content will be refined, and additional conduits will be sought by which to establish multidisciplinary dialogues across the university. More focus groups are planned and other assessments will be designed. Administrators and educators will be surveyed to ascertain levels of awareness and agreement on the university's role in delivering IT competencies. The long-term objective is to shrink yet another digital divide – the often pronounced gaps that exist between the most and least technologically savvy of our students.

References

Bartholomew, K. C. (2004 October). Computer literacy: Is the emperor still exposed after all these years? *Journal of Computing Sciences in Colleges*, *20*(1), 323-331.

Ehmann, S. (2004). Beyond computer literacy: Implications of technology for the content of a college education. *Liberal Education*. Retrieved November 30, 2005, from http://www.aacu-edu.org/liberaleducation/le-fa04/le-fa04feature1.cfm

George Mason University. (2005). Technology across the curriculum. Retrieved November 30, 2005, from http://cas.gmu.edu/tac/index.html

Hoffman, M. & Blake, J. (2003 May). Computer literacy: Today and tomorrow. *Journal of Computing Sciences in Colleges*, *18*(5), 221 - 233.

Hoffman, M., Blake, J., McKeon, J., Leone, S. & Schorr, M. (2005 May). A critical computer literacy course. *Journal of Computing Sciences in Colleges*, *20*(5), 163-175.

Holisky, D. A. (n.d.). Ten IT goals: Information technology goals for liberal arts students. George Mason University. Retrieved November 30, 2005, from http://cas.gmu.edu/tac/goals/tenitgoals.html

Harvey, B. (1983). Stop saying "Computer Literacy"! Retrieved November 30, 2005, from http://www.cs.berkeley.edu/~bh/stop.html

Tek.Xam. (2005). Retrieved November 30, 2005, from http://www.tekxam.com

Biographies

Jorge Pérez is an Assistant Professor in the Computer Science and Information Systems Department at Kennesaw State University. He holds a Ph.D. in Information Systems and has over nineteen years of experience in the field as a consultant, systems analyst, web developer and educator. Professor Pérez teaches e-business, web development and informatics at the undergraduate and graduate levels. He has published and presented research on information security, diffusion of innovations, and organizational learning. His current research focuses on identifying, assessing and imparting competencies that are needed by any informed user of information technology and the Internet.

Meg Murray is an Associate Professor in the Department of Computer Science and Information Systems at Kennesaw State University, part of the higher education system of the state of Georgia. She holds a PhD in Information Systems, an MBA in Finance and a MS in Computer Science. She has been in the field of computing for more than twenty years and has served both in higher education and industry. Dr. Murray specializes in the area of emerging technologies and the development and implementation of those technologies to meet business and organizational needs with a special interest in technology infusion in healthcare. Her current work has been in the area of Web services, including exploring the supporting technologies of XML, SOAP, .Net and J2EE, and she has been an author and presenter on the technical and societal implications of the evolving software paradigm referred to as 'Software as a Service.' Her focus in teaching is to inspire students to create and devise new and innovative ways to implement information technologies to solve real-world problems. Her most recent work is in the area of devising strategies to assess and remediate IT skills needed by an educated workforce to ensure they are able to use the power of technology as a means for innovation * the driver necessary to sustain economic growth in the state and in the country.

The page left blank intentionally.

Development of Scoring Rubrics for IS Projects as an Assessment Tool

Doncho Petkov
Eastern Connecticut State University, Willimantic, CT, USA

petkovd@easternct.edu

Olga Petkova
Central Connecticut State University, New Britain, CT, USA

petkovao@ccsu.edu

Abstract

This paper describes the experience of the authors with the development of scoring rubrics for projects in the core subjects of an Information Systems program. It presents an overview of student learning assessment issues in professional courses and the role of educational projects for that purpose. Then the steps of deriving project rubrics in different subjects across the Information Systems program are shown along with some suggestions for future work.

Keywords: Project Assessment, Program Assessment, Information Systems Education

Introduction

This paper describes the process of development of scoring rubrics for projects in the core subjects in an Information Systems (IS) program. Projects are a suitable direct vehicle for assessment of student learning in professional disciplines. Assessment work in any academic program needs to be placed in the context of the broader issues related to curriculum design and continuous quality improvement (Heywood, 2000). Projects are very important teaching tools in vocational disciplines. They can be used as a way to demonstrate the technical proficiency of the students and how well they are prepared for their future profession.

According to Ewell (2002, p. 9), assessment as a term refers to the processes used to determine an individual's mastery of complex activities, generally through observed performance. It can be seen also as a special kind of program evaluation, whose purpose is to improve curricula and pedagogy. The process of assessment starts with identification of the goals and objectives for learning, understanding of how these are addressed in the curriculum, followed by data gathering and evaluation of the results to improve educational programs. Other aspects of assessment and the related terminology are discussed in Heywood (2000, pp. 16-32).

Why assessment is necessary in an IS program? The most important reason is the need to measure student learning and define ways for its boosting. A by-product of this process can be an overall improvement of academic performance of the program, increase of its contribution to departmental goals and finally but not least, it can be a vehicle leading to program accreditation. Assessment is an essential part of the daily activities of academics but often it is not appreciated enough (see Wright, 2002).

With the exception of one effort in IS program assessment at another US university (see Petkova & Jarmoszko, 2006), the existing publications on assessment of student learning in Information Systems have focused only on single aspects of the assessment process in this discipline, like the use of surveys of graduates from a specific program (Pick & Kim, 2000), or the role of a comprehensive exit exam conducted at national level (Reynolds, Longenecker, Landry, Pardue & Applegate, 2004).

The purpose of this paper is to develop an approach to designing rubrics for projects in various IS subjects that can be easily adapted to the goals of a particular educational program. The need to boost the practical skills of the students and the concern for developing a mechanism to improve student learning in the IS program at the universities where the authors work were the motivations for this research. To the best knowledge of the authors, there has been no published work on issues of assessment of student learning through project rubrics within diverse subjects across an IS program.

The paper proceeds with a discussion on issues related to assessment of student learning in an academic program, followed with an exploration of the theoretical aspects of using rubrics in project assessment. A case study on the design of rubrics for projects in different IS subjects follows, which is concluded with possible directions for future research.

On the Assessment of Student Learning in an IS Academic Program

An overview of academic program assessment methods is presented in Palomba & Banta (1999). According to them these include:

- Direct methods: exams; performance measures (demonstrating student competence in one or more skills), including oral presentations, projects, demonstrations, case studies, simulations and portfolios; juried activities with outside panels, rating student work; involvement in internships, national licensure or professional exams.
- Indirect methods: providing proxy information about student learning through questionnaires for students to reflect on what they have learned, Interviews or focus groups.

The information gathered using the above methods may be either quantitative or qualitative in nature. Initiating a relevant assessment process within an academic program requires a careful consideration of the needs of the students, as well as of the resources available for data gathering and processing of the relevant information. A valuable collection of hints on academic program assessment issues is presented in Stassen, Doherty and Poe (2002).

Course-embedded assessment has the advantages of easy implementation, cost and time effectiveness and student acceptance. Performance appraisal is the natural choice of assessment method to be used when assessing problem solving, communication and team working skills. Here we will concentrate on an issue that is not widely researched in IS program assessment literature: using scoring rubrics for the assessment of student performance in projects in IS subjects. Since such an approach provides a direct measure for student learning, it is preferred to other indirect methods for program assessment (see Palomba & Banta, 1999), especially in a professional field like Information Systems.

Some Theoretical Issues in Project Assessment and the Use of Rubrics

According to Heywood (2000, p. 329), a student is asked in an educational project to plan, specify, make, test and evaluate an artifact or an idea. Usually the instructor provides the students with guidelines for the structure of a project outline. Typically such guidelines, according to Heywood (2000:330), include: title; analysis of the problem; practical problems to be solved; possible solutions; resources; references; future work.

A detailed review of past research on project work is presented in Brown, Bull & Pendleburry (1997, pp. 121-122). According to Brown et al (1997)., projects provide good, all around ability testing, potential for sampling wide range of practical, analytical and interpersonal skills, wider application of knowledge, understanding and skills to real/simulated situations, provide a measure of project and time management, a measure of team work skills and leadership. They stress the importance of monitoring project progress. According to the same authors, an instructor may choose from a wide variety of ways to assess a project: assessing artifacts; assessing the report; poster presentation/exhibition; presentations; logbooks.

It can be noted that classroom assessment for every subject in a program is left to the preferences of the individual instructor and typically includes quizzes, home assignments, exams and a team project. The selection of a particular set of methods for assessing an IS project will depend on its nature. Thus in an introductory subject on IS fundamentals it is usually the report that is assessed, while in a systems analysis or a database class, it is the design (the artifact).

Rubrics tell potential performers what elements of performance matter most and how the work to be judged will be distinguished in terms of relative quality (Wiggins, 1998, p. 153). Scoring rubrics are descriptive scoring schemes that are developed by teachers or other evaluators to guide the analysis of products or processes of students' efforts (Brookhart, 1999).

Rubrics are not checklists. They are associated with the development of criteria and rating scales for evaluation of the product against these criteria. There are two types of rubrics: holistic and analytic. According to Nitko (2001), a holistic rubric requires the teacher to score the overall process or product as a whole, without judging the component parts separately. With an analytic rubric the teacher scores separate, individual parts of the product or performance first, and then sums the individual scores to obtain a total score. The benefit of using a scoring rubric rather than weighted scores is that scoring rubrics provide a description of what is expected at each score level (Moskal & Leydens, 2002)

According to Moskal & Leydens (2002) whether a scoring rubric is an appropriate evaluation technique depends upon the purpose of the assessment and whether the following expected benefits are consistent with that purpose: rubrics support the examination of the extent to which the specified criteria have been reached and they provide feedback to students concerning how to improve their performance. Rubric design needs to consider the appropriateness and validity of the performance task and also the appropriateness and validity of the criteria and descriptors for discrimination in relation to the task (Wiggins, 1998, p. 164). Rubrics have been used in practice by various IS educators in the past but there is no published research on the advantages that they provide.

Apart from the descriptive role of a rubric, it has a potential for use in grading student achievement. The arithmetic calculations to obtain the corresponding percentage grade are deceptively simple but the field application of rubrics is an insufficiently researched issue in general. Mertler (2001) points out that a potentially frustrating aspect of scoring student work with rubrics is the issue of finding some way of converting them to "grades". The process of converting rubric scores to grades or categories according to him is more a process of logic and typically there are more scores at the average and above average categories than there are below average categories

(Mertler, 2001). This issue is an open question in the theory of multiple criteria decision making and in the educational assessment literature.

Criteria to Evaluate a Project

A possible scheme for evaluation of projects according to Heywood (2000, p. 330) may include the following criteria: Planning, Execution, Originality of the design, Use of resources, Critical review or self assessment and Personal contribution. Another scheme, quoted by the same author includes: Comprehension of concepts and aims, Background information, Initiatives, Motivation/application, Appropriateness of methods and/or experimental design, Organizational skills, Competence and Independence, Ability to problem solve. A set of criteria for evaluating an experimental project is presented in Brown et al (1997). It pays attention to such dimensions as Introduction, Review, Design, Methods used, Presentation of the results, Interpretation and discussion, Conclusion drawn, Layout and referencing. With respect to an arts based project, the same authors suggest a different set of criteria: Information gathering, Structure and organization, Use of evidence, Historical analysis and argument, Presentation, Overall impression from the project. It is evident that various sets of categories might be defined depending on the nature of the project work within a specific subject.

The degree to which the content of the project is taken into account or whether the assessment focuses on process issues depends on the focus of the assessor on product or process. However, in the case of a process emphasis, it is assumed that the content would have to be correct if high scores are to be obtained (Heywood, 2000, p. 333).

A new dimension to project assessment is introduced when one needs to deal with a group effort. Such aspects are the evaluation of working together and team building, while others might be assessment of development of leadership skills and project management skills (Brown et al, 1997, p. 136).

Wiggins (1998) discusses also expectations, another important issue in assessment. According to him, it looks at the pattern of overall past performance of an individual or a group that set up the norms. Hence students can exceed norms and expectations but still not perform up to standard according to Wiggins (1998, p. 157).

What criteria need to be considered in a rubric depends on what the students should know. Without claiming that every performance needs to be assessed against all five types, Wiggins (1998, p. 168) suggests five categories of criteria to be used in rubrics, relating to the impact, the craftsmanship, the methods, the content and the sophistication of the performance. Another important distinction is between rubrics assessing generic skills or specific subject matter understanding. According to Wiggins (1998, p. 176) reliability is served by using a rubric that is unique to a task and to the samples of performance that relate to that task.

Before specifying any criteria for assessment, it is essential to define clearly the purpose of assessment, the level and type of knowledge associated with a particular task (Brualdi, 2002, p. 65). This relates to the importance of understanding the taxonomy of learning outcomes defined by Bloom (1956).

General guidelines for project scoring rubrics are suggested by Moskal & Leydens (2002). Brualdi (2002) and Mertler (2001) provide almost similar practical guidelines for creating rubrics. According to Brualdi (2002), the steps in developing a scoring rubric are: Identify qualities for the highest score; Select analytic or holistic scoring; If analytic scoring is used, develop scoring schemes for each factor; Define criteria for the lowest level; Contrast the lowest and highest level to develop middle level; Contrast other levels for finer distinctions.

Very useful guidelines for designing rubrics can be found also in Mertler (2001). He suggests levels for a template for a holistic scoring rubric (one that does not take into account different criteria for the evaluation of a project): complete understanding of the problem, considerable understanding, partial, little and no understanding of the problem.

Mertler (2001) provides further an example of an analytic rubric, where for every chosen evaluation criterion is suggested the same set of four possible levels: beginning, developing, accomplished and exemplary. The next section discusses how the above concepts were applied in project assessment process in IS subjects.

An Account of Defining Information Systems Project Assessment Rubrics

Definition of a Standard Set of Criteria for the Projects in Every Information Systems Subject

The first step in creating rubrics for a group of subjects is to define a uniform set of project assessment criteria. The derived criteria for projects within the IS program at ECSU are shown in Table 1.

Table 1: Suggested project assessment criteria for subjects in an IS program

ECSU Information Systems program goals	Corresponding literature findings on criteria for assessment of projects	Proposed general criteria for assessment of IS projects reflecting the ECSU IS program goals
Technical skills (IS program goal 1)	Craftsmanship is the term used by (Wiggins, 1998)	Technical level of proficiency demonstrated through application of the technical knowledge associated with the subject.
Intellectual skills (IS program goal 3)	Method used, content (Wiggins, 1998)	Problem solving skills and ability to organize information, ability to compare a problem situation against best business practices or to select and justify the best alternative solution.
Interpersonal skills (IS program goal 4)	Impact (Wiggins, 1998), Project management skills (Brown, 1997)	Organizational, interpersonal and time management skills demonstrated in the execution of the project and its recommendations (some of it is evident from the project recommendations while some is evident from project logbooks and team member reports).
Communication skills (IS program goal 2)	Sophistication of performance (Wiggins, 1998)	Communication skills, demonstrated through the organization of the project and its presentation (sometimes it can be a project walk through instead of a presentation).

Having a standard set of project assessment criteria contributes to the faster diffusion of assessment in individual subjects. The dimensions of assessing a project within the ECSU IS program (column 3 in Table 1) were derived from the four goals of the program. They are similar to those in the standard curricular recommendations for IS programs (see Gorgone, Davis, Topi, Feinstein & Longenecker, 2003).

The general set of criteria for assessment of IS projects was developed partly from the existing literature on the use of projects in education (see Table 1, column 2). These were applied to the design of project rubrics for two IS subjects as is shown in Appendices 1 and 2. Further details on the design process are provided in the next sub-section.

On the Design of a Project Rubric for the Introductory Information Systems Course

Management of Business Information (BUS205) is the introductory course in the Business Information Systems major, serving also the Business program. It combines the content of the module on Personal Productivity Tools as defined in the IS2002 Curriculum Recommendations (see Gorgone et al., 2003) with some issues on Organizational IS. The small group project involves the analysis of information system implementation problems within a particular organization.

The BUS205 project description includes the following generic tasks:

1. Analyze the usage of a particular information system within a given work system. Analyze the problem within the framework provided by the work system model (see Alter, 2004); identify what potential sources of data (internal and external, including legislation, market research reports and specific research papers that may be relevant to it). Provide your assumptions characterizing the problem situation in the respective real organization for which the report is prepared.
2. Using relevant library databases provide an overview of the best relevant practices in industry regarding solutions to the problem on hand. Suggest what changes in the company information systems or its infrastructure would be needed to help provide assistance in the solution of such a problem.
3. Produce a business report that will show to the management of the organization how the problem can be effectively improved or resolved with relevant resources, including a schedule and deadlines.

Combining the above information and the content of Table 1, we derived the specific criteria to be used in the rubrics for projects in this subject:

- Ability to analyze a business and the IT in it as a work system.
- Ability to identify best business practices in the use of IT for the particular type of business and information systems.
- Ability to present the findings of the project within the report including time management issues
- Ability to provide a convincing presentation.

Following Mertler (2001), we have accepted the same four levels of distinction for student competency discussed earlier: beginning, developing, accomplished and exemplary. Thus the criteria and the grading of performance on each of them were derived on the basis of what is known about evaluation of projects in the educational literature in general and also taking into account the goals of the particular IS program and the specifics of a given subject. Appendix 1 contains the resulting rubric.

Using a similar approach, we formulated rubrics for other subjects like Systems Analysis and Design, Database Design and Security and IS Strategy. For example, the rubrics for Systems Analysis and Design (see Appendix 2) contain criteria that have the same structure and similar explanations for the levels of performance. To reflect better the nature of the content in that subject, an adjustment of the first two criteria was necessary as is shown below:

- Ability to define user requirements of an information system and to document the analysis and design of the system.
- Ability to apply techniques for feasibility analysis, requirements analysis and Unified Modeling Language (UML) modeling in practice.

The rubrics shown in Appendices 1 and 2 were introduced in the fall of 2005 at the IS program at Eastern Connecticut State University (ECSU). A similar type of rubric for the Database Design course was introduced also the IS program at Central Connecticut State University (CCSU). The following subsection deals with the impact that rubrics may have on student learning.

An Exploratory Field Experiment on the Impact of Using Rubrics in an Introductory Information Systems Course

To illustrate the impact of using a rubric for project assessment a simple field experiment was carried out. A similar type of project on the analysis of IS implementation problems was assigned to single sections of 20 students in Management of Business Information (BUS205) during the spring and fall semesters of 2005. Both sections were taught in two sessions a week by one of the authors. The project assignments had the same goals as specified earlier in this section. The only difference in the treatment of the groups was the fact that the fall group was provided at the beginning of the semester also with the project assessment rubric shown in Appendix 1. The students in that group were urged to examine it as a guideline to the expectations towards the quality of their work while working on the project.

The spring section was divided into eight project teams. These achieved a mean percentage grade of 95.125. The fall section was split in nine teams. Those had a mean grade of 96%.

The *null hypothesis* was that the mean percentage grade for the group not using rubrics (spring) was higher than the mean for the group that was using rubrics.

The one tail t-test for the means of two independent samples was applied. The resulting t-statistic was 1.8495444, while the critical t-value for this test corresponding to 15 degrees of freedom was 1.7530503. Since $|t|>t_{crit}$ we may conclude that the null hypothesis is rejected at the 0.05 level of confidence and that the use of rubrics has a positive impact on improving student performance.

A limitation of the above finding is the small sample and hence its exploratory nature. Further field statistical results from a larger study will be needed to support this claim.

Our preliminary experiences from using the rubrics and the qualitative analysis of student projects in this subject over three semesters demonstrate the usefulness of rubrics. They help the students focus their attention on the essential issues when working on projects. The average rating for all team projects along each criterion may serve as an indication for potential problem areas that need to be addressed by the instructor. The results could be used for deriving measures towards improvement of student learning, reaching an emphasis balance between the four types of outcomes at the various levels of the IS program and for curriculum improvement. More insights on the potential of project rubrics for the purposes of assessing student learning in individual IS subjects will be derived after processing project assessment data from several semesters.

Concluding Remarks and Possible Future Work

The suggested rubrics allow a uniform way of evaluation of projects across most subjects in an IS program. Rubrics support the standardization of the way for assessing projects in subjects with several sections like introductory level courses.

The suggested approach to designing rubrics in individual IS subjects may lay the foundation for long term assessment of student learning combining project rubrics and portfolios. Having a uniform structure of the project rubrics will allow the measurement of student progress through their studies within the program. This is one of our lines for future research in this area.

Another open question is the role of an overall evaluation indicator as part of the criteria for which we have designed rubrics. A further interesting issue relates to comparing analytic and holistic rubrics.

This paper extends further the work in Jarmozsko, Petkova, & Gendron (2003) and Petkova & Jarmozsko (2006) towards improvement of student learning in Information Systems programs through using project artifacts as direct indicators of students' theoretical and practical skills.

Acknowledgements

The authors are very grateful for the cooperation to their departmental colleagues and to the anonymous referees for their insightful and helpful comments on improving the paper.

References

Alter, S. (2004). Making work system principles visible and usable in systems analysis and design. *Proceedings of AMCIS 2004, the Americas Conference on Information Systems*, New York, NY, Aug. 8-10, 2004, 1604-1611.

Bloom, B.S. (1956). Taxonomy of educational objectives: The classification of educational goals: *Handbook I, cognitive domain*. New York; Toronto: Longmans.

Brown, G., Bull, J., & Pendleburry, M. (1997). *Assessing student learning in higher education*. London and New York: Routledge.

Brookhart, S. M. (1999). Teaching about communicating assessment results and grading. *Educational Measurement: Issues and Practice, 18*(1), 5-13.

Brualdi A. (2002). Implementing performance assessment in the classroom. In C. Boston (Ed.), *Understanding scoring rubrics: A guide to teachers* (pp. 1-4). Clearing House on Education and Assessment, University of Maryland.

Ewell, P.T., (2002). An emerging scholarship: a brief history of assessment. In T.W.Banta (Ed), *Building a scholarship of assessment*. Jossey- Bass Publishers.

Gorgone, J. T., Davis, G. B., Topi, H., Feinstein, D. L. & Longenecker, H. E. (2003), IS 2002: model curriculum and guidelines for undergraduate degree programs in information systems, *Database*, *34*(1).

Heywood, J. (2000). *Assessment in Higher education: Student learning, teaching, programmes and institutions.* Jessica Kingsley Publishers.

Jarmoszko, A., Petkova, O., & Gendron, M. (2003).Toward assessment of information systems programs: Evaluating learning outcomes in systems analysis and design courses, *Proceedings of Informing Science and Information Technology Education Joint Conference,* Pori, Finland, June 2003. Retrieved October 10, 2005 from http://proceedings.informingscience.org/IS2003Proceedings/docs/166Jarmo.pdf

Mertler, C.A. (2001). Designing scoring rubrics for your classroom, *Journal of Practical Assessment, Research and Evaluation, 7*(25).

Moskal, B. M. & Leydens, J. A. (2002). Scoring rubric development: Validity and reliability. In C. Boston (Ed), *Understanding scoring rubrics: A guide to teachers* (pp. 25-33). Clearing House on Education and Assessment, University of Maryland.

Nitko A. (2001). *Educational assessment of students.* Prentice Hall.

Palomba C. & Banta T. (1999). *Assessment essentials.* Jossey-Bass Publishers.

Petkova, O & Jarmoszko, T. (2006). Assessment loop for the MIS program at Central Connecticut State University: A practice of learning, reflection and sharing. *Information Systems Education Journal, 4*(11).

Pick, J. B., & Kim., J. (2000). Program assessment in an undergraduate information systems program: Prospects for curricular and programmatic enhancement. *Proceedings of the 15th Annual Conference of the IAIM*, Brisbane, Australia, 2000.

Reynolds, J.H., Longenecker Jr, H.E., Landry, J.P., Pardue J.H. & Applegate. B. (2004). Information systems national assessment update: the results of a Beta-test of a new information systems exit exam based on the IS 2002 model curriculum. *Information Systems Education Journal, 2*(24).

Stassen, L.A.M., Doherty, K., & Poe, M. (2001). *Program based review and assessment: Tools and techniques for program improvement.* Office of Academic Planning and Assessment, University of Massachusetts, Amherst.

Wiggins, G. (1998). *Educative assessment. Designing assessments to inform and improve student performance.* Jossey Bass Publishers.

Wright, B. D. (2002). Accreditation and the scholarship of assessment, in Banta T and associates. *Building a scholarship of assessment*, Jossey-Bass Publishers.

Appendix 1. Rubrics for Project Assessment in Management of Business Information

The criteria that are used in this subject reflect the four general criteria for evaluation of IS projects by measuring the following learning outcomes:

1. Ability to analyze a business and its information system as a work system.
2. Ability to identify best business practices in the use of IT for the particular type of business and information systems.
3. Ability to present the findings of the project within the report including time management issues
4. Ability to provide a convincing presentation.

Hence the following rubrics were defined for the evaluation of the project report:

Criterion	Definition of rubrics on a scale of proficiency (1-4)			
	Beginning 1	**Developing 2**	**Accomplished 3**	**Exemplary 4**
1. Ability to analyze a business as a work system				
1.1. Correct application of the work system model	Inappropriate	Partial	Well-defined	Results analyzed
1.2. Appropriate data collection	No evidence	Secondary	Interviews	Integrated sources
1.3. Are the conclusions in line with the factors for success or failure of IS	No evidence	Occasional	Good evidence	Evidence and good analysis
2. Review of best business practices:				
2.1. To what extent is the review relevant	No sources	Up to 2 sources	At least 5 sources-no justification	Sources well justified
2.2. Is there evidence of critical appraisal of other work or is it just descriptive	No appraisal	Occasional	Attempted minor errors	Critical appraisal no errors
2.3. Is there a summary linking the review to the problem on hand	No attempt	Somewhat	Attempted	Well defined
3. Recommendations of the project				
3.1. Have the main points to emerge from the project being picked up for discussion?	No evidence	Occasional	Good evidence	Evidence and analysis
3.2. Is there a consideration on the resources needed for the suggested transformation and the schedule?	No appraisal	Occasional	Attempted minor errors	Well defined - no errors

3.3. Was the project developed within the time allocated for the phases?	No	Mostly on time	On time	On time and with no errors
4. Presentation				
4.1. Clarity of explanation and conclusions	Lacking	Satisfactory	Good	Excellent
4.2. Visual impact of the presentation	No	Only text	A plan is evident	Excellent
4.3.Use of audio visual aids, body language	Poor	Satisfactory	Good	Excellent
4.4. Response to questions	Poor	Satisfactory	Good	Excellent

Appendix 2. Rubrics for Project Assessment in Systems Analysis and Design

The criteria used in the subject Systems Analysis and Design reflect the four general criteria for evaluation of projects by measuring the learning outcomes covered in the course and the project specific goals:

1. Ability to define user requirements of an information system and to design a system in the Unified Modeling Language (UML).
2. Ability to apply techniques for feasibility analysis, requirements analysis and UML modeling in practice.
3. Ability to present the findings of the project within the report including time management issues
4. Ability to provide a convincing presentation.

Hence the following rubrics were defined for the evaluation of the design project:

Criterion	**Definition of rubrics and scale (1-4)**			
	Beginning 1	**Developing 2**	**Accomplished 3**	**Exemplary 4**
1. Ability to define user requirements of an information system and to design a system				
1.1. Correct application of analysis and design principles	Inappropriate	Partial	Well-defined	Results analyzed
1.2. Appropriate requirements gathering	No evidence	Secondary	Interviews	Integrated sources
1.3. Is the final product relevant for a practical implementation of the information system	No evidence	Occasional	Good evidence	Evidence and good analysis
2. Ability to apply feasibility analysis, requirements analysis and UML modeling in practice:				
2.1. How are requirements assumptions relevant	No sources	Up to 2 sources	At least 5 sources-no justification	Sources well justified
2.2. Is there evidence of application of the covered analysis and design principles	No appraisal	Occasional	Attempted minor errors	Critical appraisal no errors
2.3. Is there a evidence of knowing UML	No attempt	Somewhat	Attempted	Well defined
3. Project findings				
3.1. Have the main points to emerge from the project being picked up for discussion?	No evidence	Occasional	Good evidence	Evidence and analysis
3.2. Is there a consideration on the resources needed for the suggested system and the schedule	No appraisal	Occasional	Attempted minor errors	Well defined - no errors
3.3. Was the project developed within the time allocated for the analysis and design phases?	No	Mostly on time	On time	On time and with no errors
4. Presentation				
4.1. Clarity of explanation and conclusions	Lacking	Satisfactory	Good	Excellent
4.2. Visual impact of the project walk-	No	Only text	A plan is evi-	Excellent

through			dent	
4.3.Use of audio visual aids, body language	Poor	Satisfactory	Good	Excellent
4.4. Response to questions	Poor	Satisfactory	Good	Excellent

Biographies

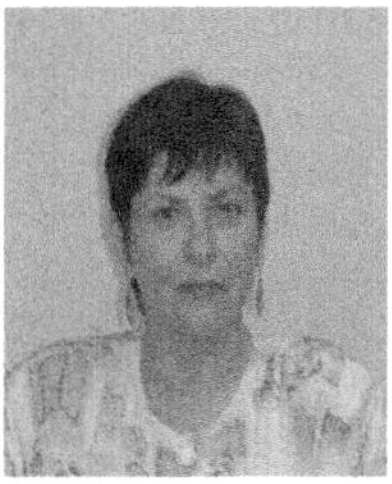

Dr Olga Petkova is an Associate Professor in MIS at Central Connecticut State University. Previously she worked at several universities in South Africa and Zimbabwe and at the Bulgarian Academy of Sciences in Sofia. Her publications are in the areas of software development productivity, systems thinking and IS education and have appeared or are accepted in Decision Support Systems, JITCA, Journal of Informatics Education Research, JITTA and elsewhere.

Dr. Doncho Petkov is an Associate Professor and Coordinator in BIS at the Eastern Connecticut State University. Previously he taught at the University of Natal in South Africa and in Zimbabwe. His publications in IS management, OR and Software Engineering have appeared or are accepted in the Journal of Systems and Software, DSS, Telecommunications Policy, International Journal on Technology Management, JITCA, JITTA and elsewhere.

The page left blank intentionally.

Information Retrieval Systems: A Perspective on Human Computer Interaction

Panagiotis Petratos
California State University, Stanislaus, Turlock, CA, USA

ppetratos@csustan.edu

Abstract

Traditional information systems design and development methodologies tend to overly focus on the technical details of the system such as memory management, system internals, algorithms and modules. It is not unusual for system designers and developers to often completely omit from the thought process the human element. This article offers a new information systems perspective particularly for information retrieval systems with a focus on human computer interaction.

Keywords: Information retrieval, human computer interaction, relevance feedback

Introduction

During the last few decades the amount of digital information has been constantly increasing at an accelerating rate. This condition is often referred to as the information overload problem. The reasons for this information overload problem are of technological as well as of social and economic nature.

Technological reasons include the recent advances in high density information storage as well as high speed telecommunications. Currently there are four types of media for the storage of information, magnetic, optical, film and the good old paper. Analogously, at present there are four types of streams for the dissemination of electronic information, the Internet, telephone, television and radio. A more traditional non-electronic but still very powerful source of information is the formal printed press which includes periodic publications such as newspapers and journals and non-periodic publications such as books.

It is interesting to note that the majority of new information created during 2002, or more than 98% of the total of all information transmitted in electronic information flows was exchanged between individuals during communication sessions including email, peer to peer file exchanges, and the telephone including both voice and data such as fax on land lines and instant messaging on wireless mobiles (Lyman & Varian, 2003).

Currently in the well-developed countries found in the continents of North America and Western Europe there is a digital convergence trend evident. Telecommunications companies such as Vonage are currently attempting to offer a flat fee model by diverting the enormous amount of information from telephone communications through the Internet and routing it as Internet packet traffic primarily due to economic reasons as the per minute charges are eliminated. It is only a matter of time before the Internet becomes the primary backbone for telephone communications and the principal information flow infrastructure for all information transmitted.

Information Storage Technologies

Furthermore, recent magnetic storage technology advances are offering an alternative to the rapidly approaching physical limit of magnetic disk storage density. During the last fifty years the traditional storing process for magnetic disks has been utilizing longitudinal recording technology. The data bits of hard disks are microscopic magnetic grains that are aligned horizontally on the surface of the disk and are magnetized according to the longitudinal recording; please see Figure 1.

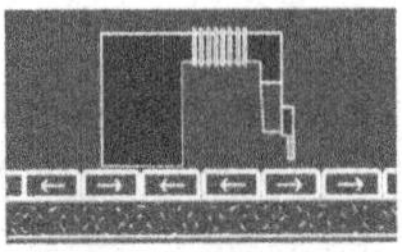

Figure 1: Longitudinal recording (Grochowski, 2005).

Based on this technology there is only one way to increase the data density of hard disks. This approach has been used successfully for the last fifty years steadily increasing data density by continuous miniaturization of the data bits. However, there are practical as well as physical limits to miniaturization, just as it is evident now to the microprocessor industry where the strategy of manufacturing ever smaller transistors, in order to pack as many as possible inside a single chip, is beginning to encounter its physical limits.

For the hard disk industry the practical as well as the physical limits are elucidated by a natural phenomenon called superparamagnetism, which occurs when the microscopic magnetic grains on the disk surface become so minute that haphazard thermal vibrations at room temperature are the aetiology for them to lose their ability to hold their magnetic orientations. The corollary is instant damage to data integrity that occurs as the microscopic magnetic grains whose north and south poles suddenly and arbitrarily reverse and experience magnetic anastrophe leading to data corruption and storage device unreliability.

A different approach from the existing data storing strategies is the new perpendicular recording technology; please see Figure 2. Perpendicular recording utilizes the depth of the disk, not just the surface of the circular platter, by aligning the microscopic magnetic grains vertically and thus allows for more data bits to be stored in the same space, which under longitudinal recording it was occupied by much fewer horizontal data bits (Mallary, Torabi, & Benakli, 2002). Perpendicular recording not only enables higher data densities but also overcomes the problem presented by the superparamagnetic effect.

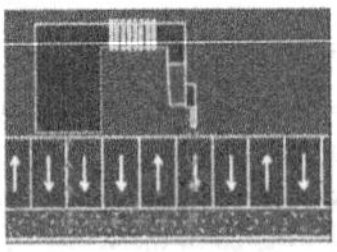

Figure 2: Perpendicular recording (Grochowski, 2005).

In March 2005, a data density of 230 gigabits per square inch (Gb/in^2) was demonstrated by Hitachi Global Storage Technologies utilizing the new perpendicular recording technology (Grochowski, 2005). This is the highest data density achieved heretofore based on perpendicular recording. This information storage accomplishment represents a twofold increase of the contemporary highest data densities in existence, which currently utilize longitudinal recording technology.

All these recent technological advances such as perpendicular recording and high speed internet access which enable people to store and disseminate increased amounts of information and the contemporary social trends which reveal that users are spending most of their time with electronic communications and exchange of information, they all indicate that information will continue increasing and more efficient systems for the search, organization, management and retrieval of information will be required.

Information Retrieval Systems

Information retrieval research and development over the years have produced a plethora of methods for locating information of interest utilizing robust text processing techniques. A number of these methods take advantage of the text characteristics, automatically create categorized clusters of documents, search entire collections of documents and retrieve pertinent information based on incisive characterizations of their texts as shown in Figure 3 (Paice, 1990; Van Rijsbergen, 1979).

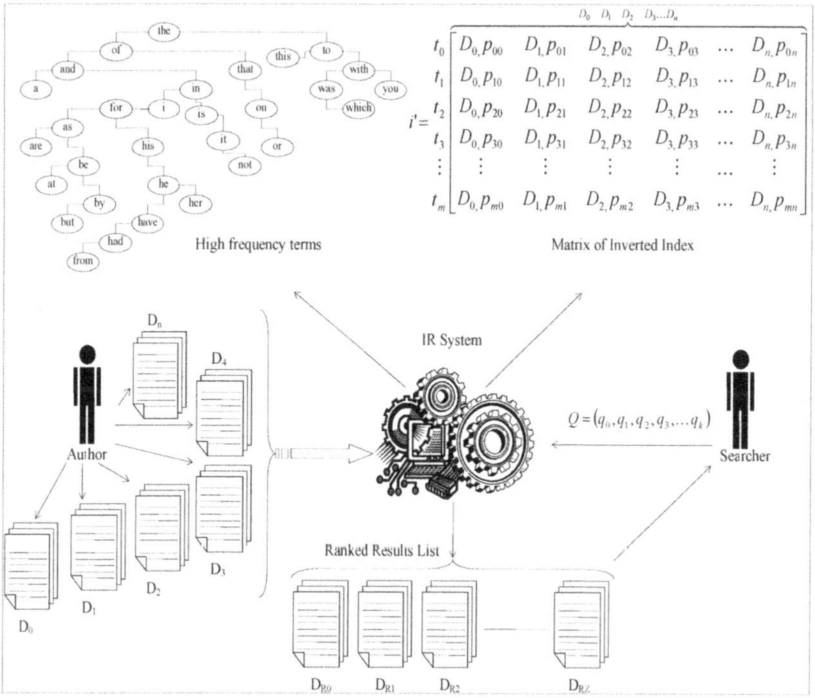

Figure 3: Traditional information retrieval system.

The more traditional, pure information retrieval approaches focus on the statistical data at the level of terms eschewing any further symbolic abstract semantic representations. This research approach presents some advantages as well as some interesting dilemmas (Mauldin, 1991; Rillof & Lehnert, 1994).

Although statistical term level techniques are axiomatically unambiguous and they have been well developed and applied in numerous practical information systems applications there are certain cases where semantic concepts diverge from simple word sequence expressions. For instance, if a semantic concept is expressed by different words such as cycle, bicycle, tricycle which all can refer to a vehicle or a geometric shape then this is called synonymy (Hudson, 1995).

Furthermore polysemy occurs if one word has several meanings such as life cycle, bicycle and vicious cycle. If a cycle query is issued then documents containing all the above will be returned. Another instance of polysemy is linked to syntheses of verbs. For instance, look after means take care of, look back on means remember nostalgically, look down on means feel superior to others, look forward to means anticipate, look up to means respect and admire, look at a painting, look familiar, look happy.

If a look query is issued then documents containing all the above will be returned. Finally phrases can have different meanings from the words they are consisted of, such as, man hunts shark, or an alleged murderer is not a murderer until proven guilty, or Lily has a beautiful Lotus automobile, or Jane slept away from lethal danger. In the first instance the information retrieval system returns an equivalency result that ensues if a query of a shark hunts man is issued.

In the second instance the information retrieval system returns an equivalency result which ensues if a query of a guilty murderer is issued. In the third instance the information retrieval system returns an equivalency result that ensues if a query of Lotus water Lily species is issued. In the third instance if a sleep disorder query is issued the paradigmatic documents will be returned.

Term dependencies, semantic phrases, synonymy, polysemy, are all concerns related to semantics. These concerns attracted the interest of researchers and numerous approaches are developed relating these issues. One approach is to utilize an approximation to world knowledge consisting of pre-compiled, pre-existing online semantic knowledge sources such as word lists, thesauri and dictionaries.

For instance synonymy can be identified through the use of a thesaurus and a sense disambiguation algorithm can select the correct sense of a polysemous word (Yarowsky, 1992). Another approach is to identify phrase segments and use them as synonymous terms by employing a syntactic parser (Lewis, 1992). Another approach to address specifically term dependencies is to employ latent semantic indexing (Deerwester et al., 1990).

All these research endeavours have encouraged other researchers to continue and expand this work by synthesizing term level statistical techniques with epiphanic semantic processing in order to improve efficiency and effectiveness of automatic text categorization systems (Liddy, Paik & Yu, 1994). All these approaches are noteworthy efforts to address the differences between term expressions and term meanings however machine understanding and learning still rudimentarily remains an approximation of the anthropologic ability to read and understand.

Information retrieval experimental data analysis

In order to carry out a series of experiments an appropriate environment must be in place. Hence the development of the experimental information retrieval system *ANACALYPSE*. The architectonic model of the experimental information retrieval system *ANACALYPSE* is designed according to distributed object oriented architecture. A plethora of components are esoteric among didymous exoteric entities that coordinate the interactions and communication of their esoteric collections of objects. The didymous distinct exoteric entities are the server and the client(s), which can be arranged to operate in a parallel configuration in order for a plethora of simultaneous clients to interact synchronously in parallel with a monadic server.

Each client consists of a plethora of objects such as interactive dialogue and user input components, user historical data preservation modules, graphical user interfaces, output displays, bidirectional fuzzy relevance feedback controls, such that all the interactions between the experts and the machines are automated without the requirement for intervention by knowledge engineers.

The monadic server is designed in such a way that it can be either esoteric or exoteric to the machine(s) where the client(s) are hosted. Furthermore, the monadic server consists of a plethora of modules for various operations. A few of these operations include the following:

Locating and transferring from distributed machines a plethora of relevant documents to the searcher's request.

Performing the metamorphosis of tag bearing text to pure text, whilst preserving the text descriptive fields of hyper media objects such as photographs, acoustic and cinematographic files. Identifying and extracting undesired high frequency terms. Discovering and preserving the types and roots of words.

Esoterically preserving the machine's historical data. Performing the analysis and metamorphosis of documents into vectors. Automatically presenting the machine training sample of documents to the experts for reading and automatically eliciting their bidirectional fuzzy relevance feedback based on the event activated human computer interaction model.

Automatically performing the syntheses of experts' bidirectional fuzzy relevance feedback with the machine training sample of corresponding document vectors in a new *Metagramma* matrix vector structure. Automatically computing the term weights of the *Metagramma* matrix vector structure according to the experts' bidirectional fuzzy relevance feedback on the machine training sample of documents.

Automatically computing the similarity of the *Metagramma* matrix vector structure with all the term vectors of all the documents that have not been read or seen by the experts, etc. Also, for evaluation purposes another object in the server selects a uniform random sample of documents from the ranked results list for inspection by the experts.

After the selection of the evaluation sample of documents from the ranked results list is complete another object in the server transfers the evaluation sample of documents to an object in the client for expert inspection and ranking evaluation. This object in the client automatically presents the evaluation sample of documents to the experts for reading and based on the event activated human computer interaction model automatically elicits the experts' bidirectional fuzzy relevance feedback and returns it to the originating object in the server. The designated object in the server computes the relative ranks of both *ANACALYPSE* and Google, compared to the expert ranking evaluation and computes all the corresponding Spearman correlation coefficients.

In synopsis, on document relevance issues of information retrieval a series of experiments can be conducted with interactive expert supervised relevance feedback in order to rank the retrieved information from irrelevant to highly relevant and to rank the retrieved information having negative impact or positive impact ergo the group impact for a particular system can then be precisely computed. The expert supervised training of the bidirectional fuzzy information retrieval system can be conducted in order to eventually achieve unsupervised system document relevance classification based on the initial small training sample and a relevance function which is morphed through syntheses of the supervised training, the document similarity measure and the term weighting function.

Dyads of supervised training modes are possible such as unidirectional and bidirectional fuzzy relevance supervised training. Firstly, the standard unidirectional fuzzy interval is [0, 1] and the documents which score 0 are completely irrelevant, the documents that score ½ are neutral and the documents that score 1 are highly relevant. Secondly, the bidirectional fuzzy interval is [-1, 1] and the documents which score -1 have high negative impact in the antithesis pole, the documents that score 0 are neutral and the documents that score 1 are highly relevant in the thesis pole.

The gradient from one stage to another can be further attributed a linguistic characterization which would illustrate the inclination from one stage to the next such as, possibly relevant, applicable, pertinent, important, etc. The queries are selected in the area of expertise by the expert supervisor in order for the relevance training to be accurate and a few of the queries selected by the expert supervisors are for instance "Itanium instruction set", "California commercial insurance laws", "Itanium source code porting methodologies", "Artificial intelligence algorithms", "Fuzzy logic techniques", "Data mining methodologies", etc. The experimentation occurred in a controlled environment with eight subject matter experts from the University of Luton to assess and evaluate the effectiveness of various possible search and analysis strategies. The present study summarizes the results obtained with the *ANACALYPSE* information retrieval system based on the processing of *2,000* documents and presents evaluation output in comparison to Google a commercial information retrieval system as shown next.

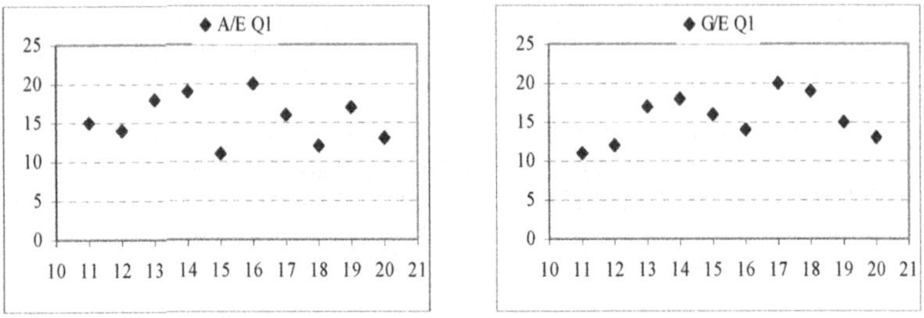

Figure 4. Scatter plots for q1 Anacalypse/Expert (left), Google/Expert (right) correlations.

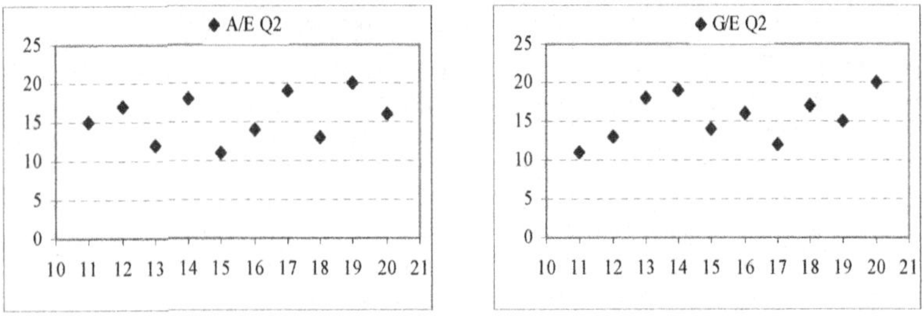

Figure 5. Scatter plots for q2 Anacalypse/Expert (left), Google/Expert (right) correlations.

In synopsis, the primary scope of this research is to propose methodologies of increased effectiveness for automatic information retrieval systems, with semantically relevant output compared to the subject matter expert's evaluation of relevance. Furthermore the experiments have two objectives:

1. To automatically compute the relevance of a large number of unseen documents based on expert relevance feedback on a small number of evaluated documents.

2. Moreover, to perform a triadic comparison and evaluate the effectiveness of the experimental information retrieval system *ANACALYPSE* and Google, the commercial information retrieval system compared to the expert's relevance standard.

The expert-supervised training of the bidirectional fuzzy information retrieval system is conducted in order to eventually achieve unsupervised system document relevance classification based on an initial small training sample and a relevance function which is morphed through a combination of the supervised training, the document similarity measure, and the term weighting function. In order to measure the convergence of the experimental and the commercial information retrieval systems with respect to the experts' relevance standard, the Spearman's correlation coefficient is used.

The procedure is based on a set of queries, which are selected in the research area (i.e. artificial intelligence, bioinformatics, software engineering, information retrieval, decipherment, etc.) of expertise by the experts who are researchers at the University of Luton in order for the relevance training and Metagramma generation to be accurate. The closer Spearman's correlation coefficient is to +1 the more linear is the relationship of the two ranks compared. For each query the experimental system retrieved and processed 100 documents, hence for the sum of 20 queries a grand total of 2,000 documents were retrieved and processed by *ANACALYPSE* for which the average Spearman's correlation to the experts' relevance judgments was 0.46542 whilst for Google the average Spearman's correlation to the experts' relevance judgments was 0.256995. According to these experimental results *ANACALYPSE*, the experimental information retrieval system is closer to the expert's relevance ranks with an average 10% positive change over Google, the commercial information retrieval system.

Conclusion

While current commercial information retrieval systems provide quite adequate methods of general heuristic for information they can be limited in effectiveness and some times restrictive in query elasticity, conditions that represent additional effort in time and reading for the information seeker. In this study syntheses of bidirectional fuzzy logic and information retrieval methodologies have been developed, analyzed and evaluated by subject matter experts. The novel methodologies have been designed and implemented in an experimental information retrieval system. According to the experimental results the academic information retrieval system is closer to the expert's relevance judgments with an average 10% positive auxesis over Google, the commer-cial information retrieval system. The proposed methodologies elucidate the bases for improved effectiveness and efficiency of information retrieval.

References

Deerwester, S., Dumais, S.T., Landauer, T.K., Furnas, G.W. & Harshman, R.A. (1990). Indexing by latent semantic analysis. *Journal of the American Society for Information Science, 41*(6), 391-407.

Grochowski, E. (2005). *Hard disk technology overview.* Hitachi Global Storage Technologies, San Jose Research Center. Retrieved January 9, 2006, from http://www.hitachigst.com/hdd/hddpdf/tech/hdd_technology2003.pdf

Hudson, R. (1995). *Word Meaning.* London, England: Routledge.

Lewis, D.D. (1992). An evaluation of phrasal and clustered representations of a text categorisation task. *Proceedings of the ACM SIGIR Conference on research and development in information retrieval*, 37-50. New York, New York: ACM.

Liddy, E., Paik, W. & Yu, E.S. (1994). Text categorization for multiple users based on semantic features from a machine readable dictionary. *ACM Transactions on Information Systems (TOIS), 12*(3), 278-295.

Lyman, P. & Varian, H. R. (2003). *How much information*? UC Berkeley School of Information Management & Systems. Retrieved January 9, 2006, from http://www.sims.berkeley.edu/research/projects/how-much-info-2003

Mallary, M., Torabi, A., & Benakli, M (2002). One terabit per square inch perpendicular recording conceptual design. *IEEE Transactions on Magnetics, 38*(4 I), 1719-1724.

Mauldin, M.L. (1991). *Conceptual information retrieval – A case study in adaptive partial parsing*. Boston, Massachusetts: Kluwer Academic Publishers.

Paice, C. (1990). Constructing literature abstracts by computer: Techniques and prospects. *Information Processing and Management, 26*(1), 171-186.

Riloff, E. & Lehnert, W.G. (1994). Information extraction as a basis for high precision text classification. *ACM Transactions on Information Systems (TOIS), 12*(3), 296-333.

Van Rijsbergen, C.J. (1979). *Information Retrieval* (2nd ed.). London, England: Butterworths.

Yarowsky, D. (1992). Word sense disambiguation using statistical models of Roget's categories trained on large corpora. *Proceedings of the International Conference on Computational Linguistics*, 454-460, Nantes, France.

Biography

Panagiotis Petratos is Assistant Professor of Computer Information Systems at California State University, Stanislaus. His research interests include object oriented system design, information retrieval systems, database systems, computer security, biometrics enabled computer systems. Email: ppetratos@csustan.edu

Collaborative Learning: A Connected Community Approach

John Rae, Carole Roberts, and Gary Taylor
University of Salford, Salford, UK

j.m.rae@salford.ac.uk c.a.roberts@salford.ac.uk
g.d.taylor@salford.ac.uk

Abstract

Collaborative Learning in group settings currently occurs across a substantial portion of the UK Higher Education curriculum. This style of learning has many roots including: Enterprise in Higher Education, Action Learning and Action Research, Problem Based Learning, and Practice Based Learning. As such our focus on Collaborative Learning development can be viewed as an evolutionary. This collaborative and active group learning provides the foundation for what can be collectively called connectivist 'Learning Communities'. In this setting a primary feature of a 'Learning Community' is one that carries a responsibility to promote one another's learning.

This paper will outline a developmental collaborative learning approach and describe a supporting software environment, known as the Salford Personal Development Environment (SPDE), that has been developed and implemented to assist in delivering collaborative learning for post graduate and other provision. This is done against a background of much research evidence that group based activity can enhance learning. These findings cover many approaches to group based learning and over a significant period of time.

This paper reports on work-in-progress and the features of the environment that are designed to help promote individual and group or community learning that have been influenced by the broad base of research findings in this area.

Keywords: Learning, collaborative learning, learning communities, VLE, connectivity, groups, action learning, learning environment, coaching, mentors, team work, learning technology, knowledge management

Introduction

The developing HE Environment is being influenced by a number of drivers that require us to address what we teach, how, when and where – and importantly how we support our students' learning. The drivers include:

i.) The continuing Government pressure to expand the HE experience to 50% of the population by 2010, notwithstanding the current growth rates are too low to achieve this;

ii.) The increasing financial pressures particularly on home students leading to an increasing number of students who are effectively "part-time" but following full-time courses of study;

iii.) The continuing change of status from "accepting student" to that of a fee-paying customer and lifelong learner with growing expectations of service to meet career needs and financial constraints;

iv.) The pressures on further education institutions to continuously improve success rates leading to students being provided with more and more information to complete coursework and pass examinations and thus less likely to develop the skills for lifelong learning or to cope with HE challenges;

v.) The impact of ICT on what is expected by learners and of what can be provided by institutions – and what rethinking of HE organisations has to follow to provide flexible and responsive modes of blended learning with integrated learning support.

Following from this last driver there is an underlying imperative to provide flexible and responsive student support structures, with institution-wide mechanisms that are capable of managing face-to-face, blended and distance learning options. These must increasingly allow students to be able to choose when, where and how they learn. Hence the support must accommodate the full diversity of study patterns and ideally be capable of personalisation to individual student level.

Coupled with the changing nature of students and their demands for flexible learning support, is the ever increasing stress on education for employability, capability and lifelong learning. Given the rapid development of knowledge anyway, we should primarily be striving for learning that lasts and preparing our students for life-long updating with more emphasis on the process of learning.

Meeting the Challenges

With the increasing emphasis on employability and capability, there is the need for students to learn how to create knowledge, as they will find it created in the real world. This will involve collaboration, consultation, teamwork and connectivism. Bruffee (1999) suggests that probably the most important lesson students should learn during their HE experience is mature, elective interdependence – social maturity with intellectual maturity.

There is a growing awareness that collaborative learning in learning communities during their time in education will help students to improve their critical thinking (Gokhale, 1995) and to learn to work effectively together, an attribute much valued in the real world with benefits to both their professional and personal lives. As Edwin Mason (1971. p. 16) wrote:

> "I cannot think of any part or moment of life in which we are not reacting to the presence of other people, or carrying over into relationship with everything else, what we have learned (by no means all of it consciously) from collaborating with other people while exploring the world with them."

But given the increasing tendency for our students to be "part-time" even while following full-time courses and to be on campus for the minimum time necessary, how can we provide an environment where they can learn collaboratively in learning communities? At Salford our developing approach to this problem is to bring together and apply three essential curriculum elements: current PDP know-how, current collaborative learning practice and a curriculum core for integrating principal subjects with PDP based reflection and planning. An integral part of this proposed approach is the development of a learning management system – the Salford Personal Development Environment (SPDE). By adapting and extending the environment using learning communities connected remotely rather than face-to-face we are striving to simultaneously engage students in the real world approach to knowledge creation, promote reflective learning and enhance their ability to learn how to learn.

Collaborative Learning, Learning Communities and Connectivity

Collaborative learning is a philosophy of teaching in which learners work together on a common goal, exchange their opinions on a subject, clarify the meanings of concepts or jointly address a problem (Hron & Friedrich, 2003).

As well as preparing students for the "real world", there is evidence that collaborative learning helps students learn better. Richard Light's (1990) studies of Harvard undergraduate education support this assertion. Light reports that dividing students into small groups tends to increase their "enthusiasm and their pursuit of topics to a more advanced level". The Russian psychologist L.S. Vygotsky (Cole, 1978) invented the term "zone of proximal development" which refers to understanding that lies just beyond current knowledge and ability – what we cannot learn on our own but can do with help from friends. Collaborative learning allows the prior knowledge that each brings to the community to be used on the problem at hand and to construct new knowledge from it. Further, collaborative learning has as one of its goals to help students acknowledge disagreement and cope with difficulties within the community. This can be hard but again prepares students for the "real world" experience.

As described by Bruffee (1999) collaborative learning actually has a long history. For example, when Benjamin Franklin was young in the 18th century he organised autonomous learning groups to promote his own informal learning. Up until the 1930s there was continued interest in educational peer influence but then it nearly died out. A revival in the 1960s was followed by another decline in the 70s and 80s. Its value is once again becoming more widely appreciated. Throughout modern times important studies have demonstrated the importance of peer-group influence (e.g. Astin, 1993; Coleman, 1973; Newcomb, 1962; Tang; 1998). Initially Astin had simply concluded that student satisfaction increased if friendships were encouraged but by 1993 he had decided that the peer group produces "some of the strongest and certainly the most widespread effects on student development" and that they seem to "learn course material in greater depth because they are involved in helping to teach it to fellow students". Indeed Tank found that the characteristics of the learning approach of a collaborating group of students were very similar to the characteristics of a deep approach to learning while students who did not collaborate in their learning displayed characteristics which were typical of a surface approach.

Notwithstanding the growing awareness of the benefits of collaborative learning, it is still frowned upon as part of the educational process by some HE teachers. Hence one factor that may constrain engagement in a learning community can be students' perception of what constitutes a "good" student, namely being independent and clever (Read, Archer, & Leathwood, 2003). However Thomas Kuhn (1970) asserted that "knowledge is intrinsically the common property of a group or else nothing at all". Oakeshott (1962) further argued that we can think because we can talk with one another, underlying the importance of conversation. Modern learning technologies have facilitated not only the dissemination of information to individuals but also the ability of groups of individuals in different geographical locations to engage in "conversation". Thus collaborative learning is now not restricted to situations where individuals can meet face-to-face at the same time and in the same place.

As we have learned in the last 10 – 15 years, asynchronous computer mediated communication whilst overcoming barriers of time and place does not automatically overcome the potentially alienating constraints posed by face-to-face learning environments. Students do not always engage with the community. Building a sense of belonging is likely to enhance students' motivation and engagement. But a successful critical community of learners will recognise the importance of "cognitive independence" as well as "social interdependence" (Garrison & Anderson, 2003). Mann (2005) also argues that as well as building a sense of belonging it may be important to consider the learning community as a "communicative event" and to focus more on supporting dialogue within the learning environment.

At Salford we are pursuing a collaborative learning approach to support Salford post graduate and other provision. Our approach places learners on the same footing as tutors thus addressing, at least in part, one of the other factors that may alienate and isolate learners, namely the effects of unequal power relations within a learning community. As will be seen, the use of the SPDE also seeks to support the development of both cognitive independence and social interdependence.

We may further ask whether working within a single community is now sufficient when learning and knowledge rests in a diversity of opinions and learning is a process of connecting specialised nodes or information sources. Siemens (2004) argues that learning theories such as behaviourism do not address learning that occurs outside of people (i.e. learning that is stored and manipulated by technology). They also fail to describe how learning happens within organisations. This is not surprising since indeed the theories were developed before technology reorganised how we live, communicate and learn. Siemens proposes "connectivism" as a learning theory for the digital age. He says:

> "Connectivism is the integration of principles explored by chaos, network, and complexity and self-organization theories. Learning is a process that occurs within nebulous environments of shifting core elements – not entirely under the control of the individual. Learning (defined as actionable knowledge) can reside outside of ourselves (within an organization or a database), is focused on connecting specialized information sets, and the connections that enable us to learn more are more important than our current state of knowing.
>
> Connectivism is driven by the understanding that decisions are based on rapidly altering foundations. New information is continually being acquired. The ability to draw distinctions between important and unimportant information is vital. The ability to recognize when new information alters the landscape based on decisions made yesterday is also critical."

Thus, it may be argued, that learning communities, as we view them, also share attributes of Siemens' connectivist entities: learning here encourages a diversity of opinions and sharing. Specialized sources of information in different communities can be connected, with the focus on capacity building and not just on current knowledge. The groups are supportive of each other which facilitates future learning. Such notions that have been outlined in this section of the paper have influenced the design of the SPDE learning environment. In short, our view of learning communities recognizes that there is much evidence that groups and group interaction can promote learning and development. Indeed we view a learning community as a group or set of groups that carry a responsibility to promote one another's learning at an individual and group level. Our objective with the SPDE was to attempt to provide an ICT based tool to promote collaborative learning amongst our learning communities.

"Collaborative Learning with Salford"

The initiative being developed at Salford goes under the banner of "Collaborative Learning with Salford" and is being facilitated by the development of the SPDE.

Collaborative Learning in group settings occurs across the majority of the Salford curriculum and at all levels. This style of learning has many roots including: Enterprise in Higher Education (EHE), Action Learning and Action Research, Problem Based Learning, and Practice Based Learning. This collaborative and active group learning provides the foundation for what are the learning communities. In this approach, a learning community is one that carries a responsibility to promote one another's learning. This is an active process, where learners are included in the development of **Learning Content,** as appropriate, and share their knowledge and experience as members of the community. The concept of a learning community can apply to staff development, curriculum development teams, subject groups, researchers, distance learners, applicants, alumni, colleges and schools, regional groups and more.

We have affixed **'with Salford'** simply because with a flexible learning approach you may be learning **with** Salford but not necessarily **at** Salford[1].

Every day the University has a wealth of knowledge pass through it that becomes lost to the ether. For example, imagine a room of managers from a variety of industries sharing their work-based knowledge and applying and evaluating concepts to their practice. This is an everyday occurrence, in another setting the consultancy bill for getting that shared knowledge and experience would be very large. But do we always systematically manage that knowledge and could we?

The management of the learning process and the resulting knowledge has led to the development of particular functionality in the SPDE. The SPDE enables an identified group of learners (a learning community) to be arranged around structured knowledge bases to enable quick access to and the sharing of experience and learning – both formal and informal. The community can also utilise a tutor or coach to help support community interactions; guiding members and moderating contributions. It brings informal and formal learning together, combining knowledge management and information sharing whilst building up learning through learning communities.

The SPDE also has other features that recognise the needs in a variety of circumstances for tracking skill development. For example, UK funding bodies now require that we evidence research skills development and so it provides a skill-based record of achievement as well as progress tracking. The design also recognises that many learners may wish to continue learning when they are mobile or not able to connect to the Internet. So it combines a mobile learning environment and a compatible centrally hosted facility. Learners can synchronize individual learning from their laptop or home PC. Finally, to better enable learning at the individual level the interface can adapt to suit a learners preferred approach to learning based around the Kolb learning cycle.

The Salford Personal Development Environment

In this section we shall briefly look at the features that have been included in the SPDE to help fulfill our learning community ambitions. The main operational elements are shown in Figure 1.

Figure 1 shows the notion of connected learning communities and the manner in which the SPDE interacts with the communities and the role of the Structured Knowledge Repository (SKR). The SKR is essentially a collection of knowledge and experience submitted by learners in the community in electronic format (e.g. a Word document or as an IMS/SCORM compliant learning object) and which is made accessible to other members of the community and the tutor or coach. This process enables the capture, sharing and dissemination of community generated knowledge and experience. Via a process of moderation this new learning can be added to the server content so that others may benefit.

---

1 Derived from comments by Bernard Lisewski, Salford University Learning Technology Group Feb 2004

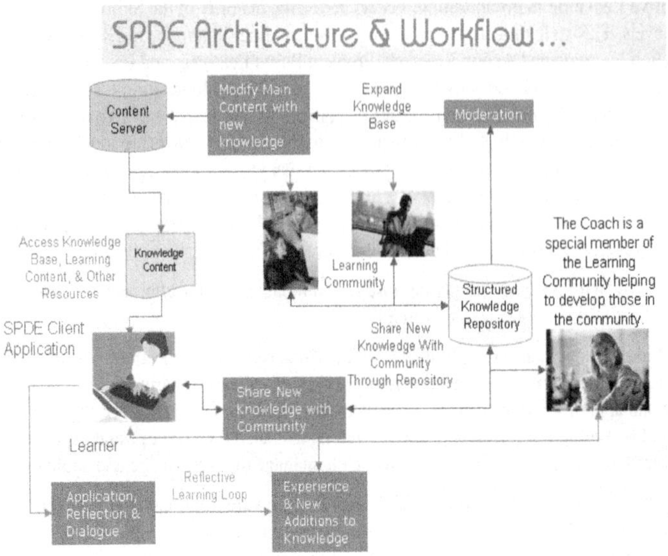

Figure 1. How SPDE interacts with connected learning communities and the role of the Structured Knowledge Repository

In summary, the SPDE enables learners and tutors, based around learning communities, to do the following:

- Tutors and learners can use the SPDE Client to easily assemble learning objects that can be structured to address a range of approaches to learning
- Tutors and learners may access a web based knowledge repository which, when used in conjunction with the SPDE, enables the collaborative development and sharing of learning content that has been enhanced by the addition of the groups experience and knowledge. Students can view and contribute to the development of such content developed and shared by staff or other students, both locally and remotely, through the Salford Shareable Knowledge Repository.
- Tutors and learners can engage in learning with the Salford PDE making use of developed content or purchased third party learning content. The Salford PDE is IMS and SCORM 1.2 compliant.
- Through engaging in learning with the Salford PDE a personal Record of Achievement is created. This can link to learning outcomes and skills framework development for auditing purposes such as PG R and T research skills or the NHS Knowledge and Skills Framework. This can link to PDPs.

The features that are essential to deliver a functioning learning community are those that allow the interaction with and the structuring and sharing of existing and new experience and knowledge. This interaction is based around members of the community and their experience as opposed to being focussed upon existing content. In the SPDE Tutors and learners have equality in the sense that both may structure and add experience and knowledge. The inbuilt functionality of the system enables this to happen. In a technical sense, to allow learners to create learning resources, the system has a simple content assembly tool that automatically packages resources (of any browser compatible format), should they wish to, to international e-learning standards. This means that other learners may load such content packages from the repository to share the experience of others. Ultimately such moderated packages can be placed on the server.

Reflection, Sharing and the Virtual Learning Environment?

The previous sections briefly describe the stimulus for and the developments of a learning environment to address what we consider are essential aspects of group-based learning. The SPDE does have some other features that address individual learning approaches by adapting the interface and delivery of the learning resources to match the preferred approach of the learner. The SPDE continuously monitors and adapts the interface based upon user metrics that are captured from the ordinary use of the system. This again arises from the desire to build upon what we know about individuals when learning. However, the focus of this paper is the group learning characteristics. To develop further the nature of some of the concerns for building the SPDE the following section explores aspects of related learning environment issues.

"What do virtual learning environments know about learning?" In a literal sense, absolutely nothing, just as a spreadsheet knows nothing of accountancy. However, both should have functionality that is supportive of the task they were designed for, and herein lies the rub. Are learning environments really designed for learning? Or, are they mostly the result of a set of historical and administratively convenient bits?

The answer is probably somewhere between the two all mixed in with a poor separation of subsystems within the overall system. In most learning environments there appears to be a mix'n'match of content management, learner management, and administrative processes. Within this mix there is also confusion over the functionality required to support learning, what it is and where it is. They are containers, more or less structured, for content that may or may not be tracked for access to some level. Linked to this is email. Add a collection of utilities like notepads and depositories, and probably a mechanism for synchronous and/or asynchronous discussion. These functional capabilities represent a set of useful tools under certain circumstances, but were they specifically designed for supporting learning? Of course not. So how and when should we use them and what is missing?

Simpson (2001) argues it is the interaction with the academic staff that puts the 'L' into VLE (Virtual Learning Environment). We would not dispute this. However, is this the only way of earning the 'L' kite mark? This paper does not try to address the overall issue of the range of functionality required to support learning, it is too big a topic for one paper. However, we do focus on a part of this domain, that of reflective learning and the role of a community within this. The importance of reflection and reflective practice has permeated individual learning and classroom practice for many years (see Dewey, 1910; Schön, 1983, and for a critique see Bleakey, 1999), not all proponents agree about the detail but most agree that reflection is an important aspect of learning.

What do we mean by being reflective? Osterman (1990) suggested:

> "Reflective practice is the mindful consideration of one's actions, specifically one's professional actions and is a challenging, focused, and critical assessment of one's behavior as a means towards developing one's craftsmanship." (p.134).

Reflective practice has also been described as a form of higher level cognitive activity. Valli (1992) states:

> "Reflection is the capacity to 'notice oneself noticing' that is, to step back and see one's mind working in relation to its projects." (p.99).

The first is related to teaching and professional development, the second could apply to any activity, and they both equally apply to learning of any description.

Most definitions involve the personal exploration of the experience of learning to better develop an understanding of how to learn and so, hopefully, improve their future learning. Such characteristics as increased self-awareness and objectivity, a greater openness of approach, increased motivation, and greater independence are eschewed on the successful reflective learner.

Our approach in utilising connected Learning Communities has been to adapt and extend the environment to place learners on a similar footing to tutors. In the postgraduate taught and research arena, where we are currently exploring this development at Salford, there is much to share and to learn from each other. This approach is being piloted on a small sample of postgraduate research students this session and their tutors. Early work with research students and their supervisors, around the PhD Learning Agreement, has been encouraging in engaging both supervisors and students in a more interactive and meaningful dialogue. The benefits of this early work in sharing good practice and ideas about an effective learning agreement can now be re-cycled to future generations of supervisors and students via the SCR.

Increasingly research students are required to demonstrate progress against a set of skills. The collaborative approach is adding value by involving students in their learning approach and by adding to the sharing of knowledge that can be linked to the required skill sets in the SPDE and then tracked in terms of use and application for the purposes of supporting progress and evidencing engagement via a record of achievement linked to PDP.

The Developing HE Environment

An underlying imperative is to provide flexible and responsive student support structures, with institution-wide mechanisms that are capable of managing face-to-face, blended and distance learning options. This support must accommodate the full diversity of study patterns and ideally be capable of personalisation to individual student level. Alongside this will go the introduction of specific packages to support learners. The aim must be to deliver effective programmes providing learners with the opportunity to develop knowledge and skills both meaningfully and efficiently and with opportunities to effectively communicate and collaborate with others.

There will be a greater role than hitherto for self-directed learning, for peer group interactions, and for learning outcomes which relate to higher-level cognitive and interpersonal outcomes. This is judged desirable because of the ever-increasing stress on education for capability and lifelong learning, and the greater range of prior learning that mature students bring to their studies.

Conclusions

We started by identifying the drivers that we believe are powering the change in the nature of learning in HE. These also indicate that part-time and work based approaches to learning will probably grow. We have a long history at Salford, as indeed so do other HEIs, of utilising the power of group learning, and such experience may be highly relevant to the greater diversity of study modes and patterns of learning where many may not be present at Salford but working more remotely with Salford. These factors have led us to explore further the nature of a learning environment that would help enable and support the community based learning that we believe will grow.

This is work in progress and the environment is new and just being established in pilots. Early qualitative results indicate a willingness to continue to explore this approach by both staff and tutors. There is still much to do and we are using the feedback from these pilots to help review and revise the practice and the system. It is early days.

The Salford PDE enables learners to engage with learning objects in their own ways and order, and at their own pace. Here again, however, we envisage a rather different form of learning community, in which essentially individual learners meet with those engaged on similar quests, to discuss problems and report successes, and engage with the demands of learning in this way. All of this can build upon Salford's experience over many years of collaborative learning.

PDPs are a priority development area leading to work to tie in skills and competencies and skills gap analysis. This has been implemented to allow the mapping of Skills and Skill Sets to e-learning created through the Collaborative Learning Communities, and to allow the further development of career mapping and skills gap analysis. This approach thus embodies the virtuous cycle of T&L research driving active experimentation, by students as well as staff, which will return benefits to the practice of T&L at Salford in terms of both providing better support for student learning and preparing students more effectively for the "real world".

References

Astin, A. W. (1993). *What matters in college? Four critical years revisited.* San Francisco: Jossey-Bass.

Bleakey, A. (1999). From reflective practice to holistic reflexivity. *Studies in Higher Education, 24*(3), 315-330.

Bruffee, K. A. (1999). *Collaborative learning* (2nd ed.). Baltimore & London: John Hopkins University Press.

Cole, M., John-Steiner, V, Scribner, S. & Souberman, E. (Eds.). (1978). *L. S. Vygotsky. Mind in Society: The Development of Higher Psychological Processes.* Cambridge, MA: Harvard University Press.

Coleman, J. S. (1973). Youth: Transition to adulthood. Report of the *Panel on Youth of the President's Science Advisory Committee*, Washington, D.C: Office of Science and Technology

Dewey, J. (1910). *How we think.* Boston, MA: Heath and Co.

Garrison, D. R., & Anderson, T. (2003). *E-learning in the 21st century: A framework for research and practice.* London & New York: Routledge & Falmer.

Gokhale, A. A. (1995). Collaborative learning enhances critical thinking. *Journal of Technology Education, 7*(1), 22-30.

Hron, A. & Friedrich, H. F. (2003). A review of web-based collaborative learning: Factors beyond technology. *Journal of Computer Assisted Learning, 19*(1), 70-79.

Kuhn, T. S. (1970). *Second thoughts on paradigms. The structure of scientific revolutions* (2nd ed.). Chicago: University of Chicago Press.

Light, R. J. (1990). *The Harvard assessment seminars* (First report). Cambridge, Massachusetts: Harvard University Graduate School of Education and Kennedy School of Government.

Mann, S. J. (2005). Alienation in the learning environment. *Studies in Higher Education, 30*(1), 43-55.

Mason, E (1970). *Collaborative learning.* London: Ward Lock Educational.

Oakeshott, M (1962). *The voice of poetry in the conversation of mankind. Rationalism in politics.* New York: Basic Books.

Osterman, K. (1990). Reflective practice: A new agenda for education. *Education and Urban Society, 22*(2), 133 – 152.

Read, B., Archer, L. & Leathwood, C (2003). Challenging cultures? Student conceptions of 'belonging' and 'isolation' at a post-1992 university. *Studies in Higher Education, 28*(3), 261-277.

Schön, D. A. (1983): *The reflective practitioner.* Basic Books. [Reprinted in 1995].

Simpson, V (2001): VE or VLE Don't forget the L! *Teaching and Learning Support Unit, 5*(1), Spring term, University of Surrey. Also in *Association for Learning Technology Newsletter, 31*, October 2000.

Siemens, G. (2004). Connectivism: A learning theory for the digital age. Retrieved October 2005 from http://www.elearnspace.org/Articles/connestivism.htm

Tang, C. (1998). Effects of collaborative learning on the quality of assignments. In B. C. Dart & G. M. Boulton-Lewis (Eds.), *Teaching and learning in higher education.* Melbourne: Australian Council for Educational Research.

Valli, L. (Ed.). (1992). *Reflective teacher education: Cases and critiques.* Albany: State University of New York Press.

Biographies

John Rae is Professorial Fellow and Associate Dean (Teaching) in the Faculty of Business and Informatics at the University of Salford. His work is in the area of lifelong learning, educational technology, and information systems. His work is focussed on the integration teaching and learning, applied learning research, and academic enterprise activities. For many years John has worked with mature learners in workbased settings and much of the learning environment development concepts stems from this experience. John is the co-developer, with Gary Taylor, of the SPDE.

Carole Roberts is a Professor and Dean of the Faculty of Business and Informatics at the University of Salford. Her teaching interests include statistics, business forecasting and marketing research. In the past her area of research included the application of system dynamics modelling and she is a past winner of the OR Society's President's Medal. She has developed an interest in educational research and established the University's Learning & Teaching Research Network (2001) and the Higher Education Research Centre (2002) of which she is Director.

Gary Taylor is a Project Manager and Lead Developer on several e-learning and information management projects based around the University's academic enterprise developments. His experience of learning technologies goes back over a decade and he was for several years the Team Leader of the Information Systems Institute's Flexible Learning Team. His roles have always involved the applied research and application of technology to reinforce and enhance the learning experience of staff and students, including the Salford Personal Development Environment currently in use at Salford. Gary is the co-developer, with John Rae, of the SPDE.

The Emotional State of Technology Acceptance

Raafat George Saadé & Dennis Kira
John Molson School of Business, Concordia University
Montreal, Quebec, Canada

rsinfo@sympatico.ca kira@vax2.concordia.ca

Abstract

Computer-phobic university students are easy to find today especially when it come to taking online courses. Affect has been shown to influence users' perceptions of computers. Although self-reported computer anxiety has declined in the past decade, it continues to be a significant issue in higher education and online courses. More importantly, anxiety seems to be a critical variable in relation to student perceptions of online courses. A substantial amount of work has been done on computer anxiety and affect. In fact, the technology acceptance model (TAM) has been extensively used for such studies where affect and anxiety were considered as antecedents to perceived ease of use. However, few, if any, have investigated the interplay between the two constructs as they influence perceived ease of use and perceived usefulness towards using online systems for learning. In this study, the effects of affect and anxiety (together and alone) on perceptions of an online learning system are investigated. Results demonstrate the interplay that exists between affect and anxiety and their moderating roles on perceived ease of use and perceived usefulness. Interestingly, the results seem to suggest that affect and anxiety may exist simultaneously as two weights on each side of the TAM scale.

Keywords: Affect; Anxiety; TAM; Perceived Usefulness; Ease of Use; Online Learning

Introduction

Recently, interest in the use of online learning tools has increased significantly. The value of online learning has become widely accepted as an approach to enhance the classroom environment. Ever since Ivari and Ervasti, (1994) stated that productivity gains and benefits to students and academic institutions promised by learning technologies cannot be realized unless they are effectively used. In fact, little research today is being done on effectiveness in online learning. Most of this research is done on acceptance which has also been identified as a critical issue in the successful usage of the learning technologies (Deci & Ryan, 1985).

Many theoretical frameworks have been used to measure technology usage satisfaction, however relatively few have been used in the online learning context. The technology acceptance model (TAM), has been recently used to study the acceptance of computer-assisted applications (Saadé, 2003, 2005). In general, the TAM theorizes that perceived usefulness (PU) influences attitudes towards technology usage (ATT) and is an important determinant of individuals' intentions to use the technology. The goal of TAM is "to provide an explanation of the determinants of computer acceptance that is in general, capable of explaining user behavior across a broad range of end-user computing technologies and user populations, while at the same time being both parsimonious and theoretically justified" (Davis, 1986, 1989; Davis, Bagozzi, & Warshaw, 1989).

Many researchers have worked on the extension of TAM model to fit different contexts. We follow that line of investigation to further provide additional understanding of the role of anxiety (ANX) and affect (AFF) as antecedents to the perceived ease of use and perceived usefulness constructs in TAM. We provide results related to the impact of affect and anxiety on perceived ease of use. Our study involves 114 students that used an online learning system (OLS) (developed in-house) as part of an introductory course in management information systems (MIS). Prior research in information systems has investigated the TAM constructs with affect and anxiety (Agarwal & Karahanna, 2000; Howard & Smith, 1986; Vallerand, 1997; Venkatesh & Davis, 2000), however, few studies, have applied it to an online learning system and have directly compared and contrasted the impact of anxiety and affect constructs on PU and PEU to further understand the PU-PEU relationship in TAM.

Theoretical Background and Research Hypothesis

The Technology Acceptance Model - TAM

Online learning is perceived by many to be a significant breakthrough in teaching and learning (Debourgh, 1995; Johanson, 1999; Keeney, 1999; Keller, 1983; & LaRose, Gregg, & Eastin, 1998). The Internet allows educators to provide learners with new and innovative virtual environments in an attempt to stimulate and enhance their learning process (Brown, 2002). In addition, Internet or web technologies are important because they support manipulation of information, facilitate/enhance communications among instructors and learners and provide tools to encourage creativity and initiative (Conlon, 1997; Mioduser et al., 2000).

Studies of learners' satisfaction are typically limited to one-dimensional post-training perceptions of learners (Johnson, Aragon, Shaik, & Palma-Rivas, 2000). Acceptance and satisfaction however, is multidimensional and includes a wide variety of critical variables including (but not limited to) perceptions, beliefs, attitudes, learners' characteristics, and level of involvement with the online course material (Chang & Cheung, 2001). If Internet-based learning environments are to benefit students then it is important from the student's perspective that they are not seen as overly complex and hard to use. The introduction of Internet-based learning environments may hinder the learning process if the technology is perceived as being complex and not useful to enhanced performance, and thus a distraction to learning. In line with acceptance and satisfaction studies, TAM is used as the basic theoretical foundation for this research work.

According to TAM, a student's intention to use a specific OLS is jointly determined by one's attitude toward using the system and PU of the system. This implies that when the OLS is perceived to be easier to use, the greater will be the student's perceived ability to use the OLS successfully and hence perform better in the course. TAM also emphasizes the importance of how external variables can affect the student's internal decision process when it comes to using an OLS within the university. External variables affect PU directly or indirectly through PEU since it influences the student's near-term perception of usefulness and to the lesser extent long-term (Compeau, Higgins, & Huff, 1999). Extrapolating from the study by Lucas and Spitler (1999) study, interaction between the different OLSs, direct experience with an OLS, OLS characteristics (Chau, 1996), and level of domain pre-requisite knowledge determine the student's perception of ease of use of an OLS. According to previous studies efficacy, intrinsic motivation, cognitive absorption and computer anxiety were all determinants of PEU (Gefen, Karahanna, & Straub, 2003a, 2003b; Gefen & Straub 1997: Pedersen and Nysveen 2003). Saadé (2003, 2005) considered student traits to study their mediating effects on the impact of perceived usefulness on attitudes to learning tools usage as well as the explanatory capability of the technology acceptance model. In addition to these findings they have observed that PEU and PU, to some extent, are influenced by external variables. Extensions to TAM have been introduced by Venkatesh and Davis (2000), and Venkatesh and Morris (2000) with comprehensive study of the determinants of perceived ease of use. Extension to the theory, proposed control, intrinsic motivation (playfulness), and emotion (anxiety) as anchors that influence users' early perceptions about system ease of use. These models were strongly supported by the empirical results and indicated that up to 60% of the variability of PEU is explained in this model (Venkatesh & Morris, 2000).

Affect

The term *Affect* consists of four dimensions: cognitive, affective, behavioral and perceived control. The cognitive component focuses on belief, for example, whether or not a person believes that computers can increase significantly the quality of their output. The affective component is the emotion or feeling concerned with how much the computer is liked, and the behavioral component of the attitude relates to what an individual actually does or intends to do with the technology. The fourth dimension considers the perceived control dimensions of computer attitudes, that is, "the perceived ease or difficulty of performing a particular behavior". By taking affect into account we should be able to explain more variance in users' intention and behavior (e.g. Davis, Bagozzi & Warshaw, 1992). In this study we consider the affective component. Affective refers to an individual's feelings of joy, elation, pleasure, depression, distaste, discontentment, or hatred with respect to a particular behavior (Triandis, 1980). Triandis argued that previous research showed a strong relationship between affect and behavior. Positive affect towards a learning tool leads to gaining experience, knowledge and self-efficacy regarding usage, and negative affect causes students to avoid the leaning tool, thereby not developing actual control (Arkkelin, 2003).

Smith Caputi, Crittenden, Jayasuriya, and Rawstone (1999) show evidence indicating support for the bi-dimensional conceptualization of the computer experience construct. They suggest that the objective computer experience and subjective computer experience measures are to be explored independently. In the same study, however, the difficulties in separating the subjective computer experience and computer attitude measures due to their similar content are indicated.

Anxiety

Use of technology in general often has unpleasant side effects, which may include strong, negative emotional states that arise during interaction with computers. Frustration, confusion, anger, anxiety and similar emotional states can affect not only the interaction itself, but also productivity, learning, social relationships, and overall well-being. There are a number of related definitions explaining as to what is anxiety. Other researchers define computer anxiety as a state of mind of being fearful or apprehensive when using or considering the use of a computer. Evidently, factors such as who may have initiated the person to the computer technology (Brosnan, 1998) past failure or successes with hardware or software; and the current tasks being attempted including the new computer applications. These researchers have attempted to predict those who will experience computer anxiety by identifying factors that correlate with its occurrence. Frequently, such factors as age, gender, ethnicity, previous computer experience, mathematics anxiety, self-efficacy, learning styles, and computer attitude are posited as factors influencing the computer anxiety.

There are three types of anxieties: trait, state, and concept-specific. Trait anxiety is defined as a general pervasive anxiety that is experienced by a person over the entire range of life experience. People who exhibit trait anxiety are chronically anxious and constantly under tension regardless of their situation. This anxiety is frequently used as a construct for personality, learning theory, and psychopathology. Trait anxiety has been studied because of the possible correlation between it and computer anxiety. Since several studies found a significant correlation between math anxiety and trait anxiety the natural extension is to consider a possible correlation between trait and computer anxieties. Concept-specific anxiety is the range between the trait and state anxieties. It is an anxiety that is associated with a specific situation. Therefore, computer anxiety is a concept-specific anxiety because it is a feeling that is associated with a person's interaction with computers. In fact, Howard (1986) defines computer anxiety as the tendency of a person to experience a level of uneasiness over his or her impending use of a computer.

Understanding the variables that cause students to hold certain beliefs about an OLS would be of substantial value to students, institutions, businesses and instructors alike. It would also provide valuable insight for the successful design, implementation, and deployment of OLSs.

The research model used here is shown in Figure 1. This captures affect and anxiety as antecedents to PU and PEU for OLS. The two belief constructs in turn influence attitudes towards using different OLSs.

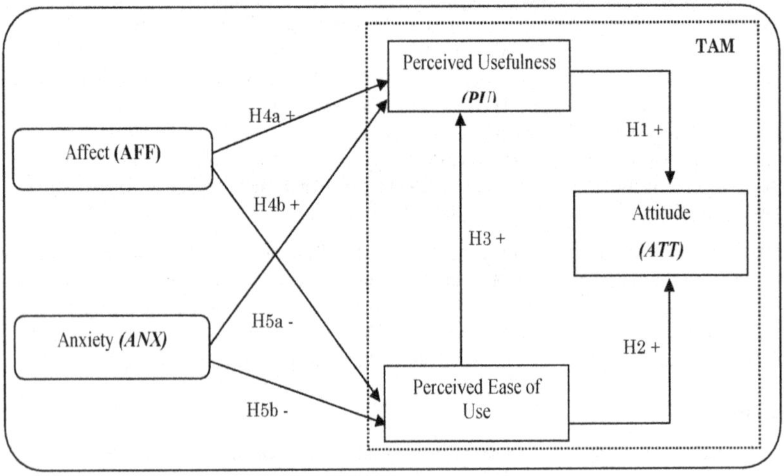

Figure 1. The Research model.

Based on the discussion above and considering that affect and anxiety may impact PU and PEU and that this impact varies depending on the characteristics of the IS (in the present case the IS is the OLS) used and the context it is used, we hypothesize that

H1. *PU will have a positive relationship with ATT.*

H2. *PEU will have a positive relationship with ATT.*

H3. *PEU will have a positive relationship with PU*

H4a. *AFF will have a positive relationship with PU.*

H4b. *AFF will have a positive relationship with PEU.*

H5a. *ANX will have a negative relationship with PU.*

H5b. *ANX will have a negative relationship with PEU.*

The Study

The study was conducted in an undergraduate course setting spanning one semester, using a web-based learning system which was developed in-house. Throughout one semester, students in an introductory management of information systems course at the John Molson School of Business used the OLS as part of the course requirements. The use of the OLS was therefore mandatory and was worth 5% of the final grade. The objective of the OLS was to help students practice course topics via interactive multiple choice and true or false questions. The system monitored the students' activities by storing the time spent on the system, the chapters practiced, and scores.

At the end of the semester, a survey instrument was administered containing 18 items shown in table 1 below for the 5 constructs given in Figure 1. One hundred and fourteen students participated in this study. The students were practically equally distributed among gender with a mean age of 23 years. The students had an average of 2 years of work experience, use the Internet close to one hour a day and claim to have strong knowledge of basic software utilization.

Items (presented in Table 1) used to measure the constructs were adopted from prior research work. The wording of the items was changed to account for the context of using the OLS. All items were measured using a five-point Likert-type scale with anchors from "Strongly disagree" to "Strongly agree".

Table1. Measures of study variables

Construct	Item	Measure
Perceived Usefulness (PU)	PU1	Using the OLS would reduce my ability to perform well in the course?
	PU2	I think that an OLS such as this one should be part of each and every course in the university.
	PU3	Using the OLS in the course would enhance my performance in the course.
Perceived Ease of Use (PEU)	PEU1	I think that learning to navigate the OLS will be easy for me.
	PEU2	I think that I will find it easy to get the OLS to do what I want them to do.
	PEU3	I think that it would be easy for me to become skillful at using the OLS.
	PEU4	I think that I will find the OLS easy to use.
Attitudes (ATT)	ATT1	The advantages of the OLS outweigh the disadvantages.
	ATT2	OLSs are not helpful for understanding better the course content.
Affect (AFF)	AFF1	I like working with computers.
	AFF2	I look forward to those aspects of my course work that require me to use a computer.
	AFF3	Once I start working on a computer, I find it hard to stop.
	AFF4	Using a computer is frustrating for me.
	AFF5	I get bored quickly when working on a computer.
Anxiety (ANX)	ANX1	I feel apprehensive about using computers.
	ANX2	It scares me to think that I could cause the computer to destroy a large amount of information by hitting the wrong key.
	ANX3	I hesitate to use a computer for fear of making mistakes I cannot correct.
	ANX4	Computers are somewhat intimidating to me.

Results, Analysis and Findings

The Cronbach's alpha coefficient for internal consistency reliability was ***first*** assessed. As summarized in Table 2, the reliability of most of all constructs was acceptable with values above 0.7 (Nunnally, 1978).

Table 2. Reliability assessment.

Variables	Cronbach alpha,	Mean	SD
Perceived Ease of Use (PEU)	0.929	3.60	1.00
Perceived Usefulness (PU)	0.821	3.76	0.67
Attitude (ATT)	0.823	3.16	0.48
Affect (AFF)	0.901	3.59	1.14
Anxiety (ANX)	0.879	2.34	1.21

Second, reliabilities of individual items were assessed by examining the loadings of the items on their respective constructs (table 3). These loadings should be higher than 0.5, following the criterion indicated by Pedersen and Nysveen (2003) to indicate that significant variance was shared between each item and the construct. It is expected that the loadings of all items within a construct should be high on that construct, indicating high convergent validity, and low on the others. The factors were extracted using the principal components method (varimax rotation) which is an optimum approach to condensation prior to rotation. Table 3 clearly shows that the five-factor solution is appropriate and the items display desirable convergent and discriminant validity.

Table 3. Factor analysis

	Factor 1	Factor 2	Factor 3	Factor 4	Factor 5
PEU1	0.291	**0.780**	0.206	0.270	0.270
PEU2	0.169	**0.917**	0.189	0.095	0.095
PEU3	0.319	**0.716**	0.104	0.156	0.156
PEU4	0.133	**0.825**	0.211	0.225	0.225
PU1	-0.040	0.107	0.170	**0.558**	-0.188
PU2	0.061	0.032	0.020	**0.880**	-0.109
PU3	0.053	0.314	0.032	**0.814**	-0.093
ATT1	0.041	0.276	0.108	0.413	**-0.536**
ATT2	0.067	0.083	0.200	0.280	**-0.728**
AFF1	0.363	0.199	**0.724**	0.316	0.316
AFF2	0.401	0.207	**0.811**	-0.027	-0.027
AFF3	0.149	0.128	**0.764**	0.097	0.097
AFF4	0.498	0.335	**0.450**	0.272	0.272
AFF5	0.517	0.175	**0.593**	0.191	0.191
ANX1	**-0.580**	0.638	-0.276	-0.121	-0.121
ANX2	**-0.774**	0.810	-0.226	-0.156	-0.156
ANX3	**-0.812**	0.848	-0.057	-0.191	-0.191
ANX4	**-0.822**	0.814	-0.105	-0.139	-0.139

In specific, Table 3 highlights in bold style the values higher than 0.5 (in each column), thereby indicating that the items used for the specific construct belong together and measure the same variable. For example, if we consider PU, we find that PU1 loads low with respect to PU2 and PU3 but can still be accepted based on the criteria explained above. The shaded part in the table identifies items that did not meet the criteria of factor analysis. The loading of AFF4 falls below 0.5 at a value of 0.45 and AFF5 loads above 0.5 on two factors namely factor 1 and 3. In this case if further analysis is to be done AFF4 and AFF5 can be dropped.

Third, the partial least squares (PLS) method was used for the assessment of the structural model of Figure 1. Each hypothesis was tested using PLS Graph and by looking at the path coefficients. All estimated path effects were found to have a degree of significance of less than or equal to 0.05. A bootstrapping procedure was used to assess the level of significance of the paths computed by PLS.

In our PLS analysis, we ran the model four times: TAM alone, complete model as per Figure 1 (TAM ±), excluding the effect of anxiety (TAM +) and excluding the effect of affect (TAM -).

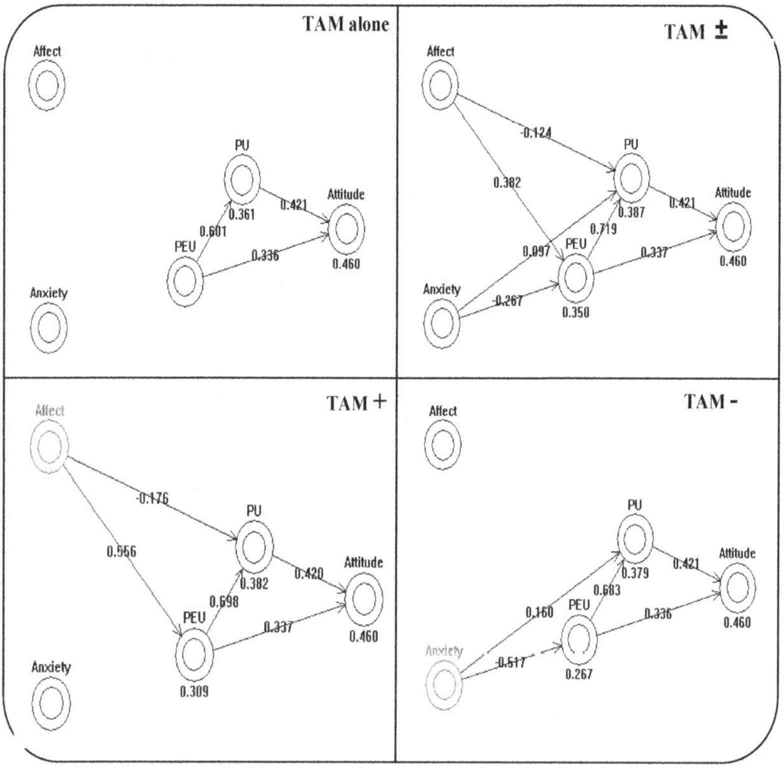

Figure 2. PLS simulations.

Together perceived ease of use and perceived usefulness explain 46% of the variances measured in relation to the students attitudes towards the OLS. It is evident though that perceived usefulness have contributed significantly more to attitudes than perceived ease of use. These results support hypotheses 1 and 2. Furthermore, hypothesis 3 which posited that PEU would influence PU was also supported with a strong path coefficient (PC) = 0.601. Adding the impact of affect alone (TAM +) on the TAM shows a strong influence of AFF on PEU with a PC = 0.556. Doing the same thing but looking at the impact of anxiety alone (TAM -) we obtain a practically equally strong influence of ANX on PEU, with PC = -0.517. In both cases, the impact of PEU on PU is strengthened by approximately 15%. Also, the influence of AFF and ANX on PEU was found to be positive and negative respectively as expected, therefore supporting hypotheses H4b and H5b.

Figure 2 also shows the influence of AFF and ANX on PU and in both cases this effect is small but significant with PC = -0.176 and 0.16 respectively. What is interesting is the sign of the path coefficient which may suggest that the more a students felt good about the OLS the less they perceived it to be useful and the more they felt anxiety about the OLS the more they perceived it to be useful. This begs the questions: Do we have to limit the level at which students may like the OLS? Is liking an OLS bad for you? In any case, hypotheses H4a and H5a were not supported.

Discussion and Conclusions

The primary objective of this study was to investigate the influence that affect and anxiety have on perceived ease of use and perceived usefulness of an online learning system and the role they play in moderating the impact of perceived ease of use on perceived usefulness. All hypotheses with the exception of H4a and H5a were supported. In specific, the results seem to indicate that the emotional state of a student (whether that may be positive or negative) has no direct impact on perceived usefulness of an online learning system. In context, student's beliefs about the usefulness of the online learning system are not determined or influenced by their emotions towards that system. However, structured equation modeling simulations suggest that the influence of emotions on perceived usefulness is indirect through the perceived ease of use construct.

To that effect, four PLS runs (presented in figure 2) show that in the context of online learning system's usage, affect and anxiety work hand in hand. Their influence on PEU is practically equal and in opposite direction thereby implying that students using an online learning system under a mandatory setting and where their performance may influence their grade may feel anxiety and affect at the same time. This concept of "I like it but I am anxious" merits further investigation. This has major significant impact on how educational information systems in general and online learning systems in specific should be designed, implemented, used and evaluated. Designers should consider the use of an online learning system within an instructional and pedagogical setting. Too much fun using an online learning system may make students feel that it is not useful. Students may be thinking: "If I am enjoying it then it is not useful" and question the learning value of a game. Students in general may view learning as a not-so-fun thing to do. On the other extreme they may be thinking: "If I have anxiety in using the online learning system then it must be useful". Whatever rational we may use, results lead us to a specific interesting conclusion: In a mandatory setting and while using an OLS, there seems to be a balance between affect (positive) and anxiety (negative) emotions occurring simultaneously. The balance or imbalance of the two is determined by the design of the online learning system and the pedagogy it is embedded in. With proper evaluation such as the model presented herein, one can optimize the impact to the effects/objectives that the designer is seeking.

Few limitations to this study exist and should be noted. First, the questionnaire approach is not free of subjectivity in the respondent and was taken at one point in time. User reactions change in time and may depend on the environment such as the classroom location and time of course. Second, caution must be taken in generalizing the results due to the fact that participants in this study were from different cultural background with different cultural beliefs influencing their perceptions and attitudes. In fact, what we are suggesting is a process of evaluation and understanding of the design-pedagogy-impact triangle for any online learning system. Most importantly, objective data on the usage of different components of online learning systems are rare. Future research should aim at designing controlled online learning environments where certain components of the course can be monitored with respect to frequency and duration of usage. This can provide greater credibility to future studies.

References

Agarwal, R. & Karahanna, E. (2000). Time flies when you're having fun: Cognitive absorption and beliefs about information technology usage. *MIS Quarterly 24*(4), 665-694.

Arkkelin, D. (2003). Putting Prometheus' feet to the fire: Student evaluations of Prometheus in relation to their attitudes towards and experience with computers, computer self-efficacy and preferred learning style. *Syllabus2003 Proceedings*.

Brosnan, M.J. (1998a). *Technophobia: The psychological impact of information technology*. New York: Routledge.

Brosnan, M.J. (1998b). The impact of computer anxiety and self-efficacy upon performance. *Journal of Computer Assisted Learning, 14*, 223-234.

Brown, I. J. T. (2002). Individual and technological factors affecting perceived ease of use of web-based learning technologies in a developing country. *EJISDC, 9* (2), 1-15.

Chang, K. M., & Cheung, W. (2001). Determinants of the intention to use internet/www at work: A confirmatory study. *Information and management, 39* (1), 1-14.

Colley, A. M. & Gale, T. M. (1994). Effects of gender role identity and experience on computer attitudes. *Journal of Educational Computing Research, 10*(2), 129-137.

Compeau, D. R., Higgins, C. A., & Huff, S. (1999). Social cognitive theory and individual reactions to computing technology: A longitudinal study. *MIS Quarterly, 23*(2), 145-158.

Conlon, T. (1997). The Internet is not a panacea. *Scottish Educational Review 29* (1), 30-38.

Davis, F. D. (1986). A technology acceptance model for empirically testing new end-user information systems: Theory and results. Doctoral Dissertation, Sloan school of management, Massachusetts Institute of Technology.

Davis, F. D. (1989). Perceived usefulness, perceived ease of use, and user acceptance of information technology. *MIS Quarterly, 13*(3), 319-339.

Davis, F. D., Bagozzi, R. P., & Warshaw, R. P. (1989). User acceptance of computer technology: A comparison of two theoretical models. *Management science, 35*(8), 982-1003.

Debourgh, G. A. (1995). Learner and instructional predictors of student satisfaction in a graduate nursing program taught via interactive video conferencing and world wide web/internet. Doctoral dissertation, University of San Francisco.

Deci, E. L., & Ryan, R.M. (1985). *Intrinsic motivation and self-determination in human behavior*. New York: Plenum.

Gefen, D., Karahanna, E. & Straub, D. W. (2003a). Trust and TAM in online shopping: An integrated model. *MIS Quarterly, 27*(1), 51-90

Gefen, D., Karahanna, E. & Straub, D. W. (2003b). Inexperience and experience with online stores: The importance of TAM and trust. *IEEE Transactions on Engineering Management, 50*(3), 1-15.

Gefen, D. & Straub, D. W. (1997). Gender difference in the perception and use of e-mail: An extension to the technology acceptance model. *MIS Quarterly, 21*(4), 389-400.

Howard, S. G. & Smith, D. R. (1986). Computer anxiety in management: Myth or reality? *Communications of the ACM, 29*(7), 611-615.

Ivari, J., & Ervasti, I. (1994). User information satisfaction: IS implementability and effectiveness. *Information and management, 27*(4), 205-220.

Johanson, T. L. (1999). The virtual community of an online classroom: Participant's interactions in a community college writing class by computer mediated communication. Doctoral dissertation, Oregon State University.

Johnson, D. S., Aragon, S. R., Shaik, N., & Palma-Rivas, N. (2000). Comparative analysis of learners satisfaction and learning outcomes in online and face-to-face learning environments. *Journal of Interactive Learning Research, 11*(1), 29-49.

Keeney, L. R. (1999). The value of Internet commerce to the customer. *Management Science, 45*(4), 533-542.

Keller, J. (1983). Motivational design of instruction. In C. Reigeluth (Ed.), *Instructional design theories and models: An overview of their current status* (pp. 386-434). Hillsdale, NJ: Erlbaum.

LaRose, R., Gregg, J., & Eastin, M. (1998). Audiographic telecourses for the web: An experiment. *Journal of Computer-Mediated Communications, 4* (2).

Lucas, H.C. & Spitler, V.K. (1999). Technology use and performance: A field study of broker workstations. *Decision Sciences, 30*, 291-311.

Lucas, H.C. & Spitler, V.K. (2000). Implementation in a world of workstations and networks. *Information & Management, 38*(2), 119-128.

Nunnally, J.C. (1978). *Psychometric theory* (2nd ed.). New York: McGraw-Hill.

Pedersen, P., & Nysveen, H. (2003). Usefulness and self-expressiveness: Extending TAM to explain the Adoption of a mobile parking Services. In the proceeding of the *16th Bled eCommerce Conference*, Bled, Slovenia, June 9-11.

Saadé, R. (2003). Web based educational information system for enhanced learning, EISEL: Student assessment. *Journal of Information Technology Education, 2*, 267-277. Available at http://jite.org/documents/Vol2/v2p267-277-26.pdf

Saadé, R. & Bahli, B. (2005) The impact of cognitive absorption on perceived usefulness and perceived ease of use in on-line learning: an extension of the technology acceptance model. *Information & Management, 42*(2), 317-327.

Smith, B., Caputi, P., Crittenden, N., Jayasuriya, R. & Rawstone, P. (1999). A review of the construct of computer experience. *Computers in Human Behaviour, 15*, 227-242.

Triandis, H. C. (1980). Values, attitudes and interpersonal behavior. *Nebraska symposium on motivation, 1979: Beliefs, attitudes, and values*, University of Nebraska Press, Lincoln, NE, 195-259.

Vallerand, R. J. (1997). Towards a hierarchical model of intrinsic and extrinsic motivation. *Advances in Experimental Social Psychology, 29*, 271-374.

Venkatesh, V. & Davis, F. D. (2000). A theoretical extension of the technology acceptance model: Four longitudinal field studies. *Management science, 46*(2), 186-204.

Venkatesh, V. & Morris, M. G. (2000). Why don't men ever stop to ask for directions? Gender, social influence, and their role in technology acceptance and usage behavior. *MIS Quarterly, 24*(1), 115-139.

Biographies

Dr. **Raafat Saadé** is an assistant professor at the DSMIS department, John Molson School of Business, Concordia University, Canada. Dr. Saadé obtained his Ph.D. in 1995 from Concordia University. He subsequently received the Canadian National Research Council postdoctoral fellowship, which he completed at McGill University in Montreal. He has been recognized twice as a North Atlantic Treaty Organization ASI award winner. Dr. Saadé has over 15 years of industrial experience (engineering, elearning and ehealth). He very active in research with over 25 peer refereed journal articles. Dr. Saadé has published in Information and Management, JITE, JIST, Computers in Human Behavior, IJIKM and Expert Systems with Applications. Dr. Saadé is also a co-founder of a non-profit organization (Viéquilibré) targeting the health, educational and spiritual needs of seniors, for a balanced life.

Dr. **Dennis Kira** is an associate professor at the DSMIS department, John Molson School of Business, Concordia University, Canada. He has been with the Faculty since 1983. He obtained his Ph.D. from University of British Columbia. Dr. Kira teaches System design, decision support systems, data management, data mining, internet related programming, and e-commerce His research activities include E-commerce, web design, distance learning, decision making under uncertainty, neural networks, machine learning, and financial modeling. Dr. Kira has published in IEEE, ORQ and management science among other journals.

The page left blank intentionally.

Openness to Experience: An HCI Experiment

Raafat George Saadé, Dennis Kira, Fassil Nebebe, and Camille Otrakji
John Molson School of Business, Concordia University, Montreal, Quebec, Canada

rsinfo@sympatico.ca kira@vax2.concordia.ca
fnebebe@jmsb.concordia.ca otrakji@sympatico.ca

Abstract

Today's market continues to introduce many and different information communications technologies. As a result, end users are faced with a variety of interfaces which they need to learn and use in a short period of time. The motivation to learn a new interface is subject to many variables most importantly is level of computer competencies, and openness to experience. The aim of this study was to explore end-users' overall computer competencies, competencies using software with graphical interfaces and openness to experiencing new software interfaces. In a controlled experiment, participants were asked to perform five tasks using an image editing icon based interface software for the first time. We identify possible personality trait construct in modeling better interfaces.

Keywords: User Interfaces, computer competencies, openness to experience, performance

Introduction

End-users in today's digital world have to utilize a variety of information and communications technologies (ICT) to perform basic daily tasks. In fact, during the same day a typical North American end-user would utilize office applications for word processing, spreadsheet, and presentations, as well as mobile applications and internet applications (email, forums and chat), many of which have been designed with significantly different interfaces. Information systems managers, designers and software developers need to understand how end-users adapt to the ever changing environment of the ICTs and how they interact with them. End-users' performance and acceptance of new ICTs usage depends strongly on various constructs mainly computer skill, beliefs and self efficacy.

The issue of computer-user interface has been a major topic among computer related industries during the last two decades. There have been a significant amount of human-computer interfaces (HCI) related works as it applies to the management of information system's (MIS) field, however most of them were within the context of end-user training and in a corporate setting (Davis, Bagozzi, & Warshaw, 1992; Marcus, 2000; Shneiderman, 1998; Shneiderman & Plaisant, 2004). Due to today's daily technology-related demands there is a need to better understand the role that different user interfaces play in end-user performance and acceptance. It is recognized that acceptance of a new ICT is dependent on behavioral and personality traits such as perceptions, attitudes, openness to experiment or ones willingness to simply try new things.

In this study, we consider the factors that tend to affect the user's performance with regards to human-computer interface. That is, factors contributing to the user's behaviors in terms of clicking on buttons, icons or menus are addressed. The paper reports the results of an exploratory study of end-user on openness to experience as it relates to the end-user's overall computer competencies in general and graphic competencies in specific, while using an icon based software. In personality trait study, the psychologists have posited prominent model called the five-factor model of personality. This theory consists of five personality trait constructs in describing personality. These five different factors are referred to as the "Big 5" (Digman, 1990). The five factors were derived from factor analyses of a large number of self- and peer reports on personality-relevant adjectives and questionnaire items. One of these five dimensions is named 'Openness to Experience' by the researchers (Costa & McCrae, 1992, Digman, 1990). Openness encompasses a general disposition that is receptive to entertaining new and challenging facets of cultural life, as well as personal thoughts and emotions (Costa & McCrae, 1992). We believe that such a personality trait affects the end-user preference of software interface type. The main contribution of this research to HCI studies is to further investigate the relationship between interface design and openness to experience.

Openness to Experience

In many ways, we are all similar but when faced with the same situation different people might act very differently. Personality psychologists have been trying to classify these tendencies to feel or behave a certain way into organized models of personality (trait theories). The goal of the theory has been to find a small number of independent dimensions called factors (traits) that would account for as much of the variation in personality as possible. Cattell (1990) generally is credited with an original short list consisting 16 traits (Sixteen Personality Traits). The list consists of Reserved/Outgoing; Less intelligent/More intelligent; Stable, ego strength; Emotionality/neuroticism; Humble/Assertive; Sober/Happy-go-lucky; Expedient/Conscientious; Shy/Venturesome; Tough-minded/Tender-minded; Trusting/Suspicious; Practical/Imaginative; Forthright/Shrewd; Placid/Apprehensive; Conservative/Experimenting; Group-dependant/Self-sufficient; Undisciplined/Controlled; Relaxed. Cattell (1990) identifies these traits by considering Allport and Odbert's (1931, 1936) 17000 words and reduced them to 171 traits. On these 171 traits, observed and behavioral data was collected. The final 17 trait list was produced using these data and conducting factor analysis to them (Gray, 1999).

There is a tradeoff between including enough factors in the model to make it explanatory enough and keeping the model simple. A good example of a factor is Eysenck's (1959, 1975) extraversion: a person who is outgoing and cheerful is classified as high in extraversion, while someone who keeps mostly to himself/herself would be less extraverted (more introverted). This is independent of whether the person is responsible, conservative or, say, aggressive, because these behaviors are determined by different traits.

Many psychologists have tried to reduce many traits to few essential ones. Amongst the best known essential trait approaches are: Cattell (1990) (16 traits), Eysnck (1955, 1975) (3 traits) and Costa and McCrae (1992) (5 traits). The Five Factor Model is currently the most widely accepted trait theory and has been independently arrived at by many different studies. On one hand, this shows that the model is robust; on the other hand, because each researcher used slightly different definitions and names for each factor, several versions of the Five Factor Model exist, all with subtle differences from one another (McCrae & Costa, 1997; McCrae & John, 1992).

The Five Factor Model was argued to be robust because it can provide a strong basis to interpret most other personality models. This interpretation is not perfect. Not all other models cover all the five areas while some models may have factors beyond the Big Five. Table 1 presents a brief summary of different studies interpreting the models discussed above in terms of the Five Factor Model (Zuckerman, Kuhlman, Joireman, Teta, & Kraft, 1993):

Table 1. Different five factor model studies.

Five Factor Model	Eysenck	Cattell's five higher-order factors	MBTI
Neuroticism	Neuroticism	Anxiety	--
Extraversion	Extraversion	Extraversion	Extraversion-Introversion
Conscientiousness	Psychoticism	Self-control	Judging-Perception
Agreeableness		Toughness/Will?	Feeling-Thinking
Openness to Experience		Independence	Intuition-Sensing

We note that MBTI (Myers-Briggs Type Indicator) is a personality test to assist a person in identifying their personality preferences. It was developed by Katharine Briggs and her daughter Isabel Briggs and follows from the theories of Carl Jung laid out in his work.

There is certainly not one single personality type which would form ideal information to a literate person. On the contrary, different personality traits may prove useful in different situations. An understanding of how different traits come into play in information search would increase our understanding of users of information services as well as the acceptance of information systems. To that effect, the aim of this study is to reflect over individual differences in information behavior with a particular focus on how and why personality traits (more specifically openness to experience) relate to human computer interface design. We are primarily interested in the relationship between openness to experience and computer/graphic competencies. This interest stems from our belief that person with a personality trait closer to "Openness to experience" is more likely to accept new interfaces. In past studies, a person whose personality trait is closely associated with openness to experience was shown to have a tendency to agree with having an active imagination, is original, and values artistic, as well as aesthetic experiences (Costa& McCrae, 1992) hence be more accepting to use a software with an iconic type of interface.

Methodology

Subjects and Procedure

Students from a School of Business in a Canadian University were asked to use a commercial off-the-shelf photo editing software. Specialized software was selected for this study such that its interface is completely iconic. The experiment was conducted as follows:

1. Students were given an appointment to perform the experiment. The experiment was performed in a controlled environment with the same moderator running the experiment in the same room, on the same computer and with the same software version, for the same period of time.
2. The moderator would then give the student an information sheet and would ask him/her to read it carefully. This sheet explains what the experiment is all about and in general what would the student be required to do.

3. The moderator would then give the student an instructions sheet which asked him/her to complete 5 tasks. Two tasks were simple and of general nature and three were of specific nature to graphics. These tasks entailed opening a file containing a picture, converting the colored picture to black and white, flipping the picture horizontally, adding noise to the picture and finally saving it in JPG format. While the student was doing the tasks, the moderator was logging the time at which he/she completed each task.
4. Upon completion of the tasks, the student was asked to complete a questionnaire containing 12 items about their experiences with the software.

Questionnaire

Validated constructs adopted from different relevant prior research work (Davis et al., 1989) were operationalized such that the wording of the items in the questionnaire was changed to account for the software used in the study. All the items used were measured using a 7-point likert-type scale and are shown in the figures below. The items used are: Openness to experience (OE): I would be motivated to try the latest version of my favorite software, or even a different company version and I would feel uncomfortable if I wear the latest in fashion clothing. In previous studies, similar questions such as "I see myself as someone who is original, comes up with new ideas", or "I see myself as someone who values artistic, aesthetic experiences" were used (Llewellyn & Wilson, 2003). Computer competencies (CC): My general computer skills are: (Novice – Expert). The number of Internet sites I usually visit is (small – very large) and I have (little – considerable) knowledge about at least one of the following software products: MS Word for windows, MS Excel, Word Perfect for windows, Visual Basic. Graphic competencies (GC): My computer graphic skills are: (Novice – Expert) and I am familiar with at least one of the following software: MS Encarta (or other encyclopedias), Kai power tools, Fractal Design Painter, Fractal Design Dabbler, Softimage Digital Studio.

Data Analysis & Discussion

Demographics

A total of 33 undergraduate students in the John Molson School of Business, Concordia University, participated in this study. The age of students ranged from 18 to 34 years old (76% of their age was between 18 to 24 years old and 24% of them were between 25 to 34 years old, and none were more than 35 years old). The students reported high proficiency in English. The scale of the proficiency in English is from 1 (I manage) to 7 (I am very comfortable). The highest proficiency in English was reported by 52% of the students, and 30% of the students reported the proficiency level of 6. The subjects' educational background was distributed as follows. The 64% percent finished CEGEP (Junior College), 18% of them finished high school, and the rest were doing their second university degree.

Perceived Computer Knowledge

In Figures 1 and 2, we report subjects' perceived familiarity with computer related skills. These figures are representative of two of the questions measuring the construct "Computer Competency".

In general, most of the students claimed to be familiar with the Internet environment. Forty six percent of the students reported that they visit many Internet site regularly (Figure 1). Moreover, more than 90% of them reported that they have considerable knowledge (greater then 4 with the scale ranging from 1 (little) to 7 (considerable)) about more than one of Microsoft Word, Microsoft Excel, Word Perfect for windows, and Visual Basic.

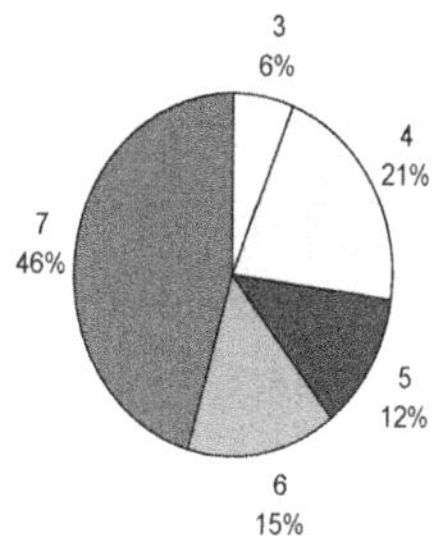

Fig 1: Knowledge of Internet sites.

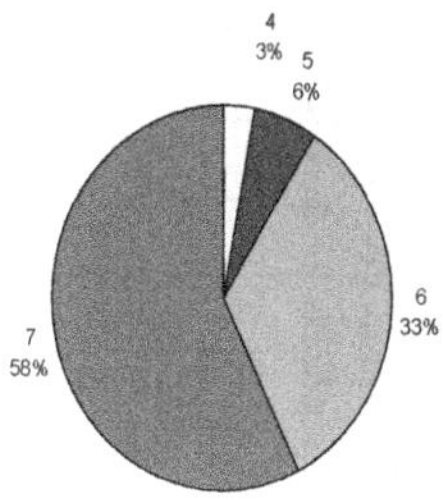

Fig 2: Knowledge of MS office application.

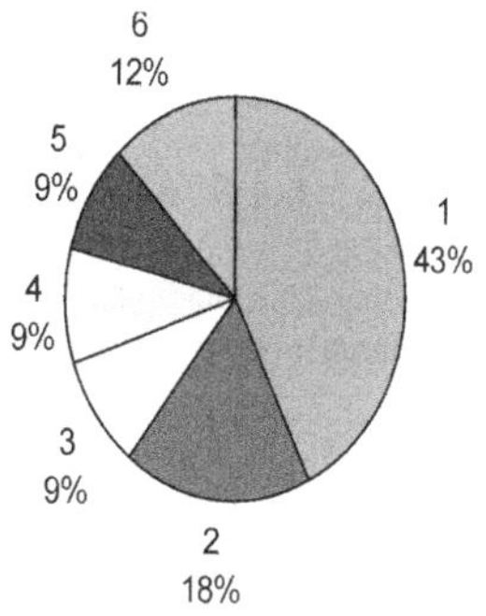

Fig 3: Knowledge to computer graphic.

Forty three percent of the students reported to have no knowledge of computer graphics software (Figure 3); however the remaining 57% indicated that their knowledge on computer graphics in general ranges from very little to expert level.

Factor Analysis

We can broadly classify factor analysis into exploratory and confirmatory. Exploratory factor analysis (EFA) is a method of discovering the number and nature of latent variables (factors) that explain the variation in a set of measured variables. Its purpose is to determine how many underlying factors are necessary to explain most of the correlations in the data; to determine the relationship through rotation between each of these underlying factors with each of the observed variables in a meaningful way so that the factors can be interpreted and named; to weed out observed variables that do not tend to measure well the underlying factors shared by the other variables; to propose blocks of variables that may be subsequently be used to create a simple sum scale and to propose a confirmatory factor analysis model (Field 2000; Hair, Anderson, Tatham, & Black, 1998).

In this study, exploratory factor analysis was run using maximum likelihood (MI) analysis with varimax rotation as well as a scree plot to assess the factor structure. For this method to provide statistically reliable results, underlying distribution need be multivariate normal. We used only the univariate check for some of the variables but for more statistically sound text one can apply skewness and kurtosis test proposed by Mardia (1974). Three factors identified through the exploratory factor analysis (each with an eigenvalue greater than 1.0) were selected as the best data reduction strategy. The factors were carefully named as Computer Competency (CC), Graphic Competency (GC), and Openness to Experience (OE). These three factors emerged with Cronbach's coefficient alpha ranging from 0.65 to 0.88 (0.67, 0.85, 0.65, respectively). And they accounted for 70% of the variance. With a cutoff of 0.5, 3 items were removed from the loading and table 2 presents the final accepted loading for the three constructs.

Table 2: Factor loading

Variable	Graphic Competencies	General Computer Competencies	Openness to Experience
OE1	0.036	0.078	**0.616**
OE2	0.367	0.208	**0.577**
CC1	0.660	**0.540**	0.246
CC2	0.277	**0.832**	0.098
CC3	0.199	**0.527**	0.299
GC1	**0.979**	0.123	-0.123
GC2	**0.555**	0.077	0.292
Eigenvalue	1.992	1.525	1.050

Computer Competency

The response of the students to the items measuring computer competencies is given on Fig. 4. The figure shows that students in general (90%) seem to feel that they have a good amount of knowledge in using Microsoft applications and close to 70% reported that they visit a large number of internet sites. With respect to general computer competencies few (4%) rated themselves as experts with approximately 65% claiming to have a reasonable computer competencies level.

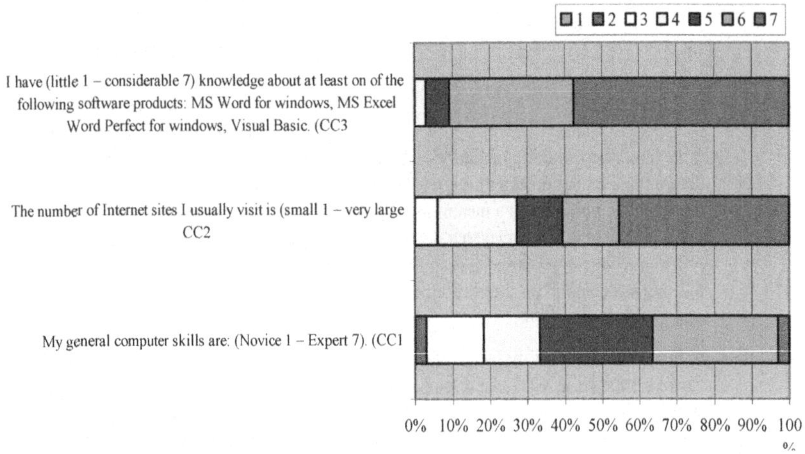

Fig 4: Response to computer competencies

Graphic Competency

The response of the students to the items measuring graphics competencies is given in Fig. 5. In general, students did not rate their computer graphic competencies high. Close to 80% of the students felt that they are a little or not at all familiar with graphics and image editing software such as MS Encarta, kai's power tools, fractal design painter/dabbler and softimage digital studio.

When asked to rate themselves in relation to general computer graphics skills, we found that the same percentage of the students felt that they were beginners at best. What is interesting is that none of the students claimed to be experts in computer graphics skills.

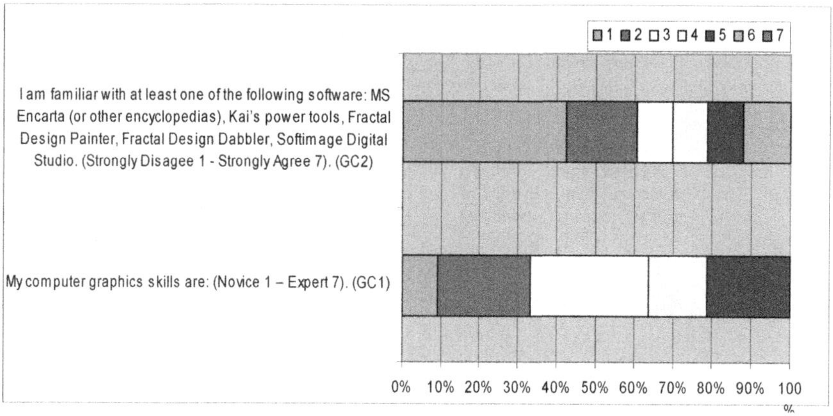

Fig 5: Students' response to GC

Openness to Experience

Openness to experience is a measure of depth, breadth and variability in a person's imagination and urge for experiences. The factor relates to intellect, openness to new ideas, cultural interests, educational aptitude and creativity as well as an interest in varied sensory and cognitive experiences. People with a high openness to experience have broad interests, are liberal and like novelty. The preservers with low openness to experience are conventional, conservative and prefer familiarity (Howard & Howard, 1995).

The response of the students to the items measuring openness to experience is given in Fig 6. These items attempt to measure the propensity or level of willingness that an individual would be willing to perform some tasks that may be out of their norm. This construct was measured using two items where one is non-technology related and the other is. What is interesting is that both items load acceptably on one factor, which is indicative that they belong together as measuring the same construct. In specific, the feeling of being comfortable to wear the latest in fashion clothing and being motivated to try new software measure the same construct.

To that effect, questionnaire results further confirm that association. Close to 60% of the students reported that they feel comfortable wearing the latest in fashion clothing. Approximately the same percent of the students also reported that they are motivated to use the latest version of their favorite software. These results seem to suggest that openness to experience in the ICT context can also be measured using non-ICT related items. This may be attributed to the possibility that the same behavioral mechanisms are in place and identify the feeling of comfort and openness to try new things irrelevant of what they are. It may be interesting to consider possible gender differences to this question. We did not perform the difference test due to small sample size.

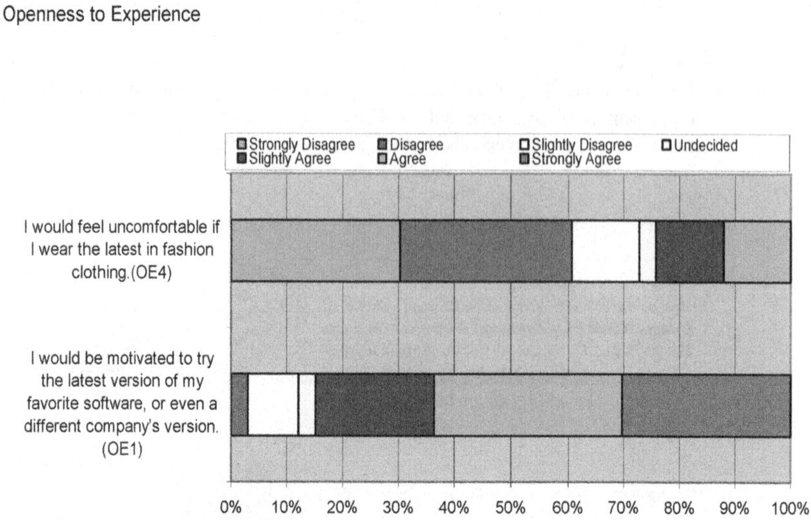

Fig 6: Students' response to openness to experience.

Influence of Competencies on Openness to Experience

As a final set of analysis we have regressed both computer competencies and graphic competencies on openness to experience as shown in Fig. 7. The influence of general CC on OE is approximately 30% more than that of GC. Additionally, the OE explains 10% of the variance from CC and only 4.5% that of GC.

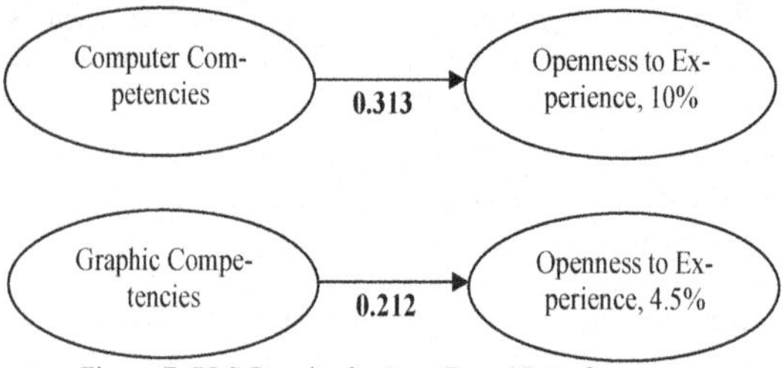

Figure 7: PLS Results for Icon Based Interface

It is evident that more research is needed to identify better items to explain and help us understand openness to experience in the ICT domain and from an HCI perspective. This field of research is ignored and has few published studies. Most of us experience numerous emotions when we are faced with trying new ICTs. One of the first things we experience is the level of difficulty to learn to use this new ICT (such as a mobile phone). Subsequently, it seems that our decision to adopt followed by our satisfaction is strongly dictated by our openness to experience/experiment and corresponding attitude.

Conclusion

It is shown that information behavior of interface usage could be connected to one of the personality dimensions, openness to experience in big five personality theory. Possible explanations for how personality traits can be a factor influencing the design of computer interfaces is discussed. It is posited that openness to experience as a personality trait can be used as one of the factors in explaining why icon based interface matches well with users with high scores on openness to experience in personality tests. Although this is an exploratory study, it shows a good promise toward developing how understanding of different personality traits can be used to increase the understanding of users of information systems and the designing of acceptable and useable interfaces.

References

Allport, G.W., & Odbert, H. S. (1936).Trait-names: A psycholexical study. *Psychological Monographs, 47* (Whole No. 211).

Allport, G.W. & Vernon, P.E. (1931). *The study of values.* Boston: Houghton Mifflin Company.

Cattell, R. B. (1990). Advances in Cattellian personality theory. In L. A. Pervin (Ed.), *Handbook of personality: Theory and research* (pp. 101-110). New York: Guildford.

Davis, F.D., Bagozzi, P.R., & Warshaw, P.R. (1992). User acceptance of computer technology: A comparison of two theoretical models. *Management Science, 35*(12), 982-1003.

Digman, J. M. (1990). Personality structure: Emergence of the five-factor model. *Annual Review of Psychology, 41,* 417-440.

Eysenck, H. J. (1959). *Manual of the Maudsley personality inventory.* London: University of London Press.

Eysenck, H. J., & Eysenck, S. B. G. (1975). *Manual of the Eysenck personality questionnaire.* London: Hodder & Stoughton.

Field, A. (2000). *Discovering statistics using SPSS for Windows.* London ,Thousand Oaks ,New Delhi: Sage.

Gray, P. (1999). *Psychology* (3rd ed.). New York: Worth Publishers.

Hair, J.E, Anderson, R.E., Tatham, R.L., & Black W.C (1998). *Multivariate data analysis* (5th ed.). Prentice-Hall

Howard, P.J. & Howard, J. M. (1995). *The Big Five quickstart: An introduction to the Five-Factor Model of Personality for human resource professionals.* Charlotte, NC: Centre for Applied Cognitive Studies.

Lawley, D., & Maxwell, A. (1965). *Factor analysis as a statistical method.* London: Butterworth.

Llewellyn, D.J. & Wilson, K.M. (2003). The controversial role of personality traits in entrepreneurial psychology. *Education + Training, 45*(6), 341-345.

Mardia, K.V. (1974) Applications of some measures of multivariate skewness and kurtosis in testing normality and robustness studies. *Sankhya B, 36*, 115-128.

McCrae, R.R. & Costa, P.T. (1997). Conceptions and correlates of openness to experience. In Hogan, J. Johnson & S. Briggs (Eds.), *Handbook of personality psychology* (pp. 825-847). London: Academic Press.

McCrae, R.R., & John, O.P. (1992). An introduction to the five-factor model and its applications. *Journal of Personality, 60*, 175-215.

Marcus, A. (2000). International and intercultural user-interface design. In C. Stephanidis (Ed.)., *User interfaces for all.* New York: Lawrence Erlbaum.

Shneiderman, B. (1998). *Designing the user interface: Strategies for effective human-computer interaction* (3rd ed.). Reading, MA: Addison Wesley.

Shneiderman, B. & Plaisant, C. (2004). *Designing the user interface: Strategies for effective human-computer interaction* (4th ed.). Reading, MA: Addison Wesley.

Solomon, P. (2002). Discovering information in context. In B. Cronin, (Ed.). *Annual Review of Information Science and Technology, 36*, 229-264.

Zuckerman, M., Kuhlman, D.M., Joireman, J., Teta, P., & Kraft, M. (1993). A comparison of three structural models for personality: The big three, the big five and the alternative five. *Journal of Personality and Social Psychology, 65*, 757-768.

Biographies

Dr. **Raafat Saadé** is an assistant professor at the DSMIS department, John Molson School of Business, Concordia University, Canada. Dr. Saadé obtained his Ph.D. in 1995 from Concordia University. He subsequently received the Canadian National Research Council postdoctoral fellowship, which he completed at McGill University in Montreal. He has been recognized twice as a North Atlantic Treaty Organization ASI award winner. Dr. Saadé has over 15 years of industrial experience (engineering, elearning and ehealth). He very active in research with over 25 peer refereed journal articles. Dr. Saadé has published in Information and Management, JITE, JIST, Computers in Human Behavior, IJIKM and Expert Systems with Applications. Dr. Saadé is also a co-founder of a non-profit organization (Viéquilibré) targeting the health, educational and spiritual needs of seniors, for a balanced life.

Dr. **Dennis Kira** is an associate professor at the DSMIS department, John Molson School of Business, Concordia University, Canada. He has been with the Faculty since 1983. He obtained his Ph.D. from University of British Columbia. Dr. Kira teaches System design, decision support systems, data management, data mining, internet related programming, and e-commerce His research activities include E-commerce, web design, distance learning, decision making under uncertainty, neural networks, machine learning, and financial modeling. Dr. Kira has published in IEEE, ORQ and management science among other journals.

The Application of Semantic Enablers in the Context of Content Management Systems

Samuel Sambasivam
Azusa Pacific University, Azusa, CA, USA

ssambasivam@apu.edu

Tilemachos Kanakis
First Consulting Group (FCG) Manhattan, NY, USA

tkanakis@fcg.com

Abstract

Content management can be viewed as the concepts, processes, technologies and practices that deal with the development, management and publishing of information. Traditionally, a Content Management System (CMS) does not offer the means for content classification, management and retrieval of data based on dynamically defined information models. Furthermore, Content Management Systems usually rely on indexed text, syntactic and/or structural metadata for content classification and retrieval. The paper discusses the design of an experimental Semantic CMS (SCMS), which exercises the application of semantic enablers – ontologies, classification & metadata – in order to achieve capture and utilization of content meaning. Lastly, it suggests that the application of semantic enablers in the context of Content Management Systems can provide the means for better information organization and retrieval as well as enhanced machine interoperability.

Keywords: Content Management, Semantic enablers, Classification, Ontology, Metadata, OWL, Relational Database

Introduction

Content management can be viewed as the concepts, processes, technologies and practices that deal with the development, management and publishing of information. However, traditional Content Management Systems rely on indexed text and syntactic or/and structural metadata for information classification and retrieval. It is argued (Fisher & Sheth, 2003) that these techniques do not promote the use of contextual meaning of stored information and they point out three basic challenges for Content Management Systems. Firstly, the heterogeneous data sources that many large-scale information systems have to comprise, where the stored data differ structurally and syntactically. This reveals a need for normalizing the representation of data in order to enable their interoperability and also make it equally accessible by humans and machines. Secondly, data is not only stored in heterogeneous data sources but many times in distributed data sources among various machines on possible different networks. Any system that aims to share content will need to take into consideration technologies that can securely provide generic transport methods and allow information integration, such as Extensible Markup Language (XML), Simple Object Access Protocol (SOAP) and Web Services. Lastly, it is the relevance factor. Probably, the most demanding challenge is to provide the means to the users of a CMS to drill down to the most relevant for the task information, which can exist in large data storages. Ideally, a CMS should provide the same or increased quality of data management as the data grows. However, it appears that this is not often the case. As the data grows the quality of retrieved information usually degrades due to the inability of the system to retain and use contextual meaning about its content and/or explicitly define and interpret the intentions of the user. As a result, information retrieval is inefficient and users are expected to act upon irrelevant results in order to locate the information of interest. It could be argued that the inability of traditional Content Management Systems to organize content in a manner where content can carry meaning and not only data is the major missing element from the current CMS model. This paper presents the design of an experimental software solution to the problem of content management via the application of semantic enablers. In particular, the solution utilizes metadata and ontology based classification technique to achieve better information organization and retrieval.

Motivation

Ideally, a CMS should provide appropriate mechanisms to organize and publish content in structures that can carry meaning and not simply data. Ironically, the World Wide Web (WWW), which could be considered as the largest and continuously growing source of data that is not structural consistent, has faced the same challenge. One of the proposed solutions for this problem is to represent Web content in a form where content can carry machine-understandable meaning and use intelligent techniques to take advantage of these content representations. This revolutionizing plan is known as the Semantic Web initiative (Berners-Lee, Hendler, & Lassila, 2001). The proponents of Semantic Web have proposed Web Ontology Language (OWL) that is an XML based technology capable to describe contextual information and capture referential knowledge representation. This in turn can allow machine-based agents to utilize this representation, operate upon the Web content and retrieve information within particular domains of knowledge, transforming in this way the Web in a more powerful and intelligent resource.

Furthermore, classification techniques are usually employed to increase the relevancy factor of information. Several classification techniques for textual and non-textual content are based on statistical analysis, pattern recognition, machine learning and rule-based methods to address content classification (Breen, Khan, Kumar & Wang, 2002; Frasconi, Soda & Vullo, 2002; Ipeirotis, Gravano & Sahami, 2000; Joachims, 1998; Yang, 1998). Moreover, ontology-based classification techniques can be used for information classification too. Studies have shown how classification results can be more precise when classified documents have XML based metadata that conform to predefined schemas (Fisher & Sheth, 2003; Sheth et al, 2003). The role of XML based semantic metadata could be considered invaluable. It could be viewed as the building block of semantic content and offer the means for better classification of information, high-precision information retrieval and increased interoperability among heterogeneous systems.

Content Management systems could clearly benefit from semantic enablers such as ontology based classification and XML based metadata. The fundamental idea behind ontology oriented modeling of an information domain is the ability to explicitly and efficiently represent classes of a domain and important associations among these classes. These associations can be utilized to traverse or search a content storage according to predefined content classes whose structure of properties can be much deeper than the basic taxonomy. The "labeling" of relationships offered in ontology based classification gives the opportunity to associate classes of content in meaningful ways and provide the necessary for information retrieval ambiguity resolution. As a result, information about the context and relationships of a content piece can be preserved and increase the relevance factor among different content pieces enabling more efficient information retrieval.

Synopsis of the SCMS

It was envisioned that a SCMS should enable ontology engineering as the means to model an information domain, and also support creation, storage and retrieval of content according to the underlying ontology concepts. In addition, it should facilitate machine interoperability. This should be achieve by exposing both the information model and stored content in OWL format, preferably via a Web Service, where other applications can utilize to retrieve and process information. Lastly, demonstration of reasoning mechanisms, which could allow process of content in meaningful for the users' manner, should also be supported, but this feature fell outside the scope of this experimental development.

In particular, the system was composed of six sub systems providing with the following assigned responsibilities:

- *Presentation Subsystem*
  Encapsulates graphical user interface and presentation services that allow to a) carry out an Ontology engineering process in order to model an information domain, b) a content form editor to adjust the presentation aspect of available content classes, c) create, modify, browse and search content according to the underlying ontology concepts and their associations.
- *Content Model Management Subsystem*
  Concepts in an information domain can be described utilizing semantic axioms adopted from OWL DL. This subsystem encapsulates business rules that enforce these semantic formalisms and maintain model integrity. It is also responsible for the synchronization of content metadata with actual content storage structure.
- *Content Modification Subsystem*
  It provides the necessary functionality for the creation and management of content based on a predefined information model. It enforces business rules necessary to maintain content versioning and integrity.
- *Content Delivery Subsystem*
  It provides access to content in order to browse and search for stored information. A web service wraps this functionality where content and metadata are delivered in OWL DL format.
- *Security Management Subsystem*
  It provides mechanisms for user authentication and authorization. It also manages user accounts, roles and role permissions on different classes of content.
- *Data Management Subsystem*
  It provides data access mechanisms in order to store and retrieve metadata and content. It is also responsible for the generation of appropriate SQL code utilized to dynamically create the underlying relational database schema for the information domain being model.

In addition, this experimental development was carried out using C#, MS.Net Framework and MS SQL Server 2000 as the backend database.

Adopting OWL Formalisms

OWL DL formalisms (Bechhofer, Harmelen, Hendler, Horrocks, McGuiness, & Patel-Schneider, 2004; McGuinness & Harmelen, 2004; Smith, Welty, & McGuinness, 2004) were adopted for the design of the system. The main purpose of this approach was to enable modeling of an information domain utilizing semantic formalisms that can be easily transformed and exposed for machine processing. In brief, the system enables the user to create taxonomies of content classes. A content class can be one of the following types:

- *General content class*, which is similar to an OWL class.
- *Abstract class*, serve as the base of more specific classes of information and without any direct instances.
- *Enumeration class*, are used to define a class of information with a finite set of class instances, which is similar to an OWL Enumeration class.
- *Boolean combination of classes* that are Union class, Intersection class, and Complement class. These types do not have any direct instances but the concept deviates from OWL formalisms.

A Boolean class is always a subclass of another general content class. Their purpose is to create meaningful Boolean combination classes that can efficiently group together instances of their base content class. Boolean combination classes represent a more advanced class constructor in Description Logic, which is a representation of AND, OR and NOT logical operators on classes. The definition of a union class includes a list of other classes, the union members. The union members are used to define a class of content where its instances will be all those instances that appear at least once in the union members. The members of an intersection class define a new content class where its instances will be all those direct instances that are common to all intersection members. Finally, a complement class defines a content class where its instances are all the direct and indirect instances of its base class except those of its complement. An abstract class cannot not be part of Union, Intersection or Complement class definition since the purpose of these classes is to group together (or exclude) direct instances from other content classes. Furthermore, properties can be added to taxonomies and used to state relationships between class instances and data values. Adopting again OWL DL formalisms two types of properties were identified:

- *Data type property* that defines a relationship between an instance of a class and an XML Schema data type.
- *Object property* that defines a relationship between two class instances.

The system allows the user to view the property's *domain* and define property's *range*, *characteristics*, its *base* property and synonyms used for the property. D*omain* is used to limit the classes where the property is applied. This feature can be viewed as a global restriction because the domain of a property is stated on the property and not on the class that is associated with it. Properties are applied to classes by defining a property facet for the class. In addition, property facets encapsulate cardinality restrictions and other facet information. Considering that an object property aims to define a relationship between class instances, there was a need to define ownership of this relationship in order to facilitate appropriate data integrity. In other words, it must be explicitly defined whether the object property facet determines a relationship owned by the class where the property is applied or it simply links two class instances. Using this ownership construct the system enforces creation of a new class instance when a new value is created for the applied *object property*. When the value is removed then the system cascades deletion of instances the removed value owns. The system also deletes any links other instances may have to the instance being deleted. This ownership construct, not apparent in OWL DL, has been considered essential in order to maintain content integrity. *Range* defines the type of property's value. If it is a data type property then it will link the property to a single XML Schema data type. In a hierarchy of data type properties a child property and its base have the same *range*. If it is an object property then the range links the property to a content class that defines the property's value type. Object properties inherit and extend the range of their base.

Property characteristics provide a powerful mechanism in order to enhance reasoning about properties and their values. They can be applied in order to provide more meaningful semantics, which could be used by other applications to carry out inferences about stored content. The system allows defining property characteristics according to OWL DL formalisms. In OWL Full data-type properties are a subclass of object properties. However, in OWL DL data-type and object-type properties are disjoint by definition. This implies that property characteristics *inverse-of, inverse-functional, symmetric* and *transitive* can be only specified for object properties. Moreover, both data type and object properties can be characterized as functional.

Meta-Model Principal Design Classes

The class model in Figure 1 illustrates principal system classes that aim to describe metadata information. Although the class model has adopted some semantic formalisms from OWL DL, it is not a precise illustration of these formalisms.

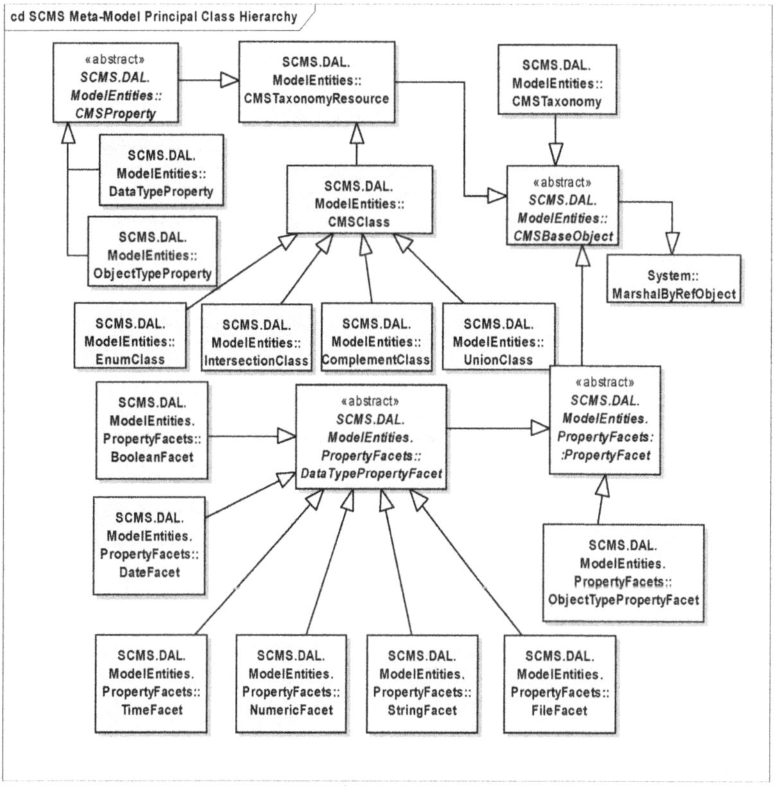

Figure 1 – Meta-Model Principal Class Hierarchy

Figure 2 represents relationships between the principal system's classes. These associations reveal several differences between OWL DL formalisms and what has been applied to cover the needs of this project. Firstly, the system is designed to support only single inheritance for content classes and properties. Moreover, *CMSClass, DataTypePropety* and *ObjectTypeProperty* classes explicitly define their subclasses and sub-properties respectively, which is not the case in OWL DL. Also, the class model does not capture the concept of equivalent classes and properties, but rather defines simple text based synonyms. Another basic difference is in the design of Boolean combination classes, *ComplementClass*, *UnionClass* and *IntersectionClass*, that they represent only named classes with a cardinality constraint on *base class* attribute to be explicitly set to one (a design feature not visible in Figure 2). This design decision was taken in order to provide Boolean combination classes with a more specific interface and facilitate meaningful grouping of class instances. The purpose of a Boolean combination class in the system is to group together instances of two or more content classes. In order to achieve this in a meaningful way, the classes being grouped together need to have a common base (which implies a common set of properties). This is achieved by enforcing Boolean combination classes to always have a valid base class, or in other words never be the root in a class hierarchy. In this way, the system can always infer properties for a Boolean combination class, as defined by its base, and allow Boolean combination of those classes that exist under its base.

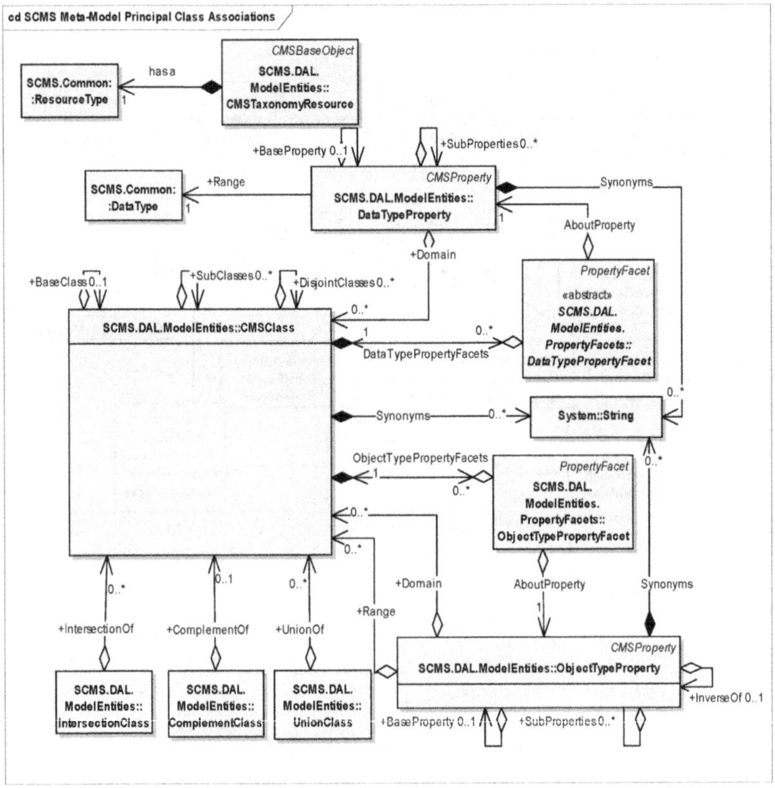

Figure 2 – Meta-Model Principal Class Associations

Implementation – An Overview

One of the design goals was to dynamically extend the database schema for content storage according to the information domain being modeled. This involved the creation of a mechanism for automatic mapping of the model to a database schema. The implementation involves the creation of two tables for each content class, one for content class instances and one for the instance versions. Also, the class instance table structure is static, meaning that it remains the same through out the class's life. The instance version table contains attributes that reflect data type properties applied to the class and therefore it can change accordingly. The code also implements generation of a table for each class's multi-value data type property. A single table is also generated for each object property in order to store relationships between class instances. In particular, the structure of an object property table facilitates the need for an instance version to always reference the active version of another instance. Database views are generated for each Boolean combination class. Figure 3 illustrates the mapping of taxonomy's classes and properties to a generalized database model.

Another interesting aspect of the implementation was the development of the system's search capabilities. The underlying database schema is not static and therefore queries are composed on the fly using content metadata and user defined filters on data type properties. The system decides what database tables need to be queried depending on the classes and data type properties the user has selected. Finally, the query is translated to an appropriate SQL statement in order to retrieve results from the database.

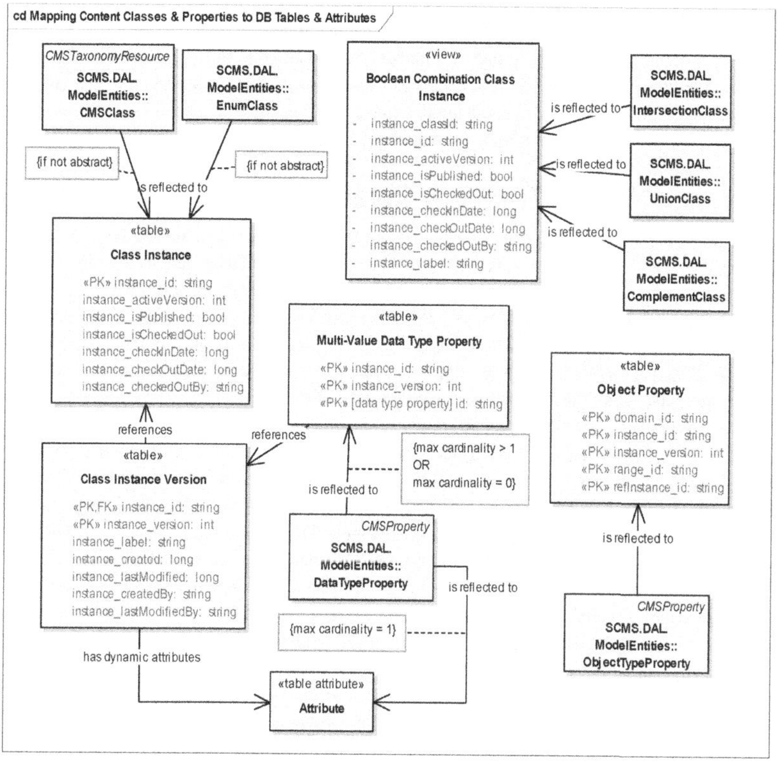

Figure 3 – Mapping Content Classes & Properties to DB Tables & Attributes

Different types of searches generate different query structures, meaning that the structure of an SQL statement for a search through the class hierarchy will be different from the one generated to search content via object property hierarchy. A user can traverse and query content using either a class hierarchy or data type property hierarchy or an object property hierarchy. These search capabilities could be summarized as it follows:

- Search of content utilizing a class hierarchy: Filter data type properties applied on a selected class. If the class is defined as abstract then the results include all instances from its subclasses.
- Search of content utilizing a data type property's domain: The user can submit a query for a single data type property and select to retrieve results only from specific content classes where the property has been applied.
- Query an Object Property: The user can query content by filtering data type properties applied on the *range* of an object type property and retrieve those class instances that reference the results of the query. For example, let's assume a scenario where we have defined a relationship between classes *Course* and *Professor* using the object property *TeachesCourses* (where *Course* is the range and *Professor* the domain). The user can filter data type properties applied on *Course* class in order to retrieve those instances of *Professor* class that reference one or more instances of *Course* class in the query's results.

Furthermore, it should be highlighted at this point that the execution cost of a query might vary depending on the type of the class and the number of classes used to retrieve the results. For example, querying a class means that the results can be a union of queries on that particular class and each child class. This in turn could imply a linear relationship between the execution cost of a query and the depth of class hierarchy (or number of classes) being queried.

Trends & Related Work

The primary driving forces behind semantic technologies, which aim to make the vision of Semantic Web a reality, is to juxtapose web enabled content and content semantics in order to bring information processing closer to human thinking. Researchers and organizations have realized the importance of semantics in several ways. They have been involved, among other things, in the development of domain specific ontologies and metadata standards, organization of content according to such taxonomies and annotation of content with semantic metadata. Antoniou and Harmelen (2004) point out the contribution of semantic Web technologies in businesses such as Audi and Swiss Life for content organization and retrieval as well as data integration. The concept of ontology as the context for semantics and its use to access content has been discussed before. Semantic Content Organization and Retrieval Engine (SCORE) (Sheth, Bertram, Avant, Hammond, Kochut & Warke, 2003) technology supports automatic semantic metadata extraction out of content and ontology-based content classification. Another important aspect of SCORE is that provides information retrieval in XML format, however, not in standard OWL format. OntoWeb (Spyns, Oberle, Volz, Zheng, Jarrar & Sure, 2002) that is a semantic portal where knowledge can be gathered and retrieved using ontology based annotated information. OntoWeb offers content provision, which is achieved using automated content syndication or manual content creation by portal users. The portal also offers content browsing and search according to the underlying concepts in OntoWeb ontology. Furthermore, Haystack (Huynh, Karger, & Quan, 2002) is a Resource Description Framework (RDF) based information management system. It provides users with a flexible way to describe, organize and retrieve information as well as to delegate processing tasks to software agents. The system provides an ontology to support collection-based organization, semantic categorization, and collaboration and trust management. Gauch, Chaffee & Pretschner (2003) report on research on technology that adapts to user web browsing habits. Users can create their own concept hierarchy in order to access content, or the system can create an ontology by observing the user's navigation habits. Lastly, it has been claimed (Bussler, Fensel, & Maedche, 2002) that semantic enabled Web Services can transform the Web from a static collection of information into a machine process-able and machine interpretable distributed device.

They propose a design for such a system, which is based on a Web Service Modeling Framework that provides a model for describing and developing semantic Web Services. Ontologies are in the hurt of this model used to describe linked concepts and to achieve the required machine inter-operability.

Conclusion & Future Directions

In conclusion, it could be claimed that ontology based techniques can be utilized for classification of content in order to increase the relevance factor of information. Content Management Systems can implement such techniques to gain an advantage over their traditional counterparts that simply rely on indexed text and syntactic and/or structural metadata for information classification and retrieval. A CMS can support ontology engineering to model an information domain and use model's metadata to generate and query the content storage. OWL can be utilized to publish model and content in a standard XML format. OWL could be considered as the means to represent data, data structures and important relationships among them in a machine process-able format in order to enhance systems interoperability.

It could be claimed that from a knowledge-acquisition perspective it would be very convenient to exploit semantic information, such as class and property hierarchies as well as property characteristics. An inverse, symmetric or/and transitive relationship could definitely be utilized to infer property values that have not been explicitly applied to a class instance. Further work is required in order to determine how such functionality could be added. Furthermore, it could be claimed that the application of semantic enablers gives an obvious advantage for information retrieval. In this development, a semantic layer was created and used to generate appropriate database tables for content storage. It could be assumed that the inverse should be feasible too. Building a semantic layer on top of one or more existing databases in order to provide a normalized view of content from different database tables should be also a realistic scenario. This could be viewed, to a certain extent, as the reverse process of what the current system carries out. That hypothetical process could involve gathering tables and their attributes from a database schema. Tables could be mapped to content classes and their attributes to appropriate data type properties. Object properties could reflect relationships between tables. More general content classes and properties can be defined and utilized to create class and property hierarchies, where classes and properties directly derived from the database schema are the leaves in these hierarchies. A content portal could use such semantic layers to provide access to content from different databases and enable users to drill down to the most relevant information for a specific task.

References

Antoniou, G., & Harmelen, F. (2004). *A semantic Web primer*. Cambridge: MIT Press.

Bechhofer, S., Harmelen, F., Hendler, J., Horrocks, I., McGuiness, D. L., & Patel-Schneider, P. F. et al, (2004). OWL Web ontology language reference. Retrieved February 10, 2005, from http://www.w3.org/TR/2004/REC-owl-ref-20040210/

Berners-Lee, T, Hendler, H. & Lassila, O. (2001). The semantic Web: A new form of Web content that is meaningful to computers will unleash a revolution of new possibilities. Retrieved February 15, 2005, from http://www.scientificamerican.com/article.cfm?articleID=00048144-10D2-1C70-84A9809EC588EF21&catID=2

Breen, C., Khan, L., Kumar, A. & Wang, L. (2002). Ontology-based image classification using neural networks. Retrieved January 29, 2006, from http://escsb2.utdallas.edu/ORES/papers/Spie_Paper2.pdf

Bussler, C., Fensel, D. & Maedche, A. (2002). A conceptual architecture for semantic enabled web services. Retrieved January 29, 2006, from http://www.sice.umkc.edu/~leeyu/class/CS690L/Reference/4.Bussler1.pdf

Fisher, M. & Sheth, A. (2003). Semantic enterprise content management. Retrieved October 21, 2004, from http://wwwt.semagix.com/documents/ SemanticEnterpriseContentManagement.pdf

Frasconi, P., Soda, G. & Vullo, A. (2002). Hidden Markov models for text categorization in multi-page documents. Journal of Intelligent Information Systems. Retrieved January 29,2006, from http://www.dsi.unifi.it/~paolo/ps/jiis-02-multipage.pdf

Friedlein, A. (2003). *Maintaining & evolving successful commercial Web sites: Managing change, content, customer relationships, and site measurement.* San Francisco: Morgan Kaufmann.

Gauch, S., Chaffee, J. & Pretschner, A. (2003). Ontology-based personalized search and browsing, Web intelligence and agent system. Retrieved January 29, 2006, from http://www.ittc.ku.edu/~sgauch/selectedpapers/WIAS2003.pdf

Huynh, D., Karger, D. & Quan, D. (2002). Haystack: A platform for creating, organizing and visualizing information using RDF. Retrieved December 5, 2004, from http://semanticweb2002.aifb.uni-karlsruhe.de/proceedings/Research/huynh.pdf

Ipeirotis, P., G., Gravano, L. & Sahami, M. (2000). Automatic classification of text databases through query probing. Retrieved January 30, 2006, from http://persival.cs.columbia.edu/papers/webdb2000.pdf

Joachims, T. (1998). Text categorization with support vector machines: Learning with many relevant features. Retrieved January 29, 2006, from http://www.cs.cornell.edu/People/tj/publications/joachims_98a.ps.gz

McGuinness, D. L. & Harmelen, F. (2004). OWL Web ontology language overview. Retrieved January 16, 2005, from http://www.w3.org/TR/owl-features/

Sheth, A., Bertram, C., Avant, D., Hammond, B., Kochut, K. & Warke, Y. (2003). Semantic content management for enterprize and the Web. University of Georgia. Retrieved January 20, 2005, from http://lsdis.cs.uga.edu/SemWebCourse_files/SCORE-draft.pdf

Smith, M. K., Welty, C. & McGuinness, D. L. (2004). OWL Web ontology language guide. Retrieved January 15, 2005, from http://www.w3.org/TR/2004/REC-owl-guide-20040210/

Spyns, P., Oberle, D., Volz, R., Zheng, J., Jarrar, M., & Sure, Y. et al (2002). OntoWeb – A semantic web community portal. Retrieved January 16, 2005, from http://www.starlab.vub.ac.be/staff/mustafa/publications/2002_pakm_ontoweb.pdf

Yang, Y. (1998). An evaluation of statistical approaches to text categorization. Retrieved January 28, 2006, from http://reports-archive.adm.cs.cmu.edu/anon/usr/ftp/usr0/ftp/1997/CMU-CS-97-127.ps

Biographies

Dr. Samuel Sambasivam is the chairman of the Department of Computer Science of Azusa Pacific University. Professor Sambasivam has done extensive research, publications, and presentations in both computer science and mathematics. His research interests include optimization methods, expert systems, Fuzzy Logic, client/server, Databases, and genetic algorithms. He has taught computer science and mathematics courses for over 20 years. Professor Sambasivam has run the regional Association for Computing Machinery (ACM) Programming Contest for six years. He has developed and introduced several new courses for computer science majors. Professor Sambasivam teaches Database Management Systems, Information Structures and Algorithm Design, Microcomputer Programming with C++, Discrete Structures, Client/Server Applications, Advanced Database Applications, Applied Artificial Intelligence, JAVA and others courses. Professor Sambasivam coordinates the Client/Server Technology emphasis for the Department of Computer Science at Azusa Pacific University.

Tilemachos Kanakis is an IT professional and currently an associate with First Consulting Group (FCG) in Manhattan, NY, USA. He has seven years of experience in analysis, design and development of desktop standalone and distributed applications utilizing Microsoft Technologies. His professional background is focused on Internet technologies and development of content management, workflow and reporting systems in banking and health sector. He has practical exposure to several development methodologies, processes and tools, such as RUP, XP, Iconix Process, UML, C++, C#, VB, ASP, MS .NET Framework, MS SQL Server, DB2, etc. He has a great interest in Semantic Web and emerging technologies as well as applications of AI and traditional statistical techniques for data analysis. During his academic pursuit for M.Sc. at Liverpool University he had the opportunity to further study and explore a variety of interrelated IT areas such as AI, Internet development, metadata technologies and current trends in software engineering.

The page left blank intentionally.

Advanced Data Clustering Methods of Mining Web Documents

Samuel Sambasivam
Azusa Pacific University
Azusa, CA, USA

ssambasivam@apu.edu

Nick Theodosopoulos
London, UK

london1@rocketmail.com

Abstract

The aim of this paper is to evaluate, propose and improve the use of advanced web data clustering techniques, allowing data analysts to conduct more efficient execution of large-scale web data searches. Increasing the efficiency of this search process requires a detailed knowledge of abstract categories, pattern matching techniques, and their relationship to search engine speed.

In this paper we compare several alternative advanced techniques of data clustering in creation of abstract categories for these algorithms. These algorithms will be submitted to a side-by-side speed test to determine the effectiveness of their design. In effect this paper serves to evaluate and improve upon the effectiveness of current web data search clustering techniques.

Keywords: Web mining, database, data clustering, algorithms, web documents.

Introduction

This paper examines the use of advanced techniques of data clustering in algorithms that employ abstract categories for the pattern matching and pattern recognition procedures used in data mining searches of web documents. With the rapid advances in data mining software technology now taking place, website managers and search engine designers have begun to struggle to maintain efficiency in "mining" for patterns of information and user behaviour. Part of the problem is the enormous amount of data being generated, making the search of web document databases in real time difficult. Real-time searching are critical for real time problem solving, high-level documentation searches and prevention of database security breaches.

The analysis of this problem will be followed by a detailed description of weaknesses in data mining methods, with suggestions for a reduction of pre-processing to improve performance of search engine algorithms, and recommendation of an optimum algorithm for this task.

The first investigators who gave a serious thought to the problem of algorithm speed were persons conducting researching in the area of database searches. The field is still in its infancy; most of the tools and techniques used for data mining today come from other related fields such as pattern recognition, statistics and complexity theory. Only recently have the researchers of these various fields been interacting to solve mining and timing issues. (Oliver & Armin, 2002)

Overview of the Methodology

The methodology employed in this paper will be experimental analysis, with the objective of testing the feasibility of abstract category data clustering algorithms for a real world web application. In order to perform this test, a group of five linear time clustering algorithms will be applied to a sample group of online web documents, simulating the activities of a web search engine looking for similar words, phrases or sequences in a large database set of web articles, publications and records. The six techniques compared will be the K-Means, Single Pass, Fractionation, Buckshot, Suffix Tree and AprioriAll clustering algorithms.

The procedure will be to measure the execution time of the test algorithms in clustering data sets consisting of whole documents, excerpts and key words of a fixed quantity and size.

Purpose of the Study

The purpose of this study is to conduct research that will analyze and improve the use of data clustering techniques in creating abstract categories in algorithms, allowing data analysts to conduct more efficient execution of large-scale searches. Increasing the efficiency of the search process requires a detailed knowledge of abstract categories, pattern matching techniques, and their relationship to search engine speed.

Data mining involves the use of search engine algorithms looking for hidden predictive information, patterns and correlations within large databases. The technique of data clustering divides datasets into mutually exclusive groups. The distance between groups is measured with respect to all the available variables, versus variables that are specific predictors, to produce "abstract categories" for analysis. Search engine algorithms and user audit trails are complex, leading to time-consuming quests for specific information. It is anticipated that the proposed study will identify the most efficient and effective data clustering algorithms for this purpose.

Background of the Problem

Data Clustering is a technique employed for the purpose of analyzing statistical data sets. Clustering is the classification of objects with similarities into different groups. This is accomplished by partitioning data into different groups, known as clusters, so that the elements in each cluster share some common trait, usually proximity according to a defined distance measure. Essentially, the goal of clustering is to identify distinct groups within a dataset, and then place the data within those groups, according to their relationships with each other. Document Clustering automatically groups documents into sets. There is no predetermined taxonomy - the taxonomy of the clusters is determined at run time (Han & Kamber, 2005).

One of the main points of document clustering is that it isn't so much a matter of finding the documents off of the web- that's what search engines are for. Search engines do a fantastic job by themselves, when the user has a specific query, and knows exactly what words will get the desired results. But the user gets a ranked list that has questionable relevance because it turns up anything that has the word in it, and the only metric is the number of times that word appears in the document. With a good clustering program, the user will instead be presented with multiple avenues of inquiry organized into broad groups that get more specific as selections are made.

Clustering exploits similarities between the documents to be clustered. The similarity of two documents is computed as a function of distance between the corresponding term vectors for those documents. Of the various measures used to compute this distance, the cosine-measure has proved the most reliable and accurate. (Meyer Zu Eissen & Stein, 2002).

Data clustering algorithms come in two basic types: hierarchical and partitional. In partitions, searches are matched against the designated clusters, and the documents in the highest scoring clusters are returned as a result. When a hierarchy processes a query, it moves down the tree along the highest scoring branches until it achieves the predetermined stopping condition. The sub tree where the stopping condition is satisfied is then returned as the result of the search.

Both strategies rely on variations of the near-neighbour search. In this search, nearness is determined by the similarity measure used to generate the clusters. Cluster search techniques are comparable to direct near-neighbour searches. Both are evaluated in terms of precision and recall. The evidence suggests that cluster search techniques are only slightly better than direct near-neighbour searches and the former can even be less effective than the latter in certain circumstances. Because of the quadratic running times necessary, clustering algorithms are often slow and unsuitable for extremely large volume tasks.

Hierarchical algorithms start with established clusters, and then create new clusters based upon the relationships of the data within the set. Hierarchical algorithms can do this one of two ways, from the bottom up or from the top down. These two methods are known as agglomerative and divisive, respectively. Agglomerative algorithms start with the individual elements in the set as clusters, and then merge them into successively larger clusters. Divisive algorithms start with the entire dataset in one cluster, and then break it up into successively smaller clusters. Because hierarchical algorithms must analyze all the relationships inherent in the dataset, they tend to be costly in terms of time and processing power.

Partitional algorithms determine the clusters at one time, in the beginning of the clustering process. Once the clusters have been created, each element of the dataset is then analyzed and placed within the cluster that it is the closest to. Partitional algorithms run much faster than hierarchical ones, which allows them to be used in analyzing large datasets, but they have their disadvantages as well. Generally, the initial choice of clusters is arbitrary, and does not necessarily comprise all of the actual groups that exist within a dataset. Therefore, if a particular group is missed in the initial clustering decision, the members of that group will be placed within the clusters that are closest to them, according to the predetermined parameters of the algorithm. In addition, partitional algorithms can yield inconsistent results- the clusters determined this time by the algorithm probably won't be the same as the clusters generated the next time it is used on the same dataset.

Algorithms of this Study

Of the six algorithms under scrutiny in this paper, three are hierarchical and three are partitional. The three hierarchical methods are suffix tree, single pass and AprioriAll.

The suffix tree, as defined by Black (2005), is "a compact representation of a trie (retrieval) corresponding to the suffixes of a given string where all nodes with one child are merged with their parents." It is a divisive method; it begins with the dataset as a whole and divides it into progressively smaller clusters, each composed of a node with suffixes branching off of it like leaves.

Single-pass clustering, on the other hand, is an agglomerative, or bottom-up, method. It begins with a single cluster, and then analyzes each element in turn to determine if it falls within a current cluster, or places it in a new cluster, depending on the similarity threshold set by the analyst.

The AprioriAll algorithm builds upon a principle called Learning Associations (Giraud-Carrier, 2004). Learning Associations consists of discovering strong associations among transactions' items, or by extension, among objects' variables and attributes. Examples include: Customers who bought product A also bought product B, or Children of 4-5 yrs old with younger siblings are more likely to be kind to others. The purpose of association learning is to find rules that meet two user defined conditions: minimum support and minimum confidence.

The three partitional algorithms are k-means, buckshot, and fractionation. K-means derives its clusters based upon longest distance calculations of the elements in the dataset then it assigns each element to the closest centroid (the data point that is the mean of the values in each dimension of a set of multi-dimensional data points). Buckshot partitioning starts with a random sampling of the dataset, then derives the centres by placing the other elements within the randomly chosen clusters. Fractionation is a more careful clustering algorithm which divides the dataset into smaller and smaller groups through successive iterations of the clustering subroutine. Fractionation requires more processing power, and therefore time (Cutting, Karger, Pedersen, & Tukey, 1992).

Clustering is a methodology for more effective search and retrieval functions pertaining to datasets. The principle is simple enough- documents with a high degree of similarity will automatically be sought by the same query. By automatically placing the documents in groups based upon similarity (e.g. clusters), the search is effectively broadened.

The buckshot algorithm is simple in design and intent. It chooses a small random sampling of the documents in the database, and then applies the cluster routine to them. The centres of the clusters generated by the subroutine are returned. This use of a rectangular time clustering algorithms makes the buckshot method fast. The trade off is that buckshot is not deterministic, since it initially relies on a random sampling process. Repeated use of this algorithm can return different clusters than previous searches, although it is maintained that repeated trials generate clusters that are similar in quality to the previous set of clusters (Cutting, et. al. 1992).

Fractionation algorithms find centres by initially breaking the corpus of documents into a set number of buckets of predetermined size. The cluster subroutine then is applied to each bucket individually, breaking the contents of the bucket into yet smaller groups within the bucket. This process is repeated until a set number of groups are found, and these are the k centres.

This method is like building a branching tree from bottom up, with leaves as individual documents and the centres (clusters) as the roots. The best fractionation methods sort the dataset based on a word index key (e.g. based on words in common between two documents).

It is important to note that both buckshot and fractionation rely on a clustering subroutine. Both algorithms are designed to find the initial centres, but rely on a separate algorithm to do the actual clustering of individual documents. This subroutine can itself be agglomerative, or divisive. However, in practice, the subroutine tends to be an agglomerative hierarchical algorithm. Buckshot applies the cluster subroutine to a random sampling of the dataset to determine the centres, while the fractionation algorithm uses repeated applications of the subroutine over groups of fixed size in order to find the centres. Fractionation is considered more accurate, while buckshot is much faster, making it more suitable for searching in real time on the Web (Cutting, et. al. 1992).

The original k-means algorithm presented by MacQueen (1967 cited in Cheung, 2003) has since been refined. The new version can deal with ellipse shaped data clusters as well as ball shaped ones, and does not suffer from the dead unit problem that plagued the earlier k-means algorithm. In addition, the new k-means algorithm performs proper clustering without pre-determining the exact cluster number. In experimental runs, it has proven to be efficient and accurate.

Suffix trees were introduced in a paper by Zamir and Etzioni (1998). It is an incremental algorithm that runs in linear time. Instead of treating a document as a collection of words, Suffix Tree Clustering treats each document as a string. The string analogy allows suffix tree to analyze relationships between word proximities from document to document. Therefore, documents are grouped together by common phrases and words, and delivered in the form of a suffix tree for ease of browsing. This results in a highly relevant hierarchy of documents.

The primary characteristics of AprioriAll algorithm are that it generates all frequent item sets that satisfy the condition of minimum support. All possible rules are then checked against condition of confidence. All rules above that threshold (minimum confidence) are considered significant. Authors claim it to be a true data mining algorithm. (Giraud-Carrier, 2004) One particular advantage of AprioriAll is that it is easy to implement with a sparse matrix and simple sums. However, it is computationally expensive- the run time depends on the minimum support. It is not strictly an association's learner- as it induces rules which are inherently unidirectional. The basic assumption is that the items under consideration are in sets, and are not in a specific order.

Since the primary focus of this paper is on clustering as a means of searching the web, then there are criteria to be considered when this is kept in mind. There are several important criteria to take into account when analyzing algorithms for use on the web (Zamir & Etzioni, 1998).

Relevance: the method ought to produce clusters that group documents relevant to the user's query separately from irrelevant ones.

- Browsable summaries: The user needs to determine at a glance whether a cluster's contents are of interest. We do not want to replace sifting through ranked lists with sifting through clusters. Therefore the method must produce concise and accurate descriptions of the clusters.
- Overlap: Since documents have multiple topics, it is important that documents not be confined to a single cluster.
- Snippet-tolerance: The method ought to produce high quality clusters even when it only has access to the snippets returned by the search engine, as most users are unwilling to wait for the original documents to be downloaded from the web by the system.
- Speed: A patient user might sift through 100 ranked documents in a set of returned results. A clustering method to allow the user to browse through at least an order of magnitude more documents. Therefore the clustering method ought to be able to cluster up to one thousand snippets in a few seconds. For the impatient user, every second counts.
- Incrementality: To save time, the method should start to process each snippet as it is received from the web.

Of the six algorithms under scrutiny, the only one that treats a document as a string is the Suffix Tree. The other five treat each document as a collection of disjointed words- the order of the words has no importance. This causes a lot of important information to be lost in the search process. Phrases have been used to supplement word-based indexing in IR projects. Lexical atoms and syntactic phrases have been shown to improve accuracy without a corresponding cost in recall. Simple statistical approaches have also been used successfully to generate phrases (Zamir & Etzioni, 1998).

Suffix Tree Clustering is organized into three logical steps:

- The first step is document cleaning, where a light stemming algorithm is used to reduce prefixes and suffixes, turn plural form to singular form, and non-word tokens such as numbers and symbols are stripped. The original document strings are preserved so that the full document can be displayed on command.
- The second step is to identify the base clusters. This phase is equated with creating an inverted index of phrases for the document collection. These results in the Suffix Tree (first introduced by Zamir and Etzioni (1998)), a data structure that can be constructed in a time linear to the number of documents in the dataset, and can also be constructed incrementally, as the documents are being read.
- The third step of the process is to combine base clusters that have many similarities between their respective sets.

Since documents can have multiple phrases in common, it is imperative for the algorithm to recognize nearly identical clusters and merge them to prevent a proliferation of redundant clusters. This step is accomplished by merging clusters that have a high level of overlap.

The Suffix Tree algorithm is incremental. Each document is read, cleaned, and then inserted into the appropriate base cluster, or placed in a newly created cluster if the similarity threshold is exceeded. Then each base cluster is recalculated and redistributed according to the same principles of similarity.

The final clusters created by the Suffix Tree Clustering method are scored and sorted by the scores of their base clusters and the amount of overlap. Each cluster is then displayed according to the number of documents it contains and the phrases of the base clusters.

Suffix Tree Clustering algorithm does not require the user to specify the number of clusters before the search- the clusters are produced incrementally according to the dictates of the algorithm. It does require the specification of the similarity threshold. Suffix Tree Clustering has a markedly less sensitive response to the similarity threshold, as opposed to AHC methods. In this way, Suffix Tree Clustering is much more forgiving concerning the initial specifications of the search.

Data Clustering Problems and Solutions

Data Clustering algorithms are basically designed to address one or more problematic factors, such as high dimensionality, efficiency, scalability with data size, sensitivity to noise in the data, and identification of clusters in various shapes. K-means (and other partitioning methods) result in the break-up of genuine clusters. Hierarchical approaches fail to handle convex and elongated shapes of clusters. Density-based algorithms are extremely sensitive to noise in the data (Foss & Zaiane, 2002). A database may constitute up to 30%-40% of Noisy data. Pre-processing data to remove the noise typically takes more time than the execution time of the algorithm (Joshi, 1997).

The need for input parameters is the most pressing problem in clustering methods. Many algorithms, especially hierarchical ones, need the number of clusters to be arbitrarily selected at the beginning of the process. Even when this is not the case, the parameters of the algorithm can greatly influence the outcome of the process.

The basic idea of partitioning is intuitive in nature, and the process of partitioning is generally to achieve an optimal performance through iterative means. All partitioning methods have comparable clustering qualities, and the major difficulties of these methods are:

- the number of clusters to be found needs to be specified before the process, requiring at least some domain knowledge beforehand (which is often unavailable),
- difficulty in determining clusters with a large variance in size, and
- the method is only suitable for conclave clusters (Foss & Zaiane, 2002).

A hierarchical clustering algorithm produces a dendogram representing the nested grouping relationship of objects in the dataset. The main distinguishing characteristic among hierarchical approaches is the measure of similarity between individual clusters and the underlying modelling of the clusters. These algorithms are costly in terms of time and computational powers, so many are initiated with a sampling of the dataset that is then clustered. This leaves the end results as a direct function of the initial sampling. While this certainly helps with the problem of computational speed, if there are many small clusters within the dataset, the sampling is likely to miss them. (Foss & Zaiane, 2002)

Dennis et. al. (cited in Meyer Zu Eissen & Stein, 2002) placed current web searching technology into four broad classifications:

Unassisted keyword search: One or more search times are entered and the search engine returns a ranked list of document summaries. (ex: Google or AltaVista)

Assisted keyword search: The search engine produces results based on the user's initial inquiry. (ex: Vivisimo)

Directory-based Search: Here, the information space is divided into a hierarchy of categories, where the user navigates from broad to specific classes. (ex: yahoo)

Query –by-example: The user selects an interesting document snippet, which is then used as the basis for a new query.

Meyer zu Eissen and Stein (2002) specify the major criteria for a successful search engine. The ideal search engine process has three stages.

- First, an initialization phase according to the plain unassisted keyword search paradigm.
- Second, a categorization phase similar to the directory based search paradigm.
- Third, a refinement phase that may combine aspects from assisted keyword search and query-by-example paradigm.

As shown in the work of Zamir and Etzioni (1998) the feasibility of searching web results is heavily influenced by the ability to preserve accuracy when clustering based only upon the snippets returned to a search engine. In their results, it was found that almost the same accuracy was present in the use of snippets only, as opposed to the whole document. This alleviates the computer from downloading the entire document for the express purpose of measuring similarities with other documents. In general, each algorithm was slightly more accurate when using the entire document, but the accuracy of the snippets was much higher than expected. In the case of the k-means algorithm, it actually performed better using the snippets instead of the whole document.

Sequential pattern mining is the mining of frequently occurring patterns related to time or other sequences (Han & Kamber, 2005).

Sequential Data mining can be confined to the data within a specified time frame. This can be set time allotments, by the month or year, etc. They can also be tied to specific parameters, such as the weeks directly following a hurricane (Han & Kamber, 2005).

The Apriori algorithm is mainly concerned with the mining of sequential patterns, or sequential analysis (Giraud-Carrier, 2004). The basic method to mine sequential patterns (based upon Apriori) is to count all large sequences (including non maximal ones.

The Apriori Algorithm operates in five phases: Sort phase, large item set phase, transformation phase, sequence phase, maximal phase. In the Sort Phase, the algorithm sorts the database with customer ID as major key and transaction time as minor key. Large item set phase is where the algorithm finds large item sets and maps them to integers. Following this is the Transformation phase, where the algorithm deletes non-large item datasets and then transforms them using integer mapping. In the Sequence phase, the algorithm uses the set of large item sets to find the desired sequences. For the Maximal phase, it is necessary to find the maximum sequences among the large item sets.

This phase is sometimes combined with sequence phase, depending on algorithm. When the two are separate, the algorithm wastes a lot of time counting non-maximal sequences which cannot be sequential patterns. A possible solution to this problem is the AprioriSome algorithm (Giraud-Carrier, 2004). It generates candidates for a pass using only the large sequences found in the previous pass. It also employs forward and backward passes.

The facts revealed in the literature review can be summarized in a few key points. Data clustering is an essential step in making web- based searches more user friendly and productive. Data Clustering operates by attempting to measure how alike documents are, then sorting them into groups based upon content. The more accurate a Clustering algorithm is, the slower it works, because it must examine more relationships in greater detail. There are many different algorithms to choose from this study encompasses a review of five of the most successful and popular clustering algorithms.

K-means clustering is a partitional algorithm that works in linear time. It calculates the centres to be used in clustering through an analysis of maximum distance relationships between documents in the dataset. Single pass clustering is an incremental algorithm that develops its clusters through calculations based upon the vector differences ascribed to the documents in the dataset.

Buckshot is a clustering method that takes a random sampling of documents to use as the centres. Fractionation is an algorithm that divides the entire dataset into fixed size buckets that are then each clustered by the clustering subroutine, then the clusters are merged or split according to similarity. Suffix Tree Clustering is a hierarchical algorithm that runs in linear time, and provides an intuitive platform in the form of the suffix tree.

Proposed Solution & Methodology

Speed versus Accuracy

The natural trade-off that exists is between the speed of the algorithm and its accuracy at returning highly relevant results. This is simply because more accurate clustering techniques require more analysis of the data set, which translates into a higher number of calculations to be performed in order to accomplish the task. The more accurate algorithms require so much time to construct the clusters that they are rendered impractical for online real time searching. Fractionation, for instance, performs excellently when allowed to cluster data offline, but the high computational cost would make its usefulness in searching the web suspect.

The suffix tree clustering method provides an avenue for exploration. In previous tests, Suffix Tree Clustering outperformed the other methods in terms of speed (Zamir & Etzioni, 1998). It also provides an intuitive visual for presenting the data, thereby allowing the user to sort through the documents for the most relevant ones pertaining to the search.

Another strong point is that it is incremental- this allows it to begin sorting documents into clusters as soon as they are received, then to add new documents as they come. In the tests from the study, the results were that the clustering program was finished clustering the last files received just .01 seconds after the search engine had delivered them.

Large Datasets and Noisy Data

The sheer size of data is a serious impediment to data mining techniques. Most existing algorithms have not addressed the issue of out of core data structures. Parallel algorithms, and other newer techniques, have begun to address this problem (Joshi, 1997).

The use of snippets seems to detract from the amount of "noise" a document can generate. These excerpts of web documents represent a search engine's attempt at extracting the distinguishing phrases of a web document. This reduction in noise could have a positive effect on low accuracy techniques, such as k-means and buckshot. In the case of k-means, this streamlines the calculations a great deal because of the reduced number of relational analyses that need to be performed.

The four primary types of web-based search are the unassisted keyword search, the assisted keyword search, the directory search, and the query-by-example. The algorithms presented here fit some or all of these functions. The unassisted keyword search is straightforward, and presents the results returned from the search engine as is, in their ranked positions. This has, proven to be a difficult and time consuming process for sifting through to find specific information on a given subject (hence the need for data clustering).

The assisted keyword search is an advancement in terms of relevancy- it provides links based upon words with similar meanings. This increases the chance of finding the right kind of information, but still leaves the sorting and sifting to the user- there is very little categorization involved, and the search still results in ranked lists. The directory search is much more closely similar to the results of clustering at least. It is a hierarchical approach, allowing the user to begin in broad categories as yielded by the search, then to progressively narrow the search and find smaller groups of more specific documents. The query-by-example is another method that closely simulates the clustering approach. By selecting a snippet and deriving a new search around it, the search becomes iterative, allowing the user to further refine the search based upon the excerpt of a highly relevant site.

When considering these four points, the need for clustering algorithms becomes clearer. The often intimidating number of results that can be found via a search engine can frustrate many users. It also creates a large obstacle to efficient sifting and sorting of data. The major focus of the clustering algorithm is to display those search results in a sensible fashion. By grouping similar documents together, the user is given a much friendlier working environment in which to search.

Based upon the research, it seems that the hierarchical algorithms have a much better platform from which to satisfy those four essential types of web- search. Certainly, the more favourable searches are the directory based and query-by-example, which are both functions that are facilitated by the suffix tree, as a hierarchical, string-based algorithm. While there will certainly be those times when the keyword search is desired, such as when you know the exact title of the document you're looking for, the more generalized search options are fitting for the average user's needs.

Since the focus of this paper is to measure the speeds of the various algorithms and produce a conclusion based upon the results, there is little attention paid to the functionality or accuracy of the algorithms. In general, it is known that there is a trade-off between speed and accuracy when using algorithms. In that case, it should be expected that the fastest algorithm is not going to be the most accurate one. Due to the nature of web-based search, however, speed is essential. Therefore, the objective is to find the fastest algorithm, then to find ways to improve its accuracy. Since the introduction of the k-means algorithm, there have been several significant advances and permutations of it that have improved performance and speed. This can also be accomplished with other algorithms as well.

Implementation

The procedure of the experiment was to measure the execution time of the test algorithms in clustering data sets consisting of whole documents, excerpts and key words of a fixed quantity and size. Times were recorded for a series of 10 tests repeated for the same group size and numbers of files, in order to determine the optimum clustering algorithm for real time online web document searches. The dataset consisted of 1000 documents pertaining to classic literature. Each document contained on average 710 words, while the excerpts averaged 50 words. The documents were results of searches for the keywords "classic" and "literature." The source of the documents was from the internet. Google search engine was used to locate and download them.

The PC was an AMD Athlon 1500+, 60 GB HD, 1024MB Ram, an intel 100Mb network card, ADSL line 2000Mb/s and a home made router/firewall (Smoothwall).

There are three series of tests. Each series is a compilation of the time taken by each of the chosen clustering algorithms to sort the documents of the dataset. The first series consists of each algorithm analyzing the entire content of the document. The second series compares the speed of searches based upon excerpts, or snippets. The third and final series of tests measures the speed of searches based upon keywords only.

Throughout the experiment, the suffix tree consistently outperformed the other algorithms with respect to speed. This proved true for all three levels of the experiment. The second best performer was the buckshot algorithm. The worst performer overall was the fractionation algorithm. Although it still runs at acceptable speeds, it is by far the slowest of the algorithms that see common usage. K-means and Single Pass reside in the middle ground between the two extremes. The following charts show a complete breakdown of each algorithms performance in each series of tests.

Table 1 Full document comparison

Trial No.	k-means	single pass	buckshot	fractionation	suffix tree	AprioriAll
1	142.6s	156.2s	116.8s	221.9s	102.9s	180.1s
2	144.8s	164.9s	113.1s	224.7s	101.5s	180.2s
3	140.5s	159.8s	118.3s	223.2s	97.9s	180.0s
4	144.8s	160.1s	111.5s	218.8s	100.1s	180.3s
5	139.2s	160.2s	110.1s	219.9s	102.2s	179.9s
6	137.2s	158.4s	109.3s	217.1s	103.6s	180.4s
7	137.6s	161.2s	118.9s	220.2s	108.0s	179.8s
8	140.6s	162.4s	115.8s	215.8s	104.4s	180.5s
9	136.7s	165.6s	108.5s	220.4s	103.0s	179.7s
10	142.2s	165.3s	112.4s	220.1s	99.4s	180.6s

Table 1 illustrates the performance of each algorithm when using the entire content of the document for clustering. The suffix tree handled the document load efficiently and beat the nearest competitor by an average of 11.2 seconds. The slowest algorithm, fractionation is more than twice as slow as the suffix tree in finishing the clustering task. In each case, the mean value of the range was within 1 second of the actual calculated average. In this series of tests, the algorithms each performed in accordance with the expectations as presented in the literature.

Table 2 Comparative results

Algorithm	Avg. Value	Range (low-high)	Mean Value
k-means	140.6	136.7- 144.8	140.75
Single pass	161.4	156.2- 165.6	160.9
buckshot	113.5	108.5- 118.9	113.7
fractionation	220.2	215.8- 224.7	220.25
suffix tree	102.3	97.9- 108.0	102.95
AprioriAll	180.1	179.7-180.6	180.1

Table 2 gives a breakdown of the comparative results of the first series of tests. The listing includes the average speed of each algorithm, the range of values from lowest to highest, and the mean value of that range. As expected the means stay close to the average values. The suffix tree came at the lowest average, beating the competition by as much as 117.9 seconds. While k-means and single pass both perform well, they are outperformed by buckshot, which comes in at a close second.

Having now run the first series of tests, it is possible to begin to formulate a basic idea of what the other two series will bring. Keep in mind that the next two series will run in just a fraction of the time of the first test. In each instance, however, the basic pattern established by the initial series of tests should be corroborated by the results of the other tests. Throughout the experiment, there will be a continuous examination of the possible ramifications of the data. It is expected that the other two series of tests are going to produce results in line with the first series. Each series of tests was recorded in the same fashion, with the only metric being speed of the operation.

Table 3 Clustering by excerpts

Trial No.	k-means	single pass	buckshot	fractionation	suffix tree	AprioriAll
1	9.8s	11.0s	8.0s	15.2s	7.2s	13.3s
2	10.0s	11.3s	7.8s	15.5s	7.1s	13.2s
3	10.2s	11.1s	8.1s	15.5s	6.9s	13.4s
4	9.7s	11.2s	7.8s	15.2s	7.1s	13.1s
5	9.7s	11.4s	7.7s	15.6s	7.0s	13.5s
6	9.7s	11.0s	7.7s	15.4s	7.3s	13.0s
7	10.2s	11.4s	8.2s	15.4s	7.4s	13.6s
8	9.9s	11.2s	8.1s	15.2s	7.2s	12.9s
9	9.9s	11.5s	7.7s	15.1s	7.1s	13.7s
10	10.0s	11.4s	7.7s	15.5s	7.0s	12.8s

Table 3 shows the results of the test when applied to the excerpts of the documents. This search highlights certain strengths for the clustering algorithms- the reliance on key phrases instead of the document as a whole has allowed each algorithm to perform much faster. Not surprisingly, however, the suffix tree is still on top with a lead ranging from .8 seconds to 7.3 seconds. Buckshot comes in a strong second place, with an average of 7.9 seconds. Fractionation lags far behind the others in terms of speed- it is still 4 full seconds away from the next in line, the single pass. At this level, the gap between the k-means and buckshot methods becomes more apparent. Also, this type of test is a comparable representation of the sort of search that a librarian or researcher would be performing regularly.

Table 4 Comparative results

Algorithm	Avg. Value	Range	Mean Value
k-means	9.9	9.7-10.2	10.0
single pass	11.4	11.0-11.5	11.3
buckshot	7.9	7.7-8.2	8.0
fractionation	15.4	15.1-15.6	15.4
suffix tree	7.1	6.9-7.4	7.2
AprioriAll	13.3	12.9-13.8	13.3

Table.4 shows the average values again stay very close to the mean value, according to range. In the case of fractionation, the mean and the average coincide. The results continue to place the suffix tree at the top of the list, followed in order by buckshot, k-means, single pass and fractionation. The shortest gap is between the first two, buckshot and the suffix tree, with a mere .8 seconds separating them. The largest gap is between the last two (single pass and fractionation) with a full 4.0 seconds between them.

Table 5 presents the results of the search by keyword series. The small running times are indicative of the simplicity of the search- after all, the algorithm is going to find the keywords in every single document in the dataset. As before, the suffix tree continues to dominate the proceedings, while the fractionation algorithm trails far behind. The relative places of each algorithm that were established in the first two series are maintained, validating the hypothesis. Since the search is faster overall the result difference between the algorithms is noticeably less.

Table 5 Keywords "classic" and "literature"

Trial No.	k-means	single pass	buckshot	fractionation	suffix tree	AprioriAll
1	.40s	.44s	.32s	.60s	.28s	.50s
2	.39s	.44s	.31s	.62s	.28s	.49s
3	.39s	.44s	.32s	.63s	.27s	.51s
4	.41s	.45s	.31s	.61s	.28s	.48s
5	.38s	.46s	.31s	.62s	.28s	.49s
6	.39s	.44s	.30s	.62s	.29s	.51s
7	.38s	.46s	.30s	.61s	.29s	.50s
8	.40s	.45s	.33s	.60s	.28s	.52s
9	.40s	.46s	.31s	.61s	.28s	.49s
10	.39s	.46s	.30s	.62s	.28s	.50s

The patterns that have been seen so far continue to be reinforced in the third series. The relative positions of the algorithms continue to remain stable with respect to one another. The suffix tree continues to be the strongest performer, while fractionation lags behind. The largest gap in this series is between single pass and fractionation, at .16 seconds. The smallest gap is a mere .3 seconds between the suffix tree and buckshot. At this level of operation, the time increments are exceedingly small, but proportionately, they stay within the same ranges as seen in the previous two series of tests. The mean values continue to stay within a short range of the average for each algorithm.

The range of lowest to highest for each algorithm is in the order of .3 seconds, giving an average variance of .15 seconds for this series.

Table 6 Comparative results

Algorithm	Avg. Value	Range	Mean Value
k-means	.39	.38-.41	.395
single pass	.45	.44-.46	.45
buckshot	.31	.30-.33	.315
fractionation	.61	.60-.63	.615
suffix tree	.28	.27-.29	.28
AprioriAll	.50	.48- .52	.50

The tests performed were designed solely to test clustering algorithms in their speed. From the results recorded, it can be seen that the suffix tree is the fastest performing algorithm. In all cases the relative ranking of the algorithms remained the same throughout all three series of tests. The ranking of the algorithms according to average speed is summarized in Table 7. The values given are for the averages of the algorithm in each of the three series of tests. The algorithms are also listed in order from fastest to slowest.

Table 7 Rankings of the six algorithms

Algorithm	1st series	2nd series	3rd series
suffix tree	102.3	7.1	.28
Buckshot	113.5	7.9	.31
k-means	140.6	9.9	.39
single pass	161.4	11.4	.45
AprioriAll	180.1	13.3	.50
fractionation	220.2	15.4	.61

Conclusion of Results

The World Wide Web is huge, widely distributed and global. It is too huge for effective data mining and data warehousing. It has no standards and structure, making it heterogeneous and complex to the point of being prohibitive (Han & Kamber, 2005). The World Wide Web grows and changes rapidly. There is a highly diverse group of users, and thus an equally diverse cross section of topics. Only a relatively small portion of web content is useful to a given user (on the order of 1%).

Web Search engines operate on a few common principles (Han & Kamber, 2005). Index based searches alternately search the web, index the web pages, and build and store huge keyword-based indices. The deficiencies of this approach are twofold: a topic of appreciable breadth is likely to return hundreds or thousands of documents, and many documents that are highly relevant may not contain the keyword of the search, and thereby be missed by the search engine. Web mining includes mining web link structures to identify authoritative web pages, the automatic classification of web documents, building a multilayered web information base, and web-log mining.

The results of the experiment clearly indicate that the suffix tree is the fastest clustering algorithm in terms of real time processing speed. It far outstrips fractionation in terms of speed. It maintains a healthy margin over both k-means and single pass methods. Buckshot runs a close second, but the suffix tree consistently outperforms it as well. The suffix tree also provides an excellent interface for the user, giving the results of the search with an intuitive bent. This allows for quick and easy browsing of categories until the desired objective is obtained.

However, the other algorithms are far from dead. Buckshot is not too far off- with a little work, or possibly a new suffix tree subroutine, the time gap could be closed. There are several versions of the k-means algorithm in existence, and the k-means has certainly improved greatly since its introduction in 1967.

The AprioriAll algorithm has some interesting points, but overall, its slow run time makes it impractical for real time web searches. While other uses of Apriori, like AprioriSome, result in a faster run time, they also reinforce the trade off between time and accuracy that is prevalent in the algorithms being studied.

When weighed against other features, the suffix tree still produces strong results. It has the ability to define similarities through strings of words, instead of just the words themselves. This makes the relevancy of its results much higher than the other algorithms. This, coupled with its speed, make it the ideal algorithm for web-based data clustering.

Earlier in this paper, the criteria for a web-based clustering algorithm were discussed. The suffix tree successfully fits all the criteria as expressed herein. The points are repeated below, with additional commentary on how the Suffix Tree fulfils the requirements of each step.

Relevance: the method ought to produce clusters that group documents relevant to the user's query separately from irrelevant ones.

This is one of the suffix tree's strongest points. While every algorithm presumably has this as its goal; the point is that some do it better than others. Some of the older algorithms, such as k-means have been known to produce questionable results when grouping documents according to relevancy.

Browsable Summaries

The user needs to determine at a glance whether a cluster's contents are of interest. Replacing sifting through ranked lists with sifting through clusters is not desirable. Therefore the method must produce concise and accurate descriptions of the clusters.

This is another aspect that the suffix tree fulfils. The suffix tree provides a concise yet accurate description of each cluster, thereby allowing the user to easily determine whether or not the cluster has relevant documents to the search. While other algorithms do produce clusters that can be browsed through, there is no guarantee that the cluster will contain all the most relevant documents.

Overlap

Since documents have multiple topics, it is important that documents not be confined to a single cluster.

This is also a feature that the suffix tree performs well. Since it relies on strings of words, and it is highly likely that documents that have the same phrase in them will be closely related in content, theme and context. This is important, because without the overlap, it is easy to miss an appropriate search result because the algorithm happened to place it in the wrong cluster.

Snippet-Tolerance

The method ought to produce high quality clusters even when it only has access to the snippets returned by the search engine, as most users are unwilling to wait for the original documents to be downloaded from the web by the system.

The results have shown that snippets are almost as effective as the full documents in the process of clustering accurately. The suffix tree was no exception to this, and still outperformed the others in terms of absolute speed. While entire document searches have shown themselves to be more accurate overall, the degree of relevance delivered by excerpts from documents has been surprisingly high.

Speed

A patient user might sift through 100 ranked documents in a set of returned results. It would be better to use clustering, allowing the user to browse through at least an order of magnitude more documents. Therefore the clustering method ought to be able to cluster up to one thousand snippets in a few seconds. For the impatient user, every second counts.

As the results of this experiment indicate, it is indeed possible for a clustering algorithm to process 1000 documents in just a few seconds when snippets are used. While snippets are in fact not as accurate as the full document, the increases in speed of computation will more than make up for the loss of accuracy. Most users would rather wait seven seconds to get their results than nearly two minutes.

Incrementality

To save time, the method should start to process each snippet as it is received from the web. Of all the algorithms that were tested, the suffix tree is the only one that performed incrementally. This provides it with the advantage of being able to begin the clustering process before all the results have been returned by the search engine. Incrementality also allows the algorithm to process more results as they are returned and place them in the appropriate cluster one at a time. This has provided a significant speed advantage for the Suffix Tree clustering algorithm.

Conclusion

When weighed by these criteria, the suffix tree stands out as not only the fastest data clustering algorithm, but it is also the most accurate and easy to use. While the focus of the research in this paper is based upon the speed of the operation, there is no significant effort to qualitatively investigate the accuracy of the algorithms in producing relevant clusters.

After this study we think a new concept of data mining pattern has to be developed. Search engine capable of automatic data mining, relationship building abilities and "smart engine". This new concept will be able to accurately find relevant information. This should be the focus of further research. The effectiveness and increased efficiency of "smart engine" will lead to a greater productivity and more satisfying end user experience.

References

Black, P. (2005). *Dictionary of Algorithms and Data Structures*. National Institute of Standards and Technology web site. Retrieved April 23 2005 from: http://www.nist.gov/dads/

Cheung, Y. (2003). k*-means: A new generalized k-means clustering algorithm. *Pattern Recognition Letters, 24*(15), 2883-2893. Retrieved 16 August 2005, from: www.comp.hkbu.edu.hk/~ymc/papers/journal/PATREC_3261_publication_version.pdf

Cutting, D. R., Karger, D. R., Pedersen, J. O., & Tukey, J. W. (1992). Scatter/Gather: A cluster-based approach to browsing large document collections. *Proceedings of the Fifteenth Annual International ACM SIGIR Conference*, June 1992, 318-329. Retrieved August 9 2005, from: http://www2.parc.com/istl/projects/ia/papers/sg-sigir92/sigir92.html

Foss, A., & Zaiane, O.R. (2002). A parameter less method for efficiently discovering clusters of arbitrary shape in large datasets. *Proceedings of the IEEE International Conference on Data Mining* (ICDM'2002), pp 179-186. Retrieved August 2 2005, from: http://doi.ieeecomputersociety.org/10.1109/ICDM.2002.1183901

Giraud-Carrier, C., (2004). From *CS 478- Association Rule Learning.ppt* Department of Computer Sciences, Brigham Young University. Retrieved August 2 2005 from: http://faculty.cs.byu.edu/~cgc/Teaching/CS_478_Su05/Lectures/CS%20478%20-%20Association%20Rule%20Learning.ppt

Han, J., & Kamber, M. (2005). *Data Mining: Concepts and Techniques* (Chapter 9). Intelligent Database Systems Research Lab. School of Computing Science, Simon Fraser University, Canada. Retrieved August 19 2005, from: http://www.cs.sfu.ca/~han/bk/9cmplx.ppt

Joshi, K. P. (1997). *Analysis of Data Mining Algorithms*. University of Minnesota. Retrieved July 25 2005, from: http://www-users.cs.umn.edu/~desikan/research/dataminingoverview.html#apriori

Meyer zu Eissen & Stein. (2002). *Analysis of Clustering Algorithms for Web-based Search*. Paderborn University, pp. 168-178. Retrieved September 2 2005, from: http://www-ai.upb.de/aisearch/pakm02-frame.pdf

Oliver W. & Armin W. (2003). *Data Mining for Ontology Building Data Mining Concepts*. HSR Hochschule Für Technik Rapperwil (University). Retrieved April 1 2005, from: http://informatik.hsr.ch/Content/Gruppen/Doz/jjoller/diplom/DataMiningForOntologyBuilding/DataMining/DataMiningConcepts.pdf

Zamir, O. & Etzioni, O. (1998). Web document clustering: A feasibility demonstration. *Proceedings of ACM SIGIR'98*. Retrieved May 15 2005, from: www.cs.washington.edu/homes/etzioni/papers/sigir98.pdf

Biographies

Dr. Samuel Sambasivam is the chairman of the Department of Computer Science of Azusa Pacific University. Professor Sambasivam has done extensive research, publications, and presentations in both computer science and mathematics. His research interests include optimization methods, expert systems, Fuzzy Logic, client/server, Databases, and genetic algorithms. He has taught computer science and mathematics courses for over 20 years. Professor Sambasivam has run the regional Association for Computing Machinery (ACM) Programming Contest for six years. He has developed and introduced several new courses for computer science majors. Professor Sambasivam teaches

Database Management Systems, Information Structures and Algorithm Design, Microcomputer Programming with C++, Discrete Structures, Client/Server Applications, Advanced Database Applications, Applied Artificial Intelligence, JAVA and others courses. Professor Sambasivam coordinates the Client/Server Technology emphasis for the Department of Computer Science at Azusa Pacific University.

Mr. Nick Theodosopoulos has a proven and successful educational background, along with over 10 year's commercial experience in the IT sector. He is currently working as an independent software consultant serving the financial institutions in the city of London. He has performed several roles including software development, in a variety of languages and operating systems. He specializes in data manipulation, migration and database design. He has recently read a Masters in Computer science at Liverpool University. His current pursuits and interests are database performance tweaking, data striping and enhancing mathematical empirical formulae all to speed up database transaction processes and overall performance.

The page left blank intentionally.

Entropy: Form Follows Function

Samuel Sambasivam
Azusa Pacific University
Azusa, CA, USA

ssambasivam@apu.edu

Vijay D. Bodas
University of Liverpool
Bahrain

vdbodas@batelco.com.bh

Abstract

Many definitions of entropy are discussed in intimacy with Boltzmann-Gibbs exponential distribution and measure theory. Tsallis introduced a definition that collapses to other definitions when parameter 'q' reaches unity limit. In this definition, Levy statistics are said to be used instead of Boltzmann distribution. Working with the hypothesis *"are we not wrong in being obsessed with the form of entropy functional?"* aim was to assess if Tsallis definition can be an alternate basis for Shannon's information entropy. A mix of analogy, comparison, both inductive and deductive reasoning were employed as research enquiry tools. The process of enquiry touched many fields to which entropy is related, including quantum information theory. The enquiry concluded that entropy additivity is adopted axiomatically in most fields for good reasons, mainly emanating from measure theory, conforming to the view that the entropy has more to do with topology and volume growth rather than statistics and distributions.

Keywords: Entropy, Tsallis, Levy and Boltzmann-Gibbs distributions, topology, volume growth, additivity, quantum information theory, information theory

Introduction

A debate rages amongst the scientific community, and two distinct camps argue the functional forms of entropy they support. Entropies have been used in thermodynamics, information theory and many other fields. Kolmogorv introduced entropy of a measure preserving transformation on probability space; viz. measure theoretic entropy. In dynamic systems entropy is taken to measure rate of divergence of function orbits. In topology, volume growth, invariant measure theoretic and topological entropies are defined Gerhard Knieper. (1995). The last decade has been replete with published works that relate Tsallis entropy to every conceivable domain of science, Information Science complexity theory included.

Relevance

All debates that relate to entropy allow us to explore solution mechanisms adopted using the so-called entropy maximization concept. Many of these relate to computer science and its quest for problem solving techniques. For example phase transition is observed in a 3-SAT problem (Ke Xu & Wei Li (2000). If phase transition is understood well, then the methods evolved in the process could be used for speedily solving 3-SAT like problems and we have P=NP. The interactions are very much a part of growing literature on Multi-agent systems and are an evolving area as in works of Liau, C. J. (2002). Particles in a box model of statistical mechanics has been applied to evidence, belief by Saul L. K., Jaakkola T., & Jordan M. I. (1996), to product distribution by Wolpert, D. (2003), in cooperative and non cooperative game theories, bounded rationality by Wolpert, D. (2004), for multi criteria decision making and control of multi agent systems by Lee, C. F. & Wolpert, D. (2004). Tsallis entropy has been purportedly used in scaling phenomena in Sociology, Language, Biology by West, B. J. (2004); in physics, chemistry, economics, medicine, geophysics, computer science by Gell-Mann, M. & Tsallis (Eds). (2004), by Abe S. & Okamoto Y. (Eds). (2001), and by Yamano, T. (2004); to Internet Seismic sciences by Abe S. & Suzuki N. (2003), in Chaos by Tsallis C., Plastino, & Zhang. (1997), Tsallis, Rapisarda, Baranger, & Latora. (2000). and Tsallis, Baldovin, & Schulze. (2003); in Quantum information theory by Abe S. (2004 December), and by Tsallis C., Lambert P. W., & Prato D. (2001); seemingly in everything under the sun. We notice a few have started to adopt Tsallis functional form and thought in Information theory (Kojadinovic, I., Marichal, J. L., & Roubens, M. (2005)).

Invariance and Scaling

By covering some aspects of scale variations by some very simple examples, formal aim below is to search an answer to the question: Can we relate the concept of entropy to scales and invariance? Change is the nature of things. What does not change when a reference point of view is changed is an invariant measure. Shannon used logarithm as a measure of communicable information. Usual first example of scale issues in linear systems is scaled partial pivoting in Gaussian elimination. Use of relative coefficient magnitudes is important to preclude overflow. An interesting example applying the concept of invariance is that of rotation of axes. Chemists plot triangle diagrams to show flammability envelopes. These diagrams can be easily plotted as right angle triangle diagrams in excel. Commercial triangle graph paper is equilateral triangular. The right triangular Graph 1 can be rotated to obtain an equilateral triangular Graph 2

Graph 1

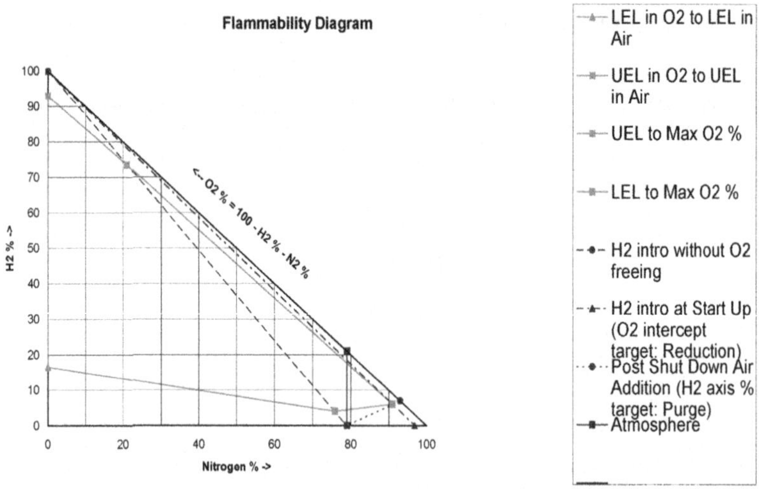

Graph 2

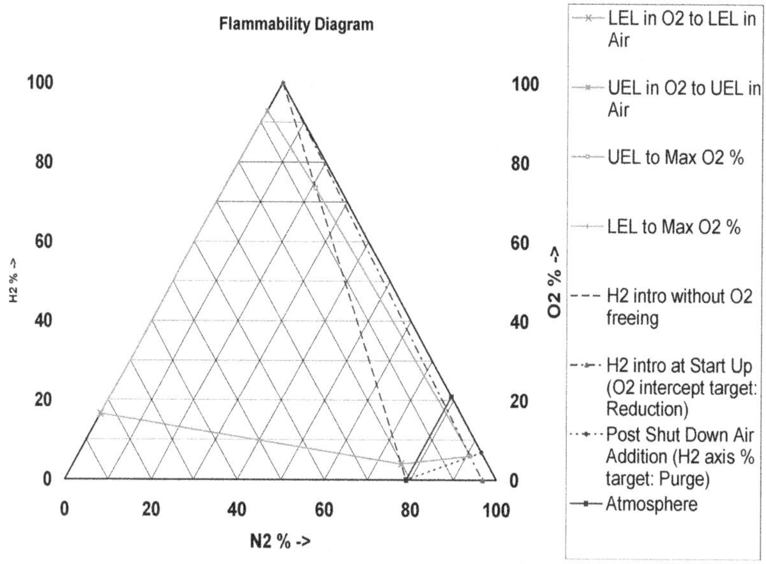

Solution of quartic is an example that comes from theory of invariance group relationships between coefficients of polynomials that evolved while Galois proved that polynomials with non prime compositional indices could not be solved. Feedback control systems that translate initiator signals from units of current to disparately different indicated units like those of temperature use "scaling over the signal band width" to change figures between completely differing signal carrier channel units. What is not apparent to casual observation is that unless additivity holds in each carrier domain, this translation is impossible. Phenomenological scaling is used to establish links and analogy between phenomena that differ in scales using invariants. Several such phenomenological models follow non BG distributions and Levy statistics.

Phase Transition

Supporters of Tsallis, C. (1988) entropy originally suggested that his form enables describing phase transitions and characterize them by a parameter q. Phase transitions were being used to characterize hardness of problems. Thus Tsallis q parameter came to be known as a measure of complexity; Yamano, T. (2004). According to Occam's razor (http://en.wikipedia.org/wiki/Occam%27s_razor), when alternate explanations are available to describe a phenomenon, the simpler one that explains all facets involved is to be accepted. Since Occam's razor is a non-mathematical statement; it is untenable to accept it as the justification of Tsallis, C. (1988) entropy as the claimant that describes phase transitions. Phase transitions have topological origin as investigated by Angelani et al (2004). Thus for a statistical mechanics model without non-homogenous interactions, it could be unreasonable to accept that Tsallis, C. (1988) entropy contributes anything of substance over Shannon-Gibbs-Boltzman formulation. In the same vein Tsallis 'q' parameter interpreted as a measure of complexity by Yamano, T. (2004) becomes questionable. However Occam's razor; itself is without a proof.

Topology and Projective Geometry

Kiehn, R. M. (2004) has detailed explanations of non-equilibrium stationary states and entropy based on thermodynamics, topology and geometry. Thermodynamics is a topological science. This is clear from a few examples below.

(1) One of the oldest results in topology is that number of vertices and two dimensional faces of a bounded convex polyhedron exceeds the number of edges by two (Dey, G. & Edelsbrunner, n.d.). Compare this to the famous Gibb's phase rule that is often introduced with the memory aid as below:

Police Force is Chief plus two, where P stands for phases, F stands for degrees of freedom, and C stands for components.

(2) Thermodynamic varieties such as Free energies and Entropies are independent of path; they depend only on the end states. In Cartan's topology and projective geometry, the path goes around the infinity and returns to another point. Thus the absence of the concept of in-betweenness is shared by Thermodynamics and projective geometry and topology.

Entropy is an extensive variable. Additivity of extensive variables is a property of projective transformations: Kiehn, R. M. (2004). Projective geometry is at the upper most level of geometric generalizations. It has its invariants in the six cross ratios with one functionally independent ratio k (Show Table of cross ratios and graph). Let us formally define a measure to grasp what additivity of a projective transformation is: "*A measure on a topological space X is just any function m from the family of subsets of space X to non-negative real numbers satisfying the property of countable additivity*": Amenta N., Bern M., Eppstein D., & Teng S. H. (2000), Projective transformations are countably additive. This situation happens to fit perfectly to Boltzmann-Planck's choice of logarithm and unfortunately, does not fit at all to Tsallis's choice of a non-additive deformed logarithm. It is clear that in above arguments we first called entropy an extensive variable and then invoked additivity of extensive variables in projective geometry. This is *a circular logic and hence in reality, entropy is extensive (additive) by axiom. The axiomatization of countable additivity was the fundamental contribution of Kolmogorov's measure theory.*

Novelty, Generalization and Innovation

In Appendix 1, a somewhat provocative extension of Tsallis generalization defines an entire and novel new branch of mathematics called "q deformed mathematics" including a "q deformed projective geometry". The purpose of this novelty is to demonstrate the connotations of rejecting additivity in entropy definition. It shows how easy it is to innovate and generalize to get a q deformed world. For example a chemist could obtain q deformed pH of acids and bases using the q deformed logarithm. Without doing any experiment, we can confidently state that no physical experiment will validate the q deformed pH measure. We accept countable additivity in the real world and reject the novelty of all generalizations and innovations like Appendix 1.

However, whatever happens to the complex world? In fine print that we did not state or reproduce, Angelani et al (2004) use a complex number in the partition function exponential to derive phase transition and conventional entropy. However, they forget to address the imaginary part and it is left dangling in free or phase space, after they had no use remaining for it.

Is it possible that we have states in the partition function that are sums of logical states with complex coefficients?

Can we then define a countable additivity on real and imaginary parts separately? Or at least map the imaginary part on to real domain and continue using something akin to conventional countably additive measure?

Can we use both the available probabilities in the projective geometry, but use one for the real variable and the other for the imaginary variable? Of course we just innovated another projective geometry in complex space, and have to radically alter Kolmogorov's concept of measure telling us about mappings to positive real numbers to address complex numbers as well. The answer to first of the above questions is yes. This space is used to define the Qubit in Quantum Computing. The remaining two questions are also answered yes (may be in a modified form), that must logically flow from the first yes. All this brings us to a rather hard to answer question, is Tsallis entropy then suited for the job in the Quantum arena? Unfortunately in the above two answers we already implicitly answered this in the negative. We shall expand on this topic a bit, later in this work under the heading quantum information theory.

Measure Theory

Measure theory is at the foundation of information science and perhaps most of the science. This fact is usually not apparent, due to years of schooling in determinism. Probability involves random occurrence of events. Two successive events can be independent or dependent on each other or be a sequence of an exhaustive search process. The dependent events could further be mutually exclusive or second could relate to the prior one in some other way. Kolmogorov re-enunciated the laws of probability on a geometric foundation, formally called measure theory. These laws and current challengers that bring additivity into question are listed below:

The total compound probability of instantiations of events A, B and C of the possible states of the world is shown in Table 1.

Table 1. The laws of probability

Event type	The total probability law
Any two events	P(AUB)=P(A)+A(B)-P(A∩B)
Disjoint events	As above, but P(A∩B)=0.0, Countable additivity
Dependent events	As above, but P(A∩B)=P(A)P(B|A)=P(B)P(A|B), dependence may relate to non additivity
Three events	P(AUBUC)=P(A)+A(B)+P(C)-P(A∩B)-P(B∩C)-P(A∩C)+P(A∩B∩C)

If and only if either P(A) or P(B) is zero then the events are said to be mutually exclusive and complimentary and the compound probability is additive (http://mathworld.wolfram.com/CountableAdditivityProbabilityAxiom.html). If it is not the case and P(A,B) exists and the compound probability is non-additive. In terms of logic symbolism

{{Pa==0} ∨ {Pb==0}} ↔ {P is additive}

¬{{Pa==0} ∨ {Pb==0}} ↔ {P is not additive}

P(A∩B)=P(A)P(B) if events are independent

When additivity is allowed and used, the belief is evidence. When combination is allowed, belief is a generalized probability, Halpern & Fagin. (1992). Halpern and Fagin apparently conclude to leave the decision as to which one to use on domain specialists. Information entropy was derived in thermodynamics under the assumptions disjoint events, factorizability and a not well-clarified " homogeneity " assumption. These assumptions about events make the compound probability used in the occurrence of events in thermodynamics additive. Dependent events mean a term that caters to any interaction between two events must be taken into consideration. Central theme in the issue of entropy functional form is the assumption of additive probabilities and independence of events. It can be easily misconstrued from the Tsallis form that the definition of compound probability is what Tsallis followed and his work caters to interactions, but that is not so.

Fuchs, C. A. (1995) gives very detailed derivations of the following on Information theoretic and probabilistic grounds in his thesis:

Error probability quantum and classical;
Fidelity, quantum and classical;
Renyi overlaps, quantum and classical;
Kullback Information, quantum and classical;
Accessible Information, quantum and classical;
Shannon's entropy.

It becomes clear from derivations reproduced by Fuchs, C. A. (1995), Appendix 2 that his so called q factor tending to unity needed to develop Shannon's entropy asymptotically from probability theory has inspired the Tsallis q factor. However, the effort in the information theory derivations is about finding a true distribution from a host of false distributions and only one of them is true. That happens to be the one when q factor is at its unity limit. And then it is Shannon-Boltzmann-Gibbs distribution. In all of Fuchs, C. A. (1995) set of probability based information theory derivations, the issue of compound probability is not approached with homogeneity & heterogeneity or interactions in mind. Thus it is clear that Tsallis entropy definition emanates from an incomplete derivation of Shannon's entropy embedded in information theory. And Tsallis definition, even according to information theory can be true only in the unity limit of the q factor; there it collapses to Shannon's definition. Thus we conclude that in fact we have no "new" definition of entropy that emanates from Information theory.

Quantum information theorists have advocated two further approaches to probability theory due to its internal debates.

Khrennikov. A. (2005) calls any two quantum measurements as those of vectors. He then uses law of vector addition to develop a probability law as below (bold face is a vector):

C=A+B;

C.C=(A+B).(A+B)

$|C^2|=|A^2|+|B^2|-2|ABCos(\theta)|$

The last form has been analogously compared to Born's rule and is used to define a probability law as: P(C)=P(A)+P(B)-P(A∩B)

The cosine term is normalized in some way. When angle between vectors changes quadrants, the sign of cos term goes positive and use of Euler's exponential-trignometric relation results in hyperbolic cosine in place of cos term. Andrei calls this "hyperbolic representation" of probabilities and calls all of this work as "contextual probability", i.e. a euphemism for compound conditional probability. However such a contrived description is not justified. Remember that the entropy and probabilities arrived on the scene due to interaction issues and while minimizing thermodynamic free energy. The interaction term can have either a positive or negative sign, based on energy balance of the system. Hyperbolic behavior does indeed exist in physically real non-homogeneous systems. We will visit this by giving physical examples in liquid mixture at a later stage.

Salgado, R. (2002) evolve a new line of thought. Citing failure of additivity for the famous double slit experiment, they propose a generalization of classical probability measure and state that a quantum probability is not additive at two event level and define an interaction non zero term I2 in the compound summand of event probabilities. However from three events (each taken as set having sum of the square norms of additive quantities) onwards, they state that quantum mechanics follows normal classical probability law. This has an analogy throwback to Gleason's theorem (Caves C., C. Fuchs C., Manne K., Rennes J. (2003) that states quantum measurements for dimensions greater than two are feasible, notwithstanding Hiesenberg's uncertainty principle. But beyond that, Salgado, Sorkin generalization of measure appears to be artificial and contrived as well.

Interactions and Theories of Liquid's

When interactions and heterogeneity are involved there is one true "mixture" distribution that includes interaction between more than one dis-similar entities participating in the chance. And there are false "mixture distributions".

Within the true mixture distribution itself, compound probability must apply and yet the overall probability has to be bounded by unity. When mixtures shift to pure states, the probabilities should remain bounded by unity. Since this starts to get confusing, it is time to turn to an area of science that has had the debates about this ongoing for years. Such discussions are about Entropy of mixing in liquid's theory. We of course begin with a clear understanding that science does not yet understand entropy of mixing very well and we are all still learning.

Liquids, solids, social teamwork, extreme programming pairing, HCI, biological systems, macro-economy's are physically the easiest examples of interactions. We shall address quantum entanglements as an example at a later stage. This section draws practitioner's ideas into the world of Information theorists.

It is known for long that theories of liquids and solids are far from perfect. However, engineers have had to deal with predictions for liquid systems, even when as we know, basic thermodynamics handled interactions and phase transitions unsatisfactorily. Applied literature on liquids is far ahead of Information theorist's literature. Engineers skirted the entropy debate completely and moved ahead with their work. Let us see how. Liquids theories of applied domain do not introduce the interactions by modifying or using Shannon's entropy definition, but by separately adding functional terms to the upper level, the system configuration free energy. The entropy as gets derived from *free energy minimization* (*the principle of least effort in team works*) is simply, accepted.

The interactions can be basically grouped into two categories, those that are homogenous and those that are not. An excellent example of interactions in biological social systems is a flock of birds flying in an arrowhead formation. It is now common knowledge that if the birds fly in an arrowhead, the effect of flapping wings of neighbor reduces energy required to fly and the flock can take longer flights than individual birds due to this energy minimization. (See Figure 1.)

Figure 1. A flock of geese flying in an arrowhead V
Retrieved from http://www.loc.gov/rr/scitech/mysteries/geese.html

What Information theorists call as "entropy maximization" is in reality, not entropy maximization but "energy minimization". Social scientists frequently quote this example in collaborative leadership and as a justification for encouraging teamwork and it is perhaps the model example for collaboration and cooperation in a Multi agent system. The homogenous interactions arise from topology of a problem and are related to entropy and information loss. Topology and entropy are intimately linked as shown by Angelani et al (2004). Homogenous interactions can also be multi-entity interactions and can be categorized again on the basis of number of entities involved in the interaction. Probability theory incorporates many body interactions as well. For example:

$P(A \cup B \cup C)=P(A)+A(B)+P(C)-P(A \cap B)-P(B \cap C)-P(A \cap C)+P(A \cap B \cap C)$; if events are pair wise mutually exclusive, then ternary interaction terms vanish. The transition order and number entities involved delink themselves for first and second order transitions, however for greater than second order transition the order and number of entities is linked by Euler characteristics as shown by Percus, A. G. & Martin, O. (1998).

The non-homogenous interactions are the ones that were introduced as application example in case of liquids, solids, social team work, terrorism etc. at the beginning. Heterogeneous interactions can be further classified into three categories viz. attractive, neutral and repulsive. The involvement of only two agencies in interactions makes them binary interactions. If the interaction between two is effected via a third party, then it is a ternary interaction. This is akin to " k nearest neighbour " ideas of Percus, A. G. & Martin, O. (1998). Heterogeneous interactions modify system models like the statistical mechanics model. However the manner in which they get introduced into the entropy of the system is very different than homogenous interactions. Though such interactions also operate with and through the system topology, they are present owing to heterogeneity's own inherent nature and behaviour and specifically not only due to mathematics of the topological space. Heterogeneous interactions must be configured and added externally to the system model function and computed and checked separately for their information loss contribution. The overall picture of interactions is shown in Figure 2.

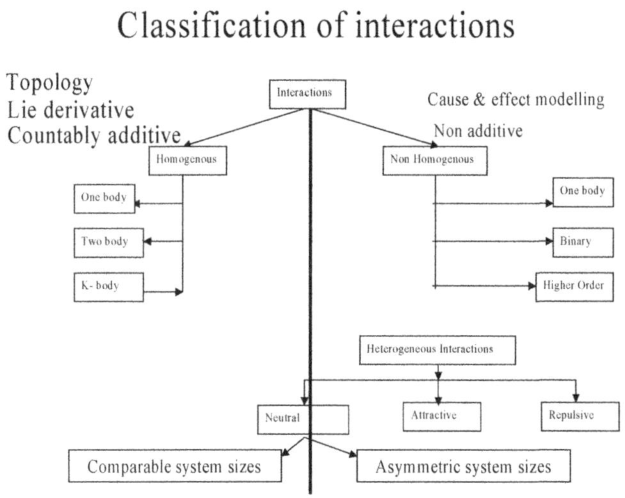

Figure 2. Interactions

In agent systems, when multi-goal programming is desired, these interactions can be introduced as normalized objectives that approach a goal. Two useful points from the theories of liquids are firstly making goals and variables bounded at both ends and expressing them as scaled variables within the bounded range as shown below and secondly to normalize the contributions to the goals so that probabilities add to one, this is a way of ensuring finite additivity instead of a countable one and it ensures that proper weights are given to the interactive goals with non interactive ones.

Scaled Goal = (Unscaled goal – Lower Bound)/(Upper Bound-Lower Bound), similarly for variables.

The need for this normalization arises because pure liquid specie need to obey additivity and probabilities must lie between zero and one. However, predicted interactions may some times end up leaving a residual in the pure liquid state when purified from an initially mixed state or the other way round. This is very analogous to what quantum information theorists are now finding in experimental data on pure and mixed states and entanglement distillation. Two molecules of same liquid may have attractive or repulsive parts, bringing neighbours close or repulsing them leading to an element of non additivity in the Interactions. This is where compound probability could be used, but through energy balance; not in any other purely mathematical way.

Let us close this part with two quick examples of liquid systems (Shown in Table 2) that involve heterogeneous interactions (Gmehling & Onken. (1977) and graph their behaviour.

Table 2. The deviant liquid mixtures

Mixture	Substances involved
1	Acetone (1-1), Chloroform(1-2)
2	Acetone (2-1), Methanol (2-2)

The liquid activity coefficient is a measure of deviation of the mixture from ideal behaviour where perfect countably additive Boltzmann Gibbs entropy applies. Values greater than unity are reported for mixture 1, less than unity for mixture two. This graph (Figure 3) shows physical example of what is termed hypothetically existent hyperbolic probability law by Khrennikov. A. (2005). But the mixture specificity of the extent of hyperbolicity indicated by the data says, one could not state hyperbolic probability law was the causal set for this behaviour, but other complex system characteristics are. There are voluminous further weird (eg two liquid phases like Kerosene-water, azeotropy etc.) and very varied real physical data in the Dechema series gathered in Gmehling & Onken. (1977).

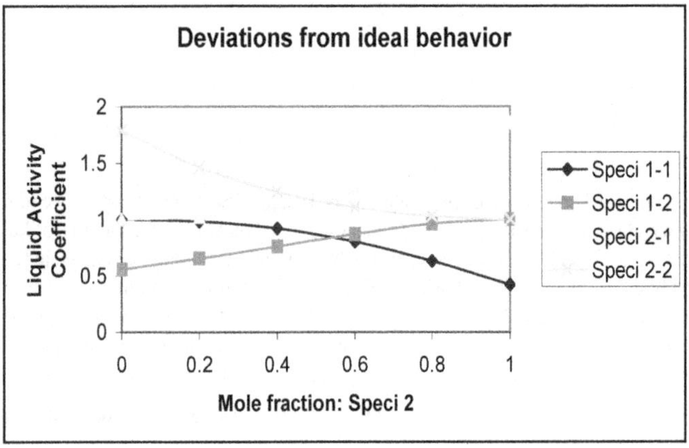

Figure 3 The plot of deviant liquid mixtures

The real world is far from ideal and above analogies we made here rather speculatively relying on Tsallis, C. & Souza A. M. C. (2003). Stability of entropy for superstatistics. *Physics Letters A 319*, 273-278.

Van der Waals (1894) theories are gradually turning out to be true in quantum domain as found by Castorina, Riccobene, & Zappala (2005). How are such observations going to be addressed within quantum information theory?

Quantum Information Theory

It is clear that for Tsallis entropy to be valid, non additivity must be valid. We will look into the evolution of additivity aspect in Quantum Information theory.

The Qubit

Quantum information is fundamentally different in character to classical computing information. Classical computing information is in bits, probabilistic information works in pbits and quantum information is in qubits. (See Figure 4.)

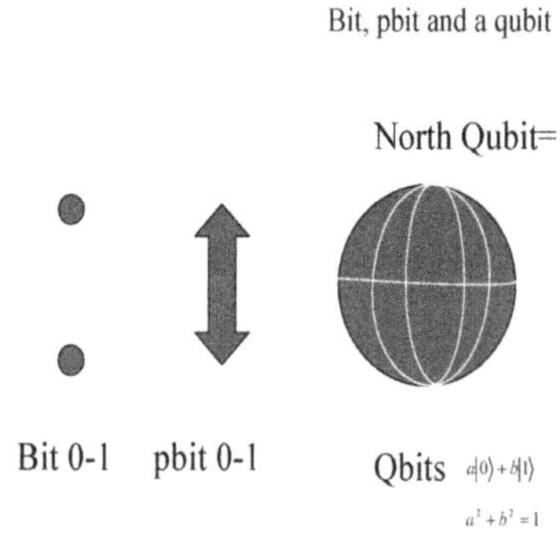

Figure 4 The bit, pbit and qubit

Visually, the qubits can be shown on a Bloch sphere, where infinitely many values between zero and one could be taken up, whereas a pbit takes only fractional values on the strip from zero to one and bit just takes two very limited values, zero and one. Due this fundamental difference in the representation of information, Shannon's proof that a communication channel has a well defined information carrying capacity and the formula he gives for it have to be modified.

Significance of Entanglement

The fields of quantum computing, teleportation and cryptography are feasible only because of what is called quantum entanglement. (See Table 3.) Keyl M. (2002) gives a vivid demonstration of this.

Table 3 Significance of entanglement

SR NO	QUANTUM OPERATION	WITHOUT ENTANGLEMENT	WITH ENTANGLEMENT
1	JOINT MEASURING DEVICE (E.G. MOMENTUM, POSITION): HISENBERG'S PRINCIPLE	NO	YES, WHEN POVM AVERAGES ARE USED; VIOLATION OF BELL INEQUALITIES,
2	QUANTUM CLONING OR COPYING	1 IS NO HENCE NO	YES, BECAUSE 1 IS YES
3	TELEPORTATION	1 IS NO HENCE NO	YES, BECAUSE 1 IS YES
4	DENSE CODING	1 IS NO HENCE NO	YES, BECAUSE 1 IS YES
5	ERROR CORRECTION	1,2,3,4 NO HENCE NO	YES, BECAUSE 1 IS YES

Measurement of State

More correct statement of Hisenberg's principle is that velocity and momentum cannot be projectively measured together. By Gleason's theorem (Caves C., C. Fuchs C., Manne K., Rennes J. (2003) and Born's rule, measurements of quantum variables are possible on Hilbert spaces of dimension greater than two. This measurement is usually made as a positive operator valued measurement (POVM). Those who utilize quantum computing usually resort to its operational vision. That is:

1 Probability is interpreted in a Bayesian manner; in a non-contextual fashion. Frequency interpretation is not used.

2 There is no attempt to insist on mixed state being convex as were the pure states;

There is no attempt made to defend use of many world's interpretation of quantum mechanics that is involved. The wave function collapse issue in this approach is handled by making the observer a part of the superposition of states. The state vector is objective and inclusion of observer keeps the whole system objective as far as probabilities are concerned. Though objective, the measurement cannot say what was measured or the outcome in each branch of the many worlds. This is an instance of the axiom of choice (http://en.wikipedia.org/wiki/Axiom_of_choice).

Distinguishability

To use the quantum information one must be able to distinguish between two different states of it. This can only be done by statistical comparison of distributions of measurement results. Thus methods as tabulated in Table 4 are needed.

Table 4 The measures of distinguishability

Measures of distinguishability	For Probability Distributions	For Quantum states
Probability of error	$P_e = \sum_{b=1}^{n} \min\{\pi_0 p_0(b), \pi_1 p_1(b)\}$	$P_e(\rho_0 \vert \rho_1) = \min_{E_b} \sum_{b=1}^{n} \min\{\pi_0 tr(\rho_0 E_b), \pi_1 tr(\rho_1 E_b)\}$
Relative information	$K(p_0 / p_1) = \sum_{b=1}^{n} p_0(b) \ln\left(\frac{p_0(b)}{p_1(b)}\right)$	$K(\rho_0 / \rho_1) = \max_{E_b} \sum_{b=1}^{n} tr(\rho_0 E_b) \ln\left(\frac{tr(\rho_0 E_b)}{tr(\rho_1 E_b)}\right)$
Renyi overlaps	$F_\alpha(p_0 / p_1) = \sum_{b=1}^{n} p_0(b)^\alpha p_1(b)^{1-\alpha}$	$F_\alpha(\rho_0 / \rho_1) = \min_{E_b} \sum_{b=1}^{n} (tr(\rho_0 E_b))^\alpha (tr(\rho_1 E_b))^{1-\alpha}$
Fidelity	$F_{0.5}(p_0 / p_1) = \sum_{b=1}^{n} \sqrt{p_0(b)}\sqrt{p_1(b)}$	$F_{0.5}(\rho_0 / \rho_1) = \min_{E_b} \sum_{b=1}^{n} \sqrt{tr(\rho_0 E_b)}\sqrt{tr(\rho_1 E_b)}$
Mutual information	$= H(\pi_0 p_0 + \pi_1 p_1) - \pi_0 H(p_0) - \pi_1 H(p_1)$	
Accessible information		$I(\rho_0 \vert \rho_1) = \max_{E_b} \sum_{b=1}^{n} (\pi_0 tr(\rho_0 E_b) \ln\left(\frac{tr(\rho_0 E_b)}{tr(\rho E_b)}\right) +$ $+ \pi_1 tr(\rho_1 E_b) \ln\left(\frac{tr(\rho_1 E_b)}{tr(\rho E_b)}\right))$

The accessible information is bounded above and below. The upper bound of accessible information is the Holevo bound. Accessible information is limited by Von Neumann entropy. It equals Shannon's entropy only when the qubits are orthogonal in the quantum state space; for non-orthogonal qubits, it is less than Shannon's entropy. Both Von Neumann and Shannon entropies are additive.

It is clear from Table 3 **Significance of entanglement** that entanglement is what enables quantum computing, teleportation, dense coding, error correction and cryptography. It is necessary to have a measure of entanglement to assess if entanglement in a certain system is sufficient for a given task. Qualities expected of an ideal entanglement measure are introduced through a series of axioms below.

Axioms and Additivity

To quantify entanglement is to associate a positive real number to each state of finite dimensional bipartite system. This is an axiom A0 and has obvious connection to measure defined by Amenta N., Bern M., Eppstein D., & Teng S. H. (2000) and measure as in functional analysis and that of Kolmogorov. (See Table 5)

Table 5 The axioms of quantum information theory

Axiom	Quantum Information theory	Measure theory
A1	Entanglement vanishes on separable and takes a maximum on maximally entangled states.	
A2	measure of entanglement has to be monotonic i.e. cannot increase under Local operations and classical two way communications.	Measure be monotonic
A2a	The measure be invariant under local unitaries.	Do
A3	a convex function	a convex function
A4	It is continuous	it is continuous
A5	Additive	Additive
5a	Sub additive	
5b	Weak additivity	
5c	a regularization exists for it Daubechies I. & Klauder J. R. (1985).	a regularization exists Wiener, N. (1923)

Table 6 shows status of all entanglement measures currently around in the literature vis-à-vis axioms A0-5. Y stands for valid, X for not valid and ? for unproven.

Table 6 Measures of entanglement vis-à-vis axioms

		A_0	A_1	A_2	A_3	A_4	A_5	A_{5a}	A_{5b}
E_D	Entanglement of distillation	Y	Y	Y	?	?	X	Y	Y
E_C	Entanglement cost	Y	Y	Y	?	?	?	?	Y

E_F	Entanglement of formation	Y	Y	Y	Y	Y	?	Y	?
E_R	Relative entropy of entanglement	Y	Y	Y	Y	Y	?	Y	X

It is clear that additivity A5 is not explicitly listed as a proven.

A Holevo channel can be defined using Von Neumann entropy functional. Maximizing the Holevo capacity over all probabilistic ensembles of a set of quantum states gives the information carrying capacity of that set of quantum states. When inputs entangled between different channel uses are allowed, the question of additivity arises. The additivity issues presented in various entries in Tables 4, 5 & 6 in several different forms, have been shown to be equivalent by Shor, P. W. (2003).

Equivalence of additivity questions in Quantum Information Theory

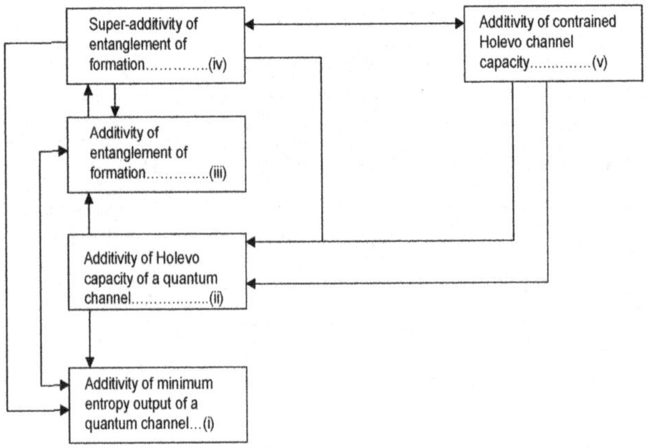

Figure 5 Tautologies of Additivity

Statement equalities (ii)=(i), (ii)=(iii), (iii)=(iv), (iv)=(iii), (i)=(iii), (iii)=(i), (iv)=(i), (iv)=(ii), (v)=(ii), (v)=(iv) and (iv)=(v) have been proven so far. If any one of the statements is true, all five are true. That makes them all tautologies. Interestingly, Table 5 shows sub-additivity of the entanglement of formation and only the entanglement of distillation to be non-additive. Other three measures are conjectured to be additive, but not proven.

Interaction and Entanglement

It is clear from liquids theory that for interacting systems, the entropy may not be additive. A normalization step that is specific to the system concerned is then needed to ensure that probabilities add up to unity. In case of quantum entanglement, the situation could be claimed to be different. But is it? Do we have extensive data on many qubit systems? The interaction here is between subsystems in the phase plane rather than between two different interacting participants. This means the entropies can potentially be thought to form from incomplete q deformation that tends to unity to eventually recover the Von Neumann entropy and obey Holevo bound.

This somehow suggests non additivity is valid in quantum domain. This has been the justification for those staking claims that Tsallis entropy is valid in quantum mechanics domain. However, as we have seen already the additivity is axiomatic. Extensive numerical search has thus far supported additivity axiom Hayashi, H., Maysumoto, K., Ruskai. M. B. et al. (2004). Perhaps the key to this is energy balance in the quantum domain. Where do the interactions between fermions and bosons fall i.e. to the right or to the left side of the interactions picture showed before?

Conclusion

No experimentation is yet documented in support of Tsallis entropy in the pure science domain. Frank, T. D. & Friedrich, R. (2004). have suggested one experiment. Interactions and their impact should be explicitly introduced into the system and analyzed. Entropy in non-homogeneous systems is not additive. Theorizations in quantum information theory are still based on few qubits. It is not clear what will be the impact of many body interactions on theories. Based on Cartan's topology, measure theory and projective geometry, for non-interacting and homogeneous reversible or irreversible continuous systems, the entropy form of Shannon-Gibbs-Boltzmann is the correct form.

In quantum information theory, the additivity issue is unresolved but Kolmogorov's measure theory is philosophically clear that non additivity means non measurable sets and any theory without additivity is simply not admissible. In function spaces unless small infinitesimal increment is "yet finitely non zero, quantized… discrete; infinities are regularized away, continuity and countable additivity hold", not all integrals that have non zero answers can be worked out.

In the non-interacting as well as interacting processes, functionally more important than the form of entropy is the concept of information loss (free energy) minimization. Form follows function.

References

Abe S. & Suzuki N. (2003) Gutenberg Richter Law for Internetquakes, *Physica A, 319*, 552-556. Retrieved 1 September 2005 from http://www.loc.gov/rr/scitech/mysteries/geese.html

Abe S. (2004 June 15). Stability analysis of generalized entropies and *q*-exponential distributions. *Physica D, 193*(1-4), 84-89.

Abe S. (2004 December). Quantum q-divergence. *Physica A , 344*, 359-365.

Abe S. & Okamoto Y. (Eds). (2001). *Nonextensive statistical mechanics and its applications*. Berlin, Heidelberg: Spinger Verlag.

AIChE CCPS. (2000). *Guidelines for chemical process quantitative risk analysis* (2nd ed.). AIChE, The Center for Chemical Process Safety.

Amenta N., Bern M., Eppstein D., & Teng S. H. (2000). Regression depths and center point, discrete and computational geometry 23:305-323. Retrieved 1 September 2005 from http://math.stanford.edu/comptop/references/abet.pdf

Angelani L., Casetti L., Pettini M., Ruocco G., & Zamponi F. (2004). Topology and phase transitions: from an exactly solvable model to a relation between topology and thermodynamics. Retrieved 1 September 2005 from http://arxiv.org/pdf/cond-mat/0406760 v1 30 June

Balasubramanian, V. (1996). Geometric formulation of Occam's razor for inference of parametric distributions, Available at http://arxiv.org/adap-org/PS_cache/9601/9601001.pdf v1 8 Jan [Accessed 1 Sep 05]

Boswell, C. & Glasser, M. L. (2005). solvable sextic equations; Available at http://arxiv.org/PS_cachee/math-ph/pdf/0504/0504001.pdf v1, 1 Apr [Accessed 1 Sep 05]

Boyden III, E. S. (1999). Quantum computation: theory and implementation. (BS physics, BS Electrical engineering and computer science, MS Electrical engineering and computer science multiple degree thesis, pp 15 of 181, MIT, 7 May. Available at http://www.media.mit.edu/physics/publications/theses/99.05.esb.pdf [Accessed 1 Sep 05]

Castorina, Riccobene, & Zappala (2005). Non commutative dynamics and roton like spectra of bosonic and fermionic and condensates. *Physics letters A 337*, 437-468.

Caves C., C. Fuchs C., Manne K., Rennes J. (2003). Gleason type derivations of the quantum probability rule for generalized measurements available at http://arxiv.org/abs/quant-ph/0306179 v1 26 Jun [Accessed 1 Sep 05].

Cheeseman, P. & Kanefsky, T. (1991). Where the hard problems really are. Proceedings of the *12th international joint conference on Artificial Intelligence* IJCAI-91, Vol 1, pp 331-337, Morgan Kaufmann

Cheney, W. & Kincaid, D. (1985). *Numerical mathematics and computing.*

Daubechies I. & Klauder J. R. (1985). Quantum mechanical path integrals with Wiener measures for all polynomial Hamiltonians. *Journal of Mathematics and Physics, 26*, 2239-2256.

Dey, G. & Edelsbrunner. (n.d.). Computational Topology available at http://citeseer.ist.psu.edu/cache/papers/cs/128/http:zSzzSzwww.ics.uci.eduzSz~eppsteinzSzginazSzDeyEdelsbrunnerGuha.pdf/dey99computational.pdf [Accessed 1 Sep 05]

Devetak I., & Staples A. E. (2004). Towards a unification of physics and information theory. Available at http://arxiv.org/PS_cache/quant-ph/pdf/0112/0112166.pdf v5, 3 April [Accessed 1 Sep 05]

Frank, T. D. & Friedrich, R. (2004). Estimating the nonextensivity of systems from experimental data: a nonlinear diffusion equation approach. *Physica A.*

Fuchs, C. A. (1995). Distinguishability and accessible information in quantum theory, doctoral dissertation, University of New Mexico, Albuquerque, Dec pp 44 of 174 http://arxiv.org/pdf/quant_ph/9601020[Accessed 1 Sep 05]

Fuchs, C. A. (1996), Distingusihability and accessible information in quantum theory; PhD Dissertation available at http://arxiv.org/pdf/quant_ph/9601020 v1, 23 Jan [Accessed 1 Sep 05]

Gell-Mann, M. & Tsallis (Eds). (2004). *Non extensive entropy: interdisciplinary applications.* New York: Oxford University Press.

Gerhard Knieper. (1995). Volume growth, entropy and the geodesic stretch. *Mathematical Research Letters, 2*, 39-58

Gmehling & Onken. (1977). Vapour liquid equilibrium data collection. *DECHEMA Chemistry Data Series, vol ,1* (parts 1-10), Frankfurt.

Gross, D. H. E. (2004), Classical equilibrium thermo-statistics, "Sancta sanctorum of statistical mechanics from nuclei to stars." *Physica A 340*, 76-84

Gupta, R. & Kundu. (2003). Discriminating between Weibull and generalized exponential distributions. *Computational Statistics and DataAanalysis, 43*, 179-196

Halpern & Fagin. (1992). Two views of belief: belief as generalized probability and belief as evidence. In Halpern & Fagin, *Artifical Intelligence 54*, 275-317 available at http://www.almaden.ibm.com/cs/people/fagin/ai92.pdf [Accessed 1 Sep 05]

Hayashi, H., Maysumoto, K., Ruskai. M. B. et al. (2004). Qubit channels which require four inputs to achieve capacity: implications for additivity conjectures. Available at http://arxiv.org/PS_cache/quant-ph/pdf/0403/0403176.pdf v2 26 Aug [Accessed 1 Sep 05]

Kaniadakis, Lissia, & Scarfone. (2004). Two parameter deformations of logarithm, exponential and entropy: a consistent framework for statistical mechanics. Available at http://arxiv.org/pdf/cond-mat/0409683 v1 26 Sept [Accessed 1 Sep 05]

Ke Xu & Wei Li (2000). The SAT phase transition, National laboratory of Software Development Environment; NNSF Grant 69433030. Available at http://www.cs.cmu.edu/afs/cs/project/jair/pub/volume12/xu00a.pdf [Accessed 1 Sep 05]

Keyl M. (2002) Fundamentals of quantum information theory. *Physics Reports 369*, 431-538. Retrieved from www.elsevier.com/locate/phyreps

Khrennikov. A. (2005). Reconstruction of quantum theory on the basis of the formula of total probability. Available at http://arxiv.org/PS-cache/pdf/quant-ph/0302/0302194 v4 24 Mar [Accessed 1 Sep 05]

Kiehn, R. M. (2004). Entropy production and irreversible processes –from the perspective of continuous topological evolution. Available at mdpi.org, Entropy, 6, 262-292 http://www.mdpi.org/entropy/papers/e6030262.pdf [Accessed on 1Sep 05]

Kiehn, R. M. (2005). Non equilibrium systems and irreversible processes, adventures in applied topology, Vol 1, non equilibrium thermodynamics from the perspective of continuous topological evolution. [Self published].

Kiehn, R. M. (n.d.), Point set topology. Available at Cartan's corner http://www22.pair.com/csdc/car/carhomep.htm[Accessed 1 Sep 05]

Kojadinovic, I., Marichal, J. L., & Roubens, M. (2005). An axiomatic approach to the definition of the entropy of discrete Choquet capacity. *Information Sciences, 172*, 131-153.

Lee, C. F. & Wolpert, D. (2004). Product distribution theory for control of multi-agent systems, AAMAS04, July 19-23, 2004, New York. Available at http://www.aamas2004.org/proceedings/065_leec_product_distribution.pdf [Accessed 1 Sep 05]

Liau, C. J. (2002). A modal logic framework for multi agent belief fusion. Available at http://arxiv.org/pdf/cs.AI/0201020 v1, 23 Jan, section 5.3 of the article [Accessed 1 Sep 05]

Lovejoy, S. & Schertzer, D. (2004). Space time complexity and multi fractal predictability. *Physica A 338*, 73-186.

Monasson, R., Zecchina, S., Kirkpatrick, B., Selman, L. & Troyansky. (1999). Determining computational complexity from characteristic phase transitions, *Nature, 400*, 133-137. Available at http://www.lpt.ens.fr/~monasson/Articles/a25.pdf.gz

Percus, A. G. & Martin, O. (1998). Scaling universalities of kth-nearest neighbour distances on closed manifolds. Available at http://arxiv.org/pdf/math.DG/9802117 v1 25 Feb [Accessed 1 Sep 05]

Salgado, R. (2002). Some identities for the quantum measure and its generalizations. Available at http://arxiv.org/pdf/gr-qc/9903015 v2 14 Jun [Accessed 1 Sep 05]

Saul L. K., Jaakkola T., & Jordan M. I. (1996). Mean field theory for sigmoidal belief networks. *Journal of Artificial Intelligence Research, 4*, 61-76 available at http://www-2.cs.cmu.edu/afs/cs/project/jair/pub/volume4/saul96a.pdf [Accessed 1 Sep 05]

Shor, P. W. (2003). Equivalence of additivity questions in quantum information theory. Available at http://arxiv.org/pdf/quant-ph/0305035 v4 3 Jul [Accessed 1 Sep 05]

Tsallis, C. (1988). Possible generalization of Boltzmann-Gibbs statistics. *Journal of Stat Physics, 52*, 479.

Tsallis, Baldovin, & Schulze. (2003). Non standard entropy production in the standard map. *Physica A, 320*, 184-192.

Tsallis C., Lambert P. W., & Prato D. (2001). A non extensive critical phenomenon scenario for quantum entanglement. *Physica A, 295*, 158-171.

Tsallis C., Plastino, & Zhang. (1997). Power law sensitivity to initial conditions – new entropic representation. *Chaos, Solitons and Fractals, 8*(6), 885-891.

Tsallis, Rapisarda, Baranger, & Latora. (2000). The rate of entropy increase at the edge of chaos. *Physics Letters A, 273*, 97-103

Tsallis, C. & Souza A. M. C. (2003). Stability of entropy for superstatistics. *Physics Letters A 319*, 273-278.

Van der Waals Diderik Johannes (1894) Z. Phys. Chem. Vol 13, 716

Wali, K. C. (1991). *Chandra: A biography of S. Chandrasekhar.* Chicago: University of Chicago Press.

West, B. J. (2004). Comments on the renormalization group, scaling and measures of complexity. *Chaos, Solitons and Fractals, 20*, 33-144.

Westerberg, Hutchison, Motard, & Winter. (1985). *Process flowsheeting*, (pp. 36-42). Cambridge University Press, reprint.

Wiener, N. (1923). Differential space. *Journal of Mathematics and Physics, 2*, 131-174.

Williamson, J. (1999). Countable additivity and subjective probability, March22, available at http://citeseer.ist.psu.edu/cache/papers/cs/28876/http:zSzzSzwww.kcl.ac.ukzSzipzSzjonwilliamsonzSz1999zSzpai_jw_99_a.pdf/williamson99countable.pdf [Accessed 1 Sep 05]

Wolpert, D. (2003). Product distribution field theory. Available at http://arxiv.org/pdf/cond-mat/0307630 v1 25 Jul [Accessed 1 Sep 05]

Wolpert, D. (2004). Information theory – The bridge connecting bounded rationality game theory and statistical physics. http://arxiv.org/pdf/cond-mat/0402508 v1 19 Feb [Accessed 1 Sep 05]

Yamano, T. (2004). A statistical measure of complexity with nonextensive entropy, *Physica A 340*, 131-137.

Zhang. (2004). Phase transitions and backbones of the asymmetric travelling salesman problem. *Journal of Artificial Intelligence Research, 21*, 471-497, available at http://www-2.cs.cmu.edu/afs/cs/project/jair/pub/volume21/zhang04b.pdf [Accessed 1 Sep 05]

Appendix 1

The q deformed logarithm and its inverse function are defined as below:

$Ln_q(x)=(x^{1-q}-1)/(1-q)$; Inverse $e_q=(1+(1-q)x)^{1/(1-q)}$, when $1+(1-q)x>0$ and $e_q=0$, otherwise.

Tsallis entropy is S_q=Sum up [$p_i Ln_q(1/p_i)$]

In order to introduce the q generalization into the mean field theory, an entire branch called "q deformed mathematics" needs to be evolved on following mathematical functional lines:

The q Trignometric functions: $Cos_q\theta = \dfrac{e_q^{i\theta} + e_q^{-i\theta}}{2}$; $Sin_q\theta = \dfrac{e_q^{i\theta} - e_q^{-i\theta}}{2i}$

A q Complex number : $Z_q = re_q^{i\theta} = r(Cos_q\theta + iSin_q\theta)$

A q gamma function: $\Gamma_q = \int_0^\infty x^{-1} e_q^{n-x} dx; n > 0$

A q Bessel function: $J_{pq}(x) = (\frac{x}{2})^p \sum_{k=0}^{\infty} \frac{(-1)^k (x/2)^{2k}}{k!\Gamma_q(p+k)}$ when p is an integer.

It is clear that "q generalized projective geometry" will result from the q generalized sin functions above introduced into Pascal's Hexagram (http://www.mathpages.com/home/kmath543/kmath543.htm). These q generalizations fall back to their respective standard mathematical counterpart functions as q tends to unity.

These functions follow standard Lemma as applicable to such functions.

Appendix 2

This appendix lists the probable source of Tsallis's inspiration in evolving his formula listed in Appendix 1. Predictably, it is the derivation of the entropy based on information theory. We will not reproduce the derivation that has been reproduced in many theses. e. g. Fuchs, C. A. (1996), Boyden III, E. S. (1999). but display two of its key steps and state that this derivation is not complete unless the unity limit of q factor of Tsallis is taken.

$$H(p(x) = (2^{1-q} - 1)^{-1} \left\{ \sum_{i=1}^{n} p_i^q - 1 \right\}$$

$$\underset{q->1}{Lt}[H(p(x)] = \underset{q->1}{Lt}[(2^{1-q} - 1)^{-1} \left\{ \sum_{i=1}^{n} p_i^q - 1 \right\}]$$

$$H(p) = -\sum_{x} p(x) Lg_2(p(x))$$

Then we have no new entropy other than that of Boltzmann-Gibbs-Von Neuman. Incomplete derivation, when limit is not taken cannot make a new definition. Neither is this incompleteness very Goedelian nor is it any improvement over Prigogine who talked about self-organized multiple stationary states far from equilibrium (Forman Robin's home page How many equilibria are there: An introduction to Morse Theory, available at http://math.rice.edu/~forman/.). The historical root cause of the problem is neither Herr Planck nor Herr Boltzmann justified their choice of logarithm by a derivation. A logarithm links topological volume to additivity making it a true measure. Choice of form follows the functional need, and did not need a derivation. Shannon's work is chronologically latest, prior to that is Von Neuman's quantum mechanics based definition. Boltzmann Planck's work was the earliest. The definition of entropy is about topological volume growth, not about statistics or distributions.

Biographies

Dr Samuel Sambasivam is the Chairman of the Department of Computer Science of Azusa Pacific University. Professor Sambasivam has done extensive research, publications, and presentations in both computer science and mathematics. His research interests include optimisation methods, expert systems, fuzzy logic, client/server, Databases and genetic algorithms. He has taught computer science and mathematics courses for over 24 years. Professor Sambasivam has run the regional Association of Computing Machinery (ACM) Programming Contest for six years. He has developed and introduced several new courses for computer science majors. Prof Sambasivam teaches Database Management Systems, Information Structures, and Algorithm Design, Microcomputer Programming with C++, Discrete Structures, Client/Server Applications, Advanced Database Applications, Applied Artificial Intelligence, JAVA and other courses. Professor Sambasivam coordinates the Client/Server Technology.

Vijay D. Bodas is Technical Services Manager with Sud-chemie AG's Bahrain office. He has a well-diversified background as a Professional Engineer registered in the state of Oregon, USA and a member of the Chartered Institute of Management Accountants. His work background includes multi-country exposure to construction and start up of grass roots chemical production facilities, process engineering, process control and systems engineering, process safety, hazard and risk management and strategic business evaluations in chemical manufacturing sector. The work here is continuation of the work carried out towards partial fulfilment of MS (IT) requirements of the University of Liverpool.

Effectiveness of Self-selected Teams: A Systems Development Project Experience

Elsje Scott and Michael Pollock
University of Cape Town, Cape Town, South-Africa

escott@commerce.uct.ac.za mpollock@commerce.uct.ac.za

Abstract

The third year systems development group project forms an essential part of the Information Systems major at the University of Cape Town. The field of Information Technology / Information Systems requires the maintenance or development of large information systems which often involves complex tasks. As effective teams are at the core of high performance organizations exposure to teamwork is important in the preparation of students for the real world environment. To ensure high quality products and limit high failure rates of projects, teams should be carefully selected. This paper explores existing team selection approaches and discusses the mechanisms put in place in the systems development group project with the emphasis on self-selected teams as a sound base for team formation. It further reports on the incorporation of the criteria defining effectiveness and effective teams into the course to prepare individual members for the rigours of industry.

Keywords: Group projects, self-selected, effectiveness, productivity, student enjoyment, performance, skills.

Introduction

The challenges of a fast-changing and competitive environment compel organizations across all business sectors to be pro-active and adapt. In many cases team-working has been introduced to cope effectively with these changes (Partington & Harris, 1999). Teams in the workplace not only have a profound effect on productivity, but also make organizations more responsive and have several intrinsic benefits for both the employees and customers (HR Focus, 2002; Katzenbach & Smith, 1993). According to Katzenbach & Smith (1993) "teams will become the primary unit of performance in high-performance organizations".

The field of Information Systems (IS) is heavily reliant on teamwork to improve the quality of information systems (Jones & Harrison, 1996). Many tasks that must be performed are unique and complex and thus require teams to possess a unique set of skills and knowledge (Waker, 2001). Most software projects in industry are accomplished by teams of professionals rather than by individuals due to the size of these projects but also because teams tend to perform better than individuals (Brown & Dobbie, 1999). Often technological issues receive most of the focus in an effort to improve IS project performance, while soft issues such as team dynamics receive little attention. The high failure rate of IS projects also provides an indication that the performance of IS team members is dependent on other members of the team and not on technical skills alone (De Marco & Lister, 1999). Finding innovative ways of designing IS project development teams to improve teamwork could thus result in more effective teams and thus higher performance overall (Leonard & Swap, 1999; Waker, 2001). Often organizations use one of many personality typing approaches to ensure diversity in team roles that may influence effectiveness and thus have a positive impact on task performance (Campion, Medsker & Higgs, 1993).

The importance of teamwork in industry demands universities to better prepare students for real life projects. One of the main benefits of team projects in tertiary education is to provide students with a unique experience of the multiple and diverse disciplines that are characteristic of the daily life of an Information Technology / Information Systems (IT/IS) specialist in industry (Scott, 2004). In addition to technical skills students also develop soft skills, like mutual respect for other team members, presentation and communication (Brown & Dobbie, 1999).

This paper explores the team selection structures and approaches as discussed in the literature in order to derive a sound base to support team selection from the perspective of the systems development group project course. Although students who have completed the course are of the opinion that the group project is one of their best and rewarding learning experiences – in over 90% of course evaluations students agreed very strongly that this was the case – during their undergraduate studies, it remains a demanding course with many deliverables and deadlines. Project teams should be supported and carefully monitored to ensure success. For this reason it is important to understand and investigate team effectiveness and the impact it has on performance. The paper will refer to the systems development group project as a *group project*, but the group of students working together on a specific project will be referred to as a team. The paper reports on the implementation of some of the guidelines for team effectiveness found in the literature, in the project course. Finally it highlights some limitations that currently exist, and proposes approaches and future research to address these limitations.

Teams

Team Structuring and Selection

DuBrin (2002) defines a group as "*a collection of people who interact with one another, are working towards a common purpose, and perceive themselves to be a group*". Katzenbach & Smith (1993) go further and define a team as a group that has a high degree of commitment from its members to achieving its goals and given objectives.

Much debate exists around the effective structuring of teams in a work environment. Teams can be structured in a variety of ways, and many formal structures have been developed for different purposes. Five distinct structures suggested by Mankin, Cohen & Bikson (1996) are shown below in Table 1.

Table 1: Team Structures (adapted from Mankin, Cohen & Bikson, 1996)

TEAM STRUCTURE	USES	CHARACTERISTICS
Work Teams	Designed to produce a specific product	Relatively permanent
Project Teams	Designed for once-off tasks	Systems Development Projects
Parallel Teams	Designed to deal with organizational issues without affecting structure.	Usually temporary.

Management Teams	Designed to guide the organization towards its objectives.	Usually permanent
Ad Hoc Network	Used by people sharing similar interests.	Usually an informal group

When deciding which structure to use for a team, the team morale, productivity and quality of product to be developed should also be taken into account (McLeod & Smith, 2001). From Mankin et al.'s (1996) study it seems natural that the once off student projects would fall under the Project Team structure.

The project teams are further more encouraged to be self-managed to a large degree. The Work in America Institute defines a self-directed work team as a "*small, semi-autonomous, interdependent group working towards shared goals, with [a] significant degree of cross training, and responsible for a relatively complete unit of work*" (HR Focus, 2002, p. 18). DuBrin (2002), similarly, defines self-managed work teams as a "*formally recognised group of employees ... responsible for an entire work process ... that delivers a product or service to an internal or external customer*". DuBrin (2002) further explains that self-managed teams tend to be far more productive with a higher level of overall performance due to the feeling of "ownership" instilled in each team member. Various instruments have been developed to identify characteristics of individual members of a team and the implementation of these to improve the effectiveness of the team (Broucek & Randell, 1996).

In IS, teams are an integral part of the systems development process, thus it is important to pay attention to the way teams are selected. There are various different approaches available to assist in the selection of team members and the forming of teams. These approaches include the Myers-Briggs Type Indicator, Belbin's Team Role theory, random selection, students' selection and lecturer selection.

The Myers-Briggs Type Indicator uses a questionnaire to measure an individual's personality. This measurement of four personality types focuses on how individuals direct their energy, how they view or receive information, how they make decisions, and how they organize their environment (Gifford, Henry & Schoenhof, 2003; Kaiser & Bostrom, 1982; Mason & Mitroff, 1973). The Myers-Briggs Type Indicator is regarded as a highly effective method of determining dominant personality traits within individuals. Research indicates that a team is likely to perform more effectively when it is formed by balancing the four Jungian personality types (Kaiser & Bostrom, 1982).

R. Meredith Belbin developed a similar method that measures how an individual's personality tends to fill each of the different roles in a team (Belbin, 1981; Henry & Stevens, 2002a, 2002b). This method helps to create balanced teams, which Gifford et al. (2003) believe potentially perform at a higher level. Belbin further argues that team members' sense of commitment grows stronger as they better understand their own roles within the team.

In a study by Henry (2000), it was found that personality testing is most effective when selecting members for student teams. Gifford et al. (2003) found that many student teams with similar skills and experience performed with varying levels of success. The lack of performance was believed to be a result of poor team development, which occurred due to the incompatibility of team members' personalities. This was a key finding as it showed that technical skills alone will not see a team performing well; the team selection and structure needs to be managed too. Gifford et al. (2003) state that it is not enough to simply place several highly skilled programmers and analysts together, but one must consider the "*personality characteristics ... that advance or impair the team effort and ultimately the final outcome of the project team*". There has been some research contradictory to Gifford et al. (2003), by Partington & Harris (1999) who found that highly diverse teams did not necessarily perform better, and Winter (2004) who found little correlation between role diversity and performance in his study on team role diversity in student computer science teams.

The other team selection approaches include random selection, which can be seen as unfair by students and result in ineffective teams due to students being unhappy with the selection; student selection, which can result in some very strong teams and some very weak teams; and lecturer selection, which is difficult to do well due to the amount of work involved in the process.

Despite this debate on best practices to support the diverse nature of teams, Scott et al. (1994) state that no single selection method is the best and that the selection criteria depend on the specific course, the demands placed on students and lecturers, the length of the course and the ability of the students involved.

The Impact of Team Effectiveness on Performance

A core element in evaluating and measuring teams is effectiveness. The 1998 Advanced Learner's Oxford dictionary defines effectiveness as: "*having the desired effect; producing the intended result... making a strong and pleasing impression*". Gibson, Zellmer-Bruhn & Schwab (2003) describe effectiveness as "*the number of errors made*". Thus, effectiveness can be defined as the product of clear goals and objectives whereby a pleasing impression has been created through competent labor, and where there has been a minimization of the number of errors made during the course of completing an objective. Further, effectiveness can also be understood as the team's ability to perform.

Belbin (2004) states that the effectiveness of a team is determined by the extent to which it "*meets its goals, maintains the satisfaction of its members and survives*". Cohen & Bailey (1997) add that effectiveness also encompasses the quality of the final product and the degree of enjoyment the members had of the project experience. Campion et al. (1993) confirm this by stating that effectiveness incorporates three important criteria, namely: productivity, employee satisfaction and manager judgement. In using productivity as a measure of effectiveness Campion et al. (1993) refer to the collection and the regular monitoring of different measures as indicators of the amount of work completed. Therefore, it can be concluded that team effectiveness can be determined by:

- **Enhanced productivity as a result of the increased levels of interaction between team members arising from teamwork**
- **The degree to which team members enjoy the project experience**
- **The quality of the final product produced by the team in achieving the desired goal**

But just knowing what encompasses effective teams is not enough to achieve them; effective management is needed. This is echoed by Hackman (1987) who suggests that "*many types of behavior can be productive; therefore, those who create and lead teams should focus on creating the right conditions for them to succeed, rather than trying to manage their behavior*". Thus, creating the correct environment for teams is crucial in providing an atmosphere in which effective teamwork is possible.

In this study, team effectiveness is measured by an instrument adapted from a survey developed by Francis & Young (1992), (see adapted questionnaire given in the Appendix). Through an extensive interviewing process Francis & Young (1992) established the main characteristics of effective teams and concurred that "*effective teamwork is the synthesis of apparently contrary forces*". They explain that the effectiveness and well-being of teams should be assessed by the teams themselves and developed a team-review survey to examine 12 key aspects of a team's effectiveness.

The Experience

The Systems Development Group Project

The third year systems development group project is the main deliverable of the capstone course of the IS major at the University of Cape Town. It has been developed and refined over a period of six years to integrate soft and hard skills. A comprehensive assessment strategy to enhance student learning and aid objective assessment of group performance forms an important component of this course (Scott & Van Der Merwe, 2003). In addition to the initiation of the group projects and the completion of the analysis and design phases, the first half of the course is also dedicated to a more formal skills transfer approach. During this time lectures, project management workshops, practical programming sessions and sessions on group conflict resolution take place. The second half of the course is dedicated to the building of the product. The project starts in February and has its final hand-in date in September. The project comprises eight interim deliverables culminating into three milestone deliverables and the final product. The project teams are expected to adhere to strict deadlines to complete the regular deliverables in order to monitor the progress of the team and enhance the quality of the final product. During the lifecycle of the project, teams have the opportunity to improve interim deliverables before re-working them into related milestone deliverables. The final product, which includes extensive documentation and the corresponding software application, is showcased to the public at an exhibition event once the final assessment procedures are completed. For many students this project is a first experience of a major team project and it is essential to pay attention to factors that impact the effectiveness and overall performance of the teams.

The group project mainly uses the self-selection approach whereby students select their own teams. This selection approach does not compromise too much on team diversity as it seems that diverse groups can be formed naturally. When problems are encountered with this approach, such as a number of students being left without teams, the lecturer selection approach is used. The skills of these remaining students are assessed and the students are assigned to teams by the lecturer.

In 2005 each of the 25 teams completed a team contract that included statements on code of conduct, participation, communication, meeting guidelines and problem solving at the offset of the project; as recommended by Schwalbe (2003). Every year teams use a two week period to find a sponsor in industry with a business problem that best fits the generic project brief. Student teams may tender for existing projects, should there be any available. Each team chooses roles for each of its members, including a project leader, head programmer, head documenter, communications officer and quality controller and is also assigned a faculty member acting as a project manager.

Instruments and Data Collection

Questions in the Francis & Young (1992) survey were posed initially to identify blockages that will inhibit the flow of energy and therefore hamper the performance of the teams. This survey was adapted to measure the effectiveness of the third year student project teams. For this purpose only nine of the question sections of the Francis & Young survey were included from the original twelve aspects; the remaining three sections were either not relevant or were contained within the nine sections. Some questions pertaining explicitly to corporate institutions were omitted. Specific questions on technical skills were included under the Skills heading as students are still in the process of developing these skills. Although vital for the success of the project a high level of competency in these skills cannot always be assumed for all students. In an educational environment mentors play an important role and some questions under the heading Team Support were used to establish the impact of the support of project manager and the sponsor on the effectiveness of the team. Table 2 exhibits the mapping of 9 headings of the team effectiveness survey used in the third year project onto the 12 aspects of the Francis & Young (1992) survey (see appendix for the questionnaire).

Table 2: Effectiveness measures mapped onto 12 aspects of Francis & Young (1992)

HEADINGS OF ADAPTED QUESTIONNAIRE	ASPECTS OF FRANCIS & YOUNG QUESTIONNAIRE
Clarity of roles, goals and objectives (CL)	Role clarity; Team achievement; Relevant corporate role
Leadership (L)	Effective team leadership
Competence (COMP)	Team achievement
Commitment (CMT)	Commitment; Positive climate; Team achievement
Communication (COMM)	Positive climate
Skills (S)	Choosing the members of a team
Team Support (TS)	Inter-team relationships
Creativity (Cr)	Team creativity
Achieving learning goals (ALG)	Positive climate; Team achievement; Effective meetings

This paper reports on data collected from 123 students, represented by 24 project teams of 5 members each and one team with only 3 members (see Table 3 below). The student survey, course evaluations and Francis & Young (1992) effectiveness questionnaire were sent to each individual student, while the six weekly update reports were sent to each group.

Table 3: Data collection instruments responses

INSTRUMENT	WHEN	SENT	RESPONSES	%
Student survey	April	123	123	100 %
Course evaluation 1	May	123	75	61 %
Course evaluation 2	September	123	112	91 %
6 x Weekly team update reports	July - August	150	126	84 %
Francis & Young effectiveness questionnaire	October	123	34	28 %
Performance results	April - October	123	123	100 %

To measure performance, marks composed of all the deliverables and assessment opportunities from the course were used (see Table 4).

Table 4: Assessment opportunities (adapted from Scott & van der Merwe, 2003)

COMPONENT	OCCURRENCE	GROUP / INDIVIDUAL	CONTRIBUTE TO FINAL MARK
Interim deliverables	8 - approx every 2 weeks	Group	Yes
Milestone deliverables	3 - approx every 6 weeks	Group	Yes
Weekly reports	Weekly	Group	No
Weekly project management meeting	Bi-weekly	Group	No
Sponsor meetings	When required	Group	No
Sponsor evaluations	Twice	Group	Yes
Course evaluation	Twice	Individual	No
Peer and self evaluations	When required and once as part of final assessment	Individual and Group	Yes (Final assessment)
Weekly Update reports	6 - from July to August	Group	No
Final presentation	Once	Group	Yes
Code review	Once	Group	Yes

Team Effectiveness

The Composition of Semi Self-Selected Teams

Although teams are mostly self-selected a faculty member in the department of Industrial Psychology facilitates and finalizes the team formation process. Student surveys filled out prior to the team selection process are used to assist the facilitator. In these surveys students are mainly required to list their strengths, weaknesses, skills and what they intend to contribute to the project and the team. The survey requires each respondent to rate him/herself on a scale from 1 to 10 (10 being best) on each of the following skills: Real Project Experience (RPE); Customer Interaction (CI); Research Skills (RS); Writing Skills (WS); Presentation Skills (PS); Programming Skills (PRGS); Project Management Software (PMS); Website Creation (WC) Leadership (L); Teamwork Facilitation (TF).

The data on each individual survey was captured and then grouped into the different teams. For every team all ratings greater than 6 (7 and more) in each skill category were counted to provide an indication of the diversity and competence of a team. Twelve teams indicated that they had one or more members per skills category with a rating above 6. The numbers in Table 5 indicate how many teams had no members with a rating of 7 or more for a specific skills category.

Five teams indicated that they lacked real project experience (RPE). This can be justified as the group project is a first encounter of a real life project for most of the teams. The lack in programming (PRGS), project management software (PMS) and web creations (WC) skills were addressed during the first half of the course by means of lectures, workshops and practical programming sessions. To empower students with advanced programming skills, a carefully guided pilot system was developed over eight programming sessions. Students obtained web development skills in a parallel e-Commerce course. Although the teams showed some diversity of the skills and experience that they had, the teams were generally on a balanced playing-field.

Table 5: The number of teams lacking skills in a specific skills category

RPE	CI	RS	WS	PS	PRGS	PMS	WC	L	TF
5	0	0	1	1	4	7	9	0	0

In order to gain insight into the effectiveness of each team involved in the study, a self-assessment survey was distributed to each member of that team. The survey focused on the core criteria, which according to Francis & Young (1992) contribute to an effective team. The team's level of effectiveness was then assessed by calculating their mean scores from the questionnaires. A high mean indicates that the team is highly effective, while a low mean indicates inherent weaknesses.

From the effectiveness questionnaire it was found that the *leadership* section had the highest mean across teams, with a mean of 82%, while the section on *creativity* followed some distance behind with a mean across teams of 64%. The section with the lowest mean across teams was found to be *achieving learning goals* with a mean of 42%. The means across teams for all of the sections can be seen in Table 6 below.

Table 6: Effectiveness means across teams

CL	L	COMP	CMT	COMM	S	TS	Cr	ALG
56%	82%	45%	52%	56%	58%	47%	64%	42%

Enhanced Productivity and Increased Levels of Interaction between Team Members

Campion et al. (1993) associated productivity measures with amount of work finished on a weekly basis. The third year group project uses an assessment strategy as depicted in Table 4 to assist students to complete tasks and deliverables on time and enhance productivity. The opportunity to improve interim deliverables before submitting them as milestone deliverables simultaneously enhances the quality of the product.

In addition to assessment opportunities several mechanisms are implemented throughout the course to make teams productive. Once a team has identified a sponsor and the related documents specifying the terms of reference and responsibilities are completed, students set up regular meetings with sponsors to understand the business problem and obtain the user requirements. It is required that they conduct regular team meetings and also meet with their respective project managers on a weekly or bi-weekly basis. Weekly reports are used to keep track of these meetings, reporting on new ideas, problems and resolutions. Microsoft (MS) Project Server 2003 is used with Microsoft Project 2003 to develop the individual project plans and to provide a secure environment for each team. Through its MS Project Web Access Interface, MS Project Server enables team members and stakeholders to collaborate, get access to project related documents and keep their project plans updated.

During the build phase, at least one representative of each team attends weekly class meetings and submits a weekly update report. All the teams except one, *Tri-Communications*, attended the meetings. *Tri-Communications* was the only team with less than 5 members, it had 3; but they appeared to be on track with their project as they obtained a 66% final project result. Advanced topics that might assist the building phase are also discussed. In 2005 each team had 6 opportunities to submit these reports that served as a "wellness" check and provided valuable information on the effectiveness and current performance of the respective teams. Teams reported on resolved and unresolved issues. They also indicated whether they were on target to finish the project within schedule, and whether they had team, project manager or sponsor problems. In those cases where problems existed, immediate action was taken after the meeting. Table 7 shows whether the teams were on target to finish the project within schedule during the build phase.

From the weekly update reports it was also found that 5 of the teams had consistent internal problems with team members. Three of these teams did not resolve these problems by the end of the project and team members were negatively affected by peer evaluations, which subtract marks from students who were judged by their fellow team members not to have performed adequately.

Table 7: Number of teams on target through the project build phase

NUMBER OF TEAMS	ON TARGET?
4	Yes
9	No
1	No, then Yes
3	Yes, then No
7	Combination of Yes and No
1	Didn't attend

The Team Members' Enjoyment of the Project Experience

A controlled and well-managed environment is necessary to create a safe space for creative development of project teams. A positive atmosphere is furthermore conducive to the productivity of teams, encourages enjoyment of the project experience, motivates teams to commit and achieve their goals.

At the end of the first and second halves of the course a course evaluation was conducted. Each student was handed an evaluation questionnaire to be completed individually. In Table 8 below, some of the questions that relate to the paper and their responses are listed. The questionnaire made use of a 6 point Likert scale, which is standardized across the department. The response percentages listed in Table 8 below indicate the percentage of students that answered the questions with the top two Likert scales, i.e. *excellent* and *very good*. In other words, the percentage of students that agreed most strongly with the statements in the questionnaires.

Table 8: Course evaluation responses

QUESTION	EVALUATION 1 RESPONSES	EVALUATION 2 RESPONSES
Usefulness of the project as a learning experience	91 %	90 %
Preparation for the IS profession	69 %	66 %
People and communication skills required	75%	62 %

Experience gained in handling project management issues	75 %	68 %
Effectiveness of course communication with regards to resolving project related issues	73 %	53 %

Numerous comments in the course evaluations indicated that despite the huge challenge of the project, students were highly motivated and committed and thoroughly enjoyed the experience. Many commented that the most positive aspect of the course was the learning experience with regard to communication with the sponsor, systems development, group conflict and work attitudes. The responses in Table 8 also reflect these opinions.

Quality of the Final Product Produced

In Figure 1 below it can be seen that all of the teams passed the project, scored above 50%, except for *Logix Solutions*, which scored 47%. 13 teams, over half of the total teams, scored above 65% for the project which points towards a high level of overall quality of the 2005 projects.

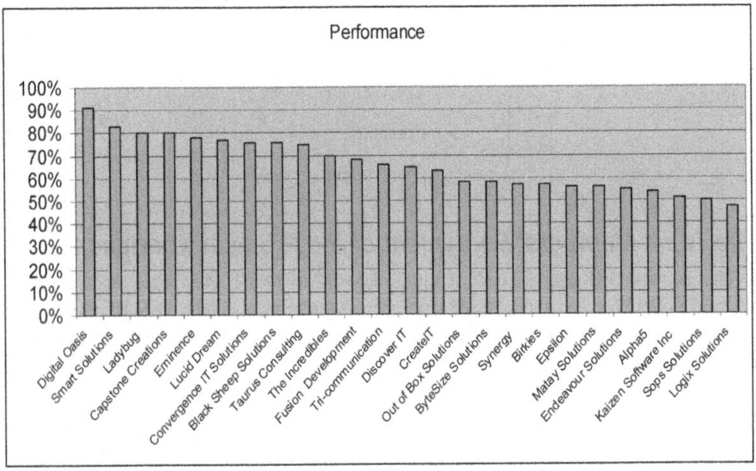

Figure 1: Final project results for each team

Sunstrom, De Meuse & Futrell, (1990) concur that one of the aspects of effectiveness is performance and therefore performance has a direct relationship to effectiveness (Katzenbach & Smith, 1992). To determine why the teams performed well and produced quality projects, the performance data was analyzed with the effectiveness data.

A correlation analysis between performance, taken from the final project result scored by each team, and the elements of effectiveness, from the Francis & Young (1992) questionnaire, revealed the strongest correlations to be between performance and competence being 0.68, followed by performance and skills with a score of 0.58, performance and creativity with 0.55, and performance and commitment with 0.52. This correlation matrix can be seen in Figure 2 below, where correlations below 0.5 can be disregarded as insignificant (Keller & Warrack, 2003).

	Clarity Of Roles, Goals and Objectives	Leadership	Competence	Commitment	Communication	Skills	Team Support	Creativity	Achieving Learning Goals	Performance
Clarity Of Roles, Goals and Objectives	1.00	-0.18	0.10	0.10	0.37	0.12	-0.06	0.17	0.48	0.03
Leadership	-0.18	1.00	-0.03	0.05	0.01	-0.37	-0.06	-0.15	0.33	-0.31
Competence	0.10	-0.03	1.00	0.92	0.07	-0.51	0.24	-0.71	0.32	-0.68
Commitment	0.10	0.05	0.92	1.00	-0.01	-0.35	0.29	-0.74	0.46	-0.52
Communication	0.37	0.01	0.07	-0.01	1.00	-0.07	0.21	-0.01	0.09	0.12
Skills	0.12	-0.37	-0.51	-0.35	-0.07	1.00	-0.07	0.44	0.04	0.58
Team Support	-0.06	-0.06	0.24	0.29	0.21	-0.07	1.00	-0.63	0.01	-0.19
Creativity	0.17	-0.15	-0.71	-0.74	-0.01	0.44	-0.63	1.00	-0.23	0.55
Achieving Learning Goals	0.48	0.33	0.32	0.46	0.09	0.04	0.01	-0.23	1.00	-0.27
Performance	0.03	-0.31	-0.68	-0.52	0.12	0.58	-0.19	0.55	-0.27	1.00

Figure 2: Correlation matrix of performance and elements of effectiveness

Of the fifteen teams that answered the effectiveness questionnaire, it can be seen in Figure 3 below that *Epsilon* rated itself that most effective, followed by *Kaizen Software Inc.* and *Fusion Development. Birkies* rated itself the least effective. Figure 3 below illustrates that there is no clear correlation between effectiveness, taken as a whole from all of the sections of the Francis & Young (1992) effectiveness questionnaire, and performance, taken as the final project result. While it does appear that the weaker teams rate themselves as highly effective, as in the cases of *Epsilon*, *Kaizen Software Inc.* and, to a lesser extent, *Endeavour Solutions*, this is not always the case, as can be seen by the teams of *Out Of Box Solutions* and *Birkies*. The teams that performed the best, i.e. the top six teams that answered the questionnaires, all rated themselves as having moderate to low effectiveness, i.e. within the lower half of the effectiveness rankings. These teams include *Smart Solutions*, *Ladybug*, *Capstone Creations*, *Eminence*, *Black Sheep Solutions* and *Convergence IT Solutions*.

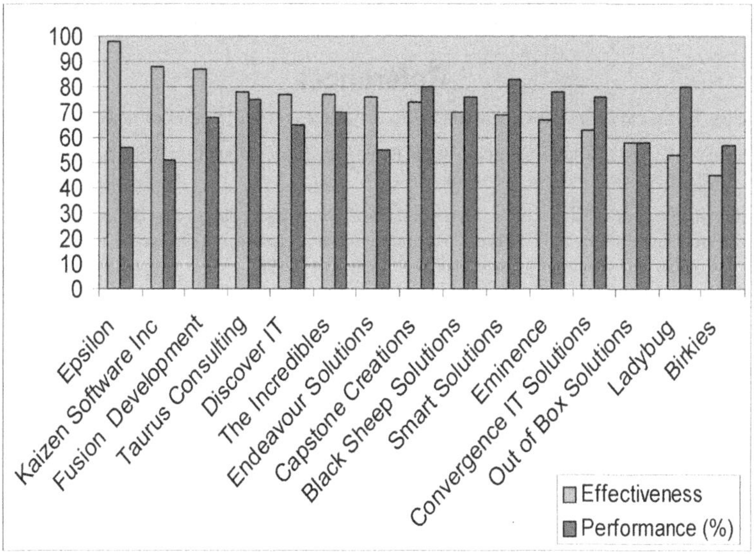

Figure 3: Effectiveness versus performance

From the data collected there is no indication as to why this occurs. But it could be that the weaker teams have unrealistic perceptions of their own abilities and tend to be over-optimistic about how well they work and the quality of their work. Stronger teams may be more restrained about their perceptions of their ability to work and their quality of work. This may lead to an overly pessimistic view of their abilities and thus a lower self-rating of their effectiveness.

Conclusion

The research presented in this paper has confirmed that the systems development group project creates a positive learning environment, provides a real-world experience and prepares students effectively for the rigours of industry.

Although there is merit in using the different approaches available to assist in the selection of teams, this paper has shown that self-selected team can be effective and that despite of team being self-selected a diverse range of skills were present in all the teams. The facilitation process during team formation has proved to be valuable and helped to complete the process timeously and efficiently.

Several sources in the literature agreed that team morale, productivity and the quality of the product to be developed are important elements of team work. These elements are represented in effectiveness criteria as defined by Campion et al. (1993) and were used to gauge the effectiveness of the student teams. A controlled and well-managed environment with regular assessment opportunities and reporting mechanisms encouraged increased levels of interactions between team members and enhanced the productivity of the teams. Despite the demanding nature of the group project the students coped with and enjoyed the challenges they were confronted with. The good performance of the teams overall and the quality of the final products led to a high level of effectiveness in the self-selected project teams. The students described the project experience with the keywords: vision, commitment and excellence.

This study opens the door for future research on teams with effectiveness, performance, role diversity and different selection approaches as key features.

References

Belbin, R.M. (1981). *Management teams: Why they succeed or fail.* Butterworth-Heinemann, Oxford.

Belbin, R.M. (2004). Belbin Team Roles. Belbin Home Page. Retrieved April 16, 2004 from http://www.belbin.com/belbin-team-roles.htm

Broucek, W.G. & Randell, G. (1996). An Assessment of the construct validity of the Belbin Self-Perception Inventory and Observer's Assessment from the perspective of the five-factor model. *Journal of Occupational and Organizational Psychology*, 69, 389-405.

Brown, J.& Dobbie, G. (1999). Supporting and evaluating team dynamic in group projects, *ACM SIGCSE Bulletin*, 31(1), 281-285.

Campion, M.A, Medsker, G.J. & Higgs, C.A. (1993). Relationships between work group characteristics and effectiveness: implications for designing effective work groups, *Personnel Psychology*, 46, 823-843.

Cohen, S.G. & Bailey, D.E. (1997). What makes teams work: group effectiveness research from the shop floor to the executive suite, *Journal of Management*, 23 (3), 239-290.

DeMarco, T. & Lister, T. (1999). *Peopleware, productive projects and teams.* 2nd Ed., Dorset House Publishing Corporation Inc., New York.

DuBrin, A.J. (2002). '1-15' in Fundamentals of Organizational Behavior, eds. Szilagyi, J., South-Western College Publishing, United States of America, 1-372.

Five Case Studies on Successful Teams. (2002). HR Focus , 79 (4), 18-19.

Francis, D. & Young, D. (1992). *Improving work groups: A practical manual for team building.* Pfeiffer & Co.

Gerstmann, P. (2004). Team roles: Individual & group effectiveness – FIRO Team Roles and Belbin Team-Roles contrasted. Retrieved November 7, 2005 from http://www.pgagroup.com/team-roles.cfm

Gibson, C.B., Zellmer-Bruhn, M.E. & Schwab, D.P. (2003). Team effectiveness across contexts, *Group & Organizational Management*, 28 (4), 444-474.

Gifford, S.S, Henry, S.M. & Schoenhof, P.K. (2003). Personality type considerations for programming teams in computer science classes. Retrieved April 16, 2004 from http://csgrad.cs.vt.edu/~sgifford/research/ptcpt.pdf

Hackman, J.R. (1987). *The design of work teams, Handbook of Organizational Behaviour.* Englewood Cliffs, NJ: Prentice Hall, 315-342.

Henry, S. (2000). Using software development teams in a classroom environment, *EBSCO Online Journal.*

Henry, S.M. & Stevens, K.T. (2002a). Analyzing software teams using Belbin's Innovative Plant Role. Retrieved November 7, 2005 from http://www.radford.edu/~kstevens2/ISTall.pdf

Henry, S.M. & Stevens, K.T. (2002b). Using Belbin's Leadership Role to improve team effectiveness. Retrieved November 7, 2005 from http://courses.cs.vt.edu/~cs4704/jss.pdf

Jones, M.C. & Harrison, H.W. (1996). Project team performance: An empirical assessment, *Information and Management*, 13, 57-65.

Kaiser, K.M. & Bostrom, R.P. (1982). Personality characteristics of MIS project teams: An empirical study and action-research design, *MIS Quarterly*, December 1982, 43-60.

Katzenbach, J.R. & Smith, D.K. (1992). Why teams matter, *McKinsey Quarterly*, 3, 3-27.

Katzenbach, J.R. & Smith, D.K. (1993). The discipline of teams, *Harvard Business Review*, 71 (2), 111-120.

Keller, G. & Warrack, B. (2003). Statistics for management and economics, Brooks/Cole, Division of Thomson Learning Inc., U.S.A.

Leonard D.A. & Swap W.C., (1999). *When sparks fly – Igniting creativity in groups.* Harvard Business School Press, Boston.

Mankin, D., Cohen, S.G. & Bikson, T.K. (1996). *Teams and technology: Fulfilling the promise of a new organization.* Boston, MA: Harvard Business School Press.

Mason, R. & Mitroff, I. (1973). A program of research on MIS, *Management Science*, 19 (5), 475-485.

McCloed, G. & Smith, D. (2001). *Managing Information Technology projects.* eds. Edwards, J, Inspired Press, South Africa.

Partington, D. & Harris, H. (1999). Team role balance and team performance: an empirical study, *Journal of Management Development*, 18 (7/8), 694-705.

Schwalbe, C. (2003). *Information Technology project management*, Course Technology; 3rd Bk&Cdr.

Scott, E.C. (2004). Systems development group project: A real world experience, *Proceedings of the Information Systems Education Conference*, Newport, Rhode Island, USA.

Scott, E.C. & Van Der Merwe, N. (2003). Using multiple assessment approaches to enhance objectivity and student learning. A special conference edition of the *Electronic Journal of Information Systems Evaluation*, 6 (2), 182-186.

Scott, T.J., Tichenor, L.H., Bisland, R.B. & Cross, J.H. (1994). Team dynamics in student programming projects, *ACM SIGCSE Bulletin*, 26 (1), 111-115.

Sundstrom, E., De Meuse, K.P. & Futrell, D. (1990). Work teams, *American Psychologist*, Feb 1990, 120-133.

Waker, L. (2001). Enhancing Information Systems project team performance: Team member selection strategies, Masters Dissertation, Department of Information Systems. University of Cape Town, Cape Town, South Africa.

Winter, M. (2004). Developing a group model for student software engineering teams, Graduate Studies and Research, Department of Computer Science, University of Saskatchewan, Saskatoon.

Wynekoop, J.L. & Walz, D.B. (1998). Revising the perennial question: Are IS people different?, *The DATA BASE for Advances in Information Systems*, 29 (2), 62-72.

Appendix

Modelling Effective IS Teams

Francis & Young (1992) Team Effectiveness Survey

Team Name [ ]

Please indicate:

[ ] Team Member

[ ] Team Leader

Please consider each of the following statements in relation to your systems development project teams and answer to the best of your knowledge. The accuracy of this survey depends on your openness and honesty in answering the questions

Please indicate your level of agreement (by highlighting in RED, as shown) with the following statements, where:

1	2	3	4	5
Agree	Agree Somewhat	Neutral	Disagree Somewhat	Disagree

1 **SECTION A: CLARITY of Roles, Goals, and Objectives**

Team roles are clearly defined	1	2	3	4	5
Team members are clear about goals	1	2	3	4	5
Leadership is clear and unambiguous	1	2	3	4	5
We are clear about how individual and team performance will be measured	1	2	3	4	5
The objectives of some team memebers conflict with others	1	2	3	4	5
Members of the team do not fully understand one anothers roles	1	2	3	4	5
Team members are uncertain about their individual roles in relation to the team	1	2	3	4	5
I could not, with complete confidence, define my own role within the team	1	2	3	4	5

2 **SECTION B: LEADERSHIP**

The leader and team members spend little time clarifying what they expect and need from one another	1	2	3	4	5
The leader rarely tolerated leadership efforts by other team members	1	2	3	4	5
The leader gives his or her own view before other members of the team have contributed their views	1	2	3	4	5

The leader does not welcome feedback about how the team sees his/her performance	1	2	3	4	5
The team leader makes decisions without talking them over with the team members	1	2	3	4	5
The leader is not willing to have his or her ideas challenged	1	2	3	4	5

3 SECTION C: COMPETENCE

We often achieve our goals	1	2	3	4	5
Rate the team members' skills and abilities in being able to carry out their tasks	1	2	3	4	5
We use resources effectively	1	2	3	4	5
Our team has a good balance and mix of skills, abilities and personalities	1	2	3	4	5
Correct people, with the correct skills are assigned to the correct tasks	1	2	3	4	5
Does the team experiment with untried ideas that may have potential benefits?	1	2	3	4	5
Does the team utilise individuals' experience and integrate it with team knowledge?	1	2	3	4	5
Does the team have a healthy self-belief in themselves and their team identity?	1	2	3	4	5

4 SECTION D: COMMITMENT

We are highly committed to the team's objectives	1	2	3	4	5
We always fulfil our objectives	1	2	3	4	5
We always fulfil our objectives on time	1	2	3	4	5
Support for members within the team is strong	1	2	3	4	5
Energy is used to solve problems rather than competitive struggles	1	2	3	4	5
Conflict is discussed openly and managed constructively	1	2	3	4	5
Participation a team responsibility	1	2	3	4	5
Team members count on one another	1	2	3	4	5
We are continuously improving group interaction and performance	1	2	3	4	5
We often celebrate successes	1	2	3	4	5
We often achieve collective goals or tasks through a concentrated action	1	2	3	4	5
I am proud to be a member of my team	1	2	3	4	5
I feel supported by the rest of the team	1	2	3	4	5
Our team lacks a sense of energy an excitement	1	2	3	4	5
We often fail to finish things in a satisfactory manner	1	2	3	4	5
Some of the team members feel that the aims of the team are hardly worthwhile	1	2	3	4	5
I do not feel a strong sense of belonging to this team	1	2	3	4	5

5 SECTION E: COMMUNICATION

Communication open and honest	1	2	3	4	5
We use effective methods to communicate within and outside of formal team meetings	1	2	3	4	5
Our team leader always keeps us informed of the latest developments	1	2	3	4	5
Team performance is reviewed regularly	1	2	3	4	5
Team meetings are highly focused	1	2	3	4	5
Attempts to critically review events are negative to progress	1	2	3	4	5
I am weary of suggesting new ideas	1	2	3	4	5
Members restrain their critical remarks to avoid rocking the boat	1	2	3	4	5
Team meetings lack a methodical approach	1	2	3	4	5
Our meetings do not resolve all of the issues that should be addressed	1	2	3	4	5
Performance would improve if constructive critism were encouraged	1	2	3	4	5
People in this team sometimes do not say what they really feel	1	2	3	4	5

6 SECTION F: SKILLS

Please rate your ability regarding the following programming languages and skills where:

1 - Little or no knowledge

5 - Highly proficient and knowledgeable

Visual Basic.Net	1	2	3	4	5
ASP.Net	1	2	3	4	5
JavaScript	1	2	3	4	5
Php	1	2	3	4	5
HTML	1	2	3	4	5
UML and documentation	1	2	3	4	5
Systems analysis and design	1	2	3	4	5
Graphic design	1	2	3	4	5

The quality of the team's work would improve if team members improved their technical abilities	1	2	3	4	5
Some team members may be unable to handle the current requirements of their work	1	2	3	4	5
Our mix of skills is inappropriate for the work that we are doing	1	2	3	4	5
We need an infusion of new knowledge and skills to make our team complete	1	2	3	4	5
We lack the skills to review our effectiveness constructively	1	2	3	4	5
We have the necessary skills to develop our project and achieve our goals successfully	1	2	3	4	5

7 SECTION G: TEAM SUPPORT

We have all the necessary information and technology available to us	1	2	3	4	5
Our environment is conducive to productive working conditions	1	2	3	4	5
Our project manager is highly supportive and knowledgeable	1	2	3	4	5
Our sponsor is highly supportive	1	2	3	4	5
Our sponsor is clear about his/her requirements	1	2	3	4	5
We meet with our sponsor regularly (i.e every 2 - 3 weeks)	1	2	3	4	5
Team members sometimes put down others in the team	1	2	3	4	5

8 SECTION H: CREATIVITY

Not many new ideas are generated by the team	1	2	3	4	5
Team members are weary about suggesting new ideas	1	2	3	4	5
Good ideas seem to get lost	1	2	3	4	5
The team needs the stimulus of more radical and creative people	1	2	3	4	5
Creative ideas often are not followed up with definite action	1	2	3	4	5

9 SECTION I: ACHIEVING LEARNING GOALS

Excellent quality of work for each group member *on individual projects*	1	2	3	4	5
Excellent quality of work for group projects	1	2	3	4	5
Unanimous understanding and mastery: Everyone's learning is the priority: When someone is having difficulty, the group will provide extra time and support until material is master	1	2	3	4	5
OR					

Each person is on his/her own. Group has only so much time. Only group tasks should addressed in group meetings. They should be achieved in the quickest and most expedient way (i.e. the most skilled person does what s/he does best and the others need not	1	2	3	4	5
Addressing learning needs and gaining in-depth understanding and ability to apply concepts and strategies learned	1	2	3	4	5
Improving interpersonal styles of communication. Involves asking for feedback on how well we express ourselves and interact in the small group setting	1	2	3	4	5

Biographies

Elsje Scott is a Senior Lecturer in the Department of Information Systems at the University of Cape Town and has 21 years experience in teaching computer programming at tertiary institutions.

The author's main research interest is systems development group projects which involve knowledge areas like project management, people management and software engineering. Specific focus areas are software testing, object-oriented programming concepts, general issues concerning the development of efficient computer systems in Information Systems and assessment strategies and software standards. Other interests are Discrete Mathematics, with a specific interest in Graph Theory and the applications thereof.

Michael Pollock is an assistant lecturer in the Information Systems Deptartment at UCT, and has worked in the department for 3 years. He has a BCOM (Hons) and MCOM in Information Systems from UCT. His research interests include technology adoption, IS project evaluation and IS teams.

The page left blank intentionally.

Concept and Rule Based Naming System

Chakkrit Snae and Michael Brückner
Naresuan University, Phitsanulok, Thailand

chakkrits@nu.ac.th michaelb@nu.ac.th

Abstract

Names are important in many societies, even in technologically oriented ones which use e.g. ID systems to identify individual people. There are many elements of personal names which vary in different cultures. Names such as surnames are the most important as they are used in many processes, such as identifying of people and genealogical research. On the other hand variation of names can be a major problem for the identification and search for people, e.g. web search or security reasons. We show name variations for different cultures to guide the implementation of a rule based naming system, currently worked out for Thai names. We characterize the LIG (Levenshtein, Index of Similarity Group (called ISG), and Guth) algorithms which help to find reasonable variants of names and use an ontology of names to capture the meaning of the variants which are based on Thai naming methodologies and rules. A further benefit of this process is an optimized name searching.

Keywords: personal names, name variations, name matching, ontology, rule based system

Introduction

Names are used for identifying persons, places, things and even ideas or concepts. Names serve for labelling of categories or classes and for individual items. They are properties of individuals which are of greater importance in most communities. In technologically oriented societies such as modern Western the reference between a name as a label and the person is not as obvious as in small tribal societies. This is especially true where names are stored within large information systems. This includes government, medical, educational and even commercial records which are kept about individuals. Names are the most important referrer to a person even if there are numbering systems like ID numbers because such systems are not universal. Names are often queried in a different way than they were entered. Personal names lead to many problems with regard to data retrieval because names are also subject to multiple variations not only between different cultures and writing systems but in a specific culture as well. Names represent complex lexical structures which have to be handled systematically for data entry, storage and retrieval in order to get sufficient recall or precision in the retrieval process.

In this paper we present a first account of our findings on elements of personal names in different cultures with their respective conventions and variations, ontology of names, rules for constructing Thai names, and algorithms of name matching to overcome name variations. Here we present a hybrid name matching procedure which is based on probabilistic phonetic and sound variation recognition with the help of an expert system and which can deal with multicultural names as well. This procedure is used in the Thai naming system.

This paper is organized as follows: Section 2 contains a description of names and their variation. In Section 3 we outline the basic term of ontology which is used in Section 4 for the conceptualisation of names. In Section 5 we present some basic characteristics of the name matching algorithms of our choice, the LIG algorithms, as well as the rule based system for naming applied to Thai names. Section 6 shows the conclusions of our study and further work which has to be performed.

What is a Name?

Names for individuals are often called proper names, for humans sometimes also anthroponyms. Names for places are called toponyms, for bodies of water hydronyms, for ethnic groups ethnonyms, for metaphors metonyms and so on. Names are more than just strings of characters. Names show important information such as titles, gender, marital status, and even birthplace. For this reason names provide different elements, which may differ amongst cultures. They also undergo variations such as phonetic and alternate spellings. This problem can be made clear in this way: how do we know that differently spelled or pronounced names belong to the same person?

Each culture has a set of conventions which govern the appearance and function of names as well as a range of permitted variations in its naming system, e.g. surname inheritance. Some cultures show the marital status very clearly, others do not refer to it, cf. Thai and German differences in stating the marital status for female. The categories of name variation are generally the same across all cultures; the difference is in the realization of the variation.

Naming for Identity and Security

From the technical point of view we want to link and match as many names as possible with the correct individuals. If we deal with individuals of the same name, e.g. John Smith, we have to establish a second identifier at least. This can be – and is in many cases – a temporal element, like the date of birth, which is an individual and unchanging property of the person. Another way to circumvent the problem is to establish numbering systems, like ID numbers. Systems of numbers or other ciphers can be generated within individual organizations. It is not likely that the resulting ID numbers will be the same in different organizations. The numbering may have limitations as well, e.g. the individual health care setting (e.g. within a hospital or district) or, in principle, more widely (e.g. the National Health Service number). In the past, the National Health Service number in England and Wales had serious limitations as a matching variable, and it was not widely used on health-care records. With the allocation of the new ten-digit number throughout the NHS all this has been changed (Gill, 1997).

Although numbering systems are simple to implement they can lead to different errors in recording, transcription, and keying. So we have to take into account methods which reduce these errors and facilitate good quality of data entry and retrieval. One such method uses a checking device such as check-digits (Wild, 1968; Hamming, 1986). When we are not able to use unique numbers or ciphers, natural matching variables are the person's name, date of birth, sex and perhaps other supplementary variables such as the address with postal code and place of birth, which are used in combination for matching. Recently, it has been suggested that this simple code could be extended for security critical places (e.g. airports, checkpoints etc.) with biometric marker information extracted from person identifier information e.g. fingerprints/iridograms.

Elements of Personal Names

Figure 1 shows typical elements of personal names together with potential variations and sources of choices, e.g. dictionary of given names.

1. Initial and feudal names
- for male–Mr.
- for female
  - -single female –Ms
  - -married female – Mrs
- professional Occupation–Dr., Prof., ranking career
- honorary titles and feudal names for social status in society - Lord, Sir, Knight, Baron, etc.

2. First name, given name
- mixture of parent names
- monks
- naming system
- astrology
- family, e.g. great grandparents
- book/ dictionary of names
- using name that matches character e.g. actor/actress

3. Middle name
- grandparents or great grandparents
- parents

4. Surname
- inherited from family
- the king or Royal family
- parents surnames
- grandparents
- using name that matches character e.g. actor/actress

5. Nickname
- last syllable of given names, e.g. Chakkrit → Krit
- first syllable of given names, e.g. Robert→ Rob
- called by family
- called by friend / local community

6. Artist name and pseudonyms
- first name only, like Sasha
- surname only, like Chernyim (Thai comedian)
- only nickname, like Prince
- only abbreviation, like -ky
- for artists, monks, etc.

Figure 1: The elements of names

Ontology of Names

The term ontology has been widely used in recent years in the field of Artificial Intelligence, computer and information science especially in domains such as, cooperative information systems, intelligent information integration, information retrieval and extraction, knowledge representation, and database management systems (Andrade & Saltz, 1999, 2000; Guarino, 1998). Many different definitions of the term are proposed. One of the most widely quoted and well-known definition of ontology is Gruber's (Gruber, 1993): An ontology is an explicit specification of a conceptualization.

The term is borrowed from philosophy, where an ontology is a systematic account of existence. Here in this paper we adopt the following definition: Ontology is the study or concern about what kinds of things exist - what entities or things are there in the universe (Blackburn, 1996). Our work on ontologies will comprise: a terminological component where we lay down the concepts and an assertional component (or Knowledge Base) which contains the individual instances (entities).The level of description will be taxonomies with hierarchically related terms and controlled vocabularies (thesaurus) with the help of semantic networks.

In this research we use ontologies for different reasons. Firstly, we want to find out the gender for a specific Thai given name. We captured the meaning of approximately 10,000 Thai given names in a database and can therefore derive the gender to which it belongs with the help of an ontology. Secondly, we use the same strategy for naming baby girls and baby boys. Here the users can check for appropriate given names according to the gender of their babies and for names with a helpful meaning and good sound. An ontology can help to combine different names, e.g. parents' names, into a new name with a meaning. For example father's name Suchat, mother's name Wipada, and so a baby girl can take the syllables Sucha- from father and -da from mother to become Suchada. This new name means "beautiful girl". Thirdly we want to capture given names belonging to the same person and which have many variations. For example, we have the name Chakkrit with the spelling variations Jakkrit, Chakrid, Chakkrid, Jagrid, Chakkit, etc. In Thai these different spellings result in the same sound. Ontologies are used when we Romanize Thai characters into Latin alphabet. Ontologies help the user to choose the appropriate Romanized version of the Thai name. This works also the other way. Consider the name Peter and its short form Pete. By using an ontology we find that both names can refer to the same person. In this case ontologies work like a thesaurus for given names.

An ontology of names can be worked out in many different forms, but every ontology will include a dictionary, some definition of the terms (semantics), and indications how they depend on each other, e.g. in hierarchies and semantic networks. For example, an ontology of names can be defined as what kinds of names exist, e.g. first name, surname, nickname, etc. This typically comprises definitions of different names, the elements of names and their structures. In this section we show how an ontology of names can be captured and defined.

An ontology can also be used to establish the network of synonyms, e.g. using spelling norms to determine whether two names are the same/similar or not. For example, two names: Totie and Totiey can be defined based on assumption that they are the same as Totty. This attempts to tackle the seemingly irreducible conventions of surname. In compositional semantics let us consider the name "Gutensohn". This name will be used to illustrate the various semantic considerations in German naming. The name is a composition of the two strings Godith and Sohn, which have unambiguous, meaningful interpretations. The interpretation of Godith is god or good battle and Sohn is interpreted as a male child in relation to his parent. The composition Gutsohn, Gudzon, or in other cultures: Guditson, Godyeson and Godithson and Godison (Reaney & Wilson 1997).

Identifying and searching result in a list of many names with variations and meanings. In order to find the correct person with a name we have to adopt ontologies of names, e.g. based on place of birth or relationship of people. The typical origins of surnames which can be a basis for ontologies of names can be classified as follows: local surnames - surnames of relationship - surnames of occupation or office.

Local surnames, that are most widely used, stem from toponyms, we can call them toponymic. They reflect land owners, place of birth, or the center of life. For example, Richard de Tonebridge was named after his castle of Tonbridge, but he was also called Richard de Clara from the Suffolk Clare, which became his chief seat and the family's definitive surname. Also Richard de Hadestoke, a London alderman, had left Hadstock (Essex) and settled in London (Reaney & Wilson, 1997). These local surnames derive (with occasional exceptions) from English, Scottish or French places (e.g. de, at, in). Toponymic Thai names are derived from Thai places and took originally a preposition na, for example, Prapas na Ranong is a person from a Southern province in Thailand called Ranong.

Surnames which come from family relation are often called patronymic, but we have to introduce a more elaborate term, because we encounter names from females and other relations than just father, such as Gilbert Fathevedsteppeson, Richard Hannebrothir, America Ibbotdoghter, and John Prestebruther.

Surnames of occupation and office refer to actual office holders like clergy names or state offices. Some of these, such as steward, constable, marshal, etc., became hereditary and gave rise to hereditary surnames, but the terms were also commonly used of lesser offices, whilst marshal was a common term for a farrier and such names frequently denoted the actual occupation. However,

Nuns, Abbots, Priors, Monks and other clerical people were bound by vows of celibacy and thus did usually not have families which adopted their respective surname.

We have to bear in mind that a full and accurate classification of surnames is impossible as there is a significant number of overlap between the different classes of names. People did not follow special rules in the naming process rather they wanted to solve an immediate problem: identifying and characterizing themselves or others. Nicknames, in particular, are even today often the result of a spontaneous reaction in a particular situation. Local surnames may be occupational, for example, John atte Gate may have lived near the town-gate, or he may have been a gate-keeper or porter. Surnames of office, such as Abbot, Bishop, Cardinal and King, are often nicknames. Ralph Vicar was a glass worker, not a clergyman, and is also called Verrer. A single modern name may belong to more than one class. For instance, Mew may be a patronymic, a nickname from the sea-mew, or occupational, either metonymic for Mewer, keeper of the hawks, or from a local surname, with the same occupational meaning. It is impossible to fit surnames into a strait-jacket (Reaney & Wilson, 1997).

Variation of Names

Name variation is one of the major problems in identifying people, because it is not easy to determine whether a name variation is a different spelling of the same name or a name for a different person. Most of these variations can be mainly categorized as mentioned in the Sections below (Bouchard and Pouyez, 1980; Branting, 2002; Dematteis, Lutz & McCallum-Bayliss, 1998).

From searching on the Internet for some personal names, e.g. in Thailand, we have found many variants of them which refer to the same names. Table 1 shows the results of variants of the personal name called "Somchai" using Google search in many search processes.

Table 1: Variants of "Somchai" using Google search

Personal name	Variation	Number of results
Somchai	Somchai	200,000
	Som Chai	149,000
	Somchay	1,640
	Somshai	231
	Somchia	77
	Somchair	48
	Somchaiy	35
	Somcai	17

As can be seen from Table 1, personal name like Somchai, Som Chai, and Somchay are the most similar but names like Somchair, Somchaiy, and Somcai exhibit the least similarity. With the help of name matching methods we find reasonable alternatives of the original name, e.g. Somchai. Then all alternative names of Somchai can be used in one single search process which covers all variants at once.

Spelling variations

Spelling variations rely on the assumption that the source and target names are strings which differ because of errors or transcription differences (e.g. different pronunciation). Spelling error patterns can be taken into consideration and single-error misspellings (mistyping) can be categorized as follows (Jurafsky & Martin, 2000): (1) insertion, e.g. BROWN as BROWMN, and MCMANUS as MACMANUS; (2) deletion or omission, e.g. BROWN as BOWN, and ROBBIN as ROBIN; (3) substitution, e.g. BROWN as BTOWN, and SMYTH as SMITH; (4) transposition, e.g. BROWN as BRONW, and BREADLEY and BRAEDLEY. Generally such variations do not affect the phonetic structure of the name but still cause problems in matching names. These variations mainly arise from misreading or mishearing, by either a human or an automated device. These can include interchanged or misplaced letters due to vowel replacement (EVANTUREL as EVENTUREL), consonant replacement (LEBRE as LETRE), consonant doubling (MAUFET as MAUFFET), very different spellings (LEWIS as LOUIS), and problematic transcription (GARWOOD as YARWOOD) (Winchester, 1973).

Phonetic variations

Phonetic variations depend on the dialect or pronunciation conventions of the speaker. For example, the nickname Pooh, as it is spelled in English, would be spelled in German as Puh. Where the phonemes of the name are modified, e.g. through mishearing, the structure of the name may be substantially altered. MAXIME and MAXIMIEN are related names but their phonetic structure is very different. Indeed, phonetic variations in first names can be very large as illustrated by ADELINE and its shortened form LINE.

Other variations

Character Variation. The problem created by capitalization, punctuation, spacing, qualifiers and abbreviations (Branting, 2001) can be shown as follows:

- Capitalization, e.g. brown and Brown; SMITH and Smith
- Punctuation, e.g. WILL SMITH and WILL-SMITH; SMIT and S.M.I.T
- Spacing, e.g. YOUNGSMITH and YOUNG SMITH
- Qualifiers, e.g. WILL SMITH and WILL SMITH YOUNG
- Abbreviations, e.g. ROB and ROBBIN; BOB and BOBBY

Double Names. There are some cases where surnames and first names are composed of two elements but both are not always shown. For example, a double surname such as PHILIPS-MARTIN may be given in full or sometimes as single names, such as PHILIPS and MARTIN. Double first names although are not common in the English language, when considering German, for example, given names such as Klaus-Dieter can be transformed like Klaus and Dieter.

Alternate First Names. It can cause major problems for identifying people when a person changes the name during the course of life or is called by one of the first names during a period of life and another later on. An example: in German culture you can get more than one first name, but only one is the caller name (Rufname). This name must not be the first given name and it can even change in the course of life. A name like Jochen Peter Spohn consists of two given names and the family name. During a certain period of time the person may have adopted Jochen as Rufname, later may be changed to Peter. In this situation an algorithm that recognizes simple variations in spelling or phonetics would not be able to identify two such names as referring to the same person. Another example is the Christian tradition of wives taking her husband's surname such as "Mrs. Totty the former Miss Penket" or "Mrs. Totty nee Haggart".

Culture of Names / Naming Conventions and Customs in Different Cultures

The issue of name variations becomes more problematic when dealing with names from other cultures because the sorts of variation that are permitted may not be the same as those permitted in English. Names vary between cultures which for a long time has been an obstacle for creating a single method for automatic name processing.

For example, within each of the following cultures (Korean, Arabic, Hispanic, and Hungarian) all the names given are permitted variants of the same name except the last one (Dematteis et al., 1998). How to find out which of the examples below are given names and surnames?

PARK DOE REE / PAG TO NI / TO NI PAG (Korean),

MOHAMMAD ALI ABD EL NADIR NUR EL DIN / IMHEMED ABDUNADEER NOOREDDINE / MHMD NUR ABD AL NADER (Arabic),

ENRIQUE CESAR VELEZ ARGUETA ENRIQUE BELES, QUIQUE VELEZ A. E. C. ARGUETA (Hispanic),

Eoetvoes Lorant / Roland Eoetvoes / Eoetvoes Roland (Hungarian)

In each case, the final name would be considered an unacceptable variation of the name under consideration; it would be another name (Dematteis et al., 1998).

Another example, in French names you sometimes cannot differ between male and female variations relying only on phonetics. Consider the male first name MICHEL which pronounced the same way as the female MICHELLE, whereas German uses two different names both in spelling and pronunciation: MICHAEL and MICHAELA.

Naming Methodology for Given Names

The way of naming can vary, e.g. naming by monks, grandparents. Since antiquity names have been very important to people. Naming from the past to the present has been continuously developed and has evolved into a variety of patterns. Each pattern has its own rules depending on local belief and language that has been developed until the present. The basic goal of naming is to provide a good fortune and progress during life. Most first names have a meaning. Three methodologies are briefly described in the following.

- Principal naming using Thai astrology is widely used since antiquity as it involves the birth day in order to form the name. This is a belief that the individual has a set of 8 attributes called name of the angles referred to in Thai astrology. These attributes influence each person's livelihood, fortune, etc. The attributes refer to Servant > Age > Power > Honor > Property > Diligence > Patron > Misfortune. Each attribute has it own letters which can be used for constructing names.
- Principal naming using numeric methodology: Each letter has distinct numbers which can be added and have according values. These values represent low or high characteristics. The method can always be used along with naming both first names and surnames by increasing the value of first name and surname. Thus using numeric methodology can be used to increase "power" in names and check for better names.
- Principal naming which uses the traditional calendar is considered by Thai fortune tellers as the best method of anticipating the horoscope or destiny of people. This methodology takes day, month and year of birth including the time of birth to calculate the personality according to astrology. The results of this prediction are defined to tell the fate and personality thoroughly in the future.

In many cultures naming is not only important because every individual needs to have a name but to have helpful names or names with a good sound. Thai parents always try to choose names which they feel will bring good luck to their offsprings and to the family. The choice of appropriate names bases on the rules of available letters that can influence the destiny of the individuals as described in the following. Letters and days refer to Thai astrology. In that process the fortune depends on the day of birth and the related letters shown in Figure 2. Note that Wednesday occurs twice. This is because counting of the Thai dates is different from the Western style. Thai people start a week on Sundays and a new day at 6 a.m. Thus naming using dates has to consider timing as well, especially on Wednesdays, which is the middle of the week and can be divided into daytime (from 06:00 to 17:59) and nighttime (18:00 to 05:59 the next day).

Figure 2: Naming rules using letters of the angles referred to in Thai astrology

The method for naming according to the available letters shown in Figure 2 is as follows. Starting with the weekday of birth we have a set of letters available which refer to 8 basic properties.

Servant > Age > Power > Honor > Property > Diligence > Patron > Misfortune

Related concepts with these attributes as they are used in Thai astrology are shown in Table 2.

Table 2: Personal attributes and related concepts

Servant	Children, Husbands, wives, including people who we support within family
Age	Life, livelihood, including the way of living
Power	Destiny, honor, fame, position, including education and love
Honor	Asset, money, appliance fortune which can be gained in the future
Property	Properties that inherited and still exist in the present including status of relatives
Diligence	Diligence, success from working, including creative and hard working
Patron	Supporters, such as parents , teachers, bosses and helpers
Misfortune	Evil, enemies, sins, including any obstacles

For example, in Figure 3 people who are born on a Sunday and need to add fortune in the attribute Servant need to use a set of vowels in naming process. For a boy the first letter must only be one of the letters in the attribute "Power" e.g. จ ฉ ช ฌ ญ. If they want a long life they need to choose one of those letters in the attribute "Age". The same applies for the attribute "Property" if the offsprings should have properties in their life. However the parents will not use letters from the set of letters in "Misfortune", in the example that is ศ ษ ส ห ฬ ฮ in order to avoid evil, enemies, sins including any obstacles.

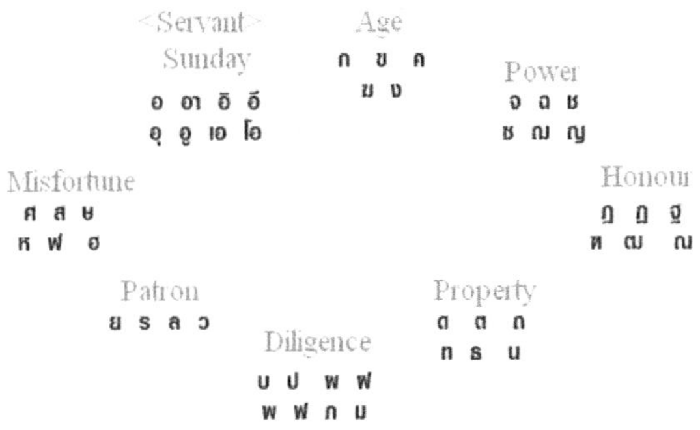

Figure 3: An example for people who were born on Sunday according letters according to Thai astrology

An example of naming using an attribute "Servant" from Thai astrology as is illustrated and described in Table 3.

Table 3: Possible letters in attribute "Servant" according the Birthday

Date of birth	Servant attribute
Sunday	All vowels
Monday	ก ข ค ฆ ง
Tuesday	จ ฉ ช ซ ฌ ญ
Wednesday (daytime)	ฎ ฏ ฐ ฑ ฒ ณ
Thursday	บ ป ผ ฝ พ ฟ ภ ม
Wednesday (nighttime)	ย ร ล ว
Friday	ศ ษ ส ห ฬ ฮ
Saturday	ด ต ถ ท ธ น

In the past, the Thai culture widely used letters in "Power" interval (attribute) for boys' names and letters in "Honor" for girls' names. Nowadays there is no limit in choosing letters for genders but letters from "Misfortune" attribute are generally avoided in the naming process.

Order of Names

Name order is crucial; although the spelling variants of the name elements in the final name are acceptable, their order is not. In Eastern naming system, e.g. Korean, Japanese, and Chinese, the family name appears in the leftmost position and cannot move to the rightmost position. This applies to Hungarian personal names as well. In Western system, e.g. English, German, French, Spanish, Italian, and American, the family name appears in the rightmost position.

For example, in Hispanic names, the family name is the next to the last element (VELEZ); the rightmost name (ARGUETA) may be dropped, but not the family name. ARGUETA would therefore refer to another family, if it occurs alone (Dematteis et al., 1998).

As the function of personal names is not only to distinguish between individuals but also to serve as a help for indexing we have to mention the different conventions for ordering names. In Western order we change the position of given names and family names for indexing. In Eastern we do not have to change because the order for family names is already there. Thai ordering of names is distinct to these because Thai names are sorted according to the first names. There is no need to change the order of first name and family name as well.

Transcription of Names

English spelling with its many-to-many sound/letter correspondences contributes to the problem of Romanization of non Western names. Dialectal differences, historical and phonetic spellings make the English names somewhat unpredictable. The latter is even the case for English names. The following examples are given by (Reaney & Wilson, 1997).

COLWELL, COLWILL, COLLWELL

LEA, LEE, LEGH, LEIGH, LEY, LEYS, LAY, LAYE, LYE

THOMPSON, THOMSON, TOMSEN, TOMSON

WORCESTER, WORSTER, WOOSTER, WOSTEAR

Spelling variations are especially prominent in names from non-Roman writing cultures when such names have been transcribed to Roman characters, e.g. the Romanized form of an Arabic name: NOOR EL DIN, NURELDIN, NUREDDINE.

For the Thai writing system which is very complicated there exists an official standard called Royal Thai General System of Transcription (Wikipedia, 2005) which is used for rendering Thai names into the Roman alphabet. It uses only straight letters for vowels, diphthongs and aspirated consonants. It does not indicate the length of a vowel and the five different tones. From Chulalongkorn University, Bangkok, there is also an automated tool available (<http://www.arts.chula.ac.th/%7Eling/tts/>) which transcripts Thai names or terms into Roman letters. It is called "Thai Romanization."

In many cultures, available standard transcription systems are not used or are used inconsistently. The range of variation found in distinct instances of the same name is therefore not fully predictable from such systems. In Arabic, for example, although there are transcription systems used by libraries and other official agencies, transcription tends to be far less predictable and highly inconsistent, even with a single individual. For example, an individual whose name is "ABD EL NADIR" may Romanize the name on one occasion as ABDUL NADEER and on another as ABDUNNADIR. Both name representations are "correct" and can be said to be accurate Romanization of the same Arabic name. Even in cultures in which transcription systems provide a reliable standard, personal interpretation, accommodation to the spelling of another culture or perceptual confusion can cause the spelling to deviate from the standard. Thus, for example, the Thai name GOFF will vary with KOFF, because G and K are Romanization alternatives from different transcriptions systems. An observed variant of GOUGH, however, are GOFF and GOFFE, representing the influence spelling of English surnames by Reaney and Wilson (1997). The Thai Romanization tool gives KOP, on the other hand KOP is a correct transliteration of two different Thai names: กอฟ and กอล์ฟ.

Implementation of Hybrid Algorithms and System Concept

Many techniques have been used to cope with the important problem of matching variant names. However, most of these techniques were developed for general word matching and as a result they are not optimized for personal names matching. Spelling as well as phonetic variations combined with cultural aspects are the more challenging problems for automated multicultural name matching systems.

Most systems today use specific techniques for name matching rules and specific variations, e.g. Guth, 1976 and Levenshtein, 1965 algorithms are spelling/string analysis based, whereas Soundex (Winchester, 1970) and Phonex (Lait & Randell, 1998) are phonetic/sound based algorithms. However, most researchers have tried to implement a method which can deal with the culture of names and naming system which are meant to overcome the ethnic problems, e.g. NameX (<http://www.namethesaurus.com/Thesaurus/FAQ.htm>) and Varispell (<http://www.alphabic.com>).

Matching Algorithms for Names

The difficulty of the name matching task and the requirements for an effective algorithm to perform this task, both depend on the type and degree of name variations which occur. More recently published name matching techniques are either of the composite or hybrid form (Snae & Diaz, 2002) and several novel hybrid algorithms (e.g. LIG2, and LIG3) have been developed for specific purposes. All the name matching algorithms encountered in the literature and presented in this paper are based on alphabetic and/or phonetic similarity and/or name transformations (e.g. forename abbreviations) but may use a variety of distance and other metrics for representing the match. From an initial search of the literature, we distinguished four types of algorithms and implemented them using the C programming language:

1. spelling/string analysis based algorithms (e.g. Guth and Levenshtein),
2. phonetic/sound based algorithms (e.g. Soundex, Metaphone, NYSIIS, and Phonex),
3. composite methods (spelling or sound, e.g. SIMPLEX, and ISG),
4. hybrid approaches (spelling and sound, e.g. LIG algorithms).

A hybrid algorithm combines phonetic and spelling based approaches using similarity measure as probability is called LIG1, LIG2, and LIG3 (LIG algorithms). The LIG algorithms are a combination of three name matching methods: Levenshtein, Index of Similarity Group (called ISG), and Guth. The LIG algorithms have the best performance in term of producing most accurate true matches, overcoming name variations, and increasing the hit rate. They have proved to be more accurate than other methods in the literature (Snae & Diaz, 2002). The advantageous characteristics of these algorithms can be summarized as follows: (1) simple design, which can lead to accuracy improvements without decreasing the performance, (2) use of probabilistic similarity measures based on distance and weight, (3) increase correct positive and reduce negative matches to maximize the overall accuracy, (4) provide phonetic tuning to address multi-cultural names without depending on the language.

For these reasons we will use LIG algorithms for name variations and matching in the proposed naming systems, e.g. Thai naming system. For that we use a dictionary database of more than

8.000 Thai names which contains not only the spelling, but also the meaning and correct pronunciation. In situations where names follow the rules but do not have a meaning we compare the name with similar names in a dictionary database and check for similarity above a specific threshold. Then the user can select the best name from the resulting list of names.

Rule Based Naming System for Thai Names

In this section we will show the basic rules for Thai given names.

Thai Transcription

For consonants, the transcription is different depending on the location of the letter within the syllable. In the column showing the vowels in Figure 4 a dash ("–") indicates the relative position of the initial consonant belonging to the vowel.

Consonants

Letter	Initial	Final
ก	k	k
ข	kh	k
ฃ	kh	k
ค	kh	k
ฅ	kh	k
ฆ	kh	k
ง	ng	ng
จ	ch	t
ฉ	ch	t
ช	ch	t
ซ	s	t
ฌ	ch	t
ญ	y	n
ฎ	d	t
ฏ	t	t
ฐ	th	t
ฑ	d	t
ฒ	th	t
ณ	n	n
ด	d	t
ต	t	t
ถ	th	t
ท	th	t
ธ	th	t
น	n	n
บ	b	p
ป	p	p
ผ	ph	p
ฝ	f	p
พ	ph	p
ฟ	f	p
ภ	ph	p
ม	m	m

Consonants

Letter	Initial	Final
ย	y	-
ร	r	n
ฤ	rue, ri, roe	-
ฤๅ	rue	-
ล	l	n
ฦ	lue	
ฦๅ	lue	-
ว	w	-
ศ	s	t
ษ	s	t
ส	s	t
ห	h	-
ฬ	l	n
ฮ	h	-

Vowels

Letter	Romanisation
-ะ, -ั, รร (with final), -า	a
รร (without final)	an
-ำ	am
-ิ, -ี	i
-ึ, -ื	ue
-ุ, -ู	u
เ-ะ, เ-็, เ-	e
แ-ะ, แ-	ae
โ-ะ, -, โ-, เ-าะ, -อ	o
เ-อะ, เ-ิ, เ-อ	oe
เ-ียะ, เ-ีย	ia
เ-ือะ, เ-ือ	uea
-ัวะ, -ัว, -ว-	ua
ใ-, ไ-, -ัย, ไ-ย, -าย	ai
เ-า, -าว	ao
-ุย	ui
โ-ย, -อย	oi
เ-ย	oei
เ-ือย	ueai
-วย	uai
-ิว	io
เ-็ว, เ-ว	eo
แ-็ว, แ-ว	aeo
เ-ียว	iao

Figure 4 Thai Transcription according to the Royal Thai General System, (Wikipedia, 2005)

Basic rules of forming syllables

Syllables are aggregated to names which sound good or aimed at good fortune according to the three methodologies mentioned above. As a consonant can not stand alone in Thai language and personal names we consider rules for vowels only. (See examples in Table 4.) The order is:

- Rule 1: Vowels can come first or can be followed by a first consonant, e.g. Ek
- Rule 2: Vowels can follow a first consonant without a final consonant, e.g. Ka
- Rule 3: Vowels that can not have final consonant, e.g. Tua
- Rule 4: Vowels that need final consonant, e.g. Kak

Table 4 Examples of Classification of Thai letter

Rules of vowels	Classification of vowels	Romanization	Examples
Rule 1	เ–, โ, แ–	E, o, ae	Ek
Rule 2	(รร), (–า), (–ิ, –ี), (–ึ, –ื) (–ุ, –ู),	(An), (a), (I), (ue), (u)	Ka
Rule 3	ะ, –ำ, เ–ะ, –ัว	A, am, e, ua	Tua, Tam
Rule 4	–ั, เ–็,	A, e	Kek

Example of construction of Thai syllables using Thai Romanization 1.10 Unicode (CU 2004) according to Figure 5: กา (Ka) = CV, เอก (Ek) = VC, กก (Kok) = CF, กัก (Kak) = CVF, เอก (Ek) = VF.

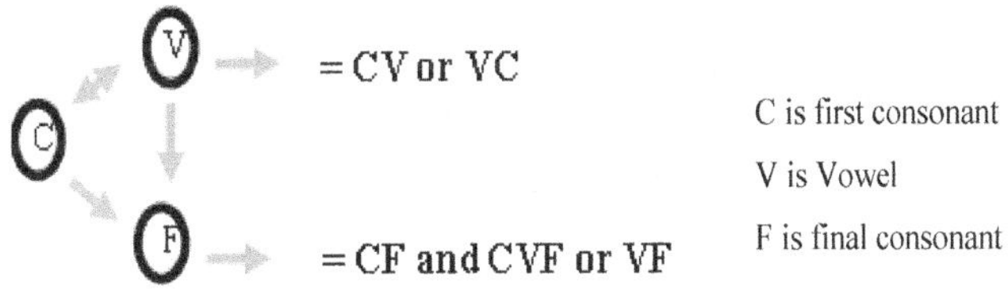

Figure 5 Forming of Thai syllables

Thai names are built from one or more syllables, which may or may not have a meaning. In the following it is shown how to construct Thai names with the help of ontologies that convey a meaning. Syllables are built from consonants (either C or F) and vowels. A name consists of one or more syllables. One syllable can have a meaning of its own, which leads in case of two or more syllables in a name to more complex meanings.

The process of constructing names according to the naming rules and methodology begins with a leading consonant or vowel that can be the only letter in the name. If we continue to add more letters we come either to a valid name (a name which has a meaning) or to an invalid name (a name without a meaning). Invalid names will be discarded in such a way that the last letter will be replaced by another or will be added with more letters.

In Figure 4 it is shown that a name comprises *n* syllables with a reasonable number of letters. The meanings of the syllables as well as of the name are found with the help of an ontology of names.

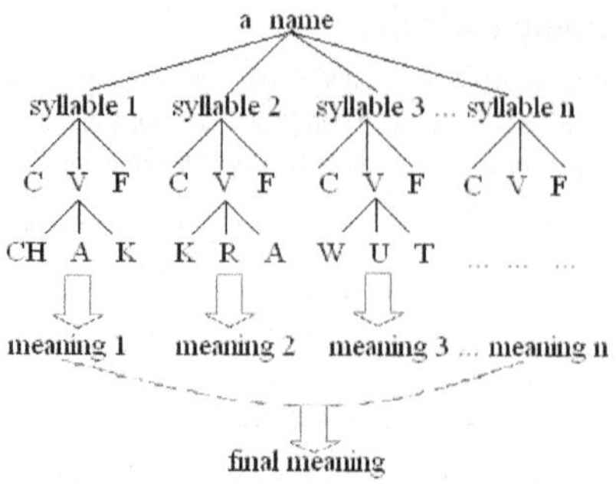

Figure 6: Representation and construction of Thai names

The meaning of the name chak-kra-wut in the example (see Figure 6) is "a man who carries a discus as a weapon".

Currently we are constructing and implementing a web-based naming expert system (see Figure 7) which offers two basic ways to come to acceptable Thai names according to the first naming methodology mentioned above. The system will first display the letters for each date of birth (as we then know the day of the week). The system uses these letters to construct names based on the basic rules (see Figure 5). It will display the names in a user readable list, so that the user will be able to choose from it taking into account their respective meaning and sound.

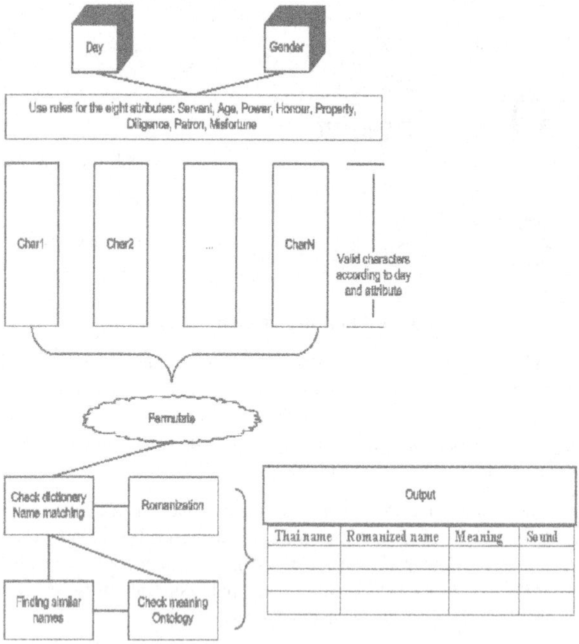

Figure 7. Architecture of Thai Naming Expert System

A second way to come to names is by using ontologies instead of basic spelling rules which are used according to the gender and date of birth. For this we check the different names against the date of birth by implementing an indexed database system of names from Thai dictionary for every day of a week.

Conclusion and Further Work

We have used Thai astrology as a naming methodology, an ontology of names, the LIG algorithms for personal name matching and the basic rules for forming syllables in Thai to construct the rule based naming system. Our proposed system will use name matching algorithms to return the variants of names from a dictionary with the relative probability of their similarity. The advantage of this process is to improve searching algorithms for multicultural names in databases as well as in the internet.

Currently we are developing a system called IT-TELLS (Interactive Transcription Tools for Explanation Level Language System) which will be a Romanization tool for names in Thai characters into Roman fonts.

A primary objective here would be to study how ontologies and algorithms can help in deciding which rules of naming system have to be implemented. This will also require an investigation into how ontologies which cover the different elements of names can be merged.

We want to extend our work to cover naming according to the birth day of the person to name. If we would know that a given name stems from the naming system using Thai astrology we can even derive the day of birth of a person with the help of ontology.

References

Andrade, H & Saltz, J. (1999). Towards a knowledge base management system (KBMS): An ontology-aware database management system (DBMS). *Proceedings of the 14th Brazilian Symposium on Databases*, Florianopolis, Brazil.

Andrade H. & Saltz, J. (2000). Query optimization in Kess – An ontology-based KBMS. *Proceedings of the 15th Brazilian Symposium on Databases* (SBBD'2000). João Pessoa, Brazil.

Blackburn, S. (1996). *The Oxford dictionary of philosophy.* Oxford: OUP.

Bouchard, G. & Pouyez, C. (1980). Name variations and computerised record linkage. *Historical Methods, 13*(2), 119-125.

Branting, L. K.. (2002). Name-matching algorithms for legal case-management systems. *The Journal of Information, Law and Technology (JILT).*

Dematteis, K., Lutz, R., & McCallum-Bayliss, H. (1998). Whose name is it: Names, ownership and databases. Originally written for: 1998 Annual Meeting American Name Society San Francisco, CA.

Gill, L. E. (1997). OX-LINK: The Oxford medical record linkage system, Complex linkage made easy, Record Linkage Techniques. *Proceedings of an International Workshop and Exposition*, 15-33.

Gruber, T. R. (1993). A translation approach to portable ontology specification. *Knowledge Acquisition, 5*(2), 199-220.

Guarino, N. (1998). Formal ontology and information systems. In N. Guarino (Ed.), *Proceedings FOIS'98*, Amsterdam.

Guth, G. J. A. (1976). Surname spellings and computerized record linkage. *Historical Methods Newsletter, 10*(1), 10-19.

Hamming, R. W. (1986). *Coding and information theory* (2nd ed.). Englewood Cliffs, NJ: Prentice Hall.

Jurafsky, D. & Martin, J. H. (2000). *Speech and language processing.* Prentice Hall.

Lait, A. J. & Randell, B. (1998). An assessment of name matching algorithm. *Society of Indexers Genealogical Group, Newsletter Contents, SIGGNL issues 17*.

Levenshtein, V. I. (1965). Binary codes capable of correcting deletions, insertions and reversals. *Doklady Akademii Nauk SSSR. 163*, 845-848. [Translation: *Soviet Physics Doklady, 10*, 707-710].

Reaney, P. H. & Wilson, R. M. (1997). *A dictionary of English surnames*. Oxford: OUP.

Snae, C. & Diaz, B. M. (2002). An interface for mining genealogical nominal data using the concept of linkage and a hybrid name matching algorithm. *Journal of 3D-Forum Society, 16*(1), 142-147.

Wikipedia. (2005). <http://en.wikipedia.org/wiki/Royal_Thai_General_System_of_Transcription> (Nov. 19, 2005)

Wild, W. G. (1968). The theory of modulus *N* check digit systems. *The Computer Bulletin, 12*, 308-311.

Winchester, I. (1973). On referring to ordinary historical persons. In E. A. Wrigley (Ed.), *Identifying People in the Past* (pp. 17-40).

Winchester, I. (1970). The linkage of historical records by man and computer: Techniques and problems. *Journal of Interdisciplinary History, 1*, 107-124.

Biographies

Chakkrit Snae. Ph.D. in Computer Science, University of Liverpool, England. M.Sc. in Computer Science, University of Newcastle Upon Tyne , England. B.Sc. in Mathematics, Naresuan University , Phitsanulok, Thailand. Since 2005 Lecturer at Department of Computer Science and Information Technology, Naresuan University, Thailand, mainly for Software Engineering and Artificial Intelligence. Research interests: Web Based Technologies, Hybrid Name Matching Algorithms, Data Mining, Intelligent System, and Expert System

Michael Brückner. Diploma in Physics from Technical University Munich, worked for many companies like Siemens and Deutsche Telephonwerke Berlin in SW Quality Assurance. Since 2004 Lecturer at Department of Computer Science and Information Technology, Thailand, mainly for Information Science. Research interests: Personal Information Management, Information Literacy, Thesaurus construction, Intelligent web search tools

Towards Building Secure Software Systems

A. S. Sodiya, S. A. Onashoga, and O. B. Ajayi
University of Agriculture, Abeokuta, Nigeria

sinaronke@yahoo.co.uk bookyy2k@yahoo.com
tayoajayi@yahoo.co.uk

Abstract

Software security breaches are now very extremely common and a larger percentage is caused by software design defects. Since individuals and organizations now completely depend on software systems for their day-to-day operations, it is then important to produce secure software products. This paper discusses the problems of producing secure software products and provides a model for improving software security. The model – Secure Software Development Model (SSDM), is unified model that integrates security engineering with software engineering so as to ensure effective production of secure software products. Supporting structure in form of laws is also presented to guide developers throughout the development process. We then present our experience that validates the model.

Keywords: Security breaches, Software system, Software security, Software design, Design defects

Introduction

Computer software systems are increasingly faced with both internal and external penetrations. One major reason for this is the fact that software systems are still with development defects which still make them to be vulnerable. This has brought issue of security into sharp focus because organisations, including governments, depend largely on software systems for their day-to-day operations. The case is even more sensitive in environments where software systems are used for critical missions. This is why building secure software is gaining attention of today's business world and researchers in field of security. In addition, because customers (organizations) have experienced unfortunate security incidence, there is increase awareness and agitation for secure software products.

However, in building secure software systems, a lot has to be done. Security techniques have to be implemented in all the stages of the software engineering. Devanbu and Stubblebine (2000) stated that security concerns must inform every phase of software development, from requirements to design, implementation, testing and deployment. This is necessary because software developer might unknowingly inject defects in all stages of the development process. Microsoft found out that 50% of software security problems were caused by design flaws (McGraw, 2003). Wilander and Gustavsson (2005) reported that, in 2004, more than new security vulnerabilities were found in commercial and open source software everyday. Jones (2000) reported the software benchmark studies conducted on hundreds of software projects and stated that the average specification, design, and implementation defects content of released software varies from 1 to 7 defects per thousand lines of new and changed code produced. Commonly computer systems are hacked by exploiting software bugs. Redwine and Davis, (2004) stated that no existing processes or practices have currently shown to consistently produce secure software. If there is no adequate security, the availability, reliability and safety of the software are not guaranteed.

Consequently, software development process must be carefully engineered and integrated with security requirements. Common development practices must change so as to produce software with few or no security weaknesses. The ultimate challenge for software engineers is then to develop software systems with desired quality, within the reasonable time and budget, and the software must be secure. Wilander and Gustavsson (2005) stated that to build more secure software, accurate and consistent security requirements must be specified. It is therefore important to continue to seek for ways of improving security of software systems. In this paper, we discuss the technical issues of software security and provided the model and support for improving software security.

The rest of this paper is organized as follows. The next section presents review of existing literature in software security. Software security issues are presented after that, followed by a discussion of the architecture for improving security of software systems. Supporting structures for secure software systems are discussed in the fifth section. A case study follows, and future work and conclusions are presented in the last section.

Overview of Existing Literature

Recently, there has been a lot of interest in building software securely. Pauli and Xu (2005) provided a threat-driven architectural design of secure information systems. The work presented threat modeling using misuse cases and stated that the findings can be used in detailed design and validation of implementation of software system. Wilander and Gustavsson (2005) mentioned in their own work that security requirements are normally poorly specified due to these three things: inconsistency in the selection of requirements, inconsistency in the level of detail and almost no standard requirements on some security solutions. The result of the study shows that security mainly treated as a functional aspect composed of security features such as login, backup, and access control. They stated that requirement on systems through assurance measures are left out. Devanbu and Stubblebine (2000) in their work emphasized that software engineering and security engineering must be integrated in order to have secure software systems. The two software articles of Ghosh, Howell, and Whittacker (2002) and Mead and McGraw (2003) also emphasized the need to build software securely from the ground.

Apart from stating and emphasizing the security needs of software system, many researchers have actually proposed methods for improving software security. One method is the correctness-by-construction proposed by Praxis Critical Systems Limited (Hall & Rod, 2004). The method operates on the principles that errors should not be introduced in first place and that errors should be removed as close as possible to the point they are introduced. The method also incorporates formal notations to specify system and design components with review and analyses for consistency and correctness. Hall and Rod (2004) reported that correctness-by-correction method produced defect densities ranging from 0.04 to 0.75 defects per thousand lines of code. Another method for achieving secure software system is the Cleanroom (Linger & Stacy, 2004). Cleanroom incorporates incremental development, functional-based specification and design, correctness verification, and statistical testing. Redwine and Davis (2004) reported the overall performance of application of cleanroom as ranging from 0.1 errors/KLOC (KLOC means Kilos of Lines of Codes) with full application to 0.4 defects/KLOC with partial application. Capability Maturity Models (CMMs) have also been used as process models to guide organizations in improving the capability to perform a particular process. An example of security related CMM is Systems Security Capability Maturity Model (SSE-CMM), which was presented in Hefner (1997). Golderson and Gibson (2003) reported that CMMs have also helped in the overall reduction in design and implementation defects of software products.

Similar to CMM is threat modeling. Threat modeling is used to analyse potential threat to computer systems in order to guide against attacks or penetrations. The usefulness of threat modeling has demonstrated in some previous works (Mogilevsky, Lee, & Yurcik, 2005; Myagmar, Lee, & Yurcik 2005). Attack trees or graphs have also been used in determining what security measures to deploy in a system (Schneir, Lippman, & Wing, 2002; Sheyner & Wing, 2004). However, attack trees model a selected set of attacks via a finite state machine and feasible only in small scenarios. They also require compiling a list of potential threats before generating attack trees. The empirical performance of both threat modeling and attack trees are not readily available.

Another method for improving security of software is the Software Engineering Institute's Team Software Process (TSP) (Davis & Mullaney, 2003). The process incorporates the idea of managing and removing specification, design and implementation defects throughout development lifecycle, controlling and monitoring of process, and using predictive measures of removing defects. Davis and Mullaney (2003) reported an average of 0.06 delivered design and implementation defects per thousand lines of codes produced.

It has shown from the literature that software systems are still with defects (though minimal in some situations). The fact is that an attacker only needs to find one security flaw to compromise the whole system. It is therefore important to design a bug-free software because the implication of a bug might be catastrophic and results in loss of large amounts of money.

Software Security Issues

Software security is concerned with protection of software and its resources. A security risk is the probability of sustaining a loss of a specific magnitude during a specific time period due to a failure of security system (Rodgers, 2002).

Software Security Goals

The three security goals of computer system are Confidentiality, Integrity and Availability. These goals are commonly referred as the CIA of computer security (Sodiya, Longe, & Akinwale, 2004) and these goals also apply to computer systems.

a. ***Confidentiality***:- This has to do with the prevention of unauthorized disclosure of software resources such as codes, data, documents, files, GUI, and so on.

b. ***Integrity***:- This is prevention of unauthorized modification of software resources.

c. ***Availability***:- This is concerned with the unauthorized denial of the services of software resources.

Over the years, there have been several security mechanisms to achieve these goals. Some of these mechanisms are authentication and authorization, access control, encryption, and so on, but the rate and magnitude of attacks on computer system is increasingly alarming. Some of the interests of attacker are financial and knowledge gains, malicious intention, competitive edge and so on. The situation is even worse now that we have mobile codes in distributed network and exposure to Internet.

Problems of Producing Secure Software

Producing secure software is complex and requires high integration of security and software engineering. Based on our experience, we present the problems of producing secure software as follows:-

a. ***Attackers' Knowledge***:- As software security continue to gain the attention of security experts and organizations, the tools and techniques used by attackers are becoming increasingly sophisticated and invasive.

b. ***Complexity of software***:- Software development is a complex process because it involves many activities and specialties. It involves different units, stages and personalities, and all these have to be integrated to achieve successful software production. The situation is even worse with the connection to Internet and the use of mobile codes.

c. ***Security Education***:- Producing secure software requires a lot of security training, education and experience. Many software developers are not well grounded in computer security. To what extent of the techniques and tools of attackers do they understand? Also, many programming books do not teach how to write secure programs. Many curricular of schools offering computer science do not properly address computer security.

d. ***Attitude of Software Engineers***:- In the past, software developers were only interested in producing software product with the desired quality. Little attention was paid on making secure products. But, the situation is changing now that everybody is aware of the implications of vulnerabilities in software.

e. ***Inadequacy of Computer Security Models***:- Many security models are still not adequate for producing secure software products. Implementing some of them is complex and difficult to realize.

Secure Software Development

It has been said that producing software requires integrating Software Engineering (SE) process with Security Engineering. In doing this, a careful understanding of software development process is important. We now present an overview of software development process.

Overview of Software Development Stages

The summary of stages of software development is:

a. Requirement definition

- ❖ Fact findings
- ❖ Investigating the current system
- ❖ Modeling the current system
- ❖ Logical models of the required system

Result: Requirement specification

b. Design

- ❖ Structuring and partitioning of the design into software sub-components
- ❖ Detailed design of the components
- ❖ Formation of the system structure and relationships

Result: Design document containing system abstraction and their relationships

c. Coding

- ❖ Programming components of the system
- ❖ Unit testing

Result: Tested software subcomponents

d. System testing

- ❖ Integrating subcomponents together
- ❖ Integration testing
- ❖ System testing to ensure that the system meets its requirements

Result: Software product

e. Implementation and Maintenance

- ❖ Installing the system in `live` environment
- ❖ Training the users
- ❖ Maintenance
- ❖ Implementing enhancements as demanded by changes in the environment and users

Result: Working software product

Secure Software Development Model (SSDM)

SSDM is a model that integrates security engineering with software development process. As shown in Figure 1, it is a unified model that combines some existing software security techniques. It is structured towards creating secure software products. The dotted lines in Figure 1, shows continuous links along an engineering path. The model shows clearly how software development should be linked to security engineering in order to produce secure software products.

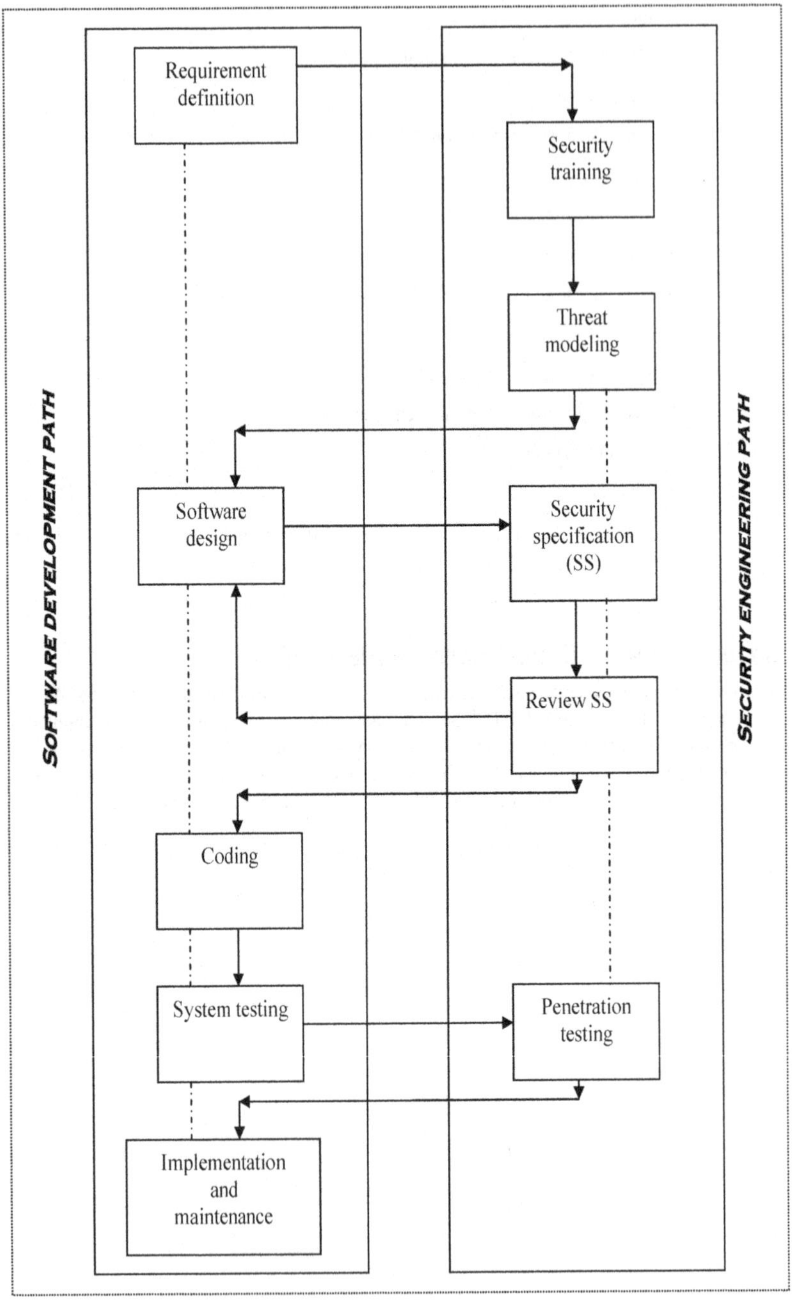

Figure 1: Secure Software Development Model (SSDM)

SSDM security engineering process

As shown in Figure 1, the security engineering path is divided into five stages.

a. ***Security Training***

Not all software engineers have adequate knowledge of computer security. The essence of security training is to provide adequate security education to stakeholders in software development. The key training requirements are:

- *Security awareness*:- This involves educating software engineers on general security concepts. Cases on previous security breaches and their consequences should be presented to them in order to appreciate the need for adequate protection of software products.
- *Knowledge of attackers on previous related applications*:- Software engineers should be educated on nature of previous attacks. There is need to understand attackers' techniques and tools and implications so as to properly understand attackers' behaviours. There is also need to understand penetration techniques of actions like logic bombs, trojans, virus, worms, and so on.
- *Understanding attackers' interests on software being developed*:- Software developers must be able to study a software system and identify software resources that might be of interest to potential attackers. This is important so as to develop techniques for protecting these resources.
- *Knowledge about secure development practices*:- Software developers should also be educated on previous practices on secure software development and their strengths and weaknesses so as to move secure software development forward.

b. ***Threat Modeling***

A threat model is used to effectively and comprehensively identify attackers and their capabilities. Every software development that must be secure must have it own threat model because the common security criteria might not be suitable for all software products.

SSDM threat model is divided into three parts. The classification is similar to what is presented in Myagmar et al., 2005, but our own seems to be more detailed.

i. <u>Understand the nature of the software</u>

This requires understanding:

- *The type of the software*:- The type of a software system determines the magnitude and nature of resources on the software system.
- *Complexity of the software*:- Provision of adequate security to big and complex system is a huge challenge. Complex software systems need more comprehensive threat analysis and modeling in order to capture potential attacks effectively.
- *Other associating software*:- The type and complexity of other software systems that are handshaking with the software under consideration must be investigated. The level of security of the associating software must be ascertained.

ii. <u>Identify attackers/threats</u>

The major issues here are:

- *Assessing the operating environment*:- There is need to study the environment in which the software must operate in order to identify the possible potential attackers and their categories.

- *Identifying the goals/targets of different category*:- Based on previous experience, we must be able to identify the possible interests and goals of attackers in the software.
- *Identifying techniques and tools used by attackers*:- It is also important to know the possible techniques and tools to be used by these attackers in order to develop techniques to block them.
- *Identifying possible future patterns/behaviours of attackers*:- Ensuring that software product are secured is not to think about the present situation alone, but to continue to plan ahead because of the changing nature of attackers' techniques and tools. There is need to identify future behaviours of attackers and undertake some measures to prevent them.
- *Constructing attack profile*:- An attack profile consisting of potential attacks, goals or target of attackers, techniques and tools of attackers and future behaviours of attackers, should be constructed.

iii. Identify possible vulnerabilities

Based on the information on the previous attacks, all likely vulnerabilities that may be introduced into the system must be identified. This will enable the software engineers not to carryout the design in a way that the vulnerabilities would be avoided.

c. ***Security Specification (SS)***

This entails stating the guidelines and procedures that guarantee security of the system The SS should contain the following:-

i. ***Security needs***:- This involves stating list of attacks to guide against and construction of vulnerability profile

ii. ***State security policies***:- This involves a clear definition of how to guide against attacks. Some specific issues to be included are:

- Avoiding errors through out the development
- Correct all errors at the time of first notice
- Employing programming tactics that prevent vulnerabilities
- Employing module integration method that guarantee security

iii. How to coordinate security implementation

iv. How to make the system to adapt to the changing landscape of security

v. How to monitor security postures of the software system

d. ***Review SS***

This is to check whether the design content of the software is in accordance with the SS. This is important because if the design is defective, then the software design must incorporate the security specifications. If the design has not guaranteed the items in the SS, then the design will be reviewed.

e. ***Penetration Testing***

Capabilities of the software in preventing attacks are tested here. It is important so as to:

- Test the security of the software and its resources

- Determine if the current security posture of the software is actually detecting and preventing attacks.

Penetration testing is carried out in a way that all identified attacks and future attack patterns are initiated on-line into the software, and the capability of the software in preventing these attacks is monitored.

Laws of Software Security

Based on our experience from the literature, and as security researchers and consultants, we present some basic laws as supporting structure towards producing secure software products. All stakeholders in software development must obey these laws in order not to introduce vulnerabilities into the system and ensure the production of secured software system. It is believed that if the software engineers have these laws at the back of their minds throughout the stages of the software production, it will ensure efficient production of secure software product. These 10 proposed laws are:-

a. ***Awareness law***:- It states that software developers must constantly update their security knowledge with new information about security.

b. ***Do- it- correct law***:- It states that any activity or process or task to be carried out by any developer should be done correctly first time and every time.

c. ***Patching law***:- It states that no error must be patched. Any error must be removed immediately it is recognized and it must be ascertained that the error will not resurface again.

d. ***Self Evaluation law***:- It states that every software developer should evaluate his/her work at the end of each process or task.

e. ***Security Inclusion law***:- It states that software engineers should bear in mind that security is a subset of quality.

f. ***None Rigidity law***:- It states that security requirements must not be rigid but must be realized. It must be rigid in the sense that suggestions about security issues should be welcomed. The details of the security specifications must be realized.

g. ***Protection law***:- It states that security engineering process itself must be secured. SS must be secret and known only to concerned individuals alone. SS must be guarded with integrity throughout the software engineering process.

h. ***Explicit law***:- It states that the details of SS must be clear and concise for easy implementation. Software developers must be able to understand clearly all issues in the SS.

i. ***Total Security law***:- It states that if software product P is secure, then all other software that must interact with P must also be secure.

Case Study

An accounting system called "Standard Accounting" or "SA" implements SSDM security engineering principles. Standard Accounting was an in-house design, which was implemented on intranet of an organization in Nigeria. The components of Standard are general ledger, sales and purchase ledger, and payroll. The development of Standard was conceived and started when the organization realized there were frequent security breaches on the old accounting package. The Accounting system of the organization operates in a way that different personnel from different units of the organization have access to it. The users of SA have privileges to use some resources of the package and some of them misuse their privileges. Consequently, there were several security breaches reported with the old accounting package. Some of these security breaches are:

- Change of information in the salary table
- Stoppage of loans
- Cancellation of purchase records
- Total collapse of the system (Denial-of-service)

A nine-member team developed and implemented SA. This comprises of 6 internal staff of the organization and 3 external consultants for supervision of the project and as security experts. The software was designed using Oracle.

During the use of the old package, the security breaches recorded were collected and categorized according to computer security goals - CIA. There were total of 129 security breaches recorded at this time. The design of SA was completed about a year ago and was implemented at the same time. We have been monitoring the implementation of SA and have not recorded any security breaches since that time. Table 1 shows the summary of the security improvement by the implementation of SSDM.

Table 1: Performance validation of SSDM

S/No	Security threats classification	Old package	New (Standard)
1	Confidentiality	69	-
2	Integrity	42	-
3	Availability	18	-
	Total	129	

It can be seen that there were 129 records of security breaches for almost three years of usage. With the new accounting system that implemented SSDM principles, no incidence of security breach has been recorded in about one years9 of usage.

Future Work and Conclusions

In this paper, we examined the problem of producing secure software. The research in software security is gaining much attention because of the implication of security breaches. Problems towards producing secure software products were identified and stated in this work. This is important for researchers so as to know the real problems and the direction to follow in providing the methodologies for providing secure software product. We also proposed an integrated model for providing secure software products and presented a case study to ascertain that the model works. The model has some interesting features that guarantee the successful production of secure software products. SSDM has shown a way of separating security specification from functional specification. It is believed that if this model is carefully implemented; it will result in the production of secure software products. It was shown in this work that implementing SSDM improves the security of software systems.

The model presented in this work still needs to be more tested so as to really ascertain its performance. Some of the components of SSDM are still major areas of research that should be studied.

References

Davis, N. & Mullaney, J. (2003). The team software process in practice: A summary of recent results. *Technical Report CMU/SEI-TR-014*, September.

Devanbu, P. T. & Stubblebine (2000). Software engineering for security: A roadmap. *Proceedings of International Conference on Software Engineering (ICSE' 2000), Special volume on "Future of Software Engineering", 2000.*

Ghosh, A. K., Howell, C. & Whittacker, J. A. (2002). Building software securely from ground up. *IEEE Software magazine*, January/February.

Goldenson, D. R. & Gibson, D. L. (2003). Demonstrating the impact and benefits of CMMI. *Special Report CMU/SEI-2003-SR-009.* The Software Engineering Institute, Carnegie Mellon University.

Hall, A & Rod, C. (2004). Correctness-by-construction. Paper written for *Cyber Security Taskforce Subgroup on Software Process*, January.

Hefner, R. (1997). Lesson learned with the systems security engineering capability model. *Proceedings of the Conference on Software Engineering*, Boston, Massachusetts, USA.

Jones, C. (2000). *Software assessments, benchmarks, and best practices.* Reading, MA: Addison-Wesley.

Linger, R. & Stacy, P. (2004). Developing secure software with Cleanroom software engineering. Paper prepared for *Cyber Security Summit Task Force Subgroup on Software Process*, February.

McGraw, G. E. (2003). On the horizon: The DIMACS workshop on software security. *IEEE Security and Privacy*, March/April.

Mead, N. R. & McGraw, G. (2003). From the ground up: The DIMACS software security workshop. *IEEE Security and Privacy*, March/April.

Mogilevsky, D., Lee, A. J. & Yurcik, W. (2005). Defining a comprehensive threat model for high performance computational clusters. *ACM Computing Research Repository (CoRR),* Technical Report cs.CR/0510046, October 16, 2005. Retrieved from http://www.ncassr.org/projects/threatmodeling/mogilevskyCorr05-threatmodel.pdf

Myagmar, S., Lee, A. J. & Yurcik, W. (2005). Threat modeling as a basis for security requirements. *Symposium on Requirements Engineering for Information Security (SREIS)* in conjunction with *13th IEEE International Requirements Engineering Conference (RE), Paris, France,* August 29.

Pauli, J. & Xu, D. (2004). Threat-driven architectural design on secure information systems. Presented at the *International Conference on Enterprise Information System, Miami, Florida, USA.*

Redwine, S. T. & Davis, N. (2004). Processes to produce secure software. *National Cyber Security Summit*, March.

Rodgers, D. H. (2002). Implementing a project security review process within the project management methodology. *GIAC Security Essentials Certification (GSEC), SANS Institute.*

Schneir, J. H., Lippman, J. R. & Wing, J. (2002). Automated generation and analysis of attack graphs. *Proceeding of IEEE Symposium on Security and Privacy, April.*

Sheyner, O. & Wing, J. (2004). Tools for generating and analysing attack graphs. *Proceeding of Formal Methods for Components and Objects.*

Sodiya, A. S., Longe, H. O. D. & Akinwale A. T. (2004). A new two-tiered strategy to intrusion detection. *Journal of Information Management and Computer Security, 12*(1).

Wilander, J. & Gustavsson, J. (2005). Security requirements – A field study of current practice. Presented at the *Symposium on Requirement Engineering for Information Security (SREIS' 2005)*, Paris, France.

Bibliographies

Dr. **A. S. Sodiya** is presently a lecturer in the department of Computer Science, University of Agriculture, Abeokuta, Nigeria. He completed his PhD in the same university in 2004. His areas of research interest are Computer Security, Computer Network, Artificial Intelligence and Software Engineering. He has published both in local and international journals. He has also attended and presented papers in several conferences.

Mrs. **S. A. Onashoga** (formerly Mrs. Ibrahim, nee OKUNLAYA) is a Lecturer in the Department of Computer Science, University of Agriculture, Abeokuta, Nigeria. She graduated with B.Sc. degree in Mathematical Sciences (Computer Science option). She had a M.Sc. in Computer Science. She has publications in local and international journals. Her areas of research interest are Data Mining and Network Security. She is currently a Ph.D. student in Computer Science.

Mr. **O. B. Ajayi** is the e-Learning/Network Administrator of the Computing Centre of the University of Agriculture, Abeokuta. His primary responsibility is in the area of System Programming and Analysis. He graduated with B.Sc (Honours) degree in Mathematical Sciences (Computer Science Option). He later obtained his M.Sc in Computer Science from the same University and postgraduate diploma in Petroleum Engineering from the University of Ibadan, Ibadan. He is blessed with two kids and a lovely wife.

Information Systems Field at the Forks: Relish Diversity or Perish

Bob Travica
University of Manitoba, Canada

btravica@ms.umanitoba.ca

Abstract

This article discusses the relationship between the informing science and information view of organization. Both approaches are described, similarities and differences between them demonstrated, and the contribution of the latter to the former discussed.

Keywords: Informing science, information view of organization, information, communication, information technology, organization theory, cognitive theory

Introduction

This article discusses the relationship between informing science and information view of organization (IVO). Both of these approaches endorse different disciplines that are orthogonal or tangent to the study of information systems (IS), while departing from slightly different theoretical premises. Information view of organization was recently introduced (Travica, 2003) as a new way of looking at organizations from the IS perspective. IVO aims at bringing together the streams of research that have traditionally addressed information and information technology (IT) independently from each other. Another integration direction concerns strengthening the links between the IS field, organization theory and cognitive theory. IVO intends to advance theory of IS and provide a guidance for practicing managers and professionals for understanding issues pertaining to the intersection of ISs and the organizational context. In addition to conceptual works on IVO, the framework has been initially tested in several case studies.

Informing science was introduced by Cohen (1999). Informing science also aims at a theoretical integration with communication and organization theory as primary targets. The main goal of informing science is defined in terms of ensuring that needs of organizational users of information are effectively served. Informing science intends primarily to provide a practical guidance to organizations. The framework of informing science has been advanced through recent efforts of its proponents.

In this article, I will describe premises, goals, and the scope of IVO and informing science, critically appraise the latter one, and define similarities and differences between the two approaches. The article will conclude with a proposal on how IVO can be used to broaden informing science.

Information View of Organization

IVO has been introduced in several recent articles (Travica, 2003, 2004,

2005a, 2005b). IVO is a conceptual and analytical framework intended to aid in explaining and managing ISs in organizations. IVO draws on the IS field, organization/management theory, and cognitive theory. In particular, IVO aims at bridging the gaps between the IS fields and organization theory. In its multidisciplinary and reconciliatory approach, IVO sides with informing science (Cohen, 1999) and similar recent initiatives (Orlikowski & Barley, 2001; social informatics). The background rationale is that organization at various levels (firm, group, individual-task/process) is presumed to be the natural habitat for ISs. By bridging the gap, both sides can gain: the IS field can better contextualize and situate its key concept of IS, and organization theory can gain better insight into modern ISs that typically are not differentiated from other organization technologies, knowledge, organizations of work, and management techniques. In addition, IVO intends to bridge a gap between different academic streams of research addressing ISs. These are split into two camps. One focuses on IT while obscuring information issues (e.g., the way information systems are usually taught in business schools in North America). The other camp does the opposite (e.g., schools of library and information science and the descendents of these). IVO insists on studying both information and IT. In addition, in approaching the IT artifact, IVO takes a more specific look that accounts for systems functionality, user interface and other material particulars. The background assumption is that the time has come to contribute to understanding IT beyond the accustomed black boxed, abstract approaches based on proxy measures (e.g., the time expended in using IT) (see Orlikowski & Iacono, 2001). An exhaustive discussion of these issues is in Travica (2005b).

IVO uses a broader understanding of information, IT, and organization. In particular, IVO conceives *information* as an informing agency, that which shapes human cognition. This concept is consistent with lexical definitions of information that draw on the Latin root of the word "information." This informing agency can take on different forms, starting with *data*—sense data as well as data as human-created artifacts (letters, numbers, image, sound). Data are processed and interpreted with assistance of *knowledge* in human mind, which results in *meaning*. Different knowledge bases can engender different meanings of the same data. Meaning, in turn, can add to the previous knowledge. IVO takes interest in data, meaning, and knowledge as forms of information that are interrelated although clearly distinguishable from each other in terms of location, complexity, portability, truth value, etc. For example, data can reside both inside and outside of the human brain (e.g., in paper records and in electronic databases), while meaning and knowledge cannot be external to the brain.

Knowledge can be externalized in various representations that are nothing but organized data. Only these data can be communicated. The same applies to meaning: it cannot be simply "transmitted" but only communicated via data. Forms of information differ in terms of the truth value as well. While data and meaning are susceptible to formal metrics of truth applicable to various frameworks (e.g., formal logic, and measurement systems), knowledge evades such precise validations. For example, competing theories based on opposed premises can coexist. This is the *modus operandi* of physics and other natural sciences as much as it is of social sciences (which sometimes are unjustly blamed for their "inexact nature"). Implications of this differentiating between different forms of information are paramount for the study of ISs in organizations. Beyond its simplest form of data, information becomes a complex cognitive phenomenon that is prone to subjective variation and evades precise validation. Also, transmission/exchange models of communication may pertain only to data and not to the higher forms of information.

With respect to understanding *IT*, IVO strives to reach beyond abstract approaches that the mainstream IS research exhibits. This research often operates with opaque operationalizations of IT in the form of surrogate measure (e.g., the frequency of usage, or the amount of investment in it). Or even less enlightening, IT is treated as a black box (see Orlikowski & Iacono, 2001). These approaches neglect particular characteristics of particular types of IT and/or corresponding ISs. Another sort of abstraction occurs with sociologizing of IT, when IT is "dissolved" in social relationships as is the case with recent institutional approaches (e.g., Orlikowski, 1992). In contrast to these abstractions, IVO pledges for reach accounts on material characteristics of IT, including functionality, usability of user interface, capabilities and limitations. Research on design, adoption, use, and evaluation of ISs should aim at understanding how these characteristics of particular technologies interact with particular users in the organizational context. To illustrate with an example from a study I currently run based on the IVO approach (further, a utility company case). Modules of an Enterprise Resource Planning (ERP) system for human resource (HR) management were released in the utility company under a tight schedule, and with some half-baked functionality. One such feature concerns the fact that data entry screens "flash" every time the user enters a piece of data. These screens run within a browser window, which in turn runs on a corporate intranet. The screen "flashing" has been identified as a big shortcoming ("annoying," "disturbing," etc.) by a number of users belonging to different departments and hierarchical positions. An interesting finding is that many users do not know why the "flashing" happens, while those claiming to know why provide differing explanations. In any case, the flashing fact appears to be a factor in the system adoption. Another finding is that the "flashing" has been cited as a downside along with other usability issues as well as with process-related issues.

The cited process issues seem to be of a particular significance for the HR management applications studied. Namely, the applications were accompanied with a change in the process of approving work hours and monetary expenses. In the past, the process combined electronic and paper records. A clerk would enter time and expenses data by using then available HR modules in the ERP system, and then the approval would be done either by the same clerk or by a manager, who would use a printout of electronic records. With the new HR modules, clerks have become limited to the role of data entry, while approval procedures are now reserved for managers. However, my investigation so far has shown that managers may not be willing to adopt the new process. One justification made is that the system "unloads more work" on managers (which indeed is true), and that this work does not add value. Another justification is that the system disables delegating approval responsibility down, and just allows it to be delegated across (both true). The users-complainers argue that this method makes it impossible to ensure that the approvals are done in absence of managers (e.g., when they attend meetings or are on a business trip or vacation). Since even the most trusting person cannot be assigned to do online approvals if such a person is not flagged with management responsibility in the system's database, approvals can only be made by other temporarily assigned managers who may not be well informed for performing this task (e.g., they reside on a remote location). My investigation reveals that radical rejections of the system typically cite this new work process as a significant problem. In short, these examples indicate advantages of using a rich account of IT that IVO advocates. The important facts of screen "flashing" (refreshment) and changed approval process may play a significant part in explaining the system adoption, evaluation, and use.

Organization is a different entity for an interpretive, modernist or postmodern theorist (Clegg, Hardy, & Nord, 1996; Hatch, 1997; Westwood & Clegg, 2003). How one understands information, communication and IT, their relationships, and organizational roles is likely to depend on the ontology of organization used. For example, for a modernist thinker an organization is usually a system with clear goals, while information, communication and IT are instruments for achieving the goals. All these aspects as well as the progress toward goals are susceptible to measurement, contend the modernist. Contrary, postmodernists break with the assumption of a driving organizational paradigm and can show tolerance for different paradigms and traditionally marginal topics, such as emotion and esthetics. Thus, organizations can also be viewed as organisms, brains, mental prisons, the context of chaos, and so on. On their part, interpretivists may turn to political and cultural/symbolist perspectives, and render the roles of information, communication and IT in this light. So for example, a system adoption failure may be interpreted through the prism of job security, hidden political agendas, and communication of unintended meanings (Sarker & Lee, 1999).

IVO advocates an ontological pluralism. Rather than being an intellectual fad, I believe that a pluralist approach is needed in order to make sense of the complexity challenging contemporary organizations (Clegg & Hardy, 1996; Davidow & Malone, 1992; Handy, 1993; Hatch, 1997; Heckscher & Donnellon, 1994; Peters, 1992; Thietart & Forgues, 1995). Bureaucratic organization is not the only organizational design, and it has been challenged by the network, virtual, adhocratic and other new designs (Travica, 1999). Organizational environments also change, become global in scale, and engender unprecedented levels of uncertainty and ambiguity. Owing to the electronically networked character of today's global economy, the social forces we create evade our comprehension and control (Castells, 1996). In this situation, it appears to be misleading to portray organizations exclusively in terms of a machine, parts of which are information and IT, and that effectiveness can be reached by greasing well and occasionally repairing the organizational machine.

In brief, there is a correspondence between conceptualizations of information, communication, IT and organization, and IVO advocates a broader approach to each of these and to their relationships.

Topical Areas in IVO

IVO incorporates several topical areas that are shown in Table 1. These topics have been discussed in several articles (Travica, 2003, 2005b; also see the articles cited separately in the following discussion).

Table 1. Topical Areas in IVO

IVO Topic	Coverage
Homoinformaticus	Individual cognition, individuals as creators and users of information and of ISs.
Groupomatics (Group Informatics)	Group cognition, decision making, collaborative work and group support systems.
Infostructure	Patterns of relationships between information segments and the arrangement of IT that complement social structure.
Infoprocesses	Interrelated information activities that altogether deliver an outcome to a customer.
Infoculture	Beliefs, behaviors and artifacts that are related to information and IT.
Infopolitics	Power, agendas, and fight/flight behaviors related to information and IT.
Infoeconomics	The value and costs of information and IT.
IS Management Areas	Issues/challenges/problems of design, adoption, use, and evaluation of IS approached from the stance of IVO aspects above.

From the IVO perspective, individual organizational members are *creators* and *users* of both information and ISs. This omnipotent individual is called *homoinformaticus.* That individuals are creators of information follows from IVO's concept of information discussed above. Whereas it is trivial that individuals create data (e.g., documents), IVO points out that individuals are also agents of developing meaning and knowledge. It is important to understand these processes on both the sender and receiver side in various communication settings in organizations. For example, while a system designer may believe that "logical" closing steps in an online approval procedure are "Send" and then "Save and Close," users may find this order to be counterintuitive (as one of the respondents in the utility company case put it: "You first save a record, then you email it"). Different knowledge perspectives engender different understandings of proper order of steps. Technologists are concentrated on a big picture of the business process (view data, make decision and record it in the system, send the decision to the payroll and the employee, permanently store new data, exit the application). What matters first is that a decision is made and sent. In contrast, users apply experience from using other applications, perhaps somewhat fueled by incomplete trust in technology (view data, make decision and record it in the system, permanently store the decision, send the decision, exit the application). What matters first is to make and save the decision. Another facet of the creativity of organizational members refers to IS development life cycle. Users can provide a valuable input for designing and implementing a system, as exemplified in participatory design (Iivari & Lyytinen, 1999), and they can modify systems functions in the adoption stage. The homoinformaticus segment of IVO draws heavily on individual and cognitive psychology.

The next topic in IVO refers to groups approached from a cognitive perspective. This is the area of *group informatics* or *groupomatics*. Specifically, of interest are the processes of perception, learning memorizing, retrieval, and thinking/problem solving. These topics parallel topics studied within individual cognitive psychology. Cognitive psychology reminds us again of a differentiated character of information. For example, perception involves both external stimuli and internal mental activity (Eysenck and Keane, 1995, pp. 80-81). An individual gathers sense data, organizes it, and, with help of previous knowledge (mental imagery, schemas, mental models), attributes a meaning to it. Perception is, thus, a process of active creation of meaning. IVO implements these assumptions in the concept of homoinformaticus and raises them again in the area of group informatics. IVO also builds on the remarkable research in the area of group support systems (e.g., Ciborra, 1996; Nunamaker, Briggs, Mittleman, Vogel, & Pierre, 1996/7; Turoff, Hiltz, Bahgat, & Rana, 1993). Another point of interest is recently advanced research into transactive memory and collective mind (Shaila & Saunders, 1995; Shepherd, Briggs, Reining, &Yen, 1995).

The next set of topical areas within IVO draws on centering the well-known views of organization around information and IT. The classical structural view is modified into *infostructure* (Table 1). For example, Weber's (1946) concept of hierarchy (the levels of graded authority) is modified into "levels of information and IT." The background assumption is that structuring of information and IT is a necessary condition for the social structuring of organizations. For example, an ERP system provides different views of data and different data manipulation capabilities depending on the hierarchal position of users. The rights of data access are a segment in the entire bundle of rights that define a level in organizational hierarchy. For instance, decision making authority of management levels strongly depends on the former rights. In addition to the vertical dimension, infostructure includes a horizontal, formalization, and centralization aspect.

The part of organizational culture that relates to information and IT is the domain of *infoculture*. Davenport and Prusak (1997) have previously proposed a concept of information culture but narrowed it down to "behaviors and attitudes that express an organization's orientation toward information" (p. 84). In an infoculture, assumptions, values, symbols, and rituals have a clear, narrower focus rather than the broad one that pertains to the concept of organizational culture. An apparent example of infoculture is core beliefs and behaviors characterizing the use of modern ISs (e.g., the etiquette of an email system). Early studies of computer mediated communication discovered that people behave differently when using email (e.g., Kiesler, Siegel, & McGuire,

1984). An aberration from usual social norms and an expression that is more honest were some of the changes (for better or for worse) discovered. Although organizations may try to channel this infoculture according to the mainstream organizational culture, it appears that every new communication technology/system repeats the story of email. A tension between paper and electronic forms of information can characterize values, attitudes and work practices in older organizations that make a transition toward modern ISs. This is true of the utility company implementing HR modules in the ERP system. Another example of infocultural artifacts, is indicated by the company's managers that tend to characterize the method of online approvals as a penetration of clerical (non-value adding) work into their turf. Symbolically, they associate the system to inappropriate work and waste of time.

Infopolitics refers to issues of power, agendas, and fights/flights that concern organizational information and IT. Making the core of contemporary organizations, information and IT constitute high political stakes. In the organizational literature, it has long been maintained that control over professional knowledge can be a source of power (Crozier, 1964; Pfeffer, 1981). Barley (1986, 1990) related power changes to knowledge of manipulating new computer-based medical technology, and Zuboff (1984) identified a possibility of power gains on the side of professionals who adopted new digital IT in different kinds of organizations. In a case study of a festival venue in Canada, I found that a monopoly of knowledge on organizing and management represented the main lever of power (Travica, 2005a). Yet, another example comes from our utility company, where new HR applications prevented clerks from making decisions they used to make before with a blessing of supervisors. Thus, the new system reasserted the formal distribution of decision making authority. Indeed, organizations can be highly politicized contexts (depending on their design). If so, words and other communication codes are more likely to have double than single, denotative meanings, and one can seek in vain to achieve the fidelity of information beyond the sheer level of data.

IVO recognizes significant merits of the process view of organization and incorporates it into its coverage through the concept of *infoprocess*. IVO's focus is on information components of business processes and fully-fledged infoprocess that consist solely of information activities. In accord with the notion of business process, infoprocess refers to interrelated information activities that deliver an outcome to a customer (cf. Hammer and Champy, 1993). IVO takes interest in various aspects of the process approach to organizations, including coordination theory (Malone and Crowston, 1994), business process reengineering (Hammer and Champy, 1993), new organizational forms, and the study of ERP systems. Infoprocesses exist at different levels, ranging from processes that manipulate data at the micro level of interconnected tasks to macro-organizational and inter-organizational infoprocesses. There are connections and dependencies between infoprocesses at different levels. The highest level infoprocesses give rise to a new organizational design—the virtual organization, since they interpenetrate organizational boundaries. In a case of Internet service in a four-star hotel, I discovered that a dysfunctional infoprocess at the micro level unraveled the related upstream infoprocess, with the end result being a dissatisfied process customer—the guest (Travica, 2004).

Finally, *infoeconomics* refers to valuing and costing issues pertaining to information and IT. This aspect is important because it relates directly to organizational economics and other aspects of the bottom line of organizations. While the cost side yields to inquiry (e.g., Snyder & Davenport, 1987), the valuing of information and IT is bound to paramount challenges. What is the economic contribution of meaning and knowledge to a particular organizational task or to the organizational bottom line (profit, quality of service)? In spite of a number of methodologies tried, success of teasing out the contribution of information are rather meager, particularly when one tries to reach beyond intangible benefits (e.g., more complete and timely information) to tangible benefits (monetary payoffs). The core of the problem may be in the character of the information phenomenon. Information appears to be one of those things whose value can be assessed only retroactively at use time. Knowledge accumulated through education is a typical example: students acquire knowledge *a priori* (before the fact), and understand its value *a posteriori* (after the fact). The payback from IT or more appropriately IS also evades analysis based on tangible figures. This is so in spite of certain properties of IT/IS that reverse classical economic laws, such as the law of diminishing returns.

One apparent reason for the challenges of valuing is that, in a typical scenario, IT/IS are in service of information; they are the means of manipulating data that can become meaning and knowledge. Therefore, the problem of valuing IT/IS boils down to valuing information. Another challenging issue is a variety of contexts of using IT/IS. IT may not be deployed directly in production but in support of functions that are not considered value adding (e.g., accounting control, HR management, communications).From this perspective, IT/IS does not add value to the organizational output, although it could help avoid or reduce administrative labor costs (a tangible benefit). When IT/IS is deployed in information industry whose output—partly or entirely—is information (e.g., mass media, education, financial and insurance industries), tracking tangible payoffs from IT is difficult to do beyond the level of data transactions. For example, to what extent and how a financial information system helps a bank analyst to design new bank services is a question for empirical research rather than an evaluation task susceptible to formalized metrics. In contrast to these examples, more automated organizational contexts dispose IT/IS closer to other production technologies, or to commodity (Carr, 2004) whose benefits may be easier to track.

The level of analysis poses another sort of challenge in valuing IT/IS and associated information. If benefits from these show up at the task level, they may not necessarily occur at the process or organizational level of analysis. The reverse is also true: process benefits may not show at the level of each individual participating task. Further, the same IT/IS can result in more benefits in one organization than in another; organizational context (structure, culture management) can make a difference (Brynjolfsson & Hitt, 1998). At the level of economic sectors, no contribution of IT/IS to the office work productivity has been detected yet. This phenomenon, known as "IT productivity paradox" (Roach, 1987), has been a subject of a heated discussion in recent years.

All these are important and interesting issues that chart the territory of infoeconomics. IVO provides a framework for analyzing relationships of infoeconomics with other IVO aspects and with the bottom line (organizational economics or effectiveness in some other respect). For example, one may investigate how infoculture does/can contribute to changes in infoprocesses that, in turn, have effect on infoeconomics and economics. Illustrating by the case of the utility company: an infoculture of paperless office ties into new infoprocesses of managers' online approvals of employees' time and expenses, which improves infoeconomics (faster data flows, higher integration of electronic data on human resources). But, impacts on organizational economics are uncertain, since savings in clerical work (for approvals) are countered by expenditures in managerial work.

The IVO topics or aspects discussed so far represent the backdrop for certain aspects of managing ISs. These are the issues of design, adoption, use, and evaluation of IS approached from the stance of IVO aspects above. So, in order to understand and manage IS adoption, one needs to look into IVO aspects that are relevant for the given situation. Establishing this relevance is an empirical question and it cannot be determined beforehand. This follows from the character of IVO: it is a framework, not a finalized research model.

In summary, IVO places information and IT at the nexus of organization. IVO uses a differentiated concept of information, strives to bring for rich accounts of IT, and operates with different models of organization. IVO consists of seven topical areas reflecting the organizational context, and intersects these with issues of IS design, adoption, use, and evaluation.

Informing Science

The term informing science and the related framework has been introduced by Cohen (1999). Drawing on Mason and Mitroff's (1973) work, Cohen defines informing science as a set of fields that have the goal to "**provide** their **clientele** with **information** in a **form, format, and schedule** that maximizes its effectiveness" (p. 4, 5; the emphases are original).

The theoretical foundation of the informing science framework consists of three models: Shannon and Weaver's (1949) mathematical model of communication, Leavitt's (1965) model of organization, and a three level-analysis (Cohen, 1999). The Shannon and Weaver model of communication was developed with the purpose of explaining data communications in telephone networks. Over time, the model was adopted by social researchers for studying human communication. The model defines and relates several concepts: sender, signal, channel, noise, information, and receiver. The sender element (e.g., a phone set) transmits a signal over a channel (e.g., a wire) to a receiver element (e.g., another phone set). While traveling, the signal loses some energy (e.g., due to resistance of the wire), which is conceived as noise or entropy. To compensate for the loss, new energy has to be added. This energy is conceived as negative entropy or *information*. Therefore, information is the measure of negative entropy that is needed for accurate transmission of electrical signals. In the later use of this model by social and behavioral scientists, there is a significant shift in the concepts and their relationships (more below). Cohen (1999) suggests that the model is useful for understanding that communication is synonymous with informing; in turn, informing reduces uncertainty on the receiver's side. Similarly, the purpose of informing science is to design, manage, and use communication systems that effectively inform/reduce uncertainty.

The Leavitt (1965) model of organization and organizational change conceives of organization in terms of people, task, technology, and structure. Organization members perform on organizational tasks, while using different technologies and following rules, lines of reporting and other structural properties. In addition to providing analytical lenses on organization at a micro level of analysis, the purpose of this model is to alert on a brittle character of organizational equilibrium. Leavitt (1965.) has assumed that the four aspects of organization are inter-related so that a change in any of them causes changes in others. Equilibrium (stability or, in Leavitt's terms, a "freeze state") is difficult to achieve. Once any aspect is tilted off balance ("unfrozen"), the other aspects follow the suit, and changes trigger new changes. It takes management effort to bring the organization system back to equilibrium, or to "re-freeze" organization and, thus, make the changes achieved permanent. The third basis of the informing science framework refers to different levels of analysis or abstraction.

Drawing on the theoretical basis described above, Cohen (1999) defines three components of the informing science framework: informing environment, delivery system, and task-completion system. The backbone is Shannon and Weaver's (1949) model (furthermore, the model), which is combined with elements from the other two theoretical bases. Specifically, informing environment corresponds to the sender part, and it is approached at three levels of analysis—the use of existing informing practices, creation of new standard practices of informing, and creation of new types of informing practices (e.g., using an IS for sending information, designing a new IS, and creating a new type of IS). (Note: The term "practice" is mine.) Delivery system refers to transmitting information, which can be done by means of an IS, and this corresponds to communication channel in the model. Finally, task-completion system refers to accomplishing a task with help of information received, which corresponds to the receiver part in the model. The provision of information for accomplishing tasks is informing process' reason for existence. Therefore, the primary goal of this modeling and of informing science in general is to inform clients (those at the receiving end of information, or user of ISs) in an effective way.

Informing science is a new framework, and attempts at advancing it have been made quite recently (e.g., Gackowski, 2005; Roussev and Rousseva, 2004). Gackowski (2005) also draws on Shannon and Weaver's model and explores characteristics of data and information (i.e., meaning) in the business context (e.g., accuracy, timelines, completeness, and economic aspects). In a critical appraisal of the original informing science framework, Gackowski points out that information does not only reduce uncertainty but can increase it as well; an example is information on environmental threats to an organization. He also proposes a set of characteristics to extend the concept of information used in informing science. In addition, Roussev and Rousseva (2004) have used propositions from the informing science framework to analyze the process of software engineering (this area of computer science largely overlaps with what is called systems analysis and design in the IS field). It could be said that many ideas the authors have discussed parallel system development methodologies that involve users more deeply. These range from participatory design and other methodologies created in Scandinavia (Iivari & Lyytinen, 1999) to today's efforts to the same end (Majchrzak, Beath, Lim, & Chin, 2005).

Informing Science and Information View of Organization

This section will provide a critical appraisal of informing science and an analysis of the relationship between informing science and IVO. The first apparent characteristic of Cohen's (1999) framework on informing science is its interdisciplinary focus. A primary motivation behind informing science is in integrating various streams of research in the IS field. Another key characteristic is that informing science takes a practitioner's approach to ISs (see Table 2, the Informing Science column). Put another way, informing science manifests a consulting and service orientation. This is indicated in the teleological definition of informing science is—the purpose of delivering effective information is framed as the key definitional point. This characteristic also indicates that information is a central concept in the framework, although an explicit conceptualization of information is missing. In addition, the definition of informing science is broad enough to encompass (a) various organized contexts in which informing can take place and (b) various categories of clients.

The Leavitt model of organization and organizational change provides a good point of departure for inquiry into informing issues in organizations. The same applies to the prescript on a multilevel analysis. In addition, a strong emphasis is placed on human communication, which is viewed exclusively through the prism of the anthropomorphic Shannon-Weaver (1949) model. Indeed, this model is the backbone of the entire informing science framework. Before turning to appraising this model, let me list some other important characteristics of informing science. The emphasis on communication is somewhat overwhelming as it obscures to some extent distinctions between communication and ISs. While the emphasis on communication has merits of bringing to the fore information, the often neglected aspect in the mainstream IS research, it is unclear why should inquiry give up the distinctions between communication and ISs. In keeping with traditions of human communication theory, communication is to be considered a particular aspect of or process in organization. Similarly, in the IS field IS is usually conceptualized as a separate whole that consists of data, IT and procedures, and which delivers processed (organized, "meaningful") data. ISs are used for various purposes, including communication. It is not clear why informing science does not use explicitly this concept of IS and integrates it with the chosen model of communication instead of bringing the model of communication and the implicit concept of IS into a parent-child relationship. Also, the goal of effective informing of clients can be equally reached if the relationship between system developers and users is placed in a service provider—customer model rather than in the communication model. In such a model, communication could still play a big role, but other aspects would be accounted for as well (budget, technology trade-offs, organizational context, vendor management, change management, etc.).

Erasing the distinction between communication and ISs has led to another questionable choice: face-to-face communication is undistinguishable from mediated communication, and IT becomes any thing and any symbolic entity. For example, Gackowski (2005) explicates that IT includes voice, personal and impersonal contacts (e.g., displays of merchandise) (p. 119). On the other hand, although IT is conceived so broadly, automated ISs are not listed as a kind of IT or IS. This choice locks out a whole slate of important systems, such as those supply chains, knowbots, software agents in online exchanges, control rooms in automated factories, and software intensive systems for the production in mass media, aircrafts and weaponry. This reduction is consequent to the driving purpose of informing human clients, but it runs (again) counter the commonly accepted definition of IS and the real world ISs.

Limitations of Shannon and Weaver's Model

Shannon and Weaver's (1949) mathematical model of communication (further, the model) makes the backbone in the informing science works discussed above (Cohen, 1999; Gackowski, 2005: Roussev & Rousseva, 2004). In the larger field of ISs, the model has achieved prominence with the proliferation of communication systems in the 1980s. According to Putnam, Phillips, and Chapman (1996), the model had for long been the most frequently used model in the study of organizational communication. In the area of organization theory, information processing view of organization (Galbraith, 1973) has most directly applied the model. It could be that the model has had the large acceptance because of its intuitive character: it outlines a common process of communication that occurs across contexts—in interpersonal as well as in mass communication, in face-to-face as well as in mediated communication, and in classical commercial publishing as well as in one-to-many publishing on the Internet (Web sites, blogging).

The trade-off side of the model, however, is paramount. First of all, the interpretation of the model in social sciences, including the IS field, is more arbitrary than formalized.[1] The ultimate roots lie in the shift of meanings that accompanied the importation of the model into social sciences. Specifically, sender and receiver have became social actors that can communicate face-to-face or via some communication technology (e.g., the telephone). Signal has become message or information, and channel is whatever medium happens to enable the exchange of messages between the sender and receiver (e.g., the air for transferring verbal messages and a computer network for email messages). In addition, noise or entropy is any loss in a message—in the content, clarity, etc. Being social actors rather than machines, both the sender and the receiver have become imbued with intention: the sender intends to send ("communicate") a certain message (information), and the receiver intends to receive the message (information) and act upon it. The shift in meanings of the core concepts in the original model also applies to "information," the key concept. No longer representing the compensation for the entropy caused by the communication channel, information is now given the role of reducing entropy that is relocated into the receiver's mind. Entropy is conceived as uncertainty—a shortage in cognition or simply ignorance, which exists prior to an act of communication. The receiver misses data or lacks knowledge, and information "comes" to him from the sender to add to his cognition, and thereby reduce his uncertainty.

The "upgrades" of the original model discussed above are of such magnitude that the resulting model qualifies indeed as a new one, deserving to be called "anthropomorphized Shannon-Weaver model." The initial arbitrariness at the point of importing the model was expanded to incorporate axioms behind the anthropomorphized variant. For example, uncertainty is approached from a deterministic perspective, which appears to be connected with an assumption that information is an object transferable from person to person (see Putnam et al., 1996). Taking again our example of the utility company and its ERP system, it is apparent that a supervisor cannot know how much time an hourly worker has put in (uncertainty) before collecting data on the hours the worker has logged (information). Then, a clerk tabulates a worker's hours (information) in an electronic spreadsheet and transfers this electronically (communication) to the supervisor for online approval. The anthropomorphized model works well in these examples of simple informing, where information poses in its simplest form of data. However, as the discussion on IVO above demonstrated, information also comes in the more complex forms of meaning and knowledge.

Consider the perspective of a developer of the ERP system in the utility company case. This system supports data entry, reporting, and approval of work hours. I would argue that it is unlikely that the developer can identify the entire domain of uncertainty associated with the system's specifications, even with a full participation of users. The scope of uncertainty includes the content and format of data records and of reports, manners in which the records and reports will be interpreted by individual users, design of screens (the navigation and esthetics characteristics desired by different users), and the system response time. The last item is complex in itself since in today's distributed, multi-tiered system architectures the system response time is a compound of response times of a database server, application server, and Web server, plus transfer times between these servers, minus slowdowns due to records locking, load imbalance, and network throughput, and so on. It is also true that the historical aspect adds to uncertainty. For example, users may not know what they really need or if what they thought they needed is what they really need unless they try the system. Foresight is a young parent of learning, and hindsight is its mature parent. If the pool of uncertainty accompanying systems design were determinate, we would have much better ISs in general and ERP systems in particular with a less dramatic failure rate than it is (the estimates of failure of ERP systems vary, but most of them put the rate above 50%; e.g., IT Cortex 2001; Karaian, 2005).

The discussion above suggests that deterministic concepts of uncertainty may not suffice. Enter complexities of information taken at the level of meaning. To what extent do technologists and end users understand each other's language? Do the same words trigger same meanings in their minds? Do they reside in comparable organizational contexts that make impacts on the creation of meaning (e.g., comparable on the IT-related goals and on understanding of business and timing priorities)? What are the effects of contextual factors, individual psychology (personal, cognitive), and situational factors (e.g., intentions and other factors that are captured in Searle's (1979) theory of speech acts)?

Realistic answers to these questions or the lack thereof are likely to underline difficulties of the deterministic approach to uncertainty. The anthropomorphized Shannon-Weaver model is incapable of dealing with the complexities of communicating meaning that pertain to both the sender and receiver because the model suits merely data transfer scenarios and focuses on the sender side (see Putnam et al., 1996).

In addition to being inherently imperfect and so coupled with uncertainty, information can even generate uncertainty. In their critique of the applications of Shannon and Weaver's model, Huber and Daft (1987) have proposed that "information can increase uncertainty if it contradicts previously believed truths" (p. 156). Gackowski's (2005) critical remark cited above is in agreement with this proposition, in contrast to other informing science works cited above. IVO is also agreeable, and it takes this proposition a step further by proposing a concept of "spiral of uncertainty" (Travica, 2006). In brief, "spiral of uncertainty" relates information (in the broad sense), uncertainty and time, and it proposes that information can reduce uncertainty with regard to the past, while it can simultaneously create uncertainty with respect to the future. For example, by learning that a worm infected corporate mail servers (information), a network administrator resolves the uncertainty regarding the state of the servers, while this realization can prompt him to question the breadth and depth of damage (uncertainty). Whereas Shannon and Weaver's original model operated with a definitive resolution of finite uncertainty, organizational and social worlds are rather like flows in which the past, present and future can only analytically be separated. Living with uncertainty indeed is the *modus vivendi* in the world of ours that behaves as a highly complex system.[2] This world has been intellectually constructed through contributions that lie on the other side of Cartesian-Newtonian certainty and predictability, such as Einstein's theories of relativity, Heizenberg's principle of uncertainty, Saussure's linguistics, Wittgenstein's language games, and contemporary philosophy (e.g., Austin, 1962; Rorty, 1982) and sociology (e.g., Giddens, 1979, 1984; Latour, 2005). Unfounded optimism or *info-optimism* characterizes the expectation that information is exclusively the means of resolving uncertainty in such a world.

Finally, the anthropomorphic Shannon-Weaver model is being abandoned among communication scholars. In the field of organizational communication, the long reign of this model and its underlying modernist paradigm has recently been challenged by the naturalistic (cultural) and critical (political) perspectives (Redding & Tompkins, 1988). The modernist view portrays organization as a purposeful instrument for achieving certain goals is no longer considered adequate. The perspective change has also been reflected in cardinal reviews of organizational communication research (cf. Jablin & Putnam, 2001; Jablin, Roberts, Putnam, & Porter, 1987). In their taxonomy of communication metaphors, Putnam and colleagues (1996) use the term "conduit model" for Shannon-Weaver model in order to point out the assumed model of organization. The authors argue that the conduit model conceives organization as a container in which transmissions of messages take place. Communication within this container is "linear and effortless," and "miscommunication occurs when no information is received or when the information received is not what the sender intended" (Putnam et al., 1996: 380). Cognate to the conduit metaphor are the metaphors of lens and linkages. The lens metaphor focuses on transmission characteristics (routing, searching, filtering, gate-keeping, distorting information). The configuration and usage of transmission channels ("communication networks") is the subject of the linkages metaphor. The contemporary study of organizational communication exhibits a radical departure from these metaphors (more further below).

In brief, the use of Shannon and Weaver's (1949) mathematical model of communication in social sciences is bound to arbitrary definitions of key terms and their relationships, deterministic assumptions, a focus on data and the sender as opposed to problems of meaning that occur at both ends of communication, and *info-optimism* regarding challenges of uncertainty. Students of organizational communication increasingly abandon the model. Given these circumstances, it is questionable if the model is the best guide for meeting the prudent goal of informing science to effectively inform clients.

Similarities and Differences between IVO and Informing Science

The discussion in the previous sections has indicated numerous connections between informing science and IVO. These are shown in Table 2. In particular, both IVO and informing science take an interdisciplinary and integrationist approach, have a practitioner/service orientation, exhibit an information, organization, and communication focus, and apply multi-level analyses.

On the difference side, IVO is more pronounced in terms of reference disciplines, communication contexts, distinctions between communication, IS and IT, and differences between mediated and face-to-face communication. Also, IVO adds a theoretical academic orientation to the practitioner's one. While service to users of information, IT and IS motivates IVO as much as service to information users motivates informing science, IVO balances this with the goal of advancing theory of ISs. It could be argued that the goal of "effective informing" put forward in the definition of informing science is not a criterion for defining an area of academic study but rather is a consequence of a practitioner's and consulting approach. ISs can be more or less effective, but this does not make or break the fact that they are ISs. Once a system is understood (the contribution of theory), effectiveness goals can be addressed.

IVO operates with a broader concept of information, organization and communication, and explicitly addresses IT in its various functional and historical forms. In contrast, informing science puts a stronger emphasis on human communication than IVO. Finally, analysis in IVO involves individual, group, organizational, and interorganizational levels, and adds the issues of systems adoption to the list of otherwise overlapping IS-related issues. As for organizational issues, IVO has somewhat a broader coverage that accounts for thus far addressed issues in informing science. For example, Gackowski's (2005) economic analysis fits into the rubric of infoeconomics (although relations between the two in terms of premises and results of analysis is a different topic that cannot be addressed in this article).

Table 2. Informing Science and Information View of Organization

Informing Science	Information View of Organization
Interdisciplinary integrationist position	Interdisciplinary integrationist position, where the core reference disciplines are organization/management theory and cognitive theory
Practitioner focus with service orientation	Practitioner/service and academic orientation
Information focus (data focus and some attention to meaning ("information"))	Information focus based on complex model of information (data, meaning, knowledge)
Broadening spectrum of information teleology (reduction of uncertainty, increase of uncertainty)	Broad spectrum of information teleology (Spiral of uncertainty)
IT implicit in the notion of delivery	IT explicit and treated broadly—from electronic to paper
Concern for organizational context using Leavitt's (1965) model	Strong concern for organizational context, aspects represent major views of organization and different philosophical paradigms
- Strong concern for human communication regardless context, goal to inform clients - Shannon & Weaver's (1949) model exclusive - Face-to-face and mediated communication undifferentiated - Communication undifferentiated from IS and IT	- Concern for human communication in the individual, group, inter-unit, and interorganizational context - Different communication models, stress on meaning and knowledge on the receiver's side - Face-to-face and mediated communication clearly differentiated - Communication, IS and IT clearly differentiated
Multi-level analysis of informing models' use, design, and creation of new designs; analysis of economic aspects	Multi-level analysis (individual, group, organizational, interorganizational) intersected with issues of IS design, adoption, use, and evaluation

In summary, there are fundamental similarities as well as certain differences between informing science and IVO. Typically, IVO is broader and more inclusive, which is particularly visible in the way IVO conceives information, IT, organization and communication.

Expanding Informing Science

Informing science is new, evolving, and open to change and self-improvement (cf. Cohen, 1999). IVO is even a newer framework that developed independently of informing science. I tried to show in the discussion above that there are significant overlaps between the two frameworks.[3]

Indications of the directions in expanding informing science are presented in Table 2.

Informing science could benefit from pronouncing clearly the differences between communication, IS and IT. Also, explanatory power could be raised by bringing IT to the fore and dealing with it in a detail-rich way as it has been attempted in case studies based on IVO. It is also important to clarify the position with regard to ontology of IT. Neither the mainstream IS field nor the organizational communication field provide support to the thesis that the concept of IT includes human voice or interpersonal contacts (Gackowski, 2005). IVO proposes that IT be conceived of in terms of material artifacts designed for manipulating data, and that this IT is part of ISs. Informing science might want to broaden this definition with institutional or some other elements. In any case, IT needs to be distinguished from definitional elements of human communication. Otherwise, informing science may turn out to be a stream of research within the communication rather than the IS field.

Another line of conceptual differentiation concerns the need to separate face-to-face and mediated communication. This separation is connected with bringing up the IT perspective since mediation comes from using IT in communication. Furthermore, it might be instructive to examine possibilities for strengthening a theoretical orientation of informing science. While providing service to users of information is a prudent goal that IVO shares, the goal would be more achievable with aid of adequate theory.

Broadening the concepts of information, organization and communication may be another area for informing science to explore. In the preceding discussion, I tried to elaborate on shortcomings of the Shannon and Weaver's (1949) model of communication as it has been used in social sciences. Also, I pointed to the dependence between models/metaphors of communication and ontology of organization. The rationale of this discussion is that informing science may be truer to its key goal if it anchors itself into broader conceptualizations of communication and organization.

The field of organizational communication, for example, provides alternatives to the conduit model. As Putnam and colleagues (1996) elaborate in their taxonomy, one option is the *metaphor of performance* (communicative performance). Advocated by Weick (1979), the performance metaphor focuses on action, reaction, interpretation, equivocality, reflection and sense making in the interpersonal context. Senders and receivers are accounted for, but in a rather non-linear fashion, and the receiver's side is prominent. The performance metaphor does not assume that organization is a given entity (structure, culture, etc.). Instead, organization is an ongoing process of organizing that unfolds via communication. Organizations present contexts of equivocality where people act and then reflect on their actions to make sense of organizing (Putnam et al., 1996).

The *symbols metaphor* focuses on organizational culture embodied in stories, metaphors, rituals, irony and other cultural artifacts (Czarniawska-Joerges, 1992). Thus, cultural artifacts and behaviors, including interactions of purposive rational informing, communicate key organizational beliefs to the "receiver." This metaphor implies that organization is created and maintained via the processes of constructing shared meanings, or by "fostering and developing (…) shared interpretive schemes that create and recreate (…) meaning" (Morgan, 1986: 135). In other words, what matters is a connotative cultural meaning rather than a denotative informing content.

Next is the *metaphor of voice*, which renders communication in a political light, by concentrating on who, when, and how an option can be voiced. (Deetz, 1992). Since some voices are expressed and others are suppressed, it is important to know what cannot be sent via communication channels and not only what is sent. Also, information accuracy (message fidelity in the conduit model) becomes secondary because information typically has a political bias—communication is "distortion" (Redding & Tompkins, 1988). This thesis strikes directly into the plexus of the model of organization as a rational instrument/machine that fits with the conduit metaphor of communication. The political metaphor embraces a model of organization in which self interest paints each aspect. Self-interest agendas range from protecting a "turf" that everyone has to imposing domination over others. Interests paint rationality as well, and so rationality of any act (including informing one) is inherently political (Morgan, 1986, p. 195).

Finally, the *metaphor of discourse* makes language the subject of study, covering many topical areas, such as speech acts, language games, conversational analysis, dialogue, and properties and patterns of interaction (see Putnam et al., 1996: 391-394). Thus, the core medium of communication—language—constitutes the domain of research problems. The organization model this metaphor espouses is the one in which organization is constructed through the use of language. But language is not just a neutral tool for encoding and decoding messages/information as the conduit metaphors suggests. As the preceding metaphors of communication suggest, language is also the means to political and cultural ends.

The analysis of the relationship between IVO and informing science also revealed that the latter prefers a deterministic approach to challenges of uncertainty. This is coupled with an expectation that information always reduces uncertainty, which appears as unwarranted optimism in this complex and probabilistic world. Instead of succumbing to such *info-optimism,* informing science may do better if it takes information for what it is—both a creator and reducer of uncertainty. Then, energy can be committed to more realistic goals of dealing with the world in which uncertainty is a *modus vivendi.* The goal shift may help to realize that uncertainty is the engine of movement, change and development without which the knowledge development would stop. It may even be useful to create uncertainty in order to mobilize the potential for creativity in organization members, as the Japanese executives use to do by uttering ambiguous statements (Nonaka & Takeuchi, 1995).

One way of assisting informing science in nearing to the changes proposed above is by the means of the Journal of Information, Information Technology, and Organizations (JIITO) that was recently launched. The mission and editorial policy of this publishing outlet complies with basic premises of IVO. A notable difference is that JIITO is supposed to cover a broader range of organizational contexts (not only firms and non-profit institutions, but communities as well). Empirical and conceptual contributions of JIITO are expected to demonstrate advantages of broadening the horizons in investigating the ways of informing information clients in organized contexts. Specifically,

> "JIITO encourages articles that use rich, detailed accounts of information and IT" and "empirical studies that explain how organizations cope, prosper, change, fail with respect to using, managing, designing and adopting information systems. In the conceptual realm, JIITO encourages articles that take a critical look at advent, genesis and uses of models that have influenced IS research for considerable time." (JIITO, 2005)

As for the influences of informing science on IVO, the demonstrated significant overlap between the two frameworks with regard to goals, premises and topics lay the ground for introducing the label "Informing View of Organization," which can be used in parallel with the original label.

Summary

This article discussed premises, goals, and the scope of IVO (Travica, 2003, 2004, 2005a, 2005b, 2006) and of informing science (Cohen, 1999; Gackowski, 2005; Roussev and Rousseva, 2004). Each approach was defined and their main conceptual characteristics were discussed. The IVO approach was also illustrated with evidence from several case studies and an ongoing investigation. Further, informing science was critically appraised, and its similarities with and differences from IVO analyzed. The article identified several ways in which IVO can contribute to advancing informing science.

Notes

(1) Note that Shannon and Weaver are not responsible for later deviations of their model, except perhaps for the choice of the keyword. The model has been widely used within the appropriate domains of application (e.g., telephone networks). However, Shannon admitted having a regret for using the term "information" to signify the notion of negative entropy. Even at their time, the term was associated with a plethora of meaning. "Information" had a formalized meaning in information theory developed under the auspices of the 19th century thermodynamics, became involved in a wide circulation with the advent of daily press, radio and TV, and was used in biology and some other areas.

(2) Even in the modern telephone systems, which descended from the telephone networks Shannon and Weaver studied, the theory of chaos appears to be a necessary addition in network management. These networks have been transformed into highly complex, dynamic systems that call for new theories and analytical models.

(3) Drawing on accustomed meanings of the terms "science" ("a department of systematized knowledge as an object of study") and "framework" ("a basic conceptual structure, as of ideas"), I prefer to use the term "informing science framework" rather than "informing science." (Merriam-Webster Online, 2005)

References

Austin, J. (1962). *How to do things with words.* Oxford, UK: Clarendon.

Barley, S. (1986). Technology as an occasion for structuring: Evidence from observations of CT scanners and the social order of radiology departments. *Administrative Science Quarterly, 31*, 78-108.

Barley, S. (1990). The alignment of technology and structure through roles and networks. *Administrative Science Quarterly, 35*, 61-103.

Brynjolfsson, E., & Hitt, L. (1998). Beyond the productivity paradox. *Communications of the ACM, 41*(8), 49-55.

Castells, M. (1996). *The rise of the network society.* Malden, MA: Blackwell.

Carr, N. (2004). IT doesn't matter. *HBR*, May.

Ciborra, C. (Ed.). (1996). *Groupware and teamwork: Invisible aid or technical hindrance?* Chichester: John Wiley & Sons.

Clegg, S., Hardy, C., & Nord, W. (Eds.). (1996). *Handbook of organization studies.* London: SAGE.

Clegg, S., & Hardy, C. (1996). Organizations, organization and organizing. In S. Clegg, C. Hardy, & W. Nord (Eds.), *Handbook of organization studies* (pp. 1-28). London: SAGE.

Cohen, E. (1999). Reconceptualizing information systems as a field of the transdiscipline informing science: From ugly duckling to swan. *Journal of Computing and Information Technology, 7*(3), 213-219.

Crozier, M. (1967). *The bureaucratic phenomenon* (2nd ed.). Chicago, IL: University of Chicago Press.

Czarniawska-Joerges, B. (1992). *Exploring complex organizations: A cultural perspective*. Newbury Park: SAGE.

Davenport, T., & Prusak, L. (1997). *Information ecology: Mastering the information and knowledge environment.* New York-Oxford: Oxford University Press.

Davidow, W. H., & Malone, M. S. (1992). *The virtual corporation.* New York: Harper.

Deetz, S. (1992). *Democracy in an age of corporate colonization: Developments in communication and the politics of everyday life.* Albany, NY: State University of New York Press.

Eysenck, M., & Keane, M. (1995). *Cognitive psychology: A student handbook.* Jove, UK: Lawrence Erlbaum Associates.

Gackowski, Z. (2005). Informing systems in business environments: A purpose-focused view. *Informing Science Journal, 8*, 101-122. Retrieved from http://inform.nu/Articles/Vol8/v8p101-122Gack.pdf.

Galbraith, J. (1973). *Designing complex organizations.* Reading: Addison-Wesley.

Giddens, A. (1979) *Central problems in social theory: Action, structure and contradiction in social analysis.* London: Macmillan.

Giddens, A. (1984) *The constitution of society. Outline of the theory of structuration.* Cambridge: Polity Press.

Hammer, M, & Champy, J. (1993). *Reengineering the corporation: A manifesto for business revolution.* New York: HarperBusiness.

Handy, Charles. (1993) *Understanding organizations.* Oxford: Oxford University Press.

Hatch, M. J. (1997). *Organization theory: Modern, symbolic, and postmodern perspectives.* Oxford-New York: Oxford University Press.

Heckscher, C., & Donnellon, A. (Eds.). (1994). *The post-bureaucratic organization: New perspectives on organizational change.* Thousand Oaks: SAGE.

Huber, G., & Daft, R. (1987). The information environments of organizations. In F. Jablin, L. Putnam, K. Roberts & L. Porter (Eds.), *Handbook of organizational communication: An interdisciplinary perspective* (pp. 130-164). Newbury Park, CA: SAGE.

Iivary, J., & Lyytinen, K. (1999). Research on information systems development in Scandinavia: Unity in plurality. In W. Currie & B. Galliers, *Rethinking management information systems* (pp. 57-100). Oxford: University Press.

IT Cortex. (2001). Statistics over IT projects failure rate. Retrieved from http://www.it-cortex.com/Stat_Failure_Rate.htm#The%20Robbins-Gioia%20Survey%20(2001) .

Jablin, F. M., & Putnam, L. L. (Eds.). (2001). *The new handbook of organizational communication: Advances in theory, research, and methods.* Thousand Oaks, CA: Sage.

Jablin, F., Roberts, K., Putnam, L., & Porter, L. (Eds.). (1987). *The handbook of organizational communication*, Newbury Park, CA: SAGE.

JIITO. (2005). Editorial statement. Accessed: 11/25/2005. Available: http://www.jiito.org/statement.html

Karaian, J. (2005). CFO Europe. Accessed: 11/28/2005. Available at http://www.cfoeurope.com/displayStory.cfm/3929294

Kiesler, S., Siegel, J., & McGuire, T. W. (1984). Social psychological aspects of computer-mediated communication. *American Psychologist, 39*(10), 1123-1134.

Latour, B. (2005). *Reassembling the social: An introduction to actor-network- theory.* Oxford University Press.

Leavitt, H. (1965). Applied organizational change in industry - Structural, technological and humanistic approaches. In J. March (Ed.), *Handbook of organizations* (pp. 1144 – 1170). Chicago: Rand McNally.

Malone, T., & Crowston, K. (1994). The interdisciplinary study of coordination. *Computing Surveys, 26*(1), 87-119.

Majchrzak, A., Beath, C., Lim, R., & Chin, W. (2005). Managing client dialogues during information systems design to facilitate client learning. *MIS Quarterly, 29*(4).

Mason, R., & Mitroff, I. (1973). A program for research in management information systems. *Management Science, 19*(5), 475-485.

Morgan, G. (1986). *Images of organization*. Newbury Park: SAGE.

Merriam-Webster Online. (2005). Dictionary units "science" and "framework." Available at http://www.m-w.com/dictionary/

Nonaka, I., & Takeuchi, H. (1995). *The knowledge creating company: How Japanese companies create the dynamics of innovation*. New York: Oxford University Press.

Nunamaker, J., Briggs, R., Mittleman, D., Vogel, D. & Pierre, B. (1996/7). Lessons from a dozen years of group support systems research: A discussion of lab and field findings. *Journal of Management Information Systems, 13*(3), 163-207.

Orlikowski, W. (1992). The duality of technology: Rethinking the concept of technology in organizations. *Organization Science, 2*(3), 398-427.

Orlikowski, W. & Barley, S. (2001). Technology and institutions: What can research on information technology and research on organizations learn from each other? *MIS Quarterly, 25*(2), 145-65.

Orlikowski, W. & Iacono, S. (2001). Research commentary desperately seeking the "IT" in research - A call to theorizing the IT artifact. *Information Systems Research, 12*(2), 121-134.

Peters, T. (1992). *Liberation management: Necessary disorganization for the nanosecond nineties*. New York: Alfred A. Knopf.

Pfeffer, J. (1981). *Power in organizations*. Marshfield, MA: Pitman Publishing Inc.

Putnam, L., Phillips, N., & Chapman, P. (1996). Metaphors of communication and organization. In S. Clegg, C. Hardy, & W. Nord (Eds.), *Handbook of Organization Studies* (pp. 375-408). London: SAGE.

Redding, W. C., & Tompkins, P. K. (1988). Organizational communication—past and present tenses. In G. M. Goldhaber & G. A. Barnett (Eds.), *Handbook of organizational communication* (pp. 5-33). Norwood, NJ: Ablex.

Roach, S. S. (1987). America's technology dilemma: A profile of the information economy. Morgan Stanley Special Economic Study, April.

Rorty, R. (1982).*Consequences of pragmatism*. Minneapolis, MN: University of Minnesota Press.

Roussev, B., & Rousseva, Y. (2004). Software development: Informing sciences perspective. *Journal of Issues in Informing Science and Information Technology, 1*, 237-245. Available at http://articles.iisit.org/040rouse.pdf

Sarker, S. & Lee, A. (2000). Using a case study to test the role of three key social enablers in ERP implementation. In S. Ang, H. Krcmar, W. Orlikowski, P. Weill, & J. I. DeGross (Eds.), *Proceedings of the 21st International Conference on Information Systems* (pp. 414-425), December 10-13, 2000 Brisbane, Australia.

Searle, J. (1979). *Expression and meaning: Studies in the theory of speech acts*. Cambridge, MA: Cambridge University Press.

Shaila, M., & Saunders, C. (1995). Group support systems: An organization development intervention to combat groupthink. *Public Administration Quarterly, 19*(2), 193-217.

Shannon, C., & Weaver, W. (1949). *The mathematical theory of communication*. Urbana, IL: University of Illinois Press.

Shepherd, M., Briggs, R., Reining, B. A., &Yen, J. (1995). Social loafing in electronic brainstorming: Invoking social comparison through technology and facilitation techniques to improve group productivity. *Proceedings of the Twenty-Eighth Hawaii International Conference on Systems Sciences, 4*, 523-532.

Snyder, H., & Davenport, E. (1997). *Costing and pricing in the digital age: A Practical guide for information services*. New York: Neal-Schuman Publishers.

Thietart, R., &. Forgues, B. (1995). Chaos theory and organization. *Organization Science, 6*(1), 19-31.

Travica, B. (1999). *New organizational designs: Information aspects*. Stamford: Ablex.

Travica, B. (2003). Information view of organizations: Contextualizing technology - Technologizing context. *Proceedings of 2003 AMCIS*, August 4-6, 2003, Tampa, FL. Nominated for the Best Papers Award.

Travica, B. (2004). Organizations as information processes. In J. Akoka (Ed.), *Proceedings of the Pre-ICIS Conference*, Washington, D.C., December 2004.

Travica, B. (2005a). Information politics and information culture: Case Study. *Informing Science Journal, 8*, 211-245. Available at http://inform.nu/Articles/Vol8/v8p211-244Travica.pdf

Travica, B. (2005b). Information view of organization. *Journal of International Technology and Information Management, 14*, 1-20.

Travica, B. (2006). *Information view of organization*. [forthcoming].

Turoff, M., Hiltz, S. R., Bahgat, A., & Rana, A. (1993). Distributed group support systems. *MIS Quarterly, 17*(4), 399-417.

Weber, M. (1946). *Essays in sociology*. Oxford University Press.

Weick, K. (1979). *The social psychology of organizing*. Reading, MA: Addison-Wesley.

Westwood, R. & Clegg, S. (Eds.). (2003). *Debating organization: point-counterpoint in organization studies*. Malden, MA: Blackwell.

Zuboff, S. (1984). *In the age of the smart machine: The future of work and power*. Basic Books.

Biography

Bob Travica teaches information systems at University of Manitoba, Canada. He taught at Indiana University, studied in the United States, lived and worked in Europe and Latin America. Bob metamorphosed through several careers including journalism and software development. His research interests include information view of organization, new organizational designs, e-commerce, and international issues.

The page left blank intentionally.

ICT Experiences in Two Different Middle Eastern Universities

Abdallah Tubaishat
Zayed University, Abu Dhabi, United Arab Emirates

Abdallah.Tubaishat@zu.ac.ae

Arif Bhatti
GIFT University, Chowk, Gujranwala, Pakistan

drbhatti@gift.edu.pk

Eyas El-Qawasmeh
Jordan University of Science and Technology
Irbid, Jordan

eyas@just.edu.jo

Abstract

This research explores the impact of technology and culture on higher education in two Arab countries. In western countries where higher education is common, individuals regardless of their gender can meet, communicate, and collaborate at anytime at any place of their choice. This may not be true in Arab countries due to the social, cultural, and religious reasons. We argue that adoption of technology could provide a comparable learning environment to students in these countries. We present results of a case study based on surveys conducted in two universities, Jordan University of Science and Technology (JUST) in Jordan and Zayed University (ZU) in United Arab Emirates (UAE). Survey results show that adoption of technology has (a) improved the motivation and confidence level of students, (b) improved their communication and technical skills, (c) encouraged students to collaborate using Information and Communication Technology (ICT) tools, and (d) allowed students to be more independent. These improvements would not have been possible without technology in a gender-segregated society.

Keywords: Technology mediated learning environment, Social and cultural issues, Implementation of technology, Collaborative learning.

Introduction

The importance of higher education to gain prosperity and to develop human resources is understood by under-developed countries. Three quarters of Arab universities were established in the last 25 years of the 20th century (UNDP: Arab Human Development Report, 2003). Students in higher education require a very flexible environment to communicate and collaborate with their peers to accomplish tasks needed to succeed.

Social and cultural values of a society do impose different rules based on gender. Females in Arab society are usually subject to different sets of rules as compared to their male counterparts in the same society. These rules may severely limit the learning opportunities for females.

In western society, culture and social values do not impose any restriction on individuals based on their gender. Students in higher education regardless of their gender can meet, communicate, and collaborate at anytime at any place of their choice. In contrast, most Middle Eastern society is based on gender segregation that permits limited interaction between genders. Culture and social values in UAE and Saudi Arabia strictly enforce gender segregation, while countries such as Jordan and Lebanon are moderately liberal in this matter.

Advances in networking technologies and the Internet can have a significant impact on teaching and learning in higher education (Hodges, 2004; Muhlhauser & Trompler, 2002; Smith & Winking-Diaz, 2004). In a technology mediated learning environment, students and teachers use a wide range of ICT tools to communicate, collaborate and share resources; these tools provide anytime anywhere learning opportunities.

We begin by providing an overview of how ICT could be used to enhance traditional instructor-led teaching to alleviate the impact of social and cultural values on higher education; to make the learning environment a place to pass information and knowledge from teacher to students, from students to teacher, and from students to students; and a place for creative thinking and learning. Next, we discuss education and learning environment in two Middle Eastern countries. We then discuss their ICT infrastructure and its impact on higher education. We conclude by presenting the findings from a case study based on surveys conducted at JUST in Jordan and at ZU in the UAE.

Education and Learning Environment

The UAE secondary schooling system remains very traditional with teacher-led classes where memorization is emphasized (Sanders & Quirke, 2002). Students prefer all-knowing teachers who provide them answers to all questions. Only the UAE citizens can attend the public education system that has separate schools for boys and girls. The private education system is mainly for ex-patriots and is usually not segregated by gender at the school level. Some private higher education institutions have a co-education environment while others have separate arrangements for male and female students. The UAE provides free education for its citizens at all levels of education. United Nations (UN) statistics indicates that the UAE is among the most developed nations in educating female students (Information in the UAE, 2005). Each major center of population within the country has two colleges of technology, one for males, and another for females.

ZU was established for the national female population. The University has five colleges and most of the faculty members are western educated. Its faculty endeavor to provide students learning opportunities in an American style of teaching ensuring a very high quality of education. ZU's operations and policies reflect the impact of social and cultural values on higher education.

Women enroll in higher education more than men and their ratio is 6:2. In UAE, 20% of the total work force is now women. Women have gained access to higher education, though they are still largely excluded from government decision making. More women are enrolled in higher education, partly because men tend to travel overseas to foreign universities (UNDP: POGAR, 2005). Adult male illiteracy exceeds female illiteracy (20% to 21% in 2002). National Admission and Placement Office (NAPO) indicated that 90% of females and 73% of males goes to federally funded higher colleges and universities (Women in the UAE, 2005). There are more female students than male students in UAE universities. In Higher Colleges of Technologies (HCT), there are 70% female students. In United Arab Emirates University (UAEU), there are 60% female students.

Education system in Jordan is co-education at kindergarten, college, and university levels. There are separate schools for boys and girls at elementary, primary, and secondary level. Few public schools have computer labs. Only 1.4% of public school teachers are computer literate. 60% of schools in Jordan are public (government owner/run) (World Economic Forum: Jordan Educational ICT pilot initiative, 2005). The development of Jordan's educational system can be described as dynamic, which means that it is evaluated and re-structured almost every year. Jordan has forged a comprehensive, high quality system to develop the human capital of its citizens. Currently almost one third of all Jordanians are enrolled in educational facilities. Women comprise a large percentage of Jordan's higher education attendees, accounting 66.6% of community college students, and 44.7% of the university populations.

In Jordan, there are public and private universities in all major centers of population. Most faculty members in science and engineering colleges are Jordanians who are western educated. The education system is more flexible and students usually improve their critical thinking skills in secondary schooling. Each student enrolled in higher education system must study two courses where one of them is computer skills course and the other is a programming course. This is regardless of the major of the student.

The Table 1 shows some educational facts about female education in Jordan and UAE (Technology and Equity, 2005).

Table 1. Educational and learning environment for females in Jordan vs. UAE

	Jordan	UAE
Female Adult Literacy	84.4%	76.8%
Female Secondary School Enrollment	55%	79.9%
Female Tertiary Students	42%	72%
Female Tertiary Students in Natural Sciences	35.5%	42.3%

JUST consists of eleven colleges, including 55 academic departments offering 52 undergraduate programs, and 95 graduate programs. It is considered a large university with an enrollment of approximately 16,000 students. It has highly qualified staff members in diverse fields of knowledge. All academic programs are open to Jordanians and students from other Arab countries resulting in a culturally diverse environment. Some students come from moderately liberal cultures such as Syria, and Lebanon, while others come from more conservative cultures such as Saudi Arabia and Oman. All courses use English as the language of instructions (JUST Website, 2005).

Culture and Higher Education

In their paper "Toward a Theory Based Measurement of Culture" Straub, Loch, Evaristo, Karahanna, and Srite (2002) argued that in IS research, the culture of subjects and respondents is problematic because it is typically an overly simplistic categorization. IS research nearly always assumes that an individual living in a particular place and time belongs to a single "culture". This may explain why cross cultural research has been so extremely difficult to conduct!"

Most social and cultural values in Gulf society do not allow free mixing and interaction of members of opposite genders. A strong influence of these values on students, student teacher interaction and in university policies is visible in day-to-day activities at ZU and other public universities in UAE.

ZU policy requires students to be on-campus during the normal operating hours. Students are not allowed to be on-campus after these hours. An electronic check-in and check-out system is used to ensure that students remain on-campus once they arrive. Students are not allowed to leave the campus without their family's permission. Attendance is required during each teaching session to ensure that students participate in class activities. During off-campus educational activities, students must be accompanied by chaperones. Normal working hours are 8:00 to 5:00 and students are not allowed to be on campus outside of this period for cultural and social reasons.

Cultural and social values in Jordan are moderately liberal. Unlike many other Arab countries, in Jordan there is a very small disparity in primary school attendance rates between urban and rural areas. Higher education institutions have co-education environment. The university environment in Jordan provides students regardless of their gender, significantly more opportunities to meet, communicate and collaborate. In Jordan, women participate in the work force in most jobs (e.g. military, nursing, technology). Women can travel freely after 18 years of age, which is not true in UAE. It is also safe to say that using technology in Jordanian society is easier than UAE due to the fact that the country is relatively liberal.

Technology Infrastructure at ZU and JUST

Advances in networking technologies and the Internet can have a significant impact on teaching and learning in higher education (Hodges, 2004; Muhlhauser & Trompler, 2002; Smith & Winking-Diaz, 2004). In our opinion, universities in the UAE have significantly better technology infrastructure than universities in Jordan. In UAE, students have more access to technology but they are less effective in using technology. For social and political reasons, many Internet sites are banned in UAE; and all home and Internet cafes traffic goes through a proxy.

ZU has an excellent technology infrastructure. ZU campuses are fully networked and allow students to connect to the University network and Internet from anywhere on campus. Each student is required to purchase a very recent laptop for use while on campus. Each faculty member receives a laptop with a three-year replacement schedule.

Students have a wealth of technology available to assist them in the learning process. Actually, ZU is known as the laptop university in this region. For the College of Information Systems, students having their own laptop loaded with software used in the courses help them to complete their work independently without coming to campus during after hours. The College of Information Systems has an independent network infrastructure for teaching and research, in addition to the University network. This infrastructure allows students to login remotely into Linux servers to use tools needed for programming languages, databases, and web development related courses. Students can also use Linux-based communication tools to collaborate with each other and with instructors. ZU students can access their university email accounts and Blackboard, a learning management system, from anywhere at anytime using a web client. Students have to be on campus to access all other computing and non-computing resources.

In Jordan, students have less access to technology but they are efficient in the use of it. The Internet is not considered as a threat to local culture, morals or religious sensibilities in general (Straub et al., 2002). Internet cafes and homes are not proctored by government and therefore there is free access to any Internet source. Introducing a new technology is easier to adopt, as the society is more liberal.

The Table 2 shows some technology facts about the two countries (UNDP: POGAR, 2005).

Table 2. Technology facts in Jordan vs. UAE

	Jordan	UAE
Telephone mainlines	127/1000	291/1000
Cellular mobile subscribers	229/1000	647/1000
Internet users	57/1000	313/1000

In Jordan, JUST laboratories are fully equipped with the latest hardware and software programs. The college of Computer and Information Technology (CIT) has 12 laboratories. All labs are fully networked, and open for teaching, research, and development purposes only during university working hours, i.e. from 8:00 to 5:00. Students have limited access to computer labs as the labs are used for different purposes. Courses that require a lab component are assigned no more than four hours per week (JUST website, 2005).

Impact of Technology on Higher Education

Distance education today is generally used to accommodate those students who are unable to physically attend regular school to learn in a traditional learning environment. Invention and adoption of the Internet has a significant impact on distance education and traditional classroom based teaching.

Web-based learning (WBL) has become a major trend in teaching and learning. There are two major classes of these systems: *synchronous* and *asynchronous* (Kinshuk & Young, 2003; Neubauer & Lobel, 2003). Synchronous WBL systems are used to create virtual classroom environment where all students in a class are accessing the same information. Computer Supported Collaborative Work (CSCW) systems are synchronous in nature and designed to replace physical classrooms with the virtual ones (Litiu, 2003; Marsic, Dorohoceanu & Tremaine, 2002). Most commonly available WBL systems are asynchronous in nature. In these systems, a web server hosts course contents and other teaching material. Learners have access to this material at anytime from anywhere using any web-browser (Linge, 2003).

Principe, Eulianno, and Lefebvre (2004) identify two basic levels in the utilization of computers in education: computer-based presentation, and computer-based instruction. They differ in the level of changes required in the teaching methodology. Use of multimedia presentations and web searching tools belong to the first category since they just make conventional classroom delivery more efficient and appealing; and they leave the teaching methodology largely unchanged. On the other hand, computer-based instructions imply a change in the traditional way of thinking about the discipline. It exploits the computer as added dimension to bridge the gap between the professor's knowledge, and how the students attain and retain the material.

Based on the mode of content delivery, a learning environment could be classified in one of the following three categories: (1) distance education completely online using web-based technologies, (2) traditional learning completely on-campus without web-based technologies and (3) Technology mediated learning where on-campus teaching is complemented with web-based teaching.

In technology mediated learning environment systems, the following factors contribute to effective online learning: using relevant and challenging assignments, having coordinated learning environment, adequate and timely feedback from instructors, developing rich environments for student-to-student interaction, flexibility in teaching and learning. In a good technology mediated learning system, students must be able to read, critically reflect, discuss, argue, generate and present new interpretations, share and exchange information ideas.

Case Study

To understand the impact of ICT on higher education in a Middle Eastern society, we conducted a survey at JUST and ZU. All surveyed students were enrolled in Computer Science/Information Systems courses. Participating students were enrolled in Information Technology, Computer Networks, Computer Architecture, and Operating Systems courses at JUST and a Database Systems course at ZU. In total 149 students, 73 female and 76 male, from JUST and 14 female students from ZU participated in this survey. It should be noted that the small size of ZU sample is due to the small sizes of classes in ZU. The survey was conducted by filling a hardcopy questionnaire. Table 3 shows the questionnaire and results.

It should be noted that in Table 3, the total of agree/disagree answers does not come to 100%. For this reason, neutral responses were excluded.

In addition to ICT tools, we used online assessment tools to provide timely feedback. *Unix and Oracle tools* are also used that enable students to do their homework online remotely from home.

Technology

The effective use of technology in education depends on the quality of infrastructure and support available to students. At ZU, students have an excellent technology infrastructure where all students have their own laptops and have Internet connectivity from campus as well as from home. In Jordan, students have access to computing resources in relevant labs and availability of personal computers is much lower than students in UAE.

To learn about the quality of technology infrastructure, we asked students' opinion. 85% students from ZU and 59% students from JUST said that they did not have any problem in accessing Learning Management Systems (LMS) from home. 5% from ZU and 14% from JUST mentioned that they had problem in accessing the online resources.

Communication

Higher education in UAE is segregated based on gender while universities in Jordan have coeducation learning environment. Even outside university, culture and social values does not allow students to freely meet, have a discussion and exchange ideas in both countries. This factor affects communication skills and confidence level of students. How can the use of technology mitigate the impact of this factor to help students to improve their communication skills and confidence level?

We asked three questions to learn the impact of technology on students' communication with their fellow students, with their instructors, and overall communication skills. 56% of students from JUST and 71% from ZU said that they use email to communicate with their fellow students. 26% from JUST and 14% from ZU disagree on the usage of email. Response from female students at both universities was higher than male students' response. The difference in responses from ZU and JUST students could be explained by the quality and availability of infrastructure for educational technology available to students at both universities.

Table 3 Impact of ICT on higher education: a comparative study between JUST and ZU

Survey Question	**Agree**		**Disagree**	
Technology	**JUST**	**ZU**	**JUST**	**ZU**
I had no problem to access LMS from home.	59%	85%	14%	5%
Communication				
I used email to communicate with fellow students.	56%	71%	26%	14%
I used email to communicate with my instructor in this class.	38%	71%	31%	14%
I developed the ability to communicate clearly.	59%	78%	9%	0%
Collaboration				
I checked the discussion board often to see what questions/answers people had.	50%	21%	20%	28%
Using communication tools such as discussion board improved my productivity.	57%	42%	13%	55%
I learned a lot from other students using the discussion board.	51%	42%	23%	21%
I was more interested in the subject by using the discussion board.	44%	28%	21%	7%
Technical Skill Development				
Using online learning improved my technical skills.	60%	64%	15%	7%
The web resources mentioned on course web pages allowed me to learn more about courses.	54%	74%	15%	6%
Confidence Development				
Using online learning allowed me to be more independent.	52%	64%	19%	28%
I felt more comfortable in posting my opinion on discussion board rather than to speak up in class.	58%	64%	20%	7%
Using Online Learning Environment made me not dependent on my teacher for help.	50%	57%	25%	7%
I became more confident in expressing my ideas using communication technologies such as email, chat, and discussion forum.	75%	71%	7%	0%
Online Assessment				
I regularly check my online grade book.	77%	99%	9%	1%
Online grade book kept me informed of my grades, and my expectation of my final grade in this course.	79%	99%	8%	0%
I liked the idea of having online exams, quizzes, class activities, etc.	59%	50%	21%	43%

The second question was related to the use of email to communicate with class instructors. 38% from JUST and 71% from ZU used email to communicate with their teachers while 31% from JUST and 14% from ZU did not use email for communication with their teachers. UAE is a very conservative society while Jordan is comparatively liberal. One author who taught in UAE and in Jordan have observed that ZU students are usually very shy, and lack confidence in face-to-face communication. JUST students on the other hand, are less shy and more confident due to co-education and frequent interaction with the members of the opposite gender. The difference in responses could also be explained based on the availability of technology and infrastructure. 59% from JUST and 78% from ZU students responded positively to the question "I developed the ability to communicate clearly using discussion forum". Only 9% from JUST responded negatively.

Overall, ZU students showed more appreciation of communication technology that helped them develop and improve their communication skills and overcome their shyness.

Collaboration

Class size at ZU has an average of 11 students per class and students are female only while class size at JUST has an average of 40 students per class and are usually large and students are both male and female. ZU students, once on-campus, cannot leave until the end of day. This policy provides lots of time on-campus with their class fellows and friends to communicate and collaborate. Environment in JUST University is very similar to any North American university campus. Students can come and go as they wish; this may result in limited face-to-face interaction and communication opportunities.

50% from JUST and 21% from ZU responded positively to the statement "I check the discussion board often to see what questions/answers people had". 19% from JUST and 28% from ZU disagree with this statement. 57% from JUST and 42% from ZU agree with "discussion board improved my group work productivity" statement. 13% from JUST and 55% from ZU disagree with this statement.

The discussion board helped students to learn from their peers. 51% from JUST and 42% from ZU agree with it while 23% and 21% from JUST and ZU respectively disagree with it. 44% from JUST and 28% from ZU agree with "I was more interested in the subject because of discussion board " statement. 21% from JUST and 7% from ZU disagree with the statement.

JUST students used technology more effectively to collaborate than ZU students. These results are inline with our observations in the first paragraph of this section. ZU students did not use discussion forums effectively because they had enough time and opportunity to collaborate on-campus. JUST students have a more flexible and liberal environment. The larger class sizes and less time for face-to-face collaboration motivated JUST students to use discussion board to collaborate.

Technical Skill Development

Availability of online learning resources and computational tools could help students to improve their technical skills. Responses from the students are inline with our observations. This is more true in the case of ZU students living in a society with conservative cultural and social values.

60% and 64% from JUST and ZU respectively agree to "online learning improved my technical skills" while 15% and 7% disagree with it. 54% from JUST and 74% from ZU responded positively to the statement "The web resources mentioned on course web pages allowed me to learn more about courses" and 15% and 6% disagree with this statement.

Confidence Development

In the Middle Eastern culture, students often lack opportunity to freely meet, communicate, and collaborate. This results in shyness and lack of confidence to express opinion in front of members of the opposite gender. This is particularly true for female students. Technology allows students to meet, communicate, and collaborate in a virtual academic environment where most of the cultural and social limitations disappear. Interaction in the virtual world helps students to be more expressive and improve their confidence level. It also helps them to be more analytical and independent individuals.

52% from JUST and 64% from ZU agreed with "using online learning allowed me to be more independent" statement while 19% and 28% disagreed with it. More students from ZU agreed than disagreed with this statement.

58% from JUST and 64% from ZU agreed with following statement: "I felt more comfortable in posting my opinion on discussion board rather than to speak up in class". 20% from JUST and 7% from ZU disagree with it. Technology helped students to overcome their shyness and gave them confidence to present their opinion and views.

75% and 71% of students from JUST and ZU respectively agreed to "I became more confident in expressing my ideas using communication technologies such as email, chat, and discussion forum." statement.

Online Assessment

Students in both universities appreciated the posting of their grades online. 77% from JUST and 99% from ZU indicated they regularly check their online grade book. Almost the same percentage of 79% from JUST, and 99% from ZU agreed with the following statement "Online grade book kept me informed of my grades, and my expectation of my final grade in this course". The higher percentage of ZU compared to JUST students who used the online grade book could be explained by the availability of infrastructure for educational technology.

Students' opinion on having online exams, quizzes, and class activities were 59% from JUST compared to 50% from ZU. 21% from JUST and 43% from ZU indicated they liked to have offline exams.

Social Aspect

It was very interesting to learn that all students felt that the use of online learning environment removed the cultural and social limitations imposed by restrictive learning environment at ZU and JUST (e.g. opportunities to discuss with friends and to access resources after campus hours).

The use of technology helped ZU students who live in a conservative Arab society to overcome family restrictions and to collaborate with their peers after campus hours, which was not possible without technology. Typical responses and comments from ZU are the following:

> "Some students can't get together because they are living far away from each other or their families wouldn't allow them to go out by themselves. Using technology allow us to access materials from anywhere anytime"

> "When students use technology they will not be limited by place (only campus) and time (during 5 days a week) to learn or study for this course. For example, on last Oracle exam even though one of the questions was difficult to answer but I used Unix to talk with other student on class. Also I looked for the power points on Blackboard, and searched on the internet for similar exercise"

> "Sometimes we do not have the time to sit with friends after campus hours. Most of my friends live far away from our house. Using online communication overcomes this problem because most of the students can access the internet anytime"

> "Some students' families do not allow their daughters to go out evening even to go to a general library. Online teaching environment helps us overcome these limitations and to do the work at home"

The use of technology helped JUST students who live in a relatively liberal Arab country to be more socially active and to express their ideas effectively and more openly with others. Typical responses and comments from JUST include:

> "Technology helped us to be more confident in ourselves. It helped us to study alone and without asking the teacher all the time"

> "It helped me to communicate with people outside the university and talk with them about their experiences"

> "According to me as a girl, it is more comfortable to access course materials from home and use Internet at home even if it was late rather than going to Internet Cafe"

Conclusions

Cultural and social values in Middle Eastern countries are usually based on gender segregation. This factor results in a lack of interaction, lack of confidence in communication and a lack of opportunity to meet and exchange ideas with members of the opposite gender. Society in general has stricter rules of interaction and communication for females. We think that technology could help overcome these cultural limitations by providing alternate means of interaction, communication, and collaboration without changing the existing social and cultural norms.

The results of our case study reassured our observations that studying in a technology mediated learning environment could improve motivation and the confidence level of students. Some of the important findings from the case study are: (a) use of technology improved students communication skills, (b) use of technology allowed students to be more independent, (c) it also improved motivation and confidence levels of students, and (d) allowed students to express their feelings and ideas more openly with others. ZU students in a conservative society used technology to develop their communication skills, gain confidence, and overcome their shyness. They did not use collaboration tools effectively. JUST students in a moderately liberal country used technology to communicate with their peers and relied heavily on collaboration technology.

References

Galpin, V. (2002). Women in computers around the world. *ACM SIGCSE Bulletin, 34*(2), 94 – 100.

Hodges, C. (2004, Winter). Designing to motivate: Motivational techniques to incorporate in e-learning experience. *The Journal of Interactive Online Learning, 2*(3).

Information in the UAE, (2005). Retrieved March 23, 2005 from http://homepages.ius.edu/BPEKINPA/web4.htm

Jordan University of Science and Technology web site. (2005). Retrieved April 20, 2005 from http://www.just.edu.jo

Kinshuk & Young, A. (2003, April). Web-based asynchronous synchronous environment for online learning. *Journal of the USDLA*.

Kurzban, S. (1982). Societies' adaptation to computing. *ACM SIGCAS Computers and Society, 12*(2), Spring, 14-20.

Linge, R. (2003). The good, the bad, and the ridiculous: Putting a course online with Blackboard. *The Consortium for Computing in Small Colleges.*

Litiu, R. & Prakash, A. (2000). Developing adaptive groupware applications using a mobile component framework. *Proceedings of the ACM 2000 Conference on Computer Supported Cooperative Work (CSCW 2000)*, Philadelphia, PA, USA.

Marsic, A. Krebs, B. Dorohonceanu, & Tremaine, M. (2002). Designing and examining PC to Palm collaboration. *Proceedings of the 35th Annual Hawaii International Conference on System Sciences (HICSS'02).*

Muhlhauser, M. & Trompler, C. (2002). Learning in the digital age: Paving a smooth path with digital lecture halls. *Proceedings of HiCSS 35th Hawaii Intl. Conference*, Waikola, HI, Jan. 7-12, 2001, IEEE CS press, Los Alamitos, CA, pp. 352-361.

Neubauer, M. & Lobel, M. (2003). The learning by doing eClassroom. *Journal of the USDLA, 17*(2), 5-17.

Principe, J., Eulianno, N. & Lefebvre, C. (2004). An interactive learning environment for adaptive systems instruction. Retrieved April 20, 2005 from http://www.cnel.ufl.edu/files/1023120351.pdf

Saunders, B. & Quirke, P. (2002). Let my laptop lead the way: A Middle Eastern study. *Educational Technology and Society, 5*(1). ISSN 1436-4522.

Smith, M. & Winking-Diaz, A. (2004). Increasing students' interactivity in an online course. *The Journal of Interactive Online Learning, 2*(3).

Straub, D. (1994). The effect of culture on IT diffusion: E-mail and fax in Japan and the US. Information *Systems Research, 5*(1), 23-47.

Straub, D., Loch, K., Evaristo, J. R., Karahanna, E., & Srite, M. (2002). Toward a theory based measurement of culture. Journal of Global Information Management. Vol. 10, No. 1, 2002, pp. 13-23

Technology and Equity: Case studies, (2005). Retrieved April 2005 from http://projects.aed.org/techequity/index.html

UNDP Arab Human Development Report, (2003). Retrieved March 29, 2005 from http://www.undp.org/

United Nations Development Programme (UNDP): POGAR, (2005). Retrieved March 23, 2005 from http://www.undp-pogar.org/countries/

Walton, M., & Vukovic, V. (2003). Cultures, literacy, and the web: Dimensions of information "scent". *Interactions SPECIAL ISSUE: HCI in the developing world, 10*(2), 64-71.

Women in the United Arab Emirates, (2005). Retrieved March 23, 2005 from http://www.findarticles.com/p/articles/mi_m2242/is_1651_283/ai_107897410

Wong, Y., Shi, Y., & Wilson, D. (2004). Impact of computers on society and organization: Experience, gender composition, social presence, decision process satisfaction and group performance. *ACM International Conference Proceedings Series; 58* : Proceedings of the Winter International Symposium on Information and Communication Technologies WISICT '04. pp. 1- 10.

World Economic Forum, (2005). Jordan educational ICT pilot initiative. Retrieved April 13, 2005 from http://www.weforum.org/pdf/DigitalDivide/Jordan_Country_Report_100902.pdf

Zayed University web site, (2005). Retrieved April 20, 2005 from http://www.zu.ac.ae

Biographies

Abdallah Tubaishat is an assistant professor in the College of Information Systems at Zayed University, United Arab Emirates. He received his PhD degree in Software engineering from the from Illinois Institute of Technology, USA in 1994. Dr. Tubaishat has around eleven Years of experience in teaching and research. His research interests include e-learning, and software engineering. He has published a book with others entitled "Computer Skills", and has around eighteen Journal and conference publications.

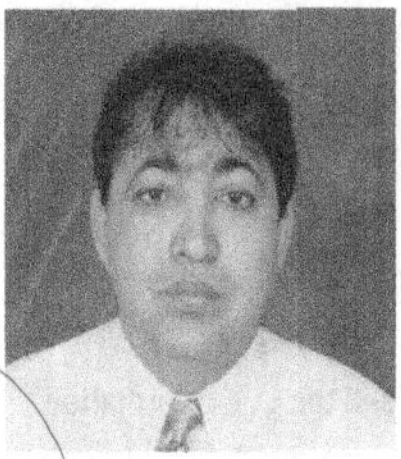

Arif Bhatti is an assistant professor at GIFT University, Pakistan. He received his PhD degree in Computer Science from the Boston University, USA in 1997. He joined the industry as senior software engineer and worked on several projects related to the parallel computing for business and web applications for mobile users. He is interested in applied research and his research interests include parallel computing, wireless computing, and distributed online learning technologies. He is a member of the ACM.

Eyas El-Qawasmeh is an assistant professor in the department of the Computer Science at Jordan University of Science and Technology, Jordan. He received his PhD degree from George Washington University, USA in 1997. In 2001, he joined George Washington University as visiting researcher through a Fulbright Commission grant. In 2001, he won Hijjawi research prize for Computer Science (best computer researcher in 2001, Jordan and Palestine). His areas of interest include multimedia databases, information retrieval, and object-oriented. He is a member of the ACM and IEEE.

Are Universities to Blame for the IT Careers Crisis?

Glen L. Van Der Vyver and Michael S. Lane
University of Southern Queensland
Department of Information Systems
Toowoomba, Australia

vandervy@usq.edu.au lanem@usq.edu.au

Abstract

At a time when the IT industry in general and the IT academy in particular face major challenges, some accuse universities of producing graduates with poor or inappropriate skills. This qualitative study, based on interviews with fifteen senior IT executives and managers in the Australian financial services industry, examines what employers seek when they recruit new graduates. We find that employers now expect much more from IT graduates. They require a blend of technical, business and people skills combined with the right attitude. Furthermore, requirements are highly mediated by contextual factors such as company size and corporate culture. We also find that universities are not perceived as negatively as some would have it. Universities face a significant challenge in producing graduates with much wider skill sets. Although this study was conducted in Australia, we are of the opinion that the issues discussed are relevant in the wider international context.

Keywords: IT Education; skills crisis; graduate employment; outsourcing; graduate attributes

Introduction

As is the case throughout the developed world, these are troubled times for the Information Technology profession in Australia. For IT academics, the situation has degenerated markedly in the last 18 months and now threatens to take on crisis proportions. Restructuring and retrenchment, which would have been unthinkable a few years ago, have besieged the IT academy and there is little to indicate that the worst is not yet to come.

Unfortunately, there are those within the profession who choose to ignore or obfuscate the real and apparent causes of the crisis and choose to blame IT academics for causing some (or most) of the problem. The common cry of these people is that the jobs are out there but the IT departments at Australian universities are simply not producing candidates with the correct skills. This cry is as likely to come from within the profession as from without and a few of those whose clarion call this has become are themselves academics.

Recently, the national president of the Australian Computer Society issued what amount to a position statement: *Our migration and university systems are not producing the skills we need. Both are churning out bulk programmers, who remain oversupplied when we really need competent broadly based technology specialists. The lack of such professionals represents a major obstacle to growth . . .* (The Australian, June 14, 2005, p. 31). The ACS is clearly of the opinion that a new skills crisis is emerging and that universities are part of the problem rather than part of the solution.

This study seeks to critically examine the so-called skills crisis and the quality of graduates produced by Australian universities. We enter the debate with open minds, even conceding that it is possible that the position of the ACS as regards the skill sets which are in demand is fundamentally correct. We interviewed fifteen executives and senior managers in the financial services industry, focusing on graduate attributes. Our point of departure is that one of the most important concerns facing IT academics today is the issue of graduate employment for their students.

The Information Technology Career in Crisis

Since the end of the dot-com boom, times have been tough for Information Technology professionals (Malykhina, 2004). Smith (2004, p. 1) argues that not only is the job market much tighter but employers are expecting much more. She sums up the situation as follows: *Structural changes in the economy have created an employment environment that dictates hiring selectivity in the Information Technology field.* Unemployment has soared amongst established professionals and new graduates are finding it difficult to obtain employment in the field (Chabrow, 2003; Chen, 2003). Trends in outsourcing, offshoring, migration and the continued demands on corporations to cut costs suggest that things are likely to get worse before they get better, if indeed they ever do (Fang, Lee, Lee & Huang, 2004). Given the problems faced in areas such as engineering (see below) it is ominous that there are warnings (Costlow, 2003) that the software area is likely to suffer more than most technical areas.

Fang, Lee, Lee, and Huang (2004) conducted an empirical study using IT graduates in the USA and conclude that, in a tight job market, various factors improve the chance of securing a job offer. These include gender, whether an internship was completed and the nature of the internship, double majors, GPA, time of declaration of the major and what type of courses were completed in the major. It is clearly no longer sufficient to simply have completed an IT major. Employers are interested in specific courses and double majors with a business subject. Essentially, employers seem to be seeking a balance between technical, communication and business skills.

Smith (2004) points out that graduates in general, and those who have majored in IT in particular, now face substantial career barriers when attempting to establish themselves in the field. Swanson and Woitke (1997, p. 434) defined career barriers as *events or conditions, either within the person or in his or her environment, that make career progress difficult.* Career barriers often have a pervasive influence on the process of career choice and establishment. They have a strong influence on cognitive and affective processes and the ultimate choices made by the individual (Swanson, Daniels, & Tokar, 1996). Career barriers operate insidiously, undermining even the best, most motivated and most confident of students (Albert & Luzzo, 1999; Brown & Brooks, 1996). Many students find themselves making decisions based on their perceptions of career barriers and organizations like the ACS hardly instill confidence in potential students with their pronouncements.

Weber (2004) argues that the current downturn in the IT profession is a purge after years of excess: He argues that the dot-com boom was an aberration and what followed was a situation where companies refused to continue investing heavily in IT. In tandem with the wave of downsizing which followed, many jobs moved offshore, particularly to China and India, where there are many highly skilled but cheap IS professionals. Weber also points out that the shock of these events has of necessity had a major influence on people teaching ICT because there is now more capacity than is required.

Weber identifies five trends which should not be ignored by IT educators, students and practitioners, namely: IT occupations will remain prominent, there will be fluctuations in demand for IT professionals, the IT employment marketplace will be global, change will be rapid, and IT will be the bellwether for other occupations. He urges educators in particular to be open to the needs of the global market, eschew regulation, and design curriculum that delivers skills and knowledge that are resistant to change,

Weber's analysis of the current state of play in IT employment (and IT education) is insightful and penetrating. There are, however, a number of issues which must be addressed. Weber's apparent point of departure is that of a firm believer in economic rationalism and globalization. We argue that his analysis must be viewed in terms of its point of departure and we argue that his vision of unencumbered IT professionals freely roaming the globe in search of job opportunities is perhaps overly optimistic. Clearly, there are many barriers that make this very difficult, for example:

- We are still a very long way from the situation where national labour markets are open to all and sundry. Australians, for example, cannot simply arrive in any foreign country of their choice and apply for IT jobs.
- The salary structures in some countries are so low that it would be impossible for the worker to return home.
- There is immense opportunity cost associated with constant relocation.
- The emotional and social overheads of this type of peripatetic life come at a cost to society and the individual.

The reality of the situation is that jobs move more frequently than people. We argue that the global IT jobs market may better be characterized as one where jobs are continually on the move, seeking cheap (and cheaper) human resources. In our opinion, the greatest strength of Weber's analysis is his detailed advice for a new IT curriculum, which he believes will prepare students for the demands of the new paradigm. Effectively, he recommends that 'softer' skills drive the curriculum but are backed up with 'vocational' courses in the technology of the day. We concur that this is the way forward – teach students fundamental skills but also allow them to hit the ground running. That being said, while there has been much talk about the need for IT graduates to be taught more 'soft' skills, empirical justification for such an approach is tenuous at best and the word 'soft' is often ambiguously defined. So, for example, a recent major study used a content analysis of newspaper advertisements and discovered that recruitment continues to focus on 'hard' skills (Gallivan, Truex & Kvasny, 2004). We argue that the approach suggested by Weber provides us with a middle way but it could mean that we need to extend the curriculum.

Research Questions and Method

The two research questions investigated in this interpretative study of graduate attributes are:

- RQ1: What attributes are you looking for in new graduates?
- RQ2: How well are Australian universities preparing IT graduates for the workplace?

The qualitative method of a series of in-depth interviews allowed the researchers to explore and identify the key issues associated an open ended set of research questions in an interpretative manner in line with the research objectives of this study (Miles & Huberman, 1994; Yin, 1994).

Data Analysis

Table 1 shows a summary of the key graduate attributes identified in the analysis of the interview data. For each attribute we note the number of interviewees who mentioned that attribute:

Table 1: Key graduate attributes

Graduate Attribute	Number of respondents
1. Communication Skills	10
2. Understand Business	10
3. Work Ethic	9
4. Technical Skills	9
5. Database	8
6. Java	7
7. Business Analysis	7
8. .Net	6
9. Adaptability / Learning	6
10. Cultural fit	5
11. People Skills	5
12. Logic	5
13. Adaptability / Learning	5
14. Problem solving	5
15 Conscientious	4
16. Understand Technology	4
17. GPA	4
18. Honesty	2
19.Leadership Potential	2
20.Proven Development Skills	2
21. C++	2
22.Open Source	1

RQ1: What attributes are you looking for in new graduates?

We were struck by the number and diversity of attributes which emerged. So-called 'soft' skills have clearly become more important but the overriding impression is that of a graduate who needs to be well-rounded and comfortable in the business and technical arenas. In short, the bar has been raised and employers expect a lot.

The idea of a generalised ideal IT graduate does not exist. Ideal graduate types varied significantly by organization type. An interviewee from a medium-sized company which develops software and offers outsourcing services offers the follow vision:

The old technological requirements are out . . . The Business Analysts are the IT guns . . .they need to be good communicators, understand current technology and business . . .and, they need to leverage technological skills.

It is interesting to note that in a company which values flair, creativity and people skills the ability to leverage technological skills is still important. This company is not looking for technological illiterates. An interviewee from a smaller software house with a similar profile and values takes up the argument:

We rarely hire people on technological skills. . . We rate people and business skills and want team players who fit in

At the other extreme, one outsourcing vendor prefers to employ engineering graduates because they value structure and very strong technical skills. The interviewee mentioned softer skills almost in passing. An interviewee from a financial institution which does a lot of development in-house has the following perspective:

I look for technically capable people, for example .Net, Java, C++,Oracle who can make a business case. I want front-end and back-end skills from requirements analysis to coding. I like to see proven development skills . . .

An interviewee from another outsourcing vendor takes a similar approach:

The work is varied . . . some of it legacy. We need highly specialised technical skills for a lot of it. We look for people who are logical . . . problem solvers . . . who can debug . . . everything from UNIX scripts to .Net and Java.

We found that larger, more formalised organizations placed more emphasis on technical skills while smaller, decentralised organizations valued softer skills more highly. The majority of organizations value both sets of skills, however. One interviewee chose identified the three skill sets, in order of importance:

- Technical Skills.
- Business Skills.
- A realistic outlook on life.

Several other interviewees would have broadly agreed with this but might have changed around the order of importance. Most of the interviewees favoured a balanced set of hard and soft skill while a few tended to the extremes.

RQ2: How well are Australian universities preparing IT graduates for the workplace?

In many cases this question naturally progressed into a broader discussion of problems that have been experienced with IT graduates. We found little evidence of a sense of deep dissatisfaction with the quality of graduates emerging from Australian universities. On the other hand, it is undeniable that there are issues which must be addressed but it is our conviction that many of these issues are perennial.

A number of interviewees identified attitude as a key problem, for example:

What we need is people who understand the meaning of R – C = P/L, i.e. Revenue – Cost = Profit or Loss . . . Too many graduates sit around and wait for things to happen . . they don't understand the costs of keeping them in their seats . . they are not proactive.

Several interviewees were critical of the general communication skills of IT graduates, for example:

A lot of these people can't write a decent note . . . forget about a report . . . and presentation skills . . . well! But I have a feeling this applies to people from other areas as well.

A relatively common theme was the problems associated with recruiting graduates with the correct combination of attitudes, technical skills and business skills:

Good A/P's are hard to find . . . it tends to be one or the other, strong tecchy or strong analyst . . . yes, I suppose this is not new . . . in my day it was the same.

A few interviewees spoke of a reticence to hire graduates because of the time lag before they were productive, for example:

Recruitment mistakes are expensive . . . we want to hire people with proven development skills who understand the SDLC. We hire analyst / programmers who can take on a variety of roles . . . (from) requirements analysis to coding.

Although these interviewees were the most critical of the level of expertise of graduates and had the least positive views of the quality of Australian IT graduates, we are not dealing with attitudes which have emerged recently. For decades, employers have wanted graduates who are ready to take on the most complex of projects with no training and for all that time universities have pointed out that they can only do so much. Even where the university has a capstone project course it cannot replicate the environment of a real project. There are certain skills that can only be learned in the workplace.

The majority of interviewees felt that Australian universities were doing a reasonably good job in terms of turning out decent IT graduates. Indeed, several interviewees who are involved in offshoring commented that the quality of Australian IT staff was significantly higher than that of the offshore staff. In some cases, this disparity had so dissipated the perceived cost advantages that work was coming back onshore:

We offshore lower skilled work . . . they are not as good as the locals . . . a lot of it has come back . . . and when it comes to understanding the business and there's obviously no comparison.

We must concede that this viewpoint was by no means universal. While it was widely acknowledged that the quality of Australian staff was highly competitive some of the interviewees felt that cost imperatives would drive the lower skilled jobs offshore. One respondent presented a somewhat apocalyptic viewpoint:

There is a tidal wave of offshoring to come. Even if I have a small job, say $100, I send it off to India late afternoon and the code is waiting for me in the morning. Sure, standards can be variable but the key is <u>specification</u>. No Australian programmer can compete on cost.

There was no indication amongst interviewees that they thought the IT academy is responsible for the current problems graduates are experiencing in finding work. Rather, the problems are rooted in structural changes associated with the dot com bust, new economic imperatives, and offshoring.

Conclusions and Implications

Australian companies require adaptable IT staff with a wide range of skills. Although 'soft' skills are much more important than was the case even a few years ago, there is little evidence of the extinction of demand for technical skills. Indeed, the ideal IT employee would offer the company a blend of technical, business and personal skills.

Our study once again exposes some of the dangers of 'survey aggregation'. We argue that there is no such thing as the ideal IT graduate. Requirements are highly contextualised and vary by type and size of company, corporate culture, project type, whether outsourcing is prevalent and a host of other factors. The methodology employed in this study has limitations of its own, of course, and we concede that the fact we interviewed fifteen people from one sector (financial services) does raise the issue of generalizability.

We note that there was little mention of skills which are often touted by those who argue that there are too many technical, programming courses in the curriculum. These people frequently favor programs which produce systems integrators and ERP specialists, neither of which was mentioned by the interviewees. This does not surprise us because we argue that it is difficult to produce good systems integrators who do not have a good technical and business background. Furthermore, these types of skills are best learned on the job and grow with experience.

Although there may be scope for improvement, we argue that Australian universities are doing a reasonable job in producing good quality IT staff. Given the constraints imposed upon universities in recent years, they are adapting well to the changed requirements. Universities face significant challenges in that they are now asked to produce IT graduates with a far wider range of skills at a time when there are severe pressures to cut costs and constrain curricula. It is a difficult task indeed to produce a graduate who is technically strong, a good communicator, and a savvy businessperson with the right attitudes and values. Indeed, some of these desirables are probably not within the domain of what people can reasonably expect universities to produce.

We do not claim this study is in any way definitive and we readily acknowledge that our information comes from a small number of people operating in a specific industry. We acknowledge that that this study may not be generalizable but we argue that the results are sufficient to stimulate debate about the claims of some that the failure of Australian universities to produce graduates with the correct skills is a key reason for the problems faced in the Australian IT sector.

In conclusion, based on the information obtained in this study, we find that there is much to support Weber's vision of an IT professional who is multi-skilled, flexible and adaptable but less to support the ACS vision of an academy wholly out of touch with the realities of the marketplace.

References

Albert, K. A., & Luzzo, D. A. (1999). The role of perceived barriers in career development: A social cognitive perspective. *Journal of Counselling and Development, 77*(4), 431-436.

Brown, D. & Brooks, L. (1996). *Career choice and development.* San Francisco: Josey-Bass.

Chabrow, E. (2004). Fewer IT workers standing in the unemployment line. *Information Week, 943*, 16.

Chen, C. (2003). Grads aren't seeing green. *Fortune, 147*(13), 29.

Costlow, T. (2003). Globalization drives changes in software careers. *IEEE Software, 20*(8), 14-16.

Fang, X., Lee, S., Lee, T. & Huang, W. (2004). Critical factors affecting job offers for new MIS graduates. *Journal of Information Systems Education, 15*(2), 189-204.

Gallivan, M. J., Truex, D. P. & Kvasny, L. (2004). Changing patterns in IT skill sets 1988-2003: A content analysis of classified advertising. *DATA BASE for Advances in Information Systems, 35*(3), 65-87.

Malykhina, E. (2004, April 19). IT job market causes concern. *InformationWeek, 985*, 76.

Miles, MB & Huberman. (1994), *Qualitative data analysis: An expanded sourcebook.* Thousand Oaks, CA: Sage Publications.

Smith, S. (2004). Career barriers among information technology undergraduate majors. *Information Technology, Learning and Performance Journal, 22*(1), 49-57.

Weber, R. (2004). Some implications of the Year-2000 era, dot-com era and offshoring for information systems pedagogy. *MIS Quarterly, 28*(2), iii-xi.

Yin, R. K. (1994). *Case study research: Design and methods* (2nd ed., vol. 5 of 14 vols). Thousand Oaks, CA: Applied Social Research Methods Series, Sage Publications.

Biographies

Glen Van Der Vyver is a senior lecturer in Information Systems at the University of Southern Queensland. He worked at the 'coalface'in Human Resources and IT (mostly) for around fifteen years before becoming an academic some years ago. Glen teaches primarily in the database area and is currently working on research relating to IT careers, outsourcing, offshoring, the function of the CIO and risk perception.

Michael Lane is a lecturer in the Division of Information Systems, Faculty of Business, University of Southern Queensland. He holds an Honours in Information Technology and a PhD with a focus in E-Commerce Development. He has published widely in Information Systems and Electronic Commerce but has varied interests in research and teaching including outsourcing, corporate governance and the function of the CIO. He has run a postgraduate course on E-Business Strategy at the Australian Graduate School of Business at USQ for the last four years.

Integrating Industrial Practices in Software Development through Scenario-Based Design of PBL Activities: A Pedagogical Re-Organization Perspective

Kam Hou VAT
University of Macau, Macau SAR, China

fstkhv@umac.mo

Abstract

This paper investigates a pedagogic model appropriate to the integration of the industrial practices in software development into the learning activities of our undergraduate students, especially in the context of group-based project work. Specifically, we are interested in the potentialities of this model enhanced from the problem-based learning context, such that people collaborating in the peculiar scenario of project development, are empowered to be more sensitive and reflective of their learning experiences. Our discussion describes a practical framework of course enactment taking into account the suggestions of the latest curriculum guidelines stipulated in the final draft of the "Computing Curriculum – Software Engineering" created by the Joint Task Force on Computing Curricula of the IEEE Computer Society and the Association for Computing Machinery. Namely, software engineering education in the 21st century needs to move beyond the lecture format, and should consider the incorporation of a variety of teaching and learning approaches, one example of which includes the constructivist model of problem-based learning (PBL) considered as appropriate to supplement or even largely replace the lecture format in certain cases. In the paper, a pedagogical re-organization perspective is presented as a way to conduct teaching in the area of software engineering. In particular, the connotation of problem-based learning in the education of future software practitioners is explored from a teacher-researcher's position, through the practice of action research. The paper concludes by emphasizing the contextualized learning scenarios involved in PBL, which have been observed to enable our students to experience the real-world practice of software development, and acquire valuable learning through teamwork that should remain with their future careers.

Keywords: Collaboration, design scenarios, problem-based learning, software engineering education.

Introduction

In the traditional model of education (Vat, 2002, 2003, 2004e, 2004f), learning design proceeded in a linear fashion from defining objectives to lesson planning to course delivery. Educators first engaged in a comprehensive learning needs analysis process, often based on assessments done by others about competencies and learning objectives. Comprehensive syllabi were developed. Finally, the course was delivered as planned. In fact, most computing courses involve setting "problems" which students are required to complete. We often refer to these problems as exercises because they are small and well defined. We used them extensively in our conventional course: there were weekly exercises, each focused on particular detailed aspects of the course, usually one that had been center-stage in the recent lectures; there were larger assignments which integrated many aspects of the course, but were still quite tightly defined, to the point where their correctness can somehow be assessed using automatic grading system. Undoubtedly, content is important, but more attention should be paid to the process. Today, a renewed mindset (Vat, 2006) is needed for education, especially when it is offered through the perspective to achieve collaborative learning, an important ingredient in the education of an engineering professional. Within the context of a computing curricula, class time should also be devoted to such generic problem-solving skills as defining a learning plan, brainstorming to get started on a problem, reflection, articulation of problems and solutions, self-assessment, practice in active listening, and other communication skills. These aspects must be assessed and contribute to the grade awarded. Besides, teaching and learning must be seen as an ongoing process rather than a program with a fixed starting and ending point. The importance of widespread participation by learners in the design of their own learning must be emphasized (Kimball, 1995). The key is to design a framework for collaborative work, which requires students to grapple with roles, protocols for working inter-dependently and mutual accountability. In this regard, problem-based learning (PBL) serves as a very good instrument to experience group learning, which is also essential to fulfill the industrial expectation in the field of software development. Our discussion in the paper elaborates on a teacher-researcher's experience in delivering a junior core course through a pedagogic model re-organized from the constructivist viewpoint of PBL. The course involves the industrial transfer of software engineering practices into classroom learning, which is fostered through a teamwork atmosphere. The model incorporates a framework of course enactment, which demonstrates the importance of contextualized learning scenarios of PBL activities, which enable students' learning through group-based project work that should remain an important asset in their future careers.

The Industrial Practices in Software Development

According to a survey done by Vaughn (2001) on the software industry's expectation of new college graduates, the following twelve characteristics were repeatedly identified: the ability to work as a member of a team, a solid work ethic, ability to work under stress, professional demeanor, communication skills, ability to follow process, technical proficiency, desire for continuous learning, project management skills, customer focus, appreciation for the dynamics of requirements, and good citizenship qualities. Tellingly, the industrial practices that have to be accommodated in any course of software engineering education, to help students acquire such qualities expected in the software industry, are many. The following items selected by Vaughn (2001) represent some typical examples: process focus, team dynamics, planning, performance evaluation, customer relationship management, delivery on time, accountability for time and billing, and product rollout.

The Focus on Process

One of the important milestones in the journey of software professionals is the encounter of the pragmatics of a process. A process characterizes the activities of people and tools, as well as the rules for organizing those activities. The software engineering community in particular has been a leader in developing new process technologies and practices for use by large, diverse organizations. These range from process improvements strategies, such as the Software Engineering Institute's Capability Maturity Model (CMM), to notations for describing software engineering processes, to tools and environments for automating software process execution, to techniques for collecting and analyzing process data. One of the lessons learned (Fuggetta &

Wolf, 1996) from experience with software process technologies and practices, is that they can be more broadly applied to other domains in which process is an important concern. For instance, software processes are currently applied to organizational contexts where there is a need to describe the complex interactions among humans, and between humans and tools. It is true that the average student has little experience in accomplishing process steps through lectures alone. Within the PBL context, it is possible for students to adopt a process for their development exercise and the team members need to learn keeping the team focused on it during the product development.

The Dynamics on Team

Working in teams is almost a fact of life in the software industry today. Most professional programming projects require individuals to be organized as members of a team or sometimes, of more than one teams. This has been the practice in contemporary software development. Still, one important factor of teamwork is whether the team has jelled. This refers to when the members of the team work so well together, they are more than the sum of their parts. In other words, their output is greater than they could have achieved individually. In practice, whether a team jells is often a function of individual attitudes, especially of egos. It is true that software developers need egos. They probably need a big one to maintain an attitude of perfection while solving difficult problems. Yet, they must find a way to submerge their egos in forming a team or the team will never jell. The dynamics of teams relative to egos is sometimes referred to as the "Bozo Effect" (Bozo was a clown character) (Tomayko & Hazzan, 2004, pp.50-51). People who disrupt teams are often called "Bozos." The Bozo effect is a function of how many Bozos can be part of the team and still have it deliver reasonably working software.

The Essence on Planning

The schedules created for a development project can make or break the project, the product, and the people involved. The attention and forethought applied to this critical activity of planning can mean the difference between: management in control and management in pain; on-time (or early) delivery and late (or no) delivery; a full-function product and a limited-function product; high employee morale (productivity) and low employee morale (productivity); customer satisfaction and customer dissatisfaction; product success and product failure. Oftentimes, the single most important plan of a project is the project schedule plan (Whitten, 1995, pp. 89-94). It defines the roadmap of activities that affect virtually every member of a project and is the keystone for communications across a project. If the schedules defined by the project schedule plan are unreasonable, then the expected progress on the project soon will become blocked. This blockage will cause project challenges to emerge, which must then be met to deal with the obstructions. It is important to realize that the failure of a major activity to be completed on schedule eventually will impact the schedules of subsequent project activities. The domino effect could continue until the project topples.

The Evaluation on Performance

In the software industry, personal contributions to the organization are kept track of, and recognized normally through an annual or semi-annual evaluation. In particular, one's individual performance is often evaluated in the context of peer evaluations, management observation, and team contribution to success. Peer evaluations are a powerful tool in determining one's contribution to the success of the organization and support to those with whom one works. In the PBL model of course enactment (Barrows, 1985, 1988; Vat, 2000, 2001, 2004f), this industrial practice of performance evaluation can be modeled by creating a peer evaluation practice which allows for the rating of each member of a PBL team by the other members on a simple 1-to-5 or 1-to-10 scale. It is also advisable to ask the rater to rate his or her own self alongside each of the other team members. Typically, at least three evaluations are performed during a semester in order to obtain a valid sampling of true contributions. The idea of performance evaluation could also be exercised as a form of feedback mechanism. Early feedback is useful to a team member in his or her desire to succeed and affords the whole team to correct problems perceived internally among team members.

The Importance of Customer Relationships

Today, commercial and IT organizations alike realize that to be competitive and to achieve the goals of their businesses, they must drive an understanding of their customer right into the center of their development processes: how customers work, how they buy, and what they will be doing in the future. They are aware that the future success of their businesses necessitates a commitment to understanding the customers and understanding their businesses. Thereby, relationships with one's customer and the ability to communicate openly and frankly is as important to project success as any element of a software lifecycle. Yet, this is a difficult lesson to teach in a classroom environment through lectures. Engineers used to making what they are interested in often feel constrained by having to think about what the customer wants. Their design conversations barely touch on how to match the structure of user work to the structure of the system. Yet, today's challenge is in front-end design – the idea that the voice of the customer must be heard before developers start to build.

The Delivery on Time

Every software project has a date for delivery. It marks the end of a project with the completion of a number of important milestones each of which has its own target delivery date. The important thing to remember is that every team slip on a milestone delivery compresses the available delivery time for subsequent deliverables. To avoid any slip, each team needs to perform periodic reviews on the work in progress, be it done through cooperating or collaborating. The former means different portions of the work done by different members before integration occurs, whereas the latter means the same portion of work being jointly performed by two or three members. There is a need to identify the major problems that haunt the project, and work out the possible solutions as soon as necessary; thus, project tracking in order to stay in control becomes an important issue in project development.

The Rollout of Product

Once the hard and fast due date for delivery of product to the customer is set. It is incumbent upon each project team to establish a meeting with the customer on or prior to this date to present a final product demonstration and provide all necessary documentation. A formal briefing is expected during which the product is presented, features are demonstrated, requirements not incorporated are addressed, documentation is provided, and a maintenance plan is discussed. The customer is the focus of this meeting and is expected to formally accept the project. The importance of this meeting cannot be overemphasized. It brings the project to closure and provides a certain amount of jobs stress on the team in that the delivery must occur on time, be professionally conducted, be complete, and is an important record for performance evaluation.

Empowering Students in Software Engineering Education

In order to enable our students to get familiar with the industrial practices in software development, we have tried adapting the problem-based learning (PBL) experience into different scenarios of real-world problem solving (Vat, 2004b, 2005a, 2005b). These learning scenarios of PBL activities are designed to allow students to experience the team-based process of software development in a suitable course whose context is flexible enough to accommodate the educational formalism and the practical innovations involved. It could be considered as the industrial transfer of the software engineering experience to the classroom environment. The key lies in the appropriate design of the learning scenarios to accommodate this experimental transfer. In the following discussion, the ongoing curriculum design of SFTW300 Software Psychology is delineated, in order to discuss how the industrial practices could be incorporated.

The Course Context

The teaching of *Software Psychology*, or more properly renamed as human-computer interactions (HCI) (Vat, 2000, 2001) in the undergraduate curriculum has always been a challenge as it is composed of such a mix of elements as human factors, user expectations, man-machine interfaces construction, cognitive psychology, computer science, and those latest developments on contextual design in interactive systems. In the case of the author's teaching experience, since 1998, the pedagogy adopted to deliver such a course has been shifted from a conventional instructivist approach to the constructivist method of problem-based learning (PBL) (Albanese & Mitchell 1993; Engel 1991; Greening, 2000; Ryan, 1993). Besides, with the increasingly accumulated course material to cover in a single semester, the idea of scenario-based design (Carroll, 2000) has also been incorporated in 2000 with an attempt to help undergraduate Software Engineering students deepen the idea that HCI is concerned with understanding, designing, evaluating and implementing interactive computer systems to match the needs of people. It is the author's experience that the constructivist's ideas of problem-based learning (PBL) (Barrows, 1986) revolving around a focal problem, group work, feedback, skill development and iterative reporting, with the instructor playing the coach by the side, guiding, probing, and supporting student-groups' initiatives along the way, could help students develop a unified team-based approach to better manage the underlying software requirements. Methodically, we need some working scenarios to try out some iterative process involving researchers (instructor) and practitioners (students) acting together on a particular cycle of development activities, including problem diagnosis, action intervention, and reflective learning. Particularly, the action research approach should involve evaluating how well the students playing the role of practitioners, could function as self-directed work teams (SDWTs) (Fisher, 2000) of software professionals, following the constructivist's tenets of PBL, in performing group-based software development for a specific user scenario. Against this backdrop, the use of soft systems methodology (SSM) (Checkland & Holwell, 1998; Checkland & Scholes, 1999; Vat, 2006) has demonstrated quite a promise in enhancing the student-practitioners' learning to deal with the design difficulties typified in the complex domain of ill-defined problem situations.

The Course Goals

Software Psychology is offered annually in the fall semester as a compulsory subject for Software Engineering majors affiliated with the Department of Computer and Information Science, at the Faculty of Science and Technology. The goals of the class used to include the following: (1) to help students become HCI-literate by developing fundamental understanding of HCI in relation to human factors, usability engineering, cognitive psychology, and computer science; (2) to encourage students to formulate and express their views on user interface design of interactive systems, through project development, written work, oral presentations and classroom discussions; and (3) to raise students' awareness of the HCI impact on computer industry, and the wide-spread focus of HCI from human factors, to usability engineering, to user-centered design, in constructing systems that support human activity. Besides, in view of incorporating more industrial practices into students' learning, different scenarios of team-based project development based on the PBL cycle of activities (Vat, 2000, 2001), have to be enhanced.

The Course Design of Group-work Activities

In each semester when *Software Psychology* is offered, students embark on the PBL cycle of learning through organized groups of 4-6 members (one being the team leader). Each PBL group will be given a project scenario to explore within a specified period of time. Individual PBL groups are each assigned a project client from other teams. Namely, each team, acting as developers, is to complete an interactive system design and prototype for another team. Yet, the same team is the client of another group, responsible for clarifying the project, and resolving ambiguities as they arise, typically through a liaison member in the developer's team. Meanwhile, each PBL team is required to present their work in progress, and lead class forums to elicit students' discussions. The team leader, equivalent to project leader, has to coordinate the team activities, and ensure effective team communications. And the team members have to help set the project goals, accomplish tasks assigned, meet deadlines, attend team meetings and participate in editing project documents to be combined as the final project report. At the end of the project, each member of the respective PBL teams is required to make a presentation of his or her project involvement, with a question and answer session for the whole class. The instructor, being the project sponsors for all client teams and project supervisors for all developer teams, design the necessary scenarios to guide, motivate and provide feedback to the teams. Also, the instructor has to evaluate how well students perform in the PBL groups, and how well such groups behave as self-directed work teams in managing software requirements, and provide the necessary adjustments.

The Course Scenarios for HCI

The coursework of *Software Psychology* is based on designing learning scenarios of PBL activities in group-based project work. According to Carroll (2000), scenarios are useful in coordinating the central task of system development which includes understanding people's needs, envisioning new activities and technologies, designing effective software and drawing general lessons from systems as they are developed and used. In particular, scenarios evoke task-oriented reflection in design work. They make human activity the starting point and the standard for design work. They help designers identify and develop correct problem requirements, seeing their work as artifacts-in-use, and bearing in mind the external constraints in the design process. Moreover, scenarios help designers analyze the varied possibilities through many alternative views of usage situations. It is believed that scenario-based design in HCI could be considered as a framework approach to manage the flow of design activity and information in a rubric of task-oriented abstractions. It draws on the incrementally accrued knowledge and experience of the designers, who, in our course context, happen to be our PBL students. Essentially, our learning scenario begins when the instructor, acting as the project sponsor, invites our PBL teams to embark on a journey to develop quality software that meets customers' real needs in Web-based development. Our teams need to encounter different roles (users, stakeholders, developers) and understand the diverse languages spoken in this journey. The general idea is to construct a dynamic class Web site where individual PBL groups have to participate in sharing information by maintaining their individual Web presence. Each PBL group has two roles to play: a client to express its own Web site requirements, and a developer to fulfill other group's Web site requirements. The class Web site is to be built by a joint effort of the PBL groups. It is designed that the first thing our PBL teams have to learn is a systematic approach to eliciting, organizing, and documenting the requirements of the system to be built (Leffingwell & Widrig, 2000). Also important is a process that establishes and maintains agreement between the customer and the project team on the changing requirements of the system. Individual PBL teams have to understand users' problems in their culture and their language and to build systems that meet their needs. They need to identify the services the system provides to fulfill users' needs, through different methods of software development.

The Course Review Web Sites for HCI

A very important tool for individual PBL team is the review Web site to keep clients apprised of the project progress and to keep all team members up-to-date on all aspects of the site. It is also where the PBL team will work collaboratively on the site. Through the review Web sites, our PBL teams can conduct remote reviews with their clients or stakeholders, who can view the site in progress, give feedback on a design, get in touch with the PBL team, and check the project schedule. The review Web site of each PBL team contains such information as the roles and responsibilities of the project team, contact information for all team members, the project mission, the vision document, site architecture, schematics, all design reviews, the project schedule, and a link to the staging site (site where the work-in-progress system can be demonstrated). The vision document defines the objective of the project along with a description of the audience and the key insight into their mindset. It is what the Web team uses to design and build the site. A site-architecture is a diagram showing how the Web pages link to one another, giving an overall view of the entire site's content. Schematics are associated with individual Web pages and they each show what elements of content live on each page. Overall, we have five to six Web sites for five to six PBL groups' review, plus one extra site for the whole class, created jointly by all the PBL groups through the efforts of the liaison members from each of the project groups.

The Course Assessment for Project Work

There are a number of milestones set for project teams throughout the semester. Typically, there will be a milestone for all client teams to present their systems of interest, followed by the milestones for all developer teams to fulfill the system design, prototyping, and final delivery. At the completion of each milestone, each PBL team will be assessed according to their performance, in terms of the necessary deliverables produced, and the presentation made by the whole team. Records of the team's work should also be available from the team's review Web site for evaluation purpose. There will be a group grade and an individual grade for each member of the team. The group grade is the same for all members, but the individual grade is different. The group grade is given by the instructor and by the whole class, except for the group being evaluated. The individual grade is given through peer evaluation among the team members. Typically, a peer evaluation form is created by the group, which is used by each member of the team to rate every other member in the same team. The rating is often divided into three aspects: qualitative comments of the member's work throughout the milestone, the ranking of the member among the group including the evaluator-member, using the scale of 1-to-5 if there are five members (5: highest performance; 1: lowest performance), and the bonus distribution among all the members, of a specific amount, say, how much each member gets allocated out of 1000 dollars of bonus. In the specific instance of client-developer pair, each developer-team should also be evaluated by the client-team using a more detailed format because of the direct relationship between the two PBL teams.

The Course Enactment for Problem-Based Learning

In a semester of about 15 weeks, spanning three and a half month, it is designed that a total of four milestones are planned for students' project work. Since *Software Psychology* is offered once a year in the fall of each calendar year, the general layout of the course activities, developed around the theme that HCI is concerned with understanding, designing, evaluating, and implementing interactive computer applications, are as follows:

September

PBL teams formation – an even number is needed to facilitate client-developer pairing;
Client PBL teams each have about three weeks to conceive a system of interest;
Milestone #1: Each client team is to present its idea on system of interest;

Evaluation done for each PBL client team by the remaining teams and the instructor;
Internal evaluation performed within each client team.

October

Developer teams paired with their respective client teams;
No two teams become the client and developer of each other;
Client-developer relationship building, with client's requirements gathered for developer's elaboration;
Milestone #2: Developer's presentation of systems to be developed, with client's yes to prototype.
Evaluation done for each PBL developer team by the remaining teams (based on presentation); by the client team (based on presentation, design documents and other developer-initiated contacts and follow-ups); and by the instructor
Internal evaluation performed by each PBL developer team, (based on project management, overall work done, and personal contributions).

November

Ongoing client-developer's requirements workshops for clarification with skeletal prototypes;
Memorandum developed to accommodate changes to be incorporated and not yet completed;
Milestone #3: Developer's presentation of system prototypes with client's consent to change or continue;
Evaluation done for each PBL developer team by remaining teams, by client team; and by instructor;
Internal evaluation performed by each PBL developer team.

December

Client-developer meeting to prepare for system rollout (final prototype);
Negotiation leading to agreement on project delay or closure;
Milestone #4: Developer's final presentation of system to be delivered with client's acceptance.
Evaluation done for each PBL developer team by remaining teams, by client team; and by instructor;
Internal evaluation performed by each PBL developer team.

The Course Time Investment from Instructor and Students

September

12 hours of upfront lecture-discussion sessions to get set for group-based project work in October-November-December

October

6 hours of group-based presentation of client problems (one hour per group and six groups altogether);
6 hours of individual group meetings for feedback on client problems (one hour per group);
6 hours of individual group meeting for follow-up on developer's work in gathering client's requirements for first client-developer meeting (one hour per group);
6 hours of group-based presentation of developers' first feedback meeting with clients (first formal client-developer one-hour meeting with signing of working agreement);

6 hours of feedback lectures conducted over four sessions each of 1.5 hour

November

9 hours of individual group meetings for feedback on developer's first formal session with client (1.5 hours per group);
9 hours of individual group meetings for follow-up on developer's work in progress to prepare client's first prototype (1.5 hours per group);
9 hours of group-based presentation of developer's first prototype of client's system (1.5 hours per group);
3 hours of feedback lectures conducted over three sessions each of 1 hour

December

9 hours of individual group meetings for feedback on developer's first prototype of client's system (1.5 hours per group)
9 hours of individual group meeting for follow-up on developer's work in progress to prepare client's second prototype (final delivery) (1.5 hours per group);
12 hours of group-based presentation of developer's second prototype of client's system plus client's onsite feedback (2 hours per developer-client pair);
9 hours of individual group meetings for feedback to developer and semester-score wrap-up session (1.5 hours per group).

Lessons Elaborated for Group-Based Project Work

Throughout the years of helping students in SFTW300 to get used to group-based project work, especially those related to prototyping for collaborative Web development, the following topics of interest have become the core lessons to be elaborated in every semester of *Software Psychology*.

The Project

Defining a project means understanding and communicating on paper the project's mission, objectives, risks, and requirements. Typically, writing a project mission statement is the first job to handle, which is decomposable to three essential tasks: identify the project's objectives; identify the users; and identify the project scope. Put it briefly, a mission statement describes the solution to the problem that the project is going to solve. There are three questions to answer: what are we going to do? For whom are we doing it? How do we go about it?

• Identify Objectives

Identifying objectives for a specific project is to define some attainable desired outcome at the end of the project. The important question is to establish criteria for objectives so that we know when we achieve the desired outcome. In particular, objectives for a Web project help the creative team to design the best graphics (look and feel) for the site, they help the programmers understand how the Web site might grow, and they tell the writers what tone or information is critical to the site.

• Identify Targeted Users

Identifying targeted users for a specific project, especially a Web project, is always important because the kinds of content that will be created for the Web site are often determined by such users whom we want to visit the site (Gause & Weinberg, 1989). The issue here is how we go about learning what the targeted users want to see on the Web site. The obvious answer is to ask them directly. There are many ways to gather user data (or requirements) such as interviewing, holding requirements workshop, and inviting users to join the development team as a liaison for ongoing changes.

- **Identify Project Scope**

Identifying project scope at the beginning of the project, with proper supporting documentation and client approval, is always important. In order to nail down the scope, the project team must determine the key elements required in the project, which are often extracted from the objectives document of the project, namely, the document that states the project objectives. Starting from the project objectives, the team will need to investigate what functional and non-functional features the Web site must have to satisfy the objectives. Examples of functional features include providing information systems (IS) support for online learning, and allowing links to use broadcast services to a number of group members. Examples of non-functional features include site design, navigation architecture, copywriting, and quality assurance testing. This process often called developing the work breakdown structure (WBS) is to break down each element into tasks, analyzing the tasks and the time it will take to complete them and making some decisions about how to implement the features so as to stay on schedule. The culmination of this effort is to produce the scope document, which reiterates the mission and objectives of the Web project including a sign-off agreement for the developer team and the client to put in writing the stated features (functional and non-functional) of the project (Web site).

The Project Team

The project team is the team that will fulfill the project objectives. This team is often composed of some core members with specific roles and responsibilities. Example roles include the project coordinator, the project tracker, the team secretary, the team liaison, and other technical members such as, in the context of a Web project, the technical lead, the creative lead, the information architect, and other support roles such as the interface designers, and the Web production specialists.

- **Identify Roles and Responsibilities**

It is important to indicate the responsibilities of specific roles in a team of members in order to fulfill the project objectives, such as planning, designing, prototyping a Web site. The following describes the roles and responsibilities of team members in the SFTW300 course scenarios.
The Project Coordinator. This role is responsible for seeing and communicating the big picture to the team and the client. Within the team, the coordinator needs to work with the team members to accomplish such tasks as scoping the project work, developing the project plan, scheduling, and allocating resources, budgeting, as well as building up the team. Without the team, the coordinator needs to handle client management, keeping the client in touch with project development, and keeping track of client's emergent requirements clarification.

The Project Tracker. This role is responsible for keeping track of the work designated among the team members during a specific period (say, in between two team meetings, or two project milestones) and overseeing that they have been accomplished timely, and with the quality expected. The idea is to ensure that any work product produced should meet the criteria specified in the scope document, and be produced on schedule. The tracker also keeps a good record of the performance of individual team members for evaluation purpose.

The Team Secretary. This role is responsible for the administrative details of project work, such as scheduling meetings for team members, collecting agenda items from team members before each meeting, keeping records of meetings minutes, issuing summary of actions items to be followed up at next meeting. The secretary is keeping a good record of rationale management (Dutoit & Paech, 2001) throughout the project. Essentially, rationale includes such details at the end of each meeting as the issues that were addressed, the alternatives that were considered, the decisions that were made to resolve the issues, the criteria that were used to guide decisions, and the debate team members went through to reach a decision.

The Team Liaison. This role is to assist the project coordinator in communicating with the client. In the SFTW300 design of inter-team communications, however, since each team is to play both the client and the developer roles, the role of the liaison becomes important in communicating with the client team, the ongoing development of their project. Meanwhile, the same liaison in each team could also serve as the spokes-person of his or her team in communicating with the developer team, the team's own project requirements. It is designed that two teams could not be the client and developer of each other.

The Technical Members. In the context of Web project, the technical members include the following roles: technical lead, creative lead, information architect, and other support staff. The technical lead oversees the project from a technical point of view. He or she assists the project coordinator in ensuring that the technical strategy is sound, and manages other technical staff such as programmers (Web or database) and systems integrators. The creative lead determines the creative concept for the Web site and is responsible for the site's design. He or she interacting with the technical lead to determine what is technically possible, often reports status to the project coordinator. The information architect designs a usable and useful interface that facilitates how the user will interact with the site and find the information they need. He or she is responsible for site architecture, navigation, search and data retrieval, as well as interaction design, such as messages to users regarding errors, service, and technical needs of the site. Other support staff includes the graphic designers and Web production specialists. The former create the look and feel of the Web site, transforming the information design into a visual design, whereas the latter transforms the artwork that the graphic designers create into Web-ready art. In practice, the Web production specialist is the person who codes the HTML pages, integrates Java or Shockwave applications, integrates images and animations, and hands the project off to the Project Tracker for quality assurance.

• Build up a Team

It certainly takes time and discipline to transform a PBL team of student members to a self-directed work team of promising software professionals. In the short span of each SFTW300's semester of about three and a half months, there are many soft skills a PBL team needs to acquire. The following serves as a useful set of selected concerns I find to be particularly important in the team buildup process.

Process Focus. The average student has little background in actually accomplishing process steps over a period of time and more often no background in doing so in a team with the added requirements of several milestones of prototyping and an inflexible delivery date, as well as a client who is generally not process oriented. During the early stages of the class, each PBL team is exposed to some typical software development processes, such as the spiral process, the unified process, and the extreme programming process. The students are asked to adopt a process for their development exercise and the team coordinator is required to attempt to keep the team focused on it during prototyping for the milestones. Students' feedback indicates that the pressure of the delivery schedule, client involvement, and prototypes development, has taught them that the chosen process has to be flexible enough to accept change but the balance between consistent application of a process and responsiveness to the client is difficult to maintain and this is impossible to learn through lectures alone. The client experience during the semester demonstrates to each team the difficulty one encounters after graduation and the lessons learned through the project tend to remain with them far longer than their readings and individual examinations.

Team Dynamics. Students embarking on SFTW300 have had one semester's PBL style of collaboration in SFTW241 Programming Language Architectures (I). However, the grouping arrangements of SFTW300 require each newly formed PBL group to discover whom they can rely on, capitalize on individual skill sets, and find a way to work together. Students still tend to be mistrusting at first and very comfortable with individual efforts but leery of having to rely on others. The early stages of class become essential occasion to conduct what will be the first of many activities that promote positive group interactions. Examples of such activities include: writing a group portfolio expressing the profiles of individual team members in terms of their individual technical expertise; engaging in mental games that require the skillful use of teamwork to complete or that make a point about the distinction between person-centered and group-centered learning/working styles. This understanding becomes instrumental when different roles are being taken by members of the group: one role taken up by one member, or one role shared by two or three members, or roles are taken by members through rotating turns. The idea is to achieve coordination to get the project work done through a suitable mix of individual work, cooperating work (different tasks done by different members so as to integrate the pieces), and collaborating work (same portions of work done jointly by different members).

Planning Concerns. Throughout the semester's work, there are several essential milestones (essential due dates) that have to be met by each PBL group. Yet, the only hard and fast date that must be met is the final delivery. Deliverables required of each PBL team include a concept of operations document, a design document, a test plan, and the final prototype comprising site architecture, schematics, and navigation guide in the specific case of a Web project. In the client-developer relationship established by the instructor, each team coordinator is permitted to make arguments for extension of any deliverable due date (except for final delivery) knowing that each extension granted added additional difficulties later in the course for an on time delivery of other documents. This procedure forced each team to evaluate their scheduling philosophy and to perform an informal risk assessment for the entire project. The policy of assigning the same project grade to each member of the team is seen as a strong motivator for each student to take seriously the project activities. Following the industrial model of shared responsibility (the team fails or the team succeeds) seems to provide a far more memorable learning experience with respect to the planning process and maintaining a schedule. Rigorous discussions have often been observed over issues of planning milestones and still leaving enough time to produce the remaining deliverables with reasonable quality and timeliness.

Meeting Routines. In a project environment, nobody likes to go to a meeting that has no agenda. These kinds of meetings seem like wastes of time to team members who have deadlines to meet. Thereby, effective meetings (Doyle & Straus, 1982) must have an agenda sent out to each participating members, so that people know what to expect. At the meetings, PBL teams have to make sure going over the schedule and determine if milestones will be hit on time. Meanwhile, asking team members for any issues or red flags that they see is important. This will help them anticipate risks as the project moves forward. Also important is to ensure that people leave with clear action items. People should know what they are supposed to be doing and what to do next either by day or by week. The main point is to keep the meeting quick and focused, and then follow up the meeting with a summary of points that were discussed. Overall, there are many steps PBL students have to learn in leading an effective team meeting.

The Project Client

Dealing with the project client is an important lesson for the PBL groups of students in SFTW300. We have a number of skills to develop in client management and these take time. So, students have to learn them incrementally throughout the semester.

- **Understanding Client's Point of View**

The client is the person or organization who has contracted the developer team to complete the project. In the case of SFTW300, the client team has this request to construct a staging Web site, demonstrating the team's topics of interest in interactive system design. It is important for each PBL developer team to take time to understand the client's project position; namely, what is at stake for the client. This is actually the beginning of a requirements gathering process, characterized by such activities as interviewing, storyboarding, and workshops of requirements elicitation.

Interviewing. Interviewing is one of the most important and straightforward ways to understand the client's concerns. Yet, before an interview is conducted, the developer team needs to do some hard thinking about what they need to learn. The process often involves preparing some thoughtful questions about the nature of the user's problem without any context for a potential solution. Examples include: Who is the user? Who is the client? Are their needs different? Where else can a solution to this problem be found? Namely, we are trying to find out what the users need in order to meet the objectives set forth by the stakeholders. Oftentimes, the use of a questionnaire to help strategize the interview is also necessary. Besides, it is suggested that a tape or a video recording of the interview is arranged to help capture the details of the interview, pending the approval of the client. In the case of SFTW300, each developer team is required to video-tape the interview as an important project item of all possible development records.

Storyboarding. The idea of storyboarding is to gain an early understanding from the users on the concepts proposed for the project system. Typically, with storyboarding, the user's reaction can be observed very early in the development cycle, well before concepts are committed to code and, in many cases, even before detailed specifications are developed. In fact, when the users do not know what they want, even a poor storyboard is likely to elicit a response of "No, that is not what we meant, it's more like the following," and the game is on. Basically, a storyboard can be anything the developer team wants it to be, and the team should feel free to use its imagination to think of ways to storyboard a specific application. Yet, depending on the mode of interaction with the users, storyboards can be categorized into three types: passive, active, or interactive (Leffingwell & Widrig, 2000, p.126). *Passive storyboards* include sketches, pictures, screen shots, PowerPoint presentations, or sample outputs. In a passive storyboard, the analyst plays the role of the system and simply walks the user through the storyboard, with a "When you do this, this happens" explanation. *Active storyboards* try to make the user see "a movie that has not been produced yet." They are animated or automated, perhaps by an automatically sequencing slide presentation or an animation tool or even a video. They provide an automated description of the way the system behaves in a typical usage or operational scenario. *Interactive storyboards* let the user experience the system in as realistic a manner as practical. They require participation by the user in order to execute. They can be simulations or mock-ups or can be advanced to the point of throwaway prototype.

Requirements Workshop. The requirements workshop (Leffingwell & Widrig, 2000, pp.103-111) is perhaps the most powerful technique for eliciting requirements. It is designed to encourage consensus on the requirements of the application and to gain rapid agreement on a course of action, all in a very short time frame. With this technique, key stakeholders of the project are gathered for a short, intensive period, typically no more than one or two days. The workshop is facilitated by a team member or by an experienced outside facilitator and focuses on the creation or review of the high-level features to be delivered by the new application. A properly run requirements workshop has many benefits: It assists in building an effective team, committed to one common purpose, i.e., the success of the project. All stakeholders get their say; no one is left out. It forges an agreement between the stakeholders and the developer team as to what the application must do. It can express and resolve political issues that are interfering with project success. The output, a preliminary system definition at the features level, is available immediately.

- **Setting Clear Expectations**

It is important to take time to communicate the developer team's work process to the client, including setting clear expectations and providing rationale for these expectations. In particular, we need to flesh out what the client's and the developer's expectations are for the following:

Deliverables. What will the developer deliver to the client? What does the client need to deliver to the developer in order to move forward? Who in the client's team is delivering content to the developer? The developer generally does not want to be inundated with requests from all over the client's organization. If the client is delivering assets (precious items, say, master copy), it is also important to keep a good record as to what and when the item has been delivered. It is also good to specify the format in which the developer needs to obtain such items.

Approvals. How will approvals be handled? Does the developer need a 24-hour turnaround for approval? The client's approval should always be in writing, no matter how good a relationship the developer has with the client. It is better to have a policy in place to handle approvals than to loose a client as a result of a dispute about what exactly was approved. It has been observed that good relationship between developer and client teams could end abruptly over a dispute.

Policies. Once available, policies such as the change-order process or approvals process should be jointly verified by both the client and the developer. The client should be able to ask questions about the policies. It is also essential not to make exceptions in policies for a client. Such exceptions could easily create disputes later in the developer-client relationship. It is an important policy to write a contact report each time the developer has a conversation with the client in which aspects of the project have been discussed, such as issues raised, and changes negotiated. A copy of this contact report should be sent to the client. It is a good way to document the project and to keep track of things being discussed informally with your client.

- **Communicating throughout the Project**

As the relationship between client and developer develops, it is important that the developer remains consistent in the approach to communication so that the client's trust of the developer should become strengthened. There are often several issues to watch for in order to keep communications clear between the developer and the client.

Assumptions. PBL students are reminded that every project has assumptions. All the deliverables that the developer determines in the scope document are made with certain assumptions. It is essential to give the client the developer's assumptions early on, when the scope document is delivered. Students are advised to take time to review the document, going over each assumption carefully to make sure the client understands what the developer expects. When the client and the developer both have their own deadlines to meet, they can truly become partners of the same team, and the client could see firsthand how their participation can affect the success of the project.

Scope and Approval Document. The questions of scope, cost, and what can be done by the deadline are ongoing issues in project work. In most Web project, the developer determines the scope of a project after a discovery phase in which both the client and the developer discuss the project's objectives and requirements. Once the requirements are determined, the developer can enter the design phase with a sense of the project scope. However, the client may not be on the same page as the developer. Experience indicates that most clients can come away with very different expectations. That is why a full explanation of scope, with the time and cost considerations clearly defined, say in the approval document, is critical to getting the client on the same page as the developer moves forward with the project. The approvals document is a document in which the client signs off on features that make up the project. In the case of a Web site, line items in the document might be navigation, visual design, forms, data schema, network configuration, site architecture, and any relevant pseudo-code. It is important to get sign-offs after each design milestone is hit.

Effective Reviews. Conducting effective reviews is a skill PBL students need to acquire through experience. Before meeting with the client, it is important to perform an internal review first, by writing down the essential points to hit, and by anticipating the client's reactions. Any point raised by the client must be responded by going back to the logic behind the decision, and the logic must also be traceable to an objective of the project. In case the client dislikes anything, the strategy is: Always be prepared to offer an alternative, and never to argue with the client. If the client approves a concept, the next step must be to get the sign-off on the design. Preparing a contact report carrying fields for signatures can help.

Enacting SSM as a Scenario-Based Learning Process

If HCI-based project development of software support is concerned with understanding, designing, evaluating and implementing interactive systems (IS) to match the needs of people (Vat, 2004a, 2004b, 2004c), a very important activity for each developer PBL team is to actively engage its client PBL team (Curtis, Krasner, & Iscoe, 1988) in ensuring the quality and timeliness of the software outcomes. Undeniably, setting up interactive IS support is a social act in itself, requiring some kind of concerted action by both the developer and the client teams (Conklin & Burgess-Yakemovic, 1991); and the operation of an IS entails such human phenomena as attributing meaning to and making judgments about what constitutes a relevant category. It is convinced (Vat, 2005a, 2005b, 2005c) that through maintaining a continuous focus on situations of and consequences for human work and activities, IS developers could become more informed of the problem domains, seeing usage situations from different perspectives, and managing trade-offs to reach usable and effective design outcomes. However, getting users' work right involves capturing and accommodating users' emergent (or subject-to-change) analytical activities, which are open-ended yet integrated and opportunistic yet coherent. IS developers must understand the intertwined regularities and idiosyncrasies of human activities and create software that support the right moves and degrees of agility at the right times and places and for specific purposes. In this regard, the problem of designing IS support for any human-centered knowledge work should never be thought of as something to be defined once and for all, and then implemented. Instead, it must be based on the observation that all real-world organizational problem situations contain people interested in trying to take purposeful action (Checkland, 1981; 1999).

And the idea of a set of activities linked together so that the whole, as an entity called the human activity systems (HAS) from the viewpoint of Soft Systems Methodology (SSM) (Checkland & Holwell, 1998; Checkland & Scholes, 1999; Wilson, 2001) could prove useful. In fact, as far as pursuing a purpose is concerned, a HAS model could be considered as a representative organizational scenario for exploring any situation-specific IS support, which is never fixed once and for all. Still, the important point is that we must be conscious of the fact that any scenario of HAS (human activity systems) models created are merely abstract logical machines for pursuing a purpose (Checkland, 1979, 1984), defined in terms of declared worldviews, which can generate insightful debate (or rational discussion) when set against actual purposeful action in the real-life situation. The implicit belief behind constructing the HAS models is that social reality – what counts as facts about the social world inside an organization, say the client PBL teams of students – is the ever changing outcome of a social process in which human beings (individual client team members) continually negotiate and re-negotiate, and so construct with others (members of the developer team) their perceptions and interpretations of the world outside themselves (expected

IS support for specific activities), and the dynamic rules for coping with it (cooperating or manipulating). In the process, the context of IS development actually becomes an organized discovery of how human agents (both the client and developer team members) make sense of their perceived worlds, and how those perceptions change over time and differ from one person or group to another.

Nevertheless, the basic shape of the scenario-based learning approach for the developer PBL team could be described as follows: Find out about the problem situation that has provoked concern; Select relevant concepts that may be integrated into different human activity systems; Create HAS models from the relevant accounts of purposeful activity; Use the models to question the real-world situation in a comparison phase. The debate initiated by the comparison normally entails the findings of accommodations between conflicting interests, that is to say, situations that may not satisfy everyone, but could still be lived with, enabling action to be taken. Oftentimes, the purpose of the debate is to collectively learn a way to possible changes (improvements) to the problem situations, by activating in the people involved (client PBL team), a learning cycle, which counts on their ability to articulate problems, to engage in collaboration, to appreciate multiple perspectives, to evaluate and to actively use their knowledge. It is worthwhile to notice that taking the purposeful action would itself change the situation, so that the whole cycle could begin again, and is in principle never ending. Likewise, through scenarios of HAS models, IS architects could provide help in articulating the requirements of specific technical support through operating the learning cycle from meanings to intentions to purposeful action among the specific group of organizational members.

Re-conceptualizing Teaching and Learning through PBL

Today, there is a growing tendency away from a conventional transmissive pedagogy in higher education, towards a pedagogy that can broadly be characterized as constructivist (Booth, 2001). The transmissive pedagogy refers to teaching based on an assumption that students receive information from the teacher and slot it straight into an empty place in their knowledge base, or at best, work on it later to make it their own. The constructivist pedagogy renders an approach to learning through a variety of knowledge building processes, and that teaching should encourage students to work actively towards understanding within a framework of personal responsibility and institutional freedom. Within the culture of transmissive teaching, what constitutes good learning has largely been based on success in examinations designed to test the quantity and the quality of what individual students have learned, in the sense of giving back, in an appropriate form, that which the teachers taught and the text-books told. The constructivist shift brings new dimensions to the notion of good learning, such as being able to find information and knowledge by oneself; of being able to look critically at what one finds; of being able to question one's teachers; of being able to collaborate with colleagues; and of being able to discuss what one knows with one's peers and with the public. Accordingly, as the need to look at the student's work as a whole is increasingly emphasized, the notion of good teaching shifts away from the role of presenter and towards the much more complex role of a guide and a coach. In this regard, problem-based learning (PBL) addresses these issues and offers an attractive alternative to traditional education by shifting the focus of education from what faculty teaches to what students learn. Content remains important, but emphasis shifts more to the process. Indeed, Greening (1998, 2000) describes PBL as a vehicle for encouraging student ownership of the learning environment. There is an emphasis on contextualization of the learning scenario, providing a basis for later transference, and learning is accomplished by reflection as an important meta-cognitive exercise. Besides, the execution of PBL, often done via group-based project work, reflects the constructivist focus on the value of negotiated meaning. More importantly, PBL being not confined by discipline boundaries encourages an integrative approach to learning, which is based on requirements of the problem as perceived by the learners themselves. Consequently, my re-conceptualized view of teaching and learning identifies with a learner-centered perspective of PBL based on the idea of collaborative learning, where it is necessary to clarify the new roles of the teachers and the students, and the renewed pedagogical organization consistent with the philosophy of a collaborative learning environment in support of PBL.

• A New Role of the Teacher

Instead of performing as the sage on the stage transmitting knowledge to a class of innocent students, in the collaborative learning environment of PBL, teachers' roles are often defined in terms of mediating learning through dialogue and collaboration where knowledge is created in the community rather than being transferred from the individual. More specifically, the idea of mediating could include such aspects of facilitating, modeling, and coaching (Chickering & Gamson, 1987; Chung, 1991; Mayer, 1988). Facilitating involves creating rich activities for linking new information to prior knowledge, providing opportunities for cooperative work and collective problem solving, and offering students a multiplicity of authentic learning tasks. Modeling serves to share with students not only the perceived content to be learned, but also the important meta-cognitive skills of higher-order thinking, in the process of communication and collaboration. Coaching involves giving hints or cues, providing feedback, redirecting students' efforts, and helping them use a strategy. A major principle of coaching is to provide help only when students need it so that students retain as much responsibility as possible for their own learning. In fact, we need to teach students to rely less on teachers as the source of knowledge. We need to help them learn to learn as self-directed groups of active, autonomous, and responsible individuals. One of the specific goals in the PBL setting is to have students rely more heavily upon their classmates for assistance in doing a task and in evaluating a possible solution. Only after they have checked with everyone in the group should they ask their teacher for help. Operationally, it is the teacher's job to specify the instructional objectives, usually in discussion with the learning (PBL) groups; explain the cooperative goal structure; observe students' interactions in terms of the learning process, and social relationships within the group; feedback on the group-based evaluation of the learning products; and also maximize social interaction among groups through suitable design of inter-group interacting patterns, to create the expected community of learners among the students in the class.

• A New Role of the Students

In collaborative learning settings, students are expected to assume their new roles as collaborators and active participants. It may be useful to think how these new roles influence processes and activities before, during, and after learning. For example, before learning, students set goals and plan learning tasks. During learning, they work together to accomplish tasks and monitor their progress. And, after learning, they assess their performance and plan for future learning. In practice, students constantly need help from the teachers to help them fulfill such new roles. Specifically, students need to learn to share, rather than compete for, recognition, and evaluate the learning outcomes rather than hurry to finish the task. It is important to nurture a group-based atmosphere for comfortable trial and error as well as for asking questions and expressing opinions. Students must learn to become teachers of their own, and the group-based interaction should serve as the incubator for co-development of ideas. Indeed, a frequent formula (Dilworth, 1998) that action learning proposes has been quite useful in constantly reminding students of their new role in collaborative learning. Namely, $L = P + Q + R$, where L (learning) equals P (programmed instruction) plus Q (questioning) plus R (reflection). Here P represents the knowledge coming through textbooks, lectures, case studies, computer-based instructions, and many others. This is an important source of learning but carries with it an embedded caution flag. That is, P is all based in the past. Q means continuously seeking fresh insight into what is not yet known. This Q helps avoid the pitfall of imperfectly constructed past knowledge. By going through the Q step first, we are able to determine whether the information available is relevant and adequate to our needs. It will point to areas that will require the creation of new P. R simply means rethinking, taking apart, putting together, making sense of facts, and attempting to understand the problem. Following the use of this formula, action steps are planned and carried out with constant feedback and reflection as the learning takes place. In short, what this formula can provide for PBL students is elevated levels of discernment and understanding through the interweaving of action and reflection.

- **A Renewed Pedagogical Organization**

It is understood that collaborative learning will not take place with students sitting in rows facing the teacher. At least, tables or desks must be pushed together in small groups to facilitate group interaction. Materials and resources should best be made readily accessible. Indeed, the basic requirements for PBL group-based activities are often beyond the capacities of many a classroom in our university environment today. Preferably, we could have access to a multi-function hall in the library (with easy access to other resources such as computers and Internet), with enough floor area to accommodate the setup of a workspace environment with re-configurable facilities such as: a number of conference desks each of which is good for at least six people; an open area with a wall-size screen for LCD-projection, for large gathering or presentation or briefing for the whole class. The idea is that sharing and working together even in a less-than-perfect environment will be louder than in an environment where isolated students work silently from textbooks. More importantly, to make collaborative learning work, there are major tasks that the instructor should address in organizing the PBL group learning activities. First, we need to clearly specify the objectives for the lesson lest the students always guess what the professor wants: academic objectives or collaborative skills objectives. Second, we need to make decisions or devise innovative strategies about placing students in learning groups before the PBL episode begins. Third, we need to carefully explain the task, goal structure, and the learning activity. Fourth, we need to monitor the effectiveness of the PBL collaborative learning groups and intervene when necessary to re-orient the learning efforts toward pinpointed tasks, or to increase students' interpersonal and group skills. Lastly, we need to evaluate student achievement and help them discuss how well they collaborated with one another. It is also important to understand that while groups work to achieve common goals, each member should fulfill a particular role or accomplish an individual task within the group project. The teacher needs to assess both the group and the individual work.

Remarks for Continuing Challenge

The software engineering workplace of this century requires professionals who not only have an extensive store of knowledge, but who also know how to keep that knowledge up-to-date, apply it to solve problems, and function as part of a team. This view of the software industry compels educators to rethink and reinvent the ways in which software professionals are prepared. In particular, schooling must extend beyond the traditional preparatory goal of establishing a knowledge base. Concomitantly, it must actively engage our students in opportunities for knowledge seeking, for problem solving, and for the collaborating necessary for effective practice. To realize such experiences, educators have looked to constructivist pedagogical designs that are based on the assumption that learning is a product of both cognitive and social interactions in problem-centered environments (Greeno, Collins, & Resnick, 1996; Savery & Duffy, 1994). Problem-based learning (PBL) is an example of such a design (Vat, 2005d, 2006). Today, what has become known as a classic version of PBL is described by Barrows (1985, 1988), in the educational context of medical students (Spaulding, 1991). This model has two key features: a rich problem is involved to afford free inquiry by students, and learning is student-centered. In this approach, a group of five to seven medical students and a facilitator meet to discuss a problem (Barrows, 1986). The facilitator provides the students with a small amount of information about a patient's case, and then the group's task is to evaluate and define different aspects of the problem and to gain insight into the underlying causes of the disease process. This is accomplished by extracting key information from the case, generating and evaluating hypotheses, and formulating learning issues. Learning issues are topics that the group deems relevant and in need of further explication. The group members divide up the learning issues among themselves and research them. They then share their information and use it to explain the patient's disease process. At the completion of the cycle, the students reflect on what they learned from the problem. The facilitator's role is to help the students' learning processes by modeling hypothesis-driven reasoning for the students and by encouraging them to be reflective. In fact, both cognitive constructivist and socio-cultural theories provide insights into the learning mechanisms of PBL (Greeno, Collins, & Resnick, 1996). In terms of individual learning, PBL situates learning within the context of professional (medical) practice. Problems give rise to epistemic curiosity (Schmidt, 1993) that will, in turn, trigger the cognitive processes of accessing prior knowledge, establishing a problem space, searching for new information, and reconstructing information into knowledge that both fits into and shapes new mental models. Meanwhile, proceeding through the PBL process requires the learner's meta-cognitive awareness of the efficacy of the process. In this regard, PBL is inherently self-directed. However, PBL does not exist in a vacuum. Rather, it is a social system within a larger cultural context. The knowledge that the learner seeks is embedded in and derives from social sources – in Barrows' case, the world of medical practice, and in our discussion, the community of software practitioners. From this perspective, the learner is seen as both transforming and being transformed as the processes of practice and their underlying symbol systems are internalized through dialectical activity (John-Steiner & Mahn, 1996). In this sense, learning is not an accumulation of information, but a transformation of the individual who is moving toward full membership in the professional community. This identity-making is marked by observing the facility with which cultural tools, or the ways of thinking and using language, are invoked, especially in the socio-cultural context of PBL group meetings, which stimulate the social process of professional problem solving often done through the scaffolding support of PBL students themselves.

To conclude this chapter, I hereby render some of my perspectives behind adopting problem-based learning (PBL) in teaching industrial practices of software engineering. The educational literature warns against compartmentalized units of study that produce students who cannot integrate the different parts of their knowledge. Although a fully integrated degree was beyond our scope of discussion, many of our conventional courses had compartments that bore out the literature's predictions. Any new course designed must be as integrated as possible especially in the context of software development, if we want our students to bring all their knowledge to bear on solving real-world problems. In this regard, the nurture of independence and initiative becomes important. Indeed, our conventional courses were widely criticized for stifling students' independence and initiative. Yet, through PBL, the problems we offer are loosely specified, leaving plenty of scope for student initiative. Students should discover they can learn by themselves, using a range of resources. They are aided in learning to do this by the PBL cycle of collaboration, which develop in them their social and mega-cognitive skills. Consequently, students' critical thinking and problem-solving abilities are sharpened. These are crucial to effective project (software) development, especially at the higher levels of analysis and design. In the specific case of SFTW300, students have to go through the process of understanding, designing, implementing and evaluating interactive computer systems to match the needs of client. This is a teamwork development exercise requiring students to work in groups. This is important for their future careers because employers nowadays expect their fresh graduates to have the ability and experience to perform in group-based project work. SFTW300 supports groups by identifying specific roles for group members, providing class time and guidelines on group management, monitoring group planning and progress, and assigning marks for group management and reflection on group processes. Students working in a group naturally learn to communicate with one another, which is another goal highly valued by employers. In particular, at the end of each problem, PBL students need to give a demonstration, during which each student must speak, and present a written report, followed by a session on question and answer. All these require the students to have good command of communications skills. Overall, PBL fosters such generic skills as group work, planning, problem-solving, independent learning, research skills, writing, and oral presentation. These are university goals and also highly valued by employers in the computing industry.

References

Albanese, M., & Mitchell, S. (1993). Problem-based learning: A review of literature on its outcomes and implementation issues. *Academic Medicine, 68* (1), 52-81.

Barrows, H. S. (1985). *How to design a problem-based curriculum for the pre-clinical years.* New York: Springer.

Barrows, H. S. (1986). A taxonomy of problem-based learning methods. *Medical Education, 20* (6), 481-486.

Barrows, H. S. (1988). *The tutorial process.* Springfield, Illinois: Southern Illinois University School of Medicine.

Booth, S. (2001). Learning computer science and engineering in context. *Computer Science Education, 11* (3), 169-188.

Carroll, J. M. (2000). *Making use: Scenario-based design of human-computer interactions.* MIT Press.

Checkland, P. (1981). *Systems thinking, systems practice.* Chichester: Wiley.

Checkland, P. (1979). Techniques in soft systems practice, Part 2: Building conceptual models. *Journal of Applied Systems Analysis, 6*, 41-49.

Checkland, P. (1999). Systems thinking. In W. L. Currie & B. Galliers (Eds.), *Rethinking management information systems.* Oxford University Press.

Checkland, P. & Holwell, S. (1998). *Information, systems, and information systems: Making sense of the field.* John Wiley and Sons: Chicheser.

Checkland, P. & Scholes, J. (1999). *Soft systems methodology in action.* Chichester: Wiley.

Checkland, P. (1984). Systems theory and information systems. In Th. M. A. Bemelmens (Ed.), *Beyond productivity: Information systems development for organizational effectiveness.* North- Holland, Amsterdam.

Chickering, A. W., & Gamson, A. (1987). Seven principles for good practice in undergraduate education. *AAHE Bulletin, 39* (7), 3-7.

Chung, J. (1991). Collaborative learning strategies: The design of instructional environments for the emerging new school. *Educational Technology, 31* (12), 15-22.

Conklin, J. & Burgess-Yakemovic, K. C. (1991). A process-oriented approach to design rationale. *Human-Computer Interaction, 6*, 357-391.

Curtis, B., Krasner, H. & Iscoe, N. (1988). A field study of the software design process for large systems. *Communications of the ACM, 31* (11), 1268-87.

Dilworth, R. L. (1998). Action learning in a nutshell. *PIQ, 11* (1), 28-43.

Doyle, M. & Straus, D. (1982). *How to make meetings work.* New York, NY: The Berkeley Publishing Group.

Dutoit, A.H. & Paech, B. (2001). Rationale management in software engineering. In S.K. Chang (Ed.), *Handbook of software engineering and knowledge engineering* (Volume. 1). World Scientific Publishing.

Engel, J. (1991). Not just a method but a way of learning. In D. Bould & G. Felletti (Eds.), *The challenge of problem-based learning* (pp. 21-31). New York, NY: St. Martin's Press.

Fisher, K. (2000). *Leading self-directed work teams: A guide to developing new team leadership skills.* McGrawHill.

Fuggetta, A. & Wolf, A. (Eds.) (1996). *Software process.* New York: John Wiley & Sons.

Gause, D. & Weinberg, G. (1989). *Exploring requirements: Quality before design.* Dorset House Publishing.

Greening, T. (2000). Emerging constructivist forces in computer science education: Shaping a new future? In T. Greening (Ed.), *Computer science education in the 21st century* (pp. 47-80). Springer.

Greening, T. (1998). Scaffolding for success in problem-based learning. *Medical Education Online, 3* (4): 1-15. Retrieved from http://www.utmb.edu/meo/

Greeno, J. G., Collins, A. M. & Resnick, L. (1996). Cognition and learning. In R. G. Calfee & D. C. Berliner (Eds.), *Handbook of educational psychology* (pp. 15-46). New York: Simon & Schuster Macmillan.

John-Steiner, V. & Mahn, H. (1996). Socio-cultural approaches to learning and development: A Vygotskian framework. *Educational Psychologist, 31,* 191-206.

Kimball, L. (1995). Ten ways to make online learning groups work. *Educational Leadership, 53* (2), 54-56.

Leffingwell, D. & Widrig, D. (2000). *Managing software requirements: A unified approach.* Reading, Massachusetts: Addison Wesley.

Mayer, R. (1998). Cognitive theory for education: What teachers need to know. In N. Lambert & B. McCombs (Eds.), *How students learn: Reforming schools through learner-centered education,* (pp. 353-378). Washington, DC: American Psychological Association.

Ryan, G. (1993). Student perceptions about self-directed learning in a professional course implementing problem-based learning. *Studies in Higher Education, 18,* 53-63.

Savery, J. R. & Duffy, T. M. (1994). Problem-based learning: An instructional model and its constructivist framework. *Educational Technology, 35* (5), 31-38.

Schmidt, H. G. (1993). Foundations of problem-based learning: Some explanatory notes. *Medical Education, 27,* 422-432.

Tomayko, J. E. & Hazzan, O. (2004). *Human aspects of software engineering.* Hingham, Massachusetts: Charles River Media.

Vat, K.H. (2000). Teaching software psychology: Expanding the perspective. In *Proceedings of the Thirsty-first SIGCSE Technical Symposium on Computer Science Education*, Austin, TX, Mar. 8-12, pp. 392-396.

Vat, K.H. (2001). Teaching HCI with scenario-based design: The constructivist's synthesis. In *Proceedings of the Sixth Annual ACM Conference on Innovation and Technology in Computer Science Education (ITiCSE2001)*, Canterbury, U.K., Jun. 25-27 pp. 9-12.

Vat, K.H. (2002). Teaching architectural approach to quality software development through problem-based learning. In *Proceedings of the 2002 Informing Science + IT Education Conference (IsITE2002)*, in Cork, Ireland: Informing Science Institute, Jun. 19-21. Also available at http://proceedings.informingscience.org/IS2002Proceedings/papers/vat043Teach.pdf

Vat, K.H. (2003). Conceiving architectural aspects for quality software education through the constructivist perspective. In T. McGill (Ed.), *Current issues in IT education* (pp.98-116). Hershey, PA: IRM Press (Idea Group Inc.).

Vat, K.H. (2004a). Conceiving a learning organization model for sustainable development: The IS Manager's perspective based on soft systems methodology. In *Proceedings of the IEEE International Engineering Management Conference 2004 (IEMC2004)* (pp. 500-504), Oct. 18-21, Singapore.

Vat, K.H. (2004b). Conceiving scenario-based IS support for knowledge synthesis: The organization architect's design challenge in systems thinking. In *Proceedings of the 10th International Conference on Information Systems Analysis and Synthesis (ISAS2004)* (pp.101-106), Orlando, Florida, USA, July 21-25.

Vat, K.H. (2004c). On the idea of soft systems methodology for IS development: A perspective based on purposeful action. In *Proceedings of the International Conference on Computing, Communications and Control Technologies (CCCT2004)* (pp. 227-232), August 14-17, Austin, Texas, USA.

Vat, K.H. (2004e). Towards a learning organization model for PBL: A virtual organizing scenario of knowledge synthesis. In *Proceedings of the Seventh Annual Conference of the Southern Association for Information Systems (SAIS2004)*, Feb. 27-28, Savannah, Georgia, USA.

Vat, K.H. (2004f). Toward a learning organization model for student empowerment: A teacher-designer's experience as a coach by the side. In *Proceedings of the 2004 IADIS International Conference on Cognition and Exploratory Learning in Digital Age (CELDA2004)* (pp. 131-140), Dec. 15-17, Lisbon, Portugal.

Vat, K.H. (2005a). Modeling human activity systems for collaborative project work: An IS development perspective. *Journal of Issues in Informing Science and Information Technology, 2*, 49-65. Available at http://2005papers.iisit.org/I05f65Vat.pdf

Vat, K.H. (2005b). On the importance of human activity systems in organization modeling for IS development. In *Proceedings of the Eighth Annual Conference of the Southern Association for Information Systems (SAIS2005)*, Feb. 25-26, Savannah, Georgia, USA.

Vat, K.H. (2005c). Systems architecting of IS support for learning organizations: The scenario-based design challenge in human activity systems. *Information Systems Education Journal (ISEDJ), 3* (2). Available at http://isedj.org/3/2/

Vat, K.H. (2005d). Teaching a collaborative model of IS development through problem-based learning. In the *Proceedings of the 2005 Information Systems Education Conference (ISECON2005)*, Oct. 6-9, Columbus, Ohio, USA.

Vat, K.H. (2006). Developing a learning organization model for problem-based learning: The emergent lesson of education from the IT trenches. *Journal of Cases on Information Technology, 8* (2).

Vaughn, Jr., R. B. (2001). Teaching industrial practices in an undergraduate software engineering course. *Computer Science Education, 11* (1), 21-32.

Whitten, N. (1995). *Managing software development projects* (2nd ed.). John Wiley & Sons.

Wilson, B. (2001). *Soft systems methodology: Conceptual model building and its contribution.* New York: John Wiley & Sons.

Biography

Kam Hou VAT is currently a lecturer in the Department of Computer and Information Science, under the Faculty of Science and Technology, at the University of Macau, Macau SAR, China. His current research interests include learner-centered design with constructivism in Software Engineering education, architected applications developments for Internet software, information systems for learning organization, information technology for knowledge synthesis, and collaborative technologies in electronic organizations.

Where Else Have You Been? The Effects of Diaspora Consciousness and Transcultural Mixtures on Ethnic Identity

Niranjala D Weerakkody
Faculty of Arts, Deakin University, Geelong, VIC, Australia

nina.weerakkody@deakin.edu.au

Abstract

In social science research, the demographic categories of ethnicity are linked to what the census bureau considers as a person's ethnic heritage. However, these categories are based on the societal assumption that members of a given category share the same characteristics and life experiences, even though the heterogeneity between members within a category may be as diverse as between categories.

The paper examines the 15 interview subjects of a research study drawn from 10 minority migrant groups, where seven of them indicated significant transcultural experiences before migrating to Australia. It argues that their lived experiences and subjectivity vary from others who migrated directly from their native countries. The formers' diaspora consciousness and transcultural mixtures may introduce an artifact to a research study's design, affecting the validity of the data collected. The paper examines other situations where this anomaly can occur and proposes precautions to minimize its negative effects.

Keywords: Demographic categories, ethnic identity, cultural identity, diaspora consciousness, transcultural mixtures, ethnic minorities, validity of research data, cultural identification, confounding variables, qualitative research.

Introduction

> "The problem of origin ... (is) no longer a question of starting or finishing. The question (is) rather what happens in between" (Deleuze, 1995, p. 121).

> "The effect of mass migration has been the creation of radically new types of human beings: people who root themselves in ideas rather than places, in memories as much as in material things- because they are so defined by others- by their otherness. (For) people in their deepest selves, strange fusions occur ... unprecedented unions between what they were and where they find themselves. The migrant suspects reality. Having experienced several ways of being, he (sic) understands their illusory nature. To see things plainly, you have to cross a frontier" (Salman Rushdie, 1991, p. 24).

Between 1965 and 2000, the number of people moving from their native country to others as legal migrants had doubled from 75 million to 150 million (IOM, 2000). The 'classical countries of immigration' receiving the bulk of this number since the late 1940s are the USA, Canada, Australia, New Zealand and Argentina. Since the 1980s, southern European countries such as Greece, Italy and Spain have moved from being emigration to immigration areas. The globalization of migration has seen a diversification of areas of origin as well as receiving countries for migrants, resulting in a broad spectrum of economic, cultural and social backgrounds being represented by these new immigrants (Castles & Miller, 2003). Generally, such migrants will report their ethnic identity by their national or ethnic origin. International and local census bureaus as well as social researchers will classify them under fairly wide demographic categories under ethnicity or national origin. These migrants also make up the official minority groups in their receiving countries.

Julie Andsager (2001; p. 1) argues that when categorizing all those born between 1946 and 1965 as 'Baby Boomers' or lumping together all those over 65 years of age for the purpose of research, we are oversimplifying a demographic variable, based on certain societal assumptions. Such categorizations assume that all those belonging to the category share the same characteristics and life experiences. This situation is the same for minority groups in multicultural societies where people are categorized based on their ethnic identity alone, assuming that all members within each group are alike and have undergone the same or similar life experiences. For examples, since the events of September 11, 2001, Muslims worldwide find themselves so categorized, profiled and negatively stereotyped which has proven extremely problematic and a disadvantage to them. This assumption also applies to other demographic categories such as gender, class and race. In an era of globalization where people move around the world as refugees, guest workers, tourists, students and migrants as part of *ethnoscapes* (movement of people) (Appadurai, 1990), their ethnic or national identity alone will not indicate the various life experiences gained in different countries other than the one of their birth, migration and settlement, causing heterogeneity of characteristics between members of the same ethnic group. Such assumptions of homogeneity pose problems for the validity of the category of 'ethnicity' in social science research (Kirk & Miller, 1991), when collecting data from individuals identifying themselves as belonging to a particular ethnic group. This is because there is probably a broader range of characteristics and cultural ambiguity represented by individuals within groups than between groups (Kaplan, 1973). Therefore, one needs to recognise that the socially constructed demographic variables such as ethnic identity or ethnic group membership, may impose differences between people where none may exist (eg. Children born in Australia and socialized as Australians but still categorized under their parents' ethnicity instead of as 'Australians') or impose homogeneity when it is not really so (eg. Categorising all those as belonging to Chinese ethnicity irrespective of their country of origin- such as Singapore, Malaysia, China and Hong Kong, with different social, cultural, economic and political systems and historical realities experienced by those individuals). Therefore, sub categories may be needed to understand and acknowledge these differences (Andsager, 2001; p. 8) to account for the anomalies where a migrant may have lived in a third or even a fourth country before their arrival in Australia as a migrant. Failing to address or at least acknowledge such anomalies and heterogeneity of characteristics within group members can introduce 'artifacts' (confounding or an extraneous variables) to a research design, which can contaminate the findings and affect the internal validity (Wimmer & Dominick, 2006) or accuracy of the data collected.

Demographic categories represent products of socialization (as being of a particular ethnic group even though a person may have never lived in what that ethnic group considers as their mother land). Therefore, it will be useful to discern individual traits and life experiences of group members instead of reifying stereotypical explanations or demographic categories set out in society (Andsager, 2001; p. 8). It is also necessary to avoid the unquestioned acceptance of self reported ethnic identities of research participants, when conducting social science or communication research with ethnic minority members.

Background

In 2000, the author conducted 15 depth interviews with individuals identifying themselves as members of the ten largest ethnic minority groups in a regional city in Australia during the preliminary stage of a research project that examined how people who are members of minorities frame their discourses when talking about the majority and other minorities, while discussing their experiences of living in Australia as migrants and members of minority ethnic groups. The project being funded by a research grant, allowed for an honorarium of $50 to be paid to each interviewee as an incentive to participate in a 1-2 hour depth interview. The latest census data (from 1996) for the city were used as the operational definition (Wimmer & Dominick, 2006) to identify its 10 largest ethnic groups and the 15 subjects were chosen to proportionately represent them in a stratified sample. The sample consisted of eight (8) females and seven (7) males belonging to various age groups. The ten ethnic groups which qualified as the largest in the city and the number of subjects chosen from each group based on their proportion in the population, were three Italians and two Russians and one each from those identifying themselves as Croatian, Chinese, Cambodian, Greek, Serbian, Polish, Spanish, German/Austrian, Czechoslovakian and Dutch. The author also endeavored to recruit interviewees who had arrived in Australia during different decades to obtain a mix of subjects and selected individuals previously unknown to her.

A call for volunteers was sent to the local Ethnic Communities Centre for posting on their notice board. The various social clubs and associations of the selected ethnic groups in the area were identified with the help of the local telephone directory and were contacted and requested to help the author in publicizing the call for volunteers. Many colleagues and contacts of the author helped distribute the advertisement by passing it on to members of the relevant ethnic groups of their acquaintance.

In response to the advertisement, many individuals telephoned to express their interest. The author noted their declared ethnic identity, age, when they arrived in Australia, and their sex and selected the 15 participants to meet the specifications of the sample. In some cases, participants helped locate other suitable individuals from among their acquaintances, when suitable volunteers from a particular ethnic group had not responded to the advertisement or had done so in insufficient numbers.

Before the interviews, the author contacted each subject about twice over the phone to collect their basic information and to schedule the interviews. Of the 15 interviewees, three were conducted at the author's workplace, and the others at the subjects' residences. Before each interview, the author made small talk with the interviewee to put them at ease in talking to a stranger about their life experiences and opinions. The purpose of the interview and the rights of the subjects were explained to them via a Plain Language Statement and a Consent Form, required and approved by the Ethics Committee of the author's organization.

The author used a semi-structured interview protocol or a set of questions, which asked the interviewees to state where they were born and when and how they arrived in Australia, before requesting them to express their opinions about their life experiences as migrants in Australia. However, in the process of answering these questions, it became apparent that seven (7) of the 15 participants had lived part of their lives outside the country of their birth, the one identified as their original nationality or the one linked to their ethnicity.

The details of these seven participants are as follows:

Subject No. 3: Female, 70 years of age.

Ethnic identity declared as Chinese. Born in Bendigo, VIC, Australia in 1930 and lived in Australia her entire life. Is a descendent of Chinese immigrants of the gold rush era and the secretary of the Chinese Cultural Association in the city.

Subject No. 4: Male, born in 1959.

Cambodian ethnicity. Arrived in Australia in 1999 and is a survivor of 'the killing fields'. Lived in Cuba from 1982-1988 undergoing tertiary study on a Cuban government scholarship. Speaks French, Spanish and English fluently.

Subject No. 5: Female, age 33 years.

Born in Yugoslavia (today's Serbia) and identifies as of Serbian ethnicity. Arrived in Australia in 1999 (only 7 months in Australia at the time of the interview). Lived in Serbia with her grandparents but visited her parents who were guest workers in Switzerland during school holidays. Parents have been living in Switzerland for 30 years. Married to a Serbian-Australian she met in Serbia.

Subject No. 6: Female, Age 76 years.

Identifies herself as Italian. Born in Egypt in 1924 and migrated directly to Australia in 1955. Never lived in Italy but learnt Italian, French and English in school and speaks Italian as her first language.

Subject No. 11: Male, Age 64 years.

Born in Spain and identifies as Spanish. As a teenager, moved to Switzerland and then to Germany where he lived and worked until the age of 33, when he migrated to Australia.

Subject No. 13: Female, age 40 years.

Lithuanian ethnicity. Married a Polish person and lived in Poland for two years before migrating to Australia with him at the age of 22. Considers herself as one on the 'young' Polish migrants in the city as the others are either Australian-born or arrived in Australia 40-50 years ago.

Subject No. 14: Female, born in 1949.

Identifies as Russian but was born in China. Lived in a segregated and self-sufficient (White) Russian community in Mongolia. Grandparents moved to China to live in exile in 1922 after the Russian Revolution of 1917. Lived in China till she was 14 when they migrated to Australia in 1963. Visited Russia as a tourist a few years ago. Never lived in Russia but is fluent in Russian and teaches the language to the children of her local Russian community.

Issues of Validity in Social Science Research

Validity refers to the degree to which a measure taps into what we think it is measuring (Adler & Clark, 2003; p. 150). But Cope (2004) points out the contentious and unresolved nature of the issue of 'rigor'- especially in qualitative research, in terms of validity and reliability (p. 5) of the data collected. Therefore, any social science researcher should anticipate and be aware of the challenges that may arise in relation to issues of validity in one's research projects (Cope, 2004). It is quite accepted that a researcher brings his or her subjectivity based on one's own background (Burns, 1994), and that his or her subject position (in society as either powerful / dominant or powerless /marginalized) and self-reference (autobiography or life experiences) come into play when interpreting and collecting data in a qualitative research process, which provides a context to the findings (Cope, 2004; p. 8). This would be the same for research subjects when they express their views and opinions, which are colored by their own unique and even idiosyncratic life experiences, which can in no way be anticipated before the research commences. For example, the three Italian subjects selected for the preliminary study were very different from each other as one was born in Italy and migrated to Australia in the late 1940s as a young man, while another was a 76 year old born and living in Egypt before arrival in Australia in 1955. She had never visited Italy before migrating to Australia. The third Italian was in his early 30s, was born and lived his entire life in the same city in Australia and speaks English as his first language. This indicated the heterogeneity of the three subjects and their life experiences, even though they claimed to have the same ethnic identity.

Stratified sampling

According to Wimmer & Dominick (2006) and Baxter & Babbie (2004), stratified sampling – the procedure used in this study to select the interview subjects based on census figures for the various ethnic groups, was expected to ensure that the sample was drawn from a homogeneous subset of the population (the ethnic minorities living in this city) that has similar characteristics. Homogeneity is considered to help reduce sampling error. According to Daymon and Holloway (2002), 'The members of a sample (e.g. drawn from the same ethnic group) generally share certain characteristics and experiences which are important for the development of the study' (p. 159). Had this study in question been the project proper involving a much larger number of subjects instead of being a preliminary one where only a few or only one subject was chosen to be interviewed from each ethnic group, the sample would have ended up being heterogeneous for each ethnic group without the researcher realizing it until after a good number of the interviews had been completed.

Validity and theory

Kirk and Miller (1991) argue that all measurements are to the same degree suspect and the issue of validity (accuracy) is a fundamental problem of theory- in this case the assumption that those belonging to the same ethnic group or demographic category will be homogeneous in their characteristics and life experiences. A theory may assert that a measurement may be valid under all circumstances when in fact it may not. In other words, the question of *repeatable regularities* will be an issue to be kept in mind with validity of interview data collected from members of demographic groups (Kaplan, 1973; p. 67) as they can be heterogeneous in characteristics within the group, as much as between groups. Therefore, in social science research, the issue of validity is a question of whether the researcher sees what he or she thinks he or she sees (Kirk & Miller, 1991; p. 21).

Identity

The concept of identity, as linked to the modernist understanding of the world is that it is singular and unitary. But the postmodern view argues that identities are multiple, complex and continuously changing (Grieshaber & Canella, 2001). Identities are also linked to society, power and circumstance, which in turn are linked to a person's lived experiences, which are shaped by their various group memberships based on gender, ethnicity, religion, class, race, sexual orientation, nationality, education, occupation etc., which result in multiple lived experiences (Canella & Grieshaber, 2001). Postmodernism highlights the historical, political and societal grounding of individuals and groups, which recognizes the complex nature of individuals as members of complicated, heterogeneous societies, giving us an opportunity to examine individuals and groups in their wider discourses and less confined identities (Canella & Grieshaber, 2001; p. 173).

Identity provides us with a location in the world and presents the link between us and the society in which we live, and provides a conceptual tool with which to understand and make sense of social, cultural, economic and political changes (Woodward, 2003; p. 1). But 'identity is never a static location and contains traces of its past, and what it is to become. It is a contingent, a provisional full stop in the play of differences and the narratives of our own lives' (Rutherford, 1990; p. 24).

Identity examines how a person fits in (belongs) to the community and the social world and is the interface between one's subjective positions and social cultural situations (Woodward, 2003). It gives a person a sense of personal location (Weeks, 1990). Identity tells us who we are and how we relate to others and the world we live in. Identity tells us how and in what ways we are the same as or different from others (Woodward, 2003; p. 2). Identities are not neutral because when saying who we are, we also indicate what we believe and what we desire, which may be in conflict between different communities as well as within individuals themselves (Weeks, 1990; p. 89).

Gilroy (2003) argues that even though race, ethnicity and nationality may seem to appear to offer a secure sense of identity, it is illusionary and problematic because due to its rigidity and constraints involved in establishing absolute and fixed divisions between peoples. Identities of persons are communicatively constituted in two senses- discursively and interactively (Mokros, 1996).

Issues of Cultural/Ethnic Identity

Identity is complex and multifaceted- especially in relation to diaspora identities. Therefore, conceiving national or ethnic identities as fixed, closed, and unchanging, has negative consequences (Gilroy, 2003; p.303). Identity and culture are shaped by common historical experiences and memories (Smith, 1990). Cultural identity on the other hand is one's sense of belonging to a given society or to the global cultural supermarket (Matthews, 2000). It is also the 'identification with a group that has shared systems of symbols and meanings as well as norms and rules for conduct' (Collier & Thomas, 1988; p 188).

A key factor in cultural identity is national identity. Most people today are socialized and propagandized to hold a national or cultural identity (eg. Protecting our way of life, values etc.). But national cultural identity is eroded by the cultural supermarket with globalized mass media and multinational corporations such as McDonalds, contributing towards homogenizing of our cultural experiences (Matthews, 2000). Under the postmodernist view, 'Identities are ...points of temporary attachments to the subject positions which discursive practices construct for us' (Hall, 1996; p. 6). According to this definition, identities are not fixed. Anthony Giddens defines identity as 'how the self conceives of itself and labels itself (Giddens, 1991; p 53).

Some researchers argue that cultural identities are studied in the absence of consistent categories for defining various types of cultural communities, which are based on arbitrary categories of classification used differently by different scholars to define different groups as cultural communities. These parameters include nationality, ethnicity, race, gender, social class, 'subculturalism', and oganizational systems (Belay, 1992).

The three main features contributing to cultural identity are: temporality (as historically emergent and evolved through time, a shared history of the group handed down through generations); territoriality (claimed and linked to a territory); constrastivity (collective consciousness and contrasting themselves against other groups); interactivity (cultural identity as created through social interaction and being enduring and resistant to change); and multiplicity (an individual having a variety of identities such as ethnicity, race, gender, and class.) (Belay, 1996).

Belay (1996) also discusses the impact of globalisation on cultural identity as part of global and international interactional processes and the challenges and opportunities posed due to the growing interconnectedness and interdependence between nations in the negotiation of identities. These multidirectional shifts of cultural identification result in tensions and transformations (p. 320). Globalisation has exposed individuals, communities and nations to diverse 'interactional conditions of utmost cultural ambiguity', which they are ill prepared or unable to handle, that it may lead people to seek the security of their ethnicity or religion such as some migrants holding on to their own, without integrating into the new culture. At the same time, the new globalized interactional context can lead to a withering away of certain types of cultural identity (Belay, 1996; p. 320).

Globalization also introduces new territorialities and temporalities to cultural identity. They in turn influence contrastivity, interactivity and multiplicity in individual identities. Exposure to multiple 'others' in a globalized world (say via travel or while living in another country), may contribute to individuals becoming less parochial and able to compare and contrast one's identity with those of others and be able to understand the concepts of 'self' and 'others' better. This means that interview subjects who were exposed to other cultures may interpret and understand their life experiences in Australia in a manner different from those who had not been exposed to other cultures before coming to Australia.

Types of cultural identification

Cultural identity is how people culturally construct and present themselves (Matthews, 2000; p. 122). Many scholars have argued the ambiguities of the categories used in the classification of various cultural communities in the research literature. For example, Asian Australians may come from a variety of countries with diverse cultural, ethnic, racial, linguistic, religious and social systems. At the same time, the English, Scottish and Welsh (migrants in Australia) are classified as a single group for census purposes as coming from the United Kingdom (Belay, 1996). This leaves no room for other categories of classification such as Indian- Australians who may come from the different states in India with diverse cultural characteristics and identities.

Belay (1996) introduces the six types of cultural identities evident in today's global interactional processes. They are: sociological (based on demographics, including religion, sexual orientation, disabilities etc.); occupational (linked to formal occupations and related institutions); geo-basic (related to cultures that evolved in different geographic regions such as Asia and Africa, assuming common cultural legacies that predates nations and based on racial characteristics); national (the most powerful parameter of cultural identification and linked to legally defined rights and responsibilities of citizenship); co-cultural (multiracial nations that represent different geo-basic groups but belong to the same nation such as the USA or Australia); and ethnic (designating a variety of collectivities within a larger national culture) (p. 325).

Ethnic identities

Used often in everyday language, the term 'ethnic identity' creates complications when used in academic contexts, with reference to studying cultures and cultural identification (Belay, 1996). This is because, the term is used to label a variety of collectivities within a large national culture, including 'racial groups', minorities and immigrant groups- which can mean either everything or nothing at all (Cohen, 1993; Jaipaul, 1977). Belay (1996) uses the term 'ethnic identity' to refer to sub-national groups in 'racially' homogeneous societies as opposed to geo-basic and co-cultural identities where ethnic identification is not related to differences in physical characteristics. He sees ethnic identity as based on cultural elements such as community, physical contiguity, religious affiliation, language / dialect, and blood or kinship relationships among members. These different classifications indicate how the demographic categorization of ethnicity generally used in census and research contexts can be problematic and inadequate to represent the heterogeneity of research subjects used to study various phenomena in multicultural societies. Ethnic identity is generally based on the idea of particular people belonging to a particular place (eg. A particular province of a country) and can also become an adjunct to one's existing national identity or serve as a counterforce to national identity (Matthews, 2000; p. 9).

Diaspora, Diaspora Consciousness and Transcultural Mixtures

A *diaspora* results in the scattering of people due to war, oppression, poverty, enslavement, indenture, pogroms, genocide and the search for better economic and social opportunities (via migration), which results in opening the diaspora culture to new influences and pressures. These new influences will vary based on where they 'scatter' in their search for a 'haven' or a new location to settle. Diaspora as a concept offers new possibilities for understanding identity to visualize a future to form social solidarity not necessarily determined by place or nationality (Gilroy, 2003; p. 304).

Diaspora Consciousness

Diaspora Consciousness is reproduced when identity is focused on the social dynamics of remembrance and communication, linked to a strong sense of the dangers involved in forgetting the location of one's origin and the process of diaspora or 'scattering' (Gilroy, 2003; p. 318). Members of a diaspora could end up with a mix or hybrid or even a recombination of cultures and identities, with aspects retained from its 'parent' culture. This would be called a *Transcultural mixture*. Texts such as narratives of their life experiences (eg. given during interviews) of these hybrid individuals should be seen as complex, compound formations and observed in terms of the durability of their original culture and identity. In other words, one should consider the experiences of these migrants or members of a diaspora who had been exposed to other cultures as different from those who were not (Gilroy, 2003).

Transcultural Mixtures

Transcultural mixtures alert us to the language/s, cultures and everyday life experiences these migrants may have been exposed to during some part of their life or time spent 'in transit' before moving to Australia from their original countries. Transcultural mixtures also tell us to recognize the changes or metamorphoses undergone by individuals who may claim a particular national or ethnic identity, due to their various lived experiences. Identity is the compound result of many accretions. Its protean (changes in shape randomly and continuously) constitution is not under the control of ethnic, racial, cultural or national absolutism (Gilroy, 2003; p. 323). However, like the (White) Russian subject in the study who grew up in a segregated Russian community while living in China, a person can be considered to have been able to maintain their culture in a form frozen at the time of their community's exile from Russia, without being mixed or influenced by the Chinese/Mongolian culture of their hosts. However, this would be a unique situation, which would have been possible only within the context of the Cold War, where her Russian community had been protected (according to the interviewee, presumably by both the US and Chinese governments) and allowed live in that location under special circumstances due to the political nature of their exile.

Not 'peas in a pod'

The concepts of diaspora consiousness and transcultural mixtures highlight the issue of sameness within differentiation and differentiation within sameness. It argues against the assumption that political and cultural identity can be described and understood with the analogy of the indistinguishable 'peas in a pod'. Apart from sharing a common genealogy and geography, members subscribing to a common ethnic or national identity who are part of a diaspora, may find that the pressure to associate, remember or forget their original culture may vary with the changes they face within the political and economic environment the members of the diaspora live in, which creates differences between members' lived experiences (Gilroy, 2003; p. 332). For example, living in an environment where one is free or not free to practice one's original culture or religion would influence how strongly the members would want to practice or preserve it or how easy or difficult it will be for them to maintain it.

Discussion

This paper argues that the varying life experiences of subjects who belong to the same ethnic group or claim the same ethnic or national identity can create an artifact or introduce a confounding variable to a study design, due to their heterogeneous nature, individual characteristics, and diverse lived experiences, within the sample. The way to control this shortcoming would be to be aware of the phenomenon that not all migrants from the same ethnic or national group will have the same life history. Therefore, a researcher must endeavor to seek information on their life experiences before recruiting them for a study. Thereafter, individuals can be recruited to make the sample as homogeneous as possible. In other words, internal validity of the data can be guarded by controlling the 'artifact' or confounding / extraneous variables, of not having subjects who are too different from each other in terms of their life experiences or are comparable to each other. It will also help rule out the alternative explanations based on the natural differences among people. This may be achieved by a) randomizing the sample, b) 'matching' (making sure subjects with the confounding variable are chosen along with ones that do not) or c) by incorporating the confounding variable into the study design (Wimmer & Dominick, 2006; p. 139).

Controlling the Confounding Variable

Randomization may not be possible in some research studies with ethnic minorities, due to the inability of the researcher to reach the entire population of the required ethnic minority group members in the research location /city and / or due to the English language skills required of the interview subjects as not all ethnic minority members- especially the older ones lack fluency in the language. Using interpreters and translators for interviews conducted with non-English speaking subjects may not always be affordable to a researcher without the required funding. *Matching* of the confounding variable may be carried out in two ways. It may be achieved with *constancy* where the variable is made uniform to all subjects. eg. Select subjects who had all been living in third countries at least for X number of years, before arriving in Australia / were born in Australia to migrant parents but had not lived anywhere else for more than two years / had arrived in Australia directly from their native country etc. The other method is *matching by pairing.* This could be done by matching a subject of a given ethnic group who has come straight to Australia from one's own country with one who has spent time in a third country before their arrival in Australia. (This had already been achieved with the Italian group in the study where one was born in Italy and arrived in Australia in the 1940s, the other was born in Egypt and never lived in Italy, and the third was born and raised in Australia by Italian migrant parents.) However, matching by constancy limits the generalizability of the findings and restricts the size of the population available for sampling. Both forms of matching require some prior knowledge about the subjects (Wimmer & Dominick, 2006; p. 139).

Improving Validity

The third option for improving the validity of the data collected will be to *include the confounding variable in the research design.* This method helps control the impact of the artifact or confounding/extraneous variable by using it as an independent variable in the study. For example, choose a subject for each of the selected ethnic groups who had lived in a third country before migrating to Australia. However, this process will increase the costs and time taken for the study by increasing the number of subjects required for interviewing.

Conclusion

The narratives of members of diasporas such as migrants in Australia, indicate the complex nature of a person's national, ethnic or cultural identity, which are far different from the old views based on religious, racial, national and ethnic identities. This preliminary study with only 15 subjects indicates that even migrants who arrived in Australia in the 1940s and 1950s may have voluntarily lived in third or even fourth countries, contrary to the belief that ethnoscapes are a phenomenon of the global village or globalization of the 1970s and beyond. With the Middle East, Southern Europe and Africa attracting guest workers from Asia, who later decide to migrate to the classical migrant countries such as Australia, New Zealand, the USA and Canada, the effects of diaspora consciousness and transcultural mixtures on research involving ethnic minorities will remain a factor for qualitative as well as quantitative researchers, who will continue to use the official categorizations for ethnic groups set by census bureaus and social research groups in these countries.

Heuristic Value of the Study

The findings of this study also has heuristic value (Littlejohn, 2002) in the sense that the findings and the theorizing about the limitations of the demographic category of ethnicity in social science research can be extended and applied to research and theorizing in the discipline of education and communication involving ethnic minority students as well as international students. Most Australian universities today enroll a significant number of ethnic minority students who may be either born overseas or in Australia to migrant parents and currently are Australian citizens or permanent residents. They may be inadvertently categorized by their original nationalities for purposes of research and official statistics. They too may have been living in third countries such as in the Middle East, Africa or even the West where their professional parents worked as guest workers, before migrating to Australia.

Anecdotal evidence also suggests that many international students currently studying in Australia are in reality those who grew up in third countries such as in the Middle East or Africa, where their parents worked as professionals or guest workers, which actually made it more affordable or even possible for them to study overseas in the first place. Even though these students may carry passports of their country of birth or the original country of their parents, they would have spent little time in their 'native' countries. Such students will be officially categorized under their legal nationality even though they will possess the characteristics of transcultural mixtures and will be different from students who arrive directly from their native countries as international students having been born, raised and undergone their secondary education in their native countries. Therefore, any researchers carrying out studies involving ethnic minority or international students in Australia, (or Argentina, Canada, New Zealand and the USA for that matter), will need to be aware of this phenomenon.

In conclusion, this paper would argue that the demographic categorisation used for grouping ethnic minorities or migrants in Australia may be inadequate as they can include heterogeneous individuals who indicate differences within a category as much as between categories due to their diverse lived experiences, which serve as artifacts or confounding or extraneous variables to social science research studies, involving ethnic minorities.

Note: This paper is based on a research study funded by a Priming Grant from the Faculty of Arts at Deakin University, VIC, Australia, where the author served as Chief Investigator of the project.

References

Adler, E. S. & Clark, R. (2003). *How it is done: An invitation to social research,* (2nd edition). Belmont, CA: Wadsworth-Thomson.

Andsagar, J. (2001). Defining individual differences in research. *CTM Concepts-The Newsletter of the Communication Theory and Methodology Division of the AEJMC, 29*(2), Spring, 1, 8.

Appadurai, A. (1990). Disjuncture and difference in the global cultural economy, *Public culture, 2*(2), Spring, 1-24.

Baxter, L. A. & Babbie, E. (2004). *The basics of communication research*. Belmont, CA: Wadsworth-Thomson.

Belay, G. (1992). Conceptual strategies for operating multicultural curricula, *Journal for Library and Information Science, 33*, 295-306.

Belay, G. (1996). The (re)construction and negotiation of cultural identities in the age of globalization. In H. B. Mocros (ed), *Interaction and identity: Information and behavior* (Vol. 5, pp. 320-346). New Brunswick, NJ: Transaction Publishers.

Burns, J. (1994). Extending critique within phenomenography. In R. Ballantyne & C. Bruce (Eds.), *Proceedings of phenomenography: Philosophy and practice* (pp. 71-76). Brisbane, QLD: Queensland University of Technology Publications and Printing.

Canella, G. S. & Grieshaber, S. (2001). Identities and possibilities. In S. Grieshaber & G. S. Canella (Eds.), *Embracing identities in early childhood education: Diversity and possibilities* (pp. 173-187). New York: Teachers' College Press.

Castles, S. & Miller, J. M. (2003). *The age of migration: International population movements in the modern world* (3rd ed.). New York: Pelgrave Macmillan.

Cohen, A. P. (1993). Culture as identity and intercultural communication. In L. A. Samovar & R. E. Porter (Eds.), *Intercultural communication: A reader* (pp. 36-44). Belmont, CA: Wadsworth Publishing Company.

Collier, M. J. & Thomas, A. (1980). Cultural identity: An interpretive perspective. In Y. Y. Kim & W. B. Gudykunst (Eds.), *Theories in intercultural communication* (pp. 99-122). Newbury Park, CA: Sage.

Cope, C. (2004). Ensuring validity and reliability in phenomenographic research using the analytical frameworks of a structure of awareness, *Qualitative Research Journal, 4*(2), 5-18.

Daymon, C. & Holloway, I. (2002*). Qualitative research methods in public relations and marketing communications.* London: Routledge.

Deleuze, G. (1995). *Negotiations 1972-1990.* (Trans. M Joughlin), New York: Columbia University Press.

Denzin, N. (1970). *Sociological methods*. Chicago, IL: Aldine.

Giddens, A. (1991). *Modernity and self-identity: Self and society in the late modern age.* (pp. 53-54). Stanford, CA: Stanford University Press.

Gilroy, P. (2003). Diaspora and the detours of identity. In K. Woodward (Ed.), *Identity and difference.* (pp. 301-342). London: Sage.

Gireshaber, S. & Canella, G. S. (2001). From identity to identities: Increasing possibilities in early childhood education. In S. Grieshaber & G. S. Canella (Eds.), *Embracing identities in early childhood education: Diversity and possibilities* (pp. 3-22). New York: Teachers' College Press.

Hall, S. (1996). Introduction: Who needs identity? In S. Hall & P. du Gay (Eds.), *Questions of cultural identity* (p. 6). London: Sage.

IOM (2000). *World migration report* 2000. Geneva: International Organisation for Migration.

Jaipaul, A. (1977). *Politics of ethnicity*. Philadelphia, PA: Ethnic Heritage Affairs Institute.

Kaplan, A. (1973). *The conduct of inquiry: Methodology for behavioural sciences.* Aylesbury: Intertext.

Kirk, J. & Miller, M. L. (1991). *Reliability and validity in qualitative research.* Newbury Park, CA: Sage.

Littlejohn, S. W. (2002). *Theories of human communication* (7th ed.). Belmont, CA: Wadsworth Thomson Learning.

Matthews, G. (2000). *Global culture/Individual identity: Searching for home in the cultural supermarket.* London: Routledge.

Mokros, H. B. (1996). Introduction: From information and behavior to interaction and identity. In H. B. Mokros (Ed.), *Interaction and identity: Information and behavior* (Vol. 5, pp. 1-22). New Brunswick, NJ: Transaction Books.

Rushdie, S. (1991). *Imaginary homelands.* London: Granta.

Rutherford, J. (1990). A place called home: Identity and the cultural politics of difference. In J. Rutherford (Ed.), *Identity, community, culture, difference* (pp. 9-27). London: Lawrence and Wishart.

Smith, A. (1990). Towards a global culture. *Theory, Culture & Society, 7,* 171-191.

Weeks, J. (1990). The value of difference. In J. Rutherford (Ed.), *Identity, community, culture, difference* (pp. 88-100). London: Lawrence Wishart.

Wimmer, R. D. & Dominick, J. R. (2006). *Mass media research: An introduction,* (8th ed.). Belmont, CA: Wadsworth-Thompson.

Woodward, K. (2003). Introduction. In K. Woodward (Ed.), *Identity and difference* (pp. 1-6). London: Sage.

Biography

Niranjala D Weerakkody (Ph D, Rutgers U, NJ, USA) is a Senior Lecturer in Media and Communication at Deakin University. She teaches qualitative and quantitative research methods at both undergraduate and postgraduate levels, in addition to units in media effects and organizational communication.

The Power of Normalised Word Vectors for Automatically Grading Essays

Robert Williams
School of Information Systems, Curtin University of Technology
Perth, Australia

Bob.Williams@cbs.curtin.edu.au

Abstract

Latent Semantic Analysis, when used for automated essay grading, makes use of document word count vectors for scoring the essays against domain knowledge. Words in the domain knowledge documents and essays are counted, and Singular Value Decomposition is undertaken to reduce the dimensions of the semantic space. Near neighbour vector cosines and other variables are used to calculate an essay score. This paper discusses a technique for computing word count vectors where the words are first normalised using thesaurus concept index numbers. This approach leads to a vector space of 812 dimensions, does not require Singular Value Decomposition, and leads to a reduced computational load. The cosine between the vectors for the student essay and a model answer proves to be a very powerful independent variable when used in regression analysis to score essays. An example of its use in practice is discussed.

Keywords: Automated Essay Grading, Latent Semantic Analysis, Singular Value Decomposition, Normalised Word Vectors, Electronic Thesaurus, Multiple Regression Analysis.

Introduction

Automated Essay Grading (AEG) systems are now appearing in the educational marketplace, and are increasingly being accepted as a way of efficiently grading large numbers of essays (Shermis & Burstein, 2003). There are many theoretical constructs underpinning the various AEG systems (Williams, 2001; Valenti, Neri & Cucchiarelli, 2003). One of the major systems, the Intelligent Essay Assessor (Pearson Knowledge Technologies, 2005), makes use of a mathematical technique known as Latent Semantic Analysis (LSA) (Landauer, Foltz & Laham, 1998). This system is interesting because of the way it derives the knowledge contained in an essay from the words comprising the essay. The MarkIT system (Williams & Dreher, 2005), being developed by the author and colleagues, uses an alternative way of deriving content from an essay, but still based on the words making up the essay. This paper discusses these two alternative word-based content representations, presents new material on the grading algorithm for MarkIT, and compares the performances of the two systems.

In this paper we do not have space to give a detailed coverage of the issues associated with AEG systems. For a comprehensive coverage of AEG systems, their algorithms, and performance details, see Hearst (2000), Williams (2001), and Valenti, Neri and Cucchiarelli (2003).

Latent Semantic Analysis

LSA is a mathematical technique based on vector algebra. It is used to derive a representation of the content of a collection of text documents in a particular domain of knowledge. This content representation is generally termed the semantic space. This space is built from text segments that may consist of the complete documents, or subsets of the documents, such as paragraphs or sentences. Each word in the segment is represented as a row in a matrix, and each segment is represented as a column in the same matrix. The counts of the number of times the words appear in the segments are entered in the corresponding elements in the matrix.

The following example, taken from Landauer, Foltz, and Laham (1998) and used with permission from the authors and Lawrence Erlbaum Associates, the publishers, illustrates the technique. The titles of five documents relating to human computer interaction and four relating to mathematical graph theory are shown below.

c1: *Human* machine *interface* for ABC *computer* applications
c2: A *survey* of *user* opinion of *computer system response time*
c3: The *EPS user interface* management *system*
c4: *System* and *human system* engineering testing of *EPS*
c5: Relation of *user* perceived *response time* to error measurement
m1: The generation of random, binary, ordered *trees*
m2: The intersection *graph* of paths in *trees*
m3: *Graph minors* IV: Widths of *trees* and well-quasi-ordering
m4: *Graph minors*: A *survey*

The matrix below shows the word count for the selected words occurring in at least two of the titles. These words are shown in italics in the document titles.

	c1	c2	c3	c4	c5	m1	m2	m3	m4
human	1	0	0	1	0	0	0	0	0
interface	1	0	1	0	0	0	0	0	0
computer	1	1	0	0	0	0	0	0	0
user	0	1	1	0	1	0	0	0	0
system	0	1	1	2	0	0	0	0	0
response	0	1	0	0	1	0	0	0	0
time	0	1	0	0	1	0	0	0	0
EPS	0	0	1	1	0	0	0	0	0
survey	0	1	0	0	0	0	0	0	1
trees	0	0	0	0	0	1	1	1	0
graph	0	0	0	0	0	0	1	1	1
minors	0	0	0	0	0	0	0	1	1

A vector algebra technique, known as Singular value Decomposition (SVD) is then applied to this matrix. SVD breaks the matrix into 3 component matrices that can be matrix multiplied to produce the original matrix. However the dimensions of these 3 matrices are reduced before the remultiplication. The remultiplied matrix is now approximately equivalent to the original matrix in terms of its element values, but now contains values for elements that were previously zero. In other words, the reconstituted matrix now has relationships for words and segments that were not explicitly displayed in the original matrix, but have been induced by the SVD process from the hidden or latent relationships amongst the words and segments. The reconstructed approximation to the original matrix, based upon the first two columns in the three component matrices (not shown), is

	c1	c2	c3	c4	c5	m1	m2	m3	m4
human	0.16	0.40	0.38	0.47	0.18	-0.05	-0.12	-0.16	-0.09
interface	0.14	0.37	0.33	0.40	0.16	-0.03	-0.07	-0.10	-0.04
computer	0.15	0.51	0.36	0.41	0.24	0.02	0.06	0.09	0.12
user	0.26	0.84	0.61	0.70	0.39	0.03	0.08	0.12	0.19
system	0.45	1.23	1.05	1.27	0.56	-0.07	-0.15	-0.21	-0.05
response	0.16	0.58	0.38	0.42	0.28	0.06	0.13	0.19	0.22
time	0.16	0.58	0.38	0.42	0.28	0.06	0.13	0.19	0.22
EPS	0.22	0.55	0.51	0.63	0.24	-0.07	-0.14	-0.20	-0.11
survey	0.10	0.53	0.23	0.21	0.27	0.14	0.31	0.44	0.42
trees	-0.06	0.23	-0.14	-0.27	0.14	0.24	0.55	0.77	0.66
graph	-0.06	0.34	-0.15	-0.30	0.20	0.31	0.69	0.98	0.85
minors	-0.04	0.25	-0.10	-0.21	0.15	0.22	0.50	0.71	0.62

What was originally a sparsely populated matrix of relationships amongst words and segments is now a rich array of associations. This is now the semantic space for this collection of document titles.

"This text segment is best described as having so much of abstract concept one and so much of abstract concept two, and this word has so much of concept one and so much of concept two, and combining those two pieces of information (by vector arithmetic), my best guess is that word X actually appeared 0.6 times in context Y." (Landauer, et al., 1998, p 264)

Essays on a particular topic are graded as follows. The appropriate semantic space is built – this can be done by processing electronic texts on the topic, or from a collection of several hundred human graded essays on the topic. The essay to be graded is then processed using the SVD technique to build a document vector in this space. An essay score is then computed from near neighbour human scored essay vectors in this space, and other variables.

The IEA is a commercial implementation of the LSA approach to AEG. Landauer indicates that this system builds the semantic space as follows:

> "IEA/LSA always starts from a reduced dimensional space based on a large relevant corpus to which it adds text special to the topic and the student essays" (personal email communication, 16 November, 2005).

Evaluation of LSA and Essay Grading

Nichols has evaluated the IEA. He concludes

> "All four of the measures of the relationship between essay scores and expert scores (percent agreement, Spearman rank-order correlation, kappa statistic and Pearson correlation) indicated a stronger relationship between the IEA and experts than between readers and experts. In addition, the results of examining the scoring processes used by the IEA showed that the IEA used processes similar to a human scorer. Furthermore, the IEA scoring processes were more similar to processes used by proficient human scorers than to processes used by non-proficient or intermediate human scorers." (Nichols, 2005, p 21).

Vector Representation of Documents using a Thesaurus to Normalise Document Words

The MarkIT AEG system is a software system that automatically grades essays against an ideal content answer at the same level of accuracy as human graders (MarkIT, 2005; Williams & Dreher, 2005). This section explains how vector algebra techniques are used to represent similarities in content between documents in MarkIT. In order to build this vector representation, a thesaurus is used to "normalise" words in the documents by reducing all words to a thesaurus root word appropriate to the concept the word belongs to. Counts of these concepts are then used for the vector representation. Consider the following start of sentence fragments from successive sentences in 3 separate documents:

Document Number	Document Text
(1)	The little boy… A small male…
(2)	A minor boy… A funny girl…
(3)	The large boy… Some minor day…

Suppose a thesaurus exists with the following root concept numbers and words:

Concept Number	Words
1.	the, a
2.	little, small, minor
3.	boy, male
4.	large
5.	funny
6.	girl
7.	some
8.	day

Three dimensional vector representations of the above document fragments on the first 3 concept numbers (1-3) can be constructed by counting the number of times a word in that concept number appears in the document fragments. These vectors are:

Document Number	Vector on first 3 concepts	Explanation
(1)	[2, 2, 2]	[The, a; little, small; boy, male]
(2)	[2, 0, 1]	[A, a; ; boy]
(3)	[1, 1, 1]	[The; minor; boy]

Figure 1 shows these 3 dimensional vectors pictorially.

Computing the Variable CosTheta

If we assume that document 1 is the model answer, then we can see how close semantically documents 2 and 3 are to the model answer by looking at the closeness of their corresponding vectors. The angle between the vectors varies according to how "close" the vectors are. A small angle indicates that the documents contain similar content, a large angle indicates that they do not have much common content. Angle Theta1 is the angle between the model answer vector and the vector for document 2, and angle Theta2 is the angle between the model answer vector and the vector for document 3.

The cosines of Theta1 and Theta2 can be used as measures of this closeness. If documents 2 and 3 were identical to the model answer, their vectors would be identical to the model answer vector, and would be collinear with it, and have a cosine of 1. If on the other hand, they were completely different, and therefore orthogonal to the model answer vector, their cosines would be 0.

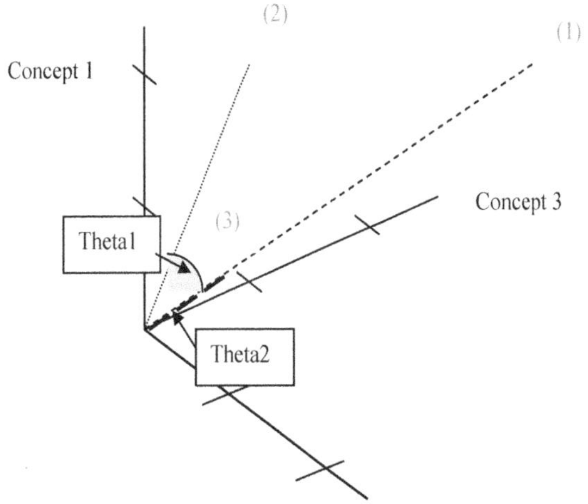

Figure 1. Vector representation (dashed lines) of documents

Generally in practice, a document's cosine is between these upper and lower limits.

The variable CosTheta used in the scoring algorithm is this cosine computed for the document being scored.

In general, these ideas are extended to the 812 concepts in the Macquarie Thesaurus from Macquarie Library Pty Ltd (Macquarie Library, 2005), and all words in the documents. This means that the vectors are constructed in 812 dimensions, and the vector theory carries over to these dimensions in exactly the same way – it is of course hard to visualise the vectors in this hyperspace. (The system developers approached a number of thesaurus publishers with a view to obtaining a research licence to use an electronic thesaurus, and Macquarie Library Pty Ltd was the only company willing to grant one; hence its usage).

Computing the Variable VarRatio

We now discuss another powerful essay grade predictor, VarRatio, which is based on these concept vectors. The number of concepts that are present in the model answer (document 1) above is 3. This can be determined from the number of non-zero counts in the numerical vector representation.

The number of concepts that are present in document 2 above is 2 – the second vector index is 0. To compute the VarRatio for this document 2 we divide the non-zero concept count for document 2 by the non-zero concept count in the model answer i.e. VarRatio = 2/3 = 0.67. The corresponding VarRatio for document 3 is 3/3 = 1.00.

This simple variable provides a remarkably strong predictor of essay scores, and is generally present as one of the components in the scoring algorithm.

Scoring Student Essays by Matching a Model Answer against Student Answers

MarkIT makes use of a multiple regression equation to assign a grade to a student essay. The regression equation is developed from about 100 human graded training essays and an ideal or model answer. The document vectors described above are constructed. Values are then computed for many variables from the relationships between the content and vectors of the model answer and the training essays. Once the training has been performed, and the grading algorithm built, each unmarked essay is processed to obtain the values for the independent variables, and the regression equation is then applied. Generally CosTheta and VarRatio are significant predictors in the scoring equation. An example taken from a trial of the system is now discussed.

In the trial, Year 10 high school students hand wrote essays on paper on the topic of "The School Leaving Age". Three trained human graders then graded these essays against a marking rubric. The essays, 390 in total, were then transcribed to Microsoft Word document format. The essay with the highest average human score was selected as the model answer. It had a score of 48.5 out of a possible 54, or 90%. In one test of the system, 100 essays were used to build the scoring algorithm. The scoring algorithm was built using the first 100 essays in the trial when ordered in ascending order of the identifier. Table 1 shows the results of the multiple regression procedure built upon the output of the MarkIT system for these 100 essays. The multiple R is 0.89 and the prediction equation is

Student Grade = -22.35 + 11.00*CosTheta + 15.70*VarRatio +7.64*Characters Per Word + 0.20 Number of NP Adjectives

Table 1. Multiple Regression Analysis for First 100 Essays

SUMMARY OUTPUT

Regression Statistics	
Multiple R	0.89
R Square	0.79
Adjusted R Square	0.78
Standard Error	4.16
Observations	100.00

ANOVA

	df	*SS*	*MS*	*F*	*Significance F*
Regression	4.00	6079.76	1519.94	87.71	0.00
Residual	95.00	1646.21	17.33		
Total	99.00	7725.97			

	Coefficients	*Standard Error*	*t Stat*	*P-value*
Intercept	-22.35	6.67	-3.35	0.00
CosTheta	11.00	3.74	2.94	0.00
VarRatio	15.70	2.86	5.49	0.00
Characters Per Word	7.64	1.74	4.40	0.00
Number of NP Adjectives	0.20	0.08	2.41	0.02

- CosTheta is computed as per the explanation above.
- VarRatio is computed as per the explanation above.
- Characters Per Word is the average number of characters in the words in the essay
- Number of NP Adjectives is the number of Adjectives in Noun Phrases in the essay

Notice that only 4 independent variables are needed for the predictor equation in this example.

Once this scoring algorithm was coded into the scoring program, the remaining 290 essays were graded by it. Figure 2 shows the results.

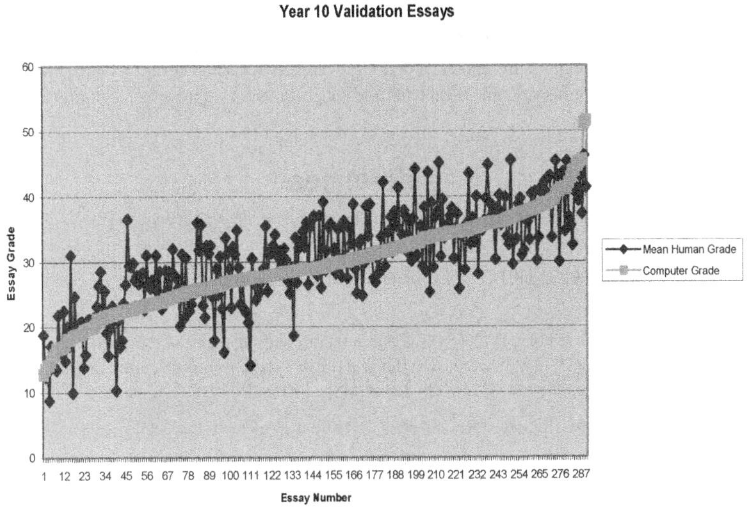

Figure 2. Results of Computer Scoring of Last 290 Essays

The mean score for the human average grade for these 290 essays was 30.34, while the mean grade given by the computer was 29.45, a difference of 0.89. The correlation between the human and computer grades was 0.79. The mean absolute difference between the two was 3.90, representing an average error rate of 7.23% when scored out of 54 (the maximum possible human score).

The correlations between the three humans amongst themselves were 0.81, 0.78 and 0.81.

The benefits of averaging the scores from the human graders are shown by the fact that the correlation between the computer and the mean score of the three humans is higher, at 0.79, than the individual correlations at 0.67, 0.75 and 0.75.

Conclusion

LSA makes use of SVD to reduce the large number of dimensions generated when each word in a document is counted as a separate dimension. Typically the dimensions are reduced to about 300 (Landauer, 2005). The processing involved for the SVD takes a few hours on a common small Linux cluster (Landauer, personal email communication, 16 November 2005).

While the number of dimensions resulting from normalising words against thesaurus index numbers is 812, much less processing is involved – typically the training session to build the scoring algorithm for a prompt using 100 essays takes 5 minutes on a Pentium 3.4GHz machine under Windows XP. Similar accuracy of the resultant scores, when compared to human scores, is maintained. For example, IEA achieved a correlation of 0.81 with human scores for GMAT essays (Landauer, Laham & Foltz, 2003), compared to the 0.79 achieved by MarkIT for the Year 10 High School essays reported above.

The power of the resultant document vectors to represent the essay content is also impressive, as only the cosine of the model and student essay vectors, and three other predictors, are needed for scoring the student essay, in the example discussed. This low number of predictors appears to be unique to MarkIT. Other documented systems appear to require substantially more (Shermis & Burstein, 2003).

Acknowledgement

The author wishes to express his appreciation to Professor Tom Landauer of the University of Colorado, Boulder, for his valuable comments and suggestions for improvements during the writing this paper.

References

Hearst, M. (2000). The debate on automated essay grading. *IEEE Intelligent Systems, 15* (5), 22-37, IEEE CS Press.

Landauer, T., Foltz, P., & Laham, D. (1998). An introduction to latent semantic analysis. *Discourse Processes, 25*, 259-284.

Landauer, T., Laham, D. & Foltz, P. (2003). Automated scoring and annotation of essays with the Intelligent Essay Assessor™. In M. Shermis & J. Burstein (Eds.), *Automated essay scoring: A cross-disciplinary perspective* (pp 87–112). New Jersey, USA: Lawrence Erlbaum Associates.

Macquarie Library. (2005). Retrieved November 29, 2005 from http://www.macquariedictionary.com.au/

MarkIT (2005). Retrieved November 28, 2005 from http://www.essaygrading.com/

Nichols, P. (2005). Evidence for the interpretation and use of scores from an automated essay scorer. *PEM Research Report 05-02,* Retrieved November 28, 2005 from http://www.pearsonedmeasurement.com/downloads/research/RR_05_02.pdf

Pearson Knowledge Technologies (2005). Retrieved November 28, 2005 from http://www.knowledge-technologies.com/

Shermis, M. & Burstein, J. (2003). *Automated essay scoring: A cross-disciplinary perspective.* New Jersey, USA: Lawrence Erlbaum Associates.

Valenti, S., Neri, F., & Cucchiarelli, A. (2003). An overview of current research on automated essay grading, *Journal of Information Technology Education*, 2, 319 – 330. Retrieved January 30, 2006 from http://jite.org/documents/Vol2/v2p319-330-30.pdf

Williams, R. (2001) Automated essay grading: an evaluation of four conceptual models. In M. Kulski & A. Herrmann (Eds.), *New horizons in university teaching and learning: Responding to change.* Perth, Australia: Curtin University of Technology.

Williams, R. & Dreher, H. (2005). Formative assessment visual feedback in computer graded essays. *Journal of Issues in Informing Science and Information Technology*, *2*, 23-32. Retrieved from http://proceedings.informingscience.org/InSITE2005/I03f95Will.pdf

Biography

Robert Williams has over 25 year's experience in the Information Systems industry, as a practitioner, researcher and lecturer. He currently is a lecturer in the School of Information Systems at Curtin University of Technology in Perth, Western Australia. He has extensive experience in systems analysis and design, and programming, on a variety of mainframe, mini and personal computers, and a variety of operating systems and programming languages. Applications he has worked with include mathematical, statistical, bridge and road engineering, financial, corporate resource allocation, business simulation and educational systems. He has published a number of articles on system users' personalities and satisfaction, decision support systems, and automated essay grading systems. In 2001 he led a team of researchers in the School of Information Systems at Curtin University of Technology which conducted what is believed to be the first trial in Australia of an Automated Essay Grading system. Robert holds a Bachelor of Arts degree with double majors in Mathematics and Economics from the University of Western Australia, a Graduate Diploma in Computing from the Western Australian Institute of Technology, and a Master of Information Systems degree from Curtin University of Technology.

The page left blank intentionally.

Quality of Informing: Bias and Disinformation Philosophical Background and Roots

(Research in Progress)

Zbigniew J. Gackowski
California State University, Stanislaus, CA, USA

ZGackowki@.csustan.edu

Abstract

This is an inquiry into the background and the origins of bias and disinformation as viewed from the philosophical perspective. This paper demonstrates the undeniable analogy between the philosophical framework defined by Schopenhauer and the informational model of decision situations as viewed today in operations research, management sciences, and decision sciences. Bias, and disinformation—the main concerns of informing science are not aberrations or deviations—are the very nature of all communications among living entities. Within the realm of informing science, research that ignores this fact may produce unreliable results. One must face this reality head on. The inquiry contributes to the theoretical foundations of informing science. The results are presented for challenge, critique, and discussion.

Keywords: Informing, bias, misinformation, disinformation, theoretical foundations, entity informed

Introduction

Eli Cohen (1999) defines informing sciences as "the field of inquiry that attempts to provide a client with information in a form, format, and schedule that maximizes its effectiveness" (p.5). This paper examines the dynamic process of informing with respect to the credibility of its content (information value) in addition to the form and format that play an *indirect* role in determining its quality. In contrast to a different paper, "Quality of informing: Credibility—a provisional model of functional dependencies," this one focuses on the philosophical background and the inherent roots of bias and disinformation. They are the greatest risks associated with informing. Thoughts about mitigation strategies are discussed. According to Eli Cohen, **bias** is a failure to fully inform, and **disinforming** is reporting untrue information as true, with knowledge that it is not true. Its purpose is to deceive.

This inquiry attempts to identify the underlying cause(s) of bias and disinformation and to demonstrate that bias is more than "failure to fully inform." The latter is the least harmful kind of bias, which is caused by ignorance, and belongs to misinforming, which is not a subject of this paper. This inquiry deals with the bias rooted in human nature, in its subconscious and intentions, which make it part of disinforming.

This paper refers to the theoretical operations research-based approach to informing and to operations quality of data and information values as proposed by Gackowski (2004; 2005a; 2005b). The philosophical background and roots of bias and disinformation are based on Schopenhauer's opus vitae, "*The world as will and representation,*" which was critically presented to English readers by Hamlyn (1980).

The main contributions of this paper are

- the modified concepts of informing
- the role of credibility in <u>passive</u> informing
- the role of credibility in <u>active</u> informing where bias and disinformation reign
- some thoughts about mitigating disinformation and intentional bias

For focused reading, key terms in paragraphs are in **bold** font, emphasis in *italics,* highest emphasis <u>underlined</u>, and terms followed by a definition in ***bold italics***.

Informing Systems as We Know

Concepts of Informing

In Nadler's (1970) terminology on work systems, "***informing systems*** are a class of work systems whose **basic output** is **information** that affects recipients' actions" as defined by Gackowski (1982, p. 108). Since that time, a separate discipline of informing science emerged that was fostered by the incessant efforts of the Informing Science Institute, led by Eli Cohen, with an established tradition of annual international conferences, journals, and other forms of publication not horded by always shared on the Web.

Informing models comprise basic components: **information source**(s), **communication channel**(s), and **informed entities.** In informing science, the latter are referred to as **clients.** In the conventional meaning of the term in commerce, networked computers, or program objects, however, they may not always be clients. The term "entities informed" renders better their role and position in informing.

Information sources may be active or passive.

- ***Active information sources—informing entities*** by their nature or design transmit, disseminate, or broadcast signals conveying information. When by design, sources are active agents—senders or disseminators of information, such as advertisers, professional information providers, politicians, preachers, etc.--the entities inform or try to affect them in a desired manner.
- ***Passive information sources*** yield information when observed, examined, and/or measured.

Communications channels link information sources and entities informed. The sets and sequences of signal transformations constitute the ***informing processes.*** They may be performed by any component of the informing model: informing entities, and/or communication channels, and/or entities informed. Usually they are functions of **information delivery and distribution systems** that constitute one of the three major components of **the informing science** framework as defined by Cohen (1999).

Clients or ***entities informed*** (marketing prospects, competitors, adversaries, students, voters, public, robotic devices, etc.) must be capable of acting autonomously so that the incoming information may make them behave differently than otherwise. Entities informed may be simple or composite entities, individuals or organizations, even robotic devices that are controlled numerically or by artificial intelligence. Within entities informed, division of labor may result in specialized sub-entities that deal with information acquisition and its presentation, decision-making and implementation, and the acting agents. Entities informed may be **targeted intentionally** by disseminators of information, or they may **actively gather information** from sources. Hence, they may be interested in being provided with some information products or services. They may pay for being informed or seek only information offered seemingly free. They may also be inclined to enter into a dialog to refine the informing process or refuse to participate in it.

There are several universal conditions for successful informing. For informing to take place, there must be a difference in states of the information source and the entity informed with regard to the transmitted signals. In communications theory, the difference is measured by ***entropy***[1]. With no difference in the states of sources and the entities informed (they know the same), their respective levels of entropy are the same. After informing has occurred, the respective states of the source and the entity informed are equal, hence, the received ***information values***[2]—their content was not known to them. The information values must meet several quality requirements to become first operationally ***usable***[3] and, next, ***useful***[4] by becoming effectively operationally complete to a degree that triggers a transition of the operations state (to act or not) (Gackowski, 2005b).

There is always a defined or at least implied purpose of informing viewed from the perspective of the informing entities and/or the entities informed. The purpose may constitute any utility value of commercial, administrative, military, and educational, entertainment, social, or even only personal nature. Whatever the purpose, one is interested in high-fidelity transmission of signals, which is a technical problem. With the exception of entertainment, all informing is of problematic credibility. Even entertainment fostering, conveying (directly or indirectly) life styles, attitudes, and behaviors of the entertaining entity is not without bias.

Problems with credibility of data or information values are mostly *non-technical.* They are inherent to all communication among living entities, including humans—usually deceptive but always biased for their purposes. Some bias may be attributed to ignorance; however, most of the bias or lack of objectivity is deeply rooted in all living nature. It is a conscious or subconscious deviation from the truth—only truth and the entire truth. Bias, except the unintended, should not be described as "failure to fully inform." The term "failure" implies that one intended to be objective and truthful but somehow failed in this respect. Even most of the unintended misinformation comes from various human imperfections and fallibility, much less from technical problems. Simply the purpose of communications taints them with bias and tempts to disinform.

Informing may be direct or indirect, solicited or unsolicited, by entities informed.

- In ***direct informing,*** information flows directly between information sources and entities informed.
- In ***indirect informing,*** intermediary acquisition, processing, retrieval, delivery, and presentation of information takes place between information sources and entities informed. In

[1] A measure of the disorder or randomness in a closed system that consists of the source and the client—the number of bits necessary to transmit a message as a function of the probability that the message will consist of a specific set of symbols.

[2] Represent things, events, and unknown states that are yet to be acquired, which change the decision situations per se, and/or the actions that implement the decisions, and/or the results of operations.

[3] A data or information value becomes operationally usable when it jointly meets all of its universal (acquisition interpretable, of significant impact, operationally timely available, actionably credible), and situation-specific (for instance, exclusively available) mandatory quality requirements. Usability does not imply effectively usable.

[4] A usable data or information value can become operationally useful only as a member of an operationally effectively complete activity-specific cluster of required operationally usable data or information values.

an advanced environment, data are organized in databases or data warehouses. These may be run by informing entities or by entities informed for them.

The design and examination of informing systems differs considerably for active and passive informing. In case of active informing, informing entities try to provide gainfully some information service and/or influence the behavior of the targeted entity informed. Usually, their perspective carries more weight than the perspective of entities informed, because the former affect the behavior of *many* entities informed. In passive informing, the entity informed may purposefully try to gather intelligence about the environment or obtain some feedback about the state of the situation under consideration if the results differ or may differ significantly when acting without the obtained information. In either situation, informing entities and entities informed aim at measurable or at least perceivable results of some utility value or payoff. Hence, in cost-aware business environments, when one aims at achieving the best results, one should carefully examine the expected cost effectiveness of the respective informing systems. A graphical schema of informing is in Gackowski (2005a).

Up to this point, the basics of informing are rather clear and not controversial; however, once one touches the purpose of informing, the issue becomes murky. The entire problem can be divided into the purpose of passive and the purpose of active informing. In both cases, credibility remains the main issue. For most cases of passive informing, credibility may be examined in a relatively objective manner. In active informing, a new source of problems emerges—intentionality. The latter requires different methods of examination, which belong to higher planes of a philosophical inquiry.

Credibility in Passive Informing—Overview

A provisional model of credibility exists that is based on and derived from the model of operations quality of data and information values. It was presented at the 10th Anniversary ICIQ-2005 Conference at MIT by Gackowski (2005b, 2006a). It identified the universal quality requirements and the universal principles governing operations quality. The latter publication presents a **credibility model** that attempts to identify all functional dependencies of the direct quality requirement of **actionable credibility** on the indirect operations quality attributes with the corresponding entity-relationship diagrams.

Credibility of a data/information value means whether it is true—whether one may rely on the value. The adjective ***true*** means consistent with reality. Complete credibility is hence rarely to never attainable. If it is Boolean (true, false), its degree is measured by the probability of its veracity (0–1). While probing for veracity of data or information values, users/entities informed face dramatic options, less with data of well-established roles and more with unknown recently acquired information values. The question is whether they received disinformation, misinformation, or valid information. To this end, outright disinformation must be excluded first, and the degree of misinformation assessed next. Only then must the concerned value be tested for validity.

Disinformation intentionally misinforms. On the one hand, it may not be clear who the originator is due to omission of contact addresses, when it was originated or updated, what methods of collection or acquisition were used, etc. On the other hand, all the above may be available. Now, however, the entity informed faces two extremes of **deception** with many possibilities in between. All indicators of validity are given to legitimize the value, but one or more of them are false, or they all are true to convince and trap the gullible in a desired manner.

Misinformation unintentionally misrepresents reality. It may be distorted at its acquisition, communication, storing, processing, presentation, and its interpretation. It may be of lesser or higher materiality, as required and defined by FASB (1983). In operations, it is determined by the impact a value exerts on them.

Valid information faithfully represents reality. To this end, it should be well defined, of known variability, objective (unbiased), accurate (error free), precise, and current (up to date). Usually, the above is attributed to the reputation of the source; can be traced back to the responsible originator, where the level of responsibility is adequate to the potential consequences (in operations) of the expected errors; and when information is of proven authorship, can be replicated, or can be confirmed otherwise.

Affecting factors may be classed into positive and negative ones. It seems that only the **variety** or the **number of independent sources** increases credibility of data/information values. ***Sources of data or information*** values may be observers, sensors, processes, tests, etc. Any data/information value acquired from a specific source inherits credibility from the reputation of its source labeled **source-specific credibility. Joint credibility** may be impaired by imperfections in **mapping quality** of values, as defined by Wand and Wang (1996), within the data and information delivery system and its **presentation credibility** to entities informed.

Actionable credibility of data or information values is attained when joint credibility equals or exceeds the threshold for a state transition of operations (to act or not) as defined by the policy in effect. Economical actionable credibility imposes additional economical requirements (Gackowski, 2005b); for instance, the cost of attaining it should not exceed the benefit the value adds to operations.

This overview covers only the *direct* functional dependencies of the joint credibility. Most of the direct factors depend again on indirect quality attributes of the first order. Many of the latter may again functionally depend on other indirect attributes of the second and subsequent orders (Gackowski, 2006).

Credibility in Active Informing—Roots of Bias and Disinformation

All the aspects of credibility of data/information values discussed in passive informing should also be taken into account in active informing. However, two major differences pertain to disinformation and bias as defined before. Bias may occur in all types of informing, although in passive informing its source is ignorance; hence, it is classed as an aspect of misinformation. It is unthinkable that individuals and organizations seeking out information values would on purpose introduce bias for themselves, although subconsciously, they may do it. Being delusional, they may seek or accept only information that is music to their ears. This aspect is not a subject of this paper.

The main subject of this section is the natural tendency of anything living toward *bias* and *outright disinformation.* In active informing, bias and disinformation reign. They are the natural *all-pervasive* features of active informing. Once one enters the realm of intentions, one literally descends into murky, foggy realms of human spirit, aspirations, and drives that are difficult to fathom. Informing science is fortunate that these most difficult problems seem to be satisfactorily elucidated within the philosophical framework developed by Arthur Schopenhauer. The edifice of Schopenhauer's philosophical thought seems to be adequate to this human non-technological realm of informing science. From the decision-science and informing-science perspective, there is a striking analogy between the contemporary model of decision situations and Schopenhauer's "*The World as Will and Representation*"—between the world of data and information values that represent the reality and the will of decision makers or decision-making bodies. It pertains to all kinds of informing, active informing in particular.

The world as will and representation

This is the title of Schopenhauer's opus vitae, which is critically presented by Hamlyn (1980). It contains the essence of his views of how the world functions. The model consists of **will** and **representation.** All processes are interplays between them. The model applies to all subjects. It is a logical equivalent to a contemporary information model of decision situations in which one takes inventory of what is already known by the decision maker **(data)**, what is not yet known and must be acquired **(information),** and the applicable rules of reasoning **(knowledge)**. These are the equivalents of Schopenhauer's **representations**. Subjects, here decision-makers, never act on the basis of the actual reality, for it is never fully known. They act based on the available purported representations of that reality. Schopenhauer's model is clearly bipolar and very incisive with regard to bias and disinformation, which are subjects of this paper. All representations are conditioned by other representations. There exists, however, an unconditioned awareness of willing. We can learn a lesson from Schopenhauer concerning the nature of action and the will and thereby concerning the place of human beings in the scheme of things. The governing principle of human existence is the will to live; i.e., egoism. The all-dominant force of the will looms large in his model, where only intellect plays the role of quieter of the will (Hamlyn, 1980).

Representation—In operations, decision-makers and/or acting agents become aware of the situation they are in by using **direct** and **indirect** sources. The ***direct sources*** comprise everything that is perceived by their senses or sensors. The ***indirect sources*** comprise values (the content) of symbolic representations (data values, information values, and knowledge meant as rules of reasoning) available to them. Decision-makers consider them in the situation they are in and the challenges they face and must deal with.

According to Schopenhauer, however, for the subjects (decision-makers in operations), *representations* are the only objects, the only empirical reality to them (Hamlyn, 1980, p. 65). They are in no casual relationship with the subject. Causality applies only to and within representations. All representations are subject to conditions, which constitute one of the four forms of the principle of sufficient reason, as defined by Schopenhauer in his doctoral dissertation (Hamlyn, 1980, p. 7). Every representation is relative to another representation that is its condition, ground, or reason. At the same time, Schopenhauer stands on the ground of "realistic dogmatism" (there really is an object separate from the subject and the representation that exists for it) and skepticism (we can never know of any real thing that lies behind representations). Nevertheless, the conditioned nature of all representation is an a priori truth in general and in detail.

We know, however, that at the lowest level of the operations hierarchy, actors or acting agents are in direct contact with tangible elements of reality—the means and objects of their actions. The higher the level of management or command (supervisory, tactical, strategic), the lesser the direct contact with reality and the higher the dependency on their substitutes—representations. At the highest level of operations, subjects act indeed only within a virtual reality of the representations available to them and their will. Schopenhauer claims that even the direct sensations, in the process of their understanding, are converted into perceptions that, in turn, provide subjects with the corresponding representations. Even when one does not accept Schopenhauer's argument that all sensations appear to the human mind as representations, it still holds true for the higher levels of decision-making in particular, where subjects live in the virtual world of representations and the will of their chief executive officer or commander-in-chief.

When one excludes incidents when decision-makers directly witness events or directly act to implement their decisions, there is nothing more left than the representations in the form of available data values, obtained information values, and known rules of reasoning. When one also considers the phenomenological aspects of reality, even intuition can be added. This, however, brings us beyond the purely rational decision-making. Thus, within the realm of operations, one cannot deny the strong analogy of Schopenhauer's world of representations and the contemporary reality in which decision-making takes place. The same holds true in one or other form to all *devices controlled numerically* or by *artificial intelligence.*

Will–Schopenhauer views and defines will in a much broader manner than usual. He identifies all force with will, whether gravity or the will to live. It is the governing principle of the universe and the human existence. It leads to egoism. ***Will***—the all-dominant force comprises all the forces of life, urges, drives, desires, ambitions, etc. (with the exclusion of reason or intellect)—permeates all nature and governs all phenomena (Hamlyn, 1980, p. 95). It is the driving force of all nature, most vividly observed in all living entities, the life force that drives all their behavior, including their autonomously functioning systems that sustain their basic physiological functions. Schopenhauer goes even further and claims that an insight into our nature is an insight into the nature of reality in general.

According to Schopenhauer, will, as thing in itself, cannot be subject to space and time and the principle of sufficient reason. Will is only one; it lies outside the possibility of plurality. However, it objectifies itself in human beings, animals, and organic life, and even in inorganic matter. This part again lies beyond the boundaries of informing science and operations.

Will is a sufficient reason to act, but it also is subject to causality, called motivation. It implies that a force is not a cause; it is what gives cause a possibility of acting (Hamlyn, 1980, p. 77). Will has no end or purpose; the latter are products of the intellect. Motives are causes seen from within. A chain of representations experienced by a decision-maker may lead to the ultimate motive of the decision to trigger a system of operations aimed at attaining a defined purpose. This represents causality viewed from the inside. The ultimate motif is another form of sufficient reason of human actions called the principle of motivation. It is the major guide in history, politics, pragmatic psychology, etc. in human endeavors and operations. Motive, if studied from the viewpoint of its value and sources, is a guide in ethics. Due to the fact that human beings have a direct and unconditional awareness of the will, they act in a true sense; animals and controlled devices only react to stimuli. The will of acting subjects has many degrees, beginning with the most silent wishes up to unchecked passions; not only the subjects' feelings but also the slightest movements of their mood are *states* of will.

The will is absolutely egoistic and directly opposed to morality. It is untiring and incessant. Its only objective or end is its continuity; thus, it promotes self-deception and deception of others (ibid., pp. 98–100). It manifests itself in growth, expansion, and preservation of individuals and species in fierce competition for resources (territory, water, food, etc.). It leads to eternal universal clash of divergent interests. There also is no absolute necessity, only necessity relative to something else. The principle of sufficient reason is the sole support of all necessity. This is Schopenhauer's rationalism. Thus, the will (as defined before) is also the source of inevitability of bias and disinformation, as we know. They are not exceptions; they are the actual reality that must be expected and faced head on. When will is a sufficient reason to act, then by the same token, the same will that blindly tries to impose itself on other subjects is a sufficient reason for all intentional (the conscious and subconscious) bias and disinformation. There also exists, however, biases due to ignorance—not a subject of this paper.

Such a consistent model based on incisive observations of reality of the human conditions and behavior possesses some explanatory and predictive features. On the one hand, Schopenhauer repudiates Kant's practical reason because of its connection to morality. He leaves room for practical reason whenever one acts from abstract principles, goals, or ends abstractly conceived, which fully applies to purposive operations. On the other hand, Schopenhauer's philosophy is very ethical and moral, but it is based on the principle of checks and balances that the human intellect may exert upon the blind drives of the will. The concept is similar to blind economic forces of free markets channeled by the framework of a proper legal system and the checks and balances, as in the American constitutional order that launched one of the most productive societies. Both were developed based on the pessimistic assumption of the egoistic nature of humans and succeeded better than other societies that proclaimed idealistic goals and natural goodness of humans. Schopenhauer considers even optimism as an *immoral* way of thinking.

Due to the incisiveness, adequacy, rigor, and consistency of his framework, most of Schopenhauer's contemporaries preferred to remain silent. Some recognition was given to him only at the end of his life. He was held in the highest esteem by Nietzsche, but in the next century, his works became necessary reading for everyone who was interested in the humanities. Of course, today's critiques of philosophical arguments raise many objections to his worldview. One of the objections is that Schopenhauer claims that the will (as defined by him) pertains to all objects of the universe, which is beyond the realm of informing science. Certainly, his view pertains to the entire animal world. Schopenhauer claims that any attempt to portray any object (representation) that did not conform to the principle of sufficient reason in one of its four forms, as defined by him, would be unintelligible. He freely admitted the impossibility of proof of it. The argument is dialectical only. But from the more limited perspective of operations, as long no one can find any example to the contrary, it is a *sufficient* proof. As long as it holds true, any labeling of his model as indicative of rationalism or idealism is irrelevant in operations. Hamlyn (1980, p. 163) concludes that none of the philosophical objections means that we have no reason to listen to what he has to say about human beings, although they are pessimistic. Philosophy is not merely an academic discipline that only extends our understanding of things. It can bring with it a form of resolution of the inevitable conflicts; Schopenhauer even claims the possibility of salvation from the will. Hamlyn (1980) concedes that "Schopenhauer's philosophy remains a magnificent intellectual construction, from which there is still much to learn" (p. 170).

Freedom of the will

In 1839, the Norwegian Scientific Society organized a competition. The question set was whether it is possible to prove the freedom of the human will from its own consciousness. Schopenhauer gave a resounding "No." He won the competition. There is no such thing as an absolute free will. He sets against it his own view of necessity as expounded in his doctoral dissertation in the "*Fourfold root of sufficient reason*" (Schopenhauer, 1974). All phenomena are subject to the principle of sufficient reason—causality. Similarly, our actions are determined by motives. Will alone, as defined by Schopenhauer, is not. It "knows no necessity" and "is not determined as consequent through a reason" (Hamlyn, 1980, p. 132).

There is, however, a relative freedom that we humans find in our consciousness. By deliberations, our intellect enables us to reflect on our motives and put off immediate actions. Thoughts that deliberations produce still function as motives. A mere image created by thoughts can act as a motive. There is no final freedom from the causal necessity that motives provide even here. At least in part, people confuse this relative freedom with real absolute freedom. What we do is subject to motives, but which motives we follow or respond to is a reflection of our individual character. According to Schopenhauer, the freedom of the will does not warrant attribution of responsibility to our deeds, but because they are a reflection of our individual character. At all times a man does what he wills, but he does it necessarily (Hamlyn, 1980, p. 127). In the realm of action, causality is all-pervasive and all-operative. We do not always act on the immediate motive but on the strongest motive, even when it requires thought for it. What a man is will determine how he acts. Cannot people change? According to Schopenhauer, people can change only with respect to knowledge, not of will (Hamlyn, 1980, p. 128). And here lies the key to some constructive solutions.

According to Schopenhauer, only contemplation of art and knowledge acts as quieter of the will as defined by him. The will cannot be abolished by anything else except knowledge (Hamlyn, 1980, p. 150). By deliberation, knowledge enables men to shift their focus from the immediate to the less immediate but frequently stronger motives, from their individual egoism to an enlarged form of egoism (Hamlyn, 1980, p. 145). In his ethics (knowledge of morals) (Hamlyn, 1980, p. 136), *wrong* is a matter of an individual will being overridden by another, while the doctrine of *right* is simply one concerned with the limits that should be put on that, given that there is, in the end and in reality, no difference between wills in society (Hamlyn, 1980, p. 138). Thus, Schopenhauer leaves room for knowledge in her role as quieter of the will, with some hope of channeling its energy from the destructive toward the constructive end of its spectrum; this leaves room for political philosophy, social sciences, public administration, and politics.

Thoughts about Politics and Informing

"The central problem of political philosophy is how to deploy or limit public power so as to maintain the survival and enhance the quality of human life. ... Political philosophy is more theoretical and normative than descriptive..... It is concerned with what ought, on various assumptions to be. It is one of the most intellectual disciplines, for it sets standards of judgment and defines the constructive purposes for the use of public power. This aspect is more urgent today than it has been in earlier periods, because mankind has at its disposal the power either to create a world civilization, where technology can benefit the human race, or destroy itself in pursuit of political myths" (Encyclopedia Britannica, Political philosophy, 2006, p. 1).

Before Schopenhauer, Hobbes stated that, without public power due to the "competitive nature of men that once more than subsistence has been achieved ... there is a war of all against all." After Schopenhauer, in the "Ruling Class," Mosca (2006) reasserted that, "in various forms there will always be a struggle for predominance" (p. 40); hence, "public laws are necessary to regulate it. Only within a framework of tolerably well-organized constitutionalism that is gradually extended to relations between states can the swiftly mounting opportunities provided by applied science be taken so that the human specie, instead of being thwarted and deformed by its institutions, can realize its full potentialities" (Encyclopedia Britannica, Political philosophy, 2006, p. 47).

When the analogy is close to perfect, one may expect that many of Schopenhauer's conclusions, once sounding as abstract as Einstein's conclusions about the physical universe, can now be empirically explored and either validated or rejected. It may represent interesting opportunities for more research.

Individual actions and massive operations, including all communications of living entities, reflect always their particular self-interest, hence intentional bias and disinformation. They are the rule, not the exception. Therefore, one must finally expect them and face them head on. One cannot eliminate but only mitigate them—channel them into a productive rather than a destructive force as one deals with economic forces and other forms of energy. Let's see what Schopenhauer, the great pessimist, says in this respect.

First, he stands firm on the position that all phenomena are subjects to the principle of sufficient reason, but will (as defined by him) alone is not. Life force and will, like any flow of any kind of energy, must be harnessed and channeled to utilize their constructive aspects while limiting their destructive aspects. The energy of the will objectified in humans is above any other known form of energy in the universe, for it is the source of all creativity, development, and progress.

To face reality means to study how, under controlled conditions, a relative equilibrium of interests of the objectified will in subjects can be maintained to mitigate the negative consequences of their conflicts. The end is to avoid unnecessary waste of resources and to encourage productiveness leading to security and a better life for all. This is the stated goal of the positivist philosophy.

Such equilibrium is very fragile but must be attempted to maximize the productive aspects and minimizing the negative of aspects of conflicts of interest. Some imagined that it can be attained by outright equality, but this leads to death of incentives and stagnation similar to the thermal death of any closed system with all levels of energy equalized. Physicists know that any equalization means cessation of all processes and activities, including communication, hence informing.

At the highest levels of decision-making, the virtual reality (the decision-makers are in) consists of self-interested individuals (courtiers, lobbyists, accountants, lawyers, consultants, etc.) who are flexible and smart enough to bend and skew the representations at hand to their liking and interests. Thus, all interactions and communications are subject to bias at least or deadly disinformation at most. With offices and agencies staffed with well-positioned agents of adversarial interests, the situation is always open to outright disinformation. This is the real world of the FBI, CIA, M-6, ENRON, WORLDCOM, Arthur Anderson, etc.

Informing should be viewed from the perspective of informing entities and/or the entities informed. The utility value of any data or information value should be considered from either side of the supply chain. For lasting business relations, the benefits of each side are equally important. One should not overlook, however, that in active informing, the informing entities are always in a stronger position than the targeted entities informed. The latter are in an extremely vulnerable situation. They may be simply distracted, controlled, taken advantage of, damaged, hurt, and even destroyed. Their perspective is not necessarily more important, but certainly they deserve all the protection a society can afford. On the other hand, the informing entities deserve a different type of protection from piracy and other forms of theft. An excellent example in this respect is the emergence of ESBN.ORG, which provides for authors, publishers, and distributors of electronic content and media a unique Electronic Standard Book Number (ESBN). It is recognized worldwide by electronic publishing companies and electronic content providers (ESBN, 2006) and can be used to track searches, visits, downloads, transfers, copies, etc.

When looking back at the many functional dependencies of credibility that are identified in the provisional model (Gackowski, 2006, Figure 2a and 2b) what practical measures can be taken to improve the situation with regard to bias and disinformation in human communications? The provisional model identified factors that directly affect the joint credibility of D/I values: **variety of sources, source-specific credibility, mapping quality**, and **presentation credibility**. The latter two play a significant role only in indirect informing, which presently is the prevalent mode of operations.

Variety of sources turns out to be the only direct factor (but an indirect quality dimension in operations quality) that is capable of increasing credibility. It implies that, whether within society or any private domain, main efforts should be focused on creating and maintaining a viable variety of competitive sources of information. The uncertainty related to source-specific credibility or lack thereof is its complement to one (1 – SSC). With additional sources, the uncertainty about a data/information value declines fast (Gackowski, 2006a). One should always search for alternative or competitive data/information sources to increase the **variety of independent sources** and subsequently increase not one but even two direct primary mandatory quality requirements of any data/information value: **operational timely availability** and its **joint credibility**. A ***variety of independent sources*** that yield the same or similar value for the same aspect of reality reduces one's uncertainty regarding its credibility. Even when all sources are inaccurate, there is a research in progress on a **theory of complementarity** of extracting accurate data from inaccurate sources through integration (Gelman, 2005). Lack of access to alternative sources of D/I values and corresponding channels of communication makes anyone and any organization extremely vulnerable to bias, disinformation, and disruption of any communication. Because credibility is rarely to never fully attainable, one should try *not to rely* on a single source. The variety of the potential sources of data or information values must be examined with regard to their **external** and **intrinsic** reputation.

The ***external reputation*** of individual sources encompasses **traceability** of individual data/information values to their respective sources, the **availability of reliable communication channels–communicable sources**, the **alignment of attitudes,** and the **alignment of interests** between active informing sources and the entities informed.

Specific data/information sources must be identified first. In many cases, they may remain unknown or questionable. In non-routine operations, one may be compelled to act even without knowledge of the source(s). Otherwise, **traceability** of data/information values to specific sources is a **mandatory** prerequisite for examining their reputation, which is particularly important for repetitive operations. ***Traceability*** of data/information values means they can be unambiguously attributed to specific sources. The more important, valuable, dangerous, litigation-prone, subject of personal accountability and responsibility, and/or vulnerable to criminal activities a value is, responsible managers or commanders preserve its traceability and transparently document its handling (audit trails). "Information systems are designed so that every financial transaction can be traced. In other words, an audit trail must exist that can establish where each transaction originated and how it was processed. Aside from financial audits, operational audits are used to evaluate the effectiveness and efficiency of information systems operations" (Encyclopedia Britannica, Information systems, 2005).

Similarly, **availability and reliability of communication** channels between the **communicable source** and the entity informed is a mandatory prerequisite for further examination of their reputation. Regardless of whether informing is passive or active, there may be no viable communication channels available, or they may be vulnerable to disruption or interference. This may render some of the potential sources unsuitable or unreliable due to intermediary circumstances, which precludes their further consideration. Here, the main defense against possible interference relies on maintaining alternative channels of communication and encryption of messages. Once, the main domains of disinformation and bias were personal relationships, fraudulent activities, propaganda, and high-flying intelligence operations. With the proliferation of the Internet, networked computers, use of e-mail, and websites, entities informed are vulnerable not only to bias but also to all kinds of disinformation and destructive invasions of their computers. Under the protection of academic freedom and freedom of expression, everybody, including students, are exposed to all kinds of bias and outright disinformation, not only by unscrupulous politicians but also by teachers and professors with nearly complete impunity—no responsibility and accountability.

In active informing particularly, the reputation of D/I sources and the implied subsequent source-specific credibility of the values provided may be severely affected by a variety of factors of biological, personal psychological, sociological, economical, and political nature. All of them may become consciously and subconsciously reasons for disinformation and bias in all types of communications—called here **alignment of attitudes and interests**. Both may decrease or increase the reputation of any source. They are of paramount overriding importance and determine the source-entity informed specific bias and disinformation. They may even preclude some of them from becoming legitimate and admissible sources of information. It works in two ways. On the one hand, the active source may exclude certain entities from providing them with information when they have been blacklisted for good or bad reasons. On the other hand, entities informed and other entities informed may outright exclude certain sources as not reputable, too questionable, or suspect.

Alignment of attitudes frequently plays such a strong role that it overrides even obvious conflicts of interest. Their intensity may vary from an irreconcilable armed death-and-life conflict through neutrality to a love-to-death affair. It may play a role in personal, family, tribal, ethnic, religious, racial, and national affairs, and even on an interplanetary level in the future. The resulting disinformation and bias may aim simply at distraction of the targeted entity or at gaining a partial, even absolute, control over the entities informed.

With regard to **alignment of interests,**

- The very first question to be asked is what kind of alignment of interest exists between the source and the entity informed—whether there is any open (declared), implied, or only a potentially adversary conflict of interest, even only an association of the source with entities that may have conflicting interests with the entity informed.
- A similar question must be asked about whether there is any divergence or disparity of interests. The purpose of such a question is to asses the likelihood of disinformation or intentional bias in the information value provided.
- A milder version of the same types of questions is whether there is any history of outright disinformation of a general nature, such as fabrication of new or intentional bias in their presentation but not necessarily targeting a specific entity informed. It may come from greed, longing for vain glory, etc., as it can be easily observed in all mass media.

In court proceedings, there are many legally prescribed precautions. Certainly, all commercials, particularly from companies without established brands and tradition, must be subject to a special scrutiny with respect to the level of bias.

Next, one must test the more ***intrinsic factors*** of the source's **reputation,** such as its **reliability** in yielding the value of interest with a **source-specific credibility** that depends on the offered **verifiability**, **replicability**, or **warranty** that increases the source's reputation, and any imperfections in **definition, variability, objectivity, accuracy, precision,** and **currency** that decreases it (Gackowski, 2006). The latter six imperfections affect **presentation credibility** in indirect informing the same way; however, only **definitions** and **objectivity** are subject to bias and are less likely to be outright disinformation.

Verifiability takes various forms. One of them is **accreditation** of the source by a reputable professional body, which periodically verifies the source's eligibility for its accreditation status. Another form is whether the source is subject to a legally mandated **periodical audit** as it applies to public corporations. Similarly, a source is verifiable when it is **bonded** or **legally responsible** for the information service it provides. For instance, all commercial offers on Web sites and by e-mail could be voluntarily registered with a commercial unit (never a government agency) that, in case of a dispute, guarantees to a certain level that the claims are legitimate. Entities informed should know to what extend their risk is limited when dealing with each partner and that commercial deals with non-registered partners are completely at their own risk.

Replicability may be another form of assurance of quality in a credible manner when the source enables replication of some tests. For instance, a specimen might be preserved for additional testing later when doubts may arise or claims are challenged.

Warranty is another form of quality assurance. It is particularly convincing when combined with bonding. Usually it assures that proper seriously observed procedures are in place. The amount of warranty offered indicates by how much the entity's informed risk is diminished in case of quality defects.

Uncertainties associated with the **definition** of what specific data represent in the real world automatically decrease by this much the final credibility of the concerned value.

Loss of **objectivity,** meant as free of bias, may happen in the process of data/information acquisition due to the approaches and methods used in selecting the primary sources, measuring and observation points, measuring instruments, and, finally, when collecting, processing, and presenting data. The resulting bias may be either unintended due to ignorance or introduced intentionally. The results of distortions may be significant, hence deceptive, and damaging to the source's reputation. To rectify the bias and compensate for it may require engagement of substantial additional resources. Whether it is economically justified can be assessed only when its impact on operations is known. As in other cases, this will affect the direct secondary operations quality requirement of **economically actionable credibility** (Gackowski, 2005b).

Mapping quality is a function of the design and operations of any data/information delivery system. As long as it is fully automated with a minimum of human intervention, it is an unlikely source of intentional bias and disinformation as long it is securely kept, run, and protected against intrusion from outside and inside of the organization. In today's networked environments with access to the Internet, it becomes more and more doubtful. Error self-detection and error self-correction codes, firewalls around networked computers, and detection of and protection from software viruses and worms are some of the possible counter measures.

Each of the discussed factors *directly* and *independently* impairs the final level of credibility of the affected value, and *none of them compensates* for the losses of credibility caused by other factors

Conclusions

In everyday life, commerce, and politics, bias and disinformation is not an exception or aberration. It is inherent to all communications among living entities and systems controlled by them. Any society capable of preventing or at least satisfactorily limiting abuses in public communications by either side of the communication channels, informing entities, and entities informed will reap the benefits from sharing the achievements of human creativity and avoid the waste from abuse of the free exchange of information. All informing systems should be designed with appropriate counter measures that protect both sides from bias, disinformation, and piracy to an economically acceptable degree.

It seems that there is also a need to extend the current Informing Science Framework introduced by Eli Cohen (1999) to the following: "Informing science is a field of inquiry that attempts to provide entities informed with **quality** information with regard to **content**, form, format, and schedule that maximize the effectiveness **of operations of informing entities and entities informed**" (added words in **bold**). The term "client" should be broadened to "entities informed." The term "clients" in its meaning in commerce, client/server computing, and program objects relationships do not cover all situations of interest.

These conclusions, certainly incomplete, are presented for critique, challenge, and discussion and for sharing of better ideas that may limit bias and outright disinformation in the free exchange of information.

References

Cohen, E. (1999). Reconceptualizing information systems as a field of the transdiscipline informing science: From ugly duckling to swan. *Journal of Computing and Information Technology,* 7(3), 213–219. Retrieved from http://inform.nu/WhatsIS.htm

Electronic Standard Book Number (ESBN). (2006). Retrieved from http://numly.com/esbn/default.asp

Encyclopedia Britannica. (2005). Information system. Retrieved April 22, 2005, from Encyclopedia Britannica Online. http://search.eb.com/eb/article?tocId=218074

Encyclopedia Britannica. (2006). Political philosophy. Retrieved January 6, 2006, from encyclopedia Britannica Online http://search.eb.com/eb/article-10229

Financial Accounting Standard Board (FASB). (1983). *Accounting standard: Statement of financial accounting concepts*. New York, NY: McGraw-Hill.

Gackowski, Z. J. (1982). An approach to categorization of information systems. *Proceedings of the ASIS (American Society for Information Science) Annual Meeting, Volume 19*, Columbus, OH.

Gackowski, Z. J. (2004). Logical interdependence of data/information quality dimensions—A purpose-focused view on IQ. *Proceedings of the Ninth International Conference on Information Quality (ICIQ-04), Cambridge, Massachusetts*. Retrieved from http://www.iqconference.org/Documents/IQ Conference 2004/Papers/LogicalInterdependence.pdf

Gackowski, Z. J. (2005a). Informing systems in business environment: A purpose-focused view. *Informing Science Journal, 8*, 101–122. Retrieved June 27, 2005, from http://inform.nu/Articles/Vol8/v8p101-122Gack.pdf

Gackowski, Z. J. (2005b). Operations quality of data and information: Teleological operations research-based approach, call for discussion. *Proceedings of the 10th Anniversary International Conference on Information Quality—ICIQ-05* at Massachusetts Institute of Technology (MIT), Cambridge, MA.

Gelman, I. A. (2005). A theory of complementarity of extracting accurate data from inaccurate sources through integration. *Proceedings of the 10th International Conference on Information Quality (ICIQ-05)*, Cambridge, Massachusetts.

Hamlyn, D. W. (1980). *Schopenhauer: The arguments of philosophers*. London, UK: Routeledge & Kegan Paul.

Mosca, G. (2006). *Encyclopedia Britannica*. Retrieved March, 8, 2006, from Encyclopedia Britannica Online http://search.eb.com/eb/article-9053877

Nadler, G. (1970). *Work systems design: The IDEAL concept*. Homewood, IL: Richard D. Irwin.

Schopenhouer, A. (1974). *The fourfold root of the principle of sufficient reason* (E. G. Payne, Trans.). La Salle, IL: Open Court.

Wand, Y., & Wang R. Y. (1996). Anchoring data quality dimensions in ontological foundations. *Communications of the ACM, 39*(11), 86–95. Retrieved from https://www.crg2.com/iqconference/documents/publications/TDQMpub/WandWangCACMNov96.pdf

Biography

Zbigniew J. Gackowski has extensive experience in industry, public administration, and universities. His teaching and research bridge the gap between Central European and US experience in Computer Information Systems (Warsaw Polytechnic, the University of Michigan [*Fulbright Research Scholarship*], Purdue University [Visiting Associate Professor], Baruch College [Visiting Professor], California State University, Stanislaus [Professor], and the University of Melbourne [Visiting Professor]). His research has received much recognition. While in Poland, he published more than 120 items, among them, 4 books, and 6 papers in refereed journals, 12 papers presented across Europe, the United States, the Middle East, and South America. While in the USA, he taught at three universities and presented 15 research papers published in the proceedings of ASIS, ACM, DSI, *Information Systems Educators Conference*, *The Informing Science Institute*, and the *International Conference on Information Quality* at MIT. He is a member of ACM and DSI and is a charter member of the *Association for Information Systems* and *the Institute of Informing Science*. His resent research focuses on quality of data and information values in informing.

Index of Authors

Made in United States
Orlando, FL
04 November 2026

90207235R00413